PSYCHOLOGICAL PROCESSES THAT AFFECT CRITICAL THINKING

Psychological research has helped to clarify how people think critically—and why, often, they do not. Here are a few of the topics relevant to critical thinking that are discussed in this book, and the chapters in which they appear.

FACTORS THAT ENHANCE CRITICAL THINKING

Scientific methods and reasoning (chapter 2)

Conditions promoting independent action and nonconformity (chapter 8)

Conditions promoting individuation (chapter 8)

Inductive, deductive, and dialectical reasoning (chapter 9)

Reflective judgment (chapter 9)

Creative problem solving (chapter 9)

Algorithms, heuristics (chapter 9)

Intelligence (chapter 9)

Metacognition (chapter 9)

Improving memory (chapter 10)

Reducing negative emotions (chapter 11)

Cognitive development (chapter 14)

Wisdom derived from life experiences (chapter 14)

Role of appraisals and rethinking in coping with stress and illness (chapter 15)

Attributions that affect feelings and behavior (chapters 8, 11, 12)

Cognitive therapy (chapter 17)

BARRIERS TO CRITICAL THINKING

Pseudoscientific thinking (chapters 1 and 2)

Conformity (chapter 8)

Deindividuation (chapter 8)

Diffusion of responsibility (chapter 8)

Entrapment (chapter 8)

Groupthink (chapter 8)

Coercive persuasion (chapter 8)

Prejudice and ethnocentrism (chapter 8)

Stereotypes (chapter 8)

Self-serving bias (chapter 8)

Mindlessness (chapter 9)

Cognitive biases (e.g., confirmation and hindsight biases) (chapter 9)

Cognitive dissonance (chapter 9)

Mental sets (chapter 9)

Nonreflective judgment (chapter 9)

Fallibility of memory (chapter 10)

Emotional reasoning (chapter 11)

Defense mechanisms (chapter 13)

Vulnerability to the "Barnum Effect" (chapter 13)

Cognitive distortions in mood disorders (chapters 11, 16)

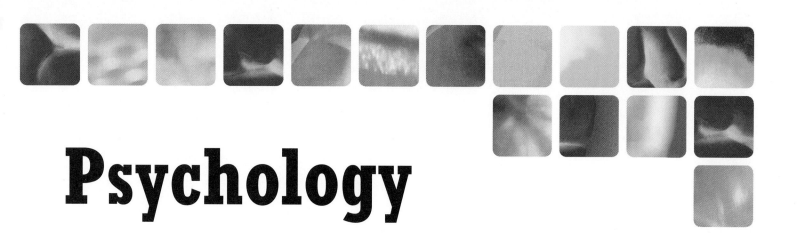

Psychology

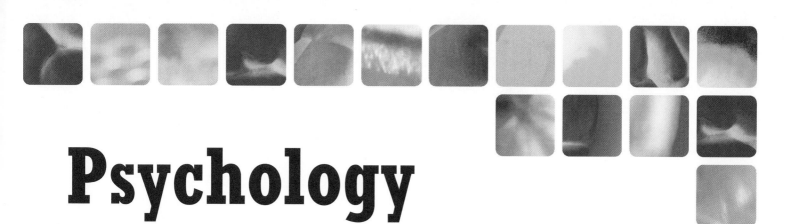

Psychology

SEVENTH EDITION

Carole Wade
Dominican University of California

Carol Tavris

UPPER SADDLE RIVER, NJ 07458

Library of Congress Cataloging-in-Publication Data

Wade, Carole.
    Psychology / Carole Wade, Carol Tavris.—7th ed.
      p. cm.
    Includes bibliographical references and index.
    ISBN 0-13-098263-6
    1. Psychology.   I. Tavris, Carol.   II. Title.

BF121.W27 2002
150—dc21
                    2002017098

VP/Editorial Director: Leah Jewell
Sr. Acquisitions Editor:
  Jennifer Gilliland
Editorial Assistant: Nicole Girrbach
Associate Editor in Chief,
  Development: Rochelle Diogenese
Development Editor: Leslie Carr
AVP/Director of Production and
  Manufacturing: Barbara Kittle
Sr. Project Manager: Maureen
  Richardson
Sr. Managing Editor: Mary Rottino
Manufacturing Manager: Nick Sklitsis
Prepress and Manufacturing Buyer:
  Tricia Kenny
Creative Design Director: Leslie Osher
Interior Design: Tom Nery
Cover Design: Ximena Tamvakopoulos

Cover Art: Courtesy of Jennifer and
  Elaine Bass and the estate of Saul Bass
Photo Researcher: Barbara Salz
Interior Image Specialist: Beth Boyd
Image Permission Coordinator:
  Joanne Dippel
Manager, Rights & Permissions:
  Zina Arrabia
Director, Image Resource Center:
  Melinda Reo
Illustrator: Electra Graphics
Production/Formatting/Art Manager:
  Guy Ruggiero
Electronic Art Creation: Maria Piper
Director of Marketing:
  Beth Gillett Mejia
Marketing Manager: Jeff Hester
Marketing Assistant: Ron Fox

Photo and text credits appear on pp. 731–734, which constitute a
continuation of the copyright page.

This book was set in 10/12.5 Sabon by TSI Graphics and was printed and bound
by RR Donnelley & Sons Company. The cover was printed by Phoenix Color Corp.

© 2003, 2000 by Pearson Education, Inc.
Upper Saddle River, New Jersey 07458

Printed in the United States of America
10 9 8 7 6 5 4 3 2 1

ISBN 0-13-098263-6

Pearson Education LTD., London
Pearson Education Australia PTY, Limited, Sydney
Pearson Education Singapore, Pte. Ltd
Pearson Education North Asia Ltd, Hong Kong
Pearson Education Canada, Ltd., Toronto
Pearson Educaión de Mexico, S. A. de C. V.
Pearson Education-Japan, Tokyo
Pearson Education Malaysia, Pte. Ltd

Contents at a Glance

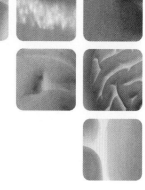

Contents

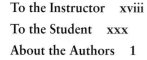

Part Two   Biology and Behavior

3   Evolution, Genes, and Behavior   68

4   Neurons, Hormones, and the Brain   100

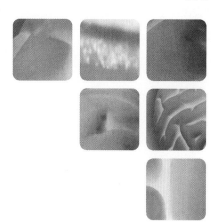

5 Body Rhythms and Mental States   140

6 Sensation and Perception   180

Part Three   The Environment and Behavior

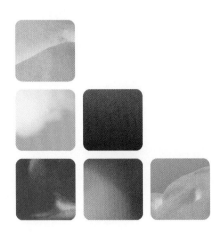

7 Learning and Conditioning   228

10 Memory 352

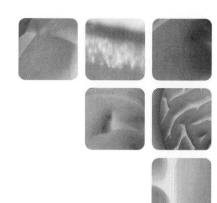

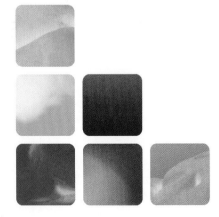

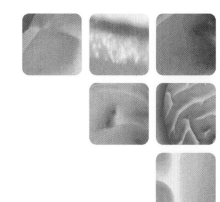

Part Six   Health and Disorder

15   Health, Stress, and Coping   548

16   Psychological Disorders   578

17 Approaches to Treatment and Therapy 620

Epilogue 655

To the Instructor

When we began work on the first edition of this textbook in the mid-1980s, we had five goals, some of which then were considered quite daring: (1) to make critical thinking integral to the introductory psychology course; (2) to represent psychology as the study of *all* human beings by mainstreaming research on culture and gender; (3) to keep ahead of the curve in coverage of new research and directions in the field; (4) to acknowledge forthrightly the many controversies in psychology; and (5) to foster active learning, so that students would become involved with the material and see how it applies to their personal and social lives.

Thinking Critically about Critical Thinking

Our first ambition, unique to textbooks at the time, was to get students to reflect on what they were learning—to show them what it is like to think like a psychologist. Psychology is not just a body of knowledge; it is also a way of approaching and analyzing the world. From the beginning, therefore, our approach has been based on critical thinking, the understanding that knowledge is advanced when people resist leaping to conclusions on the basis of personal experience alone (so tempting in psychological matters), when they apply rigorous standards of evidence, and when they listen to competing views. Because many students equate the word "critical" with "negative," we later added an emphasis on the creative, forward-moving aspects of critical thinking—the importance of generating alternative explanations of events, asking questions, and using one's imagination.

In a textbook, true critical thinking cannot be reduced to a set of rhetorical questions or to a formula for analyzing studies; it is a process that must be woven seamlessly into the narrative. The primary way we "do" critical and creative thinking, therefore, is by modeling it in our evaluations of research and popular ideas. In this book, we encourage critical thinking about concepts that many students approach uncritically, such as astrology, "premenstrual syndrome," and the "instinctive" nature of sexuality. And we also apply it to some ideas that many psychologists have

Thinking Critically and Creatively about Psychological Issues

ASK QUESTIONS; BE WILLING TO WONDER
After the collapse of the World Trade Center, rescuers like this one inspired millions by searching tirelessly to find survivors. Why do some people risk their lives to help their fellow human beings, whereas others watch from the sidelines? Social psychologists explore these and many other questions raised by the events of September 11, 2001, as we will see in Chapter 8.

DEFINE YOUR TERMS
People refer to intelligence all the time, but what is it exactly? Does the musical genius of a world-class violinist like Anne-Sophie Mutter count as intelligence? Is intelligence captured by an IQ score, or does it also include wisdom and practical "smarts"? We will consider some answers in Chapter 9.

EXAMINE THE EVIDENCE
When demonstrating "levitation" and other supposedly magical phenomena, illusionists such as André Kole exploit people's tendency to trust the evidence of their own eyes even when such evidence is misleading, as discussed in Chapter 6.

ANALYZE ASSUMPTIONS AND BIASES
Many North Americans assume that men are by nature less emotionally expressive than women. But this Palestinian man, grieving over his dead son, does not fit Western stereotypes of male emotionality. Cultural rules have a powerful influence on how men and women express their feelings, as we will see in Chapter 11.

accepted unquestioningly, such as the decisive importance of childhood to later life, Maslow's motivational hierarchy, and the disease model of addiction. By probing beneath assumptions and presenting the most recent evidence, we hope to convey the excitement and open-ended nature of psychological research and inquiry.

The first chapter starts with an extended discussion of what critical thinking is and what it isn't, and why critical thought is particularly relevant to the study of psychology. Here we introduce eight **guidelines to critical thinking,** which we draw on throughout the text as we evaluate research and popular ideas. (These guidelines are also listed and described briefly on the inside front cover of the book.)

Many, though by no means all, of our critical-thinking discussions are signaled by the lightbulb symbol shown in the margin, along with "signposts" containing provocative questions. We have explicitly identified the relevant guidelines in each signpost so that students can see more easily how the guidelines are actually applied. *The questions in the signposts are not, in themselves, illustrations of critical thinking;* rather, they serve as pointers to critical analyses in the text and invite the reader into the discussion.

> **THINKING CRITICALLY**
> **Avoid Emotional Reasoning**
>
> Many people get upset at the idea that their earliest experiences are lost to memory and angrily insist that memories from the first two years must be true. How can research help us think clearly about this issue?

Mainstreaming Culture, Gender, and Biology

Of course, all introductory textbooks are divided into chapters that cover particular topics or subfields, such as the brain, emotion, developmental psychology, and social psychology. Increasingly, however, some areas of investigation can no longer be squeezed into a single chapter, because they are relevant to topics throughout the course. This is especially true of findings from the "bookends" of human behavior—culture and biology—as well as research on gender.

At the time of our first edition, some considered our goal of incorporating research on gender and culture into introductory psychology to be quite radical—either a sop to political correctness or a fluffy and superficial fad. Today, the issue is no longer whether to include these topics, but how best to do it. From the beginning, our own answer has been to include studies of gender and culture in the main body of the text, wherever they are relevant to the larger discussion, rather than relegating these studies to an intellectual ghetto of separate chapters or boxed features.

> **Gender**
>
> **For examples of how we treat gender issues, see our discussions of:**
> - Evolutionary theories of sexual behavior (pp. 82–86)
> - Sex differences in the brain (pp. 132–134)
> - Gender and emotion (pp. 417–421)
> - Weight and eating disorders in women and men (pp. 432–435)
> - Male-female similarities in moral reasoning (p. 521)

Gender. We cover many kinds of gender differences in this book—differences in pain perception, sexual attitudes and motives, body satisfaction, depression, antisocial personality disorder, children's play preferences, and ways of expressing love, intimacy, and emotion, to mention just a few. (You will find many other gender-related topics in the index.) We do not equate "gender" with "women," either! We have been particularly attentive to research on the psychology of men, for example in discussing the underdiagnosis of male depression and the rise of eating disorders and distorted body images in young men. In many cases, we have tried to go beyond mere description of differences, by examining competing explanations for them: biological influences, evolutionary influences, social roles, gender socialization, gender schemas, and the power of current situations and experiences to shape people's choices and lives.

Nor do we focus exclusively on gender *differences.* Many differences, though reliable, are trivial in terms of real-life importance. And gender *similarities,* though they are often overlooked, are every bit as important and interesting as the eternal search for differences. We therefore include findings on similarities, too—for example, that men and women do not, overall, differ in moral reasoning (Chapter 14), obedience to authority (Chapter 8), or mood swings in the course of an average month (Chapter 5).

Culture. In recent years—and certainly in the aftermath of 9/11—most psychologists have come to appreciate the profound influence of culture on all aspects of life, from nonverbal behavior to the deepest attitudes towards how the world should be. Thus we report empirical findings about culture and ethnicity throughout the book—for example, in our discussions of addiction, anxiety symptoms, differing cultural norms (e.g., for cleanliness, risk, and conversational distance), emotional expression, group differences in IQ scores and academic achievement, motivational conflicts, personality, psychotherapy, rules about time, attitudes toward weight and the ideal body, and the effectiveness of medication. (Again, we refer you to the index for a complete listing of topics.) In addition, Chapter 8 highlights the sociocultural perspective in psychology and includes extended discussions of ethnocentrism, prejudice, and cross-cultural relations. However, the scientific study of cultural diversity is not synonymous with the popular movement called multiculturalism. The study of culture, in our view, should increase students' understanding of what culture means, how and why ethnic and national groups differ, and why no group is inherently better than another. Thus we try to apply critical thinking to our own coverage of culture, avoiding the twin temptations of ethnocentrism and stereotyping.

> **Culture**
>
> **For examples of how we treat culture, see our discussions of:**
>
> - Ethnocentrism and stereotyping (pp. 292–295)
> - Attitudes toward achievement (pp. 340, 477)
> - Cultural influences on personality (pp. 480–485)
> - Ethnic identity and acculturation (pp. 531–533)
> - Addiction rates and drug abuse (pp. 603–604)

Biology. Anyone who is awake and conscious knows that we are in the midst of a biomedical revolution that is transforming science and psychology. Findings from the Human Genome Project, studies of behavioral genetics, astonishing discoveries about the brain, the development of technologies such as PET scans and fMRIs, the proliferation of medications for psychological disorders—all have had a profound influence on our understanding of human behavior and on interventions to help people with chronic problems. This work, too, can no longer be confined to a single chapter; accordingly, we report new findings from the biological front wherever they are relevant: for example, in our discussions of neurogenesis in the brain, memory, emotion, stress, child development, aging, mental illness, personality, and many other topics (again, we refer you to the index for a full list). But just as we do with culture and gender, we apply principles of critical thinking to this domain of research, too. Thus we caution students about the dangers of reducing complex behaviors solely to biology, overgeneralizing from limited data, failing to consider other explanations, and oversimplifying solutions (e.g., as promises of "miracle" drugs often do).

> **Biology**
>
> **For examples of how we cover biological research, see our discussions of:**
>
> - Stem cells and neurogenesis (pp. 108–109)
> - Weight and body shape (pp. 428–435)
> - Sexual desire, orientation, and behavior (pp. 440–443, 447–448)
> - Genetics and personality (pp. 471–474, 479)
> - Schizophrenia (pp. 612–614)

Facing the Controversies

Psychology has always been full of lively, sometimes angry, debates, and we feel that students should not be sheltered from them. They are what make psychology so interesting! Sociobiologists and feminist psychologists often differ

> **Controversies**
>
> **For examples of our in-depth treatment of important controversies in psychology, see our discussions of:**
>
> - The contributions and limitations of evolutionary psychology (pp. 72–86)
> - The extent of parental influence on children's personalities (pp. 474–476)
> - The adult repercussions of childhood abuse and trauma (pp. 541–543)
> - Medication in the treatment of psychological disorders (pp. 624–627)
> - The "scientist–practitioner gap" (pp. 639–640, 646–648)

strongly in their analyses of gender relations (Chapters 3 and 12). Psychodynamic clinicians and experimental psychologists differ strongly in their assumptions about memory, child development, and trauma; these differences have heated repercussions for, among other things, "recovered memory" therapy and the questioning of children as eyewitnesses (Chapter 10). The "scientist–practitioner gap" between researchers and psychodynamic psychotherapists is continuing to widen (Chapter 17). Developmental psychologists are hotly debating the extent and limits of parental influence on children (Chapters 13 and 14). And psychologists continue to argue among themselves about the genetic and cultural origins of addiction, in a debate that has profound importance for the treatment of drug abuse (Chapters 5 and 16). In this book we candidly address these and other controversies, try to show why they are occurring, and suggest the kinds of questions that might lead to useful resolutions.

Applications and Active Learning: Getting Involved

Throughout this book, we have kept in mind one of the soundest findings about learning: that it requires the active encoding of material. You can't just sit there and expect it to happen. Several pedagogical features in particular encourage students to become actively involved in what they are reading.

What's Ahead consists of a brief set of questions introducing each major section within a chapter. These questions are not merely rhetorical; they are intended to be provocative and intriguing enough to arouse students' curiosity about the material to follow: Why are people all over the world getting fatter? What part of the anatomy do psychologists think is the "sexiest sex organ"? How are your beliefs about love affected by your income? What is the difference between ordinary techniques of persuasion and the coercive techniques used by cults? What is the "Big Lie"?

Looking Back, at the end of each chapter, lists all of the What's Ahead questions along with page numbers to show where the material for each question was covered. Students can check their retention and can easily review if they have trouble answering a question. This feature has another purpose as well: It gives students a sense of how much they are learning about matters of personal and social importance, and helps them appreciate that psychology offers more than "common sense." Some instructors may want to turn some of the Looking Back questions into essay or short-answer test items or written assignments.

Get Involved exercises in each chapter make active learning entertaining. Some consist of quick demonstrations (e.g., clasping your hands together to find out if you are genetically a "right thumb over left" person or the reverse). Some are simple mini-studies (e.g., observing seating patterns in the school cafeteria). Some help students relate

WHAT'S AHEAD

- Why does a note played on a flute sound different from the same note played on an oboe?
- If you habitually listen to loud music through headphones, what kind of hearing impairment are you risking?
- To locate the source of a sound, why does it sometimes help to turn or tilt your head?

LOOKING BACK

- What kind of "code" in the nervous system helps explain why a pinprick and a kiss feel different? (p. 184)
- Why does your dog hear a "silent" doggie whistle when you can't? (p. 186)
- What kind of bias can influence whether you think you hear the phone ringing when you're in the shower? (pp. 186–187)
- What happens when people are deprived of all external sensory stimulation? (pp. 187–188)
- How does the eye differ from a camera? (pp. 193–194)
- Why can we describe a color as bluish green but not as reddish green? (p. 196)
- If you were blind in one eye, why might you misjudge your distance from a painting on the wall but not the distance to buildings a block away? (p. 199)
- As a friend approaches, her image on your retina grows larger; why do you continue to see her as the same size? (p. 200)
- Why are perceptual illusions so valuable to psychologists? (p. 202)
- Why does a note played on a flute sound different from the same note played on an oboe? (pp. 204–205)
- If you habitually listen to loud music through headphones, what kind of hearing impairment are you risking? (p. 206)

Get Involved

Thumbs Up!

Ask the members of your family, one person at a time, to clasp their hands together. Include aunts and uncles, grandparents—as many of your biological relatives as possible. Which thumb does each person put on top? About half of all people fold the left thumb over the right and about half fold the right thumb over the left, and these responses tend to run in families. Do your own relatives show one tendency over the other? (If your family is an adoptive one, of course, there is less chance of finding a trend.) Try the same exercise with someone else's family; do you get the same results? Even for behavior as simple as thumb folding, the details of how genes exert their effect remain uncertain (Jones, 1994).

course material to their own lives (e.g., if they drink, listing their own motives for doing so). Instructors may want to assign some of these exercises to the entire class and then discuss the results and what they might mean.

Conceptual graphics help students visualize material in order to understand and retain it better. Students can see at a glance, for example, the various types of attachment, distinctions between different types of memories, the difference between positive and negative reinforcement, the elements of successful therapy, and how a self-fulfilling prophecy is created. We have tried to keep these visual summaries simple, straightforward, and appealing.

Review tables summarize and contrast theories and approaches discussed in the text—for example, methods used in brain research, theories of dreaming, theories of personality, and the factors that lead to health or illness. The Reviews help students extract main points, organize what they have learned, and study for exams.

Quick Quizzes are periodic self-tests that encourage students to check their progress, and to go back and review if necessary. These quizzes do more than just test for memorization of definitions; they tell students whether they comprehend the issues. Mindful of the common tendency to skip quizzes or to peek at the answers, we have used various formats and have included engaging examples in order to motivate students to test themselves.

Many of the quizzes also include critical-thinking items, identified by the critical-thinking symbol. These items invite the student to reflect on the implications of findings and to consider how psychological principles might illuminate real-life issues. For example: What kinds of questions should a critical thinker ask about a new drug for depression? How might a hypothetical study of testosterone and hostility be improved? How should a critical consumer evaluate someone's claim that health is entirely a matter of "mind over matter"? Although we offer some answers to these questions, students may have valid, well-reasoned answers that differ from our own.

Other pedagogical features designed to help students study and learn better include a **running glossary** that defines boldfaced technical terms on the pages where they occur; a **cumulative glossary** at the back of the book; a list of **key terms** at the end of each chapter that includes page numbers so students can find the sections where the terms are first mentioned; **chapter outlines**; and **chapter summaries** in paragraph form to help students review.

Taking Psychology with You, a feature that concludes each chapter, illustrates the practical implications of psychological research for individuals, groups, institutions, and society. This feature tackles topics of personal interest and relevance to many students, such as managing pain (Chapter 6), getting along with people from other cultures (Chapter 8), managing anger (Chapter 11), rearing children (Chapter 14), and assessing self-help books (Chapter 17).

The final "Taking Psychology with You" feature in the book is an **Epilogue**, a unique effort to show students that the vast number of seemingly disparate studies and points of view they have just read about are related. The Epilogue deals with a typical problem that everyone can be expected to encounter:

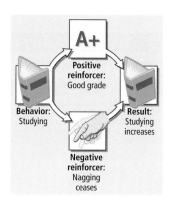

REVIEW 1.2 FIVE MAJOR PSYCHOLOGICAL PERSPECTIVES

Perspective		Major Topics of Study	Sample Finding on Violence
Biological		The nervous system, hormones, brain chemistry, heredity, evolutionary influences	Brain damage caused by birth complications or child abuse might incline some people toward violence.
Learning		Environment and experience	
	Behavioral	Environmental determinants of observable behavior	Violence increases when it pays off.
	Social-cognitive	Environmental influences, observation and imitation, beliefs and values	Violent role models can influence some children to behave aggressively.
Cognitive		Thinking, memory, language, problem solving, perceptions	Violent people are often quick to perceive provocation and insult.
Sociocultural		Social and cultural contexts	
	Social Psychology	Social rules and roles, groups, relationships	People are often more aggressive in a crowd than they would be on their own.
	Cultural Psychology	Cultural norms, values, and expectations	Cultures based on herding rather than agriculture tend to train boys to be aggressive.
Psychodynamic		Unconscious thoughts, desires, and conflicts	A man who murders prostitutes may have unconscious conflicts about his mother and about sexuality.

QUICK QUIZ

Is all this information about eating making you hungry for knowledge?

1. *True or false:* Emotional problems explain why fat people are heavy.
2. Falling and rising levels of leptin help the brain regulate appetite and _____ and play a role in maintaining a person's genetically influenced _____.
3. Rising rates of obesity can best be explained by (a) genetic changes over the past few decades, (b) a lack of will power, (c) an abundance of high-fat food and sedentary lifestyles, (d) the increase in eating disorders.
4. Bill, who is thin, reads in the newspaper that genes set the range of body weight and shape. "Oh, good," he exclaims, "now I can eat all the junk food I want; I was born to be skinny." What's wrong with Bill's conclusion?

Answers:

1. false 2. metabolism, set point 3. c 4. Bill is right to recognize that there may be limits to how heavy he can become. But he may also be oversimplifying and jumping to conclusions. Many people who have a set point for leanness will gain considerable weight on fatty foods and excess calories, especially if they don't exercise. Also, rich junk food is unhealthy for reasons that have nothing to do with becoming overweight.

Taking Psychology with You

FOOD FOR THOUGHT: DIET AND NEUROTRANSMITTERS

"Vitamin improves sex!" "Sugar makes kids wild!" "Chocolate chases the blues!" Claims like these have given nutritional theories of behavior a bad reputation. In the late 1960s, when Nobel laureate Linus Pauling proposed treating some mental disorders with mas- sive doses of vitamins, few researchers lis- tened. Mainstream medical authorities classified Pauling's vitamin therapy with such infamous cure-alls as snake oil and leeches.

Today, most mental-health profes- sionals remain skeptical of nutritional cures for mental illness. But the under- lying premise of nutritional treat- ments, that diet affects the brain and therefore behavior, is no longer con- sidered a loony idea. Diet may indeed make a difference in cognitive function and in some types of disorders. In one

conflicts in a close relationship. We show how topics discussed in previous chapters can be applied to understanding and cop- ing with such conflicts. The Epilogue can be a useful tool for helping students inte- grate the diverse approaches of contempo- rary psychology. Asking students to come up with research findings that might apply to other problems also makes for a good term paper assignment.

A Note to Users of Previous Editions

We have added up-to-date research in every chapter, from the latest findings on neu- ronal growth throughout life to new theories of schizophrenia. We have also made a few organizational changes, such as moving the discussion of weight and obesity from the genetics chapter (Chapter 3) to the motivation chapter (Chapter 12). As for content updates, a detailed explanation of all deletions, additions, and modifications in the Seventh Edition is available to adopters of the Sixth Edition, so that no one will have to guess why we made particular changes. We hope this support will make the transition from one edition to the next as painless for instructors as possible. You can obtain this description from your Prentice Hall representative or by writing to: Marketing Manager, Psychology, Prentice Hall Publishers, One Lake Street, Upper Saddle River, New Jersey 07458.

Instructor and Student Supplements

Psychology, Seventh Edition's supplements package has gone through extensive re- vision and refinement to provide you and your students with the best teaching and learning materials, both in print and media formats.

Print and Media Supplements for the Instructor

NEW Instructor's Resource Binder Created by Barbara Brown of Georgia Perimeter College, Kerri Goodwin of Loyola College, and Alan Swinkles of St. Edwards University, this exhaustive collection of resources will appeal to new and experienced instructors alike. Each chapter in the IRB includes the following resources, organized in an easy-to-reference Keyed Chapter Outline: Introducing the Chapter; Learning Objectives; Lecture Suggestions and Discussion Topics; Class- room Activities, Demonstrations, and Exercises; Out-of-Class Assignments and Pro- jects; Multimedia Resources; Video Resources; Transparencies; and Handouts. Designed to make your lectures more effective and to save you preparation time, this comprehensive set of materials gathers together the most effective activities and strategies for teaching your introductory psychology course.

NEW Media Portfolio CD-ROM Included with the Instructor's Resource Binder, this valuable, time-saving supplement provides you with a wealth of teach- ing resources in one place so that you may customize your lecture notes and media presentations. It includes PowerPoint slides customized for the Seventh Edition, electronic versions of the artwork in the text chapters, electronic versions of the overhead transparencies, and electronic files for the material in the Instructor's Resource Binder and the Test Item File. It also contains clips from Prentice Hall's Video Classics in Psychology CD-ROM, formatted for in-class presentation.

Test Item File Created by Kathleen McGreal of Michigan State University, this test bank contains over 4,500 multiple-choice, true/false, and short-answer essay questions. For each question, there is a reference to the relevant section and page number in the text; a key designating each item as easy, moderate, or difficult; and a descriptor of the question as factual, conceptual, or applied.

Prentice Hall's Custom Test for Windows and Macintosh Now available on one dual-platform CD-ROM, this best-selling test-generating software program includes a gradebook, online network testing capability, and many tools to help you edit and create tests. The program comes with full technical support and telephone "Request a Test" service.

PowerPoint Slides for Psychology, Seventh Edition Created by Krista Forrest of the University of Nebraska at Kearny, these slides highlight the key points covered in the text. They are provided in two versions, one with the chapter graphics and one without, to give you flexibility in preparing your lectures. Available on the *Media Portfolio* CD-ROM or on Prentice Hall's **PsychologyCentral** Web site described below.

NEW Prentice Hall's Introductory Psychology Transparencies, 2002 Designed to be used in large lecture settings, this set of over 130 full-color transparencies includes illustrations from the text as well as images from a variety of other sources. Available in acetate form, online at **PsychologyCentral,** or on the *Media Portfolio* CD-ROM.

NEW PsychologyCentral Web Site at www.prenhall.com/psychology Password protected for instructors' use only, this site allows you online access to all of Prentice Hall's psychology supplements. You'll find a multitude of resources for teaching introductory psychology. From this site you can download any of the key supplements available for *Psychology, Seventh Edition,* including the following: Instructor's Resource Binder, Test Item File, PowerPoint slides, chapter graphics, and electronic versions of the Introductory Psychology Transparencies, 2002. Contact your Prentice Hall representative for the user ID and password to access this site.

Online Course Management with WebCT, BlackBoard or Course-Compass This feature is *free* upon adoption of the text. Instructors interested in using online course management have their choice of options. Each version comes preloaded with text-specific quizzes and tests and can be fully customized for your course. Contact your Prentice Hall representative or visit **www.prenhall.com/demo** for more information.

Video Resources for Instructors

NEW Prentice Hall Custom Video for Introductory Psychology Adopters can receive this new videotape, which includes five- to eight-minute clips covering all major topics in introductory psychology. The videos have been carefully selected from the *Films for Humanities and Sciences* library, and then edited to provide brief and compelling video content for enhancing your lectures. Contact your local Prentice Hall representative for a full list of video clips on this tape.

The Brain Video Series Qualified adopters can select videos from this series of eight, 1-hour programs that blend interviews with world-famous brain scientists and dramatic reenactments of landmark cases in medical history. Programs include

The Enlightened Machine; The Two Brains; Vision and Movement; Madness; Rhythms and Drives; States of Mind; Stress and Emotion; and Learning and Memory. Contact your local representative for more details.

The Discovering Psychology *Video Series* Qualified adopters can select videos from this series produced in association with the American Psychological Association. The series includes thirteen tapes, each containing two half-hour segments. Contact your local sales representative for a list of videos.

ABC News Videos for Introductory Psychology, Series III Qualified adopters can obtain this selection of segments from ABC's *World News Tonight* with Peter Jennings, *Nightline, 20/20, Prime Time Live,* and *The Health Show.*

Films for the Humanities and Sciences *Video Library* Qualified adopters can select videos on various topics in psychology from the extensive library of *Films for the Humanities and Sciences.* Contact your local sales representative for a list of videos.

Print and Media Supplements for the Student

Companion Web Site at www.prenhall.com/wade Designed to reinforce student learning, this online study guide allows students to review each chapter's material, take practice tests, research topics for course projects, and more. The *Psychology, Seventh Edition* companion Web site includes the following resources for each chapter: Chapter Objectives; Interactive Lectures; five different types of quizzes that provide immediate, text-specific feedback and coaching comments; WebEssays; WebDestinations; NetSearch; *NEW* FlashCards; and *NEW Live!Psych* Media Labs (described below). Access to the *Psychology, Seventh Edition* Web site is free and available to all students.

NEW Live!Psych Media Labs This series of 33 interactive media simulations, animations, and assessments was developed to teach key concepts—often the concepts students find most challenging. Designed to get students to interact with the material and to appeal to different learning styles, these *Live!Psych* Media Labs were created in consultation with psychology instructors and carefully reviewed by a board of experts to ensure accuracy and pedagogical effectiveness. Each *Live!Psych* Media Lab is integrated into the presentation of the text material through the use of the *Live!Psych* icon. Chapter-specific *Live!Psych* Media Labs can be found on the Companion Website at **www.prenhall.com/wade.** A special thank you goes to Lynne Blesz-Vestal, the content author, and to the members of our *Live!Psych* review board: Kim Ainsworth-Darnell (Georgia State University); Eric J. Chudler (University of Washington); Margaret Gatz (University of Southern California); Karen Hoblit (Victoria Community College); Gail Knapp (Mott Community College); John Krantz (Hanover College); Nancy Simpson (Trident Technical College); and Chuck Slem (California Polytechnic State University, San Luis Obispo).

NEW Video Classics in Psychology CD-ROM: Using the power of video to clarify key concepts presented in the text, this CD-ROM offers original footage of some of the best-known classic experiments in psychology. It shows, among other things, Milgram's obedience study, Watson's Little Albert, Bandura's Bobo doll experiment, Pavlov's dog, and Harlow's monkeys. In addition, students can see interviews with renowned contributors to the field, such as B.F. Skinner, Carl Rogers, and Erik Erikson. Each video is preceded by background information on the importance of the experiment or researcher, and is followed by questions that connect the video to concepts presented in the text. The ***Video Classics in Psychology*** CD-ROM can be packaged free with *Psychology, Seventh Edition*. Contact your local sales representative for the value pack ISBN.

NEW Prentice Hall Guide to Evaluating Online Resources: Psychology, 2003 This guide provides students with a hands-on introduction to the Internet, features numerous Web sites related to psychology, and gives students guidelines on how to evaluate online resources. It now comes with *free* access to **ContentSelect,** a customized research database for students of psychology. Created by Prentice Hall and EBSCO, the world leader in online journal subscription management, this site provides students access to many peer-reviewed publications and popular periodicals in psychology.

Study Guide Written by Jody Davis of California State University, Fullerton and Jeffrey Green of Soka University, this student study guide helps students master the core concepts presented in each chapter. Each chapter of the guide includes learning objectives, a brief chapter summary, a preview outline of the text chapter, and three different practice tests.

Mind Matters CD-ROM: Free when packaged with a new text, *Mind Matters* features interactive learning modules on history, methods, biological psychology, learning, memory, sensation and perception. Each module combines text, video, graphics, simulations, games and assessment to reinforce key psychological concepts.

Supplementary Texts

Contact your Prentice Hall representative to package any of these supplementary texts with *Psychology, Seventh Edition* at a reduced price:

Psychobabble and Biobunk, Second Edition by Carol Tavris. This expanded and updated collection of opinion essays written for *The Los Angeles Times, The New York Times, Scientific American,* and other publications encourages debate in the classroom by applying psychological research and the principles of scientific and critical thinking to issues in the news.

Forty Studies that Changed Psychology, Fourth Edition by Roger Hock (Mendocino College). Presenting the seminal research studies that have shaped modern psychological study, this brief supplement provides an overview of the environment that gave rise to each study, its experimental design, its findings, and its impact on current thinking in the discipline.

The Psychology Major: Careers and Strategies for Success by Eric Landrum (Idaho State University), Stephen Davis (Emporia State University), and Terri Landrum (Idaho State University). This 160-page paperback provides valuable information on career options available to psychology majors, tips for improving academic performance, and a guide to the APA style of research reporting.

Experiencing Psychology by Gary Brannigan (State University of New York at Plattsburgh). This hands-on activity book contains 39 active learning experiences corresponding to major topics in psychology to provide students with hands-on experience in "doing" psychology.

How to Think Like a Psychologist: Critical Thinking in Psychology, Second Edition by Donald McBurney (University of Pittsburgh). This unique supplementary text uses a question-answer format to explore some of the most common questions students ask about psychology.

Acknowledgments

Like any other cooperative effort, writing a textbook requires a support team. We are indebted to the following reviewers and consultants, who made many valuable suggestions during the development of this and previous editions of *Psychology*. (Please note that affiliations of some individuals may have changed since they reviewed our book.)

Benton E. Allen, *Mt. San Antonio College*

Susan M. Andersen, *University of California, Santa Barbara*

Lynn R. Anderson, *Wayne State University*

Emir Andrews, *Memorial University of Newfoundland*

Richard Anglin, *Oklahoma City Community College*

Alan Auerbach, *Wilfrid Laurier University*

Lynn Haller Augsbach, *Morehead State University*

Harold Babb, *Binghamton University*

Brian C. Babbitt, *Missouri Southern State College*

MaryAnn Baenninger, *Trenton State College*

Patricia Barker, *Schenectady County Community College*

Ronald K. Barrett, *Loyola Marymount University*

Allan Basbaum, *University of California, San Francisco*

Carol Batt, *Sacred Heart University*

William M. Baum, *University of New Hampshire*

Gordon Bear, *Ramapo College of New Jersey*

Peter A. Beckett, *Youngstown State University*

Bill E. Beckwith, *University of North Dakota*

Helen Bee, *Madison, Wisconsin*

David F. Berger, *SUNY at Cortland*

Michael Bergmire, *Jefferson College*

Philip J. Bersh, *Temple University*

Randolph Blake, *Vanderbilt University*

Richard Bowen, *Loyola University of Chicago*

Laura L. Bowman, *Kent State University*

Edward N. Brady, *Belleville Area College*

Ann Brandt-Williams, *Glendale Community College*

John R. Braun, *University of Bridgeport*

Sharon S. Brehm, *SUNY at Binghamton*

Sylvester Briggs, *Kent State University*

Gwen Briscoe, *College of Mt. St. Joseph*

Barbara L. Brown, *Georgia Perimeter College*

Robert C. Brown, Jr., *Georgia State University*

Linda L. Brunton, *Columbia State Community College*

Stephen R. Buchanan, *University of South Carolina, Union*

Peter R. Burzvnski, *Vincennes University*

Frank Calabrese, *Community College of Philadelphia*

Jean Caplan, *Concordia University*

Bernardo J. Carducci, *Indiana University Southeast*

Sally S. Carr, *Lakeland Community College*

Michael Catchpole, *North Island College*

Paul Chance, *Seaford, Delaware*

Herbert H. Clark, *Stanford University*

Job B. Clément, *Daytona Beach Community College*

Samuel Clement, *Marianopolis College*

Eva Conrad, *San Bernardino Valley College*

Richard L. Cook, *University of Colorado*

Robert Cormack, *New Mexico Institute of Mining and Technology*

Wendi Cross, *Ohio University*

David Crystal, *Georgetown University*

Gaylen Davidson-Podgorny, *Santa Rosa Junior College*

Robert M. Davis, *Purdue University School of Science, IUPUI*

Michael William Decker, *University of California, Irvine*

Geri Anne Dino, *Frostburg State University*

Thomas Estrella, *Lourdes College*

Susan H. Evans, *University of Southern California*

Fred Fahringer, *Southwest Texas State University*

Ronald Finke, *SUNY at Stony Brook*

Deborah Finkel, *Indiana University Southeast*

John H. Flowers, *University of Nebraska Lincoln*

William F. Ford, *Bucks County Community College*

Donald G. Forgays, *University of Vermont*

Sheila Francis, *Creighton University*

William Rick Fry, *Youngstown University*

Charles A. Fuller, *University of California, Davis*

Grace Galliano, *Kennesaw State College*

Mary Gauvain, *Oregon State University*

Ron Gerrard, *SUNY at Oswego*

David Gersh, *Houston Community College*

Jessica B. Gillooly, *Glendale Community College*

Margaret Gittis, *Youngstown State University*

Carlos Goldberg, *Indiana University-Purdue University at Indianapolis*

Carol Grams, *Orange Coast College*

Patricia Greenfield, *University of California, Los Angeles*

Richard A. Griggs, *University of Florida*

Sarmi Gulgoz, *Auburn University*

Robert Guttentag, *University of North Carolina, Greensboro*

Jimmy G. Hale, *McLennan Community College*

Pryor Hale, *Piedmont Virginia Community College*

Len Hamilton, *Rutgers University*

Constance Hammen, *University of California, Los Angeles*

George Hampton, *University of Houston*

Eddie Harmon-Jones, *University of Wisconsin, Madison*

Algea Harrison, *Oakland University*

Elaine Hatfield, *University of Hawaii*

Neil Helgeson, *The University of Texas at San Antonio*

John E. Hesson, *Metropolitan State College*

Robert Higgins, *Oakland Community College*

John P. Hostetler, *Albion College*

Kenneth I. Howard, *Northwestern University*

Allen Huffcutt, *Bradley University*

John Hunsley, *University of Ottawa*

William G. Iacono, *University of Minnesota*

David E. Irwin, *University of Illinois*

Andrew Johnson, *Park University*

David A. Johnson, *Ohio University*

James Johnson, *University of North Carolina at Wilmington*

Robert D. Johnson, *Arkansas State University*

Timothy P. Johnston, *University of North Carolina at Greensboro*

Susan Joslyn, *University of Washington*

Chadwick Karr, *Portland State University*

Yoshito Kawahara, *San Diego Mesa College*

William Kelemen, *University of Missouri, St. Louis*

Michael C. Kennedy, *Allegheny University*

Geoffrey Keppel, *University of California, Berkeley*

Harold O. Kiess, *Framingham State College*

Gary King, *Rose State College*

Jack Kirschenbaum, *Fullerton College*

Donald Kline, *University of Calgary*

Stephen M. Kosslyn, *Harvard University*

Janet E. Keubli, *St. Louis University*

Michael J. Lambert, *Brigham Young University*

George S. Larimer, *West Liberty State College*

Herbert Leff, *University of Vermont*

Patricia Lefler, *Lexington Community College*

S. David Leonard, *University of Georgia*

Jacqueline Lerner, *Boston College*

Robert Levy, *Indiana State University*

Lewis Lieberman, *Columbus College*

Scott Lilienfeld, *Emory University*

R. Martin Lobdell, *Pierce College*

Walter J. Lonner, *Western Washington University*

Nina Lott, *National University*

Bonnie Lustigman, *Montclair State College*

Marlowe Mager, *Stanly Community College*

James E. Maddux, *George Mason University*

G. Alan Marlatt, *University of Washington*

Marc Marschark, *University of North Carolina at Greensboro*

Monique Martin, *Champlain Regional College*

Debra Moehle McCallum, *University of Alabama at Birmingham*

D. F. McCoy, *University of Kentucky*

C. Sue McCullough, *Texas Woman's University*

Elizabeth McDonel, *University of Alabama*

Susanne Wicks McKenzie, *Dawson College*

Mark B. McKinley, *Lorain County Community College*

Ronald K. McLaughlin, *Juniata College*

Frances K. McSweeney, *Washington State University*

Maty Jo Meadow, *Mankato State University*

Linda Mealey, *College of St. Benedict*

Ronald Melzack, *McGill University*

Dorothy Mercer, *Eastern Kentucky University*

Laura J. Metallo, *Five Towns College*

Daniel J. Miller, *Wayne State College*

Denis Mitchell, *University of Southern California*

Timothy H. Monk, *University of Pittsburgh Medical Center*

Maribel Montgomery, *Linn-Benton Community College*

Douglas G. Mook, *University of Virginia*

T. Mark Morey, *SUNY College at Oswego*

Joel Morgovsky, *Brookdale Community College*

Micah Mukabi, *Essex County College*

Sarah Murray, *Kwantlen University College, Vancouver*

James S. Nairne, *University of Texas at Arlington*

Michael Nash, *University of Tennessee, Knoxville*

Douglas Navarick, *California State University, Fullerton*

Robert A. Neimever, *University of Memphis*

Todd Nelson, *California State University, Stanislaus*

Nora Newcombe, *Temple University*

Jack Nitschke, *University of Wisconsin, Madison*

Linda Noble, *Kennesaw State College*

Keith Oatley, *Ontario Institute for Studies in Education, Toronto*

Peter Oliver, *University of Hartford*

Patricia Owen Smith, *Oxford College*

Elizabeth Weiss Ozorak, *Allegheny College*

David Page, *Nazareth College*

M. Carr Payne, Jr., *Georgia Institute of Technology*

Letitia Anne Peplau, *University of California, Los Angeles*

Dan G. Perkins, *Richland College*

Gregory Pezzetti, *Rancho Santiago Community College*

Robert Plomin, *Institute of Psychiatry, King's College London*

Wayne Poniewaz, *University of Arkansas, Monticello*

Debra Poole, *Central Michigan University*

Paula M. Popovich, *Ohio University*

Lyman Porter, *University of California, Irvine*

Robert Prochnow, *St. Cloud State University*

Janet Proctor, *Purdue University*

Richard L. Rapson, *University of Hawaii*

Eric Ravussin, *Obesity Research & Clinical Investigation, Lilly Research Laboratories*

Reginald L. Razzi, *Upsala College*

Sheena Rogers, *University of Wisconsin, Madison*

Jayne Rose, *Augustana State College*

Gary Ross-Reynolds, *Nicholls State University*

Peter J. Rowe, *College of Charleston*

Gerald Rubin, *Central Virginia Community College*

Joe Rubinstein, *Purdue University*

Karen P. Saenz, *Houston Community College, Southeast*

Nancy Sauerman, *Kirkwood Community College*

H. R. Schiffman, *Rutgers University*

Lisa Schneiter, *Jefferson Community College*

Lael Schooler, *Indiana University*

David A. Schroeder, *University of Arkansas*

Marvin Schwartz, *University of Cincinnati*

Shelley Schwartz, *Vanier College*

Joyce Segreto, *Youngstown State University*

Kimron Shapiro, *University of Calgary*

Phillip R. Shaver, *University of California, Davis*
Arthur Shimamura, *University of California, Berkeley*
Susan A. Shodahl, *San Bernardino Valley College*
Dale Simmons, *Oregon State University*
Art Skibbe, *Appalachian State University*
William P. Smotherman, *SUNY at Binghamton*
Samuel Snyder, *North Carolina State University*
Barbara A. Spellman, *University of Texas at Austin*
Larry R. Squire, *University of California, San Diego*
Granville L. Sydnor, *San Jacinto College North*
Tina Stern, *Georgia Perimeter College*
A. Stirling, *John Abbott College*
Milton E. Strauss, *Johns Hopkins University*
Judith Sugar, *Colorado State University*
Shelley E. Taylor, *University of California, Los Angeles*
Andrew Kurt Thaw, *Millsaps College*
Dennis C. Turk, *University of Washington*

Barbara Turpin, *Southwest Missouri State University*
Ronald J. Venhorst, *Kean College of New Jersey*
Wayne A. Viney, *Colorado State University*
Benjamin Wallace, *Cleveland State University*
Phyllis Walrad, *Macomb Community College*
Charles R. Walsmith, *Bellevue Community College*
Phillip Wann, *Missouri Western State College*
Thomas J. Weatherly, *DeKalb College-Central Campus*
Mary Wellman, *Rhode Island University*
Gary L. Wells, *University of Alberta*
Warner Wilson, *Wright State University*
Loren Wingblade, *Jackson Community College*
Judith K. Winters, *DeKalb College*
Rita S. Wolpert, *Caldwell College*
James M. Wood, *University of Texas at El Paso*
Phyllis Zee, *Northwestern University Medical School*

We are also grateful to the many talented and hardworking people who were involved in planning and producing this edition of *Psychology*. Our special thanks go to our inspiring and skilled senior acquisitions editor, Jennifer Gilliland, and to development editor Leslie Carr for their enormously helpful and insightful editorial suggestions during this revision. Editorial assistant Nicole Girrbach made our lives so much easier, thanks to her meticulous attention to detail and speedy response to all our requests. And our heartfelt appreciation to our calm and brilliantly organized production editor, Maureen Richardson, for so accurately and efficiently coordinating the book's many elements (including its authors) through production. We also thank executive marketing manager Sheryl Adams and psychology marketing manager Jeff Hester for their innovative contributions to the launching of this edition.

We are beholden to the art and production team at Prentice Hall for creating this beautiful edition. Our special thanks to art director Ximena Tamvakopoulos, interior designer Tom Nery, and electronic artist Maria Piper for their artistic contributions to the overall appearance of the book. Photo researcher Barbara Salz earned our undying gratitude because of her genius at finding knockout photographs and cartoons. We would like to applaud our copy editors Kathryn Beck and Kathryn Graehl for their guidance with our prose, and permissions specialist Tracy Metivier for her quick and efficient handling of all permission-related matters. And our special kudos to Connie Blacker and her formatting team at TSI Graphics, who did the layouts with their usual unsurpassed care and attention to quality.

Finally, our thanks and affection to Jennifer Bass, daughter of the late Saul Bass, for permission to use the stunning cover image created by her father, who designed the award-winning covers and distinctive look of our textbook.

Most of all, we once again thank our patient partners, Howard Williams and Ronan O'Casey, who from the first edition to this one have bolstered us with their love, sense of humor, and good cheer as we battled deadlines.

We have enjoyed writing this book, and we hope you will enjoy reading and using it. Your questions, comments, and reactions on earlier editions helped us make many improvements. Please let us hear from you.

Carole Wade
Carol Tavris

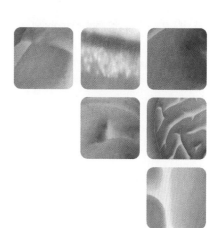

To the Student

I f you are reading this introduction, you are starting your introductory psychology course on the right foot. It is always a good idea to get a general picture of what you are about to read before charging forward.

Our goal in writing this book is to guide you to think critically and imaginatively about psychological issues, and to help you apply what you learn to your own life and the world around you. We ourselves have never gotten over our initial excitement about psychology, and we have done everything we can think of to make the field as absorbing for you as it is for us. However, what you bring to this book is as important as what we have written—we can pitch ideas to you, but you have to step up to the plate to connect with them. This text will remain only a collection of pages with ink on them unless you choose to read actively.

Getting Involved

To encourage you to read and study actively, we have included some special features.

In the first chapter, we will introduce you to the basic guidelines of **critical and creative thinking**—the principles we hope will help you learn the difference between unsupported claims or "psychobabble" and good, scientific reasoning. The identifying symbol for critical thinking is a lightbulb, like the one in the margin. Throughout the book, some (but not all) of our **critical-thinking discussions** are signaled by a "signpost" in the margin that includes this lightbulb and one of the critical-thinking guidelines. We will be telling you about many lively and passionate debates in psychology—over gender differences, psychotherapy, memory, multiple personality disorder, and many other topics—and we hope our coverage of these debates will increase your involvement with the ongoing discoveries of psychology.

Before each major section in a chapter, a feature called **What's Ahead** lists some preview questions designed to stir your curiosity and give you an overview of what the section will cover. For example: Why does paying children for good grades sometimes backfire? Do people remember better when they're hypnotized? Do men and women differ in the ability to love? When you finish the chapter, you will encounter these questions again, under the heading **Looking Back.** Use this list as a self-test; if you can't answer a question, you can go to the page indicated after the question and review the material.

Each chapter also contains several **Get Involved** exercises, entertaining little experiments or explorations you can do that relate to what you are reading about. In Chapter 3, for instance, you can find out immediately whether you are genetically disposed to cross your right thumb over your left or vice versa when you clasp your hands together; and in Chapter 11 you can find out how your own thoughts affect your emotions. Some of these exercises take only a minute; others are "mini-studies" that you can do by observing or interviewing others.

Every chapter contains several **Quick Quizzes** that permit you to test your understanding and retention of what you have just read and give you practice in applying the material to examples. Do not let the word "quiz" give you a sinking feeling. These quizzes are for your practical use and, we hope, for your enjoyment. When you have trouble with a question, do not go on; pause right then and there, review what you have read, and then try again.

Some of the Quick Quizzes contain a *critical-thinking item,* denoted by the light-bulb symbol. The answers we give for these items are only suggestions; feel free to come up with different ones. Quick Quizzes containing critical-thinking questions are not really so quick, because they ask you to reflect on what you have read and to apply the guidelines to critical thinking that are introduced in Chapter 1. But if you take the time to respond thoughtfully to them, we think you will learn more and become a more sophisticated user of psychology.

At the end of each chapter, a feature called **Taking Psychology with You** draws on research to suggest ways you can apply what you have learned to everyday problems and concerns, such as how to improve your memory or get a better night's sleep, as well as more urgent ones, such as how to live with chronic pain or help a friend who seems suicidal. The very last "Taking Psychology with You," at the end of the book, is an **Epilogue** that shows how you might integrate and use the findings and theories you have read about to solve problems in your own relationships.

How to Study

In our years of teaching, we have found that certain study strategies can vastly improve learning, and so we offer the following suggestions. (Reading Chapter 7, on learning, and Chapter 10, on memory, will also be helpful.)

Before you even start the book, we suggest you read the Table of Contents to get an overall view of the book's organization and coverage. Likewise, before starting a chapter, read the chapter title and outline to get an idea of what is in store. Browse through the chapter, looking at the pictures and reading the headings.

Do not try to read the text the same way you might read a novel, taking in large chunks at a sitting. To get the most from your studying, we recommend that you read only a part of each chapter at a time.

Instead of simply reading silently, nodding along saying "hmmmmm" to yourself, try to restate what you have read in your own words at the end of each major section. Some people find it helpful to write down main points. Others prefer to recite them aloud to someone else, or even to a patient pet. Do not count on getting by with just one reading of a chapter. Most people need to go through the material at least twice, and then revisit the main points several times before an exam. Special tables called **Reviews** will help you summarize, integrate, and compare psychological theories and approaches discussed in the chapter.

When you have finished a chapter, read the **Summary.** Use the list of **Key Terms** at the end of each chapter as a checklist. Try to define and discuss each term to see how well you understand and remember it. If you need to check your recall, the page number that follows each term refers you to the term's first mention in the chapter. Finally, go over the **Looking Back** questions to be sure you can answer them.

Important new terms in this textbook are printed in **boldface** and are defined in the margin of the page on which they appear, or on the facing page. The **marginal glossary** permits you to find all key terms and concepts easily, and will help you when you study for exams. A complete glossary appears at the end of the book.

The **Study Guide** for this book, available at your bookstore, is an excellent resource. It contains review material, exercises, and practice tests to help you understand and apply the concepts in the book.

If you are assigned a term project or a report, you may need to track down some references we provide or do further reading. Throughout the book, all studies and theories include *citations* in parentheses, like this: (Aardvark and Zebra, 2002). A citation tells you who the authors of a book, article, or paper are and when the work was published. The full reference can then be looked up in the alphabetical **bibliography** at the end of the book. At the back of the book you will also find a **name index** and a **subject index.** The name index lists the name of every author cited and the pages where the person's work is discussed. If you remember the name of a psychologist but not where he or she was mentioned, look for the person in the name index. The subject index lists all the major topics mentioned in the book. If you want to review material on, say, depression, you can look up "depression" in the subject index and find each place it is mentioned.

We have done our utmost to convey our own enthusiasm about psychology, but in the end, it is your efforts as much as ours that will determine whether you find psychology to be exciting or boring, and whether the field will matter in your own life. We welcome your ideas and reactions so that we will know what works for you and what doesn't. In the meantime, welcome to psychology!

Carole Wade

Carol Tavris

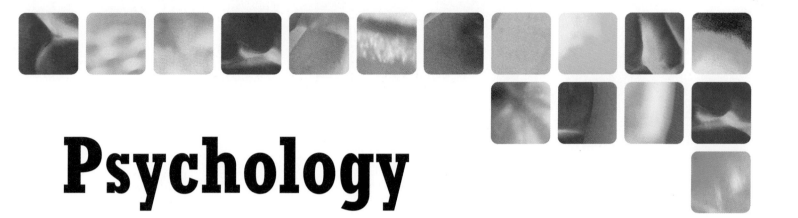

Psychology

About the Authors

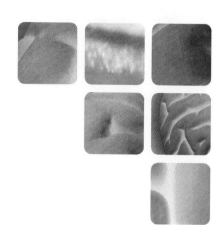

Carole Wade earned her Ph.D. in cognitive psychology at Stanford University. She began her academic career at the University of New Mexico, where she taught courses in psycholinguistics and developed the first course at the university on the psychology of gender. She was professor of psychology for ten years at San Diego Mesa College, then taught at College of Marin, and is now affiliated with Dominican University of California. She is coauthor, with Carol Tavris, of *Invitation to Psychology, Psychology in Perspective,* and *The Longest War: Sex differences in perspective.* Dr. Wade has a long-standing interest in making psychology accessible to students and the general public. For many years she has focused her efforts on the teaching and promotion of critical-thinking skills, diversity issues, and the enhancement of undergraduate education in psychology. She chaired the APA Board of Educational Affairs's Task Force on Diversity Issues at the Precollege and Undergraduate Levels of Education in Psychology, as well as the APA's Public Information Committee; has been a G. Stanley Hall lecturer at the APA convention; and served on the steering committee for the National Institute on the Teaching of Psychology. Dr. Wade is a Fellow of the American Psychological Association and a charter member of the American Psychological Society. When she isn't busy with her professional activities, she can be found riding the trails of northern California on her Arabian horse, Condé, or his stablemate, Dancer.

Carol Tavris earned her Ph.D. in the interdisciplinary program in social psychology at the University of Michigan, and as a writer and lecturer she has sought to educate the public about the importance of critical and scientific thinking in psychology. She is author of *The Mismeasure of Woman; Anger: The misunderstood emotion;* and, with Carole Wade, *Invitation to Psychology, Psychology in Perspective,* and *The Longest War: Sex differences in perspective.* She has written on psychological topics for a wide variety of magazines, journals, edited books, and newspapers. Many of her book reviews and opinion essays for *The Los Angeles Times, The New York Times Book Review, Scientific American,* and other publications have been collected in *Psychobabble and Biobunk: Using psychology to think critically about issues in the news.* Dr. Tavris lectures widely on, among other topics, pseudoscience in psychology and psychiatry, anger, and the science and politics of research on gender. She has taught in the psychology department at UCLA and at the Human Relations Center of the New School for Social Research in New York. She is a Fellow of the American Psychological Association and a charter Fellow of the American Psychological Society; a member of the board of the Council for Scientific Clinical Psychology and Psychiatry; and a member of the editorial board of the APS journal *Psychological Science in the Public Interest.* When she is not writing or lecturing, she can be found walking the trails of the Hollywood Hills with her border collie, Sophie.

1

What Is Psychology?

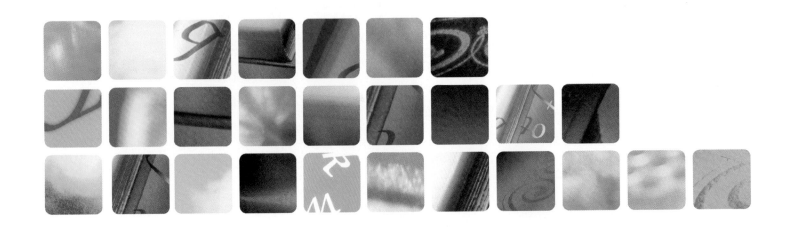

The purpose of psychology is to give us a completely different idea of the things we know best.

PAUL VALÉRY

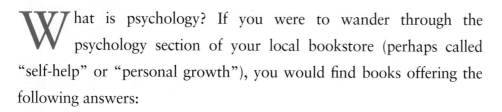

hat is psychology? If you were to wander through the psychology section of your local bookstore (perhaps called "self-help" or "personal growth"), you would find books offering the following answers:

▶ Psychology is all about finding happiness. It will teach you that *You Can Be Happy No Matter What*, presumably if you also read *I Don't Have to Make Everything All Better*. And if you are feeling that nothing will ever get better, you might be cheered up by *The Joy of Stress* and *The Joy of Failure*.

▶ Psychology will make you rich and successful if you read *Baby Steps to Success* or *Giant Steps* or *How to Succeed in Life*. You can learn *How to Make the Impossible Possible* and also how to *Get What You Deserve*.

▶ Psychology will help you fall in love, stay in love, or get over love. *Love Is the Answer*, but only if you are *Learning to Love Yourself* first and don't develop *Obsessive Love*. You can learn *How to Make Anyone Fall in Love with You* as long as you *Don't Say Yes When You Want to Say No*. Once you're in love, of course, you will need *The Art of Intimacy* and *The Art of Staying Together*.

▶ Psychology is full of contradictory advice. It provides *Toughness Training for Life* and will show you how to say *Good-bye to Guilt* but will also teach you *How to Turn the Other Cheek and Still Survive in Today's World*. You can develop your inner child, *The Animal in You*, or maybe even *Grow Up!*

The psychology that you are about to study, however, bears little relation to the popular psychology ("pop psych") found in many self-help books. It is more complex, more informative, and, we think, far more helpful because it is based on scientific research and **empirical** evidence—evidence gathered by careful observation, experimentation, and measurement.

The psychology you will be studying also addresses a far broader range of issues than does popular psychology. When people think of psychology, they usually think of mental and emotional disorders, abnormal acts, personal problems, and psychotherapy. But psychologists take as their subject the entire spectrum of brave and cowardly, intelligent and foolish, beautiful and brutish things that people do. They want to know how ordinary human beings—and other animals, too—learn, remember, solve problems, perceive, feel and get along (or fail to get along) with others.

3

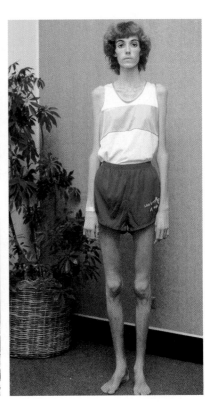

Psychologists use scientific methods to study many puzzles of human behavior. Why do people lose their inhibitions when they dress up in funny outfits? Why do people strive to become champion athletes in spite of physical disabilities? What causes people to become anorexic, and in some cases even starve themselves to death? And what could motivate terrorists to kill themselves and thousands of innocent people?

They are therefore as likely to study commonplace experiences—rearing children, gossiping, remembering a shopping list, daydreaming, making love, and making a living—as exceptional ones.

Psychology can be defined generally as *the discipline concerned with behavior and mental processes and how they are affected by an organism's physical state, mental state, and external environment.* This definition, however, is a little like defining a car as a vehicle for transporting people from one place to another, without explaining how a car differs from a train or a bus, how a Ford differs from a Ferrari, or how a catalytic converter works. To get a clear picture of what psychology is, you are going to need to know more about its methods, its findings, and its ways of interpreting information. We will begin by looking more closely at what psychology is *not*.

WHAT'S AHEAD▶

- How does "psychobabble" differ from serious psychology?
- How accurate are psychology's nonscientific competitors, such as astrologers and psychics?

empirical Relying on or derived from observation, experimentation, or measurement.

psychology The discipline concerned with behavior and mental processes and how they are affected by an organism's physical state, mental state, and external environment; the term is often represented by ψ, the Greek letter psi (usually pronounced "sy").

Psychology, Pseudoscience, and Popular Opinion

In recent decades, the public's appetite for psychological information has created a huge market for what R. D. Rosen (1977) called "psychobabble": pseudoscience and quackery covered by a veneer of psychological language. The examples that Rosen analyzed in the 1970s included group encounters designed to transform a person's rotten life in one weekend; "primal scream therapy," in which people are supposed to link their current unhappiness to the trauma of being born (this therapy still exists); and "Theta," whose leader asserted that "no one dies if they don't want to"—certainly the ultimate belief in mind over matter!

The particular programs and groups based on psychobabble have changed their names and leaders since Rosen wrote, but the common elements remain. All promise simple, quick fixes for emotional problems and needs. All rely on vaguely psychological and scientific-sounding language, such as "getting in touch with your real self," "reprogramming your brain," or "identifying your unconscious talents." Some forms of psychobabble play on the modern consumer's love of technology. All sorts of electrical gizmos have been marketed with the promise that they will get both halves of your brain working at their peak (Chance, 1989): the Graham Potentializer, the Tranquilite, the Floatarium, the Transcutaneous Electro-Neural Stimulator, the Brain SuperCharger, and the Whole Brain Wave Form Synchro-Energizer. (We are not making these up.) And today you can find all sorts of psychobabble on the Internet, where promoters promise that a higher IQ or a perfect love life or a better personality is just a click away.

Nonscientific and pseudoscientific approaches to psychological problems promise easy answers and quick solutions. Fortune tellers claim they can analyze your personality and foresee your future just from the lines on your palm. And the marriage of old-fashioned pseudoscience and modern technology has produced gizmos like the "Synchro-Energizer," which supposedly alters consciousness, boosts intelligence, and enhances sexual functioning, all by simply bombarding you with lights and sounds of different frequencies and intensities.

Because so many pop-psych ideas have filtered into public consciousness, the media, education, and even the law, we all need to distinguish between psychobabble and serious psychology, and between unsupported *popular opinion* and findings based on *research evidence*. Are unhappy memories "repressed" and then accurately recalled years later, as if they had been tape-recorded? Do most women suffer from emotional symptoms of "PMS"? Do policies of abstinence from alcohol reduce rates of alcoholism? Do abused children inevitably become abusive parents, caught in a "cycle of abuse"? As you will learn in this book, all of these common beliefs and many others are contradicted by the evidence.

Psychology has many nonscientific competitors: palm reading, graphology, fortune-telling, numerology, and the most popular, astrology. Like psychologists, promoters of these competing systems try to explain people's problems and predict their behavior. If you are having romantic problems, for example, an astrologer may advise you to choose an Aries instead of an Aquarius as your next love, and a "past-lives channeler" may say it's because you were jilted in a former life. Belief in the paranormal and pseudoscience are widespread, even in scientifically advanced countries; between one-third and one-half of Americans and Canadians believe in astrology, and 17 percent of Americans have sought out a fortuneteller or psychic for advice (De Robertis & Delaney, 2000; National Science Board, 2000).

"Sometimes the future is bright, sometimes it's dark—it's all cyclical."

Yet whenever the claims of psychics and astrologers are put to the test, those claims turn out to be so vague that they are meaningless—or just plain wrong (Park, 2000; Rowe, 1993). The world's most noted psychics predicted that in the year 2000, Prince Charles of England would fly in the space shuttle, a large flesh-eating dinosaur would be discovered in Africa, an earthquake would destroy Los Angeles and San Francisco, and people would be able to order dinner via interactive TV and find it on their tables by the next commercial (except, we suppose, for the unlucky inhabitants of Los Angeles or San Francisco) (Emery, 2001). Obviously, those famous psychics were mistaken! Moreover, no psychic has ever found a missing child, identified a serial killer, or helped police solve any other crime solely by using "psychic powers," in spite of frequent reports in the mass media that psychics do this all the time (Rowe, 1993; Shermer, 1997).

But what should be the fatal blow to psychic claims occurred on September 11, 2001, when the World Trade Center was destroyed. Not one psychic had predicted the most devastating tragedy ever to occur on American soil.

Perhaps the ultimate difference between psychobabble and scientific psychology is that psychobabble *confirms* our existing beliefs and prejudices (which is why it is so appealing), whereas psychology often *challenges* them. You do not have to be a psychologist to know that people don't always take kindly to having their beliefs challenged. You rarely hear someone say, cheerfully, "Oh, thank you for explaining to me why my lifelong philosophy of child rearing is wrong! I'm so grateful for your facts!" The person is more likely to say, "Oh, buzz off, and take your stupid ideas with you." (In Chapter 9 you will learn why this is so.)

However, although psychologists often challenge prevailing beliefs, psychological findings do not have to be surprising to be important. Psychologists, like scientists in other fields, strive not only to discover new phenomena, but also to deepen our understanding of an already familiar world—for example, by identifying the varieties of love, the origins of violence, or the reasons that a great song can lift our hearts.

WHAT'S AHEAD▷

- **Are "critical thinkers" always critical?**
- **Are all opinions created equal?**
- **What guidelines can help you evaluate psychological claims?**

Thinking Critically and Creatively about Psychology

Most people know that you have to exercise the body to keep it in shape, but they may not realize that clear thinking also requires effort and practice. All around us we can see examples of flabby thinking. Sometimes people justify their mental laziness by proudly telling you they are "open-minded." It's good to be open-minded, many scientists have observed, but not so open that your brains fall out.

In this book, you will gain practice in distinguishing scientific psychology from pseudoscience by thinking critically. **Critical thinking** is the ability and willingness to assess claims and make objective judgments on the basis of well-supported reasons and evidence, rather than emotion and anecdote. Critical thinkers are able to look for flaws in arguments and to resist claims that have no support. Critical thinking, however, is not merely negative thinking. It includes the ability to be creative and constructive—the ability to come up with alternative explanations for events, think of implications of research findings, and apply new knowledge to social and personal problems.

One prevalent misreading of what it means to be open-minded is the idea that all opinions are created equal and that everybody's beliefs are as good as everybody else's. On matters of personal preference, that is true; if you prefer the look of a Ford Taurus to the look of a Honda Accord, no one can argue with you. But if you say, "The Ford is a better car than a Honda," you have uttered more than mere opinion. Now you have to support your belief with evidence of the car's reliability, track record, and safety (Ruggiero, 1997). And if you say, "Fords are the best in the world and Hondas do not exist; they are a conspiracy of the Japanese government," you forfeit the right to have your opinion taken seriously. Your opinion, if it ignores reality, is *not* equal to any other.

Many people do not use critical-thinking skills until they are in their mid-20s, or until they have had many years of higher education. Yet even young children have the basic capacity to think critically, although they may not get much credit for it. We know one fourth-grader, who, when told that ancient Greece was the "cradle of democracy," replied, "But what about women and slaves, who couldn't vote and had no rights? Was Greece a democracy for them?" That's critical thinking!

Many educators, philosophers, and psychologists believe that contemporary education shortchanges students by not encouraging them to think critically and creatively. Too often, say these critics, teachers and students view the mind as a bin for storing "the right answers" or a sponge for "soaking up knowledge." The mind is neither a bin nor a sponge. Remembering, thinking, and understanding require judgment, choice, and the weighing of evidence. Many high school and college graduates have learned to memorize the "right" answers, but without the ability to think critically, they are unable to formulate a rational argument or see through misleading advertisements that play on their emotions. They may not know how to assess a political proposal or candidate, decide whether or when to have children, or come up

critical thinking The ability and willingness to assess claims and make judgments on the basis of well-supported reasons and evidence, rather than emotion or anecdote.

with constructive solutions to their problems. Many spend huge amounts of money on medical remedies that lack any evidence of effectiveness and that can even be life-threatening (Halpern, 1998).

Critical thinking is not only indispensable in ordinary life, it is also fundamental to all science, including psychological science. By exercising critical thinking, you will be able to distinguish serious psychology from psychobabble. To do so, you will need to exercise logical skills, but other kinds of skills are also important (Halpern, 1995; Levy, 1997; Paul, 1984; Ruggiero, 1997). Here are eight essential critical-thinking guidelines that we will be emphasizing throughout this book.

 Ask Questions; Be Willing to Wonder. What is the one kind of question that most exasperates parents of young children? "Why is the sky blue, Mommy?" "Why doesn't the plane fall?" "Why don't pigs have wings?" Unfortunately, as children grow up, they tend to stop asking "why" questions. (Why do you think this is?)

"The trigger mechanism for creative thinking is the disposition to be curious, to wonder, to inquire," observed Vincent Ruggiero (1988). "Asking 'What's wrong here?' and/or 'Why is this the way it is, and how did it come to be that way?' leads to the identification of problems and challenges." Psychologist Bob Perloff (1992) once reflected on a few questions he would like to have answered. "Why are moths attracted to wool but indifferent to cotton?" he wondered. "Why is a rainbow arched? I used to feel foolish, even dumb, because I didn't know why or how the sun shines until I learned very recently that the astrophysicists themselves are in a quandary about this."

We hope that you will not approach psychology as received wisdom but will ask many questions about the theories and findings presented in this book. Be on the lookout, too, for questions about human behavior that have not yet been asked. If you do that, you will be not only learning psychology, but also learning to think the way psychologists do.

"I still don't have all the answers, but I'm beginning to ask the right questions."

 Define Your Terms. Once you have raised a general question, the next step is to frame it in clear and concrete terms. "What makes people happy?" is a fine question for midnight reveries, but it will not lead to answers until you have defined what you mean by "happy." Do you mean being in a state of euphoria most of the time? Do you mean feeling pleasantly contented with life? Do you mean the absence of serious problems or pain?

Vague or poorly defined terms in a question can lead to misleading or incomplete answers. For example, have you ever wondered whether animals can use language? The answer depends on how you define "language." If you mean "a system of communication," then birds do it, bees do it, and even trees do it. But if you define language as "a system of communication that combines sounds or gestures into an infinite number of structured utterances that convey meaning" (which is the way linguists define it), then as far as anyone can tell, only people use language, though some animals are able to acquire some aspects of language in special settings (see Chapter 9). Or here's another example, one that has been much in the news lately: How common is it for schoolchildren to be bullied? The answer depends on how you define "bullying." If you mean "ever mistreated in any way by another child," then nearly every child has been bullied. If you mean "subjected to repeated verbal harassment and taunting," the numbers are lower. And if you mean "physically attacked and threatened," the numbers are lower still. The definition makes all the difference (Best, 2001).

Examine the Evidence. Have you ever heard someone in the heat of argument exclaim, "I just know it's true, no matter what you say" or "That's my opinion; nothing's going to change it"? Have you ever made such statements yourself? Accepting a conclusion without evidence, or expecting others to do so, is a sure sign of lazy thinking. A critical thinker asks, "What evidence supports or refutes this argument and its opposition? How reliable is the evidence?" If checking the reliability of the evidence directly is not possible, the person considers whether it came from a reliable source.

Some pop-psych ideas have been widely accepted on the basis of poor evidence or even no evidence at all. For example, many people think it is healthy to ventilate their anger at the first person, pet, or piece of furniture that gets in their way. Actually, studies across many fields suggest that sometimes expressing anger is beneficial, but more often it is not. Often it makes the angry person angrier, makes the target of the anger become angry in return, lowers everybody's self-esteem, and fosters hostility and aggression (Bushman, Baumeister, & Stack, 1999; Tavris, 1989). Yet the belief that expressing anger is always healthy persists, despite the evidence to the contrary. Perhaps you can think of some reasons that this might be so.

 Analyze Assumptions and Biases. *Assumptions* are beliefs that are taken for granted. Critical thinkers try to identify the unspoken assumptions on which claims and arguments may rest. The assumption might be "All Democrats (or Republicans) are idiots," or "You have a need for the product we are selling," or "People have free will, and are entirely responsible for any crimes they commit" (or, conversely, "People's behavior is a result of their biology or upbringing, so they aren't responsible for anything they do"). Everyone, of course, makes assumptions about how the world works; we could not function otherwise. But if we do not make our own and other people's assumptions explicit, our ability to judge an argument's merits may be impaired.

When an assumption or belief keeps us from considering the evidence fairly, or causes us to ignore the evidence completely, it becomes a *bias.* Often a bias remains hidden until someone challenges our belief and we get defensive and angry. For instance, most of us, psychologists included, believe that parents are the most important influence in shaping a child's personality. Could anything be more obvious? Isn't that what parenting books, therapists, and magazine articles have been telling us for years? In 1998, in her book *The Nurture Assumption,* Judith Rich Harris dared to question that assumption. Genes and peers, she argued, are more important influences on a child's personality and behavior than how the parents raise the child. Because this idea challenged a widespread bias, it immediately provoked a storm of disbelief, outrage, and scorn. Some critics focused on Harris's lack of credentials instead of her facts or her logic (she does not have a Ph.D.), and many attacked the book without even bothering to read it. That is the nature of a bias: It creates intellectual blinders. (You may be wondering whether Harris is right about parents and peers. In Chapter 13 we will look more closely at her argument—in as unbiased a manner as possible.)

 Avoid Emotional Reasoning. Emotion has a place in critical thinking. Passionate commitment to a view motivates people to think boldly, to defend unpopular ideas, and to seek evidence for creative new theories. But when "gut feelings" replace clear thinking, the results can be dangerous. "Persecutions and wars and lynchings," observed Edward de Bono (1985), "are all a result of gut feeling."

Because our feelings feel so *right,* so natural, we may not realize that people who hold an opposing viewpoint feel just as strongly as we do. But they usually do, which means that emotional conviction alone cannot settle arguments. You probably hold strong feelings about many topics of psychological interest, such as drugs, the causes of crime, racism, the origins of intelligence, gender differences, and homosexuality. As you read this book, you may find yourself quarreling with findings that you dislike. Disagreement is fine; it means that you are reading actively. All we ask is that you think about why you are disagreeing: Is it because the evidence is unpersuasive or because the results make you feel anxious or annoyed?

 Don't Oversimplify. A critical thinker looks beyond the obvious, resists easy generalizations, and rejects either/or thinking. For instance, is it better to feel you have control over everything that happens to you, or to accept with tranquility whatever life serves up? Either position oversimplifies. As we will see in Chapter 15, a sense of control has many important benefits, but sometimes it is best to "go with the flow."

One common form of oversimplification is *argument by anecdote*—generalizing from a personal experience or a few examples to everyone: One crime committed by a paroled ex-convict means that parole should be abolished; one friend who hates her school means that everybody who goes there hates it. Anecdotes are often the source of stereotyping as well: One dishonest welfare mother means they are all dishonest; one encounter with an unconventional Californian means they are all flaky.

Thinking Critically and Creatively about Psychological Issues

ASK QUESTIONS; BE WILLING TO WONDER

After the collapse of the World Trade Center, rescuers like this one inspired millions by searching tirelessly to find survivors. Why do some people risk their lives to help their fellow human beings, whereas others watch from the sidelines? Social psychologists explore these and many other questions raised by the events of September 11, 2001, as we will see in Chapter 8.

DEFINE YOUR TERMS

People refer to intelligence all the time, but what is it exactly? Does the musical genius of a world-class violinist like Anne-Sophie Mutter count as intelligence? Is intelligence captured by an IQ score, or does it also include wisdom and practical "smarts"? We will consider some answers in Chapter 9.

Critical thinkers want more evidence than one or two stories before drawing such sweeping conclusions.

Consider Other Interpretations. Critical thinkers creatively generate as many reasonable explanations of the topic at hand as possible before settling on the most likely one. Suppose a news magazine reports that chronically depressed people are more likely than nondepressed people to develop cancer. Before concluding that depression causes cancer, you would need to consider some other possibilities. Perhaps depressed people are more likely to smoke and drink too much, and it is those unhealthful habits that increase their cancer risk. Or perhaps, in studies of depression and cancer, early, undetected cancers were responsible for patients' feelings of depression. Alternative explanations such as these must be ruled out by further investigation before we can conclude that depression is a direct cause of cancer.

Once several explanations of a phenomenon have been generated, a critical thinker chooses the one that accounts for the most evidence and makes the fewest unverified assumptions. Thus, if a fortune-teller reads your palm and predicts that soon you will fall in love on a blind date, travel to Zanzibar, and have twins, then one of two things must be true (Steiner, 1989):

EXAMINE THE EVIDENCE

When demonstrating "levitation" and other supposedly magical phenomena, illusionists such as André Kole exploit people's tendency to trust the evidence of their own eyes even when such evidence is misleading, as discussed in Chapter 6.

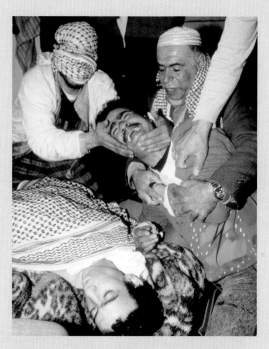

ANALYZE ASSUMPTIONS AND BIASES

Many North Americans assume that men are by nature less emotionally expressive than women. But this Palestinian man, grieving over his dead son, does not fit Western stereotypes of male emotionality. Cultural rules have a powerful influence on how men and women express their feelings, as we will see in Chapter 11.

▶ The fortune-teller can actually sort out the infinite number of interactions among people, animals, events, objects, and circumstances that could affect your life and can know for sure the outcome. Moreover, this fortune-teller is able to alter all the known laws of physics and defy the hundreds of studies showing that no one, under proper procedures for validating psychic predictions, has been able to predict the future for any given individual.

OR

▶ The fortune-teller is faking it.

A critical thinker would prefer the second alternative because it requires fewer assumptions and has the most supporting evidence.

Tolerate Uncertainty. Ultimately, learning to think critically teaches us one of the hardest lessons of life: how to live with uncertainty. Sometimes there is little or no evidence available to examine. Sometimes the evidence permits only tentative conclusions. Sometimes the evidence seems strong enough to permit conclusions . . . until, exasperatingly, new evidence throws our beliefs into disarray. Critical thinkers are willing to accept this state of uncertainty. They are not afraid to say, "I don't know" or "I'm not sure." This admission is not an evasion but a spur to further creative inquiry.

The desire for certainty often makes people uncomfortable when experts cannot give them "the" answer to a question. Patients may demand of their doctors, "What

AVOID EMOTIONAL REASONING

Intense feelings about controversial issues can keep us from considering other viewpoints. The resolution of differences requires that we move beyond emotional reasoning and instead weigh point and counterpoint, as discussed in Chapter 9.

DON'T OVERSIMPLIFY

Is the left side of the brain entirely analytic, rational, and sensible and the right side always intuitive, emotional, and spontaneous? The two hemispheres of the brain do have some specialized talents, but it is easy to exaggerate the differences, as we will see in Chapter 4.

do you mean you don't know what's wrong with me? Find out and fix it!" Students may demand of their professors, "What do you mean it's a controversial issue? Just tell me the answer!" Critical thinkers know that the more important the question, the less likely it is to have a single simple answer.

The need to accept a certain amount of uncertainty does not mean that we must abandon all beliefs and convictions. That would be impossible, in any case: We all need values and principles to guide our actions. As Vincent Ruggiero (1988) wrote, "It is not the embracing of an idea that causes problems—it is the refusal to relax that embrace when good sense dictates doing so. It is enough to form convictions with care and carry them lightly, being willing to reconsider them whenever new evidence calls them into question."

Of course, critical thinking cannot provide answers to all of life's quandaries. Some questions, such as whether there is a God and what the nature of God might be, are ultimately matters of faith. Moreover, critical thinking is a process, not a once-and-for-all accomplishment. No one ever becomes a perfect critical thinker, entirely unaffected by emotional reasoning and wishful thinking. We are all less open-minded than we think; it is always easier to poke holes in another person's argument than to critically examine our own position. As philosopher Richard W. Paul (1984) observed, critical thinking is really "fair-mindedness brought into the heart of everyday life."

CONSIDER OTHER INTERPRETATIONS

The Rastafarian church regards marijuana as a "wisdom weed." Will these young Jamaican members react to the drug in the same way as someone who buys it on the street and smokes it alone or at a party? Although people commonly attribute the effects of psychoactive substances solely to the drugs, an alternative explanation emphasizes the impact of setting, motives, and cultural practices, as we will see in Chapters 5 and 16.

TOLERATE UNCERTAINTY

Many questions currently have no firm answers. For example, several explanations of sexual orientation have been offered, but no one theory can account for the many variations of both homosexuality and heterosexuality, as we will see in Chapter 12.

As you read this book, keep in mind the eight guidelines we have described, which are summarized for you in Review 1.1. You will have many opportunities to apply these guidelines to psychological theories and to the personal and social issues that affect us all. From time to time, questions in the margin, accompanied by a lightbulb symbol, will draw your attention to a discussion where one of the guidelines is especially relevant. In Quick Quizzes, the lightbulb will identify questions that give you practice in applying the guidelines yourself. Keep in mind, however, that critical thinking is important throughout every chapter, not just where the lightbulb appears.

REVIEW 1.1	GUIDELINES TO THINKING CRITICALLY ABOUT PSYCHOLOGICAL ISSUES	
	Guideline	**Example**
	Ask questions; be willing to wonder	"Can I recall events from my childhood accurately?"
	Define your terms	"By 'childhood' I mean ages 3 to 12; by 'events' I mean things that happened to me personally, like a trip to the zoo or a stay in the hospital; by 'accurately' I mean the event basically happened the way I think it did."
	Examine the evidence	"I *feel* I recall my fifth birthday party perfectly, but studies show that people often reconstruct past events inaccurately."
	Analyze assumptions and biases	"I've always assumed that memory is like a tape recorder—perfectly accurate for every moment of my life—but maybe this is just a bias, because it's so reassuring."
	Avoid emotional reasoning	"I really *want* to believe this memory is true, but that doesn't mean it *is*."
	Don't oversimplify	"Some of my childhood memories could be accurate, others mistaken, and some partly right and partly wrong."
	Consider other interpretations	"Some 'memories' could be based on what my parents told me later, not on my own recall."
	Tolerate uncertainty	"I may never know for sure whether some of my childhood memories are real or accurate."

Note: You will be reading a lot more about the reliability of memory in Chapter 10.

WHAT'S AHEAD ▶

- **What is the lesson of phrenology for modern psychology?**
- **How old is the science of psychology?**
- **Was Sigmund Freud the official founder of scientific psychology?**

Psychology's Past: From the Armchair to the Laboratory

Now that you know what psychology is and what it isn't, and why studying it requires critical thinking, let us see how psychology developed into a modern science.

Until the nineteenth century, psychology was not a formal discipline. Of course, most of the great thinkers of history, from Aristotle to Zoroaster, raised questions that today would be called psychological. They wanted to know how people take in information through their senses, use information to solve problems, and become motivated to act in brave or villainous ways. They wondered about the elusive nature of emotion, and whether it controls us or is something we can control. Like today's psychologists, they wanted to *describe, predict, understand,* and *modify* behavior in order to add to human knowledge and increase human happiness. But unlike modern psychologists, scholars of the past did not rely heavily on empirical evidence. Often, their observations were based simply on anecdotes or descriptions of individual cases.

This does not mean that the forerunners of modern psychology were always wrong. On the contrary, they often had insights and made observations that were verified by later work. Hippocrates (c. 460 B.C.–c. 377 B.C.), the Greek physician known as the founder of modern medicine, observed patients with head injuries and inferred that the brain must be the ultimate source of "our pleasures, joys, laughter, and jests as well as our sorrows, pains, griefs, and tears." And so it is. In the first century A.D., the Stoic philosophers observed that people do not become angry or sad or anxious because of actual events, but because of their explanations of those events. And so they do. In the seventeenth century, the English philosopher John Locke (1643–1704) argued that the mind works by associating ideas arising from experience, a notion that continues to influence many psychologists today.

But without empirical methods, the forerunners of psychology also committed some terrible blunders. A good example comes from the early 1800s, when the theory of **phrenology** (Greek for "study of the mind") became wildly popular in Europe

phrenology The discredited theory that different brain areas account for character and personality traits, which can be "read" from bumps on the skull.

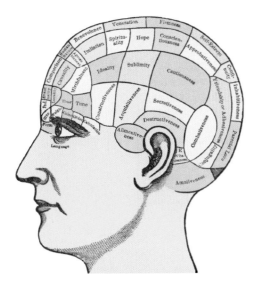

On this nineteenth-century phrenological "map," notice the tiny space allocated to self-esteem and the large one devoted to cautiousness!

and America. Inspired by the writings and lectures of Austrian physician Joseph Gall (1758–1828), phrenologists argued that different brain areas accounted for specific character and personality traits, such as "stinginess" and "religiosity," and that such traits could be "read" from bumps on the skull. Thieves, for example, supposedly had large bumps above the ears. When phrenologists examined people with "stealing bumps" who were *not* thieves, they explained away this counterevidence by saying that other bumps on the skull represented positive traits that must be holding the person's thieving impulses in check.

In the United States, all sorts of people eagerly sought the services of phrenologists. Parents used them to make decisions about child rearing and to decide whether their children could benefit from music lessons; schools used them to decide which teachers to hire; young people used them when deciding on a career or a mate; and businesses used them to find out which employees were likely to be loyal and honest (Benjamin, 1998). Some phrenologists offered classes or self-study programs for people who wanted to overcome their deficiencies—the forerunners of today's many self-improvement programs and seminars. Enthusiasm for phrenology did not disappear until well into the twentieth century, even though phrenology was a classic pseudoscience—sheer nonsense.

The Birth of Modern Psychology

At about the time that phrenology was reaching the peak of its popularity, several pioneering men and women in Europe and America were starting to study psychological issues using scientific methods. In 1879, the first psychological laboratory was officially established in Leipzig, Germany, by Wilhelm Wundt [VIL-helm Voont]. Wundt (1832–1920), who was trained in medicine and philosophy, wrote many volumes on psychology, physiology, natural history, ethics, and logic. But he is especially revered by psychologists because he was the first person to announce (in 1873) that he intended to make psychology a science and because his laboratory was the first to have its results published in a scholarly journal. Although it started out as just a few rooms in an old building, the Leipzig laboratory soon became the place to go for anyone who wanted to become a psychologist. Many of America's first psychologists got their training there.

Researchers in Wundt's laboratory did not study the entire gamut of topics that modern psychologists do. Most concentrated on sensation, perception, reaction times, imagery, and attention, and avoided learning, personality, and abnormal behavior. One of Wundt's favorite research methods was *trained introspection,* in which volunteers were taught to carefully observe, analyze, and describe their own sensations, mental images, and emotional reactions. This was not as easy as it sounds. Wundt's introspectors had to make 10,000 practice observations before they were allowed to participate in an actual study. Once trained, they might take as long as 20 minutes to report their inner experiences during a 1.5-second experiment.

Although Wundt hoped that trained introspection would produce reliable, verifiable results, most psychologists eventually rejected this method as too subjective. But Wundt still gets the credit for initiating the movement to make psychology a science.

Three Early Psychologies

During the early decades of psychology's existence as a formal discipline, three schools of psychological thought became popular. One soon faded, another disappeared as a separate school but continued to influence the field, and the third remains

Wilhelm Wundt (1832–1920), on the right, with co-workers.

Looking Inward

How reliable is introspection as a method for arriving at generalizations about human experience? Find out for yourself by asking some friends what they experience mentally when they think of a chair. Tell them to be specific about color, shape, size, style, orientation, and so on. Which aspects of the experience do they agree on, and which do they report differently?

alive today, despite passionate debate about whether it belongs in scientific psychology at all.

Structuralism. In America, Wundt's ideas were popularized in somewhat modified form by one of his students, E. B. Titchener (1867–1927), who gave Wundt's approach the name **structuralism**. Like Wundt, structuralists hoped to analyze sensations, images, and feelings into basic elements, much as a chemist might analyze water into hydrogen and oxygen atoms. For example, a person might be asked to listen to a metronome clicking and to report exactly what he or she heard. Most people said they perceived a pattern (such as, CLICK click click CLICK click click), even though the clicks of a metronome are actually all the same. Or a person might be asked to break down all the different components of taste when biting into an orange (sweet, tart, wet, etc.).

Despite an intensive program of research, however, structuralism soon went the way of the dinosaur. After you have discovered the building blocks of a particular sensation or image and how they link up, then what? Years after structuralism's demise, Wolfgang Köhler (1959) recalled how he and his colleagues had responded to it as students: "What had disturbed us was . . . the implication that human life, apparently so colorful and so intensely dynamic, is actually a frightful bore."

The structuralists' reliance on introspection also got them into trouble. Despite their training, introspectors often produced conflicting reports. When asked what image came to mind when they heard the word *triangle,* most respondents said they imagined a visual image of a form with three sides and three corners, but one person might report a flashing red form with equal angles, whereas another reported a revolving colorless form with one angle larger than the other two. Some people even claimed they could think about a triangle without forming any visual image at all (Boring, 1953). It was hard, therefore, to know what mental attributes of a triangle were basic.

Functionalism. Another early approach to scientific psychology, called **functionalism**, emphasized the function or purpose of behavior, as opposed to its analysis and description. One of functionalism's leaders was William James (1842–1910), an American philosopher, physician, and psychologist who argued that searching for building blocks of experience, as Wundt and Titchener tried to do, was a waste of time. The brain and the mind are constantly changing, he noted. Permanent ideas—of triangles or anything else—do not appear periodically before the "footlights of consciousness." Attempting to grasp the nature of the mind through introspection, wrote James (1890/1950), is "like seizing a spinning top to catch its motion, or trying to turn up the gas quickly enough to see how the darkness looks."

Where the structuralists asked *what* happens when an organism does something, the functionalists asked *how* and *why*. They were inspired in part by the evolutionary theories of British naturalist Charles Darwin (1809–1882). Darwin had argued that a biologist's job is not merely to describe, say, the brilliant plumage of a peacock

structuralism An early psychological approach that emphasized the analysis of immediate experience into basic elements.

functionalism An early psychological approach that emphasized the function or purpose of behavior and consciousness.

William James (1842–1910).

or the drab markings of a lizard, but also to figure out how these attributes enhance survival. Do they help the animal attract a mate or hide from its enemies? Similarly, the functionalists wanted to know how specific behaviors and mental processes help a person or animal adapt to the environment, so they looked for underlying causes and practical consequences of these behaviors and processes. Unlike the structuralists, they felt free to pick and choose among many methods, and they broadened the field of psychology to include the study of children, animals, religious experiences, and what James called the "stream of consciousness"—a term still used because it so beautifully describes the way thoughts flow like a river, tumbling over each other in waves, sometimes placid, sometimes turbulent.

As a school of psychology, functionalism, like structuralism, was short-lived. It lacked the kind of precise theory or program of research that wins recruits, and it endorsed the study of consciousness just as that concept was about to fall out of favor. Yet the functionalists' emphasis on the causes and consequences of behavior was to set the course of psychological science.

Psychoanalysis. The nineteenth century also saw the development of various psychological therapies. In the United States, for example, the wildly popular "Mind Cure" movement lasted from 1830 to 1900; "mind cures" were efforts to correct the "false ideas" that were said to make people anxious, depressed, and unhappy (Caplan, 1998; Moskowitz, 2001). The Mind Cure movement was the forerunner of modern cognitive therapies (see Chapter 17).

However, the form of therapy that would have the greatest impact worldwide for nearly a century had its roots in Vienna, Austria. While researchers in Europe and America were working in their laboratories, struggling to establish psychology as a science, Sigmund Freud (1856–1939), an obscure neurologist, was in his office, listening to his patients' reports of depression, nervousness, and obsessive habits. Freud became convinced that many of his patients' symptoms had mental, not physical, causes. Their distress, he concluded, was due to conflicts and emotional traumas that had occurred in early childhood and that were too threatening to be remembered consciously, such as forbidden sexual feelings for a parent.

Freud argued that conscious awareness is merely the tip of a mental iceberg. Beneath the visible tip, he said, lies the unconscious part of the mind, containing unrevealed wishes, passions, guilty secrets, unspeakable yearnings, and conflicts between desire and duty. Many of these urges and thoughts are sexual or aggressive in nature. We are not aware of them as we go blithely about our daily business, yet they make themselves known—in dreams, slips of the tongue, apparent accidents, and even jokes. Freud (1905a) wrote, "No mortal can keep a secret. If the lips are silent, he chatters with his fingertips; betrayal oozes out of him at every pore."

Freud's ideas were not an overnight sensation; his first book, *The Interpretation of Dreams* (1900/1953), managed to sell only 600 copies in the eight years following its publication. Eventually, however, his ideas evolved into a broad theory of personality and a method of psychotherapy, both of which became known as **psychoanalysis**. Most Freudian concepts were, and still are, rejected by most empirically oriented psychologists, as we will see. But they had a profound influence on the philosophy, literature, and art of the twentieth century, and Freud's name is now as much a household word as Einstein's.

From these early beginnings in philosophy, natural science, and medicine, psychology has grown into a complex discipline encompassing many different specialties, perspectives, and methods. Today the field is like a large, sprawling family. The members of this family share common great-grandparents, but some of the cousins have formed alliances, some are quarreling, and a few are barely speaking to one another.

Sigmund Freud (1856–1939).

psychoanalysis A theory of personality and a method of psychotherapy, originally formulated by Sigmund Freud, which emphasizes unconscious motives and conflicts.

QUICK QUIZ

Make sure psychology's past is still present in your memory by choosing the correct response from each pair of terms in parentheses.

1. Psychology has been a science for more than (2,000/100) years.
2. The forerunners of modern psychology depended heavily on (casual observation/empirical methods).
3. Credit for founding modern psychology is generally given to (William James/Wilhelm Wundt).
4. Early psychologists who emphasized how behavior helps an organism adapt to its environment were known as (structuralists/functionalists).
5. The idea that emotional problems spring from unconscious conflicts originated with (the Mind Cure movement/psychoanalysis).

Answers:

1. 100 2. casual observation 3. Wilhelm Wundt 4. functionalists 5. psychoanalysis

WHAT'S AHEAD

- **What are the five major perspectives in psychology?**
- **Why is psychoanalysis the "thumb on the hand of psychology"?**
- **How have humanism and feminism influenced psychology?**

Psychology's Present: Behavior, Body, Mind, and Culture

If you had a noisy, rude, surly neighbor, and you asked a group of psychologists to explain why this guy was such a miserable person, they might give you different answers. Depending on their theoretical perspective, they might cite your neighbor's biological makeup, his belligerent attitude toward the world, the way he was brought up, an environment that encourages his nasty temper, or the influence of his unconscious motives. Modern psychologists tend to examine human behavior through several lenses.

The Major Psychological Perspectives

The five lenses that predominate in psychology today are the *biological, learning, cognitive, sociocultural,* and *psychodynamic* perspectives. These approaches reflect different questions about human behavior, different assumptions about how the mind works, and, most important, different ways of explaining why people do what they do.

1 **The** biological perspective *focuses on how bodily events affect behavior, feelings, and thoughts.* Electrical impulses shoot along the intricate pathways of the nervous system. Hormones course through the bloodstream, telling internal organs to slow down or speed up. Chemical substances flow across the tiny gaps that separate one microscopic brain cell from another. Biological psychologists want to know how these physical events interact with events in the external environment to produce perceptions, memories, and behavior.

biological perspective A psychological approach that emphasizes bodily events and changes associated with actions, feelings, and thoughts.

Researchers in this perspective study how biology affects learning and performance, perceptions of reality, the experience of emotion, and vulnerability to emotional disorder. They study how the mind and body interact in illness and health. They investigate the contributions of genes and other biological factors in the development of traits and abilities. And in a popular new specialty, *evolutionary psychology,* which follows in the tradition of functionalism, researchers have been studying how our species' evolutionary past may help explain the functions of many of our present behaviors and psychological traits (see Chapter 3). The message of the biological approach is that we cannot really know ourselves if we do not know our bodies.

2 *The* learning perspective *is concerned with how the environment and experience affect a person's (or a nonhuman animal's) actions.* Within this perspective, *behaviorists* focus on the environmental rewards and punishers that maintain or discourage specific behaviors. Behaviorists do not invoke the mind or mental states to explain behavior. They prefer to stick to what they can observe and measure directly: acts and events taking place in the environment. *Social-cognitive learning theorists,* on the other hand, combine elements of behaviorism with research on thoughts, values, expectations, and intentions. They believe that people learn not only by adapting their behavior to the environment, but also by imitating others and by thinking about the events happening around them.

The learning perspective has many practical applications. Behavioral programs have helped people get rid of unwanted habits and acquire better ones; social-cognitive learning techniques have helped people boost their motivation and become more self-confident. Historically, the behaviorists' insistence on precision and objectivity has done much to advance psychology as a science, and learning research in general has given psychology some of its most reliable findings.

3 *The* cognitive perspective *emphasizes what goes on in people's heads*—how people reason, remember, understand language, solve problems, explain experiences, and form beliefs. (The word *cognitive* comes from the Latin for "to know.") One of this perspective's most important contributions has been to show how people's thoughts and explanations affect their actions, feelings, and choices. Cognitive researchers do not rely on the structuralists' method of introspection; instead, they have developed clever ways to infer mental processes from observable behavior. With these methods, they have been able to study phenomena that were once only the stuff of speculation, such as emotions, motivations, and insight. They are designing computer programs that model how humans perform complex tasks; discovering what goes on in the mind of an infant; and identifying types of intelligence not measured by conventional IQ tests. The cognitive approach is one of the strongest forces in psychology, and it has inspired an explosion of research on the intricate workings of the mind.

4 *The* sociocultural perspective *focuses on social and cultural forces outside the individual,* forces that shape every aspect of behavior, from how (and whether!) we kiss to what and where we eat. Most of us underestimate the impact of other people, the social context, and cultural rules on nearly everything we do. We are like fish that are unaware they live in water, so obvious is water in their lives. Sociocultural psychologists study the water—the social and cultural environment that people "swim" in every day.

Within this perspective, *social psychologists* focus on social rules and roles, how groups affect attitudes and behavior, why people obey authority, and how each of us is affected by other people—spouses, lovers, friends, bosses, parents, and strangers. *Cultural psychologists* examine how cultural rules and values— both explicit and unspoken—affect people's development, behavior, and feelings. They might study how culture influences people's willingness to help a stranger

learning perspective A psychological approach that emphasizes how the environment and experience affect a person's or animal's actions; it includes *behaviorism* and *social-cognitive learning theories.*

cognitive perspective A psychological approach that emphasizes mental processes in perception, memory, language, problem solving, and other areas of behavior.

sociocultural perspective A psychological approach that emphasizes social and cultural influences on behavior.

in distress, or how it influences what people do when they are angry. Because human beings are social animals who are profoundly affected by their different cultural worlds, the sociocultural perspective has made psychology a more representative and rigorous discipline.

5 *The* psychodynamic perspective *deals with unconscious dynamics within the individual, such as inner forces, conflicts, or instinctual energy.* It has its origins in Freud's theory of psychoanalysis, but many other psychodynamic theories also exist. Psychodynamic psychologists try to dig below the surface of a person's behavior to get to its unconscious roots; they think of themselves as archeologists of the mind.

Psychodynamic psychology is the thumb on the hand of psychology—connected to the other fingers, but also set apart from them because it differs radically in its language, methods, and standards of acceptable evidence. Although some psychological scientists are doing empirical studies of psychodynamic concepts, many others believe that psychodynamic approaches belong in philosophy or literature rather than in academic psychology. You are unlikely to find psychoanalysis mentioned much in mainstream journals of psychological science (Robins, Gosling, & Craik, 1999). Outside of empirical psychology, however, many psychotherapists, novelists, and laypeople are attracted to the psychodynamic emphasis on such grand psychological issues as relations between the sexes, the power of sexuality, and the universal fear of death. Later in this book, we will candidly discuss the many controversies surrounding psychodynamic ideas.

What makes us who we are? Psychologists approach questions about human behavior from five major perspectives: biological, learning, cognitive, sociocultural, and psychodynamic.

Review 1.2 on page 22 presents a summary of these five perspectives and shows you how they might be applied to a concrete issue, the problem of violence. See if you can apply these perspectives to another issue of your own choosing.

Two Influential Movements in Psychology

Throughout psychology's history, various movements and intellectual trends have emerged that do not fit neatly into any of the major perspectives. In the 1960s, **humanist psychologists** rejected the two dominant psychological approaches of the time, psychoanalysis and behaviorism. Humanists regarded psychoanalysis, with its emphasis on dangerous sexual and aggressive impulses, as too pessimistic a view of human nature, one that overlooked human resilience and the capacity for joy. And humanists regarded behaviorism, with its emphasis on observable acts, as too mechanistic and "mindless" a view of human nature, one that ignored what really matters to most people—their uniquely human hopes and aspirations. In the humanists' view, human behavior is not completely determined by either unconscious conflicts or the environment. People are capable of free will and therefore have the ability to make more of themselves than either psychoanalysts or behaviorists would predict. The goal of humanist psychology was, and still is, to help people express themselves creatively and achieve their full potential.

Although humanism is no longer a dominant movement in psychology, it has had considerable influence both inside and outside the field. Many psychologists across all perspectives embrace some humanist ideas, although most regard humanism as a philosophy of life rather than a systematic approach to psychology. Further, many topics raised by the humanists, such as creativity, joy, humor, and courage, are now

psychodynamic perspective A psychological approach that emphasizes unconscious dynamics within the individual, such as inner forces, conflicts, or the movement of instinctual energy.

humanist psychology A psychological approach that emphasizes personal growth and the achievement of human potential, rather than the scientific understanding and assessment of behavior.

REVIEW 1.2 FIVE MAJOR PSYCHOLOGICAL PERSPECTIVES

	Perspective	Major Topics of Study	Sample Finding on Violence
	Biological	The nervous system, hormones, brain chemistry, heredity, evolutionary influences	Brain damage caused by birth complications or child abuse might incline some people toward violence.
	Learning	Environment and experience	
	Behavioral	Environmental determinants of observable behavior	Violence increases when it pays off.
	Social-cognitive	Environmental influences, observation and imitation, beliefs and values	Violent role models can influence some children to behave aggressively.
	Cognitive	Thinking, memory, language, problem solving, perceptions	Violent people are often quick to perceive provocation and insult.
	Sociocultural	Social and cultural contexts	
	Social Psychology	Social rules and roles, groups, relationships	People are often more aggressive in a crowd than they would be on their own.
	Cultural Psychology	Cultural norms, values, and expectations	Cultures based on herding rather than agriculture tend to train boys to be aggressive.
	Psychodynamic	Unconscious thoughts, desires, and conflicts	A man who murders prostitutes may have unconscious conflicts about his mother and about sexuality.

being studied by scientific psychologists from many fields. A contemporary research specialty known as "positive psychology" follows in the footsteps of humanism (Taylor, 2001). It focuses on the qualities that enable people to be happy, optimistic, and resilient in times of stress (Fredrickson, 2001; Seligman & Csikszentmihaly, 2000). But humanism has had its greatest direct influence in psychotherapy and in the human potential and self-help movements.

Another important movement, which emerged in the early 1970s, was **feminist psychology.** As women began to enter psychology in greater numbers, they documented evidence of a pervasive bias in the research methods used and in the very questions that researchers had been asking (Bem, 1993; Crawford & Marecek, 1989; Hare-Mustin & Marecek, 1990). They noted that many studies used only men as subjects—and usually only young, white, middle-class men, at that—and they showed why it was often inappropriate to generalize to everyone else from such a narrow research base. They spurred the growth of research on topics that had long been ignored in psychology, including menstruation, motherhood, the dynamics of power and sexuality in relationships, definitions of masculinity and femininity, gender roles, and sexist attitudes. They critically examined the male bias in psychotherapy, starting with Freud's own case studies (Hare-Mustin, 1991). And they analyzed the social consequences of psychological findings, showing how research has often been used to justify the lower status of women and other disadvantaged groups.

Critics, both outside and within feminist psychology, are concerned that some feminists have replaced a male bias in research with a female bias—for example, by doing studies of women only and then drawing conclusions about gender differences, or by replacing the "women are inferior to men" stereotype with a "women are superior to men" stereotype (Yoder & Kahn, 1993). They also note that the goal of gender equality sometimes leads feminist psychologists to embrace conclusions that are appealing to many women—such as the notion that women are "naturally" kinder, more empathic, less aggressive, or more compassionate than men—but that lack solid empirical support (Mednick, 1989; Peplau & Conrad, 1989; Stimpson, 1996).

Nonetheless, feminist psychology has greatly advanced psychology as a field because it has had such an impact on efforts to make psychology the study of all human beings. Other groups have made similar contributions; in 1976, black psychologist Robert Guthrie, in *Even the Rat Was White,* wrote a searing and influential indictment of racism in psychological research. Since the 1970s, African-American, Latino, and Asian psychologists, gay and lesbian psychologists, and disabled psychologists have hugely expanded the theoretical and empirical vistas of psychology, as we will see throughout this book.

feminist psychology A psychological approach that analyzes the influence of social inequities on gender relations and on the behavior of the two sexes.

QUICK QUIZ

Anxiety is a common problem. To test your understanding of the five major perspectives in psychology, match each possible explanation of anxiety on the left with a perspective on the right.

1. Anxious people often think about the future in distorted ways.
2. Anxiety is due to forbidden, unconscious desires.
3. Anxiety symptoms often bring hidden rewards, such as being excused from exams.
4. Excessive anxiety can be caused by a chemical imbalance.
5. A national emphasis on competition and success promotes anxiety about failure.

a. behavioral
b. psychodynamic
c. sociocultural
d. biological
e. cognitive

Answers:

1.e 2.b 3.a 4.d 5.c

WHAT'S AHEAD

- **If someone tells you that he or she is a psychologist, why can't you assume that the person is a therapist?**
- **If you decided to call yourself a "psychotherapist," would you be breaking the law?**
- **What's the difference between a clinical psychologist and a psychiatrist?**

What Psychologists Do

Now you know the main viewpoints that guide psychologists in their work. But what do psychologists actually do with their time between breakfast and dinner?

To most people, the word *psychologist* conjures up an image of a therapist listening intently while a client, perhaps stretched out on a couch, pours forth his or her troubles. Many psychologists do in fact fit this image (though chairs are more common than couches these days). Many others, however, do not. The professional activities of psychologists generally fall into three broad categories: (1) teaching and doing research in colleges and universities; (2) providing health or mental health services, often referred to as *psychological practice;* and (3) conducting research or applying its findings in nonacademic settings such as business, sports, government, law, and the military (see Review 1.3). Some psychologists move flexibly across these areas. A researcher might also provide counseling services in a mental-health setting, such as a clinic or a hospital; a university professor might teach, do research, and serve as a consultant in legal cases.

REVIEW 1.3	WHAT IS A PSYCHOLOGIST?

Not all psychologists do clinical work. Many do research, teach, work in business, or consult. The professional activities of psychologists with doctorates fall into three general categories.

Academic/Research Psychologists	Clinical Psychologists	Psychologists in Industry, Law, or Other Settings
Specialize in areas of pure or applied research, such as:	*Do psychotherapy and sometimes research; may work in any of these settings:*	*Do research or serve as consultants to institutions on, for example:*
Human development	Private practice	Sports
Psychometrics (testing)	Mental health clinics	Consumer issues
Health	General hospitals	Advertising
Education	Mental hospitals	Organizational problems
Industrial/organizational psychology	Research laboratories	Environmental issues
Physiological psychology	Colleges and universities	Public policy
Sensation and perception		Opinion polls
Design and use of technology		Military training
		Animal behavior
		Legal issues

Psychological Research

Most psychologists who do research have doctoral degrees (Ph.D.s or Ed.D.s, doctorates in education). Some, seeking knowledge for its own sake, work in **basic psychology,** doing "pure" research. Others, concerned with the practical uses of knowledge, work in **applied psychology.** The two approaches are complementary: Applied psychology has direct relevance to human problems, but without basic psychology, there would be little knowledge to apply. A psychologist doing basic research might ask, "How does peer pressure influence people's attitudes and behavior?" An applied psychologist might ask, "How can knowledge about peer pressure be used to reduce binge drinking in colleges?" A psychologist doing basic research might ask, "Can a chimpanzee or a gorilla learn to use sign language?" An applied psychologist might ask, "Can techniques used to teach language to a chimpanzee be used to help mentally impaired or disturbed children who do not speak?"

Research psychology is the aspect of psychology least recognized or understood by the public. Ludy Benjamin (2003), bemoaning the fact that psychology has never had a United States postal stamp commemorating the discipline or its founders (unlike dozens of other fields, including poultry farming and truck driving), notes that the public "has minimal understanding of psychology as a science and even less appreciation for what psychological scientists do" or how psychological research contributes to human welfare.

We hope that by the time you finish this book, you will have a greater appreciation of what research psychologists do and of how their work contributes to human welfare. Here are just a few of the major nonclinical specialties in psychology:

▶ *Experimental psychologists* conduct laboratory studies of learning, motivation, emotion, sensation and perception, physiology, and cognition. Do not be misled by the term *experimental,* though; other psychologists also do experiments.

▶ *Educational psychologists* study psychological principles that explain learning and search for ways to improve educational systems. Their interests range from the application of findings on memory and thinking to the use of rewards to encourage achievement.

▶ *Developmental psychologists* study how people change and grow over time—physically, mentally, and socially. In the past, their focus was mainly on childhood, but many now study adolescence, young adulthood, the middle years, or old age.

▶ *Industrial/organizational psychologists* study behavior in the workplace. They are concerned with group decision making, employee morale, work motivation, productivity, job stress, personnel selection, marketing strategies, equipment design, and many other issues.

▶ *Psychometric psychologists* design and evaluate tests of mental abilities, aptitudes, interests, and personality. Nearly all of us have had firsthand experience with one or more of these tests in school, at work, or in the military.

Psychological Practice

Psychological practitioners, whose goal is to understand and improve people's physical and mental health, work in mental hospitals, general hospitals, clinics, schools, counseling centers, and private practice. Since the 1970s, the proportion of psychologists who are practitioners has steadily increased; practitioners now

basic psychology The study of psychological issues in order to seek knowledge for its own sake rather than for its practical application.

applied psychology The study of psychological issues that have direct practical significance; also, the application of psychological findings.

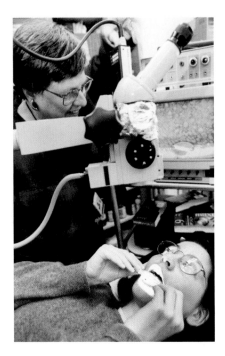

Some psychologists are researchers, others are practitioners, and some are both. On the left, researcher Linda Bartoshuk uses technology to study how the anatomy of the tongue influences the way we experience different tastes. On the right, a clinical psychologist helps a couple in therapy.

account for over two-thirds of new psychology doctorates and members of the American Psychological Association (APA), psychology's largest professional organization (APA Research Office, 1998).

Some practitioners are *counseling psychologists,* who generally help people deal with problems of everyday life, such as test anxiety, family conflicts, or low job motivation. Others are *school psychologists,* who work with parents, teachers, and students to enhance students' performance and resolve emotional difficulties. The majority, however, are *clinical psychologists,* who diagnose, treat, and study mental or emotional problems. Clinical psychologists are trained to do psychotherapy with severely disturbed people, as well as with those who are simply troubled or unhappy or who want to learn to handle their problems better.

In almost all states, a license to practice clinical psychology requires a doctorate. Most clinical psychologists have a Ph.D., some have an Ed.D., and a smaller but growing number have a Psy.D. (doctorate in psychology, pronounced "sy-dee"). Clinical psychologists typically do four or five years of graduate work in psychology, plus at least a year's internship under the direction of a practicing psychologist. Clinical programs leading to a Ph.D. or Ed.D. are usually designed to prepare a person both as a scientist and as a clinical practitioner; they require completion of a dissertation, a major scholarly project (usually involving research) that contributes to knowledge in the field. Programs leading to a Psy.D. focus on professional practice and do not usually require a research dissertation, although they typically require the student to complete a major study, literature review, or other scholarly project.

People often confuse *clinical psychologist* with three other terms: *psychotherapist, psychoanalyst,* and *psychiatrist.* But these terms mean different things:

▶ A *psychotherapist* is simply anyone who does any kind of psychotherapy. The term is not legally regulated; in fact, in most states, anyone can say that he or she is a "therapist" of one sort or another without having any training at all.

▶ A *psychoanalyst* is a person who practices one particular form of therapy, psychoanalysis. To call yourself a psychoanalyst, you must get specialized training at a psychoanalytic institute and undergo extensive psychoanalysis yourself. Until recently, admission to a psychoanalytic institute required an M.D. or a Ph.D., but increasingly this requirement is being waived; clinical social workers with master's degrees, and even interested laypeople, are often now admitted.

▶ A *psychiatrist* is a medical doctor (M.D.) who has done a three-year residency in psychiatry to learn how to diagnose and treat mental disorders under the supervision of more experienced physicians. Like some clinical psychologists, some psychiatrists do research on mental problems instead of, or in addition to, working with patients. In private practice, psychiatrists may treat any kind of emotional disorder; in hospitals, they treat the most severe disorders, such as major depression and schizophrenia. Although psychiatrists and clinical psychologists often do similar work, because of their medical training psychiatrists tend to focus more on possible biological causes of mental disorders, and they often treat these problems with medication. They can write prescriptions, and, at present, clinical psychologists in all but one state cannot. (In 2002, New Mexico granted psychologists this privilege and other states are considering doing so.) Psychiatrists, however, are often untrained in current psychological theories and methods (Luhrmann, 2000).

Other mental-health professionals include licensed clinical social workers (LCSWs) and marriage, family, and child counselors (MFCCs). These professionals ordinarily treat general problems in adjustment and family conflicts rather than severe mental disturbance, although their work may also bring them into contact with people who have serious problems—violent delinquents, people with drug addictions, sex offenders, individuals involved in domestic violence or child abuse. Licensing requirements vary from state to state but usually include a master's degree in psychology or social work and one or two years of supervised experience. (For a summary of the types of psychotherapists and the training they receive, see Review 1.4.) As if this weren't complicated enough, there are thousands of counselors who specialize in treating all kinds of problems, from sexual abuse to alcoholism; there is, however, no uniform set of standards regulating their training. Some may have nothing more than a weekend "certification" course.

Many research psychologists, and some practitioners, are worried about the increase in the number of counselors and psychotherapists who are unschooled in research methods and the empirical findings of psychology, and who use unvalidated therapy techniques (Beutler, 2000; Dawes, 1994; Poole et al., 1995). In 1987, such concerns contributed to the formation of the American Psychological Society (APS), an organization devoted to the needs and interests of psychology as a science. Many practitioners, on the other hand, argue that psychotherapy is an art, and that research findings are largely irrelevant to the work they do with clients. In Chapter 17, we will return to the important issue of the widening gap in training and attitudes between scientists and many therapists.

Partly because of these tensions, and partly because the media and the public persist in equating "psychologist" with "psychotherapist," some psychological scientists think it is time to use other labels to describe what they do and to yield the word *psychologist* to its popular meaning. Research psychologists, they say, should call themselves "cognitive scientists," "behavioral scientists," "neuroscientists," and so forth, depending on their area of study. This change in language is already underway. At present, however, the word *psychologist* still embraces all the cousins in psychology's sprawling family.

REVIEW 1.4	TYPES OF PSYCHOTHERAPISTS

Just as not all psychologists are psychotherapists, not all psychotherapists are clinical psychologists. Here are the major terms used to refer to mental-health professionals:

Psychotherapist	A person who does psychotherapy; may have anything from no degree to an advanced professional degree; the term is unregulated.
Clinical psychologist	Diagnoses, treats, and/or studies mental and emotional problems, both mild and severe; has a Ph.D., an Ed.D., or a Psy.D.
Psychoanalyst	Practices psychoanalysis; has specific training in this approach after an advanced degree (usually, but not always, an M.D. or a Ph.D.); may treat any kind of emotional disorder or pathology.
Psychiatrist	Does work similar to that of a clinical psychologist but is likely to take a more biological approach; has a medical degree (M.D.) with a specialty in psychiatry.
Licensed clinical social worker (LCSW); marriage, family, and child counselor (MFCC)	Typically treats common individual and family problems, but may also deal with more serious problems such as addiction or abuse. Licensing requirements vary, but generally has at least an M.A. in psychology or social work.

Psychologists work in all sorts of settings, from classrooms to courtrooms. On the left, sports psychologist Sean McCain helps an Olympic athlete relax and rehearse mentally what he would do physically during an actual athletic event. On the right, Louis Herman studies a dolphin's ability to understand an artificial language consisting of hand signals. In response to the gestural sequence "person" and "over," the dolphin will leap over the person in the pool.

Psychology in the Community

Since World War II, psychology has expanded rapidly in terms of scholars, publications, and specialties. The American Psychological Association now has 53 divisions. Some represent major fields such as developmental psychology or physiological psychology. Others represent specific research or professional interests, such as the psychology of women, the psychology of men, ethnic minority issues, sports, the arts, environmental concerns, gay and lesbian issues, peace, psychology and the law, and health.

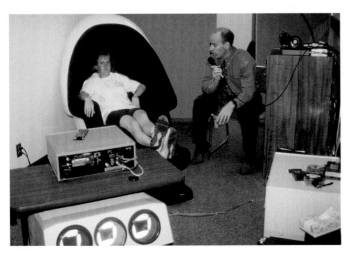

As psychology has grown, psychologists have found ways to contribute to their communities in about as many fields as you can think of. They consult with companies to improve worker satisfaction and productivity. They establish programs to improve race relations and reduce ethnic tensions. They advise commissions on how pollution and noise affect mental health. They do rehabilitation training for people who are physically or mentally disabled. They educate judges and juries about eyewitness testimony. They assist the police in emergencies involving hostages or disturbed persons. They conduct public-opinion surveys. They run suicide-prevention hotlines. They advise zoos on the care and training of animals. They help coaches improve the athletic performance of their teams. And on and on.

Is it any wonder that people are a little fuzzy about what a psychologist is?

QUICK QUIZ

Can you match the specialties on the left with their defining credentials and approaches on the right?

1. psychotherapist
2. psychiatrist
3. clinical psychologist
4. research psychologist
5. psychoanalyst

a. Trained in an approach started by Freud

b. Has Ph.D., Psy.D., or Ed.D. and does research on, or psychotherapy for, mental-health problems

c. May have any credential or none

d. Has an advanced degree (usually a Ph.D. or Ed.D) and does applied or basic research

e. Has an M.D.; tends to take a medical approach to emotional problems

Answers:

1.c 2.e 3.b 4.d 5.a

The Mosaic of Psychology

The differences we have described among the psychological perspectives have produced many passionate arguments. These differences are compounded by the fact that psychologists earn their livelihoods in many ways and are often trying to achieve different goals: knowledge for its own sake, practical knowledge, the application of knowledge in real-life settings, the ability to help people in distress. Not all psychologists, however, feel they must swear allegiance to one approach or another. Many, if not most, are *eclectic*, using what they believe to be the best features of diverse schools of thought.

Today, the field of psychology is like a giant mosaic made up of many fragments, yielding a rich, multicolored, psychological portrait. Psychologists may argue about which part of the portrait is most important, but most psychological scientists and scientist-clinicians agree on certain basic guidelines about what is and what is not acceptable in their discipline. Most believe in the importance of gathering empirical evidence instead of relying on hunches. And one thing will always unite psychologists: a fascination with the unending mysteries of human behavior and the human mind.

If you have ever wondered what makes people tick; if you love a mystery and want to know not only who did it but also why they did it; if you are willing to reconsider what you think you think . . . then you are in the right course. We invite you now to step into the world of psychology, the discipline that dares to explore the most complex topic on earth: *you.*

Taking Psychology with You

WHAT PSYCHOLOGY CAN DO FOR YOU—AND WHAT IT CAN'T

If you intend to become a research psychologist or a mental-health professional, you have an obvious reason for taking a course in psychology. But psychology can contribute to your life in many ways, whether you plan to work in the field or not. Here are a few things psychology can do for you:

▶ *Make you a more informed person.* One purpose of education is to acquaint people with their cultural heritage and with human achievements in literature, the arts, and the sciences. Because psychology plays a large role in contemporary society, being a well-informed person requires knowing something about psychological methods and findings.

▶ *Satisfy your curiosity about human nature.* When the ancient Greek philosopher Socrates admonished his students to "know thyself," he was only telling them to do what most people want to do anyway. Psychology—along with the other social sciences and with the aid of

literature, history, and philosophy—can help you better understand yourself and others.

▶ *Help you increase your control over your life.* Psychology cannot solve all your problems, but it does offer techniques that may help you handle your emotions, improve your memory, and eliminate unwanted habits. It can also foster an attitude of objectivity that is useful for analyzing your behavior and your relationships with others.

▶ *Help you on the job.* Many people who get a bachelor's degree in psychology go on to study other fields (see Figure 1.1). A background in psychology is useful for getting a job in a helping profession, for example as a welfare caseworker or a rehabilitation counselor. Anyone who works as a nurse, doctor, religious adviser, police officer, or teacher can also put psychology to work on the job. So can waiters, flight attendants, bank tellers, salespeople, reception-

ists, and others whose jobs involve customer service. Finally, psychology can be useful to those whose jobs require them to predict people's behavior—labor negotiators, politicians, advertising copywriters, managers, product designers, buyers, market researchers, magicians. . . .

▶ *Give you insights into political and social issues.* Crime, drug abuse, discrimination, and war are not only social issues but also psychological ones. Psychological knowledge alone cannot solve the complex political, social, and ethical problems that plague every society, but it can help citizens make informed judgments about them. If you know how social and cultural practices affect rates of drug use and abuse, this knowledge may affect your views about the war on drugs, and if you know how punishment affects recidivism rates, this knowledge may affect your views about mandatory sentencing of criminals.

We are optimistic about psychology's role in the world, but we want to caution you that sometimes people expect things from psychology that it cannot deliver. Psychology can't tell you the meaning of life. A philosophy of life requires not only knowledge but also reflection and a willingness to learn from life's experiences. Nor does

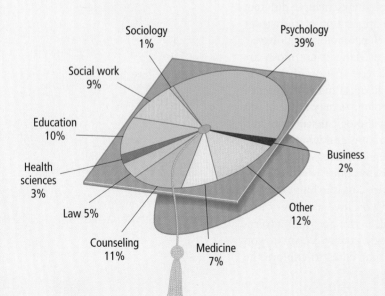

Sociology 1%
Psychology 39%
Social work 9%
Education 10%
Health sciences 3%
Law 5%
Counseling 11%
Medicine 7%
Other 12%
Business 2%

Figure 1.1

WHAT PSYCHOLOGY MAJORS GO ON TO STUDY IN GRADUATE SCHOOL

This chart, from a 1995 APA survey, shows graduate fields of study reported by students who had earlier received a bachelor's degree in psychology.

psychological understanding relieve people of responsibility for their faults and misdeeds. Knowing that your short temper is a result, in part, of your unhappy childhood does not give you a green light to yell at your family or mistreat your own kids.

Many people look to psychology for simple answers to complex questions. But as we have repeatedly emphasized, serious psychology, unlike pop psychology, does not offer simple answers or one-note explanations. Instead it offers research findings from many perspectives, which the critical thinker will try to evaluate and integrate. (In the epilogue to this book, we suggest how such an integration might apply to problems in love.)

Many years ago, George Miller, in a presidential address to the American Psychological Association (1969), called on his colleagues to "give psychology away" and to pass out psychological facts "to all who need and can use them." Ever since, critics have complained that psychologists don't know enough to "give it away." We disagree. Human behavior is complicated, but psychologists have made enormous progress in unraveling the secrets of the human brain, mind, and heart. At the end of each chapter, starting with the next one, the "Taking Psychology with You" feature will suggest ways to apply psychological findings to your own life—at school, on the job, in your relationships, and in your community.

Summary

Psychology, Pseudoscience, and Popular Opinion

▶ *Psychology* is the discipline concerned with behavior and mental processes and how they are affected by an organism's external and internal environment. Psychology's methods and reliance on *empirical evidence* distinguish it from pseudoscience and "psychobabble."

▶ Psychologists have many pseudoscientific competitors, such as astrologers and psychics. But when put to the test, the claims and predictions of these competitors have only chance-level accuracy. Psychobabble is appealing because it confirms our beliefs and prejudices; in contrast, psychology often challenges them, although it also seeks to extend our understanding of familiar facts.

Thinking Critically and Creatively about Psychology

▶ One benefit of studying psychology is the development of *critical thinking* skills and attitudes. These skills and attitudes can help people evaluate competing findings on psychological issues that are personally and socially important.

▶ The critical thinker asks questions, defines terms clearly, examines the evidence, analyzes assumptions and biases, avoids emotional reasoning, avoids oversimplification, considers alternative interpretations, and tolerates uncertainty. Critical thinking is an evolving process rather than a once-and-for-all accomplishment.

Psychology's Past: From the Armchair to the Laboratory

▶ Psychology's forerunners made some valid observations and had useful insights, but without rigorous empirical methods, they also made serious errors in the description and explanation of behavior, as in the case of *phrenology*.

▶ The official founder of scientific psychology was Wilhelm Wundt, who formally established the first psychological laboratory in 1879, in Leipzig, Germany. His work led to *structuralism*, the first of many approaches to the field. Structuralism emphasized the analysis of immediate experience into basic elements. It was soon abandoned because of its reliance on *introspection*.

▶ Another early approach, *functionalism*, was inspired in part by the evolutionary theories of Charles Darwin; it emphasized the purpose of behavior. One of its leading proponents was William James. Functionalism, too, did not last long as a distinct school of psychology, but it greatly affected the course of psychological science.

▶ Psychology as a method of psychotherapy has roots in Sigmund Freud's theory of *psychoanalysis*, which emphasizes unconscious causes of mental and emotional problems.

Psychology's Present: Behavior, Body, Mind, and Culture

▶ Five points of view predominate today in psychology. The *biological perspective* emphasizes bodily events associated with actions, thoughts, and feelings. The *learning perspective* emphasizes how the environment and a person's history affect behavior; within this perspective, *behaviorists* reject mentalistic explanations and *social-cognitive learning theorists* combine elements of behaviorism with the study of thoughts, values, and intentions. The *cognitive perspective* emphasizes mental processes in perception, problem solving, belief formation, and other human activities. The *sociocultural perspective* explores how social contexts and cultural rules affect an individual's beliefs and behavior. And the *psychodynamic perspective,* which originated with Freud's theory of psychoanalysis, emphasizes unconscious motives, conflicts, and desires; it differs greatly from the other approaches in its methods and standards of evidence.

▶ Not all approaches to psychology fit neatly into one of the five major perspectives. For example, two important movements, *humanist psychology* and *feminist psychology,* have influenced the questions researchers ask, the methods they use, and their awareness of biases in the field.

What Psychologists Do

▶ Psychologists do research and teach in colleges and universities; provide mental-health services *(psychological practice);* and conduct research and apply findings in a wide variety of nonacademic settings. *Applied psychology* is concerned with the practical uses of psychological knowledge. *Basic psychology* is concerned with knowledge for its own sake. Among the many psychological specialties are experimental, educational, developmental, industrial/organizational, psychometric, counseling, school, and clinical psychology.

▶ *Psychotherapist* is an unregulated term for anyone who does therapy, including persons who have no credentials or training at all. Licensed therapists differ according to their training and approach. *Clinical psychologists* have a Ph.D., an Ed.D., or a Psy.D.; *psychiatrists* have an M.D.; *psychoanalysts* are trained in psychoanalytic institutes; and licensed clinical social workers, counselors with various specialties, and marriage, family, and child counselors may have a variety of postgraduate degrees. Many psychologists are concerned about an increase in poorly trained psychotherapists who lack credentials or a firm understanding of research methods and findings.

The Mosaic of Psychology

▶ Many, if not most, psychologists are eclectic, drawing on more than one school of psychology. Although psychologists differ in their perspectives and goals, psychological scientists and scientist-practitioners generally agree on which methods of study are acceptable, and all psychologists are united by their fascination with the mysteries of behavior.

Key Terms

Use this list to check your understanding of terms and people in this chapter. If you have trouble with a term, you can find it on the page listed.

◀ LOOKING BACK

Now that you have read this chapter, see whether you can answer the "What's Ahead" questions that preceded each major section. By using these questions to "look back," you can find out how much you have learned—and what you may need to review.

- How does "psychobabble" differ from serious psychology? (pp. 3–6)

- How accurate are psychology's nonscientific competitors, such as astrologers and psychics? (p. 6)

- Are "critical thinkers" always critical? (p. 7)

- Are all opinions created equal? (p. 7)

- What guidelines can help you evaluate psychological claims? (pp. 8–13)

- What is the lesson of phrenology for modern psychology? (pp. 15–16)

- How old is the science of psychology? (p. 16)

- Was Sigmund Freud the official founder of scientific psychology? (p. 16)

- What are the five major perspectives in psychology? (pp. 19–21)

- Why is psychoanalysis the "thumb on the hand of psychology"? (p. 21)

- How have humanism and feminism influenced psychology? (pp. 21–23)

- If someone tells you that he or she is a psychologist, why can't you assume that the person is a therapist? (p. 24)

- If you decided to call yourself a "psychotherapist," would you be breaking the law? (p. 26)

- What's the difference between a clinical psychologist and a psychiatrist? (p. 27)

Possible answers for the Get Involved *exercise on p. 5:* "Opposites attract"; "He who hesitates is lost"; "The pen is mightier than the sword"; "Winning isn't everything, it's the only thing" (often attributed to Vince Lombardi); and "You're never too old to learn."

Go to *Live!* psych **WWW.PRENHALL.COM/WADE** for activities, practice tests, and review material.

2

How Psychologists Do Research

The negative cautions of science are never popular.

MARGARET MEAD

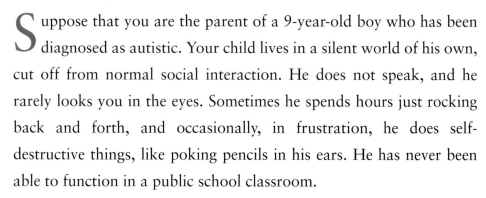

S uppose that you are the parent of a 9-year-old boy who has been diagnosed as autistic. Your child lives in a silent world of his own, cut off from normal social interaction. He does not speak, and he rarely looks you in the eyes. Sometimes he spends hours just rocking back and forth, and occasionally, in frustration, he does self-destructive things, like poking pencils in his ears. He has never been able to function in a public school classroom.

You are ecstatic, then, when you hear about a new technique called "facilitated communication," which promises to release your child from his mental prison. According to proponents of this technique, when autistic or mentally impaired children are placed in front of a keyboard and an adult "facilitator" gently places a hand over the child's hand or forearm, amazing things happen. Children who have never used words are suddenly able to peck out complete sentences, answer questions, and divulge their thoughts. One child reportedly typed, "I amn not a utistivc on thje typ" (I am not autistic on the typewriter). Some children, through their facilitators, have supposedly even mastered high-school level subjects, or have written poetry of astonishing beauty. The fee is steep, but it certainly seems worth it.

Or is it?

The situation we have described is not hypothetical; thousands of hopeful parents have been drawn to the promise of facilitated communication. Psychological scientists, however, have been more cautious. Before accepting claims and testimonials about any program or therapy, they put those claims and testimonials to the test. In the case of facilitated communication, they have done experiments involving hundreds of autistic children and their facilitators (Eberlin et al., 1993; Jacobson, Mulick, & Schwartz, 1995; Mulick, 1994). Their techniques have been simple: They show the child a picture to identify but show the facilitator a different picture, or no picture at all; or they keep the facilitator from hearing the questions being put to the child. Under these conditions, the child types out only what the facilitator sees or hears—not what the child does.

This research shows that what happens in facilitated communication is exactly what happens when a medium guides a person's hand over a Ouija board to help the

Using "facilitated communication" (FC), Betsy Wheaton, a child with autism, appeared to type that she had been sexually abused by her family; she was removed from her home. But when researcher Howard Shane tested her by showing pictures of different objects separately to Betsy and her facilitator, Betsy typed only what the facilitator saw. If Betsy saw a cup but the facilitator saw a hat (left), Betsy typed "hat" (right). Because of these results, the facilitator stopped using FC and Betsy was reunited with her family.

person receive "messages" from a "spirit": The person doing the "facilitating" is unconsciously nudging the other person's hand in the desired direction (Burgess et al., 1998; Spitz, 1997). Facilitated communication, on closer inspection, turns out to be *facilitator* communication. This finding is vitally important, because if parents waste their time and money on a treatment that doesn't work, they may never get genuine help for their children, and they will suffer when their false hopes are finally shattered by reality.

You can see why research methods matter so much to psychologists. Some students would rather not study research methods; "let's just cut straight to the findings," they say. But these methods are the tools that allow psychologists to separate truth from unfounded belief, to sort out conflicting views, and to correct false ideas that may cause people harm. We hope that when you hear and read about psychological issues, you will consider not only what the findings say, but also how the information was obtained and how the results were interpreted, using information in this chapter.

WHAT'S AHEAD

- Where do psychological scientists get their hypotheses?
- In what way are scientists risk takers?
- Why is secrecy a big "no-no" in science?

What Makes Psychological Research Scientific?

When we refer to psychologists as scientists, we do not mean that they work with complicated gadgets and machines or wear white lab coats (although some do). The scientific enterprise has more to do with attitudes and procedures than with apparatus and apparel. Here are a few key characteristics of the ideal scientist:

1 *Precision.* Scientists sometimes launch an investigation because they have a hunch about some behavior, based on previous findings or casual observations. Often, however, they start out with a general theory, an organized system of assumptions and principles that purports to explain certain phenomena and how they are related. A scientific theory is not just someone's personal opinion, as people imply when they say "It's only a theory." Theories that come to be accepted by the scientific community are those that account for many empirical findings.

From a hunch or theory, the psychological scientist derives a **hypothesis**, a statement that attempts to describe or explain a given behavior. Initially, this statement may be quite general, as in, say, "Misery loves company." But before any research can be done, the hypothesis must be made more precise. For example, "Misery loves company" might be rephrased as "People who are anxious about a threatening situation tend to seek out others facing the same threat."

theory An organized system of assumptions and principles that purports to explain a specified set of phenomena and their interrelationships.

hypothesis A statement that attempts to predict or to account for a set of phenomena; scientific hypotheses specify relationships among events or variables and are empirically tested.

A hypothesis, in turn, leads to predictions about what will happen in a particular situation. In a prediction, terms such as *anxiety* or *threatening situation* are given operational definitions, which specify how the phenomena in question are to be observed and measured. "Anxiety" might be defined operationally as a score on an anxiety questionnaire; "threatening situation" might be defined as the threat of an electric shock. The prediction might be, "If you raise people's anxiety scores by telling them they are going to receive electric shocks, and then give them the choice of waiting alone or with others in the same situation, they will be more likely to choose to wait with others than they would be if they were not anxious." The prediction can then be tested, using systematic methods.

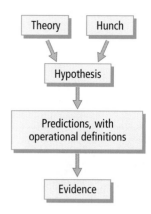

2 *Skepticism.* Scientists do not accept ideas on faith or authority; their motto is "Show me!" Some of the greatest scientific advances have been made by those who dared to doubt what everyone else assumed to be true: that the sun revolves around the earth, that illness can be cured by applying leeches to the skin, that madness is a sign of demonic possession. In the world of the researcher, skepticism means treating conclusions, both new and old, with caution. Caution, however, must be balanced by an openness to new ideas and evidence. Otherwise, the scientist may wind up as shortsighted as the famous physicist Lord Kelvin, who at the end of the nineteenth century reputedly declared with great confidence that radio had no future, X rays were a hoax, and "heavier-than-air flying machines" were impossible.

3 *Reliance on empirical evidence.* Unlike plays and poems, scientific theories and hypotheses are not judged by how pleasing or entertaining they are. An idea may initially generate excitement because it is plausible, imaginative, or appealing, but eventually it must be backed by empirical evidence if it is to be taken seriously. A collection of anecdotes or an appeal to authority will not do. Nor will the "intuitive" appeal of the idea, or its popularity. As Nobel Prize–winning scientist Peter Medawar (1979) once wrote, "The intensity of the conviction that a hypothesis is true has no bearing on whether it is true or not."

4 *Willingness to make "risky predictions."* A related principle is that a scientist must state an idea in such a way that it can be *refuted*, or disproved by counterevidence. This principle, known as the principle of falsifiability, does not mean that the idea *will* be disproved, only that it *could be* if contrary evidence were to be discovered. Another way of saying this is that a scientist must risk disconfirmation by predicting not only what will happen, but also what will *not* happen. In the "misery loves company" study, the hypothesis would be refuted if most anxious people went off alone to sulk and worry, or if anxiety had no effect on their behavior (see Figure 2.1 on page 38). A willingness to make "risky" predictions forces the scientist to take such negative evidence seriously. Any researcher who refuses to go out on a limb and risk disconfirmation is not a true scientist, and any theory that purports to explain everything that could conceivably happen is unscientific.

The principle of falsifiability plays a central role in science, because all of us—even scientists—are vulnerable to the confirmation bias: the tendency to look for and accept evidence that supports our pet theories and assumptions and ignore or reject evidence that contradicts our beliefs. The principle of falsifiability compels researchers to resist the confirmation bias and to consider counterevidence.

If you keep your eyes open, you will find many violations of the principle of falsifiability in everyday life. For example, during the 1990s, some police officers and therapists argued that murderous satanic cults were widespread, even though research psychologists, the FBI, and police investigators were never able to substantiate this claim (Goodman et al., 1995; Hicks, 1991). Believers said they were not

operational definition A precise definition of a term in a hypothesis, which specifies the operations for observing and measuring the process or phenomenon being defined.

principle of falsifiability The principle that a scientific theory must make predictions that are specific enough to expose the theory to the possibility of disconfirmation; that is, the theory must predict not only what will happen, but also what will not happen.

confirmation bias The tendency to look for or pay attention only to information that confirms one's own belief.

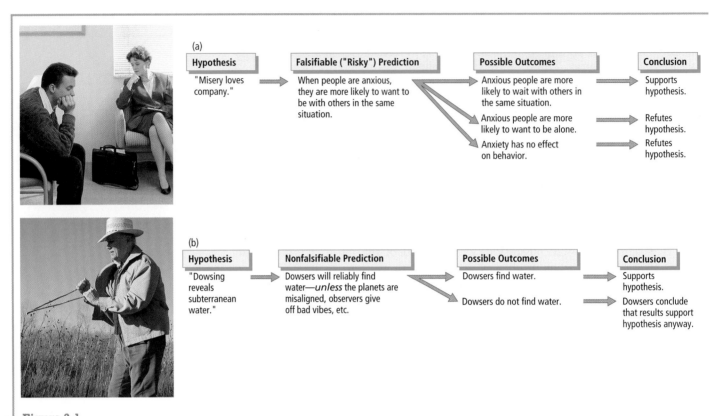

Figure 2.1

THE PRINCIPLE OF FALSIFIABILITY

The scientific method requires researchers to expose their ideas to the possibility of counterevidence, as in row (a). In contrast, people claiming psychic powers, such as dowsers (who say they can find underground water with a "dowsing rod" that bends when water is present), typically interpret *all* possible outcomes as support for their assertions, as in row (b). Their claims are therefore untestable.

surprised by the lack of evidence because satanic cults covered up their activities by eating bodies or burying them. The FBI's failure to find the evidence was "proof," they said, that the FBI itself was part of a conspiracy to support the satanists. To believers, then, the lack of evidence was actually a sign of the cults' success. But think about that claim. If a lack of evidence can count as evidence, then what could possibly count as counterevidence? What could ever get believers to change their minds, to admit they were wrong?

5 *Openness.* Science depends on the free flow of ideas and full disclosure of the procedures used in a study. Scientists must be willing to tell others where they got their ideas, how they tested them, and what the results were. They must do this clearly and in detail so that other scientists can repeat, or *replicate,* their studies and verify—or challenge—the findings. Secrecy is a big "no-no" in science.

Sometimes replication shows that an apparently fabulous phenomenon was just a fluke. A famous example occurred many years ago, when a team of researchers trained flatworms to cringe in response to a flashing light. They then killed the worms, ground them into a mash, and fed the mash to a second set of worms. This cannibalistic diet, the researchers reported, sped up acquisition of the cringe response in the second group of worms (McConnell, 1962). As you can imagine, this finding caused tremendous excitement. If worms could learn faster by ingesting the "memory molecules" of their fellow worms, what might this mean for human memory? Students joked about grinding up professors' brains; professors joked about inserting memory molecules in students. But, alas, other researchers were never able to replicate the results.

If you think about it, you will see that these principles of good science correspond to the critical thinking guidelines described in Chapter 1. Formulating a prediction with operational definitions corresponds to "define your terms."

Openness to new ideas encourages scientists to "ask questions" and to "consider other interpretations." Reliance on empirical evidence is a hallmark of critical thinking, and helps scientists avoid the temptation to oversimplify. The principle of falsifiability forces scientists to "analyze assumptions and biases" in a fair-minded fashion. And until their results have been replicated and verified, scientists must "tolerate uncertainty."

Do psychologists and other scientists always live up to the lofty standards expected of them? Of course not. For one thing, when research is sponsored by private, for-profit businesses, such as drug manufacturers, the scientific requirement of full disclosure may come smack up against a company's desire to keep its competitors from learning about research on a potentially lucrative product. Moreover, scientists, being only human, may not always follow the "rules" the way they should. They may put too much trust in their personal experiences. They may permit ambition to interfere with openness. They may fail to put their theories fully to the test: It is always easier to be skeptical about someone else's ideas than about your own.

Commitment to one's theories is not in itself a bad thing. Passion is the fuel of progress. It motivates researchers to think boldly, defend unpopular ideas, and do the exhaustive testing that is often required to support an idea. But passion can also cloud perceptions and in some sad cases has even led to deception and fraud. That is why science is a communal activity. Scientists are expected to share their evidence and procedures with others. They are also expected to submit their results to professional journals, which send the findings to experts in the field for evaluation and suggested revisions before publishing them. This process, called *peer review,* ensures that the work lives up to accepted scientific standards. Peer review is supposed to precede any announcements to the public through press releases, Internet postings, or popular books. The research community—in our case, the psychological community—acts as a jury, scrutinizing and sifting the evidence, approving some viewpoints and relegating others to the scientific scrap heap.

The peer review process is not perfect, but it does give science a built-in system of checks and balances. Individuals are not necessarily objective, honest, or rational, but science forces them to subject their findings to scrutiny and to justify their claims.

QUICK QUIZ

Can you identify which rule of science was violated in each of the following cases?

1. For years, writer Norman Cousins told how he had cured himself of a rare, life-threatening disease through a combination of humor and vitamins. In a best-selling book about his experience, he recommended the same approach to others.

2. Benjamin Rush, an eighteenth-century physician, believed that yellow fever should be treated by bloodletting. Although many of his patients died, Rush did not lose faith in his approach; he attributed each recovery to his treatment and each death to the severity of the disease (Stanovich, 1996).

Answers:

1. Cousins offered only a personal account and did not gather or cite empirical evidence from scientific studies or consider cases of sick people who were not helped by humor and vitamins. 2. Rush violated the principle of falsifiability: He interpreted a patient's survival as support for his treatment and explained away each death by saying that the person had been too ill for the treatment to work. Thus there was no possible counterevidence that could refute the theory (which, by the way, was dead wrong—the "treatment" was actually as dangerous as the disease).

- When are psychological case studies informative, and when are they useless?
- Why do psychologists often observe people's behavior in laboratories instead of in everyday situations?
- Why should you be skeptical about psychological tests you find in magazines and newspapers, or on the Internet?
- What's the difference between a psychological survey and a poll of listeners conducted by a radio talk-show host?

Descriptive Studies: Establishing the Facts

Psychologists gather evidence to support their hypotheses by using different methods, depending on the kinds of questions they want to answer. These methods are not mutually exclusive, however. Just as a police detective may use a magnifying glass *and* a fingerprint duster *and* interviews of suspects to figure out "who done it," psychological sleuths often draw on different techniques at different stages of an ongoing investigation. As you read about these methods, you may want to list their advantages and disadvantages so you will remember them better, then check your list against the one in Review 2.1 on page 55.

We will begin with **descriptive methods,** which allow researchers to describe and predict behavior but not necessarily to choose one explanation over competing ones.

Case Studies

A **case study** (or *case history*) is a detailed description of a particular individual, based on careful observation or on formal psychological testing. It may include information about a person's childhood, dreams, fantasies, experiences, relationships, and hopes—anything that will provide insight into the person's behavior. Case studies are most commonly used by clinicians, but sometimes academic researchers use them as well, especially when they are just beginning to study a topic or when practical or ethical considerations prevent them from gathering information in other ways.

For example, suppose you want to know whether the first few years of life are critical for acquiring a first language. Can children who have missed out on hearing speech (or, in the case of deaf children, seeing signs) "catch up" later? Obviously, psychologists cannot answer this question by isolating children and seeing what happens! So instead they have studied unusual cases of language deprivation.

One such case involved a 13-year-old girl who had been cruelly locked up in a small room since the age of 1½, strapped for hours to a potty chair. Her mother, a battered wife, barely cared for her, and although the child may have heard some speech through the walls of her room, no one in the family spoke a word to her. If she made the slightest sound, her severely disturbed father beat her with a large piece of wood. When she was finally rescued, "Genie," as researchers called her, did not know how to chew or stand erect, was not toilet trained, and spat on anything that was handy, including other people. Her only sounds were high-pitched whimpers. Eventually, she was able to learn some rules of social conduct, and she began to understand short sentences and to use words to convey her needs, describe her moods, and even lie. Yet even after many years, Genie's grammar and pronunciation remained abnormal. She never learned to use pronouns correctly, ask questions, produce proper negative sentences, or use the little word endings that communicate tense, number, and possession (Curtiss, 1977, 1982; Rymer, 1993). This

This picture, drawn by Genie, a young girl who endured years of isolation and mistreatment, shows one of her favorite pastimes, listening to researcher Susan Curtiss play the piano. Genie's drawings were used along with other case material to study her mental and social development.

sad case, along with similar ones, suggests that a critical period exists for language development—a window of opportunity for acquiring language—with the likelihood of fully mastering a first language declining steadily after early childhood and falling off drastically at puberty (Pinker, 1994).

Case studies illustrate psychological principles in a way that abstract generalizations and cold statistics never can, and they produce a more detailed picture of an individual than other methods do. In biological research, cases of patients with brain damage have yielded important clues to how the brain is organized (see Chapter 4). But in most instances, case studies have serious drawbacks. Information is often missing, or is hard to interpret; for example, no one knows what Genie's language development was like before she was locked up, or whether she was born with mental deficits. The observer who writes up the case is bound to have certain biases that influence which facts he or she notices and includes—or omits. And the subject of the case study may have selective and inaccurate memories of his or her past experiences, making the observer's conclusions somewhat unreliable (see Chapter 10). Most important, this method has limited usefulness for deriving general principles of behavior because the person who is the focus of the case study may be *unrepresentative* of the group that a researcher is interested in. For all these reasons, case studies are usually only sources, rather than tests, of hypotheses.

> **THINKING CRITICALLY**
>
> **Don't Oversimplify**
>
> Case studies are often enormously compelling, which is why talk shows love them. But often they are merely anecdotes. What are the dangers in using case studies to draw general conclusions about human nature?

When people do draw conclusions solely on the basis of case studies, the results can be disastrous. For example, many clinicians once believed that autism in children was caused by rejecting, cold, "refrigerator" mothers. This belief was based on the writings of psychoanalyst Bruno Bettelheim (1967), who drew his conclusions from three published cases of autistic children whose mothers had psychological problems, and from a few other unpublished cases whose number he exaggerated (Pollak, 1997). When proper studies were finally done, using objective testing procedures and a larger, representative group of autistic children and their parents, scientists learned that parents of autistic children are as psychologically healthy as any other parents. Today we know that autism stems from a neurological problem rather than from any psychological problems of the mothers, and that certain genes may increase susceptibility to the disorder (Ingram et al., 2000). But because so many people accepted Bettelheim's claims, thousands of women blamed themselves for their children's disorder and suffered needless guilt and remorse.

Be wary, then, of the compelling cases reported in the media by individuals ("I was a multiple personality") or therapists. Often, these stories are only "arguing by anecdote," and they are not a basis for drawing firm conclusions about anything.

Observational Studies

In **observational studies,** the researcher observes, measures, and records behavior, taking care to avoid intruding on the people (or animals) being observed. Unlike case studies, observational studies usually involve many participants ("subjects"). Often an observational study is the first step in a program of research; it is helpful to have a good description of behavior before you try to explain it.

The primary purpose of *naturalistic observation* is to find out how people or animals act in their normal social environments. Ethologists such as Jane Goodall and the late Dian Fossey used this method to study apes and other animals in the wild. Psychologists use naturalistic observation wherever people happen to be—at home, on playgrounds or streets, in schoolrooms, or in offices. In one study, a social psychologist and his students ventured into a common human habitat: bars. They

descriptive methods Methods that yield descriptions of behavior but not necessarily causal explanations.

case study A detailed description of a particular individual being studied or treated.

observational study A study in which the researcher carefully and systematically observes and records behavior without interfering with the behavior; it may involve either naturalistic or laboratory observation.

Get Involved ⫶⫶

A Study of "Personal Space"

Try a little naturalistic observation of your own. Go to a public place where people voluntarily seat themselves near others, such as a movie theater or a cafeteria with large tables. If you choose a setting where many people enter at once, you might recruit some friends to help you; you can divide the area into sections and give each observer one section to observe. As individuals and groups sit down, note how many seats they leave between themselves and the next person. On the average, how far do people tend to sit from strangers? Once you have your results, see how many possible explanations you can come up with.

wanted to know whether people in bars drink more when they are in groups than when they are alone. They visited all 32 pubs in a midsized city, ordered beers, and recorded on napkins and pieces of newspaper how much the other patrons imbibed. They found that drinkers in groups consumed more than individuals who were alone. Those in groups did not drink any faster; they just lingered in the bar longer (Sommer, 1977).

Note that the students who did this study did not rely on their impressions or memories of how much people drank. In observational studies, researchers count, rate, or measure behavior in a systematic way. These procedures help to minimize the tendency of observers to notice only what they expect or want to see. Careful record keeping ensures accuracy and allows different observers to cross-check their observations for consistency. Observers must also take pains to avoid being obvious about what they are doing and to disguise their intentions so they can see people as they really are. If the researchers who studied drinking habits had marched in with video cameras and announced that they were psychology students, the bar patrons might not have behaved naturally.

Sometimes psychologists prefer to make observations in a laboratory setting. In *laboratory observation*, psychologists have more control of the situation. They can

Psychologists using laboratory observation have gathered valuable information about brain and muscle activity during sleep. Psychologists using naturalistic observation have studied how people in crowded places modify their gaze and body position to preserve a sense of privacy.

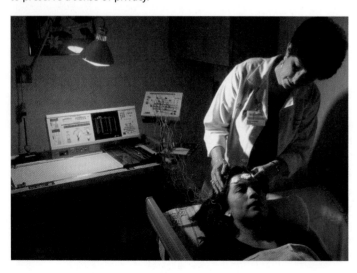

use sophisticated equipment, maintain a clear line of vision, remain hidden behind a one-way mirror, and so forth. Suppose that you wanted to know how infants of different ages respond when left with a stranger. The most efficient approach might be to have parents and their infants come to your laboratory, observe them playing together for a while through a one-way window, then have a stranger enter the room and, a few minutes later, have the parent leave. You could record signs of distress, interactions with the stranger, and other behavior. If you did this, you would find that very young infants carry on cheerfully with whatever they are doing when the parent leaves. However, by the age of about 8 months, many children will burst into tears or show other signs of what child psychologists call "separation anxiety."

One shortcoming of laboratory observation is that the presence of researchers and special equipment may cause subjects to behave differently than they would in their usual surroundings. Further, observational studies, like other descriptive studies, are more useful for describing behavior than for explaining it. For example, the barroom results we described do not necessarily mean that being in a group makes people drink a lot. People may join a group because they are already interested in drinking and find it more comfortable to hang around the bar if they are with others. Similarly, if we observe infants protesting whenever a parent leaves the room, we cannot be sure *why* they are protesting. Is it because they have become attached to their parents and want them nearby? Is it because they have learned from experience that crying brings an adult with a cookie and a cuddle? Observational studies alone cannot answer such questions.

 2.1

Tests

Psychological tests, sometimes called *assessment instruments,* are procedures for measuring and evaluating personality traits, emotional states, aptitudes, interests, abilities, and values. Hundreds of psychological tests are used in industry, education, the military, and the helping professions, and many tests are also used in research studies. Typically, tests require people to answer a series of written or oral questions. The answers may then be totaled to yield a single numerical score, or a set of scores. *Objective tests,* also called "inventories," measure beliefs, feelings, or behaviors of which an individual is aware; *projective tests* are designed to tap unconscious feelings or motives (see Chapter 16).

At one time or another, you no doubt have taken a psychological test, such as an intelligence test, an achievement test, or a vocational-aptitude test. These measures help clarify differences among people, as well as differences in the reactions of the same person on different occasions or at different stages of life. Tests may be used to promote self-understanding, to evaluate psychological treatments, or, in scientific research, to draw generalizations about human behavior. Well-constructed psychological tests are a great improvement over simple self-evaluation, because many people have a distorted view of their own abilities and traits.

One test of a good test is whether it is **standardized**—that is, whether uniform procedures exist for giving and scoring the test. It would hardly be fair to give some people detailed instructions and plenty of time and others only vague instructions and limited time. Those who administer the test must know exactly how to explain the tasks involved, how much time to allow, and what materials to use. Scoring is

psychological tests Procedures used to measure and evaluate personality traits, emotional states, aptitudes, interests, abilities, and values.

standardize In test construction, to develop uniform procedures for giving and scoring a test.

Reliability
How consistent are
the test's results?

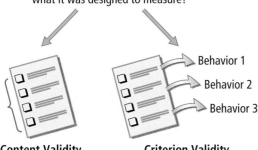

**Test–Retest
Reliability**
Are scores similar
from one session to
another?

**Alternate-forms
Reliability**
Are scores similar on
different versions
of the test?

Validity
Does the test measure
what it was designed to measure?

Behavior 1

Behavior 2

Behavior 3

Content Validity
Do items broadly
represent the
trait in question?

Criterion Validity
Do the test results
predict other measures
of the trait?

norms In test construction, established
standards of performance.

reliability In test construction, the
consistency of scores derived from a test, from
one time and place to another.

validity The ability of a test to measure
what it was designed to measure.

usually done by referring to **norms,** or established standards of
performance. The usual procedure for developing norms is to
give the test to a large group of people who resemble those for
whom the test is intended. Norms determine which scores can be
considered high, low, or average.

Test construction presents many challenges. For one thing,
the test must be **reliable:** that is, it must produce the same results from one time and place to the next. A vocational-interest
test is not reliable if it says that Tom would make a wonderful
engineer but a poor journalist, but then gives different results
when Tom retakes the test a week later. Psychologists can measure *test-retest reliability* by giving the test twice to the same
group of people, then comparing the two sets of scores statistically. If the test is reliable, individuals' scores will be similar
from one session to another. This method has a drawback,
however: People tend to do better the second time they take a
test, after they have become familiar with the strategies required and the actual test
items used. A solution is to compute *alternate-forms reliability,* by giving different
versions of the same test to the same group on two separate occasions. The items
on the two forms are similar in format but are not identical in content. With this
method, performance cannot improve because of familiarity with the items, although people may still do somewhat better the second time around because they
have learned the procedures expected of them.

To be useful, a test must also be **valid;** that is, it must measure what it
sets out to measure. A creativity test is not valid if what it actually measures is verbal sophistication. If the items broadly represent the trait in
question, the test is said to have *content validity.* If you were using a test
to study employees' job satisfaction, and your test tapped a broad array
of relevant beliefs and behaviors (e.g., "Do you feel you have reached a
dead end at work?" "Are you bored with your assignments?"), it would
have content validity. If the test asked only how workers felt about their
salary level, it would lack content validity and would be of little use; after all, highly paid people are not always satisfied with their jobs, and
people who earn low wages are not always dissatisfied.

Most tests are also judged on *criterion validity,* the ability to predict
other, independent measures, or criteria, of the trait in question. The criterion for a scholastic aptitude test might be college grades; the criterion
for a test of shyness might be behavior in social situations. To find out
whether your job-satisfaction test had criterion validity, you might return a year later to see whether it correctly predicted absenteeism, resig-
nations, or requests for job transfers.

Unfortunately, teachers, parents, and employers do not always stop to question a
test's validity, especially when the results are summarized in a single, precise-sounding
number, such as an IQ score of 115 or a job applicant's ranking of 5. But among psychologists and educators, controversy exists about the validity of even some widely
used tests. For example, the Scholastic Assessment Test (SAT), taken by hundreds of
thousands of college applicants every year, has come under fire. Undergraduates can
do pretty well on the SAT's reading-comprehension section even without reading the
passages (although not as well as when they do read them) (Katz & Lautenschlager,
1994). This finding suggests that the items measure general knowledge and test-taking
skills, and not just reading comprehension. Moreover, disagreement exists about how
well the test predicts college performance, and how fair it is to women and minorities.

Standard IQ tests also have their critics. As we will see in Chapter 9, the content validity of such tests—the extent to which they tap the broad trait known as "intelligence"—has been hotly debated. This issue is important in research, because most studies of intelligence have relied on IQ tests.

Criticisms and reevaluations of psychological tests keep psychological assessment honest and scientifically rigorous. In contrast, the pop-psych tests found in magazines, newspapers, and on the Internet usually have not been evaluated for either validity or reliability. These questionnaires have inviting headlines, such as "Are You Self-Destructive?" or "How Smart Are You?" or "The Seven Types of Lovers," but they are merely lists of questions that someone thought sounded good.

Surveys

Psychological tests usually generate information about people indirectly. In contrast, **surveys** are questionnaires and interviews that gather information by asking people *directly* about their experiences, attitudes, or opinions. Most of us are familiar with national opinion surveys, such as the Gallup and Roper polls. Surveys have been done on hundreds of topics, from consumer preferences to sexual preferences.

Surveys produce bushels of data, but they are not easy to do well. The biggest hurdle is getting a **representative sample,** a group of subjects that accurately represents the larger population that the researcher wishes to describe. Suppose you wanted to know about drug use among college sophomores. Questioning every sophomore in the country would obviously not be practical; instead, you would need to recruit a sample. You could use special selection procedures to ensure that this sample contained the same proportion of women, men, blacks, whites, poor people, rich people, Catholics, Jews, and so on as in the general population of college sophomores. Even then, a sample drawn just from your own school or town might not yield results applicable to the entire country, or even state.

Most people do not realize that a sample's size is less critical than its representativeness. A small but representative sample may yield extremely accurate results, whereas a survey or poll that fails to use proper sampling methods may yield questionable results, no matter how large the sample. For example, when a talk-radio host surveys listeners about a political issue, or a magazine surveys its readers about their sexual habits, the results are not likely to generalize to the population as a whole—even if thousands of people respond. Why? As a group, people who listen to talk radio or read *Cosmo* are likely to hold different opinions than those who prefer, say, a classical music station or read *Scientific American.*

Popular polls and surveys also suffer from a **volunteer bias:** People who feel strongly enough to volunteer their opinions may differ from those who remain silent. When you read about a survey (or any other kind of study), always ask who participated. A biased, nonrepresentative sample does not necessarily mean that a survey is worthless or uninteresting, but it does mean that the results may not hold true for other groups.

Another problem with surveys is that people sometimes lie—especially when the survey is about a touchy topic ("What? Me do that disgusting/illegal/dishonest thing? Never!"). The likelihood of lying is reduced when respondents are guaranteed anonymity. Computer technology can help in this regard, because many people feel more anonymous when they "talk" to a computer than when they fill out a paper-and-pencil questionnaire. In one national study of HIV-risk sexual behaviors, violence, and drug use, teenage boys who responded on a computer keyboard to digitally recorded questions played through headphones were far more likely to admit to risky

> **THINKING CRITICALLY**
>
> **Analyze Assumptions**
>
> A magazine has just published a survey of its female readers, called "The Sex Life of the American Wife." It reports that "Eighty-seven percent of all wives like to make love in rubber boots." Is the assumption that the sample represents all married American women justified? What would be a more accurate title for the survey?

surveys Questionnaires and interviews that ask people directly about their experiences, attitudes, or opinions.

representative sample A group of subjects, selected from a population for study, which matches the population on important characteristics such as age and sex.

volunteer bias A shortcoming of findings derived from a sample of volunteers instead of a representative sample; the volunteers may differ from those who did not volunteer.

"Are you (a) contented, (b) happy,
(c) very happy, (d) wildly happy,
(e) deliriously happy?"

behaviors than were boys who filled out questionnaires (Turner et al., 1998). Researchers also have ways to check for lying—for example, by asking the same question several times with different wording and checking for consistency in the answers. But not all surveys use these techniques, and even when respondents are trying to be truthful, they may misinterpret the survey questions or misremember the past.

Finally, when you hear about the results of a survey or opinion poll, you need to consider which questions were (and were not) asked and how the questions were phrased. The questions a researcher asks may reflect his or her assumptions about the topic or may be designed to further a particular agenda (Ericksen & Steffen, 1999). And the phrasing of a question can affect how people respond to it (as political pollsters know well). Many years ago, famed sex researcher Alfred Kinsey, in his pioneering surveys of sexual habits (Kinsey, Pomeroy, & Martin, 1948; Kinsey et al., 1953), made it his practice always to ask, "*How many times have you* (masturbated, had nonmarital sex, etc.)?" rather than "*Have you ever* (masturbated, had nonmarital sex, etc.)?" The first way of phrasing the question tended to elicit more truthful responses than the second, because it removed the respondent's potential self-consciousness about having done any of these things. The second way of phrasing the question would have permitted embarrassed respondents to reply with a simple but dishonest "No."

As you can see, although surveys can be extremely informative, they must be conducted and interpreted carefully.

QUICK QUIZ

A. Which descriptive method would be most appropriate for studying each of the following topics? (All of them, by the way, have been investigated by psychologists.)

1. Ways in which the games of boys differ from those of girls

2. Changes in attitudes toward nuclear disarmament after a television movie about nuclear holocaust

3. The math skills of children in the United States versus Japan

4. Physiological changes that occur when people watch violent movies

5. The development of a male infant who was reared as a female after his penis was accidentally burned off during a routine surgery

a. case study
b. naturalistic observation
c. laboratory observation
d. survey
e. test

B. Professor Flummox gives her new test of aptitude for studying psychology to her psychology students at the start of the year. At the end of the year, she finds that those who did well on the test averaged only a C in the course. The test lacks _____.

C. Over a period of 55 years, a British woman sniffed large amounts of cocaine, which she obtained legally under British regulations for the treatment of addicts. Yet she appeared to show no negative effects, other than drug dependence (Brown & Middlefell, 1989). What does this case tell us about the dangers or safety of cocaine?

Answers:

A. 1. b 2. d 3. e 4. c 5. a B. validity (more specifically, criterion validity) C. Not much. Snorting cocaine may be relatively harmless for some people, such as this woman, but extremely harmful for others. Also, the cocaine she received may have been less potent than cocaine purchased on the street. Critical thinking requires that we resist generalizing from a single case.

WHAT'S AHEAD▶

- **If two things are "negatively" correlated, like grades and TV watching, what is the relationship between them?**
- **If watching television and behaving aggressively are positively correlated, does that mean that TV causes violence?**

Correlational Studies: Looking for Relationships

In descriptive research, psychologists often want to know whether two or more phenomena are related and, if so, how strongly. For example, are students' grade-point averages related to the number of hours they spend watching television? To find out, a psychologist would do a **correlational study.**

Measuring Correlations

The word **correlation** is often used as a synonym for relationship. Technically, however, a correlation is a numerical measure of the *strength* of the relationship between two things. The "things" may be events, scores, or anything else that can be recorded and tallied. In psychological studies, such things are called **variables** because they can vary in quantifiable ways. Height, weight, age, income, IQ scores, number of items recalled on a memory test, number of smiles in a given time period—anything that can be measured, rated, or scored can serve as a variable.

Correlations always occur between *sets* of observations. In psychological research, these sets of observations usually come from many individuals or are used to compare groups of people. For example, in research on the origins of intelligence, psychologists look for a correlation between the IQ scores of parents and those of their children. To do this, the researchers must gather scores from a set of parents and from the children of these parents. You cannot compute a correlation if you know the IQs of only one particular parent–child pair. To say that a relationship exists, you need more than one pair of values to compare.

A **positive correlation** means that high values of one variable are associated with high values of the other, and that low values of one variable are associated with low values of the other. Height and weight are positively correlated, for example; so are IQ scores and school grades. Rarely is a correlation perfect, however. Some tall people weigh less than some short ones; some people with average IQs are superstars in the classroom and some with high IQs get poor grades. Figure 2.2a shows a positive correlation between men's educational level and their annual income. Each dot represents a man; you can find each man's educational level by drawing a horizontal line from his dot to the vertical axis. You can find his income by drawing a vertical line from his dot to the horizontal axis.

A **negative correlation** means that high values of one variable are associated with *low* values of the other. Figure 2.2b shows a negative correlation between average income and the incidence of dental disease for groups of 100 families. Each dot represents one group. In general, as you can see, the higher the income, the fewer the dental problems. In the automobile business, the older the car, the lower the price (except for antiques and models favored by collectors). As for human beings, in general, the older adults are, the fewer miles they can run, the fewer

correlational study A descriptive study that looks for a consistent relationship between two phenomena.

correlation A measure of how strongly two variables are related to one another.

variables Characteristics of behavior or experience that can be measured or described by a numeric scale.

positive correlation An association between increases in one variable and increases in another—or between decreases in one and in another.

negative correlation An association between increases in one variable and decreases in another.

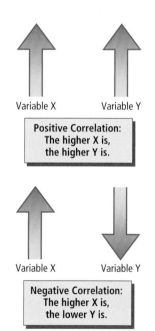

Variable X   Variable Y

Positive Correlation: The higher X is, the higher Y is.

Variable X   Variable Y

Negative Correlation: The higher X is, the lower Y is.

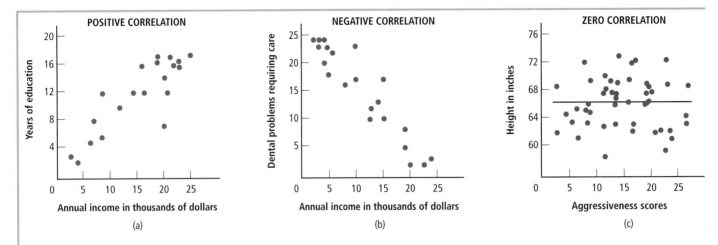

Figure 2.2

CORRELATIONS

Graph (a) shows a positive correlation: In general, income rises with education. Graph (b) shows a negative correlation: In general, the higher people's incomes, the fewer dental problems they have. Graph (c) shows a zero correlation between height and aggressiveness.

crimes they are likely to commit, and the fewer hairs they have on their heads. And remember that correlation between hours spent watching TV and grade-point averages? It's a negative one: Lots of hours in front of the television are associated with lower grades (Potter, 1987; Ridley-Johnson, Cooper, & Chance, 1983). See whether you can think of other variables that are negatively correlated. Remember that a negative correlation means that a relationship exists: the *more* of one thing, the *less* of another. If there is no relationship between two variables, we say that they are *uncorrelated* (see Figure 2.2c). Shoe size and IQ scores are uncorrelated.

The statistic used to express a correlation is called the **coefficient of correlation.** This number conveys both the size of the correlation and its direction. A perfect positive correlation has a coefficient of +1.00, and a perfect negative correlation has a coefficient of −1.00. Suppose you weighed ten people and listed them from lightest to heaviest, then measured their heights and listed them from shortest to tallest. If the names on the two lists were in exactly the same order, the correlation between weight and height would be +1.00. If the correlation between two variables is +.80, it means that they are strongly related. If the correlation is −.80, the relationship is just as strong, but it is negative. When there is no association between two variables, the coefficient is zero or close to zero.

Cautions about Correlations

Correlational findings are common in psychology and are often reported in the news. But beware; many supposed "correlations" in the media or on the Internet are based on rumor and anecdote, and turn out to be small, nonexistent, or meaningless. For example, when some parents of autistic children reported that their children first showed symptoms of the disorder after being vaccinated for measles, mumps, and rubella, many parents panicked and refused to have their children immunized. Subsequent studies, however, showed that the supposed "correlation" between vaccinations and autism had no scientific justification; it was just coincidence. Children are vaccinated at about the time that autistic symptoms become apparent (Ashrof, 2001; Vastag, 2001).

coefficient of correlation A measure of correlation that ranges in value from −1.00 to +1.00.

Keep in mind, too, that correlations, even when they are real, can be misleading because *a correlation does not show causation*. It is easy to assume that if variable A predicts variable B, A must be causing B—that is, making B happen—but that is not necessarily so. The number of storks nesting in some European villages is positively correlated with the number of human births in those villages. Therefore, knowing when the storks nest allows you to predict when more births than usual will occur. But that doesn't mean that storks bring babies or that babies attract storks! Human births seem to be somewhat more frequent at certain times of the year (you might want to speculate on the reasons), and the peaks just happen to coincide with the storks' nesting periods.

No one would assume, of course, that storks and babies "cause" each other. But in other cases, unwarranted conclusions about causation are more tempting. For example, children's television watching is moderately correlated with their aggressiveness. What does this positive correlation mean? One answer is that violent programs make some children more aggressive; indeed, many psychologists have come to that conclusion (Bushman & Anderson, 2001). But another answer is that aggressive children are drawn to television violence. And a third answer is that some other factor, such as growing up in a family where physical violence is common, accounts for *both* children's aggressiveness and their attraction to violent programs. Indeed, as we will see in Chapter 7, the association between TV violence and aggression is not a simple one.

Similarly, the negative correlation between TV watching and grades might exist because heavy TV watchers have less time to study, but it is also possible that they have some personality trait that causes an attraction to TV and an aversion to studying, or that they use TV as an escape when their grades are low, or that TV is especially appealing to people who are not academically inclined . . . you get the idea.

The moral of the story: When two variables are associated, one variable may or may not be causing the other.

THINKING CRITICALLY

Consider Other Interpretations

If stork nesting periods and human births are correlated, does that mean that storks bring babies after all? What else could be going on?

2.2

QUICK QUIZ

A. Are you clear about correlations? Find out by identifying each of the following as a positive or negative correlation.

1. The higher a male monkey's level of the hormone testosterone, the more aggressive he is likely to be.

2. The older people are, the less frequently they tend to have sexual intercourse.

3. The hotter the weather, the more crimes against persons (such as muggings) tend to occur.

 B. Now see whether you can generate two or three possible explanations for each of the preceding findings.

Answers:

A. 1. positive 2. negative 3. positive B. 1. The hormone may cause aggressiveness, acting aggressively may stimulate hormone production, or some third factor, such as age or dominance, may influence aggressiveness and hormone production independently. 2. Older people may have less interest in sex than younger people, have less energy or simply have more trouble finding partners. 3. Hot temperatures may make people edgy and cause them to commit crimes; potential victims may be more plentiful in warm weather because more people go outside; criminals may find it more comfortable to be out committing their crimes in warm weather than in cold. (Our explanations for these correlations are not the only ones possible.)

WHAT'S AHEAD

● **Why do psychologists rely so heavily on experiments?**
● **What, exactly, do control groups control for?**
● **In a double-blind experiment, who is "blind," and what aren't they supposed to "see"?**

2.3 **Live! psych**

Experiments: Hunting for Causes

Researchers gain plenty of illuminating information from descriptive studies, but when they want to actually track down the causes of behavior, they rely heavily on the experimental method. An **experiment** allows the researcher to *control*, or manipulate, the situation being studied. Instead of being a passive recorder of what is going on, the researcher actively does something that he or she believes will affect people's behavior and then observes what happens. These procedures allow the experimenter to draw conclusions about cause and effect—about what causes what.

Experimental Variables

Imagine that you are a psychologist and you come across reports suggesting that cigarette smoking improves reaction time on simple tasks. You have a hunch that nicotine has the opposite effect, however, when the task is as complex and demanding as driving a car. You know that on average, smokers have more car accidents than nonsmokers. But you realize that this relationship does not prove that smoking *causes* accidents. Smokers may simply be greater risk-takers than nonsmokers, whether the risk is lung cancer or trying to beat a red light. Or perhaps the distraction of lighting up accounts for the increased accident risk, rather than smoking itself. So you decide to do an experiment to test your hypothesis.

In a laboratory, you ask smokers to "drive" using a computerized driving simulator equipped with a stick shift and a gas pedal. The object, you tell them, is to maximize the distance covered by driving as fast as possible on a winding road while avoiding rear-end collisions. At your request, some of the subjects smoke a cigarette immediately before climbing into the driver's seat. Others do not. You are interested in comparing how many collisions the two groups have. The basic design of this experiment is illustrated in Figure 2.3, which you may want to refer to as you read the next few pages.

The aspect of an experimental situation manipulated or varied by the researcher is known as the **independent variable**. The reaction of the subjects—the behavior that the researcher tries to predict—is the **dependent variable**. Every experiment has at least one independent and one dependent variable. In our example, the independent variable is nicotine use: one cigarette versus none. The dependent variable is the number of collisions.

Ideally, everything in the experimental situation *except* the independent variable is held constant—that is, kept the same for all participants. You would not have some people use a stick shift and others an automatic, unless shift type were an independent variable. Similarly, you would not have some people go through the experiment alone and others perform in front of an audience. Holding everything but the independent variable constant ensures that whatever happens is due to the researcher's manipulation and nothing else. It allows you to rule out other interpretations.

Understandably, students often have trouble keeping independent and dependent variables straight. You might think of it this way: The dependent variable—the outcome of the study—*depends* on the independent variable. When psychologists set up

experiment A controlled test of a hypothesis in which the researcher manipulates one variable to discover its effect on another.

independent variable A variable that an experimenter manipulates.

dependent variable A variable that an experimenter predicts will be affected by manipulations of the independent variable.

an experiment, they think, "If I do X, the subjects in my study will do Y." The "X" represents manipulation of the independent variable; the "Y" represents the dependent variable:

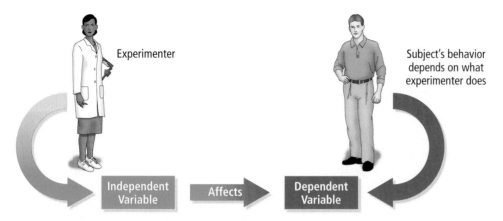

Most variables may be either independent or dependent, depending on what the experimenter wishes to find out. If you want to know whether eating chocolate makes people nervous, then the amount of chocolate eaten is the independent variable. If you want to know whether feeling nervous makes people eat chocolate, then the amount of chocolate eaten is the dependent variable.

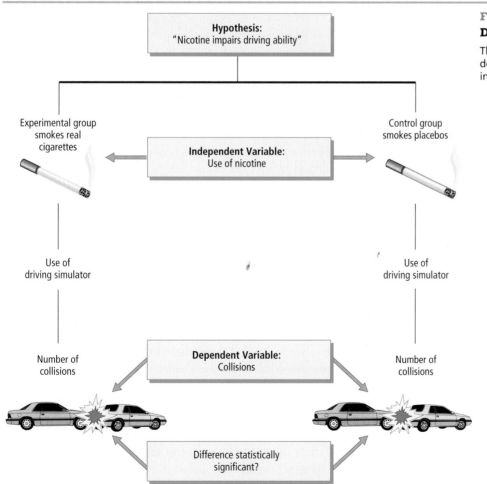

Figure 2.3

DO SMOKING AND DRIVING MIX?

The text describes this experimental design to test the hypothesis that nicotine in cigarettes impairs driving skills.

THINKING CRITICALLY

Consider Other Interpretations

You have developed a new form of therapy that you believe cures anxiety. Sixty-three percent of the people who go through your program improve. What else, besides your therapy, could account for this result? Why shouldn't you rush out to open an anxiety clinic?

Experimental and Control Conditions

Experiments usually require both an experimental condition and a comparison, or **control condition.** In the control condition, subjects are treated exactly as they are in the experimental condition, except that they are not exposed to the same treatment, or manipulation of the independent variable. Without a control condition, you cannot be sure that the behavior you are interested in would not have occurred anyway, even without your manipulation. In some studies, the same subjects can be used in both the control and the experimental conditions; they are said to serve as their own controls. In other studies, subjects are assigned to either an *experimental group* or a *control group*.

In our nicotine experiment, the people who smoke before driving make up the experimental group, and those who refrain from smoking make up the control group. We want these two groups to be roughly the same in terms of average driving skill. It would not do to start out with a bunch of reckless roadrunners in the experimental group and a bunch of tired tortoises in the control group. We probably also want the two groups to be similar in age, education, smoking history, and other characteristics so that none of these variables will affect our results. One way to accomplish this is to use **random assignment** of people to one group or another—for example, by randomly assigning them numbers and putting those with even numbers in one group and those with odd numbers in another. If we have enough participants in our study, individual characteristics that could possibly affect the results are likely to be roughly balanced in the two groups, so we can ignore them.

Sometimes, researchers use several experimental or control groups. For example, in our nicotine study, we might want to examine the effects of different levels of nicotine by having people smoke one, two, or three cigarettes before "driving," and then comparing each of these experimental groups to each other and to a control group of nonsmokers as well. For now, however, let's focus just on experimental subjects who smoked one cigarette.

We now have two groups. We also have a problem. In order to smoke, the experimental subjects must light up and inhale. These acts might set off certain expectations—of feeling relaxed, nervous, confident, or whatever. These expectations, in turn, might affect driving performance. It would be better to have the control group do everything the experimental group does except use nicotine.

Therefore, we will change the experimental design a bit. Instead of having the control subjects refrain from smoking, we will give them a **placebo,** a fake treatment. Placebos, which are critical when testing new drugs, often take the form of pills or injections containing no active ingredients (see Chapter 17). In our study, we will use phony cigarettes that taste and smell like the real thing but contain no nicotine. Our control subjects will not know their cigarettes are fake and will have no way of distinguishing them from real ones. Now if they have substantially fewer collisions than the experimental group, we will feel safe in concluding that nicotine increases the probability of an auto accident.

Control groups, by the way, are also important in nonexperimental studies. In one highly publicized descriptive study, clinical researchers followed the development of 80 children whose parents divorced when the children were young (Wallerstein, Lewis, & Blakeslee, 2000). The children, who are now in their thirties, revealed many psychological problems and difficulties in relationships, and the researchers interpreted these results as a strong indictment of divorce. But these children all grew up in one extremely affluent county in California, so the sample was not representative. Even more important, the study did not include control subjects: children growing up with unhappy parents in an intact family or, for that matter, children growing up in happy intact families. Without such control groups, the results cannot tell us much.

control condition In an experiment, a comparison condition in which subjects are not exposed to the same treatment as in the experimental condition.

random assignment A procedure for assigning people to experimental and control groups in which each individual has the same probability as any other of being assigned to a given group.

placebo An inactive substance or fake treatment used as a control in an experiment or given by a medical practitioner to a patient.

Perhaps growing up with parents who are constantly fighting and abusing one another is worse than having one's parents divorce. For the record, better designed, large-scale studies find that the psychological effects of divorce on children depend on many factors, such as the amount of conflict between the parents before and after the separation (Amato, 1994; Amato & Keith, 1991). Most children of divorce overcome their problems and go on to live well-adjusted lives.

Experimenter Effects

Because expectations can influence the results of a study, participants should not know whether they are in an experimental or a control group. When this is so, the experiment is said to be a **single-blind study.** But subjects are not the only ones who bring expectations to the laboratory; so do researchers. And researchers' expectations and hopes for a particular result may cause them to inadvertently influence the participants' responses through facial expressions, posture, tone of voice, or some other cue.

Many years ago, Robert Rosenthal (1966) demonstrated how powerful such **experimenter effects** can be. He had students teach rats to run a maze. Half the students were told that their rats had been bred to be "maze bright," and half were told that their rats had been bred to be "maze dull." In reality, there were no genetic differences between the two groups of rats, yet the supposedly brainy rats actually did learn the maze more quickly, apparently because of the way the students treated them. If an experimenter's expectations can affect a rodent's behavior, reasoned Rosenthal, surely they can affect a human being's. He went on to demonstrate this point in many other studies (Rosenthal, 1994). Even an experimenter's friendly smile (or lack of one) can affect people's responses in a study.

One solution to the problem of experimenter effects is to do a **double-blind study.** In such a study, the person running the experiment, the one having actual contact with the subjects, also does not know which subjects are in which groups until the data have been gathered. Double-blind procedures are standard in drug research. Different doses of a drug are coded in some way, and the person administering the drug is kept in the dark about the code's meaning until after the experiment. To run our nicotine study in a double-blind fashion, we would keep the person dispensing the cigarettes from knowing which ones were real and which were placebos.

single-blind study An experiment in which subjects do not know whether they are in an experimental or a control group.

experimenter effects Unintended changes in subjects' behavior due to cues inadvertently given by the experimenter.

double-blind study An experiment in which neither the subjects nor the individuals running the study know which subjects are in the control group and which are in the experimental group until after the results are tallied.

Experimenter   Subject

Single-blind Study
Experimenter knows who is in which group; subjects do not.

Experimenter   Subject

Double-blind Study
Neither experimenter nor subjects know who is in which group.

Get Involved ▪▪

The Power of a Smile

Prove to yourself how easy it is for experimenters to affect the behavior of a study's participants by giving off nonverbal cues. As you walk around campus, quickly glance at individuals approaching you and either smile or maintain a neutral expression, then observe the other person's expression. Try to keep the duration of your glance the same whether you smile or not. You might record the results as you collect them instead of relying on your memory. Chances are that people you smile at will smile back, whereas those you approach with a neutral expression will do the same. What does this tell you about the importance of doing double-blind studies?

Advantages and Limitations of Experiments

Because experiments allow conclusions about cause and effect, and because they permit researchers to distinguish real effects from placebo effects, they have long been the method of choice in psychology.

However, like all methods, the experiment has its limitations. Just as in other kinds of studies, the participants are not always representative of the larger population. Most volunteers in academic experiments are college students, who differ in many ways from people who are not in school. Moreover, in an experiment, the researcher determines which questions are asked and which behaviors are recorded, and the participants try to do as they are told. In their desire to cooperate with the experimenter or present themselves in a positive light, they may act in ways that they ordinarily would not (Kihlstrom, 1995).

Thus, research psychologists confront a dilemma: The more control they exercise over the situation, the more artificial the situation—and the results obtained from it—may be. For this reason, many psychologists have called for more **field research,** the careful study of behavior in natural contexts such as schools and the workplace, using both descriptive and experimental methods. For example, a psychologist interested in ways of reducing prejudice might study that problem not just in the laboratory, but also in offices and schools. As we will see in Chapter 8, field research on prejudice has led to successful strategies for reducing hostility among children and adults of different ethnicities.

Every research method has both its strengths and its weaknesses. Now that we have come to the end of our discussion of these methods, how did you do on your list of their advantages and disadvantages? You can find out by comparing your list with the one in Review 2.1.

field research Descriptive or experimental research conducted in a natural setting outside the laboratory.

QUICK QUIZ

A. Name the independent and dependent variables in studies designed to answer the following questions:

1. Whether sleeping after learning a poem improves memory for the poem
2. Whether the presence of other people affects a person's willingness to help someone in distress
3. Whether people get agitated from listening to heavy-metal music

B. On a talk show, Dr. Blitznik announces a fabulous new program: Chocolate Immersion Therapy. "People who spend one day a week doing nothing but eating chocolate are soon cured of eating disorders, depression, and poor study habits," claims Dr. Blitznik. What should you find out about C.I.T. before signing up?

Answers:

1. Opportunity to sleep after learning is the independent variable; memory for the poem is the dependent variable. 2. The presence of other people is the independent variable; willingness to help others is the dependent variable. 3. Exposure to heavy-metal music is the independent variable; agitation is the dependent variable. B. Some questions to ask: Is there research showing that people who go through C.I.T. did better than those in a control group who did not have the therapy, or who had a different therapy—say, Broccoli Immersion Therapy? If so, how many people were studied? How were they selected, and how were they assigned to the therapy and no-therapy groups? Did the person running the experiment know who was getting C.I.T. and who was not? How long did the "cures" last? Has the research been peer reviewed? Has it been replicated?

REVIEW 2.1   RESEARCH METHODS IN PSYCHOLOGY: THEIR ADVANTAGES AND DISADVANTAGES

Method	Advantages	Disadvantages
Case study	Good source of hypotheses. Provides in-depth information on individuals. Unusual cases can shed light on situations or problems that are unethical or impractical to study in other ways.	Vital information may be missing, making the case hard to interpret. The person's memories may be selective or inaccurate. The individual may not be representative or typical.
Naturalistic observation	Allows description of behavior as it occurs in the natural environment. Often useful in first stages of a research program.	Allows researcher little or no control of the situation. Observations may be biased. Does not allow firm conclusions about cause and effect.
Laboratory observation	Allows more control than naturalistic observation. Allows use of sophisticated equipment.	Allows researcher only limited control of the situation. Observations may be biased. Does not allow firm conclusions about cause and effect. Behavior may differ from behavior in the natural environment.
Test	Yields information on personality traits, emotional states, aptitudes, abilities.	Difficult to construct tests that are reliable and valid.
Survey	Provides a large amount of information on large numbers of people.	If sample is nonrepresentative or biased, it may be impossible to generalize from the results. Responses may be inaccurate or untrue.
Correlational study	Shows whether two or more variables are related. Allows general predictions.	Does not permit identification of cause and effect.
Experiment	Allows researcher to control the situation. Permits researcher to identify cause and effect, and to distinguish placebo effects from treatment effects.	Situation is artificial, and results may not generalize well to the real world. Sometimes difficult to avoid experimenter effects.

WHAT'S AHEAD ▶

- In psychological studies, why are averages sometimes misleading?
- How can psychologists tell whether a finding is impressive or trivial?
- Why are some findings significant statistically but unimportant in practical terms?

Evaluating the Findings

If you are a psychologist who has just done an observational study, a survey, or an experiment, your work has just begun. Once you have some results in hand, you must do three things with them: (1) describe them, (2) assess how reliable and meaningful they are, and (3) figure out how to explain them.

Descriptive Statistics: Finding Out What's So

Let's say that 30 people in the nicotine experiment smoked real cigarettes, and 30 smoked placebos. We have recorded the number of collisions for each person on the driving simulator. Now we have 60 numbers. What can we do with them?

The first step is to summarize the data. The world does not want to hear how many collisions each person had. It wants to know what happened in the nicotine group as a whole, compared to what happened in the control group. To provide this information, we need numbers that sum up our data. Such numbers, known as **descriptive statistics,** are often depicted in graphs and charts.

A good way to summarize the data is to compute group averages. The most commonly used type of average is the **arithmetic mean.** (For two other types, see the Appendix.) The mean is calculated by adding up all the individual scores and dividing the result by the number of scores. We can compute a mean for the nicotine group by adding up the 30 collision scores and dividing the sum by 30. Then we can do the same for the control group. Now our 60 numbers have been boiled down to 2. For the sake of our example, let's assume that the nicotine group had an average of 10 collisions, whereas the control group's average was only 7.

We must be careful, however, about how we interpret these averages. It is possible that no one in our nicotine group actually had 10 collisions. Perhaps half the people in the group were motoring maniacs and had 15 collisions, whereas the others were more cautious and had only 5. Perhaps almost all the subjects had 9, 10, or 11 collisions. Perhaps the number of accidents ranged from 0 to 15. The mean does not tell us about such variability in the subjects' responses. For that, we need other descriptive statistics. For example, the **standard deviation** tells us how clustered or spread out the individual scores are around the mean; the more spread out they are,

descriptive statistics Statistical procedures that organize and summarize research data.

arithmetic mean An average that is calculated by adding up a set of quantities and dividing the sum by the total number of quantities in the set.

standard deviation A commonly used measure of variability that indicates the average difference between scores in a distribution and their mean.

Averages can be misleading if you don't know the extent to which events deviated from the statistical mean and how they were distributed.

the less "typical" the mean is. (See Figure 2.4, and, for more details, the Appendix.) Unfortunately, when research is reported in newspapers or on the nightly news, you usually hear only about the mean.

Inferential Statistics: Asking "So What?"

At this point in our nicotine study, we have one group with an average of 10 collisions and another with an average of 7. Should we break out the champagne? Try to get on TV? Call our mothers?

Better hold off. Perhaps if one group had an average of 15 collisions and the other an average of 1, we could get excited. But rarely does a psychological study hit you between the eyes with a sensationally clear result. In most cases, there is some possibility that the difference between the two groups was due simply to chance. Despite all our precautions, perhaps the people in the nicotine group just happened to be a little more accident-prone, and their behavior had nothing to do with the nicotine.

To find out how impressive the data are, psychologists use **inferential statistics.** These statistics do not merely describe or summarize the data; they permit a researcher to draw *inferences* (conclusions based on evidence) about how meaningful the findings are. Like descriptive statistics, inferential statistics involve the application of mathematical formulas to the data. (Again, see the Appendix for details.)

The most commonly used inferential statistics are **significance tests,** which tell researchers how likely a result was to have occurred by chance. In our nicotine study, a significance test will tell us how likely it is that the difference between the nicotine group and the placebo group occurred by chance. It is not possible to rule out chance entirely, but if the likelihood that a result occurred by chance is extremely low, we can say that the result is *statistically significant.* This means that the probability that the difference is "real" is overwhelming—not certain, mind you, but overwhelming.

By convention, psychologists consider a result to be significant if it would be expected to occur by chance 5 or fewer times in 100 repetitions of the study. Another way of saying this is that the result is significant at the .05 ("point oh five") level. If the difference could be expected to occur by chance in 6 out of 100 studies, we would have to say that the results failed to support the hypothesis—that the difference we obtained might well have occurred merely by chance—although we might still want to do further research to be sure. You can see that psychologists refuse to be impressed by just any old result.

Statistically significant results allow psychologists to make general predictions about human behavior. These predictions are usually stated as probabilities ("On average, we can expect 60 percent of all students to do X, Y, or Z"). However, they usually do not tell us with any certainty what a particular individual will do in a particular situation. Probabilistic results are typical not only in psychology but in all of the sciences. Medical research, for example, can tell us that the odds are high that someone who smokes will get lung cancer, but because many variables interact to produce any particular case of cancer, research cannot tell us for sure whether Aunt Bessie, a two-pack-a-day smoker, will come down with the disease.

By the way, a nicotine study similar to our hypothetical example was actually done some years ago, using somewhat more complicated procedures (Spilich, June, & Renner, 1992). Smokers who lit up before driving got a little farther on the simulated road, but they also had significantly more rear-end collisions on average (10.7) than did temporarily abstaining smokers (5.2) or nonsmokers (3.1). The lead researcher in this study told us that after hearing about these findings, the head of Federal Express banned smoking on the job among all of the company's drivers.

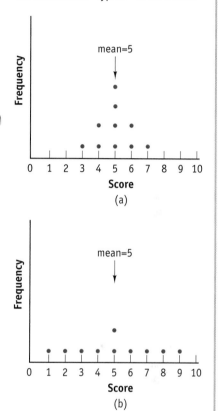

Figure 2.4

SAME MEAN, DIFFERENT MEANING

In both distributions of scores, the mean is 5, but in (a) the scores are clustered around the mean, whereas in (b) they are widely dispersed, so the standard deviations for the distributions will be quite different. In which distribution is the mean more "typical" of all scores?

2.4

inferential statistics Statistical procedures that allow researchers to draw inferences about how statistically meaningful a study's results are.

significance tests Statistical tests that show how likely it is that a study's results occurred merely by chance.

Interpreting the Findings

The last step in any study is to figure out what the findings mean. Trying to understand behavior from uninterpreted findings is like trying to become fluent in Swedish by reading a Swedish–English dictionary. Just as you need the grammar of Swedish to tell you how the words fit together, the psychologist needs hypotheses and theories to explain how the facts that emerge from research fit together.

Choosing the Best Explanation. Sometimes it is hard to choose between competing explanations. Does nicotine disrupt driving by impairing coordination, by increasing a driver's vulnerability to distraction, by interfering with the processing of information, by distorting the perception of danger—or by some combination of these factors? In interpreting any study, we must not go too far beyond the facts; several explanations may fit those facts equally well, which means that more research will be needed to determine the best one. Rarely does one single study prove anything, in psychology or any other field.

Sometimes the best interpretation of a finding does not emerge until a hypothesis has been tested in different ways. Although the methods we have described tend to be appropriate for different questions (see Review 2.2 on page 60), sometimes one method can be used to confirm, disconfirm, or extend the results obtained with another. If the findings of studies using various methods converge, there is greater reason to be confident about them. If they conflict, researchers must modify their hypotheses or do more research.

Here is an example. When psychologists compare the mental-test scores of young people and old people, they usually find that younger people outscore older ones. This type of research, in which groups are compared at a given time, is called **cross-sectional:**

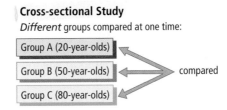

Cross-sectional Study
Different groups compared at one time:

Group A (20-year-olds)
Group B (50-year-olds)   compared
Group C (80-year-olds)

But **longitudinal studies** can also be used to investigate mental abilities across the life span. In a longitudinal study, the same people are followed over a period of time and are reassessed at regular intervals:

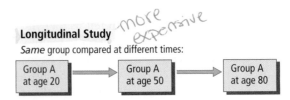

Longitudinal Study
Same group compared at different times:

Group A at age 20   Group A at age 50   Group A at age 80

cross-sectional study A study in which subjects of different ages are compared at a given time.

longitudinal study A study in which subjects are followed and periodically reassessed over a period of time.

In contrast to cross-sectional studies, longitudinal studies find that as people age, they sometimes perform as well as they ever did on certain mental tests. A *general* decline in ability may not occur until people reach their 70s or 80s (Salthouse, 1998; Schaie, 1993). Why do results from the two types of studies conflict? Probably because cross-sectional studies measure generational differences; younger generations tend to outperform older ones because they are better educated or are more familiar with the tests used. Without longitudinal studies, we might falsely conclude that all types of mental ability inevitably decline with age.

Judging the Result's Importance. Sometimes psychologists agree on the reliability and meaning of a finding, but not on its ultimate relevance for theory or practice. Statistical significance alone does not provide the answer. A result may be statistically significant at the "point oh-five level" yet be small and of little consequence in everyday life because the independent variable does not explain most of the variation in people's behavior. On the other hand, a result may not quite reach statistical significance yet be worth following up on (Falk & Greenbaum, 1995; Hunter, 1997). Because of these problems, many psychologists now prefer other statistical procedures that reveal the **effect size**—that is, procedures that tell them how powerful the independent variable really is (how much of the variation in the data the variable accounts for). If the independent variable explains 5 percent of the variation, it's not very powerful, but if it explains 40 percent, it's very impressive. An effect size might turn out to be small, even when the results were statistically significant.

One popular statistical technique, called **meta-analysis,** combines and analyzes data from many studies, instead of assessing each study's results separately. Meta-analysis tells the researcher how much of the variation in scores across *all* the studies examined can be explained by a particular variable. For example, a meta-analysis of nearly 50 years of research found that gender accounts for a good deal of the variance in performance on certain spatial-visual tasks, with males doing better on the average (Voyer, Voyer, & Bryden, 1995). In contrast, other meta-analyses have shown that gender accounts for only 1 to 5 percent of the variance on tests of verbal and math ability (Feingold, 1988; Hyde, 2000; Hyde, Fennema, & Lamon, 1990; Hyde & Linn, 1988). Although gender differences on these tests are reliable, they are small, and scores for males and females greatly overlap. Meta-analysis has been useful for identifying overall patterns in data on dozens of other topics as well.

effect size The amount of variance among scores in a study accounted for by the independent variable.

meta-analysis A procedure for combining and analyzing data from many studies; it determines how much of the variance in scores across all studies can be explained by a particular variable.

QUICK QUIZ

A. Check your understanding of the descriptive-inferential distinction by placing a check in the appropriate column for each phrase:

	Descriptive statistics	Inferential statistics
1. Summarize the data	____	____
2. Give likelihood of data occurring by chance	____	____
3. Include the mean	____	____
4. Give measure of statistical significance	____	____
5. Tell you whether to call your mother about your results	____	____

B. If a researcher studies the same group over many years, the study is said to be _____.

C. On the Internet, you read a posting about a "Fantastic Scientific Breakthrough in Treating Shyness." Why should you be cautious about this announcement?

Answers:

A. 1. descriptive 2. inferential 3. descriptive 4. inferential 5. inferential B. longitudinal C. Scientific progress, in psychology or any field, usually proceeds gradually, not all at once. And besides, anyone can post any old claim on the Internet, so you will want to ask, "What's the original source of this claim?"

REVIEW 2.2	PSYCHOLOGICAL RESEARCH METHODS CONTRASTED

Psychologists may use different methods to answer different questions about a topic. To illustrate, this table shows some ways in which the methods described in this chapter can be used to study different questions about aggression. The methods listed are not mutually exclusive. That is, sometimes two or more methods can be used to investigate the same question. As discussed in the text, findings based on one method may extend, support, or disconfirm findings based on another.

Method	Purpose	Example
Case study	To understand the development of aggressive behavior in a particular individual; to formulate research hypotheses about the origins of aggressiveness	Developmental history of a serial killer
Naturalistic observation	To describe the nature of aggressive acts in early childhood	Observation, tallying, and description of hitting, kicking, etc., during free-play periods in a preschool
Laboratory observation	To find out whether aggressiveness in pairs of same-sex and different-sex children differs in frequency or intensity	Observation through a one-way window of same-sex and different-sex pairs of preschoolers; pairs must negotiate who gets to play with an attractive toy that has been promised to each child
Test	To compare the personality traits of aggressive and nonaggressive persons	Administration of personality tests to violent and nonviolent prisoners
Survey	To find out how common domestic violence is in the general population	Questionnaire asking anonymous respondents (in a sample representative of the population) about the occurrence of slapping, hitting, etc. in their homes
Correlational study	To examine the relationship between aggressiveness and television viewing	Administration to college students of a paper-and-pencil test of aggressiveness and a questionnaire on number of hours spent watching TV weekly; computation of correlation coefficient
Experiment	To find out whether high air temperatures elicit aggressive behavior	Arrangement for individuals to "shock" a "learner" (actually a confederate of the experimenter) while seated in a room heated to either 72°F or 85°F

WHAT'S AHEAD

- Why do psychologists often lie to their subjects?
- Why do psychologists study nonhuman animals?

Keeping the Enterprise Ethical

Rigorous research methods are the very heart of science, so it is not surprising that psychologists spend considerable time discussing and debating their procedures for collecting and evaluating data. They are also concerned about the ethics of their activities—the moral principles of conduct governing research. In nearly all colleges and universities, a review committee must approve all studies and be sure they conform to federal regulations. In addition, the American Psychological Association (APA) has a code of ethics that all members must follow.

The Ethics of Studying Human Beings

The APA code calls on psychological scientists to respect the dignity and welfare of human subjects. People must participate voluntarily and must know enough about the study to make an intelligent decision about participating, a doctrine known as *informed consent*. Researchers must also protect participants from physical and mental harm, and if any risk exists, they must warn the subjects in advance and give them an opportunity to withdraw at any time. (In the case of the nicotine study used as an example in this chapter, we would have to use only people who were already smokers; exposing nonsmokers to the risks associated with smoking—a risk they would ordinarily not choose to run—would be unethical.)

However, the policy of informed consent sometimes clashes with an experimenter's need to keep subjects in the dark about the true purpose of the study. In such cases, if the purpose were revealed in advance, the results would be ruined because the participants would not behave naturally. In social psychology, especially, a study's design sometimes calls for an elaborate deception, as we will see in Chapter 8. For example, a confederate might pretend to be having a seizure. The researcher can then find out whether bystanders—the uninformed subjects—will respond to a person who needs help. If the participants knew that the confederate was only acting, obviously they would not bother to intervene or call for assistance.

Sometimes people have been misled about procedures intentionally designed to make them uncomfortable, angry, guilty, ashamed, or anxious so that researchers can learn what people do when they feel this way. In anxiety studies, for instance, participants have been led to believe, falsely, that they failed a test or were about to get a painful shock. In studies of embarrassment and anger, people have been made to look clumsy in front of others, or have been called insulting names, or have been told they were incompetent. In studies of dishonesty, participants have been entrapped into cheating, and then confronted with evidence of their guilt.

As the use of deception escalated during the 1970s, so did debate about its morality (Korn, 1998). Today, the APA's ethical guidelines require researchers to show that any deceptive procedures are justified by a study's potential value, to consider alternative procedures, and to thoroughly debrief participants about the true purpose and methods of the study afterward. When people are debriefed and told why deception is necessary, they usually are not resentful and they are willing to take part in further studies. But the issues raised by deception are still with us, and the APA frequently re-evaluates its ethical code to deal with them.

Psychologists sometimes use animals to study learning, memory, emotion, and other topics. Here a rat learns to find food in a radial maze.

The Ethics of Studying Animals

Another ethical issue concerns the use and treatment of animals in research. Animals have always been used in only a small percentage of psychological studies, and in recent years, the number has declined further. Nonetheless, in certain areas of psychological research, animals still play a crucial role. Usually they are not harmed (as in research on mating in hamsters, which is fun for the hamsters), but sometimes they are (as in research on vision in kittens, when part of the animals' visual systems must be surgically removed). Some studies require the animal's death, as when rats brought up in deprived or enriched environments are sacrificed so that their brains can be examined for any effects.

Psychologists study animals for many reasons:

▶ *To conduct basic research on a particular species.* For example, researchers have learned a great deal about the unusually lusty and cooperative lives of bonobo apes.

▶ *To discover practical applications.* For example, behavioral studies have shown farmers how to reduce crop destruction by birds and deer without resorting to their traditional method—shooting the animals.

▶ *To study issues that cannot be studied experimentally with human beings because of practical or ethical considerations.* For example, research on monkeys has demonstrated the effects of maternal deprivation on emotional development—and the effects of later experience in overcoming early deprivation.

▶ *To clarify theoretical questions.* For example, we might not attribute the longer life spans of women solely to lifestyle factors and health practices if we discover that a male–female difference exists in other mammals as well.

▶ *To improve human welfare.* For example, animal studies have helped researchers develop ways to reduce chronic pain; rehabilitate patients with neurological disorders; and understand the mechanisms underlying memory loss and senility—to name only a few benefits.

Animal research, however, has provoked angry disputes. Many animal-rights activists want to eliminate all research using animals. On the other side, some defenders of animal research have refused to acknowledge that confinement in laboratories can be psychologically and physically harmful for some species. A bitter debate is now raging over proposed federal legislation that would expand the Animal Welfare Act to cover not just animals such as primates, cats, and dogs (as it currently does) but also birds, mice, and rats. Many animal researchers themselves—according to one survey, a majority—favor the law's expansion (Plous & Herzog, 1999). But others do not, and many colleges and universities fear a costly, bureaucratic nightmare.

This conflict has motivated psychologists to find ways to improve the treatment of research animals. In recent years, the APA's ethical code covering the humane treatment of animals has been made more comprehensive, and federal laws governing the housing and care of research animals have been strengthened. Many researchers have developed less invasive procedures that take advantage of new technology. The difficult task for scientists is to balance the many benefits of animal research with an acknowledgment of past abuses and a compassionate attitude toward species other than our own.

Now that you have finished the first two chapters of this book, you are ready to explore more deeply what psychologists have learned about human behavior. The methods of science are designed not only to help us learn new things, but also to illuminate our errors and biases and help us seek knowledge with an open mind. Biologist Thomas Huxley put it well: The essence of science, he said, is "to sit down before the fact as a little child, be prepared to give up every preconceived notion, follow humbly wherever and to whatever abyss nature leads, or you shall learn nothing."

Taking Psychology with You

LYING WITH STATISTICS

In this chapter, we have emphasized that statistical procedures are essential tools for assessing research. Without them, scientists would wallow around in numbers, not knowing if they had found anything important. But statistics can also be manipulated, exaggerated, misrepresented, and even made up by people hoping to promote a particular political or social agenda. That is why an essential part of critical and scientific thinking is learning not only how to use statistics correctly, but also how to identify their misuse.

One misuse of numbers is the effort to convey a false impression of certainty when the true state of affairs is uncertainty or ignorance. Sometimes people will toss around a number that is just someone's wild guess. For example, no one really knows how many homeless people or missing children there are, but that hasn't kept people from making up numbers, no doubt out of a well-intentioned effort to drum up public compassion (and funding) on these issues.

Another misuse of statistics results from confusion or "innumeracy" (mathematical illiteracy). In his excellent book *Damned Lies and Statistics,* Joel Best (2001) tells of a graduate student who copied this figure from a professional journal: "Every year since 1950, the number of American children gunned down has doubled."

Sounds pretty scary, right? But if the claim were true, then by 1987 the number of children gunned down would have surpassed 137 billion, more than the total human population throughout history; and by 1995, the annual number of victims would have been 35 *trillion!*

Where did this wildly inaccurate number come from? The author of the article cited by the graduate student misrepresented a statistic from the Children's Defense Fund (CDF), which claimed in 1994 that "The number of American children killed each year by guns has doubled since 1950." Notice the difference: the CDF was saying that there were twice as many deaths in 1994 as in 1950, not that the number had doubled every year. But even the CDF's claim was misleading, because the U.S. population also nearly doubled during that period, so we would expect child gunshot deaths to have increased considerably just because the population grew.

We don't want you to distrust all statistics. Statistics don't "lie"; people do—or, more likely, they misinterpret what the numbers mean. When statistics are used correctly, they neither confuse nor mislead. On the contrary, they can expose unwarranted conclusions, promote clarity and precision, and protect us from our biases and blind spots. You need to be careful, though. Here are a few things you can

do when you hear that "two million people do this" or "one out of four people are that":

▶ *Ask how the number was computed.* Suppose someone on your campus gives a talk about a hot social issue and cites some big number to show how serious and widespread the problem is. You should ask the speaker how the number was calculated. Was it based on government data, such as the census? Did it come from just one small study? Is it from a meta-analysis of many studies? Or is it pure conjecture?

▶ *Check to see how terms have been defined.* As Best notes, before we can decide that more and more children are being killed by guns, we need to ask: How is "child" defined? Persons under age 10, 16, or, as in some cases, 25? And what is meant by "killed by guns"—murders only, or does the number also include suicides and accidents? Similarly, if we hear that "one out of every four women" will be raped at some point in her life, we need to ask: How was "rape" defined? If women are asked if they have ever experienced any act of unwanted sex, the percentages will be higher than if they are asked specifically whether they have been forced or coerced into intercourse against their will.

▶ *Look for the control group.* You will often encounter claims for the success of some new therapy, intervention, self-improvement method, or "alternative" medication that are based on anecdotes, case studies, or self-reports. For instance, we read an article in a magazine in which women claimed that taking Viagra had improved their sex lives dramatically. Impressed? In a controlled study of 583 women, 43 percent of women taking a placebo pill said *their* sex lives had also improved—they were no different from the Viagra group (Basson et al., 2002). If a study does not report results from a control group of people with the same problem who did *not* go through the same program or treatment, then, as they say in New York, "fuhgeddaboudit."

▶ *Separate politics from statistics.* At a conference of child-development psychologists in 2001, researchers announced the newest findings from an ongoing longitudinal study of the effects of daycare. They reported that 17 percent of kindergartners who had spent more than 30 hours a week in daycare, compared to 9 percent of the children who spent most of their early years with their mothers, were aggressive (NICHD 2001). Many people took this to mean that "daycare makes kids more aggressive," and the media had a field day.

The researchers conducting this daycare study are themselves sharply divided. One, Jay Belsky, was accused by his co-researchers of having an anti-childcare agenda; he has, in fact, been arguing for years that daycare often has bad effects on children, recommending that mothers stay home if possible. Belsky, of course, thinks it is his co-researchers who have the political agenda. "They're so busy trying to protect mothers from feeling guilty, they've lost track of the science," he told the *Los Angeles Times*. On topics like this, where findings are divisive and have important implications for the decisions people make about child care, it is especially important to try to examine the data dispassionately, as best you can. In this case, the 17 percent figure for the aggressive children turns out to be well within the normal range for children and adolescents. Moreover, the children who had spent their early years in high-quality daycare showed better language and memory skills than children kept at home.

▶ *Be cautious about correlations.* We said this before, but we'll say it again: Many statistics in the news are correlational, so you can't be sure what's causing what. In the daycare study, for example, the children were not randomly assigned to two groups, daycare and home care; the aggression statistic was a corre-

lation. We can't conclude, then, that daycare makes kids aggressive. Maybe the children who spent more time at home with their mothers simply had fewer kids around to be aggressive *with!*

Arguments over public policy often take the form of shouting matches about numbers. People on the right and left are equally likely to misuse numbers to promote their political causes. Many gay men and lesbians protested new evidence that homosexuality is statistically much less common than Alfred Kinsey reported in 1948. Many conservatives protested the evidence in the U.S. Surgeon General's 2001 report showing that "abstinence-only" sex-education programs do not lower rates of teen pregnancy; birth-control information does.

In sum, the statistics that most people like best are the ones that support their prejudices. Unfortunately, as Joel Best writes, bad statistics, repeated mindlessly and uncritically, "take on lives of their own"—they infiltrate popular culture and become almost impossible to eradicate. The information in this chapter will get you started on learning to tell the difference between numbers that are helpful and those that mislead or deceive. In future chapters, we will try to give you other guidelines for thinking critically and scientifically about popular claims and findings that make the news.

Summary

What Makes Psychological Research Scientific?

▶ Research methods provide a way for psychologists to separate well-supported conclusions from unfounded belief. An understanding of these methods can also help

people think critically about psychological issues and become astute consumers of psychological findings and programs.

▶ The ideal scientist states hypotheses and predictions precisely, is skeptical of claims that rest solely on faith or authority, relies on empirical evidence, resists the *confirmation bias* and complies with the *principle of falsifiability*, and is open about methods and results so that findings can be replicated. In contrast, pseudoscientists ignore these requirements. The public nature of science and the *peer review* process give science a built-in system of checks and balances.

Descriptive Studies: Establishing the Facts

▶ *Descriptive methods* allow psychologists to describe and predict behavior but not necessarily to choose one explanation over others. Such methods include case studies, observational studies, psychological tests, and surveys, as well as correlational methods.

▶ *Case studies* are detailed descriptions of individuals. They are often used by clinicians, and they can be valuable in exploring new research topics and addressing questions that would otherwise be difficult to study. But because the person under study may not be representative of people in general, case studies are typically sources rather than tests of hypotheses.

▶ In *observational studies,* the researcher systematically observes and records behavior without interfering in any way with the behavior. *Naturalistic observation* is used to find out how subjects behave in their natural environments. *Laboratory observation* allows more control and the use of special equipment; behavior in the laboratory, however, may differ in certain ways from behavior in natural contexts.

▶ *Psychological tests* are used to measure and evaluate personality traits, emotional states, aptitudes, interests, abilities, and values. A good test is one that has been *standardized* and is both *valid* and *reliable*. Critics have questioned the reliability and validity of even some widely used tests.

▶ *Surveys* are questionnaires or interviews that ask people directly about their experiences, attitudes, and opinions. Researchers must take precautions to obtain a sample that is *representative* of the larger population that the researcher wishes to describe and that yields results that are not influenced by a *volunteer bias*. Findings can also be affected by the fact that respondents sometimes lie, misremember, or misinterpret the questions.

Correlational Studies: Looking for Relationships

▶ In descriptive research, studies that look for relationships between phenomena are known as *correlational*. A *correlation* is a measure of the strength of a positive or negative relationship between two variables. Many correlations reported in the media or on the Internet are based on rumor and anecdote, and are not supported by data. Even when a correlation is real, it does *not* show a causal relationship between the variables.

Experiments: Hunting for Causes

▶ *Experiments* allow researchers to control the situation being studied, manipulate an *independent variable,* and assess the effects of the manipulation on a *dependent variable.* Experimental studies usually require a comparison or *control condition. Single-blind* and *double-blind* procedures can be used to prevent the expectations of the subjects or the experimenter from affecting the results. Because experiments allow conclusions about cause and effect, they have long been the method of choice in psychology. However, like laboratory observations, experiments create a special situation that may call forth behavior not typical in other environments.

Evaluating the Findings

▶ Psychologists use *descriptive statistics,* such as the *arithmetic mean* and the *standard deviation,* to summarize data. They use *inferential statistics* to find out how impressive the data are. *Significance tests* tell the researchers how likely it is that the results of a study occurred merely by chance. The results are said to be *statistically significant* if this likelihood is very low. Statistically significant results allow psychologists to make predictions about human behavior, but, as in all sciences, probabilistic results do not tell us with any certainty what a particular individual will do in a situation.

▶ Choosing among competing interpretations of a finding can be difficult, and care must be taken to avoid going beyond the facts. Sometimes the best interpretation does not emerge until a hypothesis has been tested in more than one way—for example, by using both *cross-sectional* and *longitudinal* methods.

▶ Statistical significance does not always imply real-world importance because the amount of variation in the data accounted for by the independent variable—the *effect size*—may be small. Conversely, a result that does not quite reach significance may be potentially useful. Therefore, many psychologists are now turning to other inferential measures. The technique of *meta-analysis,* for example, reveals how much of the variation in scores across many different studies can be explained by a particular variable.

Keeping the Enterprise Ethical

▶ The APA's ethical code requires researchers to obtain the *informed consent* of human subjects, protect them from harm, and warn them in advance of any risks. Many studies require deceptive procedures. Concern about the morality of such procedures has led to guidelines to protect participants.

▶ Psychologists study animals in order to gain knowledge about particular species, discover practical applications of psychological principles, study issues that cannot be studied with human beings for practical or ethical reasons, clarify theoretical questions, and improve human welfare. Debate over the use of animals in research has led to more comprehensive regulations governing their treatment and care.

▶ Statistics help scientists to understand the complexities of human behavior, but laypeople need to keep in mind that statistics are often misrepresented or misused to support particular social or political goals.

Key Terms

theory 36
hypothesis 36
operational definition 37
principle of falsifiability 37
confirmation bias 37
replicate 38
peer review 39
descriptive methods 40
case study 40
observational studies 41
naturalistic observation 41
laboratory observation 42
psychological tests 43
standardization 43
norms 44
reliability 44
   test-retest reliability 44
   alternate-forms reliability 44

validity 44
   content validity 44
   criterion validity 44
surveys 45
representative sample 45
volunteer bias 45
correlational study 47
correlation 47
variable 47
positive correlation 47
negative correlation 47
coefficient of correlation 48
experiment 50
independent variable 50
dependent variable 50
control condition 52
experimental and control groups 52
random assignment 52

placebo 52
single-blind study 53
experimenter effects 53
double-blind study 53
field research 54
descriptive statistics 56
arithmetic mean 56
standard deviation 56
inferential statistics 57
significance tests 57
statistical significance 57
cross-sectional study 58
longitudinal study 58
effect size 59
meta-analysis 59
informed consent 61

◀LOOKING BACK

• Where do psychological scientists get their hypotheses? (p. 36)

• In what way are scientists risk takers? (p. 37)

• Why is secrecy a big "no-no" in science? (p. 38)

• When are psychological case studies informative, and when are they useless? (pp. 40–41)

• Why do psychologists often observe people's behavior in laboratories instead of in everyday situations? (pp. 42–43)

• Why should you be skeptical about psychological tests in magazines and newspapers or on the Internet? (p. 45)

• What's the difference between a psychological survey and a poll of listeners conducted by a radio talk-show host? (p. 45)

- If two things are "negatively" correlated, like grades and TV watching, what is the relationship between them? (p. 47)

- If watching television and behaving aggressively are positively correlated, does that mean that TV causes violence? (p. 49)

- Why do psychologists rely so heavily on experiments? (p. 50)

- What, exactly, do control groups control for? (p. 52)

- In a double-blind experiment, who is "blind," and what aren't they supposed to "see"? (p. 53)

- In psychological studies, why are averages sometimes misleading? (p. 56)

- How can psychologists tell whether a finding is impressive or trivial? (p. 57)

- Why are some findings significant statistically but unimportant in practical terms? (p. 59)

- Why do psychologists often lie to their subjects? (p. 61)

- Why do psychologists study nonhuman animals? (p. 62)

Go to **WWW.PRENHALL.COM/WADE to reinforce these key concepts, and more.**

2.1 Observational studies	**2.3 Experiments**
2.2 Correlational studies	**2.4 Stats: Descriptive (mean) vs. inferencial (tests of significance)**

3

Evolution, Genes, and Behavior

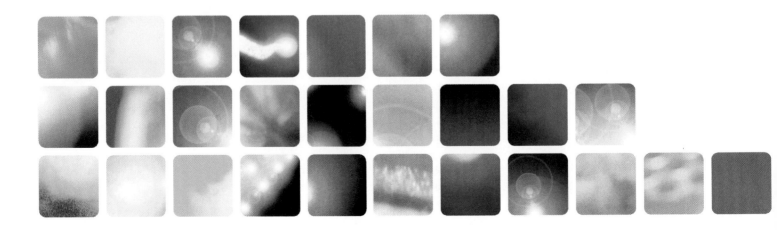

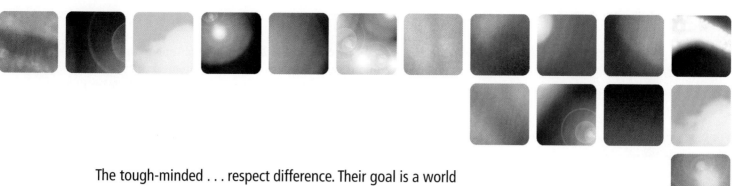

The tough-minded . . . respect difference. Their goal is a world
made safe for differences.

RUTH BENEDICT

Think of all the ways that human beings are alike. Everywhere, no matter what their backgrounds or where they live, people love, work, argue, dance, sing, complain, and gossip. They rear families, celebrate marriages, and mourn losses. They reminisce about the past and plan for the future. They help their friends and fight their enemies. They smile with amusement, frown with displeasure, and glare in anger. *Where do all these commonalities come from?*

Think of all the ways that human beings differ. Some are extroverts, always ready to throw a party, make new friends, or speak up in a crowd; others are shy and introverted, preferring the safe and familiar. Some are trailblazers, ambitious and enterprising; others are placid, content with the way things are. Some take to book learning like a cat to catnip; others struggle in school but have lots of street smarts and practical know-how. Some are overwhelmed by even the most petty of problems; others remain calm and resilient in the face of severe difficulties. *Where do all these differences come from?*

For many years, psychologists addressing these questions tended to fall into two camps. On one side were the *nativists,* who emphasized genes and inborn characteristics, or *nature;* on the other side were the *empiricists,* who focused on learning and experience, or *nurture.* Edward L. Thorndike (1903), one of the leading psychologists of the early 1900s, staked out the first position when he claimed that "in the actual race of life . . . the chief determining factor is heredity." But in words that became famous, his contemporary, behaviorist John B. Watson (1925), insisted that experience could write virtually any message on the blank slate of human nature: "Give me a dozen healthy infants, well-formed, and my own specified world to bring them up in and I'll guarantee to take any one at random and train him to become any type of specialist I might select—doctor, lawyer, artist, merchant-chief and yes, even beggar-man and thief, regardless of his talents, penchants, tendencies, abilities, vocations, and race of his ancestors."

In this chapter, we focus mostly on the contribution of nature to our human commonalities and our individual differences, and on findings from two related areas.

The long and short of it: Human beings are similar and different.

Researchers in **evolutionary psychology** emphasize the evolutionary mechanisms that might help explain commonalities in language learning, attention, perception, memory, sexual behavior, emotion, reasoning, and many other aspects of human psychology. Researchers in **behavioral genetics** study the contribution of heredity to individual differences in personality, mental ability, and other characteristics. You should keep in mind, however, that today no one argues in terms of nature *or* nurture; scientists understand that heredity and environment interact to produce not only our psychological traits but even most of our physical ones. Children can inherit a tendency to be nearsighted, for instance, but whether nearsightedness actually develops may depend on whether a child reads a lot or sits for hours staring at a TV set or computer monitor (Gwiazda et al., 1993). A teenager with a natural aptitude for sports may be more likely than other students to get on a school team and to get sports equipment as birthday presents, experiences that reward and encourage the development of that aptitude.

WHAT'S AHEAD ▶

- **What does the chemical code in our genes encode *for*?**
- **What can a complete map of the human genes reveal—and not reveal?**

Unlocking the Secrets of Genes

Let's begin by looking at what genes are and how they operate. **Genes,** the basic units of heredity, are located on **chromosomes,** rod-shaped structures found in the center (nucleus) of every cell of the body. Each sperm cell and each egg cell (ovum) contains 23 chromosomes, so when a sperm and egg unite at conception, the fertilized egg and all the body cells that eventually develop from it (except for sperm cells and ova) contain 46 chromosomes, arranged in 23 pairs.

Chromosomes consist of threadlike strands of **DNA** (deoxyribonucleic acid) molecules, and genes consist of small segments of this DNA. Each human chromosome contains thousands of genes, each with a fixed location. Collectively, all the genes together—current estimates put the number around 35,000, fewer than once thought—are referred to as the human **genome.** Many of these genes are found in other animals as well; others are uniquely human, setting us apart from chimpanzees, wasps, and plants. Many genes are inherited in the same form by everyone; others vary, contributing to our individuality.

evolutionary psychology A field of psychology emphasizing evolutionary mechanisms that may help explain human commonalities in cognition, development, emotion, social practices, and other areas of behavior.

behavioral genetics An interdisciplinary field of study concerned with the genetic bases of individual differences in behavior and personality.

genes The functional units of heredity; they are composed of DNA and specify the structure of proteins.

chromosomes Within every cell, rod-shaped structures that carry the genes.

DNA (deoxyribonucleic acid) The chromosomal molecule that transfers genetic characteristics by way of coded instructions for the structure of proteins.

genome The full set of genes in each cell of an organism (with the exception of sperm and egg cells).

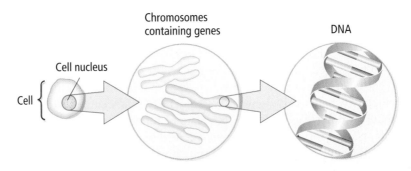

Within each gene, four basic chemical elements of DNA—identified by the letters A, T, C, and G, and numbering in the thousands or even tens of thousands—are arranged in a particular order: for example, ACGTCTCTATA. . . . This sequence forms a code that helps determine the synthesis of one of the many proteins that affect virtually every aspect of the body, from its structure to the chemicals that keep it running.

Identifying even a single gene is a daunting task; biologist Joseph Levine and geneticist David Suzuki (1993) once compared it to searching for someone when all you know is that the person lives somewhere on Earth. Researchers must usually *clone* (produce copies of) several stretches of DNA on a chromosome, then use indirect methods to locate a given gene.

One method, which has been used to search for the genes associated with many physical and mental conditions, involves doing **linkage studies.** These studies take advantage of the tendency of genes lying close together on a chromosome to be inherited together across generations. The researchers start out by looking for **genetic markers,** DNA segments that vary considerably among individuals and whose locations on the chromosomes are already known. They then look for patterns of inheritance of these markers in large families in which a condition—say, depression or impulsive violence—is common. If a marker tends to exist only in family members who have the condition, then it can be used as a genetic landmark: The gene involved in the condition is apt to be located nearby on the chromosome, so the researchers have some idea where to search for it. The linkage method was used, for example, to locate the gene responsible for Huntington's disease, a fatal neurological disorder that affects motor control, intellectual functioning, and memory (Huntington's Disease Collaborative Research Group, 1993). Although in this instance only one gene was involved, the search took a decade of painstaking work.

In 2000, after years of heated competition, an international collaboration of researchers called the Human Genome Project and a private company, Celera Genomics, both announced that they had completed a rough draft of a map of the entire human genome. Using high-tech methods, the researchers were able to identify the sequence of nearly all 3 billion units of DNA (those A's, C's, T's, and G's) and to determine the boundaries between genes and how the genes are arranged on the chromosomes (see Figure 3.1). This project has been enormously costly and time consuming, but it reflects the view among many scientists that the twenty-first century will be the century of the gene.

It is important to understand, however, that even when researchers locate a gene on a chromosome, they do not automatically know its role in physical or psychological functioning. Usually, locating a gene is just the first step in understanding what it does and how it works. Also, be wary of media reports implying that some gene is the *only* factor involved in a complex psychological ability or trait, such as intelligence or shyness. In 1998, for example, newspapers announced the discovery of a "worry gene." Don't worry about it. Unlike disorders such as Huntington's, most human traits—even such seemingly straightforward ones as height and eye

linkage studies Studies that look for patterns of inheritance of genetic markers in large families in which a particular condition is common.

genetic marker A segment of DNA that varies among individuals, has a known location on a chromosome, and can function as a genetic landmark for a gene involved in a physical or mental condition.

Figure 3.1
The human chromosomes on the left have been magnified almost 55,000 times. On the right, a small portion of the map for chromosome 10 shows 52 genes identified by the Human Genome Project, including some that have been linked to prostate cancer, leukemia, and obesity.

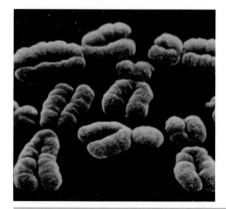

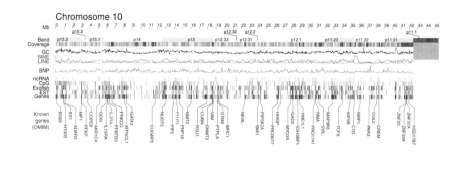

Get Involved

Thumbs Up!

Ask the members of your family, one person at a time, to clasp their hands together. Include aunts and uncles, grandparents—as many of your biological relatives as possible. Which thumb does each person put on top? About half of all people fold the left thumb over the right and about half fold the right thumb over the left, and these responses tend to run in families. Do your own relatives show one tendency over the other? (If your family is an adoptive one, of course, there is less chance of finding a trend.) Try the same exercise with someone else's family; do you get the same results? Even for behavior as simple as thumb folding, the details of how genes exert their effect remain uncertain (Jones, 1994).

color—are influenced by more than one gene pair. Psychological traits are especially likely to depend on multiple genes, with each one accounting for just a small part of the variance among people. Conversely, any single gene is apt to influence many different behaviors.

3.1

To make the picture even more complicated, when it comes to psychological qualities, genetic and environmental influences are inextricably intertwined. Thus, there is no simple, direct line between a single gene and any given behavior. New methods have been developed to tease out the small contribution that a specific gene is likely to make to a particular trait (Plomin & Crabbe, 2000), but at this point, all announcements of a "gene for this" or a "gene for that" should be viewed with extreme caution.

QUICK QUIZ

The Human Genome Project has not discovered any quiz-taking genes.

1. The basic unit of heredity is called a (a) gene, (b) chromosome, (c) genome, (d) DNA molecule.
2. What does the code within a gene encode for?
3. *True or false:* Most human genetic traits depend on a single gene.

Answers:

1. a 2. the synthesis of a particular protein 3. false

WHAT'S AHEAD

- **During evolution, why do some traits become more common and others less common?**
- **In the evolutionary view, why is the capacity to read faces innate, but not the capacity to read books?**
- **Why do so many people ignore signs saying "Don't touch"?**

The Genetics of Similarity

One of the questions that opened this chapter was, how can we explain our human similarities—the experiences and behaviors that seem to be universal, such as loyalty to a family or clan, or the capacity for language? Evolutionary psychologists believe the answer lies partly in genetic dispositions that developed during the evolutionary history of our species. As British geneticist Steve Jones (1994) wrote, "Genetics is the key to the past. Every human gene must have an ancestor. . . . Each gene is a message from our forebears and together they contain the whole story of human evolution."

Evolution and Natural Selection

To read the messages from the past that are locked in our genes, we must first understand the nature of evolution itself. Evolution is basically a change in gene frequencies within a population, a change that typically takes place over many generations. As particular genes become more common in the population or less common, so do the characteristics they influence.

Why do gene frequencies in a population change? Why don't they stay put from one generation to another? One reason is that during the division of the cells that produce sperm and eggs, if an error occurs in the copying of the original DNA sequence, genes can spontaneously change, or *mutate*. In addition, during the formation of a sperm or an egg, small segments of genetic material cross over (exchange places) from one member of a chromosome pair to another, prior to the final cell division. As genes spontaneously mutate and recombine during the production of sperm and eggs, new genetic variations—and therefore potential new traits—keep arising.

But that is only part of the story. According to the principle of **natural selection**, first formulated in general terms by the British naturalist Charles Darwin in *On the Origin of Species* (1859/1964), the fate of these genetic variations depends on the environment. (Darwin did not actually know about genes, as their discovery had not yet been widely publicized, but he realized that a species' characteristics must somehow be transmitted biologically from one generation to the next.)

The fundamental idea behind natural selection is this: If, in a particular environment, individuals with a genetically influenced trait tend to be more successful than other individuals in finding food, surviving the elements, and fending off enemies—and therefore better at staying alive long enough to produce offspring—their genes will become more and more common in the population. Their genes will have been "selected" by success, and over many generations, these genes may even spread throughout the species. In contrast, individuals whose traits are not as adaptive in the struggle for survival will not be as "reproductively fit": They will tend to die before reproducing, and therefore their genes, and the traits influenced by those genes, will become less and less common and eventually may even become extinct.

Scientists debate how gradually or abruptly such changes occur and whether competition for survival is always the primary mechanism of change. But they agree on the basic processes of evolution. Over the past century and a half, Darwin's ideas have been resoundingly supported by findings in anthropology, botany, and molecular genetics (Jones, 2000). Scientists have watched evolutionary developments occurring before their very eyes in organisms that change rapidly, such as microbes, insects, and various plants, and evolutionary principles such as natural selection now guide all of the biological sciences.

Evolutionary biologists often start with an observation about some characteristic and then try to account for it in evolutionary terms. For example, why do male peacocks have such fabulous and flamboyant feathers, whereas females look so drab and dull? Because during the evolution of peacocks, males who could put on the flashiest display got the attention of females, and such males therefore had a better chance of reproducing. In contrast, all females had to do was hang around and pick the guy with the fanciest feathers; they didn't even have to dress up.

Evolutionary psychologists work in the same way as biologists, but some take a slightly different tack: They start by asking what sorts of challenges human beings

evolution A change in gene frequencies within a population over many generations; a mechanism by which genetically influenced characteristics of a population may change.

natural selection The evolutionary process in which individuals with genetically influenced traits that are adaptive in a particular environment tend to survive and to reproduce in greater numbers than do other individuals; as a result, their traits become more common in the population.

 3.2

Many people at first ridiculed Darwin's notion that humans share a common ancestor with other primates. In this nineteenth-century cartoon, a monkeylike Darwin shows an ape how closely he resembles people. Today, evolutionary principles, which have long guided the biological sciences, are having a growing influence on psychological science as well.

might have faced in their prehistoric past—having to decide which foods were safe to eat, for example, or needing to size up a stranger's intentions quickly. Then they draw inferences about the behavioral tendencies that might have been selected because they helped our forebears solve these survival problems and enhanced reproductive fitness. (They make no assumption about whether the behavior is adaptive or intelligent in the *present* environment.) Finally, they do research to see if those tendencies actually exist throughout the world.

For example, our ancestors' need to avoid eating poisonous or rancid food might have led eventually to an innate dislike for bitter tastes and rotten smells; those individuals who happened to be born with such dislikes would have stood a better chance of surviving long enough to reproduce. Similarly, it made good survival sense for our ancestors to develop an innate capacity for language and an ability to recognize faces and emotional expressions. But they would not have had much need for an innate ability to read or drive, inasmuch as books and cars had not yet been invented (Pinker, 1994).

For many evolutionary psychologists, a guiding assumption is that the human mind is not a general-purpose computer waiting to be programmed. Instead, they say, it developed as a collection of specialized and independent "modules" to handle specific survival problems, such as the need to find food or find a mate (Buss, 1995, 1999; Cosmides, Tooby, & Barkow, 1992; Mealey, 1996). A particular module may involve several dispersed but interconnected areas of the brain, just as a computer file can be fragmented on a disk (Pinker, 1997).

Critics worry that the idea of mental modules is no improvement over instinct theory, the once-popular notion in psychology that virtually every human activity and capacity, from cleanliness to cruelty, is innate. Frans de Waal (2001b), an evolutionary theorist who believes that someday all psychology departments will have a picture of Darwin hanging on the wall, has accused some of his colleagues of mistakenly assuming that if a trait exists, then it must be adaptive and must correspond to a mental module. This assumption, he points out, is incorrect: Male pattern baldness and pimples, for example, are not particularly adaptive! Some traits can even be costly; the problems that many people have with aching backs are no doubt an

Baldness may be beautiful, but it is not necessarily adaptive!

unfortunate consequence of our ability to walk on two feet. To understand our evolutionary legacy, de Waal argues, we must consider not just individual traits in isolation, but the whole package of traits that characterize the species. This is as true for psychological traits as for physical ones.

Those who subscribe to the modules approach respond that evidence from psychology and other disciplines can distinguish behavior that has a biological origin from behavior that does not. As Steven Pinker (1994) explains, if a mental module for some behavior exists, then neuroscientists should eventually discover the brain circuits or subsystems associated with it. Further, he adds, "When children solve problems for which they have mental modules, they should look like geniuses, knowing things they have not been taught; when they solve problems that their minds are not equipped for, it should be a long hard slog." Be careful, though, to avoid the common error of assuming that if something exists, it must be adaptive.

Innate Human Characteristics

Because of the way our species evolved, many abilities, tendencies, and characteristics are either present at birth in all human beings or develop rapidly as a child matures. These traits include not just the obvious ones, such as the ability to stand on two legs or to grasp objects with the forefinger and thumb, but also less obvious ones. Here are just a few examples:

1 *Infant reflexes.* Babies are born with a number of reflexes—simple, automatic responses to specific stimuli (see Chapter 14). For example, all infants will suck something put to their lips; by aiding nursing, this reflex enhances their chances of survival.

2 *An attraction to novelty.* Novelty is appealing to human beings and many other species. If a rat has had its dinner, it will prefer to explore an unfamiliar wing of a maze rather than the familiar wing where food is. Human babies reveal a surprising interest in looking at and listening to unfamiliar things—which, of course, includes most of the world. A baby will even stop nursing if someone new enters his or her range of vision.

3 *A desire to explore and manipulate objects.* All birds and mammals have this innate inclination. Primates, especially, like to "monkey" with things, taking them apart and scrutinizing the pieces, apparently for the sheer pleasure of it

All primates, including human beings, are innately disposed to explore the environment, manipulate objects, play, and "monkey around."

(Harlow, Harlow, & Meyer, 1950). Human babies shake rattles, bang pots, and grasp whatever is put into their tiny hands. For human beings, the natural impulse to handle interesting objects can be overwhelming, which may be one reason why the command "Don't touch" is so often ignored by children, museum-goers, and shoppers.

4 *An impulse to play and fool around.* Think of kittens and lion cubs, puppies and pandas, and all young primates, who will play with and pounce on each other all day until hunger or naptime calls. Play and exploration may be biologically adaptive because they help members of a species find food and other necessities of life and learn to cope with their environments. Indeed, the young of many species enjoy *practice play,* behavior that will be used for serious purposes when they are adults (Vandenberg, 1985). A kitten, for example, will stalk and attack a ball of yarn. In human beings, play teaches children how to get along with others and gives them a chance to practice their motor and linguistic skills (Pellegrini & Galda, 1993).

5 *Basic arithmetic skills.* Incredibly, by the age of only 1 week, infants show an understanding that a set of three items differs from a set of two items, indicating a rudimentary understanding of number. Of course, 1-week-old babies cannot count. However, they will spend more time looking at a novel set of three items after getting used to a set of two items, or vice versa, which means that they can recognize the difference. By 18 months, infants know that 4 is more than 3, which is more than 2, which is more than 1—suggesting that the brain is designed to understand "more than" and "less than" relationships for small numbers. Evolutionary psychologists believe that these and other fundamental arithmetic skills evolved because they were useful to our ancestors (Geary, 1995).

In other chapters, we consider the adaptive and evolutionary aspects of sensory and perceptual abilities (Chapter 6), learning (Chapter 7), cognitive abilities (Chapter 9), emotions and emotional expressions (Chapter 11), the tendency to gain weight when food is plentiful (Chapter 12), attachment (Chapter 14), and stress reactions (Chapter 15). For now, let us look more closely at two areas of particular interest to evolutionary psychologists: the development of language and the nature of mating practices around the world.

QUICK QUIZ

How evolved is your understanding of evolutionary psychology?

1. What two processes during the formation of sperm and eggs help explain genetic changes within a population?

2. Which is the best statement of the principle of natural selection? (a) Over time, the environment naturally selects some traits over others. (b) Genetic variations become more common over time if they are adaptive in a particular environment. (c) A species constantly improves as parents pass along their best traits to their offspring.

3. Many evolutionary psychologists believe that the human mind evolved as (a) a collection of specialized modules to handle specific survival problems; (b) a general-purpose computer that adapts to any situation; (c) a collection of specific instincts for every human activity or capacity.

4. Which of the following is *not* part of our biological heritage? (a) a sucking reflex at birth; (b) a motive to explore and manipulate objects; (c) an avoidance of novel, unfamiliar objects; (d) a love of play

Answers:

1. spontaneous genetic mutations and crossover of genetic material between members of a chromosome pair, which occur before the final cell division 2. b 3. a 4. c

- **What does language allow us to do that other animals can't?**
- **What evidence suggests that evolution has equipped infants' brains with a module for acquiring language?**
- **How do parents help children acquire language?**

Our Human Heritage: Language

Try to read this sentence aloud:

Kamaunawezakusomamanenohayawewenimtuwamaanasana.

Can you tell where one word begins and another ends? Unless you know Swahili, the syllables of this sentence will sound like gibberish.*

Well, to a baby learning its native tongue, *every* sentence must, at first, be gibberish. How, then, does an infant pick out discrete syllables and words from the jumble of sounds in the environment, much less figure out what the words mean and how to combine them? Is there something special about the human brain that allows a baby to discover how language works? Darwin thought so: Language, wrote Darwin (1874), is an instinctive ability unique to human beings. Many modern researchers think he was right.

The Nature of Language

To evaluate Darwin's claim, we must first appreciate that a **language** is not just any old communication system; it is a set of rules for combining elements that are inherently meaningless into utterances that convey meaning. The elements are usually sounds, but they can also be the gestures of American Sign Language (ASL) and other manual languages used by deaf and hearing-impaired people.

Some nonhuman animals are able to acquire aspects of language if they get help from their human friends (see Chapter 9). However, we seem to be the only species that acquires language naturally. Other primates use grunts, screeches, and gestures to warn each other of danger, attract attention, and express emotions, but the sounds are not combined to produce original sentences (at least, as far as anyone can tell). Bongo may make a sound of delight when he encounters food, but he cannot say, "The bananas in the next grove are a lot riper than the ones we ate last week and sure beat our usual diet of termites."

In contrast, language, whether spoken or signed, allows human beings to express and comprehend an infinite number of novel utterances, created on the spot. This ability is critical; except for a few fixed phrases ("How are you?" "Get a life!"), most of the utterances we produce or hear over a lifetime are new. For example, in this book you will find few, if any, sentences that you have read, heard, or spoken before in exactly the same form. Yet you can understand what you are reading, and you can produce new sentences of your own about the material.

language A system that combines meaningless elements such as sounds or gestures to form structured utterances that convey meaning.

Human beings acquire language even when they cannot hear speech. In North America, many hearing-impaired people use American Sign Language (ASL) to express not only everyday meanings but also poetic and musical ones. Deaf children learn to sign in ASL as easily as hearing children learn to speak.

Kama unaweza kusoma maneno haya, wewe ni mtu wa maana sana, in Swahili, means "If you can read these words, you are a remarkable person."

The Innate Capacity for Language

At one time, most psychologists assumed that children acquired language by imitating adults and paying attention when adults corrected their mistakes. Then along came linguist Noam Chomsky (1957, 1980), who argued that language was far too complex to be learned bit by bit, as one might learn a list of world capitals.

Children, said Chomsky, must not only figure out which sounds or gestures form words; they must also take the *surface structure* of a sentence—the way the sentence is actually spoken or signed—and infer an underlying *deep structure*—how the sentence is to be understood. For example, although "Mary kissed John" and "John was kissed by Mary" have different surface structures, any 5-year-old knows that the two sentences have essentially the same underlying meaning, in which Mary is the actor and John gets the kiss:

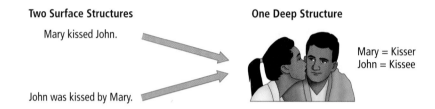

Two Surface Structures

Mary kissed John.

John was kissed by Mary.

One Deep Structure

Mary = Kisser
John = Kissee

Conversely, "Bill heard the trampling of the hikers," a single surface structure, can have two different underlying meanings: one in which the hikers are actors doing the trampling, and one in which they are the unfortunate objects of the trampling. Your ability to discern two different deep structures tells you that the sentence's meaning is ambiguous.

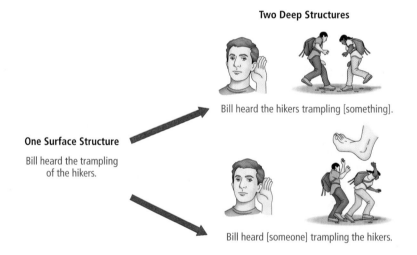

Two Deep Structures

Bill heard the hikers trampling [something].

One Surface Structure

Bill heard the trampling of the hikers.

Bill heard [someone] trampling the hikers.

To transform surface structures into deep ones, said Chomsky, children must apply rules of grammar (*syntax*). These rules govern word order and other linguistic features that determine the role a word plays in a sentence (such as, say, kisser or kissee). Most people, even adults, cannot actually state the grammatical rules of their language (e.g., "In English, adjectives usually precede the noun they describe"), yet we are able to apply thousands of such rules without even thinking about it. No native speaker of English would say, "He threw the ball big."

Because no one actually teaches us grammar when we are toddlers, the human brain, Chomsky argued, must contain a **language acquisition device**, an innate mental

language acquisition device According to many psycholinguists, an innate mental module that allows young children to develop language if they are exposed to an adequate sampling of conversation.

module that allows young children to develop language if they are exposed to an adequate sampling of conversation; just as a bird is designed to fly, human beings are designed to use language. Another way of saying this is that children are born with a *universal grammar*—that is, their brains are sensitive to the core features common to all languages, such as nouns and verbs, subjects and objects, and negatives. These common features occur even in languages as seemingly different as Mohawk and English, or Okinawan and Bulgarian (Baker, 2001; Cinque, 1999; Pesetsky, 1999).

Over the years, linguists and *psycholinguists* (researchers who study the psychology of language) have gathered much evidence in support of the Chomskyan position:

1 *Children in different cultures go through similar stages of linguistic development.* For example, they will often form their first negatives simply by adding "no" or "not" at the beginning or end of a sentence ("No get dirty"); and at a later stage, they will use double negatives ("He don't want no milk"; "Nobody don't like me"), even when their language does not allow such constructions (Klima & Bellugi, 1966; McNeill, 1966).

2 *Children combine words in ways that adults never would.* They reduce a parent's sentence ("Let's go to the store!") to their own two-word version ("Go store!") and make many charming errors that an adult would not ("The alligator goed kerplunk"; "Daddy taked me"; "Hey, Horton heared a Who") (Ervin-Tripp, 1964; Marcus et al., 1992). Such errors, which linguists call *overregularizations,* are not random; they show that the child has grasped a grammatical rule (e.g., add the *t* or *d* sound to make a verb past tense, as in *walked* or *hugged*) and is merely overgeneralizing it (*taked, goed*).

3 *Adults do not consistently correct their children's syntax, yet children learn to speak or sign correctly anyway.* Learning explanations of language acquisition assume that children are rewarded for saying the right words and are punished for making errors. But parents do not stop to correct every error in their children's speech, so long as they can understand what the child is trying to say (Brown, Cazden, & Bellugi, 1969). Indeed, parents often *reward* children for incorrect statements! The 2-year-old who says "Want milk!" is likely to get it; most parents would not wait for a more grammatical (or polite) request.

4 *Children not exposed to adult language may invent a language of their own.* Deaf children who have never learned a standard language, either signed or spoken, have made up their *own* sign languages, and across cultures, these languages show similarities in sentence structure (Goldin-Meadow & Mylander, 1998). The most astounding case comes from Nicaragua, where a group of deaf children of hearing parents, sent to two special schools, eventually created a home-grown but grammatically complex sign language that is unrelated to Spanish (Senghas & Coppola, 2001). Scientists have had a unique opportunity to observe the evolution of this language as it developed from a few simple signs to a full-blown linguistic system.

5 *Infants as young as 7 months can derive simple linguistic rules from a string of sounds.* If babies are repeatedly exposed to artificial "sentences" with an ABA pattern, such as "Ga ti ga" or "Li na li," until they get bored, they will then prefer new sentences with an ABB pattern (such as "Wo fe fe") over new sentences with an ABA pattern (such as "Wo fe wo"). (They indicate this preference by looking longer at a flashing light associated with the novel pattern than one associated with the familiar pattern.) Conversely, when the original sentences have an ABB structure, babies will prefer novel ones with an ABA structure. These responses suggest to many researchers that babies can discriminate the different types of structures (Marcus et al., 1999). Astonishingly, this ability emerges even before they can understand or produce any words.

Chomsky's ideas so revolutionized thinking about language and human nature that some linguists refer to the initial publication of his ideas as The Event (Rymer, 1993). Chomsky changed the questions researchers asked about language development, and even the terms they used (language "acquisition" replaced language "learning"). Although Chomsky himself avoided the evolutionary implications of his argument, others maintain that an innate facility for language evolved in human beings because it permitted our ancestors to convey precise information about time, space, objects, and events, and to negotiate alliances that were necessary for survival (Pinker, 1994).

The next logical step might be to identify the specific brain modules and genes that contribute to our ability to acquire language. Clues come from a large three-generation British family with a rare genetic disorder that prevents normal language acquisition. Family members who are affected with this disorder have pronunciation problems and also have trouble applying grammatical rules for changing tenses or constructing plurals—rules that normal children learn easily and unconsciously. For example, they can learn the distinction between *mice* and *mouse* but they cannot learn the general rule about adding an *s*, *z*, or *iz* sound to make a noun plural, as in *bikes* (*s*), *gloves* (*z*), and *kisses* (*iz*). Instead, they must learn each plural as a separate item, and they make many errors (Gopnik & Goad, 1997; Matthews, 1994).

Linkage studies recently led British researchers to a mutation in a specific gene that seems to contribute to this syndrome, possibly by orchestrating the activity of

---

Get Involved

A Grammar Test Everyone Can Pass

How would you complete these sentences, spoken aloud?

This morning I saw one sik. Later I saw two more _____.
This morning I saw one wug. Later I saw two more _____.
This morning I saw one litch. Later I saw two more _____.

Think about the sounds you added to these nonsense words; they differed, didn't they? In English, the plural form of most nouns depends on the last sound of the singular form. The precise rules are quite complicated, yet every speaker of English has an implicit knowledge of them and will correctly add an *s* sound to *rat* to make *rats*, a *z* sound to *rag* to make *rags*, and an *iz* sound to *radish* to make *radishes*. (The only exceptions are people with a rare genetic disorder, as described in the text.) When 5- and 6-year-olds are asked for the plural versions of nonsense words, they easily apply the appropriate rules (Berko, 1958). Such evidence has helped to convince many psychologists that human beings have an innate ability to infer the rules of grammar.

other genes during prenatal brain development (Lai et al., 2001). Scientists are still debating whether the gene's ultimate influence is on pronunciation, specific grammar circuits in the brain, or some general intellectual or perceptual process necessary for speech or language. Nonetheless, this research is an important first step in isolating possible genetic influences on language.

Learning and Language

Despite the evidence for Chomsky's view, some theorists still give experience a greater role. Using computers, they have been able to design *neural networks*, mathematical models of the brain that can "learn" some aspects of language, such as regular and irregular past-tense verbs, without the help of a language acquisition device or preprogrammed rules. Neural networks simply adjust the connections among hypothetical "neurons" in response to incoming data, such as repetitions of a word in its past tense form. The success of these computer models, say their designers, suggests that children, too, may be able to acquire linguistic features without getting a head start from inborn brain circuits (Rodriguez, Wiles, & Elman, 1999; Rumelhart & McClelland, 1987). Some theorists argue that instead of inferring grammatical rules, children learn the probability that any given word or syllable will follow another—something that infants as young as eight months are able to do (Saffran, Aslin, & Newport, 1996; Seidenberg, 1997). In this view, infants are more like statisticians than grammarians.

Although the capacity for language may be innate, parents can foster their children's language development by talking and reading with them.

Even theorists who emphasize an inborn grammatical capacity acknowledge that in any behavior as complex as language, nurture must also play a role. Although there are commonalities in language acquisition around the world, there are also some major differences. This means that language does not merely unfold biologically but also depends on the environment (Gopnik, Choi, & Baumberger, 1996; Slobin, 1985, 1991).

Further, although most children have the capacity to acquire language from mere exposure to it, parents help things along. They may not go around correcting their children's speech all day, but neither do they ignore their children's errors. For example, when a child makes a mistake or produces a clumsy sentence, parents almost invariably respond by recasting the sentence or expanding its elements ("Monkey climbing!" "Yes, the monkey is climbing the tree") (Bohannon & Stanowicz, 1988). In turn, children are more likely to imitate adult recasts and expansions, suggesting that they are learning from them (Bohannon & Symons, 1988). It is likely, therefore, that language development depends on both biological readiness and social experience. Some aspects of language imply a genetic capacity for acquiring grammatical rules. But children may also learn, from experience, the statistical patterns among words, as well as irregular constructions (Marcus, 1999; Pinker, 1999).

The importance of both heredity and the environment is apparent in the tragic cases of abandoned and abused children who have been completely isolated from normal social interaction until late childhood—such as Genie, whom we mentioned in Chapter 2. After they are rescued, these children may learn words and be able to use simple sentences, but they rarely speak normally or catch up grammatically. Such sad evidence suggests the existence of a biologically determined *critical period* in language development during the first few years of life or possibly the first decade (Curtiss, 1977; Lenneberg, 1967; Tartter, 1986). During these make or break years, children need exposure to language and opportunities to practice their emerging linguistic skills in conversation with others.

QUICK QUIZ

Use your human capacity for language to answer these questions.

1. The central distinction between human language and other communication systems is that language (a) allows for the generation of an infinite number of new utterances, (b) is spoken, (c) is learned only after explicit training, (d) expresses meaning directly through its surface structure.
2. What did Chomsky mean by a "language acquisition device"?
3. What five findings support the existence of an innate "universal grammar"?
4. Those who reject Chomsky's ideas believe that instead of figuring out grammatical rules when acquiring language, children learn _____.

Answers:

1. a 2. an innate mental module that permits young children to develop language if they are exposed to an adequate sampling of conversation 3. Children everywhere go through similar stages of linguistic development; children combine words in ways that adults would not; adults do not consistently correct their children's syntax; groups of children not exposed to adult language may make up their own; and even infants only a few months old appear to distinguish different sentence structures 4. the probability that any given word or syllable will follow another one

WHAT'S AHEAD ▶

- **How do evolutionary psychologists explain male–female differences in courtship and sexuality?**
- **What basic issue divides evolutionary psychologists and their critics?**

Our Human Heritage: Courtship and Mating

Most psychologists agree that the evolutionary history of our species has made certain kinds of learning either difficult or easy. Most acknowledge that simple behaviors, such as smiling or a preference for sweet tastes, resemble instincts, behaviors that are relatively uninfluenced by learning and that occur in all members of the species. And most agree that human beings inherit some of their cognitive, perceptual, emotional, and linguistic capacities. But social scientists disagree heartily about whether biology and evolution can help account for complex social customs, such as warfare, cooperation, and altruism (the willingness to help others). Nowhere is this disagreement more apparent than in debates over the origins of male–female differences in sexual behavior, so we are going to focus on that endlessly fascinating topic.

Evolution and Sexual Strategies

In 1975, one of the world's leading experts on ants, Edward O. Wilson, published a little book that had a big impact. It was titled *Sociobiology: The New Synthesis*, the "synthesis" being the application of biological principles to the social and sexual customs of both nonhuman animals and human beings. **Sociobiology** became a popular topic for researchers and the public, generating great controversy.

Sociobiologists contend that evolution has bred into each of us a tendency to act in ways that maximize our chances of passing on our genes, and to help our close biological relatives, with whom we share many genes, do the same. In this view, just as nature has selected physical characteristics that have proved adaptive, so it has selected

sociobiology An interdisciplinary field that emphasizes evolutionary explanations of social behavior in animals, including human beings.

psychological traits and social customs that aid individuals in propagating their genes. Customs that enhance the odds of such transmission survive in the form of kinship bonds, dominance arrangements, taboos against female adultery, and many other aspects of social life.

In addition, sociobiologists believe that because the males and females of most species have faced different kinds of survival and mating problems, the sexes have evolved to differ profoundly in aggressiveness, dominance, and sexual strategies (Symons, 1979; Trivers, 1972). In many species, they argue, it is adaptive for males to compete with other males for access to young and fertile females, and to try to win and then inseminate as many females as possible. The more females a male mates with, the more genes he can pass along. (The human record in this regard was achieved by a man who fathered 899 children [Daly & Wilson, 1983]. What else he did with his time is unknown.) But according to sociobiologists, females need to shop for the best genetic deal, as it were, because they can conceive and bear only a limited number of offspring. Having such a large biological investment in each pregnancy, females cannot afford to make mistakes. Besides, mating with a lot of different males would produce no more offspring than staying with just one. So females try to attach themselves to dominant males who have resources and status and are likely to have "superior" genes.

"It's a guy thing."

The result of these two opposite sexual strategies, in this view, is that males generally want sex more often than females do; males are often fickle and promiscuous, whereas females are devoted and faithful; males are drawn to sexual novelty and even rape, whereas females want stability and security; males are relatively undiscriminating in their choice of sexual partners, whereas females are cautious and choosy; and males are competitive and concerned about dominance, whereas females are less so.

Evolutionary psychologists generally agree with these conclusions, but they differ from sociobiologists in some respects. One difference is that sociobiologists often study nonhuman species and argue by analogy, but most evolutionary psychologists consider such analogies to be simplistic and misleading. For example, because male scorpion flies force themselves on females, sociobiologists have drawn an analogy between this behavior and human rape, and have concluded that human rape must have the same evolutionary origins (Thornhill & Palmer, 2000). But this analogy does not bear scrutiny. Human rape has many motives, including, among others, revenge, sadism, and conformity to peer pressure (see Chapter 12). It is often committed by high-status men who could easily find consenting sexual partners, and all too frequently its victims are children or the elderly, who do not reproduce. In general,

This Kenyan man has 40 wives and 349 children. Although he is unusual, in societies around the world it is far more common for men to have many wives than for women to have many husbands. Sociobiologists and evolutionary psychologists attribute this difference to the evolution of different sexual strategies in males and females.

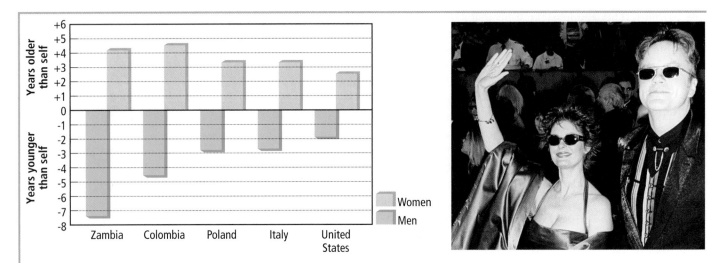

Figure 3.2
PREFERRED AGE IN A MATE

In most societies, men say they prefer to marry women younger than themselves, whereas women prefer men who are older (Buss, 1995). Evolutionary psychologists attribute these preferences to male concern with a partner's fertility and female concern with a partner's material resources and status. When the man is much older than the woman, people rarely comment, but when the woman is older, as in the case of actors Susan Sarandon and Tim Robbins, people take notice.

therefore, evolutionary psychologists rely less on comparisons with other species than sociobiologists do, focusing instead on commonalities in human mating and dating practices around the world.

Evolutionary psychologists and sociobiologists also disagree on some theoretical matters that are beyond the scope of our discussion here. Nevertheless, both groups emphasize the evolutionary origins of many human sex differences that appear to be universal, or at least very common. In one massive project, 50 scientists studied 10,000 people in 37 cultures located on six continents and five islands (Buss, 1994). Around the world, they found, men are more violent than women and more socially dominant. They are more interested in the youth and beauty of their sexual partners, presumably because youth is associated with fertility (see Figure 3.2). They are more sexually jealous and possessive, presumably because males can never be 100 percent sure that their children are really theirs genetically. They are quicker than women to have sex with partners they don't know well and more inclined toward polygamy and promiscuity, presumably so that their sperm will be distributed as widely as possible. Women, in contrast, tend to emphasize the financial resources or prospects of a potential mate, his status, and his willingness to commit to a relationship. Many studies have reported similar results (Bailey et al., 1994; Buss, 1996; Buunk et al., 1996; Daly & Wilson, 1983; Mealey, 2000; Sprecher, Sullivan, & Hatfield, 1994).

Culture and the "Genetic Leash"

THINKING CRITICALLY

Avoid Oversimplification

Sex differences in courtship and mating are common in cultures around the world and among nonhuman mammals as well. But human sexual behavior also varies in many ways. Do genes hold culture on a tight leash, a long and flexible one, or none at all?

Sociobiological and evolutionary views of sex differences have become enormously popular. Newsmagazines regularly run cover stories about the supposed evolutionary advantages for males of sowing their seeds far and wide and the supposed evolutionary advantages for females of finding a man with a good paycheck.

But critics—including some evolutionary theorists—argue that current evolutionary explanations of infidelity and monogamy are based on simplistic *stereotypes* of gender differences. The actual behavior of humans and other animals often fails to conform to images of sexually promiscuous males and coy, choosy females (Barash & Lipton, 2001; Birkhead, 2001; Fausto-Sterling, 1997; Hrdy, 1994). In species after species—birds, fish, and mammals, including human beings—females are sexually ardent and often have many male partners. The female's sexual behavior does not seem to depend only on the goal of being fertilized by the male: Females have sex when they are not ovulating and even when they are already pregnant. And in many species, from penguins to primates, males do not just mate and run. They stick around, feeding the infants, carrying them on their backs, and protecting them against predators (Hrdy, 1988; Snowdon, 1997).

These findings have sent evolutionary theorists scurrying to figure out the evolutionary benefits of female promiscuity and male nurturance. For example, by having many partners, perhaps a female increases the number of males who will support her offspring. This motive is quite explicit among the Barí people of Venezuela. A man who impregnates a woman is considered the child's primary father. But if she takes a lover during her pregnancy (an approved practice), he is considered a secondary father, and he is expected to supply mother and baby with extra food (Beckerman et al., 1998).

Critics, however, argue that all evolutionary explanations, whether of female fidelity or female promiscuity, are inadequate when applied to human beings, because human sexual behavior is so amazingly varied and changeable. Cultures range from those in which women have many children to those in which they have very few, from those in which men are intimately involved in child rearing to those in which they do nothing at all, from those in which women may have many lovers to those in which women may be killed for having sex outside of marriage (Hatfield & Rapson, 1996). In many places, the chastity of a potential mate is much more important to men than to women; but in other places, it is important to both sexes—or to neither one (see Figure 3.3). Sexual attitudes and practices also vary tremendously within a culture, from extremely traditional to extremely unconventional, as is immediately apparent to anyone surveying the panorama of sexual attitudes and behaviors within the United States and Canada (Laumann et al., 1994; Levine, 2002).

On questionnaires, when people (usually undergraduates) are asked to rank the qualities they most value in a potential mate, sex differences appear, just as evolutionary theory would predict (Kenrick et al., 2001). However, *both* sexes usually rank kindness, intelligence, and understanding over physical qualities or financial status. Plenty of women are not attracted to rich men, nor are all men attracted to stereotypically beautiful women.

Finally, a serious problem with the prevailing evolutionary view of mate selection is that our prehistoric ancestors, unlike the undergraduates in these studies, did not exactly have 5,000 fellow students to choose from. They lived in small

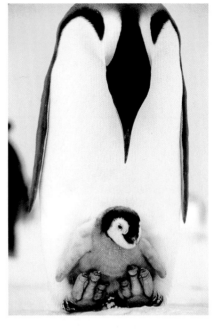

A basic assumption of evolutionary approaches to sexuality is that females across species have a greater involvement in child rearing than males do. But there are many exceptions. Female emperor penguins, for example, take off every winter, leaving behind males like this one to care for the kids.

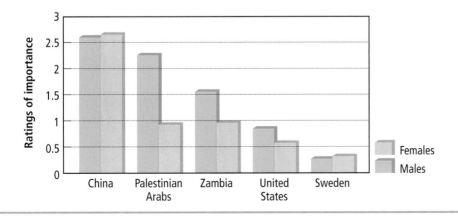

Figure 3.3
ATTITUDES TOWARD CHASTITY

In many places, men care more about a partner's chastity than women do, as evolutionary psychologists would predict. But culture has a powerful impact on these attitudes, as this graph shows. Notice that in China, both sexes prefer a partner who has not yet had intercourse, whereas in Sweden, chastity is a nonissue. (From Buss, 1995.)

bands, and if they were lucky they might get to choose between Urp and Ork, and that's about it; they could not hold out for some knockout or millionaire down the road. Because there wasn't a great range of potential partners to choose from, there would have been no need for the development of the kinds of sexual strategies described by evolutionary theorists (Hazan & Diamond, 2000). Instead, evolution might have instilled in us a tendency to select a mate based on similarity (the person's genes are like our own) and proximity (the person is around a lot). Indeed, similarity and proximity are among the strongest predictors today of the mates people actually choose, whatever they may say on questionnaires (see Chapter 12).

Debate over these matters can become quite heated because of worries that evolutionary arguments will be used to justify social and political inequalities and even violent behavior. In the past, evolutionary ideas have been used to promote *social Darwinism,* the notion that the wealthy and successful are more "reproductively fit" than other people. Such arguments have also led some people to conclude that men, with less investment in child rearing and more interest in status and dominance, are destined to control business and politics. Edward Wilson (1975) thinks so. "Even with identical education and equal access to all professions [for both sexes]," he wrote, "men are likely to continue to play a disproportionate role in political life, business, and science." This is not a message that people who hope for gender equality welcome!

Ultimately, what evolutionary scientists and their critics are quarreling about is the relative power of biology and culture. In *On Human Nature* (1978), Wilson argued that genes hold culture on a leash. The big question, replied paleontologist Stephen Jay Gould (1987), is how long and tight is that leash? Is it too tight to allow much change, or is it long enough to permit many possible customs? To sociobiologists, the leash is short and tight. To evolutionary psychologists, it is elastic enough to permit culture to modify evolved biological tendencies, although those tendencies can be pretty powerful (Kenrick & Trost, 1993). To critics of both sociobiology and evolutionary psychology, cultural variations mean that no single, genetically determined sexual strategy exists for human beings. What evolution has bestowed on us, they say, is an amazingly flexible brain. Therefore, in matters of sex and love, as in all other human behaviors, the leash is long and flexible.

QUICK QUIZ

Males and females alike have evolved to be able to answer these questions.

1. Which of the following would an evolutionary psychologist expect to be more typical of males than of females? (a) promiscuity, (b) choosiness about sexual partners, (c) concern with dominance, (d) interest in young partners, (e) emphasis on physical attractiveness of partners

2. What major issue divides evolutionary theorists and their critics in debates over courtship and mating?

 3. A friend of yours, who has read some sociobiology, tells you that men will *always* be more sexually promiscuous than women because during evolution, the best reproductive strategy for a male primate has been to try to impregnate many females. What kind of evidence would you need in order to evaluate this claim?

Answers:

1. all but b   2. the relative influence of biology and culture   3. You would not want to look just for confirming evidence (recall the principle of falsifiability). You would want to look also for evidence of female promiscuity and male monogamy among humans and other species and changes in human sexual customs in response to changing social conditions.

WHAT'S AHEAD

- **If you have a highly heritable trait, does that mean you are stuck with it forever?**
- **What kinds of studies allow psychologists to estimate a trait's heritability?**

The Genetics of Difference

We have been focusing on the origins of human similarities. We turn now to the second great issue in the nature–nurture debate: the origins of the differences among us. We begin with a critical discussion of what it means to say that a trait is "heritable." Then, to illustrate how behavioral geneticists study differences among people that might be influenced by genes, we will examine in detail a single, complex issue: the genetic contribution to intelligence. Throughout this book, you will be reading about behavioral–genetic findings on many other topics, including these:

▶ Biological rhythms (Chapter 5)
▶ Taste perception (Chapter 6)
▶ Weight and body shape (Chapter 12)
▶ Sexual orientation (Chapter 12)
▶ Personality and temperament (Chapter 13)
▶ Addiction (Chapter 16)
▶ Mental disorders (Chapter 16)

The Meaning of Heritability

Suppose you want to measure flute-playing ability in a large group of music students, so you have some independent raters assign each student a score, from 1 to 20. When you plot the scores, you find that some people are what you might call melodically disadvantaged and should forget about a musical career; others are flute geniuses; and the rest fall somewhere in between. What causes the variation in this group of students? Why are some so musically talented and others so inept? Are these differences primarily genetic, or are they the result of experience and motivation?

To answer such questions, behavioral geneticists compute a statistic called **heritability**, which gives an estimate of the *proportion of the total variance in a trait that is attributable to genetic variation within a group*. Because the heritability of a trait is expressed as a proportion (such as .60, or 60/100), the maximum value it can have is 1.0 (equivalent to "100 percent of the variance"). Height is highly heritable; that is, within a group of equally well-nourished individuals, most of the variation among them will be accounted for by their genetic differences. In contrast, table manners have low heritability because most variation among individuals is accounted for by differences in upbringing. Our guess is that flute-playing ability—and musical ability in general—falls somewhere in the middle. Differences in the ability to correctly perceive musical pitch and melody appear to be highly heritable; some people, it seems, really are born with a "tin ear" (Drayna et al., 2001). Nonetheless, musical training can enhance normal musical ability, and lack of musical training can keep a person with normal ability from tuning in to the nuances of music.

Many people hold completely mistaken ideas about heritability. But as genetic findings pour in, the public will need to understand this concept more than ever. You

THINKING CRITICALLY

Define Your Terms

What does it mean to say that some trait is "highly heritable"? If you want to improve your flute playing and someone tells you that musical ability is heritable, should you stop practicing?

heritability A statistical estimate of the proportion of the total variance in some trait that is attributable to genetic differences among individuals within a group.

cannot understand the nature–nurture issue without understanding the following important facts about heritability:

Similar Environments

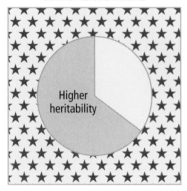

Diverse Environments

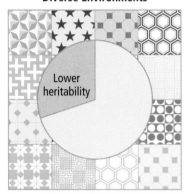

1 *An estimate of heritability applies only to a particular group living in a particular environment.* Heritability may be high in one group and low in another. Suppose that all of the children in Community A are affluent, eat plenty of high-quality food, have kind and attentive parents, and go to the same top-notch schools. Because their environments are similar, any intellectual differences among them will have to be due largely to their genetic differences. In other words, mental ability in this group will be highly heritable. In contrast, the children in Community B are rich, poor, and in between. Some of them have healthy diets; others live on fatty foods and cupcakes. Some attend good schools; others go to inadequate ones. Some have doting parents, and some have unloving and neglectful ones. These children's intellectual differences could be due to their environmental differences, in which case the heritability of intelligence for this group will be low.

2 *Heritability estimates do not apply to individuals, only to variations within a group.* You inherited half your genes from your mother and half from your father, but your *combination* of genes has never been seen before and will never be seen again (unless you have an identical twin). You also have a unique history of family relationships, intellectual training, and life experiences. It is impossible to know just how your genes and your personal history have interacted to produce the person you are today. For example, if you are a great flute player, no one can say whether your ability is mainly a result of inherited musical talent, living all your life in a family of devoted flute players, a private obsession that you acquired at age 6 when you saw the opera *The Magic Flute*—or a combination of all three. For one person, genes may make a tremendous difference in some aptitude or disposition; for another, the environment may be far more important. Scientists can only study the extent to which differences among people *in general* are explained by their genetic differences.

3 *Even highly heritable traits can be modified by the environment.* Although height is highly heritable, malnourished children may not grow to be as tall as they would with sufficient food, and children who eat an extremely nutritious diet may grow up to be taller than anyone thought they could. Hair color is genetically determined, but a trip to a hair stylist can transform you from a brunette to a blond, or vice versa. The same principle applies to psychological traits, although biological determinists sometimes fail to realize this. They argue, for example, that because IQ is highly heritable, IQ and school achievement cannot be boosted much (Herrnstein & Murray, 1994). But even if the first part of the statement is true, the second part does not necessarily follow, as we will see.

Computing Heritability

Scientists have no way to estimate the heritability of a trait or behavior directly, so they must *infer* it by studying people whose degree of genetic similarity is known. You might think that the simplest approach would be to compare blood relatives within families; everyone knows about families that are famous for some talent or trait. But family traits do not tell us much because close relatives usually share environments as well as genes. If Carlo's parents and siblings all love lasagna, that does not mean a taste for lasagna is heritable! The same applies if everyone in Carlo's family has a high IQ, is mentally ill, or is moody.

A better approach is to study adopted children (e.g., Loehlin, Horn, & Willerman, 1996; Plomin & DeFries, 1985). Such children share half their genes with each birth parent, but they grow up in a different environment, apart from their birth parents. On the other hand, they share an environment with their adoptive parents and siblings, but not their genes:

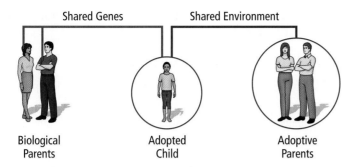

Researchers can compare correlations between the traits of adopted children and those of their biological and adoptive relatives and can use the results to compute an estimate of heritability.

Another approach is to compare identical twins with fraternal twins. Identical (monozygotic) twins develop when a fertilized egg (zygote) divides into two parts that then develop as two separate embryos. Because the twins come from the same fertilized egg, they share all their genes. (Identical twins may be slightly different at birth, however, because of differences in the blood supply to the two fetuses or other chance factors.) In contrast, fraternal (dizygotic) twins develop when a woman's ovaries release two eggs instead of one and each egg is fertilized by a different sperm. Fraternal twins are wombmates, but they are no more alike genetically than any other two siblings (they share, on average, only half their genes), and they may be of different sexes:

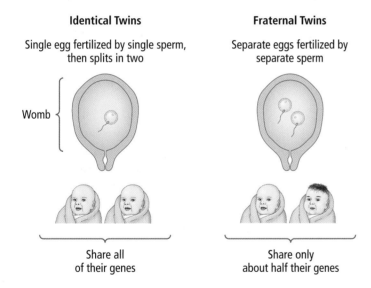

Behavioral geneticists can estimate the heritability of a trait by comparing groups of same-sex fraternal twins with groups of identical twins. The assumption is that if identical twins are more alike than fraternal twins, then the increased similarity must be due to genetic influences.

Perhaps, however, identical twins are treated differently than fraternal twins. People may treat identical twins, well, identically—or they may go to the other extreme, emphasizing the twins' differences. To avoid these problems, investigators have studied identical twins who were separated early in life and reared apart. (Until recently, adoption policies and attitudes toward births out of wedlock permitted such separations to occur.) In theory, separated identical twins share all their genes but not their environments. Any similarities between them should be primarily genetic and should permit a direct estimate of heritability.

identical (monozygotic) twins Twins that develop when a fertilized egg divides into two parts that develop into separate embryos.

fraternal (dizygotic) twins Twins that develop from two separate eggs fertilized by different sperm; they are no more alike genetically than are any other pair of siblings.

QUICK QUIZ

We hope you will treat this quiz identically to all others—by taking it.

1. Diane hears that basket-weaving ability is highly heritable. She assumes that her own low performance must therefore be due mostly to genes. What is wrong with her reasoning?

2. Bertram hears that basket-weaving ability is highly heritable. He concludes that schools should not bother trying to improve the skills of children who lack this talent. What is wrong with his reasoning?

3. Basket-weaving skills seem to run in Andy's family. Why shouldn't Andy conclude that his own talent is genetic?

4. Why do behavioral geneticists find it useful to study twins?

Answers:

1. Heritability applies only to differences among individuals within a group, not to particular individuals. 2. A trait may be highly heritable *and* still be susceptible to modification. 3. Family members share not just genes but also environments 4. Identical twins growing up together share an environment, and so do fraternal twins. So if identical twins are more alike than fraternal twins, then the increased similarity is assumed to be genetic. Identical twins reared apart share only their genes, not their environment, so similarities between them should also be primarily genetic.

WHAT'S AHEAD

- **To what extent is intelligence heritable?**
- **What error do many people make when arguing that one group is genetically smarter than another?**
- **How does the environment nurture or thwart mental ability?**

Our Human Diversity: The Case of Intelligence

Behavioral–genetics research has transformed our understanding of many aspects of behavior that were once explained solely in psychological terms (Plomin et al., 2001). Sometimes the findings have been reassuring, such as the discovery that overweight is not just a matter of "failed willpower" or "repressed anger" but also involves genetic tendencies. Some findings, such as the discovery that some mental illnesses have a genetic component, have been accepted readily. But other findings have inflamed political passions and upset people. No topic has aroused more controversy than the nature of intelligence.

Genes and Individual Differences

In heritability studies, the usual measure of intellectual functioning is an **intelligence quotient,** or IQ score. Scores on an IQ test reflect how a child has performed compared with other children of the same age, or how an adult has performed compared with other adults. The average score for each age group is arbitrarily set at 100. The distribution of scores in the population approximates a normal bell-shaped curve, with scores near the average (mean) most common and very high or very low scores rare. Two-thirds of all test-takers score between 85 and 115.

Most psychologists believe that IQ tests measure a general quality that affects all aspects of mental ability, but the tests have many critics. Some argue that intelligence comes in many varieties, more than are captured by a single score. Others argue that IQ tests are culturally biased, tapping mostly those abilities that depend on

intelligence quotient (IQ) A measure of intelligence originally computed by dividing a person's mental age by his or her chronological age and multiplying the result by 100; it is now derived from norms provided for standardized intelligence tests.

experiences in a middle-class environment and favoring white people over people of other ethnicities. We discuss the measurement of intelligence and debates surrounding this concept more fully in Chapter 9. For now, keep in mind that most heritability estimates apply only to those mental skills that affect IQ test scores and that these estimates are likely to be more valid for some groups than for others.

Despite these important qualifications, it is clear that the kind of intelligence that produces high IQ scores is highly heritable. For children and adolescents, heritability estimates average around .50; that is, about half of the variance in IQ scores is explainable by genetic differences (Chipuer, Rovine, & Plomin, 1990; Devlin, Daniels, & Roeder, 1997; Plomin, 1989). For adults, the estimates are higher—in the .60 to .80 range (Bouchard, 1995; McClearn et al., 1997; McGue et al., 1993).

In studies of twins, the scores of identical twins are always much more highly correlated than those of fraternal twins, a difference that reflects the influence of genes. In fact, the scores of identical twins reared *apart* are more highly correlated than those of fraternal twins reared *together,* as you can see in Figure 3.4. In adoption studies, the scores of adopted children are more highly correlated with those of their birth parents than with those of their biologically unrelated adoptive parents; the higher the birth parents' scores, the higher the child's score is likely to be. As adopted children grow into adolescence, the correlation between their IQ scores and those of their biologically unrelated family members diminishes; and in adulthood, the correlation falls to *zero* (Bouchard, 1997b; Scarr, 1993; Scarr & Weinberg, 1994).

Just a few years ago, a research team led by psychologist Robert Plomin identified the first marker for a gene that might influence performance on IQ tests (Chorney et al., 1998). DNA analysis showed that one form of the gene occurred twice as often in groups of children with very high IQ scores as in groups of children with average scores. But the gene accounted for less than 2 percent of the variance among individuals, which translates to about 4 IQ points.

Since then, a few other genes that may influence cognitive ability have been identified (Fisher et al., 1999; Hill et al., 1999). Each of these genes—if confirmed—is likely to contribute just a tiny piece to the puzzle of genetic variation. Special methods, beyond the scope of this book, are now being used in research with animals and humans to try to track down these and other genes that might be involved in

Separated at birth, the Mallifert twins meet accidentally.

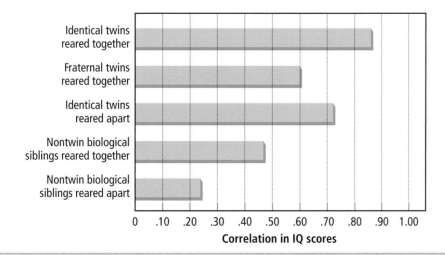

Figure 3.4

CORRELATIONS IN SIBLINGS' IQ SCORES

The IQ scores of identical twins are highly correlated, even when they are reared apart. The figures represented in this graph are based on average correlations across many studies (Bouchard & McGue, 1981).

intellectual performance, mental disorders, and personality traits, and to figure out just how those genes might produce their effects (Plomin & Crabbe, 2000).

Overall, the research on the heritability of IQ-test performance is pretty impressive. But remember: If heredity accounts for only part of why people differ in their IQ scores, then the environment (and random errors in measurement) must account for the rest.

The Question of Group Differences

If genes influence individual differences in intelligence, do they also help account for differences between groups, as many people assume? Unfortunately, the history of this issue has been marred by ethnic, class, and gender prejudice. As Stephen Jay Gould (1996) noted, genetic research has often been bent to support the belief that some groups are destined by "the harsh dictates of nature" to be subordinate to others. Because this issue has enormous political and social importance, we are going to examine it closely.

Most of the focus has been on black–white differences in IQ, because African-American children score, on average, some 10 to 15 points lower than do white children. (We are talking about *averages*; the distributions of scores for black children and white children overlap considerably.) A few psychologists have proposed a genetic explanation of this difference (Jensen, 1969, 1981; Rushton, 1988). In their much-discussed book *The Bell Curve: Intelligence and Class Structure in American Life* (1994), the late psychologist Richard Herrnstein and conservative political theorist Charles Murray cited heritability studies to imply that the gap in IQ scores between the average white and the average black child can never be closed.

> ### THINKING CRITICALLY
> **Examine Assumptions**
>
> Most behavioral-genetics studies show the heritability of intelligence to be high. A popular book argues that heredity must play a similarly large role in average IQ differences between ethnic groups. What's wrong with the assumption behind that reasoning?

You can see why heritability research provokes much more controversy than does research on, say, the sex lives of sea lions. Racists have used theories of genetic differences between groups to justify their own hatreds, and politicians have used them to argue for cuts in programs that would benefit blacks and other minorities. Herrnstein and Murray themselves concluded that there was little point in spending money trying to raise the IQs of low-scoring children.

Genetic explanations, however, have a fatal flaw: They use heritability estimates based mainly on white samples to estimate the role of heredity in *group* differences, a procedure that is not valid. This problem sounds pretty technical, but it is not too difficult to understand, so stay with us.

Consider, first, not people but tomatoes. (Figure 3.5 will help you visualize the following "thought experiment.") Suppose you have a bag of tomato seeds that vary genetically; all things being equal, some will produce tomatoes that are puny and tasteless, and some will produce tomatoes that are plump and delicious. Now you take a bunch of these seeds in your left hand and another bunch from the same bag in your right hand. Though one seed differs genetically from another, there is no *average* difference between the seeds in your left hand and those in your right. You plant the left hand's seeds in pot A, with some enriched soil that you have doctored with nitrogen and other nutrients, and you plant the right hand's seeds in pot B, with miserable, depleted soil from which you have extracted nutrients. You sing to pot A and put it in the sun; you ignore pot B and leave it in a dark corner.

When the tomato plants grow, they will vary *within* each pot in terms of height, the number of tomatoes produced, and the size of the tomatoes, purely because of genetic differences. But there will also be an average difference between the plants in pot A and those in pot B: The plants in pot A will be healthier and bear more tomatoes. This difference *between* pots is due entirely to the different soils and the care that has been given to them—even though the heritability of the *within*-pot differences is 100 percent (Lewontin, 1970). The same is true for real plants, by the way;

if you take identical, cloned plants and grow them at different elevations, they will develop differently (Lewontin, 2001).

The same principle applies to people as to tomatoes. Although intellectual differences *within* groups are at least partly genetic in origin, that does not mean differences *between* groups are genetic. Blacks and whites do not grow up, on the average, in the same "pots" (environments). Because of a long legacy of racial discrimination and de facto segregation, black children, as well as Latino and other minority children, often receive far fewer nutrients—literally, in terms of food, and figuratively, in terms of education, encouragement by society, and intellectual opportunities. Ethnic groups also differ in countless cultural ways that affect their performance on IQ tests. And negative stereotypes about ethnic groups may cause members of these groups to doubt their own abilities, become anxious and self-conscious, and perform more poorly than they otherwise would on tests (see Chapter 9).

Doing good research on the origins of group differences in IQ is extremely difficult in the United States, where racism affects the lives of even affluent, successful African-Americans (Cose, 1994; Parker, 1997; Staples, 1994). However, the handful of studies that have overcome past methodological problems fail to reveal any genetic differences between blacks and whites in whatever it is that IQ tests measure. For example, one study found that children fathered by black and white American soldiers in Germany after World War II and reared in similar German communities by similar families did not differ significantly in IQ (Eyferth, 1961). Another showed that degree of African ancestry (which can be roughly estimated from skin color, blood analysis, and genealogy) is not related to measured intelligence, as a genetic theory of black–white differences would predict (Scarr et al., 1977). And white and black infants do equally well on a test that measures their preference for novel stimuli, a predictor of later IQ scores (Fagan, 1992).

An intelligent reading of the research on intelligence, therefore, does not direct us to conclude that differences among cultural, ethnic, or national groups are permanent, genetically determined, or signs of any group's innate superiority. On the contrary, the research suggests that we should make sure that all children grow up in the best possible soil, with room for the smartest and the slowest to find a place in the sun.

Figure 3.5
THE TOMATO PLANT EXPERIMENT

In the hypothetical experiment described in the text, even if the differences among plants within each pot were due entirely to genetics, the average differences *between* pots could be environmental. The same general principle applies to individual and group differences among human beings.

The Environment and Intelligence

By now you may be wondering what kinds of experiences hinder intellectual development and what kinds of environmental "nutrients" promote it. Here are some of the influences associated with reduced mental ability:

▶ *Poor prenatal care.* If a pregnant woman is malnourished, contracts infections, takes certain drugs, smokes, drinks excessively, or is heavily exposed to pollutants, her child is at risk of having learning disabilities and a lower IQ.

▶ *Malnutrition.* The average IQ gap between severely malnourished and well-nourished children can be as high as 20 points (Stoch & Smythe, 1963; Winick, Meyer, & Harris, 1975).

▶ *Exposure to toxins.* Lead, for example, can damage the nervous system, producing attention problems, lower IQ scores, and poorer school achievement (Needleman et al., 1996). Many children in the United States are exposed to dangerous levels of lead from dust, contaminated soil, lead paint, and old lead pipes, and the concentration of lead in black children's blood is 50 percent higher than in white children's (Lanphear et al., 2002).

▶ *Stressful family circumstances.* Factors that predict reduced intellectual competence include a father who does not live with the family, a mother with a history

The children of migrant workers (left) often spend long hours in backbreaking field work and may miss out on the educational opportunities and intellectual advantages available to middle-class children (right).

of mental illness, limited parental work skills, and a history of stressful events during the child's early life (Sameroff et al., 1987). On average, each risk factor reduces a child's IQ score by 4 points. Children with seven risk factors score more than *30 points lower* than those with no risk factors.

In contrast, a healthy and stimulating environment can raise mental performance, sometimes dramatically (Guralnick, 1997; Ramey & Ramey, 1998). In one longitudinal study called the Abecedarian Project, inner-city children who got lots of mental enrichment at home and in child care or school, starting in infancy, had much better school achievement than did children in a control group (Campbell & Ramey, 1995).

Perhaps the best evidence for the importance of environmental influences on intelligence is the fact that IQ scores in developed countries have been climbing steadily for at least three generations (Flynn, 1987, 1999) (see Figure 3.6). Genes in these countries cannot possibly have changed enough to account for this rise in scores. The causes are still being debated, but most cognitive psychologists believe they include improvements in education, an increasing emphasis on the skills required by technology, and better nutrition (Neisser, 1998).

We see, then, that although heredity may provide the range of a child's intellectual potential—a Homer Simpson can never become an Einstein—many other factors affect where in that range the child will fall.

Figure 3.6

CLIMBING IQ SCORES

Raw scores on IQ tests have been rising in developed countries for many decades, at a rate much too steep to be accounted for by genetic changes. Because test norms are periodically readjusted to set the average score at 100, most people are unaware of the increase. On this graph, average scores are calibrated according to 1989 norms. As you can see, performance was much lower in 1918 than in 1989. (Adapted from Horgan, 1995.)

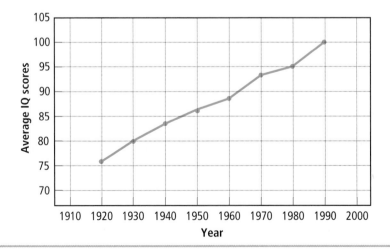

QUICK QUIZ

Are you thinking intelligently about intelligence?

1. On average, behavioral–genetic studies estimate the heritability of intelligence to be (a) about .90, (b) low at all ages, (c) about .50 for children and adolescents.
2. *True or false:* If a trait such as intelligence is highly heritable within a group, then differences between groups must also be due mainly to heredity.
3. The available evidence (does/does not) show that ethnic differences in average IQ scores are due to genetic differences.
4. Name four environmental factors associated with reduced mental ability.

Answers:

1. c 2. false 3. does not 4. poor prenatal care, malnutrition, exposure to toxins, and stressful family circumstances

In Praise of Human Variation

This chapter opened with two questions: What makes us alike as human beings, and why do we differ? Today, a prevalent but greatly oversimplified answer is: It's all in our genes. Genes, it's claimed, make men sexually adventurous and women sexually choosy. You either "have" a gene for smartness, musical ability, math genius, friendliness, or any other trait, or you don't. When researchers announced that they might have found a gene involved in mouse intelligence, *Time* magazine lost no time in putting the news on its cover with the headline "The IQ Gene?" (September 13, 1999). In this climate, many people who believe in the importance of learning, opportunities, and experience feel that they must take an equally oversimplified position: Genes don't matter at all.

As we have seen, however, heredity and environment always interact to produce the unique mixture of qualities that make up a human being. Moreover, once genetic and environmental influences become a part of us, they blend and become indistinguishable. We can no more speak of genes, or of the environment, "causing" personality or intelligence than we can speak of butter, sugar, or flour individually causing the taste of a cake (Lewontin, Rose, & Kamin, 1984). Many people do speak that way, however, out of a desire to make things clearer than they actually are, and sometimes to justify prejudices about ethnicity, gender, or class.

An unstated assumption in many debates about nature and nurture is that the world would be a better place if certain kinds of genes prevailed. This assumption overlooks the fact that nature loves genetic diversity, not similarity. The ability of any species to survive depends on such diversity. If every penguin, porpoise, or person had exactly the same genetic strengths and weaknesses, these species could not survive changes in the environment; a new virus, or a change in weather, would wipe out the entire group. With diversity, at least some penguins, porpoises, or people have a good chance of making it.

When we see the world through an evolutionary lens, we realize that psychological diversity is adaptive, too. Each of us has something valuable to contribute, whether it is artistic talent, academic ability, creativity, social skill, athletic prowess, a sense of humor, mechanical aptitude, practical wisdom, a social conscience, or the energy to get things done. In our complicated, fast-moving world, all of these qualities are needed. The challenge, for any society, is to promote the potential of each of its members.

THINKING CRITICALLY

Tolerate Uncertainty

Many people would like to specify precisely how much genes and the environment independently contribute to human qualities. But is this goal achievable? Is a human being like a jigsaw puzzle made up of separate components, or more like a cake, with blended ingredients that interact to produce its unique taste?

Taking Psychology with You

GENETIC TESTING AND YOU

Imagine that you have been feeling depressed and you go to a clinical psychologist for help. The psychologist interviews you, gives you a battery of psychological tests, lets you talk about your problems—and then has your blood drawn to check your DNA, to find out if you have a genetic predisposition for depression.

Has your blood drawn? Right now, this scenario is purely hypothetical—but maybe not for long. Two leading experts in behavioral genetics, Robert Plomin and John Crabbe (2000), predict that in the not-so-distant future, therapists will routinely have DNA tested to gather information for use in diagnosis and treatment. This is already possible, they note, for Alzheimer's disease: Having a DNA marker for a gene that codes for a particular protein heightens an individual's risk of developing the disease.

Genetic testing may be used not only to assess an individual's risk for a disorder, but also to screen large groups of people in order to take preventive action. In the case of Alzheimer's, a genetic vulnerability is especially likely to lead to the disease if the person suffers head injury or trauma (Mayeux et al., 1998). As a result, there have been calls for boxers to be routinely tested for the DNA marker involved (Jordan et al., 1997).

If you could be tested for a gene that increases your risk of developing Alzheimer's, would you do it? If you or your partner were pregnant, and you could have the fetus tested for genes that increase the risk of a reading disability, would you do it? What if the condition were homosexuality, which is not a disorder at all but which some people fear; or being very short, which in some quarters is a social disadvantage but is hardly a disability? It is natural, if you are going to be a parent, to want to avoid having a child who will suffer the agonies of a fatal or painful disease. But what if prenatal genetic testing reveals that your child has a somewhat increased chance of being gay or short; would you consider aborting the fetus then?

In coming years, as genetic testing becomes more widespread, all of us are going to have to think long and hard about such questions. You can use information from this chapter to evaluate the pros and cons of such testing for yourself or a family member. Here are some things to keep in mind:

▶ *Genes are not destiny.* It is true that some diseases, such as Huntington's, are caused by a single gene. However, as we've seen, most traits are influenced by many genes and by many environmental factors as well. Even at the cellular level of development, random developmental factors influence how an organism actually develops, regardless of genes (Lewontin, 2001). That is why knowing that you have markers for one or two genes that *may* contribute to a trait or disorder does not tell you much in practical terms.

▶ *Genetic information could be used to discriminate against individuals.* Critics of genetic testing worry that insurance companies will refuse coverage to adults and children who are currently healthy but who, their DNA reveals, have some genetic predisposition for developing a physical or psycho-logical disorder later in life. Employers who pay insurance premiums for their workers may be reluctant to hire such individuals. Some bioethicists worry that current laws are not adequate to protect the privacy of genetic information.

▶ *Knowing your genetic risk does not necessarily tell you what to do next.* If your child has a physical disorder called phenylketonuria (PKU), which prevents the body from assimilating protein and causes mental retardation, the solution is obvious: Limit the intake of protein. (All children in the United States are screened for PKU at birth.) But in the case of behavioral, cognitive, or emotional problems, the answer is usually not so straightforward. Often we simply don't yet know how to treat problems that have a genetic component, or many possible approaches exist and we don't know which one is best.

"I've been looking over your genetic code, Stockard, and I like what I see!"

▶ *Genetic testing can be liberating or stigmatizing.* Knowing that a condition or trait is "not your fault" may help you live with it or accept the limitations it causes. For example, knowing that your child's autism is genetic and not caused by bad parenting will keep you from feeling unnecessary guilt. On the other hand, genetic testing can activate prejudices against anyone with less than ideal looks or abilities. In the past, such prejudices have led to the discredited social movement called *eugenics,* which aimed to "improve" the species through forced sterilization of low-IQ people. Today, the desire to "improve" children reflects a view of children as products, to be "perfected" instead of appreciated for their own unique strengths and weaknesses (Rothman, 1989).

▶ *Knowing about a genetic disposition can create a self-fulfilling prophecy or premature diagnosis.* For example, if parents and school officials know that a child is at risk of developing a learning disorder, they may treat the child as cognitively impaired even though the child has not yet shown any signs of a problem. Similarly, if a therapist knows that a client has a DNA marker for depression, the therapist may jump too quickly to a diagnosis of depression, without considering alternatives.

▶ *Genes don't absolve you of responsibility.* "My genes made me do it" is not a good excuse for bad behavior. The flexible human brain allows us to do an end run around many of our genetic tendencies, by modifying them, ignoring them, or controlling them. As David Barash (2001), an evolutionary psychologist, put it, a strong case can be made that "we are never so human as when we behave contrary to our natural inclinations, those most in tune with our biological impulses."

We hope we have given you some food for thought. Would you be tested if some of your relatives had a disease that was influenced by heredity? How would you cope if the results were unfavorable? How serious and how likely would an inherited condition have to be before you would consider aborting a fetus: Would a 10 percent likelihood be enough, or 50 percent, or would you require near certainty? Would you want to know, while you are still young, that you carry genes associated with some disorder that usually doesn't strike until middle or old age? How might this information change your life? Think about it.

Summary

Unlocking the Secrets of Genes

▶ Genes can help us understand the qualities that unite human beings as a species and the qualities that differentiate us as individuals. In general, *evolutionary psychologists* study our commonalities and *behavioral geneticists* study our differences. Historically, *nativists* have emphasized "nature" and *empiricists* "nurture," but scientists today understand that heredity and environment interact to produce our psychological traits and even most physical ones.

▶ *Genes,* the basic units of heredity, are located on *chromosomes,* which consist of strands of *DNA.* Within each gene, a sequence of four elements of DNA constitutes a chemical code that helps determine the synthesis of a particular protein. In turn, proteins affect virtually all the structural and biochemical characteristics of the organism.

▶ Most human traits depend on more than one gene pair, which makes tracking down the genetic contributions to a trait extremely difficult. One method for doing so involves the use of *linkage studies,* which look for patterns of inheritance of *genetic markers* whose locations on the genes are already known.

▶ Researchers have recently completed a rough draft of a map of the entire human *genome.* However, this map does not automatically tell us what a particular gene does or how it does it, or how multiple genes interact and influence behavior.

The Genetics of Similarity

▶ Evolutionary psychologists argue that many fundamental human similarities can be traced to the processes of *evolution,* especially *natural selection.* They draw inferences about the behavioral tendencies that might have been selected because they helped our forebears solve survival problems and enhanced reproductive fitness, then do research to see if such tendencies actually exist throughout the world.

▶ Many evolutionary psychologists believe that the mind is not a general-purpose computer, but instead involved as a collection of specialized mental modules to handle specific survival problems. Among the candidates for such modules are inborn reflexes, an attraction to novelty, a motive to explore and manipulate objects, an impulse to play, and the capacity for simple arithmetic operations. However, the fact that some behavior or trait exists does not necessarily mean that it is adaptive or the product of natural selection.

Our Human Heritage: Language

▶ Human beings are the only species that uses language to express and comprehend an infinite number of novel utterances. Noam Chomsky argued that the ability to take the *surface structure* of any utterance and apply rules of syntax to infer its underlying *deep structure* must depend on an innate faculty for language, a *language acquisition device* sensitive to a *universal grammar* (features common to all languages). Many findings support this view: Children from different cultures go through similar stages of language development; children's language is full of *overregularizations* reflecting grammatical rules; adults do not consistently correct their children's syntax; children who have never been exposed to adult language often invent their own; and young infants can derive linguistic rules from strings of sounds. An innate capacity for language may have evolved in humans because it enhanced the chances of survival.

▶ Some scientists, however, have devised models of language acquisition that do not assume an innate capacity (*neural networks*). Some argue that instead of inferring grammatical rules, children learn the probability that any given word or syllable will follow another. Moreover, it seems clear that parental practices, such as repeating correct sentences verbatim and recasting incorrect ones, aid in language acquisition. Biological readiness and experience thus interact in the development of language. This is apparent in cases of children deprived of exposure to language. Such cases suggest that a *critical period* exists for acquiring a first language.

Our Human Heritage: Courtship and Mating

▶ *Sociobiologists* and evolutionary psychologists argue that males and females have evolved different sexual and courtship strategies in response to survival problems faced in the distant past. In this view, it has been adaptive for males to be promiscuous, to be attracted to young partners, and to want sexual novelty, and for females to be monogamous, to be choosy about partners, and to prefer security to novelty.

▶ Cross-cultural studies and animal studies support some evolutionary predictions about courtship and mating, but critics argue that human sexual behavior is too varied and changeable to fit a single evolutionary explanation. Moreover, our ancestors probably did not have a wide range of partners to choose from; what may have evolved is mate selection based on similarity and proximity. Many critics take exception to the entire line of evolutionary reasoning. The central issue dividing evolutionary theorists and their critics is the length of the "genetic leash."

The Genetics of Difference

▶ Behavioral geneticists often study differences among individuals by using data from studies of adopted children and of *identical and fraternal twins*. These data yield an estimate of the *heritability* of traits and abilities—the extent to which differences in a trait or ability within a group of individuals are accounted for by genetic differences.

▶ Heritability estimates do not apply to specific individuals or to differences between groups, and they apply only to differences within a particular group living in a particular environment. Even highly heritable traits can often be modified by the environment.

Our Human Diversity: The Case of Intelligence

▶ Heritability estimates for intelligence (as measured by IQ tests) average about .50 for children and adolescents and .60 to .80 for adults. Identical twins are more similar in IQ-test performance than fraternal twins, and adopted children's scores correlate more highly with those of their biological parents than with those of their nonbiological relatives. These results do not mean that genes determine intelligence; the remaining variance in IQ scores must be due largely to environmental influences.

▶ Researchers have recently identified markers for genes that may influence IQ performance. But each of these genes, if confirmed, is likely to contribute just a tiny piece to the puzzle of genetic variation in intelligence.

▶ It is not valid to draw conclusions about *group* differences from heritability estimates based on differences *within* a group. The available evidence fails to support genetic explanations of group differences in performance on IQ tests.

▶ Environmental factors such as poor prenatal care, malnutrition, exposure to toxins, and stressful family circumstances are associated with lower performance on intelligence tests; and a healthy and stimulating environment can improve performance.

In Praise of Human Variation

▶ Neither nature nor nurture can entirely explain people's similarities or differences. Genetic and environmental influences blend and become indistinguishable in the development of any individual.

Key Terms

nativists 69

empiricists 69

evolutionary psychology 70

behavioral genetics 70

genes 70

chromosomes 70

DNA (deoxyribonucleic acid) 70

genome 70

linkage studies 71

genetic markers 71

evolution 73

mutate 73

natural selection 73

Charles Darwin 73

language 77

surface structure 78

deep structure 78

syntax 78

language acquisition device 78

universal grammar 79

psycholinguists 79

overregularizations 79

neural networks 81

critical period (for language acquisition) 81

sociobiology 82

social Darwinism 86

heritability 87

identical (monozygotic) twins 89

fraternal (dizygotic) twins 89

intelligence quotient (IQ) 90

▶LOOKING BACK

- What does the chemical code in our genes encode *for*? (p. 70)

- What can a complete map of the human genes reveal—and not reveal? (pp. 71–72)

- During evolution, why do some traits become more common and others less common? (pp. 73–74)

- In the evolutionary view, why is the capacity to read faces innate, but not the capacity to read books? (p. 74)

- Why do so many people ignore signs saying "Don't touch"? (p. 76)

- What does language allow us to do that other animals can't? (p. 77)

- What evidence suggests that evolution has equipped infants' brains with a module for acquiring language? (pp. 79–80)

- How do parents help children acquire language? (p. 81)

- How do evolutionary psychologists explain male-female differences in courtship and sexuality? (pp. 83–84)

- What basic issue divides evolutionary psychologists and their critics? (p. 86)

- If you have a highly heritable trait, does that mean you are stuck with it forever? (p. 88)

- What kinds of studies allow psychologists to estimate a trait's heritability? (pp. 88–89)

- To what extent is intelligence heritable? (p. 91)

- What error do many people make when arguing that one group is genetically smarter than another? (pp. 92–93)

- How does the environment nurture or thwart mental ability? (pp. 93–94)

Go to **WWW.PRENHALL.COM/WADE** to reinforce these key concepts, and more.

     3.1 **Genes, chromosomes, and DNA**

     3.2 **Evolution and natural selection**

4

Neurons, Hormones, and the Brain

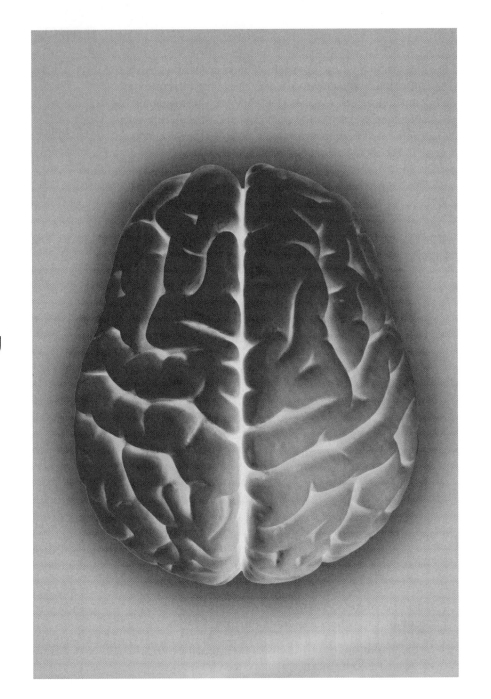

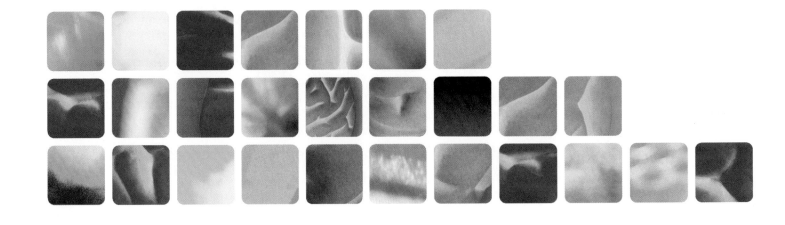

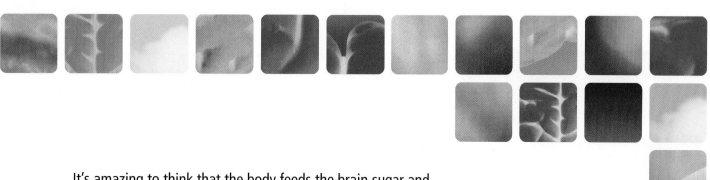

It's amazing to think that the body feeds the brain sugar and amino acids, and what comes out is poetry and pirouettes.

ROBERT COLLINS

After suffering damage to the front part of the right side of the brain, a stroke patient in Zurich, Switzerland, developed a puzzling symptom. Although the left side of his body was weak and he had trouble seeing objects in his left field of vision, what concerned him most was the blandness of the hospital food. In fact, he had become obsessed with fine dining—a phenomenon his neuropsychologist later dubbed "gourmand syndrome." In his diary, the patient wrote, "It is time for . . . a good sausage with hash browns or some spaghetti Bolognese, or risotto and a breaded cutlet, nicely decorated, or a scallop of game in cream sauce with spaetzle. . . . What a connoisseur I am, and now I am dried-up here, just like in the desert. Where is the next oasis?" After recovering, he quit his job as a political journalist and became a food columnist (Regard & Landis, 1997).

Another brain-injured man, who had been in a nearly fatal car crash in Arizona, gradually emerged from a five-month coma. With great effort, he relearned to speak, read, work at his computer, and get around in a wheelchair. Before the accident, he had managed to hold down a job as a special-education teacher while working on a doctorate. Afterwards, however, his behavior became increasingly erratic and strange. One morning he telephoned the police to report that he had lost a cereal bowl (Winslade, 1998).

A former English teacher and poet had a tumor in a part of the brain that processes the expressive qualities of speech, such as rhythm and intonation. Although she could understand words and sentences perfectly well, she could not tell whether a speaker was indignant, cheerful, or dejected unless she carefully analyzed the person's facial expressions and gestures. She was deaf to the emotional nuances of speech, the variations of tone and cadence that can move a listener to laughter, tears, or outrage. But she had one skill that many people lack. Because she could not be swayed by verbal theatrics or tone of voice, she could easily spot a liar (Sacks, 1985).

The mysterious brain.

These fascinating cases, and thousands like them, teach us that the modest-looking 3-pound organ inside our skulls is the bedrock of all behavior and mental activity. When injury or disease affects the brain's functioning, life is inevitably changed, either physically or mentally. Sometimes the changes are subtle and even benign, as in the case of "gourmand syndrome." All too often, though, they are not.

Neuropsychologists, along with neuroscientists from other disciplines, study the brain and the rest of the nervous system in hopes of gaining a better understanding of human and animal behavior. Among their many interests are the biological foundations of consciousness (Chapter 5), perception (Chapter 6), memory (Chapter 10), emotion (Chapter 11), stress (Chapter 15), and mental disorders (Chapter 16). In this chapter, we will examine the structure of the brain and the rest of the nervous system as background for our later discussions of these and other topics.

At this moment, your own brain, assisted by other parts of your nervous system, is busily taking in these words. Whether you are excited, curious, or bored, your brain is registering some sort of emotional reaction. As you continue reading, your brain will (we hope) store away much of the information in this chapter. Later on, your brain may enable you to smell a flower, climb the stairs, greet a friend, solve a personal problem, or chuckle at a joke. But the brain's most startling accomplishment is its knowledge that it is doing all these things. This self-awareness makes brain research different from the study of anything else in the universe. Scientists must use the cells, biochemistry, and circuitry of their own brains to understand the cells, biochemistry, and circuitry of brains in general.

Because the brain is the site of consciousness, people disagree about what language to use in discussing it. If we say that your brain stores events or registers emotions, we imply a separate "you" that is "using" that brain. But if we leave "you" out of the picture and just say the brain does these things, we risk implying that brain mechanisms alone explain behavior, which is untrue; we lose sight of the person—and the motives, choices, and personality traits that shape behavior. No one has ever been able to resolve this dilemma.

William Shakespeare called the brain "the soul's frail dwelling house." Actually, this miraculous organ is more like the main room in a house filled with many alcoves and passageways—the "house" being the nervous system as a whole. Before we can understand the windows, walls, and furniture of this house, we need to become acquainted with the overall floor plan. It's a pretty technical plan, which means that you will be learning many new terms, but you will need to know these terms in order to understand how biological psychologists go about explaining psychological topics.

WHAT'S AHEAD

- Why do you automatically pull your hand away from something hot, "without thinking"?
- In an emergency, which part of your nervous system whirls into action?

The Nervous System: A Basic Blueprint

The function of a nervous system is to gather and process information, produce responses to stimuli, and coordinate the workings of different cells. Even the lowly jellyfish and the humble worm have the beginnings of such a system. In very simple organisms that do little more than move, eat, and eliminate wastes, the "system" may be no more than one or two nerve cells. In human beings, who do such complex things as dance, cook, and take psychology courses, the nervous system contains billions of cells. Scientists divide this intricate network into two main parts: the central nervous system and the peripheral (outlying) nervous system (see Figure 4.1).

The Central Nervous System

The **central nervous system (CNS)** receives, processes, interprets, and stores incoming sensory information—information about tastes, sounds, smells, color, pressure on the skin, the state of internal organs, and so forth. It also sends out messages destined for muscles, glands, and internal organs. The CNS is usually conceptualized as having two components: the brain, which we will consider in detail later, and the **spinal cord.** The spinal cord is actually an extension of the brain. It runs from the base of the brain down the center of the back, protected by a column of bones (the spinal column), and it acts as a bridge between the brain and the parts of the body below the neck.

The spinal cord produces some behaviors on its own, without any help from the brain. These *spinal reflexes* are automatic, requiring no conscious effort. For example, if you accidentally touch a hot iron, you will immediately pull your hand away, even before your brain has had a chance to register what has happened. Nerve impulses bring a message to the spinal cord (hot!), and the spinal cord immediately sends out a command via other nerve impulses, telling muscles in your arm to contract and to pull your hand away from the iron. (Reflexes above the neck, such as sneezing and blinking, involve the lower part of the brain, rather than the spinal cord.)

The neural circuits underlying many spinal reflexes are linked to neural pathways that run up and down the spinal cord, to and from the brain. Because of these connections, reflexes can sometimes be influenced by thoughts and emotions. An example is erection in men, a spinal reflex that can be inhibited by anxiety or distracting thoughts, and initiated by erotic thoughts. Some reflexes can be brought under conscious control. If you concentrate, you may be able to keep your knee from jerking when it is tapped, as it normally would. Similarly, most men can learn to voluntarily delay ejaculation, another spinal reflex.

The Peripheral Nervous System

The **peripheral nervous system (PNS)** handles the central nervous system's input and output. It contains all portions of the nervous system outside the brain and spinal cord, right down to the nerves in the tips of the fingers and toes. If your brain could not collect information about the world by means of a peripheral nervous system, it would be like a radio without a receiver. In the peripheral nervous system, *sensory nerves* carry messages from special receptors in the skin, muscles, and other internal and external sense organs to the spinal cord, which sends them along to the brain. These nerves put us in touch with both the outside world and the activities of our own bodies. *Motor nerves* carry orders from the central nervous system to muscles, glands, and internal organs. They enable us to move, and they cause glands to contract and to secrete substances, including chemical messengers called *hormones*.

central nervous system (CNS) The portion of the nervous system consisting of the brain and spinal cord.

spinal cord A collection of neurons and supportive tissue running from the base of the brain down the center of the back, protected by a column of bones (the spinal column).

peripheral nervous system (PNS) All portions of the nervous system outside the brain and spinal cord; it includes sensory and motor nerves.

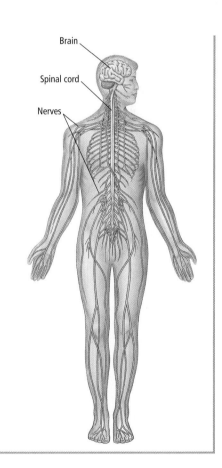

Brain

Spinal cord

Nerves

Figure 4.1

THE CENTRAL AND PERIPHERAL NERVOUS SYSTEMS

The central nervous system includes the brain and the spinal cord. The peripheral nervous system consists of 43 pairs of nerves that transmit information to and from the central nervous system. Twelve pairs of cranial nerves in the head enter the brain directly; 31 pairs of spinal nerves enter the spinal cord at the spaces between the vertebrae of the spine.

somatic nervous system The subdivision of the peripheral nervous system that connects to sensory receptors and to skeletal muscles; sometimes called the *skeletal nervous system*.

autonomic nervous system The subdivision of the peripheral nervous system that regulates the internal organs and glands.

sympathetic nervous system The subdivision of the autonomic nervous system that mobilizes bodily resources and increases the output of energy during emotion and stress.

parasympathetic nervous system The subdivision of the autonomic nervous system that operates during relaxed states and that conserves energy.

Scientists further divide the peripheral nervous system into two parts: the somatic (bodily) nervous system and the autonomic (self-governing) nervous system. The **somatic nervous system,** sometimes called the *skeletal nervous system,* consists of nerves that are connected to sensory receptors—cells that enable you to sense the world—and also to the skeletal muscles that permit voluntary action. When you feel a bug on your arm, or when you turn off a light or write your name, your somatic system is active. The **autonomic nervous system** regulates the functioning of blood vessels, glands, and internal (visceral) organs such as the bladder, stomach, and heart. When you see someone you have a crush on, and your heart pounds, your hands get sweaty, and your cheeks feel hot, you can blame your autonomic nervous system.

The autonomic nervous system is itself divided into two parts: the **sympathetic nervous system** and the **parasympathetic nervous system.** These two parts work together, but in opposing ways, to adjust the body to changing circumstances (see Figure 4.2). The sympathetic system acts like the accelerator of a car, mobilizing the body for action and an output of energy. It makes you blush, sweat, and breathe more deeply, and it pushes up your heart rate and blood pressure. As we will see in Chapter 15, when you are in a situation that requires you to fight, flee, or cope, the sympathetic nervous system whirls into action. The parasympathetic system is more like a brake: It does not stop the body, but it does tend to slow things down or keep them running smoothly. It enables the body to conserve and store energy. If you have to jump out of the way of a speeding motorcyclist, sympathetic nerves increase your heart rate. Afterward, parasympathetic nerves slow it down again and keep its rhythm regular.

Figure 4.2

THE AUTONOMIC NERVOUS SYSTEM

In general, the sympathetic division of the autonomic nervous system prepares the body to expend energy, and the parasympathetic division restores and conserves energy. Sympathetic nerve fibers exit from areas of the spinal cord shown in red in this illustration; parasympathetic fibers exit from the base of the brain and from spinal cord areas shown in green.

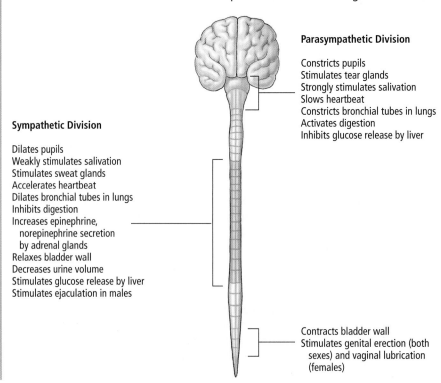

Sympathetic Division

Dilates pupils
Weakly stimulates salivation
Stimulates sweat glands
Accelerates heartbeat
Dilates bronchial tubes in lungs
Inhibits digestion
Increases epinephrine,
  norepinephrine secretion
  by adrenal glands
Relaxes bladder wall
Decreases urine volume
Stimulates glucose release by liver
Stimulates ejaculation in males

Parasympathetic Division

Constricts pupils
Stimulates tear glands
Strongly stimulates salivation
Slows heartbeat
Constricts bronchial tubes in lungs
Activates digestion
Inhibits glucose release by liver

Contracts bladder wall
Stimulates genital erection (both
  sexes) and vaginal lubrication
  (females)

QUICK QUIZ

Pause now to test your memory by mentally filling in the missing parts of the nervous system "house." Then see whether you can briefly describe what each part of the system does.

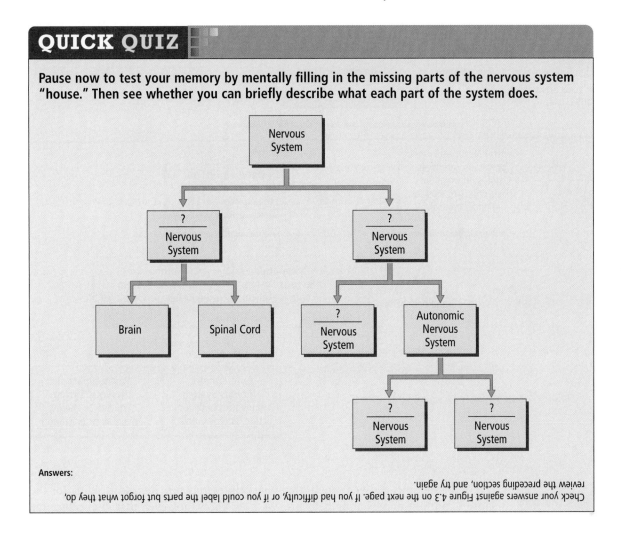

Answers:

WHAT'S AHEAD

- Which cells are the nervous system's "communication specialists," and how do they "talk" to each other?
- Are you born with all the brain cells you'll ever have?
- How do learning and experience alter the brain's circuits?
- What happens when levels of brain chemicals called neurotransmitters are too low or too high?
- Which substances in the brain mimic the effects of morphine by dulling pain and promoting pleasure?
- Do men and women have different "sex hormones"?

Communication in the Nervous System

The blueprint we just described provides only a general idea of the nervous system's structure. Now let's turn to the details.

The nervous system is made up in part of **neurons,** or *nerve cells.* Neurons are the brain's communication specialists, transmitting information to, from, and within the central nervous system. They are held in place by **glia,** or *glial cells* (from the Greek for "glue"), which make up 90 percent of the brain's cells.

neuron A cell that conducts electrochemical signals; the basic unit of the nervous system; also called a nerve cell.

glia [GLY-uh or GLEE-uh] Cells that support, nurture, and insulate neurons, remove debris when neurons die, enhance the formation and maintenance of synapses, and modify neuronal functioning.

Figure 4.3

HOW THE NERVOUS SYSTEM IS ORGANIZED

Use this diagram to check your answers to the Quick Quiz on page 105.

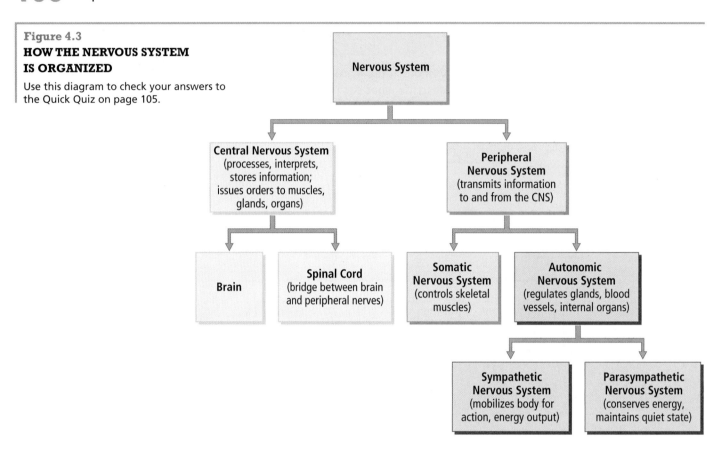

For a long time, people thought that glial cells merely provided scaffolding for the more important and exciting neurons. We now know, however, that glial cells have many vital functions: They provide the neurons with nutrients, insulate them, protect the brain from toxic agents, and remove cellular debris when neurons die. Glial cells also communicate chemically with each other and with neurons, and without them, neurons probably could not function effectively (Gallo & Chittajallu, 2001; Netting, 2001). For example, one kind of glial cell, shaped like a star, appears to give neurons the go-ahead to construct and maintain connections called *synapses* and to start "talking" to each other (Ullian et al., 2001). Without glial cells, then, neurons could not do their job. In coming years, we will be learning a great deal more about the still poorly understood role of glial cells in learning, memory, and other processes.

At present, however, much more is known about neurons. Although often called the building blocks of the nervous system, in structure neurons are more like snowflakes than blocks, exquisitely delicate and differing from one another greatly in size and shape (see Figure 4.4). In the giraffe, a neuron that runs from the spinal cord down the animal's hind leg may be 9 feet long! In the human brain, neurons are microscopic. No one is sure how many neurons the human brain contains, but a typical estimate is 100 billion, about the same number as there are stars in our galaxy—and some estimates go much higher.

The Structure of the Neuron

As you can see in Figure 4.5, a neuron has three main parts: *dendrites*, a *cell body*, and an *axon*. The **dendrites** look like the branches of a tree; indeed, the word *dendrite* means "little tree" in Greek. Dendrites act like antennas, receiving messages

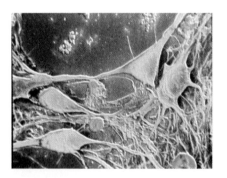

Neurons in the outer layers of the brain.

dendrites A neuron's branches that receive information from other neurons and transmit it toward the cell body.

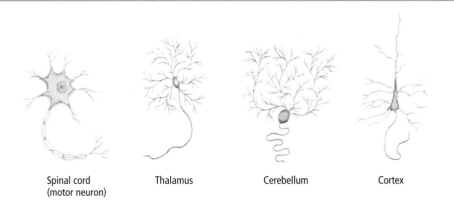

Figure 4.4
DIFFERENT KINDS OF NEURONS

Neurons vary in size and shape, depending on their location and function. More than 200 types of neurons have been identified in mammals.

Spinal cord (motor neuron)   Thalamus   Cerebellum   Cortex

from as many as 10,000 other nerve cells and transmitting these messages toward the cell body. They also do some preliminary processing of those messages. The **cell body,** which is shaped roughly like a sphere or a pyramid, contains the biochemical machinery for keeping the neuron alive. It also plays the key role in determining whether the neuron should "fire"—that is, transmit a message to other neurons—depending on inputs from other neurons. The **axon** (from the Greek for "axle") transmits messages away from the cell body to other neurons or to muscle or gland cells. Axons commonly divide at the end into branches, called *axon terminals*. In adult human beings, axons vary from only 4 thousandths of an inch to a few feet in length. Dendrites and axons give each neuron a double role: As one researcher put it, a neuron is first a catcher, then a batter (Gazzaniga, 1988).

Many axons, especially the larger ones, are insulated by a surrounding layer of fatty material called the **myelin sheath,** which is derived from glial cells. This covering is divided into segments that make it look a little like a string of link sausages (see Figure 4.5 again). One purpose of the myelin sheath is to prevent signals in adjacent cells from interfering with each other. Another, as we will see shortly, is to speed up the conduction of neural impulses. In individuals with multiple sclerosis, loss of

cell body The part of the neuron that keeps it alive and determines whether it will fire.

axon A neuron's extending fiber that conducts impulses away from the cell body and transmits them to other neurons.

myelin sheath A fatty insulation that may surround the axon of a neuron.

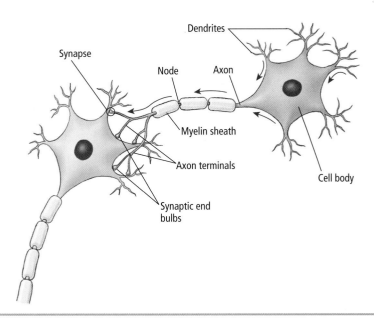

Synapse
Node
Dendrites
Axon
Myelin sheath
Axon terminals
Cell body
Synaptic end bulbs

Figure 4.5
THE STRUCTURE OF A NEURON

Incoming neural impulses are received by the dendrites of a neuron and are transmitted to the cell body. Outgoing signals pass along the axon to terminal branches.

nerve A bundle of nerve fibers (axons and sometimes dendrites) in the peripheral nervous system.

neurogenesis The production of new neurons from immature stem cells.

stem cells Immature cells that renew themselves and have the potential to develop into mature cells; given encouraging environments, stem cells from early embryos can develop into any cell type.

myelin causes erratic nerve signals, leading to loss of sensation, weakness or paralysis, lack of coordination, or vision problems.

In the peripheral nervous system, the fibers of individual neurons (axons and sometimes dendrites) are collected together in bundles called **nerves,** rather like the lines in a telephone cable. The human body has 43 pairs of peripheral nerves; one nerve from each pair is on the left side of the body, and the other is on the right. Most of these nerves enter or leave the spinal cord, but 12 pairs in the head, the *cranial nerves,* connect directly to the brain. In Chapter 6, we will discuss the cranial nerves that are involved in the senses of smell, hearing, and vision.

Neurons in the News

Until recently, neuroscientists assumed that if neurons in the central nervous system were injured or damaged, they could never regenerate (grow back). But then the conventional wisdom got turned upside down. Animal studies showed that severed axons in the spinal cord *can* regrow if you treat them with certain nervous-system chemicals (Schnell & Schwab, 1990). Researchers are now working to fine-tune this process, and are hopeful that regenerated axons will someday enable people with spinal-cord injuries to use their limbs again.

Another entrenched assumption also recently bit the dust. Scientists used to think that in mammals no new CNS cells were produced after infancy. This assumption was accepted as dogma throughout most of the twentieth century, despite evidence challenging it (Gross, 2000). But then Canadian neuroscientists, working with mice, immersed immature cells from the animal's brains in a growth-promoting protein and showed conclusively that these cells could give birth to new neurons, in a process called **neurogenesis.** What astonished the scientists even more, the new neurons then continued to divide and multiply (Reynolds & Weiss, 1992). One of the researchers, Samuel Weiss, said that this result "challenged everything I had read; everything I had learned when I was a student" (quoted in Barinaga, 1992).

Since then, scientists have discovered that the human brain and other body organs also contain such cells, which are now usually referred to as **stem cells,** or sometimes *precursor cells.* These, too, give rise to new neurons when treated in the laboratory. And stem cells involved in learning and memory seem to divide and mature throughout adulthood—a discovery of tremendous promise for human well-being. The evidence comes primarily from studies of rodents and monkeys, but also from a small autopsy study of five elderly people (Erikkson, 1998; Gage et al., 1998; Gould et al., 1998; Gould, Reeves, et al., 1999). Animal studies suggest that we have some control over the generation of stem cells, because physical and mental exercise promote

In an area associated with learning and memory, new cells develop from immature "precursor" cells, and physical and mental stimulation promotes their production and survival. These mice, who have toys to play with, tunnels to explore, wheels to run on, and other mice to share their cage with, will grow more cells than mice living in standard cages.

the production and survival of new cells (Gould, Beylin, et al., 1999; Kempermann, Brandon, & Gage, 1998; van Praag, Kempermann, & Gage, 1999). One of the researchers, psychologist Elizabeth Gould, commented, "It is a classic case of 'use it or lose it'" (quoted in the *Los Angeles Times,* February 23, 1999). On the other hand, stress can inhibit the production of new cells (Gould et al., 1998), and nicotine can kill them (Berger, Gage, & Vijayarqhavan, 1998).

Stem-cell research is one of the hottest areas in biology and neuroscience, and also one of the most hotly debated. In the United States, federal funding for basic stem-cell research has faced strong resistance by antiabortion activists. The reason: Scientists prefer working with cells from aborted fetuses and from embryos that are a few days old, which consist of just a few cells. Embryonic stem cells, which are usually taken from "extra" embryos about to be discarded by fertility clinics, are especially useful because they can differentiate into any type of cell, from neurons to kidney cells, whereas those from adults are far more limited and are also harder to keep alive.

Currently, American researchers who rely on federal funding must get their embryonic cells from only a few, already established sources. But scientists and patient-advocacy groups feel it is important for this research to continue and expand, because transplanted stem cells may eventually help people recover from damage or disease in the brain and spinal cord, as well as other parts of the body. In the meantime, scientists are making progress in prodding stem cells taken from adult organs, such as bone marrow and skin, to transform themselves into brain cells (Brazelton et al., 2000; Toma et al., 2001; Woodbury et al., 2000). One team working with rats has reported positive results using umbilical cord cells (Sanchez-Ramos et al., 2001). Another team has even grown living cells from precursor cells taken from the brains of human cadavers (Palmer et al., 2001)! It is not yet clear, however, whether such cells will be usable in therapeutic applications.

Every year brings more incredible findings about neurons, findings that only a short time ago would have seemed like science fiction. A long road lies ahead, and many daunting technical hurdles remain to be overcome before these findings yield practical benefits. Eventually, however, new treatments for medical and psychological disorders may be among the most stunning contributions of this line of basic biological research.

How Neurons Communicate

Neurons do not directly touch each other, end to end. Instead, they are separated by a minuscule space called the *synaptic cleft,* where the axon terminal of one neuron nearly touches a dendrite or the cell body of another. The entire site—the axon terminal, the cleft, and the covering membrane of the receiving dendrite or cell body—is called a **synapse.** Because a neuron's axon may have hundreds or even thousands of terminals, a single neuron may have synaptic connections with a great many others. As a result, the number of communication links in the nervous system runs into the trillions or perhaps even the quadrillions.

When we are born, most of these synapses have not yet formed, but during infancy new synapses proliferate at a great rate (see Figure 4.6). Throughout life, axons and dendrites continue to grow, and tiny projections on dendrites, called *spines,* increase in size and number, producing more complex connections among the brain's nerve cells. Just as new learning and stimulating environments promote the production of new neurons, they also produce the greatest increases in synaptic complexity (Diamond, 1993; Greenough & Anderson, 1991; Greenough & Black, 1992; Rosenzweig, 1984). Throughout life, too, unused synaptic connections are

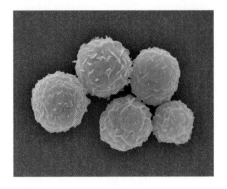

Tiny stem cells like these (magnified 1200 times in this photo) have provoked both excitement and controversy.

synapse The site where transmission of a nerve impulse from one nerve cell to another occurs; it includes the axon terminal, the synaptic cleft, and receptor sites in the membrane of the receiving cell.

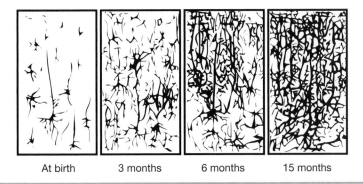

| At birth | 3 months | 6 months | 15 months |

Figure 4.6

GETTING CONNECTED

Neurons in a newborn's brain are widely spaced, but they immediately begin to form connections. These drawings show the marked increase in the number of connections from birth to age 15 months.

"pruned away" as cells or their branches die and are not replaced. Thus, the brain's circuits are continually changing in response to information, challenges, and changes in the environment.

This remarkable *plasticity* (flexibility) may help explain why people with brain damage sometimes experience amazing recoveries—why individuals who cannot recall simple words after a stroke may be speaking normally within a matter of months, and why patients who cannot move an arm after a head injury may regain full use of it after physical therapy. Their brains have rewired themselves to adapt to the damage (Liepert et al., 2000)!

Neurons speak to one another, or in some cases to muscles or glands, in an electrical and chemical language. When a nerve cell is stimulated, a change in electrical potential occurs between the inside and the outside of the cell. The physics of this process involves the sudden, momentary inflow of positively charged sodium ions across the cell's membrane, followed by the outflow of positively charged potassium ions. The result is a brief change in electrical voltage, called an **action potential,** which produces an electrical current or impulse.

If an axon is unmyelinated, the action potential at each point in the axon gives rise to a new action potential at the next point; thus, the action potential travels down the axon somewhat as fire travels along the fuse of a firecracker. But in myelinated axons, the process is a little different. Conduction of a neural impulse beneath the sheath is impossible, in part because sodium and potassium ions cannot cross the cell's membrane except at the breaks (nodes) between the myelin's "sausages." Instead, the action potential "hops" from one node to the next. (More specifically, positively charged ions flow down the axon at a very fast rate, causing regeneration of the action potential at each node.) This arrangement allows the impulse to travel faster than it could if the action potential had to be regenerated at every point along the axon. Nerve impulses travel more slowly in babies than in older children and adults because when babies are born, the myelin sheaths on their axons are not yet fully developed.

When a neural impulse reaches the axon terminal's buttonlike tip, it must get its message across the synaptic cleft to another cell. At this point, *synaptic vesicles,* tiny sacs in the tip of the axon terminal, open and release a few thousand molecules of a chemical substance called a **neurotransmitter.** Like sailors carrying a message from one island to another, these molecules then diffuse across the synaptic cleft (see Figure 4.7).

When they reach the other side, the neurotransmitter molecules bind briefly with *receptor sites,* special molecules in the membrane of the receiving neuron's dendrites (or sometimes cell body), fitting these sites much as a key fits a lock. Changes occur in the receiving neuron's membrane, and the ultimate effect is either *excitatory* (a voltage shift in a positive direction) or *inhibitory* (a voltage shift in a negative direction), depending on which receptor sites have been activated. If the effect is excitatory, the probability that the receiving neuron will fire increases; if it is inhibitory, the probability decreases. Inhibition in the nervous system is extremely important. Without it, we could not sleep or coordinate our movements. Excitation of the nervous system would be overwhelming, producing convulsions.

What any given neuron does at any given moment depends on the net effect of all the messages being received from other neurons. Only when the cell's voltage reaches a certain threshold will it fire. Thousands of messages, both excitatory and inhibitory, may be coming into the cell. The receiving neuron must essentially average them, but how it does this, and how it "decides" whether to fire, is still not well understood. The ultimate neural message in the brain depends on the rate at which individual neurons are firing, how many are firing, what types of neurons are firing, where the

action potential A brief change in electrical voltage that occurs between the inside and the outside of an axon when a neuron is stimulated; it serves to produce an electrical impulse.

neurotransmitter A chemical substance that is released by a transmitting neuron at the synapse and that alters the activity of a receiving neuron.

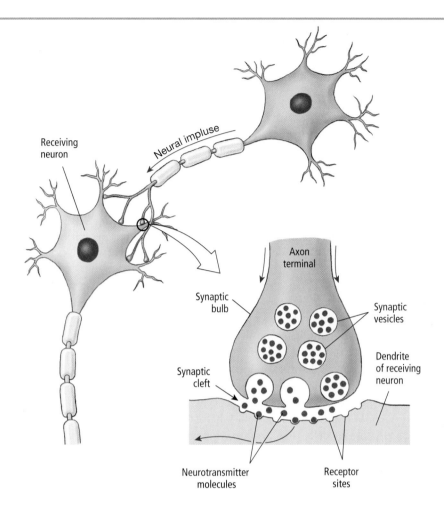

Receiving
neuron

Neural impluse

Axon
terminal

Synaptic
bulb

Synaptic
vesicles

Synaptic
cleft

Dendrite
of receiving
neuron

Neurotransmitter
molecules

Receptor
sites

Figure 4.7
NEUROTRANSMITTER
CROSSING A SYNAPSE

Neurotransmitter molecules are released
into the synaptic cleft between two
neurons from vesicles (chambers) in the
transmitting neuron's axon terminal. The
molecules then bind to receptor sites on
the receiving neuron. As a result, the
electrical state of the receiving neuron
changes, and the neuron becomes either
more or less likely to fire an impulse,
depending on the type of transmitter
substance.

neurons are located, and the degree of synchrony among different neurons. It does
not depend on how strongly the individual neurons are firing, however, because a
neuron always either fires or it doesn't. Like the turning on of a light switch, the firing of a neuron is an *all-or-none* event.

 4.1

Chemical Messengers in the Nervous System

The nervous system "house" would remain forever dark and lifeless without chemical couriers such as the neurotransmitters. Let's look more closely now at these substances, and at two other types of chemical messengers: endorphins and hormones.

Neurotransmitters: Versatile Couriers. As we have seen, neurotransmitters
make it possible for one neuron to excite or inhibit another. Neurotransmitters exist
not only in the brain, but also in the spinal cord, the peripheral nerves, and certain
glands. Through their effects on specific nerve circuits, these substances can affect
mood, memory, and well-being. The nature of the effect depends on the level of the
neurotransmitter, its location, and the type of receptor it binds with. Hundreds of
substances are known or suspected to be neurotransmitters, and the number keeps
growing. Here are a few of the better-understood neurotransmitters and some of
their known or suspected effects:

▶ *Serotonin* affects neurons involved in sleep, appetite, sensory perception, temperature regulation, pain suppression, and mood.

▶ *Dopamine* affects neurons involved in voluntary movement, learning, memory, emotion, and, possibly, response to novelty.

▶ *Acetylcholine* affects neurons involved in muscle action, cognitive functioning, memory, and emotion.

▶ *Norepinephrine* affects neurons involved in increased heart rate and the slowing of intestinal activity during stress, and neurons involved in learning, memory, dreaming, waking from sleep, and emotion.

▶ *GABA* *(gamma-aminobutyric acid)* functions as the major inhibitory neurotransmitter in the brain.

▶ *Glutamate* functions as the major excitatory neurotransmitter in the brain. It is released by about 90 percent of the brain's neurons during excitation. Star-shaped glial cells then "mop up" the excess to prevent overstimulation.

Muhammad Ali and Michael J. Fox, who both have Parkinson's, have focused public attention on the disease, which involves a loss of dopamine-producing cells.

Harmful effects can occur when neurotransmitter levels are too high or too low. Low levels of serotonin and norepinephrine have been associated with severe depression (see Chapter 16). Abnormal GABA levels have been implicated in sleep and eating disorders and in convulsive disorders, including epilepsy (Bekenstein & Lothman, 1993). People with Alzheimer's disease—a devastating condition that leads to memory loss, personality changes, and eventual disintegration of all physical and mental abilities—lose brain cells responsible for producing acetylcholine, and this deficit may help account for their memory problems. A loss of cells that produce dopamine is responsible for the tremors, rigidity, and weakness that characterize Parkinson's disease. In multiple sclerosis, immune cells produce an overabundance of glutamate, which damages or kills the glial cells that normally make myelin (Werner, Pitt, & Raine, 2001).

We want to warn you, however, that pinning down the relationship between neurotransmitter abnormalities and behavioral or physical abnormalities is extremely tricky. Each neurotransmitter plays multiple roles, and the functions of different substances often overlap. Further, it is always possible that something about a disorder leads to abnormal neurotransmitter levels, instead of the other way around. Although drugs that boost or decrease levels of particular neurotransmitters are sometimes effective in treating disorders, that does not necessarily mean that abnormal neurotransmitter levels are *causing* the disorders. After all, aspirin can relieve a headache, but headaches are not caused by a lack of aspirin!

Many of us regularly ingest things that affect our own neurotransmitters. For example, most recreational drugs produce their effects by blocking or enhancing the actions of neurotransmitters. So do some herbal remedies. St. John's wort, which many people take for depression, prevents the cells that release serotonin from reabsorbing excess molecules that have remained in the synaptic cleft; as a result, serotonin levels rise. Many people do not realize that such remedies, because they affect the nervous system's biochemistry, can interact with other medications and can be harmful in high doses. Even ordinary foods can influence the availability of neurotransmitters in the brain, as we discuss in "Taking Psychology with You."

endorphins [en-DOR-fins] Chemical substances in the nervous system that are similar in structure and action to opiates; they are involved in pain reduction, pleasure, and memory, and are known technically as *endogenous opioid peptides.*

Endorphins: The Brain's Natural Opiates. Another intriguing group of chemical messengers is known collectively as *endogenous opioid peptides,* or more popularly as **endorphins.** Endorphins have effects similar to those of natural opiates; that is, they reduce pain and promote pleasure. They are also thought to play a role in appetite, sexual activity, blood pressure, mood, learning, and memory. Some endorphins function as neurotransmitters, but most act primarily by altering the effects of neurotransmitters—for example, by limiting or prolonging those effects.

Endorphins were identified in the early 1970s. Candace Pert and Solomon Snyder (1973) were doing research on morphine, a pain-relieving and mood-elevating opiate derived from heroin, which is made from poppies. They found that morphine works by binding to receptor sites in the brain. This seemed odd. As Snyder later recalled, "We doubted that animals had evolved opiate receptors just to deal with certain properties of the poppy plant" (quoted in Radetsky, 1991). Pert and Snyder reasoned that if opiate receptors exist, then the body must produce its own internally generated, or *endogenous,* morphinelike substances, which they named "endorphins." Soon they and other researchers confirmed this hypothesis.

"PSST-ENDORPHINS. AND THEY'RE PERFECTLY LEGAL."

Endorphin levels seem to shoot up when an animal or a person is afraid or under stress. This is no accident; by making pain bearable in such situations, endorphins give a species an evolutionary advantage. When an organism is threatened, it needs to do something fast. Pain, however, can interfere with action: A mouse that pauses to lick a wounded paw may become a cat's dinner; a soldier who is overcome by an injury may never get off the battlefield. But, of course, the body's built-in system of counteracting pain is only partly successful, especially when painful stimulation is prolonged.

A link may also exist between endorphins and the pleasures of social contact. When young puppies, guinea pigs, and chicks are injected with low doses of either morphine or endorphins, the animals show much less distress than usual when separated from their mothers. (In all other respects, they behave normally.) The morphine or endorphins seem to provide a biochemical replacement for the mother, or, more precisely, for the endorphin surge presumed to occur during contact with her. Conversely, when young guinea pigs and chicks received a chemical that *blocks* the effects of opiates, their crying increases (Panksepp et al., 1980). These findings suggest that endorphin-stimulated euphoria may be a child's initial motive for seeking affection and cuddling—that, in effect, a child attached to a parent is a child addicted to love.

Hormones: Long-Distance Messengers. **Hormones,** which make up the third class of chemical messengers, are produced primarily in **endocrine glands.** They are released directly into the bloodstream, which carries them to organs and cells that may be far from their point of origin. Hormones have dozens of jobs, from promoting bodily growth to aiding digestion to regulating metabolism.

Neurotransmitters and hormones are not always chemically distinct; the two classifications are like social clubs that admit some of the same members. A particular chemical, such as norepinephrine, may belong to more than one classification, depending on where it is located and what function it is performing. Nature has been efficient, giving some substances more than one task to perform.

The following hormones, among others, are of particular interest to psychologists:

1 **Melatonin,** which is secreted by the *pineal gland,* deep within the brain, helps to regulate daily biological rhythms and promotes sleep, as we will discuss further in Chapter 5.

2 **Adrenal hormones,** which are produced by the *adrenal glands* (organs that are perched right above the kidneys), are involved in emotion and stress (see Chapters 11 and 15). These hormones also rise in response to nonemotional conditions, such as heat, cold, pain, injury, burns, and physical exercise, and in response to some drugs, such as caffeine and nicotine. The outer part of each adrenal gland

hormones Chemical substances, secreted by organs called glands, that affect the functioning of other organs.

endocrine glands Internal organs that produce hormones and release them into the bloodstream.

melatonin A hormone, secreted by the pineal gland, that is involved in the regulation of daily biological rhythms.

adrenal hormones Hormones that are produced by the adrenal glands and that are involved in emotion and stress.

sex hormones Hormones that regulate the development and functioning of reproductive organs and that stimulate the development of male and female sexual characteristics; they include androgens, estrogens, and progesterone.

produces *cortisol*, which increases blood-sugar levels and boosts energy. The inner part produces *epinephrine* (popularly known as adrenaline) and *norepinephrine*. When adrenal hormones are released in your body, activated by the sympathetic nervous system, they increase your arousal level and prepare you for action. Adrenal hormones also enhance memory, as we will see in Chapter 10.

3 **Sex hormones,** which are secreted by tissue in the gonads (testes in men, ovaries in women), and also by the adrenal glands, include three main types, all occurring in both sexes but in differing amounts and proportions in males and females after puberty. *Androgens* (the most important of which is *testosterone*) are masculinizing hormones produced mainly in the testes but also in the ovaries and the adrenal glands. Androgens set in motion the physical changes males experience at puberty—for example, a deepened voice and facial and chest hair—and cause pubic and underarm hair to develop in both sexes. Testosterone also influences sexual arousal in both sexes. *Estrogens* are feminizing hormones that bring on physical changes in females at puberty, such as breast development and the onset of menstruation, and that influence the course of the menstrual cycle. *Progesterone* contributes to the growth and maintenance of the uterine lining in preparation for a fertilized egg, among other functions. Estrogens and progesterone are produced mainly in the ovaries but also in the testes and the adrenal glands.

Researchers are now studying the possible involvement of sex hormones in behavior not linked to sex or reproduction. For example, estrogens appear to promote the formation of synapses in certain brain areas, and although the evidence has not been entirely consistent, many researchers now believe that these hormones may contribute to learning and memory (Maki & Resnick, 2000; Sherwin, 1998a; Wickelgren, 1997). But the most common belief about the nonsexual effects of sex hormones—that fluctuating levels of estrogen and progesterone make most women "emotional" before menstruation—has not been borne out by research, as we will see in Chapter 5.

4.2 *Live!* psych

Review 4.1 summarizes the three types of brain chemicals we have discussed, and their effects.

REVIEW 4.1	NERVOUS-SYSTEM CHEMICALS AND THEIR EFFECTS			
Type	**Function**	**Effects**	**Where Produced**	**Examples**
Neurotransmitters	Enable neurons to excite or inhibit each other	Diverse, depending on which circuits are activated or suppressed	Brain, spinal cord, peripheral nerves, certain glands	Serotonin, dopamine, norepinephrine
Endorphins	Usually modulate the effects of neurotransmitters	Reduce pain, promote pleasure; also linked to learning, memory, and other functions	Brain, spinal cord	(Several varieties, not discussed in this text)
Hormones	Affect functioning of target organs and tissues	Dozens, ranging from promotion of digestion to regulation of metabolism	Primarily in endocrine glands	Epinephrine, norepinephrine, estrogens, androgens

QUICK QUIZ

Get your glutamate going by taking this quiz.

A. Which word in parentheses best fits each of the following definitions?

1. Basic building blocks of the nervous system *(nerves/neurons)*

2. Cell parts that receive nerve impulses *(axons/dendrites)*

3. Site of communication between neurons *(synapse/myelin sheath)*

4. Opiatelike substance in the brain *(dopamine/endorphin)*

5. Chemicals that make it possible for neurons to communicate *(neurotransmitters/hormones)*

6. Hormone closely associated with emotional excitement *(epinephrine/estrogen)*

 B. Imagine that you are depressed, and you hear about a treatment for depression that affects the levels of several neurotransmitters thought to be involved in the disorder. Based on what you have learned, what questions would you want to ask before deciding whether to try the treatment?

Answers:

A. 1. neurons 2. dendrites 3. synapse 4. endorphin 5. neurotransmitters 6. epinephrine B. You might want to ask, among other things, about side effects (each neurotransmitter has several functions, all of which might be affected by the treatment); about evidence that the treatment works; about whether there is any reason to believe that your own neurotransmitter levels are abnormal; and about whether there may be other reasons for your depression.

WHAT'S AHEAD

- Why are patterns of electrical activity in the brain called "brain waves"?
- What scanning techniques reveal changes in brain activity while people listen to music or solve math problems?
- Is there a "gum-chewing" center in the brain?

Electrodes are used to produce an overall picture of electrical activity in different areas of the brain.

Mapping the Brain

We come now to the main room of the nervous system "house": the brain. A disembodied brain stored in a formaldehyde-filled container is unexciting, a putty-colored, wrinkled glob of tissue that looks a little like an oversized walnut. It takes an act of imagination to envision this modest-looking organ writing *Hamlet*, discovering radium, or inventing the paper clip.

In a living person, of course, the brain is encased in a thick protective vault of bone. How, then, can scientists study it? One approach is to study patients who have had a part of the brain damaged or removed because of disease or injury. Another, called the *lesion method*, involves damaging or removing sections of brain in animals, then observing the effects.

The brain can also be probed with devices called *electrodes*. Some electrodes are coin-shaped and are simply pasted or taped onto the scalp. They detect the electrical activity of millions of neurons in particular regions of the brain and are widely used in research and medical diagnosis. The electrodes are connected by wires to a machine that translates the electrical energy from the brain into wavy lines on a moving piece of paper or visual patterns on a screen. That is why electrical patterns in the brain are known as "brain waves." Different wave patterns are associated with sleep, relaxation, and mental concentration, as we will see in Chapter 5.

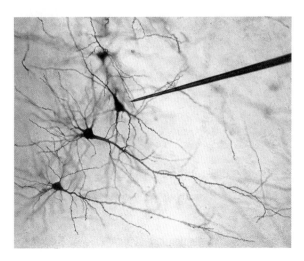

This microelectrode is being used to record the electrical impulses generated by a single cell in the brain of a monkey.

A brain-wave recording is called an **electroencephalogram (EEG).** A standard EEG is useful but not very precise because it reflects the activities of many cells at once. "Listening" to the brain with an EEG machine is like standing outside a sports stadium: You know when something is happening, but you can't be sure what it is or who is doing it. Fortunately, computer technology can be combined with EEG technology to get a clearer picture of brain activity patterns associated with specific events and mental processes; the computer suppresses all the background "noise," leaving only the pattern of electrical response to the event being studied.

For even more precise information, researchers use *needle electrodes,* very thin wires or hollow glass tubes that can be inserted into the brain, either directly in an exposed brain or through tiny holes in the skull. Only the skull and the membranes covering the brain need to be anesthetized; the brain itself, which processes all sensation and feeling, paradoxically feels nothing when touched. Therefore, a human patient or an animal can be awake and not feel pain during the procedure. Needle electrodes can be used both to record electrical activity from the brain and to stimulate the brain with weak electrical currents. Stimulating a given area often results in a specific sensation or movement. *Microelectrodes* are so fine that they can be inserted into single cells.

A more recently devised method of stimulating the brain, **transcranial magnetic stimulation (TMS),** involves delivering a large current through a wire coil placed on a person's head. The current produces a magnetic field about 40,000 times greater than the earth's natural magnetic field (Travis, 2000). This procedure causes neurons under the coil to fire. It can be used to produce motor responses (say, a twitch in the thumb or a knee jerk) and can also be used by researchers to temporarily inactivate an area and observe the effects on behavior—functioning, in effect, as a "virtual" (and temporary) lesion method. The drawback is that when neurons fire, they cause many other neurons to become active too, so it is often hard to tell which neurons are critical for a particular task. Still, TMS has produced some important findings—for example, that a brain area involved in processing visual patterns is also active when a person merely imagines the stimulus (Kosslyn et al., 1999). TMS has also been used to treat depression, as we will see in Chapter 17.

Since the mid-1970s, many other amazing doors to the brain have opened. The **PET scan (positron-emission tomography)** goes beyond anatomy to record biochemical changes in the brain as they are happening. One type of PET scan takes advantage of the fact that nerve cells convert glucose, the body's main fuel, into energy. A researcher can inject a patient with a glucoselike substance that contains a harmless radioactive element. This substance accumulates in brain areas that are particularly active and are consuming glucose rapidly. The substance emits radiation, which is a telltale sign of activity, like cookie crumbs on a child's face. The radiation is detected by a scanning device, and the result is a computer-processed picture of biochemical activity on a display screen, with different colors indicating different activity levels. Other kinds of PET scans measure blood flow or oxygen consumption, which also reflect brain activity.

PET scans, which were originally designed to diagnose abnormalities, have produced evidence that certain brain areas in people with emotional disorders are either unusually quiet or unusually active. But PET technology can also show which parts of the brain are active during ordinary activities and emotions. It lets researchers see which areas are busiest when a person hears a song, recalls a sad memory, works on a math problem, or shifts attention from one task to another. The PET scans in Figure 4.8 show what an average healthy brain looks like when a person is doing different tasks.

electroencephalogram (EEG) A recording of neural activity detected by electrodes.

transcranial magnetic stimulation (TMS) A method of stimulating brain cells, using a powerful magnetic field produced by a wire coil placed on a person's head; it can be used by researchers to temporarily inactivate neural circuits and is also being used therapeutically.

PET scan (positron-emission tomography) A method for analyzing biochemical activity in the brain, using injections of a glucoselike substance containing a radioactive element.

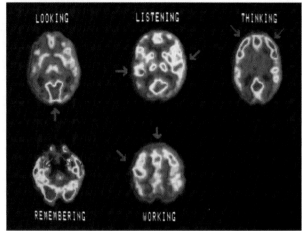

Figure 4.8

SCANNING THE BRAIN

The PET scanner on the left will detect biochemical activity in specific brain areas. In the adjacent PET scans, arrows and the color red indicate areas of highest activity and violet indicates areas of lowest activity during different tasks. At the right, an MRI shows a child's brain—and the bottle he was drinking from while the image was obtained.

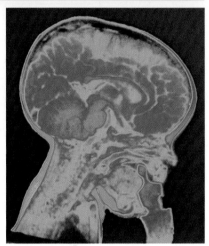

Another technique, **MRI (magnetic resonance imaging)**, allows the exploration of "inner space" without injecting chemicals. Powerful magnetic fields and radio frequencies are used to produce vibrations in the nuclei of atoms making up body organs, and the vibrations are then picked up as signals by special receivers. A computer analyzes the signals, taking into account their strength and duration, and converts them into a high-contrast picture of the organ (see Figure 4.8 again). An ultrafast version of MRI, called *functional MRI,* picks up magnetic signals from blood that has given up its oxygen to active brain cells. It can capture brain changes many times a second as a person performs a task, such as reading a sentence or solving a puzzle.

Review 4.2 summarizes the methods we have discussed. Still other scanning methods are becoming available with each passing year. Some even produce a moving picture that shows ongoing changes in the brain. These methods have allowed neuroscientists to correlate activity in specific brain areas with everything from mathematical calculations to moral reasoning to spiritual meditation. A word of caution, though: Brain scans alone do not tell us precisely what is happening inside a person's head, either mentally or physiologically. They tell us *where* things happen, but not *how* they happen—for example, how different circuits connect up to produce behavior. Enthusiasm for technology has produced a mountain of findings, but also many unwarranted conclusions about "brain centers" or "critical circuits" for this or that behavior. One scientist (cited in Wheeler, 1998) drew this analogy: A researcher scans the brains of gum-chewing volunteers, finds out which parts of their brains are active, and concludes that he or she has found the brain's "gum-chewing center"!

Descriptive studies using brain scans, then, are just a first step in understanding brain processes. Nonetheless, they are an exciting first step, providing initial clues to what goes on in the brain when we think and feel. We will be reporting many findings from PET-scan and MRI research throughout this book—findings on memory, sex differences, depression, schizophrenia, and even how psychotherapy affects brain activity. The brain can no longer hide from researchers behind the fortress of the skull. It is now possible to get a clear visual image of our most enigmatic organ without so much as lifting a scalpel.

THINKING CRITICALLY

Don't Oversimplify

Brain scans provide us with fabulous windows on the brain. But if a scan shows that a brain area is active when you're doodling, does that mean the area is a "doodling center"?

MRI (magnetic resonance imaging) A method for studying body and brain tissue, using magnetic fields and special radio receivers.

REVIEW 4.2	WINDOWS ON THE BRAIN

Method	What Is Learned
Case studies of persons with brain damage	How damage to or loss of neural circuits affects behavior and cognition
Lesion studies with animals	How damage to or loss of neural circuits affects behavior
EEGs	Patterns of electrical activity in the brain
Needle electrodes and microelectrodes	More precise information about electrical activity in small groups of neurons or single neurons
Transcranial magnetic stimulation (TMS)	What happens behaviorally when a brain area is temporarily inactivated
PET scans	Visually displayed information about areas that are active or quiet during an activity or response, and about changes associated with disorders
MRI	Images of brain structure
Functional MRI	Visually displayed information about areas that are active or quiet during an activity or response, and about changes associated with disorders

WHAT'S AHEAD

- **Which brain part acts as a "traffic officer" for incoming sensations?**
- **Which brain part is the "gateway to memory"—and what cognitive catastrophe occurs when it is damaged?**
- **Why is it a good thing that the outer covering of the human brain is so wrinkled?**
- **How did a bizarre nineteenth-century accident illuminate the role of the frontal lobes?**

A Walk Through the Brain

Most modern brain theories assume that different brain parts perform different (though overlapping) tasks. This concept, known as **localization of function**, goes back at least to Joseph Gall (1758–1828), the Austrian anatomist who thought that personality traits were reflected in the development of specific areas of the brain (see Chapter 1). Gall's theory of *phrenology* was completely wrong-headed (if you'll pardon the pun), but his general notion of specialization in the brain had merit.

To learn about what the major brain structures do, let's take an imaginary stroll through the brain. Pretend, now, that you have shrunk to a microscopic size and that you are wending your way through the "soul's frail dwelling house," starting at the lower part, just above the spine. Figure 4.9 shows the major structures we will encounter along our tour; you may want to refer to it as we proceed. Keep in mind, though, that our descriptions will necessarily be quite general, and that in any activity—feeling an emotion, having a thought, performing a task—many different structures are involved.

localization of function Specialization of particular brain areas for particular functions.

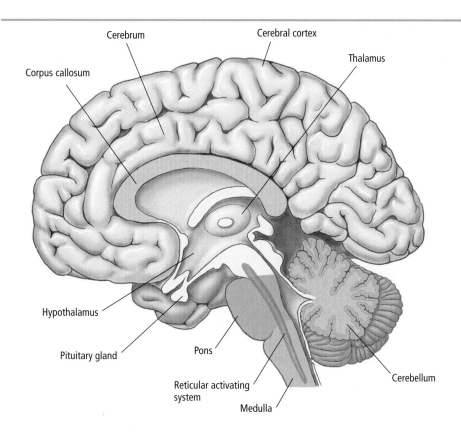

Figure 4.9
THE HUMAN BRAIN

This cross-section depicts the brain as if it were split in half. The view is of the inside surface of the right half, and shows the structures described in the text.

The Brain Stem

We begin at the base of the skull with the **brain stem,** which began to evolve some 500 million years ago in segmented worms. The brain stem looks like a stalk rising out of the spinal cord. Pathways between the spinal cord and upper areas of the brain pass through the brain stem's two main structures: the medulla and the pons. The **pons** is involved in (among other things) sleeping, waking, and dreaming. The **medulla** is responsible for bodily functions that do not have to be consciously willed, such as breathing and heart rate. Hanging has long been used as a method of execution because when it breaks the neck, nervous pathways from the medulla are severed, stopping respiration.

Extending upward from the core of the brain stem is the **reticular activating system (RAS).** This dense network of neurons, which extends above the brain stem into the center of the brain and has connections with areas that are higher up, screens incoming information and arouses the higher centers when something happens that demands their attention. Without the RAS, we could not be alert or perhaps even conscious.

The Cerebellum

Standing atop the brain stem and looking toward the back part of the brain, we see a structure about the size of a small fist. It is the **cerebellum,** or "lesser brain," which contributes to a sense of balance and coordinates the muscles so that movement is smooth and precise. If your cerebellum were damaged, you would probably become exceedingly clumsy and uncoordinated. You might have trouble using a pencil, threading a needle, or even walking. In addition, this structure is involved in remembering certain simple skills and acquired reflexes (Daum & Schugens, 1996; Krupa,

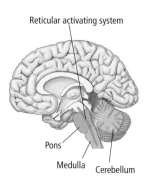

brain stem The part of the brain at the top of the spinal cord, consisting of the medulla and the pons.

pons A structure in the brain stem involved in, among other things, sleeping, waking, and dreaming.

medulla [muh-DUL-uh] A structure in the brain stem responsible for certain automatic functions, such as breathing and heart rate.

reticular activating system (RAS) A dense network of neurons found in the core of the brain stem; it arouses the cortex and screens incoming information.

cerebellum A brain structure that regulates movement and balance, and that is involved in the learning of certain kinds of simple responses.

Thompson, & Thompson, 1993). Evidence has accumulated that the cerebellum, which was once considered just a motor center, also plays a part in higher cognitive tasks, such as analyzing sensory information, solving problems, and understanding words (Fiez, 1996; Gao et al., 1996; Müller, Courchesne, & Allen, 1998).

The Thalamus

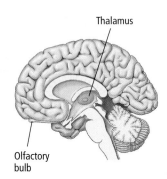

Thalamus

Olfactory bulb

Deep in the interior of the brain, roughly at its center, we can see the **thalamus,** the busy traffic officer of the brain. As sensory messages come into the brain, the thalamus directs them to higher centers. For example, the sight of a sunset sends signals that the thalamus directs to a vision area, and the sound of an oboe sends signals that the thalamus sends on to an auditory area. The only sense that completely bypasses the thalamus is the sense of smell, which has its own private switching station, the *olfactory bulb.* The olfactory bulb lies near areas involved in emotion. Perhaps that is why particular odors—the smell of fresh laundry, gardenias, a steak sizzling on the grill—often rekindle memories of important personal experiences.

The Hypothalamus and the Pituitary Gland

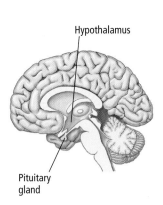

Hypothalamus

Pituitary gland

Beneath the thalamus sits a structure called the **hypothalamus** (*hypo* means "under"). It is involved in drives associated with the survival of both the individual and the species—hunger, thirst, emotion, sex, and reproduction. It regulates body temperature by triggering sweating or shivering, and it controls the complex operations of the autonomic nervous system. It also contains the biological clock that controls the body's daily rhythms (see Chapter 5).

Hanging down from the hypothalamus, connected to it by a short stalk, is a cherry-sized endocrine gland called the **pituitary gland.** The pituitary is often called the body's "master gland" because the hormones it secretes affect many other endocrine glands. The master, however, is really only a supervisor. The true boss is the hypothalamus, which sends chemicals to the pituitary that tell it when to "talk" to the other endocrine glands. The pituitary, in turn, sends hormonal messages out to these glands.

Many years ago, in a study that became famous, James Olds and Peter Milner reported finding "pleasure centers" in the hypothalamus (Olds, 1975; Olds & Milner, 1954). Olds and Milner trained rats to press a lever in order to get a buzz of electricity delivered through tiny electrodes. Some rats would press the bar thousands of times an hour, for 15 or 20 hours at a time, until they collapsed from exhaustion. When they revived, they went right back to the bar. When forced to make a choice, the hedonistic rodents opted for electrical stimulation over such temptations as water, food, and even an attractive rat of the other sex that was making provocative gestures. Today, however, researchers believe that brain stimulation activates complex neural pathways rather than discrete "centers," and that changes in neurotransmitter levels are involved. Moreover, controversy exists about just how to interpret the rats' responses (which, by the way, do not occur in people when their brains are stimulated in the same way). Were the rats really feeling pleasure, or just some kind of craving or compulsion?

The hypothalamus, along with the two structures we are about to come to, has often been considered to belong to a loosely interconnected set of structures called the **limbic system,** shown in Figure 4.10. (*Limbic* comes from the Latin for "border": These structures form a sort of border between the higher and lower parts of the brain.) Some anatomists also include parts of the thalamus in this system. Structures in this region are heavily involved in emotions, such as rage and fear, that we share with other animals (MacLean, 1993). The usefulness of speaking of the limbic system as an integrated set of structures is currently in dispute, because these structures also have other functions, and because parts of the brain outside of the

thalamus A brain structure that relays sensory messages to the cerebral cortex.

hypothalamus A brain structure involved in emotions and drives vital to survival, such as fear, hunger, thirst, and reproduction; it regulates the autonomic nervous system.

pituitary gland A small endocrine gland at the base of the brain, which releases many hormones and regulates other endocrine glands.

limbic system A group of brain areas involved in emotional reactions and motivated behavior.

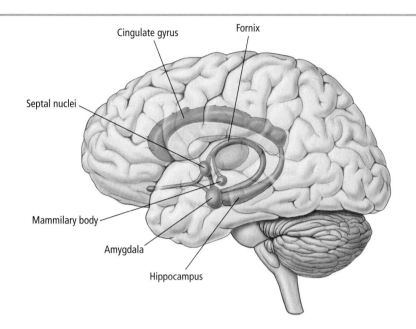

Cingulate gyrus

Fornix

Septal nuclei

Mammilary body

Amygdala

Hippocampus

Figure 4.10
THE LIMBIC SYSTEM
Structures of the limbic system play an important role in memory and emotion. The text describes two of these structures, the amygdala and the hippocampus. The hypothalamus is also often included as part of the limbic system.

limbic system are involved in emotion. However, the term "limbic system" is still in wide use among researchers, so we thought you should know it.

The Amygdala

The **amygdala** (from the ancient Greek word for "almond") appears to be responsible for evaluating sensory information, quickly determining its emotional importance, and contributing to the initial decision to approach or withdraw from a person or situation. For example, it instantly assesses danger or threat. We will be describing these functions at greater length in Chapter 11. The amygdala also plays an important role in mediating anxiety and depression; PET scans find that depressed and anxious patients show increased neural activity in this structure (Davidson et al., 1999; Drevets, 2000).

The Hippocampus

Another important area traditionally classified as "limbic" is the **hippocampus,** which has a shape that must have reminded someone of a sea horse, for that is what its name means. This structure compares sensory information with what the brain has learned to expect about the world. When expectations are met, it tells the reticular activating system to "cool it." There's no need for neural alarm bells to go off every time a car goes by, a bird chirps, or you feel your saliva trickling down the back of your throat!

The hippocampus has also been called the "gateway to memory." It enables us to form spatial memories so that we can accurately navigate through our environment (Maguire et al., 2000). And, along with adjacent brain areas, it enables us to form new memories about facts and events—the kind of information you need to identify a flower, tell a story, or recall a vacation trip. The information is then stored in the cerebral cortex, which we will be discussing shortly. For example, when you recall meeting someone yesterday, various aspects of the memory—information about the person's greeting, tone of voice, appearance, and location—are probably stored in different locations in the cortex (Damasio et al., 1996; Squire, 1987). But without the hippocampus, the information would never get to these destinations (Mishkin et al., 1997; Squire & Zola-Morgan, 1991).

amygdala [uh-MIG-dul-uh] A brain structure involved in the arousal and regulation of emotion and the initial emotional response to sensory information.

hippocampus A brain structure involved in the storage of new information in memory.

We know about the "gateway" function of the hippocampus in part from research on brain-damaged patients with severe memory problems. The case of one man, known to researchers as H. M., is probably the most intensely studied in the annals of medicine (Corkin, 1984; Corkin et al., 1997; Milner, 1970; Ogden & Corkin, 1991). In 1953, when H. M. was 27, surgeons removed most of his hippocampus, along with part of the amygdala. The operation was a last-ditch effort to relieve H. M.'s severe and life-threatening epilepsy. People who have epilepsy, a neurological disorder that has many causes and takes many forms, often have seizures. Usually, the seizures are brief, mild, and controllable by drugs, but in H. M.'s case, they were unrelenting and uncontrollable.

The operation did achieve its goal: Afterward, the young man's seizures were milder and could be managed with medication. His memory, however, had been affected profoundly. Although H. M. continued to recall most events that had occurred before the operation, he could no longer remember new experiences for much longer than 15 minutes; they vanished like water down the drain. With sufficient practice, H. M. could acquire new manual or problem-solving skills, such as playing tennis or solving a puzzle, but he could not remember the training sessions in which he learned these skills. He would read the same magazine over and over without realizing it. He could not recall the day of the week, the year, or even his last meal. Most scientists attribute these deficits to an inability to form new memories for long-term storage.

Today, many years later, H. M., now elderly, will occasionally recall an unusually emotional event, such as the assassination of someone named Kennedy. He sometimes remembers that both his parents are dead, and he knows he has memory problems. But, according to Suzanne Corkin, who has studied H. M. extensively, these "islands of remembering" are the exceptions in a vast sea of forgetfulness. This good-natured man still does not know the scientists who have studied him for decades. He thinks he is much younger than he is, and he can no longer recognize a photograph of his own face; he is stuck in a time warp from the past. We will meet H. M. again when we discuss memory in Chapter 10.

The Cerebrum

At this point in our tour, the largest part of the brain still looms above us. It is the cauliflower-like **cerebrum,** where the higher forms of thinking take place. The complexity of the human brain's circuitry far exceeds that of any computer in existence, and much of its most complicated wiring is packed into this structure. Compared with many other creatures, we humans may be ungainly, feeble, and thin-skinned, but our well-developed cerebrum enables us to overcome these limitations and creatively control our environment (and, some would say, to mess it up).

The cerebrum is divided into two separate halves, or **cerebral hemispheres,** connected by a large band of fibers called the **corpus callosum.** In general, the right hemisphere is in charge of the left side of the body and the left hemisphere is in charge of the right side of the body. As we will see shortly, the two hemispheres also have somewhat different tasks and talents, a phenomenon known as **lateralization.**

The Cerebral Cortex. Working our way right up through the top of the brain, we find that the cerebrum is covered by several thin layers of densely packed cells known collectively as the **cerebral cortex.** Cell bodies in the cortex, as in many other parts of the brain, produce a grayish tissue; hence the term *gray matter.* In other parts of the brain (and in the rest of the nervous system), long, myelin-covered axons prevail, providing the brain's *white matter.* Although the cortex is only about 3 millimeters thick, it contains almost three-fourths of all the cells in the human brain. The cortex has many deep crevasses and wrinkles, which enable it to contain its billions of neurons without requiring us to have the heads of giants—heads that would be

cerebrum (suh-REE-brum) The largest brain structure, consisting of the upper part of the brain; divided into two hemispheres, it is in charge of most sensory, motor, and cognitive processes. From the Latin for "brain."

cerebral hemispheres The two halves of the cerebrum.

corpus callosum [CORE-puhs cah-LOW-suhm] The bundle of nerve fibers connecting the two cerebral hemispheres.

lateralization Specialization of the two cerebral hemispheres for particular operations.

cerebral cortex A collection of several thin layers of cells covering the cerebrum; it is largely responsible for higher mental functions. *Cortex* is Latin for "bark" or "rind."

too big to permit us to be born. In other mammals, which have fewer neurons, the cortex is less crumpled; in rats, it is quite smooth.

Lobes of the Cortex. On each cerebral hemisphere, deep fissures divide the cortex into four distinct regions, or lobes (see Figure 4.11):

▶ The **occipital lobes** (from the Latin for "in back of the head") are at the lower back part of the brain. Among other things, they contain the *visual cortex,* where visual signals are processed. Damage to the visual cortex can cause impaired visual recognition or blindness.

▶ The **parietal lobes** (from the Latin for "pertaining to walls") are at the top of the brain. They contain the *somatosensory cortex,* which receives information about pressure, pain, touch, and temperature from all over the body. The areas of the somatosensory cortex that receive signals from the hands and the face are disproportionately large because these body parts are particularly sensitive. Parts of the parietal lobes are also involved in attention and various mental operations.

▶ The **temporal lobes** (from the Latin for "pertaining to the temples") are at the sides of the brain, just above the ears, behind the temples. They are involved in memory, perception, and emotion, and they contain the *auditory cortex,* which processes sounds. An area of the left temporal lobe known as *Wernicke's area* is involved in language comprehension.

▶ The **frontal lobes,** as their name indicates, are located toward the front of the brain, just under the skull in the area of the forehead. They contain the *motor cortex,* which issues orders to the 600 muscles of the body that produce voluntary movement. In the left frontal lobe, a region known as *Broca's area* handles speech production. During short-term memory tasks, areas in the frontal lobes are especially active (Goldman-Rakic, 1996). The frontal lobes are also involved in emotion, and in the ability to make plans, think creatively, and take initiative.

Because of their different functions, the lobes of the cerebral cortex tend to respond differently when stimulated. If a surgeon applied electrical current to your somatosensory cortex in the parietal lobes, you would probably feel a tingling in the skin or a sense of being gently touched. If your visual cortex in the occipital lobes were electrically stimulated, you might report a flash of light or swirls of color. And, eerily, many areas of your cortex, when stimulated, would do nothing at all; these "silent" areas are sometimes called the *association cortex,* because they are involved in higher mental processes.

Experiences at different times of your life can affect how specific areas in the cortical lobes are organized. For example, functional MRI studies show that bilingual people who learned both of their languages in early childhood tend to use a single, uniform Broca's area when generating complex sentences in the two languages (see Figure 4.12). But in people who learned a second language during adolescence, Broca's area is divided into two distinct regions, one for each language (Kim et al., 1997). The explanation may be that the brain's wiring process for language production occurs differently in childhood than it does later on.

Psychologists are especially interested in the forwardmost part of the frontal lobes, the *prefrontal cortex.* This area barely exists in mice and rats and takes up

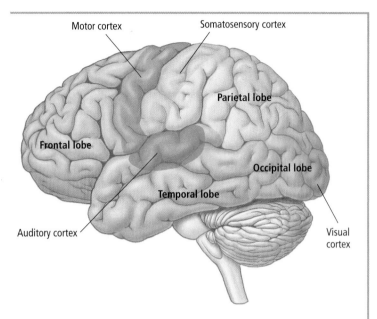

Figure 4.11
LOBES OF THE CEREBRUM

Deep fissures divide the cortex of each cerebral hemisphere into four regions.

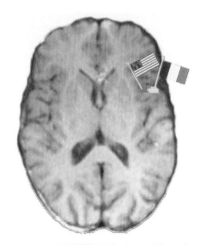

Figure 4.12
THE BILINGUAL BRAIN

While having a functional MRI done, bilingual people were asked to think about what they had done the day before, first in one language and then the other. In those who learned both of their languages in childhood, a single region in Broca's area (which manages speech production) was active. But in those who learned a second language later in life, different parts of Broca's area were activated for the two languages (Kim et al., 1997).

only 3.5 percent of the cerebral cortex in cats and about 7 percent in dogs, but it accounts for fully 29 percent of the cortex in human beings.

Scientists have long known that the frontal lobes, and the prefrontal cortex in particular, must have something to do with personality. The first clue appeared in 1848, when a bizarre accident drove an inch-thick, 3 1/2-foot-long iron rod clear through the head of a young railroad worker named Phineas Gage. As you can see in Figure 4.13, the rod (which is still on display at Harvard University, along with Gage's skull) entered beneath the left eye and exited through the top of the head, destroying much of the prefrontal cortex (H. Damasio et al., 1994). Miraculously, Gage survived this trauma and, by most accounts, he retained the ability to speak, think, and remember. But his friends complained that he was "no longer Gage." In a sort of Jekyll-and-Hyde transformation, he had changed from a mild-mannered, friendly, efficient worker into a foul-mouthed, ill-tempered, undependable lout who could not hold a steady job or stick to a plan. His employers had to let him go, and he was reduced to exhibiting himself as a circus attraction.

Today, there is some controversy about the exact details of this sad incident. For example, no one is really sure what Gage was like before his accident; perhaps the doctors exaggerated the extent of his personality transformation (Macmillan, 2000). But many other cases of brain injury, whether from stroke or trauma, support the conclusion that most scientists draw from the Gage case: that parts of the frontal lobes are involved in social judgment, rational decision making, and the ability to set goals and to make and carry through plans (Klein & Kihlstrom, 1998). Like Gage, people with damage in these areas sometimes mismanage their finances, lose their jobs, and abandon their friends. As neurologist Antonio Damasio (1994) wrote, "Observing social convention, behaving ethically, and, in general, making decisions advantageous to one's survival and progress, require both knowledge of rules and strategies and the integrity of specific brain systems." Interestingly, the mental deficits that characterize damage to these areas are accompanied by a flattening out of emotion and feeling, which suggests that normal emotions are necessary for everyday reasoning and the ability to learn from mistakes.

The frontal lobes also govern the ability to do a series of tasks in the proper sequence and to stop doing them at the proper time. The pioneering Soviet psycholo-

Figure 4.13
A FAMOUS SKULL

On the left is Phineas Gage's skull and a cast of his head. You can see where an iron rod penetrated his skull, altering his behavior and personality dramatically. The exact location of the brain damage remained controversial for almost a century and a half, until Hanna and Antonio Damasio and their colleagues (1994) used measurements of Gage's skull and MRIs of normal brains to plot possible trajectories of the rod. The reconstruction on the right shows that the damage occurred in an area of the prefrontal cortex associated with emotional processing and rational decision making.

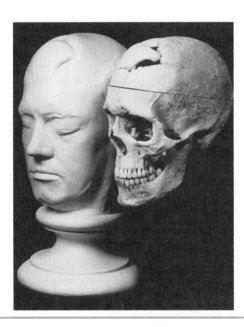
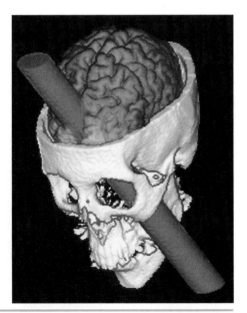

gist Alexander Luria (1980) studied many cases in which damage to the frontal lobes disrupted these abilities. One man observed by Luria kept trying to light a match after it was already lit. Another planed a piece of wood in the hospital carpentry shop until it was gone, and then went on to plane the workbench!

Review 4.3 summarizes the major parts of the brain and their primary functions.

 4.3

REVIEW 4.3	FUNCTIONS ASSOCIATED WITH THE MAJOR BRAIN STRUCTURES

The functions listed here are just some of those that have been linked with these structures.

Structure	Functions
Brain stem	
Pons	Sleeping, waking, dreaming
Medulla	Automatic functions such as breathing, heart rate
Reticular activating system (RAS) (extends into center of the brain)	Screening of incoming information, arousal of higher centers, consciousness
Cerebellum	Balance, muscular coordination, memory for simple skills and learned reflexes, possible involvement in more complex mental tasks
Thalamus	Relay of impulses from higher centers to the spinal cord, and of incoming sensory information (except for olfactory sensations) to other brain centers
Hypothalamus	Behaviors necessary for survival, such as hunger, thirst, emotion, reproduction; regulation of body temperature; control of autonomic nervous system
Pituitary gland	Under direction of the hypothalamus, secretion of hormones that affect other glands
Amygdala	Initial evaluation of sensory information to determine its importance; mediation of anxiety and depression
Hippocampus	Comparison of sensory information with expectations, modulation of the RAS; formation of new memories about facts and events
Cerebrum (including cerebral cortex)	Higher forms of thinking
Occipital lobes	Visual processing
Parietal lobes	Processing of pressure, pain, touch, temperature
Temporal lobes	Memory, perception, emotion, hearing, language comprehension
Frontal lobes	Movement, short-term memory, planning, setting goals, creative thinking, initiative, social judgment, rational decision making, speech production

QUICK QUIZ

Pause to see how your own brain is working by taking the Quick Quiz that follows.
Match each description on the left with a term on the right.

1. Filters out irrelevant information
2. Known as the "gateway to memory"
3. Controls the autonomic nervous system; involved in drives associated with survival
4. Consists of two hemispheres
5. Wrinkled outer covering of the brain
6. Site of the motor cortex; associated with planning and taking initiative

a. reticular activating system
b. cerebrum
c. hippocampus
d. cerebral cortex
e. frontal lobes
f. hypothalamus

Answers:

1.a 2.c 3.f 4.b 5.d 6.e

WHAT'S AHEAD

- **If the two cerebral hemispheres were out of touch, would they feel different emotions and think different thoughts?**
- **Why do researchers often refer to the left hemisphere as "dominant"?**
- **Should you sign up for a program that promises to perk up the right side of your brain?**

The Two Hemispheres of the Brain

We have seen that the cerebrum is divided into two hemispheres that control opposite sides of the body. Although similar in structure, these hemispheres have somewhat separate talents, or areas of specialization.

Split Brains: A House Divided

In a normal brain, the two hemispheres communicate with one another across the corpus callosum, the bundle of fibers that connects them. Whatever happens in one side of the brain is instantly flashed to the other side. What would happen, though, if the two sides were cut off from one another?

In 1953, Ronald E. Myers and Roger W. Sperry took the first step toward answering this question by severing the corpus callosum in cats. They also cut parts of the nerves leading from the eyes to the brain. Normally, each eye transmits messages to both sides of the brain. After this procedure, a cat's left eye sent information only to the left hemisphere and its right eye sent information only to the right hemisphere.

At first, the cats did not seem to be affected much by this drastic operation. But Myers and Sperry showed that something profound had happened. They trained the cats to perform tasks with one eye blindfolded; for example, a cat might have to push a panel with a square on it to get food but ignore a panel with a circle. Then the researchers switched the blindfold to the cat's other eye and tested the animal again. Now the cats behaved as if they had never learned the trick. Apparently, one side of the brain did not know what the other side was doing. It was as if the animals had two minds in one body. Later studies confirmed this result with other species, including monkeys (Sperry, 1964).

In all the animal studies, ordinary behavior, such as eating and walking, remained normal. Encouraged by this finding, a team of surgeons decided in the early 1960s to try cutting the corpus callosum in patients with debilitating, uncontrollable epilepsy. In severe forms of this disease, disorganized electrical activity spreads from an injured area to other parts of the brain. The surgeons reasoned that cutting the connection between the two halves of the brain might stop the spread of electrical activity from one side to the other. The surgery was done, of course, for the sake of the patients, who were desperate, but as a bonus, scientists would be able to find out what happens what each cerebral hemisphere can do when it is quite literally cut off from the other.

The results of this *split-brain surgery* generally proved successful. Seizures were reduced and sometimes disappeared completely. In their daily lives, split-brain patients did not seem much affected by the fact that the two hemispheres were incommunicado. Their personalities and intelligence remained intact; they could walk, talk, and in general lead normal lives. Apparently, connections in the undivided deeper parts of the brain kept body movements and other functions normal. But in a series of ingenious studies, Sperry and his colleagues (and later other researchers) showed that perception and memory had been affected, just as they had been in the earlier animal research. In 1981, Sperry won a Nobel Prize for his work.

It was already known that the two hemispheres are not mirror images of each other. In most people, language is largely handled by the left hemisphere; thus, a person who suffers brain damage because of a stroke—a blockage in or rupture of a blood vessel in the brain—is much more likely to have language problems if the damage is in the left side than if it is in the right. Sperry and his colleagues wanted to know: How would splitting the brain affect language and other abilities?

To understand this research, you must know how nerves connect the eyes to the brain. (The human patients, unlike Myers and Sperry's cats, did not have these nerves cut.) If you look straight ahead, everything in the left side of the scene before you—the "visual field"—goes to the right half of your brain, and everything in the right side of the scene goes to the left half of your brain. This is true for both eyes (see Figure 4.14 on the next page).

The procedure was to present information only to one or the other side of the patients' brains. In one early study, the researchers took photographs of different faces, cut them in two, and pasted different halves together (Levy, Trevarthen, & Sperry, 1972). The reconstructed photographs were then presented on slides. The person was told to stare at a dot on the middle of the screen, so that half the image fell to the left of this point and half to the right. Each image was flashed so quickly that the person had no time to move his or her eyes. When the patients were asked to say what they had seen, they named the person in the right part of the image (which

Get Involved ⬜

Tap, Tap, Tap

Have a right-handed friend tap on a paper with a pencil held in the right hand, for one minute. Then have the person do the same with the left hand, using a fresh sheet of paper. Finally, repeat the procedure, having the person talk at the same time as tapping. For most people, talking will decrease the rate of tapping—but more for the right hand than for the left, probably because both activities involve the same hemisphere, and there is "competition" between them. (Left-handed people vary more in terms of which hemisphere is dominant for language, so the results for them will be more variable.)

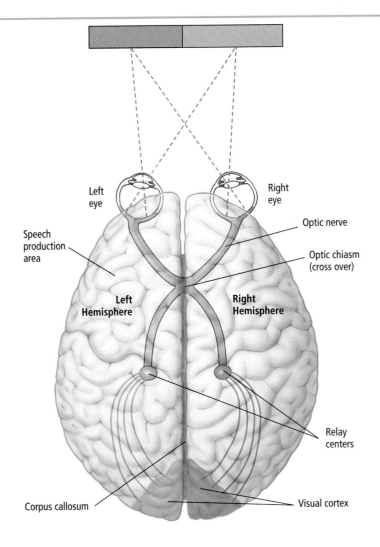

Figure 4.14
VISUAL PATHWAYS

Each cerebral hemisphere receives information from the eyes about the opposite side of the visual field. Thus, if you stare directly at the corner of a room, everything to the left of the juncture is represented in your right hemisphere and vice versa. This is so because half the axons in each optic nerve cross over (at the optic chiasm) to the opposite side of the brain. Normally, each hemisphere immediately shares its information with the other one, but in split-brain patients, severing the corpus callosum prevents such communication.

Left eye

Right eye

Optic nerve

Optic chiasm (cross over)

Speech production area

Left Hemisphere

Right Hemisphere

Relay centers

Corpus callosum

Visual cortex

would be the little boy in Figure 4.15). But when they were asked to point with their left hands to the face they had seen, they chose the person in the left side of the image (the mustached man in the figure). Further, they claimed they had noticed nothing unusual about the original photographs! Each side of the brain saw a different half-image and automatically filled in the missing part. Neither side knew what the other side had seen.

Why did the patients name one side of the picture but point to the other? Speech centers are usually in the left hemisphere. When the person responded with speech, it was the left side of the brain doing the talking. When the person pointed with the left hand, which is controlled by the right side of the brain, the right hemisphere was giving its version of what the person had seen.

In another study, the researchers presented slides of ordinary objects and then suddenly flashed a slide of a nude woman. Both sides of the brain were amused, but because only the left side has speech, the two sides responded differently. When the picture was flashed to one woman's left hemisphere, she laughed and identified it as a nude. When it was flashed to her right hemisphere, she said nothing but began to chuckle. Asked what she was laughing at, she said, "I don't know . . . nothing . . . oh—that funny machine." The right hemisphere could not describe what it had seen, but it reacted emotionally, just the same (Gazzaniga, 1967).

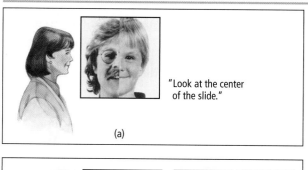

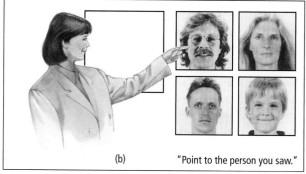

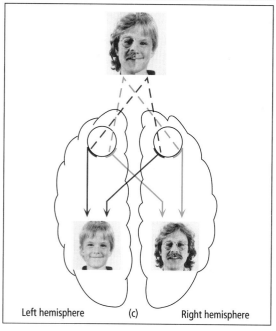

Figure 4.15

DIVIDED BRAIN, DIVIDED VIEW

When split-brain patients were shown composite photographs (a) and were then asked to pick out the face they had seen from a series of intact photographs (b), they said they had seen the face on the right side of the composite—yet they pointed with their left hands to the face that had been on the left. Because the two cerebral hemispheres could not communicate, the verbal left hemisphere was aware of only the right half of the picture, and the relatively mute right hemisphere was aware of only the left half (c).

The Two Hemispheres: Allies or Opposites?

The split-brain operation is still being performed, and split-brain patients continue to be studied. Research on left–right differences is also being done with people whose brains are intact (Springer & Deutsch, 1998). Electrodes and brain scans are used to measure activity in the left and right hemispheres while people perform different tasks. The results confirm that nearly all right-handed people and a majority of left-handers process language mainly in the left hemisphere. The left side is also more active during some logical, symbolic, and sequential tasks, such as solving math problems and understanding technical material.

Because of its cognitive talents, many researchers refer to left hemisphere *dominance.* They believe that the left hemisphere usually exerts control over the right hemisphere. One well-known split-brain researcher, Michael Gazzaniga (1983), once argued that without help from the left side, the right side's mental skills would probably be "vastly inferior to the cognitive skills of a chimpanzee." He and others also believe that a mental "module" in the left hemisphere is constantly trying to explain actions and emotions generated by brain parts whose workings are nonverbal and outside of awareness.

You can see in split-brain patients how the left hemisphere concocts such explanations. In one classic example, a picture of a chicken claw was flashed to a patient's left hemisphere, a picture of a snow scene to his right. The task was to point to a related image for each picture from an array, with a chicken the correct choice for the claw and a shovel for the snow scene. The patient chose the shovel with his left hand

"Mama and I fixed a lovely dinner. I used the right side of my brain, and she used the left side of her brain."

and the chicken with his right. When asked to explain why, he responded (with his left hemisphere) that the chicken claw went with the chicken, and the shovel was for cleaning out the chicken shed. The left brain had seen the left hand's response but did not know about the snow scene, so it interpreted the response by using the information it did have (Gazzaniga, 1988).

Other researchers, including Sperry (1982), have rushed to the right hemisphere's defense. The right side, they point out, is no dummy. It is superior in problems requiring spatial–visual ability, the ability you use to read a map or follow a dress pattern, and it excels in facial recognition and the ability to read facial expressions. It is active during the creation and appreciation of art and music. It recognizes nonverbal sounds, such as a dog's barking. The right brain also has some language ability. Typically, it can read a word briefly flashed to it and can understand an experimenter's instructions. In a few split-brain patients, right-brain language ability has been well developed, showing that individual variation exists in brain lateralization. In one unusual case, a left-handed patient could not read aloud words flashed to her right hemisphere, yet she retained the ability to write them down (Baynes et al., 1998).

Some researchers have also credited the right hemisphere with having a cognitive style that is intuitive and holistic, in contrast to the left hemisphere's more rational and analytic mode. Over the years, this idea has been oversold by books and programs that promise to make people more creative by making them more "right-brained." But the differences between the two hemispheres are relative, not absolute—a matter of degree. In most real-life activities, the two sides cooperate naturally, with each making a valuable contribution. For example, mathematical ability involves not only areas in the left frontal lobe, but also areas in both the left and the right parietal lobes. The former are needed to compute exact sums using language ("2 times 5 is 10"), and the latter are needed for using visual or spatial imagery, such as a mental "number line," to estimate quantity or magnitude ("6 is closer to 9 than to 2") (Dehaene et al., 1999).

Be cautious, then, about thinking of the two sides as two "minds." As Sperry (1982) himself once noted, "The left-right dichotomy . . . is an idea with which it is very easy to run wild."

4.4 Live! psych

QUICK QUIZ

Use as many parts of your brain as necessary to answer these questions.

1. Keeping in mind that both sides of the brain are involved in most activities, see whether you can identify which of the following is (are) most closely associated with the left hemisphere: (a) enjoying a musical recording, (b) wiggling the left big toe, (c) giving a speech in class, (d) balancing a checkbook, (e) recognizing a long-lost friend

2. Thousands of people have taken courses and bought tapes that promise to develop the "creativity" and "intuition" of their right hemispheres. What characteristics of human thought might explain the eagerness of some people to glorify "right-brainedness" and disparage "left-brainedness" (or vice versa)?

Answers:

1. c, d   2. One possible answer: Human beings like to make sense of the world, and one easy way to do that is to divide humanity into opposing categories. This kind of either-or thinking can lead to the conclusion that fixing up one brain hemisphere (e.g., making "left-brained" types more "right-brained") will make individuals happier and the world a better place. If only it were that simple!

WHAT'S AHEAD▷

- **Why do some brain researchers think a unified "self" is only an illusion?**
- **Do men talk about sports and women about feelings because their brains are different?**

Two Stubborn Issues in Brain Research

If you have mastered the definitions and descriptions in this chapter, you are prepared to read popular accounts of advances in neuropsychology. But many questions remain about how the brain works, and we will end this chapter with two of them.

Where Is the Self?

When we think about the remarkable blob of tissue in our heads that allows us to remember, to dream, and to think—the blob that can make our existence a hideous nightmare when it is damaged or diseased—we are led, inevitably, to a question that has been pondered for thousands of years: Where, exactly, is the self?

When you say, "I am feeling unhappy," your amygdala, your serotonin receptors, your endorphins, and all sorts of other brain parts and processes are active, but who, exactly, is the "I" doing the feeling? When you say, "I've decided to have a hot dog instead of a hamburger" who is the "I" doing the choosing? When you say, "My mind is playing tricks on me," who is the "me" watching your mind play those tricks, and who is it that's being tricked? Isn't the self observing itself a little like a finger pointing at its own tip?

Most religions resolve the problem by teaching that an immortal self or soul exists entirely apart from the mortal brain. But modern brain scientists usually consider mind to be a matter of matter. They may have personal religious convictions about a soul, or a spiritual response to the awesome complexity and interconnectedness of nature, but most assume that what we call "mind," "consciousness," "self-awareness," or "subjective experience" can be explained in physical terms as a product of the cerebral cortex.

Our conscious sense of a unified self may even be an illusion. Neurologist Richard Restak (1983, 1994) has noted that many of our actions and choices occur without any direction by a conscious self. He concludes that "the brains of all creatures are probably organized along the lines of multiple centers and various levels." Cognitive scientist Daniel Dennett (1991) suggests that the brain or mind consists of independent brain parts that deal with different aspects of thought and perception, constantly conferring with each other and revising their "drafts" of reality. Likewise, Michael Gazzaniga (1985, 1998) proposes that the brain is organized as a loose confederation of independent modules, or mental systems, all working in parallel. Most of these modules operate without our conscious awareness. As we saw, Gazzaniga believes that one verbal module, an "interpreter" (usually in the left hemisphere), is constantly coming up with theories to explain the actions, moods, and thoughts of the other modules. The result is the sense of a unified sense self.

Interestingly, the idea that the brain consists of modules and that the self is an illusion is consistent with the teachings of many Eastern spiritual traditions. Buddhism, for example, teaches that

THINKING CRITICALLY

Tolerate Uncertainty

We all have a sense of being a conscious "self," and brain research shows that consciousness arises from our brains. But if that is the case, where in the brain is this self located? Can this age-old question be answered?

Where in the brain is the sense of self?

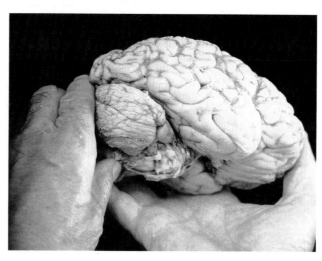

"THEN IT'S AGREED — YOU CAN'T HAVE A MIND WITHOUT A BRAIN, BUT YOU CAN HAVE A BRAIN WITHOUT A MIND."

the self is not a unified "thing" but rather a collection of thoughts, perceptions, concepts, and feelings that shift and change from moment to moment. To Buddhists, the unity and the permanence of the self are a mirage. Such notions are contrary, of course, to what most people in the West, including psychologists, have always believed about their "selves."

The mind-brain puzzle has plagued philosophers for thousands of years. Even in these days of modern technology, details about the neural circuits responsible for our sense of self remain hazy. Many researchers believe that the frontal lobes play a critical role, but not all accept the idea of modules. And no one understands yet how the inner life of the mind, or our sense of subjective experience, is linked to the physical processes of the brain. Some brain-injured patients who, like H. M., are unable to store new memories about their experiences can nonetheless describe what kind of person they have been since the brain damage occurred (Klein & Kihlstrom, 1998). Where in the brain does this capacity to reflect on one's own personality reside?

Over a century ago, William James (1890/1950) described the "self-as-knower," the inner sense we all have of being a distinct person who thinks, feels, and acts. Psychologists, neuroscientists, cognitive scientists, and philosophers all hope to learn more about how our brains and nervous systems give rise to the self-as-knower. What do you think about the existence and location of your "self" . . . and who, by the way, is doing the thinking? Think about it!

Are There "His" and "Hers" Brains?

A second stubborn issue concerns the existence of sex differences in the brain. Historically, findings on male–female brain differences have often flip-flopped in a most suspicious manner, a result of the biases of the observers rather than the biology of the brain (Shields, 1975). For example, in the 1960s, scientists speculated that women were more "right-brained" and men were more "left-brained," which supposedly explained why men were "rational" and women "intuitive." Then, when the virtues of the right hemisphere were discovered, such as creativity and artistic ability, some researchers decided that men were more right-brained. But it is now clear that the abilities popularly associated with the two sexes do not fall neatly into the two hemispheres of the brain. The left side is more verbal (presumably a "female" trait), but it is also more mathematical (presumably a "male" trait). The right side is more intuitive ("female"), but it is also more spatially talented ("male").

To evaluate the issue of sex differences in the brain intelligently, we need to ask two questions: Do male and female brains differ physically? And if so, what, if anything, does this difference have to do with behavior?

Let's consider the first question. Many anatomical and biochemical sex differences have been found in animal brains, especially in areas related to reproduction. And of course, we would expect to find male–female brain differences that are related to the regulation of sex hormones and other aspects of reproduction in human beings, too. But many researchers want to know whether there are differences that affect how men and women think or behave—and here, the picture is murkier.

For example, in 1982, an autopsy study of 14 human brains reported an average sex difference in the size and shape of the *splenium*, a small section at the end of the corpus callosum, the bundle of fibers dividing the cerebral hemispheres (de Lacoste-Utamsing & Holloway, 1982). This finding quickly made its way into newspapers, magazines, and even textbooks, before anyone had replicated it. But a decade later,

THINKING CRITICALLY

Examine the Evidence

Perhaps no topic in brain research generates as much muddy thinking and as many premature conclusions as that of sex differences in the brain. Does the existing evidence tell us much about men and women's behavior in their everyday lives?

a thorough review of the literature found that the 1982 results were an anomaly: Two very early studies (in 1906 and 1909) found that the splenium was *larger* in men, and 21 later studies found no sex difference at all (Byne, 1993). Similarly, a Canadian analysis of 49 studies found only trivial differences between the two sexes, differences that paled in comparison with the huge individual variations *within* each sex (Bishop & Wahlsten, 1997). These findings, unlike the 1982 results, never made the headlines.

Researchers have also looked for sex differences in other ways, such as by examining the density of neurons in specific areas. One team, examining nine autopsied brains, found that the women had an average of 11 percent more cells in areas of the cortex associated with the processing of auditory information; in fact, all of the women had more of these cells than did any of the men (Witelson, Glazer, & Kigar, 1994).

Other researchers have used brain scans to search for average sex differences in brain activity when people work on particular tasks. In one highly publicized study (Shaywitz et al., 1995), 19 men and 19 women were asked to say whether pairs of nonsense words rhymed, a task that required them to process and compare sounds. MRI scans showed that in both sexes an area at the front of the left hemisphere was activated. But in 11 of the women and none of the men, the corresponding area in the right hemisphere was also active. In a more recent MRI study, 10 men and 10 women listened to a John Grisham thriller being read aloud. Both men and women showed activity in the left temporal lobe, but women also showed some activity in the right temporal lobe, as you can see in Figure 4.16 (Phillips et al., 2001).

These findings, along with many others, provide evidence for a sex difference in lateralization: For some types of tasks, especially those involving language, men seem to rely more heavily on one side of the brain whereas women tend to use both sides. Such a difference could help explain why left-hemisphere damage is less likely to cause language problems in women than in men after a stroke (Inglis & Lawson, 1981; McGlone, 1978).

Many other intriguing sex differences have been reported—for example, that female brains have a higher proportion of gray matter than men's do (Gur et al., 1999), and that men use the right side of the amygdala while storing memories of an emotionally upsetting film whereas women use the left side (Cahill et al., 2001). In the coming years, research may reveal additional anatomical and information-processing differences in the brains of males and females. But even if sex differences exist, we are still left with our second question: *What do the differences mean for the behavior or personality traits of men and women in real life?*

Some popular writers have been quick to assume that brain differences explain, among other things, women's allegedly superior intuition, women's love of talking about feelings and men's love of talking about sports, women's greater verbal ability, men's edge in math ability, and why men won't ask for directions when they're lost. But there are at least three problems with these conclusions:

1 *These supposed gender differences are stereotypes;* in each case, the overlap between the sexes is greater than the difference between them. As we saw in Chapter 1, even when differences are statistically significant they are often quite small in practical terms (Hyde, 2000).

2 *A biological difference does not necessarily have implications for behavior or performance.* In the rhyme-judgment study, for example, both sexes did equally well, despite the differences in their MRIs. And in the emotional-film study, the two sexes reported comparable emotional reactions and had similar memories for the films' content. As for how brain differences might be related to more general abilities, speculations are as plentiful as ants at a picnic, but at present they remain just

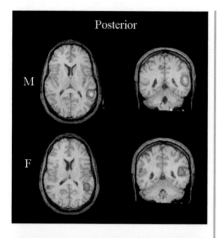

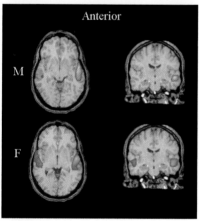

Figure 4.16

GENDER AND THE BRAIN

When women and men listened to a John Grisham thriller read aloud, they showed activity in the left temporal lobe, but women also showed some activity in the right temporal lobe (Phillips et al., 2001). (Because of the orientation of these MRI images, the left hemisphere is seen on the right and vice versa.) Along with other evidence, these results suggest a sex difference in lateralization on tasks involving language.

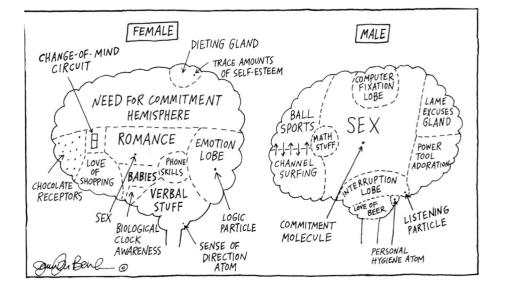

Cartoons like this one make us laugh because we all recognize that men and women often differ in things like "math stuff," "love of shopping," and "power-tool adoration." But this does not mean that all men and women differ in these ways, or that all gender differences are hard-wired in the brain.

that—speculations. As one writer noted, differences between men's and women's brains "are few, they are slight; we don't know what causes them, and in many cases we don't know what they do" (Blum, 1997).

3 *Sex differences in the brain could be the result rather than the cause of behavioral differences.* Experiences in life are constantly sculpting the circuitry of the brain, affecting the way brains are organized and how they function—and males and females often have different experiences. Thus, in discussing the results of the listening study, one of the researchers noted that "We don't know if the difference is because of the way we're raised, or if it's hard-wired in the brain" (quoted in Hotz, 2000).

In sum, the answer to our second question, whether physical differences are linked to behavior, is: "No one really knows." It is important to keep an open mind about new findings on sex differences in the brain, but because the practical significance of these findings (if any) is not yet clear, it is also important to be cautious and aware of how such results might be exaggerated and misused.

QUICK QUIZ

Men and women alike have brains that can answer these questions.

1. Many brain researchers and cognitive scientists believe that the self is not a unified "thing" but a collection of _____.

2. A new study reports that in a sample of 11 brains, 4 of the 6 women's brains but only 1 of the 5 men's brains had multiple chocolate receptors. (*Note:* We made this up; there's no such thing as a chocolate receptor!) The researchers conclude that their findings explain why so many women are addicted to chocolate. What concerns should a critical thinker have about this study?

Answers:

1. Independent modules or mental systems 2. It was based on only a few brains and has not yet been replicated. The differences may be statistically significant, but may also be trivial, and they overlook differences *within* each sex—2 women and 4 men were alike. Finally, perhaps eating chocolate affects chocolate receptors in the brain instead of the other way around.

The Lesson of Einstein's Brain

The study of the brain illuminates the capacities we all share as human beings—thought, language, memory, emotion. And yet each brain is unique, not only because a unique genetic package is present in each of us at birth, but also because a lifetime of experiences, nutrients, and sensations is constantly altering the brain's biochemistry and neural networks. Roger Sperry (1982) said it well: "The individuality inherent in our brain networks makes that of fingerprints or facial features gross and simple by comparison."

Thus, if you are a string musician, the area in your brain associated with music production is likely to be larger than that of nonmusicians; and the earlier in life you started to play, the larger it becomes (Jancke, Schlaug, & Steinmetz, 1997). If you are a cab driver, the area in your hippocampus responsible for visual representations of the environment is likely to be larger than average (Maguire et al., 2000). And, as we saw earlier, if you became bilingual in childhood, a single part of your Broca's area probably handles both languages, but if you learned a second language later in life you will probably have a separate part for each.

Because experience affects the brain, it is often hard to tease out cause-and-effect relationships between the brain and ability. For example, some people have hoped that examining parts of Einstein's brain would tell us what was special enough about it to make "Einstein" a synonym for "genius." We do know that geniuses are in all likelihood born with brains that differ in some way from other people's (see Chapter 9). A few years ago, Canadian researchers reported that a parietal area crucial for mathematical thought, three-dimensional imagery, and other mental processes was wider in Einstein's brain than in "normal" brains (Witelson et al., 1999). Might this explain Einstein's brilliance? Perhaps so. But it is also possible that a lifetime of "brain work" bulked up Einstein's parietal area. We may never know, by studying a single brain of even the greatest genius, how much his brain shaped his life, and how much his life shaped his brain.

The study of our most miraculous organ, the brain, helps us understand the abilities we all rely on and the memories and emotions that make us human. But analyzing a human being in terms of physiology alone is like analyzing the Taj Mahal solely in terms of the materials that were used to build it. Even if we could monitor every cell and circuit of the brain, we would still need to understand the circumstances, thoughts, and cultural rules that affect whether we are gripped by hatred, consumed by grief, lifted by love, or transported by joy.

Taking Psychology with You

FOOD FOR THOUGHT: DIET AND NEUROTRANSMITTERS

"**V**itamin improves sex!" "Sugar makes kids wild!" "Chocolate chases the blues!" Claims like these have given nutritional theories of behavior a bad reputation. In the late 1960s, when Nobel laureate Linus Pauling proposed treating some mental disorders with massive doses of vitamins, few researchers listened. Mainstream medical authorities classified Pauling's vitamin therapy with such infamous cure-alls as snake oil and leeches.

Today, most mental-health professionals remain skeptical of nutritional cures for mental illness. But the underlying premise of nutritional treatments, that diet affects the brain and therefore behavior, is no longer considered a loony idea. Diet may indeed make a difference in cognitive function and in some types of disorders. In one double-blind study, researchers asked depressed patients to abstain from refined sugar and caffeine. Over a three-month period, these patients showed significantly more improvement in their symptoms than did another group of patients who refrained from eating red meat and using artificial sweeteners instead (Christensen & Burrows, 1990). In another study, older people took a daily supplement containing modest amounts of vitamins, minerals, and trace elements; at the end of a year, they showed improvements in short-term memory, problem-solving ability, abstract thinking, and attention, when compared to control subjects taking a placebo (Chandra, 2001).

Some of the most exciting work on diet and behavior has looked at the role played by nutrients in the synthesis of neurotransmitters, the brain's chemical messengers. *Tryptophan,* an amino acid found in protein-rich foods (dairy products, meat, fish, and poultry), is a precursor (building block) of serotonin. *Tyrosine,* another amino acid found in proteins, is a precursor of norepinephrine, epinephrine, and dopamine. *Choline,* a component of the lecithin found in egg yolks, soy products, and liver, is a precursor of acetylcholine.

In the case of tryptophan, the path between the dinner plate and the brain is indirect. Tryptophan leads to the production of serotonin, which reduces alertness, promotes relaxation, and hastens sleep. Because tryptophan is found in protein, you might think that a high-protein meal would make you drowsy and that carbohydrates (sweets, bread, pasta, potatoes) would make you relatively alert. Actually, the opposite is true. High-protein foods contain several amino acids, not just tryptophan, and they all compete for a ride on carrier molecules headed for brain cells. Because tryptophan occurs in foods in small quantities, it doesn't stand much of a chance if all you eat is protein. It is in the position of a tiny child trying to push aside a crowd of adults for a seat on the subway.

Carbohydrates, however, stimulate the production of the hormone insulin, and insulin causes all the other amino acids to be drawn out of the bloodstream while having little effect on tryptophan. So carbohydrates increase the odds that tryptophan will make it to the brain (Wurtman, 1982). Paradoxically, then, a high-carbohydrate, no-protein meal is likely to make you relatively calm or lethargic and a high-protein one is likely to promote alertness, all

else being equal (Spring, Chiodo, & Bowen, 1987; Wurtman & Lieberman, 1982–1983). Recent research suggests that in people who tend to become frustrated, angry, or depressed in stressful situations, high-carbohydrate food can reduce these responses and help them cope (Markus et al., 2000).

Keep in mind, though, that many other factors influence mood and behavior; that nutritional effects are subtle; and that some of these effects depend on a person's age, the circumstances, and even the time of day. Further, nutrients interact with each other in complex ways. If you don't eat protein, you won't get enough tryptophan, but if you go without carbohydrates, the tryptophan found in protein will be useless. Many people try to rev themselves up with nutritional supplements, but in the United States, herbal remedies and other "dietary supplements" are currently exempt from regulation by the Food and Drug Administration. Brands vary enormously in quality and in the amount of active ingredient they contain (Angell & Kassirer, 1998).

In sum, if you're looking for brain food, you are most likely to find it not in a magic pill, but in a well-balanced diet.

Summary

▶ The brain is the bedrock of consciousness, perception, memory, emotion. Because it is the source of self-awareness, people debate how to speak about this organ: For example, where is the "you" that is using "your brain"?

The Nervous System: A Basic Blueprint

▶ The function of the nervous system is to gather and process information, produce responses to stimuli, and coordinate the workings of different cells. Scientists divide it into the *central nervous system (CNS)* and the *peripheral nervous system (PNS).* The CNS, which includes the brain and *spinal cord,* receives, processes, interprets, and stores information and sends messages destined for muscles, glands, and organs. The PNS transmits information to and from the CNS by way of *sensory* and *motor nerves.*

▶ The peripheral nervous system consists of the *somatic nervous system,* which permits sensation and voluntary actions, and the *autonomic nervous system,* which regulates blood vessels, glands, and internal (visceral) organs. The autonomic system usually functions without conscious control. The autonomic nervous system is further divided into the *sympathetic nervous system,* which mobilizes the body for action, and the *parasympathetic nervous system,* which conserves energy.

Communication in the Nervous System

▶ *Neurons* are the basic units of the nervous system. They are held in place by *glial cells*, which nourish, insulate, and protect them, and in ways still not clearly understood, enable them to function properly. Each neuron consists of *dendrites*, a *cell body*, and an *axon*. In the peripheral nervous system, axons (and sometimes dedrites) are collected together in bundles called *nerves*. Many axons are insulated by a *myelin sheath* that speeds up the conduction of neural impulses and prevents signals in adjacent cells from interfering with one another.

▶ Recent research has challenged two old assumptions: that neurons in the human central nervous system cannot be induced to regenerate and that no new neurons form after very early in life. In the laboratory, neurons have been induced to regenerate. And scientists have learned that *stem cells* in brain areas associated with learning and memory continue to divide and mature throughout adulthood. A stimulating environment seems to enhance this process of *neurogenesis*.

▶ Communication between two neurons occurs at the *synapse*. Many synapses have not yet formed at birth. During development, axons and dendrites continue to grow as a result of both physical maturation and experience with the world, and throughout life, new learning results in new synaptic connections in the brain. Thus, the brain's circuits are not fixed and immutable but are continually changing in response to information, challenges, and changes in the environment, a phenomenon known as *plasticity*.

▶ When a wave of electrical voltage *(action potential)* reaches the end of a transmitting axon, *neurotransmitter* molecules are released into the *synaptic cleft*. When these molecules bind to *receptor sites* on the receiving neuron, that neuron becomes either more or less likely to fire. The message that reaches a final destination depends on how frequently particular neurons are firing, how many are firing, what types are firing, their degree of synchrony, and where they are located.

▶ Through their effects on neural circuits, neurotransmitters play a critical role in mood, memory, and psychological well-being. Abnormal levels of neurotransmitters have been implicated in several disorders, including depression, Alzheimer's disease, and Parkinson's disease.

▶ *Endorphins*, which act primarily by modifying the action of neurotransmitters, reduce pain and promote pleasure. Endorphin levels seem to shoot up when an animal or person is afraid or is under stress. Endorphins may also be linked to the pleasures of social contact.

▶ *Hormones*, produced mainly by the *endocrine glands*, affect and are affected by the nervous system. Psychologists are especially interested in *melatonin*, which promotes sleep and regulates a "biological clock" that coordinates bodily rhythms; *adrenal hormones* such as *epinephrine* and *norepinephrine*, which are involved in emotions and stress; and the *sex hormones*, which are involved in the physical changes of puberty, the menstrual cycle *(estrogens and progesterone)*, sexual arousal *(testosterone)*, and some nonreproductive functions—including, many researchers believe, mental functioning.

Mapping the Brain

▶ Researchers study the brain by observing patients with brain damage; by using the *lesion method* with animals; and by using such techniques as *electroencephalograms (EEGs)*, *transcranial magnetic stimulation (TMS)*, *positron emission tomography (PET scans)*, and *magnetic resonance imaging (MRI)*.

▶ Brain scans reveal which parts of the brain are active during different tasks, but they do not tell us precisely what is happening, either physically or mentally, during the task. Thus, they do not automatically reveal "centers" for a particular function, and must be interpreted cautiously.

A Walk Through the Brain

▶ All modern brain theories assume *localization of function*, although a particular area may have several functions and many areas are likely to be involved in any particular activity.

▶ In the lower part of the brain, the *brain stem* controls automatic functions such as heartbeat and breathing, and the *reticular activating system (RAS)* screens incoming information and is responsible for alertness. The *cerebellum* contributes to balance and muscle coordination and may also play a role in some higher mental operations.

▶ The *thalamus* directs sensory messages to appropriate higher centers. The *hypothalamus* is involved in emotion and in drives associated with survival. It also controls the operations of the autonomic nervous system, and sends out chemicals that tell the *pituitary gland* when to "talk" to other endocrine glands. Along with other structures, the hypothalamus has traditionally been considered part of the *limbic system*, which is involved in emotions that we share with other animals. However, the usefulness of speaking of the limbic system as an integrated set of structures is now in dispute.

▶ The *amygdala* is responsible for evaluating sensory information and quickly determining its emotional importance, and for the initial decision to approach or withdraw from a person or situation. The *hippocampus* has been called the "gateway to memory" because it plays a critical role in the formation of long-term memories for facts and events. (Like the hypothalamus, these two structures have traditionally been classified as "limbic.")

▶ Much of the brain's circuitry is packed into the *cerebrum*, which is divided into two *hemispheres* and is covered by thin layers of cells known collectively as the *cerebral cortex*. The *occipital, parietal, temporal,* and *frontal lobes* of the cortex have specialized (but partially overlapping) functions. The *association cortex* appears to be responsible for higher mental processes. The *frontal lobes*, particularly areas in the *prefrontal cortex*, are involved in social judgment, the making and carrying out of plans, and decision making.

The Two Hemispheres of the Brain

▶ Studies of *split-brain* patients, who have had the *corpus callosum* cut, show that the two cerebral hemispheres have somewhat different talents. In most people, language is processed mainly in the left hemisphere, which generally is specialized for logical, symbolic, and sequential tasks. The right hemisphere is associated with spatial–visual tasks, facial recognition, and the creation and appreciation of art and music. In most mental activities, however, the two hemispheres cooperate as partners, with each making a valuable contribution.

Two Stubborn Issues in Brain Research

▶ One of the oldest questions in the study of the brain is where the "self" resides. Many brain researchers and cognitive scientists believe that a unified self may be something of an illusion. Some argue that the brain operates as a collection of independent modules or mental systems, perhaps with one of them functioning as an "interpreter." But much remains to be learned about the relationship between the brain and the mind.

▶ Although sex differences in the brains of human beings have been elusive, brain scans have revealed some differences, particularly in lateralization during tasks involving language (with females more likely to use both hemispheres). There is controversy, however, about what these differences mean in real life. Speculation has often focused on behavioral or cognitive differences that are small and insignificant. Biological differences do not necessarily explain behavioral ones, and sex differences in experience could affect brain organization rather than the other way around.

The Lesson of Einstein's Brain

▶ Because of both genetics and experience, each brain is unique. And because experience affects the brain, it is often hard to tease out cause-and-effect relationships between the brain and ability, as the study of Einstein's brain shows us. In evaluating research on the brain and behavior, it is important to remember that findings about the brain are most illuminating when they are integrated with psychological and cultural ones.

Key Terms

central nervous system 103

spinal cord 103

spinal reflexes 103

peripheral nervous system 103

sensory nerves 103

motor nerves 103

somatic nervous system 104

autonomic nervous system 104

sympathetic nervous system 104

parasympathetic nervous
  system 104

neuron 105

glia 105

dendrites 106

cell body 107

axon 107

axon terminals 107

myelin sheath 107

nerve 108

neurogenesis 108

stem cells 108

synaptic cleft 109

synapse 109

plasticity 110

action potential 110

synaptic vesicles 110

neurotransmitter 110

receptor sites 110

endorphins 112

hormones 113

endocrine glands 113

melatonin 113

adrenal hormones 113

cortisol 114

epinephrine and norepinephrine 114

sex hormones (androgens, estrogens,
  progesterone) 114

electrodes 115

electroencephalogram (EEG) 116

◀ LOOKING BACK

- Why do you automatically pull your hand away from something hot, "without thinking"? (p. 103)

- In an emergency, which part of your nervous system whirls into action? (p. 104)

- Which cells are the nervous system's "communication specialists," and how do they "talk" to each other? (pp. 105, 109–111)

- Are you born with all the brain cells you'll ever have? (p. 108)

- How do learning and experience alter the brain's circuits? (pp. 109–110)

- What happens when levels of brain chemicals called neurotransmitters are too low or too high? (p. 112)

- Which substances in the brain mimic the effects of morphine by dulling pain and promoting pleasure? (pp. 112–113)

- Do men and women have different "sex hormones"? (p. 114)

- Why are patterns of electrical activity in the brain called "brain waves"? (p. 115)

- What scanning techniques allow psychologists to view changes in the brain while people listen to music or solve math problems? (pp. 116–117)

- Is there a "gum-chewing center" in the brain? (p. 117)

- Which brain part acts as a "traffic officer" for incoming sensations? (p. 120)

- Which brain part is the "gateway to memory"—and what cognitive catastrophe occurs when it is damaged? (pp. 121–122)

- Why is it a good thing that the outer covering of the human brain is so wrinkled? (p. 122)

- How did a bizarre nineteenth-century accident illuminate the role of the frontal lobes? (p. 124)

- If the two cerebral hemispheres were out of touch, would they feel different emotions and think different thoughts? (pp. 126–128)

- Why do researchers often refer to the left hemisphere as "dominant"? (p. 129)

- Should you sign up for a program that promises to perk up the right side of your brain? (p. 130)

- Why do some brain researchers think a unified "self" is only an illusion? (p. 131)

- Do men talk about sports and women about feelings because their brains are different? (pp. 133–134)

Go to **WWW.PRENHALL.COM/WADE** to reinforce these key concepts, and more.

4.1 Neurons and neural impulses   **4.3 Major brain structures and functions**
4.2 Nervous system chemicals   **4.4 Hemispheric specialization**

5

Body Rhythms and Mental States

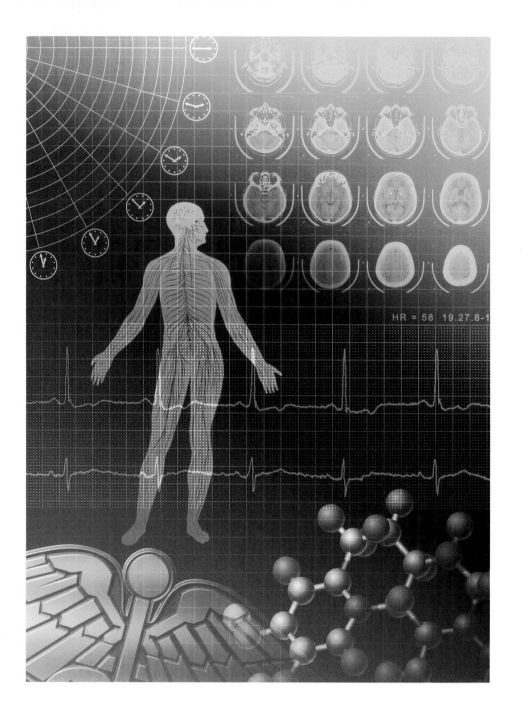

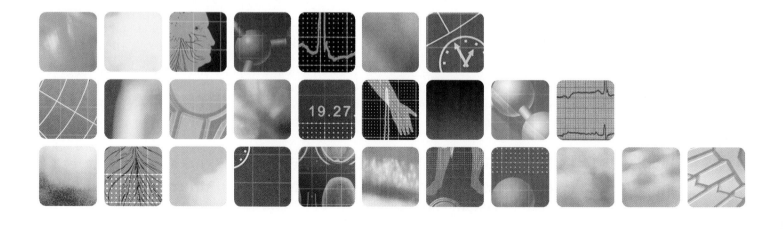

> Like a bird's life, [consciousness] seems to be made of an alternation of flights and perchings.
>
> WILLIAM JAMES

I n Lewis Carroll's immortal story *Alice's Adventures in Wonderland,* the ordinary rules of everyday life keep dissolving in a sea of logical contradictions. First Alice shrinks to within only a few inches of the ground; then she shoots up taller than the treetops. The strange antics of Wonderland's inhabitants make her smile one moment and shed a pool of tears the next. "Dear dear!" muses the harried heroine. "How queer everything is today! . . . I wonder if I've been changed in the night? Let me think: *was* I the same when I got up this morning? I almost think I can remember feeling a little different. But if I'm not the same, the *next* question is, 'Who in the world am I?' Ah, *that's* the great puzzle!"

In a way, we all live in a sort of Wonderland. For a third of our lives, we reside in a realm where the ordinary rules of logic and experience are suspended: the dream world of sleep. Throughout the day, mood, alertness, efficiency, and **consciousness** itself—our awareness of ourselves and the environment—are in perpetual flux, sometimes shifting as dramatically as Alice's height. Sometimes we are hyperalert and attentive to our own feelings and everything around us; at other times we daydream, "space out," or go on "automatic pilot."

Starting from the assumption that mental and physical states are as intertwined as sunshine and shadow, psychologists, along with other scientists, are exploring the links between fluctuations in subjective experience and changes in brain activity and hormone levels. They have come to view changing states of consciousness as part of the rhythmic ebb and flow of experience over time. For example, dreaming, traditionally classified as a state of consciousness, is also part of a 90-minute cycle of brain activity.

Examining a person's ongoing rhythmic cycles is like watching a motion picture of consciousness. Studying the person's distinct states of consciousness is more like looking at separate snapshots. In this chapter, we will first run the motion picture, to

141

see how functioning and consciousness vary predictably over time. Then we will zoom in on one specific snapshot—the world of dreams—and examine it in some detail. Finally, we will turn to two techniques that have been used to "retouch" or alter the film: the use of recreational drugs and the induction of hypnosis.

WHAT'S AHEAD ▶

- Do popular "biorhythm charts" tell you anything about what scientists call biological rhythms?
- Why do you feel "out of sync" when you fly across time zones or change shifts at work?
- How are researchers learning to reset the biological clock that governs our daily cycles?
- Does "PMS" cause most women to feel depressed or irritable before their periods?

Biological Rhythms: The Tides of Experience

Pseudoscientific ideas about biological rhythms have been around for more than a century. Nowadays, commercial "biorhythm charts" promise to predict, solely on the basis of the time and date of your birth, how your mood, alertness, and physical performance will fluctuate over your lifetime. Purveyors of these charts claim they can foresee your good days and tell when you will be susceptible to accidents, errors, and illness. Whenever researchers have taken the trouble to test such claims scientifically—for example, by examining occupational accidents in light of the charts' predictions—they have found the charts to be completely useless (Hines, 1998). Yet biorhythm charts continue to be marketed, notably on the Internet; apparently, one human characteristic that does not fluctuate much is gullibility!

It *is* true, however, that the human body changes over the course of a day, a week, a year. We all experience dozens of periodic, fairly regular ups and downs in physiological functioning. A biological clock in our brains governs the waxing and waning of hormone levels, urine volume, blood pressure, and even the responsiveness of brain cells to stimulation. Such physiological fluctuations are what scientists mean by **biological rhythms.**

Biological rhythms are typically synchronized with external events, such as changes in clock time, temperature, and daylight—a process called **entrainment.** But many of these rhythms continue to occur even in the absence of external time cues; they are **endogenous,** or generated from within. These rhythms fall into three categories:

1 **Circadian rhythms** *occur approximately every 24 hours.* The best-known circadian rhythm is the sleep–wake cycle, but there are hundreds of others that affect physiology and performance. For example, body temperature fluctuates about 1 degree centigrade each day, peaking, on average, in the late afternoon and hitting a low point, or trough, in the wee hours of the morning.

2 **Infradian rhythms** *occur less often than once a day—say, once a month, or once a season.* In the animal world, infradian rhythms are common. Birds migrate south in the fall; bears hibernate in the winter; and marine animals become active or inactive, depending on bimonthly changes in the tides. In human beings, the female menstrual cycle, which occurs every 28 days on the average, is an example of an infradian rhythm.

---

consciousness Awareness of oneself and the environment.

biological rhythm A periodic, more or less regular fluctuation in a biological system; may or may not have psychological implications.

entrainment The synchronization of biological rhythms with external cues, such as fluctuations in daylight.

endogenous Generated from within rather than by external cues.

circadian [sur-CAY-dee-un] rhythm A biological rhythm with a period (from peak to peak or trough to trough) of about 24 hours; from the Latin *circa,* "about," and *dies,* "a day."

infradian [in-FRAY-dee-un] rhythm A biological rhythm that occurs less frequently than once a day; from the Latin for "below a day."

3 Ultradian rhythms *occur more often than once a day, frequently on roughly a 90-minute schedule.* The best-studied ultradian rhythm occurs during sleep, but many other physiological responses and behaviors also follow an ultradian pattern when social customs do not intervene. They include stomach contractions, hormone levels, susceptibility to visual illusions, verbal and spatial performance, brain-wave responses during cognitive tasks, alertness, and daydreaming (Escera, Cilveti, & Grau, 1992; Klein & Armitage, 1979; Kripke, 1974; Lavie, 1976).

> **ultradian [ul-TRAY-dee-un] rhythm** A biological rhythm that occurs more frequently than once a day; from the Latin for "beyond a day."

Biological rhythms influence everything from the effectiveness of medicines taken at different times of the day to alertness and performance on the job. With a better understanding of these internal tempos, we may be able to design our days to take better advantage of our bodies' natural tempos. Let's look more closely at how these cycles operate.

Circadian Rhythms

Circadian rhythms exist in plants, animals, insects, and human beings. They reflect the adaptation of organisms to the many changes associated with the rotation of the earth on its axis, such as changes in light, air pressure, and temperature.

Usually our bodies adapt to a strict 24-hour schedule. External time cues abound, and our biological rhythms become entrained to them. To identify endogenous circadian rhythms, therefore, scientists must isolate volunteers from sunlight, clocks, environmental sounds, and all other cues to time. Some hardy souls have spent weeks or even months alone in caves and salt mines, linked to the outside world only

Stefania Follini (left) spent 4 months in a New Mexico cave (below), 30 feet underground, as part of an Italian study on biological rhythms. Her only companions were a computer and two friendly mice. In the absence of clocks, natural light, or changes in temperature, she tended to stay awake for 20 to 25 hours and then sleep for 10. Because her days were longer than usual, when she emerged she thought she had been in the cave for only 2 months.

suprachiasmatic [soo-pruh-kye-az-MAT-ick] nucleus (SCN) An area of the brain containing a biological clock that governs circadian rhythms.

melatonin A hormone secreted by the pineal gland; it is involved in the regulation of circadian rhythms.

internal desynchronization A state in which biological rhythms are not in phase (synchronized) with one another.

Travel can be exhausting, and jet lag makes it worse.

by a one-way phone line and a cable transmitting physiological measurements to the surface. More often, volunteers live in specially designed rooms equipped with stereo systems, comfortable furniture, and temperature controls.

In some studies, participants have been allowed to sleep, eat, and work whenever they wished, free of the tyranny of the timepiece. Under these circumstances, a few people have lived a "day" that is much shorter or longer than 24 hours. When people are allowed to take daytime naps, however, most soon settle into a day that averages about 24.3 hours (Moore, 1997). And when people are put on an artificial 28-hour day, in an environment free of all time cues, their body temperature and certain hormone levels follow a cycle that is very close to 24 hours—24.18 hours, to be precise (Czeisler et al., 1999). These rhythms are remarkably similar from one person to the next.

The Body's Clock. Circadian rhythms are controlled by a biological clock, or overall coordinator, located in a tiny teardrop-shaped cluster of cells in the hypothalamus called the **suprachiasmatic nucleus (SCN)**. Neural pathways from special receptors in the back of the eye transmit information to the SCN and allow it to respond to changes in light and dark. The SCN then sends out messages that cause the brain and body to adapt to these changes. Other clocks also exist, scattered around the body, and some may operate independently of the SCN, but for most circadian rhythms, the SCN is regarded as the master pacemaker.

The SCN regulates fluctuating levels of hormones and neurotransmitters, and they in turn provide feedback that affects the SCN's functioning. For example, during the dark hours, one hormone regulated by the SCN, **melatonin,** is secreted by the pineal gland, deep within the brain. The pineal gland responds to light and dark via complex connections that originate in the back of the eye. When you go to sleep in a darkened room, your melatonin level falls; when you wake up in the morning to a lightened room, it rises. Melatonin, in turn, appears to help keep the biological clock in phase with the light–dark cycle (Haimov & Lavie, 1996; Lewy et al., 1992).

Melatonin also seems to promote sleep directly. In fact, melatonin treatments have been used to treat insomnia and synchronize the disturbed sleep–wake cycles of blind people who lack light perception and whose melatonin production does not cycle normally (Sack & Lewy, 1997). But efforts to treat the insomnia of sighted people by giving them melatonin have had mixed results. Melatonin supplements sold over the counter should be used with caution, if at all. Because they are classified in the United States as a dietary supplement rather than a drug, there are no federal standards for quality or dosage, and the effectiveness and long-term safety of such treatments are not yet known.

When the Clock Is Out of Sync. Under normal conditions, the rhythms governed by the SCN are synchronized, just as wristwatches can be synchronized. Their peaks may occur at different times, but they occur in phase with one another; thus, if you know when one rhythm peaks, you can predict when another will. But when your normal routine changes, your circadian rhythms may be thrown out of phase with one another.

Such **internal desynchronization** often occurs when people take airplane flights across several time zones. Sleep and wake patterns usually adjust quickly, but temperature and hormone cycles can take several days to return to normal. The resulting jet lag affects energy level, mental skills, and motor coordination. And if jet lag is chronic, as it often is in frequent flyers and flight attendants who routinely cross many time zones on long flights, the consequences may be more serious. A British study found that flight attendants with short recovery times between flights had higher concentrations of the stress hormone cortisol in their saliva, slightly smaller temporal lobes in the right hemisphere, and lower scores on visual memory tests than flight attendants who had long periods to rest up between flights (Cho, 2001). High cortisol levels, if prolonged, can cause brain-cell damage, so they could account for the memory deficits, but other causes (such as sleep deprivation) are also possible.

Internal desynchronization also occurs when workers must adjust to a new shift. Efficiency drops, the person feels tired and irritable, accidents become more likely, and sleep disturbances and digestive disorders may occur. For police officers, emergency-room personnel, airline pilots, truck drivers, and operators of nuclear power plants, the consequences can be a matter of life and death. A National Commission on Sleep Disorders concluded that lack of alertness in night-shift equipment operators may have contributed, along with other factors, to the 1989 Exxon *Valdez* oil spill off the coast of Alaska and to disastrous accidents during the 1980s at the Three Mile Island and Chernobyl nuclear power plants.

Night work itself is not necessarily a problem: With a schedule that always stays the same, even on weekends, people often adapt and do fine. However, many swing- and night-shift assignments are made on a rotating basis, so circadian rhythms never have a chance to resynchronize. Ideally, a rotating work schedule should follow circadian principles by switching workers as infrequently as possible.

Researchers are now studying ways to hasten recovery from jet lag and ease people's adjustment to new work shifts. One approach is to use bright lights to "reset" the clock in the SCN, just as you would reset a mechanical or electronic clock forward or backward (Dawson, Lack, & Morris, 1993; Martin & Eastman, 1998). The lights fool the brain into responding on the new schedule. Another approach is to give people small amounts of melatonin on a controlled schedule, or to combine melatonin with light treatments (Arendt et al., 1997; Lewy, Ahmed, & Sack, 1995). However, procedures that seem promising in the laboratory do not always work well in the real world, where people are exposed to many natural and artificial time cues (Gallo & Eastman, 1993).

We want to emphasize that circadian rhythms are not perfectly regular and can be affected by illness, stress, fatigue, excitement, exercise, drugs, mealtimes, and ordinary daily experiences. Further, circadian rhythms differ greatly from individual to individual because of genetic differences (Hur, Bouchard, & Lykken, 1998). Some people are early birds, bouncing out of bed at the crack of dawn, whereas others are night owls who do

IF WE EVER INTEND TO TAKE OVER THE WORLD, ONE THING WE'LL <u>HAVE</u> TO DO IS SYNCHRONIZE OUR BIOLOGICAL CLOCKS."

Get Involved ⬛

Measuring Your Alertness Cycles

For at least two days, except when you are sleeping, keep an hourly record of your mental alertness level, using this five-point scale: 1 = extremely drowsy or mentally lethargic, 2 = somewhat drowsy or mentally lethargic, 3 = moderately alert, 4 = alert and efficient, 5 = extremely alert and efficient. Does your alertness level appear to follow an ultradian or circadian rhythm? If so, when does it tend to peak and plummet? Is this cycle the same on weekends as during the week? Most important, how well does your schedule mesh with your natural fluctuations in alertness?

seasonal affective disorder (SAD) A controversial disorder in which a person experiences depression during the winter and an improvement of mood in the spring.

their best work late at night and can't be pried out of bed until noon. (Schools are not designed to accommodate night owls.) You may be able to learn about your own personal pulses through careful self-observation, and you may want to try putting that information to use when planning your daily schedule.

Moods and Long-term Rhythms

According to Ecclesiastes, "To every thing there is a season, and a time for every purpose under heaven." Modern science agrees: Long-term (infradian) cycles have been observed in everything from the threshold for tooth pain to conception rates. Folklore holds that our moods follow infradian cycles, too—particularly in response to seasonal changes and, in women, menstrual changes. But do they?

Does the Season Affect Moods? Clinicians report that some people become depressed every winter, when periods of daylight are short, and improve in mood each spring, as daylight increases—a pattern that has come to be known as **seasonal affective disorder (SAD)** (Rosenthal, 1998). During the winter months, such patients report sadness, lethargy, drowsiness, increased appetite, and a craving for carbohydrates. To counteract the presumed effects of sunless days, some physicians and therapists have been treating "SAD" patients with phototherapy, having them sit in front of extremely bright fluorescent lights at specific times of the day.

Evaluating the actual prevalence of SAD and treatments for it is difficult, however. Information on SAD comes mainly from clinical case reports rather than controlled studies, and, as we saw in Chapter 2, case studies have serious drawbacks. Many clinicians, extrapolating from patients who believe they suffer from SAD, think the disorder is quite common—that as many as 20 percent of the population might have it. But a national survey suggests that in the United States, the lifetime prevalence of major seasonal depression is only 0.4 percent, and the prevalence of major or minor seasonal depression is only 1 percent (Blazer, Kessler, & Swartz, 1998).

As for the effectiveness of light treatments, research on this question, too, has been flawed. A meta-analysis of SAD studies found that phototherapy produces a

These young Norwegian women are receiving light therapy for "seasonal affective disorder (SAD)." This type of treatment is becoming increasingly popular, but fewer people actually have SAD than is commonly thought.

better outcome than no light treatment (Lee et al., 1997). But most studies have not used control groups, and it has therefore been impossible to rule out placebo effects when "SAD" patients cheer up.

Better research, though, is now being done, and this research may throw some light on the subject, so to speak. In two well-controlled studies, patients had daily sessions of one of four treatments: (a) bright light, (b) exposure to high levels of negative ions, (c) exposure to low levels of negative ions, or (d) placebo sessions in which they sat in front of a machine that they thought was generating negative ions but was not. The light treatments—and also, unexpectedly, the high levels of negative ions—were effective in alleviating the patients' symptoms, but the other two conditions were not (Eastman et al., 1998; Terman, Terman, & Ross, 1998). The effectiveness of the light treatments suggests that true SAD patients have some deficiency in the secretion of melatonin. Indeed, in another study, morning light treatments advanced the onset of daily melatonin secretion in SAD patients by nearly two hours but did not have this effect in control subjects (Lewy et al., 1998).

Nonetheless, people should be cautious about diagnosing themselves as having SAD or laying out hundreds of dollars for a light-treatment lamp. True cases of SAD may have a biological basis, but the evidence is inconsistent. When people get the winter blues, the reason could be that they hate sleet, ice, and cold weather; that they are less physically active; or that they feel lonely during the winter holidays.

Does the Menstrual Cycle Affect Moods? Controversy has also raged about another infradian rhythm, the female menstrual cycle, which occurs, on average, every 28 days. During the first half of this cycle, an increase in the hormone estrogen causes the lining of the uterus to thicken in preparation for a possible pregnancy. At midcycle, the ovaries release a mature egg, or ovum. Afterward, the ovarian sac that contained the egg begins to produce progesterone, which helps prepare the uterine lining to receive the egg. Then, if conception does not occur, estrogen and progesterone levels fall, the uterine lining sloughs off as the menstrual flow, and the cycle begins again.

The interesting question for psychologists is whether these physical changes are correlated with emotional or intellectual changes, as folklore and tradition would have us believe. Most people certainly think so. In the 1970s, a vague cluster of physical and emotional symptoms associated with the days preceding menstruation—including fatigue, headache, irritability, and depression—came to be thought of as an illness and was given a label: "premenstrual syndrome" ("PMS"). Some popular books have asserted, without any evidence whatsoever, that most women suffer from "PMS."

What does the evidence actually show? Many women do have *physical* symptoms associated with menstruation, including cramps, breast tenderness, and water retention, although women vary tremendously in this regard. And of course these physical symptoms can make some women feel grumpy or unhappy, just as pain can make men feel grumpy or unhappy. But *emotional* symptoms associated with menstruation—notably, irritability and depression—are rare, which is why we put "PMS" in quotation marks. In fact, fewer than 5 percent of all women have such symptoms predictably over their cycles (Brooks-Gunn, 1986; Reid, 1991). Just as with "SAD," more people claim to have symptoms than actually do.

If true PMS is so uncommon, then why do so many women think they have it? One possibility is that they tend to notice feelings of depression or irritability when these moods happen to occur premenstrually but overlook times when such moods are *absent* premenstrually. Or they may label symptoms that occur before a period as

"PMS" remedies line the shelves of drugstores, and most people think the "syndrome" is common—but is it?

THINKING CRITICALLY

Examine the Evidence

Many women say they become more irritable or depressed premenstrually. Does the evidence support their self-reports? How might attitudes and expectations be affecting these accounts? What happens when women report their daily moods and feelings without knowing that menstruation is being studied?

"PMS" and attribute the same symptoms at other times of the month to a stressful day or a low grade on an English paper. A woman's perceptions of her own emotional ups and downs can also be influenced by cultural attitudes and myths about menstruation.

To get around these problems, psychologists have polled women about their psychological and physical well-being without revealing the true purpose of the study (e.g., AuBuchon & Calhoun, 1985; Chrisler, 2000; Englander-Golden, Whitmore, & Dienstbier, 1978; Gallant et al., 1991; Hardie, 1997; Parlee, 1982; Rapkin, Chang, & Reading, 1988; Slade, 1984; Vila & Beech, 1980; Walker, 1994). Using double-blind procedures, they have had women report symptoms for a single day and have then gone back to see what phase of the menstrual cycle the women were in; or they have had women keep daily records over an extended period of time. Some studies have included a control group that is usually excluded from research on hormones and moods: men! Here are the major findings:

▶ *No gender differences exist in mood.* Overall, women and men do not differ significantly in the emotional symptoms they report or the number of mood swings they experience over the course of a month, as you can see in Figure 5.1 (McFarlane, Martin, & Williams, 1988).

▶ *No relation exists between stage of the menstrual cycle and emotional symptoms.* Most women do not have the typical "PMS" symptoms even when they firmly believe they do (Hardie, 1997; McFarlane & Williams, 1994). They may recall their moods as having been more unpleasant before or during menstruation, but, as you can also see in Figure 5.1, their own daily reports fail to bear them out.

▶ *No consistent "PMS" pattern exists across menstrual cycles.* Even when women know that menstruation is being studied, most do not consistently

Figure 5.1

MOOD CHANGES IN MEN AND WOMEN

In a study that challenged popular stereotypes about "PMS," college women and men recorded their moods daily for 70 days without knowing the purpose of the study. When the women were asked to recall their moods, they said their moods had been more negative premenstrually (green line)—but their daily diaries did not bear this out (purple line). Both sexes experienced only moderate mood changes, and there were no significant differences between women and men at any time of the month (McFarlane, Martin, & Williams, 1988).

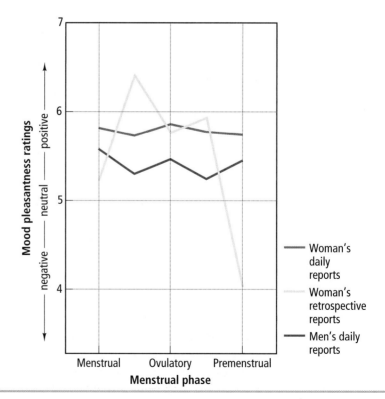

Get Involved ▪▪

A Closer Look at "PMS" Remedies

Go to your local drugstore and find the over-the-counter medications for menstrual symptoms. Do the containers mention only physical symptoms, such as water retention and cramps, or do they also mention emotional symptoms, such as mood swings? Do they refer to "PMS" or "premenstrual tension" as an illness? Are the active ingredients in these products unique to them, or are they generic painkillers such as ibuprofen? What kinds of claims are made for these remedies, and how would you evaluate those claims on the basis of the information in this chapter?

report negative (or positive) psychological changes from one cycle to the next. Their moods and emotions vary far more in degree and direction than one would expect if predictable hormone fluctuations were the main reason for these changes (Walker, 1994).

▶ *No connection exists between "PMS" and behavior.* There is no relationship between stage of the menstrual cycle and work efficiency, problem solving, motor performance, memory, college exam scores, creativity, or any other behavior that matters in real life (Golub, 1992; Richardson, 1992). In the workplace, men, premenstrual women, postmenstrual women, and nonmenstrual women all report similar levels of stress, wellness, and work performance (Hardie, 1997).

These results are unknown to most people and have usually been ignored by doctors, therapists, and the media. As a result, since the 1970s, premenstrual symptoms have come to be defined almost solely in medical and psychiatric terms (Parlee, 1994). So entrenched is the belief that most women suffer from PMS that we have occasionally been accused of bias for reporting the psychological studies that call this belief into question. In 1994, over the objections of many psychologists, the American Psychiatric Association included "premenstrual dysphoric disorder" (PMDD) in the *Diagnostic and Statistical Manual of Mental Disorders,* the bible of psychiatric diagnosis. The label is supposed to describe a rare and debilitating disorder, but its description includes the same hodgepodge of physical and emotional symptoms as "PMS" does. More recently, the antidepressant Prozac was repackaged and marketed as Sarafem, a medication supposedly just for PMDD.

Does Testosterone Affect Moods? Critics believe that the acceptance of "PMS" as a widespread problem and a psychiatric diagnosis has more to do with politics than with facts. The notion that hormones impair mood and performance, they point out, is rarely extended to men—even though levels of the masculinizing hormone testosterone rise and fall in a cyclical manner, too. Testosterone fluctuates daily in all men, usually reaching a peak in the morning, and it also follows a longer, infradian cycle in some men, varying in length from one man to another (Doering et al., 1974). Yet almost no work has been done on the relationship between testosterone cycles and mood or other psychological changes.

Researchers *have,* however, compared men who have relatively high levels of testosterone with those who have relatively low levels. High levels have been linked to a long (and sometimes contradictory) list of behaviors and traits, including criminal violence, delinquency, rambunctiousness, restlessness, elation, sadness, moodiness, sociability, aloofness—and being a trial lawyer (Dabbs et

"You've been charged with driving under the influence of testosterone."

al., 1995; Dabbs, Alford, & Fielden, 1998; Dabbs, Hargrove, & Heusel, 1996; Dabbs, Strong, & Milun, 1997; Mazur & Lamb, 1980; Susman et al., 1987). But researchers have been careful to point out that behavior affects testosterone levels as well as the reverse. For example, testosterone tends to rise after a man behaves aggressively, not before he does, and also rises after he watches a favorite team win an exhilarating sports victory (Bernhardt et al., 1998; Sapolsky, 1997). Moreover, no researcher has suggested that men are victims of hormone fluctuations or that high testosterone levels constitute a syndrome calling for treatment.

We are not suggesting that, either! We raise the issue of testosterone to point out cultural biases in thinking about hormones and behavior—biases that cause many people to reduce women's behavior to hormones but not men's. In reality, few people of either sex are likely to undergo personality shifts solely because of their hormones, except in rare cases of hormonal abnormalities. In most instances, the body only provides the clay for people's symptoms; learning and culture mold that clay, by teaching us which symptoms are important or worrisome and which are not. The impact of any bodily change—whether it is circadian, ultradian, or infradian—depends on how we interpret it and how we respond to it.

QUICK QUIZ

There are no hormonal excuses for avoiding this quiz.

1. The functioning of the biological clock governing circadian rhythms is affected by the hormone _____.

2. Jet lag occurs because of _____.

3. Which term describes the menstrual cycle? (a) circadian, (b) infradian, (c) ultradian

4. For most women, the days before menstruation are reliably associated with (a) depression, (b) irritability, (c) elation, (d) creativity, (e) none of these, (f) a and b.

5. A researcher tells male subjects that testosterone usually peaks in the morning and that it probably causes hostility. She then asks them to fill out a "HyperTestosterone Syndrome Hostility Survey" in the morning and again at night. Based on menstrual-cycle findings, what results might she get? How could she improve her study?

Answers:

1. melatonin 2. internal desynchronization 3.b 4.e 5. Because of the expectations that the men now have about testosterone, they may be biased to report more hostility in the morning. It would be better to keep them in the dark about the hypothesis, use a neutral title on the questionnaire (say, "Health and Mood Checklist"), and measure their actual hormone levels at different points in the day, because individuals vary in their biological rhythms. Also, a control group of women could be added to see whether their hostility levels vary in the same way that men's do.

WHAT'S AHEAD ▶

- **Why do we sleep?**
- **What happens when we go too long without enough sleep?**
- **Why are you likely to be dreaming when the alarm goes off in the morning?**

The Rhythms of Sleep

Perhaps the most perplexing of all our biological rhythms is the one governing sleep and wakefulness. Sleep, after all, puts us at risk: Muscles that are usually ready to respond to danger relax, and senses grow dull. As the late British psychologist

Christopher Evans (1984) once noted, "The behavior patterns involved in sleep are glaringly, almost insanely, at odds with common sense." Then why is sleep such a profound necessity?

Why We Sleep

Surprisingly, the exact functions of sleep are still uncertain (Maquet, 2001). However, generally speaking, sleep appears to provide a time-out period, so that the body can eliminate waste products from muscles, repair cells, strengthen the immune system, or recover abilities lost during the day. When we do not get enough sleep, our bodies operate abnormally. For example, levels of hormones that are necessary for normal muscle development and proper immune-system functioning decline (Leproult, Van Reeth, et al., 1997).

Although most people can still get along reasonably well after a day or two of sleeplessness, sleep deprivation that lasts for four days or longer is quite uncomfortable. In animals, forced sleeplessness leads to infections and eventually death, and the same seems to be true for people. In one tragic case, a 51-year-old man abruptly began to lose sleep. After sinking deeper and deeper into an exhausted stupor, he developed a lung infection and died. An autopsy showed that he had lost almost all the large neurons in two areas of the thalamus that have been linked to sleep and hormonal circadian rhythms (Lugaresi et al., 1986).

Sleep is also necessary for normal *mental* functioning. After the loss of even a single night's sleep, mental flexibility, attention, and creativity all suffer. In chronic sleep

Whatever your age, sometimes the urge to sleep is irresistible—especially because in fast-paced modern societies, many people do not get as much sleep as they need.

Get Involved

A Survey of Sleep Patterns

Get an idea of the variation in people's sleep patterns by asking some friends and relatives what time they typically go to sleep, what time they get up, and whether they routinely take daytime naps. Ask them, too, whether this pattern is their natural one or is simply required by their schedule (for instance, having to be at school or the office by 9:00 A.M.). Do people sleep longer on weekends, and if so, what does this fact suggest about the adequacy of their sleep during the week?

deprivation, high levels of cortisol may damage or impair the brain cells that are necessary for learning and memory (Leproult, Copinschi, et al., 1997). After several days of staying awake, people may even begin to have hallucinations and delusions (Dement, 1978).

Of course, sleep deprivation rarely reaches that point, but people frequently suffer from milder versions. Many people are plagued by insomnia—difficulty in falling or staying asleep. Insomnia can result from worry and anxiety, psychological problems, hot flashes during menopause, physical problems such as arthritis, and irregular or overly demanding work and study schedules. (For advice on how to get a better night's sleep, see "Taking Psychology with You.")

Another cause of daytime sleepiness is a disorder called **sleep apnea,** in which breathing periodically stops for a few moments, causing the person to choke and gasp. Breathing may cease hundreds of times a night, often without the person knowing it, and chronic apnea may lead to high blood pressure or irregular heartbeat. Sleep apnea has several causes, from blockage of air passages to failure of the brain to control respiration correctly. In **narcolepsy,** another serious disorder, an individual is subject to irresistible and unpredictable daytime attacks of sleepiness lasting from 5 to 30 minutes. A quarter of a million people in the United States alone suffer from this condition, many without knowing it. The cause may involve the degeneration of neurons in the hypothalamus that produce a certain brain chemical, and genetic factors seem to be involved (Lin, Hungs, & Mignot, 2001; Overeem et al., 2001; Thannickal et al., 2000).

The most common cause of sleepiness is probably the most obvious one—staying up late and not allowing yourself to get enough sleep at night. Because sleep is so vital to physical and mental well-being, many researchers are worried about the growing numbers of sleep-deprived people in modern societies. When people are sleepy, traffic and work accidents become far more likely (Coren, 1996; Maas, 1998). In 1995, the National Transportation Safety Board reported that tired truck drivers who fall asleep at the wheel are responsible for up to 1,500 road deaths a year; driver fatigue is a greater safety problem than use of alcohol or other drugs.

Two-thirds of all Americans get fewer than the recommended eight hours. American students get only about six hours of sleep a night on average, even though most people need at least eight or nine hours for optimal performance and adolescents typically need ten. Not surprisingly, lack of sleep has been linked to lower grades (Wolfson & Carskadon, 1998). According to sleep researcher James Maas (1998), many students "drag themselves through high school and college like walking zombies . . . moody, lethargic, and unprepared or unable to learn."

sleep apnea A disorder in which breathing briefly stops during sleep, causing the person to choke and gasp, and momentarily awaken.

narcolepsy A sleep disorder involving sudden and unpredictable daytime attacks of sleepiness or lapses into REM sleep.

The Realms of Sleep

Until the early 1950s, little was known about the physiology of sleep. Then a break-through occurred in the laboratory of physiologist Nathaniel Kleitman, who at the time was the only person in the world who had spent his entire career studying sleep. Kleitman had given one of his graduate students, Eugene Aserinsky, the tedious task of finding out whether the slow, rolling eye movements that characterize the onset of sleep continue throughout the night. To both men's surprise, eye movements did indeed occur, but they were rapid, not slow (Aserinsky & Kleitman, 1955). Using the electroencephalograph (EEG) to measure the brain's electrical activity (see Chapter 4), these researchers, along with another of Kleitman's students, William Dement, were able to correlate the rapid eye movements with changes in sleepers' brain-wave patterns (Dement, 1992). Adult volunteers were soon spending their nights sleeping in laboratories while scientists measured changes in their brain activity, muscle tension, breathing, and other physiological responses.

As a result of this research, today we know that during sleep, periods of **rapid eye movement (REM)** alternate with periods of fewer eye movements, or *non-REM (NREM) sleep,* in an ultradian cycle that recurs every 90 minutes or so. The REM periods last from a few minutes to as long as an hour, averaging about 20 minutes in length. Whenever they begin, the pattern of electrical activity from the sleeper's brain changes to resemble that of alert wakefulness. Non-REM periods are themselves divided into shorter, distinct stages, each associated with a particular brain-wave pattern (see Figure 5.2).

When you first climb into bed, close your eyes, and relax, your brain emits bursts of *alpha waves.* On an EEG recording, alpha waves have a regular, slow rhythm and a

rapid eye movement (REM) sleep Sleep periods characterized by eye movement, loss of muscle tone, and dreaming.

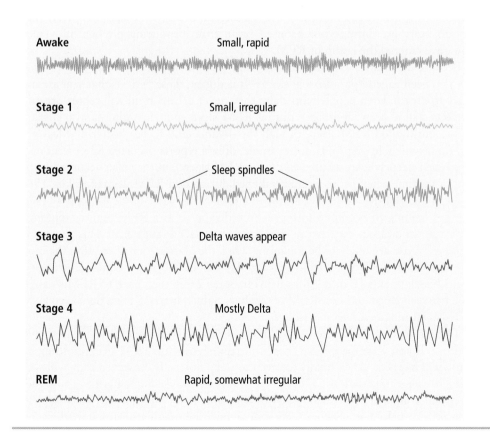

Awake — Small, rapid

Stage 1 — Small, irregular

Stage 2 — Sleep spindles

Stage 3 — Delta waves appear

Stage 4 — Mostly Delta

REM — Rapid, somewhat irregular

Figure 5.2
BRAIN-WAVE PATTERNS DURING WAKEFULNESS AND SLEEP

Most types of brain waves are present throughout sleep, but different ones predominate at different stages.

5.1 Live! psych

high amplitude (height). Gradually, these waves slow down even further, and you drift into the Land of Nod, passing through four stages, each deeper than the previous one:

▶ *Stage 1.* Your brain waves become small and irregular, and you feel yourself drifting on the edge of consciousness, in a state of light sleep. If awakened, you may recall fantasies or a few visual images.

▶ *Stage 2.* Your brain emits occasional short bursts of rapid, high-peaking waves called *sleep spindles.* Minor noises probably won't disturb you.

▶ *Stage 3.* In addition to the waves characteristic of Stage 2, your brain occasionally emits *delta waves,* very slow waves with very high peaks. Your breathing and pulse have slowed down, your muscles are relaxed, and you are hard to arouse.

▶ *Stage 4.* Delta waves have now largely taken over, and you are in deep sleep. It will probably take vigorous shaking or a loud noise to awaken you. Oddly, though, if you talk or walk in your sleep, this is when you are likely to do so. The causes of sleepwalking, which occurs more often in children than adults, are still unknown, but they may involve unusual patterns of brain activity (Bassetti et al., 2000).

This sequence of stages takes about 30 to 45 minutes. Then you move back up the ladder from Stage 4 to 3 to 2 to 1. At that point, about 70 to 90 minutes after the onset of sleep, something peculiar happens. Stage 1 does not turn into drowsy wakefulness, as one might expect. Instead, your brain begins to emit long bursts of very rapid, somewhat irregular waves. Your heart rate increases, your blood pressure rises, and your breathing becomes faster and more irregular. Small twitches in your face and fingers may occur. In men, the penis becomes somewhat erect as vascular tissue relaxes and blood fills the genital area faster than it exits. In women, the clitoris enlarges and vaginal lubrication increases. At the same time, most skeletal muscles go limp, preventing your aroused brain from producing physical movement. You have entered the realm of REM.

Because the brain is extremely active while the body is entirely inactive, REM sleep has also been called "paradoxical sleep." It is during these periods that you are most likely to dream. Even people who claim they never dream at all will report dreams if awakened in a sleep laboratory during REM sleep. But dreaming is also often reported during non-REM sleep, though the dreams tend to be shorter and less vivid and fantasy-like. In one study, for example, dream reports occurred 82 percent of the time when sleepers were awakened during REM sleep, but they also occurred 51 percent of the time when people were awakened during non-REM sleep (Foulkes, 1962).

REM and non-REM sleep continue to alternate throughout the night, with Stages 3 and 4 tending to become shorter or even disappear and REM periods tending to get longer and closer together as the hours pass (see Figure 5.3). This pattern explains why you are likely to be dreaming when the alarm clock goes off in the morning. But the cycles are far from regular. An individual may bounce directly from Stage 4 back to Stage 2 or go from REM to Stage 2 and then back to REM. Also, the time between REM and non-REM is highly variable, differing from person to person and also within any given individual.

The purpose of REM sleep is still a matter of debate, but clearly it does have a purpose. If you wake people up every time they lapse into REM sleep, nothing dramatic will happen. When finally allowed to sleep normally, however, they will spend a much longer time than usual in the REM phase, and it will be hard to rouse them. Electrical brain activity associated with REM may burst through into quiet sleep and even into wakefulness. The subjects will seem to be making up for something they were deprived of. Many people think that in adults, at least, this "something" is connected with dreaming, to which we now turn.

Because cats sleep so much—up to 80 percent of the time—it's easy to catch them in the various stages of slumber. A cat in non-REM sleep (top) remains upright, but during the REM phase (bottom), its muscles go limp and it flops onto its side.

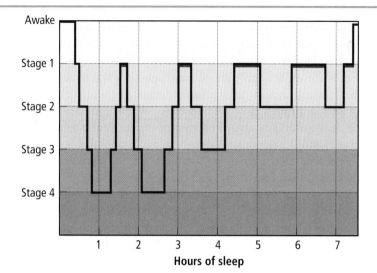

Figure 5.3
A TYPICAL NIGHT'S SLEEP FOR A YOUNG ADULT
In this graph, the thin horizontal red bars represent time spent in REM sleep. REM periods tend to lengthen as the night wears on; but Stages 3 and 4, which dominate during non-REM sleep early in the night, may disappear as morning approaches. (From Kelly, 1981.)

QUICK QUIZ

Wake up and take this quiz!

A. Match each term with the appropriate phrase.

  1. REM periods   a. delta waves and talking in one's sleep

  2. alpha   b. irregular brain waves and light sleep

  3. Stage 4 sleep   c. relaxed but awake

  4. Stage 1 sleep   d. active brain but inactive muscles

B. Sleep is necessary for normal (a) physical and mental functioning, (b) mental functioning but not physical functioning, (c) physical functioning but not mental functioning.

C. *True or false:* Most people need more than six hours of sleep a night.

Answers:

A. 1. d 2. c 3. a 4. b B. a C. true

WHAT'S AHEAD

● **Why did Freud call dreams the "royal road to the unconscious"?**

● **How might dreams be related to your current problems and concerns?**

● **How does a disruption of REM sleep affect memory?**

● **Could dreams be caused by meaningless brain-stem signals?**

Exploring the Dream World

Every culture has its theories about dreams. In some cultures, dreams are thought to occur when the spirit leaves the body to wander the world or speak to the gods. In others, dreams are thought to reveal the future. A Chinese Taoist of the third century B.C. pondered the possible reality of the dream world. He told of dreaming that he was a butterfly flitting about. "Suddenly I woke up and I was indeed Chuang Tzu. Did Chuang Tzu dream he was a butterfly, or did the butterfly dream he was Chuang Tzu?"

lucid dream A dream in which the dreamer is aware of dreaming.

In dreaming, the focus of attention is inward, though occasionally an external event, such as a wailing siren, can influence the dream's content. While a dream is in progress, it may be vivid or vague, terrifying or peaceful. It may also seem to make perfect sense—until you wake up. Then it is often recalled as illogical, bizarre, and disjointed.

Although most of us are unaware of our bodies or where we are while we are dreaming, some people report having **lucid dreams,** in which they know they are dreaming and feel as though they are conscious. A few even say that they can control the action in these dreams, much as a scriptwriter decides what will happen in a movie (LaBerge, 1986; LaBerge & Levitan, 1995). In one case, a young woman was reportedly taught to use lucid dreaming to modify her frequent nightmares and make them less frightening (Abramovitch, 1995).

One issue that has bothered sleep researchers for years is whether the eye movements of REM sleep correspond to events and actions in a dream. Are the eyes tracking these images? Some researchers believe that in adult dreamers, eye movements do resemble those of waking life, when the eyes and head move in synchrony as the person moves about and shifts his or her gaze (Herman, 1992). But others think that eye movements are no more related to dream content than are inner-ear muscle contractions, which also occur during REM sleep. Nearly all mammals, including human fetuses, experience REM sleep (the only known exceptions are the spiny anteater, the bottlenose dolphin, and the porpoise), but we might not want to credit mice, opossums, or human fetuses with what we ordinarily call dreams. Moles, which can hardly move their eyes at all, nonetheless show EEG patterns associated with REM sleep.

Why do the images in dreams arise at all? Why doesn't the brain just rest, switching off all thoughts and images and launching us into a coma? Why, instead, do we spend our nights flying through the air, battling monsters, or having weird conversations in the fantasy world of our dreams? Many explanations have been proposed; here we will cover four of them.

Dreams as Unconscious Wishes

One of the first psychological theorists to take dreams seriously was Sigmund Freud, the founder of psychoanalysis. After analyzing many of his patients' dreams and some of his own, Freud concluded that our nighttime fantasies provide insight into desires, motives, and conflicts of which we are unaware—a "royal road to the unconscious." In dreams, said Freud (1900/1953), we are able to express wishes and desires, often sexual or violent in nature, that have been forced into the unconscious part of the mind. If we did not dream, energy invested in these deep-seated wishes and desires would build up to intolerable levels, threatening our very sanity.

According to Freud, every dream is meaningful, no matter how absurd the images might seem. But if a dream's message arouses anxiety, the rational part of the mind must disguise and distort it. Otherwise, the dream would intrude into consciousness and waken the dreamer. In dreams, therefore, one person may be represented by another—for example, a father by a brother—or even by several different characters. Similarly, thoughts and objects are translated into symbolic images. A penis may be disguised as a snake, umbrella, or dagger; a vagina, as a tunnel or cave; and the human body, as a house.

To understand a dream, said Freud, we must distinguish its _manifest content,_ the aspects of it that we consciously experience during sleep and may remember upon wakening, from its

CAST OF DREAM

THE MONSTER . . . . . YOUR FATHER
KIND WOMAN . . . . . . YOUR MOTHER
POLICEMAN . . . . YOUR ANALYST
FIRST STRANGER. . . . YOUR BROTHER
SECOND STRANGER . . YOUR SISTER
LITTLE BOY . . . . . YOU

latent (hidden) _content,_ the unconscious wishes and thoughts being expressed symbolically. Freud warned against the simpleminded translation of symbols, however. Each dream had to be analyzed in the context of the dreamer's waking life, as well as the person's associations to the dream's contents. Not everything in a dream is symbolic. Sometimes, Freud cautioned, "A cigar is only a cigar."

Most psychologists today accept Freud's notion that dreams are more than incoherent ramblings of the mind—that they have psychological meaning (Fisher & Greenberg, 1996). However, many find Freudian interpretations far-fetched. They point out that there are no reliable rules for interpreting the supposedly latent content of dreams, and there is no objective way to know whether a particular interpretation is correct. Popular books and newspaper columns often give pychoanalytic interpretations of dreams, but they are only the writer's personal hunches.

Dreams as Reflections of Current Concerns

Another explanation holds that dreams reflect the ongoing _conscious_ preoccupations of waking life, such as concerns over relationships, work, sex, or health (Siegel, 1991; Webb & Cartwright, 1978). In this _problem-focused approach_ to dreaming, the symbols and metaphors in a dream do not disguise its true meaning; they convey it. For example, psychologist Gayle Delaney told of a woman who dreamed she was swimming underwater. The woman's 8-year-old son was on her back, his head above the water. Her husband was supposed to take a picture of them, but for some reason he wasn't doing it, and she was starting to feel as if she were going to drown. To Delaney, the message was obvious: The woman was "drowning" under the responsibilities of child care, and her husband wasn't "getting the picture" (in Dolnick, 1990).

The problem-focused explanation of dreaming is supported by findings that dreams are more likely to contain material related to a person's current concerns than chance would predict (Domhoff, 1996). For example, among college students, who are often worried about grades and tests, test-anxiety dreams are common: The dreamer is unprepared for or unable to finish an exam, or shows up for the wrong exam, or can't find the room where the exam is being given (Halliday, 1993; Van de Castle, 1994). (Sound familiar?) For their part, instructors often dream that they have forgotten their lecture notes at home, or that their notes contain only blank pages and they have nothing to say! Traumatic experiences can also affect people's dreams. In one cross-cultural study that had children keep dream diaries for a week, Palestinian children living in neighborhoods under threat of violence reported more themes of persecution and aggression than did Finnish or Palestinian children living in peaceful environments (Punamaeki & Joustie, 1998).

Do men and women have different dreams? Because they often have different concerns, we might expect the content of their dreams to differ—and until recently, at least, that has been true. Typically, women have been more likely than men to dream about children, family members, familiar characters, friendly interactions, household objects, clothes, and indoor events. Men have been more likely than women to dream about strangers, weapons, violence, sexual activity, achievement, and outdoor events (Domhoff, 1996; Hall et al., 1982). But as the lives and concerns of the two sexes have become more similar, so have their dreams. In one study of college students, only two differences showed up: Men were more likely to dream about behaving aggressively, and women were more likely to dream about their anxieties, especially about failing exams. Otherwise, a person's sex was not a good predictor of dream content (Bursik, 1998).

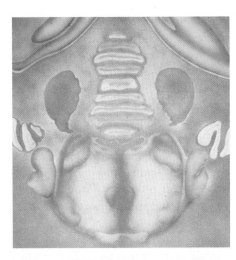

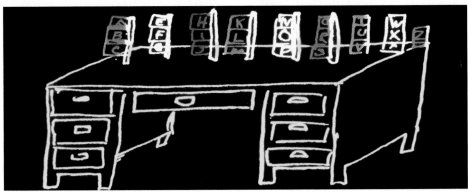

These drawings from dream journals show that the images in dreams can be either abstract or literal. The two fanciful paintings at the top represent the dreams of a person who worked all day long with brain tissue, which the drawings rather resemble. The desk was sketched in 1939 by a scientist to illustrate his dream about a mechanical device for instantly retrieving quotations—a sort of early desktop computer.

Some psychologists believe that dreams not only reflect our waking concerns but also provide us with an opportunity to resolve them. Rosalind Cartwright has been investigating this hypothesis for many years. Among people suffering from the grief of divorce, she finds, recovery is related to a particular pattern of dreaming: The first dream of the night often comes sooner than it ordinarily would, lasts longer, and is more emotional and storylike (Cartwright, 1990, 1996). Depressed people's dreams tend to become less negative and more positive as the night wears on, and this pattern, too, predicts recovery (Cartwright et al., 1998). Cartwright concludes that getting through a crisis or a rough period in life takes "time, good friends, good genes, good luck, and a good dream system."

Skeptics of this view doubt people's ability to work out their problems or conflicts while sound asleep (Blagrove, 1996; Squier & Domhoff, 1998). Dreams, they say, merely give expression to our problems; they don't solve them. The insights that people seem to gain could be occurring after they wake up and have a chance to think about what is troubling them.

Dreams as a By-product of Mental Housekeeping

A third approach explains dreams in physiological and information-processing terms. Dreams, in this view, are a by-product of mental housekeeping, in which unnecessary neural connections in the brain are eliminated and important ones are strengthened (Evans, 1984).

According to this explanation, the brain must periodically shut out sensory input so that it can process and assimilate new data and update what has already been stored. It divides new information into "wanted" and "unwanted" categories, makes new associations, and—to use a computer analogy—revises old "programs" in light of the day's experiences. The data the brain sifts through include not only recent events but also ideas, obsessions, worries, wishes, and thoughts about the past. What we recall as dreams are really only brief snippets from an ongoing process of scanning and sorting that occurs most intensely during REM sleep but possibly throughout the night. Because these snippets give us only a glimpse of the night's mental activity, they naturally seem odd and nonsensical when recalled.

Several variations on this theme have been proposed. For example, Francis Crick and Graeme Mitchison (1995) emphasize only the weakening of unused synaptic connections in the brain's vast memory network. In their view, during REM sleep a sort of "reverse learning" occurs, making memory more efficient and accurate and protecting us from becoming obsessed by unwanted thoughts and images. Dreams are merely mental garbage, and there is no point in trying to remember them or analyze them for their "meanings."

Other researchers emphasize the *strengthening* of synaptic connections associated with recently stored memories. REM sleep seems to be associated with *consolidation,* a process by which the synaptic changes associated with a recently stored memory become durable and stable (see Chapter 10). When people or animals learn a perceptual task and are allowed to get normal REM sleep, their memory for the task is better the next day, even when they have been awakened during non-REM periods; but when they are deprived of REM sleep, their memories are impaired (Karni et al., 1994; Smith, 1995). And when people learn a computerized task—hitting keys when they see a dot in different places on a screen—some of the same brain areas that are active during the task are active later during REM sleep (Maquet et al., 2000).

Further support for the role of REM sleep in memory and learning comes from a recent study with rats. Using electrodes, researchers monitored a small number of hippocampal neurons in the rats' brains while the animals learned to run a circular maze and also while the animals slept before or after running the maze. During almost half of all REM episodes, the sequence of cell activity matched the one that had occurred during the maze task. Not only that, but the results were suggestive of dreaming. By analyzing the cells' activity, the researchers said they could tell where a sleeping rat would have been in the maze if it had been awake, as well as whether the animal would have been moving or standing still (Wilson & Louie, 2001). One of the researchers told *The New York Times* (January 25, 2001) that outside the boring confines of the laboratory, rats may have far more exciting dreams. "It might be," he said, "that a wild subway rat's dreams are as exciting as our epic adventures in sleep."

But wait: Before we get too carried away about "animal dreams," we had better ask some hard questions. Perhaps the rats in this study *were* dreaming about the maze, but unfortunately, we can't ask them. Even if they were "dreaming," it is hard to imagine that a rat's dream is anything like a human being's. The same applies to human babies (not to mention fetuses). Newborns spend about 50 percent of their sleeping hours in REM sleep, versus only 20 percent for adults. Because everything that is happening to them is new, they may have a lot of consolidation of recent learning to do. But it is hard to credit them with actual dreams.

"MENTAL HOUSEKEEPING" VIEW OF DREAMS

Discarded	Retained
Price of tuna	New karate move
Traffic jam at noon	Information for exam
Dentist's phone number	Date on Saturday

THINKING CRITICALLY

Tolerate Uncertainty

After a rat learns a task, its brain activity during sleep resembles its brain activity during its training. Does this mean that animals dream the way humans do?

The notion that dreams are for "mental housekeeping" and the consolidation of memories also fails to explain why some dreams are so storylike, or why some dreams recur periodically for years. Information-processing approaches may therefore tell us more about the functions of REM sleep than they do about dreaming per se.

Dreams as Interpreted Brain Activity

A fourth approach to dreaming, the **activation–synthesis theory**, also draws heavily on physiological research. According to this explanation, first proposed by psychiatrist Allan Hobson (1988, 1990), dreams are not "children of an idle brain," as Shakespeare called them. Rather, they are largely the result of neurons firing spontaneously in the lower part of the brain, in the pons, during REM sleep. These neurons control eye movement, gaze, balance, and posture, and they send messages to sensory and motor areas of the cortex responsible during wakefulness for visual processing and voluntary action.

ACTIVATION–SYNTHESIS THEORY OF DREAMS

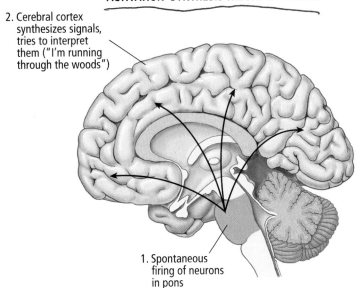

2. Cerebral cortex synthesizes signals, tries to interpret them ("I'm running through the woods")

1. Spontaneous firing of neurons in pons

According to the activation–synthesis theory, the signals originating in the pons have no psychological meaning in themselves. But the cortex tries to make sense of them by *synthesizing*, or integrating, them with existing knowledge and memories to produce some sort of coherent interpretation. (This is just what the cortex does when signals come from sense organs during ordinary wakefulness.) When neurons fire in the part of the brain that handles balance, for instance, the cortex may generate a dream about falling. When signals occur that would ordinarily produce running, the cortex may manufacture a dream about being chased. Because the signals from the pons occur randomly, the cortex's interpretation—the dream—is likely to be incoherent and confusing. And because the cortical neurons that control the initial storage of new memories are turned off during sleep, we typically forget our dreams upon waking unless we write them down or immediately recount them to someone else.

Since Hobson's original formulation, he and his colleagues have added further details and modifications (Hobson, Pace-Schott, & Stickgold, 2000). The brain stem, they say, sets off responses in emotional and visual parts of the brain. Brain-stem cells also produce acetylcholine, a neurotransmitter

---

Get Involved

Keep a Dream Diary

It can be fun to record your dreams. Keep a notebook or a tape recorder by your bedside. As soon as you wake up in the morning (or if you awaken during the night while dreaming), record everything you can about your dreams—even short fragments. After you have collected several dreams, see which theory or theories discussed in this chapter seem to best explain them. Do your dreams contain any recurring themes? Do they provide any clues to your current problems, activities, or concerns?

that boosts activity in the brain's emotional centers. At the same time, brain regions that handle logical thought and sensations from the external world shut down. These changes would account for the fact that dreams tend to be emotionally charged, hallucinatory, and illogical.

Wishes, in this view, do not cause dreams; brain mechanisms do. But that does not mean dreams are meaningless. Hobson (1988) argued that the brain "is so inexorably bent upon the quest for meaning that it attributes and even creates meaning when there is little or none to be found in the data it is asked to process." By studying these attributed meanings, you can learn about your unique perceptions, conflicts, and concerns—not by trying to dig below the surface of the dream, as Freud would, but by examining the surface itself. Or you can relax and enjoy the nightly entertainment that dreams provide.

By now you won't be surprised to learn that this theory, like all the others, has come in for criticism (Squier & Domhoff, 1998). Not all dreams are as disjointed or as bizarre as the theory predicts; some tell a coherent, if fanciful, story. Moreover, the activation-synthesis approach does not account well for dreaming that goes on outside of REM sleep. Some neuropsychologists emphasize different brain mechanisms, and many believe that dreams do reflect a person's goals and desires (Solms, 2000).

How are we to evaluate these attempts to explain dreaming? All four approaches account for some of the evidence, and each one has its drawbacks (see Review 5.1). Perhaps it will turn out that different kinds of dreams have different purposes and origins. We all know from experience that some of our dreams seem to be related to daily problems, some are vague and incoherent, and some are anxiety dreams that occur when we are tense and worried. For the time being, we are going to have to live with uncertainty about what those fascinating stories and images in our sleeping brains really mean. Clearly, much remains to be learned about the functions of dreaming and even of sleep itself.

activation–synthesis theory The theory that dreaming results from the cortical synthesis and interpretation of neural signals triggered by activity in the lower part of the brain.

REVIEW 5.1	FOUR DREAM THEORIES COMPARED	
Theory	**Purpose of Dreaming**	**Weaknesses**
Psychoanalytic	To express unconscious wishes, thoughts, and conflicts	Interpretations are often far-fetched; there is no reliable way to interpret "latent" meanings
Problem-focused	To express ongoing concerns of waking life and/or resolve current concerns and problems	Some theorists are skeptical about the ability to resolve problems during sleep
Mental housekeeping	By-product of a process of eliminating or strengthening neural connections in the brain	Says more about REM sleep than about dreaming; does not explain storylike or recurrent dreams
Activation–synthesis	None; dreams occur because of random brain-stem signals, though cortical interpretations of those signals may reflect concerns and conflicts	Does not explain coherent, storylike dreams or non-REM dreams

QUICK QUIZ

See if you can dream up an answer to this question.

In his dreams, Andy is an infant crawling through a dark tunnel looking for something he has lost. Which theory of dreams would be most receptive to each of the following explanations?

1. Andy recently misplaced a valuable watch but eventually found it.
2. While Andy was sleeping, neurons in his pons that would ordinarily stimulate leg-muscle movement were active.
3. Andy has repressed an early sexual attraction to his mother; the tunnel symbolizes her vagina.
4. Andy has broken up with his lover and is working through the emotional loss.

Answers:

1. the mental-housekeeping (information-processing) approach (the dreamer is processing information about a recent experience) 2. the activation–synthesis theory 3. psychoanalytic theory 4. the problem-focused approach

WHAT'S AHEAD▶

- **In its physiological effects, is alcohol a "downer" or an "upper"?**
- **How do recreational drugs affect the brain?**
- **Why can a glass of wine make you feel tired at one time but sociable and pepped up at another?**

Consciousness-altering Drugs

In Jerusalem, hundreds of Hasidic men celebrate the completion of the annual reading of the holy Torah by dancing for hours in the streets. For them, dancing is not a diversion; it is a path to religious ecstasy.

In South Dakota, several Lakota (Sioux) adults sit naked in the darkness of the sweat lodge, a circular hut covered with hides and blankets. When their leader throws water on a pit of red-hot rocks, a crushing wave of heat envelops them. For the Lakota, the reward will be euphoria, the transcendence of pain, and possible connection with the Great Spirit of the Universe.

Deep in the Amazon jungle, a young man training to be a shaman, a religious leader, has been starving himself. Aided by a whiff of hallucinogenic snuff made from the bark of the virola tree, he prepares to enter a trance and communicate with animals, spirits, and supernatural forces.

These three rituals, although seemingly quite different, are all aimed at release from the confines of ordinary consciousness. Cultures around the world have devised such practices, often as part of their religions. Because attempts to alter mood and consciousness appear to be universal, some writers believe they reflect a human need, one as basic as the needs for food and water (Siegel, 1989).

William James (1902/1936), who was fascinated by alterations in consciousness, would have agreed. After inhaling nitrous oxide ("laughing gas"), he wrote, "Our normal waking consciousness, rational consciousness as we call it, is but one special type of consciousness, whilst all about it, parted from it by the filmiest of screens, there lie potential forms of consciousness entirely different." James hoped that psychologists would study these other forms of consciousness, but for half a century, few took his words seriously. Then, during the 1960s, attitudes changed. During that decade of social upheaval, millions of people began to seek ways of deliberately producing *altered states of consciousness*, especially through the use of psychoactive

All cultures have found ways to alter consciousness. The Maulavis of Turkey (left), the famous whirling dervishes, spin in an energetic but controlled manner in order to achieve religious rapture. People in many cultures meditate (center) as a way to quiet the mind and achieve spiritual enlightenment. And in some cultures, psychoactive drugs are used for religious or artistic inspiration; the Huichol Indians of western Mexico (right) use peyote mushrooms to induce religious hallucinations.

drugs. Researchers became interested in the psychology, as well as the physiology, of such drugs. The "filmy screen" described by James finally began to lift.

Classifying Drugs

A **psychoactive drug** is a substance that alters perception, mood, thinking, memory, or behavior by changing the body's biochemistry. Around the world and throughout history, the most widely used drugs have been tobacco, alcohol, marijuana, opium, cocaine, peyote—and, of course, tea and coffee. The reasons for taking such drugs vary: to alter consciousness, as part of a religious ritual, for recreation, or for psychological escape. But human beings are not the only species that likes to get high on occasion; so do many other animals. Baboons ingest tobacco, elephants love the alcohol in fermented fruit, and reindeer and rabbits seek out intoxicating mushrooms (Siegel, 1989).

In Western societies, a whole pharmacopia of recreational drugs exists, and each year seems to see the introduction of new ones, both natural and synthetic. Most of these drugs can be classified as *stimulants, depressants, opiates,* or *psychedelics,* depending on their effects on the central nervous system and their impact on behavior and mood (see Review 5.2). Here we describe only their physiological and psychological effects; Chapter 16 covers addiction, and Chapter 17 reviews drugs that are used in the treatment of mental and emotional disorders.

Live! **psych** 5.2

1 Stimulants *speed up activity in the central nervous system.* They include, among others drugs, nicotine, caffeine, cocaine, amphetamines ("uppers"), and methamphetamine hydrochloride ("crank," "speed"). In moderate amounts, stimulants produce feelings of excitement, confidence, and well-being or euphoria. In large amounts, they make a person anxious, jittery, and hyperalert. In very large doses, they may cause convulsions, heart failure, and death.

Amphetamines are synthetic drugs taken in pill form, injected, smoked, or inhaled ("snorted"). Cocaine ("coke") is a natural drug, derived from the leaves of the coca plant. Rural workers in Bolivia and Peru chew coca leaf every day, without apparent ill effects. In North America, the drug is usually inhaled, injected, or smoked in the highly refined form known as crack. These methods give the drug a more immediate, powerful, and dangerous effect than when coca leaf is chewed. Amphetamines and cocaine make users feel peppy but do not actually increase energy reserves. Fatigue, irritability, and depression may occur when the effects of these drugs wear off.

psychoactive drug A drug capable of influencing perception, mood, cognition, or behavior.

stimulants Drugs that speed up activity in the central nervous system.

REVIEW 5.2	SOME PSYCHOACTIVE DRUGS AND THEIR EFFECTS		
Class of Drug	**Type**	**Common Effects**	**Results of Abuse/Addiction**
Amphetamines	Stimulant	Wakefulness, alertness, raised metabolism, elevated mood	Nervousness, headaches, loss of appetite, high blood pressure, delusions, psychosis, heart damage, convulsions, death
Cocaine	Stimulant	Euphoria, excitation, boost of energy, suppressed appetite	Excitability, sleeplessness, sweating, paranoia, anxiety, panic, depression, heart damage, heart failure, injury to nose if sniffed
Tobacco (nicotine)	Stimulant	Varies from alertness to calmness, depending on mental set, setting, and prior arousal; decreases appetite for carbohydrates	*Nicotine:* heart disease, high blood pressure, impaired circulation, erectile problems in men *Tar:* lung cancer, emphysema, mouth and throat cancer, many other health risks
Caffeine	Stimulant	Wakefulness, alertness, shortened reaction time	Restlessness, insomnia, muscle tension, heartbeat irregularities, high blood pressure
Alcohol (1–2 drinks)	Depressant	Depends on setting and mental set; tends to act like a stimulant because it reduces inhibitions and anxiety	
Alcohol (several/ many drinks)	Depressant	Slowed reaction time, tension, depression, reduced ability to store new memories or to retrieve old ones, poor coordination	Blackouts, cirrhosis of the liver, other organ damage, mental and neurological impairment, psychosis, possibly death
Tranquilizers (e.g., Valium); barbiturates (e.g., phenobarbital)	Depressant	Reduced anxiety and tension, sedation	Increased dosage needed for effects; impaired motor and sensory functions, impaired permanent storage of new information, withdrawal symptoms; possibly convulsions, coma, death (especially when taken with other drugs)
Opium, heroin, morphine	Opiate	Euphoria, relief of pain	Loss of appetite, nausea, constipation, withdrawal symptoms, convulsions, coma, possibly death
LSD, psilocybin, mescaline	Psychedelic	Exhilaration, visions and hallucinations, insightful experiences	Psychosis, paranoia, panic reactions
Marijuana	Mild psychedelic (classification controversial)	Relaxation, euphoria, increased appetite, reduced ability to store new memories, other effects depending on mental set and setting	Throat and lung irritation, lung damage (if smoked), impaired immunity; long-term effects not well established

2 Depressants *slow down activity in the central nervous system.* They include alcohol, tranquilizers, barbiturates, and most of the common chemicals that some people inhale ("huffing"). Depressants usually make a person feel calm or drowsy, and they may reduce anxiety, guilt, tension, and inhibitions. In large amounts, they may produce insensitivity to pain and other sensations. Like stimulants, in very large doses they can cause irregular heartbeats, convulsions, and death.

People are often surprised to learn that alcohol is a central nervous system depressant. In small amounts, alcohol has some of the effects of a stimulant because it suppresses activity in parts of the brain that normally inhibit impulsive behavior, such as loud laughter and clowning around. In the long run, however, it slows down nervous-system activity. Like barbiturates and opiates, alcohol can be used as an anesthetic; if you drink enough, you will eventually pass out. Over time, alcohol damages the liver, heart, and brain. Extremely large amounts of alcohol can kill, by inhibiting the nerve cells in the brain areas that control breathing and heartbeat. Every so often the news reports the death of a college student who had large amounts of alcohol "funneled" into him as part of an initiation or competition.

On the other hand, *moderate* social drinking—a drink or two of wine or liquor a day—is associated with a variety of health benefits, including a reduction in the risk of heart attacks and dementia, and increased longevity (Gaziano & Hennekens, 1995; Gronbaek et al., 1995; Locher, Suter, & Vetter, 1998; Ruitenberg et al., 2002; Thun et al., 1997).

3 Opiates *relieve pain.* They include opium, derived from the opium poppy; morphine, a derivative of opium; heroin, a derivative of morphine; and synthetic drugs such as methadone. All of these drugs mimic the action of endorphins, and most have a powerful effect on the emotions. When injected, they may produce a rush—a sudden feeling of euphoria. They may also decrease anxiety and motivation, although the effects vary.

4 Psychedelic drugs *disrupt normal thought processes,* such as the perception of time and space. Sometimes, psychedelics produce hallucinations, especially visual ones. Some psychedelics, such as lysergic acid diethylamide (LSD), are made in the laboratory. Others, such as mescaline (from the peyote cactus), *Salvia divinorum* (a plant native to Mexico), and psilocybin (from certain species of mushrooms), are natural substances. Emotional reactions to psychedelics vary from person to person and from one time to another for any individual. A "trip" may be mildly pleasant or unpleasant, a mystical revelation or a nightmare.

Some commonly used drugs fall outside these four classifications, combine elements of more than one category, or have uncertain effects. For example, *anabolic steroids,* which are synthetic derivatives of testosterone that are taken in pill form or by injection, are often taken illegally by athletes and bodybuilders to increase muscle mass and strength. Steroids have been implicated in numerous physical problems in men, including heart and liver disease, decreased testicular size, and erection difficulties (Pope & Katz, 1992). Some people claim the drugs have positive psychological effects, such as increased sex drive, increased confidence, and reduced fatigue during training. Others report negative effects, such as increased aggressiveness, irritability, anxiety, and even psychosis. But because most studies have used questionable samples or have relied on unverified self-reports, no firm conclusions can yet be drawn about the psychological effects of these drugs.

Marijuana ("pot," "grass," "weed"), which is smoked or, less commonly, eaten in foods such as brownies, is probably the most widely used illicit drug in North America and Europe. Some researchers classify it as a mild psychedelic, but others feel that its chemical makeup and its psychological effects place it outside the major

depressants Drugs that slow down activity in the central nervous system.

opiates Drugs, derived from the opium poppy, that relieve pain and commonly produce euphoria.

psychedelic drugs Consciousness-altering drugs that produce hallucinations, change thought processes, or disrupt the normal perception of time and space.

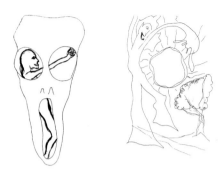

An LSD "trip" may be a ticket to agony or ecstasy. Both of these drawings were done under the influence of the drug.

classifications. The active ingredient in marijuana is tetrahydrocannabinol (THC), derived from the hemp plant, *Cannabis sativa*. In some respects, THC appears to be a mild stimulant, increasing heart rate and making tastes, sounds, and colors seem more intense. But users often report reactions ranging from mild euphoria to relaxation or even sleepiness.

In moderate doses, marijuana can interfere with the transfer of information to long-term memory, a characteristic it shares with alcohol. In large doses, it can cause hallucinations and a sense of unreality. Sometimes the drug impairs coordination, concentration, visual perception, and reaction times, though it is not clear how long these effects last. On the other hand, studies find that marijuana has some medical benefits, as we will see later when we discuss debates about legalizing drugs.

The Physiology of Drug Effects

Psychoactive drugs produce their effects primarily by acting on brain neurotransmitters, the substances that carry messages from one nerve cell to another. A drug may increase or decrease the release of neurotransmitters at the synapse; prevent the reabsorption of excess neurotransmitter molecules by the cells that have released them; block the effects of a neurotransmitter on a receiving nerve cell; or bind to receptors that would ordinarily be triggered by a neurotransmitter or a neuromodulator (see Chapter 4). Figure 5.4 shows how one drug, cocaine, increases the amount of norepinephrine and dopamine in the brain by blocking the reabsorption of these substances. Cocaine also seems to increase the transmission of serotonin (Rocha et al., 1998).

These biochemical changes affect cognitive and emotional functioning. For example, because of alcohol's effect on parts of the brain involved in judgment, drinkers often are unable to gauge their own competence. Just a couple of drinks can affect perception, response time, coordination, and balance, despite the drinker's own impression of unchanged or even improved performance. Liquor also affects memory, possibly by interfering with the work of serotonin. Information stored before a drinking session remains intact during the session but is retrieved more slowly (Haut et al., 1989). The ability to store new memories for

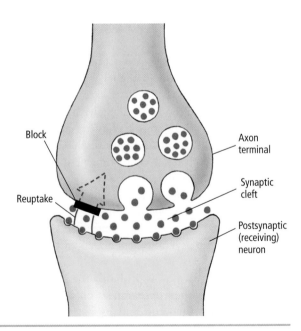

Figure 5.4
COCAINE'S EFFECT ON THE BRAIN

Cocaine blocks the brain's reabsorption ("reuptake") of the neurotransmitters dopamine and norepinephrine, so levels of these substances rise. The result is overstimulation of certain brain circuits and a brief euphoric high. Then, when the drug wears off, a depletion of dopamine may cause the user to "crash" and become sleepy and depressed.

later use also suffers after the consumption of only two or three drinks (Parker, Birnbaum, & Noble, 1976). Consuming small amounts does not seem to affect *sober* mental performance, but even occasional heavy drinking impairs later abstract thought. In other words, a Saturday night binge is potentially more dangerous than a daily drink.

As for other recreational drugs, there is no evidence that *light or moderate* use can damage the human brain enough to affect cognitive functioning, but all researchers agree that heavy or frequent use is another matter (see Chapter 16). Research with animals and humans suggests that repeated use of certain drugs, including "designer drugs" (easily synthesized variations of other drugs), can damage the brain and impair intellectual functioning. One recent study found that heavy users of methamphetamine had damage to dopamine cells and performed more poorly than other people on tests of memory, attention, and movement, even though they had not used the drug for at least 11 months (Volkow et al., 2001). Another recent study looked at the effects of Ecstasy (MDMA), a synthetic drug having properties of both a hallucinogen and a stimulant. Compared with nonusers, Ecstasy users showed memory deficits and reduced brain receptors for seratonin. The good news is that a subset of users who had abstained for at least a year did not have lasting damage to the serotonin receptors. The bad news is that these former users were still performing more poorly than nonusers on memory tests (Reneman et al., 2001).

The use of some psychoactive drugs, such as heroin and tranquilizers, can lead to **tolerance:** Over time, more and more of the drug is needed to get the same effect. When habitual heavy users stop taking a drug, they may suffer severe **withdrawal symptoms,** which, depending on the drug, may include nausea, abdominal cramps, sweating, muscle spasms, depression, and sleep problems.

The Psychology of Drug Effects

People often assume that the effects of a drug are automatic, the inevitable result of the drug's chemistry ("I couldn't help what I said—the booze made me do it"). But reactions to a psychoactive drug involve more than the drug's chemical properties. They also depend on a person's physical condition, experience with the drug, environmental setting, and mental set.

THINKING CRITICALLY

Consider Other Interpretations

One person takes a drink and flies into a rage. Another has a drink and "mellows out." What qualities of the user rather than the drug might account for this difference?

1 *Physical factors include body weight, metabolism, initial state of emotional arousal, and physical tolerance for the drug.* For example, women generally get drunker than men on the same amount of alcohol because women are smaller, on average, and their bodies metabolize alcohol differently (Fuchs et al., 1995). (Female alcoholics also seem to suffer more rapid and severe organ damage than male alcoholics.) Similarly, many Asians have a genetically determined adverse reaction to even small amounts of alcohol, which can cause severe headaches, facial flushing, and diarrhea (Cloninger, 1990). For individuals, a drug may have one effect after a tiring day and a different one after a rousing quarrel, or the effect may vary with the time of day because of the body's circadian rhythms.

2 *Experience with the drug refers to the number of times a person has used the drug.* Trying a drug—a cigarette, an alcoholic drink, a stimulant—for the first time is often a neutral or unpleasant experience. But reactions typically change once a person has become familiar with the drug's effects.

3 *Environmental setting greatly affects the response to a drug.* A person might have one glass of wine at home alone and feel sleepy but have three glasses of wine at a party and feel full of energy. Someone might feel happy and high

tolerance Increased resistance to a drug's effects accompanying continued use; as tolerance develops, larger doses are required to produce effects once brought about by smaller ones.

withdrawal symptoms Physical and psychological symptoms that occur when someone addicted to a drug stops taking it.

The motives for using a drug, expectations about its effects, and the setting in which it is used all contribute to a person's reactions to the drug.

drinking with good friends but fearful and nervous drinking with strangers. In one study of reactions to alcohol, most of the drinkers became depressed, angry, confused, and unfriendly. Then it dawned on the researchers that anyone might become depressed, angry, confused, and unfriendly if asked to drink bourbon at 9:00 A.M. in a bleak hospital room, which was the setting for the experiment (Warren & Raynes, 1972).

4 *Mental set refers to expectations about the drug's effects, as well as reasons for taking the drug.* Some people drink to become more sociable, friendly, or seductive; some drink to try to reduce feelings of anxiety or depression; and some drink in order to have an excuse for abusiveness or violence. Addicts use drugs to escape from the real world; people living with chronic pain use the same drugs in order to function in the real world (Portenoy, 1994). The motives for taking a drug greatly influence its effects.

Expectations can sometimes have a more powerful effect than the chemical properties of the drug itself. In one imaginative study, researchers compared people who were drinking liquor (vodka and tonic) with those who *thought* they were drinking liquor but were actually getting only tonic and lime juice. (Vodka has a subtle taste, and most people could not tell the real and phony drinks apart.) The experimenters found a *"think–drink" effect*: Men behaved more belligerently when they thought they were drinking vodka than when they thought they were drinking plain tonic water, *regardless of the actual content of the drinks*. And both sexes reported feeling sexually aroused when they thought they were drinking vodka, whether they actually got vodka or not (Abrams & Wilson, 1983; Marlatt & Rohsenow, 1980).

Expectations and beliefs about drugs are, in turn, shaped by the culture in which you live. Many people start their day with a cup of coffee because it increases alertness, but when coffee was first introduced in Europe, people protested against it. Women said it suppressed their husbands' sexual performance and made men inconsiderate—and maybe it did! In the nineteenth century, Americans regarded marijuana as a mild sedative with no mind-altering properties. They did not expect it to give them a high, and it didn't; it merely put them to sleep (Weil, 1972/1986). Today, motives for using marijuana have changed, and these changes have no doubt affected how people respond to it.

None of this means that alcohol and other drugs are merely placebos; drugs, as we have seen, do have physiological effects, many of them extremely potent. But an understanding of the psychological factors involved in drug use may help us think critically about the ongoing national debate about which drugs, if any, should be legal.

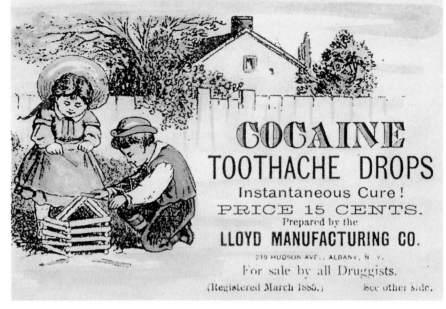

The Drug Debate

When a drug interferes with a person's functioning or disrupts the person's relationships with others, *use* turns into *abuse* (see Chapter 16). Because the consequences of drug abuse are so devastating to individuals and to society, people often have trouble thinking critically about drug laws and policies. At one extreme, some people cannot accept evidence that their favorite drug—be it coffee, tobacco, alcohol, or marijuana—might have harmful effects. At the other extreme, some cannot accept the evidence that their most hated drug—be it alcohol, morphine, marijuana, or the coca leaf—might not be dangerous in all forms or amounts and might even have some beneficial effects. Both sides often confuse potent drugs with others that have only subtle effects, and they also confuse light or moderate use of a drug with heavy or excessive use.

Once a drug is declared illegal, many people assume it is deadly, even though some legal drugs are more dangerous than illegal ones. Nicotine, which of course is legal, is as addictive as heroin and cocaine, which are illegal. Tobacco use contributes to more than 400,000 deaths in the United States every year, about 20 times the number of deaths from all other forms of drug use combined (McGinnis & Foege, 1993). Yet most people have a far more negative view of heroin and cocaine than of nicotine.

Emotions have run especially high in debates over marijuana. Heavy, prolonged use of marijuana poses some physical dangers, including lung damage and possibly a greatly increased risk of lung cancer when the drug is smoked (Barsky et al., 1998; Zhu et al., 2000). But marijuana also has some medical benefits: It reduces the nausea and vomiting that often accompany chemotherapy treatment for cancer and AIDS; it reduces the physical tremors, loss of appetite, and other symptoms caused by multiple sclerosis; it helps reduce the frequency of seizures in some patients with epilepsy; and it alleviates the retinal swelling caused by glaucoma (Grinspoon & Bakalar, 1993; Zimmer & Morgan, 1997). In the United States, voters in several states have approved the medical use of marijuana, yet the federal government has nonetheless continued its opposition to such use. In 1998, when a World Health Organization report concluded that marijuana, used in moderation, was safer than cigarettes and alcohol, United Nations officials suppressed the finding. In 1999, when a scientific panel commissioned

Cultural attitudes toward drugs vary with the times. Before it was banned in the United States in the 1920s, cocaine was widely touted as a cure for everything from toothaches to timidity. It was used in teas, tonics, throat lozenges, and even soft drinks (including, briefly, Coca-Cola, which derived its name from the coca plant). Similarly, until recent decades, cigarette smoking was promoted as healthy and glamorous.

THINKING CRITICALLY

Avoid Emotional Reasoning

In arguments over legalizing drugs, emotion runs so high that individuals and governments alike often fail to think rationally. What kinds of evidence should we consider when deciding whether to ban or permit certain drugs?

by the U.S. government called for scientific trials on marijuana's medical benefits, government officials either ignored or repudiated the recommendation.

Some people are committed to the eradication of all illegal drugs, and some think that all drugs should be decriminalized. Others would legalize narcotics for people who are in chronic pain and marijuana for recreational and medicinal use, but they would ban tobacco and most "hard drugs." Still others think that instead of punishing or incarcerating people who use drugs, society would be better off regulating where drugs are used (never at work, for example), providing treatment for addicts, and educating people about the benefits and hazards of drug use—the current approach to cigarette smoking.

Where, given the research findings, do you stand in the drug debate? Which psychoactive drugs, if any, should be legalized? Can we create mental sets and environmental settings that promote safe recreational use of some drugs, minimize the likelihood of drug abuse, and permit the medicinal use of beneficial drugs? What do you think?

QUICK QUIZ

There's no debate about whether or not you should take this quiz.

A. See whether you can name the following:
1. An illegal stimulant
2. Two drugs that interfere with the formation of new long-term memories
3. Three types of depressant drugs
4. A legal recreational drug that acts as a depressant on the central nervous system
5. Four factors that influence a person's psychological reactions to a drug

 B. A bodybuilder who has been taking anabolic steroids says the drugs make him more aggressive. What are some other possible interpretations?

Answers:

A. 1. cocaine; also some amphetamines 2. marijuana and alcohol 3. barbiturates, tranquilizers, and alcohol 4. alcohol 5. the person's physical condition, prior experience with the drug, mental set, and the environmental setting B. The bodybuilder's increased aggressiveness may be due to his expectations (a placebo effect); bodybuilding itself may increase aggressiveness; the culture of the bodybuilding gym may encourage aggressiveness; other influences in his life or other drugs he is taking may be making him more aggressive; or he may only think he is more aggressive, and his behavior may contradict his self-perceptions.

WHAT'S AHEAD

- **Can a hypnotist force you to do things against your will?**
- **Can hypnosis help you remember the past more accurately?**
- **What are the legitimate uses of hypnosis in psychology and medicine?**
- **Are hypnotized persons merely faking or playacting?**

The Riddle of Hypnosis

For many years now, stage hypnotists, "past-lives channelers," and some psychotherapists have been reporting that they can "age regress" hypnotized people to earlier years or even earlier centuries. Some therapists claim that hypnosis helps their patients accurately retrieve long-buried memories, and a few even claim that hypnosis has helped their patients recall alleged abductions by extraterrestrials. What are we to make of all this?

Hypnosis is a procedure in which a practitioner suggests changes in the sensations, perceptions, thoughts, feelings, or behavior of the subject (Kirsch & Lynn, 1995). The subject, in turn, tries to alter his or her cognitive processes in accordance with the hypnotist's suggestions (Nash & Nadon, 1997). Hypnotic suggestions typically involve performance of an action ("Your arm will slowly rise"), an inability to perform an act ("You will be unable to bend your arm"), or a distortion of normal perception or memory ("You will feel no pain," "You will forget being hypnotized until I give you a signal"). People usually report that their compliance with these suggestions feels involuntary.

To induce hypnosis, the hypnotist typically suggests that the person being hypnotized feels relaxed, is getting sleepy, and feels the eyelids getting heavier and heavier. In a singsong or monotonous voice, the hypnotist assures the subject that he or she is sinking "deeper and deeper." Sometimes the hypnotist has the person concentrate on a color or a small object, or on certain bodily sensations. People who have been hypnotized report that the focus of attention turns outward, toward the hypnotist's voice. They sometimes compare the experience to being totally absorbed in a good book, play, or favorite piece of music.

Because hypnosis has been used for everything from parlor tricks and stage shows to medical and psychological treatments, it is important to understand just what this procedure can and cannot achieve. We will begin with a general look at the findings on hypnosis; then we will consider two leading explanations of these findings.

The Nature of Hypnosis

Since the late 1960s, thousands of articles on hypnosis have appeared. Based on controlled laboratory and clinical research studies, most researchers agree on the following points (Kirsch & Lynn, 1995; Nash, 2001; Nash & Nadon, 1997).

1 *The hypnotic state is not sleep.* Whereas sleep is associated with predictable changes in brain waves and other physiological responses, comparable changes during hypnosis have not been reliably identified. The hypnotized person almost always remains fully aware of what is going on and remembers the experience later, unless explicitly instructed to forget it. Even then, the memory can be restored by a prearranged signal.

2 *Hypnotic responsiveness depends more on the efforts and qualities of the person being hypnotized than on the skill of the hypnotist.* Some people are more responsive to hypnosis than others, and this responsiveness is stable over time. Surprisingly, however, hypnotic susceptibility is unrelated to general personality traits such as gullibility, trust, submissiveness, or conformity (Nash & Nadon, 1997). People who are easily hypnotized do tend to have the ability to become easily absorbed in their activities and involved in the world of imagination, but this ability is only weakly related to hypnotic susceptibility (Council, Kirsch, & Grant, 1996; Nash & Nadon, 1997).

3 *Hypnotized people cannot be forced to do things against their will.* Like psychoactive drugs, hypnosis can be used to justify letting go of inhibitions ("I know this looks silly, but after

hypnosis A procedure in which the practitioner suggests changes in the sensations, perceptions, thoughts, feelings, or behavior of the subject.

Amazing, right? Or maybe not. This stage hypnotist's audience believes that the man he is standing on can support his weight without flinching because he's hypnotized, but most unhypnotized people can do the same thing. The only way to find out whether hypnosis produces unique results is to do research with control groups.

"THE WITNESS HAS BARKED, MEOWED AND GIVEN US FIVE MINUTES OF BABY TALK. I'D SAY HYPNOSIS IS NOT THE ANSWER."

all, I'm hypnotized"). Hypnotized individuals may even comply with a suggestion to do something that looks embarrassing or dangerous. But the individual is choosing to turn responsibility over to the hypnotist and to cooperate with the hypnotist's suggestions (Lynn, Rhue, & Weekes, 1990). There is no evidence that hypnotized people will do anything that actually goes against their morals or that constitutes a real danger to themselves or others (Laurence & Perry, 1988).

4 *Feats performed under hypnosis can be performed by motived people without hypnosis.* Hypnotic suggestions sometimes lead to feats of great strength or other seemingly surprising abilities, but hypnosis does not enable people to transcend their normal physical and mental capacities. Suggestion alone, without the special procedures of hypnosis, can produce the same results as long as people are motivated, believe they can succeed, and are encouraged to relax, concentrate, and do their best (e.g., Chaves, 1989; Spanos, Stenstrom, & Johnson, 1988).

5 *Hypnosis does not increase the accuracy of memory.* Many people assume that hypnosis can enhance the recall of forgotten experiences. Sometimes hypnosis *can* be used successfully to jog the memories of crime victims. After the 1976 kidnapping of a busload of schoolchildren in Chowchilla, California, a breakthrough in the case occurred when the bus driver, under hypnosis, was able to recall all but one of the license-plate numbers on the kidnappers' car. But in other cases, hypnotized witnesses have been completely mistaken. Although hypnosis does sometimes boost the amount of information recalled, it also increases *errors,* perhaps because hypnotized people are more willing than others to guess, or because they mistake vividly imagined possibilities for actual memories (Dinges et al., 1992; Kihlstrom, 1994). When the questioning is over, the hypnotized person is often completely convinced that his or her "memories" are true, but they are wrong (Whitehouse et al., 1988). Because pseudomemories and errors are so common in hypnotically induced recall, the American Psychological Association and the American Medical Association oppose the use of "hypnotically refreshed" testimony in courts of law.

6 *Hypnosis does not produce a literal reexperiencing of long-ago events.* When Michael Yapko (1994), a clinical psychologist who uses hypnosis in his own practice, surveyed 869 members of the American Association of Marriage and Family Therapists, he discovered that more than half believed that "hypnosis can be used to recover memories from as far back as birth." This belief is just dead wrong. When people are regressed to an earlier age, their mental and moral performance remains adultlike (Nash, 1987). Their brain-wave patterns and reflexes do not become childish; they do not reason as children do or show child-sized IQs. They may use baby talk or report that they feel 4 years old again, but the reason is not that they *are* 4; they are just willing to play the role. They will do the same when they are hypnotically *progressed* ahead—say, to age 70 or 80—or regressed to "past lives." Their belief that they are 7 or 70 or 7,000 years old may be sincere and convincing, but it is based on elaborate fantasy and role-playing.

7 *Hypnotic suggestions have been used effectively for many medical and psychological purposes.* Although hypnosis is not of much use for finding out what happened in the past, it can be useful in the treatment of psychological and medical problems. Hypnotic suggestions have been used to reduce stress, anxiety, and severe pain; anesthetize people undergoing dental work, surgery, or childbirth; eliminate unwanted habits such as smoking or nail biting; improve study skills; reduce nausea in cancer patients undergoing chemotherapy; and boost the confidence of athletes (Kirsch, Montgomery, & Sapirstein, 1995; Stam, 1989).

Theories of Hypnosis

Over the years, people have proposed many explanations of what hypnosis is and how it produces its effects. One early notion, that hypnosis is a "trance state," was eventually rejected by most researchers. Today, two competing theories predominate, with most scientists taking a position somewhere in the middle.

Dissociation Theories. One leading approach was originally proposed by the late Ernest Hilgard (1977, 1986), who argued that hypnosis, like lucid dreaming and even simple distraction, involves **dissociation**, a split in consciousness in which one part of the mind operates independently of the rest of consciousness. In many hypnotized persons, said Hilgard, while most of the mind is subject to hypnotic suggestion, one part is a *hidden observer,* watching but not participating. Unless given special instructions, the hypnotized person remains unaware of the observer.

In his research, Hilgard attempted to question the hidden observer directly. In one procedure, hypnotized volunteers had to submerge an arm in ice water for several seconds, an experience that is normally excruciating. They were told that they would feel no pain, but that the nonsubmerged hand would be able to signal the level of any hidden pain by pressing a key. In this situation, many people said they felt little or no pain—yet at the same time, their free hand was busily pressing the key. After the session, these people continued to insist that they had been pain-free, unless the hypnotist asked the hidden observer to issue a separate report.

A related theory holds that during hypnosis, dissociation occurs between an executive-control system in the brain (probably in the frontal lobes) and other brain systems that are involved in thinking and acting (Woody & Bowers, 1994). The result is an altered state of consciousness similar to that found in patients with frontal lobe disorders. Because the dissociated systems are freed from control by the executive, they are more easily influenced by suggestions from the hypnotist.

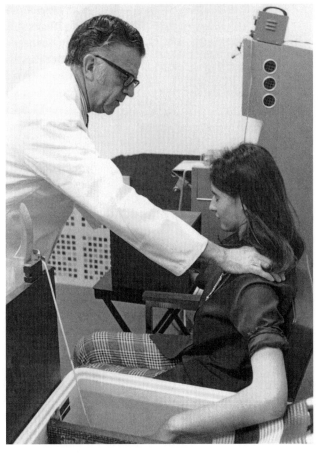

A person whose arm is immersed in ice water ordinarily feels intense pain. But Ernest Hilgard, a pioneer in hypnosis research, found that when hypnotized people are told the pain will be minimal, they report little or no discomfort. Like the young woman shown here in one of Hilgard's studies, they seem unperturbed.

DISSOCIATION THEORIES OF HYPNOSIS

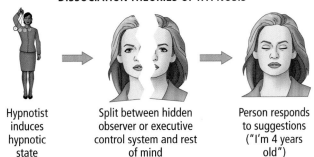

Hypnotist induces hypnotic state → Split between hidden observer or executive control system and rest of mind → Person responds to suggestions ("I'm 4 years old")

Explanations based on dissociation fit in well with findings on nonconscious mental processing (see Chapters 9 and 10). They are also consistent with modern brain theories, which propose that one part of the brain operates as an interpreter and reporter of activities carried out unconsciously by other brain parts. Nevertheless,

dissociation A split in consciousness in which one part of the mind operates independently of others.

many psychologists believe that there is less to dissociation and the hypnotic state than meets the eye. Some flat-out reject the idea that hypnosis differs from normal consciousness. They point out that when a hypnotist suggests that a person hold an arm out rigidly and the person does so, all this really tells us is that the person is suggestible and willing to go along (Barber, 1979; Weitzenhoffer, 1996). Moreover, the definition of a hypnotized "state" is circular: How do you know when people are in that state? Because they go along with the suggestions. And why do they go along? Because they are in a hypnotic state!

The Sociocognitive Approach. The second major approach to hypnosis, the *sociocognitive explanation,* holds that the effects of hypnosis result from an interaction between the social influence of the hypnotist (the "socio" part) and the abilities, beliefs, and expectations of the subject (the "cognitive" part) (Kirsch, 1997; Sarbin, 1991; Spanos, 1991). The hypnotized person is basically playing a role, one that has analogies in ordinary life, where we willingly submit to the suggestions of parents, teachers, doctors, therapists, and television commercials. Even the "hidden observer" is simply a reaction to the social demands of the situation and the suggestions of the hypnotist (Kirsch & Lynn, 1998).

The hypnotized person is not merely faking or play-acting, however. A person who has been instructed to fool an observer by faking a hypnotic state will tend to overplay the role and will stop playing it as soon as the observer leaves the room. In contrast, hypnotized subjects continue to follow the hypnotic suggestions even when they think they are not being watched (Kirsch et al., 1989; Spanos et al., 1993). Like many social roles, the role of hypnotized person is so engrossing and involving that actions required by the role may occur without the person's conscious intent.

Sociocognitive views explain why some people under hypnosis report spirit possession or "memories" of alien abductions (Baker, 1992; Spanos, 1996). Such persons may have a need to "escape the self" by turning control over to someone else (Newman & Baumeister, 1996). Often, the hypnotist readily assumes such control, shaping the person's story by giving subtle and not-so-subtle hints about what the person should say. Here is an exchange between one therapist who believes in UFO abductions and a supposed abductee who has been hypnotized (quoted in Newman & Baumeister, 1996):

SOCIOCOGNITIVE THEORIES OF HYPNOSIS

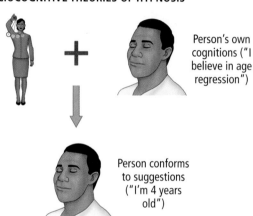

Social influence of hypnotist ("You're going back in time")

Person's own cognitions ("I believe in age regression")

Person conforms to suggestions ("I'm 4 years old")

> *Dr. Fiore:* Now I'm going to ask you a few questions at this point. You will remember everything because you want to remember. When you were being poked everywhere, did they do any kind of vaginal examination?
>
> *Sandi:* I don't think they did.
>
> *Dr. Fiore:* Now you're going to let yourself know if they put a needle in any part of your body, other than the rectum.
>
> *Sandi:* No. They were carrying needles around, big ones, and I was scared for a while they were going to put one in me, but they didn't. *[Body tenses.]*
>
> *Dr. Fiore:* Now just let yourself relax. At the count of three you're going to remember whether they did put one of those big needles in you. If they did, know that you're safe, and it's all over, isn't it? And if they didn't, you're going to remember that too, at the count of three. One . . . two . . . three.
>
> *Sandi:* They did.

The sociocognitive view can also explain apparent cases of past-life regression. In a fascinating program of research, Nicholas Spanos and his colleagues directed hypnotized Canadian university students to regress past their own births to previous lives. About a third of the students reported being able to do so. But when they were asked, while supposedly reliving a past life, to name the leader of their country, say whether the country was at peace or at war, or describe the money used in their community, the students could not do it. (One young man, who thought he was Julius Caesar, said the year was 50 A.D. and he was emperor of Rome. But Caesar died in 44 B.C. and was never crowned emperor, and dating years as A.D. or B.C. did not begin until several centuries later.) Instead, the students tried to fulfill the requirements of the role by weaving events, places, and persons from their present lives into their accounts, and by picking up cues from the experimenter. The researchers concluded that the act of "remembering" another "self" involves the construction of a fantasy that accords with the rememberer's own beliefs and also the beliefs of others—in this case, the authoritative hypnotist (Spanos, Menary, et al., 1991).

Psychologists who think hypnosis is a special state of consciousness involving dissociation and those who emphasize sociocognitive explanations agree on many issues. They agree, for example, that hypnosis does *not* create a unique state in which people can do extraordinary things, memories become sharper, or early experiences can be replayed with perfect accuracy. And many psychologists feel that both approaches have something to offer (Kihlstrom, 1998; Woody & Sadler, 1998). Whatever hypnosis is, psychologists who study it are learning much about human suggestibility, the power of imagination, and the way we perceive the present and remember the past.

> **THINKING CRITICALLY**
>
> **Consider Other Interpretations**
>
> Under hypnosis, Jim describes the chocolate cake at his fourth birthday and Joan remembers a former life as a twelfth-century French peasant. But lemon cake was served at Jim's party and Joan can't speak twelfth-century French. What explanation best accounts for these vivid but incorrect memories?

QUICK QUIZ

We'd like to plant a suggestion in your mind—that you'd be wise to take this quiz.

A. *True or false:*

1. A hypnotized person is usually aware of what is going on and remembers the experience later.

2. Hypnosis gives us special powers that we do not ordinarily have.

3. Hypnosis reduces errors in memory.

4. Hypnotized people play no active part in their behavior and thoughts.

5. According to Hilgard, hypnosis is a state of consciousness involving a "hidden observer."

6. Sociocognitive theorists view hypnosis as mere faking or conscious playacting.

B. Some people believe that hypnotic suggestions can bolster the immune system and help a person fight disease. However, support for this belief has so far been modest, and many studies have had methodological flaws (Miller & Cohen, 2001). One therapist dismissed these concerns by saying that a negative result just means that the hypnotist lacks skill or the right personality. As a critical thinker, can you spot what is wrong with his reasoning? (Think back to the qualities of the ideal scientist, discussed in Chapter 2.)

Answers:

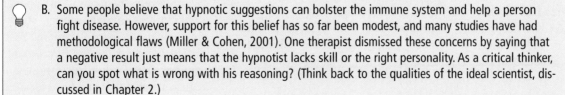

A. 1. true 2. false 3. false 4. false 5. true 6. false B. The therapist's argument violates the principle of falsifiability. If a result is positive, he counts it as evidence. But if a result is negative, he refuses to count it as counterevidence ("Maybe the hypnotist just wasn't good enough."). With this kind of reasoning, there is no way to tell whether the hypothesis is right or wrong.

As we have seen in this chapter, fluctuations and changes in consciousness, though interesting in and of themselves, also show us how people's expectations and explanations of their own mental and physical states affect what they do and how they feel. Controversy still exists about some basic issues: the prevalence of "SAD" and "PMS," the purpose of sleep, the meaning of dreams, the dangers and benefits of drugs, the best explanation of hypnosis. But the scientific scrutiny of biological rhythms, dreams, drug-induced states, and hypnotic suggestion—phenomena once thought beyond the pale of science—can deepen our understanding of the intimate relationship between body and mind.

Taking Psychology with You

HOW TO GET A GOOD NIGHT'S SLEEP

You hop into bed, turn out the lights, close your eyes, and wait for slumber. An hour later, you're still waiting. Finally you drop off, but at 3:00 A.M., to your chagrin, you're awake again. By the time the rooster crows, you have put in a hard day's night.

Insomnia affects most people at one time or another, and many people most of the time. No wonder that sleeping pills are a multimillion-dollar business. Yet most over-the-counter pills are of little use for inducing sleep, and some prescription drugs can actually make matters worse. Barbiturates greatly suppress REM sleep, a result that eventually causes wakefulness, and they also suppress Stages 3 and 4, the deeper stages of sleep. Melatonin supplements help some people, but no one knows what dosages are safe and effective, and the optimal time for taking it depends on your individual circadian cycles. Most physicians prescribe sleeping remedies for only short periods of time. Sleep research suggests some better alternatives:

▶ *Be sure you actually have a sleep problem.* Many people only *think* they don't sleep well. They overestimate how long it takes them to doze off and underestimate how much sleep they are getting. When they are observed in the laboratory, they usually fall asleep in less than 30 minutes and are awake for only very short periods during the night (Bonnet, 1990; Carskadon, Mitler, & Dement, 1974).

The amount of time spent sleeping is not a good criterion of insomnia in any case. As we saw in this chapter, most people need at least the standard eight hours of sleep. Some people, however, get by well on much less. As people age, they typically sleep more lightly, and they often break up sleep into nighttime slumber and an afternoon nap. Young people, too, can benefit from napping, which many researchers feel is biologically beneficial. The real test for diagnosing a sleep deficit is how you feel during the day. Do you doze off without intending to? Do you feel drowsy at meetings or in class? If you function well with less sleep than most people get, you probably shouldn't worry, since worrying itself can cause insomnia.

▶ *Get a correct diagnosis of the sleep problem.* Do you suffer from sleep apnea (see p. 152)? Do you have a physical disorder that is interfering with sleep? Do you live in a noisy place? (Try earplugs!) Are you fighting your personal biological rhythms by going to bed too early or too late? Do you go to bed early one night and late another? It's better to go to bed at about the same time every night and get up at the same time every morning.

▶ *Avoid excessive use of alcohol or other drugs.* Many drugs interfere with sleep. For instance, coffee, tea, cola, "energy drinks," and chocolate all contain caffeine, which is a stimulant; alcohol suppresses REM sleep; and tranquilizers such as Valium and Librium reduce Stage 4 sleep.

▶ *Don't associate the bedroom with wakefulness.* When environmental cues are repeatedly associated with some behavior, they can come to trigger the behavior. If you don't want your bedroom to trigger wakefulness, avoid reading, studying, and watching TV there. Also avoid lying awake for hours waiting for sleep; your frustration will cause arousal that can be associated with the bedroom. If you can't sleep, get up and do something else, preferably something dull and relaxing, in another room. When you feel drowsy, try sleeping again.

▶ *Take care of your health.* As your grandmother may have told you, good health habits are important for good sleep. Nutrition is one area to watch. The amino acid tryptophan promotes the onset of sleep, and other dietary elements may also influence alertness and relaxation. Exercise during the day also enhances sleep, but it should be avoided right before bedtime because in the short term it heightens alertness.

Finally, when insomnia is related to anxiety and worry, it makes sense to get to the source of your problems. Woody Allen once said, "The lamb and the lion shall lie down together, but the lamb will not be very sleepy." Like a lamb trying to sleep with a lion, you cannot expect to sleep well with stress hormones pouring through your bloodstream and worries crowding your mind. In an evolutionary sense, sleeplessness is an adaptive response to danger and threat. When your anxieties decrease, so may your sleepless nights.

Summary

Biological Rhythyms: The Tides of Experience

▶ *Consciousness* is the awareness of oneself and the environment. Changing states of consciousness are often associated with *biological rhythms*—periodic fluctuations in physiological functioning. These rhythms are typically *entrained* (synchronized) to external cues, but many are also *endogenous,* generated from within. *Circadian* fluctuations occur about once a day; *infradian* rhythms are longer; and *ultradian* rhythms are shorter, often occurring on about a 90-minute cycle.

▶ When people live in isolation from all time cues, they tend to live a day that is just slightly longer than 24 hours. Circadian rhythms are governed by a biological "clock" in the *suprachiasmatic nucleus (SCN)* of the hypothalamus. The SCN regulates, and in turn is affected by, the hormone *melatonin,* which is responsive to changes in light and dark, and which increases during the dark hours. When a person's normal routine changes, the person may experience *internal desynchronization,* in which the usual circadian rhythms are thrown out of phase with one another. The result may be fatigue, mental inefficiency, and an increased risk of accidents.

▶ Folklore holds that moods follow infradian cycles. Some people do show a recurrence of depression every winter, in a pattern that has been labeled *seasonal affective disorder (SAD),* but serious seasonal depression is rare. The causes of SAD are not yet clear. It has been difficult to rule out placebo effects in the most common treatment, phototherapy, but recent research suggests that light treatments can be effective.

▶ Another infradian rhythm is the menstrual cycle, during which various hormones rise and fall. Well controlled double-blind studies on "PMS" do not support claims that emotional symptoms are reliably and universally tied to the menstrual cycle. Overall, women and men do not differ in the emotional symptoms they report or in the number of mood swings they experience over the course of a month. Testosterone fluctuates in men, and high levels have been linked to various behaviors and moods, but no one has suggested that these behaviors and moods constitute a psychological syndrome. Expectations and learning affect how both sexes interpret bodily and emotional changes. Few people of either sex are likely to undergo dramatic monthly mood swings or personality changes because of hormones.

The Rhythms of Sleep

▶ Sleep, which recurs on a circadian rhythm, is necessary not only for bodily restoration but also for normal mental functioning. Many people get less than the optimal amount of sleep. Some suffer from insomnia, *sleep apnea,* or *narcolepsy.*

▶ During sleep, periods of *rapid eye movement,* or *REM,* alternate with non-REM sleep in an ultradian rhythm. *Non-REM sleep* is divided into four stages on the basis of characteristic brain-wave patterns. During REM sleep, the brain is active, and there are other signs of arousal, yet most of the skeletal muscles are limp; vivid dreams are reported most often during REM sleep.

Exploring the Dream World

▶ Dreams are often recalled as illogical and bizarre. Some people say they have *lucid dreams,* in which they know they are dreaming. Researchers disagree about whether the eye movements of REM sleep are related to events and actions in dreams.

▶ The psychoanalytic explanation of dreams is that they allow us to gratify forbidden or unrealistic wishes and desires that have been forced into the unconscious part of the mind. In dreams, according to Freud, thoughts and objects are disguised as symbolic images. Most psychologists today accept the notion that dreams are more than incoherent ramblings of the mind, but many psychologists quarrel with psychoanalytic interpretations.

▶ Another approach holds that dreams express current concerns or help us solve current problems by working through emotional issues, especially during times of crisis. Findings on recurrent and traumatic dreams, gender differences in dreams, and the dreams of divorced people support this *problem-focused explanation.*

▶ A third view holds that dreams are the by-product of *mental housekeeping.* According to this information-processing approach, dreams are merely random snippets from an ongoing process during which the brain scans and sort through new data, or unneeded synaptic associations in the brain are weakened. REM sleep has also been associated with the consolidation of memories, during which the synaptic changes associated with a recently stored memory become durable and stable. However, this approach seems to tell us more about REM sleep than about dreams per se.

▶ The *activation–synthesis theory* of dreaming holds that dreams occur when the cortex tries to make sense of spontaneous neural firing initiated in the pons. The dream is the resulting interpretation, or synthesis, of the signals with existing knowledge and memories. In this view, dreams do not disguise unconscious wishes, but they can reveal a person's perceptions, conflicts, and concerns.

Consciousness-altering Drugs

▶ In all cultures, people have found ways to produce *altered states of consciousness.* For example, *psychoactive drugs* alter cognition and emotion by acting on neurotransmitters in the brain. Most psychoactive drugs are classified as *stimulants, depressants, opiates,* or *psychedelics,* depending on their central nervous system effects and their impact on behavior and mood. However, some common drugs, such as Ecstasy (MDMA), anabolic steroids, and marijuana, fall outside these categories. When used regularly, some drugs

damage neurons in the brain and have a negative effect on learning or memory. The use of some psychoactive drugs leads to *tolerance,* in which increasing dosages are needed for the same effect, and *withdrawal symptoms* if an addict tries to quit.

▶ Reactions to a psychoactive drug are influenced not only by its chemical properties but also by the user's physical condition, prior experience with the drug, environmental setting, and *mental set*—the person's expectations and motives for taking the drug. Expectations can be even more powerful than the drug itself, as shown by the *"think–drink" effect.* Expectations and beliefs about drugs are in turn affected by a person's culture. People often find it difficult to distinguish abuse from use and to think critically about research findings on drug effects.

The Riddle of Hypnosis

▶ *Hypnosis* is a procedure in which the practitioner suggests changes in the sensations, perceptions, thoughts, feelings, or behavior of a subject, and the subject tries to comply. Although hypnosis has been used successfully for many medical and psychological purposes, it does not produce special abilities. Hypnosis can sometimes improve memory for facts about real events, but it also results in confusion between facts and vividly imagined possibilities. Therefore, "hypnotically refreshed" accounts are often full of errors and pseudomemories.

▶ A leading explanation of hypnosis and its effects is that hypnosis involves *dissociation,* a split in consciousness. In one version of this approach, the split is between a part of consciousness that is hypnotized and a *hidden observer* that watches but does not participate. In another version, the split is between an executive-control system in the brain and other brain systems responsible for thinking and acting.

▶ Another leading approach, the *sociocognitive explanation,* regards hypnosis as a product of normal social and cognitive processes. In this view, hypnosis is a form of role-playing in which the hypnotized person uses active cognitive strategies, including imagination, to comply with the hypnotist's suggestions. The role is so engrossing that the person interprets it as real. Sociocognitive processes can account for the apparent age and past-life "regressions" of people under hypnosis and their reports of alien abductions; these individuals are simply playing a role based on fantasy, imagination, and suggestion.

Key Terms

consciousness 141

biological rhythm 142

entrainment 142

endogenous 142

circadian rhythm 142

infradian rhythm 142

ultradian rhythm 143

suprachiasmatic nucleus (SCN) 144

melatonin 144

internal desynchronization 144

seasonal affective disorder (SAD) 146

"premenstrual syndrome" ("PMS") 147

sleep apnea 152

narcolepsy 152

rapid eye movement (REM) sleep 153

non-REM sleep 153

alpha waves 153

sleep spindles 154

delta waves 154

lucid dream 156

psychoanalytic theory of dreams 156

manifest versus latent content of dreams 156

problem-focused approach to dreams 157

mental-housekeeping approach to dreams 158

activation–synthesis theory of dreams 160

altered states of consciousness 162

psychoactive drug 163

stimulants 163

depressants 164

opiates 164

psychedelic drugs 164

anabolic steroids 164

marijuana 164

tolerance 167

withdrawal symptoms 167

"think–drink" effect 168

hypnosis 171

dissociation 173

hidden observer 173

sociocognitive explanation of hypnosis 174

◀LOOKING BACK

- Do popular "biorhythm charts" tell you anything about what scientists call biological rhythms? (p. 142)

- Why do you feel "out of sync" when you fly across time zones or change shifts at work? (pp. 144–145)

- How are researchers learning to reset the biological clock that governs our daily cycles? (p. 145)

- Does "PMS" cause most women to feel depressed or irritable before their periods? (pp. 147–149)

- Why do we sleep? (p. 151)

- What happens when we go too long without enough sleep? (pp. 151–152)

- Why are you likely to be dreaming when the alarm goes off in the morning? (p. 154)

- Why did Freud call dreams the "royal road to the unconscious"? (p. 156)

- How might dreams be related to your current problems and concerns? (pp. 157–158)

- How does a disruption of REM sleep affect memory? (p. 159)

- Could dreams be caused by meaningless brain-stem signals? (pp. 160–161)

- In its physiological effects, is alcohol a "downer" or an "upper"? (p. 165)

- How do recreational drugs affect the brain? (pp. 166–167)

- Why can a glass of wine make you feel tired at one time but sociable and pepped up at another? (p. 168)

- Can a hypnotist force you to do things against your will? (pp. 171–172)

- Can hypnosis help you remember the past more accurately? (p. 172)

- What are the legitimate uses of hypnosis in psychology and medicine? (p. 172)

- Are hypnotized persons merely faking or playacting? (p. 174)

Go to  **WWW.PRENHALL.COM** to reinforce these key concepts, and more.

5.1   The stages of sleep and their corresponding brain-wave patterns.
5.2   Psychoactive drugs and their effects.

6

Sensation and Perception

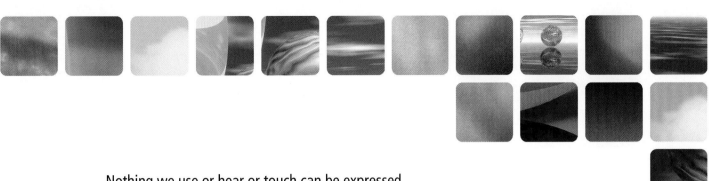

> Nothing we use or hear or touch can be expressed
> in words that equal what is given by the senses.

HANNAH ARENDT

What do you think might be going on here?

▶ A college student in Missouri reports spotting three triangular "UFOs" hovering over the highway during rush hour. Although she never put much stock in UFO stories before, she says, now she is "intrigued."

▶ An image of Jesus on a garage door draws huge crowds of people who regard the likeness with reverence. A similar image makes the news when a woman claims she sees the face of Jesus in, of all places, a tortilla.

▶ A photograph of an area on Mars, taken by a Viking 1 spacecraft, captures national attention because a mesa in the photo bears a striking resemblance to a human face. Some people maintain that the "face on Mars" is a monument constructed by an extinct Martian civilization or by beings from elsewhere in the galaxy.

▶ A photograph published shortly after the events of September 11, 2001, is widely circulated on the Internet. It appears to show a sinister face, which some people interpret as Satan's and others as Osama bin Laden's, in smoke billowing from the doomed World Trade Center.

We have all heard reports like these. Some of us scoff at them; others take them seriously. Are UFOs, visions of faces in everyday objects, and other strange sightings reported only by people who are silly or gullible, or do smart, savvy people also see alien aircraft over highways and religious figures in tortillas? If such experiences are illusions, then why are they so frequent and so detailed, and why are those who have them so confident that what they saw was real?

In this chapter, we will try to answer these questions by exploring how our sense organs take in information from the environment and how the brain uses this information to construct a model of the world. We will focus on two closely connected sets of processes that enable us to know what is happening both inside our bodies and in the world beyond our own skins. The first, **sensation,** is the detection of physical energy emitted or reflected by physical objects. The cells that do the detecting are located in the *sense organs*—the eyes, ears, tongue, nose, skin, and internal body tissues. Sensory processes produce an immediate awareness of sound, color, form, and other building blocks of consciousness. Without sensation, we would lose touch—literally—with reality. But to make sense of the world impinging on our senses, we

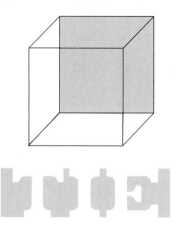

If you stare at the cube, the surface on the outside and front will suddenly be on the inside and back or vice versa, because your brain can interpret the sensory image in two different ways. The purple and white drawing can also be perceived in two ways, one involving a word. Do you see it?

also need **perception**, a set of mental operations that organize sensory impulses into meaningful patterns. Our sense of vision produces a two-dimensional image on the back of the eye, but we *perceive* the world in three dimensions. Our sense of hearing brings us the sound of a C, an E, and a G played simultaneously on the piano, but we *perceive* a C-major chord. Sometimes, a single sensory image produces two alternating perceptions, as illustrated by the examples in the margin.

Sensation and perception are the foundation of learning, thinking, and acting. Findings on these processes can often be put to practical use—for example, in the design of hearing aids and industrial robots and in the training of flight controllers, astronauts, and other people who must make crucial decisions based on what they sense and perceive. An understanding of sensation and perception can also help all of us think more critically about our own experiences. Our sensory and perceptual processes are usually astonishingly accurate—but occasionally they are not. As you read this chapter, ask yourself why people sometimes perceive things that are not there and, conversely, why they sometimes miss things that *are* there—looking without seeing, listening without hearing.

WHAT'S AHEAD ▷

- What kind of "code" in the nervous system helps explain why a pinprick and a kiss feel different?
- Why does your dog hear a "silent" doggie whistle when you can't?
- What kind of bias can influence whether you think you hear the phone ringing when you're in the shower?
- What happens when people are deprived of all external sensory stimulation?

Our Sensational Senses

At some point you probably learned that there are five senses, corresponding to five sense organs: vision (eyes), hearing (ears), taste (tongue), touch (skin), and smell (nose). Actually, there are more than five senses, though scientists disagree about the exact number. The skin, which is the organ of touch or pressure, also senses heat, cold, and pain, not to mention itching and tickling. The ear, which is the organ of hearing, also contains receptors that account for a sense of balance. The skeletal muscles contain receptors responsible for a sense of bodily movement.

All of our senses evolved to help us survive. Even pain, which causes so much human misery, is an indispensable part of our evolutionary heritage, for it alerts us to illness and injury. People who are born with a rare condition that prevents them from feeling the usual hurts and aches of life are susceptible to burns, bruises, and cuts, and they often die at an early age because they can't take advantage of pain's warning signals.

Sensory experiences contribute immeasurably to our quality of life, even when they are not directly helping us stay alive. They entertain us, amuse us, soothe us, inspire us. If we really pay attention to our senses, said poet William Wordsworth, we can "see into the life of things" and hear "the still, sad music of humanity."

The Riddle of Separate Sensations

Sensation begins with the **sense receptors**, cells located in the sense organs. The receptors for smell, pressure, pain, and temperature are extensions (dendrites) of sensory

sensation The detection of physical energy emitted or reflected by physical objects; it occurs when energy in the external environment or the body stimulates receptors in the sense organs.

perception The process by which the brain organizes and interprets sensory information.

sense receptors Specialized cells that convert physical energy in the environment or the body to electrical energy that can be transmitted as nerve impulses to the brain.

neurons (see Chapter 4). The receptors for vision, hearing, and taste are specialized cells separated from sensory neurons by synapses.

When the sense receptors detect an appropriate stimulus—light, mechanical pressure, or chemical molecules—they convert the energy of the stimulus into electrical impulses that travel along nerves to the brain. Sense receptors are like military scouts who scan the terrain for signs of activity. These scouts cannot make many decisions on their own. They must transmit what they learn to field officers—sensory neurons in the peripheral nervous system. The field officers in turn must report to generals at a command center—the cells of the brain. The generals are responsible for analyzing the reports, combining information brought in by different scouts, and deciding what it all means.

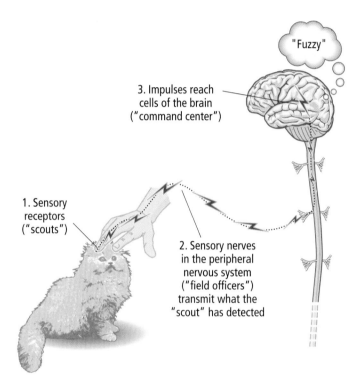

"Fuzzy"

3. Impulses reach cells of the brain ("command center")

1. Sensory receptors ("scouts")

2. Sensory nerves in the peripheral nervous system ("field officers") transmit what the "scout" has detected

The field officers in the sensory system—the sensory nerves—all use exactly the same form of communication, a neural impulse. It is as if they must all send their messages on a bongo drum and can only go "boom." How, then, are we able to experience so many different kinds of sensations? The answer is that the nervous system *encodes* the messages. One kind of code, which is *anatomical,* was first described in 1826 by the German physiologist Johannes Müller in his **doctrine of specific nerve energies.** According to this doctrine, different sensory modalities (such as vision and hearing) exist because signals received by the sense organs stimulate different nerve pathways leading to different areas of the brain. Signals from the eye cause impulses to travel along the optic nerve to the visual cortex. Signals from the ear cause impulses to travel along the auditory nerve to the auditory cortex. Light and sound waves produce different sensations because of these anatomical differences.

The doctrine of specific nerve energies implies that what we know about the world ultimately reduces to what we know about the state of our own nervous system. Therefore, if sound waves could stimulate nerves that end in the visual part of the brain, we would "see" sound. In fact, a similar sort of crossover does occur if

doctrine of specific nerve energies The principle that different sensory modalities exist because signals received by the sense organs stimulate different nerve pathways leading to different areas of the brain.

you close your right eye and press lightly on the right side of the lid: You will "see" a flash of light seemingly coming from the left. The pressure produces an impulse that travels up the optic nerve to the visual area in the right side of the brain, where it is interpreted as coming from the left side of the visual field.

Sensory crossover also occurs in a rare condition called **synesthesia,** in which the stimulation of one sense also evokes another. The person may say that the color purple smells like a rose, the aroma of cinnamon feels like velvet, or the sound of a note on a clarinet tastes like cherries. These are not merely metaphors to a synesthete; the person actually perceives the second sensation. Novelist Vladimir Nabokov said that the letter *b* made him see burnt sienna and *t* made him see pistachio green; physicist Richard Feynman saw the *n* in an equation as "mildly violet-bluish." Synesthesia is just starting to be studied with brain-scanning technology. No one knows yet why the phenomenon occurs, but many theories have been offered (Baron-Cohen & Harrison, 1997; Martino & Marks, 2001). For example, it could be that synesthetes have an unusual number of neural connections between different sensory areas of the brain.

Synesthesia, however, is an anomaly; for most of us, the senses remain separate. Anatomical encoding does not completely solve the riddle of why this is so. For one thing, linking the different skin senses to distinct nerve pathways has proved difficult. The doctrine of specific nerve energies also fails to explain variations of experience *within* a particular sense—the sight of pink versus red, the sound of a piccolo versus the sound of a tuba, or the feel of a pinprick versus the feel of a kiss. An additional kind of code is therefore necessary. This second kind of code has been called *functional*.

Functional codes rely on the fact that sensory receptors and neurons fire, or are inhibited from firing, only in the presence of specific sorts of stimuli. At any particular time, then, some cells in the nervous system are firing and some are not. Information about *which* cells are firing, *how many* cells are firing, the *rate* at which cells are firing, and the *patterning* of each cell's firing forms a functional code. You might think of such a code as the neurological equivalent of Morse code. Functional encoding may occur all along a sensory route, starting in the sense organs and ending in the brain.

Measuring the Senses

Just how sensitive are our senses? The answer comes from the field of *psychophysics*, which is concerned with how the physical properties of stimuli are related to our psychological experience of them. Drawing on principles from both physics and psychology, psychophysicists have studied how the strength or intensity of a stimulus affects the strength of sensation in an observer.

Absolute Thresholds. One way to find out how sensitive the senses are is to show people a series of signals that vary in intensity and ask them to say which signals they can detect. The smallest amount of energy that a person can detect reliably is known as the **absolute threshold.** The word *absolute* is a bit misleading because people detect borderline signals on some occasions and miss them on others. "Reliable" detection is said to occur when a person can detect a signal 50 percent of the time.

If you were having your absolute threshold for brightness measured, you might be asked to sit in a dark room and look at a wall or screen. You would then be shown flashes of light, varying in brightness, one flash at a time. Your task would be to say whether you noticed a flash. Some flashes you would never see. Some you would always see. And sometimes you would miss seeing a flash, even though you had noticed one of equal brightness on other trials. Such errors seem to occur in part because of random firing of cells in the nervous system, which produces fluctuating background noise, something like the background noise in a stereo system.

synesthesia A condition in which stimulation of one sense also evokes another.

absolute threshold The smallest quantity of physical energy that can be reliably detected by an observer.

Different species sense the world differently. The flower on the left was photographed in normal light. The one on the right, photographed under ultraviolet light, is what a butterfly might see, because butterflies have ultraviolet receptors. The hundreds of tiny bright spots are nectar sources.

By studying absolute thresholds, psychologists have found that our senses are very sharp indeed. If you have normal sensory abilities, you can see a candle flame on a clear, dark night from 30 miles away. You can hear a ticking watch in a perfectly quiet room from 20 feet away. You can taste a teaspoon of sugar diluted in two gallons of water, smell a drop of perfume diffused through a three-room apartment, and feel the wing of a bee falling on your cheek from a height of only one centimeter (Galanter, 1962).

Yet despite these impressive sensory skills, our senses are tuned in to only a narrow band of physical energies. For example, we are visually sensitive to only a tiny fraction of the electromagnetic energy that surrounds us; we do not see radio waves, infrared waves, or microwaves (see Figure 6.1). Other species can pick up signals

Figure 6.1
THE VISIBLE SPECTRUM OF ELECTROMAGNETIC ENERGY
Our visual system detects only a small fraction of the electromagnetic energy around us.

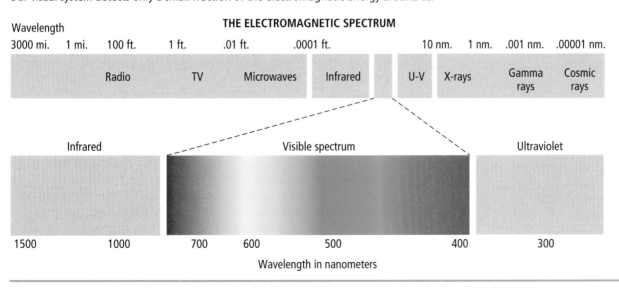

THE ELECTROMAGNETIC SPECTRUM

Wavelength

| 3000 mi. | 1 mi. | 100 ft. | 1 ft. | .01 ft. | .0001 ft. | | 10 nm. | 1 nm. | .001 nm. | .00001 nm. |

| Radio | TV | Microwaves | Infrared | | U-V | X-rays | Gamma rays | Cosmic rays |

Infrared | Visible spectrum | Ultraviolet

1500 | 1000 | 700 | 600 | 500 | 400 | 300

Wavelength in nanometers

that we cannot. Dogs can detect high-frequency sound waves that are beyond our range, as you know if you have ever called your pooch with a "silent" doggie whistle. Bats and porpoises can hear sounds two octaves beyond our range, and bees can see ultraviolet light, which merely gives human beings a sunburn. Because our sense organs evolved for particular purposes and not others, our sensory windows on the world are partly shuttered. Fortunately, by using ingenuity, technology, and the methods of science, we can pry open those shutters and measure forms of energy that our senses cannot detect directly.

Difference Thresholds. Psychologists also study sensory sensitivity by having people compare two stimuli and judge whether they are the same or different. For example, a person might be asked to compare the weight of two blocks, the brightness of two lights, or the saltiness of two liquids. The smallest difference in stimulation that a person can detect reliably (again, half of the time) is called the **difference threshold** or *just noticeable difference (jnd)*. When you compare two stimuli, A and B, the difference threshold will depend on the intensity or size of A. The larger or more intense A is, the greater the change must be before you can detect a difference. If you are comparing the weights of two pebbles, you might be able to detect a difference of only a fraction of an ounce, but you would not be able to detect such a subtle difference if you were comparing two massive boulders.

In everyday life, we may sometimes think we can detect a difference between stimuli when we cannot. Years ago, as a class project, undergraduate students at Williams College offered tasters three glasses of cola, two of one leading brand and one of the other (or vice versa), and asked them which drink they liked most and least. Each taster was given three trials. Most of the tasters were inconsistent in their preferences, indicating that they had trouble telling the two brands apart (Solomon, 1979). Apparently, the difference between the two tastes exceeded the students' difference thresholds.

Signal-Detection Theory. Despite their usefulness, the procedures we have described have a serious limitation. Measurements for any given individual may be affected by the person's general tendency, when uncertain, to respond, "Yes, I noticed a signal (or a difference)" or "No, I didn't notice anything." Some people are habitual yea-sayers, willing to gamble that the signal was really there. Others are habitual naysayers, cautious and conservative. In addition, alertness, motives, and expectations can influence how a person responds on any given occasion. If you are in the shower and you are expecting an important call, you may think you heard the telephone ring when it didn't. In laboratory studies, when observers want to impress the experimenter, they may lean toward a positive response.

Fortunately, these problems of *response bias* are not insurmountable. According to **signal-detection theory,** an observer's response in a detection task can be divided into a *sensory process,* which depends on the intensity of the stimulus, and a *decision process,* which is influenced by the observer's response bias. Methods are available for separating these two components. For example, the researcher can include some trials in which no stimulus is present and others in which a weak stimulus is present. Under these conditions, four kinds of responses are possible: The person (1) detects a signal that was present (a "hit"), (2) says the signal was there when it wasn't (a "false alarm"), (3) fails to detect the signal when it was present (a "miss"), or (4) correctly says the signal was absent when it was absent (a "correct rejection").

difference threshold The smallest difference in stimulation that can be reliably detected by an observer when two stimuli are compared; also called *just noticeable difference (jnd).*

signal-detection theory A psychophysical theory that divides the detection of a sensory signal into a sensory process and a decision process.

RESPONSES IN SIGNAL DETECTION

Stimulus Is...

Yea-sayers will have more hits than naysayers, but they will also have more false alarms because they are too quick to say, "Yup, it was there." Naysayers will have more correct rejections than yea-sayers, but they will also have more misses because they are too quick to say, "Nope, nothing was there." This information can be fed into a mathematical formula that yields separate estimates of a person's response bias and sensory capacity. The individual's true sensitivity to a signal of any particular intensity can then be predicted.

The old method of measuring thresholds assumed that a person's ability to detect a stimulus depended solely on the stimulus. Signal-detection theory assumes that there is no single "threshold" because at any given moment, a person's sensitivity to a stimulus depends on a decision that he or she actively makes. Signal-detection methods have many real-world applications, from screening applicants for jobs requiring keen hearing to training air-traffic controllers, whose decisions about the presence or absence of a blip on a radar screen may mean the difference between life and death.

Sensory Adaptation

Variety, they say, is the spice of life. It is also the essence of sensation, for our senses are designed to respond to change and contrast in the environment. When a stimulus is unchanging or repetitive, sensation often fades or disappears. Receptors or nerve cells higher up in the sensory system get "tired" and fire less frequently. The resulting decline in sensory responsiveness is called **sensory adaptation.** Such adaptation is usually useful because it spares us from having to respond to unimportant information; for example, most of the time you have no need to feel your watch sitting on your wrist. Sometimes, however, adaptation can be hazardous, as when you no longer smell a gas leak that you noticed when you first entered the kitchen.

We never completely adapt to extremely intense stimuli—a terrible toothache, the odor of ammonia, the heat of the desert sun. And we rarely adapt completely to visual stimuli, whether they are weak or intense. Eye movements, voluntary and involuntary, cause the location of an object's image on the back of the eye to keep changing, so visual receptors don't have a chance to "fatigue." But in the laboratory, researchers can stabilize the image of a simple pattern, such as a line, at a particular point on the back of a person's eye. They use an ingenious device consisting of a tiny projector mounted on a contact lens. Although the eyeball moves, the image of the object stays focused on the same receptors. In minutes, the image begins to disappear.

What would happen if our senses adapted to *most* incoming stimuli? Would we sense nothing, or would the brain substitute its own images for the sensory experiences

sensory adaptation The reduction or disappearance of sensory responsiveness when stimulation is unchanging or repetitious.

Get Involved

Now You See It, Now You Don't

Sensation depends on change and contrast in the environment. Hold your hand over one eye and stare at the dot in the middle of the circle on the right. You should have no trouble maintaining an image of the circle. However, if you do the same with the circle on the left, the image will fade. The gradual change from light to dark does not provide enough contrast to keep your visual receptors firing at a steady rate. The circle reappears only if you close and reopen your eye or shift your gaze to the *X*.

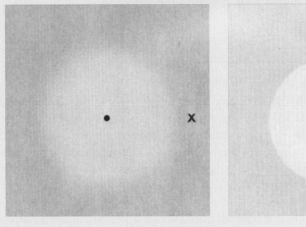

sensory deprivation The absence of normal levels of sensory stimulation.

no longer available by way of the sense organs? In early studies of **sensory deprivation,** researchers studied this question by isolating male volunteers from all patterned sight and sound. Vision was restricted by a translucent visor, hearing by a U-shaped pillow and noise from an air conditioner and fan, and touch by cotton gloves and cardboard cuffs. The volunteers took brief breaks to eat and use the bathroom, but otherwise they lay in bed, doing nothing. The results were dramatic. Within a few hours, many of the men felt edgy. Some were so disoriented that they quit the study the first day. Those who stayed longer became confused, restless, and grouchy. Many reported bizarre visions, such as a squadron of squirrels or a procession of marching eyeglasses. Few were willing to remain in the study for more than two or three days (Heron, 1957).

THINKING CRITICALLY

Don't Oversimplify

You are in a dark room, isolated from sight, sound, smell, and taste. Will you hallucinate and beg to be released, or will you find the experience restful and soothing? What might affect your reaction?

But the notion that sensory deprivation is unpleasant or even dangerous turned out to be an oversimplification (Suedfeld, 1975). In many of the studies, the experimental procedures themselves probably aroused anxiety: Participants were told about "panic buttons" and were asked to sign "release from legal liability" forms. Later research, using better methods, showed that hallucinations are less dramatic and less disorienting than at first thought. In fact, many people enjoy limited periods of deprivation, and some perceptual and intellectual abilities actually improve. Your response to sensory deprivation depends on your expectations and interpretations of what is happening. Reduced sensation can be scary if you are locked in a room for an indefinite period, but relaxing if you have retreated to that room voluntarily for a little time-out—or if you are paying for a session in a "relaxation chamber."

Still, it is clear that the human brain requires a minimum amount of sensory stimulation in order to function normally. This need may help explain why people who live alone often keep the radio or television set running continuously and why prolonged solitary confinement is used as a form of punishment or even torture.

The effects of sensory deprivation depend on the circumstances. Being isolated against your will can be terrifying, but many people have found an hour alone in a "flotation tank" to be pleasantly relaxing.

Sensory Overload

If too little stimulation can be bad for you, so can too much, because it can lead to fatigue and mental confusion. If you have ever felt exhausted, nervous, and headachy after a day crammed with hectic activities and deadlines, you know first-hand about sensory overload.

When people find themselves in a state of overload, they often cope by blocking out unimportant sights and sounds and focusing only on those they find interesting or useful. Psychologists have called this the "cocktail party phenomenon" because at a cocktail party, a person typically focuses on just one conversation, ignoring other voices, the clink of ice cubes, music, and bursts of laughter across the room. The competing sounds all enter the nervous system, enabling the person to pick up anything important—even the person's own name, spoken by someone several yards away. Unimportant sounds, though, are not fully processed by the brain.

The capacity for **selective attention** protects us in daily life from being overwhelmed by all the sensory signals impinging on our receptors. The brain is not forced to respond to everything the sense receptors send its way. The generals in the brain can choose which field officers get past the command center's gates. Those that don't seem to have anything important to say are turned back.

> **selective attention** The focusing of attention on selected aspects of the environment and the blocking out of others.

QUICK QUIZ

If you are not overloaded, try answering these questions.

1. Even on the clearest night, some stars cannot be seen by the naked eye because they are below the viewer's _____ threshold.

2. If you jump into a cold lake but moments later the water no longer seems so cold, sensory _____ has occurred.

3. If you are immobilized in a hospital bed, with no roommate and no TV or radio, and you feel edgy and disoriented, you may be suffering the effects of _____.

4. During a break from your job as a waiter, you are so engrossed in a book that you fail to notice the clattering of dishes or orders being called out to the cook. This is an example of _____.

5. In real-life detection tasks, is it better to be a "naysayer" or a "yea-sayer"?

Answers:

1. absolute 2. adaptation 3. sensory deprivation 4. selective attention 5. Neither; it depends on the consequences of a "miss" or a "false alarm" and the probability of an event occurring. You might want to be a yea-sayer if you are just out the door, you think you hear the phone ringing, and you are expecting a call about a job interview. You might want to be a naysayer if you are just out the door, you think you hear the phone ringing, and you are on your way to a job interview and don't want to be late.

- How does the eye differ from a camera?
- Why can we describe a color as bluish green but not as reddish green?
- If you were blind in one eye, why might you misjudge your distance from a painting on the wall but not the distance to buildings a block away?
- As a friend approaches, her image on your retina grows larger; why do you continue to see her as the same size?
- Why are perceptual illusions so valuable to psychologists?

Vision

Vision is the most frequently studied of all the senses, and with good reason. More information about the external world comes to us through our eyes than through any other sense organ. (Perhaps that is why people say "I see what you mean" instead of "I hear what you mean.") Because we evolved to be most active in the daytime, we are "wired" to take advantage of the sun's illumination. Animals that are active at night tend to rely more heavily on hearing.

What We See

The stimulus for vision is light; even cats, raccoons, and other creatures famous for their ability to get around in the dark need *some* light to see. Visible light comes from the sun and other stars and from lightbulbs, and it is also reflected off objects. Light travels in the form of waves, and the *physical* characteristics of these waves affect three *psychological* dimensions of our visual world: hue, brightness, and saturation.

1 **Hue,** the dimension of visual experience specified by color names, is related to the *wavelength* of light—that is, to the distance between the crests of a light wave. Shorter waves tend to be seen as violet and blue, longer ones as orange and red. (We say "tend to" because other factors also affect color perception, as we will see later.) The sun produces white light, a mixture of all the visible wavelengths. Sometimes, drops of moisture in the air act like a prism: They separate the sun's white light into the colors of the visible spectrum, and we are treated to a rainbow.

2 **Brightness** is the dimension of visual experience related to the amount, or *intensity,* of the light an object emits or reflects. Intensity corresponds to the amplitude (maximum height) of the wave. Generally speaking, the more light an object reflects, the brighter it appears. However, brightness is also affected by wavelength: Yellows appear brighter than reds and blues when physical intensities are actually equal.

3 **Saturation** (colorfulness) is the dimension of visual experience related to the *complexity of light*—that is, to how wide or narrow the range of wavelengths is. When light contains only a single wavelength, it is said to be "pure," and the resulting color is said to be completely saturated. At the other extreme is white light, which lacks any color and is completely unsaturated. In nature, pure light is extremely rare. Usually, we sense a mixture of wavelengths, and we see colors that are duller and paler than completely saturated ones.

An Eye on the World

Light enters the visual system through the eye, a wonderfully complex and delicate structure. As you read this section, examine Figure 6.2. Notice that the front part of

hue The dimension of visual experience specified by color names and related to the wavelength of light.

brightness Lightness or luminance; the dimension of visual experience related to the amount of light emitted from or reflected by an object.

saturation Vividness or purity of color; the dimension of visual experience related to the complexity of light waves.

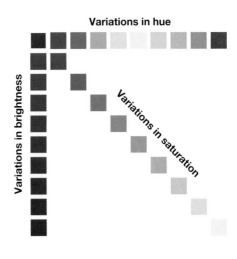

Variations in hue

Variations in brightness

Variations in saturation

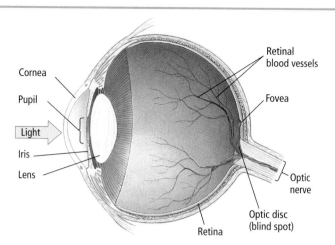

Figure 6.2

MAJOR STRUCTURES OF THE EYE

Light passes through the pupil and lens and is focused on the retina at the back of the eye. The point of sharpest vision is at the fovea.

the eye is covered by the transparent *cornea.* The cornea protects the eye and bends incoming light rays toward a *lens* located behind it. A camera lens focuses incoming light by moving closer to or farther from the shutter opening. However, the lens of the eye works by subtly changing its shape, becoming more or less curved to focus light from objects that are close by or far away. The amount of light that gets into the eye is controlled by muscles in the *iris,* the part of the eye that gives it color. The iris surrounds the round opening, or *pupil,* of the eye. When you enter a dim room, the pupil widens, or dilates, to let more light in. When you emerge into bright sunlight, the pupil gets smaller, contracting to allow in less light. You can see these changes by watching your eyes in a mirror as you change the lighting.

The visual receptors are located in the back of the eye, or **retina.** In a developing embryo, the retina forms from tissue that projects out from the brain, not from tissue destined to form other parts of the eye; thus, the retina is actually an extension of the brain. As Figure 6.3 shows, when the lens of the eye focuses light on the retina, the result is an upside-down image (which can actually be seen with an instrument used by eye specialists). Light from the top of the visual field stimulates light-sensitive receptors cells in the bottom part of the retina, and vice versa. The brain interprets this upside-down pattern of stimulation as something that is right side up.

retina Neural tissue lining the back of the eyeball's interior, which contains the receptors for vision.

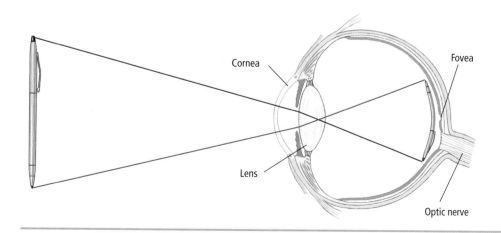

Figure 6.3

THE RETINAL IMAGE

When we look at an object, the light pattern on the retina is upside down. René Descartes (1596–1650) was probably the first person to demonstrate this fact. He cut a piece from the back of an ox's eye and replaced the piece with paper. When he held the eye up to the light, he saw an upside-down image of the room on the paper!

rods Visual receptors that respond to dim light.

cones Visual receptors involved in color vision.

dark adaptation A process by which visual receptors become maximally sensitive to dim light.

ganglion cells Neurons in the retina of the eye, which gather information from receptor cells (by way of intermediate bipolar cells); their axons make up the optic nerve.

6.1

About 120 to 125 million receptors in the retina are long and narrow and are called **rods.** Another 7 or 8 million receptors are cone-shaped and are called, appropriately enough, **cones.** The center of the retina, or *fovea*, where vision is sharpest, contains only cones, clustered densely together. From the center to the periphery, the ratio of rods to cones increases, and the outer edges contain virtually no cones.

Rods are more sensitive to light than cones are. They enable us to see in dim light and at night. (Cats see well in dim light in part because they have a high proportion of rods.) Because rods occupy the outer edges of the retina, they also handle peripheral (side) vision. That is why you can sometimes see a star from the corner of your eye even though it is invisible to you when you gaze straight at it. But rods cannot distinguish different wavelengths of light and therefore are not sensitive to color. That is why it is often hard to distinguish colors clearly in dim light. The cones, on the other hand, are differentially sensitive to specific wavelengths of light and allow us to see colors. However, the cones need much more light than rods do to respond, so they don't help us much when we are trying to find a seat in a darkened movie theater (see Review 6.1).

We have all noticed that it takes some time for our eyes to adjust fully to dim illumination. This process of **dark adaptation** involves chemical changes in the rods and cones. The cones adapt quickly, within 10 minutes or so, but they never become very sensitive to the dim illumination. The rods adapt more slowly, taking 20 minutes or longer, but are ultimately much more sensitive. After the first phase of adaptation, you can see better but not well; after the second phase, your vision is as good as it ever will get.

Rods and cones are connected by synapses to *bipolar neurons,* which in turn communicate with neurons called **ganglion cells** (see Figure 6.4). The axons of the ganglion cells converge to form the *optic nerve*, which carries information out through the back of the eye and on to the brain. Where the optic nerve leaves the eye, at the *optic disc,* there are no rods or cones. The absence of receptors produces a blind spot in the field of vision. Normally, we are unaware of the blind spot because (1) the image projected on the spot is hitting a different, "nonblind" spot in the other eye; (2) our eyes move so fast that we can pick up the complete image; and (3) the brain fills in the gap. You can find your blind spot by doing the Get Involved exercise on the next page.

REVIEW 6.1	DIFFERENCES BETWEEN RODS AND CONES	
	Rods	**Cones**
How many?	120–125 million	7–8 million
Where most concentrated?	Periphery of retina	Center (fovea) of retina
How sensitive	High sensitivity	Low sensitivity
Sensitive to color?	No	Yes

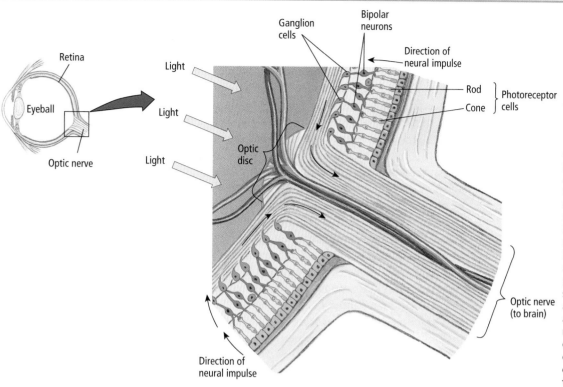

Figure 6.4
THE STRUCTURES OF THE RETINA

For clarity, all cells in this drawing are greatly exaggerated in size. In order to reach the receptors for vision (the rods and cones), light must pass through the ganglion cells and bipolar neurons as well as the blood vessels that nourish them (not shown). Normally, we do not see the shadow cast by this network of cells and blood vessels because the shadow always falls on the same place on the retina, and such stabilized images are not sensed. But when an eye doctor shines a moving light into your eye, the treelike shadow of the blood vessels falls on different regions of the retina and you may see it—a rather eerie experience.

Why the Visual System Is Not a Camera

Although the eye is often compared with a camera, the visual system, unlike a camera, is not a passive recorder of the external world. Instead of simply registering spots of light and dark, as a camera does when it takes a photo, neurons in the visual system build up a picture of the world by detecting its meaningful features.

Get Involved

Find Your Blind Spot

A blind spot exists where the optic nerve leaves the back of your eye. Find the blind spot in your left eye by closing your right eye and looking at the magician. Then slowly move the book toward and away from yourself. The rabbit should disappear when the book is between 9 and 12 inches from your eye.

feature detectors Cells in the visual cortex that are sensitive to specific features of the environment.

Ganglion cells and neurons in the thalamus of the brain respond to simple features in the environment, such as spots of light and dark. In mammals, special **feature-detector** cells in the visual cortex respond to more complex features. This fact was first demonstrated by David Hubel and Torsten Wiesel (1962, 1968), who painstakingly recorded impulses from individual cells in the brains of cats and monkeys. (In 1981, they received a Nobel Prize for their work.) Hubel and Wiesel found that different neurons were sensitive to different patterns projected on a screen in front of the animal's eyes. Most cells responded maximally to moving or stationary lines that were oriented in a particular direction and located in a particular part of the visual field. One type of cell might fire most rapidly in response to a horizontal line in the lower right part of the visual field, another to a diagonal line at a specific angle in the upper left part of the visual field. In the real world, such features make up the boundaries and edges of objects.

Since this pioneering work was done, scientists have found that other cells in the visual system have more complex specialties. For example, in primates, the visual cortex contains cells that respond maximally to bull's-eyes, spirals, or concentric circles (Gallant, Braun, & Van Essen, 1993). Even more intriguing, some cells in the right temporal lobe respond maximally to *faces* (Kanwisher, 2000; Ó Scalaidhe, Wilson, & Goldman-Rakic, 1997; Young & Yamane, 1992). The existence of a specialized "face module" in the brain could help explain why infants show a preference for looking at faces, and why a person with brain damage may continue to recognize faces even after losing the ability to recognize other objects. In one case, a patient could recognize a face made up entirely of vegetables, like the one in the painting in the margin, but he could not recognize the component vegetables (Moscovitch, Winocur, & Behrmann, 1997).

Cases of brain damage support the idea that particular systems of brain cells are highly specialized. One man's injury left him unable to identify ordinary objects, which he said often looked like "blobs." Yet he had no trouble with faces, even when they were incomplete or upside down. When shown this painting, he could easily see the face, but he could not see the vegetables comprising it (Moscovitch, Winocur, & Behrmann, 1997).

Face modules make evolutionary sense because they would have ensured our ancestors' ability to distinguish friend from foe. They could also help explain people's inclination to "see" faces in shadows, clouds, the moon, and everyday objects. Nevertheless, the existence of such modules remains a passionate topic of debate among neuroscientists (Cohen & Tong, 2001). For one thing, when you look at a face, other areas in the brain besides your "face module" cells are active; in fact, researchers can tell that you are looking at a face just by examining the overall pattern of activity in these other cells (Haxby et al., 2001). Conversely, when you look at an object that is *not* a face, such as a cat or a shoe, some of your supposed "face module" cells are active.

To complicate matters further, experience and personal interest affect what the supposed "face module" cells respond to. In one fascinating study, cells in the "face module" fired when car buffs examined pictures of classic cars but not when they looked at pictures of exotic birds, and the exact opposite was true for birdwatchers (Gauthier et al., 2000). (Cars, of course, do not have faces!) In another study by the same team of researchers, cells in the "face module" fired after people were trained to distinguish among cute—but faceless—imaginary creatures called greebles (Gauthier et al., 1999) (see Figure 6.5).

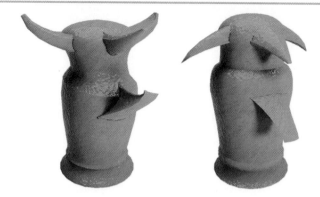

Figure 6.5
GREEBLES

Researchers trained people to recognize hypothetical "greebles" and to identify the creatures' "family" and "sex" according to subtle differences in their features. During the task, "face modules" in the participants' brains were active—yet Greebles have no faces. The researchers concluded that face modules may not be responding to faces per se, and that instead, activity in these areas may reflect certain strategies for distinguishing individuals in a category (Gauthier et al., 1999).

Figuring out the mystery of face modules may take some time. But even if face and other specialized modules do exist, the brain cannot possibly contain a special area for every conceivable object. In general, the brain's job is to take fragmentary information about edges, angles, shapes, motion, brightness, texture, and patterns, and figure out that a chair is a chair, and that it is next to the dining-room table. The perception of any given object probably depends on the activation of many cells in far-flung parts of the brain and on the overall pattern and rhythm of their activity (Bower, 1998).

How We See Colors

For 300 years, scientists have been trying to figure out why we see the world in living color. We now know that different processes explain different stages of color vision.

The Trichromatic Theory. The **trichromatic theory** (also known as the *Young-Helmholtz theory*) applies to the first level of processing, which occurs in the retina of the eye. The retina contains three basic types of cones. One type responds maximally to blue (or more precisely, to a range of wavelengths near the short end of the spectrum, which give rise to the experience of blue), another to green, and a third to red. The hundreds of colors we see result from the combined activity of these three types of cones. Subtypes of the basic cone types exist, however, and people with different subtypes for red see the color red somewhat differently (Neitz & Neitz, 1995). That is why the red sweater that you might find a warm rosy shade might seem a dull, darker red to a friend.

Total color blindness is usually due to a genetic variation that causes cones of the retina to be absent or malfunctional. The visual world then consists of black, white, and shades of gray. Many species of animals are totally color-blind, but the condition is extremely rare in human beings. Most "color-blind" people are actually *color deficient.* Usually, the person is unable to distinguish red and green; the world is painted in shades of blue, yellow, brown, and gray. In rarer instances, a person may be blind to blue and yellow and may see only reds, greens, and grays. Color deficiency is found in about 8 percent of white men, 5 percent of Asian men, and 3 percent of black men and Native American men (Sekuler & Blake, 1994). Because of the way the condition is inherited, it is rare in women.

The Opponent-Process Theory. The **opponent-process theory** applies to the second stage of color processing, which occurs in ganglion cells in the retina

trichromatic theory A theory of color perception that proposes three mechanisms in the visual system, each sensitive to a certain range of wavelengths; their interaction is assumed to produce all the different experiences of hue.

opponent-process theory A theory of color perception that assumes that the visual system treats pairs of colors as opposing or antagonistic.

A Change of Heart

Opponent-process cells that switch on or off in response to green send an opposite message—"red"—when the green is removed, producing a negative afterimage. Stare at the black dot in the middle of this heart for at least 20 seconds. Then shift your gaze to a white piece of paper or a white wall. Do you get a "change of heart"? You may see an image of a red heart with a blue border.

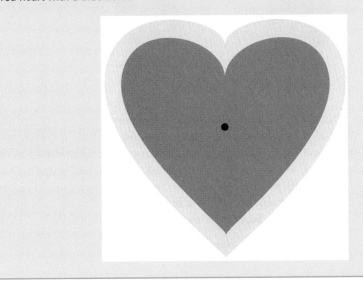

and in neurons in the thalamus and visual cortex of the brain. These cells, known as *opponent-process cells,* either respond to short wavelengths but are inhibited from firing by long wavelengths, or vice versa (DeValois & DeValois, 1975). Some opponent-process cells respond in opposite fashion to red and green; that is, they fire in response to one and turn off in response to the other. Others respond in opposite fashion to blue and yellow. (A third system responds in opposite fashion to white and black and thus yields information about brightness.) The net result is a color code that is passed along to the higher visual centers. Because this code treats red and green, and also blue and yellow, as antagonistic, we can describe a color as bluish green or yellowish green but not as reddish green or yellowish blue.

Opponent-process cells that are *inhibited* by a particular color produce a burst of firing when the color is removed, just as they would if the opposing color were present. Similarly, cells that *fire* in response to a color stop firing when the color is removed, just as they would if the opposing color were present. These facts explain why we are susceptible to *negative afterimages* when we stare at a particular hue—why we see, for instance, red after staring at green (see the Get Involved exercise above). A sort of neural rebound effect occurs: The cells that switch on or off to signal the presence of "green" send the opposite signal ("red") when the green is removed—and vice versa.

Constructing the Visual World

We do not see a retinal image; that image is merely grist for the mill of the mind, which actively interprets the image and constructs the world from the often fragmentary data of the senses. In the brain, sensory signals that give rise to vision, hearing, taste, smell, and touch are combined from moment to moment to produce a unified model of the world. This is the process of *perception*.

Form Perception. To make sense of the world, we must know where one thing ends and another begins. In vision, we must separate the teacher from the lectern; in hearing, we must separate the piano solo from the orchestral accompaniment; in taste, we must separate the marshmallow from the hot chocolate. This process of dividing up the world occurs so rapidly and effortlessly that we take it completely for granted—until we must make out objects in a heavy fog or words in the rapid-fire conversation of someone speaking a foreign language.

The *Gestalt psychologists,* who belonged to a movement that began in Germany and was influential in the 1920s and 1930s, were among the first to study how people organize the world visually into meaningful units and patterns. In German, *Gestalt* means "pattern" or "configuration." The Gestalt psychologists' motto was "The whole is more than the sum of its parts." They observed that when we perceive something, properties emerge from the whole configuration that are not found in any particular component. When you watch a movie, for example, the motion you see is nowhere in the film, which consists of separate static frames projected at 24 frames per second.

One thing the Gestalt psychologists noted was that people always organize the visual field into *figure* and *ground*. The figure stands out from the rest of the environment (see Figure 6.6). Some things stand out as figure by virtue of their intensity or size; it is hard to ignore the blinding flash of a camera or a tidal wave approaching your piece of beach. Unique objects also stand out, such as a banana in a bowl of oranges. Moving objects in an otherwise still environment, such as a shooting star, will usually be seen as figure. Indeed, it is hard to ignore a sudden change of

Figure 6.6

FIGURE AND GROUND

Do you see the goblins or angels? The woodcut *Heaven and Hell* by M. C. Escher shows both, depending on whether you see the black or white sections as figure or ground.

any kind in the environment because our brains are geared to respond to change and contrast. However, selective attention—the ability to concentrate on some stimuli and to filter out others—gives us some control over what we perceive as figure and ground.

6.2 *Live!* **psych**

Here are some other **Gestalt principles** that describe how the visual system groups sensory building blocks into perceptual units:

1 *Proximity.* Things that are near each other tend to be grouped together. Thus you perceive the dots on the left as three groups of dots, not as twelve separate, unrelated ones. Similarly, you perceive the pattern on the right as vertical columns of dots, not as horizontal rows:

2 *Closure.* The brain tends to fill in gaps in order to perceive complete forms. This is fortunate because we often need to decipher less-than-perfect images. The following figures are easily perceived as a triangle, a face, and the letter *e*, even though none of the figures is complete:

3 *Similarity.* Things that are alike in some way (for example, in color, shape, or size) tend to be perceived as belonging together. In the figure on the left, you see the circles as forming an *x*. In the one on the right, you see horizontal bars rather than vertical columns because the horizontally aligned stars share the same color:

4 *Continuity.* Lines and patterns tend to be perceived as continuing in time or space. You perceive the figure on the left as a single line partially covered by an oval rather than as two separate lines touching an oval. In the figure on the right, you see two lines, one curved and one straight, instead of two curved and two straight lines, touching at one focal point:

Gestalt principles Principles that describe the brain's organization of sensory information into meaningful units and patterns.

Since the Gestalt principles were discovered, researchers have identified other cues that help us identify which parts of what we see form objects or scenes. But consumer products are sometimes designed with little thought for these cues, which is why it can be a major challenge to find the pause button on your VCR's remote control or change from AM to FM on your car radio (Bjork, 2000; Norman, 1988). Good design requires, among other things, that crucial distinctions be visually obvious. For instance, knobs and switches with different functions should differ in color, texture, or shape, and they should stand out as "figure." How would you use this information to redesign some of the products that *you* use?

Depth and Distance Perception. Ordinarily we need to know not only what something is, but also where it is. Touch gives us this information directly, but vision does not, so we must *infer* an object's location by estimating its distance or depth.

To perform this remarkable feat, we rely in part on **binocular cues**—cues that require the use of two eyes. One such cue is **convergence**, the turning of the eyes inward, which occurs when they focus on a nearby object. The closer the object, the greater the convergence, as you know if you have ever tried to "cross" your eyes by looking at your own nose. As the angle of convergence changes, the corresponding muscular changes provide information to the brain about distance.

The two eyes also receive slightly different retinal images of the same object. You can prove this by holding a finger about 12 inches in front of your face and looking at it with only one eye at a time. Its position will appear to shift when you change eyes. Now hold up two fingers, one closer to your nose than the other. Notice that the amount of space between the two fingers appears to change when you switch eyes. The slight difference in lateral (sideways) separation between two objects as seen by the left eye and the right eye is called **retinal disparity**. Because retinal disparity increases as the distance between two objects increases, the brain can use it to infer depth and calculate distance.

Binocular cues help us estimate distances up to about 50 feet. For objects farther away, we use only **monocular cues**, cues that do not depend on using both eyes. One such cue is *interposition:* When an object is interposed between the viewer and a second object, partly blocking the view of the second object, the first object is perceived as being closer. Another monocular cue is *linear perspective:* When two lines known to be parallel appear to be coming together or converging, they imply the existence of depth. For example, if you are standing between railroad tracks, they appear to converge in the distance. These and other monocular cues are illustrated on pages 200 and 201.

Live! psych 6.3

Visual Constancies: When Seeing Is Believing. Your perceptual world would be a confusing place without still another important perceptual skill. Lighting conditions, viewing angles, and the distances of stationary objects are all continually changing as we move about, yet we rarely confuse these changes with changes in the objects themselves. This ability to perceive objects as stable or unchanging even though the sensory patterns they produce are constantly shifting is called **perceptual constancy**. The best-studied constancies are visual, and they include the following:

1 *Shape constancy.* We see objects as having a constant shape even though the shape of the retinal image produced by an object changes when our point of view changes. If you hold a Frisbee directly in front of your face, its image on the retina will be round. When you set the Frisbee on a table, its image becomes elliptical, yet you continue to identify the Frisbee as round.

binocular cues Visual cues to depth or distance requiring two eyes.

convergence The turning inward of the eyes, which occurs when they focus on a nearby object.

retinal disparity The slight difference in lateral separation between two objects as seen by the left eye and the right eye.

monocular cues Visual cues to depth or distance, which can be used by one eye alone.

perceptual constancy The accurate perception of objects as stable or unchanged despite changes in the sensory patterns they produce.

BIZARRO   By DAN PIRARO

When size constancy fails.

2 *Location constancy.* We perceive stationary objects as remaining in the same place even though the retinal image moves about as we move our eyes, heads, and bodies. As you drive along the highway, telephone poles and trees fly by—on your retina. But you know that these objects do not move on their own, and you also know that your body is moving, so you perceive the poles and trees as staying put.

3 *Size constancy.* We see an object as having a constant size even when its retinal image becomes smaller or larger. A friend approaching on the street does not seem to be growing; a car pulling away from the curb does not seem to be shrinking. Size constancy depends in part on familiarity with objects; you know people and cars don't change size from moment to moment. It also depends on the apparent distance of an object. An object that is close produces a larger retinal image than the same object farther away, and the brain takes this into account. For example, when you move your hand toward your face, your brain registers the fact that the hand is getting closer, and you correctly perceive its unchanging size despite the growing size of its retinal image. There is, then, an intimate relationship between perceived size and perceived distance.

Monocular Cues to Depth

Most cues to depth do not depend on having two eyes. Some monocular (one-eyed) cues are shown here.

LIGHT AND SHADOW

Both of these attributes give objects the appearance of three dimensions.

INTERPOSITION

An object that partly blocks or obscures another one must be in front of the other one and is therefore seen as closer.

MOTION PARALLAX

When an observer is moving, objects appear to move at different speeds and in different directions. The closer an object, the faster it seems to move; and close objects appear to move backward, whereas distant ones seem to move forward.

4 *Brightness constancy.* We see objects as having a relatively constant brightness even though the amount of light they reflect changes as the overall level of illumination changes. Snow remains white even on a cloudy day. We are not fooled because the brain registers the total illumination in the scene, and we automatically take this information into account.

5 *Color constancy.* We see an object as maintaining its hue despite the fact that the wavelength of light reaching our eyes from the object may change as the illumination changes. For example, outdoor light is "bluer" than indoor light, and objects outdoors therefore reflect more "blue" light than those indoors. Conversely, indoor light from incandescent lamps is rich in long wavelengths and is therefore "yellower." Yet objects usually look the same color in both places: An apple looks red whether you look at it in your kitchen or outside on the patio. Part of the explanation involves sensory adaptation, which we discussed earlier. Outdoors, we quickly adapt to short-wavelength (bluish) light, and indoors, we adapt to long-wavelength light. As a result, our visual responses are similar in the two situations. Also, when computing the color of a particular object, the brain takes into account *all* the wavelengths in the visual field immediately around the object. If an apple is bathed in bluish light, so, usually, is everything else around it. The increase in blue light reflected by the apple is canceled in the visual cortex by the increase in blue light reflected by the apple's surroundings, and so the apple continues to look red.

RELATIVE SIZE

The smaller an object's image on the retina, the farther away the object appears.

TEXTURE GRADIENTS

Distant parts of a uniform surface appear denser; that is, its elements seem spaced more closely together.

RELATIVE CLARITY

Because of particles in the air—from dust, fog, or smog—distant objects tend to look hazier, duller, or less detailed.

LINEAR PERSPECTIVE

Parallel lines will appear to be converging in the distance; the greater the apparent convergence, the greater the perceived distance. This cue is often exaggerated by artists to convey an impression of depth.

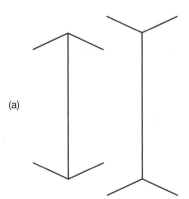
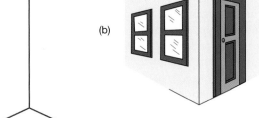
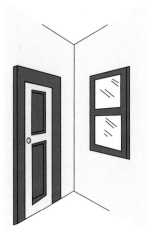

(a)

(b)

Figure 6.7
THE MÜLLER-LYER ILLUSION

The two lines in (a) are exactly the same length. We are probably fooled into perceiving them as different because the brain interprets the one with the outward-facing branches as farther away, as if it were the far corner of a room, and the one with the inward-facing branches as closer, as if it were the near edge of a building (b).

Figure 6.8
COLOR IN CONTEXT

The way you perceive a color depends on the colors around it. In this work by Joseph Albers, the adjacent Xs are actually the same color, but against different backgrounds they look different.

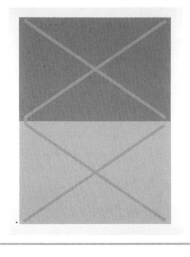

Visual Illusions: When Seeing is Misleading. Perceptual constancies allow us to make sense of the world. Occasionally, however, we can be fooled, and the result is a *perceptual illusion.* For psychologists, illusions are valuable because they are *systematic* errors that provide us with hints about the perceptual strategies of the mind.

Although illusions can occur in any sensory modality, visual illusions have been the best studied. Visual illusions sometimes occur when the strategies that normally lead to accurate perception are overextended to situations where they don't apply. Compare the lengths of the two vertical lines in Figure 6.7. If you are like most people, you perceive the line on the right as slightly longer than the one on the left. Yet they are exactly the same length. (Go ahead, measure them; everyone does.) This is the Müller-Lyer illusion, named after the German sociologist who first described it in 1889.

One explanation for the Müller-Lyer illusion is that the branches on the lines serve as perspective cues that normally suggest depth (Gregory, 1963). The line on the left is like the near edge of a building; the one on the right is like the far corner of a room (see part b of the figure). Although the two lines produce retinal images of the same size, the one with the outward-facing branches suggests greater distance. We are fooled into perceiving it as longer because we automatically apply a rule about the relationship between size and distance that is normally useful: When two objects produce the same-sized retinal image and one is farther away, the farther one is larger. The problem, in this case, is that there is no actual difference in the distance of the two lines, so the rule is inappropriate.

Just as there are size, shape, location, brightness, and color constancies, so there are size, shape, location, brightness, and color *in*constancies, resulting in illusions. For example, the perceived color of an object depends on the wavelengths reflected by its immediate surroundings, a fact well-known to artists and interior designers. Thus, you never see a good, strong red unless other objects in the surroundings reflect the blue and green part of the spectrum. When two objects that are the same color have different surroundings, you may mistakenly perceive them as different (see Figure 6.8).

Some illusions are simply a matter of physics. Thus, a chopstick in a half-filled glass of water looks bent because water and air refract light differently. Other illusions occur due to misleading messages from the sense organs, as in sensory adaptation. Still

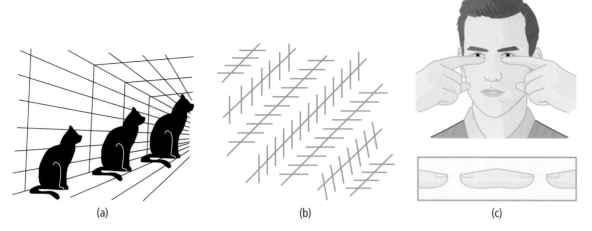

Figure 6.9

FOOLING THE EYE

Although perception is usually accurate, we can be fooled. In (a) the cats as drawn are all the same size; in (b) the diagonal lines are all parallel. To see the illusion depicted in (c), hold your index fingers 5 to 10 inches in front of your eyes as shown, then focus straight ahead. Do you see a floating "fingertip frankfurter"? Can you make it shrink or expand?

others, like the Müller-Lyer illusion, seem to occur because the brain misinterprets sensory information. Figure 6.9 shows some other startling illusions.

In everyday life, most illusions are harmless and entertaining. Occasionally, however, an illusion interferes with the performance of some skill. In baseball, two types of pitches that drive batters batty are the rising fastball, in which the ball seems to jump a few inches when it reaches home plate, and the breaking curveball, in which the ball seems to loop toward the batter and then fall at the last moment; both of these pitches are physical impossibilities. According to one explanation, they are illusions that occur when batters wrongly estimate a ball's speed and momentarily shift their gaze to where they think it will cross home plate (Bahill & Karnavas, 1993). Illusions may also lead to industrial and automobile accidents. For example, because large objects often appear to move more slowly than small ones, drivers sometimes underestimate the speed of onrushing trains at railroad crossings and think they can beat the train, with tragic results.

 6.4

QUICK QUIZ

This quiz is no illusion.

1. How can two Gestalt principles help explain why you can make out the Big Dipper on a starry night?

2. *True or false:* Binocular cues help us locate objects that are very far away.

3. Hold one hand about 12 inches from your face and the other one about 6 inches away. (a) Which hand will cast the smaller retinal image? (b) Why don't you perceive that hand as smaller?

Answers:

1. *Proximity* of certain stars encourages you to see them as clustered together to form a pattern; *closure* allows you to "fill in the gaps" and see the contours of a "dipper." 2. false 3. a. The hand that is 12 inches away will cast a smaller retinal image. b. Your brain takes the differences in distance into account in estimating size; also, you know how large your hands are. The result is size constancy.

WHAT'S AHEAD▶

- **Why does a note played on a flute sound different from the same note played on an oboe?**
- **If you habitually listen to loud music through headphones, what kind of hearing impairment are you risking?**
- **To locate the source of a sound, why does it sometimes help to turn or tilt your head?**

Hearing

Like vision, the sense of hearing, or *audition,* provides a vital link with the world around us. Because social relationships rely so heavily on hearing, when people lose their hearing they sometimes come to feel socially isolated. That is why many hearing-impaired people feel strongly about teaching deaf children American Sign Language (ASL) or other gestural systems, which allow them to communicate and forge close relationships with other signers.

What We Hear

The stimulus for sound is a wave of pressure created when an object vibrates (or, sometimes, when compressed air is released, as in a pipe organ). The vibration (or release of air) causes molecules in a transmitting substance to move together and apart. This movement produces variations in pressure that radiate in all directions. The transmitting substance is usually air, but sound waves can also travel through water and solids, as you know if you have ever put your ear to the wall to hear voices in the next room.

As with vision, *physical* characteristics of the stimulus—in this case, a sound wave—are related in a predictable way to *psychological* aspects of our auditory experience.

1 **Loudness** is the psychological dimension of auditory experience related to the *intensity* of a wave's pressure. Intensity corresponds to the amplitude, or maximum height, of the wave. The more energy contained in the wave, the higher it is at its peak. Perceived loudness is also affected by how high or low a sound is. If low and high sounds produce waves with equal amplitudes, the low sound may seem quieter.

Sound intensity is measured in units called *decibels* (dB). A decibel is one-tenth of a *bel,* a unit named for Alexander Graham Bell, the inventor of the telephone. The average absolute threshold of hearing in human beings is zero decibels. Decibels are not equally distant, as inches on a ruler are. A 60-decibel sound (such as that of a sewing machine) is not 50 percent louder than a 40-decibel sound (such as that of a whisper); it is 100 times louder. Table 6.1 shows the intensity in decibels of some common sounds.

2 **Pitch** is the dimension of auditory experience related to the frequency of the sound wave and, to some extent, its intensity. *Frequency* refers to how rapidly the air (or other medium) vibrates—that is, the number of times per second the wave cycles through a peak and a low point. One cycle per second is known as 1 *hertz* (Hz). The healthy ear of a young person normally detects frequencies in the range of 16 Hz (the lowest note on a pipe organ) to 20,000 Hz (the scraping of a grasshopper's legs).

3 **Timbre** is the distinguishing quality of a sound. It is the dimension of auditory experience related to the *complexity* of the sound wave—to the relative breadth

loudness The dimension of auditory experience related to the intensity of a pressure wave.

pitch The dimension of auditory experience related to the frequency of a pressure wave; the height or depth of a tone.

timbre The distinguishing quality of a sound; the dimension of auditory experience related to the complexity of the pressure wave.

Table 6.1	**Sound Intensity Levels in the Environment**

The following decibel levels apply at typical working distances. Each ten-point increase represents a tenfold increase in sound intensity over the previous level. Even some everyday noises can be hazardous to hearing if exposure goes on for too long a time.

Typical Level (Decibels)	Examples	Dangerous Time Exposure
0	Lowest sound audible to human ear	
30	Quiet library, soft whisper	
40	Quiet office, living room, bedroom away from traffic	
50	Light traffic at a distance, refrigerator, gentle breeze	
60	Air conditioner at 20 feet, conversation, sewing machine	
70	Busy traffic, noisy restaurant (constant exposure)	Critical level begins
80	Subway, heavy city traffic, alarm clock at 2 feet, factory noise	More than 8 hours
90	Truck traffic, noisy home appliances, shop tools, lawn mower	Less than 8 hours
100	Chain saw, boiler shop, pneumatic drill	Less than 2 hours
120	Rock concert in front of speakers, sandblasting, thunderclap	Immediate danger
140	Gunshot blast, jet plane at 50 feet	Any length of exposure time is dangerous
180	Rocket launching pad	Hearing loss inevitable

Source: Reprinted with permission from the American Academy of Otolaryngology—Head and Neck Surgery, Washington, D.C.

of the range of frequencies that make up the wave. A pure tone consists of only one frequency, but in nature, pure tones are extremely rare. Usually what we hear is a complex wave consisting of several subwaves with different frequencies. A particular combination of frequencies results in a particular timbre. Timbre is what makes a note played on a flute, which produces relatively pure tones, sound different from the same note played on an oboe, which produces very complex sounds.

When many frequencies are present but are not in harmony, we hear noise. When all the frequencies of the sound spectrum occur, they produce a hissing sound called *white noise*. Just as white light includes all wavelengths of the visible light spectrum, so white noise includes all frequencies of the audible sound spectrum. People sometimes use white-noise machines to mask other sounds when they are trying to sleep.

An Ear on the World

As Figure 6.10 shows, the ear has an outer, a middle, and an inner section. The soft, funnel-shaped outer ear is well designed to collect sound waves, but hearing would still be quite good without it. The essential parts of the ear are hidden from view, inside the head.

psych 6.5

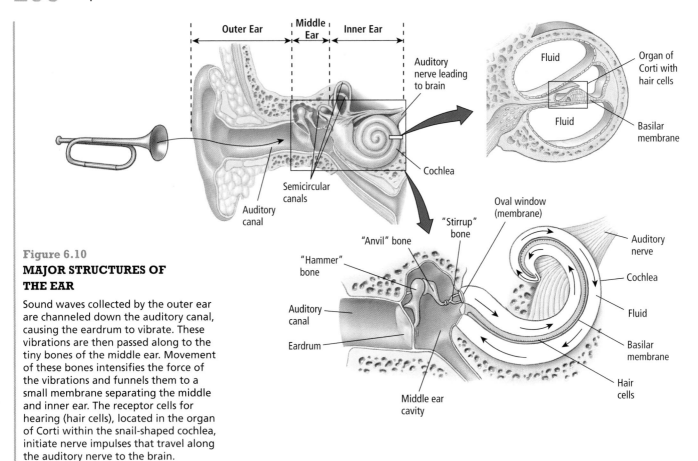

Figure 6.10

MAJOR STRUCTURES OF THE EAR

Sound waves collected by the outer ear are channeled down the auditory canal, causing the eardrum to vibrate. These vibrations are then passed along to the tiny bones of the middle ear. Movement of these bones intensifies the force of the vibrations and funnels them to a small membrane separating the middle and inner ear. The receptor cells for hearing (hair cells), located in the organ of Corti within the snail-shaped cochlea, initiate nerve impulses that travel along the auditory nerve to the brain.

organ of Corti [core-tee] A structure in the cochlea containing hair cells that serve as the receptors for hearing.

cochlea [KOCK-lee-uh] A snail-shaped, fluid-filled organ in the inner ear, containing the organ of Corti, where the receptors for hearing are located.

A sound wave passes into the outer ear and through an inch-long canal to strike an oval-shaped membrane called the *eardrum*. The eardrum is so sensitive that it can respond to the movement of a single molecule! A sound wave causes it to vibrate with the same frequency and amplitude as the wave itself. This vibration is passed along to three tiny bones in the middle ear, the smallest bones in the human body. These bones, known informally as the "hammer," the "anvil," and the "stirrup," move one after the other, which has the effect of intensifying the force of the vibration. The innermost bone, the stirrup, pushes on a membrane that opens into the inner ear.

The actual organ of hearing, the **organ of Corti,** is a chamber inside the **cochlea,** a snail-shaped structure within the inner ear. The organ of Corti plays the same role in hearing that the retina plays in vision. It contains the all-important receptor cells, which in this case look like bristles and are called hair cells, or *cilia*. Exposure to extremely loud noise for a brief period, or more moderate levels of noise for a sustained period, can damage these fragile cells (see Table 6.1 on page 205 again). They flop over, like broken blades of grass, and if the damage reaches a critical point, hearing loss occurs. In modern societies, with their rock concerts, deafening bars, and millions of automobiles, snowmobiles, power saws, leaf blowers, jackhammers, and stereos (often played at full blast and listened to through headphones), such impairment is common. Many college students already have impaired hearing because of damage to the cilia.

The hair cells of the cochlea are embedded in the rubbery *basilar membrane,* which stretches across the interior of the cochlea. When pressure reaches the cochlea, it causes wavelike motions in fluid within the cochlea's interior. These waves of fluid push on the basilar membrane, causing it to move in a wavelike fashion, too. Just above the hair cells is yet another membrane. As the hair cells rise and fall, their tips brush against it, and they bend. This causes the hair cells to initiate a signal that is passed along to the *auditory nerve,* which then carries the message to the brain. The particular pattern of hair-cell movement is affected by the manner in which the basilar membrane moves. This pattern determines which neurons fire and how rapidly they fire, and the resulting code in turn helps determines the sort of sound we hear. For example, we discriminate high-pitched sounds largely on the basis of where activity occurs along the basilar membrane; activity at different sites leads to different neural codes. We discriminate low-pitched sounds largely on the basis of the frequency of the basilar membrane's vibration; again, different frequencies lead to different neural codes.

Could anyone ever imagine such a complex and odd arrangement of bristles, fluids, and snail shells if it did not already exist?

The spiraled interior of a guinea pig's cochlea, shown here, is almost identical to that of a human cochlea.

Constructing the Auditory World

Just as we do not see a retinal image, so we do not hear a chorus of brushlike tufts bending and swaying in the dark recesses of the cochlea. Just as we do not see a jumbled collection of lines and colors, so we do not hear a chaotic collection of disconnected pitches and timbres. Instead, we use our perceptual powers to organize patterns of sound and to construct a meaningful auditory world.

For example, in class, your psychology instructor hopes you will perceive his or her voice as *figure* and the hum of a passing airplane, cheers from the athletic field, or distant sounds of a construction crew as *ground.* Whether these hopes are realized will depend, of course, on where you choose to direct your attention. Other Gestalt principles also seem to apply to hearing. The *proximity* of notes in a melody tells you which notes go together to form phrases; *continuity* helps you follow a melody on one violin when another violin is playing a different melody; *similarity* in timbre and pitch helps you pick out the soprano voices in a chorus and hear them as a unit; *closure* helps you understand a radio announcer's words even when static makes some of the individual sounds unintelligible.

Besides needing to organize sounds, we also need to know where they are coming from. We can estimate the *distance* of a sound's source by using loudness as a cue. For example, we know that a train sounds louder when it is 20 yards away than when it is a mile off. To locate the *direction* a sound is coming from, we depend in part on the fact that we have two ears. A sound arriving from the right reaches the right ear a fraction of a second sooner than it reaches the left ear, and vice versa. The sound may also provide a bit more energy to the right ear (depending on its frequency) because it has to get around the head to reach the left ear. Localizing sounds that are coming from directly in back of you or from directly above your head is hard because such sounds reach both ears at the same time. When you turn or cock your head, you are actively trying to overcome this problem. Many animals do not have to do this because the lucky things can move their ears independently of their heads.

QUICK QUIZ

How well can you localize the answers to these questions?

1. Which psychological dimensions of hearing correspond to the intensity, frequency, and complexity of the sound wave?

2. Tom Petty has a nasal voice and Bob Dylan has a gravelly voice. Which psychological dimension of hearing describes the difference?

3. An extremely loud or sustained noise can permanently damage the _____ of the ear.

4. During a lecture, a classmate draws your attention to a buzzing fluorescent light that you had not previously noticed. What will happen to your perception of figure and ground?

Answers:

1. loudness, pitch, timbre 2. timbre 3. hair cells (cilia) 4. The buzzing sound will become figure and the lecturer's voice will become ground, at least momentarily.

WHAT'S AHEAD ▶

- **Why do saccharin and caffeine taste bitter to some people but not to others?**
- **Why do you have trouble tasting your food when you have a cold?**
- **Why do people often continue to "feel" limbs that have been amputated?**

Other Senses

Psychologists have been particularly interested in vision and audition because of the importance of these senses to human survival. However, research on other senses is growing rapidly as awareness of how they contribute to our lives increases and new ways are found to study them.

Taste: Savory Sensations

Taste, or *gustation,* occurs because chemicals stimulate thousands of receptors in the mouth. These receptors are located primarily on the tongue, but some are also found in the throat, inside the cheeks, and on the roof of the mouth. If you look at your tongue in a mirror, you will notice many tiny bumps; they are called **papillae** (from the Latin for "pimple"), and they come in several forms. In all but one form, **taste buds** line the sides of each papilla (see Figure 6.11). Because of genetic differences, human tongues can have as few as 500 or as many as 10,000 taste buds (Miller & Reedy, 1990).

The taste buds, which up close look a little like a segmented orange, are commonly referred to, mistakenly, as the receptors for taste. The actual receptor cells are *inside* the buds, 15 to 50 to a bud. These cells send tiny fibers out through an opening in the bud; the receptor sites are on these fibers. The receptor cells are replaced by new cells about every 10 days. However, after age 40 or so, the total number of taste buds (and therefore receptors) declines.

Traditionally, researchers have considered fours tastes to be basic: *salty, sour, bitter,* and *sweet,* each produced by a different type of chemical. Many researchers now also include a fifth taste, *umami* (from the Japanese for "delicious"), which is the taste of monosodium glutamate (MSG) and is found in many protein-rich foods, but its inclusion remains controversial. (We know when something is bitter or salty, but

papillae [pa-PILL-ee] Knoblike elevations on the tongue, containing the taste buds. (Singular: papilla.)

taste buds Nests of taste-receptor cells.

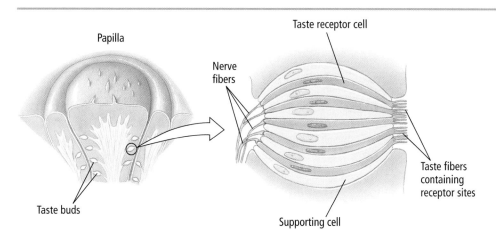

Papilla

Taste receptor cell

Nerve fibers

Taste buds

Taste fibers containing receptor sites

Supporting cell

Figure 6.11
TASTE RECEPTORS

The illustration on the left shows taste buds lining the sides of a papilla on the tongue's surface. The illustration on the right shows an enlarged view of a single taste bud.

no one ever says, "Yum, this steak sure has a great umami taste.") The basic tastes are part of our evolutionary heritage: Bitterness and sourness help us identify foods that are rancid or poisonous; sweetness helps us identify foods that are healthful or rich in calories; salt is necessary for all bodily functions; and umami (if it is basic) could have helped us identify protein-rich foods. The basic tastes can be perceived at any spot on the tongue that has receptors, and differences among the areas are small. Interestingly, the center of the tongue contains no taste buds, and so it cannot produce *any* sort of taste sensation. But, as in the case of the eye's blind spot, you will not usually notice the lack of sensation because the brain fills in the gap.

When you bite into an egg or a piece of bread or an orange, its unique flavor is composed of some combination of the four or five basic tastes, but the physiological details of taste sensation are still hazy. It has even been difficult to find the receptors for the basic tastes, although recently researchers have proposed candidates for the receptors that process bitter, sweet, and umami (Chaudhari, Landin, & Roper, 2000; Hoon et al., 1999; Huang et al., 1999; Max et al., 2001; Montmayeur et al., 2001).

Everyone knows that people live in different "taste worlds" (Bartoshuk, 1993, 1998). Some people love broccoli and others can't stand it. Some people can eat chili peppers that are killer-hot, and others cannot tolerate the mildest jalepeño. One reason for these differences is genetic. For example, in the United States, about 25 percent of people are *supertasters* who find saccharin, caffeine, broccoli, and many other substances to be unpleasantly bitter. (Women are overrepresented in this group.) "Tasters," in contrast, detect less bitterness, and "nontasters" detect none at all. Supertasters also perceive sweet tastes as sweeter and salty tastes as saltier than other people do, and they feel more "burn" from substances such as ginger, pepper, and hot chiles (Bartoshuk et al., 1998; Lucchina et al., 1998). The reason for these differences is literally on people's tongues. Supertasters have more taste buds, and certain papillae on their tongues are smaller, are more densely packed, and look different from those in nontasters (Reedy et al., 1993).

Other taste preferences are a matter of culture and learning (see Chapter 7). Many North Americans who enjoy raw oysters, raw smoked salmon, and raw herring are nevertheless put off by other forms of raw seafood that are popular in Japan, such as sea urchin and octopus. Within a given culture, some people will greedily gobble up a dish that makes others turn green. Learned taste preferences probably begin in the womb or during breast feeding. Babies whose mothers drank carrot juice while pregnant or nursing are more enthusiastic about eating porridge mixed with carrot juice than porridge mixed with water, whereas babies without this exposure show no such preference (Mennella, Jagnow, & Beauchamp, 2001).

Get Involved ⊞

The Smell of Taste

Demonstrate for yourself that smell enhances the sense of taste. Take a bite of a slice of apple, holding your nose, and then do the same with a slice of raw potato. You may find that you can't taste much difference! If you think you do taste a difference, maybe your expectations are influencing your response. Try the same thing, but close your eyes and have someone else feed you the slices. Can you still tell them apart?

The attractiveness of a food can be affected by its color, temperature, and texture ("mouthfeel"). As Goldilocks found out, a bowl of cold porridge is not nearly as delicious as one that is properly heated. And any peanut butter fan will tell you that chunky and smooth peanut butters just don't taste the same. Even more important for taste is a food's odor. Subtle flavors such as chocolate and vanilla would have little taste if we could not smell them (see Figure 6.12). Smell's influence on flavor explains why you have trouble tasting your food when you have a stuffy nose. Most people who chronically have trouble tasting things have a problem with smell, not taste.

Smell: The Sense of Scents

The great author and educator Helen Keller, who became blind and deaf as a toddler, once called smell "the fallen angel of the senses." Yet our sense of smell, or *olfaction*, although seemingly crude when compared to a bloodhound's, is actually quite good; the human nose can detect aromas that the most sophisticated machines fail to detect. And this sense is also far more useful than most people realize.

The receptors for smell are specialized neurons embedded in a tiny patch of mucous membrane in the upper part of the nasal passage, just beneath the eyes (see Figure 6.13). Millions of receptors in each nasal cavity respond to chemical molecules in the air. When you inhale, you pull these molecules into the nasal cavity, but they can also enter from the mouth, wafting up the throat like smoke up a chimney. These molecules trigger responses in the receptors that combine to yield the yeasty smell of freshly baked bread or the spicy smell of a eucalyptus tree. Signals from the receptors are carried to the brain's olfactory bulb by the *olfactory nerve*, which is made up of the receptors' axons. From the olfactory bulb, they travel to a higher region of the brain.

Figuring out the neural code for smell has been a real challenge. Of the 10,000 or so smells we detect (rotten, burned, musky, fruity, spicy, flowery, resinous, putrid . . .), none seems to be more basic than any other. Moreover, as many as a thousand kinds of receptors exist, each kind responding to a part of an odor molecule's structure (Axel, 1995; Buck & Axel, 1991). This complicated system is quite different from the one involved in vision, which uses only three basic receptor types, or in taste, which uses only four (or possibly five). But researchers are making progress; they have discovered that distinct odors activate unique combinations of receptor types, and they have succeeded in identifying some of those combinations (Malnic et al., 1999).

Figure 6.12
TASTE TEST

The red bars show the percentages of people who could identify a substance dropped on the tongue when they were able to smell it. The purple bars show the percentage who could identify the substance when they were prevented from smelling it. (From Mozell et al., 1969.)

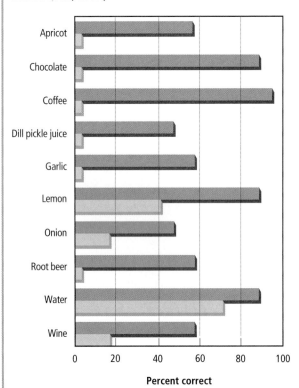

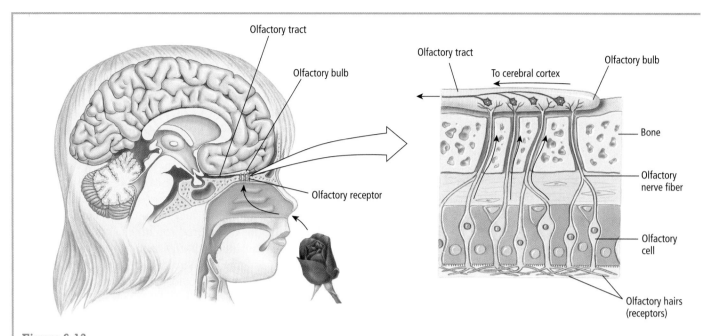

Figure 6.13
RECEPTORS FOR SMELL

Airborne chemical molecules (vapors) enter the nose and circulate through the nasal cavity, where the smell receptors are located. The receptors' axons make up the olfactory nerve, which carries signals to the brain. When you sniff, you draw more vapors into the nose and speed their circulation. Vapors can also reach the nasal cavity through the mouth by way of a passageway from the throat.

Although smell is less vital for human survival than for the survival of other animals, it is still important. We sniff out danger by smelling smoke, food spoilage, and gas leaks; thus, a deficit in the sense of smell is nothing to turn up your nose at. Such a loss can result from infection, disease, injury to the olfactory nerve, or smoking. A person who has smoked two packs a day for 10 years must abstain from cigarettes for 10 more years before the sense of smell returns to normal (Frye, Schwartz, & Doty, 1990).

Odors, of course, have psychological effects on us, which is why we buy perfumes and sniff flowers. Perhaps because olfactory centers in the brain are linked to areas that process memories and emotions, specific smells often evoke vivid, emotionally colored memories (Herz & Cupchik, 1995; Vroon, 1997). The smell of hot chocolate may trigger fond memories of cozy winter mornings from your childhood; the smell of rubbing alcohol may remind you of an unpleasant trip to the hospital.

Human odor preferences, like taste preferences, vary. In some societies, people use rancid fat as a hair pomade, but anyone in North America who did so would quickly have a social problem. Within a particular culture, context and experience are all-important. The very same chemicals that contribute to unpleasant body odors and bad breath also contribute to the pleasant bouquet and flavor of cheese.

Smell has not only evolutionary but also cultural significance. These pilgrims in Japan are purifying themselves with holy incense for good luck and health.

Senses of the Skin

The skin's usefulness is more than just skin deep. Besides protecting our innards, our two square yards of skin help us identify objects and establish intimacy with others. By providing a boundary between ourselves and everything else, the skin also gives us a sense of ourselves as distinct from the environment.

The basic skin senses include *touch* (or pressure), *warmth, cold,* and *pain*. Within these four types are variations such as itch, tickle, and painful burning. Although certain spots on the skin are especially sensitive to the four basic skin sensations, scientists have had difficulty finding distinct receptors for these sensations, except in the case of pressure. A few years ago, however, Swedish researchers found a very thin nerve fiber that seems to be responsible for some types of itching (Schmelz et al., 1997), and scientists recently identified a possible cold receptor (Seydal, 2002).

Perhaps specialized fibers will also be discovered for other skin sensations. In the meantime, many aspects of touch continue to baffle science—for example, why gently touching adjacent pressure spots in rapid succession produces tickle, and why the simultaneous stimulation of warm and cold spots produces not a luke-warm sensation but the sensation of heat. Decoding the messages of the skin senses will eventually tell us how we are able to distinguish sandpaper from velvet and glue from grease.

The Mystery of Pain

Pain, which is not only a skin sense but also an internal sense, has come under special scrutiny. Pain differs from other senses in an important way: When the stimulus producing it is removed, the sensation may continue—sometimes for years. Chronic pain disrupts lives, puts stress on the body, and causes depression and despair. (For ways of coping with chronic pain, see "Taking Psychology with You.")

The Gate-Control Theory of Pain. For many years, a leading explanation of pain has been the **gate-control theory,** which was first proposed by Canadian psychologist Ronald Melzack and British physiologist Patrick Wall (1965). According to this theory, pain impulses must get past a "gate" in the spinal cord. The gate is not an actual structure, but rather a pattern of neural activity that either blocks pain messages coming from the skin, muscles, and internal organs or lets those signals through. Normally, the gate is kept shut, either by impulses coming into the spinal cord from large fibers that respond to pressure and other kinds of stimulation or by signals coming down from the brain itself. But when body tissue is injured, the large fibers are damaged and smaller fibers open the gate, allowing pain messages to reach the brain unchecked.

Because the gate-control theory emphasizes the role of the brain in controlling the gate, it correctly predicts that thoughts and feelings can influence our reactions to pain. When we dwell on our pain, focusing on it and talking about it constantly instead of acting in spite of it, we often intensify our experience of it (Sullivan et al., 1998). Conversely, when we are distracted from our pain, we may not feel it as we usually would—which is why we hear, from time to time, of athletes who are able to finish a performance despite sprained ankles or even broken bones. The gate-control theory also correctly predicts that mild pressure, or other kinds of stimulation, can interfere with severe or protracted pain by closing the spinal gate. When we vigorously rub a banged elbow or apply ice packs, heating, or stimulating ointments to injuries, we are applying this principle.

Updating the Gate-Control Theory. The gate-control theory has been highly useful, but it does not fully explain the many instances of severe, chronic pain that

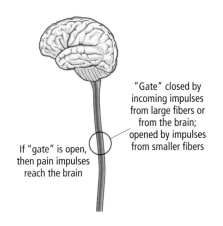

"Gate" closed by incoming impulses from large fibers or from the brain; opened by impulses from smaller fibers

If "gate" is open, then pain impulses reach the brain

gate-control theory The theory that the experience of pain depends in part on whether pain impulses get past a neurological "gate" in the spinal cord and thus reach the brain.

occur without any sign of injury or disease whatsoever. In the strange phenomenon of *phantom pain,* for instance, a person continues to feel pain that seemingly comes from an amputated limb or from an organ that has been surgically removed. An amputee may feel the same aching, burning, or sharp pain from sores, calf cramps, throbbing toes, or even ingrown toenails that he or she endured before the surgery. Even when the spinal cord has been completely severed, amputees often continue to report phantom pain from areas below the break. There are no nerve impulses for the spinal-cord gate to block or let through. So why is there pain?

These puzzles have led Ronald Melzack (1992, 1993) to revise the gate-control theory. The brain, he says, not only responds to incoming signals from sensory nerves but is also capable of *generating* pain (and other sensations) entirely on its own. An extensive matrix (network) of neurons in the brain gives us a sense of our own bodies and body parts. When this matrix produces abnormal pattern of activity, the result is pain. Such abnormal patterns can occur not only because of input from peripheral nerves, but also as a result of memories, emotions, expectations, or signals from various brain centers. In the case of phantom pain, the abnormal patterns may arise because of a lack of sensory stimulation or because of the person's efforts to move a nonexistent limb. Evidence that brain areas associated with a missing limb continue to function in its absence is consistent with this view (Davis et al., 1998).

At present, however, no general theory completely explains pain, which has turned out to be extremely complicated, both physiologically and psychologically. Pain comes in different varieties: the pain of a pinprick differs from that of a bruise, which differs from that of a stomach ulcer. These different types of pain involve different chemical changes and changes in the activity of neurons at the site of injury or disease and in the spinal cord and brain. Pain's psychological effects also vary, from the moment-to-moment unpleasantness and fear of the experience to worry about the pain's long-term implications. If the pain becomes chronic, we may begin to define ourselves in terms of our pain ("I am an ill, suffering person"), which can add to our distress and make its management more difficult (Pincus & Morley, 2001).

Pain is one of the most fascinating psychological mysteries of our time. It can rise and fall in epidemics, like the flu—as national outbreaks of back pain or whiplash or repetitive-motion injuries reveal (Gawande, 1998). The people who suffer during such epidemics are not faking it, and their pain is not "just in their heads." But it may be in their brains.

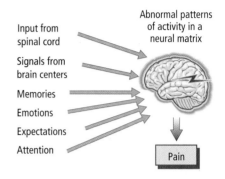

The face of pain is unmistakable.

The Environment Within

We usually think of our senses as pipelines to the "outside" world, but two senses keep us informed about the movements of our own bodies. **Kinesthesis** tells us where our body parts are located and lets us know when they move. This information is provided by pain and pressure receptors located in the muscles, joints, and tendons (tissues that connect muscles to bones). Without kinesthesis, you could not touch your finger to your nose with your eyes shut. In fact, you would have trouble with any voluntary movement. Think of how hard walking is when your leg has "fallen asleep" or how clumsy chewing is when a dentist has numbed your jaw with novocaine.

Equilibrium, or the sense of balance, gives us information about our bodies as a whole. Along with vision and touch, it lets us know whether we are standing upright or on our heads and tells us when we are falling or rotating. Equilibrium relies primarily on three **semicircular canals** in the inner ear (see Figure 6.10 on page 206). These thin tubes are filled with fluid that moves and presses on hairlike receptors

kinesthesis [KIN-es-THEE-sis] The sense of body position and movement of body parts; also called kinesthesia.

equilibrium The sense of balance.

semicircular canals Sense organs in the inner ear that contribute to equilibrium by responding to rotation of the head.

These performers from the famed Cirque du Soleil have turned their kinesthetic talents into artistry.

whenever the head rotates. The receptors initiate messages that travel through a part of the auditory nerve that is not involved in hearing.

Normally, kinesthesis and equilibrium work together to give us a sense of our own physical reality, something we take utterly for granted but should not. Oliver Sacks (1985) told the heartbreaking story of Christina, a young British woman who suffered irreversible damage to her kinesthetic nerve fibers because of a mysterious inflammation. At first, Christina was as floppy as a rag doll; she could not sit up, walk, or stand. Then, slowly, she learned to do these things, relying on visual cues and sheer willpower. But her movements remained unnatural; she had to grasp a fork with painful force or she would drop it. More important, despite her remaining sensitivity to light touch on the skin, she said she could no longer experience herself as physically embodied: "It's like something's been scooped right out of me, right at the centre. . . . "

With equilibrium, we come, as it were, to the end of our senses. Every second, millions of sensory signals reach the brain, which combines and integrates them to produce a model of reality from moment to moment. How does it know how to do this? Are our perceptual abilities inborn, or must we learn them? We turn next to this issue.

QUICK QUIZ

Can you make sense of the following sensory problems?

1. April always has trouble tasting foods, especially those with subtle flavors. What is the most likely explanation of her difficulty?

2. May has chronic shoulder pain. How might the gate-control theory and its revision explain her pain?

3. June, a rock musician, does not hear as well as she used to. What is a likely explanation?

Answers:

1. An impaired sense of smell, possibly due to disease, illness, or cigarette smoking. 2. Nerve fibers that normally close the pain "gate" may have been damaged (the gate-control theory), or a matrix of cells in the brain may be producing abnormal activity. 3. Hearing impairment has many causes, but in June's case, we might suspect that prolonged exposure to loud music has damaged the hair cells of her cochlea.

WHAT'S AHEAD ▶

- Do babies see the world the way adults do?
- What psychological motives could cause people to "see" the face of a religious figure on a cinnamon bun?

Perceptual Powers: Origins and Influences

What happens when babies first open their eyes? Do they see the same sights, hear the same sounds, smell the same smells, taste the same tastes as an adult does? Are their strategies for organizing the world wired into their brains from the beginning? Or is an infant's world, as William James once suggested, only a "blooming, buzzing confusion," waiting to be organized by experience and learning? The truth lies somewhere between these two extremes.

Inborn Abilities

In human beings, most basic sensory abilities, and many perceptual skills, are inborn or develop very early. Infants can distinguish salty from sweet and can discriminate among odors; they can even recognize their mother's unique scent—before they can recognize their mother (Montagner, 1985). They can distinguish a human voice from other sounds. They will startle to a loud noise and turn their heads toward its source, showing that they perceive sound as being localized in space.

Many visual skills are also present at birth, at least in rudimentary form, or they develop quite early, given normal experiences. For example, although human infants are born with a narrow field of vision, they can discriminate sizes and colors very early, possibly even right away. They can distinguish contrasts, shadows, and complex patterns after only a few weeks. And depth perception develops very early, during the first few months.

Testing an infant's perception of depth requires considerable ingenuity. One clever procedure that was used for decades was to place infants on a device called a *visual cliff* (Gibson & Walk, 1960). The "cliff" is a pane of glass covering a shallow surface and a deep one (see Figure 6.14). Both surfaces are covered by a checkerboard pattern. The infant is placed on a board in the middle, and the child's mother tries to lure the baby across either the shallow or the deep side. Babies as young as 6 months of age will crawl across the shallow side but will refuse to crawl out over the "cliff." Their hesitation shows that they have depth perception.

Of course, by 6 months of age, a baby has had quite a bit of experience with the world. But infants younger than 6 months, even though they are unable to crawl, can also be tested on the visual cliff. At only 2 months of age, babies show a drop in heart rate when placed on the deep side of the cliff, but no change when they are placed on the shallow side. A slowed heart rate is usually a sign of increased attention. Thus, although these infants may not be frightened the way an older infant would be, it seems they can perceive the difference between the "shallow" and "deep" sides of the cliff (Banks & Salapatek, 1984).

Figure 6.14

A CLIFF-HANGER

Infants as young as 6 months usually hesitate to crawl past the apparent edge of a visual cliff, which suggests that they are able to perceive depth.

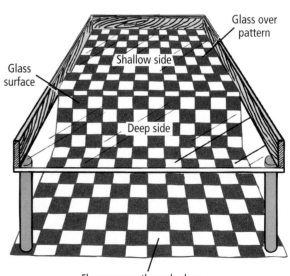

Glass over pattern

Shallow side

Glass surface

Deep side

Floor as seen through glass

Figure 6.15
VISION AND EARLY EXPERIENCE

Cats were reared in darkness for five months after birth, but for several hours each day were put in a special cylinder that permitted them to see only vertical or horizontal lines, and nothing else. Later on, cats who were exposed only to vertical lines had trouble perceiving horizontal ones, and those exposed only to horizontal lines had trouble perceiving vertical ones (Blakemore & Cooper, 1970).

Critical Periods

The fact that a perceptual capacity is inborn does not mean that experience plays no role. If an infant misses out on certain experiences during a crucial window of time—a *critical period*—perception will be impaired. Innate abilities will not survive because cells in the nervous system deteriorate, change, or fail to form appropriate neural pathways.

One way to study critical periods is to see what happens when the usual perceptual experiences of early life fail to take place. To do this, researchers usually study animals whose sensory and perceptual systems are similar to our own, such as cats. For example, like human infants, kittens are born with the ability to detect horizontal and vertical lines and other spatial orientations as well; at birth, their brains are equipped with the same kinds of feature-detector cells that adult cats have. But early experience can affect the cells sensitive to line orientations, causing them to deteriorate or change and perception to suffer accordingly (Crair, Gillespie, & Stryker, 1998; Hirsch & Spinelli, 1970).

In one famous study, kittens were exposed to either vertical or horizontal black and white stripes. Special collars kept them from seeing anything else, even their own bodies (see Figure 6.15). After several months, the kittens exposed only to vertical stripes seemed blind to all horizontal contours; they bumped into horizontal obstacles, and they ran to play with a bar that an experimenter held vertically but not to a bar held horizontally. In contrast, those exposed only to horizontal stripes bumped into vertical obstacles and ran to play with horizontal bars but not vertical ones (Blakemore & Cooper, 1970).

Fortunately, damage from early visual deprivation is not necessarily irreversible, because of the flexibility of the developing brain. Recovery depends on the animal's age when the damage occurs and how long the deprivation lasts. Kittens that have been deprived of all patterned visual stimulation begin to show new cortical connections and improvement in vision within a few hours after being exposed to normal visual input (Mitchell & Gingras, 1998).

Critical periods for sensory development also seem to exist in human beings. When adults who have been blind from infancy have their vision restored, they may see, but often they do not see well, and they cannot always make sense of what they do see. To identify objects, they may have to touch or smell them. One man, Shirl Jennings (whose story inspired the movie *At First Sight*), was confused by his own shadow, and his depth perception was so poor that he kept tripping. He found his new world strange and frightening, and when his eyesight again deteriorated, he actually seemed relieved.

But Shirl Jennings had been blind for many years. What happens to babies whose congenital blindness is corrected early? One team of researchers studied 28 infants who had been prevented by cataracts (cloudy lenses) from seeing any patterned visual input since birth. When the babies were 1 week to 9 months of age, they underwent corrective surgery and had special contact lenses inserted to focus light on the retina. At first, the infants' ability to make out visual details was no better than that of normal newborns—which is to say, poor. But improvement started to take place in as little as one hour of visual experience, and it continued over the next month (Maurer et al., 1999). These findings suggest that the critical period for the development of visual acuity extends at least to 9 months of age. It remains to be seen, however, whether all of these infants' visual abilities will return to normal.

The same pattern of findings occurs with other senses: Some abilities require sensory experiences during a critical period of development. When adults who were born deaf, or who lost their hearing before learning to speak, receive cochlear implants (devices that stimulate the auditory nerve and allow auditory signals to travel to the brain), they tend to find sounds confusing. They are unable to learn to speak normally, and often they ask to have the implants removed. In contrast, cochlear implants are often successful in restoring a fair degree of hearing to children and to adults who became deaf late in life (Rauschecker, 1999). Young children presumably have not yet passed through the critical period for processing sounds, and adults have already had years of auditory experience.

In sum, our perceptual powers are both "wired in" and dependent on experience. Because neurological connections in infants' brains and sensory systems are not completely formed, their senses are far less acute than an adult's. It takes time and experience before their sensory abilities fully develop. But an infant's world is clearly not the blooming, buzzing confusion that William James took it to be.

Psychological and Cultural Influences

The fact that some perceptual processes appear to be innate does not mean that all people perceive the world in the same way. A camera doesn't care what it "sees." A tape recorder doesn't ponder what it "hears." A robot arm on a factory assembly line holds no opinion about what it "touches." But because we human beings care about what we see, hear, taste, smell, and feel, psychological factors can influence what we perceive and how we perceive it. Here are a few of them.

1 *Needs.* When we need something, have an interest in it, or want it, we are especially likely to perceive it. For example, hungry individuals are faster than others at seeing words related to hunger when the words are flashed briefly on a screen (Wispé & Drambarean, 1953).

2 *Beliefs.* What we hold to be true about the world can affect our interpretation of ambiguous sensory signals. For example, if you believe that extraterrestrials occasionally visit the earth, and you see a round object in the sky (where there are few points of reference to help you judge distance), you may "see" a spaceship. (Impartial investigations of UFO sightings show that they are really weather balloons, rocket launchings, swamp gas, military aircraft, or ordinary celestial bodies, such as planets and meteors.) And if you believe that divine messages can be found on everyday objects, you may be fooled by ordinary sensory phenomena. Do you remember that image of Jesus on the garage door in California, in our opening story? It turned out to be caused by two streetlights that merged the shadows of a bush and a "For Sale" sign in the yard.

3 *Emotions.* Emotions can also influence our interpretation of sensory information. A small child afraid of the dark may see a ghost instead of a robe hanging on the door, or a monster instead of a beloved doll. Pain, in particular, is affected by emotion. Soldiers who are seriously wounded often deny being in much pain, even though they are alert and are not in shock. Their relief at being alive may offset the anxiety and fear that contribute so much to pain (although distraction and the body's own pain-fighting mechanisms may also be involved). Conversely, negative emotions such as anger, fear, sadness, or depression can prolong and intensify a person's pain (Fernandez & Turk, 1992; Fields, 1991).

4 *Expectations.* Previous experiences often affect how we perceive the world (Lachman, 1996). The tendency to perceive what you expect is called a **perceptual set**. Perceptual sets can come in handy; they help us fill in words in sentences, for example,

People often see what they want to see. A man in Nashville bought a cinnamon bun at a coffee shop and thought he saw a likeness of Mother Theresa in it. The bun was shellacked and enshrined at the coffee shop, and hundreds traveled to see it.

perceptual set A habitual way of perceiving, based on expectations.

when we haven't really heard every one. But perceptaul sets can also cause misperceptions. In Center Harbor, Maine, local legend has it that veteran newscaster Walter Cronkite was sailing into port one day when he heard a small crowd on shore shouting "Hello, Walter . . . Hello, Walter." Pleased, he waved and took a bow. Only when he ran aground did he realize what they had really been shouting: "Shallow water . . . shallow water."

By the way, the previous paragraph has a misspelled word. Did you notice it? If not, probably it was because you expected all the words in this book to be spelled correctly.

Our needs, beliefs, emotions, and expectations are all affected, in turn, by the culture we live in. Different cultures give people practice with different environments. In a classic study done in the 1960s, researchers found that members of some African tribes were much less likely to be fooled by the Müller-Lyer illusion and other geometric illusions than were Westerners. In the West, the researchers observed, people live in a "carpentered" world, full of rectangular structures built with the aid of straight edges and carpenter's squares. Westerners are also used to interpreting two-dimensional photographs and perspective drawings as representations of a three-dimensional world. Therefore, they interpret the kinds of angles used in the Müller-Lyer illusion as right angles extended in space—and this is just the sort of habit that would increase susceptibility to the illusion. The rural Africans in the study, living in a less carpentered environment and in round huts, seemed more likely to take the lines in the figures literally, as two-dimensional, which could explain why they were less susceptible to the illusion (Segall, Campbell, & Herskovits, 1966).

This research was followed by a flurry of replications in the 1970s, showing that it was indeed culture that produced the differences between groups (Segall, 1994; Segall et al., 1999). Since then, little work has been done on the fascinating intersection of culture and visual illusions. However, culture affects perception in many other ways: by shaping our stereotypes, directing our attention, and telling us what is important to notice and what is not. Westerners, for example, tend to focus mostly on the figure when viewing a scene, and much less on the ground. East Asians, in contrast, tend to pay attention to the overall context and the relationship between figure and ground because of a cultural inclination to see the world holistically. Thus, when Japanese and Americans were shown underwater scenes containing fish that were larger and moving faster than other objects in the scene, they reported the same numbers of details about the fish, but the Japanese reported more details about everything else in the background (Masuda & Nisbett, 2001). As one of the researchers, Richard Nisbett, likes to say, "If it ain't moving, it doesn't exist for an American" (quoted in Shea, 2001).

QUICK QUIZ

Direct your perceptual attention now to this quiz.

1. Animal studies suggest that newborns and infants (a) have few perceptual abilities, (b) need visual experiences during a critical period for vision to develop normally, (c) see as well as adults.

2. On the visual cliff, most 6-month-old babies (a) go right across because they cannot detect depth, (b) cross even though they are afraid, (c) will not cross because they can detect depth, (d) cry or get bored.

3. "Have a nice . . . " says Dewey, but then he gets distracted and doesn't finish the thought. Yet Clarence is sure he heard Dewey wish him a nice *day*. Why?

Answers:

1. b 2. c 3. perceptual set due to expectations

WHAT'S AHEAD

- Can "subliminal perception" tapes help you lose weight or reduce your stress?
- Why are most psychologists skeptical about ESP?

Puzzles of Perception

We come, finally, to two intriguing questions about perception that have captured the public's imagination for years. First, can we perceive what is happening in the world without being conscious of doing so? Second, can we pick up signals from the world or from other people without using our usual sensory channels at all?

Subliminal Perception: How Persuasive?

As we saw earlier in our discussion of the "cocktail party phenomenon," even when people are oblivious to speech sounds, they are processing and recognizing those sounds at some level. But these sounds are *above* people's absolute thresholds. Is it also possible to perceive and respond to messages that are *below* the absolute threshold—too quiet to be consciously heard (in the case of hearing) or too brief or dim to be consciously seen (in the case of vision)? Perhaps you have seen ads for products that will supposedly help you learn another language or raise your self-esteem (or, our favorite, learn to love housework) by taking advantage of such "subliminal perception." What are the facts?

> **THINKING CRITICALLY**
>
> **Examine the Evidence**
>
> For just $29.95, a "subliminal tape" promises to tune up your sluggish motivation. It is true that many perceptual processes occur outside of awareness, but does that mean that these tapes can change your behavior or improve your life?

Perceiving Without Awareness. First, a simple visual stimulus *can* affect your behavior even when you are unaware that you saw it. In one study, people subliminally exposed to a face tended to prefer that face over one they did not "see" in this way (Bornstein, Leone, & Galley, 1987). In other studies, researchers have flashed words subliminally in a person's visual field while the person focuses on the middle of a display. When the words are related to some personality trait, such as honesty, people are more likely later on to judge someone they read about as having that trait. They have been primed to evaluate the person that way (Bargh, 1999). Likewise, thirsty people who have been primed by thirst-related words are more likely to drink more of a sweet beverage than thirsty people who are not primed, and they also find ads for a thirst-quenching drink to be more persuasive (Strahan, Spencer, & Zanna, in press).

Findings such as these show that people often know more than they know they know. In fact, nonconscious processing appears to occur not only in perception

Zits

but also in memory, thinking, and decision making, as we will see in Chapters 9 and 10. However, the real-world implications of subliminal perception are not as dramatic as you might think. Even in the laboratory, where researchers have considerable control, the phenomenon is often hard to demonstrate. The strongest evidence comes from studies using simple stimuli (faces or single words such as *bread*) rather than complex stimuli such as sentences ("Eat whole-wheat bread, not white bread"). And even with single words, the influence of the subliminal stimulus is often short-lived, lasting only a few seconds (Greenwald, Draine, & Abrams, 1996).

Perception Versus Persuasion. While subliminal *perception* may occur under certain conditions, subliminal *persuasion,* the subject of many popular books and magazine articles, is quite another matter. Empirical research has uncovered no basis whatsoever for believing that advertisers can seduce us into buying soft drinks or voting for political candidates by slipping subliminal slogans and images into television and magazine ads. Nor can anyone corrupt young minds with subliminal images or messages slipped into animated movies or rock songs.

What about those subliminal tapes that promise to help you lose weight, stop smoking, relieve stress, read faster, boost your motivation, lower your cholesterol, stop biting your nails, overcome jet lag, or stop taking drugs—all without any effort on your part? In study after study, placebo tapes—tapes that do not contain the messages participants think they do—are just as "effective" as subliminal tapes (Eich & Hyman, 1992; Merikle & Skanes, 1992; Moore, 1992, 1995). In one typical study, people listened to tapes labeled "memory" or "self-esteem," but some heard tapes that were incorrectly labeled. About half showed improvement in the area specified by the label, *whether it was correct or not;* the improvement was due to expectations alone (Greenwald et al., 1991).

In sum, if advertisers want you to buy something, they would do better to spend their money on *above*-threshold messages. If you want to improve yourself or your life, we encourage you to do so, but we're afraid you will have to do it the old-fashioned way: by working at it.

Extrasensory Perception: Reality or Illusion?

Eyes, ears, mouth, nose, skin—we rely on these organs for our experience of the external world. Some people, however, claim they can send and receive messages about the world without relying on the usual sensory channels, by using *extrasensory perception (ESP).* Reported ESP experiences involve things like telepathy, the direct communication of messages from one mind to another without the usual sensory signals, and precognition, the perception of an event that has not yet happened.

Most ESP claims challenge everything we currently know to be true about the way the world and the universe operate. In the era of *The X-Files,* a lot of people are ready to accept these claims. Should they?

THINKING CRITICALLY

Examine the Evidence

ESP would certainly be useful before a tough exam or a blind date. But it's one thing to wish ESP existed and another to conclude that it does. What kind of evidence would convince you that ESP is real, and what kind is only wishful thinking?

Evidence—or Just Coincidence? Much of the "evidence" for extrasensory perception comes from anecdotal accounts. But people are not always reliable reporters of their own experiences. They often embellish and exaggerate, or recall only part of what happened. They also tend to forget incidents that don't fit their beliefs, such as "premonitions" of events that fail to occur. Many ESP experiences could merely be unusual coincidences that are memorable because they are dramatic. What passes for telepathy or precognition could also be based on what a person knows or deduces through ordinary means. If Joanne's father has had two heart attacks, her premonition that her father will die shortly (followed, in fact, by her father's death) may not be so impressive.

The scientific way to establish a phenomenon is to produce it under controlled conditions. Extrasensory perception has been studied extensively by researchers in the field of **parapsychology.** But ESP studies have often been poorly designed, with inadequate precautions against fraud and improper statistical analysis. After an exhaustive review, the National Research Council concluded that there was "no scientific justification . . . for the existence of parapsychological phenomena" (Druckman & Swets, 1988).

The issue has not gone away, however. Many people *really, really* want to believe that ESP exists. In the 1990s, social psychologist Daryl Bem made waves in the psychological community when he reported a series of ESP studies carried out with the late Charles Honorton, a British parapsychologist. Bem and Honorton (1994) studied telepathy. A sender sat in a soundproof room and concentrated on a picture or video clip selected at random by a computer. A receiver sat in another soundproof room, trying to receive the sender's imagery. Then the receiver was shown four pictures or video clips and was asked to pick out the one that most closely matched his or her mental imagery during the transmission period. If the receiver selected the stimulus that was "sent," that trial counted as a "hit." Bem and Honorton reported an overall hit rate of about 33 percent, whereas chance would predict only 25 percent. Since then, some other successes have been reported (Dalton et al., 1996; Parker, 2000).

These findings, however, have come under withering criticism. Although the methods used by Bem and Honorton were better than those used by previous researchers, possible flaws existed in the way the pictures and video clips were randomized and selected (Hyman, 1994). Moreover, a meta-analysis of 30 studies using methods as rigorous as Bem and Honorton's found no evidence whatsoever for telepathy (Milton & Wiseman, 1999, 2001). Inasmuch as negative findings often don't get published in the first place, this is strong evidence against ESP.

The history of research on psychic phenomena has been one of initial enthusiasm followed by disappointment when results cannot be replicated, and the thousands of studies done since the 1940s have failed to make a convincing case for ESP. One researcher who tried for thirty years to establish the reality of psychic phenomena finally gave up in defeat. "I found no psychic phenomena," she wrote, "only wishful thinking, self-deception, experimental error, and even an occasional fraud. I became a skeptic" (Blackmore, 2001).

Lessons from a Magician. Despite the lack of evidence for ESP, about half of all Americans say they believe in it. Perhaps you yourself have had an experience that seemed to involve ESP, or perhaps have seen a convincing demonstration by someone else. Surely you can trust the evidence of your own eyes—or can you? We will answer this question with a true story, one that contains an important lesson not only about ESP but about ordinary perception as well.

During the 1970s, Andrew Weil (who is now known for his efforts to promote alternative medicine) set out to investigate the claims of a self-proclaimed psychic named Uri Geller (Weil, 1974a, 1974b). Weil, who believed in telepathy, felt that ESP might be explained by principles of modern physics, and he was receptive to Geller's claims. When he met Geller at a private gathering, he was not disappointed. Geller correctly identified a cross and a Star of David sealed inside separate envelopes. He made a stopped watch start running and a ring sag into an oval shape, apparently

THE FAR SIDE® BY GARY LARSON

For the most part, the meeting was quite successful. Only a slight tension filled the air, stemming from the unforeseen faux pas of everyone wearing the same dress.

parapsychology The study of purported psychic phenomena such as ESP and mental telepathy.

"Seeing is believing," they say, but is it? The engraving on the left shows a "living half-woman," seemingly swinging in mid-air. The sketch on the right shows how the illusion is produced. The woman reclines on an artificial bust, her body supported by another swing and hidden by black curtains. Due to a trick of lighting, the viewer sees only the swing, the face, the necklace, and the sword beneath the swing. The moral: Be skeptical about paranormal claims, even if you "saw it with your own eyes."

without touching them. He made keys change shape in front of Weil's very eyes. Weil came away a convert. What he had seen with his own eyes seemed impossible to deny . . . until he met the Amazing Randi.

James Randi is a famous magician who is dedicated to educating the public about psychic deception. To Weil's astonishment, Randi was able to duplicate much of what Geller had done. He, too, could bend keys and guess the contents of sealed envelopes. But Randi's feats were tricks, and he was willing to show Weil exactly how they were done. Weil suddenly experienced "a sense of how strongly the mind can impose its own interpretations on perceptions; how it can see what it expects to see, but not see the unexpected."

Weil was dis-illusioned—literally. He was forced to admit that the evidence of one's own eyes is not always reliable. Even when he knew what to look for in a trick, he could not catch the Amazing Randi doing it. Weil learned that our sense impressions of reality are not the same as reality. Our eyes, our ears, and especially our brains can play tricks on us.

QUICK QUIZ

There are no subliminal messages in this quiz—trust us.

 1. A study appears to find evidence of "sleep learning"—the ability to perceive and retain material played on an audiotape while a person sleeps. What would you want to know about this research before deciding to tape this chapter and play it by your bedside all night instead of studying it in the usual way?

 2. What processes of human perception might explain why so many people interpret unexplained sensations as evidence of ESP, telepathy, and other "psychic" phenomena?

Answers:

1. You might ask about the kinds of stimuli used (in studies of other kinds of nonconscious perception, positive results have usually been obtained with very simple stimuli, not whole sentences); whether the results were large enough to have practical consequences; and how it was determined that the participants really were asleep while the tape was playing. (When brain-wave measurements are used to verify that volunteers are actually sleeping, no "sleep learning" takes place. So if you want to learn the material in this chapter, you'll have to stay awake!) 2. Psychological and cultural factors, such as perceptual sets, needs, emotions, wishes, and beliefs.

As we have seen throughout this chapter, we do not passively register the world "out there"; we mentally construct it. All of us, even those of us who are not usually gullible, have needs and beliefs that can fool us into seeing things that we *want* to see. All of us occasionally read meanings into sensory experiences that are not inherent in the experience itself; who has not seen nonexistent water on a hot highway, or felt a nonexistent insect on the skin after merely thinking about bugs?

The great Greek philosopher Plato once said that "knowledge is nothing but perception," but he was wrong. Simple perception is *not* always the best path to knowledge. The truth about human behavior is most likely to emerge if we are aware of how our beliefs, assumptions, and expectations shape and alter the way we experience the world.

Taking Psychology with You

LIVING WITH PAIN

Temporary pain is an unpleasant but necessary part of life, a warning of disease or injury. Chronic pain is another matter, a serious problem in itself. Back injuries, arthritis, migraine headaches, serious illnesses such as cancer—all can cause unrelieved misery to pain sufferers and their families. Chronic pain can also impair the immune system, putting patients at risk of further complications from their illnesses (Page et al., 1993).

At one time, the only way to combat pain was with drugs or surgery, which were not always effective. Today, we know that pain is affected by attitudes, actions, emotions, and circumstances and that treatment must take these influences into account. Even social roles can influence a person's response to pain. For example, although women tend to report greater pain than men do, a real-world study of people who were in pain for more than six months found that men suffered more psychological distress than women did, possibly because the male role made it hard for them to admit their pain (Snow et al., 1986).

Many pain-treatment programs encourage patients to manage their pain themselves instead of relying entirely on health-care professionals. Usually, these programs combine several strategies:

▶ *Painkilling medication.* Doctors often worry that patients will become addicted to painkillers or will develop a tolerance to the drugs. The physicians will therefore give a minimal dose, then wait until the effects wear off and the patient is once again in agony before giving more. This approach is ineffective and is based on outdated notions about addiction. In reality, people who take painkillers to control their pain rarely become addicted (see Chapter 16). The method now recommended by experts (although doctors and hospitals do not always follow the advice) is to give pain sufferers a continuous dose of painkiller in whatever amount is necessary to keep them pain-free, and to allow them to do this for themselves when they leave the hospital. This strategy leads to reduced dosages rather than larger ones and rarely leads to drug dependence (Hill et al., 1990; Portenoy, 1994).

▶ *Involvement by family and friends.* When a person is in pain, friends and relatives understandably tend to sympathize and to excuse the sufferer from regular responsibilities. The sufferer takes to bed, avoids physical activity, and focuses on the pain. As we discuss in Chapter 7, attention from others is a powerful reinforcer of whatever behavior produces the attention. Also, focusing on pain tends to increase it, and inactivity can lead to shortened muscles, muscle spasms, and fatigue. So sympathy and attention can sometimes backfire and may actually prolong the agony (Flor, Kerns, & Turk, 1987). For this reason, many pain experts now encourage family members to resist rewarding or reinforcing the pain and to reward activity, exercise, and wellness instead. This approach, however, must be used carefully, preferably under the direction of a medical or mental-health professional, because a patient's complaints about pain are an important diagnostic tool for the physician.

▶ *Self-management.* When patients learn to identify how, when, and where their pain occurs, this knowledge helps them determine whether the pain is being maintained by external events. Just having a sense of control over pain can have a powerful pain-reducing effect. In one study, students who monitored their pain while one hand was submerged in freezing water showed more rapid recovery from the pain than did students who had tried to suppress their awareness of pain sensations or distract themselves, apparently because the monitoring students had a sense of control (Cioffi & Holloway, 1993).

▶ *Relaxation, hypnosis, and acupuncture.* A blue-ribbon panel of experts concluded that relaxation techniques, such as meditating or focusing on reducing tension in specific muscle groups, can help reduce chronic pain from a variety of medical conditions, and that hypnosis can reduce pain due to cancer and may help in other conditions (NIH Technology Assessment Panel, 1996). Some studies find that acupuncture also helps in reducing some kinds of pain, possibly by stimulating the release of endorphins (Holden, 1997). However, the best-designed studies are the least likely to find such an effect, so many medical experts remain skeptical.

▶ *Cognitive-behavior therapy.* This form of therapy teaches people how to recognize the connections among thoughts, feelings, and pain; substitute adaptive thoughts for negative ones; and use coping strategies such as distraction, rela- beling of sensations, and imagery to alleviate suffering (see Chapter 17). Cognitive-behavioral techniques increase feelings of control and reduce feelings of inadequacy, and are effective in helping people cope with chronic pain (Morley, Eccleston, & Williams, 1999).

For further information, you can contact pain clinics or services in teaching hospitals and in medical schools. There are many reputable clinics around the country, some specializing in specific disorders, such as migraines or back injuries. But take care: There are also many untested therapies and quack practitioners who only prey on people's pain.

Summary

Our Sensational Senses

▶ *Sensation* is the detection and direct experience of physical energy as a result of environmental or internal events. *Perception* is the process by which sensory impulses are organized and interpreted.

▶ Sensation begins with the sense receptors, which convert the energy of a stimulus into electrical impulses that travel along nerves to the brain. Separate sensations can be accounted for by *anatomical codes* (as set forth by the *doctrine of specific nerve energies*) and *functional codes* in the nervous system. In a rare condition called *synesthesia*, sensation in one modality evokes a sensation in another modality, but these experiences are the exception, not the rule.

▶ Psychologists specializing in *psychophysics* have studied sensory sensitivity by measuring *absolute* and *difference thresholds*. *Signal-detection theory*, however, holds that responses in a detection task consist of both a sensory process and a decision process and will vary with the person's motivation, alertness, and expectations.

▶ Our senses are designed to respond to change and contrast in the environment. When stimulation is unchanging, *sensory adaptation* occurs. Too little stimulation can cause *sensory deprivation*, and too much stimulation can cause *sensory overload*, which is why we exercise *selective attention*.

Vision

▶ Vision is affected by the wavelength, frequency, and complexity of light, which produce the psychological dimensions of visual experience— *hue, brightness,* and *saturation*. The visual receptors, *rods* and *cones*, are located in the *retina* of the eye. Rods are responsible for vision in dim light; cones are responsible for color vision.

▶ Specific aspects of the visual world, such as lines at certain orientations, are detected by *feature-detector cells* in the visual areas of the brain. Some of these cells respond maximally to complex patterns. A heated debate is now going on about the existence of specialized "face modules." In general, however, the eye is not a camera; the brain takes in fragmentary information about lines, angles, shapes, motion, brightness, texture, and other features of what we see, and comes up with a unified view of the world.

▶ The *trichromatic* and *opponent-process* theories of color vision apply to different stages of processing. In the first stage, three types of cones in the retina respond selectively to different wavelengths of light. In the second, *opponent-process cells* in the retina and the thalamus respond in opposite fashion to short and long wavelengths of light.

▶ Perception involves the active construction of a model of the world from moment to moment. The *Gestalt principles* (e.g., *figure* and *ground, proximity, closure, similarity,* and *continuity*) describe visual strategies used by the brain to perceive forms.

▶ We localize objects in visual space by using both *binocular* and *monocular* cues to depth. Binocular cues include *convergence* and *retinal disparity.* Monocular cues include, among others, interposition and linear perspective. *Perceptual constancies* allow us to perceive objects as stable despite changes in the sensory patterns they produce. *Perceptual illusions* occur when sensory cues are misleading or when we misinterpret cues.

Hearing

▶ Hearing (*audition*) is affected by the intensity, frequency, and complexity of pressure waves in the air or other transmitting substance, corresponding to the experience of *loudness, pitch,* and *timbre* of the sound. The receptors for hearing are hair cells (cilia) embedded in the *organ of Corti* (in the *basilar membrane*), in the interior of the *cochlea.* The sounds we hear are determined by patterns of hair-cell movement, which produce different neural codes. When we localize sounds, we use as cues subtle differences in how pressure waves reach each of our ears.

Other Senses

▶ Taste (*gustation*) is a chemical sense. Elevations on the tongue, called *papillae,* contain many *taste buds.* There are four basic tastes—salty, sour, bitter, and sweet—and possibly a fifth, umami, although its inclusion is controversial. Responses to a particular taste depend in part on genetic differences among individuals; for example, some people are "supertasters." Taste preferences are also affected by culture and learning, by the texture and temperature of the food, and by a food's smell.

▶ Smell (*olfaction*) is also a chemical sense. Findings on the neural code for smell have been complicated; no basic odors have been identified, and up to a thousand differ-ent receptor types exist. But researchers have discovered that distinct odors activate unique combinations of receptor types, and they have started to identify those combinations. Cultural and individual differences also affect people's responses to particular odors.

▶ The skin senses include touch (pressure), warmth, cold, pain, and variations such as itch and tickle. Except in the case of pressure, it has been difficult to identify specialized receptors for these senses, but researchers have recently reported a receptor for one kind of itching and a possible receptor for cold.

▶ Pain is both a skin sense and an internal sense. According to the *gate-control theory,* the experience of pain depends on whether neural impulses get past a "gate" in the spinal cord and reach the brain. According to a revised version of this theory, a matrix of neurons in the brain can generate pain even in the absence of signals from sensory neurons, which may explain the puzzling phenomenon of phantom pain. Pain comes in different varieties, both physiologically and psychologically.

▶ *Kinesthesis* tells us where our body parts are located, and *equilibrium* tells us the orientation of the body as a whole. Together, these two senses provide us with a feeling of physical embodiment.

Perceptual Powers: Origins and Influences

▶ Studies of animals and human infants suggest that many fundamental perceptual skills are inborn or acquired shortly after birth. By using the *visual cliff,* for example, psychologists have learned that babies have depth perception by the age of 6 months and possibly even earlier. However, without certain experiences during *critical periods* early in life, cells in the nervous system deteriorate, change, or fail to form appropriate neural pathways, and perception is impaired. Therefore, innate abilities fail to survive.

▶ Psychological influences on perception include needs, beliefs, emotions, and expectations. These influences are affected by culture, which gives people practice with certain kinds of experiences and influences what they attend to. Because psychological factors affect the way we construct the perceptual world, the evidence of our senses is not always reliable.

Puzzles of Perception

▶ In the laboratory, simple visual subliminal messages can influence attitudes and behavior, at least briefly.

However, there is no evidence that complex behaviors can be altered by "subliminal-perception" tapes or other commercial subliminal techniques.

▶ *Extrasensory perception* (*ESP*) refers to paranormal abilities such as telepathy and precognition. Years of research have failed to produce convincing evidence for ESP. Many so-called psychics take advantage of people's desire to believe in ESP, but what they do is no different from the tricks of any good magician. The story of ESP illustrates a central fact about human perception: It does not merely capture objective reality but also reflects our needs, biases, and beliefs.

Key Terms

sensation 181

perception 182

sense receptors 182

anatomical codes 183

doctrine of specific nerve energies 183

synesthesia 184

functional codes 184

absolute threshold 184

difference threshold 186

signal-detection theory 186

sensory adaptation 187

sensory deprivation 188

selective attention 189

hue 190

brightness 190

saturation 190

retina 191

rods 192

cones 192

dark adaptation 192

ganglion cells 192

optic nerve 192

feature-detector cells 194

trichromatic theory 195

opponent-process theory 195

negative afterimage 196

figure and ground 197

Gestalt principles 198

binocular cues 199

convergence 199

retinal disparity 199

monocular cues 199

perceptual constancy 199

perceptual illusion 202

audition 204

loudness 204

pitch 204

frequency (sound wave) 204

timbre 204

organ of Corti 206

cochlea 206

basilar membrane 206

auditory nerve 207

gustation 208

papillae 208

taste buds 208

olfaction 210

gate-control theory (of pain) 212

phantom pain 213

kinesthesis 213

equilibrium 213

semicircular canals 213

perceptual set 217

subliminal perception 219

extrasensory perception 220

parapsychology 221

◀ LOOKING BACK

- What kind of "code" in the nervous system helps explain why a pinprick and a kiss feel different? (p. 184)

- Why does your dog hear a "silent" doggie whistle when you can't? (p. 186)

- What kind of bias can influence whether you think you hear the phone ringing when you're in the shower? (pp. 186–187)

- What happens when people are deprived of all external sensory stimulation? (pp. 187–188)

- How does the eye differ from a camera? (pp. 193–194)

- Why can we describe a color as bluish green but not as reddish green? (p. 196)

- If you were blind in one eye, why might you misjudge your distance from a painting on the wall but not the distance to buildings a block away? (p. 199)

- As a friend approaches, her image on your retina grows larger; why do you continue to see her as the same size? (p. 200)

- Why are perceptual illusions so valuable to psychologists? (p. 202)

- Why does a note played on a flute sound different from the same note played on an oboe? (pp. 204–205)

- If you habitually listen to loud music through headphones, what kind of hearing impairment are you risking? (p. 206)

- To locate the source of a sound, why does it sometimes help to turn or tilt your head? (p. 207)

- Why do saccharin and caffeine taste bitter to some people but not to others? (p. 209)

- Why do you have trouble tasting your food when you have a cold? (p. 210)

- Why do people often continue to "feel" limbs that have been amputated? (p. 213)

- Do babies see the world the way adults do? (pp. 215–217)

- What psychological motives could cause people to "see" the face of a religious figure on a cinnamon bun? (p. 217)

- Can "subliminal perception" tapes help you lose weight or reduce your stress? (p. 220)

- Why are most psychologists skeptical about ESP? (pp. 220–221)

Go to _Live!_ **psych** **WWW.PRENHALL.COM** **to reinforce these key concepts, and more.**

6.1 Structures of the human eye **6.4 Perceptual illusions**
6.2 Gestalt principles **6.5 Structures of the human ear**
6.3 Depth and dimension

7

Learning and Conditioning

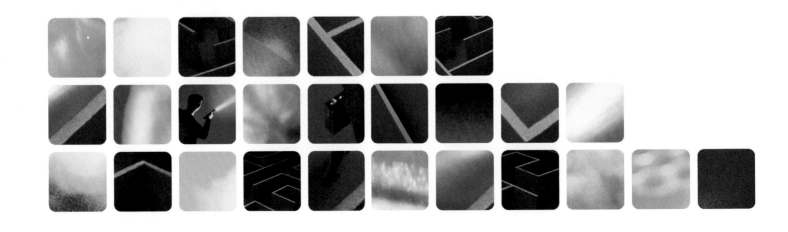

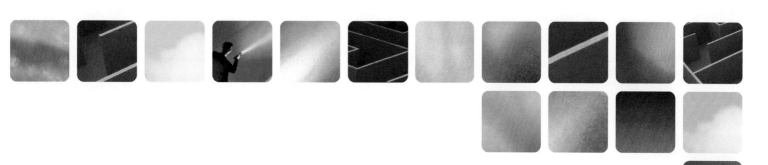

Reward and punishment . . . are the spur and reins whereby
all mankind are set on work, and guided.

JOHN LOCKE

I t's January 1, a brand-new year. The sins and lapses of the old year are behind you; the slate is clean and you're ready for a fresh start. Optimistically, you sit down to record your New Year's resolutions: to eat less fatty foods, study harder, control your temper, get more exercise, manage your spending, . . . (you can fill in the rest).

How likely are you to achieve these goals? Within weeks, days, or even hours, many people find themselves reverting to their old habits ("Well, maybe just one *small* dish of double chocolate ice cream"). They may decide that trying to mend their ways is pointless because they lack the willpower or brains or courage to do it. In this chapter, however, we will see that willpower, brains, and courage often have little to do with a person's ability to alter bad habits. Once you understand the laws of learning, you realize that behavior *can* change for the better—and you understand why it often does not.

In ordinary speech, learning usually refers to classroom activities, such as memorizing the facts of geography, or to the acquisition of practical skills, such as carpentry or sewing. But to psychologists, **learning** is *any* relatively permanent change in behavior—or the capacity for a behavior—that occurs because of experience (rather than fatigue, injury, or disease). Experience is the greatest teacher, providing the essential link between the past and the future, and enabling an organism to adapt to changing circumstances in order to survive and thrive.

Research on learning has been heavily influenced by **behaviorism,** the school of psychology that accounts for behavior in terms of observable acts and events, without reference to mental entities such as "mind" or "will." Behaviorists focus on a basic kind of learning called **conditioning,** which involves associations between environmental stimuli and responses. In fact, behaviorism is sometimes referred to informally as stimulus-response ("S-R") psychology. Behaviorists have shown that two types of conditioning, *classical conditioning* and *operant conditioning,* can explain much of human behavior. But other approaches, known as *social-cognitive learning theories,* hold that omitting mental processes from explanations of human learning is like omitting passion from descriptions of sex: You may explain the form, but you miss the substance. To social-cognitive theorists, learning is not so much a change in observable behavior as a change in *knowledge* that has the potential for affecting behavior.

229

learning A relatively permanent change in behavior (or behavioral potential) due to experience.

behaviorism An approach to psychology that emphasizes the study of observable behavior and the role of the environment as a determinant of behavior.

conditioning A basic kind of learning that involves associations between environmental stimuli and the organism's responses.

WHAT'S AHEAD

- Why would a dog salivate when it sees a lightbulb or hears a buzzer, even though it can't eat these things?
- How can classical conditioning help explain prejudice?
- If you have learned to fear collies, why might you also be scared of sheepdogs?

Classical Conditioning

At the turn of the century, the great Russian physiologist Ivan Pavlov (1849–1936) was studying salivation in dogs, as part of a research program on digestion. His work would shortly win him the Nobel Prize in physiology and medicine. One of Pavlov's procedures was to make a surgical opening in a dog's cheek and insert a tube that conducted saliva away from the animal's salivary gland so that the saliva could be measured. To stimulate the reflexive flow of saliva, Pavlov placed meat powder or other food in the dog's mouth. This procedure was later refined by others (see Figure 7.1).

Pavlov was a truly dedicated scientific observer. Many years later, as he lay dying, he even dictated his sensations for posterity! And he imbued his students with his own passion for detail. During his salivation studies, one of these students noticed something that most people would have overlooked or dismissed as trivial. After a dog had been brought to the laboratory a number of times, it would start to salivate *before* the food was placed in its mouth. The sight or smell of the food, the dish in which the food was kept, even the sight of the person who delivered the food each day or the sound of the person's footsteps were enough to start the dog's mouth watering. These new salivary responses clearly were not inborn, so they had to have been acquired through experience.

At first, Pavlov treated the dog's drooling as just an annoying secretion. But he quickly realized that his student had stumbled onto an important phenomenon, one that Pavlov came to believe was the basis of most learning in human beings and other animals (Pavlov, 1927). He called that phenomenon a "conditional" reflex—conditional because it depended on environmental conditions. Later, an error in the translation of his writings transformed "conditional" into "conditioned," the word most commonly used today.

Figure 7.1

A MODIFICATION OF PAVLOV'S METHOD

In the apparatus on the right, which was based on Pavlov's techniques, saliva from a dog's cheek flowed down a tube and was measured by the movement of a needle on a revolving drum. In the photo below, you can see Ivan Pavlov himself in the center, flanked by his students and a canine subject.

Pavlov soon dropped what he had been doing and turned to the study of conditioned reflexes, to which he devoted the last three decades of his life. Why were his dogs salivating to things other than food?

New Reflexes from Old

At first Pavlov speculated about what his dogs might be thinking and feeling to make them drool before getting their food. Was the doggy equivalent of "Oh boy, this means chow time" going through their minds? Eventually, however, he decided that speculating about his dogs' mental abilities was pointless (Todes, 1997). Instead, he focused on analyzing the environment in which the conditioned reflex arose. The original salivary reflex, according to Pavlov, consisted of an **unconditioned stimulus (US)**, food, and an **unconditioned response (UR)**, salivation. By an *unconditioned stimulus,* Pavlov meant an event or thing that elicits a response automatically or reflexively. By an *unconditioned response,* he meant the response that is automatically produced:

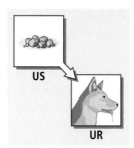

Learning occurs, said Pavlov, when a neutral stimulus (one that does not yet produce a particular response, such as salivation) is regularly paired with an unconditioned stimulus:

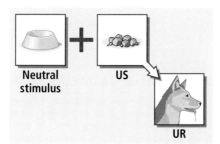

The neutral stimulus then becomes a **conditioned stimulus (CS)**, which elicits a learned or **conditioned response (CR)** that is usually similar to the original, unlearned one. In Pavlov's laboratory, the sight of the food dish, which had not previously elicited salivation, became a CS for salivation:

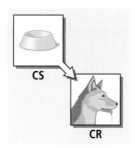

unconditioned stimulus (US) The classical-conditioning term for a stimulus that elicits a reflexive response in the absence of learning.

unconditioned response (UR) The classical-conditioning term for a reflexive response elicited by a stimulus in the absence of learning.

conditioned stimulus (CS) The classical-conditioning term for an initially neutral stimulus that comes to elicit a conditioned response after being associated with an unconditioned stimulus.

conditioned response (CR) The classical-conditioning term for a response that is elicited by a conditioned stimulus; it occurs after the conditioned stimulus is associated with an unconditioned stimulus.

classical conditioning The process by which a previously neutral stimulus acquires the capacity to elicit a response through association with a stimulus that already elicits a similar or related response.

extinction The weakening and eventual disappearance of a learned response; in classical conditioning, it occurs when the conditioned stimulus is no longer paired with the unconditioned stimulus.

spontaneous recovery The reappearance of a learned response after its apparent extinction.

The procedure by which a neutral stimulus becomes a conditioned stimulus became known as **classical conditioning**, also called *Pavlovian* or *respondent* conditioning. Pavlov and his students went on to show that all sorts of things can become conditioned stimuli for salivation if they are paired with food: the ticking of a metronome, the musical tone of a bell or tuning fork, the vibrating sound of a buzzer, a touch on the leg, a triangle drawn on a large card, even a pinprick or an electric shock. And since Pavlov's day, many automatic, involuntary responses besides salivation have been classically conditioned—for example, heartbeat, stomach secretions, blood pressure, reflexive movements, blinking, and muscle contractions. The optimal interval between the presentation of the neutral stimulus and the presentation of the US depends on the kind of response involved; in the laboratory, the interval is often less than a second.

Principles of Classical Conditioning

Classical conditioning occurs in all species, from worms to *Homo sapiens*. Let us look more closely at some important features of this process: extinction, higher-order conditioning, and stimulus generalization and discrimination.

Extinction. Conditioned responses do not necessarily last forever. If, after conditioning, the conditioned stimulus is repeatedly presented without the unconditioned stimulus, the conditioned response eventually disappears, and **extinction** is said to have occurred (see Figure 7.2). Suppose that you train your dog Milo to salivate to the sound of a bell, but then you ring the bell every five minutes and do *not* follow it with food. Milo will salivate less and less to the bell and will soon stop salivating altogether; salivation will have been extinguished. Extinction is not the same as unlearning or forgetting, however. If you come back the next day and ring the bell, Milo may salivate again for a few trials. The reappearance of the response, called **spontaneous recovery**, explains why completely eliminating a conditioned response usually requires more than one extinction session.

Figure 7.2

ACQUISITION AND EXTINCTION OF A SALIVARY RESPONSE

A neutral stimulus that is consistently followed by an unconditioned stimulus for salivation will become a conditioned stimulus for salivation (left). But when this conditioned stimulus is then repeatedly presented without the unconditioned stimulus, the conditioned salivary response will weaken and eventually disappear (right); it has been extinguished.

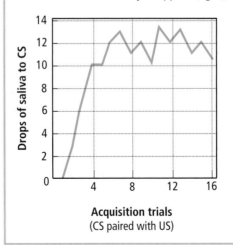

Acquisition trials
(CS paired with US)

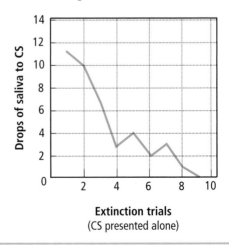

Extinction trials
(CS presented alone)

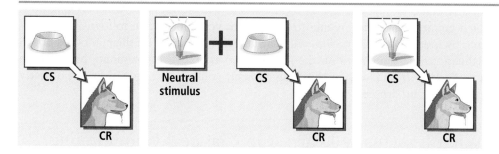

Figure 7.3
HIGHER-ORDER CONDITIONING

In this illustration of higher-order conditioning, the food dish is a previously conditioned stimulus for salivation (left). When the light, a neutral stimulus, is paired with the dish (center), the light, too, becomes a conditioned stimulus for salivation (right).

Higher-Order Conditioning. Sometimes a neutral stimulus can become a conditioned stimulus by being paired with an already established CS, a procedure known as **higher-order conditioning.** Say Milo has learned to salivate to the sight of his food dish. Now you flash a bright light before presenting the dish. With repeated pairings of the light and the dish, Milo may learn to salivate to the light. The procedure for higher-order conditioning is illustrated in Figure 7.3.

Higher-order conditioning may explain why some words trigger emotional responses in us—why they can inflame us to anger or evoke warm, sentimental feelings. When words are paired with objects or other words that already elicit some emotional response, they, too, may come to elicit that response (Chance, 1999; Staats & Staats, 1957). For example, a child may learn a positive response to the word *birthday* because of its association with gifts and attention. Conversely, the child may learn a negative response to ethnic or national labels, such as *Swede, Turk,* or *Jew,* if those words are paired with words that the child has already learned are disagreeable, such as *dumb* or *dirty.* Higher-order conditioning, in other words, may contribute to the formation of prejudices.

Stimulus Generalization and Discrimination. After a stimulus becomes a conditioned stimulus for some response, other, similar stimuli may produce a similar reaction—a phenomenon known as **stimulus generalization.** For example, if you condition your patient pooch Milo to salivate to middle C on the piano, Milo may also salivate to D, which is one tone above C, even though you did not pair D with food. Stimulus generalization is described nicely by an old English proverb: "He who hath been bitten by a snake fears a rope."

The mirror image of stimulus generalization is **stimulus discrimination,** in which *different* responses are made to stimuli that resemble the conditioned stimulus in some way. Suppose that you have conditioned Milo to salivate to middle C

higher-order conditioning In classical conditioning, a procedure in which a neutral stimulus becomes a conditioned stimulus through association with an already established conditioned stimulus.

stimulus generalization After conditioning, the tendency to respond to a stimulus that resembles one involved in the original conditioning; in classical conditioning, it occurs when a stimulus that resembles the CS elicits the CR.

stimulus discrimination The tendency to respond differently to two or more similar stimuli; in classical conditioning, it occurs when a stimulus similar to the CS fails to evoke the CR.

Get Involved

Conditioning an Eye-Blink Response

Try out your behavioral skills by conditioning an eye-blink response in a friend, using classical conditioning procedures. You will need a drinking straw and something to make a ringing sound—a spoon tapped on a water glass works well. Tell your friend that you are going to blow air in his or her eye through the straw, but don't say why. Immediately before each puff of air, make the ringing sound. Repeat this procedure ten times. Then make the ringing sound but *don't* puff. Your friend will probably blink anyway, and may continue to do so for one or two more repetitions of the sound before the response extinguishes. Can you identify the US, the UR, the CS, and the CR in this exercise?

7.1

on the piano by repeatedly pairing the sound with food. Now you play middle C on a guitar, *without* following it by food (but you continue to follow C on the piano by food). Eventually, Milo will learn to salivate to a C on the piano and not to salivate to the same note on the guitar; that is, he will discriminate between the two sounds. If you keep at this long enough, you could train Milo to be a pretty discriminating drooler!

What Is Actually Learned in Classical Conditioning?

For classical conditioning to be most effective, the stimulus to be conditioned should *precede* the unconditioned stimulus rather than follow it or occur simultaneously with it. This makes sense, because in classical conditioning, the conditioned stimulus becomes a *signal* for the unconditioned stimulus. Classical conditioning is in fact an evolutionary adaptation, one that enables the organism to anticipate and prepare for a biologically important event that is about to happen. In Pavlov's studies, for instance, a bell, buzzer, or other stimulus was a signal that meat was coming, and the dog's salivation was preparation for digesting food.

Today, therefore, many psychologists contend that what an animal or person actually learns in classical conditioning is not merely an association between two paired stimuli that occur close together in time, but rather *information* conveyed by one stimulus about another: for example, "If a tone sounds, food is likely to follow" (Davey, 1992). This view is supported by the research of Robert Rescorla (1988), who showed, in a series of imaginative studies, that the mere pairing of an unconditioned stimulus and a neutral stimulus is not enough to produce learning. To become a conditioned stimulus, the neutral stimulus must reliably signal, or *predict,* the unconditioned stimulus. If food occurs just as often without a preceding tone as with it, the tone is unlikely to become a conditioned stimulus for salivation—because the tone does not provide any information about the probability of getting food.

In everyday life, too, a potential CS may sometimes predict an unconditioned stimulus and sometimes not, so conditioning is less certain than when the CS and US always occur together in the laboratory. A friend of ours, behaviorist Paul Chance, gave us this example: Suppose you work in an office where you are allowed to receive routine phone calls only from other employees; you may take outside calls only in emergencies. One day, there are three emergencies: Your lover calls to jilt you, the police call to report that your new car was stolen, and your landlord calls to tell you that a broken water pipe has flooded your apartment. If these were the only calls you got, the next time you heard the phone ring (the CS), you might freak out (the CR). But if they occurred randomly among 50 routine business calls, the phone's ringing would probably not upset you (any more than you already are!) because it would not necessarily signal another disaster.

Rescorla (1988) concluded that "Pavlovian conditioning is not a stupid process by which the organism willy-nilly forms associations between any two stimuli that happen to co-occur. Rather, the organism is better seen as an information seeker using logical and perceptual relations among events, along with its own preconceptions, to form a sophisticated representation of its world." Not all learning theorists agree with this conclusion; an orthodox behaviorist would say that it is silly to talk about the preconceptions of a rat. The important point, however, is that concepts such as "information seeking," "preconceptions," and "representations of the world" open the door to a more cognitive view of classical conditioning.

QUICK QUIZ

Classical-conditioning terms can be hard to learn, so be sure to take this quiz before going on.

A. Name the unconditioned stimulus, unconditioned response, conditioned stimulus, and conditioned response in these two situations.

1. Five-year-old Samantha is watching a storm from her window. A huge bolt of lightning is followed by a tremendous thunderclap, and Samantha jumps at the noise. This happens several more times. There is a brief lull and then another lightning bolt. Samantha jumps in response to the bolt.

2. Gregory's mouth waters whenever he eats anything with lemon in it. One day, while reading an ad that shows a big glass of lemonade, Gregory notices his mouth watering.

B. In the view of many learning theorists, pairing a neutral and unconditioned stimulus is not enough to produce classical conditioning; the neutral stimulus must _____ the unconditioned stimulus.

Answers:

A. 1. US = the thunderclap; UR = jumping elicited by the noise; CS = the sight of the lightning; CR = jumping elicited by the lightning. 2. US = the taste of lemon; UR = salivation elicited by the taste of lemon; CS = the picture of a glass of lemonade; CR = salivation elicited by the picture. B. signal or predict

WHAT'S AHEAD

- **Why do advertisers often include pleasant music and gorgeous scenery in ads for their products?**
- **How would a classical-conditioning theorist explain your irrational fear of heights or mice?**
- **If you eat licorice and then happen to get the flu, how might your taste for licorice change?**
- **How can sitting in a doctor's office make you feel sick?**

Classical Conditioning in Real Life

If a dog can learn to salivate to the ringing of a bell, so can you. In fact, you probably have learned to salivate to the sound of a lunch bell, not to mention the phrase *hot fudge sundae*, "mouth-watering" pictures of food in magazines, and a voice calling out "Dinner's ready!" But the role of classical conditioning goes far beyond the learning of simple reflexive responses; conditioning affects us every day in many ways.

One of the first psychologists to recognize the real-life implications of Pavlovian theory was John B. Watson, who founded American behaviorism and enthusiastically promoted Pavlov's ideas. Watson believed that the whole rich array of human emotion and behavior could be accounted for by conditioning principles. For example, he thought that you learned to love another person when that person was paired with stroking and cuddling. (Watson, who was married five times, apparently tried many different pairings.) Watson turned out to be wrong about love, which is a lot more complicated than he thought (see Chapter 12). But he was right about the power of classical conditioning to affect our emotions, preferences, and tastes.

John B. Watson (1878–1958)

Learning to Like

Classical conditioning plays a big role in our emotional responses to objects, people, symbols, events, and places. It can explain why sentimental feelings sweep over us when we see a school mascot, a national flag, or the logo of the Olympic games: These objects have been associated in the past with positive feelings:

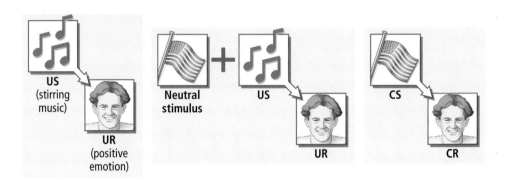

Many advertising techniques are also based on the principles first demonstrated by Pavlov, whether advertising executives realize it or not. In one study, college students looked at slides of either a beige pen or a blue pen. During the presentation, half of the students heard a song from a recent American musical film, and half heard a selection of traditional music from India. (The experimenter made the reasonable assumption that the American music would be more appealing to the young Americans in the study.) Later the students were allowed to choose one of the pens. Almost three-fourths of those who heard the popular music chose a pen that was the same color as the one they had seen in the slides. An equal number of those who heard the Indian music chose a pen that *differed* in color from the one they had seen (Gorn, 1982).

In classical-conditioning terms, the music in this study was an unconditioned stimulus for internal responses associated with pleasure or displeasure, and the pens became conditioned stimuli for similar responses. You can see why television commercials often pair their products with music, attractive people, or other appealing sounds and images.

Learning to Fear

Positive emotions are not the only ones that can be classically conditioned; so can dislikes and negative emotions such as fear. A person can learn to fear just about anything if it is paired with something that elicits pain, surprise, or embarrassment. Human beings, however, are biologically primed to be especially susceptible to certain kinds of acquired fears. It is far easier to establish a conditioned fear of spiders, snakes, and heights than of butterflies, flowers, and toasters (Öhman & Mineka, 2001). The former can be dangerous to your health, so in the process of evolution, human beings acquired a tendency to learn quickly to be wary of them.

When fear of an object or situation becomes irrational and interferes with normal activities, it qualifies as a *phobia*. To demonstrate how a phobia might be learned, John Watson and Rosalie Rayner (1920) deliberately established a rat phobia in an 11-month-old boy named Albert. For ethical reasons, no psychologist today would do such a thing to a child. Nevertheless, the study remains a classic, and its main conclusion, that fears can be conditioned, is still well accepted.

"Little Albert" was a placid child who rarely cried. When Watson and Rayner gave him a furry white rat to play with (a live one, not a toy), Albert showed no fear; in fact, he was delighted. However, like most children, Albert was afraid of loud noises. When the researchers made a loud noise behind his head by striking a steel bar with a hammer, he would jump and fall sideways onto the mattress he was sitting on. The noise made by the hammer was an unconditioned stimulus for the unconditioned response of fear.

Having established that Albert liked rats, Watson and Rayner set about teaching him to fear them. Again they offered him a rat, but this time, as Albert reached for it, one of the researchers struck the steel bar. Startled, Albert fell onto the mattress. The researchers repeated this procedure several times. Albert began to whimper and tremble. Finally, they held out the rat to him without making the noise. Albert fell over, cried, and crawled away as fast as he could; the rat had become a conditioned stimulus for fear:

counterconditioning In classical conditioning, the process of pairing a conditioned stimulus with a stimulus that elicits a response that is incompatible with an unwanted conditioned response.

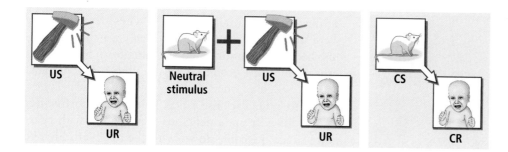

Tests done five days later showed that Albert's fear had generalized to other hairy or furry objects, including white rabbits, cotton wool, a Santa Claus mask, and even John Watson's hair.

Unfortunately, Watson and Rayner lost access to Little Albert, so they were unable to reverse the conditioning. However, Watson and Mary Cover Jones did reverse another child's conditioned fear—one that was, as Watson put it, "homegrown" rather than psychologist-induced (Jones, 1924).

Three-year-old Peter was deathly afraid of rabbits. Watson and Jones eliminated his fear with a method called **counterconditioning,** in which a conditioned stimulus is paired with some other stimulus that elicits a response incompatible with the unwanted response. In this case, the rabbit (the CS) was paired with a snack of milk and crackers, and the snack produced pleasant feelings that were incompatible with the conditioned response of fear. At first, the researchers kept the rabbit some distance from Peter, so that his fear would remain at a low level. Otherwise, Peter might have learned to fear milk and crackers! But gradually, over several days, they brought the rabbit closer and closer. Eventually Peter learned to like rabbits:

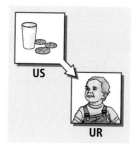

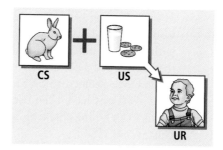

Peter was even able to sit with the rabbit in his lap, playing with it with one hand while he ate with the other. A variation of this procedure, called *systematic desensitization,* was later devised for treating phobias in adults (see Chapter 17).

Accounting for Taste

Classical conditioning can also explain how we learn to like and dislike many foods and odors. In the laboratory, researchers have taught animals to dislike foods or odors by pairing them with drugs that cause nausea or other unpleasant symptoms. One researcher trained slugs to associate the smell of carrots, which slugs normally like, with a bitter-tasting chemical that they detest. Soon the slugs were avoiding the smell of carrots. The researcher then demonstrated higher-order conditioning by pairing the smell of carrots with the smell of potato. Sure enough, the slugs began to avoid the smell of potato as well (Sahley, Rudy, & Gelperin, 1981).

Whether we say "yuck" or "yum" to a food may depend on a past experience involving classical conditioning.

Many people have learned to dislike a food after eating it and then falling ill, even when the two events were unrelated. The food, previously a neutral stimulus, becomes a conditioned stimulus for nausea or for other symptoms produced by the illness. Psychologist Martin Seligman once told how he himself was conditioned to hate béarnaise sauce. One night, shortly after he and his wife ate a delicious filet mignon with béarnaise sauce, he came down with the flu. Naturally, he felt wretched. His misery had nothing to do with the béarnaise sauce, of course, yet the next time he tried it, he found he disliked the taste (Seligman & Hager, 1972).

Notice that unlike conditioning in the laboratory, Seligman's aversion to the sauce occurred after only one pairing of the sauce with illness and with a considerable delay between the conditioned and unconditioned stimuli. Moreover, Seligman's wife did *not* become a conditioned stimulus for nausea, and neither did his dinner plate or the waiter, even though they, too, had been paired with illness. Why? In groundbreaking work, John Garcia and Robert Koelling (1966) provided the answer, which became known as the "Garcia effect." Working with rats, they showed that the animals were biologically primed to associate sickness with taste more readily than with sights or sounds. Later work established the same principle for many species, including human beings. Like the tendency to acquire certain fears, this biological tendency evolved through natural selection because it enhances a species' survival: Eating bad food is more likely to be followed by illness and death than are particular sights or sounds.

Psychologists have taken advantage of this phenomenon to develop humane ways of discouraging predators from preying on livestock, using conditioned taste aversions instead of traps and poisons. In one classic study, researchers laced sheep meat with a nausea-inducing chemical; coyotes and wolves fell for the bait, and as a result they developed a conditioned aversion to sheep (Gustavson et al., 1974, 1976). Two wolves even seemed to become afraid of sheep! Similar techniques for conditioning taste aversions have been used to deter other predators—for example, to deter raccoons from killing chickens, and ravens and crows from eating crane eggs (Garcia & Gustavson, 1997).

Reacting to Medical Treatments

Because of classical conditioning, medical treatments can create unexpected misery or relief from symptoms, for reasons that are entirely unrelated to the treatment itself.

For example, unpleasant reactions to a treatment generalize to a wide range of other stimuli. This is a particular problem for cancer patients. The nausea and vomiting resulting from chemotherapy often generalize to the place where the therapy is administered, the waiting room, the nurse's uniform, or the smell of rubbing alcohol. The drug treatment is an unconditioned stimulus for nausea and vomiting, and through association, the other, previously neutral stimuli become conditioned stimuli for these responses. Even *mental images* of the sights and smells of the clinic may become conditioned stimuli for nausea (Dadds et al., 1997; Redd et al., 1993).

Some cancer patients also acquire a classically conditioned anxiety response to anything associated with their chemotherapy. In one study, patients who drank lemon-lime Kool-Aid before their therapy sessions developed an anxiety response to the drink—an example of higher-order conditioning. They continued to feel anxious even when the drink was offered in their homes rather than at the clinic (Jacobsen et al., 1995).

On the other hand, patients may have *reduced* pain and anxiety when they take *placebos*—pills and injections that have no active ingredients, or treatments that have no direct physical effect on the problem (see Chapter 2). Placebos can be amazingly powerful, and the fancier or more impressive they are, the stronger their psychological effects. For example, a large placebo pill is more effective in reducing pain than is a small placebo pill, a placebo with a brand name is more effective than a nameless placebo, and a placebo injection of harmless saline is more effective than a placebo pill (Benedetti & Levi-Montalcini, 2001). Why do placebos work? Cognitive psychologists emphasize the role of expectations. But behaviorists would say that placebos work because the room in which the medication is given, the doctor's white coat, and pills and injections all become conditioned stimuli for relief from symptoms. The reason is that these stimuli have been associated in the past with *real* drugs (Ader, 1997, 2000). The real drugs are the unconditioned stimuli, the relief they bring is the unconditioned response, and the placebos acquire the ability to elicit similar reactions, thereby becoming conditioned responses.

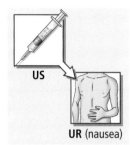

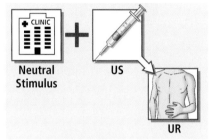

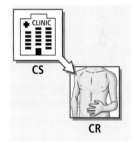

QUICK QUIZ

We hope you have not acquired a classically conditioned fear of quizzes. See whether you can supply the correct term to describe the outcome in each of these situations.

1. After a child learns to fear spiders, he also responds with fear to ants, beetles, and other crawling bugs.

2. A toddler is afraid of the bath, so her father puts just a little water in the tub and gives the child a lollipop to suck on while she is being washed. Soon, the little girl loses her fear of the bath.

3. A factory worker notices that his mouth waters whenever a noontime bell signals the beginning of his lunch break. One day, the bell goes haywire and rings every half hour. By the end of the day, the worker has stopped salivating to the bell.

Answers:

1. stimulus generalization 2. counterconditioning 3. extinction

WHAT'S AHEAD▶

- What do praising a child and ceasing your nagging have in common?
- How can operant principles account for superstitious rituals?
- What is the best way to discourage a friend from interrupting you while you're studying?
- How do trainers teach guide dogs to perform the amazing services they do for their owners?

Operant Conditioning

At the end of the nineteenth century, in the first known scientific study of anger, G. Stanley Hall (1899) asked people to describe angry episodes they had experienced or observed. One person told of a 3-year-old girl who broke out in furious, seemingly uncontrollable sobs when she was punished by being kept home from a ride. In the middle of her tantrum, the child suddenly stopped crying and asked her nanny in a perfectly calm voice if her father was in. Told no, she immediately resumed her sobbing.

Children, of course, cry for many valid reasons—pain, discomfort, fear, illness, fatigue—and these cries deserve an adult's sympathy and attention. The child in Hall's study, however, was crying for a different reason. She had learned from prior experience that an outburst of sobbing would bring her attention and possibly the ride she wanted. Her behavior, though some might call it "naughty," was perfectly understandable, because in the past crying had paid off. Her tantrum illustrates one of the most basic laws of learning: *Behavior becomes more likely or less likely, depending on its consequences.*

An emphasis on environmental consequences is at the heart of **operant conditioning** (also called *instrumental conditioning*), the second type of conditioning studied by behaviorists. In classical conditioning, it does not matter whether an animal's or person's behavior has consequences. In Pavlov's procedure, for example, the dog learned an association between two events that were not under its control (e.g., a tone and the delivery of food) and the animal got food whether it salivated or not. But in operant conditioning, the organism's response (the little girl's sobbing, for example) *operates* or produces effects on the environment. These effects, in turn, influence whether the response will occur again.

Classical and operant conditioning also tend to differ in the types of responses they involve. In classical conditioning, the response is typically reflexive, an automatic reaction to something happening in the environment, such as the sight of food or the sound of a bell. Generally speaking, responses in operant conditioning are complex and are not reflexive—for instance, riding a bicycle, writing a letter, climbing a mountain, . . . or throwing a tantrum.

The Birth of Radical Behaviorism

Operant conditioning has been studied since the start of the twentieth century, although it was not called that until later. Edward Thorndike (1898), then a young doctoral candidate, set the stage by observing cats as they tried to escape from a complex "puzzle box" to reach a scrap of fish located just outside the box. At first, the cat would scratch, bite, or swat at parts of the box in an unorganized way. Then, after a few minutes, it would chance on the successful response (loosening a bolt, pulling a string, or hitting a button) and rush out to get the reward. Placed in the box again, the cat now took a little less time to escape, and after several trials, the animal immediately made the correct response. According to Thorndike, this response had been "stamped in" by its satisfying result, getting the food. In contrast, annoying or unsatisfying results "stamped out" behavior. Behavior, said Thorndike, is controlled by its consequences.

the neighborhood. Jerry Van Amerongen

An instantaneous learning experience.

operant conditioning The process by which a response becomes more likely to occur or less so, depending on its consequences.

This general principle was elaborated and extended to more complex forms of behavior by B. F. (Burrhus Frederic) Skinner (1904–1990). Skinner called his approach "radical behaviorism" to distinguish it from the behaviorism of John Watson, who emphasized classical conditioning. Skinner argued that to understand behavior we should focus on the external causes of an action and the action's consequences. Skinner avoided terms that Thorndike used, such as "satisfying" and "annoying," which reflect assumptions about what an organism feels and wants. To explain behavior, he said, we should look outside the individual, not inside.

The Consequences of Behavior

In Skinner's analysis, which has inspired an immense body of research, a response ("operant") can lead to three types of consequences.

1 *A neutral consequence neither increases nor decreases the probability that the response will recur.* If a door squeaks each time you open it, but you ignore the sound and it has no effect on your likelihood of opening the door in the future, the squeak is considered a neutral consequence. We will not be concerned further with neutral consequences.

2 Reinforcement *strengthens the response or makes it more likely to recur.* When your dog begs for food at the table, and you give her the lamb chop off your plate, her begging is likely to increase:

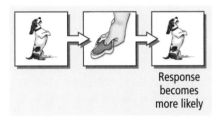

Response becomes more likely

Reinforcers are roughly equivalent to rewards, and many psychologists use *reward* and *reinforcer* as approximate synonyms. However, strict behaviorists avoid the word *reward*, because it implies that something has been earned that results in happiness or satisfaction. To a behaviorist, a stimulus is a reinforcer if it strengthens the preceding behavior, whether or not the organism experiences pleasure or a positive emotion. Conversely, no matter how pleasurable a stimulus is, it is not a reinforcer if it does not increase the likelihood of a response. It's great to get a paycheck, but if you get paid regardless of the effort you put into your work, the money will not reinforce "hard-work behavior."

3 Punishment *weakens the response or makes it less likely to recur.* Any aversive (unpleasant) stimulus or event may be a *punisher.* If your dog begs for food from the table, and you swat her nose and shout "No," her begging is likely to decrease—as long as you don't feel guilty and then give her the lamb chop anyway:

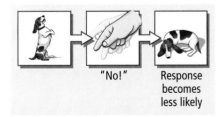

"No!" Response becomes less likely

Parents, employers, and governments resort to reinforcers and punishers all the time—to get kids to behave well, employees to work hard, and constituents to pay

reinforcement The process by which a stimulus or event strengthens or increases the probability of the response that it follows.

punishment The process by which a stimulus or event weakens or reduces the probability of the response that it follows.

primary reinforcer A stimulus that is inherently reinforcing, typically satisfying a physiological need; an example is food.

primary punisher A stimulus that is inherently punishing; an example is electric shock.

secondary reinforcer A stimulus that has acquired reinforcing properties through association with other reinforcers.

secondary punisher A stimulus that has acquired punishing properties through association with other punishers.

positive reinforcement A reinforcement procedure in which a response is followed by the presentation of, or increase in intensity of, a reinforcing stimulus; as a result, the response becomes stronger or more likely to occur.

negative reinforcement A reinforcement procedure in which a response is followed by the removal, delay, or decrease in intensity of an unpleasant stimulus; as a result, the response becomes stronger or more likely to occur.

taxes—but they do not always use them effectively. For example, they may wait too long to deliver the reinforcer or punisher. In general, the sooner a consequence follows a response, the greater its effect; you are likely to respond more reliably when you do not have to wait ages for a paycheck, a smile, or a grade. When there is a delay, other responses occur in the interval, and the connection between the desired or undesired response and the consequence may not be made.

Primary and Secondary Reinforcers and Punishers. Food, water, light stroking of the skin, and a comfortable air temperature are naturally reinforcing because they satisfy biological needs. They are therefore known as **primary reinforcers.** Similarly, pain and extreme heat or cold are inherently punishing and are therefore known as **primary punishers.** Primary reinforcers and punishers can be very powerful, but they have some drawbacks, both in real life and in research. For one thing, a primary reinforcer may be ineffective if an animal or person is not in a deprived state; a glass of water is not much of a reward if you just drank three glasses. Also, for obvious ethical reasons, psychologists cannot go around using primary punishers (say, hitting their subjects) or taking away primary reinforcers (say, starving their subjects).

Fortunately, behavior can be controlled just as effectively by **secondary reinforcers** and **secondary punishers,** which are learned. Money, praise, applause, good grades, awards, and gold stars are common secondary reinforcers. Criticism, demerits, catcalls, scoldings, fines, and bad grades are common secondary punishers. Most behaviorists believe that secondary reinforcers and punishers acquire their ability to influence behavior by being paired with primary reinforcers and punishers. (If that reminds you of classical conditioning, reinforce your excellent thinking with a pat on the head! Indeed, secondary reinforcers and punishers are often called *conditioned* reinforcers and punishers.) One secondary reinforcer, money, has considerable power over most people's behavior because it can be exchanged for primary reinforcers such as food and shelter. It is also associated with other secondary reinforcers, such as praise and respect.

Positive and Negative Reinforcers and Punishers. In our example of the begging dog, something pleasant (getting the lamb chop) followed the dog's begging response, so the response increased. Similarly, if a good grade follows your studying, your efforts to study are likely to continue or increase. This kind of process, in which a pleasant consequence makes a response more likely, is known as **positive reinforcement.** But there is another type of reinforcement, **negative reinforcement,** which involves the *removal* of something *unpleasant.* For example, if someone nags you all the time to study, but stops nagging when you comply, your studying is likely to increase—because you will then avoid the nagging:

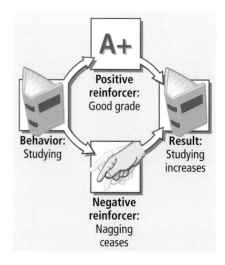

A+

Positive reinforcer: Good grade

Behavior: Studying

Result: Studying increases

Negative reinforcer: Nagging ceases

The positive–negative distinction can also be applied to punishment: Something unpleasant may occur following some behavior (positive punishment), or something *pleasant* may be *removed* (negative punishment). For example, if your friends tease you for being an egghead (positive punishment) or if studying makes you lose time with your friends (negative punishment), you may stop studying:

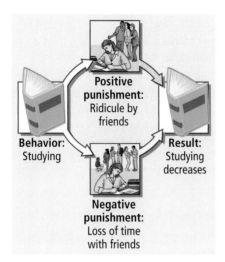

The distinction between positive and negative reinforcement and punishment has been a source of confusion for generations of students, turning many strong minds to mush. You will master these terms more quickly if you understand that "positive" and "negative" have nothing to do with "good" or "bad." They refer to *procedures*—giving something or taking something away.

In the case of reinforcement, think of a positive reinforcer as something that is added or obtained (you might picture a plus sign), and a negative reinforcer as avoidance of, or escape from, something unpleasant (you might picture a minus sign). *In either case, a response becomes more likely.* Do you recall what happened when Little Albert learned to fear rats through a process of classical conditioning? After he acquired this fear, crawling away was negatively reinforced by escape from the now-fearsome rodent. The negative reinforcement that results from escaping or avoiding something unpleasant explains why so many fears are long-lasting. When you avoid a feared object or situation, you also cut off all opportunities for extinguishing your fear.

Understandably, people often confuse negative reinforcement with positive punishment, because both involve an unpleasant stimulus. With punishment, though, you are subjected to the unpleasant stimulus, and with negative reinforcement, it is taken away. To keep these terms straight, remember that punishment—whether positive or negative—*decreases* the likelihood of a response, whereas reinforcement—whether positive or negative—*increases* it. In real life, punishment and negative reinforcement often go hand in hand. If you use a choke collar to teach your dog to heel, a yank on the collar punishes the act of walking; release of the collar negatively reinforces the act of standing by your side.

You can positively reinforce your studying of this material by taking a refreshment break. As you master the material, a decrease in your anxiety will negatively reinforce studying. But we hope you won't punish your efforts by telling yourself "I'll never get it" or "It's too hard"!

QUICK QUIZ

What kind of consequence will follow if you can't answer these questions?

1. A child nags her father for a cookie; he keeps refusing, but finally, unable to stand the nagging any longer, he hands over the cookie. For him, the ending of the child's pleas is a _____. For the child, the cookie is a _____.

2. An able-bodied driver is careful not to park in a handicapped space anymore after paying a large fine for doing so. The loss of money is a _____.

3. Which of the following are secondary reinforcers: quarters spilling from a slot machine, a winner's blue ribbon, a piece of candy, an A on an exam, frequent-flyer miles.

4. During late-afternoon "happy hours," bars and restaurants sell drinks at a reduced price and appetizers are often free. What undesirable behavior may be rewarded by this practice?

Answers:

1. negative reinforcer; positive 2. punisher—or more precisely, a negative punisher (because something desirable was taken away) 3. All but the candy are secondary reinforcers. 4. One possible answer: The reduced prices, free appetizers, and cheerful atmosphere all reinforce heavy alcohol consumption just before rush hour, thus possibly contributing to binge drinking and drunk driving.

Principles of Operant Conditioning

Thousands of operant conditioning studies have been done, many using animals. A favorite experimental tool is the *Skinner box*, a cage equipped with a device that delivers food into a dish when an animal makes a desired response (see Figure 7.4). In the original version, a machine connected to the cage automatically recorded each response and produced a graph on a piece of paper, showing the cumulative number of responses across time; nowadays, computers are used.

Early in his career, Skinner (1938) used the Skinner box for a classic demonstration of operant conditioning. A rat that had previously learned to eat from the pellet-releasing device was placed in the box. Because no food was present, the animal proceeded to do typical ratlike things, scurrying about the box, sniffing here and there, and randomly touching parts of the floor and walls. Quite by accident, it happened to press a lever mounted on one wall, and immediately, a pellet of tasty rat food fell into the food dish. The rat continued its movements and again happened to press the bar, causing another pellet to fall into the dish. With

Figure 7.4

THE SKINNER BOX

When a rat in a Skinner box presses a bar, a food pellet or drop of water is automatically released. The photo shows Skinner at work on one of the boxes.

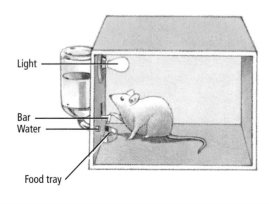

Light
Bar
Water
Food tray

additional repetitions of bar pressing followed by food, the animal began to behave less randomly and to press the bar more consistently. Eventually, Skinner had the rat pressing the bar as fast as it could. Since then, behavioral researchers have used the Skinner box and similar devices to discover many important techniques and applications of operant conditioning.

Extinction. In operant conditioning, as in classical, **extinction** is a procedure that causes a previously learned response to stop. In operant conditioning, extinction takes place when the reinforcer that maintained the response is removed or is no longer available. At first, there may be a spurt of responding, but then the responses gradually taper off and eventually cease. Suppose you put a coin in a vending machine and get nothing back. You may throw in another coin, or perhaps even two, but then you will probably stop trying. The next day, you may put in yet another coin, an example of *spontaneous recovery.* Eventually, however, you will give up on that machine. Your response will have been extinguished.

Stimulus Generalization and Discrimination. In operant conditioning, as in classical, **stimulus generalization** may occur. That is, responses may generalize to stimuli that were not present during the original learning situation but that resemble the original stimuli. For example, a pigeon that has been trained to peck at a picture of a circle may also peck at a slightly oval figure. But if you wanted to train the bird to discriminate between the two shapes, you would present both the circle and the oval, giving reinforcers whenever the bird pecked at the circle and withholding reinforcers when it pecked at the oval. Eventually, **stimulus discrimination** would occur.

Sometimes an animal or human being learns to respond to a stimulus only when some other stimulus, called a **discriminative stimulus,** is present. The discriminative stimulus signals whether a response, if made, will pay off. In a Skinner box containing a pigeon, a light may serve as a discriminative stimulus for pecking at a circle. When the light is on, pecking brings a reward; when it is off, pecking is futile. Human behavior is controlled by many discriminative stimuli, both verbal ("Store hours are 9 to 5") and nonverbal (traffic lights, doorbells, the ring of a telephone, the facial expressions of others). Learning to respond correctly when such stimuli are present is an essential part of a person's socialization.

Learning on Schedule. When a response is first acquired, learning is usually most rapid if the response is reinforced each time it occurs; this procedure is called **continuous reinforcement.** However, once a response has become reliable, it will be more resistant to extinction if it is rewarded on an **intermittent (partial) schedule of reinforcement,** which involves reinforcing only some responses, not all of them. Skinner (1956) happened on this fact when he ran short of food pellets for his rats and was forced to deliver reinforcers less often. Not all scientific discoveries are planned!

Intermittent reinforcement helps explain why people often get attached to "lucky" hats, charms, and rituals. A batter pulls his earlobe, gets a home run, and from then on always pulls his earlobe before each pitch. A student takes an exam with a purple pen and gets an A, and from then on will not take an exam without a purple pen. These rituals persist because *sometimes* they are followed, purely coincidentally, by a reinforcer—a hit, a good grade—and so they become resistant to extinction.

Skinner (1948) once demonstrated this phenomenon by creating eight "superstitious" pigeons in his laboratory. He rigged the pigeons' cages so that food was delivered every 15 seconds, even if the birds didn't lift a feather. Pigeons are often in motion, so when the food came, each animal was likely to be doing *something.* That something was then reinforced by delivery of the food. The behavior, of course, was reinforced entirely by chance, but it still became more likely to occur, and thus to be

extinction The weakening and eventual disappearance of a learned response; in operant conditioning, it occurs when a response is no longer followed by a reinforcer.

stimulus generalization In operant conditioning, the tendency for a response that has been reinforced (or punished) in the presence of one stimulus to occur (or be suppressed) in the presence of other, similar stimuli.

stimulus discrimination In operant conditioning, the tendency of a response to occur in the presence of one stimulus but not in the presence of other, similar stimuli that differ from it on some dimension.

discriminative stimulus A stimulus that signals when a particular response is likely to be followed by a certain type of consequence.

continuous reinforcement A reinforcement schedule in which a particular response is always reinforced.

intermittent (partial) schedule of reinforcement A reinforcement schedule in which a particular response is sometimes but not always reinforced.

THINKING CRITICALLY
Consider Other Interpretations

People cling to superstitious rituals because they think they work. Could this "effectiveness" be an illusion, explainable in terms of operant principles?

"Maybe you're right, maybe it won't ward off evil spirits, but maybe it will, and these days who wants to take a chance?"

reinforced again. Within a short time, six of the pigeons were practicing some sort of consistent ritual—turning in counterclockwise circles, bobbing the head up and down, or swinging their heads to and fro. None of these activities had the least effect on the delivery of the reinforcer; the birds were behaving "superstitiously." It was as if they thought their movements were responsible for bringing the food.

Many kinds of intermittent schedules have been studied (see Figure 7.5). These variations in how reinforcers are delivered have characteristic effects on the rate, form, and timing of behavior—effects that most people are not aware of. Here are four major types of intermittent schedules:

1 *On* fixed-ratio schedules, *reinforcement occurs after a fixed number of responses.* Fixed-ratio schedules produce very high rates of responding. In the laboratory, a rat may rapidly press a bar several hundred times to get a single reward. Outside the laboratory, fixed-ratio schedules are often used by employers to increase productivity. Both a salesperson who must sell a specific number of items before getting a commission and a factory worker who must produce a specific number of products before earning a given wage (a system known as "piecework") are on fixed-ratio schedules. An interesting feature of fixed-ratio schedules is that performance sometimes drops off just after reinforcement. If a writer must complete four chapters before getting a check, interest and motivation will sag right after the check is received.

2 *On* variable-ratio schedules, *reinforcement occurs after some average number of responses, but the number varies from reinforcement to reinforcement.* For example, a reinforcer might be delivered on the average after every fifth response but sometimes after one, two, six, or seven responses, or any other number, as long as the average is five. Variable-ratio schedules produce extremely high, steady rates of responding. The responses are more resistant to extinction than when a fixed-ratio schedule is used. The prime example of a variable-ratio schedule is delivery of payoffs by a slot machine. The player knows that the average number of responses necessary to win is set at a level that makes money for the house. Hope springs eternal, though. The gambler takes a chance on being in front of the machine during one of those lucky moments when fewer responses bring a payoff.

3 *On* fixed-interval schedules, *reinforcement of a response occurs only if a fixed amount of time has passed since the previous reinforcer.* For example, a rat might get a food pellet the first time it presses a bar after passage of a 10-second interval. Pressing the bar earlier does not hasten the reward. Animals on fixed-interval schedules seem to develop a sharp sense of time. After a pellet is delivered, a rat will often stop responding altogether. Then as the end of the interval approaches, responding again picks up, reaching a maximum rate right before reinforcement. Similarly, if you get an e-mail from your true love every morning at around ten, you might start checking as the hour approaches, then not check again until the next day.

fixed-ratio schedule An intermittent schedule of reinforcement in which reinforcement occurs only after a fixed number of responses.

variable-ratio schedule An intermittent schedule of reinforcement in which reinforcement occurs after a variable number of responses.

fixed-interval schedule An intermittent schedule of reinforcement in which a reinforcer is delivered for the first response made after a fixed period of time has elapsed since the last reinforcer.

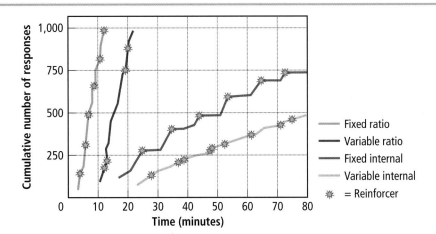

Figure 7.5
REINFORCEMENT SCHEDULES
AND BEHAVIOR

In this figure, each star represents the delivery of a reinforcer. As you can see, different schedules produce different learning curves (patterns of responding over time). A fixed-ratio schedule produces a very fast rate of responding. When a fixed-interval schedule is used, responses drop off immediately after reinforcement, resulting in a scalloped curve. (Adapted from Skinner, 1961.)

4 *On* variable-interval schedules, *reinforcement of a response occurs only if a variable amount of time has passed since the previous reinforcer.* For example, the interval might average 10 seconds but will vary from reinforcement to reinforcement. Because the animal or person cannot predict when a reward will come, responding is relatively low but steady. That is why, if your true love's e-mails come at unpredictable intervals, you might check your e-mail at a steady but slow rate—perhaps once every hour or two. You never know when you will be rewarded with the message "You've got mail!"

Now, listen up, because here comes one of the most useful things to know about operant conditioning: If you want a response to persist after it has been learned, you should reinforce it *intermittently,* not continuously. If you are continuously giving Harry, your hamster, a treat for pushing a ball with his nose, and then you suddenly stop the reinforcement, Harry will soon stop pushing that ball. Because the change in reinforcement is large, from continuous to none at all, Harry will easily discern the change. But if you have been reinforcing Harry's behavior only every so often, the change will not be so dramatic, and your hungry hamster will keep responding for quite a while. Pigeons, rats, and people on intermittent schedules of reinforcement have responded in the laboratory thousands of times without reinforcement before throwing in the towel, especially when the timing of the reinforcer varies. Animals will sometimes work so hard for an unpredictable, infrequent bit of food that the energy they expend is greater than that gained from the reward; theoretically, they could actually work themselves to death!

variable-interval schedule An intermittent schedule of reinforcement in which a reinforcer is delivered for a response made after a variable period of time has elapsed since the last reinforcer.

Get Involved ▪▪

The Well-Behaved Pet

If you have a pet, you can use operant conditioning to teach your animal something you'd like it to do. Choose something simple. One student we know taught her cat to willingly enter the garage for the night by feeding the animal a special treat there each evening at the same time. Soon the cat was "asking" to get into the garage at bedtime! Another student taught her pastured horse to come to her for haltering by rewarding the animal's occasional approach with a carrot. Soon the horse was approaching regularly and could be put on an intermittent schedule of reinforcement. Be creative, and see whether you can make your pet better behaved or more cooperative in some way.

Behavioral techniques such as shaping have many useful applications. Monkeys have been trained to assist their paralyzed owners by opening doors, helping with feeding, and turning the pages of books. Miniature "guide horses" help blind people navigate the streets of the city. Note the cool protective sneakers!

It follows that if you want to get rid of a response—your own or someone else's—you should be careful *not* to reinforce it intermittently. If you are going to extinguish undesirable behavior by ignoring it—a child's tantrums, a friend's midnight phone calls, a parent's unwanted advice—you must be absolutely consistent in withholding reinforcement (your attention). Otherwise, you will probably only make matters worse. The other person will learn that if he or she keeps up the screaming, calling, or advice giving long enough, it will eventually be rewarded. One of the most common errors people make, from a behavioral point of view, is to reward intermittently the very responses that they would like to eliminate.

Shaping. For a response to be reinforced, it must first occur. But suppose you want to train Harry the hamster to pick up a marble, a child to use a knife and fork properly, or a friend to play terrific tennis. Such behaviors, and most others in everyday life, have almost no probability of appearing spontaneously. You could grow old and gray waiting for them to occur so that you could reinforce them. The operant solution to this dilemma is a procedure called **shaping.**

In shaping, you start by reinforcing a tendency in the right direction, then you gradually require responses that are more and more similar to the final, desired response. The responses that you reinforce on the way to the final one are called **successive approximations.** In the case of Harry and the marble, you might deliver a food pellet if the hamster merely turned toward the marble. Once this response was well established, you might then reward the hamster for taking a step toward the marble. After that, you could reward him for approaching the marble, then for touching the marble, then for putting both paws on the marble, and finally for holding it. With the achievement of each approximation, the next one would become more likely, making it available for reinforcement.

Using shaping and other techniques, Skinner was able to train pigeons to play Ping-Pong with their beaks and to "bowl" in a miniature alley, complete with a wooden ball and tiny bowling pins. (Skinner had a great sense of humor.) Animal trainers routinely use shaping to teach animals to act as the "eyes" of the blind and to act as the "limbs" of people with spinal-cord injuries; these talented companions learn to turn on light switches, open refrigerator doors, and reach for boxes on shelves.

Biological Limits on Learning. All principles of operant conditioning, like those of classical conditioning, are limited by an animal's genetic dispositions and physical characteristics; if you try to use shaping to teach a fish to climb a ladder, you're going to get pretty frustrated (and wear out the fish). Operant conditioning procedures always work best when they capitalize on inborn tendencies.

shaping An operant-conditioning procedure in which successive approximations of a desired response are reinforced.

successive approximations In the operant-conditioning procedure of shaping, behaviors that are ordered in terms of increasing similarity or closeness to the desired response.

Years ago, two psychologists who became animal trainers, Keller and Marian Breland (1961), learned what happens when you ignore biological constraints on learning. They found that their animals were having trouble learning tasks that should have been easy. One animal, a pig, was supposed to drop large wooden coins in a box. Instead, the animal would drop the coin, push at it with its snout, throw it in the air, and push at it some more. This odd behavior actually delayed delivery of the reinforcer (food, which is *very* reinforcing to a pig), so it was hard to explain in terms of operant principles. The Brelands finally realized that the pig's rooting instinct—using its snout to uncover and dig up edible roots—was keeping it from learning the task. They called such a reversion to instinctive behavior **instinctive drift**.

In human beings, too, operant learning is affected by genetics and the evolutionary history of our species. As we saw in Chapter 3, human children are biologically disposed to learn language without much effort, and they may be disposed to learn some arithmetic operations as well. Further, temperaments and other inborn dispositions may affect how a person responds to rewards and punishments. For example, it will be easier to shape belly-dancing behavior if a person is temperamentally disposed to be outgoing and extroverted than if the person is temperamentally disposed to be shy. And in Chapter 16, we will see that people with antisocial personality disorder (popularly called "sociopaths" or "psychopaths") often fail to respond to punishment the way other people do.

instinctive drift During operant learning, the tendency for an organism to revert to instinctive behavior.

Skinner: The Man and the Myth

Because of his groundbreaking work on operant conditioning, B. F. Skinner has often been called the greatest of American psychologists. Certainly he is one of the best known—and also one of the most misunderstood. For example, many people (even some psychologists) think that Skinner denied the existence of human consciousness and the value of studying it. In reality, Skinner (1972, 1990) maintained that we *can* study private, internal events—what we call perceptions, emotions, and thoughts—by observing our own sensory responses, the verbal reports of others, and the conditions under which such events occur. Internal events, he said, are as real as any others. But he insisted that thoughts and feelings cannot *explain* behavior; these components of consciousness, he said, are themselves simply behaviors that occur because of reinforcement and punishment.

Skinner aroused strong passions in both his supporters and his detractors. Perhaps the issue that most provoked and angered people was his insistence that free will is an illusion. In contrast to humanist and some religious doctrines that human beings have the power to shape their own destinies, his philosophy promoted the *determinist* view that we are shaped by our environments and our genetic heritage. Skinner refused to credit personal traits (such as curiosity and perseverance) or mental events (such as intentions and motives) for anyone's accomplishments, including his own. He regarded himself not as a "self" but as a "repertoire of behaviors" resulting from an environment that encouraged looking, searching, and investigating (Bjork, 1993).

Because Skinner thought the environment should be manipulated to alter behavior, some critics have portrayed him as cold-blooded. One famous controversy regarding Skinner occurred when he invented an enclosed "living space,"

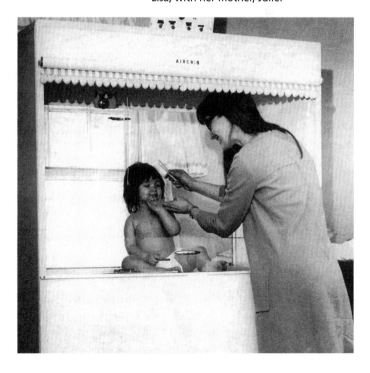

B. F. Skinner invented the Air Crib to provide a more comfortable, less restrictive infant bed than the traditional crib with its bars and blankets. The baby in this Air Crib is Skinner's granddaughter Lisa, with her mother, Julie.

the Air-Crib, for his younger daughter Deborah when she was an infant. This "baby box," as it came to be known, had temperature and humidity controls to eliminate the usual discomforts suffered by babies: heat, cold, wetness, and confinement by blankets and clothing. Skinner believed that to reduce a baby's cries of discomfort and make infant care easier for the parents, you should fix the environment. But people imagined, incorrectly, that the Skinners were leaving their child in the baby box all the time without cuddling and holding her, and rumors later circulated that she had gone insane or killed herself. Actually, both of Skinner's daughters turned out to be perfectly well-adjusted and very successful.

Skinner, who was a kind and mild-mannered man, felt that it would be unethical *not* to try to improve human behavior by applying behavioral principles. He practiced what he preached, proposing many ways to improve society and reduce human suffering. At the height of public criticism of Skinner, in 1972, the American Humanist Association recognized his efforts on behalf of humanity by honoring him with its Humanist of the Year Award.

7.2

QUICK QUIZ

Can you apply the principles of operant conditioning? In each of the following situations, choose the best alternative, and give your reason for choosing it.

1. You want your 2-year-old to ask for water with a word instead of a grunt. Should you give him water when he says "wa-wa" or wait until his pronunciation improves?

2. Your roommate keeps interrupting your studying even though you have asked her to stop. Should you ignore her completely or occasionally respond for the sake of good manners?

3. Your father, who rarely writes to you, has finally sent a letter. Should you reply quickly or wait a while so he will know how it feels to be ignored?

Answers:

1. You should reinforce "wa-wa," an approximation of *water*, because complex behaviors need to be shaped. 2. From a behavioral view, you should ignore her completely because intermittent reinforcement (attention) could cause her interruptions to persist. 3. If you want to encourage letter writing, you should reply quickly because immediate reinforcement is more effective than delayed reinforcement.

WHAT'S AHEAD ▶

● Why do efforts to "crack down" on wrongdoers often go awry?
● What's the best way to discourage a child from throwing tantrums?
● Why does paying children for good grades sometimes backfire?

Operant Conditioning in Real Life

Operant principles can clear up many mysteries about why people behave as they do, and why, in spite of all the motivational seminars they attend or resolutions they make, they have trouble changing when they want to. If life at work and at home remains full of the same old reinforcers, punishers, and discriminative stimuli (a grumpy boss, an unresponsive spouse, a refrigerator stocked with high-fat goodies), any new responses that have been acquired may fail to generalize.

To help people change unwanted, dangerous, or self-defeating habits, behaviorists have carried operant principles out of the laboratory and into the wider world of the classroom, athletic field, prison, mental hospital, nursing home, rehabilitation ward, child-care center, factory, and office. The use of operant techniques (and classical ones) in such real-world settings is called **behavior modification.**

Behavior modification has had some enormous successes (Kazdin, 2001). Behaviorists have taught parents to toilet train their children in only a few sessions (Azrin & Foxx, 1974). They have trained disturbed and mentally retarded adults to communicate, dress themselves, mingle socially with others, and earn a living (Lent, 1968; McLeod, 1985). They have taught brain-damaged patients to control inappropriate behavior, focus their attention, and improve their language abilities (McGlynn, 1990). They have developed the most effective programs available for helping autistic children improve their social, language, and academic skills (Green, 1996). And they have helped ordinary folk get rid of unwanted habits, such as smoking and nail biting, or acquire wanted ones, such as practicing the piano or studying.

Nonpsychologists have also used behavioral techniques successfully. In Berkeley, California, police officers, tired of giving tickets to punish traffic offenses, began rewarding *good* driving behavior, such as yielding the right-of-way or stopping to let a pedestrian cross the street. The reinforcers were coupons for free lattes, smoothies, and other treats. At first, drivers were apprehensive—they had been conditioned to expect bad news when an officer stops them! But eventually the program, aimed at making drivers more patient and courteous, was picked up by other communities. In one, good drivers were rewarded with $20 grocery coupons (*Los Angeles Times,* April 19, 2001).

Yet when people try to apply the principles of conditioning to commonplace problems, their efforts sometimes miss the mark. They may not have a good grasp of the principles you have been learning about; for example, they may delay the reward too long, or reinforce unwanted behavior intermittently. And both punishment and reinforcement have their pitfalls, as we are about to see.

A police officer in Palo Alto, California, reinforces law-abiding behavior by giving a gift certificate to a pedestrian.

The Pros and Cons of Punishment

In his novel *Walden Two* (1948/1976), Skinner imagined a utopia in which reinforcers were used so wisely that undesirable behavior was rare. Unfortunately, we do not live in a utopia; bad habits and antisocial acts abound, and we are faced with how to get rid of them.

An obvious solution might seem to be punishment. Nearly all Western countries have banned the physical punishment of schoolchildren by principals and teachers, but 23 American states still permit it for disruptiveness, vandalism, and other misbehavior. The United States is also far more likely than any other developed country to jail its citizens for nonviolent crimes such as drug use and to enact the ultimate punishment—the death penalty—for violent crimes. And of course in daily life, people punish one another constantly, by yelling, scolding, fining, and sulking. Does all this punishment work?

When Punishment Works. Sometimes punishment is unquestionably effective. Some highly disturbed children have been known to chew their own fingers to the bone, stick objects in their eyes, or tear out their hair. If you ignore such behavior, the children will seriously injure themselves. If you respond with concern and affection, you may unwittingly reward the behavior. But immediately punishing the self-destructive behavior eliminates it (Lovaas, 1977; Lovaas, Schreibman, & Koegel, 1974). Mild punishers, such as a spray of water in the face, or even a firm "No!", are often just as effective as strong ones, such as electric shock.

> **THINKING CRITICALLY**
>
> **Examine the Evidence**
>
> The response to wrongdoing is often punishment. People assume that fines, long prison terms, yelling, and spanking are good ways to get rid of undesirable behavior. What does the evidence show?

behavior modification The application of conditioning techniques to teach new responses or to reduce or eliminate maladaptive or problematic behavior.

Punishment can also deter some young criminals from repeating their offenses. A study of the criminal records of all Danish men born between 1944 and 1947 (nearly 29,000 men) examined repeat arrests (recidivism) through age 26 (Brennan & Mednick, 1994). After any given arrest, punishment reduced rates of subsequent arrests for both minor and serious crimes, though recidivism still remained fairly high. Contrary to the researchers' expectations, however, the severity of punishment made no difference: Fines and probation were about as effective as jail time. What mattered most was the *consistency* of the punishment. This is understandable: When lawbreakers sometimes get away with their crimes, their behavior is intermittently reinforced and therefore becomes resistant to extinction.

Unfortunately, that is exactly the situation in the United States. Young offenders are punished far less consistently than they are in Denmark, often because prosecutors, juries, and judges do not want to condemn them to mandatory prison terms. Because the courts have no other options for punishment, they may merely admonish the offenders and set them free (Brennan & Sarnoff, 1994). Ironically, then, policies that mandate severe punishment can actually lead to ineffective punishment—or to no punishment at all.

In sum, these results show that punishment can reduce recidivism, but they also show why harsh sentencing laws and simplistic efforts to "crack down" on wrongdoers often fail or even backfire. Indeed, despite its high incarceration rates, the United States has a far higher rate of violent crime than other developed countries do. And within the United States, crime rates are not consistently correlated with rates of incarceration or the imposition of the death penalty (Currie, 1998).

When Punishment Fails. What about punishment that occurs every day in families, schools, and workplaces? Laboratory and field studies find that it, too, often fails, for several reasons:

1 *People often administer punishment inappropriately or mindlessly.* They swing in a blind rage or shout things they don't mean, applying punishment so broadly that it covers all sorts of irrelevant behaviors. And even when people are not carried away by anger, they often misunderstand the proper application of punishment. One student told us his parents used to punish their children before leaving them alone for the evening because of all the naughty things they were *going* to do. Naturally, the children did not bother to behave like angels.

2 *The recipient of punishment often responds with anxiety, fear, or rage.* Through a process of classical conditioning, these emotional side effects may then generalize to the entire situation in which the punishment occurs—the place, the person delivering the punishment, and the circumstances. These negative emotional reactions can create more problems than the punishment solves. A teenager who has been severely punished may strike back or run away. A spouse who is constantly abused will feel bitter and resentful and is likely to retaliate with small acts of hostility. Being physically punished in childhood is a risk factor for depression, low self-esteem, violent behavior, and many other problems (Barrish, 1996; Straus & Kantor, 1994).

3 *The effectiveness of punishment is often temporary, depending heavily on the presence of the punishing person or circumstances.* All of us can probably remember some transgressions of childhood that we never dared commit when our parents were around but that we promptly resumed as soon as they were gone. All we learned was not to get caught.

4 *Most misbehavior is hard to punish immediately.* Punishment, like reward, works best if it quickly follows a response. But outside the laboratory, rapid punishment is often hard to achieve, and during the delay, the behavior may be

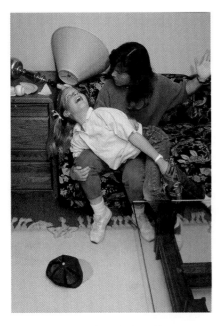

Many harried parents habitually resort to physical punishment without being aware of its many negative consequences for themselves and their children. Based on your reading of this chapter, what alternatives does this mother have?

Why do so many people ignore warnings and threats of punishment?

reinforced many times. For example, if you punish your dog when you get home for getting into the doggie biscuits and eating them all up, the punishment will not do any good: Your pet's misbehavior has already been reinforced by all those delicious treats.

5 *Punishment conveys little information.* If it immediately follows the misbehavior, punishment may tell the recipient what *not* to do, but it does not communicate what the person (or animal) *should* do. For example, spanking a toddler for messing in her pants will not teach her to use the potty chair, and scolding a student for learning slowly will not teach him to learn more quickly.

6 *An action intended to punish may instead be reinforcing because it brings attention.* Indeed, in some cases, angry attention may be just what the offender is after. If a mother yells at a child who is throwing a tantrum, the very act of yelling may give him what he wants—a reaction from her. In the schoolroom, teachers who scold children in front of other students, thus putting them in the limelight, often unwittingly reward the very misbehavior they are trying to eliminate.

Because of these drawbacks, most psychologists believe that punishment, especially severe punishment, is a poor way to eliminate unwanted behavior in most situations. When punishment must be used, these guidelines should be kept in mind: (1) It should not involve physical abuse—for example, parents can use "time-outs" and loss of privileges (negative punishers) instead of hitting; (2) it should be accompanied by information about what kind of behavior would be appropriate; and (3) it should be followed, whenever possible, by the reinforcement of desirable behavior.

Fortunately, a good alternative to punishment exists: extinction of the responses you want to discourage. Of course, the simplest form of extinction—ignoring the behavior—is often hard to carry out. It is not easy to ignore a child nagging for a cookie before dinner, a roommate interrupting your concentration, or a dog barking its lungs out. And ignoring the behavior is not always appropriate. A teacher cannot ignore a child who is hitting a playmate. The dog owner who ignores Fido's backyard barking may soon hear "barking" of another sort from the neighbors. A parent whose child is a video-game addict cannot ignore the behavior, because playing video games is rewarding to the child. One solution: Combine extinction of undesirable acts with reinforcement of alternative ones. For example, the parent of a video-game addict might ignore the child's pleas for "just one more game" and at the same time praise the child for doing something else that is incompatible with video-game playing, such as reading or playing basketball.

The Problems with Reward

So far, we have been praising the virtues of reinforcement. But like punishers, rewards do not always work as expected. Let's look at two complications that arise when people try to use them.

Misuse of Rewards. Suppose you are a fourth-grade teacher, and a student has just turned in a paper full of grammatical and punctuation errors. This child has little self-confidence and is easily discouraged. What should you do?

Many people think you should give the paper a high mark anyway, in order to bolster the child's self-esteem. Indeed, teachers everywhere are handing out lavish praise, happy-face stickers, and high grades in hopes that students' academic performance will improve as they learn to "feel good about themselves." In a new educational fad, "up-front" reinforcement, teachers are even providing rewards before students have done anything to merit them—much as our student's parents punished their children "in advance." One obvious result has been grade inflation at all levels of education. In many colleges and universities, Cs, which once meant average or satisfactory, are nearly extinct.

GABLE
THE GLOBE AND MAIL
Toronto
CANADA

The problem, from a behavioral point of view, is that to be effective, *rewards must be tied to the behavior you are trying to increase.* When rewards are dispensed indiscriminately, without being earned, they become meaningless because they no longer reinforce desired behavior; all that teachers get is minimal effort and mediocre work. Real self-esteem emerges from effort, persistence, and the gradual acquisition of skills, and is nurtured by a teacher's genuine appreciation of the *content* of a child's work (Damon, 1995). In the case of the child who turned in a poorly written paper, the teacher could praise its strengths but also give feedback on the paper's weaknesses and show the child how to correct them.

Why Rewards Can Backfire. A little girl we know came home from school one day in a huff after her teacher announced that good work would be rewarded with play money that could later be exchanged for privileges. "Doesn't she think I can learn without being bribed?" the child asked her mother indignantly.

This child's reaction illustrates another problem in the use of reinforcers. Most of our examples of operant conditioning have involved **extrinsic reinforcers,** which come from an outside source and are not inherently related to the activity being reinforced. Money, praise, gold stars, applause, hugs, and thumbs-up signs are all extrinsic reinforcers. But people (and probably some other animals, too) also work for **intrinsic reinforcers,** such as enjoyment of the task and the satisfaction of accomplishment. As psychologists have applied operant conditioning in real-world settings, they have found that extrinsic reinforcement sometimes becomes too much of a good thing: If you focus on it exclusively, it can kill the pleasure of doing something for its own sake.

Consider what happened when psychologists gave nursery-school children the chance to draw with felt-tipped pens (Lepper, Greene, & Nisbett, 1973). The children

extrinsic reinforcers Reinforcers that are not inherently related to the activity being reinforced.

intrinsic reinforcers Reinforcers that are inherently related to the activity being reinforced.

already liked this activity and readily took it up during free play. First, the researchers recorded how long each child spontaneously played with the pens. Then they told some of the children that if they would draw with felt-tipped pens for a man who had come "to see what kinds of pictures boys and girls like to draw with Magic Markers," they would get a prize, a "Good Player Award" complete with gold seal and red ribbon. After drawing for six minutes, each child got the award, as promised. Other children did not expect an award and were not given one.

A week later, the researchers again observed the children's free play. Those children who had expected and received an award were spending much less time with the pens than they had before the start of the experiment. In contrast, children who were not given an award continued to show as much interest in playing with the pens as they had initially, as you can see in Figure 7.6. Similar results have occurred in other studies, when children have been offered a reward for playing with a toy or at an activity they already enjoy (Deci et al., 1999).

Why should extrinsic rewards undermine the pleasure of doing something for its own sake? One possibility is that when we are paid for an activity, we interpret it as work. It is as if we say to ourselves, "I'm doing this because I'm being paid for it. Since I'm being paid, it must be something I wouldn't do if I didn't have to." When the reward is withdrawn, we refuse to "work" any longer. Or perhaps, because we regard extrinsic rewards as controlling, they reduce our sense of autonomy and choice ("I guess I should just do what I'm told to do—and *only* what I'm told to do") (Deci & Ryan, 1987). A third, more behavioral explanation is that extrinsic

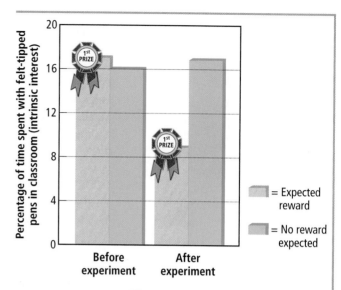

Figure 7.6

TURNING PLAY INTO WORK

Extrinsic rewards can sometimes reduce the intrinsic pleasure of an activity. When preschoolers were promised a prize for drawing with felt-tipped pens, the behavior temporarily increased. But after the children got their prizes, they spent less time with the pens than they had before the study began.

Get Involved

What's Reinforcing Your Behavior?

For each activity that you do, indicate whether the reinforcers are extrinsic or intrinsic.

Activity	Reinforcers mostly extrinsic	Reinforcers mostly intrinsic	Reinforcers about equally extrinsic and intrinsic
Studying	_____	_____	_____
Housework	_____	_____	_____
Worship	_____	_____	_____
Grooming	_____	_____	_____
Job	_____	_____	_____
Dating	_____	_____	_____
Attending class	_____	_____	_____
Reading unrelated to school	_____	_____	_____
Sports	_____	_____	_____
Cooking	_____	_____	_____

Is there an area of your life in which you would like intrinsic reinforcement to play a larger role? What can you do to make that happen?

"That is the correct answer, Billy, but I'm afraid you don't win anything for it."

reinforcement sometimes raises the rate of responding above some optimal, enjoyable level. Then the activity really does become work.

However, extrinsic rewards do not always weaken the impact of intrinsic ones. If you get money, a high grade, or a trophy for doing a task *well*, rather than for just doing it, your intrinsic motivation is not likely to decline (Dickinson, 1989; Eisenberger & Cameron, 1996, 1998). If you have always been crazy about reading or playing the banjo, you will probably keep reading or playing even when you are not getting a grade or applause for doing so (Mawhinney, 1990). In such cases, you will probably attribute your continued involvement in the activity to your own intrinsic interests and motivation rather than to the reward.

So, what is the take-home message about extrinsic rewards? First, sometimes they are necessary: Few people would trudge off to work every morning if they never got paid; and in the classroom, teachers may need to offer incentives to unmotivated students. Second, extrinsic rewards should be used sparingly, so that intrinsic pleasure in an activity can blossom. As one mother once wrote in *Newsweek*, children need to discover for themselves "the joy of music from songs, the power of mathematics from counting and all of human wisdom from reading" (Skreslet, 1987). And finally, educators and employers can avoid the trap of either-or thinking by recognizing that most people do their best when they get tangible rewards *and* when they have interesting, challenging, and varied kinds of work to do (see Chapter 12).

Effective behavior modification, as you can see, is not only a science but an art. In "Taking Psychology with You," we offer additional guidelines for mastering that art.

QUICK QUIZ ▪▪

Is the art of mastering quizzes intrinsically reinforcing yet?

A. According to behavioral principles, what is happening here?

1. An adolescent whose parents have hit him for minor transgressions since he was small runs away from home.

2. A young woman whose parents paid her to clean her room while she was growing up is a slob when she moves to her own apartment.

3. Two parents scold their young daughter every time they catch her sucking her thumb. The thumb sucking continues anyway.

B. In a fee-for-service health-care system, doctors are paid for each visit by a patient or for each service performed; the longer the visit, the higher the fee. In contrast, some health maintenance organizations (HMOs) pay their doctors a fixed amount per patient for an entire year. If the amount spent is less, the physician gets a bonus, and in some systems, if the amount spent is more, the physician must pay a penalty. Given what you know about operant conditioning, what are the advantages and disadvantages of each system?

Answers:

A. 1. The physical punishment was painful, and through a process of classical conditioning, the situation in which it occurred also became unpleasant. Because escape from an unpleasant stimulus is negatively reinforcing, the boy ran away. 2. Extrinsic reinforcers are no longer available, and room-cleaning behavior has been extinguished. Also, extrinsic rewards may have displaced the intrinsic satisfaction of having a tidy room. 3. Punishment has failed, possibly because it rewards thumb sucking with attention or because thumb sucking still brings the child pleasure whenever the parents are not around. B. In a fee-for-service system, the doctor is likely to provide the attention and tests that ill patients need. However, this system also rewards doctors for unnecessary tests and patient visits, contributing to the explosion in health-care costs. The policies of the HMOs help contain these costs, but because doctors are rewarded for reducing costs in some cases penalized for running up charges, some patients may not get the attention or services they need. (In recognition of this fact, in 2001, Blue Cross of California departed from industry practice by discontinuing its HMO cost-cutting incentive program and instituting instead a program linking physicians' bonuses to measures of patient satisfaction.)

WHAT'S AHEAD▶

- Can you learn something without any obvious reinforcement?
- Why do two people often learn different lessons from exactly the same experience?
- Does watching violence on TV make people more aggressive?

Learning and the Mind

For half a century, most American learning theories held that learning could be explained by specifying the behavioral "ABCs"— *antecedents* (events preceding behavior), *behaviors,* and *consequences.* Behaviorists liked to compare the mind to an engineer's hypothetical "black box," a device whose workings must be inferred because they cannot be observed directly. To them, the box contained irrelevant wiring; it was enough to know that pushing a button on the box would produce a predictable response. But even as early as the 1930s, a few behaviorists could not resist peeking into that black box.

Latent Learning

One behaviorist, Edward Tolman (1938), committed virtual heresy at the time by noting that his rats, when pausing at turning points in a maze, seemed to be *deciding* which way to go. Moreover, the animals sometimes seemed to be learning even without any reinforcement. What, he wondered, was going on in their little rat brains that might account for this puzzle?

In a classic experiment, Tolman and C. H. Honzik (1930) placed three groups of rats in mazes and observed their behavior daily for more than two weeks. The rats in Group 1 always found food at the end of the maze and quickly learned to find it without going down blind alleys. The rats in Group 2 never found food and, as you would expect, they followed no particular route. Group 3 was the interesting group. These rats found no food for ten days, and seemed to wander aimlessly, but on the eleventh they received food, and then they quickly learned to run to the end of the maze. By the next day, they were doing as well as Group 1, which had been rewarded from the beginning (see Figure 7.7)

Group 3 had demonstrated **latent learning,** learning that is not immediately expressed in performance. A great deal of human learning also remains latent until

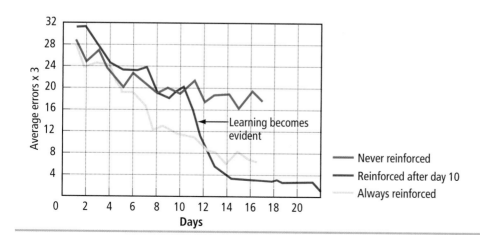

Figure 7.7

LATENT LEARNING

In a classic experiment, rats that always found food in a maze made fewer and fewer errors in reaching the food (green curve). Rats that never received food showed little improvement (blue curve). Rats in a third group got no food for ten days, and then were given food on the eleventh (red curve). These animals showed rapid improvement from then on, quickly equaling the performance of the rats that had received food from the start. This result suggests that learning involves cognitive changes that can occur in the absence of reinforcement and that may not be acted on until a reinforcer becomes available (Tolman & Honzik, 1930).

circumstances allow or require it to be expressed. A driver finds her way to Fourth and Kumquat Streets using a new route she has never used before. A little boy observes a parent setting the table or tightening a screw but does not act on this learning for years; then he finds he knows how to do these things, even though he has never done them before. Latent learning not only occurs without any obvious reinforcer; it also raises questions about what, exactly, is learned during learning. In the Tolman and Honzik study, the rats that did not get any food until the eleventh day seemed to have acquired a mental representation of the maze. They had been learning the whole time; they simply had no reason to act on that learning until they began to find food. Similarly, the driver taking a new route can do so because she already knows how the city is laid out.

What seems to be acquired in latent learning, therefore, is not a specific response, but *knowledge* about responses and their consequences. We learn how the world is organized, which paths lead to which places, and which actions can produce which payoffs. This knowledge permits us to be creative and flexible in reaching our goals.

Social-cognitive Learning Theories

The "black box" was opened further in the 1940s, when two social scientists proposed a major modification of radical behaviorism, which they called *social-learning theory* (Dollard & Miller, 1950). Most human learning, they argued, is acquired by observing other people in a social context, rather than through standard conditioning procedures. By the 1960s and 1970s, social-learning theory was in full bloom, and a new element had been added: the human capacity for higher-level cognitive processes. Its proponents agreed with behaviorists that human beings, along with the rat and the rabbit, are subject to the laws of operant and classical conditioning. But they added that human beings, unlike the rat or the rabbit, are full of attitudes, beliefs, and expectations that affect the way they acquire information, make decisions, reason, and solve problems.

These mental processes affect what individuals will do at any given moment and also, more generally, the personality traits they develop (see Chapter 13). Because people differ in their attitudes, expectations, and perceptions, they can live through the same event and come away with entirely different lessons from it (Bandura, 2001). All siblings know this. One may regard being grounded by their father as evidence of his all-around meanness, and another may see the same behavior as evidence of his care and concern for his children.

Because of this emphasis on cognitive factors, one leading theorist, Walter Mischel, has called his approach *cognitive social-learning theory* (Mischel, 1973; Mischel & Shoda, 1995); and another, Albert Bandura, calls his *social-cognitive theory* (Bandura, 1986). We will use the general term **social-cognitive theory** to include all modern social-learning approaches (Barone, Maddux, & Snyder, 1997). They share an emphasis on the importance of our beliefs and perceptions, and our observations of others' behavior, in determining what we learn and how we behave.

Learning by Observing. Late one night, a friend who lives in a rural area was awakened by a loud clattering and banging. Her whole family raced outside to find the source of the commotion. A raccoon had knocked over a "raccoon-proof" garbage can and seemed to be demonstrating to an assembly of other raccoons how to open it: If you jump up and down on the can's side, the lid will pop off.

According to our friend, the observing raccoons learned from this episode how to open stubborn garbage cans, and the observing humans learned how smart raccoons can be. In short, they all benefited from **observational learning:** learning by watching what others do and what happens to them for doing it.

latent learning A form of learning that is not immediately expressed in an overt response; it occurs without obvious reinforcement.

social-cognitive theories Theories that emphasize how behavior is learned and maintained through observation and imitation of others, positive consequences, and cognitive processes such as plans, expectations, and beliefs.

observational learning A process in which an individual learns new responses by observing the behavior of another (a model) rather than through direct experience; sometimes called *vicarious conditioning.*

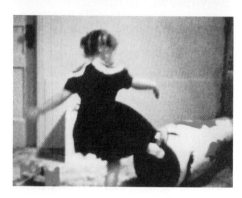

Adults and children alike learn through observation. In studies by Albert Bandura and his colleagues, children watched films of an adult kicking, punching, and hammering on a big rubber doll (top). Later, the children imitated the adult's behavior, some of them almost exactly.

Behaviorists have always acknowledged the importance of observational learning, which they call *vicarious conditioning,* and have tried to explain it in stimulus-response terms. But social-cognitive theorists believe that in human beings, observational learning cannot be fully understood without taking into account the thought processes of the learner (Meltzoff & Gopnik, 1993). They emphasize the knowledge that results when a person sees a *model*—another person—behaving in certain ways and experiencing the consequences (Bandura, 1977).

None of us would last long without observational learning. We would have to learn to avoid oncoming cars by walking into traffic and suffering the consequences or learn to swim by jumping into a deep pool and flailing around. Learning would be not only inefficient but dangerous. Parents and teachers would be busy 24 hours a day shaping children's behavior. Bosses would have to stand over their employees' desks, rewarding every little link in the complex behavioral chains we call typing, report writing, and accounting.

Many years ago, Albert Bandura and his colleagues showed just how important observational learning is, especially for children who are learning the rules of social behavior (Bandura, Ross, & Ross, 1963). The researchers had nursery school children watch a short film of two men, Rocky and Johnny, playing with toys. (Apparently the children did not think this behavior was the least bit odd.) In the film, Johnny refuses to share his toys, and Rocky responds by clobbering him. Rocky's actions are rewarded because he winds up with all the toys. Poor Johnny sits dejectedly in the corner, while Rocky marches off with a sack full of his loot and a hobby horse under his arm. After viewing the film, each child was left alone for 20 minutes in a playroom full of toys, including some of the items shown in the film. Watching through a one-way mirror, the researchers found that the children were much more aggressive in their play than a control group that had not seen the film. Some children imitated Rocky almost exactly. At the end of the session, one little girl even asked the experimenter for a sack!

Of course, people imitate positive activities that they observe, too. Matt Groening, the creator of the cartoon show *The Simpsons*, decided it would be funny if the Simpsons' 8-year-old daughter Lisa played the baritone sax. Sure enough, across the country little girls began imitating her. Cynthia Sikes, a saxophone teacher in New York, told *The New York Times* (January 14, 1996) that "When the show started, I got an influx of girls coming up to me saying, 'I want to play the saxophone because Lisa Simpson plays the saxophone.'"

The Case of Media Violence. These findings on latent learning, the role of perceptions in learning, and observational learning have added fuel to an ongoing, emotional debate: Does media violence make people behave more aggressively? Every time an American child or teenager commits a shocking murder, there is a public outcry over the countless acts of violence that children see on television, in films, and in video games. Politicians and parents blame the media, and the media claim to be blameless. What does the evidence show?

First, since Bandura's early research, hundreds of other experimental studies of children, teenagers, and adults have corroborated his findings, convincing many psychologists that observing aggression does increase aggression (APA Commission on Violence and Youth, 1993; Bushman & Anderson, 2001; Eron, 1995). Meta-analyses show that the greater the exposure to violence in movies and on television, the stronger the likelihood of a person's behaving aggressively, even after researchers control for social class, intelligence, and other factors (e.g., Anderson & Bushman, 2001). Moreover, when grade-school children cut back on their time watching TV or playing video games, which are often violent in nature, their aggressiveness declines (Robinson et al., 2001). When two researchers compared the correlation between media violence and aggression with correlations in the medical area (for example, between calcium intake and bone mass, or condom use and sexually transmitted HIV), only one effect was larger: the correlation between smoking and lung cancer (Paik & Comstock, 1994).

Of course, media violence does not cause all viewers to become aggressive, any more than cigarettes cause all smokers to get lung cancer. Some psychologists and social critics believe that the relationship between media violence and real violence is not strong enough to worry about (Freedman, 1988). Children, they note, watch many different programs and movies, and have many models to observe besides those they see in the media; their parents and peers are also influential. For every teenager who is obsessed with playing *Mortal Kombat* and who entertains violent fantasies of blowing up the world, dozens more think the game is just plain fun, and then go off to do their homework. Indeed, although the number of violent video games increased throughout the 1990s, overall rates of teenage violence actually *declined.*

Critics also point out that cause and effect work in the opposite direction: Children and adults who are habitually aggressive like to watch violent shows, and are more affected by them, than are nonaggressive people. Given a choice of films to watch, aggressive, hostile individuals prefer the violent ones. When they watch violent films, they feel angrier afterward than nonaggressive people do. And if given the chance to behave aggressively toward others after watching a violent film, they are more likely to do so than nonaggressive people are (Bushman, 1995). Moreover, a troubled person who is prone to aggression may find the "justification" to behave violently from *anything* he or she sees. Years ago, a German

Do violent video games, such as "The House of the Dead," make players more aggressive?

named Heinrich Pommerencke went to the movies, where, watching women dancing on screen, he became convinced that all women were immoral and deserved to die. He then committed four brutal rape-murders before he was caught. The film that set him off was Cecil B. DeMille's *The Ten Commandments*.

In the social-cognitive view, both conclusions about the correlation between media violence and violent behavior have merit. It is indisputable that repeated acts of aggression in the media *do* model behavior and responses to conflict that some people will imitate—just as media ads influence what many people buy and what many people think the ideal male or female body should look like. But perceptions and interpretations, along with personality dispositions such as aggressiveness (or, in the case of people like Pommerencke, mental illness), are crucial factors that intervene between what we see, what we learn, and how we respond. One person may learn from seeing people being blown away in a film that violence is cool and masculine; another may conclude that violence is ugly and stupid.

And so, ironically, both sides in the media violence debate are right: It does have an influence, *and* that influence is neither strong nor universal. Yet the social consequences of even a small influence can be enormous because the audiences for TV, movies, and video games are immense: If 10 million people watch a violent TV program and only 1 percent of them become more violent afterwards, that's 100,000 people (Bushman & Anderson, 2001)! And although the effects of one program may be short-lived, the *cumulative* effects over a period of years may be long-lasting.

What, if anything, should society do about these findings? Complete censorship would be impossible; how could anyone agree on which acts of violence to ban? *Hamlet*? Cartoons? A funny Jackie Chan martial-arts film like *Shanghai Noon*? It would also be unfair, because the vast majority of viewers are unaffected by watching violent acts. And, in the United States, censorship would violate the Constitution, which guarantees freedom of speech. As for voluntary censorship, parents already have the opportunity to install "V-chips" on their TVs to block violent programs, yet only a tiny number of parents actually use them. It seems we will have to tolerate uncertainty about how best to reduce the violence that media images inspire in some viewers until we can find a fair and equitable way of solving the problem.

> **THINKING CRITICALLY**
>
> **Tolerate Uncertainty**
>
> The evidence shows that an association exists between media violence and aggressiveness. But censorship creates its own set of problems. So what is society to do?

QUICK QUIZ

How latent is your learning?

1. A friend asks you to meet her at a new restaurant across town. You have never been to this specific address, but you find your way there anyway because you have experienced _____ learning.

2. To a social-cognitive theorist, the fact that we can learn without being reinforced for any obvious responses shows that we do not learn specific responses but rather _____.

3. After watching her teenage sister put on lipstick, a little girl takes a lipstick and applies it to her own lips. She has acquired this behavior through a process of _____.

 4. The families of victims shot at a high school by two fellow students claimed in a $5 billion lawsuit against several video-game manufacturers that the tragedy would not have happened had the killers not had access to violent games. How would you evaluate this claim?

Answers:

1. latent 2. knowledge about responses and their consequences 3. observational learning 4. Although a link has been established between media violence and aggressiveness, it is impossible to prove cause and effect in any given case. Violence has many different causes; for example, some teenagers kill because they have been taunted and rejected by their classmates. Further, a person's response to media violence is influenced by his or her perceptions and attitudes. Finally, although violent video games increased in the 1990s, overall rates of juvenile violence decreased.

Although the behavioral and social-cognitive approaches to learning differ in emphasis, they share a fundamental optimism about the possibilities of change for individuals and societies. In the learning view, we do not have to sit around hoping that people will magically have a change of heart and stop harming themselves or others. Instead, we can focus on changing the reinforcers, role models, and media images that affect people's attitudes and actions.

Skinner himself never wavered in his determination to apply learning principles to fashion better, healthier environments for everyone. Toward the end of his life, in a book called *Enjoy Old Age*, Skinner offered all sorts of useful tips on how the elderly could make their lives easier (Skinner & Vaughan, 1984). And in 1990, just a week before his death, ailing and frail, he addressed an overflow crowd at the annual meeting of the American Psychological Association, making the case one last time for the approach he was convinced could create a better society.

When you see the world as the learning theorist views it, Skinner was saying, you see the folly of human behavior, but you also see the possibility of improving it.

Taking Psychology with You

SHAPE UP!

Operant conditioning can seem deceptively simple—a few rewards here, a bit of shaping there, and you're done. In practice, though, behavior modification can be full of unwanted surprises, even in the hands of experts. You can find information on using behavioral techniques in books such as *Don't Shoot the Dog: The New Art of Teaching and Training*, by Karen Pryor (1999), and *Behavior Modification: What It Is and How to Do It*, by Garry Martin and Joseph Pear (1999). In addition, here are a few things to keep in mind if you want to modify someone's behavior.

▶ *Accentuate the positive.* Most people notice bad behavior more than good and therefore miss opportunities to use reinforcers. Parents, for example, often scold a child for bed-wetting but fail to give praise for dry sheets in the morning; or they punish a child for poor grades but fail to reward studying.

▶ *Reinforce small improvements.* A common error is to withhold reinforcement until behavior is perfect (which may be never). Has your child's grade in math improved from a D to a C? Has your favorite date, who is usually an awful cook, managed to serve up a half-decent omelette? Has your messy roommate left some dirty dishes in the sink but vacuumed the rug? It's probably time for a reinforcer. On the other hand, you don't want to overdo praise or give it insincerely. Gushing about every tiny step in the right direction will cause your praise to lose its value, and soon nothing less than a standing ovation will do.

▶ *Find the right reinforcers.* You may have to experiment a bit to find which reinforcers a person (or animal) actually wants. In general, it is good to use a variety of reinforcers because the same one used again and again can get boring. Reinforcers, by the way, do not have to be *things*. You can also use valued activities, such as going out to dinner, to reinforce other behavior.

▶ *Always examine what you are reinforcing.* It is easy to reinforce undesirable behavior just by responding to it. Suppose someone is always yelling at you at the slightest provocation, and you want it to stop. If you respond to it at all, whether by crying, apologizing, or yelling back, you are likely to reinforce it. An alternative might be to explain in a calm voice that you will henceforth not respond to complaints unless they are communicated without yelling—and then, if the yelling continues, walk away. When the person does speak civilly, you can reward this behavior with your attention and goodwill.

▶ *Analyze the reasons for a person's undesirable behavior before responding to it.* A child screaming in a supermarket may be saying, "I'm going out of my head with boredom. Help!" A lover who sulks may be saying, "I'm not sure you really care about me; I'm frightened." Once you understand the purpose of someone's behavior, you may be more effective in dealing with it.

These guidelines apply to your own behavior as well. Assume, for example, that you want to get yourself to study more. Here are some behavioral strategies for increasing the time you spend with your books:

▶ *Analyze the situation.* Are there circumstances that keep you from studying, such as a friend who is always pressuring you to go out or a rock band that practices next door? If so, you need to change your environment during study periods. Try to find a comfortable, cheerful, quiet place. Not only will you concentrate better, but you may also have positive emotional responses to the environment that may generalize to the activity of studying.

▶ *Set realistic goals.* Goals should be demanding but achievable. If a goal is too vague, as in "I'm going to work harder," you don't know what behavioral changes are necessary to reach it or how to know when you have done so (what does "harder" mean?). If your goal is focused, as in "I am going to study two hours every evening instead of one" or "I will read 25 pages instead of 15," you have specified both a course of action and a goal you can achieve (and reward).

▶ *Keep records.* Chart your progress in some way, perhaps by making a graph. This will keep you honest, and the progress you see on the graph will serve as a secondary reinforcer.

▶ *Don't punish yourself.* If you did not study enough last week, don't brood about it or berate yourself with self-defeating thoughts, such as "I'll never be a good student" or "I'm a failure." Think about the coming week instead.

Above all, be patient. Shaping behavior is a creative skill that takes time to learn. Like Rome, new habits cannot be built in a day.

Summary

▶ Research on *learning* has been heavily influenced by *behaviorism*, which accounts for behavior in terms of observable events, without reference to mental entities such as "mind" or "will." Behaviorists have focused on two types of *conditioning*: classical and operant.

Classical Conditioning

▶ *Classical conditioning* was first studied by Russian physiologist Ivan Pavlov. In this type of learning, when a neutral stimulus is paired with an *unconditioned stimulus* (US) that elicits some reflexive *unconditioned response* (UR), the neutral stimulus comes to elicit a similar or related response. The neutral stimulus is then called a *conditioned stimulus* (CS), and the response it elicits, a *conditioned response* (CR). Nearly any kind of involuntary response can become a CR.

▶ In *extinction*, the conditioned stimulus is repeatedly presented without the unconditioned stimulus, and the conditioned response eventually disappears—although later it may reappear (*spontaneous recovery*). In *higher-order conditioning*, a neutral stimulus becomes a conditioned stimulus by being paired with an already established conditioned stimulus. In *stimulus generalization*, after a stimulus becomes a conditioned stimulus for some response, other, similar stimuli may produce the same reaction. In *stimulus*

discrimination, different responses are made to stimuli that resemble the conditioned stimulus in some way.

▶ Many theorists believe that what an animal or person learns in classical conditioning is not just an association between the unconditioned and conditioned stimulus, but information conveyed by one stimulus about another. Indeed, classical conditioning appears to be an evolutionary adaptation that allows an organism to prepare for a biologically important event. Considerable evidence exists to show that a neutral stimulus does not become a CS unless it reliably signals or predicts the US.

Classical Conditioning in Real Life

▶ Classical conditioning helps account for positive emotional responses to particular objects and events, fears and phobias, the acquisition of likes and dislikes, and reactions to medical treatments and placebos. John Watson showed how fears may be learned and then may be unlearned through a process of *counterconditioning*. Human beings (and many other species) are biologically primed to acquire some adaptive responses easily, such as conditioned taste aversions and certain fears.

Operant Conditioning

▶ In *operant conditioning*, behavior becomes more likely to occur or less so, depending on its consequences.

Responses are generally not reflexive and are more complex than in classical conditioning. Research in this area is closely associated with B. F. Skinner, who called his approach "radical behaviorism."

▶ In the Skinnerian analysis, a response ("operant") can lead to neutral, reinforcing, or punishing consequences. *Reinforcement* strengthens or increases the probability of a response. *Punishment* weakens or decreases the probability of a response. Immediate consequences usually have a greater effect on a response than do delayed consequences.

▶ Reinforcers are called *primary* when they are naturally reinforcing (e.g., because they satisfy a biological need) and *secondary* when they have acquired their ability to strengthen a response through association with other reinforcers. A similar distinction is made for punishers.

▶ Reinforcement and punishment may be either positive or negative, depending on whether the consequence involves a stimulus that is presented, or one that is removed or avoided. In *positive reinforcement*, something pleasant follows a response; in *negative reinforcement*, something unpleasant is removed. In *positive punishment*, something unpleasant follows the response; in *negative punishment*, something pleasant is removed.

▶ Using the Skinner box and similar devices, behaviorists have shown that *extinction, stimulus generalization*, and *stimulus discrimination* occur in operant as well as in classical conditioning. A *discriminative stimulus* signals that a response is likely to be followed by a certain type of consequence.

▶ The pattern of responding in operant conditioning depends in part on the *schedule of reinforcement. Continuous reinforcement* leads to the most rapid learning. However, *intermittent (partial) reinforcement* makes a response resistant to extinction (and therefore helps account for the persistence of superstitious rituals). Intermittent schedules deliver a reinforcer after a given amount of time has passed since the last reinforcer (*interval schedules*) or after a given number of responses are made (*ratio schedules*). Such schedules may be *fixed* or *variable*. One of the most common errors people make is to reward intermittently the responses they would like to eliminate.

▶ *Shaping* is used to train behaviors with a low probability of occurring spontaneously. Reinforcers are given for *successive approximations* to the desired response, until the desired response is achieved.

▶ Biology places limits on what an animal or person can learn through operant conditioning. For example, animals sometimes have trouble learning a task because of *instinctive drift*.

Operant Conditioning in Real Life

▶ *Behavior modification,* the application of conditioning principles, has been used successfully in many settings, but reinforcement and punishment both have their pitfalls.

▶ Punishment, when used properly, can discourage undesirable behavior, including criminal behavior. But it is frequently misused, and may have unintended consequences. It is often administered inappropriately because of the emotion of the moment; it may produce rage and fear; its effects are often only temporary; it is hard to administer immediately; it conveys little information about the kind of behavior that is desired; and it may provide attention that is rewarding. Extinction of undesirable behavior, combined with reinforcement of desired behavior, is generally preferable to the use of punishment.

▶ Reinforcers can also be misused. Rewards that are given out indiscriminately, as in efforts to raise children's self-esteem, do not reinforce desirable behavior. An exclusive reliance on *extrinsic reinforcement* can sometimes undermine the power of *intrinsic reinforcement*. But money and praise do not usually interfere with intrinsic pleasure when a person is rewarded for succeeding or making progress rather than for merely participating in an activity, or when a person is already highly interested in the activity.

Learning and the Mind

▶ Even during behaviorism's heyday, some researchers were probing the "black box" of the mind. For example, in the 1930s, Edward Tolman studied *latent learning,* in which no obvious reinforcer is present during learning and a response is not expressed until later on, when reinforcement does become available. What seems to be acquired in latent learning is not a specific response, but *knowledge* about responses and their consequences.

▶ The 1960s and 1970s saw the increased influence of *social-cognitive theories* of learning, which focus on *observational learning* and the role played by beliefs, interpretations of events, and other cognitions. Social-cognitive theorists argue that in observational learning, as in latent learning, what is acquired is knowledge, rather than a specific response.

▶ Because people differ in their perceptions and beliefs, they may learn different lessons from the same event or situation. For example, although observing media violence does increase aggressiveness in some viewers, it does not do so in most of them. The social consequences of even a small effect, however, can be serious.

Key Terms

◀ LOOKING BACK

- Why would a dog salivate when it sees a lightbulb or hears a buzzer, even though it can't eat these things? (p. 231)

- How can classical conditioning help explain prejudice? (p. 233)

- If you have learned to fear collies, why might you also be scared of sheepdogs? (p. 233)

- Why do advertisers often include pleasant music and gorgeous scenery in ads for their products? (p. 236)

- How would a classical-conditioning theorist explain your irrational fear of heights or mice? (pp. 236–237)

- If you eat licorice and then happen to get the flu, how might your taste for licorice change? (p. 238)

- How can sitting in a doctor's office make you feel sick? (p. 239)

- What do praise and ceasing your nagging have in common? (p. 242)

- How can operant principles account for superstitious rituals? (pp. 245–246)

- What is the best way to discourage a friend from interrupting you while you're studying? (p. 248)

- How do trainers teach guide dogs to perform the amazing services they do for their owners? (p. 248)

- Why do efforts to "crack down" on wrongdoers often go awry? (pp. 252–253)

- What's the best way to discourage a child from throwing tantrums? (p. 253)

- Why does paying children for good grades sometimes backfire? (pp. 254–255)

- Can you learn something without any obvious reinforcement? (pp. 257–258)

- Why do two people often learn different lessons from exactly the same experience? (p. 258)

- Does watching violence on TV make people more aggressive? (pp. 260–261)

Go to **WWW.PRENHALL.COM/WADE** to reinforce these key concepts, and more.
7.1 Classical conditioning process   7.2 Operant conditioning process

8

Behavior in Social and Cultural Context

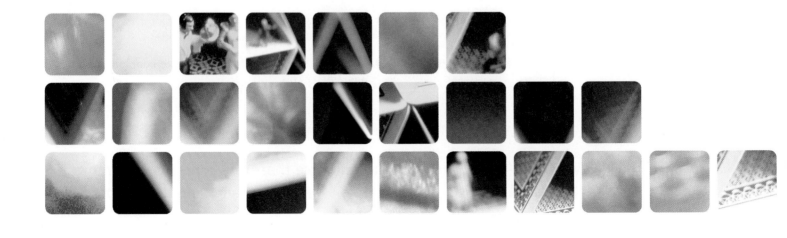

Even the most sadistic and destructive man
is human, as human as the saint.

ERICH FROMM

When Mohamed Atta was in graduate school in Germany, studying urban planning, his friends saw him as a good man who, like many students, was troubled by the social injustice he observed in the world. Atta was especially disturbed by the gap between rich and poor, although he himself came from a well-to-do family; his father was a lawyer and two sisters became university professors. "I knew Mohamed as a guy searching for justice," his German friend Volker Hauth told *The Los Angeles Times* (September 27, 2001). "Atta was very religious," said another friend. "He was very full of idealism and he was a humanist." In 2000, Atta left Germany for good. On September 11, 2001, he was one of the 19 hijackers who attacked the World Trade Center and the Pentagon, killing 3,000 people.

In Rwanda in 1994, members of the Hutu tribe shot or hacked to death hundreds of thousands of Tutsis, a rival tribe. At one point, thousands of Tutsi took refuge in a Benedictine convent, believing the nuns there would shelter them. Instead, the mother superior, Sister Gertrude, and another nun, Sister Maria Kisito—both of them Hutu—reported the Tutsi refugees to the Hutu militia. More than 7,000 Tutsi were killed in the ensuing massacre. When the two nuns were brought to trial in Belgium, where they had fled after the war, Sister Gertrude told the court she did it because "we were all going to perish." But observers testified that when 500 Tutsi fled to the convent's garage, the two nuns brought the militiamen gasoline. The garage was set afire, and anyone trying to escape the flames was hacked to death. The two women were sentenced to 15- and 12-year terms for crimes against humanity.

In 1961, Adolf Eichmann was put on trial for murder, although he personally had never killed anyone. Eichmann, a high-ranking officer of the Nazi SS (an elite

Mohamed Atta, Rwandan Hutu nuns Sister Gertrude and Sister Maria Kisito at their trial in Brussels, and Adolf Eichmann at his trial in Israel. All of these people committed barbaric crimes against humanity. Were they "monsters"?

military unit of storm troopers), supervised the deportation and death of millions of Jews during World War II. He was proud of his efficiency at his work and his ability to resist feeling pity for his victims. But when the Israelis captured him, he insisted that he was not anti-Semitic: He had had a Jewish mistress and he personally arranged for the protection of his Jewish half-cousin—two dangerous crimes for an SS officer. Shortly before his execution by hanging, Eichmann said, "I am not the monster I am made out to be. I am the victim of a fallacy" (R. Brown, 1986).

The fallacy to which Eichmann referred was the widespread belief that a person who does monstrous deeds must be a monster, someone sick and evil. Is that true? Mohamed Atta, Sisters Gertrude and Maria Kisito, and Adolf Eichmann all committed monstrous deeds leading to the deaths of thousands of innocent people. Were they crazy? Evil? Six psychiatrists examined Eichmann and pronounced him sane. His family life was normal, they said, and he had deep feelings of love for his wife, children, and parents. Two observers described him as "an average man of middle class origins and normal middle class upbringing, a man without identifiable criminal tendencies" (Von Lang & Sibyll, 1984). Psychiatrists would probably have said the same of Atta and the nuns.

So much evil and cruelty in the world—and yet, even more often, so much kindness, sacrifice, and heroism, as America saw in the aftermath of the World Trade Center disaster. How can we even begin to explain either side of human nature?

The fields of *social psychology* and *cultural psychology* approach this question by examining the powerful influence of the social and cultural environment on the actions of individuals and groups. In this chapter, we will focus on the foundations of social psychology, basic principles that can help us understand why some people who are not "crazy" or "monstrous" nonetheless do unspeakably evil things—or, for that matter, why some otherwise ordinary people reach heights of heroism when the occasion demands. In particular, we will look at roles, attitudes, and groups, including the conditions under which people conform or dissent. Then we will consider some of the social and cultural reasons for prejudice and conflict between groups.

WHAT'S AHEAD

- How do social rules regulate behavior—and what is likely to happen when you violate them?
- Do you have to be mean or disturbed to inflict pain on someone just because an authority tells you to?
- How can ordinary college students be transformed into sadistic prison guards?
- How can people be "entrapped" into violating their moral principles?

Roles and Rules

"We are all fragile creatures entwined in a cobweb of social constraints," social psychologist Stanley Milgram once said. The constraints he referred to are social **norms**, rules about how we are supposed to act. Norms are the conventions of everyday life that make interactions with other people predictable and orderly; like a cobweb, they are often as invisible as they are strong. Every society has norms for just about everything in human experience: for conducting courtships, for raising children, for making decisions, for behavior in public places. Some norms are enshrined in law, such as, "A person may not beat up another person, except in self-defense." Some are unspoken cultural understandings, such as, "A man may beat up another man who insults his masculinity." And some are tiny, unspoken regulations that people learn to follow unconsciously, such as, "You may not sing at the top of your lungs on a public bus."

In every society, people also fill a variety of social **roles**, positions that are regulated by norms about how people in those positions should behave. Gender roles define the proper behavior for a man and a woman. Occupational roles determine the correct behavior for a manager and an employee, a professor and a student. Family roles set tasks for parent and child, husband and wife. Certain aspects of every role must be carried out or there will be penalties—emotional, financial, professional. As a student, for instance, you know just what you have to do to pass your psychology course (or you should by now!).

When you violate a role requirement, intentionally or unintentionally, you will tend to feel uncomfortable—or other people will try to make you feel uncomfortable. For instance, in traditional families, it is part of the woman's role to take care of relationships—send gifts to relatives, write thank-you notes and holiday cards, organize parties, remember an aunt's birthday, and so forth. If a woman does not do these things when she is expected to, her friends and relatives will blame her (di Leonardo, 1987). And traditional male norms have required a man to be strong, reject qualities associated with women (such as emotional "weakness" and crying), keep his problems to himself, and retaliate aggressively if threatened (Fischer et al., 1998). When men violate these norms—for example, by revealing their fears and worries—they may be regarded by both sexes as being "too feminine" and poorly adjusted (Kimmel, 1995). Of course, role requirements can change, as they have for both sexes in Western cultures. Nowadays male politicians and athletes even cry in public, a "feminine" act that not long ago would have cost them their careers.

The requirements of a social role are in turn shaped by the culture you live in. **Culture** can be defined as a program of shared rules that govern the behavior of people in a community or society, and a set of values and beliefs shared by most members of that community and passed from one generation to another (Lonner, 1995).

norms (social) Rules that regulate human life, including social conventions, explicit laws, and implicit cultural standards.

role A given social position that is governed by a set of norms for proper behavior.

culture A program of shared rules that govern the behavior of members of a community or society, and a set of values, beliefs, and attitudes shared by most members of that community.

Many roles in modern life require us to give up our individuality. If one of these members of the British Coldstream Guards suddenly broke into a dance, his career would be brief—and the dazzling effect of the parade would be ruined. But when does adherence to a role go too far?

You learn most of your culture's rules and values the way you learn your culture's language—without thinking about it.

For example, cultures differ in their rules for *conversational distance:* how close people normally stand to one another when they are speaking (Hall, 1959, 1976). Arabs like to stand close enough to feel your breath, touch your arm, and see your eyes—a distance that makes white Americans, Canadians, and northern Europeans uneasy, unless they are talking intimately with a lover. The English and the Swedes stand farthest apart when they converse; southern Europeans stand closer; and Latin Americans and Arabs stand the closest (Keating, 1994; Sommer, 1969). Knowing another culture's rules, though, does not make it any easier to change your own. Caroline Keating (1994), an American cultural psychologist, told about walking on a street with a Pakistani colleague. The closer he moved toward her, seeking the closeness he was comfortable with, the more she moved away, seeking the distance *she* was comfortable with. Eventually she fell off the curb!

Naturally, people bring their own personalities and interests to the roles they play. Just as two actors will play Hamlet differently although they are reading from the same script, you will have your own "reading" of how to play the role of student, friend, parent, or employer. Nonetheless, the requirements of a social role are strong, so strong that they may even cause you to behave in ways that shatter your fundamental sense of the kind of person you are. We turn now to two famous studies that illuminate the power of social roles in our lives.

Arabs stand much closer in conversation than Westerners do, close enough to feel one another's breath and "read" one another's eyes. Most Westerners would feel "crowded" standing so close, even talking to a friend.

The Obedience Study

In the early 1960s, Stanley Milgram (1963, 1974) designed a study that would become world famous. It was, in effect, a study of Eichmann's claim that he was not a "monster," just a normal man following orders.

Design and Findings. Milgram wanted to know how many people would obey an authority figure when directly ordered to violate their own ethical standards. Participants in the study, however, thought they were part of an experiment on the effects of punishment on learning. Each was assigned, apparently at random, to the role of "teacher." Another person, introduced as a fellow volunteer, was the "learner." Whenever the learner, seated in an adjoining room, made an error in reciting a list of word pairs he was supposed to have memorized, the teacher had to give him an electric shock by depressing a lever on a machine (see

Figure 8.1). With each error, the voltage (marked from 0 to 450) was to be increased by another 15 volts. The shock levels on the machine were labeled from SLIGHT SHOCK to DANGER—SEVERE SHOCK and, finally, ominously, XXX. In reality, the learners were confederates of Milgram and did not receive any shocks, but none of the teachers ever realized this during the study. The actor-victims played their parts convincingly: As the study continued, they shouted in pain and pleaded to be released, all according to a prearranged script.

Before doing this study, Milgram asked a number of psychiatrists, students, and middle-class adults how many people they thought would "go all the way" to XXX on orders from the researcher. The psychiatrists predicted that most people would refuse to go beyond 150 volts, when the learner first demanded to be freed, and that only one person in a thousand, someone who was disturbed and sadistic, would administer the highest voltage. The nonprofessionals agreed with this prediction, and all of them said that they personally would disobey early in the procedure.

That is not the way the results turned out. Every single person administered some shock to the learner, and about two-thirds of the participants, of all ages and from all walks of life, obeyed to the fullest extent. Many protested to the experimenter, but they backed down when he calmly asserted, "The experiment requires that you continue." They obeyed no matter how much the victim shouted for them to stop and no matter how painful the shocks seemed to be. They obeyed even when they themselves were anguished about the pain they believed they were causing. As Milgram (1974) noted, participants would "sweat, tremble, stutter, bite their lips, groan, and dig their fingernails into their flesh"—but still they obeyed.

More than 1,000 people at several American universities eventually went through replications of the Milgram study. Most of them, men and women equally, inflicted what they thought were dangerous amounts of shock to another person. Researchers in other countries have also found high percentages of obedience, ranging to more than 90 percent in Spain and the Netherlands (Meeus & Raaijmakers, 1995; Smith & Bond, 1994).

Milgram and his team subsequently set up several variations of the study to determine the circumstances under which people might disobey the experimenter. They found that virtually nothing the victim did or said changed the likelihood of compliance—even when the victim said he had a heart condition, screamed in agony, or stopped responding entirely as if he had collapsed. However, people *were* more likely to disobey under the following conditions:

▶ *When the experimenter left the room.* Many people then subverted authority by giving low levels of shock but reporting that they had followed orders.

THINKING CRITICALLY

Ask Questions

Jot down your best guess in answering these three questions: (1) What percentage of people are sadistic? (2) If told by an authority to harm an innocent person, what percentage of people would do it? (3) If *you* were instructed to harm an innocent person, would you do it or would you refuse?

Figure 8.1

THE MILGRAM OBEDIENCE EXPERIMENT

On the left is Milgram's original shock machine; in 1963, it looked pretty ominous. On the right, the "learner" is being strapped into his chair by the experimenter and the "teacher."

In Milgram's study, when the "teacher" had to administer shock directly to the learner, most subjects refused—but this one continued to obey.

▶ *When the victim was right there in the room,* and the teacher had to administer the shock directly to the victim's body.

▶ *When two experimenters issued conflicting demands* to continue the experiment or to stop at once. In this case, no one kept inflicting shock.

▶ *When the person ordering them to continue was an ordinary man,* apparently another volunteer, instead of the authoritative experimenter.

▶ *When the subject worked with peers who refused to go further.* Seeing someone else rebel gave subjects the courage to disobey.

Obedience, Milgram concluded, was more a function of the situation than of the particular personalities of the participants. "The key to [their] behavior, Milgram (1974) summarized, "lies not in pent-up anger or aggression but in the nature of their relationship to authority. They have given themselves to the authority; they see themselves as instruments for the execution of his wishes; once so defined, they are unable to break free."

Evaluating the Obedience Study. The Milgram study has had its critics. Some consider it unethical because people were kept in the dark about what was really happening until the session was over (of course, telling them in advance would have invalidated the study) and because many suffered emotional pain (Milgram countered that they would not have felt pain if they had simply disobeyed instructions). Others question the conclusion that personality traits always have less influence on behavior than the demands of the situation; certain traits, such as hostility and rigidity, do increase obedience to authority in real life (Blass, 1993, 2000).

Some psychologists also object to the parallel Milgram drew between the behavior of the study's participants and the brutality of the Nazis and others who commit acts of barbarism in the name of duty (Berkowitz, 1999; Darley, 1995). The people in Milgram's study obeyed only when the experimenter was hovering right there, and many of them felt enormous discomfort and conflict. In contrast, the Nazis acted without direct supervision by authorities, without external pressure, and without feelings of anguish.

Nevertheless, this famous and compelling study has had a tremendous influence on public awareness of the dangers of uncritical obedience (Blass, 2000). As John Darley (1995) observed, "Milgram shows us the beginning of a path by means of which ordinary people, in the grip of social forces, become the origins of atrocities in the real world."

The Prison Study

Imagine that one day, as you are walking home, a police car pulls up. Two uniformed officers get out, arrest you, and take you to a prison cell. There you are stripped of your clothes, sprayed with a delousing fluid, assigned a prison uniform, photographed with your prison number, and put behind bars. You feel a little queasy but you are not panicked; you have agreed to play the part of prisoner for a two-week study and your arrest is merely part of the script. Your prison cell, while apparently authentic, is located in the basement of a university building. So began an effort to discover what happens when ordinary college students take on the roles of prisoners and guards (Haney, Banks, & Zimbardo, 1973).

Design and Findings. The young men who volunteered for this experience were paid a nice daily fee. They were randomly assigned to be prisoners or guards, but other than that, they were given no instructions about how to behave. Yet the results were dramatic. Within a short time, the prisoners became distressed, help-less, and panicky. They developed emotional symptoms and physical ailments. Some became apathetic; others became rebellious. After a few days, half of the prisoners begged to be let out. They were more than willing to forfeit their pay to gain an early release.

Within an equally short time, the guards adjusted to their new power. Some tried to be nice, helping the pris-oners and doing little favors for them. Some were "tough but fair," holding strictly to "the rules." But about a third became tyrannical. Although they were free to use any method to maintain order, they almost always chose to be harsh and abusive, even when the prisoners were not re-sisting in any way. One guard, unaware that he was being observed by the researchers, paced the corridor while the prisoners were sleeping, pounding his nightstick into his hand. Another put a prisoner in solitary confinement (a small closet) and tried to keep him there all night. He concealed this information from the researchers, who, he thought, were "too soft" on the prisoners. Not one of the less actively cruel guards, by the way, ever intervened or complained about the behavior of their more abusive peers.

Prisoners and guards quickly learn their respective roles, which usually have more influence on their behavior than their personality does.

The researchers, who had not expected such a speedy and terrifying transforma-tion of healthy students, ended this study after only six days. The prisoners were re-lieved by this decision, but most of the guards were disappointed. They had enjoyed their short-lived authority.

Evaluating the Prison Study. Critics maintain that you cannot learn much from such an artificial setup. They argue that the volunteers already knew, from movies, TV, and games, how they were supposed to behave. The guards acted their parts to the hilt in order to have fun and please the researchers. Their behavior was no more surprising than if they had been dressed in football gear and had then been found to be willing to bruise each other. The prison study made a great story, said some critics, but it wasn't *research*. That is, the researchers did not carefully inves-tigate relationships between factors; for all the study's drama, it provided no new information (Festinger, 1980).

Craig Haney and Philip Zimbardo, who designed the prison study, responded that this dramatization illustrated the power of roles in a way that no ordinary lab experiment ever could. If the guards were just having fun, why did they lose sight of the "game" and behave as if it were a real job? Twenty-five years after the prison study was done, Haney and Zimbardo (1998) reflected on its contribution to under-standing the behavior of real prisoners and guards in prisons, and also to increasing public awareness of how situations can outweigh personality and private values in influencing behavior.

The Power of Roles

The two imaginative studies we have described vividly demonstrate the power of so-cial roles and obligations to influence the behavior of individuals. When people in the Milgram study believed they had to follow the legitimate orders of authority, most of them put their private values and personality traits aside. The behavior of the prisoners and guards varied—some prisoners were more rebellious than others, some guards were more abusive than others—but ultimately what the students did depended on the roles they were assigned.

Obedience, of course, is not always harmful or bad. A certain amount of routine compliance with rules is necessary in any group, and obedience to authority has many benefits for individuals and society. A nation could not operate if all its citizens ignored traffic signals, cheated on their taxes, dumped garbage wherever they chose, or assaulted each other. An organization could not function if its members came to work only when they felt like it. But obedience also has a darker aspect. Throughout history, the plea "I was only following orders" has been offered to excuse actions carried out on behalf of orders that were foolish, destructive, or illegal. The writer C. P. Snow once observed that "more hideous crimes have been committed in the name of obedience than in the name of rebellion."

Most people follow orders because of the obvious consequences of disobedience: They can be suspended from school, fired from their jobs, or arrested. They may also obey because of what they hope to gain: being liked, getting certain advantages or promotions from the authority, learning from the authority's greater knowledge or experience. Primarily, though, people obey because they are deeply convinced of the authority's legitimacy. That is, they obey not in hopes of gaining some tangible benefit, but because they like and respect the authority and value the relationship (Tyler, 1997).

But what about all those obedient people in Milgram's study who felt they were doing wrong and who wished they were free, but who could not untangle themselves from the cobweb of social constraints? Why do people obey when it is not in their interests, or when obedience requires them to ignore their own values or even commit a crime? How do they become morally disengaged from the consequences of their actions? Researchers looking at the social context of behavior draw our attention to several factors that cause people to obey when they would rather not (Bandura, 1999; Gourevich, 1998; Kelman & Hamilton, 1989; Staub, 1999):

1 *Allocating responsibility to the authority.* One common way that people justify their behavior is to hand over responsibility to the authority, thereby absolving themselves of accountability for their actions. In Milgram's study, many of those who administered the highest levels of shock adopted the attitude, "It's his problem; I'm just following orders." In contrast, individuals who refused to give high levels of shock took responsibility for their own actions and refused to grant the authority legitimacy. "One of the things I think is very cowardly," said a 32-year-old engineer, "is to try to shove the responsibility onto someone else. See, if I now turned around and said, 'It's your fault . . . it's not mine,' I would call that cowardly" (Milgram, 1974).

2 *Routinizing the task.* When people define their actions in terms of routine duties and roles, their behavior starts to feel normal, just a job to be done. Becoming absorbed in busywork distracts them from doubts or ethical questions, and it fosters an uncritical, mindless attention to details that obscures the larger picture. In the Milgram study, some people became so fixated on the "learning task" that they shut out any moral concerns about the learner's demands to be let out. Routinization is typically the mechanism by which gov-

The routinization of torture allows people to commit or collaborate in atrocities. More than 16,000 political prisoners were tortured and killed at Tuol Sleng prison by Cambodia's Khmer Rouge, during the genocidal regime of Pol Pot. Prison authorities kept meticulous records and photos of each victim in order to make their barbarous activities seem mundane and normal. This man, Ing Pech, one of only seven survivors, was spared because he had skills useful to his captors. He now runs a museum at the prison.

ernments enlist citizens to aid and abet programs of genocide. Nazi bureaucrats kept meticulous records of every victim, and in Cambodia the Khmer Rouge recorded the names and histories of the millions of victims they tortured and killed. "I am not a violent man," said Sous Thy, one of the clerks who recorded these names, to a reporter from *The New York Times*. "I was just making lists."

3 *Wanting to be polite.* Good manners protect people's feelings and make relationships and civilization possible. But once people are caught in what they perceive to be legitimate roles and are obeying a legitimate authority, good manners ensnare them into further obedience. Most people do not want to rock the boat, appear to doubt the experts, or be rude, because they know they will be disliked for doing so (Collins & Brief, 1995).

Most people learn the language of manners ("please," "thank you," "I'm sorry for missing your birthday"), but they literally lack the words to justify disobedience and rudeness toward an authority they respect. In the Milgram study, many people could not find the words to justify walking out, so they stayed. One woman kept apologizing to the experimenter, trying not to offend him with her worries for the victim: "Do I go right to the end, sir? I hope there's nothing wrong with him there." (She did go right to the end.) A man repeatedly protested and questioned the experimenter, but he too obeyed, even when the victim had apparently collapsed in pain. "He thinks he is killing someone," Milgram (1974) commented, "yet he uses the language of the tea table."

4 *Becoming entrapped.* **Entrapment** is a process in which individuals escalate their commitment to a course of action in order to justify their investment in it (Brockner & Rubin, 1985). The first steps of entrapment pose no difficult choices, but one step leads to another, and before you realize it, you have become committed to a course of action that poses problems. In Milgram's study, once subjects had given a 15-volt shock, they had committed themselves to the experiment. The next level was "only" 30 volts. Because each increment was small, before they knew it most people were administering what they believed were dangerously strong shocks. At that point, it was difficult to explain a sudden decision to quit. Participants who resisted early in the study, questioning the procedure, were less likely to become entrapped by it and more likely to eventually disobey (Modigliani & Rochat, 1995).

Slot machines rely on the principle of entrapment, the reason that casinos win millions and most players don't. A person vows to spend only a few dollars, but, after losing them, says, "Well, maybe another couple of tries" or "I've spent so much, now I really have to win something to get back my loss."

Individuals and nations alike are vulnerable to the sneaky process of entrapment. You start dating someone you like moderately; before you know it, you have been together so long that you can't break up, although you don't want to become committed, either. Government leaders start a war they think will end quickly. Years later, the nation has lost so many soldiers and so much money that the leaders believe they cannot retreat without losing face.

A chilling study of entrapment was conducted with 25 men who had served in the Greek military police during the authoritarian regime that ended in 1974 (Haritos-Fatouros, 1988). A psychologist who interviewed the men identified the steps used in training them to use torture in questioning prisoners. First the men were ordered to stand guard outside the interrogation and torture cells. Then they stood guard in the detention rooms, where they observed the torture of prisoners. Then they "helped" beat up prisoners. Once they had obediently followed these orders and became actively involved, the torturers found their actions easier to carry out.

entrapment A gradual process in which individuals escalate their commitment to a course of action to justify their investment of time, money, or effort.

Thus even torture is not a practice only of "bad" people in enemy cultures. In a book appropriately called *Unspeakable Acts, Ordinary People: The Dynamics of Torture*, John Conroy (2000) documented cases of torture by Chicago police officers against prisoners; by the British Army against IRA suspects in Northern Ireland; and by Israeli soldiers against Palestinians. As Milgram would have predicted, the torturers were otherwise "good guys," just "doing their jobs." This is a difficult concept for people who divide the world into "good guys" versus "bad guys" and cannot imagine that good guys might do bad things. Yet in everyday life, as in the Milgram study, people often set out on a path that is morally ambiguous, only to find that they have traveled a long way toward violating their own principles. From Greece's torturers to the Khmer Rouge's dutiful clerks, from Milgram's well-meaning volunteers to all of us in our everyday lives, people face the difficult task of drawing a line beyond which they will not go. For many, the demands of the role defeat the inner voice of conscience.

QUICK QUIZ

Step into your role as student to answer these questions.

1. About what percentage of the people in Milgram's obedience study administered the highest levels of shock? (a) two-thirds, (b) one-half, (c) one-third, (d) one-tenth

2. Which of the following actions by the "learner" reduced the likelihood of being shocked by the "teacher" in Milgram's study? (a) protesting noisily, (b) screaming in pain, (c) complaining of having a heart ailment, (d) nothing he did made a difference

3. A friend of yours, who is moving, asks you to bring over a few boxes. Since you are there anyway, he asks you to fill them with books. Before you know it, you have packed up his entire kitchen, living room, and bedroom. What social-psychological process is at work here?

Answers:

1. a 2. d 3. entrapment

WHAT'S AHEAD ▷

- **What is one of the most common mistakes people make when they explain the behavior of others?**
- **Why would a person blame victims of rape or torture for having brought their misfortunes on themselves?**
- **What is the "Big Lie," and why does it work so well?**
- **What is the difference between ordinary techniques of persuasion and the coercive techniques used by cults?**

Social Influences on Beliefs

social cognition An area in social psychology concerned with social influences on thought, memory, perception, and other cognitive processes.

Social psychologists are interested not only in what people do in social situations, but also in what goes on in their heads while they are doing it. Researchers in the area of **social cognition** examine how people's perceptions of themselves and others affect their relationships, and how the social environment influences thoughts, beliefs, and values. The social environment consists not only of the people around you, but also your social circumstances, such as whether you live alone or in a family, whether you are a single parent or a partnered one, and the level of your education and income. We will consider two important topics in this area: explanations about behavior and the formation of attitudes.

Attributions

People read detective stories to find out *who* did the dirty deed, but in real life we also want to know *why* people do things—was it because of a terrible childhood, a mental illness, possession by a demon, or what? According to **attribution theory**, the explanations we make of our behavior and the behavior of others generally fall into two categories. When we make a *situational attribution,* we are identifying the cause of an action as something in the situation or environment: "Joe stole the money because his family is starving." When we make a *dispositional attribution,* we are identifying the cause of an action as something in the person, such as a trait or a motive: "Joe stole the money because he is a born thief."

When people are trying to find reasons for someone else's behavior, they reveal a common bias: They tend to overestimate personality traits and underestimate the influence of the situation (Forgas, 1998; Nisbett & Ross, 1980). In terms of attribution theory, they tend to ignore situational attributions in favor of dispositional ones. This tendency has been called the **fundamental attribution error** (sometimes called the *correspondence bias,* because of the underlying assumption that people's dispositions correspond to their behavior [E. Jones, 1990; Van Boven, Kamada, & Gilovich, 1999]). Were the hundreds of people who obeyed Milgram's experimenters cruel by nature? Were the student guards in the prison study sadistic and the prisoners cowardly? Those who think so are committing the fundamental attribution error.

The impulse to explain other people's behavior in terms of their personalities is so strong that we do it even when we know that the other person is *required* to behave that way (Yzerbyt et al., 2001). People are especially likely to overlook situational attributions when they are in a good mood and not inclined to think about other people's motives critically, or when they are distracted and preoccupied and don't have time to stop and ask themselves, "Why, exactly, *is* Aurelia behaving like such a dimwit today?" (Forgas, 1998). Instead, they leap to the easiest attribution, which is dispositional: It's all because of her dim personality. They are less likely to wonder if Aurelia has recently joined a group of friends who are encouraging dimwitted behavior, or is under unusual pressure that is making her act "out of character."

The fundamental attribution error is highly prevalent in Western nations, where middle-class people tend to believe that individuals are responsible for their own actions. In countries such as India, where everyone is embedded in caste and family networks, and in Japan, Korea, China, and Hong Kong, where people are more group oriented than in the West, people are more likely to be aware of situational constraints on behavior (Choi, Nisbett, & Norenzayan, 1999; Morris & Peng, 1994). Thus, if someone is behaving oddly, makes a mistake, or plays badly in a soccer match, a person from India or China, unlike a Westerner, is more likely to make a situational attribution of the person's behavior ("He's under pressure") than a dispositional one ("He's incompetent") (Menon et al., 1999).

Westerners do not always prefer dispositional attributions, however. When it comes to explaining their *own* behavior, they often reveal a **self-serving bias:** They

attribution theory The theory that people are motivated to explain their own and others' behavior by attributing causes of that behavior to a situation or disposition.

fundamental attribution error The tendency, in explaining other people's behavior, to overestimate personality factors and underestimate the influence of the situation.

self-serving bias The tendency, in explaining one's own behavior, to take credit for one's good actions and rationalize one's mistakes.

8.1

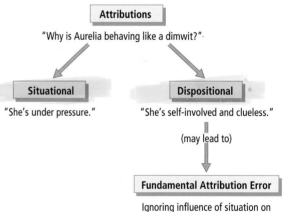

just-world hypothesis The notion that many people need to believe that the world is fair and that justice is served; that bad people are punished and good people rewarded.

tend to choose attributions that are favorable to them, taking credit for their good actions (a dispositional attribution) but letting the situation account for their bad or embarrassing actions (Campbell & Sedikides, 1999). For instance, most Westerners, when angry, will say, "I am furious for good reason—this situation is intolerable." They are less likely to say, "I am furious because I am an ill-tempered grinch." On the other hand, if they do something admirable, such as donating to charity, they are likely to attribute their motives to a personal disposition ("I'm so generous") instead of the situation ("That guy on the phone pressured me into it").

According to the **just-world hypothesis**, attributions are also affected by the need to believe that the world is fair, that justice prevails, and that good people are rewarded and bad guys punished. This belief, which is especially prevalent in North America, helps people make sense out of senseless events and feel safe in the presence of threatening events (Lerner, 1980). Unfortunately, it also leads to a dispositional attribution called *blaming the victim*. If a friend is fired, if a woman is raped, or an innocent bystander is shot 41 times by the police (as happened in the tragic case of Amadou Diallo in New York), it is reassuring to think that they all must have done something to deserve what happened or to provoke it: The friend wasn't doing his work, the woman was dressed too "provocatively," the bystander shouldn't have been standing in a dark hallway. Blaming the victim is virtually universal when people are ordered to harm others or find themselves entrapped into harming others (Bandura, 1999). In the Milgram study, some "teachers" made comments such as, "[The learner] was so stupid and stubborn he deserved to get shocked" (Milgram, 1974).

An extreme example of blaming the victim occurred in the aftermath of the World Trade Center and Pentagon attacks, when the Rev. Jerry Falwell said that America deserved the 3,000 deaths and brought this harsh punishment upon itself because God was displeased with the country's godless, secular ways. Falwell's remarks angered many people, but they showed how powerful is the desire to find a reason for something inexplicably horrible—and how desperately eager many people are to preserve their faith in a just world.

Of course, sometimes dispositional (personality) attributions do explain a person's behavior. The point to remember is that attributions, whether they are accurate or not, have tremendously important consequences. Here's an example that will apply to your own relationships. Happy couples tend to attribute their partners' occasional lapses to something in the situation ("Poor Horace is under a lot of stress"), and the partners' positive actions to stable, internal dispositions ("Horace has the sweetest nature"). But unhappy couples do just the reverse. They attribute lapses to their partner's personalities ("Henry is a hopeless mama's boy") and good behavior to the situation ("Yeah, he gave me a present, but only because his mother

---

THINKING CRITICALLY

Consider Other Interpretations

How do explanations of people's behavior affect your feelings toward them? Why is it important to "consider other explanations" when someone's actions are annoying you?

Calvin and Hobbes   by Bill Watterson

Children learn the value of self-serving attributions at an early age.

told him to"). These attributional habits, which can change over time, are strongly related to satisfaction with the partner (Karney & Bradbury, 2000). The attributions you make about your partner, your parents, and your friends will make a big difference in how you get along with them—and how long you will put up with their failings.

QUICK QUIZ

To what do you attribute your success in answering these questions?

1. What kind of attribution is being made in each case, situational or dispositional? (a) A man says, "My wife has sure become a grouchy person." (b) The same man says, "I'm grouchy because I've had a bad day at the office." (c) A woman reads that unemployment is high in inner-city communities. "Well, if those people weren't so lazy, they would find work," she says.

2. What principles of attribution theory are suggested by the items in the preceding question?

Answers:

1. a. dispositional b. situational c. dispositional 2. Item *a* illustrates the fundamental attribution error; *b*, the self-serving bias; and *c*, blaming the victim, possibly because of the just-world hypothesis.

Attitudes

People hold attitudes about all sorts of things—politics, people, food, children, movies, sports heroes, you name it. An *attitude* is a belief about people, groups, ideas, or activities. Attitudes range from the trivial (say, your attitude toward broccoli) to deeply held convictions that are often at the core of a person's motivations and behavior. Some attitudes are *explicit:* We are aware of them; they shape our conscious decisions and actions; and they can be measured on self-report questionnaires. Others are *implicit:* We are unaware of them; they may influence our behavior in ways we do not recognize; and they are measured in various indirect ways, as we will see later in discussing the attitudes involved in prejudice (Wilson, Lindsey, & Schooler, 2000).

On most topics, like movies and sports, people easily accept the fact that attitudes range from casual opinions to passionate convictions. If your best friend is neutral about baseball whereas you are an insanely devoted fan, your friendship will probably survive. But when the subject is one involving beliefs that give meaning and purpose to a person's life—most notably, politics and religion—it's another ball game, so to speak. For example, some people regard the traditions of their religion as sacred sources of guidance, which are to be taken literally and which offer the only possible route to salvation. Others regard the precepts of their religion as general guides that are open to interpretation; they accept some rituals and beliefs, but not all of them. Still others find religious beliefs and rituals to be of little personal relevance, or actively rebel against them.

Perhaps the one religious attitude that causes the most controversy and bitterness around the world is the one toward such religious diversity itself—accepting or intolerant. Some people of all religions accept a world of differing religious views and

Talk about being tolerant of different attitudes! Democrat James Carville reacts as his Republican wife, Mary Matalin, discusses her new job for the Bush administration.

practices, and believe that church and state should be separate. But for many fundamentalists, religion and politics are inseparable, and they believe that one religion should prevail. Such intolerance becomes more rigid when religiosity combines with two other personality traits, conservatism and authoritarianism, an unquestioning attitude toward tradition and authority (Saucier, 2000). You can see, then, why the irreconcilable attitudes of religious tolerance and intolerance cause continuing conflict and, in extreme cases, can be used to justify war and terrorism.

Some attitudes and convictions, such as those that arise from the conservatism-authoritarianism-religiosity cluster, are deeply ingrained and difficult to change (Olson et al., 2001). Other attitudes, however, are more flexible, depending on the groups you belong to, the experiences you have, your economic circumstances, and many other social and environmental influences.

One such influence is your *generational identity,* which reflects the characteristic attitudes and values that result from being a certain age at a certain moment in history. Each generation shares many of the same experiences, such as financial busts or booms, increases or decreases in rates of violence, job and marital opportunities (or the lack of them), technological breakthroughs, war or peace. The ages between 16 and 24 appear to be critical for the formation of a generational identity. The social and political events that occur during these years make deeper impressions and exert more lasting influence than those that happen later in life (Inglehart, 1990; Schuman & Scott, 1989). In the United States, key generational events were the Depression in the 1930s, the post-war Baby Boom, the Vietnam War, and the civil-rights and women's movements of the 1960s and 1970s. After the attacks in 2001 on New York and Washington, which shattered the sense of safety and security that most Americans had felt, many commentators observed that this devastating experience will undoubtedly shape the generational identity of young Americans.

"Take a load off, Leonard—we're watching Generations X and Y duke it out."

Our attitudes dispose us to behave in predictable ways; if you have a positive attitude toward horror movies, you'll choose to go to *Scream, The 185th Sequel.* But behavior also affects our attitudes: If a friend drags you to a horror movie, which you would normally avoid, and you have a terrific time, you might develop a more positive attitude toward such movies. And if you change your familiar social groups, your attitudes might change too. One of the most striking examples of attitude change we can think of is the story of T. J. Leyden, a former white supremacist and skinhead, whose idea of fun was once "to beat the hell" out of gay men while calling them vile names. Leyden turned his back on the supremacist world, left everyone he knew who was connected with it (including his neo-Nazi wife), and is now a consultant to the Simon Wiesenthal Center's Task Force Against Hate.

Attitudes also change because of a psychological need for consistency. In Chapter 9, we discuss **cognitive dissonance**, the uncomfortable feeling that occurs when two attitudes, or an attitude and behavior, are in conflict (are dissonant). To resolve this dissonance, one of those attitudes has to change. For example, if a celebrity you admire does something stupid, immoral, or illegal, you can restore consistency by lowering your opinion of the person. Or you can decide that the person's behavior wasn't so stupid or immoral after all . . . and besides, everyone else does it, too.

Most people think that their attitudes are based on thinking, a result of reasoned conclusions and decisions. Sometimes, of course, that's true! But some attitudes are a result of not thinking at all. Instead, they are a result of social influence—efforts by others to get us to change our minds by using subtle manipulation—and sometimes outright coercion.

cognitive dissonance A state of tension that occurs when a person simultaneously holds two cognitions that are psychologically inconsistent, or when a person's belief is incongruent with his or her behavior.

Friendly Persuasion. All around you, every day, advertisers, politicians, and friends are trying to influence your attitudes. One weapon they use is the drip, drip, drip of a repeated idea. Repeated exposure even to a nonsense syllable such as *zug* is enough to make a person feel more positive toward it (Zajonc, 1968). The attitude-boosting effect of merely seeing the same thing repeatedly is a robust phenomenon, replicated across cultures, across species, and across states of consciousness—it works even for stimuli presented below your conscious awaresesss (Monahan, Murphy, & Zajonc, 2000).

The effectiveness of familiarity has long been known to politicians and advertisers: Repeat something often enough, even the basest lie, and eventually the public will believe it. Hitler's propaganda minister, Joseph Goebbels, called this technique the "Big Lie." Its formal name is the **validity effect**.

In a series of experiments, Hal Arkes and his associates demonstrated how the validity effect operates (Arkes, 1993; Arkes, Boehm, & Xu, 1991). In a typical study, people read a list of statements, such as "Mercury has a higher boiling point than copper" or "Over 400 Hollywood films were produced in 1948." They had to rate each statement for its validity, on a scale of 1 (definitely false) to 7 (definitely true). A week or two later, they again rated the validity of some of these statements and also rated others that they had not seen previously. The result: Mere repetition increased the perception that the familiar statements were true. The same effect also occurred for other kinds of statements, including unverifiable opinions (e.g., "At least 75 percent of all politicians are basically dishonest"), opinions that subjects initially felt were true, and even opinions they initially felt were false. "Note that no attempt has been made to persuade," said Arkes (1993). "No supporting arguments are offered. We just have subjects rate the statements. Mere repetition seems to increase rated validity. This is scary."

Another effective technique for influencing people's attitudes is to have arguments presented by someone who is considered admirable, knowledgeable, or beautiful; this is why advertisements are full of sports heroes, experts, and models (Cialdini, 1993). Persuaders may also try to link their message with a nice, warm, fuzzy feeling. In one early study, students who were given peanuts and Pepsi while listening to a speaker's point of view were more likely to be convinced by it than were students who listened to the same words without the pleasant munchies and soft drinks (Janis, Kaye, & Kirschner, 1965). This finding has been replicated many times (Pratkanis & Aronson, 1992), perhaps explaining why so much business is conducted over lunch, and so many courtships over dinner!

In sum, here are three good ways to influence attitudes:

Some ads are more effective than others. The Oreo name on this cereal takes advantage of the "familiarity effect"— Oreos have been advertised since 1912. In contrast, fear tactics to get people to quit doing risky things usually backfire. But perhaps this campaign to persuade men to quit smoking will be the exception!

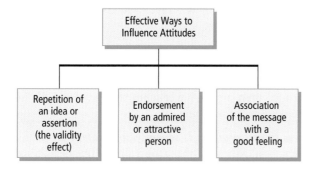

Effective Ways to Influence Attitudes

- Repetition of an idea or assertion (the validity effect)
- Endorsement by an admired or attractive person
- Association of the message with a good feeling

One of the most common ways of trying to change people's attitudes and behavior, scaring them to death, is actually the least effective. Fear tactics are often used in advertising campaigns to try to persuade people to quit smoking, drive only when

validity effect The tendency of people to believe that a statement is true or valid simply because it has been repeated many times.

sober, use condoms, check for signs of cancer, and prepare for earthquakes. But the use of fear can backfire; it can scare people so much that they become defensive and resist the message ("Don't be silly; that will never happen to me"). Fear tactics are more effective, however, when the message also provides information about how to avoid the danger and if people feel competent to take advantage of this information (Aronson, Wilson, & Akert, 2002).

Coercive Persuasion. Some manipulators use harsher tactics, not just hoping that people will change their minds but attempting to force them to. These tactics are sometimes referred to as *brainwashing,* but most psychologists prefer the phrase *coercive persuasion.* "Brainwashing" implies that a person has a sudden change of mind and is unaware of what is happening; it sounds mysterious and strange. In fact, the methods involved are neither mysterious nor unusual.

Persuasion techniques become coercive when they suppress an individual's ability to reason, think critically, and make choices in his or her own best interests. Some people may be more vulnerable than others to coercive tactics. But these techniques are powerful enough to overwhelm even mentally healthy and well-educated individuals. Studies of religious, political, and other cults have identified some of the key processes of coercive persuasion (Galanter, 1989; Mithers, 1994; Ofshe & Watters, 1994; Singer, Temerlin, & Langone, 1990; Zimbardo & Leippe, 1991):

1 *The person is put under physical or emotional distress.* The individual may not be allowed to eat, sleep, or exercise; may be isolated in a dark room with no stimulation or food; or may be induced into a trancelike state through repetitive chanting or fatigue.

2 *The person's problems are reduced to one simple explanation, which is repeatedly emphasized.* There are as many simplistic explanations as there are cults, but here are two real examples: Are you afraid or unhappy? It all stems from the pain of being born. Are you struggling financially? It's your fault for not fervently wanting to be rich. Members may also be taught to simplify their problems by blaming a particular enemy: Jews, the government, nonbelievers. . . .

3 *The leader offers unconditional love, acceptance, and attention.* The new recruit may be given a "love bath" from the group—constant praise and affection. Euphoria and well-being are intense because they typically follow exhaustion and fatigue. In exchange, the leader demands everyone's adoration and obedience.

4 *A new identity based on the group is created.* The recruit is told that he or she is part of the chosen, the elite, or the saved. To foster this new identity, many cults require their members to wear special clothes or eat special diets, and they assign each member a new name.

5 *The person is subjected to entrapment.* At first, the new member agrees only to do small things, but gradually the demands increase: for example, to spend a weekend with the group, then another weekend, then take weekly seminars, then advanced courses, then to contribute money. . . .

6 *The person's access to information is severely controlled.* As soon as a person is a committed believer or follower, the group limits the person's choices, denigrates critical thinking, makes fun of doubts, and insists that any private distress is due to lack of belief in the group. Total conformity is demanded. The person may be physically isolated from the outside world and thus from antidotes to the leader's ideas. In many groups, members are required to break all ties with their parents,

These members of the Aum Shinrikyo ("Supreme Truth") sect in Japan, wearing masks of their leader's face, take the uniformity of cult identity to an extreme. The group's founder instructed his devotees to place a nerve gas in a Japanese subway, which killed 10 and sickened thousands of other passengers. One former member said of the sect, "Their strategy is to wear you down and take control of your mind. They promise you heaven, but they make you live in hell."

who are the strongest link to the members' former world and thus the greatest threat to the leader's control.

Every few years another cult makes the news when its leader has a "vision" and, for one reason or another, calls upon his followers to kill themselves. In the 1970s, when Jim Jones told members of his "People's Temple" that the time had come to die, 800 people dutifully lined up to drink Kool-Aid mixed with cyanide. Eighty babies and infants were given the drink by their parents, who then swallowed it themselves. In the 1990s, David Koresh, leader of the Branch Dividian cult in Waco, Texas, led his followers to a fiery death in a shoot-out with the FBI. And Marshall Applewhite, leader of the Heaven's Gate cult in San Diego, persuaded his followers that if they committed suicide, they would travel to heaven in a spaceship traveling in the tail of a comet. None of these leaders ever said to new recruits, "If you follow me, you will eventually give up your marriages, homes, children, and your lives"; but by the end, that is just what all of them did.

QUICK QUIZ

Now, how can we persuade you to take this quiz without using coercive techniques?

1. Candidate Carson spends $3 million to make sure his name is seen and heard frequently and to repeat unverified charges that his opponent is a thief. What psychological process is he relying on to win?

2. Your best friend urges you to join a "life-renewal" group called "The Feeling Life." Your friend has been spending increasing amounts of time with her fellow Feelies, and you have some doubts about them. What questions would you want to have answered before joining up?

Answers:

1. the validity effect 2. A few things to consider: Is there an autocratic leader who tolerates no dissent or criticism, while rationalizing this practice as a benefit for members? ("Doubt and disbelief are signs that your feeling side is being repressed.") Have long-standing members given up their families, friends, interests, and ambitions for this group? Does the leader offer simple but unrealistic promises to repair your life and all that troubles you? Are members required to make extreme sacrifices by donating large amounts of money?

WHAT'S AHEAD▷

- Why do people in groups often go along with the majority even when the majority is dead wrong?
- How can "groupthink" lead to bad, even catastrophic, decisions?
- In an emergency, are you more likely to get help when there are lots of strangers in the area or only a few?
- What enables some people to be nonconformists, help others at risk to themselves, or blow the whistle on wrongdoers?

Individuals in Groups

In March 1998, a man named Larry Froistad admitted to his Internet support group that he had killed his 5-year-old daughter, Amanda, three years earlier. "When she was asleep," he wrote in an e-mail, he got drunk, set the house on fire, "listened to her scream twice, climbed out the window and set about putting on a show of shock and surprise and grief to remove culpability from myself." Of the more than 200 members of his on-line support group, only 3 called the police; Froistad was arrested and pleaded guilty. When members learned that the matter had been reported to the police, many of them became enraged—not at the man who cold-bloodedly murdered his child, but at the "meddlesome rat fink" who turned him in. "Frankly, I'm offended," wrote one. "This is a SUPPORT group."

The members of Froistad's group were caught between two sets of norms and values: you are supposed to report a murderer to the police, but you are also supposed to be loyal to members of your "support" group. If you were in such a situation, what do you think you would do?

All of us act differently when we are with a bunch of other people than when we are on our own, regardless of whether the group has convened to solve problems and make decisions, has gathered to have fun, consists of anonymous bystanders or anonymous members of an Internet chat room, or is just a loose collection of individuals waiting around in a room. The decisions we make and the actions we take, in groups, often depend less on our personal desires than on the structure and dynamics of the group itself.

Conformity

One thing people in groups do is conform, taking action or adopting attitudes as a result of real or imagined group pressure.

Suppose that you are required to appear at a psychology laboratory for an experiment on perception. You join seven other students seated in a room. You are shown a 10-inch line and asked which of three other lines is identical to it. The correct answer, line A, is obvious, so you are amused when the first person in the group chooses line B. "Bad eyesight," you say to yourself. "He's off by 2 whole inches!" The second person also chooses line B. "What a dope," you think. But by the time the fifth person has chosen line B, you are beginning to doubt yourself. The sixth and seventh students also choose line B, and now you are worried about *your* eyesight. The experimenter looks at you. "Your turn," he says. Do you follow the evidence of your own eyes or the collective judgment of the group?

This was the design for a series of famous studies of conformity conducted by Solomon Asch (1952, 1965). The seven "nearsighted" students were actually Asch's confederates. Asch wanted to know what people would do when a group unanimously contradicted an obvious fact. He found that when people made the line comparisons on

Test line   A   B   C

8.2

their own, they were almost always accurate. But in the group, only 20 percent of the students remained completely independent on every trial, and often they apologized for not agreeing with the group. One-third conformed to the group's incorrect decision more than half the time, and the rest conformed at least some of the time. Whether they conformed or not, the students often felt uncertain of their decision. As one participant later said, "I felt disturbed, puzzled, separated, like an outcast from the rest."

Asch's experiment has been replicated many times over the years, in the United States and other countries. According to a meta-analysis of 133 studies in 17 countries, conformity in America has declined since the 1950s, when Asch first did his work, suggesting that conformity reflects social norms, which can change over time (Bond & Smith, 1996). Conformity varies with cultural norms, too. People in **individualist cultures**, such as the United States, value individual rights and place the "self" above duty to others; people in **collectivist cultures**, such as many Asian societies, regard duty and social harmony as more important than individual rights or happiness. (In Chapter 13, we discuss this important difference between cultures in more detail.) What an individualist American would regard as normal self-expression, therefore, a collectivist Korean might regard as an appalling lack of harmony with others.

For example, as researchers Heejung Kim and Hazel Markus (1999) point out, an American in a coffee bar in San Francisco might order a decaffeinated cappuccino with nonfat milk, enjoying the pleasure of making such an individualistic choice. A person who orders the same drink in Seoul, Korea, however, is likely to feel strange about getting such a distinctive cup of coffee. "In Korea," the researchers observe, "the normal, regular, and traditional are usually the best tastes for the individual, and a particular taste that differs from the 'right' taste is typically taken to be bad taste." In their studies of Koreans and Americans, they found that uniqueness has positive connotations to Americans; it means freedom and independence. But conformity has positive connections to Koreans; it means connectedness and harmony.

Regardless of culture, however, everyone conforms under some circumstances, and they do so for all sorts of reasons. Some do so because they identify with group members and want to be like them in dress, attitudes, or behavior. Some want to be liked and know that disagreeing with a group can make them unpopular. Some believe the group has knowledge that is superior to their own. And some conform out

individualist cultures Cultures in which individual goals and wishes are prized above duty and relations with others.

collectivist cultures Cultures in which harmony with one's group is prized above individual goals and wishes.

Sometimes people like to conform in order to feel part of the group . . . and sometimes they like to assert their individuality.

groupthink In close-knit groups, the tendency for all members to think alike for the sake of harmony and to suppress disagreement.

of self-interest, to keep their jobs, get promoted, or win votes. Also, it is not so easy to be a nonconformist! Group members are often uncomfortable with deviants and will try to persuade them to conform. If pleasant persuasion fails, the group may punish, isolate, or reject the deviant (Moscovici, 1985).

Like obedience, conformity has both its positive and its negative sides. Society runs more smoothly when people know how to behave in a given situation, and when they share the same attitudes and manners. Most people like to feel that they are liked by others in their group and able to get along with them. Conformity in dress, preferences, and ideas confers a sense of being "in sync" with one's group, and marks a person as being part of that group. But conformity can also suppress critical thinking and creativity. In a group, many people will deny their private beliefs, agree with silly notions, and even repudiate their own values.

Groupthink

Close, friendly groups usually work well together. But they face the problem of getting the best ideas and efforts of their members while avoiding an extreme form of conformity called **groupthink**, the tendency to think alike and suppress dissent. According to Irving Janis (1982, 1989), groupthink occurs when a group's need for total agreement overwhelms its need to make the wisest decision. Groupthink produces the following symptoms:

▶ *An illusion of invulnerability.* The group believes it can do no wrong and is 100 percent correct in its decisions.

▶ *Self-censorship.* Dissenters decide to keep quiet rather than rock the boat, offend their friends, or risk being ridiculed.

▶ *Pressure on dissenters to conform.* The leader teases or humiliates dissenters or otherwise pressures them to go along.

▶ *An illusion of unanimity.* By discouraging dissent, leaders and group members create an illusion of consensus. They may even explicitly deny suspected dissenters the chance to say what they think.

Janis (1982) examined the records of historical military decisions and identified typical features of groups that are vulnerable to groupthink: Their members feel that they are part of a tightly connected team; they are isolated from other viewpoints; they feel under pressure from outside forces; and they have a strong, directive leader. Do you notice the similarities between these conditions and those of coercive cults?

Throughout history, groupthink has led to disastrous decisions in military and civilian life. One example occurred in 1961, when President John F. Kennedy, after meeting with his advisers, approved a CIA plan to invade Cuba at the Bay of Pigs and overthrow the government of Fidel Castro; the invasion was a humiliating defeat. Another occurred in the mid-1960s, when President Lyndon Johnson and his cabinet escalated the war in Vietnam in spite of obvious signs that further bombing and increased troops were not bringing the war to an end. A third example occurred in 1986, when NASA officials made the fatal decision to launch the space shuttle *Challenger,* which exploded shortly after takeoff. Apparently they insulated themselves from the objections of dissenting engineers who tried to warn them that the rocket was unsafe (Moorhead, Ference, & Neck, 1991).

It is not cohesion alone that inevitably causes groupthink; some cohesive groups welcome innovative and dissenting views. Recent research suggests that a key factor in determining whether a group will fall victim to groupthink has to do with *group norms:* the standards or rules governing members of the group (Postmes, Spears, & Cihangir, 2001). Some groups demand consensus; they want all members to dress, think, and behave the same way. Others not only tolerate but value nonconformity, setting norms and expectations for critical thinking and independent action.

Groupthink can therefore be counteracted by creating conditions that explicitly encourage and reward the expression of doubt and dissent and by basing decisions on majority rule instead of unanimity (Kameda & Sugimori, 1993). President Kennedy apparently learned this lesson from the Bay of Pigs decision. In his next political crisis, provoked by missiles placed in Cuba by the then-Soviet Union in 1962, Kennedy brought in outside experts to advise his inner circle, often absented himself from the group so as not to influence their discussions, and encouraged free debate between the "hawks" and the "doves" (Aronson, Wilson, & Akert, 2002). The crisis, one of the most dangerous in post-World War II history, was resolved peacefully.

The Anonymous Crowd

Suppose that you were in trouble on a city street or another public place—say, being mugged or having a sudden appendicitis attack. Do you think you would be more likely to get help if (a) one other person was passing by, (b) several other people were in the area, or (c) dozens of people were in the area? Most people would choose the third answer, on the grounds that the more people who are available to help, the more likely it is that someone will step forward. But that is not how people operate. On the contrary, the more people there are around you, the *less* likely it is that one of them will come to your aid. Why?

Diffusion of Responsibility. The answer has to do with a common group process called the **diffusion of responsibility**, in which responsibility for an outcome is diffused, or spread, among many people. In crowds, individuals often fail to take action because they believe that someone else will do so. For example, in London, England, four teenagers repeatedly stabbed a 10-year-old immigrant boy from Nigeria. As many as 10 people saw this happen but did not stop to help or call the police. The boy dragged himself to an open stairwell, where he bled to death.

The many reports of *bystander apathy* in the news, like this one, reflect the diffusion of responsibility. When others are near, people fail to call for help or come to the aid of a person in trouble. People are more likely to come to a stranger's aid if they are the only ones around to help, because responsibility cannot be diffused.

In work groups, the diffusion of responsibility sometimes takes the form of *social loafing:* Each member of a team slows down, letting others work harder (Karau & Williams, 1993; Latané, Williams, & Harkins, 1979). Social loafing occurs when individual group members are not accountable for the work they do; when people feel that working harder would only duplicate their colleagues' efforts; when workers feel that others are getting a "free ride"; or when the work itself is uninteresting (Shepperd, 1995). When the challenge of the job is increased or when each member of the group has a different, important job to do, the sense of individual responsibility rises and social loafing declines (Harkins & Szymanski, 1989; Williams & Karau, 1991).

diffusion of responsibility In organized or anonymous groups, the tendency of members to avoid taking responsibility for actions or decisions, assuming that others will do so.

People in crowds, feeling anonymous, often seem to "forget themselves" and do destructive things they would never do on their own. These soccer hooligans are kicking a fan of the opposition team during a night of violence after their team lost.

Deindividuation. The most extreme instances of the diffusion of responsibility occur in large, anonymous mobs or crowds—whether they are cheerful ones, such as sports spectators, or angry ones, such as rioters. In crowds like these, people often lose all awareness of their individuality and seem to hand themselves over to the mood and actions of the crowd, a state called **deindividuation** (Festinger, Pepitone, & Newcomb, 1952). You are more likely to feel deindividuated in a large city, where no one recognizes you, than in a small town, where it is hard to hide. Sometimes organizations actively promote the deindividuation of their members in order to enhance conformity and allegiance to the group. This is an important function of uniforms or masks, which eliminate each member's distinctive identity.

Deindividuation has long been considered a prime reason for mob violence. According to this explanation, because deindividuated people in crowds "forget themselves" and do not feel accountable for their actions, they are more likely to violate social norms and laws than they would on their own: breaking store windows, looting, getting into fights, rioting at a sports event. Their usual inhibitions against aggressiveness are weakened.

Many studies have indeed found that deindividuation increases a person's willingness to harm a stranger, cheat, or break the law (Aronson, Wilson, & Akert, 2002). Deindividuation even eliminates gender differences in aggressiveness, in spite of the belief that women are "naturally" less aggressive than men. In two studies, men behaved more aggressively than women in a competitive video war game when they were individuated—that is, when their names and background information about them were spoken aloud, heard by all participants, and recorded publicly by the experimenter. But when the men and women believed they were anonymous to their fellow students and to the experimenter—that is, when they were deindividuated—they did not differ in how aggressively they played the game (Lightdale & Prentice, 1994).

However, deindividuation does not always make people more combative. Sometimes it makes them more friendly; think of all the chatty, anonymous people on buses and planes who reveal things to their seatmates they would never tell anyone they knew. What really seems to be happening when people are in large crowds or anonymous situations is not that they become "mindless" or "uninhibited." Rather, they become more likely to conform to the norms of the *specific situation* (Postmes & Spears, 1998). College students who go on wild sprees during spring break may be violating the local laws and norms of Palm Springs or Key West, not because their "aggressiveness" has been released but because they are conforming to the "let's party!" norms of their fellow students. Crowd norms can also foster helpfulness and altruism, as they did in the aftermath of the World Trade Center attack, when countless New Yorkers anonymously came out to help victims and rescue workers, leaving food, clothes, and tributes.

deindividuation In groups or crowds, the loss of awareness of one's own individuality.

Get Involved

Losing Yourself

For this exercise in deindividuation, choose two situations: one in which you are one of many people, perhaps hundreds (as in a large classroom or a concert audience); and one in which you are one of a few (as in a small discussion group). In both situations, close your eyes and pretend to fall asleep. Is this easier to do in one context than the other? Why? In each case, what is the reaction of other people around you?

Two classic experiments illustrate the power of the situation to influence what deindividuated people will do. In one, women who wore Ku Klux Klan–like disguises that completely covered their faces and bodies (see photo) delivered twice as much apparent electric shock to another woman as did women who were not only undisguised but also wore large name tags (Zimbardo, 1970). In a second, women who were wearing nurses' uniforms gave *less* shock than did women in regular dress (Johnson & Downing, 1979). Evidently, the KKK disguise was a signal to behave aggressively; the nurses' uniforms were a signal to behave nurturantly.

Anonymity and Responsibility. Deindividuation has important legal as well as psychological implications. Should individuals in a crowd be held accountable for their harmful "deindividuated" behavior? Consider a trial held in South Africa in the late 1980s, in which six black residents of an impoverished township were accused of murdering an 18-year-old black woman who was having an affair with a hated black police officer. The woman was "necklaced"—a tire was placed around her neck and set afire—during a community protest against the police. The crowd danced and sang as she burned to ashes.

The six men were convicted of murder, but their sentence was commuted to 20 months of prison when a British social psychologist, Andrew Colman (1991), testified that deindividuation should reduce the "moral blameworthiness" of their behavior. The young men were swept up in the mindless behavior of the crowd, he argued, and hence not fully responsible for their actions. Do you agree? An African social scientist, Pumla Gobodo-Madikizela (1994), did not. She interviewed some of the men accused of the necklacing and found they were not so mindless after all. Some were tremendously upset, were well aware of their actions, had debated the woman's guilt, thought about running away, and consciously tried to rationalize their behavior. Moreover, she argued, we must remember that in every crowd, some people do not go along; they remain mindful of their own values.

And so, should the deindividuation excuse, like the "I was only following orders" excuse, exonerate a person of responsibility for looting, rape, or murder? If so, to what degree? What do you think?

Wearing a uniform or disguise can increase deindividuation.

> **THINKING CRITICALLY**
>
> **Examine The Evidence**
>
> How mindless are "mindless" crowds? Should deindividuation be a legitimate excuse for people who loot, rape, or commit murder because the mob is doing it?

QUICK QUIZ

On your own, take responsibility for identifying which phenomenon discussed in the previous section is illustrated in the following situations:

1. The president's closest advisers are afraid to disagree with his views on arms negotiations.

2. You are at a costume party wearing a silly gorilla suit. When you see a chance to play a practical joke on the host, you do it.

3. Walking down a busy street, you see that fire has broken out in a store window. "Someone must have called the fire department," you say.

Answers:

1. groupthink 2. deindividuation 3. diffusion of responsibility

Rosa Parks being fingerprinted on the day she was arrested.

Disobedience and Dissent

We have seen how social roles, norms, and pressures to obey authority and conform to one's group can cause people to behave in ways they might not otherwise do. Yet, throughout history, men and women have disobeyed orders they believed to be immoral and have gone against prevailing beliefs; their actions have changed the course of history. In 1956 in Montgomery, Alabama, Rosa Parks refused to give up her seat and move to the back of a bus, as the segregation laws of the time required. She was arrested, fingerprinted, and convicted of breaking the law. Her calm defiance touched off a boycott in which black citizens refused to ride city buses. It took them over a year, but they won—and the civil rights movement began.

Dissent and *altruism*, the willingness to take selfless or dangerous action on behalf of others, are in part a matter of personal convictions and conscience. However, just as there are situational reasons for obedience and conformity, so there are situational influences on a person's decision to speak up for an unpopular opinion, choose conscience over conformity, or help a stranger in trouble. Here are some of the steps involved in deciding to "rock the boat" or behave courageously, and some social and cultural factors involved in them:

1 *You perceive the need for intervention or help.* It may seem obvious, but before you can take independent action, you must realize that such action is necessary. Sometimes people willfully blind themselves to wrongdoing to justify their own inaction ("I'm just minding my business here"; "I have no idea what they're doing over there at Dachau"). But blindness to the need for action also occurs when a situation imposes too many demands on people's attention. Residents of densely populated cities cannot stop to offer help to everyone who seems to need it; they would never do anything else (Levine et al., 1994).

Whether you interpret a situation as requiring your aid also depends on cultural rules (see Figure 8.2). In northern European nations and in the United States, husband–wife disputes are considered strictly private; neighbors intervene at their peril. In Mediterranean and Latin cultures, however, a dispute between

Figure 8.2

CULTURE AND THE OBLIGATION TO HELP

Community-oriented Hindus in India believe that people are obligated to help anyone who needs it—parent, friend, or stranger—even if the need is minor. In contrast, individualistic Americans do not feel as obligated to help friends and strangers, or even parents who merely have "minor" needs. People in both cultures, however, share a sense of obligation to help anyone in a life-threatening situation (Miller, Bersoff, & Harwood, 1990).

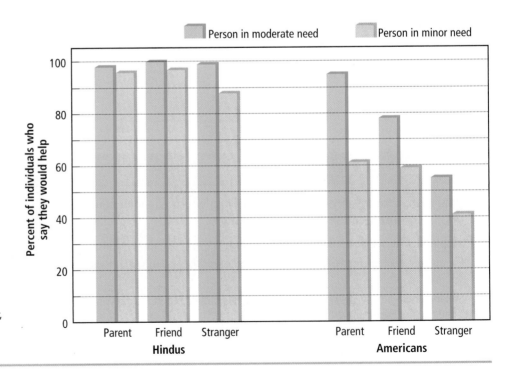

any two people is considered fair game for anyone who is passing by. In fact, two people in a furious dispute might even rely on bystanders to intervene (Hall & Hall, 1990).

2 *The situation increases the likelihood that you will take responsibility.* When you are in a large crowd of observers or in a large organization, it is easy to avoid action because of the diffusion of responsibility. In contrast, if you are in an environment that rewards independent thinking and dissent and discourages social loafing, you may behave accordingly. The decision to take responsibility also depends on the degree of risk involved. It is easier to be a whistle-blower or to protest a company policy when you know you can find another job, but what if jobs in your field are scarce and you have a family to support? People are less likely to take an independent action if situational risks are high.

3 *The cost-benefit ratio supports your decision to get involved.* The cost of help-ing or protesting might be embarrassment and wasted time or, more seriously, lost income, loss of friends, and even physical danger. The cost of not helping or remaining silent might be guilt, blame from others, loss of honor, or, in some tragic cases, the injury or death of others. Three employees of Rockwell International weighed these two sets of costs and ended up trying to convince NASA that the space shuttle *Challenger* was unsafe. The NASA authorities (perhaps influenced by groupthink, as we noted earlier) weighed the costs differently, and refused to post-pone the launch. The price of their decision was an explosion that caused the deaths of the entire crew.

4 *You have an ally.* In Asch's conformity experiment, the presence of one other per-son who gave the correct answer was enough to overcome agreement with the majority. In Milgram's experiment, the presence of a peer who disobeyed the exper-imenter's instruction to shock the learner sharply increased the number of people who also disobeyed. One dissenting member of a group may be viewed as a trouble-maker and two dissenting members as a conspiracy, but several are a coalition. An ally reassures a person of the rightness of the protest, and their combined efforts may eventually persuade the majority (Wood et al., 1994).

5 *You become entrapped.* Once having taken the initial step of getting involved, most people will increase their commitment. In one study, nearly 9,000 feder-al employees were asked whether they had observed wrongdoing at work, whether they had told anyone about it, and what happened if they had told. Nearly half of the sample had observed some serious cases of wrongdoing, such

Some people behave selflessly to help others, even at risk to their own lives or jobs. After the bombing of the Federal Building in Oklahoma City, which killed 168 people, many individuals—not only professional rescue workers—came to the aid of victims. On the left, a restaurant worker, still wearing his hair covering, rushed out to help a victim. On the right, three whistle-blowers from Rockwell International (Ria Solomon, Sylvia Robins, and Al Bray) tried to inform NASA that the space shuttle Challenger was not safe.

as stealing federal funds, accepting bribes, or creating a situation that was dangerous to public safety. Of that half, 72 percent had done nothing at all, but the other 28 percent reported the problem to their immediate supervisors. Once they had taken that step, a majority of the whistle-blowers eventually took the matter to higher authorities (Graham, 1986).

As you can see, certain social and cultural factors make altruism, disobedience, and dissent more likely to occur, just as other factors suppress them. This is why people behave inconsistently across situations. A woman may blow the whistle on her company for failing to observe worker-safety precautions, yet conform to the opinions of others when she serves on a jury, even though she disagrees with their verdict. How do you think you would behave if you were faced with a conflict between social pressure and conscience? Would you call 911 if you saw someone being injured in a fight? Would you voice your true opinion in class even though everyone else seemed to disagree? What aspects of the situation and your culture's norms would influence your responses?

QUICK QUIZ

Imagine that you are chief executive officer of a new electric-car company. You want your employees to feel free to offer their suggestions for improving productivity and satisfaction, and to inform managers if they find any evidence that your cars are unsafe, even if that means delaying production. What concepts from this chapter could you use in setting company policy?

Answers:

Some possibilities: You could encourage and acknowledge deviant ideas, and not require unanimity of group decisions (to avoid group-think); reward individual innovation and suggestions by paying attention to them and implementing the best ones (to avoid social loafing and deindividuation); stimulate commitment to the task (building a car that will solve the world's pollution problem); establish a written policy to protect whistle-blowers. What else can you think of?

WHAT'S AHEAD

- **How difficult is it to create "us–them" thinking?**
- **How do stereotypes benefit us, and how do they distort reality?**
- **Is prejudice more likely to be a *cause* of competition and war or a *result* of them?**
- **If you believe that women are naturally better than men, are you "sexist"?**
- **Why isn't mere contact between cultural groups enough to reduce prejudice between them? What does work?**

Group Conflict and Prejudice

So far, we have been discussing the effects of groups on their members. But a lot of human misery occurs when groups compete and conflict with one another, and especially when groups are operating on the basis of different cultural rules. Most of us take our own rules and norms for granted, assuming they are logical, normal, and right. The trouble starts when we assume that other people's customs are irrational, peculiar, and wrong.

Ethnocentrism, the belief that one's own culture or ethnic group is superior to all others, is universal, probably because it aids survival by making people feel attached to their own group and willing to work on the group's behalf. Ethnocentrism is even

ethnocentrism The belief that one's own ethnic group, nation, or religion is superior to all others.

embedded in some languages: The Chinese word for China means "the center of the world," and the Navajo and the Inuit call themselves simply "The People." But does the fact that we feel good about our own culture, nationality, gender, or school mean that we have to regard other groups as inferior? Social and cultural psychologists strive to identify the conditions that promote harmony or conflict, understanding or prejudice, between groups.

Group Identity: Us Versus Them

Each of us develops a personal identity that is based on our particular traits and unique history. But we also develop **social identities** based on the groups we belong to, including our national, ethnic, religious, and occupational groups (Brewer & Gardner, 1996; Tajfel & Turner, 1986). Social identities are important because they give us a feeling of place and position in the world. Without them, most of us would feel like loose marbles rolling around in an unconnected universe.

Being in a group confers an immediate social identity: Us. As soon as people have created a category called "us," however, they invariably perceive everybody else as "not-us." This in-group solidarity can be manufactured in a minute in a laboratory, as Henri Tajfel and his colleagues (1971) demonstrated in an experiment with British schoolboys. Tajfel showed the boys slides with varying numbers of dots on them and asked the boys to guess how many dots there were. The boys were arbitrarily told they were "overestimators" or "underestimators" and were then asked to work on another task. In this phase, they had the chance to award points to other boys identified as overestimators or underestimators. Although each boy worked alone in his own cubicle, almost every single one assigned far more points to boys he thought were like him, an overestimator or an underestimator. As the boys emerged from their rooms, they were asked, "Which were you?"—and the answers received a mix of cheers and boos from the others.

Us–them social identities are strengthened when two groups compete with one another. Years ago, Muzafer Sherif and his colleagues used a natural setting, a boys' camp called Robber's Cave, to demonstrate the effects of competition on hostility and conflict between groups (Sherif, 1958; Sherif et al., 1961). Sherif randomly assigned 11- and 12-year-old boys to two groups, the Eagles and the Rattlers. To build a sense of in-group identity and team spirit, he had each group work together on projects such as making a rope bridge and building a diving board. Sherif then put the Eagles and Rattlers in competition for prizes. During fierce games of football, baseball, and tug-of-war, the boys whipped up a competitive fever that soon spilled off of the playing fields. They began to raid each other's cabins, call each other names, and start fistfights. No one dared to have a friend from the rival group. Before long, the Rattlers and the Eagles were as hostile toward each other as any two gangs fighting for turf or any two nations fighting for dominance. Their hostility continued even when they were just sitting around together watching movies.

Then Sherif decided to try to undo the hostility he had created and make peace between the Eagles and Rattlers. He and his associates set up a series of predicaments in which both groups needed to work together to reach a desired goal—pooling their resources to get a movie they all wanted to see, or pulling a staff truck up a hill on a camping trip. This policy of *interdependence in reaching mutual goals* was highly successful in reducing the boys' competitiveness and hostility; the boys eventually made friends with their former enemies (see Figure 8.3).

Interdependence has a similar effect in adult groups. The reason, it seems, is that cooperation causes people to think of themselves as members of one big group—a new social identity—instead of two opposed groups, *us* and *them* (Gaertner et al., 1990).

As these bumper stickers and lapel pin show, everyone is ethnocentric!

social identity The part of a person's self-concept that is based on his or her identification with a nation, culture, or ethnic group or with gender or other roles in society.

Figure 8.3

THE EXPERIMENT AT ROBBER'S CAVE

In this study, competitive games fostered hostility between the Rattlers and the Eagles. Few boys had a best friend from the other group (top). But after the boys had to cooperate to solve various problems, the percentage who made friends across "enemy lines" shot up (bottom) (Sherif et al., 1961).

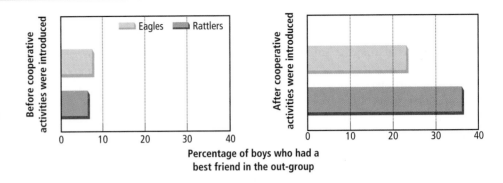

Percentage of boys who had a best friend in the out-group

Stereotypes

stereotype A summary impression of a group, in which a person believes that all members of the group share a common trait or traits (positive, negative, or neutral).

If you are like most people, you can think of a million ways that members of your family vary—Jeff is stodgy, Ruth is prissy, Farah is outgoing. But if you have never met a person from Turkey or Tibet, you are likely to *stereotype* Turks and Tibetans. A **stereotype** is a summary impression of a group of people in which all members of the group are viewed as sharing a common trait or traits. Stereotypes may be negative, positive, or neutral. There are stereotypes of people who drive Jeeps or BMWs, of men who wear earrings and of women who wear business suits, of engineering students and art students, of feminists and fraternity men.

Stereotypes play an important role in human thinking. They help us quickly process new information and retrieve memories. They allow us to organize experience, make sense of differences among individuals and groups, and predict how people will behave. They are, as some psychologists have called them, useful "tools in the mental toolbox"—energy-saving devices that allow us to make efficient decisions (Macrae, Milne, & Bodenhausen, 1994).

Although stereotypes reflect real differences among people, they also distort that reality in three ways (Judd et al., 1995). First, *they exaggerate differences between groups*, making the stereotyped group seem odd, unfamiliar, or dangerous, not like "us." Second, *they produce selective perception;* people tend to see only the evidence that fits the stereotype and reject any perceptions that do not fit. Third, *they under-estimate differences within other groups*. People realize that their own groups are made up of all kinds of individuals, but stereotypes create the impression that all members of other groups (say, all Texans or all teenagers) are the same.

Which woman is the chemical engineer and which is the assistant? The Western stereotype holds that (a) women are not engineers in the first place, but (b) if they are, they are Western. Actually, the engineer at this refinery is the Kuwaiti woman on the left.

Some stereotypes stem from a person's cultural values. For example, white Americans tend to have strongly negative stereotypes about fat people because of a cultural ideology that individuals are responsible for what happens to them and for how they look. In contrast, Mexicans (in Mexico and the United States) and African-Americans are significantly more accepting of heavy people (Crandall & Martinez, 1996; Hebl & Heatherton, 1998).

Cultural values also affect how people evaluate a particular action (Taylor & Porter, 1994). For example, Chinese students in Hong Kong, where communalism and respect for elders are valued, think that a student who comes late to class or argues with a parent about grades is being selfish and disrespectful of adults. But Australian students, who value individualism, think that the same behavior is perfectly appropriate (Forgas & Bond, 1985). You can see how the Chinese might form negative stereotypes of "disrespectful" Australians, and how the Australians might form negative stereotypes of the "spineless" Chinese. And it is a small step from negative stereotypes to prejudice.

Prejudice

A *prejudice* consists of a negative stereotype and a strong, unreasonable dislike or hatred of a group or its individual members. Feelings of prejudice violate the spirit of critical thinking because they resist rational argument and evidence. In his classic book *The Nature of Prejudice*, Gordon Allport (1954/1979) described the responses characteristic of a prejudiced person when confronted with evidence contradicting his or her beliefs:

Live! **psych** 8.3

> Mr. X: The trouble with Jews is that they only take care of their own group.
>
> Mr. Y: But the record of the Community Chest campaign shows that they give more generously, in proportion to their numbers, to the general charities of the community, than do non-Jews.
>
> Mr. X: That shows they are always trying to buy favor and intrude into Christian affairs. They think of nothing but money; that is why there are so many Jewish bankers.
>
> Mr. Y: But a recent study shows that the percentage of Jews in the banking business is negligible, far smaller than the percentage of non-Jews.
>
> Mr. X: That's just it; they don't go in for respectable business; they are only in the movie business or run night clubs.

Notice that Mr. X does not respond to Mr. Y's evidence; he just moves along to another reason for his dislike of Jews. That is the slippery nature of prejudice.

The Origins of Prejudice. When social psychologists began to study prejudice in earnest after World War II, they regarded prejudice as a form of mental illness: Only disturbed, mentally unhealthy people, they thought, could be prejudiced. (They were thinking of Hitler.) Since then, they have learned that, on the contrary, prejudice is a universal human experience that affects just about every human being (Dovidio, 2001). The reason is that prejudice has many sources and functions: psychological, social-cultural, and economic.

1 *Psychological functions.* Prejudice often serves to ward off feelings of doubt and fear. Prejudiced persons may transfer their worries onto the target group. Thus, a person who has doubts or anxieties about his own sexuality may develop a hatred of gay people. Prejudice also allows people to use the target group as a scapegoat: "Those people are the source of all my troubles." And, as research from many nations has confirmed, prejudice is a tonic for low self-esteem: People puff up their own feelings of low self-worth by disliking or hating groups they see as inferior (Islam & Hewstone, 1993; Stephan et al., 1994; Tajfel & Turner, 1986).

2 *Social and cultural functions.* Some prejudices are acquired through groupthink and other social pressures to conform to the views of friends, relatives, or associates. Rather than having deep-seated psychological roots, some social prejudices are passed along mindlessly from one generation to another, as when parents communicate to their children that "We don't associate with people like that." And some unconscious (implicit) prejudices are acquired from advertising, TV shows, and news reports that contain derogatory images and stereotypes of certain groups.

Prejudice also serves cultural purposes, bonding people to their own ethnic or national group and its ways. Indeed, this may be a major evolutionary reason for its universality and persistence (Fishbein, 1996). In this respect, prejudice is the flip side of ethnocentrism; it is not only that *we* are good and kind, but also that *they* are bad or evil. By disliking "them," we feel closer to others who are like "us."

3 *Economic functions.* Prejudice makes official forms of discrimination seem legitimate, by justifying the majority group's dominance, status, or greater wealth (Sidanius, Pratto, & Bobo, 1996). Historically, for example, white men in positions of power have justified their exclusion of women, blacks, and other minorities from the workplace and politics by claiming those minorities were inferior, irrational, and incompetent (Gould, 1996). But any majority group—of any ethnicity, gender, or nationality—that discriminates against a minority will call upon prejudice to legitimize its actions (Islam & Hewstone, 1993).

Although it is widely believed that prejudice is the primary cause of conflict and war between groups, prejudice is actually more often a *result* of conflict and war; it *legitimizes* them. When any two groups are in direct competition for jobs, or when people are worried about their incomes and the stability of their communities, prejudice between them increases (Doty, Peterson, & Winter, 1991). Social psychologist Elliot Aronson (1999b) traced the rise and fall of attitudes toward Chinese immigrants in the United States in the nineteenth century, as reported in newspapers of the time. When the Chinese were working in the gold mines and potentially taking jobs from white laborers, whites described them as depraved, vicious, and bloodthirsty. Just a decade later, when the Chinese began working on the transcontinental railroad—doing difficult and dangerous jobs that few white men wanted—prejudice against them declined. Whites described them as hardworking, industrious, and law-abiding. Then, after the railroad was finished and the Chinese had to compete with Civil War veterans for scarce jobs, white attitudes changed again. Whites now considered the Chinese to be "criminal," "crafty," "conniving," and "stupid" (Aronson, 1999b). (The white newspapers did not report the attitudes of the Chinese.)

The ultimate competition between groups, of course, is war. When two nations are at war, prejudice against the enemy allows each side to continue feeling righteous about its cause. As you can see in the propaganda images on this page, each side portrays the other in stereotyped ways to demonize and dehumanize the enemy, making it seem that the enemy is less than human and thus deserves to be killed (Keen, 1986).

The inhuman enemy: In times of conflict and war, people in every country stereotype "them," the enemy, as ugly, aggressive, brutal, and less than human—as "vermin," dogs, or pigs. After the attack on the World Trade Center, anti-American demonstrators in Jakarta portrayed George Bush as a rabid dog, and an American cartoonist lumped all Arab Muslims and nations into a "barrel of vermin."

REVIEW 8.1	SOURCES OF PREJUDICE		
Psychological	**Social**	**Economic**	**Cultural**
Low self-esteem	Groupthink	Majority's desire to preserve its status	Ethnocentrism
Anxiety	Conformity		Desire for group identity
Insecurity	Parental messages	Competition for jobs, power, resources	The justification of war
	Societal messages (ads, etc.)		
"Those people are not as moral and decent as we are."	"My parents taught me that those people are just no good."	"Those people aren't smart enough to do this work."	"We have to protect our religion/country/government from those people."

Fomenting prejudice against the enemy—calling them vermin, rats, mad dogs, traitors, heathens, baby-killers, brutes, or monsters—legitimizes the attackers' motives for war.

Review 8.1 summarizes these sources of prejudices and the many functions prejudices serve for those who hold them.

Defining and Measuring Prejudice. Prejudice is a weasel—hard to grasp and hold on to. One problem is that not all prejudiced people are prejudiced in the same way or to the same extent. Suppose that Raymond wishes to be tolerant and open-minded, but he grew up in a small homogeneous community and feels uncomfortable with members of other cultural and religious groups. Should we put Raymond in the same category as Rupert, an outspoken bigot who actively discriminates against others? Do good intentions count? What if Raymond knows nothing about Hindus and mindlessly blurts out a remark that reveals his ignorance? Is that prejudice or thoughtlessness? These questions complicate the measurement of prejudice.

Similar complexities occur in defining "sexism." In research with 15,000 men and women in 19 nations, psychologists found that "hostile sexism," which reflects active dislike of women, is different from "benevolent sexism," in which superficially positive attitudes put women on a pedestal but nonetheless reinforce women's subordination. The latter type of sexism is affectionate but patronizing, conveying the attitude that women are so wonderful, good, kind, and moral that they should stay at home, away from the rough and tumble (and power and income) of public life (Glick et al., 2000). In all 19 countries studied, men had significantly higher hostile sexism scores than women did, but in about half of the countries, women endorsed benevolent sexism as much as men did. The researchers believe that benevolent sexism is "a particularly insidious form of prejudice" because, lacking a tone of hostility to women, it

THINKING CRITICALLY

Define Your Terms

What does it mean to be "prejudiced"? Is it blatant hostility, vague discomfort with another group, a patronizing attitude of superiority, or ignorance about an unfamiliar culture?

doesn't seem like a "prejudice" to men, and also because women "may find its sweet allure difficult to resist" (Glick & Fiske, 2001). Yet both forms of sexism—whether you think women are "too good" for equality or "not good enough"—legitimize gender discrimination. (And, by the way, what about women who are prejudiced against men? Is that a form of "sexism"?)

Today, however, the hardest aspect of measuring any prejudice is that most people know they shouldn't have any (Cunningham, Preacher, & Banaji, 2001). If you ask people directly about their prejudices, most will say, in effect, "Me, prejudiced? Not at all! I love everybody equally!" Indeed, on surveys, prejudice of all kinds has

The Many Targets of Prejudice

Prejudice has a long history, everywhere in the world. Why do new prejudices keep emerging and why do some old ones persist? In the 1920s (photo at left) and during World War II, anti-Japanese feelings ran high, and returned during America's economic competition with Japan in the early 1990s. Prejudice toward gay men and lesbians has often erupted in virulent protest, anger, and violence. Antisemitism is one of the world's oldest prejudices, and still erupts among those who make Jews the scapegoats for their problems.

declined sharply in the United States and Canada. White attitudes toward integration have become steadily more favorable, and the once-common beliefs that blacks are inferior to whites, and women inferior to men, have dropped sharply (Plant & Devine, 1998; Dovidio, 2001).

This change, however, may simply reflect a growing awareness that it isn't cool to admit prejudice, rather than a real decline in prejudiced feelings. That would explain why, when white students fill out a prejudice questionnaire in the presence of a black experimenter, their prejudice scores are lower than when the experimenter is white (Fazio et al., 1995). In the presence of the black researcher, apparently, the students mask their true feelings. Similarly, studies find that most whites do not discriminate against black job candidates who have strong qualifications, but they are far more likely to choose *average* white candidates over *average* black ones (Dovidio & Gaertner, 2000). This finding suggests that old-fashioned discrimination ("We would never hire a black person") may be gone, but lives on in a subtler form ("We would hire Colin Powell and Tiger Woods in a heartbeat, but that's it . . .").

One reason that prejudice lives on, as Gordon Allport (1954/1979) observed years ago, is that "defeated intellectually, prejudice lingers emotionally." People may lose their *explicit* prejudices toward a group but retain an *implicit,* unconscious prejudice (recall the distinction we drew earlier between explicit and implicit attitudes). Implicit attitudes and prejudices are assumed to be automatic and unintentional, and hence a truer measure of a person's "real" feelings (Cunningham, Preacher, & Banaji, 2001). Researchers have developed three different ways to measure implicit prejudices:

During the economic recession of the early 1990s, Iranians and other immigrants became targets of American hostility. Native Americans have been objects of hatred since Europeans first arrived on the continent. Segregated facilities for blacks were legal until the 1950s, and even today many neighborhoods and schools remain separate and unequal. And anti-female prejudice continues.

1 *Measures of symbolic racism.* Some researchers believe that prejudice against blacks lurks behind a mask of *symbolic racism,* in which whites disguise their animosity toward black individuals by claiming they are concerned only about social issues such as "reverse discrimination" or "hard-core criminals" (Bell, 1992; J. Jones, 1997). Instead of asking respondents about feelings of prejudice toward blacks in general, therefore, researchers probe for hostile feelings that might lie beneath surface attitudes. The same whites who will not admit to disliking blacks, for example, might agree that "blacks are getting too demanding in their push for equal rights" (Brauer, Wasel, & Niedenthal, 2000).

2 *Measures of behavior rather than attitudes.* Some investigators observe how people unconsciously behave when they are with a possible object of prejudice. Some individuals sit farther away than they normally would, reveal involuntary, negative facial expressions, or have other signs of physical tension (Fazio et al., 1995; Guglielmi, 1999).

Another behavioral approach is to observe what allegedly unprejudiced people do when they are angered or stressed (J. Jones, 1991; Sinclair & Kunda, 1999). In one experiment, students thought they were giving shock to other students in a study of biofeedback. White students initially showed *less* aggression toward blacks than toward whites. But as soon as the white students were angered by overhearing derogatory remarks about themselves, they showed *more* aggression toward blacks than toward whites (Rogers & Prentice-Dunn, 1981). The same pattern appears in studies of how English-speaking Canadians behave toward French-speaking Canadians (Meindl & Lerner, 1985), straights toward homosexuals, and non-Jewish students toward Jews (Fein & Spencer, 1997).

These findings imply that people are willing to control negative feelings toward targets of prejudice under normal conditions. But as soon as they are angry or frustrated, or get a jolt to their self-esteem, their real prejudice reveals itself.

3 *Measures of unconscious associations with the target group.* In recent years, another way of measuring implicit prejudices has become popular among researchers. This method taps people's unconscious associations between a stimulus and its degree of pleasantness or unpleasantness (Cunningham, Preacher, & Banaji, 2001; Dovidio, 2001). Using this method, researchers have found that many people who describe themselves as unprejudiced nonetheless have unconscious negative associations with certain groups. For example, it takes white students longer to respond to associations between black faces and positive words (e.g., triumph, honest) or to associations between white faces and negative words (e.g., devil, failure), than it does to respond to black faces and negative words or white faces and positive words (see Figure 8.4).

This test has also been used to identify allegedly unconscious prejudices against women, the elderly, and Asians. For example, the Japanese and the Koreans have a long history of mutual antagonism. In one experiment, ethnically Korean students found it more difficult to process Japanese names associated with pleasant words than Korean names with pleasant associations, and the reverse was true for the Japanese students (Greenwald, McGhee, & Schwartz, 1998).

Unfortunately, it is difficult to know exactly what these implicit measures are measuring: actual prejudice (animosity), unfamiliarity with the target stimulus, or activation of a stereotype. As we saw earlier, people find familiar names, products, and even nonsense syllables to be more pleasant than unfamiliar ones. So are these tests measuring true prejudice toward a target or merely unfamiliarity with it? If a black student and a Korean student sit farther away from one another than they would with a student of their own ethnicity, does this reveal prejudice, discomfort, unfamiliarity with the target, or, as we also saw earlier, different cultural norms for conversational distance?

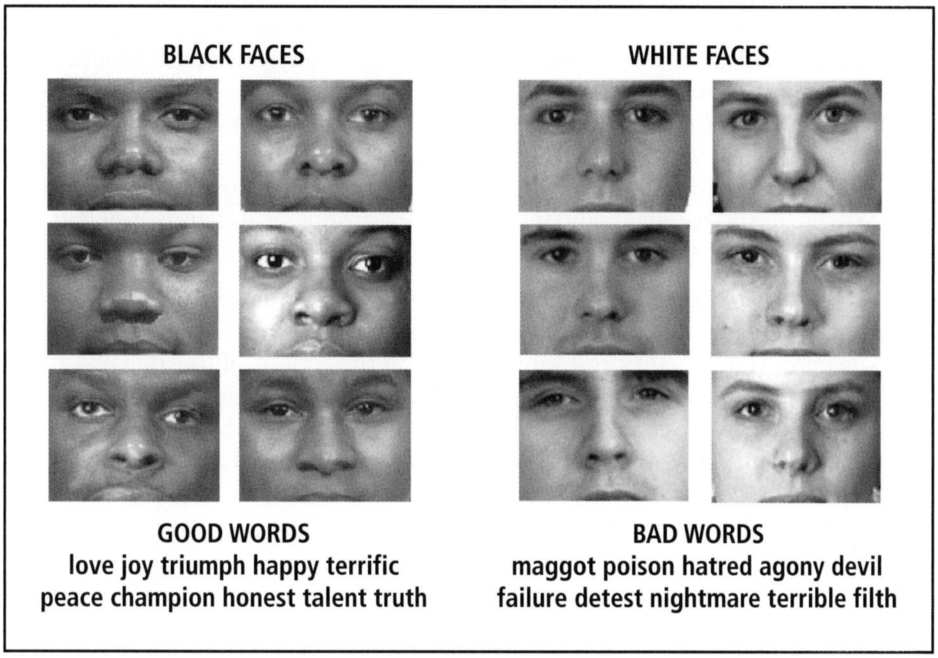

BLACK FACES   WHITE FACES

GOOD WORDS
love joy triumph happy terrific
peace champion honest talent truth

BAD WORDS
maggot poison hatred agony devil
failure detest nightmare terrible filth

Figure 8.4

AN IMPLICIT MEASURE OF PREJUDICE

In a series of experiments, participants responded to black or white faces and to positive or negative words. They used separate computer keys to indicate whether each face was black or white, and the same keys to indicate whether each word was good or bad. But half of the time, "white + good" and "black + bad" were on the same keys, and the other half, "white + bad" and "black + good" were on the same keys. Participants took longer to respond in the white + bad condition than in white + good, indicating that they had stronger unconscious associations between "white" and "good" (Cunningham, Preacher, & Banaji, 2001).

As you can see, defining and measuring prejudice are not easy tasks. They involve distinguishing explicit attitudes from unconscious ones, active hostility from simple discomfort, what people say from what they feel, and what people feel from how they actually behave (Brauer, Wasel, & Niedenthal, 2000).

Reducing Conflict and Prejudice

In the aftermath of the attacks on the World Trade Center and the Pentagon, many white Americans took out their frustrations and anger on fellow Americans who happened to be Arab, Sikh, Pakistani, Hindu, or Afghan. Two men in Chicago beat up an Arab-American taxi driver, yelling, "This is what you get, you mass murderer!"

Just as social psychologists investigate the situations that increase prejudice and animosity toward other groups—particularly, how war and economic conflict produce heightened stereotyping and ethnocentrism—they have also examined the conditions that might reduce them. Of course, given the many sources, kinds, and functions of prejudice, no one method will work in all situations. People who have psychological motives for hating another group (say, to bolster their own self-esteem, or to displace anger and fear) may change their explicit attitudes if forced to by social pressures, yet retain implicit prejudices. People who hold prejudices in order to justify their economic superiority over a poorer group are not going to give them up—at least, not until both sides have more equitable resources (Plant & Devine, 1998).

In spite of these complexities, in some situations prejudice and conflict between groups can be overcome. Social psychologists have identified four conditions that must be met for this to happen (Allport, 1954/1979; Dovidio, Gaertner, & Validzic, 1998; Fisher, 1994; Pettigrew, 1998; Rubin, 1994; Slavin & Cooper, 1999; Staub, 1996; Stephan, 1999; Wittig & Grant-Thompson, 1998):

1 *Both sides must have equal legal status, economic opportunities, and power.* This requirement is the spur behind efforts to change laws that permit discrimination. Integration of public facilities in the American South would never have occurred if civil rights advocates had waited for segregationists to have a change of heart. Women would never have gotten the right to vote, attend college, or do "men's work" without persistent challenges to the laws that permitted gender discrimination. Laws, however, do not necessarily change attitudes if all they do is produce unequal contact between groups or if competition for jobs continues.

2 *Authorities and community institutions must endorse egalitarian norms and thereby provide moral support and legitimacy for both sides.* Society must establish norms of equality and support them in the actions of its officials—teachers, employers, the judicial system, government officials, and the police. Where segregation is official government policy, as apartheid was in South Africa, obviously conflict and prejudice will not only continue, but will seem "normal" and justified.

3 *Both sides must have opportunities to work and socialize together, formally and informally.* According to the *contact hypothesis,* prejudice declines when people have the chance to get used to one another's rules, food, music, customs, and attitudes. By making friends with one another, people of different groups and cultures can discover their shared interests and shared humanity. Stereotypes are shattered once people realize that "those people" aren't, in fact, "all alike" (Garcia-Marques & Mackie, 1999).

The contact hypothesis has been supported by many diverse studies in the laboratory and in the "real world": studies of newly integrated housing projects in the American South during the 1950s and 1960s; relationships between German and immigrant Turkish children in German schools; young people's attitudes toward the elderly; healthy people's attitudes toward the mentally ill; nondisabled children's attitudes toward the disabled; and straight people's prejudices toward gay men and lesbians (Fishbein, 1996; Herek, 1999; Herek & Capitanio, 1996; Pettigrew, 1997; Wilner, Walkley, & Cook, 1955). When people make friends with members of another group, they tend to become less prejudiced toward the group as a whole.

Nevertheless, contact and friendship alone are not enough to reduce prejudice and achieve harmony between groups (Fishbein, 1996). This is sadly apparent at multiethnic high schools, where ethnic groups often form cliques and gangs, fighting other groups and defending their own ways.

4 *Both sides must cooperate, working together for a common goal.* Cooperation often reduces us–them thinking and prejudice by creating an encompassing social identity ("We're all in this together"). Many successful cooperative situations have been established in schools, businesses, and communities, requiring formerly antagonistic groups to work together for a common goal—the Eagles and the Rattlers solution.

For example, some elementary schools have experimented with the "jigsaw" method of building cooperation. Children from different ethnic groups work together on a task that is broken up like a jigsaw puzzle; each child needs to cooperate with the others to put the assignment together. Children in such classes tend to do better, like their classmates better, and become less stereotyped in

Tensions between groups often subside when people work together on a common goal. Here, volunteers from Habitat for Humanity, a group that constructs housing for low-income people, build a new home in the Watts area of Los Angeles.

their thinking than children in competitive classrooms (Aronson & Patnoe, 1997; Slavin & Cooper, 1999). However, cooperation does not work when members of a group have unequal status, blame one another for loafing or "dropping the ball," or believe that their teachers or employers are playing favorites.

Each of these four approaches to reducing prejudice is important, but none is sufficient on its own. Perhaps one reason that group conflicts and prejudice are so persistent is that all four conditions are rarely met at the same time.

QUICK QUIZ

Try to overcome your prejudice against quizzes by taking this one.

A. Which concept—ethnocentrism, stereotyping, or prejudice—is illustrated by each of the following statements?

1. Juan believes that all Anglos are uptight and cold, and he won't listen to any evidence that contradicts his belief.

2. John knows and likes the Mexican minority in his town, but he privately believes that Anglo culture is superior.

3. Jane believes that Honda owners are thrifty and practical. June believes that Honda owners are stingy and dull.

B. What strategy does the Robbers Cave study suggest for reducing hostility between groups?

C. What are four important conditions required for reducing prejudice and conflict between groups?

D. Surveys find that large percentages of African-Americans, Asian-Americans, and Latinos hold negative stereotypes of one another and resent other minorities almost as much as they resent whites. What are some reasons that people who have themselves been victims of stereotyping and prejudice would hold the same attitudes toward others?

Answers:

A. 1. prejudice 2. ethnocentrism 3. stereotypes B. fostering interdependence in reaching mutual goals C. Both sides must have equal status and power; have the moral and legal support of authorities and society at large; have opportunities to socialize, formally and informally; and cooperate for a common goal. D. ethnocentrism; low self-esteem; conformity with relatives and friends who share these prejudices; parental lessons and messages conveyed by the media; and economic competition

WHAT'S AHEAD▶

● **Are "age-old tribal hatreds" the best explanation for war and genocide?**
● **What is the "banality of evil," and what does it tell us about human nature?**

The Question of Human Nature

Throughout this chapter we have seen that "human nature" contains the potential for unspeakable acts of cruelty and inspiring acts of goodness. Nineteen men on a suicide mission caused the deaths of thousands of people at the World Trade Center. Yet in the mournful and shocked aftermath of the disaster, countless numbers of people all over the nation and world rallied to help rescue workers and the families of the victims. They offered their services—as everything from steel-workers and excavators to doctors, psychologists, and cooks. They brought hot food, flowers, tributes, and clothes. They donated so much blood that the Red Cross had to call a moratorium. They contributed millions of dollars, in sums great and small. The village of Bari, Italy, raised $500,000 to help rebuild the St. Nicholas Greek Orthodox church, destroyed during the collapse of the twin towers. An impoverished farming town of 1,600 people in Montana held a fund-raiser to help New Yorkers.

> **THINKING CRITICALLY**
>
> **Don't Oversimplify**
>
> Many people like to divide individuals and nations into those that are "good" and those that are "evil." What is wrong with thinking this way?

It's easy to believe that some cultures and individuals are just inherently good or evil. But from the standpoint of social and cultural psychology, all human beings, like all cultures, contain the potential for both. People everywhere love their families and are loyal to their friends and country, and yet virtually no country or group has bloodless hands. The Nazis systematically exterminated millions of Jews, Gypsies, homosexuals, disabled people, and anyone else not of the "pure" Aryan "race." Americans and Canadians slaughtered native peoples in North America, Turks slaughtered Armenians, the Khmer Rouge slaughtered millions of fellow Cambodians, the Spanish conquistadors slaughtered native peoples in Mexico and South America, Idi Amin waged a reign of terror against his own people in Uganda, the Japanese slaughtered Koreans and Chinese, Iraqis slaughtered Kurds, despotic political regimes in Argentina and Chile killed thousands of dissidents and rebels, the Hutu in Rwanda murdered thousands of Tutsi, and in the former Yugoslavia, Bosnian Serbs massacred Bosnian Muslims in the name of "ethnic cleansing."

Many people believe that these outbreaks of horrifying violence are a result of inner aggressive drives, the sheer evilness of the enemy, or "age-old tribal hatreds." But in the social-psychological view, they result from the all-too-normal processes we have discussed in this chapter, including ethnocentrism, obedience to authority, conformity, groupthink, deindividuation, stereotyping, and prejudice. These processes are especially likely to be activated when a government feels weakened and vulnerable. By generating an outside enemy, rulers create "us–them" thinking to impose order and cohesion among their citizens and to create a scapegoat for the country's economic problems (Smith, 1998; Staub, 1996). However, throughout history, as circumstances have changed within a culture, societies have changed from being warlike to being peaceful, and vice versa.

The philosopher Hannah Arendt (1963), who covered the trial of Adolf Eichmann, used the phrase *the banality of evil* to describe how it was possible for Eichmann and other "normal" people in Nazi Germany to commit the monstrous acts they did. (*Banal* means "commonplace" or "unoriginal.") The compelling evidence for the banality of evil is, perhaps, the hardest lesson in psychology. Of course, some people do stand out as being unusually heroic or unusually sadistic. But as we have seen, good people can do terribly disturbing things when norms and roles encourage or require them to do so—when the situation takes over and they do not stop to think critically. Otherwise healthy people may join self-destructive cults, harm others if ordered to, and go along with a violent crowd.

The research discussed in this chapter suggests that ethnocentrism and prejudice will always be with us, as long as differences exist among groups. But it can also help us formulate ways of living in a diverse world. By identifying the conditions that create the banality of evil, perhaps we can create others that foster the "banality of virtue"—everyday acts of kindness, selflessness, and generosity.

Taking Psychology with You

TRAVELS ACROSS THE CULTURAL DIVIDE

A French salesman worked for a company that was bought by Americans. When the new American manager ordered him to step up his sales within the next three months, the employee quit in a huff, taking his customers with him. Why? In France, it takes years to develop customers; in family-owned businesses, relationships with customers may span generations. The American wanted instant results, as Americans often do, but the French salesman knew this was impossible and quit. The American view was, "He wasn't up to the job; he's lazy and disloyal, so he stole my customers." The French view was, "There is no point in explaining anything to a person who is so stupid as to think you can acquire loyal customers in three months" (Hall & Hall, 1987).

Both men were committing the fundamental attribution error: assuming the other person's behavior was due to personality rather than the situation—in this case, a situation governed by cultural rules. Many corporations now realize that such rules are not trivial and that success in a global economy depends on understanding them. You, too, can benefit from the psychological research on culture, whether you plan to do business abroad, visit as a tourist, or just want to get along better in your own society.

▶ **Be sure you understand the other culture's rules, manners, and customs.** If you find yourself getting angry over something a person from another culture is doing, try to find out whether your expectations and perceptions of that person's behavior are appropriate. For example, Koreans typically do not shake hands when greeting strangers, whereas most North Americans and Europeans do. People who shake hands as a gesture of friendship and courtesy are likely to feel insulted if another person refuses to do the same, unless they understand this cultural difference.

Or suppose you are shopping in the Middle East or Latin America, where bargaining on a price is the usual practice. If you are not used to bargaining, the experience is likely to be exasperating—you will not know whether you got taken or got a great deal. On the other hand, if you are from a bargaining culture, you will feel just as exasperated if a seller offers you a flat price. "Where's the fun in this?" you'll say. "The whole human transaction of shopping is gone!"

Whichever kind of culture you come from, you may need a "translator" to help you navigate the unfamiliar system. For example, in Los Angeles, a physician we know could not persuade his Iranian patients that office fees are fixed, not negotiable. They kept offering him half, then 60 percent . . . and each time he said "no" they thought he was just taking a hard negotiating position. It took a bicultural relative of the patients to explain the odd American custom of fixed prices for service.

▶ **When in Rome, do as the Romans do—as much as possible.** Most of the things you really need to know about a culture are not to be found in the guidebooks or travelogues. To learn the unspoken rules of a culture, look, listen, and observe. What is the pace of life like? Do people regard brash individuality as admirable or embarrassing? When customers enter a shop, do they greet and chat with the shopkeeper or ignore the person as they browse?

Remember, though, that even when you know the rules, you may find it difficult to carry them out, as we noted in discussing conversational distance. For example, cultures differ in their tolerance for prolonged gazes (Keating, 1994). In the Middle East, two men will look directly at one another as they talk, but such direct gazes would be deeply uncomfortable to most Japanese and a sign of insult or confrontation to some African-Americans. Knowing this fact about gaze rules can help people accept the reality of different customs, but most of us will still feel uncomfortable trying to change our own ways.

▶ **Avoid stereotyping.** Try not to let your awareness of cultural differences cause you to overlook individual variations within cultures. During a dreary Boston winter, social psychologist Roger Brown (1986) went to the Bahamas for a vacation. To his surprise, he found the people he met unfriendly, rude, and sullen. He decided that the reason was that Bahamians had to deal with spoiled, demanding foreigners, and he tried out this hypothesis on a cab driver. The cab driver looked at Brown in amazement, smiled cheerfully, and told him that Bahamians don't mind tourists; just *unsmiling* tourists.

And then Brown realized what had been going on. "Not tourists generally, but this tourist, myself, was the cause," he wrote. "Confronted with my unrelaxed wintry Boston face, they had assumed I had no interest in them and had responded non-committally, inexpressively. I had created the Bahamian national character. Everywhere I took my face it sprang into being. So I began smiling a lot, and the Bahamians changed their national character. In fact, they lost any national character and differentiated into individuals."

Wise travelers can use their knowledge of cultural differences to expand their understanding of human behavior, while avoiding the trap of stereotyping. Sociocultural research teaches us to appreciate the countless explicit and implicit cultural rules that govern our behavior, values, and attitudes, and those of others. Yet we should not forget Roger Brown's lesson that every human being is an individual: one who not only reflects his or her culture, but who shares the common concerns of all humanity.

Summary

Roles and Rules

▶ Social psychology is the study of people in social context, including the influence of *norms, roles,* and groups on behavior and cognition. Roles and norms are affected by one's *culture.*

▶ Two classic studies illustrate the power of roles to affect individual actions. In Milgram's obedience study, most people in the role of "teacher" inflicted what they thought was extreme shock on another person because of the authority of the experimenter. In Zimbardo's prison study, college students quickly fell into the role of "prisoner" or "guard."

▶ Obedience to authority contributes to the smooth running of society, but obedience can also lead to actions that are deadly, foolish, or illegal. People obey orders because they can be punished if they do not, out of respect for authority, and to gain advantages. Even when they would rather not obey, they may do so because they hand over responsibility for their actions to the authority; because the role is *routinized* into duties that are performed mindlessly; because they are embarrassed to break the rules of good manners and lack the words to protest; or because they have become *entrapped.*

Social Influences on Beliefs

▶ According to *attribution theory,* people are motivated to search for causes to which they can attribute their own and other people's behavior. Their attributions may be *situational* or *dispositional.* The *fundamental attribution error* occurs when people overestimate per-

sonality traits as a cause of behavior and underestimate the influence of the situation. A *self-serving bias* allows people to excuse their mistakes by blaming the situation yet take credit for their good deeds. According to the *just-world hypothesis,* most people need to believe that the world is fair and that people get what they deserve. To preserve this belief, they may blame victims of abuse or injustice for provoking or deserving it, instead of blaming the perpetrators.

▶ People hold many *attitudes* about people, things, and ideas. Attitudes may be *explicit* (conscious) or *implicit* (unconscious); some are fairly ingrained aspects of personality, and others result from social influences and are more changeable. One important external influence on attitudes is the shared experiences of a person's age group, which create a *generational identity.* Some attitudes change through experience; others change because of a psychological need for consistency (the discomfort of being in a state of *cognitive dissonance*).

▶ One powerful way to influence attitudes is through the *validity effect:* Simply repeating a statement over and over again makes it seem more believable. Techniques of attitude change include associating a product or message with someone who is famous, attractive, or expert, and linking the product with good feelings. Fear tactics tend to backfire.

▶ Some methods of attitude change are intentionally manipulative. Tactics of *coercive persuasion* include putting a person under extreme distress; defining problems simplistically; offering the appearance of unconditional love and acceptance in exchange for unquestioning loyalty; creating a new identity for the person; using entrapment; and controlling access to outside information.

Individuals in Groups

▶ In groups, individuals often behave differently than they would on their own. Conformity has many benefits for the smooth running of society and allows people to feel in harmony with others like them. As the famous Asch experiment showed, most people will conform to the judgments of others even when the others are plain wrong. People in *collectivist* cultures value conformity and the sense of group harmony it creates more than do people in *individualist* cultures. But everyone conforms under some conditions.

▶ Most people conform to social pressure because they identify with a group, trust the group's judgment or knowledge, hope for personal gain, or wish to be liked. But they also may conform mindlessly and self-destructively, violating their own preferences and values because "everyone else is doing it."

▶ Groups that are strongly cohesive, are isolated from other views, are under outside pressure, and have strong leaders are vulnerable to *groupthink,* the tendency of group members to think alike, censor themselves, actively suppress disagreement, and feel that their decisions are invulnerable. Groupthink often produces faulty decisions because group members fail to seek disconfirming evidence for their ideas. However, groups can be structured to counteract groupthink.

▶ *Diffusion of responsibility* in a group can lead to inaction on the part of individuals, such as *bystander apathy* or, in work groups, *social loafing.* The diffusion of responsibility is especially likely to occur under conditions that promote *deindividuation,* the loss of awareness of one's individuality. Deindividuation increases when people feel anonymous, as in a large group or crowd, or when they are wearing masks or uniforms. In some situations, crowd norms lead deindividuated people to behave aggressively, but in others, crowd norms foster helpfulness and altruism.

▶ The willingness to speak up for an unpopular opinion, blow the whistle on illegal or immoral practices, help a stranger in trouble or perform other acts of *altruism* is partly a matter of personal belief and conscience. But several social and situational factors are also important. The person perceives that help is needed; the situation increases the likelihood that the person will take responsibility; the person decides that the costs of not doing anything are greater than the costs of getting involved; the person has an ally; and the person becomes entrapped in a commitment to help or dissent.

Group Conflict and Prejudice

▶ *Ethnocentrism,* the belief that one's own group or nation is superior to all others, promotes "us–them" thinking. People develop *social identities* based on their group affiliations, including nationality, ethnicity, religion, and other social memberships. As soon as people see themselves as "us" (members of an in-group), they tend to define anyone different as "them." Dividing the world into us and them is often fueled by competition. Conflict and hostility between groups can be reduced by teamwork and by *interdependence* in working for mutual goals.

▶ *Stereotypes* help people rapidly process new information, organize experience, and predict how others will behave. But they distort reality by (1) emphasizing differences between groups, (2) underestimating the differences within groups, and (3) producing selective perception.

▶ A *prejudice* is an unreasonable negative feeling toward a category of people. Prejudice has psychological, social-cultural, and economic functions. It wards off feelings of anxiety and doubt; provides a simple explanation of complex problems; and bolsters self-esteem when a person feels threatened. Prejudice also allows people to feel closer to their families, social groups, and culture. But the most important function of prejudice is to justify a majority group's economic interests and dominance, or, in extreme cases, to legitimize war. During times of economic insecurity and competition for jobs, prejudice rises significantly.

▶ Prejudice is complex to define and measure. For example, "hostile sexism" is different from "benevolent sexism," yet both legitimize gender discrimination. People often disagree on whether racism and other prejudices are declining or have merely taken new forms. Because many people are unwilling to admit their prejudices openly, some researchers measure *symbolic racism* (prejudice disguised in opinions about race-related social issues); people's actual behavior toward a target group when they are stressed, provoked, or insulted; or nonconscious, *implicit* prejudice as revealed in emotional associations to a target group.

▶ Four conditions are required for reducing prejudice and conflict between groups: both sides must have equal legal status, economic standing, and power; both sides must have the legal and moral support of authorities and the larger culture; both sides must have opportunities to work and socialize together (the *contact hypothesis*); and both sides must work together for a common goal.

The Question of Human Nature

▶ Although many people believe that only bad people do bad deeds, the principles of social and cultural psychology show that under certain conditions, good people are often induced to do bad things, too. All individuals are affected by the rules and norms of their cultures; and by the social processes of obedience and conformity, bystander apathy, groupthink, deindividuation, ethnocentrism, stereotyping, and prejudice.

Key Terms

social psychology 268

cultural psychology 268

norms (social) 269

role 269

culture 269

conversational distance 270

routinization 274

entrapment 275

social cognition 276

attribution theory 277

situational attributions 277

dispositional attributions 277

fundamental attribution error 277

self-serving bias 277

just-world hypothesis 278

blaming the victim 278

attitude 279

generational identity 280

cognitive dissonance 280

validity effect 281

coercive persuasion 282

individualist versus collectivist
 cultures 285

groupthink 286

diffusion of responsibility 287

bystander apathy 287

social loafing 287

deindividuation 288

altruism 290

ethnocentrism 292

social identity 293

us–them thinking 293

stereotype 294

prejudice 295

implicit versus explicit prejudice 299

symbolic racism 300

contact hypothesis 302

◀ LOOKING BACK

- How do social rules regulate behavior—and what is likely to happen when you violate them? (p. 269)

- Do you have to be mean or disturbed to inflict pain on someone just because an authority tells you to? (p. 271)

- How can ordinary college students be transformed into sadistic prison guards? (pp. 272–273)

- How can people be "entrapped" into violating their moral principles? (p. 275)

- What is one of the most common mistakes people make when they explain the behavior of others? (p. 277)

- Why would a person blame victims of rape or torture for having brought their misfortunes on themselves? (p. 278)

- What is the "Big Lie," and why does it work so well? (p. 281)

- What is the difference between ordinary techniques of persuasion and the coercive techniques used by cults? (p. 282)

- Why do people in groups often go along with the majority even when the majority is dead wrong? (pp. 285–286)

- How can "groupthink" lead to bad, even catastrophic, decisions? (p. 286)

- In an emergency, are you more likely to get help when there are lots of strangers in the area or only a few? (p. 287)

- What enables some people to disagree with a group, take independent action, or blow the whistle on wrongdoers? (pp. 290–291)

- How difficult is it to create "us–them" thinking? (p. 293)

- How do stereotypes benefit us, and how do they distort reality? (p. 294)

- Is prejudice more likely to be a *cause* of competition and war or a *result* of them? (p. 296)

- If you believe that women are naturally better than men, are you a "sexist"? (pp. 297–298)

- Why isn't mere contact between cultural groups enough to reduce prejudice between them? What does work? (p. 302)

- Are "age-old tribal hatreds" the best explanation for war and genocide? (p. 304)

- What is the "banality of evil," and what does it tell us about human nature? (p. 304)

Go to **WWW.PRENHALL.COM/WADE** to reinforce these key concepts, and more.

     8.1 Attributions
     8.2 Conformity
     8.3 Prejudice

9

Thinking and Intelligence

A great many people think they are thinking when they are merely rearranging their prejudices.

WILLIAM JAMES

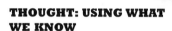

Think about what *thinking* does for you. It frees you from the confines of the immediate present: You can think about a trip taken three years ago, a party next Saturday, or the War of 1812. It carries you beyond the boundaries of reality: You can imagine unicorns and utopias, Martians and magic. Because you think, you do not need to grope your way blindly through your problems but, with some effort and knowledge, can solve them intelligently and creatively.

Each day, in the course of ordinary living, we all make plans, draw inferences, construct explanations, analyze relationships, and organize and reorganize our mental world. Descartes' famous declaration "I think, therefore I am" could just as well have been reversed: "I am, therefore I think." Our impressive powers of thought and intelligence have inspired us to call ourselves *Homo sapiens,* Latin for wise or rational man. But just how "sapiens" are we, really? Consider:

▶ Every spring, when daylight savings time begins, some people fret about tampering with "normal time." One woman in Colorado complained to a local newspaper that the "extra hour of sunlight" was burning up her front lawn!

▶ In Seal Beach, California, a visitor to a library asked whether the library had a newspaper clipping announcing the birth of Jesus.

▶ Many people confuse fictional characters in novels, movies, and soap operas with real people. The town of Nottingham, England, distributed flyers to visitors telling them Robin Hood and his pals never actually lived in nearby Sherwood Forest. Tourism plummeted and the flyers were discontinued.

▶ At a fast-food restaurant in Kentucky, a customer paid for a $2 order with a phony $200 bill depicting former President George Bush, a drawing of the White House with a lawn sign reading "We like broccoli," and, on the reverse side, an oil well. The cashier accepted the bill and gave the customer $198 in change.

The human mind, which has managed to come up with poetry, penicillin, and pantyhose, is a truly miraculous thing; but the human mind has also managed to come up with traffic jams, junk mail, and war. To better understand why the same species that figured out how to get to the moon is also capable of breathtaking bumbling here on Earth, we will examine in this chapter how people reason, solve problems, and grow in intelligence, as well as some sources of their mental shortcomings.

WHAT'S AHEAD ▶

● **When you think of a bird, why are you more likely to recall a robin than a penguin?**
● **How are visual images like images on a computer screen?**
● **What is happening mentally when you mistakenly take your geography notes to your psychology class?**

Thought: Using What We Know

To explain our mental abilities, many cognitive psychologists liken the human mind to an information processor, somewhat analogous to a computer but far more complex. Information-processing approaches capture the fact that the brain does not passively record information but actively alters and organizes it. When we take action, we physically manipulate the environment; when we think, we *mentally* manipulate internal representations of objects, activities, and situations.

The Elements of Cognition

One type of mental representation is the **concept,** a mental category that groups objects, relations, activities, abstractions, or qualities having common properties. The instances of a concept are seen as roughly similar. For example, *golden retriever, cocker spaniel,* and *border collie* are instances of the concept *dog;* and *anger, joy,* and *sadness* are instances of the concept *emotion.* Concepts simplify and summarize information about the world so that it is manageable, and so that we can make decisions quickly and efficiently. You may never have seen a *basenji* or eaten *escargots,* but if you know that the first is an instance of *dog* and the second an instance of *food,* you will know, roughly, how to respond (unless you do not like to eat snails, which is what escargots are).

Basic concepts have a moderate number of instances and are easier to acquire than those that have either few or many instances (Rosch, 1973). What is the object pictured in the margin? You will probably call it an apple. The concept *apple* is more basic than *fruit,* which includes many more instances and is more abstract. It is also more basic than *McIntosh apple,* which is quite specific. Similarly, *book* is more basic than either *printed matter* or *novel.* Children seem to learn basic-level concepts earlier than others, and adults use them more often than others, because basic concepts convey an optimal amount of information in most situations.

The qualities associated with a concept do not necessarily all apply to every instance: Some apples are not red; some dogs do not bark; some birds do not fly or perch on trees. But all the instances of a concept do share a "family resemblance." When we need to decide whether something belongs to a concept, we are likely to compare it to a **prototype,** a representative example of the concept (Rosch, 1973). For instance, which dog is doggier—a golden retriever or a chihuahua? Which fruit is more fruitlike—an apple or a pineapple? Which activity is more representative of sports—football or weight lifting? Most people within a culture can easily tell you which instances of a concept are most representative, or *prototypical.*

Concepts are the building blocks of thought, but they would be of limited use if we merely stacked them up mentally. We must also represent their relationships to one another. One way we accomplish this may be by storing and using **propositions,**

What is this?

concept A mental category that groups objects, relations, activities, abstractions, or qualities having common properties.

basic concepts Concepts that have a moderate number of instances and that are easier to acquire than those having few or many instances.

prototype An especially representative example of a concept.

proposition A unit of meaning that is made up of concepts and expresses a single idea.

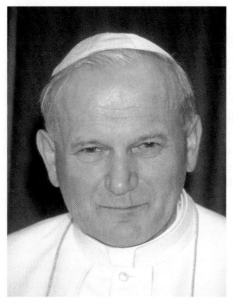

Some instances of a concept are more representative or prototypical than others. For example, Hollywood heartthrob Josh Hartnett clearly qualifies as a "bachelor," an unmarried man (at least, as of 2002). But is the Pope a bachelor? What about Robert Redford, who is divorced and has not remarried?

units of meaning that are made up of concepts and that express a unitary idea. A proposition can express nearly any sort of knowledge ("Hortense raises border collies") or belief ("Border collies are smart"). Propositions, in turn, are linked together in complicated networks of knowledge, associations, beliefs, and expectations. These networks, which psychologists call **cognitive schemas,** serve as mental models of aspects of the world. For example, gender schemas represent a person's beliefs and expectations about what it means to be male or female (see Chapter 14). People also have schemas about cultures, occupations, animals, geographical locations, and many other features of the social and natural environment.

Mental images—especially visual images, pictures in the mind's eye—are also important in thinking and in the construction of cognitive schemas. Although no one can directly "see" another person's visual images, psychologists are able to study them indirectly. One method is to measure how long it takes people to rotate an image in their imaginations, scan from one point to another in an image, or read off some detail from an image. The results suggest that visual images are much like images on a computer screen: We can manipulate them, they occur in a mental "space" of a fixed size, and small ones contain less detail than larger ones (Kosslyn, 1980; Shepard & Metzler, 1971).

Most people also report auditory images (for instance, a song, slogan, or poem you can hear in your "mind's ear"), and many report images in other sensory modalities as well—touch, taste, smell, or pain. Some even report kinesthetic images, imagined feelings in the muscles and joints. Athletes often imagine themselves performing a skill, such as diving or sprinting, and this visual and kinesthetic rehearsal seems to improve actual performance (Druckman & Swets, 1988). Mental practice of this sort activates most of the brain circuits involved in the activity itself (Stephan et al., 1995).

Here, then, is a visual summary of the elements of cognition:

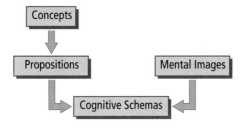

cognitive schema An integrated mental network of knowledge, beliefs, and expectations concerning a particular topic or aspect of the world.

mental image A mental representation that mirrors or resembles the thing it represents; mental images occur in many and perhaps all sensory modalities.

How Conscious Is Thought?

When we think about thinking, we usually have in mind those mental activities, such as solving problems or making decisions, that are carried out in a deliberate way with a conscious goal in mind. However, not all mental processing is conscious.

Subconscious and Nonconscious Thinking. Some of our cognitive processes lie outside of awareness but can be brought into consciousness with a little effort when necessary. These **subconscious processes** allow us to handle more information and to perform more complex tasks than if we depended entirely on conscious, deliberate thought, and they enable us to perform more than one task simultaneously (Kahneman & Treisman, 1984).

Consider all the automatic routines performed "without thinking," though they might once have required careful, conscious attention: knitting, typing, driving a car, decoding the letters in a word in order to read it. Because of the capacity for automatic processing, people can, with proper training, even learn to perform simultaneously such complex tasks as reading and taking dictation (Hirst, Neisser, & Spelke, 1978). In ordinary life, however, it can be risky to depend on automatic routines when "multitasking." For example, your risk of a car accident increases when you talk on your cell phone while driving, even if you use a hands-free phone (Strayer & Johnston, 2001). Functional MRI scans show that when a person does two tasks at once, the amount of brain activity devoted to each task decreases (Just et al., 2001). Remember this when you try to watch TV and do your homework at the same time!

Nonconscious processes remain outside of awareness. For example, you have no doubt had the odd experience of having a solution to a problem "pop into mind" after you have given up trying to find one. With sudden insight, you see how to solve an equation, assemble a cabinet, or finish a puzzle, without quite knowing how you managed to find the solution. Similarly, people will often say they rely on "intuition"—hunches and gut feelings—rather than conscious reasoning to make judgments and decisions.

Insight and intuition probably involve two stages of mental processing (Bowers et al., 1990). In the first stage, clues in the problem automatically activate certain memories or knowledge, and you begin to see a pattern or structure in the problem, although you cannot yet say what it is. This nonconscious process guides you toward a hunch or a hypothesis. Then, in the second stage, your thinking becomes conscious, and you become aware of a possible solution. This stage may feel like a sudden revelation ("Aha, now I see!"), but considerable nonconscious mental work has already occurred.

Sometimes people solve problems without ever getting to the second stage. For example, some people discover the best strategy for winning a card game without ever being able to consciously identify what they are doing (Bechara et al., 1997). Psychologists call this phenomenon **implicit learning:** You learn a rule or an adaptive behavior, either with or without a conscious intention to do so; but you don't know how you learned it, and you can't state, either to yourself or to others, exactly what it is you have learned (Lieberman, 2000; Stadler & Frensch, 1998).

Mindlessness. Usually, of course, much of our thinking is conscious, but we may not be thinking very *hard.* Like the cashier who cheerfully cashed the phony $200 bill, we may act, speak, and make decisions out of habit, without stopping to

Some well-learned skills do not require much conscious thought and can be performed while doing other things. But multi-tasking can also get you into trouble. It's not a good idea to talk on your cell phone, eat, and try to drive all at the same time.

subconscious processes Mental processes occurring outside of conscious awareness but accessible to consciousness when necessary.

nonconscious processes Mental processes occurring outside of and not available to conscious awareness.

implicit learning Learning that occurs when you acquire knowledge about something without being aware of how you did so and without being able to state exactly what it is you have learned.

analyze what we are doing or why we are doing it. This sort of *mindlessness*—mental inflexibility, inertia, and obliviousness to the present context—keeps people from recognizing when a change in a situation requires a change in behavior (Langer, 1989, 1997).

In one classic study of mindlessness, a researcher approached people as they were about to use a photocopier and made one of three requests: "Excuse me, may I use the Xerox machine?" "Excuse me, may I use the Xerox machine, because I have to make copies?" or "Excuse me, may I use the Xerox machine, because I'm in a rush?" Normally, people will let someone go before them only if the person has a legitimate reason, as in the third request. In this study, however, people also complied when the reason sounded like an authentic explanation but was actually meaningless ("because I have to make copies"). They heard the form of the request, but not its content, and they mindlessly stepped aside (Langer, Blank, & Chanowitz, 1978).

The mindless processing of information has benefits: If we stopped to think twice about everything we did, we would never get anything done ("I'm reaching for my toothbrush; now I'm putting toothpaste on it; now I'm brushing my upper-right molars"). But mindlessness can also lead to errors and mishaps, ranging from the trivial (putting the butter in the dishwasher or locking yourself out of your apartment) to the serious (driving carelessly while on "automatic pilot").

Jerome Kagan (1989) has argued that fully conscious awareness is needed only when we must make a deliberate choice, when events happen that cannot be handled automatically, and when unexpected moods and feelings arise. "Consciousness," he says, "can be likened to the staff of a fire department. Most of the time, it is quietly playing pinochle in the back room; it performs [only] when the alarm sounds." That may be so, but most of us would probably benefit if our mental firefighters paid a little more attention to their jobs. Cognitive psychologists have, therefore, devoted a great deal of study to mindful, conscious thought and the capacity to reason.

Advertisers sometimes count on mindlessness in consumers.

QUICK QUIZ

Stay conscious while taking this quiz.

1. Stuffing your mouth with cotton candy, licking a lollipop, and chewing on a piece of beef jerky are all instances of the _____ *eating*.

2. Which concept is most basic: *furniture, chair,* or *high chair*?

3. Which example of the concept *chair* is prototypical: *high chair, rocking chair, dining-room chair*?

4. In addition to concepts and images, _____, which express a unitary idea, have been suggested as a basic form of mental representation.

5. Peter's mental representation of *Thanksgiving* includes associations (e.g., to turkeys), attitudes ("It's a time to be with relatives"), and expectations ("I'm going to gain weight from all that food"). They are all part of his _____ for the holiday.

6. Zelda discovers that she has dialed her boyfriend's phone number instead of her mother's, as she intended. Her error can be attributed to _____.

Answers:

1. concept 2. chair 3. A plain, straight-backed dining-room chair will be prototypical for most people. 4. propositions 5. cognitive schema 6. mindlessness

WHAT'S AHEAD

- Mentally speaking, why is making a cake, well, a piece of cake?
- Why can't logic solve all our problems?
- What kind of reasoning do juries need to be good at?
- When people say that all opinions and claims are equally valid, what error are they making?

Reasoning Rationally

Reasoning is purposeful mental activity that involves operating on information in order to reach conclusions. Unlike impulsive or nonconscious responding, reasoning requires us to draw specific inferences from observations, facts, or assumptions.

Formal Reasoning: Algorithms and Logic

In *formal reasoning problems*—the kind you might find, say, on an intelligence test or a college entrance exam—the information needed for drawing a conclusion or reaching a solution is specified clearly, and there is a single right (or best) answer.

In some formal problems and well-defined tasks, all you have to do is apply an **algorithm,** a set of procedures guaranteed to produce a solution even if you do not really know how it works. To solve a problem in long division, you apply a series of operations that you learned in elementary school. To make a cake, you apply an algorithm called a *recipe*.

For other formal problems, the rules of formal logic are crucial tools to have in your mental toolbox. One such tool is **deductive reasoning,** which involves drawing conclusions from a set of observations or propositions (*premises*). In deductive reasoning, a conclusion *necessarily* follows from a set of observations or propositions (*premises*):

DEDUCTIVE REASONING

For example, if the premises "All human beings are mortal" and "I am a human being" are true, then the conclusion "I am mortal" must also be true.

We all use deductive reasoning all the time, although many of our premises are implicit rather than explicitly spelled out: "I never have to work on Saturday. Today is Saturday. Therefore, I don't have to work today." But the ability to apply

reasoning The drawing of conclusions or inferences from observations, facts, or assumptions.

algorithm A problem-solving strategy guaranteed to produce a solution even if the user does not know how it works.

deductive reasoning A form of reasoning in which a conclusion follows necessarily from certain premises; if the premises are true, the conclusion must be true.

Zits

Reprinted with special permission of King Features Syndicate.

deductive reasoning to abstract problems that are divorced from everyday life does not come naturally; it depends on experience, culture, and schooling (Segall et al., 1999). And even in everyday life, almost everyone has trouble thinking deductively in some situations. Many people mentally reverse a premise, and this error can have serious consequences, as one of our students recognized when he worried about the effects of confusing "All rapists are men" with "All men are rapists."

Another important form of logical thinking is **inductive reasoning,** in which a conclusion *probably* follows from certain propositions or premises but could conceivably be false:

INDUCTIVE REASONING

Premise true + Premise true + Possibility of discrepant information ▪ ▪ ▪ ➡ Conclusion probably true

People often think of inductive reasoning as the drawing of general conclusions from specific observations, as when you generalize from past experience: "I had three good meals at Joe's restaurant; they sure have great food." But an inductive argument can also have premises that are stated as general statements (Copi & Burgess-Jackson, 1992). If your premises are that all cows are mammals and have lungs, all whales are mammals and have lungs, and all humans are mammals and have lungs, you might reasonably conclude that probably all mammals have lungs. Inductive arguments can also have specific conclusions: If your premises are that most people with season tickets to the concert love music, and that Jeannine has season tickets to the concert, you might conclude that Jeannine probably loves music.

Science depends heavily on inductive reasoning because scientists make careful observations and then draw conclusions that they think are probably true. But in inductive reasoning, no matter how much supporting evidence you gather, it is always possible that new information will turn up to show you are wrong. For example, the three meals you ate at Joe's Restaurant may not be typical—everything else on the menu may be awful. And perhaps Jeannine bought those concert tickets not because she loves music but because she wanted to impress a friend. In science, too, new information may show that previous conclusions were faulty and must therefore be revised or modified.

Informal Reasoning: Heuristics and Dialectical Thinking

Useful as they are, algorithms and logical reasoning cannot solve all of life's problems. In *informal reasoning problems,* there may be no clearly correct solution (Galotti, 1989). Many approaches, viewpoints, or possible solutions may compete, and you may have to decide which one is most reasonable. Further, the information at your disposal may be incomplete, or people may disagree on what the premises should be. Your position on the controversial issue of abortion, for example, will depend on your premises about when meaningful human life begins, what rights an embryo has, and what rights a woman has to control her own body. People on opposing sides of this issue even disagree on how the premises should be phrased because they have different emotional reactions to terms such as "rights," "meaningful life," and "control over one's body."

inductive reasoning A form of reasoning in which the premises provide support for a conclusion, but it is still possible for the conclusion to be false.

Table 9.1	Two Kinds of Reasoning

In formal reasoning, we apply rules of logic to solve well-specified problems. In informal, everyday reasoning, we must solve problems that are less clearly defined. Here are some differences between the two modes of thought:

Formal	Informal
All premises are supplied.	Some premises are implicit, and some are not supplied at all.
There is typically one correct answer.	There are typically several possible answers that vary in quality.
Established methods often exist for solving the problem.	Established procedures of inference that apply to the problem rarely exist.
You usually know when the problem is solved.	It is often unclear whether the current solution is good enough.
The problem typically has limited real-world interest.	The problem is often of personal relevance.
Problems are often solved as a means of achieving other goals.	Problems are solved for their own sake.

Source: Adapted from Galotti, 1989.

Whether you are chess champion Garry Kasparov, pondering his next move in a match against a computer, or just an ordinary person solving ordinary problems, you need to use heuristics, rules of thumb that help you decide on a reasonable strategy.

The differences between formal and informal reasoning problems are summarized in Table 9.1. These two kinds of problems typically call for different approaches. Whereas formal problems can often be solved with an algorithm, informal problems often call for a **heuristic**—a rule of thumb that suggests a course of action without guaranteeing an optimal solution. Anyone who has ever played chess or a card game such as hearts is familiar with heuristics (e.g., "Get rid of high cards first"). In these games, working out all the possible sequences of moves would be impossible. Heuristics are also useful to an investor trying to predict the stock market, a renter trying to decide whether to lease an apartment, a doctor trying to determine the best treatment for a patient, and a factory owner trying to boost production: All are faced with incomplete information on which to base a decision and may therefore resort to rules of thumb that have proved effective in the past.

In thinking about real-life problems, a person must also be able to use **dialectical reasoning,** the process of comparing and evaluating opposing points of view in order to resolve differences. Philosopher Richard Paul (1984) has described dialectical reasoning as movement "up and back between contradictory lines of reasoning, using each to critically cross-examine the other":

heuristic A rule of thumb that suggests a course of action or guides problem solving but does not guarantee an optimal solution.

dialectical reasoning A process in which opposing facts or ideas are weighed and compared, with a view to determining the best solution or resolving differences.

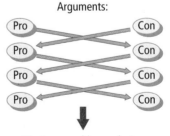

DIALECTAL REASONING
Arguments:

Most reasonable conclusion based on evidence and logic

Dialectical reasoning is what juries are supposed to do to arrive at a verdict: consider arguments for and against the defendant's guilt, point and counterpoint. It is also what voters are supposed to do when thinking about whether the government should raise taxes or lower them, or about the best way to improve public education.

Reflective Judgment

Many adults clearly have trouble thinking dialectically—they take one position, and that's that. To find out precisely how people reason and justify their conclusions, Karen Kitchener and Patricia King interviewed adolescents and adults of all ages and occupations, asking them where they stood on issues such as nuclear power, the safety of food additives, and the objectivity of the news media. Kitchener and King did not care how much people knew about these issues, or even how they felt about them; they just wanted to know how their respondents had reached their conclusions. More specifically, they wanted to know whether people use *reflective judgment* in thinking about everyday problems (King & Kitchener, 1994; Kitchener & King, 1990). Reflective judgment is basically what we have called critical thinking: the ability to question assumptions, evaluate and integrate evidence, relate that evidence to a theory or opinion, consider alternative interpretations, and reach conclusions that can be defended as reasonable or plausible, while standing ready to reassess those conclusions in the face of new information.

The researchers began by providing their interviewees with statements that described opposing viewpoints on various topics. Then the interviewer asked, What do you think about these statements? How did you come to hold that point of view? On what do you base your position? Can you ever know for sure that your position is correct? Why do you suppose disagreement exists about this issue?

Based on the responses, King and Kitchener were able to identify seven cognitive stages on the road to reflective thought, some occurring in childhood and others unfolding throughout adolescence and adulthood. At each stage, people make different assumptions about how things are known and use different ways of justifying or defending their beliefs. Each stage builds on the skills of the prior one and lays a foundation for successive ones.

We will not be concerned here with the details of these stages, but only with their broad outlines. In general, people in the two early, *prereflective stages* assume that a correct answer always exists and that it can be obtained directly through the senses ("I know what I've seen") or from authorities ("They said so on the news"; "That's what I was brought up to believe"). If authorities do not yet have the truth, prereflective thinkers tend to reach conclusions on the basis of what "feels right" at

Prereflective judgment

"I was brought up to believe..."
"I just know what I know."

the moment. They do not distinguish between knowledge and belief, or between belief and evidence, and they do not see any reason for justifying a belief (King & Kitchener, 1994):

Interviewer: Can you ever know for sure that your position [on evolution] is correct?

Respondent: Well, some people believe that we evolved from apes and that's the way they want to believe. But I would never believe that way and nobody could talk me out of the way I believe because I believe the way that it's told in the Bible.

During the three *quasi-reflective stages,* people recognize that some things cannot be known with absolute certainty, but they are not sure how to deal with these situations. They realize that judgments should be supported by reasons, but they pay attention only to evidence that fits what they already believe. They know that there are alternative viewpoints, but they seem to think that because knowledge is uncertain, any judgment about the evidence is purely subjective. Quasi-reflective thinkers will defend a position by saying that "we all have a right to our own opinion," as if all opinions are created equal. Here is the response of a college student who uses quasi-reflective reasoning:

Interviewer: Can you say you will ever know for sure that chemicals [in foods] are safe?

Student: No, I don't think so.

Interviewer: Can you tell me why you'll never know for sure?

Student: Because they test them in little animals, and they haven't really tested them in humans, as far as I know. And I don't think anything is for sure.

Interviewer: When people differ about matters such as this, is it the case that one opinion is right and one is wrong?

Student: No. I think it just depends on how you feel personally because people make their decisions based upon how they feel and what research they've seen. So what one person thinks is right, another person might think is wrong. . . . If I feel that chemicals cause cancer and you feel that food is unsafe without it, your opinion might be right to you and my opinion is right to me.

In the last two stages, a person becomes capable of reflective judgment. He or she understands that although some things can never be known with certainty, some judgments are more valid than others because of their coherence, their fit with the evidence, their usefulness, and so on. People at these stages are willing to consider evidence from a variety of sources and to reason dialectically. At the very highest stage, they are able to defend their conclusions as representing the most complete, plausible, or compelling understanding of an issue, based on currently available evidence. This interview with a graduate student illustrates reflective thinking:

Interviewer: Can you ever say you know for sure that your point of view on chemical additives is correct?

Student: No, I don't think so. . . . [but] I think that we can usually be reasonably certain, given the information we have now, and considering our methodologies.

Interviewer: Is there anything else that contributes to not being able to be sure?

Student: Yes . . . it might be that the research wasn't conducted rigorously enough. In other words, we might have flaws in our data or sample, things like that.

Quasi-reflective judgment

"Knowledge is purely subjective."
"We all have a right to our opinion."

Reflective judgment

"Based on the evidence, I believe…"
"Here are the reasons for my conclusions…"

Interviewer: How then would you identify the "better opinion"?

Student: One that takes as many factors as possible into consideration. I mean one that uses the higher percentage of the data that we have, and perhaps that uses the methodology that has been most reliable.

Interviewer: And how do you come to a conclusion about what the evidence suggests?

Student: I think you have to take a look at the different opinions and studies that are offered by different groups. Maybe some studies offered by the chemical industry, some studies by the government, some private studies. . . . You wouldn't trust, for instance, a study funded by the tobacco industry that proved that cigarette smoking is not harmful . . . you have to try to interpret people's motives and that makes it a more complex soup to try to strain out.

Most people do not show evidence of reflective judgment until their middle or late twenties, if at all. And most undergraduates, regardless of age, tend to score at only Stage 3 during their first year of college. But here's the good news: When students get support for thinking reflectively and have opportunities to practice, their thinking tends to become more complex, sophisticated, and well-grounded (Kitchener et al., 1993). Moreover, higher education gradually moves people closer to reflective judgment: By their senior year, students typically score at Stage 4; most graduate students score at Stage 4 or 5; and many advanced doctoral students perform consistently at Stage 6 (King & Kitchener, 1994). Longitudinal studies show that these differences do not occur only because lower-level thinkers are more likely to drop out along the way.

The gradual development of thinking skills among college students, said one writer (Kroll, 1992), represents an abandonment of "ignorant certainty" in favor of "intelligent confusion." It may not seem so, but this is a big step forward! You can see why, in this book, we emphasize thinking about and evaluating psychological findings, and not just memorizing them.

The mass media do not always encourage reflective judgment.

QUICK QUIZ

Reflect on the answers to these questions.

1. Most of the holiday gifts Mervin bought this year cost more than they did last year, so he concludes that inflation is increasing. Is he using inductive, deductive, or dialectical reasoning?

2. Yvonne is arguing with Henrietta about whether real estate is a better investment than stocks. "You can't convince me," says Yvonne. "I just know I'm right." Yvonne needs training in _____ reasoning.

3. Seymour thinks the media have a liberal political bias, and Sophie thinks they are too conservative. "Well," says Seymour, "I have my truth and you have yours. It's purely subjective." Which of King and Kitchener's levels of thinking describes Seymour's statement?

4. What kind of evidence might resolve the issue that Seymour and Sophie are arguing about?

Answers:

1. inductive 2. dialectical 3. quasi-reflective 4. Researchers might have raters watch a random sample of TV news shows and measure the time devoted to conservative and liberal viewpoints. Or raters could read a random sample of newspaper editorials from all over the country and evaluate the editorials as liberal or conservative. Perhaps you can think of other strategies. However, subjective ratings of *entire* TV programs or newspapers as liberal or conservative might not be as informative because people often perceive only what they want or expect to perceive.

WHAT'S AHEAD▷

- Why do people worry about dying in an airplane crash but ignore dangers that are far more likely?
- How might your physician's choice of words about alternative treatments for your illness affect which one you choose?
- When "Monday morning quarterbacks" say they knew all along who would win Sunday's big game, what bias might they be showing?
- Why will a terrible hazing make you more loyal to the group that hazed you?

Barriers to Reasoning Rationally

Although most people have the capacity to think logically, reason dialectically, and make judgments reflectively, it is abundantly clear that they don't always do so. One obstacle is the need to be right; if your self-esteem depends on being right all the time, you will find it hard to listen with an open mind to competing views. Another obstacle is plain old mental laziness. Many social critics think such laziness is on the rise because television watching has replaced reading. Reading requires you to sit still and follow extended arguments; it gives you the opportunity to examine connections among statements and to spot contradictions, and you can always go back a page and reread something you missed. When you read a book, therefore, you are usually mindfully engaged in its argument. But television programs often provide sound bites instead of fully developed arguments, encouraging viewers to form quick, impulsive opinions instead of carefully considered ones.

Human thought processes are also tripped up by many predictable biases and errors. Psychologists have studied dozens of these cognitive pitfalls; here we describe just a few of them.

Exaggerating the Improbable

One common bias is the inclination to exaggerate the probability of rare events—a bias that helps explain why so many people enter lotteries and buy disaster insurance. There are many reasons for this bias. For example, as we discuss in Chapter 7, evolution has equipped us to fear certain things, such as snakes; but the fear has outlasted the actual danger, so we overestimate the danger. The risk of a rattler sinking its fangs into you in Chicago or New York is pretty low!

People are especially likely to exaggerate the likelihood of a rare event if its consequences are catastrophic. One reason is the **availability heuristic,** the tendency to judge the probability of an event by how easy it is to think of examples or instances (Tversky & Kahneman, 1973). Catastrophes and shocking accidents stand out in our minds and are therefore more "available" mentally than are other kinds of negative events. This is why people overestimate the frequency of deaths from tornadoes and underestimate the frequency of deaths from asthma, which occur 20 times as often but do not make headlines; or why they estimate deaths from accidents and disease to be equally frequent, even though 16 times as many people die each year from disease as from accidents (Lichtenstein et al., 1978). It is why every summer there are panics about "epidemics" of shark bites, even though shark attacks on humans are extremely rare. And the availability heuristic explains why

Many of us overestimate the chances of suffering a shark attack. One reason is the availability heuristic: Shark attacks are very rare, but they are dramatic and easy to visualize and recall.

so many people became terrified of flying after the events of September 11, 2001, even though they continued to take a far higher risk by driving their cars. (In the United States, the lifetime odds of dying in a plane crash are less than 1 in 1 million.)

Because of the availability heuristic, people will also irrationally ignore dangers that are hard to visualize, such as death from cigarette smoking or a rise in skin cancer rates due to depletion of the earth's ozone layer. Parents are often more frightened about real but unlikely threats to their children, such as being kidnapped by a stranger or dying from a routine immunization (both horrible but extremely rare), than they are about more common problems, such as depression, delinquency, and poor grades, or dangers that are far more likely, such as auto accidents or accidental drownings.

availability heuristic The tendency to judge the probability of a type of event by how easy it is to think of examples or instances.

Avoiding Loss

In general, people try to avoid or minimize risks and losses when they make decisions. So when a choice is framed in terms of the risk of losing something, they will respond more cautiously than when the *same* choice is framed in terms of gain. They will, for example, choose a ticket that has a one percent chance of winning a raffle to one that has a 99 percent chance of losing. Or they will rate a condom as effective when they are told it has a 95 percent success rate in protecting against the AIDS virus, but not when they are told it has a 5 percent failure rate—which is exactly the same thing (Linville, Fischer, & Fischhoff, 1992).

Here's another example. Suppose you had to choose between two health programs to combat a disease expected to kill 600 people. Which would you prefer: a program that will definitely save 200 people, or one with a one-third probability of saving all 600 people and a two-thirds probability of saving none? (Problem 1 in Figure 9.1 illustrates this choice.) When asked this question, most people, including

PROBLEM 1

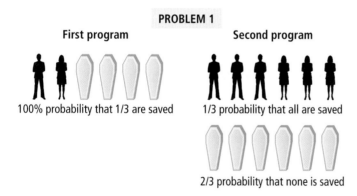

PROBLEM 2

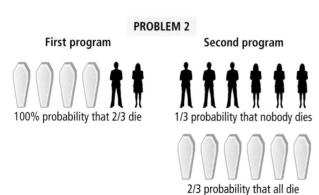

Figure 9.1

A MATTER OF WORDING

The decisions we make depend on how the alternatives are framed. When asked to choose between the two programs in Problem 1, which are described in terms of lives saved, most people choose the first program. When asked to choose between the programs in Problem 2, which are described in terms of lives lost, most people choose the second program. Yet the alternatives in the two problems are actually identical.

physicians, say they would prefer the first program. In other words, they reject the riskier though potentially more rewarding solution in favor of a sure gain. However, people *will* take a risk if they see it as a way to *avoid loss*. Suppose now that you have to choose between a program in which 400 people will definitely die and a program in which there is a one-third probability of nobody dying and a two-thirds probability that all 600 will die. If you think about it, you will see that the alternatives are exactly the same as in the first problem; they are merely worded differently (see Problem 2 in Figure 9.1). Yet, this time most people choose the second solution. They reject risk when they think of the outcome in terms of lives saved, but they accept risk when they think of the outcome in terms of lives lost (Tversky & Kahneman, 1981).

Few of us will have to face a decision involving hundreds of lives, but we may have to choose between different medical treatments for ourselves or a relative. Our decision may be affected by whether the doctor frames the choice in terms of chances of surviving or chances of dying.

Biases Due to Mental Sets

Another barrier to rational thinking is the development of a **mental set,** a tendency to try to solve new problems by using the same heuristics, strategies, and rules that worked in the past on similar problems. Mental sets make learning and problem solving efficient; because of them, we do not have to keep reinventing the wheel. But mental sets are not helpful when a problem calls for fresh insights and methods. They cause us to cling rigidly to the same old assumptions and approaches, blinding us to better or more rapid solutions. (For an illustration of this point, try the Get Involved exercise on this page.)

One general mental set is the tendency to find patterns in events. This tendency is adaptive because it helps us understand and exert some control over what happens in our lives. But it also leads us to see meaningful patterns even when they don't exist. For example, many people with arthritis think that their symptoms follow a pattern dictated by the weather. They suffer more, they say, when the barometric pressure changes, or when the weather is damp or humid. Yet when researchers followed 18 arthritis patients for 15 months, no association whatsoever emerged between

mental set A tendency to solve problems using procedures that worked before on similar problems.

Get Involved

Connect the Dots

Copy the following figure, and see whether you can connect the dots by using no more than four straight lines, without lifting your pencil or pen. A line must pass through each point. Can you do it?

Most people have difficulty with this problem because they have a mental set to interpret the arrangement of dots as a square. Once having done so, they then assume that they can't extend a line beyond the "boundaries" of the square. Now that you know this, you might try again if you haven't yet solved the puzzle. Some possible solutions are given on page 351.

weather conditions and the patients' self-reported pain levels, their ability to function in daily life, or a doctor's evaluation of their joint tenderness (Redelmeier & Tversky, 1996). Did the patients say, "Oh, thank you for pointing out that my belief was unfounded! How incredibly interesting"? No, they adamantly refused to believe the results.

The Hindsight Bias

Would you have predicted, beforehand, that hundreds of dot-com companies would crash and burn in 2001? When people learn the outcome of an event or the answer to a question, they are often sure that they knew it all along. Armed with the wisdom of hindsight, they see the outcome that actually occurred as inevitable, and they overestimate their ability to have predicted what happened. Compared with judgments made *before* an event takes place, their after-the-fact judgments about their own ability to have predicted an event are inflated (Fischhoff, 1975; Hawkins & Hastie, 1990).

This **hindsight bias** is common in political judgments ("I always knew my candidate would win"), medical judgments ("I could have told you that mole was cancerous"), and military opinions ("The generals should have known that Pearl Harbor would be attacked"). And when investors buy a stock and then it goes up in price, they are apt to think, in hindsight, that they were more confident about their purchase at the time they made it than they really were (Louie, 1999).

Like mental sets, the hindsight bias can be adaptive. When we try to make sense of the past, we focus on explaining just one outcome, the one that actually occurred, because explaining outcomes that did not take place can be a waste of time. Then, in light of current knowledge, we reconstruct and misremember our previous judgment (Hoffrage, Hertwig, & Gigerenzer, 2000). As Scott Hawkins and Reid Hastie (1990) wrote, "Hindsight biases represent the dark side of successful learning and judgment." They are the dark side because when we are sure that we knew something "all along," we are also less willing to find out what we need to know in order to make accurate predictions in the future. In medical conferences, for example, when doctors are told what the postmortem findings were for a patient who died, they tend to think the case was easier to diagnose than it actually was ("I would have known it was a brain tumor"), and so they learn less from the case than they should (Dawson et al., 1988).

Perhaps you feel that we are not telling you anything new because you have always known about the hindsight bias. But then, you may just have a hindsight bias about the hindsight bias!

The Confirmation Bias

When people want to make the most accurate judgment possible, they will usually try to consider all of the relevant information. But as we saw in Chapter 2, when they are thinking about an issue they already feel strongly about, they often succumb to the **confirmation bias,** paying attention only to evidence that confirms their belief and finding fault with evidence or arguments that point in a different direction (Edwards & Smith, 1996; Kunda, 1990; Nickerson, 1998). You rarely hear someone say, "Oh, thank you for explaining to me why my lifelong philosophy of child raising (or politics, or investing) is wrong. I'm so grateful for the facts!" The person usually says, "Oh, buzz off, and take your cockamamie ideas with you."

Once you start looking for it, you will see the confirmation bias everywhere. Politicians, for example, brag about economic reports that confirm their party's position and dismiss counterevidence as biased or unimportant. Police officers who are convinced of a suspect's guilt take anything the suspect says or does as evidence that confirms it,

hindsight bias The tendency to overestimate one's ability to have predicted an event once the outcome is known; the "I knew it all along" phenomenon.

confirmation bias The tendency to look for or pay attention only to information that confirms one's own belief.

Get Involved

Confirming the Confirmation Bias

Suppose someone deals out four cards, each with a letter on one side and a number on the other. You can see only one side of each card:

Your job is to find out whether the following rule is true: "If a card has a vowel on one side, then it has an even number on the other side." Which two cards do you need to turn over to find out?

The vast majority of people say they would turn over the E and the 6, but they are wrong. You do need to turn over the E (a vowel), because if the number on the other side is even, it confirms the rule, and if it's odd, the rule is false. However, the card with the 6 tells you nothing. The rule does not say that a card with an even number must always have a vowel on the other side. So it doesn't matter whether the 6 has a vowel or a consonant on the other side. The card you do need to turn over is the 7, because if it has a vowel on the other side, that fact disconfirms the rule.

People do poorly on this problem because they are biased to look for confirming evidence and because they ignore the possibility of disconfirming evidence. Don't feel too bad if you missed it. Most judges, lawyers, and people with doctorates do, too.

including the suspect's claims of innocence. The confirmation bias also affects jury members. In one study, people listened to an audiotaped reenactment of an actual murder trial and then said how they would have voted and why. Instead of considering and weighing possible verdicts against the evidence, many people quickly constructed a story about what had happened and then considered only the evidence that supported their version of events. These same people were the most confident in their decisions and most likely to vote for an extreme verdict (Kuhn, Weinstock, & Flaton, 1994).

The confirmation bias can also affect how you react to what you are learning in school. When students read about scientific findings that dispute one of their own cherished beliefs or that challenge the wisdom of their own actions, they tend to acknowledge but minimize the strengths of the research. In contrast, when a study supports their view, they will acknowledge any flaws (such as a small sample or a reliance on self-reports) but will give these flaws less weight than they would otherwise (Sherman & Kunda, 1989). In thinking critically, it seems, people apply a double standard: They think most critically about results they dislike.

The Need for Cognitive Consistency

THINKING CRITICALLY

Ask Questions

Time and again, doomsday predictions fail. Why don't people who wrongly predict a devastating earthquake or the end of the world feel embarrassed when their forecasts flop?

The confirmation bias enables us to avoid evidence that contradicts our beliefs. But what happens when disconfirming evidence finally smacks us in the face, and we cannot ignore or discount it any longer? For example, as the twentieth century rolled to an end, predictions of doomsday—the end of the world—escalated. Similar predictions have been made throughout history. When these predictions fail, how come we never hear believers say, "Boy, what a fool I was"?

According to the theory of **cognitive dissonance,** people will resolve such conflicts in predictable, though not always obvious, ways (Festinger, 1957). *Dissonance,* the opposite of consistency (*consonance*), is a state of tension that occurs when you simultaneously hold either two cognitions (beliefs, thoughts, attitudes) that are psychologically inconsistent with one another or a belief that is incongruent with your behavior. This tension is uncomfortable, so you will be motivated to reduce it. You may do this by rejecting or modifying one of those inconsistent beliefs, changing your behavior, denying the evidence, or rationalizing:

COGNITIVE DISSONANCE

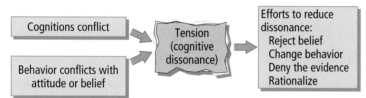

Many years ago, in a famous field study, Leon Festinger and two associates explored people's reactions to failed prophecies by infiltrating a group of people who thought the world would end on December 21 (Festinger, Riecken, & Schachter, 1956). The group's leader, whom the researchers called Marian Keech, promised that the faithful would be picked up by a flying saucer and whisked to safety at midnight on December 20. Many of her followers quit their jobs and spent all their savings, waiting for the end. What would they do or say, Festinger and his colleagues wondered, to reduce the dissonance between "The world is still muddling along on the 21st" and "I predicted the end of the world and sold off all my worldly possessions"?

The researchers predicted that believers who had made no public commitment to the prophecy, who awaited the end of the world by themselves at home, would simply lose their faith. But those who had acted on their conviction by selling their property and waiting with Keech for the spaceship would be in a state of dissonance. They would, said the researchers, have to *increase* their religious belief to avoid the intolerable realization that they had behaved foolishly and others knew it. That is just what happened. At 4:45 A.M., long past the appointed hour of the saucer's arrival, the leader had a new vision. The world had been spared, she said, because of the impressive faith of her little band.

Cognitive-dissonance theory predicts that in more ordinary situations, too, people will resist or rationalize information that conflicts with their existing ideas. For example, if you are a cigarette smoker, your behavior is dissonant with your awareness that smoking causes illness. You might try to reduce the dissonance by trying to quit; by rejecting the evidence that smoking is bad; by persuading yourself that you will quit later on ("after these exams"); by emphasizing the benefits of smoking ("A cigarette helps me relax"); or by deciding that you don't want a long life, anyhow ("It will be shorter, but sweeter").

You are particularly likely to try to reduce dissonance under three conditions (Aronson, 1998; Aronson, Wilson, & Akert, 2002):

1 *When you need to justify a choice or decision that you freely made.* All car dealers know about "buyer's remorse": The second that people buy a car, they worry that they made the wrong decision or spent too much—a phenomenon called **postdecision dissonance.** You may try to resolve this dissonance by deciding that car you chose (or the toaster, or house, or spouse) is really, truly the best in the world.

cognitive dissonance A state of tension that occurs when a person simultaneously holds two cognitions that are psychologically inconsistent, or when a person's belief is incongruent with his or her behavior.

postdecision dissonance In the theory of cognitive dissonance, tension that occurs when you believe you may have made a bad decision.

Figure 9.2

THE JUSTIFICATION OF EFFORT

The more effort you put into reaching a goal, the more highly you are likely to value it. As you can see in the graph on the left, after people listened to a boring group discussion, those who went through a severe initiation to join the group rated it most highly (Aronson & Mills, 1959). In the photo on the right, new cadets at the Virginia Military Institute are forced to crawl through mud until they are covered from head to toe. They'll probably become devoted to the military.

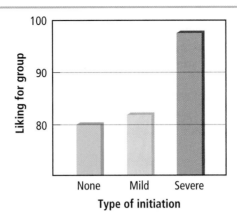

However, if someone else made your decision for you, you will not feel much dissonance if it proves misguided. There is no dissonance between "The Army drafted me; I had no choice about being here" and "I hate basic training."

2 *When you need to justify behavior that conflicts with your view of yourself.* If you have a concept of yourself as honest, cheating will put you in a state of dissonance. To avoid feeling like a hypocrite, you will try to reduce the dissonance by justifying your behavior ("Everyone else does it"; "I had to do it to get into pharmacy school and learn to save lives"). If you see yourself as a kind person and you harm someone, you may reduce your dissonance by blaming the person you have victimized (see Chapter 8) or by finding other self-justifying excuses.

3 *When you need to justify the effort put into a decision or choice.* The harder you work to reach a goal, or the more you suffer for it, the more you will try to convince yourself that you value the goal, even if the goal itself is not so great after all (Aronson & Mills, 1959). This explains why hazing, whether in social clubs or in the military, turns new recruits into loyal members (see Figure 9.2). You might think that people would hate the group that hazed them. But the cognition "I went through a lot of awful stuff to join this group" is dissonant with the cognition "only to find I hate the group." Therefore, people must decide either that the hazing was not so bad or that they really like the group. This mental reevaluation is called the **justification of effort,** and it is one of the most popular methods of reducing dissonance.

Cognitive-dissonance theory has its limitations. Some people are secure enough to own up to their mistakes instead of rationalizing them. Some people do not have a strong need for consistency, so they are less subject than others to feel cognitive dissonance (Cialdini, Trost, & Newsom, 1995). And in some cultures, such as those of East Asia, contradictions and inconsistencies are seen as inevitable in human life, and people often do not feel a great need to resolve dissonance in the way westerners do (Choi, & Nisbett, 2000; Peng & Nisbett, 1999). Still, under certain conditions, the need for cognitive consistency will often lead to irrational, self-defeating decisions and actions.

Overcoming Our Cognitive Biases

justification of effort The tendency of individuals to increase their liking for something that they have worked hard or suffered to attain; a common form of dissonance reduction.

The fact that our decisions and judgments, and the feelings of regret or pleasure that follow, are not always logical or rational has enormous implications for the legal system, business, medicine, government—in fact, in all areas of life. But before you despair about the human ability to think clearly and rationally, we should tell you that the situation is not hopeless. For one thing, people are not equally irrational in all situations. When they are doing things they have some expertise in, or are making decisions that have serious consequences, their cognitive biases often diminish (Smith & Kida, 1991).

Further, once we understand a bias, we may be able to reduce or eliminate it. For example, as we saw, doctors are vulnerable to the hindsight bias if they already know what caused a patient's death. But Hal Arkes and his colleagues (1988) were able to reduce a similar bias in neuropsychologists. The psychologists were given a case study and asked to state one reason why each of three possible diagnoses—alcohol withdrawal, Alzheimer's disease, and brain damage—might have been applicable. This procedure forced the psychologists to consider all the evidence, not just evidence that supported the correct diagnosis. The hindsight bias evaporated, presumably because the psychologists realized that the correct diagnosis had not been so obvious at the time the patient was being treated.

Some people, of course, seem to think more rationally than others all the time; we call them "intelligent." But just what is intelligence, and how can we measure and improve it? We take up that question next.

 9.1

QUICK QUIZ

In hindsight, will you say this quiz was easy?

1. Stu meets a young woman at the student cafeteria. They hit it off, start to see each other regularly, and eventually get married. Says Stu, "I knew that day, when I headed for the cafeteria, that something special was about to happen." What cognitive bias is affecting his thinking, charmingly romantic though it is?

2. In a classic study of cognitive dissonance, students did some boring, repetitive tasks and then had to tell another student, who was waiting to participate in the study, that the work was interesting and fun (Festinger & Carlsmith, 1959). Half the students were offered $20 for telling this lie and the others only $1. Which students who lied decided later on that the tasks had been fun after all?

Answers:

1. the hindsight bias 2. The students who got only $1. They were in a state of dissonance because "The task was as dull as dishwater" is dissonant with "I said I enjoyed it"—and for a mere dollar, at that." Those who got $20 could rationalize that the large sum (which was *really* large) justified the lie.

WHAT'S AHEAD

- Why do psychologists debate whether a single thing called "intelligence" even exists?
- How did the original purpose of intelligence testing change when IQ tests came to America?
- Is it possible to design intelligence tests that are not influenced by culture?
- Why do some psychologists defend traditional intelligence testing and others oppose it?

Measuring Intelligence: The Psychometric Approach

Educator Sylvia Ashton-Warner once called intelligence "the tool to find the truth—a tool that must be kept sharpened." But psychologists disagree on just what this tool is. Some equate it with the ability to reason abstractly, others with

A psychologist gives a student an intelligence test.

the ability to learn and profit from experience in daily life. Some emphasize the ability to think rationally, others the ability to act purposefully. These qualities are all probably part of what most people mean by **intelligence,** but theorists weigh them differently.

One of the longest-running debates in psychology is whether a global quality called "intelligence" even exists. A typical intelligence test asks you to do several things: provide a specific bit of information, notice similarities between objects, solve arithmetic problems, define words, fill in the missing parts of incomplete pictures, arrange pictures in a logical order, arrange blocks to resemble a design, assemble puzzles, use a coding scheme, or judge what behavior would be appropriate in a particular situation. Researchers use a statistical method called **factor analysis** to try to identify which basic abilities underlie performance on the various items. This procedure identifies clusters of correlated items that seem to be measuring some common ability, or factor. Most scientists believe that a general ability, or **g factor,** underlies the specific abilities and talents measured by intelligence tests (Jensen, 1998; Spearman, 1927; Wechsler, 1955). But others dispute the existence of a g factor, on the grounds that a person can excel in some tasks yet do poorly in others (Gould, 1994; Guilford, 1988). Disagreements over how to define intelligence led one early researcher, Edwin G. Boring (1923), to argue that intelligence is "whatever intelligence tests measure."

The traditional approach to intelligence, the **psychometric** approach, focuses on how well people perform on standardized aptitude tests. The tests you take in your courses are called *achievement tests* because they are designed to measure skills and knowledge you have already learned. *Aptitude tests,* in contrast, are designed to measure the ability to acquire skills or knowledge in the future. For example, vocational aptitude tests can help you decide whether you will do better as a mechanic or a musician, and IQ tests do a pretty good job of predicting school performance. But all mental tests are in some sense achievement tests because they assume past learning or experience with particular objects, words, or situations. The difference between achievement and aptitude tests is one of degree and intended use.

intelligence An inferred characteristic of an individual, usually defined as the ability to profit from experience, acquire knowledge, think abstractly, act purposefully, or adapt to changes in the environment.

factor analysis A statistical method for analyzing the intercorrelations among various measures or test scores; clusters of measures or scores that are highly correlated are assumed to measure the same underlying trait, ability, or aptitude (factor).

g factor A general intellectual ability assumed by many theorists to underlie specific mental abilities and talents.

psychometrics The measurement of mental abilities, traits, and processes.

mental age (MA) A measure of mental development expressed in terms of the average mental ability at a given age.

The Invention of IQ Tests

The first widely used intelligence test was devised in 1904, when the French Ministry of Education asked psychologist Alfred Binet (1857–1911) to find a way to identify children who were slow learners so they could be given remedial work. The ministry was reluctant to let teachers identify such children because the teachers might have prejudices about poor children or might assume that shy or disruptive children were mentally impaired. They wanted a more objective approach.

Binet's Brainstorm. Wrestling with the problem, Binet had a great insight: In the classroom, the responses of "dull" children resembled those of ordinary children of younger ages. Bright children, on the other hand, responded like children of older ages. The thing to measure, then, was a child's **mental age (MA),** or level of intellectual development relative to other children's. Then instruction could be tailored to the child's capabilities.

The test devised by Binet and his colleague, Theodosius Simon, measured memory, vocabulary, and perceptual discrimination. Items ranged from those that most young children could do easily to those that only older children could handle, as determined by the testing of large numbers of children. A scoring system developed later by others used a formula in which the child's mental age was divided by the child's chronological age to yield an **intelligence quotient,** or **IQ** (a quotient is the result of division). Thus a child of 8 who performed like the average 10-year-old would have a mental age of 10 and an IQ of 125 (10 divided by 8, times 100). All average children, regardless of age, would have an IQ of 100 because mental age and chronological age would be the same.

This method of figuring IQ had serious flaws, however. At one age, scores might cluster tightly around the average, whereas at another age they might be more dispersed. As a result, the score necessary to be in the top 10 or 20 or 30 percent of your age group varied, depending on your age. Also, the IQ formula did not make sense for adults; a 50-year-old who scores like a 30-year-old does not have low intelligence! Today, therefore, intelligence tests are scored differently. The average is usually set arbitrarily at 100, and tests are constructed so that about two-thirds of all people score between 85 and 115. Individual scores are computed from tables based on established norms. These scores are still informally referred to as "IQs," and they still reflect how a person compares with other people, either children of a particular age or adults in general. At all ages, the distribution of scores approximates a normal (bell-shaped) curve, with scores near the average (mean) most common and very high or very low scores rare (see Figure 9.3).

The IQ Test Comes to America. In the United States, Stanford psychologist Lewis Terman revised Binet's test and established norms for American children. His version, the Stanford–Binet Intelligence Scale, was first published in 1916 and has been updated several times since. (For some sample items, see Table 9.2.) Two decades later, David Wechsler designed another test expressly for adults, which became the Wechsler Adult Intelligence Scale (WAIS). It was followed by the Wechsler Intelligence Scale for Children (WISC). Although the Wechsler tests produce a general IQ score, they also provide specific scores for different kinds of ability. Verbal items test a person's vocabulary, arithmetic abilities, immediate memory span, ability to recognize similarities (e.g., "How are books and movies alike?"),

intelligence quotient (IQ) A measure of intelligence originally computed by dividing a person's mental age by his or her chronological age and multiplying by 100; it is now derived from norms provided for standardized intelligence tests.

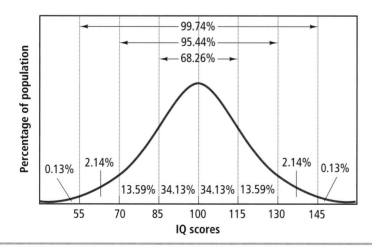

Figure 9.3
EXPECTED DISTRIBUTION OF IQ SCORES

In a large population, IQ scores tend to be distributed on a normal (bell-shaped) curve. On most tests, about 68 percent of all people will score between 85 and 115; about 95 percent will score between 70 and 130; and about 99.7 percent will score between 55 and 145. In any actual sample, however, the distribution will depart somewhat from the theoretical ideal.

Table 9.2	**Sample Items from the Stanford–Binet Intelligence Test, Form L-M**

The older the test-taker is, the more the test requires in the way of verbal comprehension and fluency.

Age	Task
4	Fills in the missing word when asked, "Brother is a boy; sister is a _____." Answers correctly when asked, "Why do we have houses?"
9	Answers correctly when examiner says, "In an old graveyard in Spain they have discovered a small skull which they believe to be that of Christopher Columbus when he was about 10 years old. What is foolish about that?" Examiner presents folded paper; child draws how it will look unfolded.
12	Completes "The streams are dry . . . there has been little rain." Tells what is foolish about statements such as "Bill Jones's feet are so big that he has to put his trousers on over his head."
Adult	Can describe the difference between *misery* and *poverty, character* and *reputation, laziness* and *idleness*. Explains how to measure 3 pints of water with a 5-pint and a 2-pint can.

Source: From Lewis M. Terman & Maud A. Merrill, *Stanford–Binet Intelligence Scale* (1972 norms ed.). Boston: Houghton Mifflin, 1973. (Currently published by The Riverside Publishing Company.) Items are copyright 1916 by Lewis M. Terman, 1937 by Lewis M. Terman and Maud A. Merrill, © 1960, 1973 by The Riverside Publishing Company. Reproduced or adapted by permission of the publisher.

and general knowledge and comprehension (e.g., "Who was Thomas Jefferson?" "Why do people who want a divorce have to go to court?"). Performance items test a range of nonverbal skills (see Figure 9.4).

Binet had emphasized that his test merely *sampled* intelligence and did not measure everything covered by that term. A test score, he said, could be useful, along with other information, for predicting school performance, but it should not be confused with intelligence itself. The tests were designed to be given to each child individually, so the test-giver could see whether a child was ill or nervous, had poor vision, or was not trying. The purpose was to identify children with learning problems, not to rank all children.

But when intelligence testing was brought from France to the United States, its original purpose got lost at sea. In America, IQ tests became widely used not to bring slow learners up to the average, but to categorize people in school and in the armed services according to their presumed "natural ability." The testers overlooked the fact that in America, with its many ethnic groups, people did not all share the same background and experience (Gould, 1996).

Can IQ Tests Be "Culture-Free"?

Intelligence tests developed between World War I and the 1960s for use in schools favored city children over rural ones, middle-class children over poor ones, and white children over nonwhite children. One item, for example, asked whether the Emperor Concerto was written by Beethoven, Mozart, Bach, Brahms, or Mahler. (The answer is Beethoven.) Critics soon complained that the tests did not measure the kinds of knowledge and skills that indicate intelligent behavior in a minority neighborhood or in the hills of Appalachia. They feared that because teachers thought IQ scores revealed the limits of a child's potential, low-scoring children would not get the educational attention or encouragement they needed.

THINKING CRITICALLY

Consider Other Interpretations

When tests find IQ differences between groups of children, many people assume that the children who score lower are inherently less intelligent. What other explanations are possible?

Picture arrangement
(Arrange the panels to make a meaningful story)

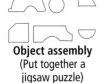

Object assembly
(Put together a
jigsaw puzzle)

Code

Test

Digit symbol
(Using the key at the top, fill in the
appropriate symbol beneath each number)

Picture completion
(Supply the missing
feature)

Block design
(Copy the design shown, using another set of blocks)

Figure 9.4

PERFORMANCE TASKS ON THE WECHSLER TESTS

Nonverbal items such as these are particularly useful for measuring the abilities of those who have poor hearing, are not fluent in the tester's language, have limited education, or resist doing classroom-type problems. A large gap between a person's verbal score and performance score on a Wechsler test sometimes indicates a specific learning problem. (Object assembly, digit symbol, and picture completion adapted from Cronbach, 1990.)

Test-makers responded by trying to construct tests that were *culture-free.* Such tests were usually nonverbal; in some, instructions were even pantomimed. They also tried to design tests that were *culture-fair:* Instead of trying to eliminate the influence of culture, they attempted to include items that incorporate knowledge and skills common to many different cultures. But both approaches were less successful than originally hoped.

One reason for the disappointing results was that cultures differ in the problem-solving strategies they emphasize (Serpell, 1994). In the West, white, middle-class children typically learn to classify things by category—to say that an apple and a peach are similar because they are both fruits, and that a saw and a rake are similar because they are both tools. But children who are not trained in middle-class ways of sorting things may classify objects according to their sensory qualities or functions. For example, they may say that an apple and a peach are similar because they taste good. We think that's a charming and innovative answer, but it is one that test-givers interpret as less intelligent (Miller-Jones, 1989).

It is also hard to eliminate the influence of culture in testing because cultural values and experiences affect a person's attitude toward exams, comfort in the settings required for testing, motivation, rapport with the test-giver, competitiveness, and ease in solving problems independently rather than with others (Anastasi & Urbina, 1997; López, 1995).

Expectations, Stereotypes, and IQ Scores. People's performance on IQ and other tests also depends on their own expectations about how they will do. Those expectations, in turn, are shaped by cultural stereotypes. Stereotypes that portray people of a certain ethnicity, age, gender, or socioeconomic group as unintelligent can actually depress the test performance of people in these groups. You might think that a woman would say, "So sexists think women are dumb at math? I'll show *them*" or that an African-American would say, "So racists believe that blacks aren't as smart as whites? Just give me that exam." But often that is not what happens.

On the contrary, such individuals commonly feel a burden of doubt about their abilities that Claude Steele (1992, 1997) has labeled **stereotype threat.** The threat occurs because they believe that if they do not do well, they will confirm the stereotypes about their group. Their anxiety may then worsen their performance. Or they may cope by "disidentifying" with the test, saying to themselves, in effect, "The outcome of this test has no bearing on how I feel about myself" (Major et al., 1998). As a result, they may not be motivated to do well:

STEREOTYPE THREAT

Stereotype threat has been shown to affect the test performance of many African-Americans, Latinos, low-income people, women, and elderly people—all of whom perform better on tests when they are not feeling self-conscious about themselves as members of negatively stereotyped groups (Aronson & Salinas, 1997; Brown & Josephs, 1999; Croizen & Claire, 1998; Levy, 1996; Steele & Aronson, 1995; Quinn & Spencer, 2001). The decline in test scores occurs both on general tests, such as the Scholastic Assessment Test (SAT), and on tests of specific abilities, such as math or verbal ability. Anything that increases the salience of group stereotypes can increase stereotype threat and affect performance, including taking the test in a setting where you are the only member from your group (Inzlicht & Ben-Zeev, 2000).

Positive stereotypes, in contrast, can *improve* test performance. When Asian women answered a questionnaire about their ethnicity, they then performed better on a math test than did Asian women who did not answer the questionnaire. Apparently, a positive stereotype—"Asians are good at math"—had been activated, and the women tried to live up to it. But when Asian women answered a questionnaire about their *gender* and then took the test, they did worse than the control group. In this case, a negative stereotype—"women are bad at math"—had been activated (Shih, Pittinsky, & Ambady, 1999).

The Dilemma of Differences. What can be done to reduce ethnic differences in IQ test scores, and to reduce the stereotype threat that contributes to them? In theory, it should be possible to establish test norms that are not based on white urban children, by throwing out items on which such children get higher scores than others. A similar strategy was actually used many years ago to eliminate sex differences in IQ (Samelson, 1979). On early tests, girls scored higher than boys at every age. No one was willing to conclude that males were intellectually inferior, so in the 1937 revision of the Stanford–Binet test, Lewis Terman simply deleted the items on which boys had done poorly. Poof! No sex differences.

But few people seem willing to do for cultural differences what Terman did for sex differences, and the reason reveals a dilemma at the heart of intelligence testing. Intelligence tests put some groups of children at a disadvantage, yet they also measure skills and knowledge useful in the classroom. How can educators recognize and accept cultural differences and, at the same time, require students to demonstrate mastery of the skills, knowledge, and attitudes that will help them succeed in school and

stereotype threat A burden of doubt a person feels about his or her performance, due to negative stereotypes about his or her group's abilities.

in the larger society? How can they eliminate bias from tests while preserving the purpose for which the tests were designed?

Beyond the IQ Test

Many social scientists believe that it is important to keep using IQ tests. The tests predict school performance fairly well, and they identify not only the mentally retarded but also gifted students who have not previously considered higher education. To supporters of IQ testing, concealing the effects of cultural disadvantage by rejecting conventional tests is "equivalent to breaking a thermometer because it registers a body temperature of 101" (Anastasi, 1988). When the tests reveal group differences, the pro-test camp maintains, the solution is to give special help to children who need it so they can do better—Binet's original goal. Indeed, many schools are already doing this.

Critics, however, point out that standardized tests tell us nothing about *how* a person goes about answering questions and solving problems. Nor do they explain why people with low scores on IQ tests often behave intelligently in real life—making smart consumer decisions, winning at the racetrack, and making wise personal choices (Ceci, 1996). Some researchers, therefore, have rejected the psychometric approach to the study and measurement of intelligence in favor of a cognitive approach, as we will discuss next.

QUICK QUIZ

What's your Quiz Quotient (QQ)?

1. In a sense, all mental tests are (aptitude/achievement) tests.
2. *True or false:* Culture-fair tests have eliminated group differences that show up on traditional IQ tests.
3. Hilda, who is 66, is about to take an IQ test, but she is worried because she knows that older people are often assumed to have diminished mental abilities. Hilda is being affected by _____.

Answers:

1. achievement 2. false 3. stereotype threat

WHAT'S AHEAD

- **What kind of intelligence allows you to master the unspoken rules for academic success?**
- **What is "EQ" and why is it as important as IQ?**
- **Why do Asian children perform so much better in school than American students do?**

Dissecting Intelligence: The Cognitive Approach

Cognitive psychologists, thinking critically, have questioned prevailing assumptions about the very meaning of intelligence and the best way to measure it. In contrast to the psychometric approach to intelligence, which is concerned with how many answers a person gets right on a test, the *cognitive approach* looks at many kinds of intelligence and emphasizes the *strategies* people use when thinking about a problem and arriving at a solution.

The Triarchic Theory

One well-known cognitive theory is Robert Sternberg's **triarchic theory of intelligence** (1988) (triarchic means "three-part"). It distinguishes three aspects of intelligence:

1 *Componential intelligence* refers to the information-processing strategies you use when you are thinking intelligently about a problem. These mental "components" include recognizing the problem, selecting a method for solving it, mastering and carrying out the strategy, and evaluating the result. This is the type of intelligence tapped by IQ tests.

Componential intelligence requires not only analytic skills but also **metacognition,** the knowledge or awareness of your own cognitive processes and the ability to monitor and control those processes. Metacognition and academic success are correlated, with each influencing the other. First, metacognitive skills help you learn. Students who are weak in metacognition fail to notice when a passage in a textbook is difficult, and they do not always realize that they haven't understood what they've been reading. As a result, they spend too little time on difficult material and too much time on material they already know (Nelson & Leonesio, 1988). In contrast, students who are strong in metacognition check their comprehension by restating what they have read, backtracking when necessary, and questioning what they are reading, so they learn better (Bereiter & Bird, 1985).

Second, the same type of intelligence that enhances academic performance can also help you develop metacognitive skills. Students with poor academic skills typically don't realize how little they know; they think they're doing fine. In one study, students who were only in the 12th percentile on a test of logical reasoning guessed that they had scored in the 62nd percentile and thought that their overall skills in logic put them in the 65th percentile. They were blissfully ignorant not only of their problems with logic but also of their own ignorance (Kruger & Dunning, 1999, 2002). In contrast, people with strong academic skills tend to be more realistic, and often they even slightly underestimate their abilities. As Thomas Jefferson said, "He who knows best knows how little he knows."

2 *Experiential intelligence* refers to your creativity in transferring skills to new situations. People with experiential intelligence cope well with novelty and learn quickly to make new tasks automatic; those who are lacking in this area perform well only under a narrow set of circumstances. For example, a student may do well in school, where assignments have specific due dates and feedback is immediate, but be less successful after graduation if her job requires her to set her own deadlines and her employer doesn't tell her how she is doing.

3 *Contextual intelligence* refers to the practical application of intelligence, which requires you to take into account the different contexts in which you find yourself. If you are strong in contextual intelligence, you know when to adapt to the environment (you are in a dangerous neighborhood, so you become more vigilant). You know when to change environments (you had planned to be a teacher but discover that you dislike working with kids, so you switch to accounting). And you know when to fix the situation (your marriage is rocky, so you and your spouse go for counseling).

Contextual knowledge allows you to acquire **tacit knowledge**—practical, action-oriented strategies for achieving your goals that usually are not formally taught but must instead be inferred by observing others (Sternberg et al., 1995).

triarchic theory of intelligence A theory of intelligence that emphasizes information-processing strategies, the ability to creatively transfer skills to new situations, and the practical application of intelligence.

metacognition The knowledge or awareness of one's own cognitive processes.

tacit knowledge Strategies for success that are not explicitly taught but that instead must be inferred.

In studies of college professors, business managers, and salespeople, tacit knowledge and practical intelligence are strong predictors of effectiveness on the job (Sternberg et al., 2000). In college students, tacit knowledge about how to be a good student actually predicts academic success as well as entrance exams do (Sternberg & Wagner, 1989).

Domains of Intelligence

Other psychologists, too, are expanding our understanding of what it means to be intelligent. They point out that someone who is intelligent in one area, or domain, is not necessarily intelligent in all others. A Nobel Prize winner in physics may be helpless when it comes to making up a budget; a biologist who is cautious and careful in his own field may uncritically accept unscientific claims about human psychology (Ceci, 1996; Shermer, 1997).

Howard Gardner (1983, 1993, 1995) has proposed that the domains of intelligence be expanded to include musical aptitude, kinesthetic intelligence (the bodily grace and physical self-awareness of athletes and dancers), and the capacity for insight into oneself, others, or the natural world. These talents, Gardner argues, are relatively independent. They may even have separate neural structures. People with brain damage often lose one domain without losing their competence in the others. And some autistic and retarded individuals with *savant syndrome* (*savant* means "learned" in French) have exceptional talents in one area, such as music, art, or rapid mathematical computation, despite poor functioning in all others.

Two of Gardner's domains, understanding yourself and understanding others, overlap with what some psychologists call **emotional intelligence:** the ability to identify your own and other people's emotions accurately, express your emotions clearly, and regulate emotions in yourself and others (Goleman, 1995; Mayer & Salovey,

Some theorists who argue for an expanded definition of intelligence would say that a surveyor has spatial intelligence, a compassionate friend has emotional intelligence, and a singer has musical intelligence.

People with emotional intelligence are skilled at reading nonverbal emotional cues. Which of these boys do you think feels the most confident and relaxed, which one is shyest, and which feels most anxious? What cues are you using to answer?

emotional intelligence The ability to identify your own and other people's emotions accurately, express your emotions clearly, and regulate emotions in yourself and others.

1997). People with high emotional intelligence—popularly known as "EQ"—use their emotions to motivate themselves, to spur creative thinking, and to deal empathically with others. People who are low in emotional intelligence are often unable to identify their own emotions; they may insist that they are not depressed when a relationship ends, for example, but meanwhile they start drinking too much, become extremely irritable, and stop going out with friends. They express emotions inappropriately, such as by acting violently or impulsively when they are angry or worried. And they misread nonverbal signals from others; for example, they will give a long-winded account of all their problems even when the listener is obviously bored.

Studies of brain-damaged adults suggest a biological basis for emotional intelligence. Neuroscientist Antonio Damasio (1994) has studied patients with prefrontal-lobe damage that makes them incapable of experiencing strong feelings. Although they score in the normal range on conventional mental tests, these patients persistently make "dumb," irrational decisions in their lives because they cannot assign values to different options based on their own emotional reactions and cannot read emotional cues from others. As we will see again in Chapter 11, feeling and thinking are not always incompatible processes, as many people assume; in fact, one requires the other.

Thinking Critically About Intelligence(s)

Not everyone is enthusiastic about the proliferation of new "intelligences." Some argue that emotional intelligence is not a special cognitive ability but a collection of personality traits, such as empathy and extroversion, and nothing is gained by giving "EQ" its own trendy label (Davies, Stankov, & Roberts, 1998). Others maintain that abilities such as Gardner's musical and kinesthetic intelligences are better thought of as talents, or else the very concept of intelligence loses all meaning. What is to prevent someone from adding "handicraft intelligence" or "financial intelligence" or "farming intelligence"?

Broadening the notion of intelligence, however, has been extremely useful, for several reasons. It has forced us to go beyond "g" and think more critically about what we mean by intelligence. It has inspired research on a promising new type of mental testing, in which the test-giver provides ongoing feedback to the test-taker so that the person can learn from the experience and improve his or her performance (Grigorenko & Sternberg, 1998). It has led to a focus on teaching children practical strategies for improving their abilities in reading, writing, doing homework, and taking tests. For example, children may learn to manage their time so they don't procrastinate, and study differently for multiple-choice versus essay exams (Sternberg et al., 1995). Most important, new approaches to intelligence encourage us to overcome the mental set of assuming that the only kind of intelligence necessary for a successful life is the kind captured by IQ tests.

For a summary of the differences between the psychometric and cognitive approaches, see Review 9.1.

Motivation and Intellectual Success

Even with a high IQ, emotional intelligence, and practical know-how, you still might get nowhere at all. Talent, unlike cream, does not inevitably rise to the top; success also depends on drive and determination.

The Lesson of the Termites. Consider a finding from one of the longest-running psychological studies ever conducted. Since 1921, researchers have studied a group of more than 1,500 people with childhood IQ scores in the top 1 percent of the distribution. As boys and girls, these people were nicknamed "Termites," after Lewis Terman, who originally directed the research. The Termites started out bright, physically healthy, sociable, and well adjusted. As they entered adulthood, most became successful in the traditional ways of the times: men in careers and women as homemakers (Sears & Barbee, 1977; Terman & Oden, 1959). However, some gifted men failed to live up to their early promise, dropping out of school or

REVIEW 9.1	THE PSYCHOMETRIC AND COGNITIVE APPROACHES TO INTELLIGENCE, COMPARED	
	Psychometric	**Cognitive**
Main focus	How well people perform on standardized tests	Strategies people use when solving problems
What intelligence is	A general intellectual ability captured by IQ scores; or a range of specific verbal and nonverbal abilities	Many different skills and talents in addition to intellectual ones
Deals with emotional intelligence?	No	Yes
Deals with practical intelligence?	No	Yes
Uses well-validated standardized tests?	Yes	Tests currently being developed

drifting into low-level work. When the researchers compared the 100 most successful men in the Stanford study with the 100 least successful, they found that motivation made the difference. The successful men were ambitious, were socially active, had many interests, and were encouraged by their parents. The least successful drifted casually through life. There was *no* average difference in IQ between the two groups.

Cultural Attitudes and Motivation. Motivation to work hard at intellectual tasks depends in turn on your attitudes about intelligence and achievement. Cultural values strongly influence these beliefs and feelings.

For many years, Harold Stevenson and his colleagues have been studying attitudes toward achievement in Asia and the United States. Since 1980 they have been comparing large samples of grade-school children, parents, and teachers in Minneapolis, Chicago, Sendai (Japan), Taipei (Taiwan), and Beijing (Stevenson & Stigler, 1992; Stevenson, Chen, & Lee, 1993). Their results have much to teach us about the cultivation of intellect.

In 1980, the Asian children far outperformed the American children on a broad battery of mathematical and reading tests. On computations and word problems, there was virtually no overlap between schools, with the lowest-scoring Beijing schools doing better than the highest-scoring Chicago schools. (A similar gap occurred in reading scores.) By 1990, the gulf between the Asian and American children had grown even greater. Only 4 percent of the Chinese children and 10 percent of the Japanese children had math scores as low as those of the *average* American child. These differences could not be accounted for by educational resources: The Chinese had worse facilities and larger classes than the Americans, and on average, the Chinese parents were poorer and less educated than the American parents. Nor did it have anything to do with intellectual abilities in general; the American children were just as knowledgeable and capable as the Asian children on tests of general information.

But this research found that Asians and Americans are worlds apart in their attitudes, expectations, and efforts:

▶ *Beliefs about intelligence.* Asian parents, teachers, and children are far more likely than Americans to believe that mathematical ability results from studying (see Figure 9.5). Americans tend to think such ability is innate: If you "have it," you don't have to work hard, and if you don't have it, there's no point in trying.

> ▶ *Standards.* American parents have far lower standards for their children's performance; they are satisfied with scores barely above average on a 100-point test. In contrast, Chinese and Japanese parents are happy only with very high scores.
>
> ▶ *Values.* American students do not value education as much as Asian students do, and they are more complacent about mediocre work. When asked what they would wish for if a wizard could give them anything they wanted, more than 60 percent of the Chinese fifth-graders named something related to their education. Can you guess what the American children wanted? A majority said money or possessions.

When it comes to intellect, then, it's not just what you've got that counts, but what you do with it. Complacency, fatalism, or low standards can prevent people from recognizing what they don't know and can reduce their efforts to learn.

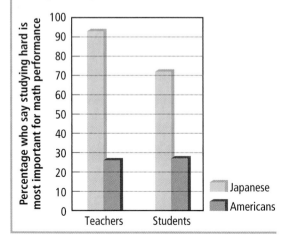

Figure 9.5

WHAT'S THE SECRET OF MATH SUCCESS?

Japanese school teachers and students are much more likely than their American counterparts to believe that the secret to doing well in math is working hard. Americans tend to think that you either have mathematical intelligence or you don't.

QUICK QUIZ

Are you feeling complacent about your quiz performance?

1. What goals do cognitive theories of intelligence have that psychometric theories do not?

2. Logan understands the material in his statistics class, but on tests, he spends the entire period on the most difficult problems and never even gets to the problems he can solve easily. According to the triarchic theory of intelligence, which aspect of intelligence does he need to improve?

3. Tracy does not have an unusually high IQ, but at work she is quickly promoted because she knows how to set priorities, communicate with management, and make others feel valued. Tracy has _____ knowledge about how to succeed on the job.

4. What is wrong with defining intelligence as "whatever intelligence tests measure"?

Answers:

1. to understand people's strategies for solving problems and use this information to improve mental performance 2. componential intelligence (which includes metacognition) 3. tacit 4. This definition implies that a low score must be entirely the scorer's fault rather than the test's. But the test-taker may be intelligent in ways that the test fails to measure, and the test may be measuring traits other than intelligence. The definition is also circular: How do we know someone is intelligent? Because he or she scored high on an intelligence test. Why did the person score high? Because the person is intelligent!

WHAT'S AHEAD ▷

● **Why do some researchers think that animals can think?**

● **People love to talk to their pets—but can their pets learn to talk back?**

Animal Minds

A green heron swipes some bread from a picnicker's table and scatters the crumbs on a nearby stream. When a minnow rises to the bait, the heron strikes, swallowing its prey before you can say "hook, line, and sinker." A sea otter, floating calmly on its back, bangs a mussel shell against a stone that is resting on its stomach. When the shell cracks apart, the otter devours the tasty morsel inside, tucks the stone under its flipper, and dives for another shell, which it will open in the same way. Incidents such as these, summarized in Donald Griffin's *Animal Minds* (1992), have convinced some biologists, psychologists, and ethologists that we are not the only animals with cognitive abilities—that "dumb beasts" are far smarter than we may think. Many best-selling books have described the amazingly humanlike emotions and "thoughts" of animals. But how humanlike are they?

How smart is this otter?

Animal Intelligence

In the 1920s, Wolfgang Köhler (1925) put chimpanzees in situations in which some tempting bananas were just out of reach, then watched to see what the apes would do. Most did nothing, but a few turned out to be quite clever. If the bananas were outside the cage, the animal might pull them in with a stick. If they were hanging overhead, and there were boxes in the cage, the chimpanzee might pile up the boxes and climb on top of them to reach the fruit. Often the solution came after the animal had been sitting quietly for a while. It appeared as though the chimp had been thinking about the problem and was struck by a sudden insight.

In an early study of animal intelligence, Sultan, a talented chimpanzee studied by Wolfgang Köhler, was able to figure out how to reach a cluster of bananas by stacking some boxes and climbing on top of them.

Behaviorists, as you might imagine, felt that this seemingly impressive behavior could be accounted for perfectly well by the standard principles of operant learning (see Chapter 7). Because of their influence, for years any scientist who claimed that animals could think was likely to get laughed at, or worse. Today, however, the study of animal intelligence is enjoying a resurgence, especially in the interdisciplinary field of **cognitive ethology.** (Ethology is the study of animal behavior, especially in natural environments.) Cognitive ethologists argue that some animals can anticipate future events, make plans, and coordinate their activities with those of their comrades—that they are, indeed, capable of thought.

When we think about animal cognition, we must be careful, because even complex behavior might be genetically prewired and automatic. The assassin bug of South America catches termites by gluing nest material on its back as camouflage, but it is hard to imagine how the bug's tiny dab of brain tissue could enable it to plan this strategy consciously. Moreover, an animal could be aware of its environment and know some things without knowing that it knows and without being able to think about its own thoughts as human beings do—in short, without having metacognition (Budiansky, 1998; Hauser, 2000).

Yet explanations of animal behavior that leave out any sort of consciousness at all and that attribute animals' actions entirely to instinct do not seem to account for some of the amazing things that animals can do. Like the otter who uses a stone to crack mussel shells, many animals are capable of using objects in the natural environment as rudimentary tools. For example, chimpanzees' mothers occasionally show their young how to use stone tools to open hard nuts (Boesch, 1991).

In the laboratory, too, nonhuman primates have accomplished some surprising things. In one study, chimpanzees compared two pairs of food wells containing chocolate chips. One pair might contain, say, five chips and three chips, the other four chips and three chips. Allowed to choose which pair they wanted, the chimps almost always chose the one with the higher combined total, showing some sort of summing ability (Rumbaugh, Savage-Rumbaugh, & Pate, 1988). Other chimps have learned to use numerals to label quantities of items and simple sums (Boysen & Berntson, 1989; Washburn & Rumbaugh, 1991). Two rhesus monkeys, Rosencrantz and Macduff, learned to order groups of one to four symbols according to the number of symbols in each group (e.g., one square, two trees, three ovals, four flowers).

cognitive ethology The study of cognitive processes in nonhuman animals.

Later, when presented with pairs of symbol groups containing five to nine symbols, they were able to point to the group with more symbols, without any further training (Brannon & Terrace, 1998) (see Figure 9.6). This is not exactly algebra, but it does suggest that monkeys have a rudimentary sense of number.

One of the hottest questions about animal cognition is whether any animals besides human beings have a **theory of mind:** a system of beliefs about the way one's own mind and the minds of others work, and an understanding of how thoughts and feelings affect behavior. A theory of mind enables you to draw conclusions about the intentions, feelings, and beliefs of others; empathize with others ("What would I experience if I were in the other person's position?"); recognize when someone is lying; engage in pretense yourself; pretend an object is something else; recognize yourself in a mirror; know when others can or cannot see you; and devise strategies for reaching a goal. In human beings, a theory of mind starts to develop in the second year and is clearly present by about age 3 or 4 (see Chapter 14).

Evidence is accumulating that the great apes—chimpanzees, gorillas, and orangutans—have at least some abilities that depend on a theory of mind (de Waal, 2001a; Suddendorf & Whiten, 2001). For example, if you put a mark on an ape's body in a place that is not visible to the animal, it may try to find the mark when looking in a mirror, suggesting self-recognition. Scientists have seen chimpanzees console other chimps who are in distress, use deceptive tactics when competing for food, and draw attention to an object by pointing, all of which imply that at least some chimps can grasp what is going on in another chimps' mind. Even nonprimates may have some of these abilities; some dolphins seem to pass the "mirror test" for self-recognition (Reiss & Marino, 2001). But scientists are still divided about how convincing such findings are (Povinelli, 2000).

Animals and Language

A primary ingredient of human cognition is *language,* the ability to combine elements that are themselves meaningless into an infinite number of utterances that convey meaning. Language is often regarded as the last bastion of human uniqueness, a result of evolutionary forces that produced our species (see Chapter 3). Do animals have anything comparable? Many people have wished they could ask their pet what it's like to be a dog, or a cat, or a horse. If only animals could speak!

To qualify as a language, a communication system must meet certain criteria (Hockett, 1960). It must use combinations of sounds, gestures, or symbols that are *meaningful,* not random. It must permit *displacement,* communication about objects and events that are not present here and now but rather are displaced in time or space; merely pointing to things is not language. And it must have a grammar (syntax) that permits *productivity,* the ability to produce and comprehend an infinite number of new utterances.

By these criteria, no nonhuman species has its own language. Of course, animals do communicate, using gestures, body postures, facial expressions, vocalizations, and odors. And some of these signals have highly specific meanings. For example, vervet monkeys seem to have separate calls to warn about leopards versus eagles versus snakes (Cheney & Seyfarth, 1985). But vervets cannot combine these sounds to produce entirely novel utterances, as in "Look out, Harry, that eagle-eyed leopard is a real snake-in-the-grass."

Perhaps, however, some animals could acquire language if they got a little help from their human friends. Dozens of researchers have tried to provide chimpanzees with just such help. Because the vocal tract of an ape does not permit speech, most

Figure 9.6
CAN MONKEYS COUNT?

Two rhesus monkeys learned to put pictures, each consisting of 1 to 4 elements, in the correct order. Later, when shown pairs of pictures selected from those above, the monkeys were able to touch the pictures in the correct order, even when they had not seen the quantities before (e.g., 5 before 7).

theory of mind A system of beliefs about the way ones' own mind and the minds of others work, and of how individuals are affected by their beliefs and feelings.

"It's always 'Sit,' 'Stay,' 'Heel'—never 'Think,' 'Innovate,' 'Be yourself.'"

THINKING CRITICALLY

Avoid Emotional Reasoning

It's easy to love apes who use symbols to apologize or lie. But emotion can sometimes get in the way of objectivity. What does research show about the ability of animals to use language?

researchers have tried innovative approaches that rely on gestures or visual symbols. In one project, chimpanzees learned to use as words geometric plastic shapes arranged on a magnetic board (Premack & Premack, 1983). In another, they learned to punch symbols on a computer-monitored keyboard (Rumbaugh, 1977). In yet another, they learned hundreds of signs from American Sign Language (ASL) (Fouts & Rigby, 1977; Gardner & Gardner, 1969).

All these animals learned to follow instructions, answer questions, and make requests. More important, they combined individual signs or symbols into longer utterances that they had never seen before. Before long, accounts of the apes' abilities were causing quite a stir. The animals were apparently using their newfound skills to apologize for being disobedient, scold their trainers, and even talk to themselves. Koko, a lowland gorilla, reportedly used signs to say that she felt happy or sad, to refer to past and future events, to mourn for her dead pet kitten, and to convey her yearning for a baby. She even lied on occasion, when she did something naughty (Patterson & Linden, 1981).

The animals in these studies were lovable, the findings appealing—so it was easy for emotional reasoning to prevail over critical thinking. But soon skeptics and some of the researchers themselves began to point out serious problems (Seidenberg & Petitto, 1979; Terrace, 1985). In their desire to talk to the animals and their affection for their primate friends, researchers had not always been objective. They had overinterpreted the animal's utterances, reading all sorts of meanings and intentions into a single sign or symbol, and unwittingly giving nonverbal cues that might enable the apes to respond correctly. Further, the animals appeared to be stringing signs and symbols together in no particular order, instead of using grammatical rules to produce novel utterances; "Me eat banana" seemed to be no different for them than "Banana eat me."

These problems still plague some projects. In 1998, America Online sponsored a live chat with Koko. Her trainer, Francine Patterson, used sign language to relay questions from the audience to the gorilla. Critics felt Patterson read much too much into Koko's "replies":

Question: Koko are you going to have a baby in the future?

Koko: Pink.

Patterson: Koko was commenting on the color of my shirt. We had an earlier discussion about colors today.

Q: Do you like to chat with people?

Koko: Fine nipple.

Patterson: Nipple rhymes with people, she doesn't sign people per se, she was trying to do a "sounds like . . ."

Q: Koko, do you feel love from the humans who have raised you?

Koko: Lips, apple give me.

Patterson: People give her favorite foods.

Today, however, most researchers have taken the criticisms to heart and have greatly improved their procedures. They have shown that with careful training, chimps can indeed acquire the ability to use symbols to refer to objects. Some animals have even used signs spontaneously to converse with each other, suggesting that they are not merely imitating or trying to get a reward (Van Cantfort & Rimpau, 1982).

Bonobos (a type of ape) are especially adept at language. One bonobo named Kanzi has learned to understand English words, short sentences, and keyboard

Kanzi, a bonobo with the most advanced linguistic skills yet acquired by a nonhuman primate, answers questions and makes requests by punching symbols on a specially designed computer keyboard. He also understands short English sentences. He is shown here with researcher Sue Savage-Rumbaugh.

symbols *without formal training* (Savage-Rumbaugh & Lewin, 1994; Savage-Rumbaugh, Shanker, & Taylor, 1998). Kanzi responds correctly to commands such as "Put the key in the refrigerator" and "Go get the ball that is outdoors," even when he has never heard the words combined in that particular way before. He picked up language as children do—by observing others using it, and through normal social interaction. He has also learned, with training, to manipulate keyboard symbols to request favorite foods or activities (games, TV, visits to friends) and to announce his intentions.

You do not even have to be a primate to acquire some aspects of language. In Hawaii, Louis Herman and his colleagues have taught dolphins to respond to requests made in two artificial languages, one consisting of computer-generated whistles and another of hand and arm gestures (Herman, 1987; Herman & Morrel-Samuels, 1996; Herman, Kuczaj, & Holder, 1993). To interpret a request correctly, the dolphins must take into account both the meaning of the individual symbols in a string of whistles or gestures and the order of the symbols (syntax). For example, they must understand the difference between "To left Frisbee, right surfboard take" and "To right surfboard, left Frisbee take."

In another fascinating project, Irene Pepperberg (2000) has been working since the late 1970s with an African gray parrot named Alex, teaching him to count, classify, and compare objects by vocalizing English words. Alex is no birdbrain, even though his brain is the size of a walnut; he shows evidence of both linguistic and cognitive ability. When he is shown up to six items and is asked how many there are, he responds with spoken (squawked?) English phrases, such as "two cork(s)" or "four key(s)." He can even respond correctly to questions about items specified on two or three dimensions, as in "How many blue key(s)?" or "What matter [material] is orange and three-cornered?" Alex also makes requests ("Want pasta") and answers simple questions about objects ("What color [is this]?" "Which is bigger?"). When presented with a blue cork and a blue key and asked "What's the same?" he will correctly respond "Color." He actually scores slightly better with new objects than with familiar ones, suggesting that he is not merely "parroting" a set of stock phrases. In informal interactions, Alex tells Pepperberg, "I love you," "I'm sorry," and "Calm down." And his education continues: He is learning the sounds of the alphabet!

Alex is one bright bird—but how bright? His abilities raise intriguing questions about the intelligence of animals and their capacity for specific aspects of language.

Thinking About the Thinking of Animals

These results on animal language and cognition are impressive, but scientists are still divided over just what the animals in these studies are doing. Do they have true language? Are they "thinking," in human terms? How intelligent are they?

On one side are those who worry about *anthropomorphism,* the tendency to falsely attribute human qualities to nonhuman beings. They tell the story of Clever Hans, a "wonder horse" at the turn of the century, who was said to possess mathematical and other abilities (Spitz, 1997). For example, Clever Hans would answer math problems by stamping his hoof the appropriate number of times. But a little careful experimentation by a psychologist, Oskar Pfungst (1911/1965), revealed that when Hans was prevented from seeing his questioners, his "powers" left him. It seems that questioners were staring at the horse's feet and leaning forward expectantly after stating the problem, then lifting their eyes and relaxing as soon as he completed the right number of taps. Clever Hans was indeed clever, but not at math or other human skills. He was merely responding to nonverbal signals that people were inadvertently providing. (Perhaps he had a high EQ.)

Clever Hans in action.

On the other side are those who warn against *anthropodenial*—the tendency to think, mistakenly, that human beings have nothing in common with other animals, who are, after all, our evolutionary cousins (de Waal, 1997, 2001a; Fouts, 1997). The need to see our own species as unique, they say, may keep us from recognizing that other species, too, have cognitive abilities, even if not as intricate as our own. Those who take this position point out that most modern researchers have gone to great lengths to avoid the Clever Hans problem.

The outcome of this debate is bound to have an effect on how we view ourselves and our place among other species. As Donald Griffin (1992) wrote, "Cognitive ethology presents us with one of the supreme scientific challenges of our times, and it calls for our best efforts of critical and imaginative investigation." Perhaps, as cognitive ethologist Marc Hauser (2000) suggests, we can find a way to study and respect animal minds and emotions without assuming sentimentally that they are just like ours.

QUICK QUIZ

Regrettably, your pet beagle can't help you answer these questions.

1. Which of the following abilities have primates demonstrated, either in the natural environment or the laboratory? (a) the use of objects as simple tools; (b) the summing of quantities; (c) the use of symbols to make requests; (d) an understanding of short English sentences.

2. A honeybee performs a little dance that communicates to other bees the direction and distance of food. Because the bee can "talk" about something that is located elsewhere, its communication system shows _____. But because the bee can create only utterances that are genetically wired into its repertoire, its communication system lacks _____.

3. Barnaby thinks his pet snake Curly is harboring angry thoughts about him because Curly has been standoffish and won't curl around his neck anymore. What error is Barnaby making?

Answers:

1. all of them 2. displacement, productivity 3. anthropomorphism

We human beings are used to thinking of ourselves as the smartest species around because of our astounding ability to adapt to change, find novel solutions to problems, invent endless new gizmos, and use language to create everything from puns to poetry. Yet, as this chapter has shown, we are not quite as wise in our thinking as we might think. We can, however, boast of one crowning accomplishment: *We are the only species that tries to understand its own misunderstandings.* We want to know what we don't know; we are motivated to overcome our mental shortcomings. Our uniquely human capacity for self-examination is probably the best reason to remain optimistic about our cognitive abilities.

Taking Psychology with You

BECOMING MORE CREATIVE

Take a few moments to answer these items from the Remote Associates Test. Your task is to come up with a fourth word that is associated with each item in a set of three words (Mednick, 1962). For example, an appropriate answer for the set *news-clip-wall* is *paper.* Got the idea? Now try these (the answers are given on page 351):

1. piggy-green-lash

2. surprise-political-favor

3. mark-shelf-telephone

4. stick-maker-tennis

5. cream-cottage-cloth

Associating elements in new ways by finding a common connection among them is an important component of creativity. People who are uncreative rely on *convergent thinking,* following a particular set of steps that they think will converge on one correct solution. Once they have solved a problem, they tend to develop a mental set and approach future problems the same way.

Creative people, in contrast, exercise *divergent thinking;* instead of stubbornly sticking to one tried-and-true path, they explore side alleys and generate several possible solutions. They come up with new hypotheses, imagine other interpretations, and look for connections that are not immediately obvious. They can think of many uses for familiar objects, such as, say, unneeded CD-ROM disks (which can be used as mobiles, Christmas tree decorations, coasters, . . .). Creative thinking can be found in the auto mechanic who invents a new tool, the mother who designs and makes her children's clothes, or the office manager who devises a clever way to streamline work flow (Richards, 1991).

A high IQ does not guarantee creativity. Personality characteristics seem more important, especially these three (Helson, Roberts, & Agronick, 1995; MacKinnon, 1968; McCrae, 1987; Schank, 1988):

1. *Nonconformity.* Creative individuals are not overly concerned about what others think of them. They are willing to risk ridicule by proposing ideas that may initially appear foolish or off the mark. Geneticist Barbara McClintock's research was ignored or belittled by many for nearly 30 years. But she was sure she could show how genes move around and produce sudden changes in heredity. In 1983, McClintock won the Nobel Prize. The judges called her work the second greatest genetic discovery of our time, after the discovery of the structure of DNA.

2. *Curiosity.* Creative people are open to new experiences; they notice when reality contradicts expectations, and they are curious about the reason. For example, Wilhelm Roentgen, a German physicist, was studying cathode rays when he noticed a strange glow on one of his screens. Other people had seen the glow, but they ignored it because it didn't jibe with their understanding of cathode rays. Roentgen studied the glow, found it to be a new kind of radiation, and thus discovered x-rays (Briggs, 1984).

3. *Persistence.* After that imaginary lightbulb goes on over your head, you still have to work hard to make the illumination last. Or, as Thomas Edison, who invented the real lightbulb, reportedly put it, "Genius is one-tenth inspiration and nine-tenths perspiration." No invention or work of art springs forth full-blown from a person's head. There are many false starts and painful revisions along the way.

In addition to traits that foster creativity, there are *circumstances* that do. Creativity flourishes when schools and employers encourage intrinsic motivation and not just extrinsic rewards (see Chapters 7 and 12). Intrinsic motives include a sense of accomplishment, intellectual fulfillment, the satisfaction of curiosity, and the sheer love of the activity. Creativity also increases when people have control over how to perform a task or solve a problem, are evaluated unobtrusively instead of being constantly observed and judged, and work independently (Amabile, 1983). Organizations encourage creativity when they let people take risks, give them plenty of time to think about problems, and welcome innovation.

In sum, if you hope to become more creative, there are two things you can do. One is to cultivate the personal qualities that lead to creativity. The other is to seek out the kinds of situations that permit you to express these qualities.

Summary

Thought: Using What We Know

▶ *Thinking* is the mental manipulation of information. Our mental representations simplify and summarize information from the environment.

▶ A *concept* is a mental category that groups objects, relations, activities, abstractions, or qualities that share certain properties. *Basic concepts* have a moderate number of instances and are easier to acquire than concepts with few or many instances. *Prototypical* instances of a concept are more representative than others. *Propositions* are made up of concepts and express a unitary idea. They may be linked together to form *cognitive schemas,* which serve as mental models of aspects of the world. *Mental images* also play a role in thinking.

▶ Not all mental processing is conscious. *Subconscious processes* lie outside of awareness but can be brought into consciousness when necessary. *Nonconscious processes* remain outside of awareness but nonetheless affect behavior and are involved in what we call "intuition" and "insight," and in *implicit learning.* Conscious processing may be carried out in a mindless fashion if we overlook changes in context that call for a change in behavior.

Reasoning Rationally

▶ *Reasoning* is purposeful mental activity that involves drawing inferences and conclusions from observations, facts, or assumptions (premises).

▶ *Formal reasoning problems* can often be solved by applying an *algorithm,* a set of procedures guaranteed to produce a solution, or by using logical processes, such as *deductive* and *inductive reasoning.*

▶ *Informal reasoning problems* often have no clearly correct solution. Disagreement may exist about basic premises, information may be incomplete, and many viewpoints may compete. Such problems may call for the application of *heuristics,* rules of thumb that suggest a course of action without guaranteeing an optimal solution. They may also require *dialectical thinking* about opposing points of view.

▶ Studies of *reflective judgment* show that many people have trouble thinking dialectically. People in the *prereflective* stages assume that a correct answer always exists; they do not distinguish between knowledge and belief, or between belief and evidence. Those in the *quasi-reflective* stages think that because knowledge is sometimes uncertain, any judgment about the evidence is purely subjective. Those who think *reflectively* understand that although some things cannot be known with certainty, some judgments are more valid than others, depending on their coherence, usefulness, fit with the evidence, and so on. Higher education moves people gradually closer to reflective judgment.

Barriers to Reasoning Rationally

▶ The need to be right is an obstacle to rational thinking, as is mental laziness, which many commentators think has increased because of the replacement of reading by television watching.

▶ The ability to reason clearly and rationally is also affected by many cognitive biases. People tend to exaggerate the likelihood of improbable events, in part because of the *availability heuristic;* to be swayed in their choices by the desire to *avoid loss;* to be mentally rigid, forming *mental sets* and seeing patterns where none exists; to overestimate their ability to have made accurate predictions (the *hindsight bias*); and to attend mostly to evidence that confirms what they want to believe (the *confirmation bias*).

▶ The theory of *cognitive dissonance* holds that people are motivated to reduce the tension that exists when two cognitions, or a cognition and a behavior, conflict—by rejecting or changing a belief, changing their behavior, or rationalizing. People are especially likely to do so when they need to justify a decision (i.e., reduce *postdecision dissonance*), when their actions violate their concept of themselves as honest and kind, and when they have put hard work into an activity (the *justification of effort*).

▶ People are not always rational, but once we understand a bias, we may be able to reduce or eliminate it.

Measuring Intelligence: The Psychometric Approach

▶ Although we all wish to think intelligently, *intelligence* is hard to define. Some theorists believe that a general ability (a *g factor*) underlies the many specific abilities tapped by intelligence tests, whereas others do not.

▶ The traditional approach to intelligence, the *psychometric* approach, focuses on how well people perform on standardized *aptitude tests*. The *intelligence quotient*, or *IQ*, represents how a person has done on an intelligence test, compared to other people. Alfred Binet designed the first widely used intelligence test for the purpose of identifying children who could benefit from remedial work. But in the United States, people assumed that intelligence tests revealed "natural ability," and they used the tests to categorize people in school and in the armed services.

▶ IQ tests have been criticized for being biased in favor of white, middle-class people. However, efforts to construct *culture-free* and *culture-fair* tests have been disappointing. Culture affects nearly everything to do with taking a test, from attitudes to problem-solving strategies. Negative stereotypes about a person's ethnicity, gender, or age may cause the person to suffer *stereotype threat*, a burden of doubt about his or her own abilities, which can lead to anxiety or "disidentification" with the test.

▶ Many social scientists consider IQ tests useful for predicting school performance and diagnosing learning difficulties. But critics would like to dispense with IQ tests because they do not provide information about *how* people solve problems or why people with low scores often behave intelligently in everyday life.

Dissecting Intelligence: The Cognitive Approach

▶ In contrast to the psychometric approach, *cognitive approaches* to intelligence emphasize several kinds of intelligence and the strategies people use to solve problems rather than merely whether they get the right answers.

▶ Sternberg's *triarchic theory of intelligence* proposes three aspects of intelligence: *componential* (including *metacognition*), *experiential*, and *contextual*. Contextual intelligence allows you to acquire *tacit knowledge*, practical strategies that are important for success but are not explicitly taught.

▶ Intelligence in one domain does not necessarily imply intelligence in another. Howard Gardner proposes that there are actually several "intelligences" besides those usually considered, including musical and kinesthetic intelligence as well as the capacity to understand the natural world, yourself, or others. The latter two intelligences overlap with what some psychologists call *emotional intelligence*, which is associated with personal, academic, and occupational success.

▶ Intellectual achievement also depends on motivation and attitudes. Cross-cultural work shows that beliefs about the origins of mental abilities, parental standards, and attitudes toward education can help account for differences in academic performance.

Animal Minds

▶ Some researchers, especially those in *cognitive ethology*, argue that nonhuman animals have greater cognitive abilities than is usually thought. Some animals can use objects as rudimentary tools. Chimpanzees have learned to use numerals to label quantities of items and symbols to refer to objects. The great apes have shown some evidence of having a *theory of mind*, which allows them to do things like recognize themselves in a mirror, empathize with others, and use deception. But not all researchers are convinced that these abilities exist in animals.

▶ Several researchers have used visual symbol systems or American Sign Language (ASL) to teach primates language skills, and some animals (even some nonprimates) seem able to use simple grammatical ordering rules to convey or comprehend meaning. However, scientists are still divided as to how to interpret these findings and the research on animal cognition, with some worrying about *anthropomorphism* and others worrying about *anthropodenial*.

Key Terms

◀LOOKING BACK

- When you think of a bird, why are you more likely to recall a robin than a penguin? (p. 312)

- How are visual images similar to images on a computer screen? (p. 313)

- What is happening mentally when you mistakenly take your geography notes to your psychology class? (pp. 314–315)

- Mentally speaking, why is making a cake, well, a piece of cake? (p. 316)

- Why can't logic solve all our problems? (p. 317)

- What kind of reasoning do juries need to be good at? (p. 319)

- When people say that all opinions and claims are equally valid, what error are they making? (p. 320)

- Why do people worry about dying in an airplane crash but ignore dangers that are far more likely? (pp. 322–323)

- How might your physician's choice of words about alternative treatments for your illness affect which one you choose? (p. 324)

- When "Monday morning quarterbacks" say they knew all along who would win Sunday's big game, what bias might they be showing? (p. 325)

- Why will a terrible hazing make you more loyal to the group that hazed you? (p. 328)

- Why do psychologists debate whether a single thing called "intelligence" even exists? (pp. 329–330)

- How did the original purpose of intelligence testing change when IQ tests came to America? (p. 332)

- Is it possible to design intelligence tests that are not influenced by culture? (pp. 333–334)

- Why do some psychologists defend traditional intelligence testing and others oppose it? (p. 335)

- What kind of intelligence allows you to master the unspoken rules for academic success? (p. 336)

- What is "EQ" and why is it as important as IQ? (pp. 337–338)

- Why do Asian children perform so much better in school than American students do? (p. 340)

- Why do some researchers think that animals can think? (pp. 341–343)

- People love to talk to their pets—but can their pets learn to talk back? (pp. 343–345)

Answers to the creativity test on page 347:

back, party, book, match, cheese

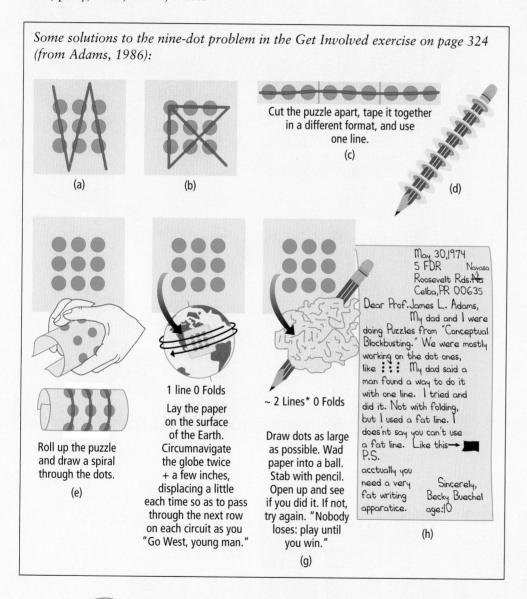

Some solutions to the nine-dot problem in the Get Involved exercise on page 324 (from Adams, 1986):

(a)

(b)

Cut the puzzle apart, tape it together in a different format, and use one line.
(c)

(d)

Roll up the puzzle and draw a spiral through the dots.
(e)

1 line 0 Folds

Lay the paper on the surface of the Earth. Circumnavigate the globe twice + a few inches, displacing a little each time so as to pass through the next row on each circuit as you "Go West, young man."
(f)

~ 2 Lines* 0 Folds

Draw dots as large as possible. Wad paper into a ball. Stab with pencil. Open up and see if you did it. If not, try again. "Nobody loses: play until you win."
(g)

May 30, 1974
5 FDR   Navasa
Roosevelt Rds. Na
Ceiba, PR 00635
Dear Prof. James L. Adams,
My dad and I were doing Puzzles from "Conceptual Blockbusting." We were mostly working on the dot ones, like ⦙⦙⦙ My dad said a man found a way to do it with one line. I tried and did it. Not with folding, but I used a fat line. I does'nt say you can't use a fat line. Like this→ ◼
P.S.
acctually you need a very fat writing apparatice.
Sincerely,
Becky Buechel
age: 10
(h)

10

Memory

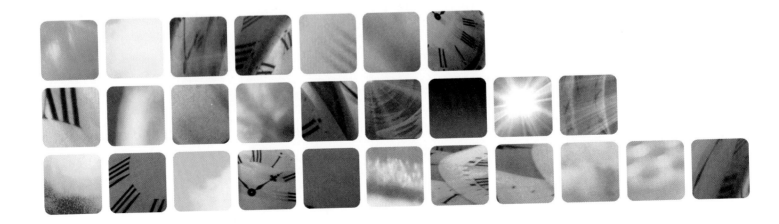

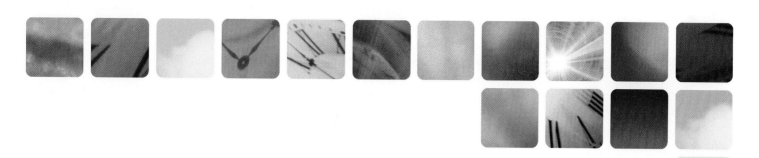

Better by far that you should forget and smile
than that you should remember and be sad.

CHRISTINA ROSSETTI

In 1987, Ronald Junior Cotton, a black man, was sentenced by a North Carolina appeals court to two life sentences for the rape of Jennifer Thompson, a young white college student. Immediately after the attack, Thompson helped police put together a composite sketch of her attacker's face. A few days later, she identified Cotton in a series of police photos, and eventually she picked him out from a lineup. At the trial, she testified that during her ordeal, as a knife was being held to her throat, she made a deliberate effort to memorize every detail of the rapist's face and to look for scars, tattoos, and other characteristics that would help her identify him later on.

During a pretrial hearing for the appeal, Thompson learned that another inmate in the prison where Cotton was being held, Bobby Poole, had boasted that he was the one who committed the rape. But Thompson remained certain that she had identified the right man. When Poole was brought into court, Thompson was asked if she had ever seen him. "I have never seen him in my life," she answered. "I have no idea who he is."

At one time, most prosecutors and juries would have dismissed Jennifer Thompson's testimony outright. For decades, it was difficult for rape victims to get justice in the legal system because public opinion tended to blame them for having "provoked" the attack or for failing to fight back strongly enough. Then, as people became more aware of the horrific nature of rape and the unfairness of blaming victims, acceptance of women's testimony increased. Today, some defendants, like Ronald Junior Cotton, are being sent to prison or even sentenced to death almost solely on the strength of the victim's testimony. But is an eyewitness's account always reliable? In the absence of corroborating evidence, should a witness's confidence in her memory be sufficient for establishing guilt? Much is at stake in our efforts to answer these questions: getting justice for rape victims, and also avoiding the false conviction of men who are innocent.

An appeals court upheld the conviction of Ronald Junior Cotton (top), identified by Jennifer Thompson as having raped her. Although a fellow inmate, Bobby Poole (bottom), boasted of committing the crime, Thompson stood by her testimony and the reliability of her memory.

The Cotton case did not end in 1987. At the conclusion of this chapter we will tell you what ultimately happened. Meanwhile, as you read, ask yourself, when should we trust our memories, and when should we be cautious about doing so? We all forget a great deal, of course: We watch the evening news and half an hour later can't recall the main story; we enjoy a meal and quickly forget what we ate. Do we also "remember" things that never happened? Are memory malfunctions the rare exception to the rule, or are they commonplace? And if memory is not always reliable, how can any of us hope to know the story of our own lives? How can we hope to understand the past?

WHAT'S AHEAD ▷

- **What's wrong with thinking of memory as a mental movie camera?**
- **Why do "flashbulb" memories of surprising or shocking events sometimes have less wattage than we think?**
- **If you have a strong emotional reaction to a remembered event, does that mean your memory is accurate?**

Reconstructing the Past

Memory refers to the capacity to retain and retrieve information, and also to the structures that account for this capacity. Human beings are capable of astonishing feats of memory. Most of us can easily remember who fought whom in World War II, the tune of our national anthem, how to use an automated teller machine, the most embarrassing experience we ever had, zillions of details about our favorite sports or films, and hundreds of thousands of other bits of information.

Memory confers competence; without it we would be as helpless as newborns, unable to carry out even the most trivial of our daily tasks. Memory also endows us with a sense of personal identity; each of us is the sum of our recollections, which is why we feel so threatened when others challenge our memories. Individuals and cultures alike rely on a remembered history for a sense of coherence and meaning; memory gives us our past and guides our future.

The Manufacture of Memory

In ancient times, philosophers compared memory to a soft wax tablet that would preserve anything that chanced to make an imprint on it. Then, with the advent of the printing press, they began to think of memory as a gigantic library, storing specific events and facts for later retrieval. Today, in the audiovisual age, many people compare memory to a video or movie camera, automatically recording every moment of their lives.

Popular and appealing though this belief about memory is, however, it is utterly wrong. Not everything that happens to us or impinges on our senses is tucked away for later use. Memory is selective. If it were not, our minds would be cluttered with mental junk—the temperature at noon Thursday, the price of turnips two years ago, a phone number needed only once. Moreover, recovering a memory is not at all like replaying a videotape of an event; it is more like watching a few unconnected frames and then figuring out what the rest of the scene must have been like.

One of the first scientists to make this point was the British psychologist Sir Frederic Bartlett (1932). Bartlett asked people to read lengthy, unfamiliar stories from other cultures and then tell the stories back to him. As the volunteers tried to recall the stories, they made interesting errors: They often eliminated or changed details that did not make sense to them, and they added other details to make the story coherent, sometimes even adding a moral. Memory, Bartlett concluded, must therefore be largely a *reconstructive* process. We may reproduce some kinds of simple information by rote, said Bartlett, but when we remember complex information, we typically alter it in ways that help us make sense of the material, based on what we already know or think we know. Since Bartlett's time, hundreds of studies have found this to be true for everything from stories to conversations to personal experiences (Schacter, 1996, 2001).

In reconstructing their memories, people often draw on many sources. Suppose, for example, that someone asks you to describe one of your early birthday parties. You may have some direct recollection of the event, but you may also incorporate information from family stories, photographs, or home videos, and even from accounts of other people's birthdays and reenactments of birthdays on television. You take all these bits and pieces and build one integrated account. Later, you may not be able to separate your original experience from what you added after the fact—a phenomenon called **source amnesia** or *source misattribution*.

A dramatic instance of reconstruction once occurred in the sad case of H. M., whom we described briefly in Chapter 4. Ever since 1953, when much of H. M.'s hippocampus and the adjacent cortex were surgically removed, he has been unable to form lasting memories for new events, facts, songs, stories, or faces, and so he does not remember much of anything that has happened since his operation (Hilts, 1995; Ogden & Corkin, 1991). To cope with his devastating condition, H. M. will sometimes resort to reconstructions. On one occasion, after eating a chocolate Valentine's Day heart, H. M. stuck the shiny red wrapping in his shirt pocket. Two hours later, while searching for his handkerchief, he pulled out the paper and looked at it in puzzlement. When a researcher asked why he had the paper in his pocket, he replied, "Well, it could have been wrapped around a big chocolate heart. It must be Valentine's Day!" But a short time later, when she asked him to take out the paper again and say why he had it in his pocket, he replied, "Well, it might have been wrapped around a big chocolate rabbit. It must be Easter!"

Sadly, H. M. *had* to reconstruct the past; his damaged brain could not recall it in any other way. But those of us with normal memory abilities also reconstruct, far more often than we realize.

If these children remember this birthday party later in life, their constructions may include information picked up from family photographs, videos, and stories. Because of source amnesia, they will probably be unable to distinguish their actual memories from information they got elsewhere.

source amnesia The inability to distinguish what you originally experienced from what you heard or were told about an event later.

The Fading Flashbulb

Of course, some unusual, shocking, or tragic events, such as earthquakes or accidents, do hold a special place in memory, especially when we were personally involved. Such events seem frozen in time, with all the details intact. Years ago, Roger Brown and James Kulik (1977) labeled these vivid recollections of emotional events "flashbulb memories" because that term captures the surprise, illumination, and seemingly photographic detail that characterize them. They speculated that the capacity for flashbulb memories may have evolved because such memories had survival

THINKING CRITICALLY

Examine the Evidence

Many of our recollections are subject to distortion. Are vivid "flashbulb" memories an exception to this rule? How accurate are our seemingly "perfect" memories of emotional or shocking events?

Do you recall where you were and what you were doing on September 11, 2001, when you learned of the attack on the World Trade Center? You probably have a "flashbulb" memory of that event. But even vivid flashbulb memories are not always complete or accurate, and they often change over time.

value. Remembering the details of a surprising or dangerous experience could have helped our ancestors avoid similar situations.

Despite their intensity, however, even flashbulb memories are not always complete or accurate records of the past. People usually remember the *gist* of a startling, emotional event they experienced or witnessed—say, a violent shoot-out, or the assassination of an admired politician—but errors creep into the details (McNally, 2003). For example, people who saw the 1986 explosion of the space shuttle *Challenger* often swear that they know exactly where they were and what they were doing when the tragedy occurred. But research done after the explosion shows otherwise. On the morning after the tragedy, college students reported how they had heard the news. Three years later, when they again recalled how they learned of the incident, not one student was entirely correct and a third of them were *completely wrong,* although they felt confident that they were remembering accurately (Neisser & Harsch, 1992). Similarly, 32 months after the announcement of the verdict in the O. J. Simpson murder trial, only 29 percent of college students' recollections remained accurate, and more than 40 percent contained major distortions (Schmolck, Buffalo, & Squire, 2000). We expect that researchers will soon report similar results for people's flashbulb memories of the events of September 11, 2001.

Even with flashbulb memories, then, facts tend to get mixed with a little fiction. The conclusion is inescapable: Remembering is an *active* process, one that involves not only dredging up stored information but also putting two and two together to reconstruct the past. And sometimes we put two and two together and get five.

The Conditions of Confabulation

In Chapter 9, we saw that rational thinking is often hampered by the confirmation bias and the need to reduce dissonance. Memory, too, is biased: For example, after making a decision, people will remember information that supported the wisdom of their choice and cleverly "forget" information that might have led them to make an alternative choice (Mather, Shafir, & Johnson, 2000). These predictable memory distortions reduce feelings of regret, but they also make it harder for people to learn from their mistakes.

Because memory is reconstructive, it is subject to **confabulation**—confusing an event that happened to someone else with one that happened to you, or coming to believe that you remember something that never happened. Such confabulations are especially likely to occur under four circumstances (Garry, Manning, & Loftus, 1996; Hyman & Pentland, 1996; Johnson, 1995):

1 *You have thought about the imagined event many times.* Suppose that at family gatherings you keep hearing about the time that Uncle Sam scared everyone at a New Year's party by pounding a hammer into the wall with such force that the wall collapsed. The story is so colorful that you can practically see Uncle Sam in your mind's eye. The more you think about this event, the more likely you are to believe that you were actually there, even if you were sound asleep in another house. This process has been called "imagination inflation," because your own active imagination inflates your belief that the event really occurred (Garry & Loftus, 2000).

2 *The image of the event contains a lot of details.* Ordinarily, we can distinguish an imagined event from a real one by the amount of detail we recall; real events tend to produce more details. However, the longer you think about an imagined

confabulation Confusion of an event that happened to someone else with one that happened to you, or a belief that you remember something when it never actually happened.

event, the more details you are likely to add—what Sam was wearing, the fact that he'd had too much to drink, the crumbling plaster, people standing around in party hats—and these details may in turn persuade you that the event really happened and that you have a direct memory of it.

3 *The event is easy to imagine.* If forming an image of an event takes little effort (as does visualizing a man pounding a wall with a hammer), then we tend to think that our memory is real. In contrast, when we must make an effort to form an image—for example, of being in a place we have never seen or doing something that is utterly foreign to us—our cognitive efforts apparently serve as a cue that the event did not really take place, or that we were not there when it did.

NEVER FORGETS

SOMETIMES FORGETS

ALWAYS FORGETS

4 *You focus on your emotional reactions to the event rather than on what actually happened.* Emotional reactions to an imagined event can resemble those that would have occurred in response to a real event, and so they can mislead us. This means that your feelings about an event, no matter how strong they are, do not guarantee that the event really happened. Consider again our Sam story, which happens to be true. A woman we know believed for years that she had been present in the room as an 11-year-old child when her uncle destroyed the wall. Because the story was so vivid and upsetting to her, she felt angry at him for what she thought was his mean and violent behavior, and she assumed that she must have been angry at the time as well. Then, as an adult, she learned that she was not at the party at all but had merely heard about it repeatedly over the years; and that Sam had not pounded the wall in anger, but as a joke—to inform the assembled guests that he and his wife were about to remodel their home. Nevertheless, our friend's family has had a hard time convincing her that her "memory" of this event is entirely wrong, and they are not sure she believes them yet.

As the Sam story illustrates, and as laboratory research verifies, false memories can be as stable over time as true ones (Brainerd, Reyna, & Brandse, 1995; Poole, 1995; Roediger & McDermott, 1995). There's just no getting around it: Memory is reconstructive.

QUICK QUIZ

Can you reconstruct what you have read now in order to answer these questions?

1. Memory is like (a) a wax tablet, (b) a giant file cabinet, (c) a video camera, (d) none of these.

2. *True or false:* Flashbulb memories are invulnerable to distortion because they are so vivid.

3. Which of the following confabulated "memories" might a person be most inclined to accept as having really happened to them, and why? (a) being lost in a shopping center at the age of 5, (b) taking a class in astrophysics, (c) visiting a monastery in Tibet as a child, (d) being bullied by another kid in the fourth grade

Answers:

1. d 2. false 3. a and d because they are common events that are easy to imagine and that contain a lot of vivid details. It would be harder to induce someone to believe that he or she had studied astrophysics or visited Tibet because these are rare events that take an effort to imagine.

WHAT'S AHEAD

- Can your memories of an event be affected by the way someone questions you about it?
- Can children's testimony about sexual abuse always be trusted?

Memory and the Power of Suggestion

The reconstructive nature of memory helps the mind work efficiently. Instead of cramming our brains with infinite details, we can store the essentials of an experience, then use our knowledge of the world to figure out the specifics when we need them. But precisely because memory is reconstructive, it is also vulnerable to suggestion—to ideas implanted in our minds after the event, which then become associated with it. This fact raises thorny problems in legal cases that involve eyewitness testimony or people's memories of what happened, when, and to whom.

The Eyewitness on Trial

Without the accounts of eyewitnesses, many guilty people would go free. But because memory is reconstructive, eyewitness testimony is not always reliable, even when the witness is dead certain about the accuracy of his or her report (Bothwell, Deffenbacher, & Brigham, 1987; Sporer et al., 1995). As a result, some convictions based solely or mostly on such testimony turn out to be tragic mistakes.

Eyewitness identification is especially vulnerable to error when the suspects' ethnicity differs from that of the witness. Whites are more apt to make errors when identifying blacks and vice versa.

Eyewitnesses are especially likely to make mistaken identifications when the suspect's ethnicity differs from their own. When people say of another group, "They all look alike to me," often, unfortunately, they are telling the truth. Because of unfamiliarity with or prejudice toward other ethnic groups, the eyewitness may focus solely on the ethnicity of the person they see committing a crime ("He's black"; "He's white"; "He's an Arab") and ignore the distinctive features that would later make identification more accurate (Levin, 2000). The witness may also rely on ethnic stereotypes to reconstruct what happened (Chance & Goldstein, 1995; Sherman & Bessenoff, 1999).

Eyewitness accounts are also heavily influenced by the way in which questions are put to the witness and by suggestive comments made during an interrogation or interview. In a classic study of leading questions, Elizabeth Loftus and John Palmer (1974) showed people short films depicting car collisions. Afterward, the researchers asked some of the viewers, "About how fast were the cars going when they hit each other?" Other viewers were asked the same question, but with the verb changed to *smashed, collided, bumped,* or *contacted.* Estimates of how fast the cars were going varied, depending on which word was used. *Smashed* produced the highest average speed estimates (40.8 mph), followed by *collided* (39.3 mph), *bumped* (38.1 mph), *hit* (34.0 mph), and *contacted* (31.8 mph).

In a similar study, the researchers asked some participants, "Did you see a broken headlight?" but asked of others "Did you see the broken headlight?" (Loftus & Zanni, 1975). The question with *the* presupposes a broken headlight and merely asks whether the witness saw it, whereas the question with *a* makes no such presupposition. People who received questions with *the* were far more likely to report having seen something that had not really appeared in the film than were those who

Figure 10.1
Misleading information can profoundly affect recall. Students saw the face of a young man with straight hair, then heard a description of the face supposedly written by another witness—one that wrongly mentioned light, curly hair. When they reconstructed the face using a kit of facial features, a third of their reconstructions contained the misleading detail, whereas only 5 percent contained it when curly hair was not mentioned. On the left is one person's reconstruction in the absence of the misleading information; on the right is another person's reconstruction of the same face after exposure to the misleading information (Loftus & Greene, 1980).

received questions with *a*. If a tiny word like *the* can lead people to "remember" what they never saw, you can imagine how the leading questions of police detectives and lawyers might influence a witness's recall.

Misleading information from other sources, too, can profoundly alter what we remember. In one study, students were shown the face of a young man who had straight hair, then heard a description of the face supposedly written by another witness—a description that wrongly said the man had light, curly hair (see Figure 10.1). When the students reconstructed the face using a kit of facial features, a third of their reconstructions contained the misleading detail, whereas only 5 percent contained it when curly hair was not mentioned (Loftus & Greene, 1980).

Leading questions, suggestive comments, and misleading information affect people's memories for their own experiences, not just events they have witnessed. Researchers have been able to induce people to "recall" complicated events from early in life that never actually happened, such as getting lost in a shopping mall, being hospitalized for a high fever, being harassed by a bully, or spilling punch all over the mother of the bride at a wedding (Hyman & Pentland, 1996; Loftus & Pickrell, 1995; Mazzoni et al., 1999). In one study, about a third of people who saw a phony Disneyland ad featuring Bugs Bunny later recalled having met a Bugs character at Disneyland (Braun, Ellis, & Loftus, 2002). Some even claimed to remember specific details, such as shaking hands with the character or seeing him in a parade. But these "memories" were impossible, because Bugs Bunny is a Warner Bros. creation and would definitely be rabbit-non-grata at Disneyland!

Children's Testimony

The power of suggestion can affect anyone, but many people are especially concerned about its impact on children being questioned about possible sexual abuse. For many years most adults believed that children's memories could not be trusted because young children confuse fantasy with reality and are easily influenced by adults. Then, as the issue of child abuse came to public attention in the 1970s and 1980s, some people began to argue that no child would ever lie about or misremember such a traumatic experience.

THINKING CRITICALLY

Don't Oversimplify

Some people claim that children's memories of sexual abuse are always accurate; others claim that children can't distinguish fantasy from reality. How can we avoid either–or thinking on this emotional issue? Is the question "Are children's memories accurate?" even the right one to ask?

Resolving this debate became critical as accusations of child abuse in day-care centers across the United States skyrocketed. The first, in the mid-1980s, involved a case against the McMartin preschool in Los Angeles, and it was soon followed by dozens of others. After being interviewed by therapists and police investigators, children in these schools claimed that their teachers had molested them in the most terrible ways: hanging them in trees, putting handcuffs on them, raping them, even forcing them to eat feces. Although in no case had parents actually seen such mistreatment, although none of the children had complained to their parents, and although none of the parents had noticed any symptoms or problems in their children, most of the accused teachers were sentenced to many years in prison—where many of them remain today. Were these people really guilty of unspeakably horrible acts, or had the children been somehow persuaded to make up fanciful stories?

After reviewing the research on this issue, Stephen Ceci and Maggie Bruck (1995) concluded that both extreme positions—"children always lie" and "children never lie"—are wrong. Ceci and Bruck found that most children *do* recollect accurately much of what they have observed or experienced. On the other hand, many children *will* say that something happened when it did not or report improbable details. Like adults, they can be influenced by leading questions and suggestions from the person interviewing them.

Therefore, instead of asking "Are children suggestible?" or "Are children's memories accurate?" Ceci and Bruck (1995) proposed asking a more useful question: "Under what conditions are children apt to be suggestible?" One such condition is being very young. Preschoolers' memories are more vulnerable to suggestive questions than are those of school-age children and adults. Preschoolers are also more likely to have source amnesia, failing to remember whether they actually saw or experienced something themselves or heard about it from an adult. And the boundary between reality and fantasy may blur for very young children, especially in emotionally charged situations, making it more likely that their accounts will include confabulations of imagined events (Poole & Lamb, 1998).

In addition, children's memories, just like adults' memories, can be influenced by pressure to conform to the interviewer's expectations and by a desire to please the interviewer. One team of researchers, having analyzed the transcripts of interrogations of children in the McMartin case, applied the same techniques in an experiment with preschool children (Garven et al., 1998). A young man visited children at their preschool, read them a story, and handed out treats. The man did nothing aggressive, inappropriate, or surprising. A week later the experimenter questioned the children about the man's visit. She asked children in one group leading questions ("Did he shove the teacher? Did he throw a crayon at a kid who was talking?"). She asked a second group the same questions but also used influence techniques used by interrogators in the McMartin case and other cases of day-care workers accused of child abuse: for example, telling the children what "other kids" had supposedly said, expressing disappointment if answers were negative, and praising children for making allegations.

In the first group, children said "yes, it happened" to about 15 percent of the false allegations about the man's visit. This finding alone refutes the notion that children never lie, misremember, or make things up. In the second group, the 3-year-olds, on average, said "yes" to *over 80 percent* of the false allegations suggested to them, and the 4- to 6-year-olds said "yes" to about half the allegations (see Figure 10.2). Note that the interviews in this study lasted only 5 to 10 minutes, whereas in actual investigations, interviewers often question children repeatedly over many weeks.

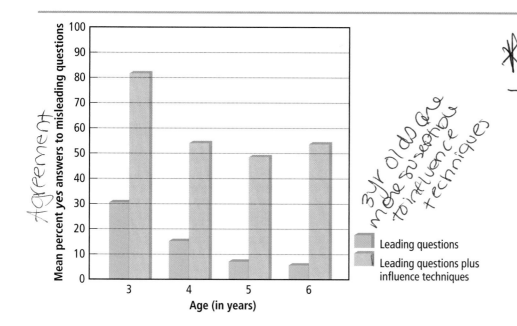

Figure 10.2

SOCIAL PRESSURE AND CHILDREN'S FALSE ALLEGATIONS

When researchers asked a group of preschoolers whether a visitor to their classroom had committed aggressive acts—acts that had not actually occurred—many said that yes, he had. And when the researchers interviewed another group of children using social influence techniques taken from real-life child-abuse investigations, *most* of the children said yes. As you can see, the younger the children, the more likely they were to agree with the interviewer's leading questions (Garven et al., 1998).

(handwritten: 3 yr olds are more susceptible to influence techniques)

(chart labels: Agreement; Mean percent yes answers to misleading questions; Age (in years); Leading questions; Leading questions plus influence techniques)

Some people argue that children cannot be induced to falsely report real-life experiences that were traumatic, but that is not the case. In one study, schoolchildren were asked for their recollections of an actual incident in which a sniper had terrorized their schoolyard. Many of the children who were not at the school during the shooting, including some who were on vacation at the time, reported memories of hearing shots, seeing someone lying on the ground, and other details they could not possibly have experienced directly. Apparently, they had been influenced by the accounts of the children who had been there (Pynoos & Nader, 1989).

In sum, children, like adults, can be accurate in what they report; and, also like adults, they can distort, forget, fantasize, and be misled. As research shows, their memory processes are only human.

QUICK QUIZ

We hope you are suggestible enough to accept our suggestion that you take this quiz.

1. *True or false:* False identifications are more likely when a suspect's ethnicity differs from that of the eyewitness, even when the witness feels certain about being accurate.

2. Research suggests that the best way to encourage truthful testimony by children is to (a) reassure them that their friends have had the same experience, (b) reward them for telling you that something happened, (c) scold them if you believe they are lying, (d) avoid leading questions.

3. In psychotherapy, hundreds of people have claimed to recall long-buried memories of having taken part in satanic rituals involving animal and human torture and sacrifice. Yet investigators have been unable to confirm any of these reports (Goodman et al., 1995). Based on what you have learned so far, how might you explain such "memories"?

Answers:

1. true 2. d 3. Therapists who uncritically assume that satanic cults are widespread may ask leading questions and otherwise influence their patients. Patients, who are susceptible to their therapists' interpretations, may then confabulate and "remember" "experiences that did not happen, borrowing details from fictionalized accounts or from other troubling experiences in their lives (Ofshe & Watters, 1994). The result may be source amnesia and the patient's mistaken conviction that the memory is real.

WHAT'S AHEAD

- In general, which is easier, a multiple-choice item or a short-answer essay item—and why?
- Can you know something without knowing that you know it?
- Why is the computer often used as a metaphor for the mind?

In Pursuit of Memory

Now that we have seen how memory *doesn't* work—namely, like a video camera, an infallible filing system, or a journal written in indelible ink—we turn to studies of how it *does* work. The ability to remember is not an absolute talent; it depends on the type of performance being called for. If you have a preference for multiple-choice, essay, or true–false exams, you already know this.

Measuring Memory

10.1 *Live! psych*

explicit memory Conscious, intentional recollection of an event or of an item of information.

recall The ability to retrieve and reproduce from memory previously encountered material.

recognition The ability to identify previously encountered material.

Conscious, intentional recollection of an event or an item of information is called **explicit memory.** It is usually measured using one of two methods. The first method tests for **recall,** the ability to retrieve and reproduce information encountered earlier. Essay and fill-in-the-blank exams and memory games such as Trivial Pursuit or Jeopardy require recall. The second method tests for **recognition,** the ability to identify information you have previously observed, read, or heard about. The information is given to you, and all you have to do is say whether it is old or new, or perhaps correct or incorrect, or pick it out of a set of alternatives. The task, in other words, is to compare the information you are given with the information stored in your memory. True–false and multiple-choice tests call for recognition.

Recognition tests can be tricky, especially when false items closely resemble correct ones. Under most circumstances, however, recognition is easier than recall. Recognition for visual images is particularly impressive. If you show people 2,500 slides of faces and places, and later you ask them to identify which ones they saw out of a larger set, they will be able to identify more than 90 percent of the original slides accurately (Haber, 1970).

Get Involved

Recalling Rudolph's Friends

You can try this test of recall if you are familiar with the poem *'Twas the Night Before Christmas* or the song *Rudolph the Red-Nosed Reindeer*. Rudolph had eight reindeer friends; name as many of them as you can. After you have done your best, turn to the Get Involved exercise on page 364 for a recognition test on the same information.

How many of your high school classmates can you recall by name? Which would be easier, recognizing their pictures and names, or recalling them?

implicit memory Unconscious retention in memory, as evidenced by the effect of a previous experience or previously encountered information on current thoughts or actions.

priming A method for measuring implicit memory in which a person reads or listens to information and is later tested to see whether the information affects performance on the same or another type of task.

relearning method A method for measuring retention that compares the time required to relearn material with the time used in the initial learning of the material.

The superiority of recognition over recall was once demonstrated in a study of people's memories of their high school classmates (Bahrick, Bahrick, & Wittlinger, 1975). The participants, ages 17 to 74, first wrote down the names of as many classmates as they could remember. Recall was poor; even when prompted with yearbook pictures, the youngest people failed to name almost a third of their classmates, and the oldest failed to name most of them. Recognition, however, was far better. When asked to look at a series of cards, each of which contained a set of five photographs, and to say which picture in each set showed a former classmate, recent graduates were right 90 percent of the time—and so were people who had graduated 35 years earlier. The ability to recognize names was nearly as impressive.

Sometimes, information encountered in the past affects our thoughts and actions even though we do not consciously or intentionally remember it—a phenomenon known as **implicit memory** (Graf & Schacter, 1985; Schacter, Chiu, & Ochsner, 1993). To get at this subtle sort of knowledge, researchers must rely on indirect methods instead of the direct ones used to measure explicit memory. One common method, **priming**, asks you to read or listen to some information and then tests you later to see whether the information affects your performance on a similar task or another type of task.

For example, suppose that you had to read a list of words, some of which began with the letters *def* (such as *define, defend,* or *deform*). Later you might be asked to complete word stems (such as *def-*) with the first word that comes to mind. Even if you could not recognize or recall the original words very well, you would be more likely to complete the word fragments with words from the list than you would be if you had not seen the list. In this procedure, the original words "prime" certain responses on the word-completion task (that is, make them more available), showing that people can retain more knowledge about the past than they realize. They know more than they know that they know (Richardson-Klavehn & Bjork, 1988; Roediger, 1990).

Another method of measuring implicit memory, the **relearning method** or *savings method,* straddles the boundary between implicit and explicit memory tests. Devised by Hermann Ebbinghaus (1885/1913) over a century ago, the relearning

PRIMING

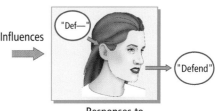

Exposure to information — Influences — Responses to *different* task

Get Involved

Recognizing Rudolph's Friends

If you took the recall test in the Get Involved exercise on page 362, now try a recognition test. From the following list, see whether you can identify the correct names of Rudolph the Red-Nosed Reindeer's eight reindeer friends. The answers are at the end of this chapter—but no fair peeking!

Blitzen	Dander	Dancer	Masher
Cupid	Dasher	Prancer	Comet
Kumquat	Donder	Flasher	Pixie
Bouncer	Blintzes	Trixie	Vixen

Which was easier, recall or recognition? Can you speculate on the reason?

method requires you to relearn information or a task that you learned earlier. If you master it more quickly the second time around, you must be remembering something from the first experience. One eminent memory researcher told us that he considers the relearning method to be a test of explicit memory. But another maintained that it can function as a test of implicit memory if the learner is unaware that the material being relearned was ever learned earlier.

Models of Memory

Although people usually refer to memory as a single faculty, as in "I must be losing my memory" or "He has a memory like an elephant's," the term *memory* actually covers a complex collection of abilities and processes. If video or movie cameras are not accurate metaphors for capturing these diverse components of memory, then what metaphor would be better?

As we saw in Chapter 9, many cognitive psychologists liken the mind to an information processor, along the lines of a computer, though more complex. They have constructed *information-processing models* of cognitive processes, liberally borrowing computer programming terms such as *input, output, accessing,* and *information retrieval*. When you type something on your computer's keyboard, the machine encodes the information into an electronic language, stores it on a disk, and retrieves it when you need to use it. Similarly, in information-processing models of memory, we *encode* information (convert it to a form that the brain can process and use), *store* the information (retain it over time), and *retrieve* the information (recover it for use). In storage, the information may be represented as concepts, propositions, images, or *cognitive schemas*, mental networks of knowledge, beliefs, and expectations concerning particular topics or aspects of the world. (If you can't retrieve these terms, see Chapter 9.)

In most information-processing models, storage takes place in three interacting memory systems. *Sensory memory* retains incoming sensory information for a second or two, until it can be processed further. *Short-term memory (STM)* holds a limited amount of information for a brief period of time, perhaps up to 30 seconds or so, unless a conscious effort is made to keep it there longer. *Long-term memory (LTM)* accounts for longer storage—from a few minutes to decades (Atkinson & Shiffrin, 1968, 1971). Information can pass from sensory memory to short-term memory, and in either direction between short-term and long-term memory, as illustrated in Figure 10.3.

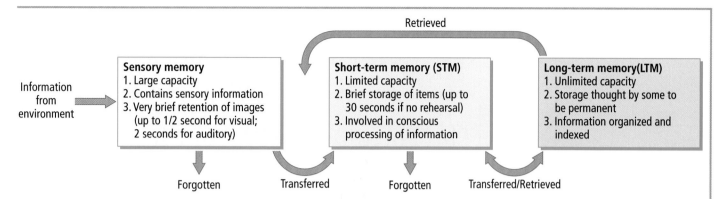

Figure 10.3
THREE MEMORY SYSTEMS

In the "three-box model" of memory, information that does not transfer out of sensory memory or short-term memory is assumed to be forgotten forever. Once in long-term memory, information can be retrieved for use in analyzing incoming sensory information or performing mental operations in short-term memory.

This model, which is often informally called the "three-box model," has dominated research on memory since the late 1960s. However, many other models also exist; for example, some psychologists argue that just one system exists, with different mental processes called on for different tasks. And some critics of the three-box model note that the human brain does not operate like your average computer. Most computers process instructions and data sequentially, one item after another, and so the three-box model has emphasized sequential operations; but the human brain performs many operations simultaneously, in parallel. It recognizes patterns all at once rather than as a sequence of information bits, and it perceives new information, produces speech, and searches memory all at the same time. It can do this because millions of neurons are active at once, and each neuron communicates with thousands of others, which in turn communicate with millions more.

Because of these differences between human beings and machines, some cognitive scientists prefer a **parallel distributed processing (PDP)** or *connectionist* model. Instead of representing information as flowing from one system to another, a PDP model represents the contents of memory as connections among a huge number of interacting processing units, distributed in a vast network and all operating in parallel—just like the neurons of the brain (McClelland, 1994; Rumelhart, McClelland, & the PDP Research Group, 1986). As information enters the system, the ability of these units to excite or inhibit each other is constantly adjusted to reflect new knowledge.

Memory researchers are still arguing about which model of memory is most useful. In this chapter, we emphasize the three-box model, but keep in mind that the computer metaphor which inspired it could one day be as outdated as the metaphor of memory as a camera.

parallel distributed processing (PDP) model A model of memory in which knowledge is represented as connections among thousands of interacting processing units, distributed in a vast network, and all operating in parallel.

QUICK QUIZ

How well have you encoded what you just learned?

1. Alberta solved a crossword puzzle a few days ago. She no longer recalls the words in the puzzle, but while playing a game of Scrabble, she unconsciously tends to form words that were in the puzzle, showing that she has _____ memories of some of the words.

2. The three basic memory processes are _____, storage, and _____.

3. Do the preceding two questions ask for recall, recognition, or relearning? (And what about *this* question?)

4. One objection to traditional information processing theories of memory is that unlike most computers, the brain performs many independent operations _____.

Answers:

1. implicit 2. encoding, retrieval 3. The first two questions both measure recall; the third question measures recognition. 4. simultaneously, or in parallel

WHAT'S AHEAD

- Why is short-term memory like a leaky bucket?
- When a word is on the tip of your tongue, what errors are you likely to make in recalling it?
- What's the difference between "knowing how" and "knowing that"?

The Three-Box Model of Memory

The information model of three separate memory systems—sensory, short-term, and long-term—remains a leading approach because it offers a convenient way to organize the major findings on memory, does a good job of accounting for these findings, and is consistent with the biological facts about memory, which we will describe later. Let us now peer into each of the "boxes."

Sensory Memory: Fleeting Impressions

In the three-box model, all incoming sensory information must make a brief stop in **sensory memory,** the entryway of memory. Sensory memory includes a number of separate memory subsystems, as many as there are senses. Visual images remain in a visual subsystem for a maximum of half a second. Auditory images remain in an auditory subsystem for a slightly longer time, by most estimates up to two seconds or so.

Sensory memory acts as a holding bin, retaining information in a highly accurate form until we can select items for attention from the stream of stimuli bombarding our senses. It gives us a brief time to decide whether information is extraneous or important; not everything detected by our senses warrants our attention. **Pattern recognition,** the identification of a stimulus on the basis of information already contained in long-term memory, occurs during the transfer of information from sensory memory to short-term memory.

sensory memory A memory system that momentarily preserves extremely accurate images of sensory information.

pattern recognition The identification of a stimulus on the basis of information already contained in long-term memory.

Get Involved

Your Sensory Memory at Work

In a dark room or closet, swing a flashlight rapidly in a circle. You will see an unbroken circle of light instead of a series of separate points. The reason: The successive images remain briefly in sensory memory.

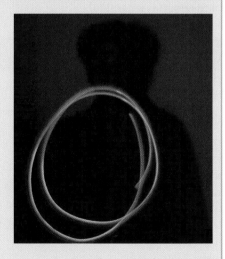

Information that does not quickly go on to short-term memory vanishes forever, like a message written in disappearing ink. That is why people who see an array of 12 letters for just a fraction of a second can only report four or five of them; by the time they answer, their sensory memories are already fading (Sperling, 1960). The fleeting nature of sensory memory is actually beneficial; it prevents multiple sensory images—"double exposures"—that might interfere with the accurate perception and encoding of information.

Short-term Memory: Memory's Scratch Pad

Like sensory memory, **short-term memory (STM)** retains information only temporarily—for up to about 30 seconds by many estimates, although some researchers think that the maximum interval may extend to a few minutes for certain tasks. In short-term memory, the material is no longer an exact sensory image but is an encoding of one, such as a word or a phrase. This material either transfers into long-term memory or decays and is lost forever.

Individuals with brain injury, such as H. M., demonstrate the importance of transferring new information from short-term memory into long-term memory. H. M., you will recall, can store information on a short-term basis; he can hold a conversation and he appears normal when you first meet him. However, for the most part, H. M., and other patients like him, cannot retain explicit information about new facts and events for longer than a few minutes. Their terrible memory deficits involve a problem in transferring explicit memories from short-term storage into long-term storage. With a great deal of repetition and drill, they can learn some new visual information, retain it in long-term memory, and recall it normally (McKee & Squire, 1992). But usually information does not get into long-term memory in the first place.

Besides retaining new information for brief periods while we are learning it, short-term memory holds information that has been retrieved from long-term memory for temporary use, providing the mental equivalent of a scratch pad. **Working memory** consists of this "scratch pad," plus mental processes that control the retrieval of information from long-term memory and interpret that information appropriately for a given task (Baddeley, 1992). When you do an arithmetic problem, your working memory contains the numbers and the instructions for doing the necessary operations, and it also carries out those operations and retains the intermediate results from each step. The ability to bring information from long-term memory into working memory is not disrupted in patients like H. M. They can do arithmetic, converse, relate events that predate their injury, and do anything else that requires retrieval of information from long-term into short-term memory. Their problem is with the flow of information in the other direction, from short-term memory to long-term.

People such as H. M. fall at the extreme end on a continuum of forgetfulness, but even those of us with normal memories know from personal experience how frustratingly brief short-term retention can be. We look up a telephone number, are distracted for a moment, and find that the number has vanished from our minds. We meet someone at a meeting and two minutes later find ourselves groping unsuccessfully for the person's name. Is it any wonder that short-term memory has been called a "leaky bucket"?

According to most memory models, if the bucket did not leak it would quickly overflow, because at any given moment, short-term memory can hold only so many items. Years ago, George Miller (1956) estimated its capacity to be "the magical

If the visual sensory register did not clear quickly, multiple images might interfere with the accurate perception and encoding of information.

short-term memory (STM) In the three-box model of memory, a limited-capacity memory system involved in the retention of information for brief periods; it is also used to hold information retrieved from long-term memory for temporary use.

working memory In many models of memory, a memory system comprising short-term memory plus the mental processes that control retrieval of information from long-term memory and interpret that information appropriately for a given task.

If you do not play chess, you probably will not be able to recall the positions of these chess pieces after looking away. But experienced chess players, in the middle of a game, can remember the position of every piece after glancing only briefly at the board. They are able to "chunk" the pieces into a few standard configurations, instead of trying to memorize where each piece is located.

number 7 plus or minus 2." Five-digit zip codes and 7-digit telephone numbers fall conveniently in this range; 16-digit credit card numbers do not. Some researchers have questioned whether Miller's magical number is so magical after all; estimates of STM's capacity have ranged from 2 items to 20, with one recent estimate putting the "magical number" at around 4 (Cowan, 2001). Everyone agrees, however, that the number of items that short-term memory can handle at any one time is small.

If this is so, then how do we remember the beginning of a spoken sentence until the speaker reaches the end? After all, most sentences are longer than just a few words. According to most information-processing models of memory, we overcome this problem by grouping small bits of information into larger units, or **chunks.** The real capacity of STM, it turns out, is not a few bits of information but a few chunks. A chunk may be a word, a phrase, a sentence, or even a visual image, and it depends on previous experience. For most Americans, the acronym *FBI* is one chunk, not three, and the date *1492* is one chunk, not four. In contrast, the number *9214* is four chunks and *IBF* is three—unless your address is 9214 or your initials are IBF. To take a visual example: If you are unfamiliar with football and look at a field full of players, you probably won't be able to remember their positions when you look away. But if you are a fan of the game, you may see a single chunk of information—say, a wishbone formation—and be able to retain it.

Even chunking cannot keep short-term memory from eventually filling up. Fortunately, much of the information we take in during the day is needed for only a few moments. If you are multiplying two numbers, you need to remember them only until you have the answer. If you are talking to someone, you need to keep the person's words in mind only until you have understood them. But some incoming information is needed for longer periods and must be transferred to long-term memory. Items that are particularly meaningful, have an emotional impact, or relate to something already in long-term memory may enter long-term storage easily, with only a brief stay in STM. The destiny of other items depends on how soon new information displaces them in short-term memory. Material in short-term memory is easily displaced unless we do something to keep it there, as we will discuss shortly.

Long-term Memory: Final Destination

The third box in the three-box model of memory is **long-term memory (LTM).** The capacity of long-term memory seems to have no practical limits. The vast amount of information stored there enables us to learn, get around in the environment, and build a sense of identity and a personal history.

Organization in Long-term Memory. Because long-term memory contains so much information, it must be organized in some way, so that we can find the particular items we're looking for. One way to organize words (or the concepts they represent) is by the *semantic categories* to which they belong. *Chair,* for example, belongs to the category *furniture.* In a classic study, people had to memorize 60 words that came from four semantic categories: animals, vegetables, names, and professions. The words were presented in random order, but when people were allowed to recall the items in any order they wished, they tended to recall them in clusters corresponding to the four categories (Bousfield, 1953). This finding has been replicated many times.

chunk A meaningful unit of information; it may be composed of smaller units.

long-term memory (LTM) In the three-box model of memory, the memory system involved in the long-term storage of information.

Evidence on the storage of information by semantic category also comes from cases of people with brain damage. In one such case, a patient called M. D. appeared to have made a complete recovery after suffering several strokes, with one odd exception: He had trouble remembering the names of fruits and vegetables. M. D. could easily name a picture of an abacus or a sphinx, but he drew a blank when he saw a picture of an orange or a carrot. He could sort pictures of animals, vehicles, and other objects into their appropriate categories but did poorly with pictures of fruits and vegetables. On the other hand, when M. D. was *given* the names of fruits and vegetables, he immediately pointed to the corresponding pictures (Hart, Berndt, & Caramazza, 1985). Apparently, M. D. still had information about fruits and vegetables, but his brain lesion prevented him from using their names to get to the information when he needed it, unless the names were provided by someone else. This evidence suggests that information about a particular concept (such as *orange*) is linked in some way to information about the concept's semantic category (such as *fruit*).

Indeed, many models of long-term memory represent its contents as a vast network of interrelated concepts and propositions (Anderson, 1990; Collins & Loftus, 1975). In these models, a small part of a conceptual network for *animals* might look something like the one in Figure 10.4. The way people use these networks, however, depends on experience and education. For example, studies of rural children in Liberia and Guatemala have shown that the more schooling children have, the more likely they are to use semantic categories in recalling lists of objects (Cole & Cole, 1993). This makes sense, because in school, children must memorize a lot of information in a short time, and semantic grouping can help. Unschooled children, having less need to memorize lists, do not cluster items and do not remember them as well (Cole & Cole, 1993). But this does not mean that unschooled children have

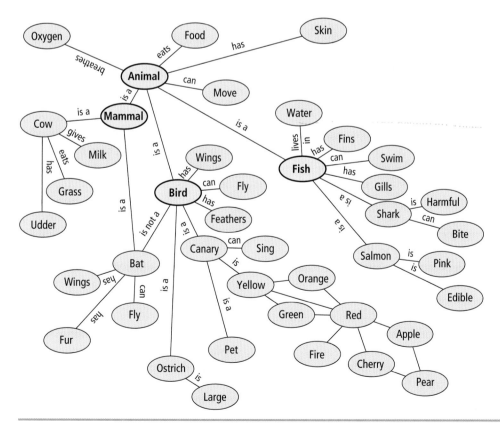

Figure 10.4

PART OF A CONCEPTUAL GRID IN LONG-TERM MEMORY

Many models of memory represent the contents of long-term semantic memory as an immense network or grid of concepts and the relationships among them. This illustration shows part of a hypothetical grid for *animals*.

Culture affects the encoding, storage, and retrieval of information in long-term memory. Navajo healers, who use stylized, symbolic sand paintings in their rituals, must commit to memory dozens of intricate visual designs because no exact copies are made and the painting is destroyed after each ceremony.

poor memories. When the task is meaningful to them—say, recalling objects that were in a story or a village scene—they remember extremely well (Mistry & Rogoff, 1994).

We organize information in long-term memory not only by semantic groupings but also in terms of the way words sound or look. Have you ever tried to recall some word that was on the "tip of your tongue"? Nearly everyone experiences such *tip-of-the-tongue (TOT) states*, especially when trying to recall the names of acquaintances or famous persons, the names of objects and places, or the titles of movies or books (Burke et al., 1991). TOT states are reported even by users of sign language, who call them tip-of-the-finger states!

One way to study this frustrating experience is to have people record tip-of-the-tongue episodes in daily diaries. Another is to give people the definitions of uncommon words and ask them to supply the words. When a word is on the tip of the tongue, people tend to come up with words that are similar in meaning to the right one before they finally recall it. For example, for "patronage bestowed on a relative, in business or politics" a person might say "favoritism" rather than the correct response, "nepotism." But verbal information in long-term memory also seems to be indexed by sound and form, and it is retrievable on that basis. Incorrect guesses often have the correct number of syllables, the correct stress pattern, the correct first letter, or the correct prefix or suffix (R. Brown & McNeill, 1966). For example, for the target word *sampan* (an Asian boat), a person might say "Siam" or "sarong."

Information in long-term memory may also be organized by its familiarity, relevance, or association with other information. The method used in any given instance probably depends on the nature of the memory; you would no doubt store information about the major cities of Europe differently from information about your first date. To understand the organization of long-term memory, then, we must know what kinds of information can be stored there.

The Contents of Long-term Memory. Most theories of memory distinguish skills or habits ("knowing how") from abstract or representational knowledge ("knowing that"). **Procedural memories** are memories of knowing how to do something—for example, knowing how to comb your hair, use a pencil, solve a jigsaw puzzle, knit a sweater, or swim. Many researchers consider procedural memories to be implicit, because once skills and habits are well learned, they do not require much conscious processing. **Declarative memories,** on the other hand, involve knowing that something is true, as in knowing that Ottawa is the capital of Canada; they are usually assumed to be explicit.

Declarative memories, in turn, come in two varieties, semantic memories and episodic memories (Tulving, 1985). **Semantic memories** are internal representations of the world, independent of any particular context. They include facts, rules, and concepts—items of general knowledge. On the basis of your semantic memory of the concept *cat,* you can describe a cat as a small, furry mammal that typically spends its time eating, sleeping, prowling, and staring into space, even though a cat may not be present when you give this description, and you probably won't know how or when you first learned it. **Episodic memories** are internal representations of personally experienced events and include information about

procedural memories Memories for the performance of actions or skills ("knowing how").

declarative memories Memories of facts, rules, concepts, and events ("knowing that"); they include semantic and episodic memories.

semantic memories Memories of general knowledge, including facts, rules, concepts, and propositions.

episodic memories Memories of personally experienced events and the contexts in which they occurred.

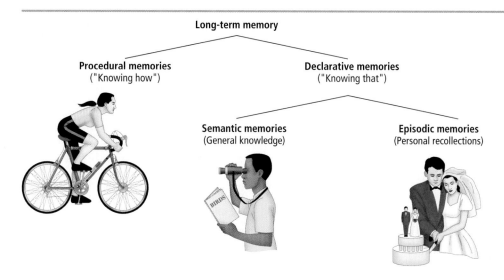

Figure 10.5

TYPES OF LONG-TERM MEMORIES

This diagram summarizes the distinctions among long-term memories. Can you come up with other examples of each memory type?

where, when, and the circumstances under which the event occurred. When you remember how your cat once surprised you in the middle of the night by pouncing on your face as you slept, you are retrieving an episodic memory. Figure 10.5 summarizes these kinds of memories.

From Short-term to Long-term Memory: A Riddle. The three-box model of memory is often invoked to explain an interesting phenomenon called the **serial-position effect**. If you are shown a list of items and are then asked immediately to recall them, your retention of any particular item will depend on its position in the list (Glanzer & Cunitz, 1966). Recall will be best for items at the beginning of the list (the *primacy effect*) and at the end of the list (the *recency effect*). When retention of all the items is plotted, the result is a U-shaped curve, as shown in Figure 10.6. A serial-position effect occurs when you are introduced to a lot of people at a party and find you can recall the names of the first few people you met and the last, but almost no one in between.

According to the three-box model, the first few items on a list are remembered well because short-term memory was relatively "empty" when they entered, so these items did not have to compete with others to make it into long-term memory. They were thoroughly processed, so they remain memorable. The last few items are remembered for a different reason: At the time of recall, they are still sitting in short-term memory. The items in the middle of a list, however, are not so well retained because by the time they get into short-term memory, it is already crowded. As a result, many of these items drop out of short-term memory before they can be stored in long-term memory.

This explanation makes sense except for one thing: Under some conditions, the last items on a list are well remembered even when the test is delayed past the time when short-term memory has presumably been "emptied" and filled with other information (Greene, 1986). In other words, the recency effect occurs even when, according to the three-box model, it should not. At present, then, the serial-position curve remains something of a puzzle.

serial-position effect The tendency for recall of the first and last items on a list to surpass recall of items in the middle of the list.

 10.2

Figure 10.6

THE SERIAL-POSITION EFFECT

When people try to recall a list of similar items immediately after learning it, they tend to remember the first and last items best and the ones in the middle worst.

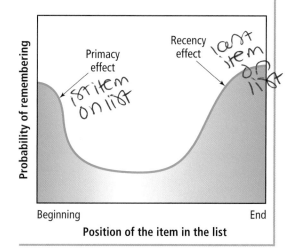

QUICK QUIZ

Find out whether the findings just discussed have transferred from your short-term memory to your long-term memory.

1. _____ memory holds images for a fraction of a second.
2. For most people, the abbreviation *USA* consists of _____ informational chunk(s).
3. Suppose you must memorize a long list of words that includes the following: *desk, pig, gold, dog, chair, silver, table, rooster, bed, copper,* and *horse.* If you can recall the words in any order you wish, how are you likely to group them in recall? Why?
4. When you roller-blade, are you relying on procedural, semantic, or episodic memory? How about when you recall the months of the year? Or when you remember falling while roller-blading on an icy January day?
5. If a child is trying to memorize the alphabet, which sequence should present the greatest difficulty: *abcdefg, klmnopq,* or *tuvwxyz?* Why?

Answers:

1. sensory 2. one 3. *Desk, chair, table,* and *bed* would probably form one cluster; *pig, dog, rooster,* and *horse* a second; and *gold, silver,* and *copper* a third. Concepts tend to be organized in long-term memory in terms of semantic categories, such as *furniture, animals,* and *metals.* 4. procedural; semantic; episodic 5. *klmnopq,* because of the serial-position effect

WHAT'S AHEAD▶

- **What changes occur in your neurons when you store a long-term memory?**
- **Where in the brain are memories for facts and events stored?**
- **Which hormones can improve your memory?**

The Biology of Memory

We have been discussing memory solely in terms of information processing, but what is happening in the brain while all that processing is going on?

Changes in Neurons and Synapses

Forming a memory involves chemical and structural changes at the level of neurons, and these changes differ for short-term memory and long-term memory.

In short-term memory, changes within neurons temporarily alter the neurons' ability to release neurotransmitters, the chemicals that carry messages from one cell to another (see Chapter 4). Evidence comes from studies with sea snails, sea slugs, and other organisms that have small numbers of easily identifiable neurons (Alkon, 1989; Kandel & Schwartz, 1982). These primitive animals can be taught simple conditioned responses, such as withdrawing or not withdrawing parts of their bodies in response to a light touch. When the animal retains the skill for only the short term, the neuron or neurons involved temporarily show an increase or decrease in readiness to release neurotransmitter molecules.

In contrast, long-term memory involves lasting structural changes in the brain. To mimic what they think may happen during the formation of a long-term memory, researchers apply brief, high-frequency electrical stimulation to groups of neurons in the brains of animals, or to brain cells in a laboratory culture. In various areas, especially the hippocampus, this stimulation increases the strength of synaptic responsiveness, a phenomenon known as **long-term potentiation** (Bliss & Collingridge, 1993; McNaughton & Morris, 1987). In other words, some synaptic pathways become more excitable.

long-term potentiation A long-lasting increase in the strength of synaptic responsiveness, thought to be a biological mechanism of long-term memory.

Most (though not all) researchers believe that long-term potentiation is the process underlying many and perhaps all forms of learning and memory, but the exact biochemical and molecular changes involved are still being debated. Some researchers think the critical changes are in receptors for the neurotransmitter glutamate on the receiving neuron (Malenka & Nicoll, 1999). Others believe that critical changes also occur in the release of glutamate by the transmitting neuron, or in other changes on the transmitting neuron (Antonova et al., 2001). Whatever the mechanism, the ultimate result is that the receiving neurons become more receptive to the next signal that comes along. It is a little like increasing the diameter of a funnel's neck to permit more flow through the funnel. In addition, during long-term potentiation, dendrites grow and branch out, and certain types of synapses increase in number (Greenough, 1984). And at the same time, in another process, some neurons become *less* responsive than they were previously (Bolshakov & Siegelbaum, 1994).

Most of these changes take time, which probably explains why long-term memories remain vulnerable to disruption for a while after they are stored—why, for example, a blow to the head may disrupt new memories even though old ones are unaffected. Just as concrete takes time to set, the neural and synaptic changes in the brain that underlie long-term memory take a while to develop fully. Memories therefore undergo a gradual period of **consolidation,** or stabilization, before they "solidify" and become stable. Consolidation can continue for weeks in animals and for several years in human beings.

Locating Memories

Scientists have used microelectrodes, brain-scan technology, and other techniques to identify the brain structures responsible for the formation and storage of specific types of memories. During short-term memory tasks, areas in the frontal lobes of the brain are especially active (Goldman-Rakic, 1996). In the formation of long-term declarative memories (memories for facts and events, or "knowing that"), the hippocampus plays a critical role: Damage to this structure causes amnesia for facts and events (Press, Amaral, & Squire, 1989). The prefrontal cortex and areas adjacent to the hippocampus in the temporal lobe are also important for the efficient encoding of pictures and words (Brewer et al., 1998; Schacter, 1999; Wagner et al., 1998).

The formation and retention of procedural memories (memory for skills and habits) seems to involve other brain structures and pathways. For example, in work with rabbits, Richard Thompson (1983, 1986) showed that one kind of procedural memory— a simple, classically-conditioned response to an unpleasant stimulus—is associated with specific changes in the cerebellum. When rabbits are conditioned to blink their eyes in response to a tone, changes in electrical activity occur in parts of the cerebellum. If the affected brain tissue is removed or destroyed, the animals immediately forget the response and cannot relearn it. Moreover, if you deaden a part of the cerebellum during initial conditioning, the rabbits will not learn the response in the first place (Krupa, Thompson, & Thompson, 1993). Human patients with damage in the cerebellum are also incapable of this type of conditioning (Daum & Schugens, 1996).

The formation of declarative and procedural memories in different brain areas could explain a curious finding about patients like H. M. Despite their inability to form new declarative memories, such patients can, with sufficient practice, acquire new procedural memories that enable them to solve a puzzle, read mirror-reversed words, or play tennis—although they do not recall the training sessions in which they learned these skills. Apparently, the parts of the brain involved in acquiring new procedural memories have remained intact.

consolidation The process by which a long-term memory becomes durable and stable.

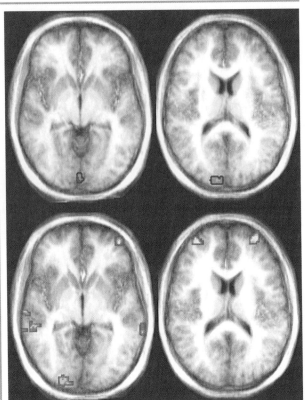

Figure 10.7

BRAIN ACTIVITY IN EXPLICIT AND IMPLICIT MEMORY

As these composite functional MRI scans show, patterns of brain activity differ depending on the type of memory task involved. When people had an explicit memory for dot patterns they had seen earlier, areas in the visual cortex, temporal lobes, and frontal lobes (indicated by orange in the lower photos) were more active. When people's implicit memories were activated, areas in the visual cortex (blue in the upper photos) were relatively inactive (Reber, Stark, & Squire, 1998).

Patients such as H. M. also retain some implicit memory for verbal material, as measured by priming tasks. For example, if H. M. sees the word *define* on a list and later has to complete the stem *def* with the first word that comes to mind, he is more likely to say "define" than some other word, just as people with normal memories are (Keane, Gabrieli, & Corkin, 1987). Some psychologists conclude that there must therefore be separate systems in the brain for implicit and explicit tasks. As Figure 10.7 shows, this view has been bolstered by brain scans, which reveal differences in the location of brain activity when normal subjects perform explicit versus implicit memory tasks (Reber, Stark, & Squire, 1998; Squire et al., 1992).

The brain circuits that take part in the *formation* of long-term memories, however, are not the same as those involved in long-term *storage* of those memories. The role of the hippocampus, for example, appears to be only temporary, and the ultimate destinations of declarative memories seem to lie in parts of the cerebral cortex. Scientists have long suspected that memories were stored in the same cortical areas that were involved in the original perception of the information (Mishkin & Appenzeller, 1987). Brain-scan studies support this view; when people remember pictures, visual parts of the brain become active, and when they remember sounds, auditory areas become active—just as they did when the information was first perceived (Nyberg et al., 2000; Thompson & Kosslyn, 2000; Wheeler, Petersen, & Buckner, 2000).

The typical "memory" is a complex cluster of information. When you recall meeting a man yesterday, you remember his greeting, his tone of voice, how he looked, and where he was. Even a single concept, such as "shovel," includes a lot of information (about its length, what it's made of, what it's used for . . .). These different pieces of information are probably processed separately and stored at different locations that are distributed across wide areas of the brain, with all the sites participating in the representation of the event or concept as a whole (Damasio et al., 1996; Squire, 1987). The role of the hippocampus may be to somehow bind together the diverse aspects of a memory at the time it is formed, so that even though these aspects are stored in different cortical sites, the memory can be retrieved as one coherent entity (Squire & Zola-Morgan, 1991).

Review 10.1 shows the structures that we have discussed and summarizes some of the memory-related functions associated with them. But we have given you just a few small nibbles from the smorgasbord of findings now available. Researchers are learning more and more about where memories are located. Someday, neuroscientists may be able to describe the entire stream of events in the brain that occur from the moment you say to yourself "I must remember this" to the moment you actually do remember (or find that you can't).

Hormones and Memory

Have you ever smelled fresh cookies and recalled a tender scene from your childhood? Do you have a vivid memory of seeing a particularly horrifying horror movie? Emotional memories such as these are often especially intense, and the explanation resides partly in our hormones.

Hormones released by the adrenal glands during stress and emotional arousal, including epinephrine (adrenaline) and certain steroids, enhance memory. If you give people a drug that prevents their adrenal glands from producing these hormones, they will remember less about emotional stories they heard than a control group will

REVIEW 10.1 SOME BRAIN AREAS INVOLVED IN MEMORY

No simple summary of brain areas associated with memory can do this complex topic justice. Here are just a few of the areas and functions that have been studied.

Brain Area	Associated Memory Function
Frontal lobes	Short-term memory tasks
Prefrontal cortex, parts of temporal lobes	Efficient encoding of words, pictures
Hippocampus	Formation of long-term declarative memories; may "bind together" diverse elements of a memory so it can be retrieved later as a coherent entity
Cerebellum	Formation and retention of simple classically conditioned responses
Cerebral cortex	Storage of long-term memories, probably in areas involved in the original perception of the information

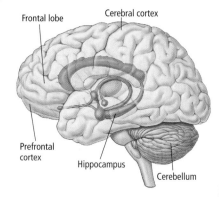

(Cahill et al., 1994). Conversely, if you give epinephrine to animals right after learning, their memories will improve (McGaugh, 1990). The link between emotional arousal and memory makes evolutionary sense: Arousal tells the brain that an event or piece of information is important enough to encode and store for future use.

When animals are given very high doses of adrenal hormones, however, their memories for learned tasks suffer instead of improving; a moderate dose is optimal. Similarly, if you are studying for a psychology exam, very high hormone levels could actually interfere with memory. If you want to remember such information well, you should aim for an arousal level somewhere between "hyper" and "laid back."

How can hormones produced in the adrenal glands affect storage of information in the brain? One possibility is that epinephrine causes the level of glucose (a sugar) to rise in the bloodstream. Although epinephrine does not readily enter the brain from the bloodstream, glucose does. Once in the brain, glucose may enhance memory either directly or by altering the effects of neurotransmitters (Gold, 1987).

This "sweet memories" effect occurs both in aged rats and mice and in elderly human beings. In one encouraging study, healthy older people fasted overnight, drank a glass of lemonade sweetened with either glucose or saccharin, and then took two memory tests. The saccharine-laced drink had no effect on their performance, but lemonade with glucose greatly boosted their ability to recall a taped passage 5 or 40 minutes after hearing it (Manning, Hall, & Gold, 1990). Glucose also enhances the ability of Alzheimer's patients to recognize words, prose passages, and faces (Manning, Ragozzino, & Gold, 1993).

However, the exact mechanisms involved in the hormone–memory link remain unclear and controversial. In this area, as in others in the biology of memory, many findings are still provisional, and we have much to learn. No one knows yet exactly how the brain actually stores information, how different memory circuits link up with one another, or how a student is able to locate and retrieve information at the drop of a multiple-choice item.

QUICK QUIZ

We hope your memory circuits will link up to help you answer this quiz.

1. Is long-term potentiation associated with (a) increased responsiveness of a receiving neuron to a transmitting neuron, (b) a decrease in receptors on a receiving neuron, or (c) reaching your true potential?

2. The cerebellum has been associated with _____ memories; the hippocampus has been associated with _____ memories.

3. *True or false:* Hormone research suggests that if you want to remember well, you should be as relaxed as possible while learning.

4. After reading about glucose and memory, should you immediately start gulping down lemonade? Why or why not?

Answers:

1. a 2. procedural, declarative 3. false 4. You probably should not pig out on sugar yet. Results from elderly people, using measures of memory on which older people show deficits, may not generalize to younger people with normal memories. Even if the results do generalize, you would need to know how much glucose is effective; in the elderly, there is an optimal dose (Parsons & Gold, 1992). Also, in some people, frequent glucose consumption may have adverse health consequences that would outweigh the benefits.

WHAT'S AHEAD ▶

● **What's wrong with trying to memorize in a rote fashion when you're studying— and what's a better strategy?**
● **Memory tricks are fun, but are they always useful?**

How We Remember

Once we understand how memory works, we can use that understanding to encode and store information so that it "sticks" and will be there when we need it. What are the best strategies to use?

Effective Encoding

Encoding classroom material for later recall usually takes a deliberate effort. Which of these students do you think will remember best?

Our memories, as we have seen, are not exact replicas of experience. Sensory information is summarized and encoded—for example, as words or images—almost as soon as it is detected. When you hear a lecture, for example, you may hang on every word (we hope you do), but you do not memorize those words verbatim. You extract the main points and encode them.

To remember information well, you have to encode it accurately in the first place. With some kinds of information, accurate encoding takes place automatically, without effort. Think about where you usually sit in your psychology class. When were you last there? You can probably provide this information easily, even though you never made a deliberate effort to encode it. But many kinds of information require *effortful encoding*—the plot of a novel, the procedures for assembling a cabinet, the arguments for and against a proposed law. To retain such information, you might have to select the main points, label concepts, or associate the information with personal experiences or with material you already know.

Unfortunately, people sometimes count on automatic encoding when effortful encoding is needed. For example, some students wrongly assume that they can encode the material in a textbook as effortlessly as they encode where they sit in the classroom. Or they assume that the ability to remember and perform well on tests is innate and that effort will not make any difference. As a result, they wind up in trouble at test time. Experienced students know that most of the information in a college course requires effortful encoding and sometimes hard work.

Rehearsal

An important technique for keeping information in short-term memory and increasing the chances of long-term retention is *rehearsal,* the review or practice of material while you are learning it. When people are prevented from rehearsing, the contents of their short-term memories quickly fade.

In an early study of this phenomenon, people had to memorize meaningless groups of letters. Immediately afterward, they had to start counting backward by threes from an arbitrary number; this counting prevented them from rehearsing the letter groups. Within only 18 seconds, the subjects forgot most of the items. But when they did not have to count backward, their performance was much better, probably because they were rehearsing the items to themselves (Peterson & Peterson, 1959). You are taking advantage of rehearsal when you look up a phone number and then repeat it over and over in order to keep it in short-term memory until you no longer need it. And, when you can't remember a phone number because you have always used speed dial to call it, you are learning what happens when you *don't* rehearse!

Short-term memory holds many kinds of information, including visual information and abstract meanings. But most people—or at least most hearing people—seem to favor speech for encoding and rehearsing the contents of short-term memory. The speech may be spoken aloud or to oneself. When people make errors on short-term memory tests that use letters or words, they often confuse items that sound the same or similar, such as *d* and *t,* or *bear* and *bare.* These errors suggest that they have been rehearsing verbally.

Elaborative Rehearsal. Some strategies for rehearsing are more effective than others. **Maintenance rehearsal** involves merely the rote repetition of the material. This kind of rehearsal is fine for keeping information in STM, but it will not always lead to long-term retention. A better strategy if you want to remember for the long haul is **elaborative rehearsal,** also called *elaboration of encoding* (Cermak & Craik, 1979; Craik & Tulving, 1975). Elaboration involves associating new items of information with material that has already been stored or with other new facts. It can also involve analyzing the physical, sensory, or semantic features of an item.

Suppose, for example, that you are studying the hypothalamus in Chapter 4. Simply memorizing the definition of the hypothalamus in a rote manner is unlikely to help much. Instead, when going over the concept, you could encode the information in the lower part of Figure 10.8. The more you elaborate the concept of the hypothalamus, the better you are likely to remember it.

Deep Processing. A related strategy for prolonging retention is **deep processing,** or the processing of meaning (Craik & Lockhart, 1972). If you process only the physical or sensory features of a stimulus, such as how the word *hypothalamus* is spelled and how it sounds, your processing will be shallow even if it is elaborated. If you recognize patterns and assign labels to objects or events ("The *hypothalamus is below* the thalamus"), your processing will be somewhat deeper. If you fully analyze the meaning of what you are trying to remember (for example, by encoding the functions and importance of the hypothalamus), your processing will be deeper yet.

maintenance rehearsal Rote repetition of material in order to maintain its availability in memory.

elaborative rehearsal Association of new information with already stored knowledge and analysis of the new information to make it memorable.

deep processing In the encoding of information, the processing of meaning rather than simply the physical or sensory features of a stimulus.

Figure 10.8
ELABORATION OF ENCODING

In elaborated encoding, you encode the features of an item and its associations with other items in memory. When you studied the hypothalamus in Chapter 4, was your encoding elaborated or impoverished?

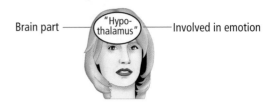

IMPOVERISHED ENCODING
(poor retention)

Brain part —— "Hypo-thalamus" —— Involved in emotion

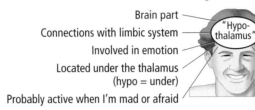

ELABORATE ENCODING
(good retention)

Brain part —— Involved in survival drives like hunger and thirst
Connections with limbic system —— "Hypo-thalamus"
Involved in emotion —— Regulates body temperature
Located under the thalamus (hypo = under) —— Sends messages to pituitary gland
Probably active when I'm mad or afraid —— Controls autonomic nervous system

Shallow processing is sometimes useful; when you memorize a poem, for instance, you will want to pay attention to (and elaborately encode) the sounds of the words and the patterns of rhythm in the poem, and not just the poem's meaning. Usually, however, deep processing is more effective. That is why, if you try to memorize information that has little or no meaning for you, the information may not stick.

Mnemonics

In addition to using elaborative rehearsal and deep processing, people who want to give their powers of memory a boost sometimes use **mnemonics** [neh-MON-iks], formal strategies and tricks for encoding, storing, and retaining information. (Mnemosyne, pronounced neh-MOZ-eh-nee, was the ancient Greek goddess of memory. Can you remember her?) Some mnemonics take the form of easily memorized rhymes (e.g., "Thirty days hath September / April, June, and November . . ."). Others use formulas (e.g., "Every **g**ood **b**oy **d**oes **f**ine" for remembering which notes are on the lines of the treble clef in musical notation). Still others use visual images or word associations.

The best mnemonics force you to encode material actively and thoroughly. They may also reduce the amount of information by chunking it, which is why in ads many companies now use words for their phone numbers instead of unmemorable numbers (for example, "Dial GET RICH"). Many mnemonics make the material meaningful and thus easier to store and retrieve, say, by having you weave unrelated facts and words into a coherent story (Bower & Clark, 1969). If you needed to remember the parts of the digestive system for a physiology course, you could construct a narrative about what happens to a piece of food from the moment it enters a person's mouth, then repeat the narrative aloud to yourself or to a study partner.

Some stage performers with amazing recall rely on more complicated mnemonics. We are not going to spend time on them here, because for ordinary memory tasks, such tricks are often no more effective than rote rehearsal, and sometimes they are actually worse (Wang, Thomas, & Ouellette, 1992). Most memory researchers do not use such mnemonics themselves (Hébert, 2001). After all, why bother to memorize a grocery list using a fancy mnemonic when you can write down what you need to buy? The fastest route to a good memory is to follow the principles suggested by the findings in this section and by research reviewed in "Taking Psychology with You."

"YOU SIMPLY ASSOCIATE EACH NUMBER WITH A WORD, SUCH AS 'TABLE' AND 3,476,029."

10.3 **Live! psych**

mnemonics Strategies and tricks for improving memory, such as the use of a verse or a formula.

WHAT'S AHEAD

- **How might new information "erase" old memories?**
- **What theory explains why you keep dialing an old area code instead of your new one?**
- **Why is it easier to recall experiences from elementary school if you see pictures of your classmates?**
- **Why are many researchers skeptical about claims of "repressed" and "recovered" memories?**

Why We Forget

Have you ever, in the heat of some deliriously happy moment, said to yourself, "I'll never forget this, never, *never*, NEVER"? Do you find that you can more clearly remember saying those words than the deliriously happy moment itself? Sometimes you encode an event, you rehearse it, you analyze its meaning, you tuck it away in long-term storage—and still you forget it. Is it any wonder that most of us have wished, at one time or another, for a "photographic memory"?

Actually, having a perfect memory is not the blessing that you might suppose. The Russian psychologist Alexander Luria (1968) once told of a journalist, S., who could reproduce giant grids of numbers both forward and backward, even after the passage of 15 years. S. also remembered the exact circumstances under which he had originally learned the material. To accomplish his astonishing feats, he used mnemonics, especially the formation of visual images. But you should not envy him, for he had a serious problem: He could not forget even when he wanted to. Along with the diamonds of experience, he kept dredging up the pebbles. Images he had formed in order to remember kept creeping into consciousness, distracting him and interfering with his ability to concentrate. At times he even had trouble holding a conversation because the other person's words would set off a jumble of associations. In fact, Luria called him "rather dull-witted." Eventually, S. took to supporting himself by traveling from place to place, demonstrating his mnemonic abilities for audiences.

Paradoxically, then, forgetting is adaptive: We need to forget if we wish to remember efficiently (Bjork, Bjork, & Anderson, 1998). Forgetting also contributes to our survival, our happiness, and our very sanity. Think back: Would you really want to recall every angry argument, every embarrassing episode, every painful moment in your life? Could it be that self-confidence and optimism depend on locking some follies and grievances in a back drawer of memory?

Nonetheless, most of us forget more than we would like to, and we would like to know why. Over a century ago, in an effort to measure pure memory loss independent of personal experience, Hermann Ebbinghaus (1885/1913) memorized long lists of

Motor skills, which are stored as procedural memories, can last a lifetime. Why don't memories of people, events, and facts always do likewise?

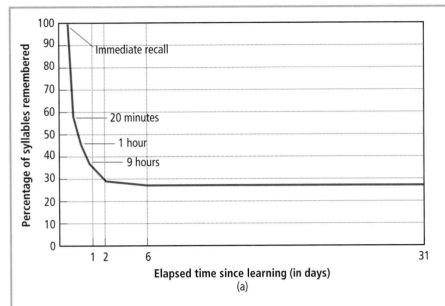

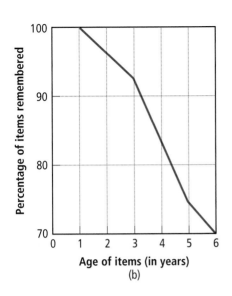

Elapsed time since learning (in days)
(a)

Age of items (in years)
(b)

Figure 10.9

TWO KINDS OF FORGETTING CURVES

When Hermann Ebbinghaus tested his own memory for nonsense syllables, forgetting was rapid at first and then tapered off (a). In contrast, when Marigold Linton tested her own memory for personal events over a period of several years, her retention was excellent at first, but then it fell off at a gradual but steady rate (b).

nonsense syllables, such as *bok, waf,* or *ged,* and then tested his retention over a period of several weeks. Most of his forgetting occurred soon after the initial learning and then leveled off (see Figure 10.9a). Ebbinghaus's method of studying memory was adopted by generations of psychologists, even though it did not tell them much about the kinds of memories that people care about most.

A century later, Marigold Linton decided to find out how people forget real events rather than nonsense syllables. Like Ebbinghaus, she used herself as a subject, but she charted the curve of forgetting over years rather than days. Every day for 12 years she recorded on a 4- × 6-inch card two or more things that had happened to her that day. Eventually, she accumulated a catalogue of thousands of discrete events, both trivial ("I have dinner at the Canton Kitchen: delicious lobster dish") and significant ("I land at Orly Airport in Paris"). Once a month, she took a random sampling of all the cards accumulated to that point, noted whether she could remember the events on them, and tried to date the events. Linton (1978) expected the kind of rapid forgetting reported by Ebbinghaus. Instead, as you can see in Figure 10.9b, she found that long-term forgetting was slower and proceeded at a much more constant pace, as details gradually dropped out of her memories.

Of course, some memories, especially those that mark important transitions, are more memorable than others. But why did Marigold Linton, like the rest of us, forget so many details? Psychologists have proposed five mechanisms to account for forgetting: decay, replacement of old memories by new ones, interference, cue-dependent forgetting, and psychological amnesia brought on by repression.

10.4

Decay

One commonsense view, the **decay theory**, holds that memory traces fade with time if they are not "accessed" now and then. We have already seen that decay occurs in sensory memory and that it occurs in short-term memory as well unless we rehearse the material. However, the mere passage of time does not account so well for forgetting in long-term memory. People commonly forget things that happened only yesterday while remembering events from many years ago. Indeed, some memories, both procedural and declarative, remain accessible for a lifetime. If you learned to swim as a child, you will still know how to swim at age 30, even

decay theory The theory that information in memory eventually disappears if it is not accessed; it applies better to short-term than to long-term memory.

Figure 10.10
When people who saw a car with a yield sign (left) were later asked if they had seen "the stop sign" (a misleading question), many said they had. Likewise, when those shown a stop sign were asked if they had seen "the yield sign," many said yes. These false memories persisted even after the participants were told about the misleading questions, suggesting that misleading information had erased their original mental representations of the signs (Loftus, 1980).

if you have not been in a pool or lake for 22 years. We are also happy to report that some school lessons have great staying power. In one study, people did well on a Spanish test some 50 years after taking Spanish in high school, even though most had hardly used Spanish at all in the intervening years (Bahrick, 1984). Decay alone, although it may play some role, cannot entirely explain lapses in long-term memory.

Replacement

Another theory holds that new information entering memory can wipe out old information, just as rerecording on an audiotape or videotape will obliterate the original material. In one study supporting this view, researchers showed people slides of a traffic accident and used leading questions to get them to think that they had seen a stop sign when they had really seen a yield sign, or vice versa (see Figure 10.10). People in a control group who were not misled in this way were able to identify the sign they had actually seen. Later, all the participants were told the purpose of the study and were asked to guess whether they had been misled. Almost all of those who had been misled continued to insist that they had *really, truly* seen the sign whose existence had been planted in their minds (Loftus, Miller, & Burns, 1978). The researchers interpreted these findings to mean that the subjects had not just been trying to please them, and that people's original perceptions had in fact been "erased" and replaced by the misleading information.

Interference

A third theory holds that forgetting occurs because similar items of information interfere or compete with one another in either storage or retrieval; the information may get into memory and stay there, but it becomes confused with other information. Such interference, which occurs in both short- and long-term memory, is especially common when you have to recall isolated facts—names, addresses, PIN numbers, area codes, and the like.

Suppose you are at a party and you meet someone named Julie. A little later you meet someone named Judy. You go on to talk to other people, and after an hour, you again bump into Julie, but by mistake you call her Judy. The second name has interfered with the first. This type of interference, in which new information interferes with the ability to remember old information, is called **retroactive interference**.

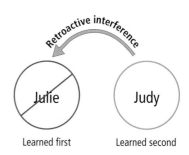

Retroactive interference

Julie — Learned first

Judy — Learned second

Retroactive interference is illustrated by the story of an absent-minded professor of ichthyology (the study of fish) who complained that whenever he learned the name of a new student, he forgot the name of a fish. But whereas with replacement, the new memory erases the old and makes it irretrievable, in retroactive interference the loss of the old memory is sometimes just temporary. With a little concentration, that professor could probably recall his new students and his old fish.

Because new information is constantly entering memory, we are all vulnerable to the effects of retroactive interference—or at least most of us are. H. M. is an exception; his memories of childhood and adolescence are unusually detailed, clear, and unchanging. H. M. can remember actors who were famous when he was a child, the films they were in, and who their costars were. He also knows the names of friends from the second grade. Presumably, these early declarative memories were not subject to interference from memories acquired since the operation for the simple reason that H. M. has not acquired any new memories.

Interference also works in the opposite direction. Old information (such as the Spanish you learned in high school) may interfere with the ability to remember new information (such as the French you are trying to learn now). This type of interference is called **proactive interference**. Over a period of weeks, months, and years, proactive interference may cause more forgetting than retroactive interference does, because we have stored up so much information that can potentially interfere with anything new.

Cue-dependent Forgetting

Often, when we need to remember, we rely on *retrieval cues,* items of information that can help us find the specific information we're looking for. For example, if you are trying to remember the last name of an actor, it might help to know the person's first name or the name of a recent movie the actor starred in.

When we lack retrieval cues, we may feel as if we are lost among the stacks in the mind's library. In long-term memory, this type of memory failure, called **cue-dependent forgetting,** may be the most common type of all. Willem Wagenaar (1986), who, like Marigold Linton, recorded critical details about events in his life, found that within a year, he had forgotten 20 percent of those details, and after five years, he had forgotten 60 percent. However, when he gathered cues from witnesses about ten events that he thought he had forgotten, he was able to recall something about all ten, which suggests that some of his forgetting was cue dependent.

Cues that were present when you learned a new fact or had an experience are apt to be especially useful later as retrieval aids. That may explain why remembering is often easier when you are in the same physical environment as you were when an event occurred: Cues in the present context match those from the past. Some people have suggested that the overlap between present and past cues may also lead to a *false* sense of having been in exactly the same situation before; this is the eerie phenomenon of *déjà vu* (which means "already seen" in French). Ordinarily, however, contextual cues help us remember the past more accurately.

Your mental or physical state may also act as a retrieval cue, evoking a **state-dependent memory.** For example, if you are intoxicated when something happens, you may remember it better when you once again have had a few drinks than when you are sober. (This is not an endorsement of drunkenness! Your memory will be best if you are sober during both encoding and recall.) Likewise, if your emotional

Proactive interference

Julie — Judy

Learned first — Learned second

retroactive interference Forgetting that occurs when recently learned material interferes with the ability to remember similar material stored previously.

proactive interference Forgetting that occurs when previously stored material interferes with the ability to remember similar, more recently learned material.

cue-dependent forgetting The inability to retrieve information stored in memory because of insufficient cues for recall.

state-dependent memory The tendency to remember something when the rememberer is in the same physical or mental state as during the original learning or experience.

arousal is especially high or low at the time of an event, you may remember that event best when you are once again in the same emotional state. When victims of violent crimes have trouble recalling details of the experience, it may be in part because they are far less emotionally aroused than they were at the time of the crime (Clark, Milberg, & Erber, 1987).

You may also be better able to retrieve a memory when your current mood matches the *kind of material* you are trying to remember. You are likely to remember happy events better when you are feeling happy than when you are sad (Mayer, McCormick, & Strong, 1995). Similarly, you are likely to remember unhappy events better and remember more of them when you are feeling unhappy, which in turn creates a vicious cycle. The more unhappy memories you recall, the more depressed you feel, and the more depressed you feel, the more unhappy memories you recall . . . so you stay stuck in your depression and make it even worse (Lyubomirsky, Caldwell, & Nolen-Hoeksema, 1998). You can break out of this trap by deliberately focusing on memories of happy events instead of unpleasant ones.

Charlie Chaplin's film *City Lights* provides a classic illustration of state-dependent memory. After Charlie saves the life of a drunken millionaire, the two spend the rest of the evening in boisterous merrymaking. But the next day, after sobering up, the millionaire fails to recognize Charlie and gives him the cold shoulder. Then, once again, the millionaire gets drunk—and once again he greets Charlie as a pal.

The Repression Controversy

A final theory of forgetting is concerned with **psychogenic amnesia**, the loss of memory for painful or disturbing events. *Amnesia,* the inability to remember important personal information, can result from organic conditions such as brain disease or head injury. Sometimes it occurs in the immediate aftermath of a physically traumatic experience, such as a car accident, and usually it is temporary. In psychogenic amnesia, however, the causes of forgetting are psychological: a need to escape intolerable feelings of embarrassment, guilt, shame, or emotional shock. The notion of psychogenic amnesia originated with the psychoanalytic theory of Sigmund Freud, who argued that the mind defends itself from unwelcome and upsetting memories through the mechanism of **repression**—the selective, involuntary pushing of threatening or upsetting information into the unconscious (see Chapter 13).

Most psychologists accept the idea that people can have psychogenic amnesia for troubling, embarrassing, and painful experiences, and that with the right cues, these memories may return. One clinician reported the case of a client who became upset when he saw several men reading X-rated magazines at a newsstand. Eventually he remembered that when he was 11, he had been sexually molested by his cousin and several other older boys—who had been reading the same kind of magazine (Nash, 1994). His cousin corroborated his memory and told him how ashamed he was of what happened.

Most memory researchers, however, reject the notion that a special mechanism called "repression" explains psychogenic amnesia. One major problem is that it is hard to identify "repression" when you see it, let alone distinguish it from normal forms of forgetting. Perhaps people who forget disturbing experiences are not repressing those experiences but are intentionally keeping themselves from retrieving

psychogenic amnesia The partial or complete loss of memory (due to nonorganic causes) for threatening information or traumatic experiences.

repression In psychoanalytic theory, the selective, involuntary pushing of threatening or upsetting information into the unconscious.

their painful memories, say, by distracting themselves when a memory is awakened or by focusing entirely on positive memories. Perhaps, understandably, they are not rehearsing unhappy memories, so the memories become more likely to fade. Perhaps they are simply avoiding the retrieval cues that would evoke the memories.

The debate over repression erupted into the public arena in the 1990s, when claims of recovered memories of sexual abuse began to occur. Many women and some men came to believe, during psychotherapy, that they could recall long-buried—"repressed"—memories of sexual victimization. Criminal charges were lodged against the alleged perpetrators, usually fathers or other relatives. In one typical case, a woman named Laura B. sued her father, claiming that he had molested her from the ages of 5 to 23 and had even raped her just days before her wedding. Laura B. said she had repressed these memories and had no recollection of them until they emerged during therapy.

For psychodynamic therapists who accept the view that painful memories can be repressed and thus remain inaccessible for years, such recovered memories are entirely believable (J. Herman, 1992; Pope, 1996). But others argue that although real abuse occurs, many false memories of victimization have been encouraged by naive therapists who are unaware of the power of suggestion and the dangers of confabulation (Lindsay & Read, 1994; Loftus & Ketcham, 1994). These critics point out that repeated experiences of trauma like those claimed by Laura B. are more likely to be remembered than forgotten, even when the victims wish they could forget (McNally, 2003; Schacter, 2001). Only rarely have "recovered" memories been corroborated by objective evidence, so it is difficult and often impossible to determine their accuracy. Most research psychologists are skeptical of the whole concept of repression, which they consider vague and ill-defined (Holmes, 1990; Schacter, 1996, 2001).

For these reasons, many courts, too, have become skeptical of accusations based solely on "repressed" and "recovered" memories. In the case of Laura B., the judge wrote that her recovered memories would not be admissible evidence because "the phenomenon of memory repression, and the process of therapy used in these cases to recover the memories, have not gained general acceptance in the field of psychology; and are not scientifically reliable" (*State of New Hampshire* v. *Joel Hungerford*, May 23, 1995).

How, then, should we respond to an individual's claim to have recovered memories of abuse? Given current research on memory, we should be skeptical if the person says that, thanks to therapy, he or she now has memories from the first year or two of life. (As we will see in the next section, this is not possible.) We should be skeptical if, over time, the person's memories become more and more implausible—for instance, the person says that sexual abuse continued day and night for 15 years without ever being remembered and without anyone else in the household noticing anything amiss. And we should hear alarm bells go off if a therapist used suggestive techniques, such as hypnosis, dream analysis, and leading questions, to "help" a patient recall the alleged abuse (see Chapter 17), because these techniques increase confabulations (Loftus, 1996). In contrast, a person's recollections are more likely to be trustworthy if there is corroborating evidence from medical records or from other family members, and if the person spontaneously recalled the event without pressure from others or the use of suggestive techniques in therapy.

THINKING CRITICALLY

Examine the Evidence

Some people think recovered memories of sexual abuse should always be trusted, and some think they should not. How can we draw on research findings when evaluating someone's claim to have recovered a memory that was long buried?

Films and novels reflect and influence popular notions about memory. When Alfred Hitchcock made *Spellbound* in 1945, psychoanalytic ideas held sway. In the film, amnesia patient Gregory Peck is suspected of murder, and the clues to the identity of the real killer appear in a dream he has. The surrealistic dream sequences, designed by artist Salvador Dali, conveyed the idea that painful memories are never forgotten but are merely locked away in the unconscious with all the details intact, waiting to be recovered—a notion that modern research has questioned.

QUICK QUIZ

If you have not repressed what you just read, try these questions.

1. When she read *Even Cowgirls Get the Blues* many years ago, Wilma fell in love with the novels of Tom Robbins. Later, she developed a crush on actor Tim Robbins, but every time she tried to recall his name, she called him "Tom." Why?

2. When a man at his twentieth high-school reunion sees his old friends, he recalls incidents he thought were long forgotten. Why?

3. What mechanisms other than repression could account for a person's psychogenic amnesia?

Answers:

1. proactive interference 2. The sight of his friends provides retrieval cues for the incidents. 3. The person could be intentionally avoiding the memory by using distraction or focusing on positive experiences; the person's failure to rehearse the memory may be causing it to fade; or the person may be avoiding retrieval cues that would evoke the memory.

WHAT'S AHEAD

- **Why are the first few years of life a mental blank?**
- **Why have human beings been called the "storytelling animal"?**
- **Which periods of life tend to stand out in memory?**

Autobiographical Memories

For most of us, our autobiographical memories—our memories about our own experiences—are by far the most fascinating. We use them to entertain ("Did I ever tell you about the time . . .?"); we modify them—some people even publish them—in order to create an image of ourselves; we analyze them to learn more about who we are.

Childhood Amnesia: The Missing Years

A curious aspect of autobiographical memory is that most adults cannot recall any events from earlier than the third or fourth year of life. A few people apparently can recall momentous experiences that occurred when they were as young as 2 years old, such as the birth of a sibling, but not earlier (Newcombe et al., 2000; Usher & Neisser, 1993). As adults, we cannot remember being fed in infancy by our parents, taking our first steps, or uttering our first halting sentences. We are victims of **childhood amnesia** (sometimes called *infantile amnesia*).

There is something disturbing about childhood amnesia—so disturbing that some people adamantly deny it, claiming to remember events from the second or even the first year of life. But like other false memories, these are merely reconstructions based on photographs, family stories, and imagination. The "remembered" event may not even have taken place. Swiss psychologist Jean Piaget (1952b) once reported a memory of nearly being kidnapped at the age of 2. Piaget remembered sitting in his pram, watching his nurse as she bravely defended him from the kidnapper. He remembered the scratches she received on her face. He remembered a police officer with a short cloak and white baton who finally chased the kidnapper away. But when Piaget was 15, his nurse wrote to his parents confessing that she had made up the entire story. Piaget noted, "I therefore must have heard, as a child, the account of this story . . . and projected it into the past in the form of a visual memory, which was a memory of a memory, but false."

THINKING CRITICALLY

Avoid Emotional Reasoning

Many people get upset at the idea that their earliest experiences are lost to memory and angrily insist that memories from the first two years must be true. How can research help us think clearly about this issue?

childhood (infantile) amnesia The inability to remember events and experiences that occurred during the first two or three years of life.

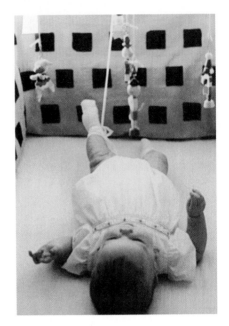

Psychologists have devised ingenious methods to measure memory in infants. This infant, whose leg is attached by a string to a colorful mobile, will learn within minutes to kick in order to make the mobile move. A week later, when tested without the string, she may still remember the trick—an example of procedural memory (Rovee-Collier, 1993). However, when she is older she will not remember the experience itself. Like the rest of us, she will fall victim to childhood amnesia.

Of course, we all retain procedural memories from the toddler stage, when we first learned to use a fork, drink from a cup, and pull a wagon. We also retain semantic memories acquired early in life: the rules of counting, the names of people and things, knowledge about objects in the world, words and meanings. Further, toddlers who are only 1 to 2 years old can often remember past experiences, and some 4-year-olds can remember experiences that occurred before age 2½ (Bauer & Dow, 1994; McDonough & Mandler, 1994). What young children do not do well is encode and retain their early episodic memories—memories of particular events—and carry them into later childhood or adulthood.

Sigmund Freud thought that childhood amnesia was another case of repression, but most memory researchers today think that repression has nothing to do with it. Biological psychologists believe that childhood amnesia occurs because brain areas involved in the formation or storage of events, and other areas involved in working memory and decision making (such as the prefrontal cortex), are not well developed until a few years after birth (McKee & Squire, 1993; Newcombe et al., 2000). Cognitive psychologists have proposed other explanations, such as the following:

1 *Lack of a sense of self.* In one view, we cannot have an autobiographical memory of our*selves* until we have a self to remember. Indeed, autobiographical memories do not begin until the emergence of a self-concept, an event that occurs at somewhat different ages for different children, but usually not before the age of 2 (Howe, Courage, & Peterson, 1994).

2 *Impoverished encoding.* Preschoolers encode experiences far less elaborately than adults do. Young children have not yet mastered the social conventions for reporting events; they do not know what is important and interesting to others. Instead, they tend to rely on adults' questions to provide retrieval cues ("Where did we go for breakfast?" "Who did you go trick-or-treating with?"), and this dependency on adults may prevent them from building up a stable core of remembered material that will be available when they are older (Fivush & Hamond, 1991).

3 *A focus on the routine.* Preschoolers tend to focus on the routine, familiar aspects of an experience, such as eating lunch or playing with toys, rather than the distinctive aspects that will provide retrieval cues and make an event memorable in the long run (Fivush & Hamond, 1991).

4 *Children's ways of thinking about the world.* The cognitive schemas used by preschoolers are very different from those used by older children and adults. Only after acquiring language and starting school do children learn to think like adults do. Their new, adultlike schemas do not contain the information and cues necessary for recalling earlier experiences, so memories of those experiences are lost (Howe & Courage, 1993).

Whatever the explanation for childhood amnesia, our first memories, even when they are not accurate, may provide useful insights into our personalities, current

Get Involved

Analyze a Childhood Memory

Write down as much as you can about an incident in your childhood that stands out in your memory. Now ask a friend or family memory who was present at the time to write a description of the same event. Do your accounts differ? If so, why? What does this exercise tell you about the nature of memory—and about your own personality or present concerns?

concerns, ambitions, and attitudes toward life (Kihlstrom & Harackiewicz, 1982). What are your first memories?

Memory and Narrative: The Stories of Our Lives

The communications researcher George Gerbner once observed that our species is unique because we tell stories—and live by the stories we tell. This view of human beings as the "storytelling animal" has had a huge impact in cognitive psychology. The *narratives* we compose to simplify and make sense of our lives have a profound influence on our plans, memories, love affairs, hatreds, ambitions, and dreams.

Thus we say, "I am this way because, as a small child, this happened to me, and then my parents. . . ." We say, "Let me tell you the story of how we fell in love." We say, "When you hear what happened, you'll understand why I felt entitled to take such cold-hearted revenge." These stories are not necessarily fictions, as in the child's meaning of "Tell me a story." Rather, they are attempts to provide a unifying theme that organizes and gives meaning to the events of our lives. But because these narratives rely heavily on memory, and because memories are reconstructed and are constantly shifting in response to present needs, beliefs, and experiences, our stories are also, to some degree, works of interpretation and imagination. Adult memories thus reveal as much about the present as they do about the past.

The nature of our autobiographical narratives depends on many of the processes discussed in this chapter. For example, elaborative encoding and deep processing help us retain memories about our own lives. This fact may help explain why girls and women tend to remember more childhood events than boys and men do, especially when the memories are emotional (Davis, 1999; Seidlitz & Diener, 1998). The two sexes are equally motivated to remember past events, equally likely to rehearse details about these events, and equally adept at describing the events, but females may encode more details in the first place, and these details may provide them with retrieval cues that enhance their recall.

Your culture may also affect how you encode and tell your "story." American college students live in a culture that emphasizes individuality, personal feelings, and self-expression, and their earliest childhood memories reflect that fact: They tend to report lengthy, emotionally elaborate memories of events, memories that focus on—who else?—themselves. In contrast, Chinese students, who live in a culture that emphasizes group solidarity, social roles, and personal humility, tend to report early memories of family or neighborhood activities, general routines, and emotionally neutral events (Wang, 2001).

Once we have formulated a story's central theme ("My parents opposed my plans," "My lover was a scheming rat"), that theme may then serve as a cognitive schema that guides what we remember and what we forget (Mather, Shafir, & Johnson, 2000). The story's theme may also influence our judgments of events and people in the present. If you have a fight with your lover, for example, the central theme in your story about the fight might be negative ("He was a jerk") or neutral ("It was a mutual misunderstanding"). This theme may bias you to blame or forgive your partner long after you have forgotten what the conflict was all about or who said what (McGregor & Holmes, 1999). You can see that the "spin" you give a story is critical—so be careful about the stories you tell!

As we age, certain periods of our lives tend to stand out. Old people remember more from adolescence and early adulthood than from midlife, a phenomenon known as the *reminiscence bump* (MacKavey, Malley, & Stewart, 1991). Perhaps the younger years are especially memorable because they are full of significant transitions: going off to college, graduating, getting a first job, falling in love, marrying or forming a committed relationship. Perhaps they are memorable because they are the period when an adult identity is forged (Conway & Pleydell-Pearce, 2000; Thorne, 2000). Or perhaps during these years, young people's changing and expanding social worlds require them to tell their stories often to others, and so they remember the details better (Pasupath, 2001).

Yet, as we have seen throughout this chapter, many details about events, even those landmarks we are sure we remember clearly, are probably distorted, forgotten, or added after the fact. Think of all the factors you have learned about that can trip us up when we try to remember things: confabulation, source amnesia, poor encoding and rehearsal strategies, interference, inadequate retrieval cues, suggestability, and biases. By now, you should not be surprised that memory can be as fickle as it can be accurate. As cognitive psychologists have shown repeatedly, we are not merely actors in our personal life dramas; we also write the scripts.

QUICK QUIZ

You can't blame childhood amnesia if you have forgotten the answers to these questions.

1. Name four possible cognitive reasons for childhood amnesia.
2. When older people look back on their lives, which periods constitute the "reminiscence bump"?

Answers:

1. lack of a sense of self in early childhood; impoverished encoding in early childhood; the tendency of preschoolers to focus on routine rather than distinctive aspects of an experience; the differences between earlier and later cognitive schemas 2. adolescence and early adulthood

---

Memory and Myth

At the start of this chapter, we promised to tell you what happened in the case of Ronald Junior Cotton, convicted of the rape of Jennifer Thompson on the strength of her eyewitness testimony.

In 1995, Thompson agreed to provide a blood sample so that DNA tests could be run on evidence that had been collected during the investigation. The tests revealed that Cotton was innocent. In fact it was Bobby Poole, the man who had bragged about the crime during Cotton's trial, who had raped her. Confronted with the evidence, Poole confessed, and Ronald Cotton, who had spent 11 years in prison, was released. In a *New York Times* editorial (June 18, 2000), Jennifer Thompson wrote, "The man I was so sure I had never seen in my life was the man who was inches from my throat, who raped me, who hurt me, who took my spirit away, who robbed me of my soul. And the man I had identified so emphatically on so many occasions was absolutely innocent."

Since Ronald Cotton was exonerated of the rape of Jennifer Thompson, the two have become friends. Thompson says she lives with constant anguish because of her mistaken identification.

How would you feel if your testimony resulted in the conviction of an innocent person? Would you be able to admit your mistake, or would you, as some have, cling more stubbornly than ever to the accuracy of your memory? Thompson decided to meet Cotton and apologize to him personally. Amazingly, they were both able to put this tragedy behind them, overcome the racial barrier that divided them, and become friends. Nevertheless, she wrote that she still lives "with the constant anguish that my profound mistake cost him so dearly. I cannot begin to imagine what would have happened had my mistaken identification occurred in a capital case." Thompson learned from personal experience what you have learned from this chapter: that eyewitnesses can and do make mistakes, that ethnic differences can increase these mistakes, that even memories for shocking or traumatic experiences are vulnerable to distortion and influence by others, and that our confidence in our memories is not a reliable guide to their accuracy.

The Cotton case is far from unique. A 1996 Justice Department report estimated that as many as 200,000 people—10 percent of America's prison population—may be innocent of the crimes for which they were convicted. When psychological scientists examined 40 cases in which wrongful conviction had been established beyond a doubt, they found that 36 of them had involved a false identification by one or more eyewitnesses (Wells et al., 1998). Obviously, not all eyewitness testimony is erroneous, and such testimony certainly needs to be heard and taken into account. But the potential for errors in identification makes it extremely important to gather evidence carefully, ensure adequate legal representation for defendants, conduct police interviews using proper procedures, and obtain a DNA analysis whenever possible.

The most important lesson to be learned from the research in this chapter, the lesson Jennifer Thompson learned to her despair and to her credit, is that human memory has both tremendous strengths and tremendous weaknesses. Because our deepest sense of ourselves relies on our memories, this is a difficult truth to accept. If we can do so, we will be able to respect the great power of memory and at the same time retain humility about our capacity for error, confabulation, and self-deception.

Taking Psychology with You

HOW TO . . . UH . . . REMEMBER

Someday in the near future, drugs may be available to help people remember better. For the time being, however, those of us who hope to improve our memories must rely on mental strategies. Some simple mnemonics can be useful, but as we have seen, complicated ones are often more bother than they're worth. A better approach is to follow some general guidelines based on the principles in this chapter:

▶ *Pay attention!* It seems obvious, but often we fail to remember because we never encoded the information in the first place. For example, which of these is the real Lincoln penny?

Most Americans have trouble recognizing the real penny because they have never attended to the details of a penny's design (Nickerson & Adams, 1979). We are not advising you to do so, unless you happen to be a coin collector or a counterfeiting expert. Just keep in mind that when you do have something to remember, such as the material in this book, you will do better if you encode it well. (The real penny, by the way, is the left one in the bottom row.)

▶ *Encode information in more than one way.* The more elaborate the encoding of information, the more memorable it will be. Use your imagination! For instance, in addition to remembering a telephone number by the sound of the individual digits, you might note the spatial pattern they make as you punch them in on the telephone.

▶ *Add meaning.* The more meaningful the material, the more likely it is to link up with information already in long-term memory. Meaningfulness

also reduces the number of chunks of information you have to learn. Common ways of adding meaning include making up a story about the material (fitting the material into a cognitive schema), thinking of examples, and forming visual images. (Some people find that the odder the image, the better.) If your license plate happens to be 236MPL, you might think of 236 maples. If you are trying to remember the concept of procedural memory from this chapter, you might make the concept meaningful by thinking of an example from your own life, such as your ability to ride a mountain bike, and then imagine a "P" superimposed on an image of yourself on your bike.

▶ *Take your time.* Leisurely learning, spread out over several sessions, usually produces better results than harried cramming (although *reviewing* material just before a test can be helpful). In terms of hours spent, "distributed" (spaced) learning sessions are more efficient than "massed" ones; in other words, three separate one-hour study sessions may result in more retention than one session of three hours.

▶ *Take time out.* If possible, minimize interference by using study breaks for rest or recreation. Sleep is the ultimate way to reduce interference. In a classic study, students who slept for eight hours after learning lists of nonsense syllables retained them better than students who went about their usual business (Jenkins & Dallenbach, 1924). Sleep is not always possible, of course, but periodic mental relaxation usually is.

▶ *Overlearn.* You can't remember something you never learned well in the first place. Overlearning—study-ing information even after you think you know it—is one of the best ways to ensure that you'll remember it.

▶ *Monitor your learning.* Test yourself frequently, rehearse thoroughly, and review periodically to see how you are doing. (A great way to test yourself is to teach the material to someone else; you will quickly discover whether you really know it!) Don't just evaluate your learning immediately after reading the material, though; because the information is still in short-term memory, you are likely to feel a false sense of confidence about your ability to recall it later. If you delay making a judgment for at least a few minutes, your evaluation will probably be more accurate (Nelson & Dunlosky, 1991).

Whatever strategies you use, you will find that active learning produces more comprehension and better retention than does passive reading or listening. The mind does not gobble up information automatically; you must make the material digestible.

Even then, you should not expect to remember everything you read or hear. Nor should you want to. Piling up facts without distinguishing the important from the trivial is just confusing. Popular books and tapes that promise a "perfect," "photographic" memory, or "instant recall" of everything you learn, fly in the face of what psychologists know about how the mind operates. Our advice: Forget them.

Summary

Reconstructing the Past

▶ Unlike a tape recorder or video camera, human memory is highly selective and is *reconstructive:* People add, delete, and change elements in ways that help them make sense of information and events. They often have *source amnesia,* the inability to distinguish information stored during an event from information added later. Even *flashbulb memories,* emotionally powerful memories that are particularly vivid, are often embellished or distorted and tend to become less accurate over time.

▶ Because memory is reconstructive, it is subject to *confabulation,* the confusion of imagined events with actual ones. Confabulation is more likely when people have thought about the imagined event many times ("imagination inflation"), the image of the event contains many details, the event is easy to imagine, and the focus of attention is on emotional reactions to the event.

Memory and the Power of Suggestion

▶ The reconstructive nature of memory makes memory vulnerable to suggestion. Eyewitness testimony is especially vulnerable to error when the suspect's ethnicity differs from that of the witness, when leading questions are put to witnesses, or when the witnesses are given misleading information.

▶ Findings on memory help clarify the issues in the debate about whether children are capable of making up accounts of sexual abuse. Children, like adults, often remember the essential aspects of an event accurately. However, like adults, they can also be suggestible, especially when they are very young, are in emotionally charged situations that blur the line between fantasy and reality, are asked leading questions, or wish to please the interviewer or conform to what they believe other children have said.

In Pursuit of Memory

▶ The ability to remember depends in part on the type of performance called for. In tests of *explicit memory* (conscious recollection), *recognition* is usually better than *recall.* In tests of *implicit memory,* which is measured by indirect methods such as *priming,* past experiences may affect current thoughts or actions even when these experiences are not consciously and intentionally remembered. The *relearning method* seems to straddle the boundary between explicit and implicit tests of memory.

▶ In *information-processing models,* memory involves the *encoding, storage,* and *retrieval* of information. In the *three-box model,* there are three interacting systems: sensory memory, short-term memory, and long-term memory. Some cognitive scientists prefer a *parallel distributed processing (PDP)* or *connectionist* model, which represents knowledge as connections among numerous interacting processing units, distributed in a vast network and all operating in parallel. But the three-box model continues to offer a convenient way to organize the major findings on memory.

The Three-Box Model of Memory

▶ In the three-box model, incoming sensory information makes a brief stop in *sensory memory,* which momentarily retains it in the form of sensory images. *Pattern recognition* occurs during the transfer of information from sensory memory to short-term memory. Sensory memory gives us a little time to decide whether information is important enough to warrant further attention.

▶ *Short-term memory (STM)* retains new information for up to 30 seconds by most estimates (unless rehearsal takes place). It also provides us with a *working memory* for the processing of information retrieved from long-term memory for temporary use. The capacity of STM is extremely limited but can be extended if information is organized into larger units by *chunking.* Items that are meaningful, have an emotional impact, or link up to something already in long-term memory may enter long-term storage easily, with only a brief stay in STM.

▶ *Long-term memory (LTM)* contains an enormous amount of information that must be organized to make it manageable. For example, words (or the concepts they represent) are often organized by semantic categories. Many models of LTM represent its contents as a network of interrelated concepts. The way people use these networks depends on experience and education. Research on *tip-of-the-tongue (TOT) states* shows that words are also indexed in LTM in terms of sound and form.

▶ *Procedural memories* ("knowing how") are memories for how to perform specific actions; *declarative memories* ("knowing that") are memories for abstract or representational knowledge. Declarative memories include *semantic memories* (general knowledge) and *episodic memories* (memories for personally experienced events).

▶ The three-box model is often invoked to explain the *serial-position effect* in memory, but although it can explain the *primacy effect,* it cannot explain why a *recency effect* sometimes occurs even when it should not.

The Biology of Memory

▶ Short-term memory involves temporary changes within neurons that alter their ability to release neurotransmitters, whereas long-term memory involves lasting structural changes in neurons and synapses. *Long-term potentiation,* an increase in the strength of synaptic responsiveness, seems to be an important mechanism of long-term memory. Neural changes associated with long-term potentiation take time to develop, which helps explain why long-term memories require a period of *consolidation.*

▶ Areas of the prefrontal cortex are especially active during short-term memory tasks. The hippocampus and adjacent areas play a critical role in the formation of long-term declarative memories. Other areas, such as the cerebellum, are crucial for the formation of procedural memories. Studies of patients with amnesia suggest that different brain systems are active during explicit and implicit memory tasks. The long-term storage of declarative memories probably takes place in cortical areas that were active during the original perception of the information or event. The various components of a memory are probably stored at different sites, with all of these sites participating in the representation of the event as a whole.

▶ Hormones released by the adrenal glands during stress or emotional arousal, including epinephrine and some steroids, enhance memory. Epinephrine causes the level of glucose to rise in the bloodstream, and glucose may enhance memory directly or by altering the effects of neurotransmitters. But very high hormone levels can interfere with the retention of information; a moderate level is optimal for learning new tasks.

How We Remember

▶ In order to remember material well, we must encode it accurately in the first place. Some kinds of information, such as material in a college course, require effortful, as opposed to automatic, encoding. Rehearsal of information keeps it in short-term memory and increases the chances of long-term retention. *Elaborative rehearsal* is more likely to result in transfer to long-term memory than is *maintenance rehearsal,* and *deep processing* is usually a more effective retention strategy than *shallow processing.*

▼ *Mnemonics* can also enhance retention by promoting elaborative encoding and making material meaningful, but for ordinary memory tasks, complex memory tricks are often ineffective or even counterproductive.

Why We Forget

▶ Forgetting can occur for several reasons. Information in sensory and short-term memory appears to *decay* if it does not receive further processing. New information may "erase" old information in long-term memory. *Proactive* and *retroactive interference* may take place. *Cue-dependent forgetting* may occur when retrieval cues are inadequate. The most effective retrieval cues are those that were present at the time of the initial experience. A person's mood or physical state may also act as a retrieval cue, evoking a *state-dependent memory*.

▶ Some lapses in memory are due to *psychogenic amnesia*, the forgetting of disturbing or shocking events, but psychologists are divided about why this occurs. The psychodynamic explanation, *repression*, has met with skepticism among psychological scientists, who consider it vague and unverified. In cases involving claims of recovered memories of repressed events, courts have also become skeptical.

Autobiographical Memory

▶ Most people cannot recall any events from earlier than the third or fourth year of life. The reason for such *childhood amnesia* may be partly biological. Cognitive explanations include the lack of a sense of self until the age of 2 or 3, young children's impoverished encoding of their experiences, their focus on routine rather than distinctive aspects of an experience, and their immature cognitive schemas.

▶ A person's *narrative* "life story" organizes the events of his or her life and gives them meaning. Narratives change as people build up a store of episodic memories, and life stories are, to some degree, works of interpretation and imagination. These narratives are affected by gender and culture. The central themes of our stories can guide recall and influence our judgments of people and events. Older people remember more from adolescence and young adulthood than from midlife, a phenomenon known as the *reminiscence bump*.

Key Terms

memory 354
reconstructive memory 355
source amnesia 355
"flashbulb memories" 355
confabulation 356
leading questions 356
explicit memory 362
recall 362
recognition 362
implicit memory 363
priming 363
relearning method 363
information-processing models 364
encoding, storage, and retrieval 364
cognitive schemas 364
"three-box model" 365
parallel distributed processing (PDP) model 365

sensory memory 366
pattern recognition 366
short-term memory (STM) 367
working memory 367
chunks 368
long-term memory (LTM) 368
semantic categories 368
tip-of-the-tongue (TOT) state 370
procedural memories 370
declarative memories 370
semantic memories 370
episodic memories 370
serial-position effect 371
primacy and recency effects 371
long-term potentiation 372
consolidation 373
effortful versus automatic encoding 376

maintenance rehearsal 377
elaborative rehearsal 377
deep processing 377
shallow processing 377
mnemonics 377
decay theory 380
retroactive interference 381
proactive interference 382
retrieval cues 382
cue-dependent forgetting 382
state-dependent memory 382
psychogenic amnesia 383
repression 383
childhood (infantile) amnesia 385
narratives 387
reminiscence bump 387

◀**L**OOKING BACK

- What's wrong with thinking of memory as a mental movie camera? (pp. 354–355)

- Why do "flashbulb" memories of surprising or shocking events sometimes have less wattage than we think? (p. 356)

- If you have a strong emotional reaction to a remembered event, does that mean your memory is accurate? (p. 357)

- Can your memories of an event be affected by the way someone questions you about it? (pp. 358–359)

- Can children's testimony about sexual abuse always be trusted? (pp. 359–361)

- In general, which is easier, a multiple-choice item or a short-answer essay item—and why? (p. 362)

- Can you know something without knowing that you know? (p. 363)

- Why is the computer often used as a metaphor for the mind? (p. 364)

- Why is short-term memory like a leaky bucket? (pp. 367–368)

- When a word is on the tip of your tongue, what errors are you likely to make in recalling it? (p. 370)

- What's the difference between "knowing how" and "knowing that"? (p. 370)

- What changes occur in your neurons when you store a long-term memory? (pp. 372–373)

- Where in the brain are memories for facts and events stored? (p. 374)

- Which hormones can improve your memory? (p. 374)

- What's wrong with trying to memorize in a rote fashion when you're studying—and what's a better strategy? (p. 377)

- Memory tricks are fun, but are they always useful? (p. 378)

- How might new information "erase" old memories? (p. 381)

- What theory explains why you keep dialing an old area code instead of your new one? (p. 382)

- Why is it easier to recall experiences from elementary school if you see pictures of your classmates? (p. 382)

- Why are many researchers skeptical about claims of "repressed" and "recovered" memories? (pp. 383–384)

- Why are the first few years of life a mental blank? (p. 386)

- Why have human beings been called the "storytelling animal"? (p. 387)

- Which periods of life tend to stand out in memory? (p. 387)

Answers to the Get Involved exercises on pages 362 and 364: Rudolph's eight friends were Dasher, Dancer, Prancer, Vixen, Comet, Cupid, Donder, and Blitzen.

Go to **WWW.PRENHALL.COM/WADE** to reinforce these key concepts, and more.

10.1 **Measuring memory**
10.2 **Information–processing model of memory**
10.3 **Mnemonics**
10.4 **Theories of forgetting**

11

Emotion

The beauty of the world has two edges, one of laughter,
one of anguish, cutting the heart asunder.

VIRGINIA WOOLF

F or the first seven years of her life, Chelsea Thomas was a happy, cheerful, normal child with an unusual problem. Chelsea had been born with Möbius syndrome, in which a nerve that transmits commands from the brain to the facial muscles is missing. As a result, the child had a perpetually grumpy look. She could not convey delight at being given a present, amusement at watching a favorite TV show, or happiness at meeting a friend. Then surgeons transplanted nerves from Chelsea's leg to both sides of her mouth, and today Chelsea can do what most people in the world take for granted—smile.

Temple Grandin (1996) is a successful scientist and writer with an unusual condition. Because she has a neurological disorder, a form of autism that can be extremely debilitating, Grandin's emotions differ in quality and kind from those of most other people. She can feel the anguish of animals, but not of human beings. She has never known romantic love or been moved by the beauty of a sunset. Unable to feel the array of normal emotions, she is unable to read the emotions of others; she is out of tune with the rest of humanity.

Cases like these are poignant reminders of how important it is to be able to feel and express emotions, and to recognize emotions in others. Emotions are the heart and soul of human experience. If you lacked emotion, your life would be easier in some ways: You would never again worry about a test result, a job interview, or a first date, and you would never be riled by injustice. But you would also be unmoved by the magic of music. You would never feel the grief of losing someone you love, not only because you wouldn't know sadness but also because you wouldn't know love. You would never laugh because nothing would strike you as funny.

People often curse their emotions, wishing to be freed from the "irrational" pain of anger, jealousy, shame, guilt, grief, and unrequited love. The belief that we are at the mercy of our irrational emotions has been part of western culture for centuries. Emotions and cognitions have been regarded as two separate, indeed warring processes, with the clash between them causing eternal muddles and miseries.

THINKING CRITICALLY

Don't Oversimplify

Many people wish they could be free of the "irrational" emotions that make them miserable. But what would our lives be like without emotions? Are they really so irrational?

Modern psychological research, however, shows that the historical distinction between our "rational" human abilities of thought and our supposedly "irrational" mammalian heritage of emotion is a false one. As we saw in the chapters on thinking (Chapter 9) and memory (Chapter 10), human cognition is not always rational; it involves many biases in what we perceive and remember. Conversely, emotions are not always irrational. They bind people together, regulate relationships, and motivate people to achieve their goals. Without the capacity to feel emotion, people have difficulty making ethical decisions and planning for the future. When you are faced with a decision between two appealing and justifiable career alternatives, for example, your sense of which one "feels right" emotionally may help you make the best choice (Damasio, 1994; Oatley, 1990).

As psychologists have moved away from regarding emotions solely as disorganizing and disruptive influences on human behavior, they have identified some of the evolutionarily adaptive and beneficial functions of emotions and their expression. Disgust, which is pretty disgusting, probably evolved as a mechanism that protects infants and adults from eating tainted or poisonous food. Even embarrassment, so painful to the individual, serves important functions: It appeases others when you feel you have made a fool of yourself, broken a moral rule, or violated a social norm. Signs of embarrassment—acting nervous and awkward, blushing, biting your tongue, withdrawing, apologizing—make other people feel sympathetic toward you, more willing to forgive your blunder (Keltner & Anderson, 2000).

In defining **emotion**, psychologists focus on three major components: *physiological* changes in the face, brain, and body, *cognitive* processes such as interpretations of events, and *cultural* influences that shape the experience and expression of emotion. If we compare human emotions to a tree, the biological capacity for emotion is the trunk and root system; thoughts and explanations create the many branches; and culture is the gardener that shapes the tree and prunes it, cutting off some limbs and cultivating others. We will begin with the trunk.

WHAT'S AHEAD ▷

- **Which facial expressions of emotion do most people recognize the world over?**
- **Why might hanging around with a depressed friend make you gloomy, too?**
- **Why don't you smile much when you are home alone?**
- **Which little structure in the brain sees to it that you cross the street fast when a truck is headed toward you?**
- **Which two hormones can make you "too excited to eat"?**
- **What do "lie detectors" actually detect?**

Elements of Emotion 1: The Body

emotion A state of arousal involving facial and bodily changes, brain activation, cognitive appraisals, subjective feelings, and tendencies toward action, all shaped by cultural rules.

primary emotions Emotions considered to be universal and biologically based; they generally include fear, anger, sadness, joy, surprise, disgust, and contempt.

Research on the physiological aspects of emotion suggests that people everywhere are born with certain basic or **primary emotions.** Although psychologists differ somewhat in the emotions they consider to be primary, the list typically includes fear, anger, sadness, joy, surprise, disgust, and contempt. These emotions have distinctive physiological patterns and corresponding facial expressions, and the situations that evoke them are the same all over the world: Everywhere, sadness follows perception of loss, fear follows perception of threat and bodily harm, anger follows perception of insult or injustice, and so forth (Scherer, 1997). In contrast,

secondary emotions include all the variations and blends of emotion that vary from one culture to another and develop gradually with increasing cognitive maturity.

Researchers in the physiological tradition are studying three major biological aspects of emotion: facial expressions, brain regions and circuits, and the autonomic nervous system.

The Face of Emotion

"There are characteristic facial expressions that are observed to accompany anger, fear, erotic excitement, and all the other passions," wrote Aristotle (384–322 B.C.). Two thousand years later, Charles Darwin added an evolutionary explanation for Aristotle's astute observation. In *The Expression of the Emotions in Man and Animals* (1872/1965) Darwin argued that certain human facial expressions—the smile, the frown, the grimace, the glare—are as "wired in" as the wing flutter of a frightened bird, the purr of a contented cat, or the snarl of a threatened wolf. Such expressions evolved, he said, because they allowed our forebears to tell at a glance the difference between a friendly stranger and a hostile one. They make it possible for us to signal our feelings and intentions to others, and they "serve as the first means of communication between the mother and her infant." He was right on all counts.

Universal Expressions of Emotion. Modern psychologists have supported Darwin's ideas by confirming that some emotional expressions are recognized the world over (see Figure 11.1). Paul Ekman and his colleagues have gathered abundant evidence for the universality of seven facial expressions of emotion—expressions that correspond to the list of emotions usually identified as primary: anger, happiness, fear, surprise, disgust, sadness, and contempt (Ekman, 1997; Ekman & Heider, 1988; Ekman et al., 1987). In every culture they have studied—in Brazil, Chile, Estonia, Germany, Greece, Hong Kong, Italy, Japan, New Guinea, Scotland, Sumatra, Turkey, and the United States—a large majority of people recognize the basic emotional expressions portrayed by those in other cultures. Even most members of isolated groups that have never watched a movie or read *People* magazine, such as the Foré of New Guinea or the Minangkabau of West Sumatra, can recognize the emotions expressed in pictures of people who are entirely foreign to them, and we can recognize theirs.

Ekman and his associates developed a special coding system to analyze and identify each of the nearly 80 muscles of the face, as well as the combinations of muscles associated with various emotions. Make an expression of disgust and notice what you are doing: You are probably wrinkling your nose, dropping the corners of your mouth, or retracting your upper lip. When people try to hide their feelings and "put on" an emotion, they use different groups of muscles than they do for authentic ones. For example, when people try to pretend that they feel sad, only 15 percent manage to get the eyebrows, eyelids, and forehead wrinkle exactly right, mimicking the way true grief is expressed spontaneously. Authentic smiles last only two seconds; false smiles may last ten seconds or more (Ekman, 1994; Ekman, Friesen, & O'Sullivan, 1988).

The Functions of Facial Expressions. Interestingly, facial expressions not only can reflect our internal feelings; they also may *influence* our internal feelings. In the process of **facial feedback,** the facial muscles send messages to the brain about the basic emotion being expressed: A smile tells us that we're happy, a frown that we're angry or perplexed (Izard, 1990). When people are told to smile and look pleased or happy, their positive feelings increase; when they are told to look angry, displeased, or disgusted, positive feelings decrease (Kleinke, Peterson, & Rutledge, 1998).

The unmistakable face of anger.

11.1

secondary emotions Emotions that develop with cognitive maturity and vary across individuals and cultures.

facial feedback The process by which the facial muscles send messages to the brain about the basic emotion being expressed.

Figure 11.1

SOME UNIVERSAL EXPRESSIONS

Can you tell what feelings are being conveyed here? Most people around the world can readily identify expressions of surprise, disgust, happiness, sadness, anger, fear, and contempt—no matter what the age, culture, sex, or historical epoch of the person conveying the emotion.

Facial feedback affects emotional states even when people are not specifically asked to imitate an emotion, but just to alter their facial muscles. For example, when people are told to contract the facial muscles involved in smiling (though not actually instructed to smile) and are then shown cartoons, they find the cartoons funnier than if they are contracting their muscles in a way that is incompatible with smiling (Strack, Martin, & Stepper, 1988). And when they are asked to contort their facial muscles into patterns associated with anger, that is often the emotion they feel. As one young man put it, "When my jaw was clenched and my brows down, I tried not to be angry but it just fit the position" (Laird, 1974). If you put on an "angry" face, your heart rate will rise faster than if you put on a "happy" face (Levenson, Ekman, & Friesen, 1990).

As Darwin suggested, facial expressions also probably evolved to help us communicate our emotional states to others and provoke a response from them—"Come help me!" "Get away!" (Fridlund, 1994). This signaling function begins in infancy. A baby's expressions of misery, angry frustration, or disgust are apparent to most parents, who respond by soothing an uncomfortable baby, feeding a grumpy one, or removing unappealing food from a disgusted one (Izard, 1994b; Stenberg & Campos, 1990). And an infant's smile of joy usually melts the heart of the weariest parent, provoking a happy cuddle. Obviously a baby's facial expressions have survival value!

Babies, in turn, react to the facial expressions of their parents, especially when their parents are happy. American, German, Greek, Japanese, Trobriand Island, and

Get Involved ▪▪

Put on a Happy Face

Great moms have always understood the importance of facial feedback, as this cartoon shows! So now see whether facial feedback works for you. The next time you are feeling sad or afraid, try purposely smiling, even if no one is around. Keep smiling. Does your facial expression affect your mood?

Yanomamo mothers all "infect" their babies with happy moods by displaying happy expressions (Keating, 1994). Babies also seem primed to respond in other ways to happy facial expressions. Tiny newborns will suck longer on a pacifier if it produces a happy face than if it produces a face with a neutral or negative expression (Walker-Andrews, 1997). (If you become a parent, remember this.)

Starting at the end of their first year, babies begin to alter their own behavior in reaction to their parents' facial expressions of emotion, and this ability, too, has survival value. Do you recall the visual-cliff studies described in Chapter 6 (p. 215)? These studies were originally designed to test for depth perception, which emerges early in infancy. But in one experiment, 1-year-old babies were put on a more ambiguous visual cliff that did not drop off sharply and thus did not automatically evoke fear, as the original cliff did. In this case, the babies' behavior depended on the mother's expression: 74 percent crossed the cliff when their mothers put on a happy, reassuring expression, but not a single infant crossed when the mother showed an expression of fear (Sorce et al., 1985). If you have ever watched a toddler take a tumble and then look at his or her parent before deciding whether to cry or to forget it, you will understand the influence of parental facial expressions, and why they have had such survival value for babies. An infant needs to be able to read the parent's facial signals of alarm or safety because young children do not yet have the experience necessary for judging danger.

Finally, facial expressions of emotion can actually generate emotions in others, creating *mood contagion*. When people see pictures of facial expressions of emotion or other nonverbal emotional signals, their own facial muscles mimic the ones they are observing, activating a similar emotional state in themselves (Dimberg, Thunberg, & Elmehed, 2000; Neumann & Strack, 2000). Have you ever been in a cheerful mood, had lunch with a depressed friend, and come away feeling vaguely depressed yourself? Have you ever stopped to have a chat with a friend who was nervous about an upcoming exam, and ended up feeling panicked yourself? That's mood contagion at work.

As you might expect, people who live or work together are especially vulnerable to mood contagion (Totterdell et al., 1998). For example, in a study of 96 pairs of college roommates, roommates of depressed students became more depressed themselves over the course of the three-week study, even when the researchers statistically controlled for upsetting life events that might be affecting them (Joiner, 1994). If you are starting to feel gloomy at school or work, perhaps you should check out your friends' or co-workers' moods and facial expressions before you decide that *you* are the one who is depressed!

Facial Expressions in Social Context. Despite the evidence for the importance and universality of certain facial expressions, these expressions, like all human behavior, occur in a social context. So the connections among your feelings, your expressions, and what other people think you are communicating are not so simple.

1 *Across and within cultures, agreement often varies on which emotion a particular facial expression is revealing.* While most people in most cultures do recognize basic emotions as portrayed in photographs, sometimes a large minority does not. Across 20 studies of Western cultures, for example, fully 95 percent of the participants agreed in their judgments of happy faces, but only 78 percent agreed on expressions of sadness and anger. And across 11 non-Western societies, 88 percent recognized happiness, but only 74 percent agreed on sadness and 59 percent on anger (Ekman, 1994). When people are not forced to select a particular emotion label in a multiple-choice item ("Is it anger or fear?"), and are simply asked what facial expression a photo is conveying, agreement drops further (Frank & Stennett, 2001).

2 *People don't usually display their emotions in facial expressions unless other people are around.* Most people do not go around scowling and clenching their jaws whenever they are angry. Most people grieve and feel enormously sad without weeping. When you are at home by yourself, you are unlikely to walk around smiling even if you are feeling happy; you will save your smiles until you have an audience (or are

Facial expressions do not always convey the emotion being felt. A posed, social smile like Gloria Vanderbilt's (left) may have nothing to do with true feelings of happiness. Conversely, you would never know from the apparently anguished face of Oksana Baiul (right) that she was actually feeling jubilant over winning an Olympic medal for figure skating.

watching a funny TV show). A study of 22 Olympic gold medalists, observed as they stood on the podium during the awards ceremonies, found that the athletes smiled only when they were interacting with officials or the public, not when they were standing alone—though presumably they were equally happy the whole time (Fernández-Dols & Ruiz-Belda, 1995).

3 *Facial expressions convey different messages depending on their circumstances.* A smile, for example, might not mean "I'm happy," but rather "I'm trying to be pleasant," "Don't be mad at me," or even "Nyahhh, I was right and you were wrong." How you interpret someone else's expression, therefore, depends on the circumstance in which it occurs. For example, look at the photograph of the woman in the margin. What emotion is she expressing? Most people would say that her staring eyes and open mouth are signs of fear. But if they have been told that she has good reason to be irritated, because a snooty maitre d' is making her wait an hour for her table, they will say she is angry. Conversely, people who see an "angry" face in a situation that would normally provoke fear tend to say that the person is afraid (Carroll & Russell, 1996).

4 *People often use facial expressions to lie about their feelings as well as to express them.* In Shakespeare's play *Henry VI*, the villain who will become the evil King Richard III says,

Can you guess her emotion?

> *Why, I can smile, and murder while I smile;*
> *And cry content to that which grieves my heart;*
> *And wet my cheeks with artificial tears,*
> *And frame my face to all occasions.*

In sum, facial expressions not only reveal and communicate our true feelings, they also disguise and deceive. Even Ekman, who has been studying them for years, concludes, "There is obviously emotion without facial expression and facial expression without emotion."

QUICK QUIZ

Smile as you take this quiz, and see whether that makes you feel better.

1. Which of the following emotions is (are) not generally considered to be among the universal, primary ones? (a) anger, (b) pride, (c) fear, (d) disgust, (e) happiness, (f) sadness, (g) embarrassment
2. What are the functions of facial expressions? (Use the whole preceding section to answer this question.)
3. What four findings show the importance of social context in understanding facial expressions?

Answers:

1. pride, embarrassment 2. They signal our intentions, reflect our feelings, permit nonverbal communication between parents and infants, provide cues to ourselves about what we are feeling (facial feedback), affect other people's emotions and behavior (as in mood contagion), and enable us to lie and deceive. 3. People don't always agree on which emotion a given expression reveals; people's facial expressions depend on the presence of others; people's ability to "read" another person's facial expression depends on circumstances; and people use facial expressions to lie about their real emotions.

The Brain and Emotion

Another line of physiological research seeks to identify parts of the brain responsible for different emotions and for specific components of emotional experience: recognizing another person's emotion, feeling an emotion, expressing an emotion, and acting on an emotion.

The capacity to feel or recognize particular emotions is associated with specific parts of the brain. For example, people who have Huntington's disease or a stroke that affects two areas involved in disgust are often unable to feel disgusted! One young man with stroke damage in these regions could recognize all of the basic facial expressions except for disgust, and he had little or no emotional response to images and ideas that would be disgusting to most people, such as feces-shaped chocolate (Calder et al., 2000). (Are you making a disgusted expression as you read that? He couldn't.) And people with damage in a particular part of the right hemisphere, important for the processing of emotional information, have trouble understanding jokes or getting the emotions portrayed in films and stories (Heller, Nitschke, & Miller, 1998).

The Role of the Amygdala. In recent years psychologists have discovered that a small structure in the brain, the *amygdala,* plays a key role in emotion, especially fear (see Chapter 4). The amygdala is responsible for evaluating sensory information, which it gets from the thalamus, quickly determining its emotional importance, and making the initial decision to approach or withdraw from a person or situation (Adolphs, 2001; LeDoux, 1996). The amygdala quickly assesses danger or threat, which is a good thing, because otherwise you could be standing in the street asking, "Is it wise to cross now, while that very large truck is coming toward me?" The amygdala's initial response may then be overridden by a more accurate appraisal from the cortex. This is why you jump with fear when you suddenly feel a hand on your back in a dark alley, and why your fear evaporates when the cortex registers that the hand belongs to a friend whose lousy idea of humor is to scare you in a dark alley.

If either the amygdala or critical areas of the cortex are damaged, abnormalities in the ability to process fear result. A rat with a damaged amygdala "forgets" to be afraid when it should be and may not be able to acquire conditioned fears. Likewise, people with damage to the amygdala often have difficulty recognizing fear in others (Adolphs, 2001; Damasio, 1994). In one fascinating case, a woman with damage to her amygdala could accurately *display* fear and other emotions herself, but she could not *perceive* or recognize expressions of fear in others (Anderson & Phelps, 2000). In contrast, rats or people with damage to the prefrontal cortex often lose the capacity to put aside their initial fear when the emotion is no longer necessary or appropriate. The result can be constant, irrational feelings of impending doom or anxiety or obsessive thoughts of danger, as we discuss in Chapter 16.

The Role of the Prefrontal Cortex. Most emotions motivate a response of some sort: to embrace or approach the person who instills joy in you, attack a person who makes you angry, withdraw from a scene that disgusts you, or flee from a person or situation that frightens you (Brehm, 1999). A growing body of research suggests that the prefrontal regions of the brain are involved in these impulses to approach or withdraw. Regions of the *left* prefrontal cortex appear to be specialized for the motivation to approach others (as with happiness, a positive emotion, and anger, a negative one). People with damage to this area often lose the capacity for joy. Even in people without brain damage, some who are clinically depressed have less activation in the left frontal regions than nondepressed people do, though no one yet knows whether this lower activation is learned, inborn—or a result of depression rather than a cause (Davidson & Henriques, 2000; Heller & Nitschke, 1997).

In contrast, regions of the *right* prefrontal region are specialized for withdrawal or escape (as in disgust and fear) (Davidson, Jackson, & Kalin, 2000; Harmon-Jones & Allen, 1998; Harmon-Jones & Sigelman, 2001). People with damage to the right prefrontal cortex may feel excessively manic and euphoric, with little counterbalancing caution.

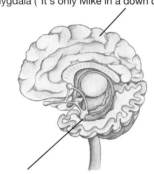

2. The cerebral cortex generates a more complete picture; it can override signals sent by the amygdala ("It's only Mike in a down coat").

1. The amygdala scrutinizes information for its emotional importance ("It's a bear! Be afraid! Run!").

Get Involved

Turn On Your Right Hemisphere

These faces have expressions of happiness on one side and sadness on the other. Look at the nose of each face: Which face looks happier? Which face looks sadder?

(a)   (b)

You are likely to see face (b) as the happier one and face (a) as the sadder one. The likely reason is that in most people the left side of a picture is processed by the right side of the brain, where recognition of emotional expression primarily occurs (Oatley & Jenkins, 1996).

These brain differences reflecting approach or avoidance tendencies occur even in infants. In one study, 10-month-old babies were briefly separated from their mothers, then monitored during the happy reunion. The babies smiled, their "happy" left frontal regions were active, and they reached out to their moms. But when the babies were only smiling socially at strangers, these areas showed no increased activation, and the babies did not reach out (Fox & Davidson, 1988). Even a baby brain reveals a difference between the warm happiness of a loving smile directed toward someone worthy of approaching (mom), and the cooler pleasure of a social smile directed toward mom's friends!

Hormones and Emotion

When the amygdala and prefrontal cortex signal "danger! Get outta here!" you need to be able to move fast. The next stage of the emotional relay is the release of hormones, which produce the energy of emotion. When you are under stress or experience an intense emotion, the sympathetic division of the autonomic nervous system spurs the adrenal glands to send out two hormones, *epinephrine* and *norepinephrine* (see Chapter 4). These chemical messengers produce a state of arousal and alertness. The pupils dilate, widening to allow in more light; the heart beats faster; breathing speeds up; and blood sugar rises, providing the body with more energy to act. Digestion slows down, so that blood flow can be diverted from the stomach and intestines to the muscles and surface of the skin. (This is why, when you are excited, scared, furious, or wildly in love, you may not want to eat.) The ultimate purpose of all these physiological changes is to prepare the body to respond quickly to danger or threat, excitement or opportunity (Frijda, 1988; Lang, 1995).

The adrenal glands produce epinephrine and norepinephrine in response to many challenges in the environment. These hormones will surge if you are laughing at a funny movie, playing a video game, worrying about an exam, cheering at a sports event, or driving on a hot day in terrible traffic. Epinephrine in particular provides the energy of an emotion—that familiar tingle, excitement, and sense of

Intense but short-lived "road anger" results in part from physiological arousal caused by the stress of driving. That's why passengers rarely get as furious as the driver does.

animation. At high levels, it can create the sensation of being "seized" or "flooded" by an emotion that is out of your control. In a sense, the release of epinephrine does cause us to lose control, because few people can consciously alter their heart rates, blood pressures, and digestive tracts. However, people *can* learn to control their actions when they are under the sway of an emotion (as we discuss in "Taking Psychology with You"). And no emotion, no matter how urgent or compelling, lasts forever. As arousal subsides, a "hot" emotion turns into its "cool" counterpart. Anger may pale into annoyance, ecstasy into contentment, fear into worry, past emotional whirlwinds into calm breezes.

Although epinephrine and norepinephrine are released during many emotional states, emotions also differ from one another biochemically. The brain has a variety of chemical messengers at its disposal—neurotransmitters, hormones, and neuromodulators—and these play different roles in different emotions (Oatley & Jenkins, 1996). Fear, disgust, anger, sadness, surprise, and happiness are also associated with somewhat different patterns of brain activity and autonomic nervous system activity, as measured by heart rate, electrical conductivity of the skin, and finger temperature (Damasio et al., 2000; Levenson, 1992; Levenson, Ekman, & Friesen, 1990). These distinctive patterns may explain why people all over the world use similar terms to describe basic emotions, saying they feel "hot and bothered" when they are angry, feel "cold and clammy" when they are afraid, and have a "lump in the throat" when they are sad. These metaphors capture what is going on in their bodies (Mesquita & Frijda, 1992; Oatley & Duncan, 1994).

In sum, the physiology of emotion involves characteristic facial expressions; activity in specific parts of the brain, notably the amygdala and specialized parts of the prefrontal cortex; and sympathetic nervous system activity that prepares the body for action (see Review 11.1).

Detecting Emotions: Does the Body Lie?

Because physiological arousal and brain activation are associated with emotional states, many people have tried to invent physiological measurements to detect what a person is feeling and whether the person is lying about it. For example, in Asia the "rice method" of lie detection was once commonly used on people accused of a crime. The suspect had to chew on a handful of dry rice and then spit it out. The belief was that an innocent person would be able to do this easily, whereas a guilty person would have grains of rice stuck to the tongue and the roof of the mouth.

The theory behind the rice method is similar to that of the modern *polygraph machine,* commonly called the lie detector, which was invented in 1915 by a Harvard professor named William Marston. (Marston went on to become famous for a *really* important creation—Wonder Woman [Zelicoff, 2001].) Both methods are based on the assumption that a person who is guilty and fearful will have increased activity in the autonomic nervous system. In the case of the guilty rice-eater, such arousal should dry the saliva in the mouth and cause grains to stick to the tongue. In the case of the guilty suspect taking a polygraph test, a lie should be revealed by increased heart rate, respiration rate, and electrical conductance of the skin, as the person responds to incriminating questions.

THINKING CRITICALLY

Analyze Assumptions

Many people assume that because physiological changes, such as elevated heart rate, are involved in emotional states, physiological measurements can tell us whether someone is afraid, guilty—or lying. Is this assumption valid? What evidence does it overlook?

REVIEW 11.1	EMOTION AND THE BODY
Facial Expressions	Reflect internal feelings, influence internal feelings (facial feedback), communicate feelings, signal intentions, affect behavior and feelings of others (mood contagion), conceal or pretend an emotion (lie).
The Brain	Specific areas are involved in specific emotions (e.g., disgust) and in different aspects of emotion (e.g., recognizing facial expressions in others, expressing an emotion oneself).
Amygdala	Determines emotional importance of incoming sensory information; is responsible for initial decision to approach or withdraw; is involved in learning, recognizing, and expressing fear.
Cortex	Appraises the significance of emotional information from amygdala. The left prefrontal cortex is associated with "approach" emotions (e.g., happiness, anger); the right prefrontal cortex with "withdrawal" emotions (e.g., fear, sadness).
Autonomic Nervous System	Activates the hormones epinephrine and norepinephrine, which produce energy and alertness. Certain emotions are associated with distinctive patterns of autonomic nervous system activity (e.g., making people feel "hot" when they are angry, "cold" when they are afraid).

A few psychologists still lobby enthusiastically on behalf of the polygraph, arguing that it is a reliable and valid way to identify a liar (Raskin, Honts, & Kircher, 1997). However, they represent a minority view. Most researchers regard polygraph tests as invalid, because *no physiological patterns of autonomic arousal are specific to lying* (Furedy, 1996; Iacono & Lykken, 1997; Lilienfeld, 1993; Saxe, 1994; Zelicoff, 2001). Machines cannot tell whether you are feeling guilty, angry, nervous, amused, or revved up from an exciting day. Innocent people may be tense and nervous about the whole procedure. They may react to the word *bank* not because they robbed a bank, but because they recently bounced a check. In either case, the machine will record a "lie." The reverse mistake is also common. Suave, practiced liars can lie without flinching, and others "beat the machine" by tensing muscles or thinking about an exciting experience during neutral questions (Lykken, 1981). This is one reason that the people who administer the tests often fail to agree among themselves on whether a test subject is lying or telling the truth.

In experiments in which federal employees were given knowledge of acts of mock espionage and told to try to hide this knowledge from investigators, many of the "guilty" respondents were able to pass polygraph tests with flying colors (Honts, 1994). This happens in real life, too. Aldrich Ames, a high-level CIA official, was convicted of spying for the former Soviet Union and selling national secrets. During the investigation, Ames passed two polygraph tests designed to detect his treasonous acts. So did Robert Philip Hanssen, an FBI agent who also spied for Russia for many years. Although the CIA, FBI, and National Security Agency have administered tens of thousands of polygraphs to their staffs, the tests have yet to uncover a single spy (Park, 1999).

The polygraph is not only poor at catching real liars; it is even more likely to accuse the innocent of lying (Kleinmuntz & Szucko, 1984; Saxe, 1994). When large numbers of people are given screening polygraph tests by employers, the government, or police (in an effort to identify cheats, spies, or criminals), the polygraph will correctly catch many liars and guilty people, but misidentify a very high number of innocent people (see Figure 11.2). As one researcher put it, "Suppose 1,000

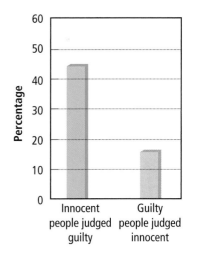

Figure 11.2
This graph shows the average percentages across three studies of *incorrect* classifications by lie detectors. As you see, nearly half of the innocent people were classified as guilty, and a significant number of guilty people were classified as innocent. The investigators independently confirmed a suspect's guilt or innocence by other means, such as confessions of other suspects (Iacono & Lykken, 1997).

"WE CAN'T DETERMINE IF YOU'RE TELLING THE TRUTH, BUT YOU SHOULD HAVE A DOCTOR CHECK YOUR PRESSURE."

people were screened, and 50 of them were liars. The polygraph would generate positive results in 38 out of 50 liars and in 351 out of 950 truthtellers, that is, more than nine false positives for every true positive" (Phillips, 1999).

Because of such findings, about half of the states in the U.S. have ruled that polygraph results are inadmissible in court. However, most police departments continue to use them, not for their accuracy but because they hope to scare people into telling the truth and induce suspects to confess—by telling them that they failed the test. Many accused people use them too, hoping the polygraph will "prove" that they are innocent.

Some researchers are now trying to find other ways of measuring physiological signs of emotional reactivity and lying. They are going high-tech, using thermal imaging to monitor brain waves and fluctuations in blood flow in the face, measuring "voice stress," designing computer programs to read "authentic" versus faked facial expressions, and using measures of brain activity to see whether they can infer whether a person possesses guilty knowledge of a crime and is lying. But if the basic *assumption* in all this work is faulty—that there are universal signs in the brain or face that reveal when a person is lying—these methods will also be unreliable. Because of the normal variability among people in their autonomic and brain reactivity, innocent but highly reactive people are still likely to be mislabeled "guilty" by these tests (Zelicoff, 2001).

The problems inherent in the persistent search for accurate "lie detectors" reveal the limitations of biological approaches to emotion. As powerful as the physical changes involved in emotion are, they are not a sure guide to what a person is feeling. You cannot know just from measuring someone's hormones or heart rate whether he or she is lying or telling the truth, feeling thrilled or frightened, sick or just in love. Nor can biology alone explain why, of two students about to take an exam, one feels psyched up and the other feels overwhelmed by anxiety. To understand emotions, you must also know what is going on in a person's mind.

QUICK QUIZ

Aren't you longing to take this quiz? Don't lie—we can tell.

1. A 3-year-old sees her dad dressed as a gorilla and screams in fear. What brain structure is probably involved in her reaction?

2. Luisa is watching an old Laurel and Hardy film, which makes her laugh and want to see more of them. Which side of her prefrontal cortex is likely to be activated?

3. Luis is watching *Horrible Hatchet Murders in the Dorm*. Which hormones cause his heart to pound and his palms to sweat when the murderer stalks an unsuspecting victim?

4. When Congressman Gary Condit was being questioned about the disappearance of his intern and lover Chandra Levy, he agreed to take a lie detector test given by an expert of his choice. He passed, but the police were unimpressed and wanted him to take another polygraph administered by *their* expert. In either case, what would the results tell us?

Answers:

1. the amygdala 2. the left 3. epinephrine, norepinephrine 4. Not much. The polygraph is not reliable, regardless of who administers it, because so many factors can affect a person's physiological responses to it.

WHAT'S AHEAD

- When people say, "The more I thought about it, the madder I got," what does that tell us about emotion?
- In a competition, who is likely to be happier, the third-place winner or the second-place winner—and why?
- Why can't an infant feel shame or guilt?

Elements of Emotion 2: The Mind

Two friends of ours returned from a mountain-climbing trip to Nepal. One said, "It was wonderful! The crystal-clear skies, the millions of stars, the friendly people, the majestic mountains, the harmony of the universe!" The other said, "It was horrible! The bedbugs and fleas, the lack of toilets, the yak-butter tea, the awful food, the unforgiving mountains!" Can you guess which traveler was ecstatic while traveling and which was unhappy?

Same trip, two different reactions to it. Why? As we saw in Chapter 1, in the first century A.D., the Stoic philosophers suggested an answer: People do not become angry or sad or anxious because of actual events, but because of their explanations of those events. Modern psychologists have verified the Stoics' ideas experimentally and are identifying the cognitive processes involved in emotions.

How Thoughts Create Emotions

In 1924, a Spanish physician named Gregorio Marañon wondered whether he could generate emotions in his subjects simply by injecting them with epinephrine (Cornelius, 1991). He got a curious result. Nearly 30 percent of the people in his research reported feeling genuine emotions. But more than 70 percent merely reported physical changes ("My heart is beating fast," "My throat feels tight") or what Marañon called "as if" emotions: "I feel *as if* I were angry," "I feel *as if* I were happy."

What caused the difference between the two groups? Marañon was able to induce genuine emotions by asking the first group to think about their sick children or their deceased parents. In short, the people who reported genuine emotions had a reason for them! Marañon concluded that emotions involve a *physical* component, consisting of the bodily changes that accompany arousal, and a psychological or *mental* component, consisting of the interpretation the individual gives them, within the context in which those changes occur.

Marañon's findings languished in a dusty journal until the 1960s, when Stanley Schachter and Jerome Singer (1962) advanced similar ideas with their **two-factor theory of emotion**. Like Marañon, they argued that bodily changes are necessary to experience an emotion, but are not enough. Emotion, they said, depends on two factors: *physiological arousal and the cognitive interpretation* of that arousal. Your body may be churning away in high gear, but unless you can interpret, explain, and label those changes, you will not feel a true emotion.

Schachter and Singer's own experiments testing their hypothesis were not successfully replicated by others. But their ideas launched scores of studies designed to investigate how emotions are created or influenced by beliefs, perceptions of the situation, expectations, and *attributions*—the explanations that people make of their own and other people's behavior (see Chapter 8). Human beings, after all, are the

two-factor theory of emotion The theory that emotions depend on both physiological arousal and a cognitive interpretation of that arousal.

Get Involved

Going Dotty

Put your finger on the dot below, and smile.

How do you feel at this moment, amused or irritated? If you followed our instructions and touched the dot, you probably feel more amused than angry. You may be laughing at yourself for doing such a silly thing, and that will make you feel happy. If you didn't put your finger on the dot, you probably feel more irked than amused. "Why are the authors of this book asking me to play stupid games?" you may be asking yourself. Notice that it is not our request that produced your emotion; it is your interpretation of what we asked you to do. Such interpretations are critical to all emotions.

---

only species that can say, "The more I thought about it, the madder I got." That common remark shows that we can think ourselves into an emotion, and, by implication, we can think ourselves out of it.

Attributions and Emotions. Perceptions and attributions are involved in every emotion, even those widely considered to be primary, such as happiness and sadness. To see how, imagine that you have had a crush for weeks on a fellow student. Finally you get up the nerve to start a conversation. Heart pounding, palms sweating, you manage to say, "Hi, there!" Before you can continue, the object of your passion has walked right past you without even a nod. Do you feel angry? Sad? Embarrassed? Your answer will depend on how you explain the student's behavior:

> *Angry:* "What a rude thing to do, to ignore me like that!"
>
> *Sad:* "I knew it; I'm no good. No one will ever like me."
>
> *Embarrassed:* "Oh, no! Everyone saw how I was humiliated!"

Notice that it is not the student's behavior, but your interpretation of it, that generates your emotional response. Or consider this example: If you get an A on your psychology midterm; how will you feel? If you get a D, how will you feel then? Most people assume that success brings happiness and failure brings unhappiness, but the emotions you feel will depend more on how you *explain* your grade than on what you actually get. Do you attribute your grade to your own efforts (or lack of them) or to the teacher, fate, or luck? In a series of experiments, students who believed they did well because of their own efforts tended to feel proud, happy, and satisfied. Those who believed they did well because of a lucky fluke or chance tended to feel gratitude, surprise, or guilt ("I don't deserve this"). Those who believed their failures were their own fault tended to feel regretful or guilty. And those who blamed others tended to feel—no surprise—angry (Weiner, 1986).

Here is a more surprising example of how thoughts affect emotions. Of two Olympic finalists, one who wins a second-place silver medal and one who wins a third-place bronze medal, which will feel happier? Won't it be the silver medalist?

Nope. In a study of athletes' reactions to placing second and third in the 1992 Olympics and the 1994 Empire State games, the bronze medalists were happier than the silver medalists (Medvec, Madey, & Gilovich, 1995). Apparently, the athletes were comparing their performance to "what might have been." The second-place winners, comparing themselves to the gold medalists, were unhappy that they didn't get the gold. But the third-place winners, comparing themselves to those who did worse than they, were happy that they had earned a medal at all! Over a century ago, William James commented on the paradox of an athlete who is "shamed to death" because he is merely the second best in the whole world: "That he is able to beat the whole population of the globe minus one is nothing; he has 'pitted' himself to beat that one; and as long as he doesn't do that nothing else counts."

Surprisingly, third-place winners tend to be happier about their performance than those who come in second. Certainly, Olympic fencing bronze medalist Jean-Michel Henry of France (left) is happier than silver medalist Pavel Kolobkov of the Unified Team (right). (Eric Strecki, center, won the gold for France.)

People are constantly appraising the events that befall them for their personal implications: Do I care about what is happening? Is it good or bad for me? Can I do anything about it? Is this matter going to get better or worse? Can I cope? If you decide that being stuck in a traffic jam is trivial and you can't do anything about it anyway, you may take it calmly. If you are on the way to your best friend's wedding, you see that the traffic is getting worse, and being late is *really* going to be bad for you because your friend will personally kill you, you are likely to feel hopping mad at those stupid cars that are blocking your way.

The cognitions involved in emotion range from your immediate perceptions of a specific event to your general philosophy of life (Lazarus, 2000a). If your guiding philosophy is that winning is everything and trying your best counts for nothing, you may feel depressed rather than happy if you "only" come in second, just like those silver medalists. If you think a friend's criticism is intentionally mean rather than well-meaning, you may respond with anger rather than gratitude. If you are a perfectionist about your work, brooding and obsessing about your occasional mistakes, you will become more anxious and depressed than if you are able to put your errors behind you (Flett et al., 1998). Cognitive appraisals are thus an essential part of the experience of emotion (Frijda, 1988; Oatley & Jenkins, 1996).

Get Involved ⠿

Examining Your Emotions After an Exam

After your next psychology test, write down the reasons you think you got the grade you did. Do you attribute the reasons to your own efforts (or lack of effort)? If you did not do as well as you hoped, do you blame yourself or the teacher? If you did do well, do you take credit, or do you think your success was a lucky fluke? How are these explanations related to your feelings about your grade?

This baby is able to feel utterly miserable—but not to feel remorse for keeping her parents up all night.

Cognitions and Emotional Complexity

As you can see, cognitions and physiology are inextricably linked in the experience of emotion—they are the Romeo and Juliet, the yin and yang, of human passion. Each affects the other in an endless loop: cognitions affect emotions, and emotional states influence cognitions. For example, blaming others for your woes can make you feel angry, but once you are angry you may be more inclined to think the worst of other people's motives (Lerner, Goldberg, & Tetlock, 1998).

Some emotions require only minimal or primitive cognitions. A conditioned sentimental response to a patriotic symbol, a conditioned disgust response to an ugly bug, and a warm fuzzy feeling toward a familiar object all involve simple, nonconscious reactions (Izard, 1994a; Murphy, Monahan, & Zajonc, 1995). An infant's primitive emotions do not have much mental sophistication: "Hey, I'm mad because no one is feeding me!"

As a child's cerebral cortex matures, however, cognitions, and therefore emotions, become more cognitively complex: "Hey, I'm mad because this situation is entirely wrong-headed and unfair!" Some emotions depend entirely on the maturation of higher cognitive capacities. Shame and guilt, for example, do not occur until after infancy because these *self*-conscious emotions require the emergence of a sense of self and the perception that you have behaved badly or let another person down (Baumeister, Stillwell, & Heatherton, 1994; Tangney et al., 1996).

Because our cognitions constantly shift as we interact with others, so do our emotions. As cognitive researcher Richard Lazarus (2000a) said, "An emotional encounter is not a single action or reaction, as in a still photo, but a continuous give and take between people"—a story as told in a movie. He describes a quarrel between a husband and wife over their morning orange juice. She has not given him freshly squeezed juice as usual, and when he asks why, the wife, still annoyed that he came home the night before in a sullen mood, tells him he can make his own $%^&* juice. Surprised and annoyed by her harsh tone, he sulks, making her angrier. Before long the quarrel has escalated into mutual accusations about other matters. Then, as the husband is about to storm out the door, he mentions that he learned yesterday that he would have to take a pay cut at work and that many employees were being fired. Suddenly the wife realizes why he was so remote the night before, and feels terrible about her outburst. She apologizes; he does, too. He admits how anxious he feels about his job; she feels guilty that she yelled at him. When each spouse feels misunderstood and mistreated, each becomes angry; when each perceives another explanation for the spouse's behavior, the anger dissipates.

Studies of the cognitive element in emotion suggest that people can learn how their thinking affects their emotions and can change their thinking accordingly. (As we will see in Chapter 17, cognitive therapy is based on this assumption.) They can ask themselves what the evidence is for their belief that the world will collapse if they get a C in biology, that no one loves them, or that they will be lonely forever. In such cases, notice that it is not emotional reasoning that prevents critical thinking; it is the failure to think critically that creates the emotion!

An individual's experience of emotion, then, combines mind and body. Yet there is still one part of the emotion "tree" missing. Thoughts may influence emotion, but where do these thoughts come from? When people feel that it is shameful for a man to dance on a table with a lampshade on his head, or for a woman to walk down a street with her arms and legs uncovered, where do their ideas about shame originate? If you punch the walls when you are angry, where did you learn how to express your feelings in that way? To answer these questions, we turn to the third major aspect of emotional experience: the role of culture.

QUICK QUIZ

Are your thoughts about quizzes affecting your feelings about taking this one?

1. What were the two factors in Schachter and Singer's two-factor theory of emotion?

2. Dara and Dinah get Bs on their psychology midterm, but Dara is ecstatic and proud and Dinah is furious. What thoughts are probably affecting their emotional reactions?

 3. At a party, a stranger is flirting with your date. You are flooded with jealousy. What cognitions might be causing this emotion? *Be specific.* What alternative thoughts might reduce your jealousy?

Answers:

1. physiological arousal and a cognitive interpretation of that arousal 2. Dara was probably expecting a lower grade and is attributing her B to her own efforts; Dinah was probably expecting a higher grade and is attributing her B to the instructor's unfairness, bad luck, or other external causes. 3. Possible thoughts causing jealousy are "My date finds other people more attractive," "That person is trying to steal my date," or "My date's behavior is humiliating me." But you could be saying, "It's a compliment to me that other people find my date attractive," or "It pleases me that my date is getting such deserved attention."

WHAT'S AHEAD ▶

- Why does one person find bugs disgusting—and another consider them a culinary treat?
- Do Germans, Japanese, and Americans always mean the same thing when they smile at others?
- Why do people show sadness at funerals even when they are not feeling sad?

Elements of Emotion 3: The Culture

A young wife leaves her house one morning to draw water from the local well as her husband watches from the porch. On her way back from the well, a male stranger stops her and asks for some water. She gives him a cupful and then invites him home to dinner. He accepts. The husband, wife, and guest have a pleasant meal together. The husband, in a gesture of hospitality, invites the guest to spend the night—with his wife. The guest accepts. In the morning, the husband leaves early to bring home breakfast. When he returns, he finds his wife again in bed with the visitor.

At what point in this story does the husband feel angry? The answer depends on his culture (Hupka, 1981, 1991). A North American husband would feel rather angry at a wife who had an extramarital affair, and a wife would feel rather angry at being offered to a guest as if she were a lamb chop. But these reactions are not universal. A Pawnee husband of the nineteenth century would be enraged at any man who dared ask his wife for water. An Ammassalik Inuit husband finds it perfectly honorable to offer his wife to a stranger, but only once. He would be angry to find his wife and the guest having a second encounter. And a Toda husband at the turn of the century in India would not be angry at all because the Todas allowed both husband and wife to take lovers. Both spouses might feel angry, though, if one of them had a *sneaky* affair, without announcing it publicly.

Although people in most cultures feel angry in response to insult and the violation of social rules, they often disagree about what an insult is or what the correct rule should be. As the wife-at-the-well story illustrates, culture determines what people feel angry, sad, lonely, happy, ashamed, or disgusted *about*. Among the Bedouins and other "shame-oriented" cultures, shame is produced by violations of a complex code of honor; on Bali and Java, shame results from perceived challenges to one's status

(Mesquita & Frijda, 1992). As we saw, disgust is universal, but the *content* of what produces disgust changes as an infant matures, and it varies from culture to culture. People in some cultures learn to become disgusted by bugs (which other people find beautiful or even tasty), unfamiliar sexual practices, dirt, death, "contamination" by casual physical contact such as a handshake, or particular foods (e.g., meat if they are vegetarian, or pork if they are Muslims or orthodox Jews). Most people feel disgust when their culture's moral rules are broken, such as the taboos against incest or sex with children (Rozin, Lowery, & Ebert, 1994).

How else might culture affect our emotions and their expression?

Culture and Emotional Variation

One interesting debate in the study of emotion is whether some emotions are specific to particular cultures and are not found elsewhere. What does it mean, for example, that some languages have words for subtle emotional states that other languages lack (Mesquita & Frijda, 1992)? The Germans have *schadenfreude,* a feeling of joy at another's misfortune. The Japanese speak of *hagaii,* helpless anguish tinged with frustration. *Litost* is a Czech word that combines grief, sympathy, remorse, and longing; the Czech writer Milan Kundera used it to describe "a state of torment caused by a sudden insight into one's own miserable self."

Conversely, some languages lack words for emotions that seem universal. For example, Tahitians lack the Western concept of and word for sadness. If you ask a Tahitian who is grieving over the loss of a lover what is wrong, he will say, "A spirit has made me ill." In contrast, Tahitians have a word for an emotion that most Westerners do not experience: *Mehameha* refers to "a sense of the uncanny," a trembling sensation that Tahitians feel when ordinary categories of perception are suspended—at twilight, in the brush, watching fires glow without heat. To Westerners, an event that cannot be identified is usually greeted with fear. Yet *mehameha* does not describe what Westerners call fear or terror (Levy, 1984).

Do these interesting linguistic differences mean that Germans are more likely than others actually to feel *schadenfreude,* the Japanese to feel *hagaii,* the Czechs to feel *litost,* and the Tahitians to feel *mehameha?* Or are they just more willing to give these subtle, multifaceted emotions a single name? (Certainly many non-German Westerners feel something like *schadenfreude* at the downfall or humiliation of their political opponents or ex-lovers!) Do Tahitians experience sadness the way Westerners do even though they identify it as illness?

> **THINKING CRITICALLY**
>
> **Ask Questions; Be Willing to Wonder**
>
> What does it mean if one language has a term for an emotion that another language lacks, like *litost* or *hagaii?* Are people who have these words actually more likely to feel the emotion, or just to have a term that describes it?

The father on the left is clearly proud of his family, and the husband on the right is clearly showing the affectionate "gaze of love" to his wife. But pride and love are not on most lists of primary emotions. Should they be, or are they just variations of happiness?

Physiological researchers would answer that all human beings are capable of feeling the primary, hard-wired emotions—by whatever name they call them—the ones that have distinctive physiological hallmarks in the brain, face, and nervous system. And they would answer that individuals might indeed differ in their abilities to experience secondary emotions, including variations such as *schadenfreude* or *hagaii*; blends of emotions such as *litost* or *mehameha*; and degrees of intensity and nuance that some cultures recognize or emphasize and others do not.

In support of this view, researchers have found that the difference between primary emotions and more complex adult variations is reflected in language, all over the world. In Chapter 9, we noted that a *prototype* is a typical representative of a class of things. People everywhere consider the primary emotions to be core examples of the concept *emotion:* For example, most people will say that "anger" and "sadness" are more representative of an emotion than "irritability" and "nostalgia" are. Prototypical emotions are reflected in the emotion words that young children learn first: *happy, sad, mad,* and *scared.* As children develop, they begin to draw emotional distinctions that are less prototypical and more specific to their language and culture, such as *ecstatic, depressed, hostile,* or *anxious* (Hupka, Lenton, & Hutchison, 1999; Russell & Fehr, 1994; Shaver, Wu, & Schwartz, 1992). In this way, they come to experience the gradations and nuances of emotional feeling that their cultures emphasize.

Cultural psychologists, however, argue that there is *no* aspect of any emotion, primary or secondary, that is not deeply influenced by culture. Thus, even if anger is universal, the way it is experienced and felt will vary from culture to culture—whether it feels good or bad, nauseating or exhilarating, useful or destructive (Tavris, 1989). Culture also affects whether people experience an emotion as arising from within themselves or from within the situation. In Chapter 8 we noted the distinction between individualist cultures, typical of North America and Europe, and collectivist (group-oriented) cultures, typical of Asia, South America, and the Middle East. In a study comparing individualist Dutch respondents with collectivist Surinamese and Turkish respondents, the latter described their emotions as stemming from, and affecting, other people. The individualists felt that their emotions were emerging from their own inner experience (Mesquita, 2001).

Finally, culture affects which emotions are even defined as basic or "primary." For example, anger is regarded as a primary emotion by individualistic Western psychologists. But in collectivist cultures, shame and loss of face are more central emotions (Kitayama & Markus, 1994). And on the tiny Micronesian atoll of Ifaluk, everyone would say that *fago* is the most fundamental emotion. *Fago,* translated as "compassion/love/sadness," reflects the sad feeling one has when a loved one is absent or in need, and the pleasurable sense of compassion in being able to care and help (Lutz, 1988). What, then, would theories of primary emotions look like from a non-Western perspective? They might start with shame and *fago,* which are just blips on the radar screen of Western emotion research.

To many cultural psychologists, therefore, "primary" emotions are those that are important within a given social and cultural context, not necessarily those that can be measured in the brain or identified on the face (Roseman, Wiest, & Swartz, 1994).

When these happy babies grow up, how will their culture and language affect their experience of joy?

The Rules of Emotional Regulation

On Sunday, April 25, in the year 1227, a knight named Ulrich von Lichtenstein disguised himself as the goddess Venus. Wearing an ornate white gown, waist-length braids, and heavy veils, Ulrich traveled from Venice to Bohemia, challenging all local warriors to a duel. By his own count (which may have been exaggerated), Ulrich

What some of us do for love: Ulrich von Lichtenstein disguised as Venus.

broke 307 lances, unhorsed four opponents, and completed his five-week journey with an undefeated record. The reason for Ulrich's knightly performance was his passion for a princess, nameless to history, who barely gave poor Ulrich the time of day. Ulrich trembled in her presence, suffered in her absence, and constantly endured feelings of longing, misery, and melancholy—a state of love that apparently made him very happy (M. Hunt, 1959/1967).

We will have a lot more to say about love in the next chapter, but for the moment consider only Ulrich's *expression* of his passion. If someone tried to win your heart by performing a modern version of such acts of bravery, would you be charmed, irritated, or alarmed?

Display Rules. In some cultures, people would find Ulrich's extravagant demonstration of love exciting and touching; in others, they would find it weird and lunatic—they would be suspicious of Ulrich's real motives. Likewise, in some cultures grief is expressed by noisy wailing and weeping; in others, by tearless resignation; and in still others, by merry dance, drink, and song. Cultures everywhere influence the **display rules** that specify when, where, and how emotions are to be expressed or when they should be squelched (Ekman et al., 1987; Gross, 1998). Once you feel an emotion, how you express it is rarely a simple matter of "I say (or show) what I feel." You may be obliged to disguise what you feel. You may wish you could feel what you say. You may convey an emotion unintentionally, through nonverbal signals.

Even the smile, which seems a straightforward signal of friendliness, has many meanings and uses that are not universal. Americans smile more frequently than Germans, not because Americans are friendlier but because they differ in their notions of when a smile is appropriate. After a German-American business session, Americans often complain that the Germans are cold and aloof. For their part, Germans often complain that Americans are excessively cheerful, hiding their real feelings under the mask of a smile (Hall & Hall, 1990). The Japanese smile even more than Americans, to disguise embarrassment, anger, or other negative emotions whose public display is considered rude and incorrect.

THINKING CRITICALLY

Consider Other Interpretations

A European who behaves in a way that conveys good manners and dignified restraint may seem cold to the average American. An American who smiles effusively may seem superficial and childish to the average European. How might each of them interpret the other's behavior more constructively?

Around the world, the cultural rules for expressing emotions (or suppressing them) differ. The display rule for a formal Japanese wedding portrait is "no expressions of emotion"—but not every member of this family has learned that rule yet.

People learn their culture's display rules as effortlessly as they learn its language. Just as they can speak without consciously knowing the rules of grammar, most people express or suppress their emotions without being aware of the rules they are following (Hall & Hall, 1990; Keating, 1994). When they try to communicate across cultures, however, not knowing the other person's display rules of emotion can lead to major misunderstandings, hostilities, and, in extreme cases, even war.

Here is a tragic example (Triandis, 1994): On January 9, 1991, the Foreign Minister of Iraq, Tariq Aziz, met with the American Secretary of State, James Baker, to discuss Iraq's invasion of Kuwait. Seated next to Aziz was the half-brother of Iraq's president, Saddam Hussein. Baker said, "If you do not move out of Kuwait we will attack you." A clear statement, right? But he followed the display rules for an American diplomat, moderate and restrained. He did not shout, stamp his feet, or wave his hands. Saddam Hussein's brother, for his part, behaved like a normal Iraqi. He paid attention to Baker's nonverbal language, which he considered the important form of communication. He reported to Saddam Hussein that Baker was "not at all angry. The Americans are just talking, and they will not attack." Saddam therefore instructed Aziz to be inflexible and to yield nothing. This misunderstanding contributed to the outbreak of a bloody war in which thousands of people died.

Body Language. Fiorello LaGuardia, who was mayor of New York from 1933 to 1945, was fluent in three languages: English, Italian, and Yiddish. LaGuardia knew more than the words of those languages; he also knew the gestures that went along with each one. Researchers who studied films of his speeches could tell which language he was speaking with the sound turned off! They could do so by reading his *body language,* the nonverbal signals of body movement, posture, gesture, and gaze that people constantly express (Birdwhistell, 1970). Italians and Jews embellish their speech with circular movements of their arms and hands, and by measuring the radius of those movements you can actually predict whether a speaker is of Italian or Jewish descent: The larger the radius, the more likely the speaker is Italian (Keating, 1994).

Some signals of body language, like some facial expressions, seem to be "spoken" universally. Across cultures, people generally recognize body movements that reveal pleasure or displeasure, liking or dislike, tension or relaxation, high status or low status, grief and anger (Buck, 1984; Matsumoto, 1996). When people are depressed, it shows in their walk, stance, and head position. However, most aspects of body language are specific to particular spoken languages and cultures, which makes even the simplest gesture subject to misunderstanding and offense. The sign of the University of Texas football team, the Longhorns, is to extend the index finger and the pinkie. Be careful where you make this gesture! In Italy and other parts of Europe, it means a man's wife has been unfaithful to him—a serious insult.

When people are talking to each other, a mismatch of body languages will make their conversation feel "out of sync"; they may feel as confused and emotionally upset as if they had had a verbal misunderstanding. In contrast, when people's gestures and body language are in synchrony, they will feel greater rapport and emotional harmony (see Figure 11.3). The ability to synchronize body language is crucial to smooth interaction between people (Bernieri et al., 1996;

display rules Social and cultural rules that regulate when, how, and where a person may express (or must suppress) emotions.

Arms and hands communicate interest, emphasis, and emotion, just as words do.

Figure 11.3
THE CONTAGION OF EMOTION

These volunteers, videotaped in a study of conversational synchrony, are obviously "in sync" with one another, even though they have just met. The degree to which two people's gestures and expressions are synchronized affects the rapport they feel with one another. Such synchrony can also create a "contagion" of moods (Bernieri et al., 1991).

emotion work Expression of an emotion that the person does not really feel, often because of a role requirement.

Smiling to convey friendliness is part of the job description for flight attendants, whether they are male or female—but not necessarily for the passengers they serve.

Hatfield, Cacioppo, & Rapson, 1994). When people feel uncomfortable with someone from another culture, the reason may simply be that their body languages are out of sync.

Emotion Work. Cultural display rules and rules governing body language tell us not only what to do when we *are* feeling an emotion, but also how and when we should show an emotion we do *not* feel. Acting out an emotion we do not really feel, or trying to create the right emotion for the occasion, is called **emotion work,** and it is part of our normal efforts to regulate our emotions when we are with others (Gross, 1998; Hochschild, 1983). Most people are expected to demonstrate sadness at funerals, happiness at weddings, and affection toward relatives. If they do not really feel such emotions, they may playact to convince others that they do.

Sometimes emotion work is actually a job requirement. Flight attendants must outwardly convey cheerfulness, even if they are privately angry about a rude or drunken passenger. Bill collectors must put on a stern face to convey threat, even if they are feeling sorry for the poor person in debt (Hochschild, 1983). Other employees do emotion work when they express agreement with an employer's infuriating decision or friendliness to annoying customers. One possible benefit of this kind of emotion work—if you remember what you read about facial feedback—is that the effort to display feelings of warmth and friendliness toward others may generate positive feelings in the sender as well as the receiver.

In sum, culture influences the content of our emotional reactions—what makes us feel angry, ashamed, and so forth. It may influence our ability to experience blends and nuances of emotions, and it affects which emotions we consider primary or central. And it determines how, when, and where we express our emotions through display rules, body language, and emotion work.

QUICK QUIZ

Please use verbal communication to answer these questions.

1. In Western theories of emotion, anger would be called a _____ emotion, whereas *fago* would be called a _____ emotion.

2. In a class discussion, a student says something that embarrasses a student from another culture. The second student smiles to disguise his discomfort; the first student, thinking he is not being taken seriously, gets angry. These students' misunderstanding reflects their different _____ for the expression of embarrassment and anger.

3. Maureen is working in a fast-food restaurant and becoming irritated with a customer who isn't ordering fast enough. "Hey, whaddaya want to order, slowpoke?" she snaps at him. To keep her job, and her temper, Maureen needs practice in _____.

Answers:

1. primary, secondary 2. display rules 3. emotion work

WHAT'S AHEAD

- **Are women really more emotional than men?**
- **What factors other than your sex predict how well you can tell what someone is feeling?**
- **What factors other than your sex predict how emotionally expressive you are?**

Putting the Elements Together: Emotion and Gender

"Women are too emotional," men often complain. "Men are too uptight," women often reply. One of the oldest gender stereotypes is that women are "more emotional" than men (Plant et al., 2000). But what do they mean by "emotional"? It's time to define our terms and examine our assumptions.

Women *are* more likely than men to suffer from severe depression, a mood disorder we discuss in Chapter 16. But if we define emotionality as the ability to feel the everyday emotions of life, men and women do not differ much (Baumeister, Stillwell, & Wotman, 1990; Brody, 1999; Fischer et al., 1993; Kring & Gordon, 1998; Oatley & Duncan, 1994; Shields, 2002). Both sexes are equally likely to feel anxious in new situations; to feel love and loneliness; to feel angry when they believe they have been insulted or treated unfairly; to feel embarrassed when they make public mistakes; and to grieve when attachments break up. So we must look elsewhere for evidence that one sex is "more emotional" than the other and the conditions under which such differences might occur.

> **THINKING CRITICALLY**
>
> **Define Your Terms**
>
> People say that women are the emotional sex, but they often fail to define their terms. What, for example, does *emotional* mean? Why is it "arguing" when he does it but "getting emotional" when she does it?

Physiology and Intensity. When men and women are asked to *recall* emotional experiences, women give more intense and vivid accounts. But when emotions are measured at the time they occur, men are "more emotional" in terms of intensity than women are (Seidlitz & Diener, 1998). And if we define emotionality in terms of reactivity to provocation, again men are often more emotional than women. Studies of hundreds of married couples have found that conflict is physiologically

"It's truly remarkable, Louis, thirty-seven years next Tuesday and never a cross word between us."

more upsetting for men than for women, which may be why many men try to avoid conflict entirely (Gottman, 1994). In studies of actual quarrels between married couples, men's heart rates, unlike women's, often soar as soon as signs of conflict begin and stay high longer. Moreover, more husbands than wives feel more negative and hostile the more agitated they are (Levenson, Carstensen, & Gottman, 1994).

One possible explanation for these differences is that the male's autonomic nervous system is generally more sensitive and reactive than the female's. When men are under stress or in a competitive situation, many show a more pronounced elevation in blood pressure, heart rate, and epinephrine than women do (Polefrone & Manuck, 1987; T. Smith et al., 1996). But another explanation is that men are more likely than women to rehearse angry thoughts, such as "I don't have to take this" or "It's all her fault." These thoughts prolong and intensify the physiological reactions involved in anger (Rusting & Nolen-Hoeksema, 1998). Women, in contrast, are more likely than men to ruminate about, and thus prolong, feelings of depression and sadness.

Sensitivity to Other People's Emotions. Sometimes women are considered more emotional because of their alleged sensitivity to other people's emotional states. On a test that measures the ability to detect emotions revealed in another person's voice, body movements, and facial expressions, women have indeed scored slightly better than men (J. Hall, 1987). But sensitivity to another person's emotions depends far more on the *context* in which the two people are interacting than on their gender. In particular, men's and women's ability to "read" emotional signals depends on the following factors:

1 *The sex of the sender and of the receiver.* Most people are better at reading the emotional signals, facial expressions, and gestures of members of their own sex than those of the other sex (Buck, 1984).

2 *How well the sender and receiver know each other.* Fortunately, affection improves cross-gender accuracy. Dating and married couples can interpret each other's facial expressions, idiosyncratic signs of lying, and other emotional signs better than strangers can (Hatfield, Cacioppo, & Rapson, 1994; Smith, Keltner, & Gonzaga, 1998).

3 *How expressive the sender is.* The receiver's gender and sensitivity to other people is less important than the sender's expressiveness. In other words, women are no better at reading the emotions of a "strong, silent" type than men are. Even among intimate couples, the best predictor of communication accuracy is the expressiveness of the sender; the sensitivity of the receiver counts for much less (Snodgrass, Hecht, & Ploutz-Snyder, 1998).

4 *Who has the power.* In any relationship in which one person has more power or authority than the other—such as parent and child, boss and employee, or teacher and student—the less powerful person is motivated to learn to read the powerful person's nonverbal signals (Fiske, 1993; Henley, 1995; Lakoff, 1990). Is Mr. Hepworth in a mood to give me a raise? Is Professor Postlethwaite mad at us for blowing the midterm? Many supposed gender differences in the ability to read emotions actually reflect power differences. As one psychologist put it, "women's intuition" is really "subordinate's intuition" (Snodgrass, 1985). In male–female pairs in which one person was randomly assigned to be the leader and the other the follower, the subordinate was more sensitive to the leader's nonverbal signals than the leader was to the follower's cues. This difference occurred whether a man or a woman was the leader or the follower (Snodgrass, 1985, 1992).

5 *Stereotypes and expectations*. People see what they expect to see, and stereotypes may guide their expectations. For example, most North Americans think it is appropriate for men to express anger and women to express sadness, but not the other way around. Therefore, they often have trouble recognizing male sadness or female anger. In one study, even unambiguous expressions of anger by women were rated as a mixture of anger and sadness (Plant et al., 2000).

Cognitions. If a male teacher compliments a female student on her appearance, is that a sign of flattery or harassment? If a woman touches a male friend on his arm, is she signaling affection or sexual interest? Men and women often differ in their perceptions of the same event (Lakoff, 1990; Stapley & Haviland, 1989). Their different interpretations, in turn, can create different emotional responses to the event.

For example, although men and women often feel angry in response to betrayal and injustice, they sometimes differ in the kinds of everyday events that provoke their anger. Women are more likely than men to become angry over things they perceive as signs of a partner's disregard, such as forgetting a birthday; men are more likely to become angry about damage to their property or affronts by a stranger (Fehr et al., 1999). When your partner blows up over something you think is trivial, it is easy to conclude that he or she is being "too emotional"!

Expressiveness. The one gender difference that undoubtedly contributes most to the stereotype that women are "more emotional" than men—their status and power being equal—is women's greater willingness to express their feelings, nonverbally and verbally. In North America, women on average do smile more than men do, gaze at their listeners more, have more emotionally expressive faces, use more expressive hand and body movements, and tend to touch others more and be touched more (DePaulo, 1992; Kring & Gordon, 1998). Women also talk about their emotions more than men do. They are far more likely than men to cry, and to acknowledge emotions that reveal vulnerability and weakness, such as "hurt feelings," fear, sadness, loneliness, shame, and guilt (Grossman & Wood, 1993; Smith & Reise, 1998; Timmers, Fischer, & Manstead, 1998).

In contrast, most North American men express only one emotion more freely than women: anger toward strangers, especially other men, when they believe they have been challenged or insulted. Otherwise, men are expected to control and mask negative feelings. When they are worried or afraid, they are more likely than women to say they feel moody, irritable, frustrated, or "on edge" (Fehr et al., 1999; Smith & Reise, 1998). If they express supposedly unmanly emotions at all, they will usually do so only to their intimate partners, and rarely to casual male friends.

An unfortunate consequence of the taboo on male expressiveness may be difficulty in recognizing when men are seriously unhappy. Many boys and men fail to be diagnosed as depressed because the tests for depression are based on typically female

Does this woman's touch signify affection, dominance, harassment, sexual interest, or simple friendliness? How do you think the man is reacting? Men and women often disagree on the meaning of another's touch. Depending on their perceptions, they may respond with anger, happiness, disgust, fear, or desire.

Both sexes feel emotionally attached to friends, but often they express their affections differently. From childhood on, girls tend to prefer "face to face" friendships, based on shared feelings; boys tend to prefer "side by side" friendships, based on shared activities.

reactions—crying and talking about their unhappiness (Riessman, 1990; Stapley & Haviland, 1989). But most North American men do not express grief this way. Instead, they try to distract themselves, work harder or quit working altogether, bury their feelings in alcohol or other drugs, or, in extreme cases, become violent. Because the sexes tend to have different ways of coping with depression, some people wrongly infer that men suffer less than women when relationships end or that men are incapable of deep feeling.

Even gender differences in emotional expressiveness, however, are strongly affected by three important factors:

1 *Gender roles.* Women *and* men who are untraditional in their gender roles are more emotionally expressive—verbally and nonverbally—than traditionalists (Kring & Gordon, 1998). Perhaps they feel freer to express their true selves because they do not feel obligated to play the "proper" male or female role.

2 *Cultural norms.* Expressive people, male or female, tend to come from cultures in which expressiveness is the rule (Kring & Gordon, 1998). Italian, French, Spanish, and Middle Eastern men can have entire conversations using highly expressive hand gestures and facial expressions; there aren't many sex differences in nonverbal expressiveness in their cultures. In contrast, in Asian cultures, both sexes are taught to control emotional expression (Matsumoto, 1996; Mesquita & Frijda, 1992). Cultures also determine which emotions men and women express most freely. Israeli and Italian men are more likely than women to mask feelings of sadness, but British, Spanish, Swiss, and German men are *less* likely than their female counterparts to inhibit this emotion (Wallbott, Ricci-Bitti, & Bänninger-Huber, 1986).

3 *The specific situation.* As we saw in the case of "subordinate's intuition," the influence of a particular situation often determines whether you will express your feelings or inhibit them, regardless of your gender or culture. An American man will be as likely as an American woman to control his temper when the target of anger is someone with higher status or power; few people, no matter how angry, will readily sound off at a professor, police officer, or employer. And you won't find many gender differences in emotional expressiveness at a football game.

Israeli parents (left) and a Palestinian father (right) react to the death of their children in the Middle Eastern conflict. Notice that the men are following different display rules for the expression of grief, rules that govern whether they should "let it out" or "keep a stiff upper lip." Your own culture's rules may affect your reactions to these scenes: Is the Israeli father "cold and uptight" or "mature and manly"? Is the Palestinian father being "hysterical" or "humanly expressive"?

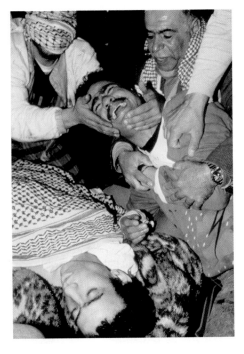

Emotion Work. Both sexes know the experience of having to hide emotions they feel and to show emotions they do not feel. Yet their emotion work, on the job and at home, is often different. On the whole, women tend to be involved in the flight-attendant side of emotion work, persuading others that they are friendly, happy, and warm, and making sure others are happy (DePaulo, 1992; Shields, 2002). Men tend to be involved in the bill-collection side, persuading others that they are stern, aggressive, and unemotional.

Again, the major reason for this difference has to do with gender roles and status. When a man expresses anger, most Americans accord him greater status than when he expresses sadness. In one clever study, people were more favorably inclined toward former President Clinton when they saw tapes of him expressing anger about the Monica Lewinsky scandal than when they saw him expressing sadness about it (Tiedens, 2001).

In contrast, women are expected to be kind and attentive to other people's feelings, often as a requirement of the female role (Fischer, 1993; Grossman & Wood, 1993). Thus, many North American women smile more often than men do as part of their emotion work—to pacify others, smooth over conflicts, or convey deference (Hecht & LaFrance, 1998). If women do *not* smile when others expect them to, they are often disliked, even if they are actually smiling as often as men would. Girls learn this lesson early; 6- to 10-year-olds show a steady increase in knowledge about when they should disguise their true feelings and put on a "polite smile"—for instance, when they are given a gift they don't like. Boys are much less likely to mask their negative feelings in this way (Davis, 1995; Saarni, 1989).

In summary, the answer to "which sex is more emotional?" is: sometimes men, sometimes women, and sometimes neither. "Being emotional" can refer to feeling an emotion, being highly reactive physiologically, being inclined to perceive events in an emotion-generating way, being sensitive to other people's emotional states, being emotionally expressive, or feeling obligated to do a particular type of "emotion work." Everyone feels emotions, but cultural norms and gender roles shape the expression of these emotions in countless ways.

QUICK QUIZ

Both sexes have the emotional stamina to take this quiz.

A. Indicate whether each of these descriptions applies (a) more to men than to women, (b) more to women than to men, or (c) to both sexes equally.
   1. Does "emotion work" to make other people feel good.
   2. Finds it difficult to express anger to a superior.
   3. Expresses anger to a stranger.
   4. Feels grief when a relationship ends.
   5. Admits feeling scared to death.
   6. Can read another person's emotions.

B. Question #6 was sneaky, because the ability to identify another person's emotions is affected by factors other than the perceiver's sex. What are they?

Answers:

A. 1. b 2. c 3. a 4. c 5. b 6. c B. Sensitivity to another person's emotions is enhanced when the sender and receiver are the same sex; the two people know each other; the sender is expressive; the receiver is in a subordinate position in relation to the sender; the receiver does not hold gender stereotypes.

As we have seen in this chapter, the emotion "tree" can take many shapes, depending on physiology, cognitive processes, and cultural rules. The case of gender and emotion shows that if we look at just one part of the tree, we come up with an incomplete or misleading picture. And it shows, too, that emotions have many purposes: They allow us to establish close bonds, threaten and warn, get help from others, reveal or deceive. The many varieties and expressions of emotion suggest that although we feel emotions physically, we use them socially. As we explore further issues in the study of motivation, personality, development, well-being, and mental disorders, we will see again and again how emotions involve thinking and feeling, perception and action—head and heart.

Taking Psychology with You

"LET IT OUT" OR "BOTTLE IT UP"? THE DILEMMA OF ANGER

What do you do when you feel angry? Do you tend to brood and sulk, collecting your righteous complaints like acorns for the winter, or do you erupt, hurling your wrath upon anyone or anything at hand? Do you discuss your feelings when you have calmed down? Does "letting anger out" get rid of it for you, or does it only make it more intense? The answer is crucial for how you get along with your family, neighbors, employers, and strangers.

Chronic feelings of anger and an inability to control anger can be as emotionally devastating and unhealthy as chronic problems with depression, panic, or anxiety. In contrast to much pop-psych advice, research shows that expressing anger does not always get it "out of your system"; often people feel worse after an angry confrontation, both physically and mentally (Bushman, Baumeister, & Stack, 1999; Tavris, 1989). When people talk incessantly about their anger or act on that feeling, they tend to rehearse their grievances and pump up their blood pressures. Conversely, when people learn to control their tempers and express anger constructively, they usually feel better, not worse; calmer, not angrier (Deffenbacher et al., 1996).

Charles Darwin (1872/1965) was right when he observed: "The free expression by outward signs of an emotion intensifies it. . . . He who gives way to violent gestures will increase his rage."

When people are feeling angry, they have a choice of doing any number of things. They can write letters, play the piano, jog, bake bread, try to solve the problem that is causing their anger, abuse their friends or family, hit a punching bag, or yell. If a particular action soothes their feelings or gets the desired response from others, they are likely to acquire a habit. Soon that habit feels "natural," as if it could never be changed; indeed, many people justify their violent tempers by saying, "I just couldn't help myself." But they can. If you have learned an abusive or aggressive habit, the research in this chapter offers practical suggestions for relearning constructive ways of managing anger:

▶ **Don't sound off in the heat of anger; let bodily arousal cool down.** Whether your arousal comes from background stresses such as heat, crowds, or loud noise, or from conflict with another person, take time to relax. Time allows you to

decide whether you are "really" angry or just tired and tense. This is the reason for that sage old advice to count to 10, count to 100, or sleep on it. Other cooling-off strategies include taking a time-out in the middle of an argument, meditating or relaxing, and calming yourself with a distracting activity.

▶ **Don't take it personally.** If you feel that you have been insulted, check your perception for its accuracy. Could there be another reason for the behavior you find offensive? People who are quick to feel anger tend to interpret other people's actions as intentional offenses. People who are slow to anger tend to give others the benefit of the doubt, and they are not as focused on their own injured pride. Empathy ("Poor guy, he's feeling rotten") is usually incompatible with anger, so practice seeing the situation from the other person's perspective. Also, be sure you understand another person's nonverbal communication before you decide that you have been insulted. In Stockton, California, a driver used a hand signal to alert a car behind him at a stoplight that his headlights were off. The driver of the second car interpreted this gesture as a sign of disrespect, shot at the first car—and killed a passenger.

▶ *If you decide that expressing anger is appropriate, be sure you use the right verbal and nonverbal language to make yourself understood.* Because cultures have different display rules, be sure the recipient of your anger understands what you are feeling and what complaint you are trying to convey. If your way of expressing anger is to sulk, expecting everyone else to read your mind and make amends to you, you are not likely to be communicating clearly.

▶ *Think carefully about how to express anger so that you will get the results you want.* What do you want your anger to accomplish? Do you just want to make the other person feel bad, or do you want the other person to understand your concerns and make amends? Shouting "You moron! How *could* you be so stupid!" might accomplish the former goal, but it's not likely to get the person to apologize, let alone to change his or her behavior. If your goal is to improve a bad situation or achieve justice, then learning how to express anger so the other person will listen is essential. People who have been the targets of injustice have learned that outbursts of anger may draw society's attention to a problem, but real change requires sustained political effort, challenges to unfair laws, and the use of tactics that persuade rather than alienate the opposition.

Of course, if you just want to blow off steam, go right ahead; but you risk becoming a hothead.

Summary

▶ Emotion and cognition are not "opposites," with one being "irrational" and the other "rational." Emotions bind people together, regulate relationships, motivate people to achieve their goals, and help them make plans and decisions. The complex experience of *emotion* involves physiological changes in the brain, face, and autonomic nervous system; cognitive processes; and cultural norms and regulations.

Elements of Emotion 1: The Body

▶ *Primary emotions* are those that appear to be inborn and universal, having corresponding physiological patterns and facial expressions. *Secondary emotions* include all the variations and blends of emotion that may vary across culture.

▶ Some basic facial expressions—anger, fear, sadness, happiness, disgust, surprise, contempt—are widely recognized across cultures. They probably evolved to foster communication with others, enhance infant survival, and signal our intentions to others. As studies of *facial feedback* show, they also help us to identify our own emotional states. Facial expressions often cause unconscious imitations in others, which can create *mood contagion.*

▶ Facial expressions always take place in a social context, which is why the connections between emotions, facial expressions, and other people's perceptions are not simple. Agreement on which emotion a given expression reveals varies considerably; people's facial expressions depend on the presence of others; people's ability to "read" another person's facial expression depends on the social context; and people use facial expressions to lie about their real emotions.

▶ Many aspects of emotion are associated with specific parts of the brain. Damage to certain areas, for example, may affect a person's ability to feel disgust. The *amygdala* is responsible for initially evaluating the emotional importance of incoming sensory information, and is especially involved in fear. The *prefrontal cortex* provides the cognitive ability to override this initial appraisal. Emotions generally involve the motivation to approach or withdraw; regions of the *left* prefrontal cortex appear to be specialized for the motivation to approach others (as with happiness and anger), whereas regions of the *right* prefrontal region are specialized for withdrawal or escape (as with disgust and fear).

▶ During the experience of any emotion, *epinephrine* and *norepinephrine* produce a state of physiological arousal to prepare the body for an output of energy. But different emotions are also associated with different biochemical responses and different patterns of autonomic nervous system activity.

▶ Many efforts have been made to detect guilt and lies by measuring changes in physiological arousal or brain activity. The most popular method is the *polygraph machine,* or "lie detector," but this method has low reliability and validity because there are no patterns of autonomic nervous system activity specific to lying.

Elements of Emotion 2: The Mind

▶ The *two-factor theory of emotion* held that emotions result from arousal and the labeling or interpretation of that arousal. Research spurred by this theory has investigated the cognitive processes involved in emotion, such as the *attributions* people make about others' behavior and the way people interpret and evaluate events. The cognitions involved in emotion range from immediate perceptions of a specific event to one's philosophy of life.

▶ Thoughts and emotions operate reciprocally, each influencing the other. Some of the primary emotions that are apparent in infancy, along with conditioned emotional responses, can occur without much cognition. But many emotions, such as shame and guilt, depend on higher cognitive processes and the emergence of a sense of self. In any emotional encounter, cognitions and appraisals are constantly changing, affecting the emotions the participants feel.

Elements of Emotion 3: The Culture

▶ Cultures affect the content of emotion: what people feel angry, ashamed, disgusted, etc. about. Physiological researchers believe that all human beings share the ability to experience primary emotions, whereas secondary emotions and blends of feeling may be culture-specific— a view supported by research on emotion *prototypes.*

But cultural psychologists believe that culture affects every aspect of emotional experience, including whether people experience emotions as originating in relationships or within themselves, and which emotions are considered primary.

▶ Culture strongly influences the *display rules* and *body language* that regulate how and whether people express their emotions. The ability to synchronize moods through body language is important for rapport and smooth interactions. *Emotion work* is the effort a person makes to display an emotion he or she does not feel but feels obliged to convey. Cultural differences in display rules, body language, and emotion work can lead to misunderstandings.

Putting the Elements Together: Emotion and Gender

▶ In everyday life, women and men are equally likely to feel a wide array of emotions, from love to anger. Many men seem to be more physiologically reactive to conflict than women are, however, and the sexes sometimes differ in the perceptions and attributions that generate emotion and emotional intensity. Although women are thought to be better than men at reading another person's emotional state, gender is less important than other factors: whether the two individuals are of the same sex, how well they know each other, the sender's expressiveness, which person has more power in the situation, and what stereotypes or expectations they have.

▶ Men and women differ primarily in expressiveness— in the display rules they follow for expressing emotions, both verbally and nonverbally. In North America, women are more likely than men to cry and to reveal feelings of fear, sadness, guilt, and loneliness; men are more likely to deny or mask such feelings of "weakness." North American men express one emotion more freely than women: anger toward strangers. These gender differences are in turn affected by gender roles, family and cultural norms, and the influence of a particular situation. Gender role requirements also often specify different emotion work for the two sexes.

▶ The example of gender and emotion shows that to understand the full experience and expression of emotion, we must understand biology, cognitive attributions and perceptions, and cultural rules. Examining just one component gives an incomplete picture.

Key Terms

emotion 396

primary emotions 396

secondary emotions 397

facial feedback 397

mood contagion 399

amygdala 402

prefrontal cortex 402

epinephrine 403

norepinephrine 403

polygraph ("lie detector") 404

two-factor theory of emotion 407

attributions 407

emotion prototypes 413

display rules 414

body language 415

emotion work 416

◀ LOOKING BACK

- Which facial expressions of emotion do most people recognize the world over? (p. 397)

- Why might hanging around with a depressed friend make you gloomy, too? (pp. 399–400)

- Why don't you smile much when you are home alone? (p. 400)

- Which little structure in the brain sees to it that you cross the street fast when a truck is headed toward you? (p. 402)

- Which two hormones can make you "too excited to eat"? (p. 403)

- What do "lie detectors" actually detect? (pp. 405–406)

- When people say, "The more I thought about it, the madder I got," what does that tell us about emotion? (pp. 407–408)

- In a competition, who is likely to be happier, the third-place winner or the second-place winner—and why? (p. 409)

- Why can't an infant feel shame or guilt? (p. 410)

- Why does one person find bugs disgusting—and another consider them a culinary treat? (p. 412)

- Do Germans, Japanese, and Americans always mean the same thing when they smile at others? (p. 414)

- Why do people show sadness at funerals even when they are not feeling sad? (p. 416)

- Are women really more emotional than men? (p. 417, p. 421)

- What factors other than your sex predict how well you can tell what someone is feeling? (p. 418)

- What factors other than your sex predict how emotionally expressive you are? (p. 420)

Go to *Live!* psych **WWW.PRENHALL.COM/WADE** to reinforce this key concept, and more.

11.1   Facial expressions of emotion

12

Motivation

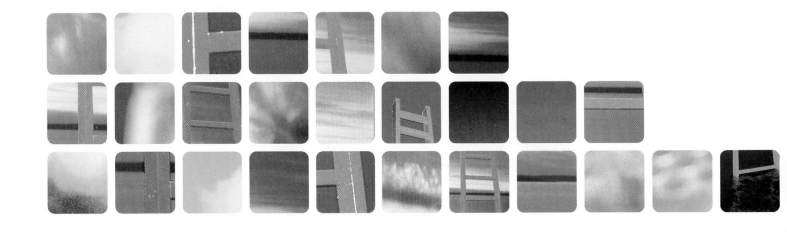

Just don't give up trying to do what you really want to do. Where there is love and inspiration, I don't think you can go wrong.

ELLA FITZGERALD

In 2001, Lance Armstrong won the three-week Tour de France for the third consecutive time. His victories in the grueling bicycle race, which covers 2,300 miles across the mountains of France, were particularly astonishing, because Armstrong had managed to recover from testicular cancer that had spread to his abdomen, lungs, and brain. The cancer, diagnosed in 1996, was arrested by two operations and intensive chemotherapy. By 1998, Armstrong was ready to retire from the sport, but eventually he came back to win this most difficult of bicycle races.

Nineteen-year-old Merrick Ryan was 5'7" tall and weighed 128 pounds when she decided she was too fat. After a visit to New York, she told her parents that all the women there were size 2 or 4, and she felt fat just walking down the sidewalk. She lost 10 pounds and, she said, began to feel "prettier." But Merrick couldn't shut off her determination to lose weight. In a few months she had dropped to 88 pounds. Therapy didn't help. One afternoon, having told her therapist and her parents that she would stop starving herself, she overdosed on antidepressants. Barely conscious, she told her mother: "I just can't live like this anymore. I don't want to be fat. I want to die." She died that evening (*People*, October 30, 2000).

In 1875, a teenager named Annie Oakley defeated Frank Butler, the star of the Buffalo Bill Wild West Show, in an arranged sharpshooting competition. "It was her first big match—my first defeat," wrote Butler. "The next day I came back to see the little girl who had beaten me, and it was not long until we married." He became her manager, and for the next 50 years, they traveled together across Europe and America, where her skills with a gun made her the toast of both continents. Throughout his life, Frank published love poems to Annie, and they remained devoted until their deaths, within 18 days of one another, in 1926 (Kreps, 1990).

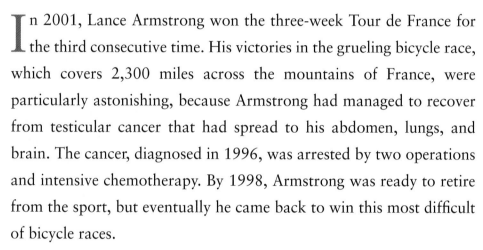

THE HUNGRY ANIMAL: MOTIVES TO EAT

The Genetics of Weight
Culture, Psychology, and Weight
Weight and Health: Biology Versus Culture

THE SOCIAL ANIMAL: MOTIVES TO LOVE

The Psychology of Love
Gender, Culture, and Love

THE EROTIC ANIMAL: MOTIVES FOR SEX

The Biology of Desire
The Psychology of Desire
The Culture of Desire
The Riddle of Sexual Orientation

THE COMPETENT ANIMAL: MOTIVES TO ACHIEVE

The Effects of Motivation on Work
The Effects of Work on Motivation

MOTIVES, VALUES, AND WELL-BEING

Taking Psychology with You
How to Lose Weight—and Whether You Should

427

motivation An inferred process within a person or animal that causes movement either toward a goal or away from an unpleasant situation.

intrinsic motivation The pursuit of an activity for its own sake.

extrinsic motivation The pursuit of an activity for external rewards, such as money or fame.

What motivated Lance Armstrong to fight not only his cancer, but also his impulse to give up racing—indeed, to triumph so dramatically over his illness? What motivated a beautiful, slim young woman to starve herself to death? What kept Annie Oakley and Frank Butler in love for 50 years, when so many other romantic passions die in five years—or five weeks?

The word *motivation*, like the word *emotion*, comes from the Latin root meaning "to move," and the psychology of motivation is indeed the study of what moves us, why we do what we do. To psychologists, **motivation** refers to a process within a person or animal that causes that organism to move *toward* a goal or *away* from an unpleasant situation. The goal may be to get married or avoid marriage. The goal may be to eat or avoid eating. The goal may be to satisfy a biological need, as in eating a sandwich to reduce hunger, or to fulfill a psychological ambition, such as being the first to row across the Atlantic in a dinghy.

For many decades, the study of motivation was dominated by a focus on *biological drives*, for example, to acquire food and water or avoid cold and pain. It was believed that organisms live in a state of physiological equilibrium; when that state is unbalanced—say, when you are thirsty, hungry, or bored—you are motivated to drink, eat, or try something new and different. But drive theories of motivation declined when it became apparent that most motives are *not* always triggered by physiological deprivation and not always terminated when deprivation ceases (McSweeney & Swindell, 1999). For example, people and other animals will eat or drink liquids long before they physically need to, and some will keep eating or drinking long after they don't need to.

All human motives, whether inborn or learned, are powerfully shaped by social and cultural forces. People are motivated to eat, for instance, but that information doesn't tell us why some individuals who hold strong political commitments will go on hunger strikes to protest injustice. Today, therefore, the study of motivation focuses on the ways in which biological, psychological, and cultural factors interact to keep people striving to reach a specific goal—or prevent them from reaching it.

In this chapter, we will examine four central areas of human motivation: food, love, sex, and achievement. We will see how happiness and well-being are affected by the kinds of goals we set for ourselves, and by whether we are spurred to reach them because of **intrinsic motivation**, pursuit of an activity for its own sake, or **extrinsic motivation**, pursuit of a goal for external rewards.

WHAT'S AHEAD ▶

- **Is overweight usually a result of psychological problems?**
- **What theory explains why it's so hard for heavy people to lose weight—and just as hard for thin people to gain it?**
- **Why are people all over the world getting fatter?**
- **Why are bright, academically motivated college women most vulnerable to eating disorders?**

The Hungry Animal: Motives to Eat

Some people are skinny; others are plump. Some are shaped like string beans; others look more like pears. Some can eat anything they want without gaining an ounce; others struggle unsuccessfully their whole lives to shed pounds. How much do genes, psychology, and environment contribute to these differences?

The Genetics of Weight

At one time, most psychologists thought that being overweight was a sign of emotional disturbance. If you were fat, it was because you hated your mother, feared intimacy, or were trying to fill an emotional hole in your psyche by loading up on rich desserts. The evidence for psychological theories of overweight, however, came mainly from self-reports and from flawed studies that lacked control groups or objective measures of how much people were actually eating (Allison & Heshka, 1993). When researchers did controlled experiments, they learned that fat people, on average, are no more and no less emotionally disturbed than average-weight people (Stunkard, 1980).

Even more surprising, studies showed that *heaviness is not always caused by overeating.* Many heavy people do eat large quantities of food, but so do some thin people. Many thin people eat very little, but so do some obese people. In one study that carefully monitored everything that subjects were eating, two 260-pound women maintained their weights while consuming only 1,000 calories a day (Wooley, Wooley, & Dyrenforth, 1979). In another study, which had volunteers gorge themselves for months, it was as hard for slender people to gain weight as it is for most heavy people to lose weight. The minute the study was over, the slender people lost weight as fast as dieters gained it back (Sims, 1974).

The leading explanation for such findings has been that a biological mechanism keeps your body weight at a genetically influenced **set point**—the weight you stay at when you are not trying to gain or lose (Lissner et al., 1991). The set point can vary about 10 percent in either direction. For example, a woman with a set point of 150 pounds might weigh anywhere from 135 to 165. But if her weight dips below 135 or goes above 165, her body will produce either an insatiable urge to eat or a loss of appetite, to bring its fat levels back into line.

Set-point theory explains why most people who diet eventually gain their weight back: They are returning to their set-point weight (Leibel, Rosenbaum, & Hirsch, 1995). Everyone has a genetically programmed *basal metabolism rate,* the rate at which the body burns calories for energy, and a fixed number of fat cells, which store fat for energy and can change in size. A complex interaction of metabolism, fat cells, and hormones keeps people at the weight their bodies are designed to be, much in the way that a thermostat keeps a house at a pre-set temperature. When a heavy person diets, the body's metabolism slows down to conserve energy and fat reserves. When a thin person overeats, metabolism speeds up, burning energy. In one study, in which 16 slender volunteers ate 1,000 extra calories every day for 8 weeks, their metabolisms sped up to burn the excess calories. They became like hummingbirds, in constant movement: fidgeting, pacing, changing their positions frequently while seated, and so on (Levine, Eberhardt, & Jensen, 1999).

Set-point theory predicts that the heritability of weight and body fat should be high, and indeed it is: In twin and adoption studies, heritability estimates fall between .40 and .70 (Comuzzie & Allison, 1998). Pairs of adult identical twins who grow up in different families are just as similar in body weight and shape as twins raised together. The early family environment has almost *no effect at all* on body shape, weight gain, or percentage of fat in the body (Stunkard et al., 1990). When identical twins gain weight, they gain it in the same place: Some pairs store extra pounds around their waists, others on their hips and thighs (C. Bouchard et al., 1990).

Genes are also involved in some types of obesity. In a study of 171 Pima Indians in Arizona, two-thirds of the women and half of the men became obese over time, and the slower their metabolisms, the greater the weight gain. After adding anywhere from 20 to 45 pounds, however, the Pimas stopped gaining weight. Their metabolism rates rose, and their weights stabilized at the new, higher level (Ravussin et al., 1988).

> **THINKING CRITICALLY**
>
> **Ask Questions**
>
> Obesity is caused mainly by psychological problems and lack of will power that drive people to overeat, isn't it? When researchers questioned this obvious assumption, they were in for a surprise.

set point The genetically influenced weight range for an individual, maintained by biological mechanisms that regulate food intake, fat reserves, and metabolism.

Body weight and shape are strongly affected by genetic factors. Set-point theory helps explain why the Pimas of the American Southwest gain weight easily but lose it slowly, whereas the Bororo nomads of Nigeria can eat a lot of food yet remain slender.

Many Pimas apparently have a set point for plumpness. A few years ago, a team of researchers isolated a genetic variation that causes mice to become obese (Zhang et al., 1994). The usual form of the gene, called "obese," or *ob* for short, causes fat cells to secrete a protein, which the researchers named *leptin* (from the Greek *leptos*, "slender"). Leptin travels through the blood to the brain's *hypothalamus*, which is involved in the regulation of appetite. Injecting leptin into mice reduces the animals' appetites, speeds up their metabolisms, and makes them more active; as a result, the animals shed weight (Halaas et al., 1995).

The story of leptin is, however, a good cautionary tale for consumers. When the effects of leptin were discovered in mice and the presence of leptin was discovered in humans, one pharmaceutical company thought it had a panacea obesity drug at hand: Take leptin, lose weight! It seemed to be too good to be true, and, alas, it was. The role of leptin in human obesity is more complicated than it is in mice. For most obese people, leptin does not play a major role, and taking more of it does not produce much weight loss (Comuzzie & Allison, 1998).

Researchers have also discovered a gene that modulates production of a protein that apparently converts excess calories into heat rather than fat. Possession of this gene may be the reason that slim people who eat a lot stay slim (Arsenijevic et al., 2000). "This is a gene that determines whether a high-fat diet makes you fat or not," one of the researchers told *The Los Angeles Times*. An editorial in *Nature Genetics*, which published the finding, said the discovery was a "major breakthrough" that "is likely to have important implications for the treatment of human obesity."

Enthusiasm is a fine quality, but critical thinkers should be wary of oversimplified claims that a gene "determines" anything, or that its discovery is "a major breakthrough." Dozens of other genes and body chemicals are involved in appetite, metabolism rates, and weight regulation. No single gene or protein is the key. You have receptors in your nose and mouth that might keep urging you to eat more ("The food is right there! It's good! Eat!"), receptors in your gut telling you to quit ("You've had enough already!"), and leptins and other chemicals telling you that you have stored enough fat or not enough. These elements often conflict, which is why many people continue to eat after they feel full. The complexity of the mechanisms governing appetite and weight explains why "appetite suppressing" drugs fail in the long run (Gawande, 2001). A drug or intervention that af-

Both of these mice have a mutation in the *ob* gene, which usually makes mice chubby (left). But when leptin is injected daily, the mice eat less and burn more calories, becoming slim (right). Unfortunately, leptin injections have not had the same results in most human beings.

fects one part of the eating-weight interaction might have an unintended influence on another.

Culture, Psychology, and Weight

Is this man heavy because of his genes, his diet, or both? Does your answer affect how you feel about him—sympathetic, neutral, or contemptuous?

Despite the obvious involvement of genes in weight and body shape, they cannot explain the recent increase in rates of overweight and extreme obesity (Pinel, Assanand, & Lehman, 2000). If most people have normal set points, why are so many people everywhere getting fatter? Half of all American adults are overweight and at least 25 percent of all Americans under age 19 are overweight or obese. Increases in obesity rates have occurred in both sexes, all social classes, and all age groups, and in many other countries (Taubes, 1998). In July 2001, the United Nations, so used to dealing with problems of starvation and malnutrition, announced that "Obesity is the dominant unmet global health issue," especially in the United States, Canada, Great Britain, Japan, Australia, and even coastal China and Southeast Asia.

The Environment and Obesity. Genes have not changed in the last decades, but the environment certainly has. The leading environmental culprits causing the worldwide weight-gain epidemic are (1) the increased abundance of low-cost, varied, high-fat foods; (2) the habit of eating high-calorie food on the run rather than leisurely meals; (3) the rise in "energy-saving" devices, such as remote controls; (4) the speed and convenience of driving rather than walking or biking; and (5) the preference for watching television and videos rather than exercising (Hill & Peters, 1998; Robinson, 1999).

Most human beings are predisposed to gain weight when rich food is abundant because, in the past, starvation was all too often a real possibility. Therefore, a tendency to store calories in the form of fat provided a definite survival advantage.

Unfortunately, evolution did not design a counter-mechanism to prevent most people—the ones without humming bird metabolisms—from gaining too much weight when food is easily available, tasty, high fat, varied, and cheap—precisely the situation today, surrounded as we are by ¾-pound burgers, fries, chips, tacos, candy bars, and pizzas (Pinel, Assanand, & Lehman, 2000). When diets are more or less routine and predictable, people habituate to what they are eating and eat less of it. As soon as food becomes more varied, however, people eat more and gain more weight (Raynor & Epstein, 2001). Moreover, in America, food portions have become gargantuan: Many Europeans and Asians regard the huge sandwiches and large servings that Americans consider normal to be gluttonous and alarming (Critser, 2002).

Many people are unaware of the fats and hidden calories in the foods they eat. For example, many Mexican-Americans born in the United States are fatter than those who were born in Mexico. Why? In Mexico, poor people eat corn tortillas,

Get Involved

Are You Fat?

One way of assessing the risks of being excessively overweight is based on one's body mass index. Although BMI is usually calculated by dividing your body weight in kilograms by your height in meters squared, Americans who don't know their metric system can do it this way: 1. Multiply your weight in pounds by 703. 2. Multiply your height in inches by your height in inches. 3. Divide the answer in Step 1 by the answer in Step 2. That is your body mass index. A BMI of 25 or more is considered overweight, and 30 or more is obese. However, some highly fit, muscular people may have a high BMI without being at elevated risk of medical problems.

which are cheap; and their diet overall is lower in fat and higher in fiber than that of their relatives in the north. But Mexican-Americans born in the United States tend to eat flour tortillas, which are made with lard and are thus much higher in calories, and they eat other high-fat foods because of acculturation to American ways. As a result, they have higher obesity rates than their kin in Mexico (Dixon, Sundquist, & Winkleby, 2000; Sundquist & Winkleby, 2000).

Another nongenetic influence on weight is exercise, which boosts the body's metabolic rate and may lower its set point. When obese women are put on severely restricted diets, their metabolic rates drop sharply, as set-point theory would predict. But when they combine the diet with moderate physical activity—daily walking—they lose weight and their metabolic rates rise (Wadden et al., 1990). This is true even for people who are genetically susceptible to obesity, like the Pima Indians. Pimas who live in Mexico are more physically active, and their weight is therefore significantly lower, than that of Pimas who live in Arizona (Esparza et al., 2000).

Cultural Attitudes. Eating habits and activity levels, in turn, are shaped by a culture's customs and standards of what the ideal body should look like: fat, thin, muscular, soft. In many places around the world, especially where famine and crop failures are common, fat is taken as a sign of health, affluence in men, and sexual desirability in women (Stearns, 1997). Among the Calabari of Nigeria, brides are put in special "fattening huts" where they do nothing but eat, so as to become obese enough to please their husbands. And at the Hangandi festival in Niger, the fattest woman wins the beauty contest. In the United States, many African-Americans and Mexican-Americans are more accepting of fat people and less concerned about being "overweight" than are white Americans (Crandall & Martinez, 1996; Hebl & Heatherton, 1998).

Ironically, while people of all ethnicities and social classes have been getting fatter, the cultural ideal for white women in the United States, Canada, and Europe has been getting thinner and thinner. The ideal of the voluptuously curvy woman, big-breasted and big-hipped, was popular before World War I and after World War II. But in the flapper era of the 1920s and again starting in the 1960s, big breasts and hips became unfashionable. Today the female ideal is an odd combination: big breasts but no hips. The cultural ideal for American men has changed, too. Until relatively recently, most heavily muscled men were laborers and farmers, so being physically strong and muscular was a sign of being working class. In the past decade, pressures have increased for middle-class men to be "buff" and strong (Bordo, 2000).

Why did these changes occur? One explanation is that white men and women associate overweight, in either sex, with softness, laziness, and weakness (Crandall & Martinez, 1996). In particular, the curvy, big-breasted female body is associated in people's minds with femininity, nurturance, and motherhood. Hence, big breasts are fashionable in eras that celebrate women's role as mothers—such as after World War II, when women were encouraged to give up their wartime jobs and have many children (Stearns, 1997). However, people also associate femininity, alas, with incompetence. Thus, whenever women have entered traditionally male spheres of education and work, as they did in the 1920s and again since the 1970s, bright, ambitious women have tried to look boyishly thin and muscular in order to avoid appearing "soft," feminine, and dumb (Silverstein & Perlick, 1995; Silverstein, Peterson, & Perdue, 1986). Today's big-breasted but otherwise skinny female ideal may reflect cultural ambivalence about whether women's proper role is domestic or professional. As for men, having a strong, muscular body is now a sign of affluence rather than poverty. It means a man has the money and the time to join a gym and work out.

Should a woman be voluptuous and curvy or slim as a reed? Should a man be thin and unmuscled or strong and buff? Genes and evolution cannot explain cultural changes in attitudes toward the ideal body. During the 1950s, actresses like Diana Dors embodied the post-war ideal: curvy, buxom, and "womanly." Today, many women struggle to look like Calista Flockhart: skinny, angular, and boyish. Men, too, have been caught up in body-image changes. The hippie ideal of the 1960s is a far cry from today's muscular, macho ideal.

Weight and Health: Biology Versus Culture

What happens when your genetic dispositions clash with your culture's notions of the ideal body? The battle between biology and culture can cause physical and emotional problems, because being extremely overweight or starving to be underweight can both be harmful.

Cultures that regard overweight as a sign of health and sexiness—the "more to love" school of thought—are obviously more accepting of people who are naturally heavy. But obesity is now a serious health problem of epidemic proportions. When combined with a lack of aerobic fitness, it is a leading risk factor in diabetes, high blood pressure, heart disease, stroke, cancer, infertility, sleep apnea, and many other disorders. Otelio Randall and his colleagues at Howard University have established a program to teach African-Americans about the risks of obesity, which are especially high among this population. About 67 percent of all black women are overweight, compared to 47 percent of white women, and 1 in 10 middle-aged black women is more than 100 pounds overweight—explaining in part why black women are four times as likely as white women to die young of heart disease (Angier, 2000).

Researchers are also trying to combat cultural pressures to be overweight among white farm families, who often eat large amounts of rich food. The reasons originally

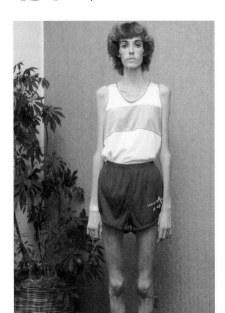

Anorexics cannot see the difference between being fashionably thin and being dangerously skeletal. This anorexic woman died.

bulimia An eating disorder characterized by episodes of excessive eating (bingeing) followed by forced vomiting or use of laxatives (purging).

anorexia nervosa An eating disorder characterized by fear of being fat, a distorted body image, radically reduced consumption of food, and emaciation.

were *intrinsic:* When you do hard, labor-intensive work, you need a lot of calories. But today many farm families eat for *extrinsic* motives: to be sociable and conform to family tradition. In the Farm Belt states of the American Midwest, people are expected to eat huge, hearty meals and plenty of sweet desserts. If you don't join in, an anthropologist from Iowa told *The New York Times,* you are being antisocial—insulting your hosts and rejecting your kin (Angier, 2000).

Efforts to match a cultural standard of excessive thinness can also pose serious risks to health. Evolution has programmed women for a reserve of fat necessary for the onset of menstruation, healthy childbearing, nursing, and, after menopause, the production and storage of estrogen. In cultures that think women should look like the TV character Ally McBeal, therefore, many women—like Merrick Ryan in our opening story—become obsessed with weight and are continually dieting, forever fighting their bodies' need for a minimum of fat. A significant minority of women develop serious eating disorders that reflect an irrational terror of being "too fat" (Walsh & Devlin, 1998). In **bulimia,** the person binges (eats vast quantities of rich food) and then purges by inducing vomiting or using laxatives. In **anorexia nervosa,** the person eats hardly anything and therefore becomes dangerously thin; anorexics have severely distorted body images, thinking they are fat even when they are emaciated.

Bulimia and anorexia are at least ten times more common in women than in men (Davison & Neale, 2001). Although many people with these disorders recover, others damage their health permanently, or, in the case of anorexia, die of heart or kidney failure or osteoporosis. Eating disorders and body-image distortions among boys and men are increasing too, though they take different forms (Bordo, 2000). Just as anorexic women see their gaunt bodies as being too fat, men with the comparable delusion, which one group of researchers calls an "Adonis complex," see their muscular bodies as being too puny. So they abuse steroids and exercise or pump iron compulsively (Pope, Phillips, & Olivardia, 2000).

Just as America exports fast food to world markets, it exports an image of the thin female ideal. One research team was able to observe directly the influence of extremely slim television stars on a culture's notions of ideal body image and on the rise of eating disorders. In the early 1990s, Anne Becker (1999) began studying women on the Pacific island of Fiji, where for many years the ideal female body was large and robust. But after television was introduced in 1995 (offering only one channel, which showed American favorites like *ER*), bulimia among teenage girls increased from 3 percent to 15 percent in only three years. One girl commented that the women on television are "slim and very tall," adding, "We want our bodies to become like that."

Genes may also play a role in the development of eating disorders, just as they do in obesity, body weight, and shape (Allison & Faith, 1997). However, genetic dispositions clearly interact with cultural pressures and with a person's psychological conflicts. Ballerinas, models, actresses, and jockeys are under enormous professional pressure to be thin; fashion models weigh 25 percent less than the average American woman (Brumberg, 2000). College women who develop eating disorders are often caught between their desires to achieve and their parents' messages about "women's place"; the body becomes a battleground to resolve this conflict. They are more likely than other women to say that their parents believe a woman's place is in the home, that their mothers are unhappy with their lives, and that their fathers think their sons are more intelligent than their daughters (Silverstein & Perlick, 1995). Perhaps this is why women who have eating disorders tend to be depressed, perfectionistic, and more self-critical than healthy eaters (Lehman & Rodin, 1989; Walsh & Devlin, 1998).

But why are many men becoming as vulnerable as women to media images of nearly impossible body shapes, devouring magazines that promise "Perfect Abs in 10 Days!" and "Fat to Flat: Drop 20 Pounds the Easy Way!" and spending billions on cosmetic surgery and gym equipment? One explanation is that, in an era of growing equality and challenges to their masculinity, men want to look strong and "manly" to distinguish themselves from "soft" women (Pope, Phillips, & Olivardia, 2000). Another is that commercial interests just know a vulnerable audience when they see one—and they also know how to create one.

In sum, within a given environment, genes interact with cultural rules, psychological needs, and individual habits to shape, sometimes quite literally, who we are.

QUICK QUIZ

Is all this information about eating making you hungry for knowledge?

1. *True or false:* Emotional problems explain why fat people are heavy.
2. Falling and rising levels of leptin help the brain regulate appetite and _____ and play a role in maintaining a person's genetically influenced _____.
3. Rising rates of obesity can best be explained by (a) genetic changes over the past few decades, (b) a lack of will power, (c) an abundance of high-fat food and sedentary lifestyles, (d) the increase in eating disorders.
4. Bill, who is thin, reads in the newspaper that genes set the range of body weight and shape. "Oh, good," he exclaims, "now I can eat all the junk food I want; I was born to be skinny." What's wrong with Bill's conclusion?

Answers:

1. false 2. metabolism, set point 3. c 4. Bill is right to recognize that there may be limits to how heavy he can become. But he may also be oversimplifying and jumping to conclusions. Many people who have a set point for leanness will gain considerable weight on fatty foods and excess calories, especially if they don't exercise. Also, rich junk food is unhealthy for reasons that have nothing to do with becoming overweight.

WHAT'S AHEAD

- **When someone says, "I love you," can you be sure what the person means?**
- **Do men and women differ in the ability to love?**
- **How are your beliefs about love affected by your income?**

The Social Animal: Motives to Love

Everybody needs somebody. In the film *Cast Away*, Tom Hanks's character, marooned on an island, paints a face on a volleyball that washed ashore—and thereby turns "Wilson" into a cherished companion. One of the deepest and most universal of human motives is the **need for affiliation,** the need to be with others, make friends, cooperate, love. Human survival depends on the infant's ability to form attachments (see Chapter 14), on parents' devotion to their children, and on adults' ability to have close partners and friends. While the need for attachment and companionship is universal, however, love—that most intense of attachments—takes various forms and has many meanings. Psychologists want to know not only why we love, but whom we love and how we love.

The Psychology of Love

Do you have a favorite love story? Is it one where the couple falls madly in love at first sight, and, after a couple of silly misunderstandings, lives happily ever after,

need for affiliation The motive to associate with other people, as by seeking friends, companionship, or love.

As this happy couple illustrates, like attracts like!

without a single quarrel or miserable moment? Or is it more like the story of Annie Oakley and Frank Butler, one of lifelong mutual respect and companionship?

Many romantics believe there is only "one true love" awaiting them. Considering that there are nearly 6 billion people on the planet, the odds of finding said person are a bit daunting! What if you're in Omaha or Winnipeg and your True Love is in Dubrovnik or Kankakee? You could wander for years and never cross paths.

Fortunately, evolution has made it possible to form deep and lasting attachments without traveling the world. In fact, the first major predictor of whom we love is plain *proximity*: The people who are nearest to you are most likely to be dearest to you, too. We choose our friends and lovers from the set of people who live closest to us, or who study or work near us. And although romantics also believe that "opposites attract," the fact is that we tend to choose friends and loved ones who are most like us. *Similarity*—in looks, attitudes, beliefs, values, personality, and interests—is the second key predictor of whom we love (Berscheid & Reis, 1998).

The Ingredients of Love. Once you have found a possible partner, *how* do you love? The oldest answer distinguishes *passionate ("romantic") love,* characterized by a turmoil of intense emotions and sexual passion, from *companionate love,* characterized by affection and trust (Hatfield & Rapson, 1996). Passionate love is the stuff of crushes, infatuations, "love at first sight," and the early stage of love affairs. It may burn out completely or subside into companionate love.

Robert Sternberg (1997) has added a third element in his *triangular theory,* which holds that the three ingredients of love are *passion* (euphoria and sexual excitement), *intimacy* (feeling free to talk about anything, feeling close to and understood by the loved one), and *commitment* (needing to be with the other person, being loyal). People combine these elements in every possible way, producing different kinds of love. For example, romantic love is intimacy and passion, without commitment; companionate love is intimacy and commitment, without passion; empty love is commitment, without passion or intimacy; and infatuation is passion alone. In Sternberg's view, ideal love integrates all three: passion, closeness, and the security that comes from commitment.

When people are asked to define the key ingredients of love, most do agree that love is a mix of passion, intimacy, and commitment (Aron & Westbay, 1996; Lemieux & Hale, 2000). However, in most relationships, over the years, romantic passion subsides and intimacy increases. Intimacy is based on deep knowledge of the other person, which accumulates gradually and thus needs time to reach a maximum degree of closeness; but passion is based on emotion, which is generated by novelty and change. That is why passion is usually highest at the beginning of a relationship, when two people begin to disclose things about themselves to each other, and lowest when knowledge of the other person's beliefs and habits is at its

JUMP START reprinted by permission of United Feature Syndicate, Inc.

maximum—when it seems that there is nothing left to learn about the beloved. The negative correlation between passion and intimacy explains why passion is often reawakened when a couple is separated or unexpected crises occur, or when the couple takes up a new shared activity that brings them closer (Baumeister & Bratslavsky, 1999).

The way we define "real" love deeply affects our satisfaction with relationships, and even whether our relationships last. After all, if you believe that the only real love is romantic love, that love is *defined* by sexual passion and hot emotion, then you may decide you are "out of love" when the initial phase of attraction fades, as it eventually must—and you will be repeatedly disappointed. Robert Solomon (1994) argued that "We conceive of [love] falsely . . . We expect an explosion at the beginning powerful enough to fuel love through all of its ups and downs instead of viewing love as a process over which we have control, a process that tends to increase with time rather than wane."

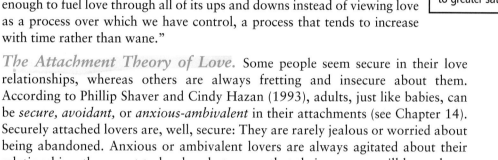

THINKING CRITICALLY

Define Your Terms

Many people define love as an overwhelming romantic passion. What are the consequences of defining love that way? What other definitions might lead to greater satisfaction in a relationship over time?

The Attachment Theory of Love. Some people seem secure in their love relationships, whereas others are always fretting and insecure about them. According to Phillip Shaver and Cindy Hazan (1993), adults, just like babies, can be *secure, avoidant,* or *anxious-ambivalent* in their attachments (see Chapter 14). Securely attached lovers are, well, secure: They are rarely jealous or worried about being abandoned. Anxious or ambivalent lovers are always agitated about their relationships; they want to be close but worry that their partners will leave them. Other people often describe them as "clingy," which may be why they are more likely than secure lovers to suffer from unrequited love (Aron, Aron, & Allen, 1998). Avoidant people distrust and avoid intimate attachments.

Where do these differences come from? In the *attachment theory of love,* people acquire their attachment styles in large part from how their parents cared for them. Starting in infancy and childhood, people form internal "working models" of relationships: Can I trust others? Am I worthy of being loved? Will my beloved leave

Get Involved

What Is Your Love Attachment Style?

Which of the following three statements, adapted from Hazan & Shaver (1987), best describes how you typically feel in your romantic relationships?

Secure style: I find it relatively easy to get close to others and am comfortable depending on them and having them depend on me. I don't often worry about being abandoned or about someone getting too close.

Avoidant style: I am somewhat uncomfortable being close; I find it difficult to trust others completely, difficult to allow myself to depend on them. I am nervous when anyone gets close, and often love partners want me to be more intimate than I feel comfortable being.

Anxious style: I find that others are reluctant to get as close as I would like. I often worry that my partner doesn't really love me or won't stay with me. I want to merge completely with another person, and this desire sometimes scares people away.

If you are currently in a dating relationship—and have the nerve!—ask your partner how he or she would reply. Are you matched?

me? If a child's parents were cold and rejecting and provided little or no contact comfort, that is how the child learns to expect other relationships will be. If children form secure attachments to trusted parents, they become more trusting of others, expecting to form other secure attachments with friends and lovers in adulthood (Levy, Blatt, & Shaver, 1998).

According to a nationally representative survey of American adults, the distribution of the three basic styles of attachment among adults is in fact very similar to that found for infants: about two–thirds secure, 25 percent avoidant, and 11 percent anxious. Further, the kinds of relationships that people have as adults are strongly related to their reports of how their parents treated them (Mickelson, Kessler, & Shaver, 1997). Securely attached adults report having had warm, close relationships with their parents. Although they recognize their parents' flaws, they describe their parents as having been more benevolent and kind than insecurely attached people do. Anxious/ambivalent people report feeling more ambivalence toward their parents, especially their mothers, and also describe their parents ambivalently—as having been both punitive and kind.

"My preference is for someone who's afraid of closeness, like me."

People with an avoidant attachment style describe their parents in almost entirely negative terms, as having been punitive and mean (Levy, Blatt, & Shaver, 1998). Avoidant individuals are most likely to report having had cold, rejecting parents, extended periods of separation from their mothers, or childhood environments that prevented them from making close ties with others (Feeney & Noller, 1990; Hazan & Shaver, 1994; Klohnen & Bera, 1998). The avoidant style is particularly resistant to change, because people who are busy avoiding one another never learn to trust someone long enough to become securely attached (Klohnen & Bera, 1998). However, even avoidant or anxiously attached people can have successful, stable relationships if they find securely attached partners who will put up with their insecurities (Kirkpatrick & Davis, 1994; Koski & Shaver, 1997).

Keep in mind, though, that a person's own temperament could also account for the consistency of attachment styles from childhood to adulthood, as well as for the "working models" of relationships that are formed during childhood. Certainly some parents are cold, punitive, and rejecting. But a temperamentally fearful and avoidant child may reject even a kind parent's efforts to console and cuddle, and eventually come to believe that all relationships are untrustworthy.

Gender, Culture, and Love

Which sex is more romantic? Which sex truly understands "true" love? Which sex falls in love but won't commit? Pop-psych books are full of answers, along with advice for dealing with all those love-impaired members of the other sex who break your heart. But all stereotypes oversimplify. Neither sex loves more than the other in terms of "love at first sight," passionate love, or companionate love over the long haul (Dion & Dion, 1993; Fehr, 1993; Hatfield & Rapson, 1996). Men and women are equally likely to suffer the heart-crushing torments of unrequited love. Both sexes suffer mightily when a love relationship ends, assuming they did not want it to.

However, women and men do differ, on average, in how they *express* love. As we saw in Chapter 11, males in many cultures learn early that revelations of emotion can be construed as evidence of vulnerability and weakness, which are considered unmasculine. Thus, men in such cultures often develop ways of expressing love that differ from women's. In contemporary Western society, many women express feelings of love in words, whereas many men express these feelings in actions—doing things for the partner, supporting the family financially, or just sharing the same activity, such as watching TV or a football game together (Baumeister & Bratslavsky, 1999; Cancian, 1987; Swain, 1989). Similarly, many women tend to define "intimacy" as shared revelations of feelings, but many men define intimacy as just hanging out together.

These gender differences in ways of expressing the universal motives of love and intimacy do not just pop up from nowhere; they reflect social, economic, and cultural forces. For example, for many years, Western men were more romantic than women in their choice of partner, and women in turn were far more pragmatic than men. One reason was that a woman did not just marry a man; she married a standard of living. Therefore, she could not afford to marry someone "unsuitable" or waste her time in a relationship that was "not going anywhere," even if she loved him. She married, in short, for extrinsic reasons rather than intrinsic ones. In contrast, a man could afford to be sentimental in his choice of partner. In the 1960s, two-thirds of a sample of college men said they would not marry someone they did not love, but only one-fourth of the women ruled out the possibility (Kephart, 1967).

As women entered the workforce and as two incomes became necessary in most families, however, the gender difference in romantic love waned, and so did economic reasons for marriage—all over the world. Nowadays, in every developed and developing nation, only tiny numbers of women and men would consider marrying someone who had all the "right" qualities if they were not in love with the person. Pragmatic reasons for marriage, with romantic love being a remote luxury, persist only in economically underdeveloped countries, such as India and Pakistan, where the extended family still controls the rules of marriage (Hatfield & Rapson, 1996).

As you can see, our beliefs about love, and the kind of love we feel, are influenced by the culture we live in, the historical era that shapes us, and something as unromantic as economic self-sufficiency.

Economic and social changes are transforming gender roles in all developed nations. But marriage for financial security is still the only option for many women from impoverished nations—like this bride, whose husband chose her from a mail-order catalogue.

QUICK QUIZ

Are you passionately committed to quizzes yet?

1. According to Sternberg's triangular theory of love, the three major ingredients of love are _____ .

2. Tiffany is wildly in love with Timothy, and he with her, but she can't stop worrying about his fidelity and doubting his love. She wants to be with him constantly, but when she feels jealous she pushes him away. According to the attachment theory of love, which style of attachment does Tiffany have?

3. *True or false:* Until recently, men in Western societies were more likely than women to marry for love.

Answers:

1. passion, intimacy, commitment 2. anxious-ambivalent 3. true

WHAT'S AHEAD

- Is one kind of orgasm better or healthier for women than another?
- What part of the anatomy do psychologists think is the "sexiest sex organ"?
- How do the sexual rules for heterosexual couples foster misunderstandings?
- Can psychological theories about smothering mothers or absent fathers explain why some men are gay?

The Erotic Animal: Motives for Sex

Most people believe that sex is a biological drive, just a matter of doing what comes naturally. It is certainly true that in most other species, sexual behavior is genetically programmed. Without instruction, a male stickleback fish knows exactly what to do with a female stickleback, and a whooping crane knows when to whoop. But as sex researcher Leonore Tiefer (1995) has observed, for human beings "sex is not a natural act." For one thing, the activities that one culture considers "natural" are often considered "unnatural" in another culture or historical time. For another, people have to learn from experience and culture what they are supposed to do with their sexual desires and how they are expected to behave sexually. Human sexuality is a blend of biological, psychological, and cultural factors.

The Biology of Desire

Biological researchers have contributed to our understanding of sexual motivation by sweeping away the cobwebs of superstition and ignorance about how the body works. They have disproved the idea that the sexes are physically opposite and have documented the capacity for sexual arousal, orgasm, and pleasure in both sexes.

Hormones and Sexual Response. One biological factor that seems to promote sexual desire in both sexes is the hormone testosterone. Its role has been documented in studies of men who have been given synthetic hormones that suppress

Desire and sensuality are lifelong pleasures.

the production of testosterone; of men and women who have abnormally low testosterone levels; of women who have taken androgens after having had their ovaries removed; and of women who kept diaries of their sexual activity while also having their hormone levels periodically measured (Bradford & Pawlak, 1993; Carani et al., 1992; Dabbs, 2000; Sherwin, 1998b).

However, hormones do not *cause* sexual behavior, or any other behavior, in a simple, direct way, even though some pop-psych books and media personalities claim that they do. Hormones and behavior travel a two-way street: Testosterone contributes to sexual arousal, but sexual activity also produces higher levels of testosterone (Sapolsky, 1997). Moreover, testosterone is almost always trumped by psychological factors. Thus, raising testosterone levels may increase sexual desire in some women who have unusually low levels of it, as might occur if their ovaries were removed, but for most women psychological factors influence sexual desire far more than hormone levels do (Bancroft et al., 1991). Conversely, sex offenders who are chemically castrated when they take a medication that suppresses production of testosterone do not always lose their sexual desires.

Arousal and Orgasm. Physiological research has also dispelled a lot of nonsense written about female sexuality. Freud, for example, claimed that when women reach puberty, their locus of sexual sensation shifts from the "childish" clitoris to the "mature" vagina, and women can then have healthy "vaginal" orgasms instead of immature "clitoral" orgasms. (Freud's theory was at least an improvement on the Victorian notion, still held in some cultures, that normal or "good" women don't have orgasms at all.) Freudian ideas caused countless women to worry that they were mentally disturbed or sexually repressed if they were not having the correct kind of orgasm (Ehrenreich, 1978).

The first modern attack on these beliefs came from Alfred Kinsey and his associates (1948, 1953), in their pioneering books on male and female sexuality. Kinsey's team surveyed thousands of Americans about their sexual attitudes and behavior, and also reviewed the existing research on sexual physiology. In *Sexual Behavior in the Human Female,* they observed that "males would be better prepared to understand females, and females to understand males, if they realized that they are alike in their basic anatomy and physiology." For example, the penis and the clitoris develop from the same embryonic tissues; they differ in size, of course, but not in sensitivity.

The idea that men and women are sexually similar in any way was extremely shocking and progressive in 1953. At that time many people believed that women were not as sexually motivated as men, that orgasm was not as important to women, that female sexuality was more "diffuse" than male sexuality, and that women cared more about affection than sexual satisfaction—notions soundly disputed by Kinsey's interviews. Kinsey did believe, however, that women overall have a "lesser sexual capacity" than men, reflected in women's lower frequency of masturbation and orgasm. Although he acknowledged that many women are taught to avoid, dislike, or feel ambivalent about sex, he tended to attribute this gender difference to biology.

The next wave of sex research began in the 1960s with the laboratory research of physician William Masters and his associate Virginia Johnson (1966). In studies of physiological changes during sexual arousal and orgasm, Masters and Johnson confirmed that male and female orgasms are indeed remarkably similar and that all orgasms are physiologically the same, regardless of the source of stimulation. But Masters and Johnson disagreed with Kinsey's assertion that women have a lesser sexual capacity than men. On the contrary, they argued, women's capacity for sexual response "infinitely surpasses that of men" because a woman, unlike most men, is physiologically able to have repeated orgasms until exhaustion or a ringing telephone makes her stop.

The "Kinsey Report" on women, officially titled *Sexual Behavior in the Human Female,* was not exactly greeted with praise and acceptance—or with clear thinking.

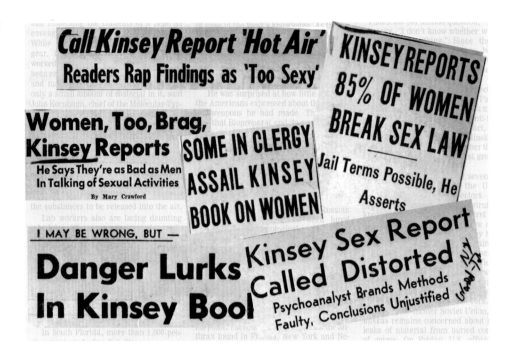

One serious limitation of Masters and Johnson's research, innovative and important though it was at the time, was that they did not investigate how people's physiological responses might vary according to their age, experience, and culture. Not all women, or even all men, are easily orgasmic, let alone multiply orgasmic, and many women do not easily achieve orgasm through intercourse, though they do in other ways. In their eagerness to show that the physiology of arousal and orgasm were the same in both sexes, Masters and Johnson tended to overlook individual differences (Irvine, 1990).

Since Masters and Johnson's studies, sex researchers have learned much more about individual variation in sexual physiology and responsiveness (Ellison, 2000; Zilbergeld, 1992). They have learned that people's *physiological* responses do not always correlate with their *subjective* experience of desire and arousal (Irvine, 1990). For example, vaginal lubrication is not always a sign of arousal; it can also be a response to nervousness, excitement, disgust, or fear. Similarly, a man's erection is not always due to sexual stimulation; it can also be a response to fear, anger, disgust, or other emotions.

The question of whether men and women are alike or different in some underlying, biologically based "sex drive" continues to provoke lively debate. Some psychologists argue that although women are certainly as capable as men of sexual *pleasure,* on average, men, testosterone-infused creatures that they are, have a greater *sex drive* than women do. Proponents of this view point out that certain behaviors, such as frequency of masturbation and orgasm, are universally higher among men than women—as Kinsey found—even when men are forbidden by social or religious rules to engage in sex of any kind (Baumeister, Catanese, & Vohs, 2001; Dabbs, 2000; Oliver & Hyde, 1993).

Many social psychologists, however, maintain that most gender differences in sexual behavior reflect women's and men's different roles and experiences in life, and have little or nothing to do with biologically based drives (Eagly & Wood, 1999). As long as large numbers of women are taught to fear, dislike, or avoid sex, they say, it is impossible to know what women's "sexual drive" would be like. A compromise view is that men's sexual behavior is more biologically influenced ("driven") than is women's, whereas women's sexual desires and responsiveness are more affected by circumstances, the specific relationship, and cultural norms (Baumeister, 2000; Peplau et al., 2000).

The Psychology of Desire

Psychologists are fond of observing that the sexiest sex organ is the brain, where perceptions begin. People's values, fantasies, and beliefs profoundly affect their sexual desire and behavior. That is why a touch on the knee by an exciting new date feels terrifically sexy, but the same touch by a creepy stranger on a bus feels disgusting. It is why a worried thought can kill sexual arousal in a second, and why a fantasy can be more erotic than reality.

The Many Motives for Sex. To most people, the primary motives for sex are pretty obvious: to enjoy the pleasure of it, to express love and intimacy, or to make babies. But there are other motives too, not all of them so positive. Studies of several hundred college students and more than 1,500 older adults identified six factors underlying the many reasons that people give for having sex (Cooper, Shapiro, & Powers, 1998):

► *Enhancement*—the emotional satisfaction or physical pleasure of sex.
► *Intimacy*—emotional closeness with the partner.
► *Coping*—dealing with negative emotions and disappointments.
► *Self-affirmation*—reassurance that one is attractive or desirable.
► *Partner approval*—the desire to please or appease one's partner, for example, to avoid the partner's anger or rejection.
► *Peer approval*—the wish to impress one's friends, be part of the group, and conform to what "everyone else" seems to be doing.

In this research, men and women did not differ in their motives for intimacy, but men more strongly endorsed all the other motives, especially peer approval. The older that people were, the more likely they were to have sex for intimacy and for self-enhancement (pleasure), and the less likely they were to have sex for peer or partner approval. White adolescents more strongly endorsed intimacy motives than black adolescents did, and black teenagers more strongly endorsed coping and peer-pressure motives.

There are many motivations for sex, including financial gain and physical lust, intimacy and love, and joyful playfulness.

Perhaps you can think of other motives for sex, too: spiritual transcendence, money, duty, power over others, submission to others, rebellion. . . . People's motives for having sex affect many aspects of their sexual behavior, including whether they engage in sex in the first place, whether they enjoy it, whether they have unprotected or otherwise risky sex, and whether they have few or many partners (Browning et al., 2000). Extrinsic motives, such as having sex for purposes of coping and gaining approval, are most strongly associated with risky sexual behavior, including having many partners and not using birth control (Cooper, Shapiro, & Powers, 1998).

Many studies of college students find that large numbers of women *and* men are having sex not for pleasure or intimacy, but because of feelings of inadequacy or peer pressure. In one survey of nearly 1,000 college students, fully two-thirds of the men reported having had unwanted intercourse (Muehlenhard & Cook, 1988). The main reasons for doing so, the men said, were peer pressure, inexperience, a desire for popularity, and a fear of seeming homosexual or "unmasculine." Women too said they "gave in," but for different reasons: because it was easier than having an argument; because they did not want to lose the relationship; because they felt obligated, once the partner had spent time and money on them; or because the partner made them feel guilty.

Sexual Coercion and Rape. One of the most persistent differences in the sexual experiences of women and men has to do with their perceptions of, and experiences with, sexual coercion. In a nationally representative survey of more than 3,000 Americans ages 18 to 59, nearly one-fourth of the women said that a man— usually a husband or boyfriend—had forced them to do something sexually that they did not want to do (Laumann et al., 1994). But only about 3 percent of the men said they had ever forced a woman into a sexual act. Obviously, what many women regard as coercion is not always seen as coercive by men. Among Canadian and American university students, too, men are far more likely than women to admit coercing a partner into sex—using alcohol or other drugs, or threats or actual physical force (O'Sullivan, Byers, & Finkelman, 1998).

The most extreme form of sexual coercion, of course, is rape. Although the public image of the rapist tends to be one of a menacing stranger, in most cases the rapist is known to the victim. They may have dated once or a few times; they may even be married (Koss, 1993; Russell, 1990). A recent survey of more than 2,000 Massachusetts high school students, ages 14 to 18, found that 11 percent of the girls said they had been sexually assaulted by someone they were dating (Silverman et al., 2001). And according to a representative survey of more than 4,000 women over the age of 18 in the United States, 14 percent of all American women have been the victims of forcible rape at least once in their lives, most by men they knew; only 22 percent of rape victims were assaulted by strangers (National Victim Center, 1992). The survey did not include women in prison or the military, or homeless women, groups especially vulnerable to rape (Koss, 1993; Merrill et al., 1998).

This ad, which is directed at men, emphasizes the importance of respect and communication in sexual relationships. Do you think it is effective? Why or why not?

What motivates some men to rape? For many, the answer is not sexual satisfaction, but peer approval. College men who have physically coerced their dates into having sex have often been pressured by male friends, since early adolescence, to prove their masculinity by "scoring" (Kanin, 1985). For other men who rape, the motive is anger, revenge, or a desire to dominate. Sexually aggressive males are characterized by insecurity, defensiveness, hostility toward women, and a preference for promiscuous, impersonal sex. They misperceive women's behavior in social situations, equate feelings of power with sexuality, and blame women for whatever happens to them (Drieschner & Lange, 1999; Malamuth et al., 1995; Zurbriggen, 2000). Some rapists have even more disturbed motives: anger at women or the world, a need for power, contempt for women, and a sadistic pleasure in inflicting pain (Knight, Prentky, & Cerce, 1994).

The argument that rape is primarily an act of dominance and aggression is supported by the widespread evidence of soldiers who rape captive women during war, and then often kill them (Olujic, 1998). Aggressive motives also occur in the rape of men by other men, usually by anal penetration (King & Woollett, 1997). This form of rape typically occurs in youth gangs, where the intention is to humiliate rival gang members, and in prison, where again the motive is to conquer and degrade the victim.

Perhaps you can see that the answer to the question "Why do people have sex?" is not obvious after all, and by no means a simple matter of "doing what's natural." In addition to the intrinsic motives of intimacy, pleasure, procreation, and love, extrinsic psychological motives include intimidation, dominance, insecurity, appeasing the partner, approval from peers, and the wish to prove oneself a real man or a desirable woman.

The Culture of Desire

Think about kissing. Westerners like to think about kissing, and to do it, too. But if you think kissing is natural, try to remember your first serious kiss—and all you had to learn about noses, breathing, and the position of teeth and tongue. The sexual kiss is so complicated that some cultures have never even gotten around to it. They think that kissing another person's mouth—the very place that food enters!—is disgusting (Tiefer, 1995). Others have elevated the sexual kiss to high art; why do you suppose one version is called "French" kissing?

As the kiss illustrates, having the physical equipment to perform a sexual act is not all there is to sexual motivation. People have to learn, from cultural norms, peers, and parental lessons, what is supposed to "turn them on" (or off), which parts of the body and what activities are erotic (or repulsive), and even how to have sexual relations (Laumann & Gagnon, 1995).

The range of cultural variations in sexuality is remarkable. To men of the Victorian era, the sight of a woman's ankle, let alone her entire leg, was highly arousing; to men of the modern era, an ankle doesn't do it. In some cultures, oral sex is regarded as a bizarre sexual deviation and may even be against the law; in others, it is not only considered normal but also supremely desirable. In some cultures, sex is seen as something joyful and beautiful, an art to be cultivated as one might cultivate the skill of gourmet cooking. In others, it is considered ugly and dirty, something to be "gotten through" as quickly as possible.

Sexual Scripts. How do cultures transmit their rules and requirements about sex to their members? During childhood and adolescence, people learn their culture's *gender roles*—collections of rules that determine the proper attitudes and behavior for men and women, sexual and otherwise (see Chapter 8). Just as an actor in the role of Hamlet needs a script to learn

Kissing is a learned skill—one that some people start practicing earlier than others.

These teenagers are following the sexual scripts for their gender—the boys, by ogling and making sexual remarks about girls in order to impress their peers, and the girls, by preening and wearing makeup to look good for boys.

his part, a person following a gender role needs a **sexual script** that teaches men and women how to behave in sexual matters (Gagnon & Simon, 1973; Laumann & Gagnon, 1995). Are women supposed to be sexually adventurous and assertive or sexually modest and passive? Are old people supposed to be sexually active or "past all that"? The answers differ from culture to culture, as members act in accordance with the sexual scripts for their gender and age.

In many parts of the world, boys acquire their attitudes about sex in a competitive atmosphere where the goal is to impress other males, and they talk and joke about masturbation and other sexual experiences with their friends. While boys are learning to value physical sex, however, girls are learning to value relationships and to make themselves attractive. They learn that their role is to be sexually desirable (which is good), but not to indulge in their own sexual pleasures (which would be bad). Britney Spears is the ultimate media symbol of these conflicting pressures on women: She promotes herself as a traditional "good girl," yet her image is flamboyantly sexual and provocative. The different sexual scripts for heterosexual couples can create conflicting motives for sexuality and misreadings of one another's behavior. Is she dressing that way to look sexy or to tell me she wants sex? Is he really interested in me or just in hooking up for tonight?

Gay men and lesbians follow sexual scripts, too. In number of sexual partners, sexual practices, and acceptance of casual sex, gay men are generally similar to heterosexual men, and lesbians are similar to heterosexual women. But lesbians and gay men tend to be more flexible than heterosexuals in establishing rules for their relationships, because neither partner is clearly the pursuer or the pursued or the one who makes the sexual decisions (Peplau & Spalding, 2000; Rose, Zand, & Cini, 1993).

Where do sexual scripts and gender differences come from? As we saw in Chapter 3, evolutionary psychologists and sociobiologists think that evolutionary processes

sexual scripts Sets of implicit rules that specify proper sexual behavior for a person in a given situation, varying with the person's age, culture, and gender.

Get Involved

Is the Double Standard Still Alive?

Think of all the words you know to describe a sexually active woman, and then think of words for a sexually active man. Is one list longer than the other? Are the two lists equally negative or positive in their connotations? What does this exercise tell you about the survival of the double standard and your culture's sexual scripts?

such as natural selection best account for gender differences in sexuality: why men often pressure women for sex, why women tend to reject casual sex, and why women "give in" and men "make a move" when they do not really want to (Buss, 1994; Gangestad & Simpson, 2000; Oliver & Hyde, 1993).

But social and cultural psychologists believe that gender roles reflect a culture's economic and social arrangements. When those arrangements change, so do people's attitudes and behavior, as we saw in the case of love. Whenever women have needed marriage to ensure their social and financial security, they have regarded sex as a bargaining chip, an asset to be rationed rather than an activity to be enjoyed for its own sake (Hatfield & Rapson, 1996). A woman cannot afford to casually seek sexual pleasure if that means risking an unwanted pregnancy, the security of marriage, her reputation in society, her physical safety, or, in some cultures, her death. When women become self-supporting and able to control their own fertility, however, they are more likely to want sex for pleasure rather than as a means to another goal.

The Riddle of Sexual Orientation

Why do most people become heterosexual, some homosexual, and others bisexual? Many psychological explanations for homosexuality have been proposed over the years, but none of them has been supported. Homosexuality is not a result of having a "smothering mother," an absent father, or emotional problems. It is not caused by same-sex sexual play in childhood or adolescence, which is actually quite common (Lamb, 2002). It is not caused by "seduction" by an older adult (Rind, Tromovitch, & Bauserman, 1998). It is not caused by parental practices or role models. Most gay men recall that they rejected the typical "boy" role and boys' toys and games from a very early age, in spite of enormous pressures from their parents and peers to conform to the traditional male role (Bailey & Zucker, 1995). Conversely, the overwhelming majority of children of gay parents do not become gay, as a learning model would predict, although they are more likely than the children of straight parents to be open-minded about homosexuality and gender roles (Bailey et al., 1995, 2000; C. Patterson, 1992, 1995).

Many researchers, therefore, have been turning to biological explanations of sexual orientation, but the evidence to date is inconclusive. In the early 1990s, a few studies of gay men reported associations between sexual orientation and specific areas of the

In Vermont, three gay couples and a lesbian couple joyfully celebrate their legal civil unions. Why are some people homosexual in spite of enormous social pressures to be heterosexual, including laws and customs that typically deny them the benefits accorded to straights? And why does the issue of legalizing gay and lesbian marriage evoke so much anger and controversey?

brain (Allen & Gorski, 1992; LeVay, 1991). These studies got lots of press at the time, but they have not been replicated (Byne, 1995). Researchers have also examined the role of prenatal exposure to androgens (Bailey & Pillard, 1995; Gladue, 1994). Female babies accidentally exposed in the womb to masculinizing hormones—androgens or other chemicals—are more likely than other girls to become bisexual or lesbian, and to prefer "boys' toys" and activities (Collaer & Hines, 1995; Meyer-Bahlburg et al., 1995). However, most of these "androgenized" women do *not* become lesbians, and most lesbians were not exposed to atypical prenatal hormones (Peplau et al., 2000).

Sexual orientation does seem to be moderately heritable, particularly in men (Bailey & Pillard, 1995; Bailey et al., 2000; Whitam, Diamond, & Martin, 1993). But genetic research too is inconclusive. One research team made national headlines when they reported finding a genetic marker on the X chromosome in pairs of gay brothers (Hamer et al., 1993; Hu et al., 1995). However, a later study of 52 pairs of gay brothers did not replicate this finding (Rice et al., 1999). And the vast majority of gay men and lesbians do *not* have a close gay relative, and their siblings, including twins, are overwhelmingly likely to be heterosexual (Peplau et al., 2000).

So we are left with a real puzzle. One problem with trying to find "the" origin of sexual orientation is that sexual identity and behavior may take many different forms. Some people are equally attracted to men and women, and some are heterosexual in behavior but have homosexual fantasies (Baumrind, 1995; Byne, 1995). Some gay men are "feminine" in interests and manner, but many are not; some lesbians are "butch," that is, "masculine" in interests and manner, but many other lesbians are not (Singh et al., 1999). Some lesbians do have an exclusively same-sex orientation their whole lives, but many others have sex with the person they fall in love with, regardless of his or her gender (Kitzinger & Wilkinson, 1995; Peplau et al., 2000). In some cultures, teenage boys go through a homosexual phase that they do not define as homosexual and that does not affect their future relations with women (Herdt, 1984). In Lesotho, in South Africa, women have intimate relations with other women, including passionate kissing and oral sex, but they do not define these acts as sexual, as they do when a man is the partner (Kendall, 1999).

Genetics cannot account for the diversity of such customs nor for the diversity of experience among homosexuals. At present, therefore, we will have to tolerate uncertainty about the origins of sexual orientation. Sexual identity and behavior involve an interaction of biology, cultural norms, and experiences; the routes to homosexual orientation may differ for males and females; and the origins of sexual orientation may differ among individuals.

THINKING CRITICALLY

Avoid Emotional Reasoning

Many people, straight and gay, have strong emotional reactions (pro and con) to biological research on homosexuality. Why? How do people's emotions and attitudes toward homosexuality affect their interpretations of this research?

How are you reacting to these findings? Your responses are probably affected by your feelings about homosexuality. Many gay men and lesbians welcome biological research on the grounds that it supports what they have been saying all along: Sexual orientation is not a matter of choice, but a fact of nature. Others fear that people who are prejudiced against homosexuals will use this research to argue that gay people have a biological "defect" that should be eradicated or "corrected" (as the talk-show host Laura Schlessinger has advocated). But people who are hostile to homosexuals can use any theory, biological or psychological, to justify their wish to eliminate homosexuality. For example, they have used learning theories to argue, mistakenly, that "if it's learned, it can be unlearned," and thus to subject gay men, and even "unboyish" boys as young as 3 years old, to harsh and punitive forms of behavior modification (Burke, 1996).

What these reactions show is that research on sexuality can be used for many contradictory purposes and political goals, depending on the values and attitudes of the popular culture in which such findings emerge. As long as a society is uncomfortable about homosexuality, preconceptions and prejudice are likely to cloud its reactions to anything that psychologists learn about it.

WHAT'S AHEAD

- Why is "doing your best" an ineffective goal to set for yourself?
- When you are learning a new skill, which should you concentrate on: mastering it or performing it well in front of others?
- Which aspects of a job are more important than money in increasing your work satisfaction and involvement?
- How is the *desire* to achieve affected by the *opportunity* to achieve?

The Competent Animal: Motives to Achieve

Almost every adult works. But "work" does not only mean paid employment. Students work at studying. Homemakers work, often more hours than salaried employees, at running a household. Artists, poets, and actors work, even if they are paid erratically (or not at all). Most people are motivated to work in order to meet the basic needs for food and shelter. Yet survival does not explain why some people want to do their work well and others want just to get it done. And it does not explain why some people work merely to make a living and put their passions for achievement into unpaid activities—learning to become an accomplished trail rider or traveling to Madagascar to add a rare helmet vanga to their list of birds sighted. What keeps everybody doing what they do?

Psychologists, particularly those in the field of *industrial/organizational psychology*, have measured the psychological qualities that spur achievement and success and also the environmental conditions that influence productivity and satisfaction. Their findings apply not only to understanding why people thrive or wilt at their jobs, but also to understanding people's aspirations and achievements in general.

"Finish it? Why would I want to finish it?"

need for achievement A learned motive to meet personal standards of success and excellence in a chosen area.

Thematic Apperception Test (TAT) A projective test that asks respondents to interpret a series of drawings showing scenes of people; usually scored for unconscious motives, such as the need for achievement, power, or affiliation.

The Effects of Motivation on Work

In the early 1950s, David McClelland and his associates (1953) speculated that some people have a **need for achievement** that motivates them as much as hunger motivates people to eat. To measure the strength of this motive, McClelland used a variation of the **Thematic Apperception Test (TAT)**, which requires the test taker to make up a story about a set of ambiguous pictures, such as a young man sitting at a desk. (The TAT is one of many *projective tests*, which are based on the assumption that a person will project unconscious motives and feelings onto an ambiguous stimulus; see Chapter 16.) The strength of the achievement motive, said McClelland (1961), is captured in the fantasies the test taker reveals. "In fantasy anything is at least symbolically possible," he explained. "A person may rise to great heights, sink to great depths, kill his grandmother, or take off for the South Sea Islands on a pogo stick."

Needless to say, people with high achievement motivation do not fantasize about taking off for the South Seas or sinking to great depths. They tell stories about working hard, inventing a cure for cancer, and clobbering the opposition with their wit and brilliance. When they are in situations that arouse their competitiveness and desire to succeed—when, for example, they are told that the TAT measures their intelligence and leadership ability—their achievement-related themes shoot up (Atkinson, 1958). High scorers are more likely to start their own businesses. They set high personal standards, and they like challenges. They prefer to work with capable colleagues who can help them succeed rather than with co-workers who are merely friendly (McClelland, 1987).

The TAT is one of the few projective tests that has modest empirical support for the measurement of achievement motivation. But it does not have strong test–retest reliability, meaning that people's responses are easily influenced by what is going on at that moment in their lives rather than by some "inner drive" to succeed. Some peo-

The Many Motives of Accomplishment

IMMORTALITY

WILLIAM FAULKNER
(1897–1962)
Novelist

"Really the writer doesn't want success . . . He wants to leave a scratch on that wall [of oblivion]—Kilroy was here—that somebody a hundred or a thousand years later will see."

KNOWLEDGE

HELEN KELLER
(1880–1968)
Blind/deaf author and lecturer

"Knowledge is happiness, because to have knowledge—broad, deep knowledge—is to know true ends from false, and lofty things from low."

JUSTICE

MARTIN LUTHER KING, JR.
(1929–1968)
Civil rights activist

"I have a dream . . . that my four little children will one day live in a nation where they will not be judged by the color of their skin but the content of their character."

AUTONOMY

GEORGIA O'KEEFFE
(1887–1986)
Artist

"[I] found myself saying to myself—I can't live where I want to, go where I want to, do what I want to . . . I decided I was a very stupid fool not to at least paint as I wanted to."

ple might tell stories of achieving against all odds not because they are determined to do so, but because they are idly daydreaming that day or just saw the movie *Against All Odds*. Also, it isn't clear that the TAT tells researchers anything they would not learn by just *asking* people about their ambitions (Lilienfeld, Wood, & Garb, 2000). But the method launched many investigations into the question of why some people seem to have a drive to "make it," no matter what, and others drift along.

The Importance of Goals. Today the predominant approach to understanding achievement motivation emphasizes goals rather than inner drives: What you accomplish depends on the goals you set for yourself and the reasons you pursue them (Barron & Harackiewicz, 2001). Not just any old goals will promote achievement, though. A goal is most likely to improve your motivation and performance when three conditions are met (Cooper, Shapiro, & Powers, 1998; Higgins, 1998; Smither, 1998):

▶ *The goal is specific.* Defining a goal as "doing your best" is as ineffective as having no goals at all. You need to be specific about what you are going to do and when you are going to do it: "I will write four pages of this paper today."

▶ *The goal is challenging but achievable.* You are apt to work harder for tough but realistic goals that make you feel gratified when you reach them, than for either easy goals that pose no challenge or impossible goals that can never be attained.

▶ *The goal is framed in terms of getting what you want rather than avoiding what you do not want.* **Approach goals** are positive experiences that you seek directly, such as "trying to be smarter" or "learning to scuba dive." **Avoidance goals** involve the effort to avoid unpleasant experiences, such as "trying not to make a fool of myself" or "trying to avoid being dependent." People who frame their goals in specific, achievable approach terms (e.g., "I'm going to lose weight by jogging three times a week") feel better about themselves, feel more competent, are more optimistic and less depressed, and even have fewer colds and other physical symptoms than people who frame the same goals in avoidance terms (e.g., "I'm going to lose weight by staying away from rich foods"). Can you

approach goals Goals framed in terms of desired outcomes or experiences, such as learning to scuba dive.

avoidance goals Goals framed in terms of avoiding unpleasant experiences, such as trying not to look foolish in public.

POWER

HENRY KISSINGER
(b. 1923)
Former Secretary of State

"Power is the ultimate aphrodisiac."

DUTY

Eleanor Roosevelt
(1884–1962)
Humanitarian, lecturer, stateswoman

"As for accomplishments, I just did what I had to do as things came along."

EXCELLENCE

FLORENCE GRIFFITH JOYNER
(1959–1998)
Olympic gold medalist

"When you've been second best for so long, you can either accept it, or try to become the best. I made the decision to try and be the best."

GREED

IVAN BOESKY
(b. 1937)
Financier, convicted of insider trading violations

"Greed is all right . . . I think greed is healthy. You can be greedy and still feel good about yourself."

performance goals Goals framed in terms of performing well in front of others, being judged favorably, and avoiding criticism.

mastery (learning) goals Goals framed in terms of increasing one's competence and skills.

guess why? Approach goals allow you to focus on what you can actively do to accomplish them, whereas avoidance goals make you focus on what you have to give up (Coats, Janoff-Bulman, & Alpert, 1996; Elliot & Sheldon, 1998).

Defining your goals is only the first step on the road to success; next you need to know what to do when you hit a pothole. Some people give up when a goal becomes difficult or they are faced with a setback, whereas others become even more determined to succeed. Talent or ambition alone does not predict who will push on and who will give up. The crucial factor is whether a person's main motivation is to perform well in front of others or to learn the task for the satisfaction of it.

People who are motivated by **performance goals** are concerned primarily with doing well, being judged favorably, and avoiding criticism (Dweck, 1992; Dweck & Sorich, 1999). When such people are focused on how well they are performing and then do poorly, they often decide the fault is theirs, and they stop trying to improve. Because their goal is to demonstrate their abilities, they set themselves up for grief when they temporarily fail—as all of us must if we are to learn anything new. In contrast, those who are motivated by **mastery (learning) goals** are concerned with increasing their competence and skills. Therefore, they regard failure as a source of useful information that will help them improve. Failure and criticism do not discourage them because they know that learning takes time.

Mastery goals are powerful motivators (Elliot & McGregor, 2001). Students who are in school primarily to master new areas of knowledge choose more challenging projects, persist in the face of difficulty, use deeper and more elaborate study strategies, and *enjoy* learning more than do students who are there only to get a degree and a "meal ticket." Mastery goals thus promote greater intrinsic pleasure in a task or goal (Barron & Harackiewicz, 2001; Rawsthorne & Elliot, 1999). However, there is an exception to this rule. For ambitious individuals who already have high achievement motivation—for example, those determined to become great athletes, scientists, or musicians—performance and mastery goals work hand in hand. Focusing on specific ways of improving their performance raises their intrinsic motivation and satisfaction (Barron & Harackiewicz, 2001).

Children acquire performance or mastery goals early, from the actions adults praise them for and from what they observe in their environments. For example, many parents believe in the importance of praising their child's intelligence and ability when the child does well ("Wow, Katie, are you smart!"). Yet, surprisingly, such praise can backfire (see Chapter 7). In several studies, children who were praised for their intelligence and ability later cared more about performance goals and less about learning goals than did children praised for their *efforts* (see Figure 12.1). After these "smart" children failed a problem-solving game, they tended to give up on subsequent ones, enjoyed them less, and lied to other kids about how well they had done. And they actually performed less well than children who had been praised for their efforts (Mueller & Dweck, 1998). The reason seems to be that most American children regard intelligence and ability as fixed traits that you can't do anything about. Therefore, if you fail, you might as well give up. But effort is subject to improvement; you can always try again, and that is the key to mastery. As one learning-oriented child said, "Mistakes are our friends" (Dweck & Sorich, 1999).

Expectations and Self-Efficacy. How hard you work for something also depends on your expectations. If you are fairly certain of success, you will work harder to reach your goal than if you are fairly certain of failure.

A classic experiment showed how quickly experience affects these expectations. Young women were asked to solve

Figure 12.1
MASTERY AND MOTIVATION

Children praised for "being smart" rather than for "working hard" tend to lose the pleasure of learning and focus on how well they are doing. Nearly 70 percent of fifth graders who were praised for intelligence later chose performance goals (doing "problems that aren't too hard, so I don't get many wrong") rather than learning goals (doing "problems that I'll learn a lot from, even if I won't look so smart") —compared to fewer than 10 percent of children who were praised for their efforts (Mueller & Dweck, 1998).

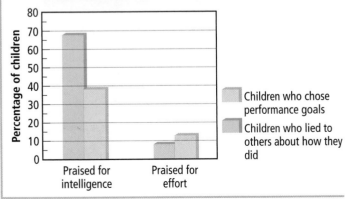

Children who chose performance goals

Children who lied to others about how they did

15 anagram puzzles. Before working on each one, they had to estimate their chances of solving it. Half of the women started off with very easy anagrams, but half began with insoluble ones. Sure enough, those who started with the easy ones increased their estimates of success on later ones. Those who began with the impossible ones decided they would all be impossible. These expectations, in turn, affected the young women's ability to actually solve the last 10 anagrams, which were the same for everyone. The higher the expectation of success, the more anagrams the women solved (Feather, 1966). Once acquired, therefore, expectations can create a **self-fulfilling prophecy** (Merton, 1948): Your expectations make you behave in ways that make the expectation come true. You expect to succeed, so you work hard—and succeed. Or you expect to fail, so you don't do much work, and as a result you do poorly.

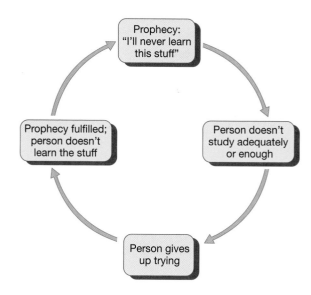

But where do expectations come from? One source is your level of confidence in your abilities. Do you feel able to handle challenges? Albert Bandura calls this feeling of confidence **self-efficacy**. No one is born with self-efficacy; you acquire it, through experience in mastering new skills, overcoming obstacles, and learning from occasional failures. Self-efficacy also comes from having successful role models who teach you that your ambitions are possible, and from having people around to give you constructive feedback and encouragement (Bandura, 1997, 2001).

People who have a strong sense of self-efficacy are quick to cope with problems, rather than stewing and brooding about them. Studies in North America, Europe, and Russia find that self-efficacy has a positive effect on just about every aspect of people's lives: how well they do on a task, how persistently they pursue their goals, the kind of career choices they make, their ability to solve complex problems, their motivation to work for political and social goals, their health habits, and even their chances of recovery from heart attack (Bandura et al., 2001; Ewart, 1995; Maddux, 1995; Stajkovic & Luthans, 1998).

The Effects of Work on Motivation

Imagine that you live in a town that has one famous company, Boopsie's Biscuits & Buns. Everyone in the town is grateful for the 3B company and goes to work there with high hopes. Soon, however, an odd thing starts happening to many employees. They complain of fatigue and irritability. They are taking lots of sick leave. Productivity declines. What's going on at Boopsie's Biscuits & Buns? Is everybody suffering from sheer laziness?

Most people would answer that something is the matter with those employees. However, many psychologists have criticized the idea that achievement depends entirely on

self-fulfilling prophecy An expectation that comes true because of the tendency of the person holding it to act in ways that bring it about.

self-efficacy A person's belief that he or she is capable of producing desired results, such as mastering new skills and reaching goals.

personality traits and motives to succeed. This notion, they say, leads to the incorrect inference that people who don't "make it" have only themselves to blame (Morrison & Von Glinow, 1990). Some people undoubtedly do lack motivation, but accomplishment does not depend on psychological motives alone. We also need to ask: How does the work we do, and the conditions under which we do it, nurture or squash our motives to succeed?

Working Conditions. Several aspects of the work environment are known to increase job involvement, motivation, and satisfaction (S. Brown, 1996; Judge et al., 2001; Kohn & Schooler, 1983):

▶ The work feels meaningful and important to employees.

▶ Employees have control over many aspects of their work—for example, they can set their own hours and make decisions.

▶ Tasks are varied rather than repetitive.

▶ The company maintains clear and consistent rules.

▶ Employees have supportive relationships with their superiors and co-workers.

▶ Employees receive useful feedback about their work, so they know what they have accomplished and what they need to do to improve.

▶ The company offers opportunities for its employees to learn and advance.

Like employees, students can have poor working conditions that affect their motivation. They may have to study in crowded quarters or may have small siblings who interrupt and distract them.

Companies that foster these conditions tend to have more productive and satisfied employees. Workers tend to become more creative in their thinking and feel better about themselves and their work than they do if they feel stuck in routine, boring jobs that give them no control or flexibility over their daily tasks (Karasek & Theorell, 1990; Locke & Latham, 1990). Conversely, when people with high achievement motivation are put in situations that frustrate their desire and ability to succeed, they become dissatisfied and stressed out, and their achievement motive declines (Jenkins, 1994).

Did you notice anything missing from that list of beneficial working conditions? Where is money, supposedly the great motivator? Actually, work motivation is related not to the amount of money you get, but to how and when you get it. The strongest motivator is *incentive pay*, bonuses that are given upon completion of a goal rather than as an automatic raise (Locke et al., 1981). Incentive pay increases people's feelings of competence and accomplishment ("I got this raise because I deserved it"). This doesn't mean that people should accept low pay so they will like their jobs better, or that they should never demand cost-of-living raises!

Opportunities to Achieve. Another important working condition that affects achievement is having the *opportunity* to achieve. When someone does not do well at work, others are apt to say it is the individual's own fault because he or she lacks the internal drive to "make it." But what the person may really lack is a fair chance to make it, and this is especially true for those who have been subjected to systematic discrimination, such as women and ethnic minorities. At one time, for example, women were said to be less successful than men in the workplace because women had an internalized "fear of success." Yet as opportunities for women improved and sex discrimination was made illegal, this apparent "motive" vanished.

Similarly, when the proportion of men and women in an occupation changes, so do people's motivations to work in that field (Kanter, 1977/1993). Many occupations are still highly segregated by gender; there are few male secretaries or female auto mechanics. As a result, many people form gender stereotypes of the requirements of such careers: "Female" jobs require kindness and nurturance, "male" jobs require strength and smarts. These stereotypes, in turn, stifle many people's aspirations to enter a non-traditional career (Cejka & Eagly, 1999). As job segregation breaks down, however, people's motivations change. When law and bartending were almost entirely male professions, few women aspired to become lawyers or bartenders. Now that women make up a large percentage of both occupations, their motivation to become lawyers or bartenders has changed rapidly.

Once in a career, people may become more motivated to advance up the ladder or less so, depending on how many rungs they are permitted to climb. Men *and* women who work in jobs with no prospect of promotion tend to play down the importance of achievement, fantasize about quitting, and emphasize the social benefits of their jobs instead of the intellectual or financial benefits (Kanter, 1977/1993). Women and members of minority groups often encounter a "glass ceiling," a barrier to promotion that is so subtle as to be transparent, yet strong enough to prevent advancement. Researchers can determine that a company has a glass ceiling when a woman or minority person's educational level, work experience, and professional accomplishments do not predict advancement as they do for white men (Graham, 1994; Valian, 1998).

As you can see, work motivation and satisfaction depend on the right fit between qualities of the individual and conditions of the work. The illustration in the margin summarizes the factors within individuals and in their environments that promote or inhibit intrinsic motivation.

QUICK QUIZ

Work on your understanding of work motivation.

1. Horatio wants to earn a black belt in karate. Which way(s) of thinking about this goal are most likely to help him reach it? (a) "I should do the best I can," (b) "I should be sure not to lose many matches," (c) "I will set specific goals that are tough but attainable," (d) "I will set specific goals that I know I can reach easily," (e) "I will strive to achieve key milestones on the way to my goal."

2. Ramón and Ramona are learning to ski. Every time she falls, Ramona says, "This is the most humiliating experience I've ever had! Everyone is watching me behave like a clumsy dolt!" When Ramón falls, he says, "&*!!@$@! I'll show these dratted skis who's boss!" Why is Ramona more likely than Ramón to give up? (a) She *is* a clumsy dolt; (b) she is less competent at skiing; (c) she is focused on learning; (d) she is focused on peformance.

3. Which of these factors significantly increase work motivation? (a) specific goals, (b) regular pay, (c) feedback, (d) general goals, (e) being told what to do, (f) being able to make decisions, (g) the chance of promotion, (h) having routine, predictable work

 4. Phyllis works at an umbrella company. Her work is competent, but she rarely arrives on time, doesn't seem as motivated as others to do well, and has begun to take an unusual number of sick days. This behavior is annoying her boss, who is thinking of firing her. What guidelines of critical thinking is the boss overlooking, and what research should the boss consider before taking this step?

Answers:

1. c, e 2. d 3. a, c, f, g 4. The boss is jumping to the conclusion that Phyllis has low achievement motivation. This may be true, but because her work is competent, the boss should consider other explanations and examine the evidence. Perhaps the work conditions are unsatisfactory; There may be few opportunities for promotion; she may get no feedback; perhaps the company does not provide child care, so Phyllis arrives late because she has child-care obligations. What other possible explanations come to mind?

WHAT'S AHEAD ▶

- **Does more money = more happiness?**
- **What kind of conflict do you have when you want to study for a big exam but you also want to go out partying?**
- **Do you have to satisfy basic needs for security and belonging before you can become "self-actualized"?**

Motives, Values, and Well-Being

Throughout this chapter we have been looking at the central motives of human life: food, love, sex, and work. In these domains and many others, a key conclusion emerges: People who are motivated by the intrinsic satisfaction of an activity are happier and more satisfied than those motivated solely by extrinsic rewards (Deci & Ryan, 1985; Kasser & Ryan, 2001).

We saw, too, how intrinsic motivation in any domain will rise or fall depending on the goals we choose and the way we think of them. Goals, in turn, are determined by *values,* beliefs about what is important in life: freedom, religion, beauty, equality, wealth, fame, wisdom, serenity, salvation, sexual passion, the desire to improve the world, or anything else. Psychology cannot tell us which values or goals to choose; individuals, cultures, and religions emphasize different ones—such as serenity or salvation, wisdom or wealth. But research does illuminate the psychological *consequences* of our choices.

For example, although American culture puts a high value on accumulating wealth, the pursuit of material things for their own sake has some dark consequences. According to studies conducted in both America (an affluent nation) and Russia (a struggling nation), people who are primarily motivated to get rich have poorer psychological adjustment and lower well-being than do people whose primary values are self-acceptance, affiliation with others, or wanting to make the world a better place (Kasser & Ryan, 1996; Ryan et al., 1999). This is especially true when the reasons for striving for money are, again, extrinsic (e.g., you do it to impress others) rather than intrinsic (e.g., you do it so you can afford to do the volunteer work you love) (Carver & Baird, 1998; Srivastava, Locke, & Bartol, 2001).

Whichever values and goals you choose, if they are in conflict, the discrepancy can produce emotional stress and unhappiness. Two motives conflict when the satisfaction of one leads to the inability to act on the other—when, that is, you want to eat your cake and have it, too. Researchers have identified three kinds of motivational conflicts (Lewin, 1948):

1 *Approach–approach conflicts* occur when you are equally attracted to two or more possible activities or goals. For example, you would like to be a veterinarian *and* a rock singer; you would like to go out Tuesday night with friends *and* study like mad for an exam Wednesday.

2 *Avoidance–avoidance conflicts* require you to choose between the lesser of two evils because you dislike both alternatives. Novice parachute jumpers, for example, must choose between the fear of jumping and the fear of losing face if they don't jump.

3 *Approach–avoidance conflicts* occur when a single activity or goal has both a positive and a negative aspect. For example, you want to be a powerful executive but you worry about losing your friends if you succeed. In culturally diverse nations, differing cultural values produce many approach–avoidance conflicts, as our students have revealed. A Chicano student said he wants to become a lawyer, but his parents, valuing family closeness, worry that if he goes to graduate school, he will become

independent and feel superior to his working-class family. An African-American student from a poor neighborhood, in college on scholarship, is torn between wanting to leave his background behind him forever and returning to help his home community. And a white student wants to be a marine biologist, but her friends tell her that only nerdy guys and dweebs go into science.

THE FAR SIDE ® By GARY LARSON

© 1985 FarWorks, Inc. All Rights Reserved/Dist. by Creators Syndicate

"C'mon, c'mon—it's either one or the other."

A classic avoidance-avoidance conflict.

Conflicts like these are inevitable, part of the price and pleasure of living. But if conflicts remain unresolved, they can take an emotional toll. In students, high levels of conflict and ambivalence about goals and values are associated with anxiety, depression, headaches and other symptoms, and more visits to the health center (Emmons & King, 1988). In contrast, students who are "true to themselves," who strive for *goals that are consistent with the qualities they value most,* are healthier and have a greater sense of meaning and purpose in life than do those who are pursuing goals discrepant with their core values (McGregor & Little, 1998; Sheldon & Houser-Marko, 2001).

Are some psychological goals more important to our well-being than others? The humanist psychologist Abraham Maslow (1970) thought so, as long as people are able to meet their physical needs for survival. Maslow envisioned people's motives as forming a pyramid, a *hierarchy of needs*. At the bottom level of the pyramid were basic survival needs for food, sleep, and water; at the next level were security needs, for shelter and safety; at the third level were social needs, for belonging and affection; at the fourth level were esteem needs, for self-respect and the respect of others; and at the top were needs for self-actualization and "self-transcendence." Maslow argued that your needs must be met at each level before you can even think of the matters posed by the level above it. You can't worry about achievement if you are hungry, cold, and poor. You can't become self-actualized if you haven't satisfied your needs for self-esteem and love. Human beings behave badly, he argued, only when their lower needs are frustrated.

This theory, which was intuitively logical and optimistic about human progress, became immensely popular. "Motivational experts" still often refer to it, using colorful pictures of Maslow's pyramid. But the theory, which was based mostly on Maslow's observations and intuitions, has had little empirical support (Sheldon et al., 2001; Smither, 1998). Can you think of some reasons this would be so? One is that people may have *simultaneous* needs for comfort and safety *and* for attachments, self-esteem, and competence. Another is that individuals who have met their "lower" needs do not inevitably seek "higher" ones, nor is it the case that people behave badly only when their lower needs are frustrated. Higher needs may even supersede lower ones. History is full of examples of people who would rather die of torture or starvation than sacrifice their convictions; or who would rather explore, risk, or create new art than be safe and secure at home.

Recently, a different conceptualization of universal psychological needs has been developed by researchers who studied large samples of students in the United States and South Korea (Sheldon et al., 2001). Although these samples were not representative of all cultures or ages (students aren't actually typical of all human beings, startling though that realization may be!), the findings are provocative and support many of the points of this chapter. The top four psychological needs turned out to be *autonomy* (feeling that you are making choices based on your "true interests and values"), *competence* (feeling able to master hard challenges), *relatedness* (feeling close to others who are important to you), and *self-esteem* (having self-respect). Other needs were of lesser importance, including pleasure, self-actualization (which was at the top of Maslow's list), popularity, and, at the bottom, once again . . . money and luxury (see Figure 12.2).

THINKING CRITICALLY

Examine the Evidence

Maslow argued that motives can be ranked from basic physical needs to higher psychological ones. This theory is intuitively appealing, but does the evidence support it? Do people's motives always form a progressive hierarchy, from lower to higher?

Figure 12.2

PSYCHOLOGICAL NEEDS AND EMOTIONAL WELL-BEING

American and South Korean students were asked to think about events that had been especially satisfying to them, and to report the specific psychological needs that these events had fulfilled. In both countries, four psychological needs—self-esteem, autonomy, competence, and relatedness—were at the top of the list. They were also the most strongly associated with positive emotions and the lack of negative emotions (the "affect balance" correlation). Notice that popularity was completely unrelated to good feeling, and money–luxury, the lowest-ranked need, was actually negatively related to well-being (Sheldon et al., 2001).

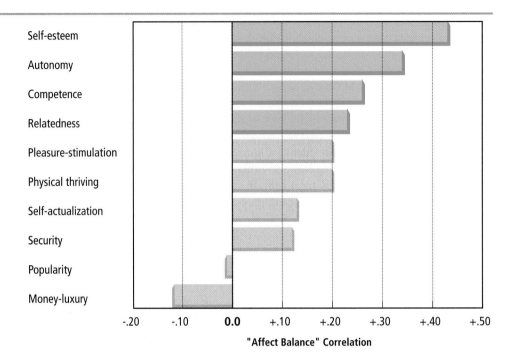

"Affect Balance" Correlation

It is interesting that autonomy was high on the list, even in South Korea, where group harmony is generally regarded as more important than individual satisfaction. But autonomy is not the same as selfishness. People who feel that their motives and goals are freely chosen and self-directed—even if they choose to be self-sacrificing—are happier and have greater intrinsic satisfaction than people who feel their goals and motives are externally controlled by social pressures and demands (Sheldon & Elliot, 1999).

In sum, psychological well-being depends on finding activities and choosing goals that are intrinsically satisfying; on being able to resolve conflicts between competing goals; and on feeling that we have the freedom to choose which goals we want to pursue.

QUICK QUIZ

Do you wish to approach or avoid this quiz?

1. A Pakistani student says she desperately wants an education and a career as a pharmacist, but she also does not want to be disobedient to her parents, who have arranged a marriage for her back home. Which kind of conflict does she have?

2. Maslow's popular hierarchy of needs has several flaws. What are they?

 3. Letitia just got her law degree. She wanted to work in environmental law, but a corporate firm specializing in real-estate contracts has offered her a job and an enormous salary that seem too good to refuse. Why should she think carefully and critically in making a decision?

Answers:

1. Approach–avoidance 2. It was not based on extensive empirical research; it has not been well supported by research; the needs he proposed could be simultaneous rather than hierarchical; "higher" needs often supersede "lower" ones. 3. Because taking a job primarily for its extrinsic benefits might suppress her intrinsic satisfaction in the work; because people motivated solely to acquire money often have poorer psychological adjustment and lower well-being; and because, while money provides material benefits, psychological needs are also important, such as autonomy, competence, self-esteem, and connection to others.

In a commencement address some years ago, Mario Cuomo, the former governor of New York, had these words of wisdom for the graduating students: "When you've parked the second car in the garage, and installed the hot tub, and skied in Colorado, and wind-surfed in the Caribbean, when you've had your first love affair and your second and your third, the question will remain: Where does the dream end for me?" The motives and goals that inspire us, and the choices we make in their pursuit, are what give our lives passion, color, and meaning. Choose your dreams wisely.

Taking Psychology with You

HOW TO LOSE WEIGHT—AND WHETHER YOU SHOULD

Western populations may be getting fatter, but so are the wallets of the people promoting "miracle" diets. Quick-fix solutions proliferate to tempt a gullible and desperate public: earplugs that curb the appetite. Diet pills. "Slimming Insoles" for your shoes that help you lose weight by pressing on nerves in the foot. Tablets that "block the absorption of fat" in the body. And even a shiny "Fat-Be-Gone" ring, said to produce the same effect as jogging six miles.

Save your money. As research in this chapter suggests, the first question dieters should ask is why they want to lose weight: to conform to a cultural ideal or to be healthier? As we saw, some people have a genetic tendency to be plump, and some kinds of extreme obesity are a result of genetic disorders. Understanding this fact may help people accept the normal diversity of body shapes and sizes, lose their prejudice against fat people, and set realistic goals for themselves. Instead of trying to conform to a pencil-thin or hypermuscular cultural ideal that is impossible for all but a minority of women and men, for example, people can find and sustain the best weight within their own set-point range.

On the other hand, obesity is associated with many health risks, so people should consider what they *can* control. The major *nongenetic* reasons for weight gain are lack of exercise; the availability of inexpensive, high-fat, high-calorie food; oversized portions; the rapid pace of life, which encourages people to eat fattening "convenience" meals and snacks on the run; and social and cultural pressures to overeat. Research therefore offers some suggestions for anyone caught up in the dieting dilemma:

▶ *Be realistic about your need to diet.* Dieting and a 10 percent reduction in weight may be of benefit to an obese older man with high blood pressure but unhealthy for a girl who is going through the normal changes of puberty and thinks she is fat (Brownell & Rodin, 1994).

▶ *Avoid fad diets* that restrict you to only a few foods or put you on starvation rations. People on these diets often become obsessed with food, get depressed and anxious when they slip off the diet, and ultimately binge, which restores the lost weight—plus some. It is far better to permanently alter your eating habits by reducing fat intake and eating more grains, fruits, and vegetables.

▶ *Get more exercise,* which will raise your metabolic rate. You do not have to become a marathon runner, but you can increase your activity level—for example, by walking instead of driving to work or school. And turn off the TV! Sitting around watching the tube and eating can add pounds rapidly (Robinson, 1999). Even people who are genetically disposed to be overweight can become physically fit, by walking or swimming 30 minutes a day, and fitness reduces the risks that accompany obesity.

▶ *Avoid yo-yo dieting,* in which you repeatedly lose and gain weight.

Yo-yo dieting is linked to a higher-than-normal risk of cardiovascular disease, hypertension, and other chronic diseases (Brownell & Rodin, 1994).

▶ *Find ways to nurture and reward yourself other than eating.* When you are feeling tired or blue, instead of heading for the refrigerator, try a soothing bath, a massage, or a funny movie.

▶ *Avoid amphetamines and other diet pills,* which can be far more dangerous to your health than a few pounds and can become addictive. Diet pills raise the metabolic rate only as long as you take them. When you stop taking them, the pounds return.

▶ *Seek treatment if you have an eating disorder.* If you are mistakenly trying to control weight by frequent vomiting and abuse of laxatives, or by starving yourself, you can break this harmful pattern by joining an eating-disorders program, preferably one based on cognitive behavior therapy (see Chapter 17). School counselors and health clinics can direct you to suitable programs.

Remember that the biological disposition to gain weight varies from person to person, and that even with exercise, genetic factors limit how much you can change. Think critically about the reasons you are dieting. Are you truly overweight? Are you trying to look like a real person or a fashion model? Whose standards are you following, and why?

Summary

▶ *Motivation* refers to an inferred process within a person or animal that causes that organism to move toward a goal—to satisfy a biological need or achieve a psychological ambition—or away from an unpleasant situation. A few primary *drives* are based on physiological needs, but all human motives are affected by psychological, social, and cultural factors. Motivation may be *intrinsic,* for the inherent pleasure of an activity, or *extrinsic,* for external rewards.

The Hungry Animal: Motives to Eat

▶ Overweight and obesity are not simply a result of failed willpower, emotional disturbance, or overeating. Hunger, weight, and eating are regulated by a set of bodily mechanisms, such as *basal metabolism rate* and number of fat cells, that keep people within a genetically influenced *set point.* Genes influence body shape, distribution of fat, and whether the body will convert excess calories into fat. Genes may also account for certain types of obesity; the *ob* gene regulates *leptin,* which enables the *hypothalamus* to regulate appetite and metabolism. However, the role of leptin in human obesity is still unclear.

▶ Set-point theory alone cannot explain why rates of overweight and obesity are rising all over the world, among all social classes, ethnicities, and ages. The reasons reflect the interaction of an evolved disposition to gain weight when rich food is plentiful, and an environment that provides cheap, varied, high-fat food and rewards sedentary lifestyles. Eating habits and activity levels are also affected by cultural standards of what the ideal body should look like—heavy or thin, soft or muscular.

▶ When genetic predispositions clash with culture, physical and mental problems can result. In cultures that foster overeating and regard overweight as a sign of attractiveness and health, obesity is acceptable, but obesity is associated with a greatly elevated risk of many diseases and disabilities. In cultures that foster unrealistically thin bodies, eating disorders increase, especially *bulimia* and *anorexia.* In women these disorders are associated with a desire for a boyish body and a conflict between the desire to achieve and parental messages about "women's place." As pressures on men to have muscular bodies have increased, body-image problems in men are increasing too.

The Social Animal: Motives to Love

▶ All human beings have a *need for affiliation*—for connection, attachment, and love. Two strong predictors of whom people will love are *proximity* and *similarity.* But love itself takes various forms and has different meanings. Traditionally, *passionate ("romantic") love* has been distinguished from *companionate love.* According to the *triangular theory of love,* love consists of different combinations of passion, intimacy, and commitment. *Attachment theory* views adult love relationships, like those of infants, as being secure, avoidant, or anxious–ambivalent. Adults' attachment styles tend to be stable from childhood throughout adulthood and affect their own close relationships.

▶ Men and women are equally likely to feel love and need attachment, but gender roles affect how they express feelings of love and how they define "intimacy." In Western societies, women often express love in words, whereas men express it in actions. But as women have entered the workforce in large numbers and pragmatic reasons for marriage have faded, the two sexes have become more alike in endorsing romantic love as a requirement for marriage.

The Erotic Animal: Motives for Sex

▶ Biological research finds that testosterone influences sexual desire in both sexes, although hormones do not "cause" sexual behavior in a simple, direct way. The Kinsey surveys of male and female sexuality and the laboratory research of Masters and Johnson showed that physiologically, male and female sexuality are more similar than different, that there is no "right" kind of orgasm for women to have, and that both sexes are capable of sexual arousal and response.

▶ Some researchers believe that men, on average, have a stronger "sex drive" than women do, accounting for men's higher frequency of many sexual behaviors. Others believe that gender differences in sexual motivation and behavior are a result of differences in cultural norms and opportunity. A compromise view is that male sexuality is more biologically influenced than is women's, whereas female sexuality is more governed by circumstances, relationships, and cultural norms.

▶ Psychological, social, and cultural approaches to sexual motivation emphasize the ways that values, beliefs, and fantasies affect sexual desire and response. Men and women have sex to satisfy many different psychological motives, including pleasure, intimacy, coping, self-affirmation, the partner's approval, or peer approval. Extrinsic motives for sex, such as sex for approval, are associated with riskier sexual behavior than intrinsic motives are. Both sexes may agree to intercourse for nonsexual motives: Men sometimes feel obligated to "make a move" to prove their masculinity, and women sometimes feel obliged to "give in" to preserve the relationship.

▶ A major gender difference in sexual experience has to do with rape and perceptions of sexual coercion: What many women regard as coercion is not always seen as such by men. Men who rape do so for diverse reasons, including peer pressure, insecurity, hostility toward women, a wish to dominate or humiliate the victim, and sometimes sadism.

▶ Cultures differ widely in determining what parts of the body people learn are erotic, which sexual acts are considered erotic or repulsive, and whether sex itself is good or bad. Cultures transmit these ideas through *gender roles* and *sexual scripts,* which specify appropriate behavior during courtship and sex, depending on a person's gender, age, and sexual orientation. Scripts for heterosexual women and men often lead to different sexual goals and misunderstandings.

▶ As in the case of love, gender differences (and growing similarities) in sexuality are strongly affected by cultural and economic factors. As gender roles have become more alike, so has the sexual behavior of men and women.

▶ The origins of sexual orientation are still unknown. Traditional psychological explanations have not been supported. Genetic and hormonal factors may be involved, although the evidence is stronger for gay men than for lesbians, whose sexuality is more varied and flexible. Biology, culture, learning, and circumstance interact in complex ways to produce a given person's orientation. Research on this issue is sensitive because people often confuse scientific questions about the origins of homosexuality with political and moral questions about the rights of gays and lesbians.

The Competent Animal: Motives to Achieve

▶ The study of achievement motivation began with research using the *Thematic Apperception Test (TAT).* People who are motivated by a high *need for achievement* set high but realistic standards for success and excellence. This method has various empirical problems, but it launched the study of the factors that motivate achievement.

▶ People achieve more when they have specific, focused goals; when they set high but achievable goals for themselves; and when they have *approach goals* (seeking a positive outcome) rather than *avoidance goals* (avoiding an unpleasant outcome). The motivation to achieve depends not only on ability, but also on whether people set *mastery (learning) goals,* in which the focus is on learning the task well, or *performance goals,* in which the focus is on performing well for others. Mastery goals lead to persistence in the face of failures and setbacks; performance goals often lead to giving up. People's expectations can create *self-fulfilling prophecies* of success or failure. These expectations reflect one's level of *self-efficacy.*

▶ Work motivation also depends on circumstances of the job itself. Working conditions that promote motivation and satisfaction are those that provide workers with a sense of meaningfulness, control, variation in tasks, clear rules, supportive relationships, feedback, and opportunities for advancement and learning. *Incentive pay* is more effective than predictable raises in elevating work motivation. One factor in the motivation to enter a career is its gender ratio. The motivation to achieve also depends on having the opportunity to be promoted, in contrast to hitting a "glass ceiling."

Motives, Values, and Well-Being

▶ Satisfaction and well-being increase when people enjoy the *intrinsic satisfaction* of an activity and when their goals and values are in harmony. In an *approach–approach conflict,* a person is equally attracted to two goals. In an *avoidance–avoidance conflict,* a person is equally repelled by two goals. An *approach–avoidance conflict* is the most difficult to resolve, because the person is both attracted to and repelled by the same goal. Prolonged conflict can lead to physical symptoms and reduced well-being.

▶ Abraham Maslow believed that human motives could be ranked along a *hierarchy of needs,* from basic biological needs for survival to higher psychological needs for self-actualization. But this popular theory has not been well supported empirically. A more recent approach suggests that people have four major psychological needs, for autonomy, relatedness, competence, and self-esteem.

Key Terms

◀LOOKING BACK

- Is overweight usually a result of psychological problems? (p. 429)

- What theory explains why it's so hard for heavy people to lose weight—and just as hard for thin people to gain it? (p. 429)

- Why are people all over the world getting fatter? (p. 431)

- Why are bright, academically motivated college women most vulnerable to eating disorders? (p. 432)

- When someone says, "I love you," can you be sure what the person means? (p. 436)

- Do men and women differ in the ability to love? (p. 438)

- How are your beliefs about love affected by your income? (p. 439)

- Is one kind of orgasm better or healthier for women than another? (p. 441)

- What part of the anatomy do psychologists think is the "sexiest sex organ"? (p. 443)

- How do the sexual rules for heterosexual couples foster misunderstandings? (p. 446)

- Can psychological theories about smothering mothers or absent fathers explain why some men are gay? (p. 447)

- Why is "doing your best" an ineffective goal to set for yourself? (p. 451)

- When you are learning a new skill, which should you concentrate on: mastering it or performing it well in front of others? (p. 452)

- Which aspects of a job are more important than money in increasing your work satisfaction and involvement? (p. 454)

- How is the *desire* to achieve affected by the *opportunity* to achieve? (pp. 454–455)

- Does more money = more happiness? (p. 456)

- What kind of conflict do you have when you want to study for a big exam but you also want to go out partying? (p. 456)

- Do you have to satisfy basic needs for security and belonging before you can become "self-actualized"? (p. 457)

Go to  **WWW.PRENHALL.COM/WADE** **for activities, practice tests, and review materials.**

13

Theories of Personality

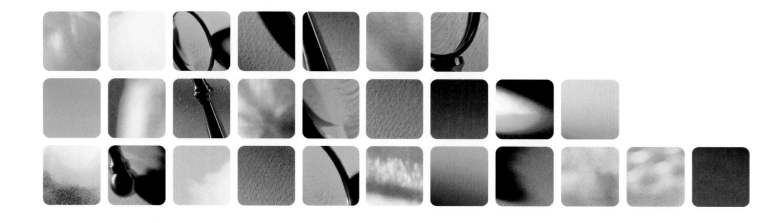

People often say that this or that person has not yet found himself. But the self is not something that one finds. It is something that one creates.

THOMAS SZASZ

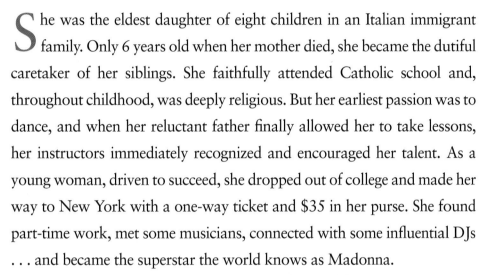

She was the eldest daughter of eight children in an Italian immigrant family. Only 6 years old when her mother died, she became the dutiful caretaker of her siblings. She faithfully attended Catholic school and, throughout childhood, was deeply religious. But her earliest passion was to dance, and when her reluctant father finally allowed her to take lessons, her instructors immediately recognized and encouraged her talent. As a young woman, driven to succeed, she dropped out of college and made her way to New York with a one-way ticket and $35 in her purse. She found part-time work, met some musicians, connected with some influential DJs . . . and became the superstar the world knows as Madonna.

Today, Madonna works tirelessly and demands total control over her shows: writing the songs, producing the music, choreographing her dances, creating her costumes, doing her own makeup. Her friends and associates have observed that she also obsessively controls her films, public appearances, and even her private life in the service of her public image. And that image is a continual work in progress. As reporter Jock McGregor (1997) observed, "She is always changing her image, whether it is from the good girl gone bad to the virgin in white; from Marilyn Monroe to the 1920s gangster moll; from androgynous, cold robot to naked sex symbol; from glamour queen to cosmic spirit and finally to doting mother."

Who is Madonna: the flamboyant performer who loves to shock or the "doting mother"? Was she born to be an exhibitionist, or did she create a persona to make herself famous? Which personality traits best describe her: extroverted, ambitious, outrageous, motherly, obsessive, funny, selfish, rebellious? Who is the "real" Madonna amid the changing public images? *Is* there a real one?

In this chapter, we will see how psychologists answer such questions—how they define and study personality. **Personality** refers to a distinctive pattern of behavior, mannerisms, thoughts, motives, and emotions that characterizes an individual over time and across different situations. This pattern consists of many distinctive **traits**, habitual ways of behaving, thinking, and feeling: shy, reliable, friendly, hostile, gloomy, confident, ambitious, and so on.

465

personality A distinctive and relatively stable pattern of behavior, thoughts, motives, and emotions that characterizes an individual throughout life.

trait A characteristic of an individual, describing a habitual way of behaving, thinking, and feeling.

For most of the twentieth century, textbooks on personality described several competing theories of personality that seemed to have no overlap. The leading perspective was Freudian psychoanalytic theory, which we will discuss later in this chapter. Its sweeping view of personality held that a person's conflicts, guilts, defenses, and ways of dealing with others could be traced to unconscious dynamics originating in early childhood. By mid-century, a second approach, behaviorism, was on the rise (see Chapter 7). Radical behaviorists held that "personality" was an illusion, a convenient fiction. In their view, people did not have internal "traits" that they carried around inside themselves like a kidney. Any consistency in a person's actions was simply a result of patterns of reinforcement over time. And because reinforcers could change from one setting to another, so could "personality"; for example, an individual might be relaxed and outgoing in one situation and shy in another. During the 1960s and 1970s, a third view emerged: Humanist psychologists rejected psychoanalytic *and* behavioral views of human nature, offering instead an approach that focused on the individual's strength and free will. To humanists, personality was the private self, the "true self" behind the many masks that people wear in daily life.

Then, in the 1990s, the revolution in behavioral-genetic research changed the conversation entirely. Researchers showed that about half of the human variation in personality traits is due to genetic variations. So compelling was this discovery, from so many lines of evidence, that few scientists think any more that babies are tiny lumps of clay, shaped entirely by how their parents treat them or the experiences they have. Few think that you can turn any infant into an adventurer, a genius, or a performer like Madonna.

On the other hand, if about half of the human variation in personality traits is due to genetics, what is responsible for the other half? Psychological theories of personality offer different answers: your parents, your experiences, your culture, your unconscious, your free will. But we think it makes more sense to focus on *interacting influences* rather than warring theories. "The nature–nurture debate is over," said one behavioral geneticist (Turkheimer, 2000). "The bottom line is that everything is heritable, an outcome that has taken all sides of the nature–nurture debate by surprise." Nonetheless, he added, the findings "do not show that genes are more fundamental than environments." In this chapter, we will show how behavior can be heritable, yet profoundly shaped by environments and experience to create the distinctive stamp of personality.

We will begin by identifying some basic traits that are the bedrock of personality. We will then consider the *genetic, environmental* (*learning*), *cultural,* and *psychodynamic* influences that shape the formation and expression of those traits. Finally, we will consider the humanist approach to the "private" personality—our inner sense of ourselves.

WHAT'S AHEAD ▶

- How reliable are those tests that tell you what "personality type" you are?
- How can psychologists tell which personality traits are more central or important than others?
- Which five dimensions of personality seem to describe people the world over?

Measuring Personality

Almost as soon as human beings noticed differences among their fellows, they started trying to fit people into different "types." Early philosophers thought our personalities fell into four categories depending on mixes of basic body fluids, or "humors": blood, phlegm, yellow bile (choler), and black bile. For example, if you were an angry, irritable sort of person, you supposedly had an excess of choler, and even now the word *choleric* describes a hothead. If you were slow-moving and unemotional, you supposedly had an excess of phlegm, making you a *phlegmatic* type.

The theory of the four humors is as dead as the dodo, but the love of typing people is as alive as ever. Today, there are many pop-psych tests of personality "types" that allegedly predict how people will do at work, whether they will get along with others, or whether they will succeed as leaders. One such test, the Myers-Briggs Type Indicator, is hugely popular in business and motivational seminars; at least a million people a year take it. The test assigns people to one of 16 different types, depending on how the individual combines various tendencies, such as being introverted or extroverted or being someone who relies on logic or intuition. However, the Myers-Briggs is not reliable; one study found that fewer than half of the respondents scored as the same type a mere five weeks later. And there is little evidence to support the test's key premise that knowledge of a person's type reliably predicts behavior on the job or in relationships (Barbuto, 1997; Pittenger, 1993).

To date, the personality-assessment industry has developed more than 2,500 "personality tests" given to people applying for jobs, tests that supposedly will indicate whether applicants are prone to stealing, taking drugs, or being disloyal (Ehrenreich, 2001). But many of these tests are nearly useless from a scientific point of view, which is why it is important to understand the difference between well-validated tests and unscientific ones. (In "Taking Psychology with You," we discuss other unreliable tests to watch out for.)

Personality researchers and clinical psychologists generally rely on two kinds of personality tests. *Projective tests* are based on the assumption that the test-taker will transfer ("project") unconscious conflicts and motives onto an ambiguous stimulus. (Because projective tests are used primarily in the diagnosis of mental disorders, we will cover them in Chapter 16.) **Objective tests (inventories)** are standardized questionnaires that require written responses, typically to multiple-choice or true-false items. These tests have better reliability and validity than do projective tests or the subjective judgments of clinicians, and they are better at predicting behavior (Anastasi & Urbina, 1997; Dawes, 1994; Lilienfeld, Wood, & Garb, 2000; Paunonen, 1998).

Objective tests provide information about literally hundreds of different aspects of personality, including needs, values, interests, and typical ways of responding to situations. For example, the Beck Depression Inventory assesses the severity of a person's depression. The Minnesota Multiphasic Personality Inventory (MMPI) is used largely to assess personality disorders (we will discuss this widely used test in Chapter 16). And the Multidimensional Personality Questionnaire (MPQ) is often used in behavioral-genetic studies of dimensions of personality and the traits that make up each dimension (Tellegen & Waller, in press; Krueger, 2000).

Using well-constructed inventories, psychologists have identified hundreds of traits, ranging from sensation seeking (the enjoyment of risk) to "erotophobia" (the fear of sex). They have gone on to ask: Are some traits more important or central to defining "personality" than others? Do some of them overlap or cluster together?

For Gordon Allport, one of the most influential psychologists in personality theory, the answers were yes. Allport (1937, 1961) recognized that not all traits have

THE FAR SIDE® **BY GARY LARSON**

The four basic personality types

objective tests (inventories)
Standardized questionnaires requiring written responses; they typically include scales on which people are asked to rate themselves.

factor analysis A statistical method for analyzing the intercorrelations among various measures or test scores; clusters of measures or scores that are highly correlated are assumed to measure the same underlying trait or ability (factor).

equal weight and significance in people's lives. Most of us, he said, have 5 to 10 *central traits* that reflect a characteristic way of behaving, dealing with others, and reacting to new situations. For instance, some people see the world as a hostile, dangerous place, whereas others see it as a place for fun and frolic. *Secondary traits,* in contrast, are more changeable aspects of personality, such as music preferences, habits, casual opinions, and the like.

Modern research has confirmed Allport's idea that traits vary in their "centrality" to the individual. Raymond B. Cattell advanced the study of this issue by applying a statistical method called **factor analysis.** Performing a factor analysis is like adding water to flour: It causes the material to clump up into little balls. When applied to traits, this procedure identifies clusters of correlated items that seem to be measuring some common, underlying factor. For example, the traits of assertiveness, willingness to tell jokes in large groups, and pleasure in meeting new people might share the common factor of extroversion.

Using questionnaires, life descriptions, and observations of thousands of people, Cattell (1965, 1973) measured dozens of personality traits, including humor, intelligence, creativity, dominance, and emotional disorders. Out of these he developed the 16 Personality Factors (PF) Questionnaire. Later in his career, he noted that only six of the 16 factors measured by the questionnaire had been repeatedly confirmed, but the 16 PF personality test has nonetheless remained popular (Digman, 1996).

By the mid-1980s, hundreds of factor-analytic studies had supported the existence of a cluster of central personality traits. Although researchers are still debating exactly how many traits belong to this inner group—some say three, others say as many as nine—most personality researchers agree on the centrality of five "robust factors," known informally as the *Big Five* (Digman, 1996; Jang et al., 1998; McCrae et al., 2000; Wiggins, 1996):

Where do you think this man would score on extroversion?

1 *Extroversion versus introversion* describes the extent to which people are outgoing or shy. It includes such traits as being talkative or silent, sociable or reclusive, adventurous or cautious, eager to be in the limelight or inclined to stay in the shadows.

2 *Neuroticism (negative emotionality) versus emotional stability* describes the extent to which a person suffers from such traits as anxiety, an inability to control impulses, and a tendency to feel negative emotions such as anger, guilt, scorn, and resentment. Neurotic individuals are worriers, complainers, and defeatists, even when they have no major problems. They are always ready to see the sour side of life and none of its sweetness.

3 *Agreeableness versus antagonism* describes the extent to which people are good-natured or irritable, cooperative or abrasive, secure or suspicious and jealous. It reflects the tendency to have friendly relationships or hostile ones.

4 *Conscientiousness versus impulsiveness* describes the degree to which people are responsible or undependable, persevering or quick to give up, steadfast or fickle, tidy or careless, self-disciplined or impulsive.

5 *Openness to experience versus resistance to new experience* describes the extent to which people are curious, imaginative, questioning, and creative, or conforming, unimaginative, predictable, and uncomfortable with novelty.

Get Involved ■■

Rate Your Traits

For each of the "Big Five" factors below, indicate on a 5-point scale where you think you fall, from 1 = describes me well to 5 = does not describe me at all. (These descriptions are just samples from the full personality inventory.)

_____ **Extroversion:** The extent to which you like most people you meet, enjoy talking with people, and are regarded as being warm and friendly.

_____ **Neuroticism:** The extent to which you worry frequently, are easily frightened, and feel fearful, anxious, or tense.

_____ **Agreeableness:** The extent to which you believe that other people are well intentioned, honest and trustworthy, rather than unreliable and likely to take advantage.

_____ **Conscientiousness:** The extent to which you are known for your common sense, and are prepared for new situations, willing to take civic duties seriously, and able to make informed decisions.

_____ **Openness to Experience:** The extent to which you have an active imagination and enjoy adventure.

Now ask a friend or relative to rate you on each of these dimensions. How closely does this rating match your own? If there is a discrepancy, what might be the reason for it?

As you might imagine, some of these traits tend to overlap; it is hard to imagine an easygoing, agreeable person who is also high in neuroticism (Jang et al., 2001). Also, culture can affect the prominence of these traits and how they are reflected in language. One team found that seven factors were needed to capture personality dimensions in Spanish (Benet-Martínez & Waller, 1997). In contrast, an Italian team found that only three of the Big Five were replicated in Italy (Di Blas & Forzi, 1999). Openness to experience did not emerge as a distinct factor, but, fortunately for Italians, neither did neuroticism! (An Italian friend of ours was not surprised. "Who among us," he said, "could remain emotionally negative in a land of such great pasta, wine, and art?")

Nonetheless, the Big Five have emerged as distinct, central personality dimensions in most places around the world. Factor-analytic evidence for the Big Five has turned up in countries as diverse as Britain, Canada, Czechoslovakia, China, Turkey, the Netherlands, Japan, Spain, the Philippines, Hawaii, Germany, Portugal, Israel, Korea, Russia, and Australia (Digman & Shmelyov, 1996; Katigbak, Church, & Akamine, 1996; Katigbak et al., 2002; Somer & Goldberg, 1999; Yang & Bond, 1990). These five traits emerge whether you ask people for self-reports or have people assessed by friends, relatives, or independent observers (Borkenau et al., 2001; Watson, Hubbard, & Wiese, 2000).

Moreover, the Big Five are remarkably stable over a lifetime, especially once a person hits 30 (Costa & McCrae, 1994; Roberts & DelVecchio, 2000). There is some good news, however, for crabby neurotics, especially young ones. Studies of thousands of people in 10 countries find that young people, ages 16 to 21, are the most neurotic (emotionally negative) and the least agreeable and conscientious. But by age 30, perhaps as a result of the responsibilities of adulthood, people tend to become more agreeable and conscientious and less negative. Unfortunately, in later adulthood older people also tend to become less extroverted and less open to

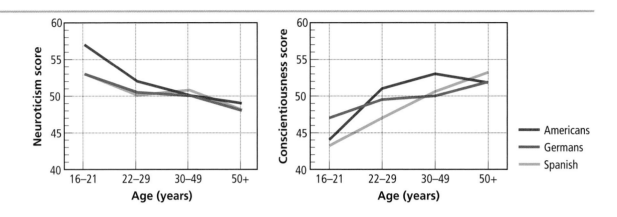

Figure 13.1

CONSISTENCY AND CHANGE IN PERSONALITY OVER THE LIFE SPAN

Studies of thousands of people in many different cultures in Europe, North America, and Asia find that although the Big Five traits remain fairly stable, changes occur over the life span. As you can see here, neuroticism (negative emotionality) is highest among young adults, and then declines; conscientiousness is lowest among young adults, and then steadily increases. These changes probably reflect common experiences that occur as young people grow up and leave home (Costa et al., 1999).

new experiences (see Figure 13.1). Because these changes have been found in many different countries, they seem to reflect common maturational changes over the life span (Costa et al., 1999; McCrae et al., 2000).

The Big Five are not a complete picture of personality, of course. Clinical psychologists note that important traits involved in mental disorders are missing, such as psychopathy (impulsivity and lack of remorse), self-absorption, and obsessionality (Westen & Shedler, 1999). Personality researchers note that other important dimensions are missing, such as religiosity, dishonesty, humorousness, and conventionality (Paunonen & Ashton, 2001). But the Big Five do seem to lie at the core of personality variations among healthy individuals. The next question is, where do these traits, and others, come from?

QUICK QUIZ

Show that you have the trait of conscientiousness by taking this quiz.

1. What is the advantage of inventories, compared with clinical judgment and projective tests, in measuring personality?

2. Raymond Cattell advanced the study of personality by (a) developing case-study analysis, (b) using factor analysis, (c) devising the Myers-Briggs Type Inventory.

3. Which of the following are *not* among the Big Five personality traits? (a) introversion, (b) agreeableness, (c) psychoticism, (d) openness to experience, (e) intelligence, (f) neuroticism, (g) conscientiousness

4. Which trait among the Big Five typically decreases by age 30? (a) agreeableness, (b) extroversion, (c) openness to experience, (d) neuroticism

Answers:

1. In general, they have better reliability and validity 2. b 3. c, e 4. d

WHAT'S AHEAD

- **Is it possible to be born irritable or easygoing?**
- **Do you have to be a person to have a personality?**
- **To what extent are personality differences among people influenced by their genetic differences?**

Genetic Influences on Personality

A mother we know was describing her two children: "My daughter has always been difficult, intense, and testy," she said, "but my son is the opposite, placid and good-natured. They came out of the womb that way." Was this mother right? Is it possible to be born touchy or good-natured? What aspects of personality might have an inherited component?

Psychologists who take a biological view of personality try to answer these questions in two ways: by studying temperaments in children (and other animals) and by doing heritability studies of twins and adopted individuals. They hope that the genes underlying temperaments and key traits will one day be discovered (Plomin et al., 2001). One research team believes it has already found one of several genes involved in neuroticism, pessimism, and anxiety (Lesch et al., 1996). Another team, using data from hundreds of twins in Canada, Germany, and Japan, has found a serotonin transporter gene that seems to be involved in both neuroticism and (non)agreeableness (Jang et al., 2001). These findings are still tentative, but the search for genes involved in particular aspects of personality is moving ahead rapidly, and you will be hearing lots more about genetic discoveries in the coming years.

Heredity and Temperament

A psychologist who was interviewed in the *Los Angeles Times* described Susie, someone he worked with, as irritable, grumpy, and manipulative. Hardly a comment to make headlines, except that Susie is a bear (Gosling & John, 1999). Many other species, including dogs, hyenas, cats, and of course our fellow primates, vary in their temperamental dispositions to respond to the environment and to one another in different ways (Gosling, 2001). Apparently you don't have to be a person to have a personality.

Human babies, too, have tiny personalities, even in the first weeks after birth. Infants differ in activity level, mood, responsiveness, "soothability," heart rate, and attention span (Belsky, Hsieh, & Crnic, 1996; Kagan, 1994; Snidman et al., 1995). Some are irritable and cranky; others are placid and sweet-natured. Some will cuddle up in an adult's arms and snuggle; others squirm and fidget, as if they cannot stand being held. Some smile easily; others fuss and cry.

These differences appear soon after birth, even when you control for possible prenatal influences such as the mother's nutrition, drug use, or problems with the pregnancy. That is one reason most psychologists believe that babies are born with genetically determined **temperaments**, dispositions to respond to the environment in certain ways. Temperaments include *reactivity* (how excitable, arousable, or responsive a baby is), *soothability* (how easy it is to calm an upset baby), and positive and negative emotionality. Temperaments are quite stable over time and may later form the basis of specific personality traits (McCrae et al., 2000; Rothbart, Ahadi, & Evans, 2000).

"THERE'S ANOTHER HEREDITARY DISEASE THAT RUNS IN THE ROYAL FAMILY. YOUR GRANDFATHER WAS A STUBBORN FOOL, YOUR FATHER WAS A STUBBORN FOOL, AND YOU ARE A STUBBORN FOOL."

temperaments Physiological dispositions to respond to the environment in certain ways; they are present in infancy and are assumed to be innate.

Extreme shyness and fear of new situations tend to be biologically based, stable aspects of temperament—both in human beings and in monkeys. On the right, a timid infant rhesus monkey cowers behind a friend in the presence of an outgoing stranger.

Here is an amazing example of temperamental stability. Researchers videotaped the full-face emotional expressions of 18-month old children who were briefly separated from, and then reunited with, their mothers. Expressions of *positive* emotions were later correlated, when the children were 3½ years old, with the mother's ratings of the child's degree of extroversion and openness to experience. But the infants' *negative* emotional expressions were correlated with continued negative emotionality (neuroticism) and inversely with agreeableness (Abe & Izard, 1999).

Jerome Kagan (1997) has spent many years studying the temperament of reactivity, following children from infancy to adolescence. About 20 percent of all children are at one extreme (highly reactive) or the other (nonreactive); the other 80 percent fall somewhere in between. Highly reactive infants, even at four months of age, are excitable, nervous, and fearful; they overreact to any little thing, even a colorful picture placed in front of them. As toddlers, they tend to be wary and fearful of new things—toys that make noise, odd-looking robots—even when their moms are right there with them. At 5 years, many of these children are still timid and uncomfortable in new situations. At 7 years, many still have symptoms of anxiety. They are afraid of being kidnapped, they need to sleep with the light on, and they are afraid of sleeping in an unfamiliar house—even if they have never experienced any sort of trauma. In contrast, nonreactive infants, Kagan (1998a) says, are "California, laid-back babies." They lie there without fussing; they rarely cry; they babble happily. As toddlers, they are outgoing and curious about new toys and events. They continue to be easygoing and extroverted throughout childhood.

Children at these two extremes differ physiologically, too (Rothbart, Ahadi, & Evans, 2000). During mildly stressful tasks, reactive children are more likely than nonreactive children to show signs of activity in the sympathetic nervous system, indicating physiological arousal. These signs include increased heart rate, dilation of the pupils, heightened brain activity, and high levels of two stress hormones, norepinephrine and cortisol. Interestingly, the same physiological attributes appear in shy, anxious infant rhesus monkeys (Suomi, 1991). Starting early in life, these "uptight" monkeys respond with anxiety to novelty and challenge, just as highly reactive children do. They too have high heart rates and elevated stress hormones.

Biologically based temperaments, then, influence later personality traits. However, biology is not a blueprint; it is more like a rough sketch. Consistency in a given temperament depends in part on how extreme that trait is in infancy. Kagan put it this way: What proportion of extremely reactive babies remain extremely shy, subdued, and fearful as older children? About 15 percent. What proportion become average, neither extremely shy nor extremely outgoing? The rest. What proportion become vivacious, fearless, and extroverted? Zero. "The environment acts on fearful children to move them toward health, toward the center," Kagan (1998a) explained, "but it's really hard to move them to the other end."

Heredity and Traits

A second way to study genetic contributions to personality is to estimate the **heritability** of specific traits within groups of children or adults. As we saw in Chapter 3, heritability refers to the proportion of the total variance in a trait that is attributable to genetic variation with a group. Estimates of heritability come from behavioral-genetic studies of adopted children and of identical and fraternal twins reared apart and together. (If you need to review these methods and how they are used to estimate the role of genetics, see pages 88–89.)

Findings from adoption and twin studies have provided compelling support for a genetic contribution to personality. Identical twins reared apart will often have unnerving similarities in gestures, mannerisms, and moods; indeed, their personalities often seem as similar as their physical features. If one twin tends to be optimistic, glum, or excitable, the other will probably be that way too (Braungert et al., 1992; Plomin et al., 2001).

Behavioral-genetic findings have shown remarkable consistency in the heritability of traits. Whether the trait in question is one of the Big Five, or many others from aggressiveness to happiness, heritability is typically around .50 (Bouchard, 1997b; Jang et al., 1998; Loehlin, 1992; Lykken & Tellegen, 1996; Waller et al., 1990). This means that within a group of people, about 50 percent of the variation in such traits is attributable to genetic differences among the individuals in the group. These findings have been replicated in many countries.

Some researchers have even reported high heritability for such specific activities as getting divorced (McGue & Lykken, 1992) and watching a lot of television in childhood (Plomin et al., 1990). But how on earth can divorce and TV watching be heritable? Our prehistoric ancestors didn't get married, let alone divorced, and they certainly didn't watch TV! Perhaps, though, certain traits or temperaments that *are* heritable could predispose a person to do these things.

We think you will agree that these findings are pretty amazing. But it is important not to leap to conclusions or oversimplify ("It's all in our genes!"). Remember that a genetic *predisposition* does not imply genetic *inevitability*. If heredity accounts for about half of the explanation of why people differ in their traits, then the environment (and errors in measurement) must account for the other half. As Robert Plomin (1989), a leading behavioral geneticist, observed, "The wave of acceptance of genetic influence on behavior is growing into a tidal wave that threatens to engulf the second message of this research: These same data provide the best available evidence for the importance of environmental influences." Let us now see what some of those influences might be.

heritability A statistical estimate of the proportion of the total variance in some trait that is attributable to genetic differences among individuals within a group.

13.1

Identical twins Gerald Levey (left) and Mark Newman were separated at birth and raised in different cities. When they were reunited at age 31, they discovered some astounding similarities. Both were volunteer firefighters, wore mustaches, and were unmarried. Both liked to hunt, watch old John Wayne movies, and eat Chinese food. They drank the same brand of beer, held the can with the little finger curled around it, and crushed the can when it was empty. The challenge is to figure out which of these traits and behaviors are influenced strongly by heredity, which result mainly from environmental factors such as social class and upbringing, and which are due merely to chance.

We hope you have a few quiz-taking genes.

1. What two broad lines of research support the hypothesis that personality differences are due in part to genetic differences?

2. In behavioral-genetic studies, the heritability of personality traits, including the Big Five, is typically about (a) .50, (b) .90, (c) .10 to .20, (d) zero.

3. A newspaper headline announces "Couch Potatoes Born, Not Made: Kids' TV Habits May Be Hereditary." Why is this headline misleading? What other explanations of the finding are possible? What aspects of TV watching *could* have a hereditary component?

Answers:

1. Research on temperaments and on heritability of traits. 2. a 3. The headline implies that there is a "TV-watching gene," but the writer is failing to consider other explanations. For example, perhaps some temperaments dispose people to be sedentary or passive, and this disposition leads to a tendency to watch a lot of television.

WHAT'S AHEAD▶

- **Are people who have highly heritable personality traits stuck with them forever?**
- **How much can parents shape their children's personalities?**
- **How consistent is your personality across situations?**

Environmental Influences on Personality

The environment may be half of the influence on personality, but what *is* the environment, exactly? The very language of the "nature–nurture" debate implied that the opposite of nature (genetics) is nurture (how your parents raised you). But environmental influences cover a lot more territory than just what parents do (Harris, 1998). In this section, we will consider three crucial aspects of the environment—parents, peers, and particular situations—and see how much each contributes to personality.

The Power of Parents

In April 1999, Dylan Klebold and Eric Harris, teenagers enraged at the popularity of school jocks and resentful about their own inadequacies, killed 12 classmates and a teacher at Columbine High School in Littleton, Colorado, in a coldly premeditated plan. Then they committed suicide. In the ensuing atmosphere of panic and blame, many people tried to find reasons for the boys' rampage. They blamed the boys' genes, the media, violent video games, the availability of guns, . . . and above all, their parents. The victims' families have since sued Dylan Klebold's parents, whom they hold responsible for Dylan's violent eruption. The Klebolds should have known, say the families. They should have done something to prevent the tragedy. Or they did something very wrong in raising their son—maybe they were neglectful or abusive.

These claims reflect the entrenched Western belief that parental child-rearing practices are the strongest influence, maybe even the *sole* influence, on children's personality development. For many decades, few psychologists thought to question this assumption, and many still accept it. Learning theorists assume that parents are busy dispensing the rewards and punishments that eventually shape the behaviors called personality traits. Psychodynamic theorists, as we will see, assume that parents exert a crucial influence on the child's unconscious mind. Either way, your personality is the result of how your parents treat you.

Yet the belief that personality is primarily determined by how parents treat their children—what Judith Harris (1998) calls "the nurture assumption"—has begun to crumble under the weight of three lines of evidence:

> **THINKING CRITICALLY**
>
> **Examine the Evidence**
>
> Most people believe that parents are almost entirely responsible for their children's personality and behavior. What evidence challenges this popular belief?

1 *The shared environment of the home has little if any influence on personality.* In behavioral-genetic research, the "shared environment" includes the family you grew up with and the experiences and background you shared with your siblings and parents. If these had as powerful an influence as commonly assumed, then studies should find a strong correlation between the personality traits of adopted children and those of their adoptive parents. In fact, the correlation is weak to nonexistent, indicating that the influence of child-rearing practices and family life is nil compared to the influence of genetics (Cohen, 1999; Plomin et al., 2001).

In contrast to the weak effects of the shared environment, the major environmental contribution to personality differences comes from the **nonshared environment:** the unique experiences you have that are not shared with other family members, such as being in Mrs. Miller's class in the fourth grade or winning the lead in the school play (Bouchard, 1997b; Hur, McGue, & Iacono, 1998; Plomin et al., 2001).

2 *Few parents have a single child-rearing style that is consistent over time and that they use with all their children.* Although developmental psychologists have tried to identify the effects of many specific child-rearing practices on children's personality traits, the problem is that parents are inconsistent from day to day and over the years, depending on their own stresses, moods, marital satisfaction, and the child's age (Harris, 1998; Holden & Miller, 1999). As one child we know said to her exasperated mother, "Why are you so mean to me today, Mommy? I'm this naughty every day." Moreover, parents tend to adjust their methods of child-rearing according to the temperament of the child; they are often more lenient with easygoing children and more punitive with difficult ones.

3 *Even when parents try to be consistent in the way they treat their children, there may be little relation between what they do and how the children turn out.* Some children of troubled and abusive parents are resilient and do not suffer lasting emotional damage; some children of the kindest and most nurturing parents succumb to drugs, mental illness, or gangs. By all accounts, the parents of Dylan Klebold were loving and involved with their son (Garbarino & Bedard, 2001).

This evidence does not mean that parents have *no* influence on their children. Most important, *parents can modify their children's dispositions and extreme traits.* For example, we saw in the previous section that *most* infants who are highly reactive and fearful eventually shift away from this extreme (Kagan, 1998, 1998b). How

nonshared environment Unique aspects of a person's environment and experience that are not shared with family members.

JUMP START reprinted by permission of United Feature Syndicate, Inc.

Do parents have total control over how their children turn out, even if they try to keep constant tabs on them?

much they do, in turn, depends on how parents and others respond to their reactivity. Imagine a high-strung parent with a baby who is fearful, quick to cry, and slow to be consoled. The parent, feeling desperate or angry, may withdraw from the child or use excessive punishment, which in turn makes the child even more timid and withdrawn. In contrast, a patient parent may have a calming effect on a frightened child, leading the child to become more outgoing. Likewise, parents may not be able to turn extremely shy children into extroverts, but they can help them become more sociable and less frightened of new situations.

Thus, even traits that are highly heritable are not rigidly fixed; experience can strengthen or diminish them. In one important longitudinal study that followed children from age 3 to age 21, those who were impulsive, undercontrolled, and aggressive at age 3 were far more likely than calmer children to grow up to be impulsive, unreliable, and antisocial, and more likely to commit crimes (Caspi, 2000). Early temperament was a strong and consistent predictor of these later personality traits. But not *every* child came out the same way. What protected some of those at risk, and helped them move in a healthier direction? One answer is having parents who made sure they stayed in school (Caspi, 2000). Boys who are at high risk of delinquency and crime are often rescued if they get consistent parental discipline and close supervision, if their parents are affectionate and maintain close attachments, and if their parents set high standards and expectations (McCord, 1992; Patterson et al., 1998; C. Smith et al., 1997). (In Chapter 14, we will consider the impact of particular child-rearing practices on children's moral behavior and aggressiveness.)

Keep in mind, too, that parents affect many things about their children other than personality traits. These influences include religious practices and beliefs, intellectual and occupational interests, feelings of self-esteem or inadequacy, adherence to traditional or modern notions of masculinity and femininity, moral standards, skills, values, attitudes, and social identities (Beer, Arnold, & Loehlin, 1998; McCrae et al., 2000). Parents also have a strong influence on how helpful or altruistic their children become (Krueger, Hicks, & McGue, 2001).

Most of all, what parents do profoundly affects the quality of their relationship with their children—whether their children feel loved, secure, and valued, or humiliated, frightened, and worthless (Harris, 1998). Surely this is the most important influence that parents have! But once children leave home, starting in preschool, parental influence on children's behavior *outside* the home begins to wane. The "nonshared environment"—peers, chance events, and circumstances—takes over.

The Power of Peers

Should the parents of Dylan Klebold have known how angry and resentful their son felt, angry enough to inflict such a bloody revenge on his classmates? Was the "real" Dylan the good son or the enraged classmate? When two psychologists surveyed 275 freshmen at Cornell University, they found that most of them had "secret lives," private selves, that they never revealed to their parents (Garbarino & Bedard, 2001). Most reported committing crimes, drinking, doing drugs, and having sex without their parents' knowing anything about it. The researchers concluded that Dylan Klebold was an extreme case of a common adolescent phenomenon: showing your parents only one facet of your personality and an entirely different one to your peers.

Children, like adults, live in two environments: their homes and their world outside the home. At home children learn how their parents want them to behave and what they can get away with; as soon as they leave home, however, they conform to

The first day of day care can be a rude awakening for an only child raised at home.

WE'RE HERE AND WE'RE PEERS... GET USED TO IT.

the dress, habits, language, and rules of their peers. Children who were law-abiding in the fifth grade may start breaking the law in high school, if that is what it takes—or what they think it takes—to win the respect of their peers. Parents lament the conformity of their children to their peer groups, but, according to Judith Harris (1998), children's attachment to their peer groups is not irrational but essential. Identification with the peer group, not identification with the parent, Harris argues, is the key to survival of the next generation. That is why children have their own traditions, words, rules, and games, and why their culture often operates in opposition to adult rules.

Adolescent culture often consists of many different peer groups, organized by interests (jocks, nerds, musicians, artists), ethnicity, or by status and popularity. Unfortunately, children and teenagers who are temperamentally fearful and shy, have few or no friends, or are physically unattractive or weak are more likely than other kids to be bullied, victimized, and rejected by their peers (Hodges & Perry, 1999). Peer acceptance is so important to children and adolescents that these experiences are often far more traumatic than is punitive treatment by parents. In one Canadian study, college students were asked, "What made you most unhappy when you were a child?" Only 9 percent mentioned their parents; 37 percent described humiliation or rejection by peers (Ambert, 1997).

Have you ever been in this situation—as the excluded student or the one doing the excluding? Being rejected by peers is one of the most painful experiences that adolescents report having.

It has been difficult to tease apart the effects of parents and peers, Harris observes, because parents usually try to arrange things so that their children's environments duplicate their own values, language, and customs. To see which has the stronger influence on behavior, therefore, we must look at situations in which these environments clash. For example, when parents value academic achievement and their child's peers do not, who wins? The answer, typically, is peers.

In a study of 15,000 students at nine different American high schools, researchers sought reasons for the average difference in school performance of Asian-Americans, African-Americans, Latinos, and whites (Steinberg, Dornbusch, & Brown, 1992). Asian-American students, who had the highest grades on the average, reported having the highest level of peer support for academic achievement. They studied together in groups, cheered one another on, and praised one another's success. But many African-American students regarded academic success as a sign of selling out to the white establishment. High-achieving black students often said they had few black friends for this reason; they felt they had to choose between doing well in school and being popular with their peers. This dilemma affects students of *any* ethnicity or gender whose peer group thinks that academic success is only for nerds and sellouts (Arroyo & Zigler, 1995; Fordham, 1991).

As the achievement example shows, peers, like parents, shape the expression of personality traits, causing us to emphasize some attributes or abilities and downplay others. Of course, our temperaments and dispositions may cause us to select particular peer groups (if they are available) instead of others, and our temperaments also influence how we behave within the group. But once we are among peers, most of us go along with them, molding facets of our personalities to the pressures of the group.

> conclusion

Situations and Circumstances

The very definition of a trait is that it is consistent across situations. But as we just saw in discussing parents versus peers, people often behave one way at home and a different way with their friends. In a study in which people kept records of their feelings and behavior five times a day for 13 days, it turned out that almost everyone routinely revealed all of the Big Five traits in their everyday behavior (Fleeson,

Get Involved

Situation and Self

Are you a different person when you are alone, with your parents, hanging out with friends, in class, or at a party? If so, in what ways? Do you have a "secret self" that you do not show to others? Use the Big Five factors (or any other aspects of your personality that are important to you) as you answer these questions.

2001). People differed in the average frequency and intensity of each of these traits, but there was also variation *within each individual* in the expression of those traits—again, depending on the situation.

The reason, in learning terms, is that some behaviors are rewarded, and others punished or ignored, in different contexts. For example, your degree of shyness or extroversion often depends on the situation. You are likely to be more extroverted at a "Liberate the Suppressed Self" weekend, where you are rewarded with smiles, praise, and hugs for dancing naked on a tabletop and telling family secrets, than at home, with relatives who would regard such behavior with alarm and condemnation.

Principles of social–cognitive learning theory also help explain why behavior is often inconsistent (Cervone & Shoda, 1999). (To refresh your memory of these principles, see Chapter 7.) According to social–cognitive theorists, personality traits result from a continual interaction between aspects of an individual and aspects of a given situation. Our temperaments, learned habits, and beliefs about our abilities influence how we respond to others, whom we associate with, and the situations we seek out (Bandura, 1986, 2001; Cervone, 1997; Mischel & Shoda, 1995). In turn, the situation influences our behavior and beliefs, rewarding some behaviors and extinguishing others. This process, called **reciprocal determinism**, looks like this:

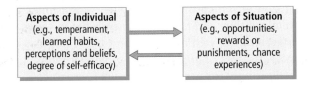

Over the course of their lives, people learn that some acts will be rewarded and others punished. Thus they develop general expectations about whether or not their actions and efforts will be successful. For example, a child who studies hard and gets good grades, attention from teachers, admiration from friends, and praise from parents will come to expect that hard work in other situations will also pay off—and become "ambitious" and "industrious." A child who studies hard and gets poor grades, is ignored by teachers and parents, and is rejected by friends for being a grind will come to expect that working hard isn't worth it—and become (in the view of others) "unambitious" or "lazy." This is how self-fulfilling prophecies are formed and maintained (see Chapter 12).

The process of reciprocal determinism (as opposed, say, to the one-way determinism of "genes determine everything" or "everything is learned") helps explain the influence of the nonshared environment on personality. What makes children

reciprocal determinism In social-cognitive theories, the two-way interaction between aspects of the environment and aspects of the individual in the shaping of personality traits.

who grow up in the same family so different, apart from their genes? The answer seems to be: An assortment of experiences that affect each child differently, chance events that cannot be predicted, and situations and peer groups that the children belong to (Plomin et al., 2001; Rutter et al., 2001). Nonshared and chance experiences might include being hospitalized, being bullied at school, joining a delinquent peer group, finding out that you excel in karate, having an unexpected encounter with a casting director. . . .

The illustration in the margin, showing very different sides of Madonna's personality as a mother and as a performer, depicts the reciprocal influence of genetic and situational influences on personality traits.

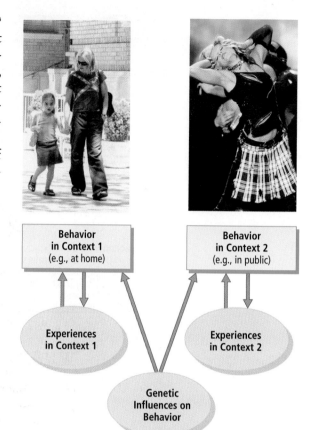

Resolving the Nature–Nurture Debate

Understandably, behavioral geneticists are excited about their findings on the heritability of personality traits. "It will doubtless seem incredible to many readers that variables such as social class, educational opportunities, religious training, and parental love and discipline have no substantial influence on adult personality," wrote Robert McCrae and Paul Costa (1988), "but imagine for a moment that it is correct. What will it mean for research in developmental psychology? How will clinical psychology and theories of therapy be changed?"

Good questions! What *do* these findings mean for education, for raising children, or for psychotherapy and the treatment of personality problems? How can we use research on genetics wisely, without reducing our traits and actions to one cause?

Some psychotherapists believe that one wise use of behavioral-genetics research is to help people in therapy realize that they cannot transform their personalities, but that they can learn to cope with their existing temperamental dispositions and limits (Efran, Greene, & Gordon, 1998). Another wise application might be to unburden parents of the sole responsibility for how their children turn out. Parents can claim some credit (and blame), while also acknowledging that children come into the world with their own predispositions and are later influenced by many environments and groups other than their families, as the Klebolds learned to their sorrow (Cohen, 1999).

Often, however, behavioral-genetic findings are misused and misunderstood by the public. When people oversimplify, claiming that "genes are everything," they overlook the role of the environment and experience in modifying traits. As a result, many people mistakenly assume that personality problems that have a genetic component are hopeless—that someone is "born to be bad" or merely a miserable grump forever. Similarly, they may assume that if a problem, such as depression, has "genetic" origins, it will respond only to medication and there is no point trying other interventions (we discuss this fallacy in Chapter 17). In Chapter 12, we saw that despite the clear role of genetics in weight and body shape, environmental changes in diet and exercise best explain the worldwide rise in obesity. Likewise, personality traits may stem from genetic dispositions, but they are profoundly shaped by learning, peers, situations, experience, and, as we will see next, the largest "environment" of all: the culture.

> **THINKING CRITICALLY**
>
> **Don't Oversimplify**
>
> Some personality traits, such as shyness, are highly heritable. Some people think that means "genes are everything"—a temperamentally shy 5-year-old will inevitably grow up to become a wall-flower. What is a more accurate way to think about the impact of heredity on personality?

QUICK QUIZ

We want to nurture your appreciation of quizzes because it's in our nature to give them to you.

1. What three lines of evidence have disputed the belief that parents are the major influence on their children's personalities?

2. Which contributes more to the variation among people in personality traits: (a) the family environment that all siblings share, or (b) the unique experiences that people have that are not shared with their families?

3. Most people believe that what parents do profoundly affects their child's personality. Behavioral geneticists believe that most personality traits have a genetic component and emerge almost regardless of what parents do. How might these two positions be reconciled?

Answers:

1. The shared family environment has little if any influence on personality; few parents have a consistent child-rearing style; and even when parents try to be consistent in the way they treat their children, there may be little relation between what they do and how the children turn out. 2. b 3. We can avoid either-or thinking by asking which qualities may be due largely to temperament (such as extroversion) and which are strongly affected or controlled by parental and cultural lessons (such as altruism). Also, the child's temperament interacts with the parents' behavior; parents are able to modify their children's inborn temperaments and predispositions.

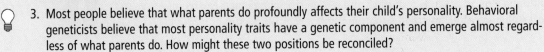

WHAT'S AHEAD

- Why are risk-taking and punctuality more than just individual personality traits?
- How does belonging to an individualist or collectivist culture influence your personality—and even whether you think you have a stable "self"?
- Why are men in the South and West more likely to get angry at personal insults than other American men are?
- What cultural practices affect the traits of altruism or selfishness?

Cultural Influences on Personality

Are you the kind of person who likes taking risks—say, by smoking cigarettes, driving 100 mph on the highway without a seat belt, or having unprotected sex with a stranger? Are you the kind of person who becomes enraged when someone calls you a rude name, or are you more likely to laugh it off?

Most Western psychologists regard risk-taking and quickness to anger as personality traits that are embedded in an individual, whether as a result of genetics or learning. But **culture** also has a profound effect on people's behavior, attitudes, and the traits they value or disdain. It provides rules that govern our behavior and values that shape our beliefs (see Chapter 8).

Until recently, most psychologists were uninterested in the influence of culture on individuals. In contrast to biology, which they treated as real and tangible, they regarded culture as merely a light veneer on human behavior, or perhaps a source of useful information for tourist travel ("In Spain, people eat dinner after midnight"). As a result, students and teachers knew little about the psychological characteristics of people living in other societies, and they assumed that they could generalize from studies of people in their own culture to people everywhere (Matsumoto, 1996; Segall, Lonner, & Berry, 1998).

Today many psychologists recognize that culture is just as powerful an influence on personality and behavior as any biological process. Cultural values, for example, affect people's feelings about risk. People in the Netherlands and Britain are more likely than Germans and Austrians to take risks and less likely

culture A program of shared rules that govern the behavior of members of a community or society, and a set of values, beliefs, and attitudes shared by most members of that community.

to favor rules and regulations intended to promote public safety, such as the requirement to carry citizen identification cards (Cvetkovich & Earle, 1994). The reason is that Germany and Austria (among other societies) place a high value on avoiding uncertainty and thus welcome laws that reduce danger to individuals and communities.

Society-wide events can also affect individual personality and behavior. Consider changes over time in a personality trait called "locus of control," which reflects how much control you feel you have over your environment and your future (see Chapter 15). During the 1960s, when the civil-rights movement was gathering steam in America, civil-rights activists and black student leaders were more likely to feel confident of their abilities to change the world and control their own lives than were their counterparts who were uninvolved in civil-rights efforts (Gore & Rotter, 1963). By the 1970s, however—after the assassinations of Martin Luther King, Jr., and John and Robert Kennedy, and after many Americans had become disillusioned with the Vietnam War—people's feelings of control began to change. They became less confident that they, as individuals, could improve the world (Strickland, 1989). Today, many Americans seem to feel even less in control of their lives, a change reflected in the rising numbers who do not vote and who believe their fates are predetermined by the stars or by destiny.

The 1960s also saw the beginning of what would be a sharp rise in crime and divorce rates (although both rates have been falling in the last decade) and other signs of social instability. Two meta-analyses comparing young Americans in 1952 and 1993 found substantially higher levels of anxiety and other negative emotions (neuroticism) in the 1990s generation. The increased social instability, it seems, had reduced young people's sense of safety (Twenge, 2000). Thus, while "neuroticism" may be a genetically influenced trait, it is also affected by larger events going on in society and culture.

In this section, we will consider several key dimensions of culture that shape the content and expression of other traits.

Culture, Values, and Traits

It is not easy to see how cultural rules affect your own personality, but here's a demonstration. Take as much time as you like to answer this question: "Who are you?" "I am _____."

Your response to "Who am I?" will be influenced by your cultural background, particularly whether your culture emphasizes individualism or community (Hofstede

Collectivist Chinese workers in Beijing do their morning T'ai Chi exercises in identical, harmonious fashion. Individualistic Americans exercise by running, walking, bicycling, and skating, all in different directions and wearing different clothes.

individualist cultures Cultures in which the self is regarded as autonomous, and individual goals and wishes are prized above duty and relations with others.

collectivist cultures Cultures in which the self is regarded as embedded in relationships, and harmony with one's group is prized above individual goals and wishes.

& Bond, 1988; Markus & Kitayama, 1991; Triandis, 1995, 1996). In **individualist cultures**, the independence of the individual takes precedence over the needs of the group, and the self is often defined as a collection of personality traits ("I am outgoing, agreeable, and ambitious") or in occupational terms ("I am a psychologist"). In **collectivist cultures**, group harmony takes precedence over the wishes of the individual, and the self is defined in the context of relationships and the community ("I am the son of a farmer, descended from three generations of storytellers on my mother's side and five generations of farmers on my father's side . . .").

As Table 13.1 shows, individualist and collectivist ways of defining the self influence many aspects of life, including which personality traits we value, how we express emotions, and how much we value having relationships or maintaining freedom (Campbell et al., 1996; Kashima et al., 1995). Individualist and collectivist outlooks even affect whether we believe that personality is stable across situations. In a revealing study comparing Japanese and Americans, the Americans reported that their sense of self changes only 5 to 10 percent in different situations, whereas the Japanese said that 90 to 99 percent of their sense of self changes (de Rivera, 1989). For the group-oriented Japanese, it is important to enact *tachiba*, to perform your social roles correctly so that there will be harmony with others. Americans, in contrast, tend to value "being true to your self" and having a "core identity." You can see that even notions of what personality means and whether it is consistent across situations are deeply affected by culture.

Customs in Context. Because people fail to understand the power of culture on behavior, they often attribute another person's mysterious or annoying actions to personality when they are really due to cultural norms. Take cleanliness. How often do you bathe—once a day, once a week? Do you regard baths as healthy and invigorating or as a disgusting wallow in dirty water? How often, and where, do you wash your hands—or feet? A person who would seem obsessively clean in one culture might seem an appalling slob in another (Fernea & Fernea, 1994).

Table 13.1	**Some Average Differences Between Individualist and Collectivist Cultures**
Members of individualist cultures	**Members of collectivist cultures**
Define the self as autonomous, independent of groups.	Define the self as an interdependent part of groups.
Give priority to individual, personal goals.	Give priority to the needs and goals of the ingroup.
Value independence, leadership, achievement, self-fulfillment.	Value group harmony, duty, obligation, security.
Give more weight to an individual's attitudes and preferences than to group norms as explanations of behavior.	Give more weight to group norms than to individual attitudes as explanations of behavior.
Attend to the benefits and costs of relationships; if costs exceed advantages, a person is likely to drop a relationship.	Attend to the needs of group members; if a relationship is beneficial to the group but costly to the individual, the individual is likely to stay in the relationship.

Source: Triandis, 1996.

Or consider tardiness. Individuals differ in whether they try to be places "on time" or are always late, but cultural norms affect how individuals regard time in the first place. In **monochronic cultures,** such as those of northern Europe, Canada, and the United States, time is organized into linear segments in which people do one thing "at a time" (Hall, 1983; Hall & Hall, 1990). The day is divided into appointments, schedules, and routines, and because time is a precious commodity, people don't like to "waste" time or "spend" too much time on any one activity. In such cultures, therefore, it is considered the height of rudeness (or high status) to keep someone waiting. But in southern Europe, in South America, and in Africa, you are more likely to find **polychronic cultures,** where time is organized along parallel lines. People do many things at once, and the needs of friends and family supersede mere appointments. People in Latin America and the Middle East think nothing of waiting all day, or even a week, to see someone. The idea of having to be somewhere "on time," as if time were more important than a person, is unthinkable.

In culturally diverse North America, the two time systems keep bumping into each other. Business, government, and other institutions are organized monochronically, but Native Americans, Latinos, Middle Easterners and others tend to operate on polychronic principles. The result is repeated misunderstandings. An Anglo judge in Miami got into hot water when he observed that "Cubans always show up two hours late for weddings"—late in his culture's terms, that is. The judge was accurate in his observation; the problem was his implication that something was wrong with Cubans for being "late." And "late" compared to what, by the way? The Cubans were perfectly on time for Cubans.

Aggressiveness and Altruism. Nowadays many people assume that male violence is mostly a matter of testosterone. The poor guys can't help it; aggressiveness is in their genes and hormones. But considerable cross-cultural evidence suggests that male aggression results more from cultural factors than biological ones. In cultures in which resources are abundant and there are no serious hazards or enemies to worry about—such as the Ifaluk, the Tahitians, and the people of Sudest Island near New Guinea—men do not feel they have to prove themselves and they are not raised to be tough and aggressive (Lepowsky, 1994; Levy, 1984). In contrast, in cultures in which competition for resources is fierce and survival is difficult (which has been true for most cultures on the planet, throughout human history), men are "toughened up" and pushed to take risks, even with their lives (Gilmore, 1990).

In a fascinating analysis of the rates of violence in different regional cultures of the United States, Richard Nisbett (1993) set out to explain why the American South, and some western regions of the country originally settled by southerners, have much higher rates of white homicide than the rest of the country. Nisbett ruled out explanations based on poverty, racial tensions, and a history of slavery. The higher rates of violence in the South, he found, derive ultimately from economic causes: They occur in cultures based on herding, rather than agriculture. Why? People who depend economically on agriculture tend to foster cooperative strategies for survival. But people who depend on their herds are extremely vulnerable; their livelihoods can be lost in an instant by the theft of their animals. To reduce the likelihood of theft, says Nisbett, herders "cultivate a posture of extreme vigilance toward any act that might be perceived as threatening in any way," and respond with force to any potential threat.

The emphasis on aggressiveness and vigilance in herding cultures, in turn, fosters a *culture of honor,* in which even apparently small disputes and trivial insults (trivial to people from other cultures, that is) put a man's reputation for toughness

monochronic cultures Cultures in which time is organized sequentially; schedules and deadlines are valued over people.

polychronic cultures Cultures in which time is organized horizontally; people tend to do several things at once and value relationships over schedules.

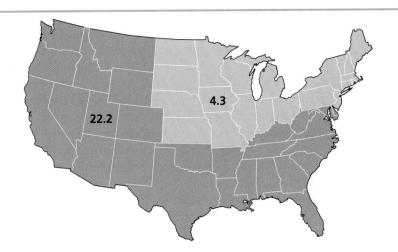

Figure 13.3

VIOLENCE AND "CULTURES OF HONOR"

This map of the United States shows that "argument-related" homicide rates—deaths caused by fights to restore status and honor among men—are five times higher in Southern and Western states, which foster "cultures of honor," than in Northern and Eastern states. The rates are per 100,000 white males ages 15 to 39, and occur independently of the general crime rate, poverty, or community instability. (Study excluded Washington, D.C., Alaska, and Hawaii.)

on the line, requiring him to respond with violence to restore his status (Cohen, 1998). Although the herding economy has become less important in the South and West, the legacy of its culture of honor remains. These regions have higher rates of honor-related homicides (such as murder to avenge a perceived insult to one's family) than other regions of the country (see Figure 13.3).

Coming from a culture of honor can literally get into your blood. In three experiments in which college men were called an offensive name, those raised in the North tended to respond calmly; they thought it was funny. But many Southerners were immediately inflamed. They felt that their masculine reputations were threatened; their stress hormones and testosterone levels shot up; and they were more likely to retaliate aggressively than Northerners were (Cohen et al., 1996).

Just as aggressiveness is shaped by culture, so is altruism, the willingness to help others. As children grow up, they learn how their culture defines moral behavior and whether or not that behavior is valued in practice. For example, does a public figure commit an illegal or immoral act and then earn a fortune from movie deals? Does a sports hero get away with breaking the law because his team needs him to win and to keep earning big bucks for them? The answers shape the behavior of those in a position to behave the same way, and the public's attitudes toward them.

One of the strongest influences on children's moral behavior comes from their cultural obligations and what others expect of them (Eisenberg, 1995; Segall et al., 1999). In a cross-cultural study of children in Kenya, India, Mexico, the Philippines, Okinawa, the United States, and five other cultures, researchers measured how often children behaved altruistically (offering help, support, or unselfish suggestions) or egoistically (seeking help and attention or wanting to dominate others) (Whiting & Edwards, 1988; Whiting & Whiting, 1975). American children were the least altruistic on all measures and the most egoistic. The most altruistic children came from societies in which children are assigned many tasks, such as caring for younger children and gathering and preparing food. These children knew that their work made a genuine contribution to the well-being or economic survival of the family. In cultures that value individual achievement and self-advancement, taking care of others has less importance.

Evaluating Cultural Theories

A woman we know, originally from England, married a Lebanese man. They were happy together but had the usual number of marital misunderstandings and squabbles. After a few years, they visited his home town in Lebanon, where she had never been before. "I

In many cultures, children are expected to contribute to the family income and to take care of their younger siblings. These experiences encourage helpfulness and empathy.

was stunned," she told us. "All the things I thought he did because of his *personality* turned out to be because he's *Lebanese*! Everyone there was just like him!"

Our friend's reaction illustrates both the contributions and the limitations of cultural studies of personality. She was right in recognizing that some of her husband's behavior was attributable to his culture—for example, his Lebanese notions of time were very different from her English notions. But she was wrong to infer that the Lebanese are all "like him": Individuals are affected by their culture, but they vary within it.

Cultural psychologists face the problem of how to describe cultural influences on personality without stereotyping (Church & Lonner, 1998). As one student of ours put it, "How come when we students speak of 'the' Japanese or 'the' blacks or 'the' whites or 'the' Latinos, it's called stereotyping, and when you do it, it's called 'cross-cultural psychology'?" This question shows excellent critical thinking! The study of culture does not rest on the assumption that all members of a culture behave the same way or have the same personality traits. Individuals vary according to their temperaments, beliefs, and learning histories, and this variation occurs within every culture.

Moreover, regional variations occur in every society. America may be an "individualist" culture overall, but the deep South, with its history of strong regional identity, is more collectivist than the rugged, independent West (Vandello & Cohen, 1999). The Chinese and the Japanese both value group harmony, but the Chinese are more likely to promote individual achievement, whereas the Japanese are more likely to strive for group consensus (Dien, 1999).

Cultural psychologists also face the risk of exaggerating the contrasts between cultures. In spite of their differences, all cultures reflect adaptations to universal human needs, such as those for love, attachment, family, work, and psychological meaning. As one cultural psychologist put it, "Human beings are not blank slates on which any cultural form can be written" (Cohen, 2001). Yet the existence of cross-cultural universals and of individual variations within cultures does not negate the importance of cultural rules that, on average, make Swedes different from Bedouins, or Cambodians different from Italians. The traits that we value, our sense of self versus community, and our notions of the right way to behave—all key aspects of personality—begin with the culture in which we are raised.

THINKING CRITICALLY

Don't Oversimplify

People often speak of "the" German personality or "the" British character. How can we think about the cultural factors that influence personality traits without stereotyping?

QUICK QUIZ

You are living in a culture that values the importance of quizzes.

1. Cultures whose members regard the "self" as a collection of stable personality traits are (individualist/collectivist).
2. Cultures whose members do many things at once and value relationships over schedules and appointments are (monochronic/polychronic).
3. Which of the terms in Items 1 and 2 apply to the majority culture in the United States and Canada?
4. Why, according to cultural psychologists, do men in the American South and West respond more aggressively to perceived insults than other American men?
5. Which cultural practice tends to foster the traits of helpfulness and altruism? (a) Every family member "does his or her own thing," (b) parents insist that children obey, (c) children contribute to the family welfare, (d) parents remind children often about the importance of being helpful.

Answers:

1. individualist 2. polychronic 3. individualist, monochronic 4. Men in these regions come from "cultures of honor." 5. c

Sigmund Freud (1856–1939).

psychoanalysis A theory of personality and a method of psychotherapy developed by Sigmund Freud; it emphasizes unconscious motives and conflicts.

psychodynamic theories Theories that explain behavior and personality in terms of unconscious energy dynamics within the individual.

intrapsychic Within the mind (psyche) or self.

WHAT'S AHEAD

- **How do psychologists regard Freud today—as a genius or a fraud?**
- **In Freud's theory of personality, why are the id and the superego always at war?**
- **When people say you're being "defensive," what defenses might they be thinking of?**
- **What would Carl Jung have had to say about Darth Vader?**
- **What are the "objects" in the object-relations approach to personality?**

Psychodynamic Influences on Personality

Of all the theories of personality, the psychodynamic approach is the one most embedded in popular culture. A man apologizes for "displacing" his frustrations at work onto his family. A woman suspects that she is "repressing" a childhood trauma. An alcoholic reveals that he is no longer "in denial" about his drinking. A teacher informs a divorcing couple that their 8-year-old child is "regressing" to immature behavior. All of this language—about displacing, repressing, denying, and regressing—can be traced to the first psychodynamic theory of personality, Sigmund Freud's theory of **psychoanalysis.**

Freud's theory is called **psychodynamic** because it emphasizes the movement of psychological energy within the person, in the form of attachments, conflicts, and motivations. Today's psychodynamic theories differ from Freudian theory and from one another, but they all share an emphasis on unconscious, **intrapsychic** processes going on within the mind. They also share an assumption that adult personality and ongoing problems are formed primarily by experiences in early childhood. These experiences produce unconscious thoughts and feelings which later form characteristic habits, conflicts, and often self-defeating behavior.

No one disputes the profound influence that Sigmund Freud had on the twentieth century. But there is enormous dispute about the lasting value of his work. Freud saw himself as one of the great geniuses of history, and many people agree with that assessment. But many modern scientists think he was a flat-out fraud whose ideas have not stood the test of time—a "dinosaur in the history of ideas" (Medawar, 1982). In this section, we will introduce you to Freud's ideas, and to two modern psychodynamic approaches. We will try to show you why attitudes toward Freud today range from reverence to contempt, and why he evokes such controversy.

Freud and Psychoanalysis

To enter the world of Sigmund Freud is to enter a realm of unconscious motives, passions, guilty secrets, unspeakable yearnings, and conflicts between desire and duty. These unseen forces, Freud believed, have far more power over our personalities than our conscious intentions do. The unconscious reveals itself, said Freud, in art, dreams, jokes, apparent accidents, and slips of the tongue. The British member of Parliament who referred to the "honourable member from Hell" when he meant to say "from Hull," said Freud (1920–1960), was revealing his actual, unconscious appraisal of his colleague.

"VERY WELL I'LL INTRODUCE YOU. EGO MEET ID. NOW GET BACK TO WORK."

The Structure of Personality. In Freud's theory, personality consists of three major systems: the id, the ego, and the superego. Any action we take or problem we have results from the interaction and degree of balance among these systems (Freud, 1905, 1920/1960, 1923/1962).

The **id,** which is present at birth, is the reservoir of unconscious psychological energies and the motives to avoid pain and obtain pleasure. The id contains two competing instincts: the life, or sexual, instinct (fueled by psychic energy called the **libido**) and the death, or aggressive, instinct. As energy builds up in the id, tension results. The id may discharge this tension in the form of reflex actions, physical symptoms, or uncensored mental images and unbidden thoughts.

The **ego,** the second system to emerge, is a referee between the needs of instinct and the demands of society. It bows to the realities of life, putting a rein on the id's desire for sex and aggression until a suitable, socially appropriate outlet for them can be found. The ego, said Freud, is both conscious and unconscious, and it represents "reason and good sense."

The **superego,** the last system of personality to develop, represents morality and parental authority; it includes the conscience, the inner voice that says you did something wrong. The superego, which is partly conscious but largely unconscious, judges the activities of the id, handing out good feelings of pride and satisfaction when you do something well and handing out miserable feelings of guilt and shame when you break the rules.

According to Freud, the healthy personality must keep all three systems in balance. Someone who is too controlled by the id is governed by impulse and selfish desires. Someone who is too controlled by the superego is rigid, moralistic, and bossy. Someone who has a weak ego is unable to balance personal needs and wishes with social duties and realistic limitations.

If a person feels anxious or threatened when the wishes of the id conflict with social rules, the ego has weapons at its command to relieve the tension. These unconscious strategies, called **defense mechanisms,** deny or distort reality, but they also protect us from conflict and anxiety. They become unhealthy only when they cause self-defeating behavior and emotional problems. Freud described 17 defense mechanisms; later, other psychoanalysts revised his list. Here are some of the primary defenses identified by Freud's daughter Anna (1967), who became a psychoanalyst herself, and by most contemporary psychodynamic psychologists (Vaillant, 1992):

1 *Repression* occurs when a threatening idea, memory, or emotion is blocked from consciousness. A woman who had a frightening childhood experience that she cannot remember, for example, is said to be repressing her memory of it.

id In psychoanalysis, the part of personality containing inherited psychic energy, particularly sexual and aggressive instincts.

libido [li-BEE-do] In psychoanalysis, the psychic energy that fuels the life or sexual instincts of the id.

ego In psychoanalysis, the part of personality that represents reason, good sense, and rational self-control.

superego In psychoanalysis, the part of personality that represents conscience, morality, and social standards.

defense mechanisms Methods used by the ego to prevent unconscious anxiety or threatening thoughts from entering consciousness.

"I'm sorry, I'm not speaking to anyone tonight. My defense mechanisms seem to be out of order."

Drawing by Joe Mirachi; © 1985 The New Yorker Magazine, Inc.

2 *Projection* occurs when a person's own unacceptable or threatening feelings are repressed and then attributed to someone else. A person who is embarrassed about having sexual feelings toward members of a different ethnic group, for example, may project this discomfort onto them, saying, "Those people are dirty-minded and oversexed."

3 *Displacement* occurs when people direct their emotions (especially anger) toward things, animals, or other people that are not the real object of their feelings. A boy who is forbidden to express anger toward his father, for example, may "take it out" on his toys or his younger sister. When displacement serves a higher cultural or socially useful purpose, as in the creation of art or inventions, it is called *sublimation*. Freud argued that society has a duty to help people sublimate their unacceptable impulses for the sake of civilization. Sexual passion may be sublimated into the creation of art or literature; aggressive impulses, he believed, may be sublimated into competitive sports.

4 *Reaction formation* occurs when a feeling that produces unconscious anxiety is transformed into its opposite in consciousness. A woman who is afraid to admit to herself that she fears her husband may instead cling to the belief that she loves him deeply. A person who is aroused by erotic images may angrily assert that pornography is disgusting. How does such a transformed emotion differ from a true emotion? In reaction formation the professed feeling is excessive, and the person is extravagant and compulsive about demonstrating it: "Of course I love him! I *never* have any bad thoughts about him! He's perfect!"

5 *Regression* occurs when a person reverts to a previous phase of psychological development. An 8-year-old boy who is anxious about his parents' divorce may regress to earlier habits of thumb sucking or clinging. Adults may regress to immature behavior when they are under pressure—for example, by having temper tantrums if they don't get their way.

6 *Denial* occurs when people refuse to admit that something unpleasant is happening, such as mistreatment by a partner; that they have a problem, such as drinking too much; or that they are feeling a forbidden emotion, such as anger. Denial protects a person's self image and preserves the illusion of invulnerability: "It can't happen to me."

The Development of Personality. Freud thought that personality develops in a series of *psychosexual stages*, in which sexual energy takes different forms as the child matures. Each new stage produces a certain amount of frustration, conflict, and anxiety. If these are not resolved properly, normal development may be interrupted, and the child may remain *fixated*, or stuck, at the current stage.

For example, said Freud, some people remain fixated at the *oral stage*, the first year of life, when babies experience the world through their mouths. As adults, they will seek oral gratification in smoking, overeating, nail biting, or chewing on pencils; some may become clinging and dependent, like a nursing child. Others remain fixated at the *anal stage*, ages 2 to 3, when toilet training and control of bodily wastes are the key issues. They may become "anal retentive," holding everything in, obsessive about neatness and cleanliness. Or they may become just the opposite, "anal expulsive"—messy and disorganized.

For Freud, however, the most crucial stage for the formation of personality was the *phallic (Oedipal) stage*, which lasts roughly from age 3 to age 5 or 6. During this stage, said Freud, the child unconsciously wishes to possess the parent of the other sex and to get rid of the parent of the same sex. Children often announce proudly that "I'm going to marry Daddy (or Mommy) when I grow up," and they reject the same-sex "rival." Freud (1924a, 1924b) labeled this phenomenon the **Oedipus complex,** after the Greek legend of King Oedipus, who unwittingly killed his father and married his mother.

Boys and girls, Freud believed, go through the Oedipal stage differently. Boys are discovering the pleasure and pride of having a penis, so when they see a naked girl for the first time, they are horrified. Their unconscious exclaims (in effect), "Her penis has been cut off! Who could have done such a thing to her? Why, it must have been her powerful father. And if he could do it to her, my father could do it to me!" This realization, said Freud, causes the boy to repress his desire for his mother and identify with his father. He accepts his father's authority and the father's standards of conscience and morality; the superego has emerged.

A Freudian would say that this woman's smoking and nail-biting are signs of an oral fixation.

Freud admitted that he did not quite know what to make of girls, who, lacking the penis, could not go through the same steps. He speculated that a girl, upon discovering male anatomy, would panic that she had only a puny clitoris instead of a stately penis. She would conclude that she already had lost her penis. As a result, Freud said, girls do not have the powerful motivating fear that boys do to give up their Oedipal feelings and develop a strong superego; they have only a lingering sense of "penis envy."

Freud believed that when the Oedipus complex is resolved, at about age 5 or 6, the child's personality is fundamentally formed. Unconscious conflicts with parents, unresolved fixations and guilts, and attitudes toward the same and the other sex will continue to replay themselves throughout life. The child settles into a supposedly nonsexual *latency* stage, in preparation for the *genital* stage, which begins at puberty and leads to adult sexuality. (Modern research, however, shows that most "latency"-age children are curious about sex, and many masturbate or experiment with sexual play [Friedrich et al., 1998; Lamb, 2002]).

In Freud's view, then, your adult personality is shaped by how you progressed through the early psychosexual stages, which defense mechanisms you have adopted to reduce anxiety, and whether your ego is strong enough to balance the conflict between the id (what you would like to do) and the superego (your conscience).

As you might imagine, Freud's ideas were not exactly received with yawns. Sexual feelings in 5-year-olds! Repressed longings in respectable adults! Unconscious meanings in dreams! Penis envy! This was strong stuff in the early years of the twentieth century, and before long psychoanalysis had captured the public imagination in Europe and America. But it also produced a sharp rift with the emerging schools of empirical psychology (Hornstein, 1992).

This rift continues to divide psychologists and other scholars today. Some revere Freud as a hero who battled public censure and ridicule in his unwavering pursuit of truth (Gay, 1988). Others acknowledge that some of Freud's ideas have proved faulty, but they believe that the overall framework of his theory is timeless and brilliant (Westen, 1998). Still others think psychoanalytic theory is nonsense, with little empirical support (Cioffi, 1998). Citing evidence from papers suppressed in Freud's lifetime and for many years after his death, these critics argue that Freud was not the

Oedipus complex In psychoanalysis, a conflict occurring in the phallic (Oedipal) stage, in which a child desires the parent of the other sex and views the same-sex parent as a rival.

brilliant theoretician, impartial scientist, or even successful clinician that he claimed to be. On the contrary, Freud often bullied his patients into accepting his explanations of their symptoms, and he ignored all evidence disconfirming his ideas (Crews, 1998; Powell & Boer, 1995; Sulloway, 1992; Webster, 1995). In one famous case, he pressured an 18-year-old patient, "Dora" (Ida Bauer), to accept the unwanted sexual advances of one of her father's friends, attributing her "hysterical" refusal to her own supposedly repressed sexual desires. Dora angrily left treatment after three months (Lakoff & Coyne, 1993).

On the positive side, Freud welcomed women into the profession of psychoanalysis, wrote eloquently about the devastating results to women of society's suppression of their sexuality, and argued, ahead of his time, that homosexuality was neither a sin nor a perversion but a "variation of the sexual function" and "nothing to be ashamed of" (Freud, 1961). Freud was thus a mixture of intellectual vision and blindness, sensitivity, and arrogance. His provocative ideas left a powerful legacy to psychology—one that others began to tinker with immediately.

QUICK QUIZ

Have Freudian concepts registered in your unconscious?

Which Freudian concepts do the following events suggest?

1. A 4-year-old girl wants to snuggle on Daddy's lap but refuses to kiss her mother.
2. A celibate priest writes poetry about sexual passion.
3. A man who is angry at his boss shouts at his kids for making noise.
4. A woman whose father was cruel to her when she was little insists over and over that she loves him dearly.
5. A racist justifies segregation by saying that black men are only interested in sex with white women.
6. A 9-year-old boy who moves to a new city starts having tantrums.

Answers:

1. Oedipus complex 2. sublimation 3. displacement 4. reaction formation 5. projection 6. regression

---

Other Psychodynamic Approaches

Some of Freud's followers stayed in the psychoanalytic tradition and modified Freud's theories from within. Women, as you might imagine, were not too pleased about "penis envy." Clara Thompson (1943–1973) and Karen Horney [HORN-eye] (1926–1973) argued that it was insulting philosophy and bad science to claim that half the human race is dissatisfied with its anatomy. When women feel inferior to men, they said, we should look for explanations in the disadvantages that women live with and their second-class status. In fact, Horney added, if anyone has an envy problem, it is men. Men have "womb envy": They envy women's ability to bear children.

Others broke away from Freud, or were actively rejected by him, and went off to start their own schools. Today, there are many psychodynamic approaches, but two are especially popular: those of Carl Jung and of the object-relations theorists.

Jungian Theory. **Carl Jung** (1875–1961) was originally one of Freud's closest friends and a member of his inner circle. But the friendship ended over a furious quarrel about the nature of the unconscious. In addition to the individual's own unconscious, said Jung (1967), all human beings share a vast **collective unconscious**, containing universal memories, symbols, and images that are the legacy of human history. (Freud sneered at this notion, calling the collective

collective unconscious In Jungian theory, the universal memories and experiences of humankind, represented in the symbols, stories, and images (archetypes) that occur across all cultures.

unconscious a "black tide of mud" [Hayman, 2001]). Examining myths, art, and folklore in cultures around the world, Jung identified many common themes, which he called **archetypes**.

An archetype can be a picture, such as the "magic circle," called a *mandala* in Eastern religions, which Jung thought symbolizes the unity of life and "the totality of the self." Or it can be a figure found in fairy tales, legends, and popular stories, such as the Hero, the nurturing Earth Mother, the Powerful Father, or the Wicked Witch. It can even be an aspect of the self. For example, the *shadow* archetype reflects the prehistoric fear of wild animals and represents the bestial, evil side of human nature. Psychologists have found that some basic archetypes, such as the Hero and the Earth Mother, do appear in the stories and images of virtually every society, taking different forms (Campbell, 1949–1968; Neher, 1996). Jung would recognize dragons, Darth Vader, and Dracula as expressions of the shadow archetype.

Two of the most important archetypes, in Jung's view, are those of maleness and femaleness, which he believed existed in both sexes. The *anima* represents the feminine archetype in men; the *animus* represents the masculine archetype in women. Problems can arise, however, if a person tries to repress his or her internal, opposite archetype—that is, if a man totally denies his softer "feminine" side or if a woman denies her "masculine" aspects. People also create problems in relationships when they expect the partner to behave like the ideal archetypal man or woman, instead of a real human being who has both sides (Young-Eisendrath, 1993).

Although Jung shared with Freud a fascination with the darker aspects of the personality, he (along with other dissenters from Freudian orthodoxy) had confidence in the positive, forward-moving strengths of the ego. He believed that people are motivated not only by past conflicts, but also by their future goals and their desire to fulfill themselves. Jung was also among the first to identify extroversion/introversion as a basic dimension of personality. Nonetheless, many of Jung's ideas were more suited to mysticism and philosophy than to empirical psychology, which may be why so many Jungian ideas became popular with New Age movements.

Jung himself had a psychotic breakdown after his split with Freud. And he revealed his own "dark side" when he supported the Nazis, writing vicious attacks on Jews and claiming that their collective unconscious differed from that of gentiles (so much for its "universality"). But he continued to treat patients and attract many worshipful followers by virtue of his charisma. Like Freud, he was notorious for inflating his own reputation and creating myths about his own life and work (Hayman, 2001). Like Freud, therefore, Jung as an individual left a troubling personal legacy along with theories that attracted legions of believers.

The Object-Relations School. Freud essentially regarded the baby as if it were an independent, greedy little organism ruled by its own instinctive desires; other people were relevant only insofar as they gratified the infant's drives or blocked them. But by the 1950s, increased awareness of the importance of human attachments led to the emergence of the **object-relations school**, developed in Great Britain by Melanie Klein, D. W. Winnicott, and others.

To object-relations theorists, the central problem in life is to find a balance between the need for independence and the need for others. This balance requires constant adjustment to separations and losses: small ones that occur during quarrels, moderate ones such as leaving home for the first time, and major ones such as divorce or death. The way we react to these separations, according to object-relations analysts, is largely determined by our experiences in the first year or two of life.

In *The Wizard of Oz*, the Wicked Witch of the West is a beloved example of the archetype of evil.

archetypes [AR-ki-tipes] Universal, symbolic images that appear in myths, art, stories, and dreams; to Jungians, they reflect the collective unconscious.

object-relations school A psychodynamic approach that emphasizes the importance of the infant's first two years of life and the baby's formative relationships, especially with the mother.

According to object-relations theory, a baby constructs unconscious representations of his or her parents, which will influence the child's relations with others throughout life.

Whereas Freud emphasized the child's fear of the powerful father, object-relations analysts emphasize the child's need for the powerful mother, who is usually the baby's caregiver in the first critical years. Whereas Freud emphasized the gratification of inner impulses, object-relations theorists believe that the most important human drive is the need to be in relationships.

The reason for the clunky word "object" in object-relations, instead of the warmer words "human" or "parent," is that the infant's attachment is not only to a real person (usually the mother) but also to the infant's evolving perception of her. The child creates a *mental representation* of the mother—someone who is kind or fierce, protective or rejecting. The child's representations of important adults, whether realistic or distorted, unconsciously affect personality throughout life, influencing how the person relates to others: with trust or suspicion, acceptance or criticism (Westen, 1998).

The object-relations school also departs from Freudian theory regarding the nature of male and female development (Sagan, 1988; Winnicott, 1957/1990). In the object-relations view, children of both sexes identify first with the mother. Girls, who are the same sex as the mother, do not need to separate from her; the mother treats a daughter as an extension of herself. But boys, to develop a masculine identity, must break away from the mother; the mother encourages a son to be independent and separate. Thus, men develop more rigid boundaries between themselves and other people than women do.

The result, in the object-relations view, is that men tend to be less secure than women because their identity is based on *not* being like women. Later in life, the typical psychological problem for women is how to increase their autonomy and assert their own needs in close relationships. In contrast, the typical problem for men is how to permit close attachments (Gilligan, 1982). Some object-relations theorists believe that this gender difference is inevitable because women are biologically suited to be the primary nurturers. Others argue that if men played a greater role in nurturing infants and small children, the sex difference in the need for separation from the mother would fade, and so would men's need to be "opposite" from women (Chodorow, 1978, 1992).

Evaluating Psychodynamic Theories

Although modern psychodynamic theorists differ in many ways, they share a general belief that to understand personality we must explore its unconscious dynamics and origins. Genetics, learning, and culture may play some role, they say, but the crucial influences are the person's unconscious reactions to parents, to anatomical differences between the sexes, and to sexuality. Many psychologists in other fields, however, regard most psychodynamic ideas as literary metaphors rather than as scientific explanations (Cioffi, 1998; Crews, 1998). Critics argue that psychodynamic theories are guilty of three scientific failings:

THINKING CRITICALLY

Analyze Assumptions

Freud and his followers assumed they could derive general principles of personality by studying patients in therapy, that childhood traumas inevitably have lifelong emotional consequences, and that memories are reliable guides to the past. What's wrong with these assumptions?

1 *Violating the principle of falsifiability.* As we saw in Chapter 2, a theory that is impossible to disconfirm in principle is not scientific. Many psychodynamic concepts, however, are impossible to confirm or disconfirm. Followers of psychody-

namic approaches often accept an idea simply because it seems intuitively right or their experience seems to support it. Anyone who doubts the idea or offers disconfirming evidence is then accused of being "defensive" or "in denial." Freud himself often accused critics of his theory of lacking his own astute observational skills (Crews, 1998; Fancher, 1995). This way of dismissing criticism is neither scientific nor fair!

2 *Drawing universal principles from the experiences of a few atypical patients.* Freud and most of his followers generalized from a few individuals, often patients in therapy, to all human beings. Of course, the problem of overgeneralizing from small samples occurs in other areas of psychology too, and sometimes valid insights about human behavior can be obtained from case studies. The problem occurs when the observer fails to confirm these observations by studying other samples and incorrectly infers that what applies to some individuals applies to all.

3 *Basing theories of personality development on retrospective accounts and the fallible memories of patients.* Most psychodynamic theorists have not observed random samples of children at different ages, as modern child psychologists do, to construct their theories of development. Instead they have worked backward, creating theories based on themes in adults' recollections of childhood. The analysis of memories can be an illuminating way to achieve insights about our lives; in fact, it is the only way we can think about our own lives! But memory is often inaccurate, influenced as much by what is going on in our lives now as by what happened in the past (see Chapter 10). If you are currently not getting along with your mother, you may remember all the times when she was hard on you and forget the counterexamples of her kindness.

Retrospective analysis has another problem: It creates an *illusion of causality* between events. People often assume that if A came before B, then A must have caused B. For example, if your mother spent three months in the hospital when you were 5 years old and today you feel shy and insecure in college, an object-relations analyst would probably draw a connection between the two facts. But a lot of other things could be causing your shyness and insecurity, as we have already seen in this chapter: your temperament, your learning history, the norms of your culture, or a particular situation, such as going to a large and impersonal college. When psychologists conduct longitudinal studies, following people from childhood to adulthood, they often get a very different picture of causality from the one that emerges by looking backward (see Chapter 14).

Freud believed that little girls suffer from "penis envy," but empirical studies find that young children of both sexes are curious about, and often imagine having, the reproductive abilities of the other sex (Linday, 1994).

In response to these scientific concerns, some psychodynamic psychologists are turning to empirical methods and research findings to reformulate and refine their theories (Westen, 1998). Some psychodynamic ideas have in fact gained empirical support. Cognitive psychologists are identifying nonconscious processes in thought, memory, and behavior (Epstein, 1994; Kihlstrom, Barnhardt, & Tataryn, 1992). Others are finding support for the object-relations idea that we carry around "mental representations" of significant others (Blatt, Auerbach, & Levy, 1997). There is also evidence for many of the major defense mechanisms (Cramer, 2000). Reaction formation, projection, and denial do seem to operate unconsciously to protect self-esteem and reduce anxiety, and people certainly do "displace" aggressive feelings onto innocent bystanders (Baumeister, Dale, & Sommer, 1998; Marcus-Newhall et al., 2000).

More generally, modern research confirms the psychodynamic idea that people are often unaware of the motives behind their own puzzling or self-defeating actions. Some aspects of personality do, indeed, lie beyond conscious awareness.

QUICK QUIZ

Are you feeling defensive about answering this quiz?

A. An 8-year-old boy is behaving aggressively, hitting classmates and disobeying his teacher. Which of the following explanations of his behavior might come from a Freudian, Jungian, or object-relations analyst?

 1. The boy has repressed his *anima* archetype.

 2. The boy is expressing the aggressive energy of the id and has not developed enough ego control.

 3. The boy has had unusual difficulty separating from his mother and is compensating by behaving aggressively.

B. What criticism of all three of the preceding explanations might be made by a psychological scientist?

C. In the 1950s and 1960s, many psychoanalysts, observing unhappy gay men who had sought therapy, concluded that homosexuality was a mental illness. What violation of the scientific method were they committing?

Answers:

A. 1. Jung 2. Freud 3. object-relations analyst B. All three explanations are nonfalsifiable; that is, there is no way to disconfirm them or confirm them. They are just subjective interpretations. C. The analysts were drawing inappropriate conclusions from atypical patients in therapy, failing to test these conclusions with gay men who were not in therapy or with heterosexuals. When such research was done, using appropriate control groups, it turned out that gay men were not more mentally disturbed or depressed than heterosexuals (Hooker, 1957).

WHAT'S AHEAD ▶

- How does the humanist vision of human nature differ from the visions of behaviorism and psychoanalysis?
- In the humanist view, what's wrong with saying to a child, "I love you because you've been good"?

The Inner Experience

A final way to look at personality starts with the person's own view of him- or herself. Psychologists who take a *humanist* approach to personality emphasize our uniquely human capacity to shape our own futures. Biology may hand us temperamental dispositions that limit us, the environment may deal us some tough experiences, our parents may treat us as we would not have wished, but we have the free will to transcend these forces.

Humanist Approaches

Humanist psychology was launched as a movement in the early 1960s. The movement's chief leaders—Abraham Maslow (1908–1970), Carl Rogers (1902–1987), and Rollo May (1909–1994)—argued that it was time to replace psychoanalysis and behaviorism with a "third force" in psychology, one that would draw a fuller picture of human potential and personality.

Abraham Maslow. The trouble with psychology, said Maslow (1970, 1971), was that it had ignored many of the positive aspects of life, such as joy, laughter, love, happiness, and *peak experiences*, rare moments of rapture caused by the attainment of excellence or the experience of beauty. The traits that Maslow thought most important to personality were not the Big Five, but rather the qualities of the *self-actualized person*—the person who strives for a life that is meaningful, challenging, and satisfying.

Abraham Maslow regarded self-actualization as a lifelong process, one you are never too old to begin. Hulda Crooks, shown here at age 91 climbing Mt. Fuji, took up mountain climbing at 54. "It's been a great inspiration for me," she said. "When I come down from the mountain, I feel like I can battle in the valley again." She died at the age of 101.

For Maslow, personality development could be viewed as a gradual progression toward self-actualization. Most psychologists, he argued, had a lopsided view of human nature, a result of their emphasis on studying emotional problems and negative traits such as neuroticism or insecurity. As Maslow (1971) wrote, "When you select out for careful study very fine and healthy people, strong people, creative people . . . then you get a very different view of mankind. You are asking how tall can people grow, what can a human being become?"

Carl Rogers. Rogers, like Freud, derived many of his ideas from observing his clients in therapy. As a clinician, Rogers (1951, 1961) was interested not only in why some people cannot function well, but also in what he called the fully functioning individual. How you behave depends on your subjective reality, Rogers said, not on the external reality around you. Fully functioning people experience *congruence,* or harmony, between the image they project to others and their true feelings and wishes. They are trusting, warm, and open, rather than defensive or intolerant. Their beliefs about themselves are realistic.

To become fully functioning people, Rogers maintained, we all need **unconditional positive regard,** love and support for the people we are, without strings (conditions) attached. This doesn't mean that Charlene should be allowed to kick her brother when she is angry with him or that Wilbur may throw his dinner out the window because he doesn't like pot roast. In these cases, a parent can correct the child's behavior without withdrawing love from the child. The child can learn that the behavior, not the child, is what is bad. "House rules are 'no violence,' Charlene," is a very different message from "You are a horrible person, Charlene."

Unfortunately, Rogers observed, many children are raised with *conditional* positive regard: "I will love you if you behave well, and I won't love you if you behave badly." Adults often treat each other this way, too. People treated with conditional regard begin to suppress or deny feelings or actions that they believe are unacceptable to those they love. The result, said Rogers, is incongruence, a sense of being out of touch with your feelings, of not being true to your "real self," which in turn produces low self-regard, defensiveness, and unhappiness. A person experiencing incongruence scores high on neuroticism, becoming bitter and negative.

Rollo May. May shared with the humanists a belief in free will and freedom of choice. But he also emphasized some of the inherently difficult and tragic aspects of the human condition, including loneliness, anxiety, and alienation. In books such as *Love and Will* and *The Meaning of Anxiety,* May brought to American psychology elements of the European philosophy of *existentialism.* This doctrine holds that free will confers on us responsibility for our actions. But freedom, and its burden of accountability, carries a price in anxiety and despair. This is why so many people try to escape from freedom into narrow certainties and blame others for their misfortunes. For May, our personalities reflect the ways we cope with the inevitable struggles of life: to find meaning in existence, to use our freedom wisely, and to face suffering and death bravely. May popularized the humanist idea that we can choose to make the best of ourselves by drawing on inner resources such as love and courage, but he added that we can never escape the harsh realities of life and loss.

Evaluating Humanist Theories

As with psychodynamic theories, the major criticism of humanist psychology is that many of its assumptions are untestable. Freud looked at humanity and saw destructive drives, selfishness, and lust. Maslow and Rogers looked at humanity and saw cooperation, selflessness, and love. May looked at humanity and saw fear of freedom, loneliness, and the struggle for meaning. These differences, say critics, may tell us more about the observers than about the observed.

humanist psychology A psychological approach that emphasizes personal growth, resilience, and the achievement of human potential.

unconditional positive regard To Carl Rogers, love or support given to another person with no conditions attached.

Existential psychologists remind us of the inevitable struggles of human existence, such as the fight against loneliness and alienation.

THINKING CRITICALLY

Define Your Terms

Unconditional positive regard sounds like a good thing, but what does it mean, exactly? Does it mean giving loved ones your total support and approval, no matter what they do? Does it permit setting limits and offering constructive criticism?

Many humanist concepts, although intuitively appealing, are hard to define operationally (see Chapter 2). How can we know whether a person is self-fulfilled or self-actualized? How can we tell whether a woman's decision to quit her job and become a professional rodeo rider represents an "escape from freedom" or a freely made choice? And what exactly is unconditional positive regard? If it is defined as unquestioned support of a child's efforts at mastering a new skill, or as assurance that the child is loved in spite of his or her mistakes, then it is clearly a good idea. But in the popular culture, it has often been interpreted as an unwillingness ever to say "no" to a child, or to offer constructive criticism and set limits, which children need.

Despite such concerns, humanist psychologists have added balance to the study of personality. Influenced in part by the humanists, psychologists are studying many positive human traits, such as courage, helpfulness to others, the motivation to excel, and self-confidence; as we saw in Chapter 1, humanists are the intellectual forebears of the "positive psychology" movement today. Stress researchers have discovered the healing powers of humor and hope. Developmental psychologists are studying ways to foster children's empathy and creativity. And some researchers are studying the emotional effects of fear of death. When people are made aware of death, they resort not only to conscious efforts to suppress frightening thoughts, but also to nonconscious defenses to make themselves feel better and safer and their lives more meaningful (Pyszczynski, Greenberg, & Solomon, 2000).

Finally, the existential argument that we have the power to choose our own destinies, even when fate delivers us into tragedy, has fostered a new appreciation of human resilience in the face of adversity.

QUICK QUIZ

Exercise free will by choosing to take this quiz.

1. According to Carl Rogers, a man who loves his wife only when she is looking her best is giving her positive regard that is (a) conditional or (b) unconditional.

2. The humanist who described the importance of having peak experiences was (a) Abraham Maslow, (b) Rollo May, (c) Carl Rogers.

 3. A humanist and a Freudian psychoanalyst are arguing about human nature. What underlying assumptions about psychology and human potential are they likely to bring to their discussion? How can they resolve their differences without either-or thinking?

Answers:

1. a 2. a 3. The Freudian assumes that human nature is basically selfish and destructive; the humanist, that it is basically loving and life-affirming. They can resolve this either-or debate by recognizing that human beings have both capacities; the situation and culture often determine which capacity is expressed at a given time.

Now that you have read about the major influences on personality (see Review 13.1), how would you "explain" Madonna? Some aspects of her character and temperament, such as extroversion and conscientiousness, seem likely to have a genetic component. Her personality was perhaps also shaped, however, by unique experiences in her childhood and young adulthood that were not shared with her siblings: having the opportunity to take dance classes, later taking a chance and running away to New York. Madonna's chameleon-like "persona," which changes every couple of years, is further shaped and rewarded by today's postmodern culture, which values image over reality, transience over permanence, style over substance, celebrity over obscurity. Psychodynamic theorists might wonder whether Madonna's unconscious

REVIEW 13.1 — THE MAJOR INFLUENCES ON PERSONALITY

	Genetic Influences	Children are born with particular temperaments and most traits are highly influenced by genes.
Experience	**Environmental Influences**	Learning, situations, and unique experiences affect which traits are encouraged and expressed.
	Parents	Modify and shape a child's temperament and genetic pre-dispositions; affect gender roles, attitudes, self-concept; affect the quality of the relationship with the child.
	Peer group	Influences an individual's values, behavior, ambitions, goals, etc.
	Situation	Determines which behaviors are rewarded and which are punished or ignored, thereby shaping the expression or suppression of particular traits.
	Chance events	May influence a person's experiences and choices in unexpected ways, thus encouraging the development of some traits over others.
	Cultural Influences	Cultural norms specify which traits are valued; affect basic notions of the "self" and "personality"; and shape behaviors, from aggressiveness to altruism.
	Psychodynamic Influences	Unconscious dynamics shape human motives, guilts, conflicts, and defenses.
	Humanist Approaches	Despite genetic, environmental, cultural, and psychodynamic influences, people can exercise free will to determine the kind of person they will become.

motivations for success and her constant changing of public personalities stem from the shock of losing her mother when she was only 6; Madonna was her mother's first name, too. And humanists might remind us that we do not know anything about the real Madonna, because the faces she presents to the public might reveal nothing at all about her inner, private self.

Each of us weaves the many dimensions of personality together in the narratives we tell to explain our lives, our inconsistencies across situations, and our failures and successes—to explain, in short, why we are the way we are. Genetic influences, learned habits, cultural norms, unconscious fears and conflicts, and visions of possibility, filtered through our interior sense of self and our life story, give each of us the stamp of our personality, the qualities that make us feel uniquely . . . us.

Taking Psychology with You

GRAPHOLOGY, HOROSCOPES, AND THE "BARNUM EFFECT"

How well does the following paragraph describe you?

Some of your aspirations tend to be pretty unrealistic. At times you are extroverted, affable, sociable, while at other times you are introverted, wary, and reserved. You pride yourself on being an independent thinker and do not accept others' opinions without satisfactory proof. You prefer a certain amount of change and variety, and you become dissatisfied when hemmed in by restrictions and limitations. At times you have serious doubts as to whether you have made the right decision or done the right thing.

When people believe that this description was written just for them, as the result of a personalized horoscope or handwriting analysis, they all say the same thing: "It's me! It describes me *exactly*!" The reason that everyone thinks this description is accurate is that it is vague enough to apply to almost everyone, and it is flattering (don't we all consider ourselves to be "independent thinkers"?).

This is why many psychologists worry about the "Barnum effect" (Snyder & Shenkel, 1975). P. T. Barnum was the great circus showman who said, "There's a sucker born every minute." He knew that the formula for success was to "have a little something for everybody"—and that is just what unscientific personality profiles, horoscopes, and handwriting analysis (graphology) have in common. They have "a little something for everyone" and hence are nonfalsifiable.

For example, graphologists claim that they can identify your personality traits from the form and distribution of your handwritten letters (Beyerstein,

1996). Wide spacing between words means you feel isolated and lonely. If you crowd your words together, you are desperate for companionship. If your lines drift upward, you are an "uplifting" optimist, and if your lines droop downward, you are a pessimist who feels you are being "dragged down." If you make large capital I's, you have a large ego.

Graphologists are not the same as handwriting experts, who are trained to determine, say, whether a document was really written by Hitler or is a forgery. Graphologists usually know little or nothing about the scientific method, how to correct for biases, or how to empirically test their claims. There are more than 30 graphological societies in the United States alone, and their methods often conflict. For example, according to one system, a certain way of crossing T's reveals someone who is vicious and sadistic; according to another, it reveals a practical joker (Beyerstein, 1996).

Whenever graphology has been tested empirically, it has failed. A meta-analysis of 200 published studies found no validity or reliability to graphology in predicting work performance, aptitudes, or personality. No school of graphology fared better than any other, and no graphologist was able to perform better than untrained amateurs making guesses (Dean, 1992; Klimoski, 1992).

If graphology were just an amusing game, no one would worry about it, but unfortunately it can have harmful consequences. Graphologists have been hired by companies to predict a person's leadership ability, attention to detail, willingness to be a good team player, and more. They pass judgment on people's honesty, generosity, jealousy, and

even criminal tendencies (Beyerstein, 1996). How would you feel if you were turned down for a job because some graphologist said your handwriting indicated you might become violent?

If you do not want to be taken in by graphology or the many other methods that rely on the Barnum effect, research offers this advice:

▶ *Beware of all-purpose descriptions that could apply to anyone.* Sometimes you doubt your decisions; who among us has not? Sometimes you feel outgoing and sometimes shy; who does not? Do you "have sexual secrets that you are afraid of confessing"? Of course you do. Such secrets are very common.

▶ *Beware of your own selective perceptions.* Most of us are so impressed when an astrologer, psychic, or graphologist gets something right that we overlook all the descriptions that are plain wrong. Be aware of the confirmation bias—the tendency to "explain away" anything that doesn't confirm your own impression of yourself.

▶ *Resist flattery.* This is a hard one! It is easy to reject a profile that describes you as selfish or stupid. Watch out for the ones that tell you how wonderful and smart you are, what a great leader you will be, or how modest you are about your abilities.

If you keep your critical faculties with you, you won't end up paying hard cash for soft answers, pawning the piano because Geminis should invest in gold this month, or taking a job you despise because it fits your "personality type." In other words, you'll have proved Barnum wrong.

Summary

▶ *Personality* refers to an individual's distinctive and relatively stable pattern of behavior, motives, thoughts, and emotions. Personality is made up of many different *traits,* characteristics that describe a person across situations.

Measuring Personality

▶ Most popular tests that divide personality into "types" are not valid or reliable. In research, psychologists typically rely on *objective tests* (*inventories*), such as the Beck Depression Inventory, the Minnesota Multiphasic Personality Inventory, or the Multidimensional Personality Questionnaire, to identify and study personality traits and disorders.

▶ Gordon Allport argued that people have a few *central traits* that are key to their personalities, and a greater number of *secondary traits* that are less fundamental. Raymond Cattell used *factor analysis* to identify clusters of traits that he considered the basic components of personality. Today there is strong evidence for the *Big Five* dimensions of personality: extroversion, neuroticism (negative emotionality), agreeableness, conscientiousness, and openness to experience. Although these traits are quite stable over time and across circumstances, some of them do change over the life span, reflecting maturational development.

Genetic Influences on Personality

▶ Individual differences in *temperaments*—ways of reacting to the environment—appear to be inborn, emerging early in life and influencing subsequent personality development. Temperamental differences in extremely reactive and nonreactive children may be due to variations in the responsiveness of the sympathetic nervous system to change and novelty. Experience can help extremely shy children become less shy and timid in new situations, but it cannot make them extroverts.

▶ Behavioral-genetic data from twin and adoption studies suggest that the *heritability* of many adult personality traits is around .50. But genes tell only half the story; the environment tells the rest.

Environmental Influences on Personality

▶ Learning theorists have studied how parents, peers, and specific situations influence the development of personality. Three lines of evidence challenge the popular assumption that parents have the greatest impact: (1) Behavioral-genetic studies find that shared family environment has little if any influence on personality; (2) few parents have a consistent child-rearing style over time and with all their children; and (3) even when parents try to be consistent, there may be little relation between what they do and how the children turn out. However, parents can modify their children's temperaments, prevent children at risk of delinquency and crime from choosing a path of antisocial behavior, influence many of their children's values and attitudes, and teach them to be kind and helpful. And of course parents profoundly affect the quality of their relationship with their children.

▶ Once children leave home, starting in preschool, parental influence on children's behavior outside the home begins to wane and the influence of the *nonshared environment* takes over. One major outside influence is the peer group. Most children and teenagers behave differently with their parents than with their peers.

▶ People often behave inconsistently in different circumstances because behaviors that are rewarded in one situation may be punished or ignored in another. According to social-cognitive learning theorists, personality results from the interaction of aspects of the environment and aspects of the individual, in a pattern of *reciprocal determinism.*

▶ The nature–nurture debate can be resolved by understanding that neither influence alone "determines" personality. Genetic influences create dispositions and set limits on the expression of specific traits. But even traits that are highly heritable are often modified throughout life by circumstances, chance, and learning.

Cultural Influences on Personality

▶ Many qualities that Western psychologists treat as individual personality traits are heavily influenced by *culture.* Events in the larger society or culture, such as war or changes in the divorce rate, can affect aspects of personality, such as people's sense of control over their lives and their levels of anxiety (neuroticism).

▶ People from *individualist cultures* define themselves in different terms than those from *collectivist cultures,* and they perceive their "selves" as more stable across situations. People from *monochronic cultures* are more concerned with punctuality and doing things "one at a time" than are people from *polychronic cultures,* who value relationships above time schedules. Men in *cultures of honor* are more likely to become angry when they feel insulted and to behave aggressively to restore their sense of honor than are men from other cultures. Altruistic children tend to come from cultures in which their families assign them many tasks that contribute to the family's well-being or economic survival.

▶ Cultural theories of personality face the problem of describing broad cultural differences and their influences on personality without promoting stereotypes or overlooking universal human needs.

Psychodynamic Influences on Personality

▶ Sigmund Freud was the founder of *psychoanalysis,* which was the first *psychodynamic* theory. Modern psychodynamic theories share an emphasis on *intrapsychic* processes and a belief in the formative role of childhood experiences and early, unconscious conflicts.

▶ To Freud, the personality consists of the *id* (the source of sexual energy, which he called the *libido,* and the aggressive instinct); the *ego* (the source of reason); and the *superego* (the source of conscience). *Defense mechanisms* protect the ego from unconscious anxiety. They include, among others, repression, projection, displacement (one form of which is sublimation), reaction formation, regression, and denial.

▶ Freud believed that personality develops in a series of *psychosexual stages,* with the *phallic (Oedipal) stage* the most crucial. During this stage, Freud believed, the *Oedipus complex* occurs, in which the child desires the parent of the other sex and feels rivalry with the same-sex parent. When the Oedipus complex is resolved, the child identifies with the same-sex parent, but females retain a lingering sense of inferiority and "penis envy"—a notion later contested by female psychoanalysts like Clara Thompson and Karen Horney.

▶ Carl Jung believed that people share a *collective unconscious* that contains universal memories and images, or *archetypes.* Personality, in this view, includes many archetypes, such as the shadow (evil) and the anima and animus.

▶ The *object-relations school* emphasizes the importance of the first two years of life, rather than the Oedipal phase; the infant's relationships to important figures, especially the mother, rather than sexual needs and drives; and the problem in male development of breaking away from the mother.

▶ Psychodynamic approaches have been criticized for violating the principle of falsifiability; for overgeneralizing from atypical patients to everyone; and for basing theories on the unreliable memories and retrospective accounts of patients, which can create an *illusion of causality.* However, some psychodynamic ideas have received empirical support, including the existence of nonconscious processes, mental representations, and defenses.

The Inner Experience

▶ *Humanist psychologists* focus on a person's subjective sense of self and free will to change. They emphasize human potential and the strengths of human nature, as in Abraham Maslow's concepts of *peak experiences* and *self-actualization.* Carl Rogers stressed the importance of *unconditional positive regard* in creating a "fully functioning" person. Rollo May brought *existentialism* into psychology, emphasizing some of the inherent challenges of human existence that result from having free will, such as the search for meaning in life.

▶ Many ideas from humanist psychology are subjective and difficult to measure, but the field has fostered research on many positive aspects of personality, including resilience, empathy, humor, and hope.

▶ Genetic influences, learned habits, idiosyncratic experiences, cultural norms, unconscious fears and conflicts, and our private sense of the "inner self" all combine in complex ways to create our distinctive personalities.

Key Terms

personality 465

trait 465

projective tests 467

objective tests (inventories) 467

Gordon Allport 467

central and secondary traits 468

Raymond Cattell 468

factor analysis 468

the "Big Five" personality traits 468

temperament 471

heritability 473

shared environment 475

nonshared environment 475

reciprocal determinism 478

culture 480

individualist versus collectivist cultures 482

monochronic versus polychronic cultures 483

culture of honor 483

Sigmund Freud 486

LOOKING BACK

- How reliable are those tests that tell you what "personality type" you are? (p. 467)

- How can psychologists tell which personality traits are more central or important than others? (p. 468)

- Which five dimensions of personality seem to describe people the world over? (p. 468)

- Is it possible to be born irritable or easygoing? (p. 471)

- Do you have to be a person to have a personality? (p. 471)

- To what extent are personality differences among people influenced by their genetic differences? (p. 473)

- Are people who have highly heritable personality traits stuck with them forever? (p. 473)

- How much can parents shape their children's personalities? (pp. 475–476)

- How consistent is your personality across situations? (pp. 477–478)

- Why are risk-taking and punctuality more than just individual personality traits? (p. 480)

- How does belonging to an individualist or collectivist culture influence your personality—and even whether you think you have a stable "self"? (p. 482)

- Why are men in the South and West more likely to get angry at personal insults than other American men are? (pp. 483–484)

- What cultural practices affect the traits of altruism or selfishness? (p. 484)

- How do psychologists regard Freud today—as a genius or a fraud? (pp. 486–487)

- In Freud's theory of personality, why are the id and the superego always at war? (p. 487)

- When people say you're being "defensive," what defenses might they be thinking of? (pp. 487–488)

- What would Carl Jung have had to say about Darth Vader? (p. 491)

- What are the "objects" in the object-relations approach to personality? (p. 492)

- How does the humanist vision of human nature differ from the visions of behaviorism and psychoanalysis? (p. 494)

- In the humanist view, what's wrong with saying to a child, "I love you because you've been good"? (p. 495)

Go to *Live! psych* **WWW.PRENHALL.COM/WADE to reinforce this key concept, and more.**

13.1 Heredity and personality

14

Development over the Life Span

Time is a dressmaker specializing in alterations.

FAITH BALDWIN

A few years ago, a 63-year-old woman gave birth to a healthy baby girl. The child was conceived through in vitro fertilization, with sperm from the woman's 60-year-old husband and an egg donated by a younger woman. The woman and her family were delighted, but some fertility experts and ethicists had misgivings. Dr. Mark Sauer, who pioneered the use of donor eggs in older women, said, "I lose my comfort level after 55 because I have to believe that there are quality-of-life issues involved in raising a child at [the parent's] age. When [the baby] is 5, her mother will be 68. And I have to believe that a 78-year-old dealing with a teenager may have some problems."

How do *you* react to the idea of a 63-year-old woman having a baby? Would it make any difference if the mother were "only" 55 years old, or 50, or 45? How do you feel about a man fathering a baby when he is in his 70s or 80s? Do you feel the same about older fathers as you do about older mothers? Is there a "right" time to become a parent? For that matter, is there a right time to do anything in life—go to school, get married, retire, . . . die?

During the first half of the twentieth century, the answer would have been a resounding *yes*. Most people shared a common life trajectory that seemed to fall into distinct stages. Childhood consisted of "formative" years that determined what kind of adult the child would become. Adolescence, the years between the physical changes of puberty and the social markers of adulthood, became longer and longer, defined by turmoil and turbulence. Adulthood was conceptualized as a series of steps from marriage to parenthood to retirement. Elderly people were increasingly separated from the rest of society on the grounds that they could not keep up with the fast-moving world.

Today we are undergoing another revolution in the way we think about the universal human journey from birth to death. Because of improvements in health care, a changing economy, a high divorce rate, and advances in reproductive technology, events over the life span are no longer as predictable as they were just a few decades ago. Millions of people are doing things out of order, if at all.

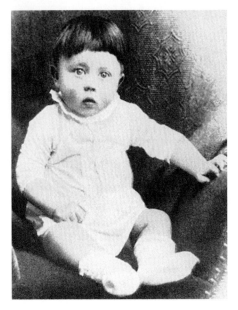

Development depends on the genetic hand you are dealt at birth, the resources and opportunities your parents provide for you, experiences that happen to you, and the unexpected events of history. What futures might you imagine for these three children? Later in this chapter, you'll see who they are.

Developmental psychologists study physiological and cognitive changes across the life span, and how these are affected by culture, circumstance, and experience. Some focus on children's mental and social development, including **socialization,** the process by which children learn the rules and behavior expected of them by society. Others specialize in the study of adolescents, adults, or aging. In this chapter, we will explore some of their major findings, starting at the very beginning of human development, with the period from conception to birth, and continuing through adulthood into old age.

WHAT'S AHEAD

- **How can a pregnant woman reduce the risk of damage to the embryo or fetus?**
- **Given a choice, what do newborns prefer to look at?**
- **Does culture affect when and whether a baby learns to crawl?**
- **Why is cuddling so important for infants (not to mention adults)?**
- **If you have a 1-year-old, why shouldn't you worry if your baby cries when left with a new baby-sitter?**
- **Do the experiences of the first years of life affect a child's brain forever?**

From Conception Through the First Year

A baby's development, before and after birth, is a marvel of *maturation,* the sequential unfolding of genetically influenced behavior and physical characteristics. In only 9 months of a mother's pregnancy, a cell grows from a dot this big (.) to a squalling bundle of energy who looks just like Aunt Sarah. In another 15 months, that bundle of energy grows into a babbling toddler who is curious about everything. No other time in human development brings so many changes, so fast.

socialization The processes by which children learn the behaviors, attitudes, and expectations required of them by their society or culture.

Prenatal Development

Prenatal development is divided into three stages: the germinal, the embryonic, and the fetal. The *germinal stage* begins at conception, when the male sperm unites with the female ovum (egg); the fertilized single-celled egg is called a *zygote*. The zygote soon begins to divide, and in 10 to 14 days it has become a cluster of cells that attaches itself to the wall of the uterus. The outer portion of this cluster will form part of the placenta and umbilical cord, and the inner portion becomes the embryo. The placenta, connected to the embryo by the umbilical cord, serves as the growing embryo's link for food from the mother. It allows nutrients to enter and wastes to exit, and it screens out some, but not all, harmful substances.

Once implantation is completed, about two weeks after conception, the *embryonic stage* begins, lasting until the eighth week after conception, at which point the embryo is only 1½ inches long. During the fourth to eighth week, the hormone testosterone is secreted by the rudimentary testes in embryos that are genetically male; without this hormone, the embryo will develop to be anatomically female. After eight weeks, the *fetal stage* begins. The organism, now called a *fetus*, further develops the organs and systems that existed in rudimentary form in the embryonic stage. The greatest gains in brain and nervous system development occur during the last 12 weeks of a full-term pregnancy.

Although the womb is a fairly sturdy protector of the growing embryo or fetus, some harmful influences can cross the placental barrier (O'Rahilly & Müller, 2001). These influences include the following:

1 *German measles* (rubella), especially early in the pregnancy, can affect the fetus's eyes, ears, and heart. The most common consequence is deafness. Rubella is preventable if the mother has been vaccinated, which can be done up to three months before pregnancy.

2 *X-rays or other radiation and toxic chemicals* such as lead can cause fetal abnormalities and deformities. Exposure to lead is also associated with attention problems and lower IQ scores.

3 *Sexually transmitted diseases* can cause mental retardation, blindness, and other physical disorders. Genital herpes affects the fetus only if the mother has an outbreak at the time of delivery, which exposes the newborn to the virus as the baby passes through the birth canal. (This risk can be avoided by having a cesarean section.) HIV, the virus that causes AIDS, can also be transmitted to the fetus, especially if the mother has developed AIDS and has not been treated.

4 *Cigarette smoking* during pregnancy increases the likelihood of miscarriage, premature birth, abnormal fetal heartbeat, and an underweight baby. The negative

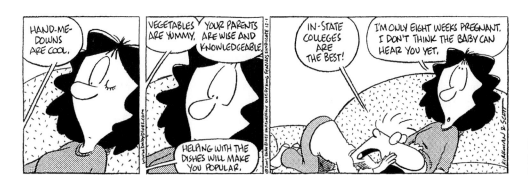

Many parents hope they can have a positive influence on their offspring even before their children are born!

effects may last long after birth, showing up in increased rates of infant sickness, sudden infant death syndrome (SIDS), and, in later childhood, hyperactivity and learning difficulties. Cigarette smoking is actually more dangerous to the fetus than cocaine use (Slotkin, 1998).

5 *Having more than two alcoholic drinks every day* significantly increases the risk of a baby's having *fetal alcohol syndrome (FAS)*. FAS infants are smaller than normal and have smaller brains, have facial deformities, are uncoordinated, and are mentally retarded; in fact, FAS is the leading cause of nonhereditary mental retardation. Even when babies do not have FAS itself, binge drinking and drinking regularly throughout pregnancy can kill neurons throughout the fetus's developing brain and impair babies' later mental abilities, attention span, and academic achievement (Ikonomidou et al., 2000; Streissguth et al., 1999). The consequences of lighter drinking—one drink on rare occasions—are not as clear. But because alcohol can affect many different aspects of fetal brain development, most specialists recommend that a pregnant woman abstain completely, to be safe.

6 *Drugs other than alcohol* can be harmful to the fetus, whether they are illicit ones such as morphine, cocaine, and heroin, or commonly used legal substances such as antibiotics, antihistamines, tranquilizers, acne medication, and diet pills. Fathers' drug use can also cause fetal defects; cocaine, for example, does so by binding to sperm (Yazigi, Odem, & Polakoski, 1991). Longitudinal studies of children exposed to cocaine in the womb have dispelled the myth of the "crack baby" who is supposedly brain damaged for life (Newman & Buka, 1991). Nonetheless, cocaine can cause small, subtle impairments in children's cognitive and language abilities (Lester, LaGasse, & Seifer, 1998).

The lesson is clear. A pregnant woman does well to stop smoking and drinking alcohol, and to take no other drugs of any kind unless they are medically necessary and have been adequately tested for safety—and then to accept the fact that her child will never be properly grateful for all that sacrifice!

The Infant's World

Newborn babies could never survive on their own, but they are far from being passive and inert. Many abilities, tendencies, and characteristics are universal in human beings and are present at birth or develop very early, given certain experiences.

Physical Abilities. Newborns begin life with several automatic *motor reflexes* (see Table 14.1). They will grasp tightly a finger pressed on their tiny palms. They will turn their heads toward a touch on the cheek or corner of the mouth and search for something to suck on, a handy "rooting reflex" that allows them to find the breast or bottle. Many of these reflexes eventually disappear, but others—such as the knee-jerk, eye-blink, and sneeze reflexes—remain.

Babies are also equipped with a set of inborn perceptual abilities. They can see, hear, touch, smell, and taste (bananas and sugar water are in, rotten eggs are out). A newborn's visual focus range is only about 8 inches, the average distance between the baby and the face of the person holding the baby, but visual ability develops rapidly. Newborns open their eyes wide to investigate what is around them, even in the dark. They can distinguish contrasts, shadows, and edges. They can discriminate their mother or other primary caregiver on the basis of smell, sight, or sound almost immediately. Within a couple of months, they show evidence of depth perception (see Chapter 6).

Social Skills. Newborns are sociable from the start. At birth, they are primed to respond to human faces. Babies who are only *9 minutes old* will turn their heads

Table 14.1	Reflexes of the Newborn Baby

Reflex	Description
Rooting	An infant touched on the cheek or the corner of the mouth will turn toward the touch and search for something to suck on.
Sucking	An infant will suck on anything suckable, such as a nipple or finger.
Swallowing	An infant can swallow, though this reflex is not yet well coordinated with breathing.
Moro or "startle"	In response to a loud noise or a physical shock, an infant will throw its arms outward and arch back.
Babinski	In response to a touch on the bottom of the foot, the infant's toes will splay outward and then curl in. (In adults, the toes just curl in.)
Grasp	In response to a touch on the palm of the hand, an infant will grasp.
Stepping	If held so that the feet just touch the ground, an infant will show "walking" movements, alternating the feet in steps.

to watch a drawing of a face if it moves in front of them, but they will not turn if the "face" consists of scrambled features or is only the outline of a face (Goren, Sarty, & Wu, 1975; Johnson et al., 1991). By the age of 4 to 6 weeks, babies are smiling regularly, even though they haven't the foggiest notion of whom they are smiling at.

Babies also have rudimentary "conversations" with those who tend them, even without words. Like many social exchanges, a baby's first "conversation" with the mother or primary caregiver often takes place over a good meal: During nursing, babies and their mothers often play little games with each other, exchanging nonverbal signals in a rhythmic pattern. This rhythmic dialogue illustrates a crucial aspect of all human exchanges: *synchrony*, the adjustment of one person's nonverbal behavior to coordinate with another's (Bernieri et al., 1994; Jaffe et al., 2001). Just as adults unconsciously modify their rhythms of speech and gestures to be "in sync" with those of a person they are speaking to, newborns and infants synchronize their behavior and attention to adult speech but not to other sounds, such as street noise or tapping. Parents in turn coordinate their movements and rhythms with those of their baby.

Culture and Maturation. Although infants everywhere develop according to the same maturational sequence, many aspects of their development depend on cultural customs that govern how their parents hold, touch, feed, and talk to them (Super & Harkness, 1994). For example, in the United States, babies are expected to sleep for eight uninterrupted hours by the age of 4 or 5 months. This milestone

This mother and baby, exchanging giggles, facial expressions, and coos, illustrate synchrony in action.

Most Navaho babies calmly accept being strapped to a cradle board (left), whereas white babies will often protest vigorously (right). Yet despite cultural differences in such practices, babies everywhere eventually sit up and walk.

is considered a sign of neurological maturity, although many babies wail when the parent puts them in the crib at night and leaves the room. But among Mayan Indians, rural Italians, African villagers, and urban Japanese, this nightly clash of wills never occurs because the infant sleeps with the mother for the first few years of life, waking and nursing about every four hours. These differences in babies' sleep arrangements reflect cultural and parental values. Mayan mothers believe it is important to sleep with the baby in order to forge a close bond with the child; many North American and German parents believe it is important to foster the child's independence as soon as possible (Kagan, 1998b; Morelli et al., 1992).

Developmental "milestones" can change quickly when there is a cultural change in baby-care practices. For example, the milestone for crawling has traditionally been about 6 to 8 months. Nowadays, however, many babies do not begin crawling at that age, or even at all; they go directly from sitting to toddling. Why? Traditionally, in the United States and England, most babies were put to sleep on their stomachs. From that position, a little squirming and a push-up led to crawling. But for the last 10 years, physicians have been advising parents to put babies on their backs to sleep, to avoid the risk of suffocation. In that position, it is more difficult for a baby to roll over and start crawling, and more and more babies never do. Yet they are perfectly normal by every other measure (Davis et al., 1998). And they all eventually get up and walk.

Attachment

Emotional attachment is a universal capacity of all primates and is crucial for health and survival all through life. The mother is usually the first, primary object of attachment for an infant, but in many cultures (and other species), babies become just as attached to their fathers, siblings, and grandparents (Hrdy, 1999). By becoming attached to their caregivers, children gain a secure base from which they can explore the environment and a haven of safety to return to when they are afraid (Bowlby, 1969).

Contact Comfort. Attachment begins with physical touching and cuddling between infant and parent. **Contact comfort**, the pleasure of being touched and held, is important throughout life. Adults who are "undertouched," such as the sick and the aged, suffer emotional and physical symptoms. In hospital settings, even the mildest touch by a nurse or physician on the patient's arm or forehead reassures and comforts (Field, 1998).

Margaret and Harry Harlow first demonstrated the importance of contact comfort by raising infant rhesus monkeys with two kinds of artificial mothers (Harlow, 1958; Harlow & Harlow, 1966). The "wire mother" was a forbidding construction of wires and warming lights, with a milk bottle connected to it. The "cloth mother" was also made of wire, but was covered in foam rubber and cuddly terry cloth (see Figure 14.1). At the time, psychologists thought that babies become attached to their mothers because mothers provide food and warmth. But the Harlows' baby monkeys ran to the terry-cloth "mother" when they were frightened or startled, and cuddling up to it calmed them down. Human children, too, often seek contact comfort when they are in an unfamiliar situation, are scared by a nightmare, or fall and hurt themselves.

Separation and Security. Once babies are emotionally attached to the mother or other caregiver, separation can be a wrenching experience. Between 6 and 8 months of age, babies become wary or fearful of strangers. They wail if they are put in an unfamiliar setting or are left with an unfamiliar person. And they show **separation anxiety** if the primary caregiver temporarily leaves them. This reaction usually con-

contact comfort In primates, the innate pleasure derived from close physical contact; it is the basis of the infant's first attachment.

separation anxiety The distress that most children develop, at about 6 to 8 months of age, when their primary caregivers temporarily leave them with strangers.

Figure 14.1
THE COMFORT OF CONTACT

Infants need cuddling as much as they need food. In Margaret and Harry Harlow's studies, infant rhesus monkeys were reared with a cuddly terry-cloth "mother" and with a bare wire "mother" that provided milk (left). The infants would cling to the terry mother when they were not being fed, and when they were frightened (as by a toy spider, right), it was the terry mother they ran to.

tinues until the middle of the second year, but many children show signs of distress until they are about 3 years old (Hrdy, 1999). All children go through this phase, though cultural child-rearing practices influence how strongly the anxiety is felt and how long it lasts (see Figure 14.2). In cultures where babies are raised with lots of adults and other children, separation anxiety is not as intense or as long-lasting as it can be in countries like Japan, where babies form attachments primarily or exclusively with the mother (Rothbaum et al., 2000).

To determine the nature of the attachment between mothers and babies, Mary Ainsworth (1973, 1979) devised an experimental method called the *Strange Situation*. A mother brings her baby into an unfamiliar room containing lots of toys. After a while a stranger comes in and attempts to play with the child. The mother leaves the baby with the stranger. She then returns and plays with the child, and the stranger leaves. Finally, the mother leaves the baby alone for three minutes and returns. In each case, observers carefully note how the baby behaves with the mother, with the stranger, and when the baby is alone.

Ainsworth divided children into three categories on the basis of their reactions to the Strange Situation. Some babies are *securely attached:* They cry or protest if the parent leaves the room; they welcome her back and then play happily again; they are clearly more attached to the mother than to the stranger. Other babies are *insecurely attached,* and this insecurity can take two forms. The child may be *avoidant,* not caring if the mother leaves the room, making little effort to seek contact with her on her return, and treating the stranger about the same as the mother. Or the child may be *anxious* or *ambivalent,* resisting contact with the mother at reunion but protesting loudly if she leaves. Anxious or ambivalent babies may cry to be picked up and then demand to be put down, or they may behave as if they are angry with the mother and resist her efforts to comfort them.

Insecure attachment worries many psychologists because it is associated with emotional and behavioral problems in childhood and even throughout life (Mickelson, Kessler, & Shaver, 1997; Shaw, Keenan, & Vondra, 1994). What causes it?

What Causes Insecure Attachment? Interest in the importance of attachment began with the work of British psychiatrist John Bowlby (1969, 1973), who observed the devastating effects on babies raised in orphanages without touches,

STYLES OF ATTACHMENT

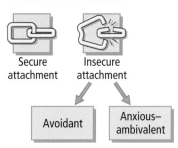

Secure attachment

Insecure attachment

Avoidant

Anxious–ambivalent

Figure 14.2

THE RISE AND FALL OF SEPARATION ANXIETY

At around 6 months of age, many babies begin to show separation anxiety when the person who is their main source of attachment tries handing them over to someone else or leaves the room. This anxiety typically peaks at about a year of age and then steadily declines. But the proportion of children responding this way varies across cultures, from a high among rural African children to a low among children raised in a communal Israeli kibbutz, where children become attached to many adults (Kagan, Kearsley, & Zelazo, 1978).

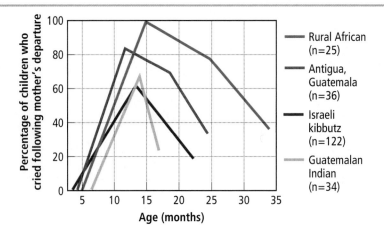

kisses, or cuddles, and on other children raised in conditions of severe deprivation or neglect. But before long psychologists were also wondering whether attachment was affected by what *normal* parents do under *normal* conditions.

Ainsworth believed that the difference between secure, avoidant, and anxious attachment lies primarily in the way mothers treat their babies in the first year. Mothers who are sensitive and responsive to their babies' needs, she said, create securely attached infants; mothers who are uncomfortable with or insensitive to their babies create insecurely attached infants. To many, the implication was that babies needed the "right kind" of mothering from the very first in order to become securely attached, and that putting a child in day care would retard this development—notions that have caused considerable insecurity among mothers!

The emphasis on maternal sensitivity, however, overlooked the facts that few mothers have the time and energy to be as sensitive to a fourth child as to a first, and that most mothers all over the world have many other time-consuming obligations. Further, differences in normal parental child-rearing practices do not affect a child's attachment style (De Wolff & van IJzendoorn, 1997). About two-thirds of all children become securely attached under a wide range of parental practices. For example, German babies are frequently left on their own for a few hours at a stretch by mothers who believe that even babies should become self-reliant (Kagan, 1998b). Among the Efe of Africa, babies spend about half their time away from their mothers, in the care of older children and other adults, and they do not develop the intense one-on-one attachment that Western

Longitudinal studies find that good day care does not affect the security of children's attachments, and indeed often produces many social and intellectual benefits.

children do (Tronick, Morelli, & Ivey, 1992). Yet German and Efe children are not insecure, and they develop as normally as children who spend more time with their mothers.

Likewise, time spent in day care has no effect on the security of a child's attachment. In a major longitudinal study of more than 1,000 children, researchers compared infants who were in child care 30 hours or more a week, from age 3 months to age 15 months, with children who spent less than 10 hours a week in child care. The two groups did not differ on any measure of attachment (NICHD Early Child Care Research Network, 1997; see also McKim et al., 1999).

What factors, then, do promote insecure attachment? One is parenting that is truly abusive, neglectful, or erratic. Another is the child's own genetically influenced temperament (see Chapter 13). Babies who are fearful and prone to crying from birth are more likely to show insecure behavior in the Strange Situation, regardless of the mother's degree of "sensitivity" (Belsky et al., 1996; Seifer et al., 1996). And a third factor is stressful circumstances in the child's family. Infants and young children may temporarily shift from secure to insecure attachment—becoming clingy and fearful of being left alone—if their families are undergoing a period of chronic stress, as during parental divorce or a family member's chronic illness (Belsky et al., 1996; Lewis, 1997).

How Critical Are the Early Years?

Many psychologists believe that the first one to three years of life are crucial to a child's mental development, largely because of the rapid growth of the brain during this time. During the baby's first 15 months, there is an explosion of new synapses, the connections among neurons in the brain (see Chapter 4). In fact, *too many* synapses are produced. As the brain integrates and consolidates early experience, unnecessary synapses are pruned away, leaving behind a more efficient neural network (Bruer, 1999).

Some psychologists and popular writers have interpreted these facts to mean that infants need maximum stimulation and crucial experiences in order to develop an optimum number of synapses. They fear that if a baby does not start out well or get "enough" mental stimulation, the baby's whole life will be influenced for the worse. This is indeed true in the sad cases of infants completely deprived of contact comfort, love, and attention, or whose developing brains are damaged in the womb or after birth by neglect or abuse.

But media accounts of research on early brain development have tended to exaggerate and oversimplify the findings, fostering alarm and worry among the public. When a small (and subsequently unreplicated) study suggested that classical music temporarily improved *adults'* scores on part of an IQ test, Georgia's governor sent parents of every newborn in the state a classical music CD. "Baby Mozart" tapes became a thriving business; one series promises that the music will "stimulate and inspire young minds, improve intelligence, and help develop IQs." We love Mozart, but alas, it isn't true (Chabris et al., 1999).

The developing brain can be profoundly affected, before and after birth, by toxins, viruses, and drugs. But the brain is not formed, once and for all, in the first three years (see Chapter 4). The process of synapse formation and pruning in different parts of the brain continues all through childhood and again in adolescence, and synapses keep developing even into the later years (Greenough, Cohen, & Juraska, 1999; Spear, 2000).

Yet many questions remain unanswered. We know that there are critical periods during the first year for the development of normal perceptual abilities, but we do not know the extent or impact of "critical periods" for intellectual development. We do not know which early experiences, if any, are essential in early brain development or when they must occur. And we do not know the relative influence of genes versus

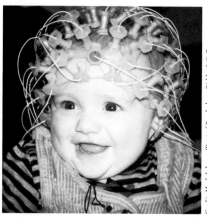

This baby is wearing a device that allows researchers to record the electrical activity of her brain as she learns. Such methods are yielding many discoveries, but some people are going overboard in interpreting them.

Credit: Mark Johnson/Dept of Psychology, Birkbeck College

experience on the proliferation and pruning of synapses. As two psychologists concluded, "This makes it difficult to provide parents with definitive guidance, based on neuroscientific research, concerning the influence of specific parental practices on the developing brain" (Thompson & Nelson, 2001).

In the absence of "definitive guidance" from research, the public would be wise to be wary of fads and exaggerated claims. Of course it's good for parents to nurture and stimulate their babies, but you don't have to read Shakespeare to your baby all day and play chess with her all night! The first three years are important in brain development, but so is prenatal care and so is what happens in a child's later years. In "Taking Psychology with You," we consider other information that might alleviate the anxieties many parents feel about whether they are doing the right thing.

QUICK QUIZ

Is your understanding of early development developing normally?

1. Name as many potentially harmful influences on fetal development as you can.
2. A mother coos and rocks her baby, who smiles and giggles back at her. Their "conversation" shows _____.
3. Melanie is playing happily on a jungle gym at her day-care center when she falls off and badly scrapes her knee. She runs to her caregiver for a consoling cuddle. Melanie seeks _____.
4. *True or false:* To develop normally, infants must sleep in their own cribs, apart from their mothers.
5. A baby left in the Strange Situation does not protest when his mother leaves the room, and he seems to ignore her when she returns. What style of attachment is this behavior said to reflect?
6. In Item 3, what else besides the child's style of attachment could account for the child's reaction?

Answers:

1. German measles early in pregnancy; exposure to radiation or toxic chemicals; sexually transmitted diseases; the mother's use of cigarettes, alcohol, or other drugs 2. synchrony 3. contact comfort 4. false 5. insecure (avoidant) 6. the child's own temperament and the child's familiarity with being temporarily left alone

---

WHAT'S AHEAD ▶

- **Why do so many parents speak "baby talk"?**
- **What important accomplishment are infants revealing when they learn to play peekaboo?**
- **Why will most 5-year-olds choose a tall, narrow glass of lemonade over a short, fat glass containing the same amount?**

Cognitive Development

Our friend Joel reports how thrilled he was when his 13-month-old daughter Alison suddenly said, for the first time, "Daddy!" His delight was deflated somewhat, though, when the doorbell rang and she ran to the door, calling, "Daddy!" Later Joel learned that there was a 2-year-old child in Alison's day-care group whose father would ring the doorbell when he picked her up. Alison acquired her friend's enthusiasm for doorbells but didn't quite get the hang of "Daddy." She will soon enough, though. She will also be able to see the world from Daddy's viewpoint.

Language

In Chapter 3 we saw that the ability to use language is an evolutionary adaptation of the human species. In only a few years, children are able to understand thousands of words, use rules of syntax to string them together in meaningful sentences, and produce and understand an endless number of new word combinations.

The acquisition of language begins in the first few months. Infants may only cry and coo, but they are already responsive to the pitch, intensity, and sound of language, and they react to the emotions and rhythms in voices. When most people speak to babies, their pitch is higher and more varied than usual and their intonation is exaggerated. Adult use of baby talk—researchers call it *parentese*—has been documented all over the world, from Sweden to Japan. Parentese helps babies learn the "melody" and rhythm of their native language (Fernald & Mazzie, 1991; Kuhl et al., 1997).

By 4 to 6 months of age, babies can often recognize their own names and other words that are regularly spoken with emotion, such as "mommy" and "daddy." They also know many of the key consonant and vowel sounds of their native language and can distinguish such sounds from those of other languages (Kuhl et al., 1992). Over time, exposure to the baby's native language reduces the child's ability to perceive speech sounds in other languages. Thus, Japanese infants can hear the difference between the English sounds "la" and "ra," but older Japanese children cannot. Because this contrast does not exist in their language, they become insensitive to it.

Between 6 months and 1 year, infants become increasingly familiar with the sound structure of their native language. They are able to distinguish words from the flow of speech. They will listen longer to words that violate their expectations of what words should sound like and even to sentences that violate their expectations of how sentences should be structured (Jusczyk, 1997; Marcus et al., 1999). They start to babble, making many "ba-ba" and "goo-goo" sounds, endlessly repeating sounds and syllables. Then, at about a year of age, though the timing varies considerably, children start to name things. They already have some concepts in their minds for familiar people and objects, and their first words represent these concepts ("mama," "doggie," "truck").

Starting at about 11 months, babies develop a repertoire of symbolic gestures, another important tool of communication. Babies gesture to refer to objects (e.g., sniffing to indicate "flower"), to request something (smacking the lips for "food"), to describe objects (blowing or waving a hand for "hot"), and to reply to questions (opening the palms or shrugging the shoulders for "I don't know"). They clap in response to pictures of things they like, from Teletubbies to baseball games. Children whose parents encourage them to use gestures acquire larger vocabularies, have better comprehension, are better listeners, and are less frustrated in their efforts to communicate than babies who are not encouraged to use gestures (Goodwyn & Acredolo, 1998). When babies begin to speak, they continue to gesture along with their words (just as adults gesture when talking), suggesting that gestures are not a substitute for language but are deeply related to its development (Mayberry & Nicoladis, 2000).

Between the ages of 18 months and 2 years, toddlers begin to produce words in two- or three-word combinations ("Mama here," "go 'way bug," "my toy"). The child's first combinations of words have been described as **telegraphic.** When people had to pay for every word in a telegram, they quickly learned to drop unnecessary articles (*a, an,* or *the*) and auxiliary verbs (*is* or *are*), but they still conveyed the message. Similarly, the two-word sentences of toddlers omit articles, word endings, auxiliary verbs, and other parts of speech, but these sentences are remarkably accurate in conveying meaning. Children use two word "telegrams" to locate things ("there toy"), make demands ("more milk"), negate actions ("no want," "all gone milk,"), describe events ("Bambi go," "hit ball"), describe objects ("pretty dress"), show possession ("Mama dress"), and ask questions ("where Daddy?"). Pretty good for a little kid, don't you think?

Say out loud, "Where is your eye?" Now repeat the question as if you were talking this baby. Chances are your voice will shift to "parentese," becoming more singsong, rhythmic, and higher in pitch. The melodic rhythms of "baby talk" help babies learn language.

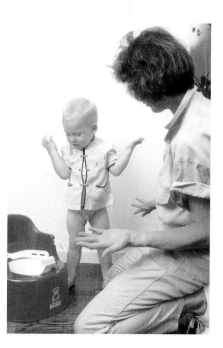

Symbolic gestures emerge early!

telegraphic speech A child's first word combinations, which omit (as a telegram did) unnecessary words.

assimilation In Piaget's theory, the process of absorbing new information into existing cognitive structures.

accommodation In Piaget's theory, the process of modifying existing cognitive structures in response to experience and new information.

By the age of 6, the average child has a vocabulary of between 8,000 and 14,000 words, meaning that children acquire about five to eight new words *a day* between the ages of 1 and 6. (When did you last learn and use eight new words in a day?) They absorb new words as they hear them, forming a quick impression of the likely meaning of the word by using their knowledge of grammatical contexts and the rules for formulating words (Rice, 1990). The process of absorbing and understanding thousands of new words continues up through adolescence.

Thinking

As anyone who has ever observed a young child knows, children do not think the way adults do. At age 2, they may call all large animals by one name (say, "horsie") and all small animals by another (say, "bug"). At 4, they may protest that a sibling has "more" fruit juice when it is only the shapes of the glasses that differ, not the amount of juice.

In the 1920s, Swiss psychologist Jean Piaget [Zhan Pee-ah-ZHAY] (1896–1980) proposed a theory of cognitive development to explain these childish mistakes. Piaget was to child development what Freud was to psychoanalysis and Skinner to behaviorism (Flavell, 1996). His keen observations of children caused a revolution in thinking about how thinking develops, and they inspired thousands of studies by investigators all over the world.

Piaget's great insight was that children's errors are as interesting as their correct responses. Children will say things that seem cute or wildly illogical to adults. But the *strategies* that children use to think and solve problems, said Piaget, are not random or meaningless. They reflect a predictable interaction between the child's maturational stage and the child's experience in the world.

Piaget's Theory of Cognitive Stages. According to Piaget (1929/1960, 1952a, 1984), as children develop, they must make constant mental adaptations to new observations and experiences. Adaptation takes two forms: assimilation and accommodation.

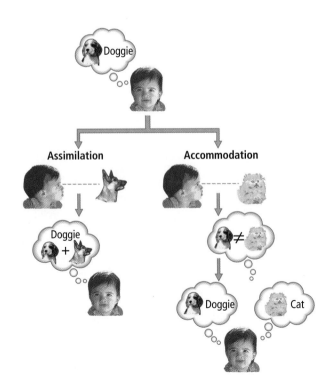

Assimilation is what you do when you fit new information into your present system of knowledge and beliefs or into your mental *schemas* (networks of associations, beliefs, and expectations about categories of things and people). Suppose that little Harry learns a schema for "dog" by playing with the family spaniel. If he then sees the neighbor's collie and says "doggie!" he has assimilated the new information about the neighbor's pet into his schema for dogs. **Accommodation** is what you do when, as a result of undeniable new information, you must change or modify your existing schemas. If Harry sees the neighbor's Siamese cat and still says "doggie!" his parents are likely to laugh and correct him. Harry will have to modify his schema for *dogs* to exclude cats, and he will have to create a schema for *cats*. In this way, he accommodates the new information that a Siamese cat is not a dog.

Using these concepts, Piaget proposed that all children go through four stages of cognitive development:

1 *The sensorimotor stage (birth to age 2).* In this stage, the infant learns through concrete actions: looking, touching, putting things in the mouth, sucking, grasping. "Thinking" consists of coordinating sensory information with bodily movements. Gradually these movements become more purposeful as the child explores the environment and learns that specific movements will produce specific results. Pulling a cloth away will reveal a hidden toy; letting go of a fuzzy toy duck will cause it to drop out of reach; banging on the table with a spoon will produce dinner (or Mom, taking the spoon away).

A major accomplishment at this stage, said Piaget, is **object permanence,** the understanding that something continues to exist even when you can't see it or touch it. In the first few months, he observed, infants seem to follow the motto "out of sight, out of mind." They will look intently at a little toy, but if you hide it behind a piece of paper they will not look behind the paper or make an effort to get the toy. By about 6 months of age, however, infants begin to grasp the idea that the toy exists whether or not they can see it. If a baby of this age drops a toy from her playpen, she will look for it; she also will look under a cloth for a toy that is partially hidden. By 1 year of age, most babies have developed an awareness of the permanence of (some) objects; even if a toy is covered by a cloth, it must be under there. This is when they love to play peekaboo.

Object permanence, said Piaget, represents the beginning of the child's capacity to use mental imagery and symbols. The child becomes able to hold a concept in mind, to learn that the word "fly" represents an annoying, buzzing creature and that "Daddy" represents a friendly, playful one.

2 *The preoperational stage (ages 2 to 7).* During this stage, the use of symbols and language accelerates. A 2-year-old is able to pretend, for instance, that a large box is a house, table, or train. But Piaget described this stage largely in terms of what (he thought) the child cannot do. Although children can think, said Piaget, they cannot reason, and they lack the mental abilities necessary for understanding abstract principles or cause and effect. Piaget called these missing abilities **operations,** by which he meant reversible actions that the child performs in the mind. An operation is a sort of "train of thought" that can be run backward or forward. Multiplying 2 times 6 to get 12 is an operation; so is the reverse operation, dividing 12 by 6 to get 2.

Piaget also believed (mistakenly, as we will see) that preoperational children cannot take another person's point of view because their thinking is **egocentric.** They see the world only from their own frame of reference and cannot imagine that others see things differently.

Further, said Piaget, preoperational children cannot grasp the concept of **conservation,** the notion that physical properties do not change when their forms or appearances change. Children at this age do not understand that an amount of liquid or a number of pennies remains the same even if you pour the liquid from one glass to another or stack the pennies (see Figure 14.3). If you pour liquid from a short, fat glass into a tall, narrow glass, preoperational children will say there is more liquid in the second glass. They attend to the appearance of the liquid (its height in the glass) to judge its quantity, and so are misled.

object permanence The understanding, which develops throughout the first year, that an object continues to exist even when you cannot see it or touch it.

operations In Piaget's theory, mental actions that are cognitively reversible.

egocentric thinking Seeing the world from only your own point of view; the inability to take another person's perspective.

conservation The understanding that the physical properties of objects—such as the number of items in a cluster or the amount of liquid in a glass—can remain the same even when their form or appearance changes.

 14.1

Get Involved

A Test of Conservation

If you know any young children, try one of Piaget's conservation experiments. A simple one is to make two rows of seven buttons or pennies, aligned identically. Ask the child whether one row has more. Now simply spread out the buttons in one row, and ask the child again whether one row has more. If the child says "Yes," ask which one, and why. Try to do this experiment with a 3-year-old and a 7- or 8-year-old. You will probably see a big difference in their answers.

Figure 14.3

PIAGET'S PRINCIPLE OF CONSERVATION

In a typical test for conservation of number (left), the number of blocks is the same in two sets, but those in one set are then spread out and the child must say whether one set has "more" blocks than another. Preoperational children think that the set that takes up more space has more blocks. In a test for conservation of quantity (right), the child is shown two short glasses with equal amounts of liquid. Then the contents of one glass are poured into a tall, narrower glass, and the child is asked whether one container now has more. Most preoperational children do not understand that pouring liquid from a short glass into a taller one leaves the amount of liquid unchanged. They judge only by the height of liquid in the glass.

3 *The concrete operations stage (ages 7 to 12).* In this stage, Piaget said, children's thinking is still grounded in *concrete* experiences and concepts, rather than in abstractions or logical deductions. However, the nature and quality of their thought processes change significantly. Children come to understand the principles of conservation, reversibility, and cause and effect. They learn mental operations, such as addition, subtraction, multiplication, and division. They learn to categorize things (e.g., oaks as trees) and to order things serially from smallest to largest, lightest to darkest, and shortest to tallest. And they understand the nature of *identity;* for example, they know that a girl does not turn into a boy by wearing a boy's hat, and that a brother will always be a brother, even if he grows up.

4 *The formal operations stage (age 12 through adulthood).* In this last stage, teenagers become capable of abstract reasoning. They understand that ideas can be compared and classified, just as objects can. They are able to reason about situations they have not experienced firsthand, and they can think about future possibilities. They are able to search systematically for answers to problems. They are able to draw logical conclusions from premises common to their culture and experience. (Review 14.1 summarizes Piaget's stages of cognitive development.)

Vygotsky's Theory of Sociocultural Influences. Piaget thought that children's cognitive development more or less developed naturally, like the blooming of a flower. He was amused by what he called "the American question"—Americans were forever asking him what they could do to speed up their children's mental development. Forget it, he would tell them. You can't rush the qualitative changes that occur as children go through each cognitive stage.

In contrast, the Russian psychologist Lev Vygotsky (1896–1934), who was born the same year as Piaget but died at the age of only 38, emphasized the *sociocultural* influences on children's cognitive development. Vygotsky (1962, 1978) believed that the child develops mental representations of the world through culture and language, and that adults do play a major role in their children's development by constantly guiding and teaching them. Once children acquire language and internalize the rules of their culture, said Vygotsky, they start using *private speech,* talking to themselves to direct their own behavior. At first, children's private speech is actually spoken aloud; you can often observe preschoolers talking to themselves when they have done something they know is naughty or when they are faced with a problem. Over time, private speech becomes internalized and truly "private"—that is, silent (although adults have been known to make choice remarks about themselves out loud when they goof, too).

REVIEW 14.1	PIAGET'S STAGES OF COGNITIVE DEVELOPMENT	
	Stage	**Major Accomplishments**
"Ball"	Sensorimotor (0–2)	Object permanence Beginning of capacity to use mental images and symbols
AB 12 DC 43	Preoperational (2–7)	Accelerated use of symbols and language
=	Concrete operations (7–12)	Understanding of conservation Understanding of identity Understanding of serial ordering
"if x then y"	Formal operations (12–)	Abstract reasoning Ability to compare and classify ideas

Vygotsky did not share Piaget's view that children go through invariant stages. Once children have language, he said, their cognitive development may proceed in any number of directions, depending on what adults teach them, what their culture makes possible for them, and the particular environment they live in.

Current Views of Cognitive Development. Piaget was a brilliant observer of children, and his major point has been well supported: New reasoning abilities depend on the emergence of previous ones—you cannot learn algebra before you can count, and you cannot learn philosophy before you understand logic. But research has changed the way developmental psychologists regard children's cognitive maturation, in the following ways:

1 *Cognitive abilities develop in overlapping waves rather than discrete steps or stages.* If you observe children at different ages, as Piaget did, it will seem that they reason differently. But if you study the everyday learning of children at any given age, you will find that a child may use several different strategies to solve a problem, some more complex or accurate than others (Siegler, 1996, 2001). Learning occurs gradually, with retreats to former ways of thinking as well as advances to new ones. Children's reasoning ability also depends on the circumstances—who is asking them questions, the specific words used, the materials used, and what they are reasoning about—not just on the stage they are in.

2 *Children understand far more than Piaget gave them credit for.* Taking advantage of the fact that infants look longer at novel or surprising stimuli than at familiar ones, psychologists have designed delightfully imaginative methods of testing what babies know (see Figure 14.4). As we discuss in Chapter 3, these methods reveal that babies may be born with "mental modules" or "core knowledge systems" about numbers, the spatial relations of objects, and other features of the physical world (Spelke, 2000). At only 4 months of age, babies even seem to understand some basic principles of physics! Babies that young will look longer at a ball if it seems to roll through a solid barrier, leap between two platforms, or hang in midair than they do when the ball obeys the laws of physics—suggesting

Figure 14.4

TESTING INFANTS' KNOWLEDGE

In this clever procedure, a baby watches as a box is pushed from left to right along a striped platform. The box is pushed until it reaches the end of the platform (a possible event) or until only a bit of it rests on the platform (an impossible event). Babies look longer at the impossible event, suggesting that it suprises them. Somehow they know that an object needs physical support and can't just float on air (Baillargeon, 1994).

Possible event

Impossible event

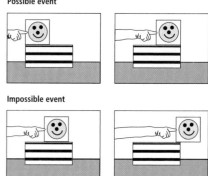

theory of mind A system of beliefs about the way one's own mind and the minds of others work, and how cognitions and feelings affect behavior.

that the unusual event is surprising to them. And infants as young as 2½ to 3½ months are aware that objects continue to exist even when masked by other objects, a form of object permanence that Piaget never imagined possible in babies so young (Baillargeon, 1994, 1999).

One team of developmental psychologists calls the infant "the scientist in the crib" (Gopnik, Meltzoff, & Kuhl, 1999). Children come into the world ready to form theories about how things work, and then test them. Imagine that your toddler throws her spoon on the floor for the sixth time as you try to feed her and you say, "That's enough! I will *not* pick up your spoon again!" The child will now test your claim. Are you serious? Are you angry? What will happen if she throws the spoon again? She is not doing this to drive you crazy, though it might feel that way. Rather, she is learning that her desires and yours can differ, and that sometimes those differences are important and sometimes they are not. Like a good scientist, she will keep testing her hypotheses and revising them with new information.

3 *Preschoolers are not as egocentric as Piaget thought.* Most 3- and 4-year-olds *can* take another person's perspective (Flavell, 1999). When 4-year-olds play with 2-year-olds, for example, they modify and simplify their speech so the younger children will understand (Shatz & Gelman, 1973). One preschooler we know showed her teacher a picture she had drawn of a cat and an unidentifiable blob. "The cat is lovely," said the teacher, "but what is this thing here?" "That has nothing to do with you," said the child. "That's what the *cat* is looking at."

By about ages 3 to 4, children also begin to understand that you cannot predict what a person will do just by observing a situation or knowing the facts; you have to know what the person is feeling and thinking—the person might even lie. They start asking why other people behave as they do ("Why is Johnny so mean?"). In short, they are developing a **theory of mind,** a system of beliefs about how their own and other people's minds work and how people are affected by their beliefs and emotions (see Chapter 9). They start using verbs like *think* and *know,* and by age 4 they understand that what another person thinks might not match their own beliefs (Flavell, 1999; Lillard, 1998). To cognitive psychologists, the ability to understand that people can have false beliefs is a major milestone, because it means the child is beginning to question how we know things. The ability to think this way is a foundation for later higher-order, scientific thinking (Kuhn, 2000).

This 3-year-old was asked to place the doll where the policeman could not find him. According to Piaget, she should be "egocentric" and therefore hide the doll from herself as well (left). On several occasions, however, she placed the doll where she, but not the policeman, could see him, suggesting that she was able to take the policeman's point of view (right).

4 *Cognitive development depends on the child's education and culture.* On this point, Vygotsky was correct and ahead of his time. Culture—the world of tools, language, rituals, beliefs, games, and social institutions—profoundly shapes and structures children's cognitive development (Tomasello, 2000). Cultures may foster some abilities and ignore others. For example, traditional nomadic hunting peoples, such as the Inuit of Canada and the Aborigines of Australia, do not quantify things and do not need to (Dasen, 1994). The Aborigines have number words only up to 5; after that, all quantities are described as "many." In such cultures, understanding the conservation of quantity develops late, if at all. But nomadic hunters excel in spatial abilities because spatial orientation is crucial for finding water holes and successful hunting routes. In contrast, children who live in settled agricultural communities, such as the Baoulé of the Ivory Coast, develop rapidly in the ability to quantify and much more slowly in spatial reasoning. In all cultures, however, education affects cognitive abilities: Many unschooled children of the Wolof, a rural group in Senegal, do not understand conservation, as do their peers who attend school, but brief training can speed its development (Greenfield, 1976).

Experience and culture influence cognitive development. Children who work with clay, wood, and other materials, such as this young potter in India, tend to understand the concept of conservation sooner than children who have not had this kind of experience.

5 *Just as Piaget underestimated the cognitive skills of young children, he overestimated those of many adults.* Not all adolescents and adults develop the ability for formal reasoning and reflective judgment (see Chapter 9). Some never develop the capacity for formal operations, and others think concretely unless a specific problem requires abstract thought.

Although, as you can see, Piaget's work has been greatly modified, modern researchers agree with him that children are not passive vessels into which education and experience are poured. Children actively interpret their worlds, using their developing schemas and abilities to assimilate new information and figure things out.

QUICK QUIZ

Please use language (and thought) to answer these questions.

1. "More cake!" and "Mommy come" are examples of _____ speech.

2. Understanding that two rows of six pennies are equal in number, even if one row is flat and the other is stacked up, is an example of _____.

3. Understanding that a toy exists even after Mom puts it in her purse is an example of _____, which develops during the _____ stage.

4. Three-year-old Tasha accidentally breaks a glass. "You bad girl!" she exclaims. Reprimanding herself is an example of Vygotsky's notion of _____.

5. A 5-year-old who tells his dad that "Sally said she saw a bunny but she was lying" has developed a _____.

6. List five findings from contemporary research on children's cognitive development that challenge Piaget's theory.

Answers:

1. telegraphic 2. conservation 3. object permanence, sensorimotor 4. private speech 5. theory of mind 6. The changes from one stage to another occur in overlapping waves rather than distinct stages; children know more and know it earlier than Piaget thought; they are less egocentric than Piaget thought; their cognitive development is affected by their culture; and not all adolescents and adults achieve the ability for formal operations.

WHAT'S AHEAD

- According to a leading theory, why is moral reasoning that is based on law, justice, and duty *not* the pinnacle of moral development?
- When reasoning about moral dilemmas, are women more compassionate and caring than men are?
- What is wrong with "because I say so" as a way of getting children to behave?

Moral Development

Piaget (1932) pioneered in the study of another important aspect of cognitive development: moral reasoning, which changes according to a child's cognitive maturity. A young child, he observed, will say that a child who breaks a vase by accident is as naughty as one who breaks it intentionally. Older children, because of their maturing cognitive abilities, are able to evaluate moral behavior in terms of a person's intentions and motives.

Moral Reasoning

In the 1960s, Lawrence Kohlberg, inspired by Piaget's work, outlined a stage theory of moral reasoning that became highly influential. Your moral stage, said Kohlberg, can be determined by the answers you give to hypothetical dilemmas. Suppose a man's wife is dying and needs a special drug. The man cannot afford the drug, and the druggist refuses to lower its price. Should the man steal the drug? If the man is caught, should the judge be lenient? To Kohlberg, as to Piaget, the reasoning behind the answers was more important than the decisions themselves.

Kohlberg (1964, 1984) proposed that children progress through three levels of moral development, each consisting of two stages:

▶ *Preconventional morality.* Very young children obey rules because they fear being punished if they disobey and later because they think it is in their best interest to obey. Their moral reasoning is hedonistic, self-centered, and lacking in empathy; what is right is what feels good.

▶ *Conventional morality.* At about ages 10 or 11, according to Kohlberg, children shift to the conventional morality of adult society, which is based at first on conformity and loyalty to others. Eventually it shifts to a "law-and-order" orientation, based on understanding law and justice.

▶ *Postconventional ("principled") morality.* Some adults, said Kohlberg, realize that certain laws—such as those that legitimize the mistreatment of minorities—are themselves immoral. They realize that people hold different values and standards, and that laws are important but can be changed. A very few postconventional individuals develop a moral standard based on universal human rights. When faced with a conflict between law and conscience, they follow conscience, even at great personal risk.

THINKING CRITICALLY

Consider Other Explanations

Do people reason differently about moral dilemmas because of the cognitive stages they are in? What else could be influencing their judgments?

Kohlberg's theory of moral reasoning generated much debate and research. Certainly, moral reasoning, like scientific reasoning, becomes more complex as the child matures. But are the answers that people give due entirely or even primarily to their unfolding cognitive abilities? There are four significant problems with cognitive stage theories of moral development:

1 *Moral reasoning is influenced by education.* College-educated people tend to give "higher-level" explanations of moral decisions than people who have not attended college, but all that shows, say Kohlberg's critics, is that college-educated people are more verbally sophisticated and have learned to think in legalistic terms (Eckensberger, 1994).

2 *Moral reasoning is profoundly affected by cultural experiences and values.* Kohlberg greatly underestimated the importance of culture (Shweder, Mahapatra, & Miller, 1990). In Iceland and Germany, for example, even very young children reveal a moral sense based on concern for others. In China, moral decisions and values based on social harmony and devotion to parents often conflict with Kohlberg's notion that "higher" moral reasoning is based on analytic, individualistic thinking (Dien, 1982). A Nigerian psychologist who interviewed 200 teenagers and young adults found that their criteria for moral reasoning involve primary values of obedience to parents, family interdependence, and the "transcendental authority of divine guidance," concepts not found on Kohlberg's measures (Okonkwo, 1997).

3 *Moral reasoning is often inconsistent across situations.* The kind of moral reasoning that people do depends on the situation and on the nature of the dilemma (Wygant, 1997). For example, you might show conventional morality by overlooking a racial slur at a dinner party because you do not want to upset anyone, but reveal postconventional reasoning by protesting a governmental policy you regard as immoral. In one study using Kohlberg's dilemmas, most of the participants gave responses spanning three to six substages; only one young man based all his judgments on the same stage (Wark & Krebs, 1996).

4 *Moral reasoning is often unrelated to moral behavior.* Moral-reasoning ability increases during the school years, but so do cheating, lying, cruelty, and the cognitive ability to rationalize these actions (Kagan, 1993). College students usually draw on lofty principles of justice and fair play to justify moral decisions, yet about one-third of American and Canadian college men say they would force a woman into sexual acts if they could get away with it—the lowest form of moral reasoning (Malamuth & Dean, 1990). As Thomas Lickona (1983) wryly summarized, "We can reach high levels of moral reasoning, and still behave like scoundrels."

Another popular approach to moral reasoning was proposed in the early 1980s by Carol Gilligan (1982). Gilligan argued that men tend to base their moral choices on abstract principles of law and justice, asking questions such as "Whose rights should take precedence here?" whereas women tend to base their moral decisions on principles of compassion and caring, asking questions such as "Who will be hurt least?" This was an appealing theory—especially to women! But a meta-analysis of the many studies that have investigated this argument found no support for Gilligan's view that women predominantly use a "care" orientation and men a "justice" orientation (Jaffee & Hyde, 2000).

The main problem with Gilligan's theory is that it implies that moral reasoning is fixed and consistent, depending primarily on your gender. But moral reasoning depends on what people are reasoning about and the situation they are in (Rest et al., 1999). Both sexes tend to use justice-based reasoning when they are thinking about abstract ethical dilemmas that have no relevance to their lives, and care-based reasoning when they are thinking about personal dilemmas (Clopton & Sorell, 1993; Walker, deVries, & Trevethan, 1987; Wygant, 1997). And, unfortunately, for women as for men, moral reasoning of either kind often has little relation to actual behavior. Both sexes can talk a good game, yet be hurtful, selfish, and uncompassionate toward others.

"It all depends on how you define 'chop.'"

You can be verbally sophisticated in rationalizing bad behavior, and still do the wrong thing!

According to Kohlberg, Mohandas Gandhi (the "Mahatma," or wise one) reached the highest level of morality because of his commitment to nonviolence. But people's moral behavior is not the same in every situation or relationship. Gandhi, for example, was aloof from his family and followers, whom he often treated in a harsh and callous manner.

Moral Behavior

Today, developmental psychologists recognize that the child's emerging ability to understand right from wrong—and to behave accordingly—depends not only on reasoning skills but also on the emergence of conscience and "moral emotions" such as shame, guilt, and empathy (Hoffman, 1990). The capacity for moral feeling, like that for language, seems to be inborn. As Jerome Kagan (1984) wrote, "Without this fundamental human capacity, which nineteenth century observers called a *moral sense,* the child could not be socialized." The moral sense and a desire to behave well with others can be nurtured or extinguished, however, by experiences in a child's life.

For example, when you did something wrong as a child, did the adults in your family spank you, shout at you, punish you, or explain the error of your ways? One of the most common methods used by parents to enforce moral standards and good behavior is **power assertion**, which includes threats, physical punishment, depriving the child of privileges, and generally taking advantage of being bigger, stronger, and more powerful. Of course, a parent may have no alternative other than "Do it because I say so!" if the child is too young to understand a rule or impishly keeps trying to break it. But when "power assertion" consists of sheer parental bullying and frequent physical punishment, it is associated with greater aggressiveness in children, reduced empathy, and failure to internalize moral standards (Gershoff, 2002; Hoffman, 1994; Lopez, Bonenberger, & Schneider, 2001). When parents are verbally abusive, insulting and ridiculing the child ("You are so stupid, I wish you had never been born"), the results are especially devastating (Moore & Pepler, 1998).

This does not mean that power assertion has the same effects on all children, in all environments, in all cultures (Collins et al., 2000). For one thing, the child's own temperament will affect how a parent treats the child, as we saw in Chapter 13 as well as earlier in this chapter. Second, cultures tend to prefer different methods of discipline; Chinese and African-American families are often sterner than middle-class white families, but the children generally regard their parents' discipline as evidence of concern, not abusiveness. Third, the *context* in which the discipline occurs makes an enormous difference. Is the parent-child relationship fundamentally loving and trusting or one full of hostility and fighting?

THINKING CRITICALLY

Avoid Emotional Reasoning

Most people hold passionate feelings about spanking: either it is good for the child or devastating for the child. Could both views be wrong?

Consider spanking. "My parents spanked me and I am fine," some people say—and they may well be. Some psychologists believe that the occasional, moderate use of spanking has no long-term detrimental outcomes for most middle-class children (Baumrind, Larzelere, & Cowan, 2002). The reason is that it typically occurs in an otherwise loving context, as a quick action of last resort when a child is misbehaving. Physical punishment backfires, however, when it is used inappropriately or harshly, causing anger and resentment in the recipient. Many parents resort to spanking whenever they don't know what else to do. If the family atmosphere is one of anger, quarreling, and constant efforts to subdue the children, the use of physical punishment can easily spiral out of control (Gershoff, 2002).

Researchers have observed how this spiral works, and its devastating consequences, in longitudinal studies of parent-child interactions in the home. The parents of aggressive children do a lot of shouting, scolding, and spanking, but they fail to connect the punishment with the child's behavior. They do not state clear rules, require compliance, consistently punish violations, or praise good behavior. Instead, they nag and shout, unpredictably tossing in a slap or a loss of privileges. This combination of power assertion with intermittent discipline causes the chil-

power assertion A method of child rearing in which the parent uses punishment and authority to correct the child's misbehavior.

dren's aggressiveness to increase and eventually get out of hand. The child becomes withdrawn, manipulative, and difficult to manage, which causes the parents to assert their power even more forcefully, which makes the child angrier . . . and a vicious cycle escalates (Patterson, Reid, & Dishion, 1992; Snyder & Patterson, 1995).

A strategy that is more successful than spanking and other forms of power assertion for teaching moral behavior is **induction**, in which the parent appeals to the child's own resources, helpful nature, affection for others, and sense of responsibility. A parent using induction might explain to a misbehaving child that the child's actions could harm or upset another person ("You made Doug cry; it's not nice to bite"; "You must never poke anyone's eyes because that could hurt them seriously"). Or the parent might appeal to the child's own helpful inclinations ("I know you're a person who likes to be good to others"), which is far more effective than citing external reasons to be good ("You'd better be nice or you won't get dessert") (Eisenberg, 1995). Children whose parents use induction tend to feel guilty if they hurt others. They are more likely to internalize standards of right and wrong and be considerate of others (Berkowitz & Grych, 2000; Hoffman, 1994).

Induction is not the same as being overly permissive—letting children do anything they want—or being uninvolved or unconcerned. Parents who use induction tend to be *authoritative* and democratic rather than arbitrarily *authoritarian* or permissive. That is, they give emotional support to the child and listen to the child's concerns and wishes, but they also require good behavior; they set high but reasonable expectations and teach their children how to meet them (Baumrind, 1989, 1991; Berkowitz & Grych, 2000).

induction A method of child rearing in which the parent appeals to the child's own resources, abilities, sense of responsibility, and feelings for others in correcting the child's misbehavior.

POWER ASSERTION

The parent uses physical force, threats, insults, or other kinds of power to get the child to obey.

Example:
"Do it because I say so"; "Stop that right now"; hitting

Result:
The child obeys, but only when the parent is present; the child often feels resentful.

INDUCTION

The parent appeals to the child's good nature, empathy, love for the parent, and sense of responsibility to others, and offers explanations of rules.

Example:
"You're too grown up to behave like that"; "Fighting hurts your little brother."

Result:
The child tends to internalize reasons for good behavior.

QUICK QUIZ

How can we induce you to take this quiz?

1. Margo says she pays her taxes because she believes in obeying the law; Manny says he pays because he is afraid of getting caught. According to Kohlberg, what level of moral reasoning has each of them achieved?

2. Which method of disciplining an aggressive child is most likely to teach empathy? (a) induction, (b) authoritarian firmness, (c) power assertion, (d) physical punishment

3. Two psychologists noted that in Kohlberg's system, the cruelest lawyer could get a higher moral-reasoning score than the kindest 8-year-old. Why might that happen?

Answers:

1. Margo is at a conventional level, Manny at a preconventional level. 2. a 3. The lawyer's score reflects verbal sophistication and education and does not indicate whether he or she actually behaves in a kind and moral way; people's moral reasoning and their behavior are often unrelated.

WHAT'S AHEAD

- **How would a biologically oriented psychologist explain why most little boys and girls are "sexist" in their choice of toys?**
- **How do teachers unintentionally make boys more aggressive?**
- **If a little girl "knows" that girls can't be doctors, does this mean she will never go to medical school?**

Gender Development

No parent ever excitedly calls a relative to exclaim, "It's a baby! It's a 7½-pound, black-haired baby!" The baby's sex is the first thing everyone notices and announces. Most babies, unless they have rare abnormalities, are born unambiguously male or female—an anatomical distinction. But how do children learn the rules of masculinity and femininity—the things that boys do that are different from what girls do? Why, as one friend of ours observed, do so many preschool children act like the "gender police," insisting, say, that boys can't be nurses and girls can't be doctors?

Many psychologists use the terms *sex* and *gender* to capture the distinction between anatomy and behavior (Deaux, 1985; Lott & Maluso, 1993). *Sex* refers to the physiological or anatomical attributes of males and females; there is a "sex difference" in the frequency of baldness or color blindness. *Gender* refers to the cultural and psychological attributes that children learn are appropriate for the sexes; there is a "gender difference" in sexual attitudes, dishwashing, and fondness for romance novels.

Toddlers can label themselves as boys or girls, but it is not until the age of 4 or 5 that most children develop a secure **gender identity,** a fundamental sense of maleness or femaleness that exists regardless of what they wear or how they behave. Only then do they understand that *what boys and girls do* does not necessarily indicate *what sex they are:* A girl remains a girl even if she can climb a tree, and a boy remains a boy even if he has long hair. In contrast, **gender typing** reflects society's ideas about which abilities, interests, traits, and behaviors are appropriately "masculine" or "feminine." A person can have a strong gender identity and not be gender typed: A man may be confident in his maleness and not feel threatened by doing "unmasculine" things such as needlepointing a pillow; a woman may be confident in her femaleness and not feel threatened by doing "unfeminine" things such as serving in combat.

gender identity The fundamental sense of being male or female; it is independent of whether the person conforms to the social and cultural rules of gender.

gender typing The process by which children learn the abilities, interests, personality traits, and behaviors associated with being masculine or feminine in their culture.

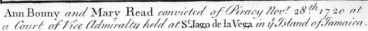

Ann Bonny *and* Mary Read *convicted of Piracy Nov.* 28th 1720 *at a Court of Vice Admiralty held at* St. Jago de la Vega *in ye Island of Jamaica.*

Influences on Gender Development

Developmental psychologists study the influence of biology, cognition, and learning in the emergence of gender identity, gender differences in behavior, and gender typing.

Biological Influences. Starting in the preschool years, boys and girls congregate primarily with other children of their sex and prefer the toys and games of their own sex (Maccoby, 1998). Boys and girls will play together if required to, but given their druthers, they usually choose to play with friends of their own sex. This preference occurs all over the world, almost regardless of how adults treat children—whether they encourage boys and girls to play together or separate them (Lytton & Romney, 1991; Maccoby, 1998). Likewise, although many parents lament that they try to give their children the same toys, often it makes no difference; their sons want trucks and their daughters want dolls.

Biological researchers believe that these play and toy preferences must have a biological basis, perhaps in prenatal hormones, genes, or brain organization. They point out that girls who were exposed to prenatal androgens (masculinizing hormones) in the womb are later more likely than nonexposed girls to prefer "boys' toys," such as cars, fire engines, and Lincoln logs (Berenbaum & Snyder, 1995). And in all primate species, young males are more likely than females to go in for physical roughhousing (Maccoby, 1998).

Cognitive Influences. Cognitive psychologists explain the mystery of children's gender segregation and toy preferences not in terms of biology but in terms of the child's own unfolding cognitive abilities. As children mature, they develop a **gender schema,** a mental network of beliefs and expectations about what it means to be male or female—and what each sex is supposed to wear, do, feel, and think (Bem, 1993; Fagot, 1985; Spence, 1985). Gender schemas even include metaphors. For example, after age 4, children of both sexes will usually say that rough, spiky, black, or mechanical things are "male" and that soft, pink, fuzzy, or flowery things are "female" (Fagot & Leinbach, 1993). As soon as children have a gender schema, they change their behavior to conform to it.

Before you can have a gender schema, of course, you have to be able to recognize that there are two genders. This ability starts to emerge even before children can speak. By the age of 9 months, most babies can discriminate male from female faces (Fagot & Leinbach, 1993), and they can match female faces with female voices (Poulin-Dubois et al., 1994). But it takes a couple of years before children label

A person's anatomical sex and the culturally assigned duties of gender do not always correspond. Throughout history, some men have chosen the roles and dress of women, sometimes with the approval of their communities. In the photo above right, taken about 1885, We-Wha, a Zuni Indian man, wears the traditional dress and decoration of a woman. Likewise, some women have dressed like men and taken on male roles, as did the eighteenth-century pirates Ann Bonny and Mary Read (left).

gender schema A cognitive schema (mental network) of knowledge, beliefs, metaphors, and expectations about what it means to be male or female.

Look familiar? In a scene typical of many nursery schools and homes, the boy builds a gun out of anything he can, and the girl dresses up in any pretty thing she can find. Psychologists (and parents) debate whether such gender typing is biologically based or a result of subtle reinforcements and the emergence of gender schemas.

themselves and others consistently as being a "boy" or "girl." Once they can do that, they begin to prefer same-sex playmates and sex-traditional toys, without being explicitly taught to do so. They become more gender typed in their toy play, games, aggressiveness, and verbal skills than children who still cannot consistently label males and females. Most notably, girls stop behaving aggressively (Fagot, 1993). It is as if they go along behaving like boys—until they know they are girls. At that moment, but not until that moment, they seem to decide: "Girls don't do this; I'm a girl; I'd better not either."

One puzzle of gender development is that virtually all over the world, boys' gender schemas are more rigid than girls' are. That is, boys express stronger preferences for "masculine" toys and activities than girls do for "feminine" ones, and boys are harsher on themselves and other boys who fail to behave in gender-typed ways (Bussey & Bandura, 1992; Maccoby, 1998). One reason may be that most societies value masculine occupations and traits more than feminine ones, and males have higher status. So when boys behave like (or play with) girls, they lose status, and when girls behave like boys, they gain status (Serbin, Powlishta, & Gulko, 1993).

With increasing experience and cognitive sophistication, older children construct their own standards of what boys and girls may or may not do. Eventually, they become aware of exceptions to their gender schemas; they understand that women can be engineers and men can be cooks. From middle childhood on, many people become more flexible about gender rules, especially if they have friends of the other sex and if their families, jobs, or cultures encourage such flexibility (Katz & Ksansnak, 1994). Other people retain rigid gender schemas throughout their lives, feeling uncomfortable with or angry about the prospect of a male nurse or female drill sergeant. You can see how cultural practices—favoring gender equality or extreme gender separation—might affect a child's and adult's gender schemas. How flexible are your own gender schemas?

Learning Influences. A third influence on gender development is the environment, which is full of subtle and not-so-subtle messages about what girls and boys are supposed to do. Behavioral and social–cognitive learning theorists study how the process of gender socialization instills these messages in children. Although many adults say they treat boys and girls equally or that sex differences are apparent right away, research disputes their claims. Gender socialization begins at the moment of birth.

Get Involved ⊞

Can You Imagine Being the Other Sex?

If you woke up tomorrow and found that you had been transformed into a member of the other sex, how would your life change, if at all? Would anything be different about your attitudes, behavior, habits, experiences, choices, preferences, and feelings? Write down your first reactions, and then ask a few of your male and female friends the same question. If possible, ask young children, too. Do their answers differ depending on their sex? If so, how? What does this exercise reveal about gender socialization and schemas?

cathy®   by Cathy Guisewite

For example, parents tend to portray their newborn girls as being more feminine and delicate than boys, and boys as more athletic and stronger than girls—although it is hard to know how athletic a newborn boy could be, because all newborns are pretty delicate (Karraker, Vogel, & Lake, 1995). And many parents are careful to dress their baby in outfits of the "correct" color and pattern for his or her sex. Clothes don't matter to the infant, of course, but they are signals to adults about how to treat the child. Adults often respond to the same baby differently, depending on whether the child is dressed as a boy or a girl (Stern & Karraker, 1989).

Adults respond to boys and girls differently even when the children are behaving in *exactly the same way*. In one observational study, 12- to 16-month-old boys and girls were equally assertive (as measured by the frequency of their efforts to get an adult's attention) and verbal (as measured by attempts to communicate with others). But teachers responded far more often to assertive boys than to shy ones, and to verbal girls than to nonverbal ones. Subtly, the teachers were reinforcing gender-typed behavior. When the researchers observed the same children a year later, a gender difference was now apparent, with boys behaving more assertively and girls talking more to teachers (Fagot et al., 1985).

Parents, teachers, and other adults convey their beliefs and expectations about gender even when they are entirely unaware that they are doing so. For example, when parents believe that boys are naturally better at math or sports and that girls are naturally better at English, they unwittingly communicate those beliefs by how they respond to a child's success or failure. They may tell a son who did well in math, "You're a natural math whiz, Johnny!" But if a daughter gets good grades, they may

Not long ago, these images had the power to startle or offend people; today, they are commonplace. Social and economic changes have required the participation of women in every kind of work, and the participation of men in family life.

say, "Wow, you really worked hard in math, Janey, and it shows!" The implication is that girls have to try hard but boys have a natural gift. Messages like these are not lost on the children, who tend to lose interest in activities that are not "natural" for them—even when they all start out with equal abilities (Frome & Eccles, 1998).

Gender over the Life Span

In today's fast-moving world, gender development has become a lifelong process, in which people's gender schemas, attitudes, and behavior shift as they have new experiences and as society itself changes. In some areas, gender rules are still being negotiated. For example, for many people, the rules governing a date are in flux: Which partner pays? Who asks out whom? Who makes sexual overtures? In other situations, such as working on an assembly line, gender is usually irrelevant.

Gender differences in personality traits and motivations are greatest in childhood and adolescence, but in North America they decline significantly in adulthood (Cohn, 1991). By middle age, many people report a "gender crossover" as they explore aspects of their personalities and interests they had previously suppressed: Women often become more achievement oriented, men more nurturant and family oriented (Franz, 1997; James & Lewkowicz, 1997; Stewart & Ostrove, 1998).

In sum, 3-year-old children may behave like sexist piglets while they are trying to figure out what it means to be male or female. Their behavior may be driven by genes and hormones, cognitive schemas, parental and social lessons, or a combination of all of these factors. But their gender-typed behavior as 3-year-olds often has little to do with how they will behave at 23 or 43. Children can grow up in an extremely gender-typed family and yet, as adults, find themselves in careers or relationships they would never have imagined for themselves (Maccoby, 1998). If 3-year-olds are the gender police, many adults end up breaking the law.

QUICK QUIZ

Quiz-taking is appropriate behavior for all sexes and genders.

1. Two-year-old Paulo thinks that if he changed from wearing pants to wearing dresses he could become a girl. He still lacks a stable _____.

2. A biological psychologist would say that a 3-year-old boy's love of going "vroom, vroom" with his truck collection is probably a result of _____; a learning theorist would say that it results from _____ by parents and teachers.

3. Which statement about gender schemas is *false?* (a) They are present in early form by 1 year of age; (b) they are permanent conceptualizations of what it means to be masculine or feminine; (c) they eventually expand to include many meanings and associations to being male and female; (d) they probably reflect the status of women and men in society.

4. Herb hopes his 4-year-old daughter will become a doctor, but she refuses to play with the toy stethoscope he bought her and insists that only boys can be doctors. What conclusions can Herb draw about gender differences?

Answers:

1. gender identity 2. biological factors such as hormones or brain processes; gender socialization 3. b 4. Not many. His daughter's rigid gender-typed behavior is typical when children are acquiring gender schemas, but it does not predict much of anything about the career she will choose as an adult.

- **What are the pros and cons of going through puberty earlier than most of your classmates?**
- **During adolescence, are extreme turmoil and unhappiness the exception or the rule?**
- **When teenagers and their parents quarrel, what is it typically about?**
- **In what ways do minority teenagers balance their ethnic identity with mainstream culture?**

Adolescence

Adolescence refers to the period of development between **puberty**, the age at which a person becomes capable of sexual reproduction, and adulthood. In some cultures, the time span between puberty and adulthood is only a few months; a sexually mature boy or girl is expected to marry and assume adult tasks. In modern Western societies, teenagers are not considered emotionally mature enough to assume the rights, responsibilities, and roles of adulthood.

puberty The age at which a person becomes capable of sexual reproduction.

menarche [men-ARR-kee] The onset of menstruation.

The Physiology of Adolescence

Until puberty, boys and girls produce roughly the same levels of "male hormones" (androgens) and "female hormones" (estrogens). At puberty, the brain's pituitary gland begins to stimulate hormone production in the adrenal and reproductive glands. From puberty on, boys have a higher level of androgens than girls do, and girls have a higher level of estrogens than boys do.

In boys, the reproductive glands are the testes (testicles), which produce sperm; in girls, the reproductive glands are the ovaries, which release eggs. During puberty, these sex organs mature and the individual becomes capable of reproduction. In girls, the development of breasts and **menarche,** the onset of menstruation, are signs of sexual maturity. In boys, the signs are the onset of nocturnal emissions and the growth of the testes, scrotum, and penis. Hormones are also responsible for the emergence of *secondary sex characteristics,* such as a deepened voice and facial and chest hair in boys and pubic hair in both sexes.

Researchers used to think that sexual attraction and behavior followed the onset of puberty; now there is evidence that the age of first sexual attraction—whether heterosexual or homosexual—usually precedes puberty. Adrenal androgens begin to rise in both boys and girls as early as age 6, and the average age of first sexual attraction to another is about age 10, years before a child's reproductive abilities have fully matured (McClintock & Herdt, 1996).

The Timing of Puberty. The onset of puberty depends on both genetic and environmental factors. Menarche, for example, depends on a female's having a critical level of body fat, which is necessary to sustain a pregnancy. Body fat triggers the hormonal changes associated with puberty (Chehab et al., 1997). An increase in body fat among children in developed countries may help explain why the average age of puberty declined in Europe and North America until the mid-twentieth century. The average age of menarche now occurs at about 12 years and 8 months in white girls and a few months earlier in black girls.

To their embarrassment, children typically reach puberty at different times. These girls are all the same age, but they differ considerably in physical maturity.

The physical changes of puberty are part of the last "growth spurt" on the child's road to adulthood. For girls, the adolescent growth spurt begins, on average, at age 10, peaks at 12 or 13, and stops at about age 16, by which time most girls are sexually mature. For boys, the average adolescent growth spurt starts at about age 12 and ends at about age 18. This difference in rates of development is often a source of misery to adolescents, because most girls mature sooner than most boys.

Early and Late Puberty. The figures we have given you are only averages; individuals vary enormously in the onset and length of puberty. If you entered puberty before most of your classmates, or if you matured much later than they did, you know that your experience of adolescence was different from that of the average teenager (whoever that is). Early-maturing boys generally have a more positive view of their bodies, and their relatively greater size and strength gives them a boost in sports and the prestige that being a good athlete brings young men. But they are also more likely to smoke, drink alcohol in binges, use other drugs, and break the law than later-maturing boys, and to have less self-control and emotional stability (Duncan et al., 1985).

Likewise, some early-maturing girls have the prestige of being socially popular. But, partly because others in their peer group regard them as being sexually precocious, they are also more likely to fight with their parents, drop out of school, have a negative body image, and be angry or depressed. Early menarche itself does not cause these problems; rather, it tends to accentuate existing behavioral problems and family conflicts. Girls who go through puberty relatively late, in contrast, have a more difficult time at first, but by the end of adolescence many are happier with their appearance and more popular than their early-maturing classmates (Caspi & Moffitt, 1991; Stattin & Magnusson, 1990).

Brain Development. When people think of physical changes in adolescence, they usually think of hormones and body maturation. But the brain undergoes significant developmental changes, too, and these occur at a comparable age of adolescence in other species. An explosion of synaptic connections and pruning occurs, just as it does during the baby's first year. One researcher compares this process to remodeling a house—the basic structure is there, but it's perked up a bit. Changes occur primarily in the prefrontal cortex, which is responsible for impulse control and planning, and the limbic system, which is involved in emotional processing (Spear, 2000). In Chapter 16 we will see that errors in the pruning process during adolescence may be involved in the onset of schizophrenia in vulnerable individuals.

The Psychology of Adolescence

In January 2002, a 15-year-old boy stole a small private plane and crashed it into a building, hoping perhaps to emulate the terrorists who destroyed the World Trade Center the previous September. He succeeded only in committing suicide. His action followed closely upon other dramatic episodes in recent years of teenagers killing classmates and teachers, and sometimes themselves. The media were quick to imply that America was in the midst of an explosion of violence among teenage males: Headlines warned of "Teenage Time Bombs" and "[Teenage] Children Without Souls" (Glassner, 2001). How typical are these stories? Are growing numbers of teenagers suicidally depressed and murderously angry?

Turmoil and Adjustment. To begin with, the rate of violent crimes committed by adolescents has actually been plummeting steadily since 1993; in 1999, teenage homicide rates were the lowest they had been since 1966. Even in 1998–1999, when the shooting spree at Columbine High School

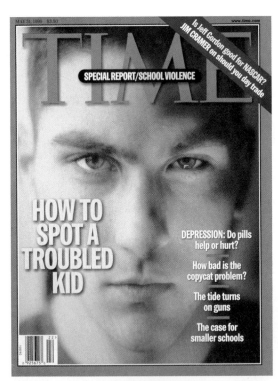

THINKING CRITICALLY

Examine the Evidence

News stories, like the one above, about "troubled," violent, or suicidal teenagers, feed the popular notion that adolescence is a time of misery, anger, and conflict with parents. What is missing from this portrait of adolescence?

occurred, the total number of violent deaths in all American schools was 30 . . . out of 52 million students (Glassner, 2001).

Studies of representative samples of adolescents find that only a small minority are seriously troubled, angry, or unhappy. Most teenagers have supportive families, a sense of purpose and self-confidence, good friends, and the skill to cope with their problems. Extreme turmoil and unhappiness are the exception, not the rule (Steinberg, 1990).

Nevertheless, three kinds of problems are more common during adolescence than during childhood or adulthood: conflict with parents, mood swings and depression, and higher rates of reckless, rule-breaking, and risky behavior (Arnett, 1999). The years of adolescence can be difficult and challenging because teenagers are developing their own standards and values, often by trying on the styles, actions, and attitudes of their peers, in contrast to those of their parents. This is one reason for the appeal of breaking adult rules. The peer group represents the values and style of the generation that they identify with, the generation that they will share experiences with as adults. The peer group teaches children crucial lessons about cooperation, friendship, and getting along with others, and thereby fosters great cognitive complexity (Bukowski, 2001; Hartup, 1999). That is why the peer group becomes especially important during adolescence. As we saw in Chapter 13, many people report that rejection by peers was more devastating than punitive treatment by parents.

Adolescents who are lonely, depressed, worried, or angry tend to express these concerns in ways characteristic of their sex. Boys are more likely than girls to *externalize* their emotional problems in acts of aggression and other antisocial behavior. Girls, in contrast, are more likely than boys to *internalize* their feelings and problems, for example, by becoming withdrawn or developing eating disorders (Zahn-Waxler, 1996).

Separation and Connection. In Western cultures, conflicts between teenagers and adults typically focus on the adolescent's increased desire for autonomy (Eccles et al., 1993). Teenagers are usually trying to *individuate,* to develop their own opinions, values, and style of dress and look; but they do not want to sever the connection entirely. In one study, adolescents described quarrels over issues like these: "Why my mother manipulates the conversation to get me to hate her"; "How much of a bastard my father is to my sister"; "How ugly my mom's taste is"; "How pigheaded my mom and dad are" (Csikszentmihalyi & Larson, 1984). But these fights—over what is important, who should set the rules, differences of opinion and taste, and the like—rarely reflected a true rift between parent and adolescent.

For these young men and women, quarrels with parents tend to signify a change from one-sided parental authority to a more reciprocal, adult relationship (Laursen & Collins, 1994). But in the many collectivist and traditionalist cultures around the world, such as India, most adolescents would not dream of rebelling against their parents, to whom they feel they owe allegiance and loyalty, nor would the goal of autonomy be more important than family harmony (Arnett, 1999; Segall et al., 1999).

Ethnic Identity and Acculturation

One of the great psychological tasks for Western adolescents, as they prepare for entrance into adult responsibilities, centers on the formation of identity: Who am I? Where do I belong in the world? What can I become? Adolescents are formulating many aspects of their identities, including their sexuality, their goals and ambitions, their sense of themselves and what they might become.

An important aspect of identity development, especially in societies that are ethnically diverse, has to do with finding a balance between **ethnic identity**, a close identification with one's religious or ethnic group, and **acculturation**, an identification with

ethnic identity A person's identification with a racial, religious, or ethnic group.

acculturation The process by which members of minority groups come to identify with and feel part of the mainstream culture.

A little adolescent rebellion is common on the road to autonomy.

Bicultural adolescents adopt aspects of mainstream culture. But like the Chicana on the left and the Ukrainian teens on the right, they also enjoy celebrating the traditions of their ethnic heritage.

Ethnic identity

	Strong	Weak
Strong	Bicultural	Assimilated
Weak	Separatist	Marginal

Acculturation

the dominant culture (Cross, 1991; Phinney, 1996; Segall et al., 1999). This process begins early in childhood and continues all through life. But the issues are often especially powerful in adolescence, when teenagers tend to cluster according to their own ethnic groups in school and struggle to find a balance between "loyalty to your own" and "making it" (or "selling out") in the larger world (Spencer & Dornbusch, 1990).

There are theoretically four ways of balancing ethnic identity and acculturation, depending on whether ethnic identity is strong or weak and whether identification with the larger culture is strong or weak (Berry, 1994; Phinney, 1990). People who are *bicultural* have strong ties both to their ethnicity and to the larger culture: They say, "I am proud of my ethnic heritage, but I identify just as much with my country." They can alternate easily between their culture of origin and the majority culture, slipping into the customs and language of each as circumstances dictate. People who choose *assimilation* have weak feelings of ethnicity but a strong sense of acculturation: Their attitude, for example, might be "I'm an American, period." *Ethnic separatists* have a strong sense of ethnic identity but weak feelings of acculturation: They may say, "My ethnicity comes first; if I join the mainstream, I'm betraying my origins." And some people feel *marginal*, connected to neither their ethnicity nor the dominant culture: They tend to feel that they do not belong anywhere.

A person's degree of acculturation may change throughout life in response to experiences and societal events. For example, many immigrants arrive in North America with every intention of becoming "true" Canadians or Americans. If they encounter discrimination or setbacks, however, they may decide that acculturation is harder than they anticipated or that ethnic separatism offers greater solace. In any case, acculturation is rarely a complete accommodation to mainstream culture. Many individuals adopt values and behaviors of the mainstream culture while also keeping aspects of their heritage that are important to their self-identity (Ryder, Alden, & Paulhus, 2000). They pick and choose among customs of their own ethnicity and those of the dominant culture, or they set limits on how far they want their own acculturation to go (Segall et al., 1999). You might become acculturated to another ethnic group's food and customs but believe in the importance of marrying within your own group.

It is a sign of our multiethnic times that increasingly, many people refuse to be pigeonholed into any single ethnic category. In the 2000 U.S. census, nearly 7 million

Get Involved ⊞

How Acculturated Are You?

Refer to the marginal illustration on this page and its categories of bicultural, assimilated, separatist, or marginal. Can you locate yourself in one of those categories, or don't you fit? Are you, say, bicultural about some things and separatist about others? Have you become more or less assimilated in recent years? Ask five friends, relatives, or acquaintances—ideally from different ethnic groups—how they would respond. If you feel that you do not have an ethnic heritage other than a national identity, why is that? Would your parents and grandparents feel the same as you?

people listed themselves as various combinations of identities. The tension over the balance between one's ethnic heritage and mainstream culture is likely to continue as ethnic groups struggle to define their place, raise their status, and secure their identity in a medley of cultures.

QUICK QUIZ

If you are not in the midst of adolescent turmoil, try these questions.

1. The onset of menstruation is called _____.

2. *True or false:* Puberty is not the same thing as adolescence.

3. Extreme turmoil and rebellion in adolescence are (a) nearly universal, (b) the exception rather than the rule, (c) rare.

4. In Western societies, conflicts between teenagers and their parents are typically over issues of _____.

5. Frank, an African-American college student, finds himself caught between two philosophies on his campus. One holds that blacks should move toward full integration into mainstream culture. The other holds that blacks should immerse themselves in the history, values, and contributions of African culture. The first group values _____, whereas the second emphasizes _____.

Answers:

1. menarche 2. true (can you say why?) 3. b 4. autonomy or individuation 5. acculturation, ethnic identity

---

WHAT'S AHEAD

- **What is wrong with thinking that life occurs in a series of predictable stages?**
- **What feelings are common during "emerging adulthood," the years from 18 to 25?**
- **Does menopause make most women depressed and irrational?**
- **Do men go through a male version of menopause?**
- **Which mental abilities decline in old age, and which ones do not?**

Adulthood

According to ancient Greek legend, the Sphinx was a monster—half lion, half woman—who terrorized passersby on the road to Thebes. The Sphinx would ask each traveler a question and then murder those who failed to answer correctly. (The Sphinx was a pretty tough grader.) The question was this: What animal walks on four feet in the morning, two feet at noon, and three feet in the evening? Only one traveler, Oedipus, knew the solution to the riddle. The animal, he said, is Man, who crawls on all fours as a baby, walks upright as an adult, and limps in old age with the aid of a staff.

The Sphinx was the first life-span theorist. Since then, many philosophers, writers, and scientists have speculated on the course of adult development. Are the changes of adulthood predictable, like those of childhood? What are the major psychological issues of adult life? Is mental and physical deterioration in old age inevitable?

Stages and Ages

One of the first modern theorists to propose a life-span approach to psychological development was psychoanalyst Erik H. Erikson (1902–1994). Just as children progress through stages, he said, so do adults. Erikson (1950/1963, 1982) wrote that all individuals go through eight stages in their lives. Each stage is characterized by a particular challenge, which he called a "crisis," that ideally should be resolved before the individual moves on. But the challenges are present in one form or another at all ages of life, and each stage depends on every other.

1 *Trust versus mistrust* is the challenge that occurs during the baby's first year, when the baby depends on others to provide food, comfort, cuddling, and warmth. If these needs are not met, the child may never develop the essential trust of others necessary to get along in the world.

2 *Autonomy (independence) versus shame and doubt* is the challenge that occurs when the child is a toddler. The young child is learning to be independent and must do so without feeling too ashamed or doubtful of his or her actions.

3 *Initiative versus guilt* is the challenge that occurs as the preschooler develops. The child is acquiring new physical and mental skills, setting goals, and enjoying newfound talents, but must also learn to control impulses. The danger lies in developing too strong a sense of guilt over his or her wishes and fantasies.

4 *Competence versus inferiority* is the challenge for school-age children, who are learning to make things, use tools, and acquire the skills for adult life. Children who fail these lessons of mastery and competence may come out of this stage feeling inadequate and inferior.

5 *Identity versus role confusion* is the great challenge of adolescence, when teenagers must decide what they are going to be and what they hope to make of their lives. The term *identity crisis* describes what Erikson considered to be the primary conflict of this stage. Those who resolve it will come out of this stage with a strong identity, ready to plan for the future. Those who do not will sink into confusion, unable to make decisions.

6 *Intimacy versus isolation* is the challenge of young adulthood. Once you have decided who you are, said Erikson, you must share yourself with another and learn to make commitments. No matter how successful you are in work, you are not complete until you are capable of intimacy.

7 *Generativity versus stagnation* is the challenge of the middle years. Now that you know who you are and have an intimate relationship, will you sink into complacency and selfishness, or will you experience generativity—creativity and renewal? Parenthood is the most common means for the successful resolution of this stage, but people can be productive, creative, and nurturant in other ways, in their work or their relationships with the younger generation.

8 *Ego integrity versus despair* is the final challenge of old age. As they age, people strive to reach the ultimate goals—wisdom, spiritual tranquility, an acceptance of their lives. Just as the healthy child will not fear life, said Erikson, the healthy adult will not fear death.

Erikson recognized that cultural and economic factors affect people's development through these stages. Some societies, for example, make the passages relatively easy. If you know you are going to be a farmer like your parents and you have no alternative, then moving from adolescence into young adulthood is not a terribly painful step (unless you hate farming). If you have many choices, however, as adolescents in urban societies often do, the transition can become prolonged. Some people put off making choices and never resolve their "identity crisis." Similarly,

According to Erik Erikson, children must resolve the challenge of generativity—as this child and her grandmother certainly are doing. But are the needs for generativity and competence important at only one stage of life?

cultures that place a high premium on independence and individualism will make it difficult for many of their members to resolve Erikson's sixth crisis, that of intimacy versus isolation.

Erikson's work reminds us that development is an ongoing process. His ideas were important because he placed adult development in the context of family, work, and society, and he specified many of the essential concerns of adulthood: trust, competence, identity, generativity, and the ability to enjoy life and accept death.

Current Approaches to Adult Development. Because Erikson discussed these themes in terms of their presumably greatest importance at different ages, many readers of his work assumed that the psychological concerns he identified occur at only one crucial time of life. Erikson was aware that they can occur "out of order," although that was not his emphasis.

Later researchers, working at a time when people's lives had become less traditional and predictable, discovered just how out of order people's psychological concerns can be. Although in Western societies adolescence *is* often a time of confusion about identity and aspirations, an identity crisis is not limited to the teen years. A man who has worked in one job all his life, and then is laid off and must find an entirely new career, may have an identity crisis too. Likewise, competence is not mastered once and for all in childhood. People learn new skills and lose old ones throughout their lives, and their sense of competence rises and falls accordingly. Moreover, people who are highly generative (in terms of being committed to helping the next generation) tend to be so throughout their lives, doing volunteer work or choosing occupations that allow them to contribute to society, rather than at only one age (Mansfield & McAdams, 1996).

Stage theories, therefore, are no longer considered an adequate way of understanding how adults grow and change (or remain the same) across the life span (Helson & Srivastava, 2001). Psychologists now regard adult development as an interaction of biological changes, personality traits, personal experiences, larger historical and cultural events, the particular environments that people live in, and the friends and relationships they have (Bronfenbrenner, 1995; Schaie & Willis, 2002). The result of this complex interaction is, as one psychologist summarized, that "there is not one process of aging, but many; there is not one life course followed, but multiple courses. . . . The variety is as rich as the historic conditions people have faced and the current circumstances they experience" (Pearlin, 1982).

Remember the cute children pictured on page 504? They are Adolph Hitler, Queen Elizabeth II, and Albert Einstein. What genetic, familial, and historical influences made these three famous people so remarkably different?

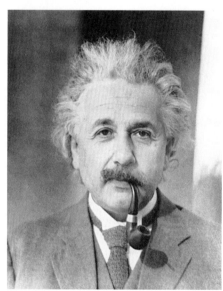

What is your reaction to these two first-time mothers? Arceli Keh (left), whose story began this chapter, became a mother at the age of 63; but the mother on the right had a child as a young teen. Do you think that either or both of these women are "off time" for the transition to motherhood, and does your answer affect your feelings about them?

The Transitions of Life

Of course, certain events do tend to occur at particular times in life: going to school, learning to drive a car, having a baby, retiring from work. In all societies, people rely on a *social clock* to determine whether they are "on time" for these transitions or "off time." The social clock consists of norms governing what people of the same age and historical generation are expected to do (Helson & McCabe, 1993; Moen & Wethington, 1999; Neugarten, 1979).

Cultures have different social clocks. In some, young men and women are supposed to marry and start having children right after puberty, and work responsibilities come later. In others, a man may not marry until he has shown that he can support a family, which might not be until his 30s. Doing the right thing at the right time, compared to your friends, is reassuring. When nearly everyone your age goes through the same experience or enters a new role at the same time, adjusting to these transitions is relatively easy. Conversely, if you *aren't* doing these things and hardly anyone you know is doing them either, you will not feel out of step.

Today, social clocks are not telling time the way they once did. Most people will face unanticipated transitions, events that happen without warning, such as being fired from a job because of downsizing. And many people have to deal with changes that they *expect* to happen that do not: for example, not getting married at the age they expected, not getting promoted, not being able to afford to retire, or realizing that they cannot have children (Schlossberg & Robinson, 1996). With this in mind, consider some of the major transitions of life.

Emerging Adulthood. In industrialized nations, major demographic changes have postponed the timing of career decisions, marriage or cohabitation, and parenthood until a person's late 20s or 30s on the average. The result has been the social creation of a new phase of life, between the ages of 18 and 25, that is distinctly different from both adolescence and adulthood. Jeffrey Arnett (2000) calls these years "emerging adulthood." When "emerging adults" are asked whether they feel they have reached adulthood, the majority answer: in some ways yes, in some ways no (see Figure 14.5). "They have no name for the period they are in—because the society they live in has no name for it—so they regard themselves as being neither adolescents nor adults," Arnett observes.

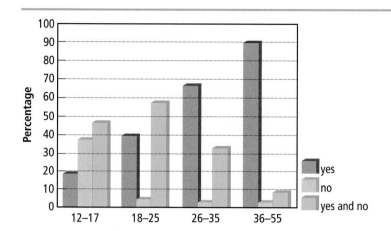

Figure 14.5

ARE YOU AN ADULT YET?

When people are asked "Do you feel that you have reached adulthood?" the percentage who answer "yes" steadily increases over time. But as you can see, people between the ages of 18 and 25, "emerging adults," are most likely to say "yes *and* no" (Arnett, 2000).

In certain respects, emerging adults have moved beyond adolescence into maturity, becoming more emotionally controlled, more confident, less dependent, and less angry and alienated (Roberts, Caspi, & Moffitt, 2001). But they are also the group most likely to live unstable lives, feel unrooted, and take risks. Emerging adults move more often than other demographic groups do—back to their parents' homes and then out again, from one city to another, from living with roommates to living on their own. And their rates of binge drinking, having unprotected sex, and drunk driving are higher than those of any other age group, including adolescents.

Of course, not all young people in this age group are alike. Some groups within the larger society, such as Mormons, promote early marriage and parenthood. And young people who are poor, who have dropped out of school, who had a child at 16, or who have few opportunities for good jobs will not have the income or leisure to "explore" many possible options. But the overall shift in all industrialized nations toward a global economy, increased education, and delayed career and family decisions, Arnett (2000) predicts, means that emerging adulthood is likely to grow in importance as a distinct phase of prolonged exploration and freedom.

The Middle Years. Most people think that the most important issues of the middle years are, for women, the misery of menopause and the "empty nest" (when grown children leave home), and, for men, a corresponding "midlife crisis."

Actually, according to a large-scale research project that has followed 8,000 Americans for 10 years, for most women and men the midlife years—between 35 and 65—are the prime of life (MacArthur Foundation, 1999). These years are often a time of reflection and reassessment; people look back on what they have accomplished, take stock of what they regret not having done, and think about what they want to do with their remaining years (Stewart & Vandewater, 1999). Far from being a time of crisis, midlife is typically a time of psychological well-being, good health, productivity, and community involvement. When midlife crises do occur (with equal likelihood for both sexes), it is for reasons not related to aging but to specific life-changing events, such as illness or the loss of a job or spouse (Wethington, 2000).

But doesn't menopause make most midlife women depressed, irritable, and irrational? **Menopause,** which usually occurs between ages 45 and 55, is the cessation of menstruation after the ovaries stop producing estrogen and progesterone. Menopause does produce physical symptoms in many women, notably "hot flashes," as the vascular system adjusts to the decrease in estrogen. But only about 10 percent of all women have unusually severe physical symptoms.

The negative view of menopause as a syndrome that causes depression and other negative emotional reactions is based on women who have had an early menopause following a hysterectomy (removal of the uterus) or who have had a lifetime history

menopause The cessation of menstruation and of the production of ova; it is usually a gradual process lasting up to several years.

of depression. But these women are not typical. According to many surveys of thousands of healthy, randomly chosen women in the general population, most women view menopause positively (with relief that they no longer have to worry about pregnancy or menstrual periods) or with no particular feelings at all. The vast majority have only a few, temporarily bothersome symptoms, and do not become depressed; only 3 percent even report regret at having reached menopause (MacArthur Foundation, 1999; Matthews et al., 1990; McKinlay, McKinlay, & Brambilla, 1987).

Although women lose their fertility after menopause and men theoretically remain fertile throughout their lives, men have a "biological clock" too. Testosterone diminishes, although it never drops as sharply in men as estrogen does in women. The sperm count may gradually drop, and the sperm still produced are more likely to have genetic mutations that can increase the risk of certain diseases in children conceived by older fathers. (The cells that become sperm divide and reproduce frequently, unlike a woman's ova, and each cell division introduces a slight risk of mutation in the DNA.) For example, fathers over age 50 have three times the risk of conceiving a child who develops schizophrenia as fathers under age 25 (Malaspina, 2001).

Although hormone levels decline in the middle years, hormones do not cause a midlife crisis in men any more than in women. For both sexes, the physical changes of midlife do not predict how people will feel about aging or how they will respond to it (Moen, 2001; Schaie & Willis, 2002).

More and more people are living not merely into old age, but past 100. This six-generation family includes Sara Knauss, age 118 (center), her daughter Kitty Sullivan, age 95 (right), her grandson Bob Butz, age 73 (center), her great-granddaughter Kathy Jacoby, age 49 (standing), her great-great-granddaughter Kristina Patton, age 27 (on floor), and her great-great-great-grandson Bradley Patton, age 3. Bradley doesn't yet know how many family relationships he will have to remember.

Old Age

In Western youth-oriented cultures, old people are typically assumed to be forgetful, somewhat senile, and physically feeble. On television and in the movies, old people are usually portrayed as objects of amusement, sympathy, or scorn. But *gerontologists*—researchers who study aging and the old— have been challenging these stereotypes.

To begin with, when does old age start? Not long ago you would have been considered old in your 60s. Today, the fastest-growing segment of the population in North America consists of people over the age of 85. There were 4 million Americans age 85 or older in 2000, and the Census Bureau projects that there may be as many as 31 million by 2050 (Schneider, 1999). And there will be more than 600,000 Americans over the age of 100. How will these people do?

First, the Bad News. Various aspects of intelligence, memory, and other forms of mental functioning decline significantly with age; older adults score lower on tests of reasoning, spatial ability, and complex problem solving than do younger adults (Verhaeghen & Salthouse, 1997).

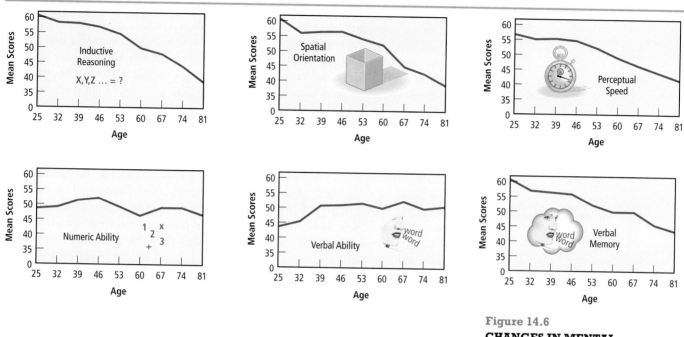

Figure 14.6

CHANGES IN MENTAL FUNCTIONING OVER TIME

As these graphs show, some intellectual abilities tend to dwindle with age, but numerical and verbal abilities remain relatively steady over the years.

It takes older people longer to retrieve names, dates, and other information; in fact, the speed of cognitive processing in general slows down significantly (Bashore, Ridderinkhof, & van der Molen, 1997).

But not all cognitive abilities worsen with age; fluency with words and numbers, for example, remains pretty constant (see Figure 14.6). Gerontologists distinguish two kinds of cognitive ability. **Fluid intelligence** is the capacity for deductive reasoning and the ability to use new information to solve problems (the kind of intelligence discussed in Chapters 3 and 9). It reflects an inherited predisposition, and it parallels other biological capacities in its growth and, in later years, its decline (Baltes & Graf, 1996; Bosworth & Schaie, 1999). **Crystallized intelligence** consists of knowledge and skills built up over a lifetime—the kind of intelligence that gives us the ability to solve math problems, define words, or take political positions. It depends heavily on education and experience, and it tends to remain stable or even improve over the life span. This is why physicians, lawyers, teachers, farmers, musicians, insurance agents, politicians, psychologists, and people in many other occupations can continue working well into old age.

Now the Good News. Fortunately, gerontologists have made great strides in separating conditions once thought to be an inevitable part of old age from those that are preventable or treatable:

▶ Apparent senility in the elderly is often caused by prescription medications, harmful combinations of medications, and even by over-the-counter drugs (such as sleeping pills and antihistamines), all of which can be hazardous to old people.

▶ Depression and passivity often result from the loss of meaningful activity, intellectual stimulation, and control over events (Langer, 1983; Schaie & Zuo, 2001).

▶ Weakness and frailty are often caused by sedentary lifestyles. Exercise and moderate levels of weight training can restore strength and flexibility (Rowe & Kahn, 1998).

Gerontologists estimate that only about 30 percent of the physical losses of old age are genetically based; the other 70 percent have to do with behavioral and psychological factors (Rowe & Kahn, 1998). A longitudinal Canadian study of 250 middle-aged

THINKING CRITICALLY

Consider Other Explanations

People assume that aging inevitably produces senility, depression, weakness, and a decline in mental abilities. What else could be causing these problems?

fluid intelligence The capacity for deductive reasoning and the ability to use new information to solve problems; it is relatively independent of education and tends to decline in old age.

crystallized intelligence Cognitive skills and specific knowledge of information acquired over a lifetime; it is heavily dependent on education and tends to remain stable over the lifetime.

and older adults found that those who remained involved in intellectually challenging activities did not show declines in cognitive ability (Hultsch et al., 1999). The researchers could not rule out the possibility that people with high cognitive functioning continue to pursue intellectual challenges because they are able to. But other research shows that mental stimulation does increase mental functioning. Older adults can sometimes do as well on memory tests as people in their 20s, when given guidance and cues for retrieving memories—for example, when they are taught to use encoding strategies rather than making lists (Loewen, Shaw, & Craik, 1990). Short-term training programs for people between 60 and 80 produce gains in mental-test scores that are as large as the losses typical for that age group (Baltes, Sowarka, & Kliegl, 1989; Willis, 1987).

Although some losses are inevitable with age, physical exercise and mental stimulation promote the growth of synapses in the human brain, even well into old age (Kleim et al., 1998). Also, as people age, their brains seem to compensate for cognitive losses by recruiting areas that previously had not been involved in a given task. In PET-scan studies comparing younger adults (ages 18 to 30) and older adults (ages 65 to 75) on memory tests, the younger people's brains showed lateralization in the frontal lobes: left hemispheric activation for verbal memory and right hemispheric activation for spatial memory. But in the older people, both halves of the frontal lobe were activated for both types of memory (Reuter-Lorenz, Stanczak, & Miller, 1999; Reuter-Lorenz et al., 2000).

Perhaps the best news is that as people get older, most become happier and their well-being improves; they learn to regulate negative feelings and emphasize the positive (Mroczek & Kolarz, 1998). The frequency of intense negative emotions is highest among people aged 18 to 34, then drops sharply to age 65. After 65, it levels off, rising only slightly among old people facing crises of illness and bereavement (Carstensen et al., 2000; Charles, Reynolds, & Gatz, 2001). Perhaps some people do grow wiser, or at least more peaceful, with age!

Some researchers who study aging are therefore optimistic. In their view, people who have challenging occupations and interests, and who adapt flexibly to change, are likely to maintain their cognitive abilities (Diamond, 1993; Kolb & Whishaw, 1998). "Use it or lose it," they say. Other researchers, however, are less optimistic.

The two images of old age: More and more old people are living healthy, active, mentally stimulating lives, but with increasing longevity, many people are also falling victim to degenerative diseases such as Alzheimer's.

"When you've lost it, you can't use it," they reply. They are worried about the growing numbers of people living into their 90s and beyond, when rates of cognitive impairment and dementia rise dramatically (Thomassen, van Schaick, & Blansjaar, 1998). The challenge for society is to make sure that the many people who will be living into advanced old age can keep using their brains instead of losing them.

QUICK QUIZ

People of any age can answer this quiz.

1. The key psychological issue during adolescence, said Erikson, is a(n) _____ crisis.

2. What new phase of life development has been created because of demographic changes, and what years does it include?

3. Most women react to menopause by (a) feeling depressed, (b) regretting the loss of femininity, (c) going a little crazy, (d) feeling relieved or neutral.

4. Which of these statements about the decline of mental abilities in old age is *false?* (a) It can often be lessened with training programs; (b) it inevitably happens to all old people; (c) it is sometimes a result of malnutrition or disease rather than aging; (d) it is slowed when people live in stimulating environments.

5. Suddenly, your 80-year-old grandmother has become confused and delusional. Before concluding that old age has made her senile, what other explanation should you rule out?

Answers:

1. identity 2. emerging adulthood, ages 18 to 25 3. d 4. b 5. You should rule out the possibility that she is taking too many medications, even nonprescription drugs, that can be hazardous in older people.

WHAT'S AHEAD

● **Do traumatic childhood experiences affect a person forever?**
● **Do most abused children become abusive parents?**

Are Adults Prisoners of Childhood?

Most people take for granted that the path from childhood to adolescence to adulthood is a fairly straight one. We think of the lasting attitudes, habits, and values our parents taught us. We continue to have deep emotional attachments to our families, even when we are fighting with them. And many people carry with them the scars of emotional wounds they suffered as children. When children have been beaten, neglected, or constantly subjected to verbal or physical abuse by their parents, they are in fact more likely than other children to have emotional problems, become delinquent and violent, commit crimes, have low IQs, drop out of school, or attempt suicide (Emery & Laumann-Billings, 1998; Malinosky-Rummell & Hansen, 1993; Maxfield & Widom, 1996).

Many clinicians therefore have accepted the psychodynamic assumption that childhood traumas have specific emotional effects that inevitably continue into adulthood. They have come to believe this because, in their work as therapists, they naturally see the people who are having trouble coping with events of the past. They do not see the people in the general population who have overcome their early experiences. Research psychologists, in contrast, have questioned the psychodynamic assumption about the effects of early trauma and have produced considerable evidence that disputes it:

THINKING CRITICALLY

Analyze Assumptions

Many people are convinced that childhood traumas always cause emotional problems in adulthood. What is wrong with this assumption, and what evidence does it overlook?

Most children who suffered troubling, painful early experiences are surprisingly resilient. Although the actress Audrey Hepburn nearly starved to death in her native Belgium during the Nazi occupation in World War II, she ultimately became a happy and successful adult. Until the end of her life, she worked tirelessly on behalf of children suffering from the effects of illiteracy, famine, and war.

▶ *Recovery from war.* After World War II, many European children, made homeless by the war, were adopted by American families. About 20 percent of the children had problems at first, but over the years they all made good progress in school, none had psychiatric problems, and all established happy, affectionate relationships with their new parents (Rathbun, DiVirgilio, & Waldfogel, 1958).

▶ *Recovery from early illness.* Researchers who followed the development of hundreds of biologically vulnerable children from birth to age 32 found that supportive home environments totally overcame any initial problems. "As we watched these children grow from babyhood to adulthood," the researchers reported, "we could not help but respect the self-righting tendencies within them that produced normal development under all but the most persistently adverse circumstances" (Werner, 1989).

▶ *Recovery from abusive or alcoholic parents.* Compared to children of healthy parents, more children of abusive or alcoholic parents become abusive or alcoholic themselves, but the majority do not (Cohen, 1999; Kaufman & Zigler, 1987; West & Prinz, 1987).

▶ *Recovery from sexual abuse.* Children who have been sexually abused have more emotional and behavioral symptoms than nonabused children, especially if the abuse is severe and repeated. Yet the research shows, much to people's surprise, that by adulthood, most victims are as well adjusted as people in the general population. Meta-analyses of studies of nearly 37,000 college students and of more than 12,000 adults have found no *overall* link between childhood sexual abuse and later emotional disorders or unusual psychological problems (Rind & Tromovitch, 1997; Rind, Tromovitch, & Bauserman, 1998).

This reassuring news does not mean that it is easy to recover from abuse and neglect or that society can afford to be indifferent to children's welfare. But as children develop, they are subject to other influences, too. Psychologists are now looking for the origins of *resilience* in the children of violent, neglectful, abusive, or alcoholic parents (Cowen et al., 1990; Garmezy, 1991); see Table 14.2. One psychologist, Ann Masten (2001), who has long studied this topic, observed that most people assume that there is something special and rare about these children. "The

Table 14.2	**Sources of Resilience in Children and Adolescents**

The following sources of resilience will vary in importance, depending on whether a child's difficulties or traumatic experiences are due to parental, enviromental, or physical factors (e.g., parental abuse, poverty and deprivation, or chronic illness).

Source	Examples
Individual	Good intellectual functioning Sociable, easygoing disposition Self-efficacy, self-confidence Talents and skills Religious faith
Family	Close relationship to caring adult Authoritative parenting: warmth, structure, high expectations Socioeconomic advantages Connections to extended family
Community	Bonds to supportive adults outside family Connections to organizations (e.g., church, sports, drama club) Safe and effective schools

Source: Based on Masten & Coatsworth, 1998

great surprise" of the research, she concludes, is how ordinary and common resilience is. Many of these children have easygoing temperaments or personality traits, such as self-efficacy, that affect how they respond to adversity; they roll with fairly severe punches. Other resilient children are rescued by love and attention from their siblings, extended family, peers, or caring adults other than their parents. And some have experiences outside the family—in schools, places of worship, or other organizations—that give them a sense of competence, moral support, solace, religious faith, and self-esteem.

Perhaps the most powerful reason for the resilience of so many children, and for the changes that adults make throughout their lives, is that we are all constantly interpreting our experiences. We can decide to repeat the mistakes our parents made or break free of them. We can decide to remain prisoners of childhood or to strike out in new directions at 20, 50, . . . or 70. In the next decades, as the world changes in countless unpredictable ways, the territory of adulthood will continue to expand, providing new frontiers as well as fewer signposts and roadmaps to guide us. Increasingly, age will be what we make of it.

Taking Psychology with You

BRINGING UP BABY

Every year or so another best-selling book arrives to tell parents they've been doing it all wrong. Years ago the public was warned that the most crucial thing is bonding: The mother must bond with the baby right away, right after birth, or dire things will happen to the baby's development. Then it turned out that although immediate bonding is certainly nice if you can do it, adopted babies will bond to parents just fine even if the adoption took place several days, months, or years after the child's birth (Eyer, 1992). Today, countless books advise parents to treat their children in very specific, if contradictory ways: Pick them up, don't pick them up; respond when they cry, don't respond when they cry; let them sleep with you, never let them sleep with you; be highly sensitive to their every need so they will securely attach to you, don't overreact to their every mood or complaint or you will spoil them.

No need to panic. As we have seen in this chapter, babies and young chil-

dren thrive under a wide variety of child-rearing methods. They bring their own temperaments to the matter, too: Some respond readily to induction; others require stricter discipline. And as children grow up, they are subject to the influences of their peers and generation and to particular experiences that shape their interests and motivation.

Well, then, how *should* you treat your children? Should you be strict or lenient, powerful or permissive? Should you require your child to stop having tantrums, to clean up his or her room, to be polite? Should you say, "Oh, nothing I do will matter, anyway" or "Children need to express themselves in any way they please"? Child-development research suggests certain overall guidelines to help parents teach children to be confident, considerate, and helpful:

▶ *Set high expectations that are appropriate to the child's age and temperament, and teach the child how to meet them.* Some parents make

few demands on their children, either unintentionally or because they believe a parent should not impose standards. Others make many demands, such as requiring children to be polite, help with chores, control their anger, be thoughtful of others, and do well in school. The children of parents who make few demands tend to be aggressive, impulsive, and immature. The children of parents who have high expectations tend to be helpful and above average in competence and self-confidence (Damon, 1995). But the demands must be appropriate for the child's age. You can't expect 2-year-olds to dress themselves, and before you can expect children to get up on time, they have to know how to work an alarm clock.

▶ *Explain, explain, explain.* Induction—telling a child why you have applied a rule—teaches a child to be responsible. Punitive methods ("Do it or I'll spank you") may result in compliance, but the child will tend to disobey as soon as you are out of sight. Explanations also teach children how to reason and understand; they reward curiosity and open-mindedness. While setting standards for your children, you can also allow them to express disagreements and feelings. This does not mean you have to argue with a 4-year-old about the merits of table manners or permit antisocial and destructive behavior. Once you have explained a rule, you need to enforce it consistently.

▶ *Encourage empathy.* Call the child's attention to the effects of his or her actions on others, appeal to the child's sense of fair play and desire to be good, and teach the child to take another person's point of view. Even very young children are capable of empathy and taking another perspective. Vague orders, such as "Don't fight," are less effective than showing the child how fighting disrupts and hurts others. For boys especially, aggression and empathy are strongly and negatively related: the higher the one, the lower the other (Eisenberg et al., 1996).

▶ *Notice, approve of, and reward good behavior.* Many parents punish the behavior they dislike, a form of attention that often is rewarding to the child. It is much more effective to praise the behavior you do want, which teaches the child how to behave.

Even the best parental practices cannot create the "ideal child"—that is, one who is an exact replica of you. You cannot control everything that happens to your child or your child's basic temperamental dispositions. "The idea that we can make our children turn out any way we want is an illusion. Give it up," advises Judith Harris (1998). But, she adds, parents do have the power to make their children's lives miserable or secure, and to affect the quality of the relationship they will have with their child throughout life: one filled with conflict and resentment, or one that is close and loving.

Summary

▶ *Developmental psychologists* study how people grow and change over the life span. Many study *socialization,* the process by which children learn the rules and behavior society expects of them.

From Conception to the First Year

▶ *Maturation* is the unfolding of genetically influenced behavior and characteristics. Prenatal development consists of the *germinal, embryonic,* and *fetal* stages. Harmful influences that can adversely affect the fetus's development include German measles and other illnesses, toxic chemicals, some sexually transmitted diseases, cigarettes, alcohol (which can cause *fetal alcohol syndrome* and cognitive deficits), illegal drugs, and even over-the-counter medications.

▶ Babies are born with *motor reflexes* and a number of perceptual abilities. Newborns are also naturally attracted to human faces, and soon after birth they develop *synchrony* of pace and rhythm with their caregivers. Cultural practices affect the timing of physical "milestones" such as crawling.

▶ Babies' survival depends on physical and emotional attachment to their caregivers. Their innate need for *contact comfort* gives rise to emotional attachment to their caregivers, and by the age of 6 to 8 months, infants begin to feel *separation anxiety.* Studies of the *Strange Situation* have distinguished *secure* from *insecure* attachment; insecurity takes two forms, *avoidant* or *anxious-ambivalent.*

▶ Styles of attachment are relatively unaffected by the normal range of child-rearing practices, and also by whether or not babies spend time in day care. Insecure attachment may be caused by parents who reject, mistreat, or abandon their infants, by the child's own fearful, insecure temperament, or by stressful family situations.

▶ The first few years of life are important for later cognitive development. But the brain develops all through childhood, adolescence, and adulthood. No one knows how much of the brain's synaptic growth in the first years is due to genetics or experience, or what kinds of experience are important.

Cognitive Development

▶ Infants are responsive to the pitch, intensity, and sound of language, which may be why adults in many cultures speak to babies in *parentese,* using higher-pitched words and exaggerated intonation. At 4 to 6 months of age, babies begin to recognize the sounds of their own language; they go through a babbling phase from age 6 months to 1 year. At about 1 year, they start saying single words and using symbolic gestures, which are important to language development. At age 2, children speak in two- or three-word *telegraphic* sentences that convey a variety of messages.

▶ Jean Piaget argued that cognitive development depends on an interaction between maturation and a child's experiences in the world. Children's thinking changes and adapts through *assimilation* and *accommodation*. Piaget proposed four stages of cognitive development: *sensorimotor* (birth to age 2), during which the child learns *object permanence; preoperational* (ages 2 to 7), during which language and symbolic thought develop, although the child remains *egocentric* in reasoning; *concrete operations* (ages 7 to 12), during which the child comes to understand *conservation,* identity, and serial ordering; and *formal operations* (age 12 to adulthood), during which abstract reasoning develops.

▶ Lev Vygotsky, working at about the same time as Piaget, emphasized a *sociocultural* approach to children's cognitive development. He noted that once children develop language, they begin speaking to themselves (using *private speech*) to direct their own behavior.

▶ Researchers have found that the changes from one stage to another are not as clear-cut as Piaget implied; that young children have more cognitive abilities, at earlier ages, than Piaget thought; and that young children are not always egocentric in their thinking. By the age of 4 or 5 they have developed a *theory of mind* to account for their own and other people's behavior. Cultural practices affect the pace and content of cognitive development, and not all adults develop the ability for formal operations.

Moral Development

▶ Lawrence Kohlberg's theory of moral development proposed three levels of moral reasoning, each with two stages: *preconventional morality* (based on rules, punishment, and self-interest), *conventional morality* (based on relationships and rules of justice and law), and *postconventional morality* (based on higher principles of human rights). Stage theories of moral reasoning have four limitations: They tend to confuse verbal sophistication, acquired through formal education, with moral reasoning ability; they overlook the power of culture; moral reasoning is often inconsistent across situations; and moral reasoning and moral behavior are often unrelated.

▶ Carol Gilligan argued that women tend to base moral decisions on principles of compassion, whereas men tend to base theirs on abstract principles of justice. Most research, however, finds no gender differences in moral reasoning.

▶ Parental methods of discipline have different consequences for a child's moral behavior. *Power assertion* is associated with children who are more aggressive and fail to internalize moral standards. The effects of physical punishment (such as spanking) depend on the family con-

text and on the severity and frequency of the punishment. *Induction* is associated with children who develop empathy and internalized moral standards and who can resist temptation. In general, *authoritative* parents, who use induction and set limits, have better results with their children than do *authoritarian* or *permissive* parents.

Gender Development

▶ Gender development includes the emerging awareness of *gender identity,* the understanding that a person is biologically male or female regardless of what he or she does or wears, and *gender typing,* the process by which boys and girls learn what it means to be masculine or feminine.

▶ Biological psychologists account for gender differences in behavior in terms of genetics, hormones, and brain organization, observing that universally, young children tend to prefer same-sex toys and playing with other children of their sex. Cognitive psychologists study how children develop *gender schemas* of "male" and "female" categories and qualities, which in turn shape their gender-typed behavior. Gender schemas tend to be inflexible at first but often become more flexible as the child cognitively matures and assimilates new information. Learning theorists study the direct and subtle reinforcers and social messages that foster gender typing.

▶ Gender development changes over the life span, depending on people's experiences with work and family life. Gender differences are greatest in childhood and adolescence, but often decline in adulthood.

Adolescence

▶ *Adolescence* begins with the physical changes of *puberty.* In girls, puberty is signaled by *menarche* and the development of breasts; in boys, it begins with the onset of nocturnal emissions and the development of the testes and scrotum. Boys and girls who enter puberty early tend to have a more difficult later adjustment than do those who enter puberty later than average. One reason may be that early puberty intensifies existing problems from childhood.

▶ Most adolescents do not go through extreme emotional turmoil, anger, or rebellion. However, conflict with parents, mood swings and depression, and reckless behavior are more common in adolescence than in childhood or adulthood. The peer group becomes especially important for teenagers. Boys tend to externalize their emotional problems in acts of aggression and other antisocial behavior; girls tend to internalize their problems by becoming withdrawn or developing eating disorders. One challenge of adolescence in Western cultures is *individuation,* breaking away from parents to develop autonomy and a more reciprocal relationship.

▶ In culturally diverse societies, many adolescents face the problem of balancing their *ethnic identity* with *acculturation* into the larger society. A person may become bicultural, assimilated, separatist, or marginal—or some combination of these, depending on the custom or attitude in question. The way people balance ethnic identity and acculturation often changes over the life span.

Adulthood

▶ Erik Erikson proposed that life consists of eight stages, each with a unique psychological challenge, or crisis, that must be resolved, such as an *identity crisis* in adolescence. Erikson identified many of the essential concerns of adulthood and showed that development is a lifelong process. However, adult stages are not universal, and psychological issues or crises are not confined to particular chronological periods. Because of the variety of experiences, cultural and historical influences, and personality traits that influence adults, modern theorists do not regard adults as moving through "stages."

▶ Adults often evaluate their development according to a *social clock* that determines whether they are "on time" or "off time" for a particular event. When most people in an age group go through the same event at about the same time, transitions are easier than when people are "out of step."

▶ In industrialized nations, major demographic changes have postponed the timing of career decisions, marriage, and parenthood until a person's late 20s or 30s on the average. The result is a new life phase during the years between 18 and 25, "emerging adulthood." For many, this phase is qualitatively different from both adolescence and adulthood.

▶ The middle years are generally not a time of turmoil or crisis, but the prime of most people's lives. In women, *menopause* begins in the late 40s or early 50s. Many women have temporary physical symptoms, but most do not regret the end of fertility or become depressed and irritable. In middle-aged men, hormone production slows down but fertility continues, although mutations in sperm increase the risk of birth defects in offspring of older fathers.

▶ *Gerontologists* have revised our ideas about old age, now that people are living longer and healthier lives. The speed of cognitive processing slows down, and *fluid intelligence* parallels other biological capacities in its eventual decline. *Crystallized intelligence*, in contrast, depends heavily on culture, education, and experience, and it tends to remain stable over the life span.

▶ Many supposedly inevitable results of aging, such as senility, depression, and physical weakness, are often the result of disease, medication, poor nutrition, and lack of stimulation, control of one's environment, and exercise. Exercise and mental stimulation promote the growth of synapses in the human brain, even well into old age, although some mental losses are inevitable.

Are Adults Prisoners of Childhood?

▶ Children who experience violence or neglect are at risk of many serious problems later in life. But the majority of children are resilient, able to overcome early traumas and even parental abuse. Psychologists now study not only the sad consequences of neglect, poverty, and violence, but also the origins of resilience under adversity, which they find more common and ordinary than was once believed.

Key Terms

developmental psychology 504

socialization 504

maturation 504

germinal, embryonic, fetal stages 505

zygote 505

fetus 505

fetal alcohol syndrome 506

motor reflexes 506

synchrony 507

contact comfort 508

separation anxiety 509

Strange Situation 509

kinds of attachment (Ainsworth): secure, avoidant, anxious-ambivalent 509

"parentese" 513

telegraphic speech 513

Jean Piaget 514

assimilation 514

accommodation 514

sensorimotor stage 514

object permanence 515

preoperational stage 515

operations 515

egocentric thinking 515

conservation 515

concrete operations stage 516

formal operations stage 516

Lev Vygotsky 516

private speech 516

theory of mind 518

preconventional, conventional, and postconventional levels of moral reasoning (Kohlberg) 520

care-based versus justice-based moral reasoning (Gilligan) 521

◄ LOOKING BACK

- How can a pregnant woman reduce the risk of damage to the embryo or fetus? (p. 506)

- Given a choice, what do newborns prefer to look at? (pp. 506–507)

- Does culture affect when and whether a baby learns to crawl? (p. 508)

- Why is cuddling so important for infants (not to mention adults)? (pp. 508–509)

- If you have a 1-year-old, why shouldn't you worry if your baby cries when left with a new baby-sitter? (p. 509)

- Do the experiences of the first years of life affect a child's brain forever? (pp. 511–512)

- Why do so many parents speak "baby talk"? (p. 513)

- What important accomplishment are infants revealing when they learn to play peekaboo? (p. 515)

- Why will most 5-year-olds choose a tall, narrow glass of lemonade over a short, fat glass containing the same amount? (p. 515)

- According to a leading theory, why is moral reasoning that is based on law, justice, and duty *not* the pinnacle of moral development? (p. 520)

- When reasoning about moral dilemmas, are women more compassionate and caring than men are? (p. 521)

- What is wrong with "because I say so" as a way of getting children to behave? (p. 522)

- How would a biologically oriented psychologist explain why most little boys and girls are "sexist" in their choice of toys? (p. 525)

- How do teachers unintentionally make boys more aggressive? (p. 527)

- If a little girl "knows" that girls can't be doctors, does this mean she will never go to medical school? (p. 528)

- What are the pros and cons of going through puberty earlier than most of your classmates? (pp. 529–530)

- During adolescence, are extreme turmoil and unhappiness the exception or the rule? (pp. 530–531)

- When teenagers and their parents quarrel, what is it typically about? (p. 531)

- In what ways do minority teenagers balance their ethnic identity with mainstream culture? (p. 532)

- What is wrong with thinking that life occurs in a series of predictable stages? (p. 535)

- What feelings are common during "emerging adulthood," the years from 18 to 25? (pp. 536–537)

- Does menopause make most women depressed and irrational? (p. 538)

- Do men go through a male version of menopause? (p. 538)

- Which mental abilities decline in old age, and which ones do not? (p. 539)

- Do traumatic childhood experiences affect a person forever? (p. 542)

- Do most abused children become abusive parents? (p. 542)

15

Health,
Stress,
and
Coping

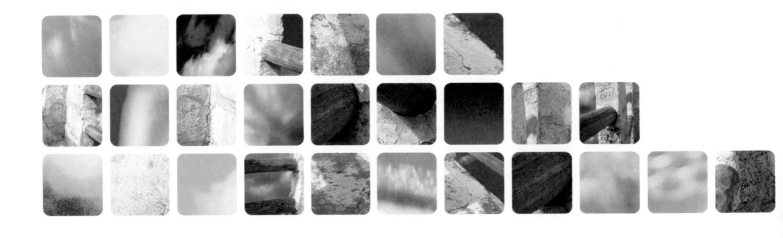

The process of living is the process of reacting to stress.

STANLEY SARNOFF

Bill and his father have been battling for years. Bill feels that his father is always ready to criticize him for the slightest flaw. After Bill left home he gained some perspective on their relationship, but every time his father comes to visit, Bill gets a migraine.

Tanya lost her apartment and most of her possessions in a hurricane. Months later, she still feels upset, can't seem to get her life back together, and finds it difficult to talk about her continuing anxieties.

Vicente is working two jobs to make ends meet. His supervisor at one job is making his life miserable, but Vicente can't afford to offend him, so he says nothing. His blood pressure is high and lately he's been having awful stomachaches, but he can't see a way of improving his situation.

Val gets caught in a massive traffic jam and is late for class. As she walks in the door, her instructor reprimands her for being late. Later, rushing to get her notes together for an overdue assignment, Val spills coffee all over herself and the papers. By noon she has a splitting headache and feels exhausted.

All of these people are certainly under "stress," but, as you see, their experiences are far from the same. The popular use of the word *stress* includes recurring conflicts (Bill and his father), a sudden traumatic experience that affects almost every part of your life (Tanya), continuing pressures that seem uncontrollable (Vicente), or small irritations that wear you down (Val). Everyone complains about stress; the big question is whether and how these "stressful" events, all normal parts of life, are linked to illness. Why does Bill get migraines during yet another miserable visit with his father? Will Tanya's traumatic experience affect her health as well as her emotions? Are Vicente's stomachaches related to the pressures of his job, or to a bad digestive

549

system? Val may be having an annoying day, but will it increase her chances of getting the flu? And can any of them, by controlling their stress levels, prevent illness and maintain good health?

We will explore these questions by looking at findings from *health psychology*, which is concerned with the biological, psychological, social, and cultural factors that influence health and illness. We will see that although good health is not "all in your mind" and not entirely under your control, your thoughts and actions do play a major role in whether you fall ill—and how quickly you recover when you do.

WHAT'S AHEAD ▶

- **Which stressors pose the greatest hazard to your health?**
- **Are you more likely to get a cold when you are "stressed out"?**

The Stress-Illness Mystery

Many years ago, a classic study got plenty of big-city dwellers worried about their health. Two identical groups of mice, both carrying a virus known to produce a type of breast cancer, were housed in two different conditions: a high-stress environment, characterized by crowding, noise, temperature fluctuations, frequent handling by the experimenters, and other unpleasant events; or a mouse-friendly, low-stress, comfortable environment. After 12 months, 92 percent of the stressed mice had developed cancerous tumors, compared to only 7 percent of the stress-free mice (Riley, Spackman, & Santisteban, 1975). These were amazing results. Soon researchers were exploring the kinds of environmental events—*stressors*—that might pose dangers for human beings, too.

First, some good news: Everyday hassles—such as traffic, lousy weather, broken plumbing, lost keys, or a computer that crashes when a deadline is near—are exasperating, but they do not pose much threat to health. But other experiences or situations do increase the risk of illness, especially when they severely disrupt a person's life, when they are uncontrollable, or when they are chronic, lasting at least six months. Here are some of them:

1 *Noise.* Loud noise becomes unhealthful (apart from what it does to your hearing) when it goes on day in and day out without relief. Constant exposure to loud noise contributes to cardiovascular problems, irritability, fatigue, and aggressiveness (Staples, 1996). Children who live or go to school near noisy airports have higher blood pressure and higher levels of stress hormones, are more distractible, and have more learning and attention difficulties than do children in quieter environments (Cohen et al., 1980; Evans, Bullinger, & Hygge, 1998).

2 *Bereavement and loss.* One of life's most powerful stressors is the loss of a loved one or close relationship, especially through divorce or death. In the two years following bereavement, widowed people, especially men, are more susceptible to illness and physical ailments, and their mortality rate is higher than would otherwise be expected (Stroebe, Stroebe, & Schut, 2001). Divorce can also take a long-term toll on health: Divorced adults have higher rates of heart disease, pneumonia, and other diseases than their counterparts who are not divorced (Laudenslager, 1988).

3 *Work-related problems.* Because work is central in most people's lives, the effects of unemployment or of a chronically stressful work environment can be more severe than the effects of other kinds of stressors. A Swedish study found that people who reported a history of severe workplace problems over the past decade had 5.5 times the normal risk of developing colon or rectal cancers, even when diet and other factors linked to these malignancies were taken into account (Courtney et al., 1993).

Work-related stress can also increase a person's vulnerability to a more mundane illness: the common cold. Heroic volunteers in the war against winter colds were given either ordinary nose drops or nose drops containing a cold virus. Everyone was then quarantined for five days. The people most likely to get a cold's miserable symptoms were those who had been underemployed or unemployed for at least a month (see Figure 15.1). They were even more likely to get a cold than people who had been recently divorced or who were having ongoing conflicts in relationships. The longer the work problems had lasted, the greater the likelihood of illness (Cohen et al., 1998).

4 *Poverty and powerlessness.* People at the lower rungs of the socioeconomic ladder have worse health and higher mortality rates for almost every disease and medical condition than do those at the top (Adler et al., 1994). In America, one obvious reason is that poor people cannot afford medical care and preventive examinations. They are also more likely to eat high-fat, high-salt fast food, which is easily available and inexpensive—and which greatly increases obesity and its many health risks, as we saw in Chapter 12. Another reason for the poorer health of low-income people is that they often live with continuous environmental stressors: higher crime rates, discrimination, fewer community services, rundown housing, and greater exposure to hazards such as chemical contamination (Taylor, Repetti, & Seeman, 1997; Wandersman & Nation, 1998). In North America, these conditions affect urban blacks disproportionately and may help account for their relatively high incidence of hypertension (high blood pressure), which can lead to kidney disease, strokes, and heart attacks (Clark et al., 1999; Krieger & Sidney, 1996).

However, before you try to persuade your instructors that the stress of chronic studying is bad for your health, consider this mystery: None of the chronic stressors we just discussed leads in a direct, simple way to illness or affects everyone in the same way. Some people's health is affected by bereavement, losing a job, poverty, or discrimination; yet *most* individuals living with these stressors do not get sick (Basic Behavioral Science Task Force, 1996; Taylor, Repetti, & Seeman, 1997). Some people exposed to a flu virus are sick all winter; others don't even get the sniffles. Some people in high-pressure careers wind up with heart disease; others work just as hard but remain healthy. Why?

To understand why prolonged stress makes trouble for some people but not others, health researchers focus on three areas that we will discuss in the rest of this

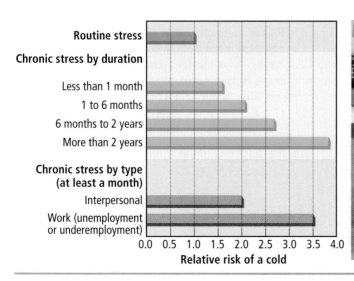

Figure 15.1

STRESS AND THE COMMON COLD

Chronic stress lasting a month or more boosts the risk of catching a cold. The risk is increased among people undergoing problems with their friends or loved ones—and is highest among people who are out of work (Cohen et al., 1998).

chapter: (1) *individual physiological differences* in the cardiovascular, endocrine, immune, and other bodily systems; (2) *psychological factors,* such as attitudes, emotions, and perceptions of events; and (3) *how people behave under stress,* which ranges from actions that increase the risk of illness or accident to constructive coping that reduces the negative effects of stress.

WHAT'S AHEAD

- **What happens to your body when you try to cross a busy street against the light?**
- **Why is being under stress not enough to make you ill?**
- **How do psychological factors affect the immune system?**

The Physiology of Stress

Throughout history, stress has been one of those things, like love, that is hard to define even though everyone has experienced it. In this section, we will see how the concept of stress has changed as researchers have learned more about its physiological effects.

Selye's Theory

15.1

The modern era of stress research began in 1956, when Canadian physician Hans Selye (1907–1982) published his book *The Stress of Life.* Selye was the first scientist to try to figure out how external stressors get "under the skin" to make us ill. Environmental stressors such as heat, cold, noise, pain, and danger, Selye wrote, disrupt the body's normal equilibrium. The body then mobilizes its resources to fight off these stressors and restore normal functioning—but it is not always successful.

Drawing largely on data from animal studies, Selye described the body's response to external stressors of all kinds as a **general adaptation syndrome,** a series of physiological reactions that occur in three phases.

1 *The alarm phase,* in which the body mobilizes to meet the immediate threat or other stressor. To prepare the body to attack back or escape from danger (a reaction that psychologist Walter Cannon decades earlier had named the "fight or flight" response), the sympathetic division of the autonomic nervous system kicks into gear. The result is a boost in energy, tense muscles, reduced sensitivity to pain, the shutting down of digestion (so that blood will flow more efficiently to the brain, muscles, and skin), a rise in blood pressure, and increased output of *adrenal hormones,* sometimes called "stress hormones" (see Chapter 4). Selye thought these responses were pretty much the same whether you are running from a rabid dog, about to take a test you haven't studied for, or trying to cross a busy street against the light.

general adaptation syndrome According to Hans Selye, a series of physiological responses to stressors that occur in three phases: alarm, resistance, and exhaustion.

Stress hormones elevated

Blood flow increases

Heart rate speeds up

Digestion slows

Muscles tense

Alas, the same stress hormones that help in the short run can have unwanted long-term consequences.

2 *The resistance phase,* in which the body attempts to resist or cope with a stressor that persists over time. During this phase, the physiological responses of the alarm phase continue, but these very responses make the body more vulnerable to *other* stressors. For example, when your body has mobilized to fight off the flu, you may find you are more easily annoyed by minor frustrations. In most cases, the body will eventually adapt to the stressor and return to normal.

3 *The exhaustion phase,* in which persistent stress depletes the body of energy and therefore increases vulnerability to physical problems and eventually illness. The same reactions that allow the body to respond effectively in the alarm and resistance phases are unhealthy as long-range responses. Tense muscles can cause headache and neck pain. Increased blood pressure can become chronic hypertension. If normal digestive processes are interrupted or shut down for too long, digestive disorders may result.

Selye did not believe that people should aim for a stress-free life. Some stress is positive and productive, he said, even if it also requires the body to expend short-term energy: competing in an athletic event, falling in love, working hard on a project you enjoy. And some negative stress is simply unavoidable; it's called life! The goal, said Selye, is to minimize wear and tear on the system, not get rid of it entirely.

Current Approaches

Many of Selye's ideas about the general adaptation syndrome proved to be extremely insightful, such as his observation that the same biological changes that are adaptive in the short run—the changes that permit the body to respond quickly to danger—can become hazardous in the long run (McEwen, 1998). Modern researchers are learning exactly how this happens, along with other details about the physiology of stress and its effects.

When you are under stress, your brain's hypothalamus sends messages to the endocrine glands along two major pathways. One, as Selye observed, activates the sympathetic division of the autonomic nervous system for "fight or flight," producing the release of epinephrine and norepinephrine from the inner part of the adrenal glands. In addition, the hypothalamus initiates activity along the **HPA axis** (HPA stands for hypothalamus–pituitary–adrenal cortex): The hypothalamus releases chemical messengers that communicate with the pituitary gland, which in turn sends messages to the outer part (cortex) of the adrenal glands. The adrenal cortex secretes cortisol and other hormones that elevate blood sugar and protect the body's tissues from inflammation in case of injury (see Figure 15.2).

One result of HPA activation is increased energy, which is crucial for short-term responses to stress. But if cortisol and other stress hormones stay high too long, they can be harmful, contributing to hypertension, other physical disorders, and possibly emotional problems such as depression and posttraumatic stress disorder (see Chapter 16).

HPA (hypothalamus–pituitary–adrenal cortex) axis A system activated to energize the body to respond to stressors. The hypothalamus sends chemical messengers to the pituitary, which in turn prompts the adrenal cortex to produce cortisol and other hormones.

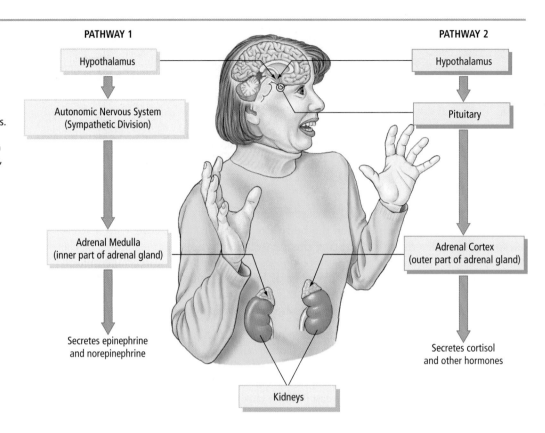

Figure 15.2

THE BRAIN AND BODY UNDER STRESS

When a person is in danger or under stress, the hypothalamus sends messages to the endocrine glands along two major pathways. In one, the hypothalamus activates the sympathetic division of the autonomic nervous system, which stimulates the adrenal medulla to produce epinephrine and norepinephrine. The result is the many bodily changes associated with "fight or flight." In the other pathway, messages travel along the HPA axis to the adrenal cortex, which produces cortisol and other hormones. The result is increased energy and protection from tissue inflammation in case of injury.

15.2

Selye thought that all stressors, from a rabid dog to an impending exam, affect the body in roughly the same ways, but we now know that different stressors may evoke somewhat different responses. In addition, individuals vary widely in their physiological responses to the *same* stressor, depending on their learning history, gender, preexisting medical conditions, and genetic predispositions for high blood pressure, obesity, diabetes, or other problems (McEwen, 2000; Taylor et al., 2000b).

For example, most people react to the stress of public speaking with a temporary increase in cortisol. With time and practice, they adapt and calm down, and cortisol declines. However, a small percentage of people do not adapt; in fact, their cortisol levels continue to increase (Kirschbaum, Prussner, & Stone, 1995). Likewise, some people respond to stressors with much greater increases in blood pressure, heart rate, and hormone levels than other individuals do (T. Smith et al., 1996; Uchino et al., 1995). These hyperresponsive and nonadapting individuals may be the ones most at risk for eventual illness.

The Mind–Body Link

Modern researchers have also made great strides in their ability to study the exact biological mechanisms that link stress and illness. Many work in an interdisciplinary specialty with the cumbersome name **psychoneuroimmunology,** or **PNI** for short. The "psycho" part stands for psychological processes such as emotions and perceptions; "neuro" for the nervous and endocrine systems; and "immunology" for the immune system, which enables the body to fight disease and infection (Ader, 2001).

PNI researchers are especially interested in the white blood cells of the immune system, which are designed to recognize

Do you see work as a bottomless pit of obligations or as a tidy stack of achievements? The answer affects how "stressed" you are.

foreign or harmful substances, such as flu viruses, bacteria, and tumor cells, and then destroy or deactivate them. The immune system deploys different kinds of white blood cells as weapons, depending on the nature of the enemy. For example, natural killer cells are important in tumor detection and rejection, and are involved in protection against the spread of cancer cells and viruses. Helper T cells enhance and regulate the immune response; they are the primary target of the HIV virus that causes AIDS. Chemicals produced by the immune cells are sent to the brain, and the brain in turn sends chemical signals to stimulate or restrain the immune system. Anything that disrupts this communication loop—drugs, surgery, or chronic stress—can weaken or suppress the immune system.

PNI researchers also study how psychological factors might affect the immune system, and thereby the onset or course of an illness. For example, peptic ulcers are usually caused by a bacterium, *Helicobacter pylori*, yet many healthy people who have *H. pylori* in their stomach linings do *not* get ulcers. The bacterium is necessary but not sufficient; psychological factors also play a role (Levenstein et al., 1999).

Psychological factors help explain why people, unlike mice, are not always stressed by environmental conditions such as crowding. Mice get really nasty when they're crowded. But many human beings love crowds. Not many other species would voluntarily choose to get squashed in Times Square on New Year's Eve or in a mosh pit at a rock concert. Human beings show signs of stress not when they are *actually* crowded but when they *feel* crowded—trapped or forced to endure unwanted interactions with others (Evans, Lepore, & Schroeder, 1996). Individuals and cultures differ in the amount of "personal space" and population density they consider normal and desirable; Asians and Latinos typically feel less crowded than Anglos do, given the same number of people. But regardless of culture, when people feel crowded, especially in their home living arrangements, they are more likely to develop emotional and physical symptoms (Evans, Lepore, & Allen, 2000).

As you can see, the scientific understanding of stress has come a long way since Selye's early formulation of the body's automatic response to environmental threat. We turn next to the emotional influences on the complex interaction between the body and the mind.

The immune system consists of fighter cells that look more fantastical than any alien creature Hollywood could design. This one is about to engulf and destroy a cigarette-shaped parasite that causes a tropical disease.

psychoneuroimmunology (PNI) The study of the relationships among psychology, the nervous and endocrine systems, and the immune system.

QUICK QUIZ

We hope these questions are not a source of stress for you.

1. Which of these statements is true? (a) Most people who suffer the death of a loved one become sick; (b) work problems and unemployment pose a greater health risk than conflicts in relationships; (c) people with high incomes often have more stressful lives than low-income people; (d) daily hassles are as hazardous to health as major stressors.

2. Steve is unexpectedly called on in class. He hasn't the faintest idea of the answer, and he feels his heart start to pound and his palms sweat. According to Selye, he is in the _____ phase of his stress response.

3. Key stress hormones released by the adrenal glands are epinephrine, norepinephrine, and _____.

Answers:

1. b 2. alarm 3. cortisol

WHAT'S AHEAD ▶

- Which emotion may be most hazardous to your heart?
- Does chronic depression lead to physical illness?
- Is confession as healthy for the body as it is for the soul?
- Why do optimists tend to live longer than pessimists?
- Why does it matter whether you think you control your own destiny or your destiny controls you?

The Psychology of Stress

Some people find traveling to China or having a heavy workload stressful, whereas others regard travel and work deadlines to be challenging opportunities. People's emotional responses to stress, and the way that they think about their lives and problems, can affect their health.

Emotions and Illness

Perhaps you have heard people say things like "She was so depressed, it's no wonder she got cancer" or "He's always so angry, he's going to give himself a heart attack one day." They take it for granted that negative emotions—especially anger and depression—are hazardous to health.

To evaluate this claim, we need, first, to distinguish between the effects of negative emotions on healthy people and on people who are ill. Many studies find that *once a person has a virus or medical condition*, negative emotions can indeed affect the course of the illness and of recovery. Feeling anxious, depressed, and helpless, for example, can delay the healing of wounds after surgery, whereas feeling hopeful can significantly speed healing (Kiecolt-Glaser et al., 1998). Loneliness and worry can suppress the immune system and permit existing viruses, such as herpes, to erupt (Kiecolt-Glaser et al., 1985a). And people who become depressed after a heart attack are significantly more likely to die from cardiac causes in the succeeding year, even controlling for severity of the disease and other risk factors (Frasure-Smith et al., 1999).

But can anger and depression *cause* illness all on their own? The answers are yes, maybe, and it depends on the illness. Let's see why.

Hostility and Heart Disease. One of the first modern efforts to link emotions and illness was research in the 1970s on the *Type A personality*, a set of qualities thought to be associated with heart disease (Friedman & Rosenman, 1974). Type A people are determined to achieve, have a sense of time urgency, are irritable, respond physiologically to threat and challenge very quickly, and are impatient at anyone who gets in their way. Type B people are calmer and less intense. It seemed logical that Type A's would be at greater risk of heart trouble than Type B's.

It turned out, however, that being highly reactive to stress and challenge is not in itself a risk factor in heart disease (Krantz & Manuck, 1984). Type A people do set themselves a fast work pace and a heavy workload, but many cope better than Type B people who have a lighter workload. Further,

A classic Type A personality.

people who are highly involved in their jobs, even if they work hard, have a low incidence of heart disease. "There would be nothing wrong with us fast-moving Type A's," said a friend of ours, "if it weren't for all those slow-moving Type B's."

The next round of research uncovered what it was about the behavior of some Type A's that *is* dangerous to health: hostility. By "hostility" we do not mean the irritability or anger that everyone feels on occasion. The toxic kind is *cynical* or *antagonistic hostility,* which characterizes people who are mistrustful of others and ready to provoke mean, furious arguments (Marshall et al., 1994; T. Miller et al., 1996). In a study of male physicians who had been interviewed as medical students 25 years earlier, those who were chronically angry and resentful were five times as likely as nonhostile men to get heart disease, even when other risk factors, such as smoking and a poor diet, were taken into account (Ewart & Kolodner, 1994; Williams, Barefoot, & Shekelle, 1985) (see Figure 15.3). These findings have been replicated in other large-scale studies, with African-Americans and whites, and with women as well as men (J. Williams et al., 2000). Proneness to anger is a significant risk factor, all on its own, for impairments of the immune system, elevated blood pressure, and heart disease (Suinn, 2001).

Depression and Disease. Can depression also lead to illness? In two studies that each followed more than 1,000 people for many years, those who had been clinically depressed at the outset were two to four times more likely to have a heart attack than nondepressed people were. This finding held up even after researchers controlled for high blood pressure, smoking, obesity, amount of exercise, and family history of heart disease (Ford et al., 1998; Pratt et al., 1996). Another study of more than 5,000 people over age 65 showed that those who had many depressive symptoms were 25 percent more likely to die of cardiovascular disorders within six years than nondepressed people, even after the researchers controlled for demographic factors, presence of disease, and risk factors like smoking (Schulz et al., 2000).

Other research, however, has failed to find a link between depression and death from heart disease (Wulsin, Vaillant, & Wells, 1999) or between depression and other causes of death, such as cancer and AIDS (Lyketsos et al., 1993; Penninx et al., 1998). All we can say at present, therefore, is that chronic depression seems to be a significant risk factor for heart disease, though probably not in a direct way. Some people may become entrapped in a downward spiral in which having an illness, feeling depressed, and therefore not taking care of oneself all feed on each other, reducing the body's physical ability to recover (Schulz et al., 2000).

Emotional Inhibition. You might assume by now that the safest thing to do when you feel angry, depressed, or worried is to try to suppress the feeling. But anyone who has tried to banish an unwelcome thought, a bitter memory, or pangs of longing for an ex-lover knows how hard it can be to do this. When you are trying to avoid a thought, you are in fact processing the thought more frequently—rehearsing it. That is why, when you are obsessed with someone you were once romantically involved with, trying not to think of the person actually prolongs your emotional responsiveness to him or her (Wegner & Gold, 1995).

Most people try to suppress their feelings some of the time, but some people, "suppressors," do so almost all of the time; they have a personality trait called *emotional inhibition* (Basic Behavioral Science Task Force, 1996). Suppressors tend to deny feelings

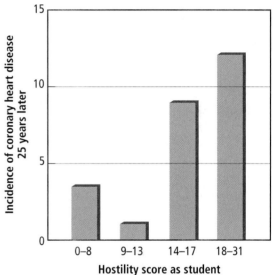

Figure 15.3
HOSTILITY AND HEART DISEASE

Anger is more hazardous to health than a heavy workload. Men who had the highest hostility scores as young medical students were the most likely to have coronary heart disease 25 years later (Williams, Barefoot, & Shekelle, 1985).

of anxiety, anger, or fear and pretend that everything is fine. Yet, when they are in stressful or emotion-producing situations, their physiological responses, such as heart rate and blood pressure, rise sharply. Suppressors are at greater risk of becoming ill than people who can acknowledge their fears, and once they contract a serious disease, they may even die sooner (Cohen & Herbert, 1996).

Emotional inhibition might increase the risk of illness because the prolonged inhibition of thoughts and emotions requires physical effort that is stressful to the body (Pennebaker, 1997; Smyth & Pennebaker, 1999). The inability or unwillingness to confide important or traumatic events also seems to place continuing stress on the immune system. People who are able to express matters of great emotional importance to them show elevated levels of disease-fighting white blood cells, whereas people who suppress such feelings tend to have decreased levels (Petrie, Booth, & Pennebaker, 1998).

Letting Grievances Go

Given the findings on the harmful effects of *feeling* negative emotions and also of *suppressing* them, what is a person supposed to do with them? Occasional feelings of anger, anxiety, and sadness are, of course, inevitable. It is only when people hold onto them too long, rehearsing them and brooding about them, that they can become harmful.

One way to let them go comes from research on the benefits of confession: divulging private thoughts and feelings that make you ashamed or depressed. Confession can even help students who are going through a normal but stressful transition: starting college. You might think there is little to "confess" about going to college, but it turns out that many freshmen feel scared that they won't do well and will disappoint their families, and anxious about being on their own. They think that they are the only ones feeling this way, of course, so few reveal their worries. In one study, freshmen who wrote about these fears reported greater short-term homesickness and anxiety, compared to students who wrote about trivial topics. But by the end of the school year they had had fewer bouts of flu and visits to the infirmary than the control group (Pennebaker, Colder, & Sharp, 1990).

Confession is also beneficial for people who are carrying the burden of painful secrets. A group of college students were asked to write about either a personal, traumatic experience or a neutral topic for 20 minutes a day for four days. Those who were asked to reveal their "deepest thoughts and feelings" about a traumatic event all had something to talk about. Many told stories of sexual coercion, physical beatings, humiliation, or parental abandonment. Yet most had never discussed these experiences with anyone. The researchers collected data on the students' physical symptoms, white blood cell counts, emotions, and visits to the health center. On every measure, the students who wrote about traumatic experiences were better off than those who did not (Pennebaker, Kiecolt-Glaser, & Glaser, 1988). Some of them showed temporary increases in anger and depression; writing about an unpleasant experience, after all, was disturbing. But over time, their health and well-being improved.

Of course, confession can make you feel worse if you reveal your secrets to a confidant who is judgmental, is unable to help, or betrays your confidence (Kelly, 1999). Even when you talk to a supportive friend or record your thoughts into a tape recorder or journal, confession's benefits occur only when it produces insight and understanding about the source or significance of the problem, thereby ending the stressful repetition of obsessive thoughts and unresolved feelings (Kennedy-Moore & Watson, 2001; Lepore, Ragan, & Jones, 2000). One young woman, who had been molested at the age of 9 by a boy a year older, at first wrote about her feelings of embarrassment and guilt. By the third day, she was writing about how angry she felt at the boy. By the last day, she had begun to see the whole event differ-

Everyone has secrets and private moments of sad reflection. But when you feel sad, anxious, or fearful for too long, keeping your feelings to yourself may increase your stress.

ently; he was a child too, after all. When the study was over, she said, "Before, when I thought about it, I'd lie to myself. . . . Now, I don't feel like I even have to think about it because I got it off my chest. I finally admitted that it happened."

Another important way of letting go of negative emotions is to give up the thoughts that produce grudges and replace them with a different perspective. In recent years, there has been a surge of research not only on anger but on anger's antidote: forgiveness. When people rehearse their grievances and hold unforgiving grudges, their blood pressure, heart rate, and skin conductance rise (see Figure 15.4). Forgiving thoughts (as in the example above—"he was a child too"—or "what she did to me was horrible, but it's over now, and it's time for both of us to move on") reduce these signs of physiological arousal and restore feelings of control (Witvliet, Ludwig, & Vander Laan, 2001). Forgiveness, like confession when it works, helps people see events in a new light. It promotes empathy, the ability to see the situation from another person's perspective. Forgiveness does *not* mean that the offended person denies, ignores, or excuses the offense, which might be serious. It does mean that the victim is able, finally, to come to terms with the injustice and let go of obsessive feelings of hurt, rage, and vengefulness. As the Chinese proverb says, "He who pursues revenge should dig two graves."

In sum, health psychology suggests a middle path between "keeping your cool" and "getting hot and bothered": learning to identify, express, and deal with negative emotions without ruminating on them and letting them erode your relationships (Richards & Gross, 2000).

Positive Emotions: Do They Help? Just as negative emotions can be unhealthy, positive emotions seem to be healthful (Folkman & Moskowitz, 2000). Consider some findings from the famous "nun study." Researchers examined handwritten autobiographies of 180 Catholic nuns, composed when the women were about 22 years old, to see whether the quality of their writing predicted the onset of Alzheimer's disease later in life. (It did.) When other researchers scored the writings for their emotional content, they found a very strong association between the extent of positive emotions described—happiness, interest, love, hope, gratitude, contentment, amusement, relief, accomplishment—and longevity six decades later (Danner, Snowdon, & Friesen, 2001). The nuns whose life stories contained the most words describing their positive emotions lived, on average, 9 years longer than nuns who reported the fewest positive feelings! These differences in longevity could not be due to, say, the stress of poverty, raising children, or particular experiences. The women had the same experiences and standard of living, at least after they entered the convent.

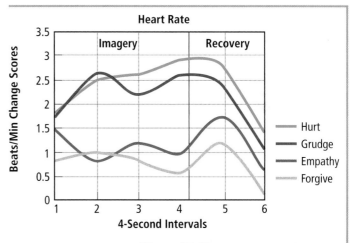

Figure 15.4
HEARTFELT FORGIVENESS

Participants in this study were asked to think of someone whom they felt had mistreated, offended, or hurt them. Then they were asked to imagine unforgiving reactions (rehearsing the hurt and harboring a grudge) and forgiving reactions (feeling empathy, forgiving). As you can see, people's heart rates increased much more sharply, and took longer to return to normal, when their thoughts were unforgiving (Witvliet, Ludwig, & Vander Laan, 2001).

Of course, this was only a correlational study, and it would be premature to conclude that joy, hope, and love directly promote longevity. Perhaps the cheerfulness of the long-lived nuns simply reflected an easygoing temperament or other genetic influences that promote long life. On the other hand, positive emotions may indeed be physically beneficial because they soften or counteract the high arousal caused by negative emotions or chronic stressors. They may dispose people to think more creatively about their opportunities and choices, and to take action to achieve their goals. People who express positive feelings are more likely to attract friends and supporters, too, than are people who are always bitter and brooding, and, as we will see, social support contributes to good health (Folkman & Moskowitz, 2000; Fredrickson, 2001; Salovey et al., 2000).

Emotion and Health: A Two-Way Street. How strong, overall, is the link between emotion and illness? Some researchers believe that the inhibition or expression of specific negative emotions can be tied to specific illnesses, such as cancer or heart disease (Eysenck, 1993). Others caution against exaggerating the role of emotional styles in health, arguing that we must not overlook the stronger influences of chronic stressors in the environment, the biology of the disease, the individual's genetically influenced temperament, and unhealthy habits such as smoking (Jorgensen et al., 1996).

Both sides, however, agree that the links between emotions and illness should not be oversimplified. Living with unresolved negative emotions can be stressful to the body, but a life of constant stress also tends to foster negative emotions. Depression and anxiety may contribute to illness in some individuals, but illness also makes some people depressed or anxious. Emotional inhibition is hazardous to some people's health, but so is constant emotional ventilation, which can alienate others and, in some cultures, violates social norms (Kelly, 1999; Wellenkamp, 1995). Positive emotions are wonderful feelings, but they are no guarantee against stress, loss, and tragedy.

Explanatory Styles

When something bad happens to you, what is your first reaction? Do you tell yourself not to panic, that you will somehow come through it okay, or do you gloomily mutter, "More proof that if something can go wrong for me, it will"?

These two responses to bad events reflect *pessimistic* and *optimistic explanatory styles,* and as far as health is concerned, optimism—the general expectation that, overall, things will go well in spite of the occasional setback—is a lot better for you (Carver & Scheier, 1999; Peterson, 2000; Seligman, 1991). In a fundamental way, of course, optimism makes life and society possible; if people believe "I am in a jam now, but things will get better eventually," they will keep working and striving to make that belief come true. As one researcher observed, even despondent fans of the Chicago Cubs and the Boston Red Sox, who have not won the World Series in living memory, maintain a lunatic optimism that "there's always next year."

Some people adopt a compromise attitude between pessimism and optimism called "defensive pessimism": "I expect the worst, but I'll work hard to avoid it, so if it happens anyway, it won't be my fault, and if something good happens, I'll be pleasantly surprised" (Norem, 2001). We don't think this is true pessimism, though; it sounds more like optimism with your fingers crossed to avoid bad luck. True pessimists don't ever expect to be pleasantly surprised by anything, and that attitude is associated with lower achievement, more illness, and slower recovery from defeats and traumas.

If you are a pessimist, you will probably protest that optimism is just a *result,* not a cause, of good health or good fortune; it's easy to think positively when you feel good! But optimism actually seems to produce good health and even prolong life, whereas "catastrophizing" pessimism is associated with untimely death (Maruta et

Explanatory style—pessimism or optimism— may affect health and longevity. Zack Wheat, an outfielder for the Brooklyn Dodgers, had an optimistic explanatory style: "I'm a better hitter than I used to be because my strength has improved and my experience has improved." Wheat lived to be 83.

Walter Johnson, a star pitcher for the Washington Senators, had a pessimistic explanatory style: "I can't depend on myself to pitch well. I'm growing old. I've had my day." Johnson died at the age of 59.

al., 2000; Peterson et al., 1998). In one imaginative study of baseball Hall-of-Famers who had played between 1900 and 1950, 30 players were rated according to their explanatory style. A pessimist would attribute a bad performance to a permanent failing in himself, as in: "We didn't win because my arm is shot, and it'll never get better." An optimist would attribute the same performance to temporary conditions, as in, "We didn't win because we got a couple of lousy calls, just bad luck in this game, but we'll be great tomorrow." The optimists were significantly more likely to have lived well into old age than were the pessimists (Seligman, 1991).

Optimists may have better health than pessimists in part because they take better care of themselves when they get sick, whether their ailment is a simple cold or a life-threatening disease like AIDS. They cope better, in all the ways we discuss later in this chapter, and draw on friends to help them through bad times (Brissette, Scheier, & Carver, 2002). Pessimists often do self-destructive things: They drink too much, smoke, fail to wear seat belts, drive too fast, and refuse to take medication for illness. This may be why pessimists, especially males, are more likely than optimists to die untimely deaths as a result of accidents or violence (Peterson et al., 1998). But optimism is also directly associated with better immune function, such as a rise in natural killer cells that fight infection (Räikkönen et al., 1999; Segerstrom et al., 1998).

What is optimism, exactly? Currently, health psychologists are debating whether optimism involves self-delusion or realistic confidence. Research amply demonstrates that sometimes health and well-being do depend on having some optimistic "positive illusions" about yourself and your circumstances, such as expecting to survive a disease with a high mortality rate (Schneider, 2001; Taylor & Brown, 1994; Taylor et al., 2000a). In one study of gay men with AIDS, those who had realistically accepted the likelihood of

THINKING CRITICALLY

Define Your Terms

It may seem obvious what "optimism" is. But what is it, exactly? Does it involve self-delusion and denial, or realistic confidence? If it involves self-delusion, is that good or bad for a person?

an early death actually died nine months earlier than did optimists who were unrealistic about their chances of survival. This result could not be accounted for by the time since the initial diagnosis, their use of the medication AZT, their age, or their alcohol and drug use (Reed et al., 1994).

Positive illusions, however, are not the same as complete denial. It is good to feel good about yourself and your prospects, but if you delusionally believe that you are the best in the world and that everything will come your way without your lifting a finger, you may set yourself up for a fall when trouble occurs or when you don't do well on a task (Robins & Beer, 2001; Schneider, 2001). Optimists maintain a positive outlook while recognizing life's realities and limitations. They do not deny their problems or avoid facing bad news. On the contrary, they are more likely than pessimists to be active problem solvers and to seek information that can help them (Aspinwall & Taylor, 1997). They do not give up at the first sign of a setback or escape into wishful thinking. They keep their sense of humor, plan for the future, and reinterpret the situation in a positive light (Aspinwall & Brunhart, 1996; Chang, 1998).

Can pessimists be "cured" of their gloomy outlook? Optimists, naturally, think so! In Chapter 17, we discuss cognitive therapy, which teaches pessimists to test their dim predictions against the evidence and change their expectations, and we report on a successful intervention that "inoculated" children against pessimism and depression. Another method worked for psychologist Rachel Hare-Mustin, whose mother cured her budding childhood pessimism with humor. "Nobody likes me," Rachel lamented. "Don't say that," her mother said. "Everybody hasn't met you yet."

QUICK QUIZ

Are you optimistic about your ability to answer these questions?

1. Which of the following aspects of Type A behavior seems most hazardous to men's health? (a) working hard, (b) being in a hurry, (c) cynical hostility, (d) high physical reactivity to work, (e) general grumpiness

2. Nguyen has many private worries about being in college that she is afraid to tell anyone. What might be the healthiest solution for her? (a) exercise, (b) writing down her feelings in a diary, (c) talking frequently to strangers who won't judge her, (d) expressing her hostility whenever she feels it

3. "I'll never find anyone else to love because I'm not good-looking; that one romance was a fluke" illustrates a(n) _____ explanatory style.

Answers:

1. c 2. b 3. pessimistic

The Sense of Control

Optimism is related to another important ingredient of health: having an internal locus of control (Chang, 1998; Marshall et al., 1994). **Locus of control** refers to your general expectation about whether you can control the things that happen to you (Rotter, 1990). People who have an *internal locus of control* ("internals") tend to believe that they are responsible for what happens to them, that they control their own destiny. People who have an *external locus of control* ("externals") tend to believe that their lives are controlled by luck, fate, or other people. The Internal/External (I/E) Scale measures these dispositions. Respondents choose the statement in each pair of items with which they most strongly agree, as in these two items:

locus of control A general expectation about whether the results of your actions are under your own control (internal locus) or beyond your control (external locus).

1. a. Many of the unhappy things in people's lives are partly due to bad luck.
   b. People's misfortunes result from mistakes they make.

2. a. Becoming a success is a matter of hard work; luck has little or nothing to do with it.
   b. Getting a good job depends mainly on being in the right place at the right time.

Over the years more than 2,000 studies based on the I/E Scale (including a version for children) have been published, with people of all ages and from many different ethnic groups. An internal locus of control emerges at an early age and is associated with many aspects of life, including health, academic achievement, political activism, and emotional well-being (Lang & Heckhausen, 2001; Nowicki & Strickland, 1973; Strickland, 1989). Where would you place your own locus of control, and do you think it affects your beliefs about the possibility of changing yourself or improving the world?

The Benefits of Control. Most people would agree that Robert James has a miserable job. He works all day long in a cramped token booth in the New York City subway—the 205th Street terminal in the Bronx, to be exact—protected by bulletproof glass (with a bullet hole in it). But Robert James is beloved by the subway passengers he meets every day. He decorates his little space cheerfully for each season. He wears a subway-map tie and blue alligator boots. He makes sure strangers get on the right trains. He passes messages, and sometimes a few bucks, between friends and family members. He once helped a young man on his way to a job interview get spruced up. He writes inspiring thoughts on his message board.

Robert James has achieved an optimal balance between what he cannot control (the requirements of his job in a subway token booth) and what he can control—how he decorates his small space, thinks about his work, and deals with people.

Robert James can't do much to control the requirements of his job, but within those confines, he certainly controls his environment: how he decorates it, how he chooses to behave with the public, how he thinks about his work. He has turned a job that would seem dreary to most into an oasis of sunlight, for himself and all who come in contact with him. He controls what he is able to control about his subterranean world.

People can tolerate all kinds of stressors if, like Robert James, they feel able to control them. The greatest threat to health and well-being occurs when people feel caught in a situation they cannot escape. Feelings of control can reduce or even eliminate the relationship between stressors and health that we described earlier in this chapter, as these examples illustrate:

▶ Among people exposed to cold viruses, those who feel in control of their lives are half as likely to actually develop colds as are people who feel that their lives are "unpredictable, uncontrollable, and overwhelming" (Cohen, Tyrrell, & Smith, 1993).

▶ Low-income people who have a strong sense of control and mastery over their lives are as healthy, and have equally high levels of well-being, as people from higher-income groups (Lachman & Weaver, 1998).

▶ People who have the greatest control over their work pace and activities—that is, executives and managers—have fewer illnesses and stress symptoms than do employees who have little opportunity to exercise initiative, who feel trapped doing repetitive tasks, and who have a low chance of promotion (Karasek & Theorell, 1990).

▶ African-American professionals who have the resources and confidence to fight discrimination, and who feel in control of their work lives, are at lower risk of hypertension than are black workers who do not (Krieger & Sidney, 1996).

▶ When elderly residents of nursing homes are given more choices and control over their activities—even small activities such as tending plants—they become more alert and happier, and they live longer (Langer, 1983).

Who has more "stress"—corporate managers in highly competitive jobs or assembly-line workers in routine and predictable jobs? Researchers find that "it is not the bosses but the bossed who suffer most from job stress"—especially if they cannot control many aspects of their work (Karasek & Theorell, 1990).

Feeling in control also helps to reduce pain and speed up recovery from surgery and from some diseases (Shapiro, Schwartz, & Astin, 1996; E. Skinner, 1996). As with optimism, feeling in control makes people more likely to take action to improve their health when necessary. In a group of patients recovering from heart attacks, for example, those who thought the heart attack occurred because they smoked, didn't exercise, or had a stressful job were likely to change their bad habits and recover more quickly. In contrast, those who thought their illness was due to bad luck or fate—factors outside their control—were less likely to generate active plans for recovery and more likely to resume their old unhealthy habits (Affleck et al., 1987; Ewart, 1995).

Cultures differ in their degree of fatalism and in their beliefs about whether it is possible to take control of one's health. For example, in Germany, which has a highly structured social welfare system, people feel more psychological control over their health and work than Americans do (Staudinger, Fleeson, & Baltes, 1999). In other cultures, people feel they have almost no control over their health and lives.

Might these cultural attitudes be related to mortality rates? The answer, remarkably, seems to be yes. In traditional Chinese astrology, certain birth years are considered unlucky, and people born in those years often fatalistically expect bad fortune. This expectation can become a self-fulfilling prophecy. In a study of many thousands of people matched by age and cause of death, Chinese-Americans who had been born in a year traditionally considered to be ill-fated died significantly earlier—one to five years earlier!—than whites who had been born in the same year and who had the same disease. The more strongly traditional the Chinese were, the more years of life they lost. These results held for nearly all causes of death studied, even when the researchers controlled for how well the patients took care of themselves and which treatments they were given (Phillips, Ruth, & Wagner, 1993).

THINKING CRITICALLY

Define Your Terms

In general, it's good to feel in control of your life, but what does that mean exactly? Control over what? How much of your life? Can believing you have total control ever be a bad thing?

The Limits of Control. Overall, then, a sense of control is a good thing. But the question must always be asked: Control over what? It is surely not beneficial for people to believe they can control absolutely every aspect of their lives; some things, such as death, taxes, or being a random victim of a crime, are out of anyone's control. Health and well-being are not enhanced by self-blame ("Whatever goes wrong with my health is my fault") or the belief that all disease can be prevented by doing the right thing ("If I take vitamins and work out nine times a week, I'll never get sick").

Eastern and Western cultures tend to hold different attitudes toward the ability and desirability of controlling one's own life. In general, Western cultures celebrate **primary control,** in which people try to influence existing reality by trying to exert control over it: If you do not like a situation, you are supposed to change it, fix it, or fight it. The Eastern approach emphasizes **secondary control,** in which people try to accommodate to reality by changing their own aspirations or desires: If you have a problem, you are supposed to live with it or act in spite of it (Rothbaum, Weisz, & Snyder, 1982).

A Japanese psychologist once offered some examples of Japanese proverbs that teach the benefits of yielding to the inevitable (Azuma, 1984): *To lose is to win* (giving in, to protect the harmony of a relationship, demonstrates the superior trait of generosity); *Willow trees do not get broken by piled-up snow* (no matter how many problems pile up in your life, flexibility will help you survive them); and *The true tolerance is to tolerate the intolerable* (some "intolerable" situations are facts of life that no amount of protest will change). You can imagine how long "To lose is to win" would survive on an American football field, or how long most Americans would be prepared to tolerate the intolerable!

People who are ill or under stress can reap the benefits of both Western and Eastern forms of control by avoiding either–or thinking: for example, by taking responsibility for future actions while not blaming themselves unduly for past ones. Those who do so adjust better than people who believe they can control everything—or nothing (Thompson, Nanni, & Levine, 1994). Among women coping with cancer, for instance, adjustment is related to a woman's belief that she is not to blame for getting sick but that she *is* in charge of taking care of herself from now on (Taylor, Lichtman, & Wood, 1984). "I felt that I had lost control of my body somehow," said a woman in one study, "and the way for me to get back some control was to find out as much as I could." This way of thinking allows a person to avoid guilt and self-blame while retaining self-efficacy—the belief that you are basically in charge of your own life and can take steps to get better when you are sick.

Many problems require us to decide what we can change and accept what we cannot; perhaps the secret of healthy control lies in knowing the difference.

primary control An effort to modify reality by changing other people, the situation, or events; a "fighting back" philosophy.

secondary control An effort to accept reality by changing your own attitudes, goals, or emotions; a "learn to live with it" philosophy.

QUICK QUIZ

You can increase your sense of control over the material in this section by answering these questions.

1. Maria has worked as a file clerk for 17 years. Which aspect of the job is likely to be most stressful for her? (a) the speed of the work, (b) the attention to many details, (c) feeling trapped, (d) the daily demands from her boss

2. Anika usually takes credit for doing well on her work assignments and blames her failures on lack of effort. Benecia attributes her successes to luck and blames her failures on the fact that she is an indecisive Gemini. Anika has an _____ locus of control whereas Benecia has an _____ locus.

3. Adapting to the reality that you are getting older is an example of (primary/secondary) control; joining a protest to make a local company clean up its hazardous wastes is an example of (primary/secondary) control.

4. On television, a self-described health expert explains that "no one gets sick if they don't want to be sick, because all of us can learn to control our bodies." As a critical thinker, how should you assess this claim?

Answers:

1. c 2. internal, external 3. secondary, primary 4. Skeptically. First, you would define your terms: What does "control" mean, and what kind of control is the supposed expert referring to? People can control some things, such as the decision to exercise and quit smoking, and they can control some aspects of treatment once they become ill; but they cannot control everything that happens to them. Second, you would examine the assumption that control is always a good thing. The belief that we have total control over our lives could lead to depression and unwarranted self-blame when illness strikes.

WHAT'S AHEAD

- When you are feeling overwhelmed, what are some good ways to calm down?
- Why is it important to move beyond the emotions caused by a problem and deal with the problem itself?
- Can tragedies and losses ever be beneficial for you?
- When do friends reduce your stress, and when do they just make matters worse?

Coping with Stress

We have noted that most people who are under stress, even in continuing, difficult situations, do not become ill. In addition to feeling optimistic and in control, and not wallowing around in negative emotions, how do they manage to cope?

Coping consists of all the things people do to control, tolerate, or reduce the effects of life's stressors—perceived threats, existing problems, or emotional losses (Aspinwall & Taylor, 1997; Lazarus, 2000). Coping is not a single strategy that applies to all circumstances; people cope differently with hassles, deaths of loved ones, traumas, and challenges. And the techniques they use change over time and circumstance, depending on the nature of the stressor and the particular situation (Cheng, 2001).

The word "coping" implies that people are behaving in ways that barely help them keep their heads above water ("How are you doing?" "Oh, I'm coping"). But some people cope in ways that not only help them *survive* adversity but actually help them *thrive*, by learning from their experiences (see Figure 15.5). In this section, we will consider what research shows about some of the most effective methods of coping with, living with, and learning from the troubles of life.

Cooling Off

The most immediate way to handle the physiological symptoms of stress is to calm down and reduce your body's physical arousal and your mind's buzz of distracting thoughts and worries. *Progressive relaxation* training—learning to alternately tense and relax the muscles, from toes to head, and to meditate by clearing your mind—lowers blood pressure, stress hormones, and feelings of anger or anxiety (Scheufele, 2000). Studies of many different groups, including elderly residents of retirement homes and women with first-stage breast cancer, find that relaxation techniques also significantly improve immune activity (Gruber et al., 1993; Kiecolt-Glaser et al., 1985b).

Figure 15.5

SUCCUMBING, SURVIVING, OR THRIVING: THE RANGE OF RESPONSES TO ADVERSITY

People may respond to tragedy and loss by giving up, surviving with some impairment, recovering fully, or thriving—learning from the experience and coming out stronger because of it. This group of disabled performers, led by polio survivor Loree Lynn (front), knows about overcoming diversity! (Carver, 1998; O'Leary & Ickovics, 1994).

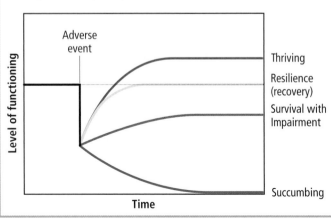

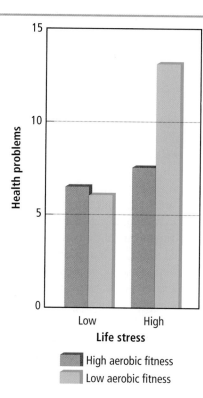

Figure 15.6
FITNESS AND HEALTH
Among people under low stress, aerobically fit individuals had about the same number of health problems as those who were less fit. But among people under high stress, fit individuals had fewer health problems (Roth & Holmes, 1985).

Another effective way to cool off is through massage, one of the oldest treatments for stress in the world. (The Chinese were recommending it in the second century B.C.) In a series of wide-ranging studies, Tiffany Field (1998, 2001) has demonstrated the benefits of deep pressure massage on human beings of every age, from premature infants to the very old, and on people with asthma and diabetes, adolescents with eating disorders, depressed elderly people, and hyperactive children. Massage lowers stress hormones; reduces depression, pain, and anxiety; improves immune function by increasing levels of natural killer cells; and increases concentration and mental alertness.

After you have scheduled meditation and massage into your busy week, go for a walk! A low level of physical activity is associated with decreased life expectancy for both sexes and contributes independently to the development of many chronic diseases (Vita et al., 1998). As you can see in Figure 15.6, when people are undergoing the same pressures, those who are physically fit have fewer health problems than people who are less fit. The more that people exercise, the less anxious, depressed, and irritable they are, and the fewer physical symptoms and colds they have (Hendrix et al., 1991).

Perhaps you can think of other ways to cool off when you are hot and bothered—listening to soothing music, writing in a journal, or baking bread. Such activities give the body a chance to recover from the "alarm phase" of its stress response and from the intensity of negative emotions. But some problems call for more than cooling off. If your house has burned down or you need a serious operation, jogging and meditating won't be enough. Sometimes other coping strategies are necessary.

Solving the Problem

A woman we know, whom we will call Nancy, was struck by tragedy when she was 22. She and her new husband were driving home when a car ran out of control and crashed into them. When Nancy awoke in a hospital room, she learned that her husband had been killed and that she herself had permanent spinal injury and would never walk again. For many months, Nancy reacted with rage and despair. "Get it out of your system," her friends said. "You need to get in touch with your feelings." "But I know I'm miserable," Nancy lamented. "What do I *do?*"

The advice Nancy's friends gave her and her reply illustrate the difference between *emotion-focused* and *problem-focused coping* (Lazarus, 2000; Lazarus & Folkman, 1984). Emotion-focused coping concentrates on the emotions the problem has caused, whether anger, anxiety, or grief. For a period of time after any tragedy or disaster, it is normal to give in to these emotions and feel overwhelmed by them, as most Americans did in the aftermath of September 11, 2001. In this stage, people often need to talk obsessively about the event in order to come to terms with it, make sense of it, and decide what to do about it (Lepore et al., 1996).

Eventually, though, most people become ready to concentrate on solving the problem itself. The specific steps in problem-focused coping depend on the nature of the problem: whether it is a pressing but one-time decision; a continuing difficulty, such as living with a disability; or an anticipated event, such as having an operation.

Once the problem is identified, the coper can learn as much as possible about it from professionals, friends, books, and others in the same predicament (Clarke & Evans, 1998). For example, when people know what to expect when they are having surgery, they often get better more quickly, and feel less pain, than do people who are unprepared (Doering et al., 2000). In Nancy's case, she learned more about her medical condition and prognosis, how other accident victims had coped, and the occupations that were possible for her (which was most of them). Nancy stayed in school, remarried, got a Ph.D. in psychology, and now does research and counseling with disabled people.

Rethinking the Problem

Some problems cannot be solved; these are the tragedies that occur out of the blue, or unavoidable facts of life, such as an inability to have children. Even when you cannot fix a problem, however, you can change the way you think about it. Here are four effective cognitive coping methods:

The ultimate example of reappraisal.

1 *Reappraising the situation.* Although you may not be able to get rid of a stressor (that nasty neighbor is unlikely to move; you cannot undo the fact that you lost your job or have a chronic illness), you can choose to think about it differently—a process called *reappraisal*. Problems can be turned into challenges, and losses into unexpected gains. Maybe that job you lost was pretty dismal but you were too afraid to quit to look for another; now you can. As we saw in Chapter 11 and in discussing the benefits of confession and forgiveness earlier, the way you think about a situation or provocation affects the emotions you feel about it. Reappraisal can turn anger into sympathy, worry into determination, and feelings of loss into feelings of opportunity (Folkman & Moskowitz, 2000).

Get Involved

Rethink Your Stresses

The next time you feel stressed by a situation you can't control, observe your thoughts. What are you saying to yourself? Are your thoughts adding to your stress ("That stupid driver just tried to kill me!")? Try to apply the lessons on "rethinking the problem" to your own situation. For example, can you think of another explanation for a family member's behavior? Can you think of something funny about your predicament—and will it make a good story later? Can you think of something good about the situation, or a lesson it might offer you?

2 *Learning from the experience.* Most victims of traumatic events and life-threatening illnesses report that the experience made them stronger, more resilient, even better human beings who grew and learned from the event (McFarland & Alvaro, 2000). For example, a study of people with spinal-cord injuries found that two-thirds of them felt the disability had had positive side effects. They named such benefits as becoming a better person, seeing the value in other people, and gaining a new appreciation of "brain, not brawn" (Schulz & Decker, 1985).

The ability to find meaning and benefits even in the worst adversity seems crucial to psychological recovery. It even slows the course of serious diseases. In a longitudinal study of men with HIV who had been recently bereaved, those who "tried not to think about it" showed sharper declines in helper T cells (the cells that attack the virus) and were more likely to die during the follow-up period than were men who found meaning and purpose in the loss. The latter said they had acquired greater appreciation of the loved one, a perception of life as being fragile and precious, or other benefits. "I would say that his death lit up my faith," said one man (Taylor et al., 2000a).

Some people emerge from adversity with newfound or newly acquired skills, having been forced to learn something they had not known before—how to cope with the medical system, say, or how to manage a deceased parent's estate. Others discover sources of courage and strength they did not know they had. Those who draw lessons from the inescapable tragedies of life and find meaning in them are far better off psychologically and physically than are people who do not. They are the ones who thrive as a result of adversity instead of simply surviving it (Davis, Nolen-Hoeksema, & Larson, 1998; Folkman & Moskowitz, 2000).

3 *Making social comparisons.* In a difficult situation, successful copers often compare themselves to others who are (they feel) less fortunate. No matter how bad off they are, even if they have fatal diseases, they find someone who is worse off (Taylor & Lobel, 1989; Wood, Michela, & Giordano, 2000). One AIDS sufferer said in an interview, "I made a list of all the other diseases I would rather not have than AIDS. Lou Gehrig's disease, being in a wheelchair; rheumatoid arthritis, when you are in knots and in terrible pain." Another said: "I really have an advantage in a sense over other people. I know there is a possibility that my life may not go on for as many years as other people's. I have the opportunity to look at my life, to make changes, and to deeply appreciate the time that I have" (Reed, 1990).

Sometimes successful copers also compare themselves to those who are doing *better* than they are (Collins, 1996). They might say, "Look at her—she's had such family troubles, and survived that awful bout with cancer, and she's happier than ever with her life. How did she do it?" or "He and I have the same kinds of problems; how come he's doing so much better in school than I am? What does he know that I don't?" Such comparisons are beneficial when they provide a person with information about ways of coping, managing an illness, or improving a stressful situation, and when the person feels able to take advantage of such information (Blanton et al., 1999).

4 *Cultivating a sense of humor.* Unfortunately, we now have to report some research that makes us very grumpy. In earlier editions of this book we reported studies that suggested that humor is not only fun, but good for your health: that it improves immune functioning, hastens recovery from surgery and serious illness, and even prolongs life (Carver et al., 1993; Martin & Dobbin, 1988).

Well, darn, science marches on, and sometimes it makes us give up our favorite notions. Rod Martin (2001), who has been studying humor for more than 20 years and has long believed in its benefits, did a meta-analysis of all research on the effects of humor and laughter on immune function, pain, blood pressure, longevity, and symptoms of illness. To his surprise (and dismay), he found that many studies had been poorly designed: For instance, they did not actually measure the "funniness" of videotapes to the people who watched them, they lacked control groups, or they did not use valid and reliable measures of "sense of humor." Many researchers did

The actor Bert Lahr, shown here as the lovable Cowardly Lion in *The Wizard of Oz*, began using humor as a way to cope with the unhappiness of his early life.

not even define their terms—what *is* a "sense of humor"? One fairly reliable finding—that laughter generated by watching funny movies increases people's tolerance for pain—had a surprising twist: People's pain tolerance also increases when they watch films that make them sad, disgusted, or horrified! The painkilling effects, therefore, might be due to general emotional arousal, not specifically to positive emotions associated with humor and laughter.

After reviewing this literature critically and examining the better-done studies, Martin (2001) concluded that overall, having a good sense of humor or watching funny movies won't help anyone live longer, avoid the flu, or recover from injury faster. On the other hand, he found, humor *does* have benefits as a style of coping with stressful situations, if it is the kind of humor that allows you to see the ridiculous aspects of the problem and gain a sense of distance from it or control over it. (Sarcastic, hostile humor just tends to make matters worse.) People who can see the absurd or whimsical aspects of a bad situation may not live longer, but they are better off mentally than are people who give in to gloom, moping, and tears (Nezu, Nezu, & Blissett, 1988; Solomon, 1996).

Drawing on Social Support

So far we have been discussing individual coping strategies—things you can do for yourself. But often these individual strategies are not enough, and it is necessary to draw on the help and support of others in your network of family, friends, neighbors, and co-workers. Your health depends not only on what is going on in your body and mind but also on what is going on in your relationships: what you take from them, and what you give to them.

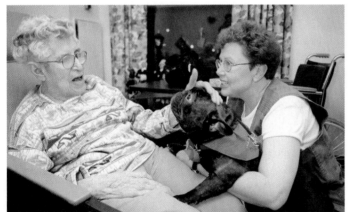

Amy, a French bulldog, is a "certified therapy dog"! Here she comforts a 90-year-old patient at a convalescent hospital. Animal companions, certified or not, provide the health benefits of contact comfort and affection.

When Friends Help You Cope . . . Think of all the ways in which people help one another. They offer concern and affection. They help evaluate problems and plan a course of action. They offer resources and services—by loaning you money or a car, by taking notes in class for you when you are sick. Most of all, they are sources of attachment and connection, which everyone needs throughout life. Perhaps this is why old people who have dogs as companions visit medical clinics less often than their peers who have no pets—or who have cats! Dogs provide devoted companionship and attachment, the two gifts of a truly best friend (J. Siegel, 1990).

Friends are not only nice to have; they also can improve your health. Remember the study we described earlier, showing that stress increases your risk of getting a cold? Well, having a lot of friends and social contacts reduces that risk. In a group of nearly 300 volunteers exposed to a flu virus, those with the most friends were the least likely to get sick (Cohen et al., 1997). Social support is even more important for people who have extremely stressful jobs that require high cardiovascular responsiveness day after day, such as firefighters. The mere presence of a reassuring friend helps heart rate and cortisol levels return to normal more quickly after a stressful episode (Roy, Steptoe, & Kirschbaum, 1998; Thorsteinsson, James, & Gregg, 1998).

People who live in a network of close connections actually live longer than those who do not. In two studies that followed thousands of adults for ten years, people who had many friends, social connections, or memberships in church and other groups lived longer on average than those who had few. The importance of having social networks was unrelated to physical health at the time the studies began, to socioeconomic status, and to risk factors like smoking (Berkman & Syme, 1979; House, Landis, & Umberson, 1988). And in another study of older men and women who had

had heart attacks, 58 percent of those who reported having no close contacts died within the year, compared with only 27 percent of those who said they had two or more people they could count on (Berkman, Leo-Summers, & Horwitz, 1992).

A more formal source of social support comes from joining with other people who have experienced the same illness, problem, or tragedy. People are particularly likely to join and benefit from such groups if they have an illness that is life-threatening or causes them embarrassment (such as AIDS), disfigurement (breast cancer), or stigma (a mental disorder) (Davison, Pennebaker, & Dickerson, 2000). Some researchers have claimed that being in a support group can extend the survival time of people with terminal illnesses, such as advanced breast cancer (Spiegel et al., 1989). However, recent, better-controlled research disputes this finding (Goodwin et al., 2001). Yet even when social support does not prolong patients' lives, it often lessens their suffering and pain.

Like the other factors we have seen that are related to health, social support affects the immune system. Lonely people have poorer immune function than people who are not lonely; students in a network of friends have better immune function before, during, and after exam periods than students who are more solitary; and spouses of cancer patients, although under considerable stress themselves, do not show a drop in immune function if they have lots of social support (Uchino, Cacioppo, & Kiecolt-Glaser, 1996).

. . . And Coping with Friends. Of course, sometimes other people *aren't* helpful. Sometimes they themselves cause unhappiness, stress, and anger. Many people at midlife, particularly women, are stressed by the responsibilities of caring for their immediate families and also for their infirm and ailing parents, who may be suffering from dementia, chronic diseases, or other debilitating conditions.

In close relationships, the same person who is a source of support can also become a source of stress, especially if the two parties are arguing all the time. A major review of 64 articles found that being in an unhappy, bitter, uncommunicative marriage can significantly impair health. It makes the partners depressed and angry, affects their diet and other health habits, and also directly influences the cardiovascular, endocrine, and immune systems (Kiecolt-Glaser & Newton, 2001). Married couples who argue in a hostile fashion—criticizing, interrupting, or insulting the other person, and becoming angry and defensive—show significant elevations of stress hormones and impairments of immune function afterward. Couples who argue in a positive fashion—trying to find common ground, compromising, listening to each other's

Friends can be our greatest source of warmth, support, and fun . . .

. . . and also sources of exasperation, anger, and misery.

concerns, and using humor to defuse tension—do not show these impairments (Kiecolt-Glaser et al., 1993). As one student of ours observed, "This study gives new meaning to the accusation 'You make me sick'!" It also suggests that learning to argue fairly and constructively may have physical as well as psychological benefits.

In addition to being sources of conflict, friends and relatives may be unsupportive in times of disaster or illness simply out of ignorance or awkwardness. They may abandon you or say something stupid and hurtful. Sometimes they actively block your efforts to change bad health habits—say, to cut down on binge drinking or smoking—by making fun of you or pressuring you to conform to what "everyone" does. And sometimes, because they have never been in the same situation and don't know what to do to help, they offer the wrong kind of support. For example, they may try to cheer you up, saying "Everything will be fine," rather than let you talk about your fears or find solutions (Bolger et al., 1996).

Healing Through Helping

A final way to cope with stress, loss, and tragedy is by *giving* support to others, rather than always being on the receiving end. Julius Segal (1986), a psychologist who worked with Holocaust survivors, prisoners of war, hostages, refugees, and other survivors of catastrophe, wrote that a key element in their recovery was compassion, "healing through helping." People gain strength, he said, by focusing less on their own woes and more on helping other people overcome theirs.

Why should this be so? The ability to look outside oneself, to be concerned with helping others, is related to virtually all of the successful coping mechanisms we have discussed (see Review 15.1). It stimulates optimism and restores feelings of control. It encourages people to solve their problems instead of blaming others or venting their emotions. It helps them reappraise the situation by seeing another person's perspective, and allows them to gain perspective on their own problems. Because it promotes forgiveness, tolerance, and empathy, "looking outward" helps people live with situations that are facts of life.

REVIEW 15.1	SUCCESSFUL WAYS OF COPING WITH STRESS	
	Category	**Examples**
	Physical strategies	Relaxation Massage Exercise
	Problem-oriented strategies	Emotion-focused coping to reduce negative emotions Problem-focused coping (e.g., gathering information)
	Cognitive strategies	Reappraising the problem Learning from the problem Making social comparisons
	Social strategies	Relying on friends and family Finding a support group of people in the same situation Helping others

QUICK QUIZ

Can you cope with these refresher questions?

1. Finding out what your legal and financial resources are when you have been victimized by a crime is an example of (a) problem-focused coping, (b) emotion-focused coping, (c) distraction, (d) reappraisal.

2. Learning deep-breathing techniques to reduce anxiety about having been victimized by a crime is an example of (a) problem-focused coping, (b) emotion-focused coping, (c) avoidance, (d) reappraisal.

3. You accidentally broke your glasses. Which response is an example of reappraisal? (a) "I am such a stupid, clumsy idiot!" (b) "I never do anything right." (c) "What a shame, but I've been wanting new frames anyway." (d) "I'll forget about it in aerobics class."

4. "This class drives me crazy, but I'm better off than my friends who aren't in college" is an example of (a) distraction, (b) social comparison, (c) denial, (d) empathy.

5. Isabel has diabetes. Her family is trying to be helpful, but they are impatient when she talks about her worries and medical needs. What lesson about social support is her family illustrating? And what might Isabel do about it?

 6. Your roommate has turned your room into a garbage dump, filled with rotten leftover food and unwashed clothes. Assuming that you don't like living with rotting food and dirty clothes, what coping strategies described in this section might help you?

Answers:

1.a 2.b 3.c 4.b 5. Isabel's family is not offering her the right kind of support, because they don't understand her worries and can't provide practical help or emotional comfort. She might seek a support group of other people with diabetes who can meet this need. 6. You might solve the problem by compromising (clean the room together), You might reappraise the seriousness of the problem ("I only have to live with this person until the end of the term") or compare your roommate to others ("At least mine is generous and friendly"). And you might mobilize some social support—offer your friends a pizza if they help you clean up.

WHAT'S AHEAD

- **What are the three best things you can do to prolong your life?**
- **How can we think critically about mainstream and alternative approaches to health?**

How Much Control Do We Have over Our Health?

It should be clear by now that the line between stress and illness is not straightforward and direct. Many factors are links in the long chain of cumulative events between stressors and illness or health, including genetic vulnerabilities to certain diseases, diet, emotions, explanatory styles, coping strategies, and social networks (see Review 15.2).

Yet to hear some people talk, health is almost entirely a matter of "mind over matter." Even the worst diseases, they say, can be cured with laughter, vitamins, and positive thinking, and if you become sick, it's your own fault. This attitude is quite recent, a result of medical advances that occurred over the past century. As industrialized societies conquered many of the environmental sources of infectious diseases, through innovations in water treatment, sewage disposal, and food storage, and through the discovery of antibiotics and vaccines, public attention turned to diseases that are affected by what we eat and how we live. Accordingly, the focus of health professionals shifted from changing the environment to changing individuals (Taylor, Repetti, & Seeman, 1997).

REVIEW 15.2 FACTORS THAT INCREASE THE RISK OF ILLNESS

	Factors	Examples
	Environmental	Uncontrollable noise, poverty, lack of access to health care, discrimination
	Experiential	Bereavement or divorce, traumatic events, chronic and severe job stress, unemployment
	Biological	Viral or bacterial infections, disease, genetic vulnerability, toxins
	Psychological	Hostility, possibly chronic depression, emotional inhibition, pessimism, external locus of control (fatalism), feeling powerless
	Behavioral	Smoking, a high-fat diet, lack of exercise, abuse of alcohol and other drugs, lack of sleep
	Social	Lack of supportive friends and relatives, low involvement in groups

Many health psychologists fear that the public is oversimplifying the message of their research, by concluding that the factors that produce good health and long life are entirely psychological or entirely under our control, and that we need not worry about the environment. Clearly, as we saw in this chapter, people do have some control over many of the psychological and social factors that are involved in the onset and course of many illnesses—such as negative emotions, pessimism, and lack of supportive friends. And people do have control over the three strongest predictors of longevity and health, which are not psychological at all: not smoking (or quitting), eating a healthy diet, and exercising regularly (Vita et al., 1998).

However, life is full of stressful experiences, chronic problems, and disastrous bolts from the blue that we cannot predict or avoid. At such times, critical thinking becomes especially important, because the temptation is great to slide into oversimplified, either–or thinking: For example, *either* you get traditional medical procedures to treat a disease *or* you use alternative psychological ones, such as visual imagery, meditation, and support groups. These are not opposite choices, of course. In fact, most physicians today, while endorsing traditional medical treatments, also recognize the role of psychological and social factors in their patients' recovery and well-being: the importance of an optimistic attitude, a good support system, and effective coping strategies. They worry, however, that some people will put off crucial medical procedures in favor of relying exclusively on alternative treatments.

Successful coping does not mean eliminating all stress. It does not mean constant happiness or a life without pain. The healthy person faces problems, deals with them, and gets beyond them, but the problems are necessary if the person is to acquire coping skills that endure. To wish for a life without stress would be like wishing for a life without friends. The result might be calm, but it would be joyless and ultimately hazardous to your health. The stresses of life—the daily hassles and the occasional tragedies—force us to grow, and to grow up.

THINKING CRITICALLY

Don't Oversimplify

Marlon and Maren are arguing about alternative vs. traditional medicine. One thinks modern medicine is cold and too commercial. The other thinks alternative methods are silly and superstitious. How might they resolve their differences about the two approaches to health?

Taking Psychology with You

HEALTH HABITS YOU CAN LIVE WITH

The marketplace is full of people who prey on the public's health worries by selling them worthless programs, pills, and devices (Angell & Kassirer, 1998). Many promoters of such products have impressive-looking but academically meaningless "credentials," often from unaccredited schools that offer mail-order degrees. At one of these places you can study "nutri-medical dentistry," for example, or "therapeutic nutri-medicine" (Raso, 1996).

Look out for unvalidated advice, and watch your wallet. The findings from health psychology offer practical, *free* guidelines for maintaining good health and coping with stressors or illness when they occur:

▶ *Follow "good old-fashioned motherly advice" and practice good health habits.* You know them: do not smoke; do not drink excessively or in binges; eat a healthful diet; wear seat belts; exercise regularly; and get enough sleep (Matarazzo, 1984; Vita et al., 1998). Healthful habits are important not only for prevention of illness but also for its treatment. When people become ill, they often stop taking care of themselves. They drink too much, stop exercising, and don't eat well, all of which can speed the course of the disease. One of the greatest challenges for health psychologists is how to persuade people to change their current bad health habits for the sake of future benefits. Who cares, many young smokers say, about getting lung cancer 20 years from now? Why exercise now, when it's easier to watch TV and there's no fitness payoff for weeks, even months? Why not indulge myself now and worry about possible problems later? One answer, of course, is that "later" may be too late.

▶ *Learn how to regulate negative emotions.* Confessing your deepest thoughts and feelings—by writing them down, speaking into a tape recorder, or talking with a trusted friend or therapist—and finding the ability to forgive may help you let go of resentment, grudges, anger, and blame. The goal is to see the experience in a new light and think about it differently. But constant rehearsal and ventilation of your negative emotions is not therapeutic if you keep talking about them endlessly to anyone who will listen. The repeated expression of your feelings will not, by itself, help you achieve insight into the origins of your problems.

▶ *Take control of what you can, such as finding the best treatment for a medical problem or the best solution to a psychological one.* If you are under stress at school because you are not doing well, learning to relax or splurging on massages might help, but ultimately you will have to decide what you can do to improve your grades. If you are under stress at home because you are constantly quarreling with your partner or parents, talking with others about the problem might make you feel temporarily better, but ultimately you will have to figure out why you are fighting so much—and how you can argue constructively.

▶ *Reappraise the situation or event to find meaning in it and see its positive aspects.* Many things happen that are out of your control: accidents, being born to particular parents, flu epidemics, natural disasters, and countless other events. But you do have control over how you cope with them. When you cannot change a fact of life, try to identify the challenges, opportunities, and "learning experiences" that it offers you.

▶ *Don't try to "go it alone"; get the social support you need.* Find individuals who understand your problems and who can offer practical as well as moral support. Whether your stress results from a one-time upsetting event or a chronic situation, try to find people who have "been there" and who can advise you on the best ways to cope.

▶ *Don't stay in a network that is not helpful; get rid of the "social support" you don't need!* Are your friends or colleagues encouraging you to maintain unhealthy practices that you would like to change? Are they preventing you from making improvements in your life? If so, you may need to think about finding new friends or new ways of sticking to your changed habits in spite of your old friends' efforts.

Health psychology offers many other practical applications of research that can improve your life. But if you find that you are not perfectly able to control every stressor that comes your way, don't get upset. After all, that will only add to your stress.

Summary

The Stress-Illness Mystery

▶ Several chronic *stressors* increase the risk of illness: constant, uncontrollable noise; bereavement and loss; unemployment and work-related problems; and poverty and powerlessness. However, most people who experience these stressors do not become ill. *Health psychologists* study the psychological, social, and biological factors that predict who gets sick and who stays healthy.

The Physiology of Stress

▶ Hans Selye argued that environmental stressors such as heat, pain, and danger produce a *general adaptation syndrome*, in which the body responds in three stages: *alarm*, which activates the "fight or flight" response of the autonomic nervous system; *resistance*; and *exhaustion*. If a stressor persists, it may overwhelm the body's ability to cope, and fatigue and illness may result.

▶ Modern research has modified and added to Selye's framework. When a person is under stress or danger, the hypothalamus sends messages to the endocrine glands along two major pathways. One activates the sympathetic division of the autonomic nervous system, releasing epinephrine and norepinephrine from the inner part of the adrenal glands. The hypothalamus also initiates activity along the *HPA axis*. Chemical messengers travel from the hypothalamus to the pituitary, and in turn to the outer part (cortex) of the adrenal glands. The adrenal cortex secretes *cortisol* and other hormones that elevate blood sugar and protect the body's tissues from inflammation. Excess levels of cortisol can become harmful in the long run. Responses to stress differ across individuals, depending on the type of stressor and the individual's own genetic predispositions.

▶ Researchers in the field of *psychoneuroimmunology (PNI)* are studying how psychological factors, the nervous and endocrine systems, and the immune system (particularly the white blood cells that destroy harmful bacteria, viruses, or tumor cells) interact to produce illness.

The Psychology of Stress

▶ Researchers have sought links between psychological factors, such as personality traits, emotions, and beliefs, and illness. Having a competitive, impatient *Type A personality* is not itself related to heart disease, but *cynical hostility*, which is often part of the Type A pattern, is. Chronic depression seems to also be a risk factor in heart disease, but its link to other illnesses remains unclear.

▶ People who are *emotionally inhibited* are at greater risk of illness than people who can acknowledge and cope with negative emotions. The effort to suppress thoughts, worries, secrets, and memories of upsetting experiences can paradoxically lead to obsessively ruminating on these thoughts and can be stressful to the body. Research finds that people benefit physiologically when they are able to let negative emotions go, through confession (expressing them on paper or to a trusted friend) or forgiveness. *Positive emotions*, such as happiness, joy, gratitude, hope, and love, are associated with better health and longevity.

▶ Other important psychological factors that affect health are having an *optimistic explanatory style* (in contrast to a pessimistic one), even when optimism involves unrealistic but positive illusions, and an *internal locus of control*. Optimism and control affect a person's ability to tolerate pain, live with ongoing illness and stress, and recover from disease. People can sometimes have too strong a sense of control; the healthiest balance is to take responsibility for getting well without blaming oneself for getting sick.

▶ Health and well-being may depend on the right combination of *primary control*, trying to change the stressful situation, and *secondary control*, learning to accept and accommodate to the stressful situation. Cultures differ in the kind of control they emphasize and value most.

Coping with Stress

▶ *Coping* involves active efforts to manage demands that feel stressful. One way to cope with stress is to reduce its physical effects, for example, through relaxation, massage, and exercise. Another is to focus on solving the problem (*problem-focused coping*) rather than focusing solely on ventilating the emotions caused by the problem (*emotion-focused coping*). A third is to rethink the problem, which involves *reappraisal*, learning from and finding meaning in the experience, comparing oneself to others, and seeing humor in the situation.

▶ *Social support*—from friends, family, and other people—is important in maintaining health and emotional well-being. People who have good friends, many social contacts, and a network of community relations have better health and actually live longer than those who do not. However, family and friends can also be a source of stress. In close relationships, couples who fight in a hostile and negative way show impaired immune function. *Giving* support—looking outside yourself to help others—is also associated with health and hastens recovery from traumatic experiences.

How Much Control Do We Have over Our Health?

▶ Psychological factors and social networks are links in a long chain that connects stress and illness. Coping with stress does not mean trying to live without pain, problems, or losses. It means learning how to live with them.

Key Terms

health psychology 550

stressors 550

Hans Selye 552

general adaptation syndrome 552

alarm/resistance/exhaustion phases of stress 552–553

adrenal hormones 552

epinephrine, norepinephrine, cortisol 553

HPA axis (hypothalamus–pituitary–adrenal cortex) 553

psychoneuroimmunology 554

Type A personality 556

cynical (antagonistic) hostility 557

emotional inhibition 557

pessimistic and optimistic explanatory styles 560

locus of control (internal versus external) 562

primary control 564

secondary control 565

coping 566

progressive relaxation 566

emotion-focused coping 568

problem-focused coping 568

reappraisal 568

social comparisons 569

social support 570

◀LOOKING BACK

- Which stressors pose the greatest hazard to your health? (pp. 550–551)

- Are you more likely to get a cold when you are "stressed out"? (p. 551)

- What happens to your body when you try to cross a busy street against the light? (p. 552)

- Why is being under stress not enough to make you ill? (p. 554)

- How do psychological factors affect the immune system? (p. 555)

- Which emotion may be most hazardous to your heart? (p. 557)

- Does chronic depression lead to physical illness? (p. 557)

- Is confession as healthy for the body as it is for the soul? (p. 558)

- Why do optimists tend to live longer than pessimists? (p. 561)

- Why does it matter whether you think you control your own destiny or your destiny controls you? (pp. 563–564)

- When you are feeling overwhelmed, what are some good ways to calm down? (pp. 566–567)

- Why is it important to move beyond the emotions caused by a problem and deal with the problem itself? (p. 568)

- Can tragedies and losses ever be beneficial for you? (p. 569)

- When do friends reduce your stress, and when do they just make matters worse? (pp. 570–572)

- What are the three best things you can do to prolong your life? (p. 574)

- How can we think critically about mainstream and alternative approaches to health? (p. 574)

 Go to **Live! psych WWW.PRENHALL.COM/WADE** to reinforce these key concepts, and more.

15.1 Stress and Selye's general adaption syndrome
15.2 The brain and the body under stress

16

Psychological Disorders

Who in the rainbow can draw the line where the violet tint ends and the orange tint begins? . . . So with sanity and insanity.

HERMAN MELVILLE, *BILLY BUDD*

Margaret Mary Ray believed with all her heart that late-night talk-show host David Letterman was in love with her. Caught up in this delusion, she stalked Letterman day and night for a decade, writing him letters and repeatedly breaking into his house. She camped out on his tennis court and once stole his car. The tabloids treated her delusions as a running joke. Finally, she gave up. She wrote to her mother, "I'm all traveled out," and put herself in front of a coal train. She was killed instantly.

A young man wandered into the counseling center at his college to seek help for his failing grades. For a year he had been a good student, but now he was depressed, skipping classes, and arguing with his parents. He had also spent hundreds of hours on the Internet that semester. According to a survey of students at eight colleges and universities, his behavior was not so unusual. "Internet addiction" is a growing problem: Some students are spending 12 to 15 hours a day online, in chat rooms and playing games, eventually flunking out of school.

You don't have to be a psychologist to know that something was terribly wrong with Margaret Mary Ray. When people think of "mental illness," they usually think of individuals like her—people with delusions, people who behave in bizarre ways, or people who plant bombs or commit random murders. But most psychological problems, like those of students with "Internet addiction," are far less dramatic and far more common. Some people go through episodes of complete inability to function, yet get along fine between those episodes. Many people function adequately every day, yet suffer constant melancholy, always feeling below par in happiness. Some cannot control their worries or tempers.

One of the most common worries that people have is "Am I normal?" It is normal to fear being abnormal—especially when you are reading about psychological problems! But it is also normal to have problems. All of us on occasion have difficulties that seem too much to handle, and it is often unclear precisely when "normal" problems shade into "abnormal" ones. In this chapter, you will learn how psychologists and psychiatrists define disorder and how they diagnose a wide range of psychological problems.

WHAT'S AHEAD ▶

- **Is insanity the same thing as having a mental disorder?**
- **What are three approaches to defining "mental disorder"?**
- **Why is the standard guide to the diagnosis of mental disorders controversial?**
- **Why were slaves who dreamed of freedom once considered to be mentally ill?**
- **How reliable are "projective" tests like the famous and popular Rorschach Inkblot Test?**

Defining and Diagnosing Disorder

Many people confuse abnormal behavior—behavior that deviates from the norm—with mental disorder, but the two are not the same. A person may behave in ways that are statistically rare (collecting ceramic pigs, being a genius at math, committing murder) without having a mental illness. Conversely, some mental disorders, such as depression and anxiety, are extremely common.

People also confuse mental disorder and insanity. In the law, the definition of *insanity* rests primarily on whether a person is aware of the consequences of his or her actions and can control his or her behavior. But insanity is a legal term only; a person may have a mental illness and yet be considered sane by the court.

If frequency of the problem is not a guide, and insanity reflects only one extreme kind of mental illness, how then should we define "mental disorder"?

Dilemmas of Definition

One problem with trying to define mental disorder is that the definition depends on whether we are taking society's point of view, the view of people who are affected by the troubled individual, or the perspective of troubled individuals themselves.

1 *Mental disorder as a violation of cultural standards.* This criterion emphasizes the roles and rules of the culture. Every society sets up standards for its members to follow, and those who break the most important rules governing appropriate behavior are usually considered deviant or disturbed. However, many of these rules are specific to a particular time or group. For example, in most North American cultural groups, having visions of a deceased relative, though not uncommon, is considered abnormal; bereaved people tend to keep their hallucinations secret, for fear of being labeled "crazy." In contrast, the Chinese, the Hopi, and members of many other cultures regard such visions as perfectly normal.

2 *Mental disorder as maladaptive or harmful behavior.* Another approach emphasizes the negative consequences of a person's behavior. Some behavior is harmful to the individual—for example, the behavior of a woman who is so afraid of crowds that she cannot leave her house, a man who drinks so much that he cannot keep a job, and a student who is so anxious that he cannot take exams. In other cases, the individual may report feeling fine and deny that anything is wrong, yet behave in ways that are disruptive, dangerous, or out of touch with reality—as when a child sets fires, a compulsive gambler loses the family savings, or a woman hears voices telling her to stalk a celebrity.

3 *Mental disorder as emotional distress.* A third approach identifies mental disorder in terms of a person's suffering, for example, from depression, anxiety, incapacitating fears, or problems with drugs. In this definition, a behavior that is unendurable or upsetting for one person, such as lack of interest in sex, may be acceptable and normal for another. But it does not cover the behavior of people who are clearly disturbed and dangerous to others, yet are not troubled about their actions.

In this chapter, we define **mental disorder** broadly, as any behavior or emotional state that causes an individual great suffering or worry, is self-defeating or self-destructive, or is maladaptive and disrupts either the person's relationships or the larger community. By this definition, many people will have some mental-health problem in the course of their lives, or their loved ones will.

People the world over paint their bodies, but what is normal for one person or one culture may not be to others. Hiromi Nakano (left), whose body has been completely tattooed, has taken body painting to an extreme rare in most societies, including her own. The Samburu tribesman of Kenya (center) has adorned his face in ways that seem odd to Westerners but that are typical of his culture. The tattoos of the American bikers (right) seem abnormal to most Americans but are perfectly normal in their biking subculture. Do you find these examples of body decoration to be beautiful, amusing, disgusting, or creepy? Your own cultural ideas of what is "normal" will affect your answers.

Dilemmas of Diagnosis

Even armed with a general definition of mental disorder, psychologists have found that classifying mental disorders into distinct categories is easier said than done. In this section we will examine why this is so.

Classifying Disorders: The DSM. The standard reference manual used to diagnose all mental disorders is the *Diagnostic and Statistical Manual of Mental Disorders* (DSM), published by the American Psychiatric Association (1994, 2000). The DSM's primary aim is *descriptive:* to provide clear diagnostic categories, so that clinicians and researchers can agree on which disorders they are talking about and then can study and treat these disorders. (For a list of the DSM's major categories, see Table 16.1.) The DSM lists the symptoms of each disorder and, wherever possible, gives information about the typical age of onset, predisposing factors, course of the disorder, prevalence of the disorder, sex ratio of those affected, and cultural issues that might affect diagnosis. In addition, clinicians are encouraged to evaluate each client according to five *axes,* or dimensions:

1. The primary clinical problem, such as depression.

2. Ingrained aspects of the client's personality that are likely to affect the person's ability to be treated, such as negative emotionality (neuroticism), a disposition to be pessimistic and bitter (see Chapter 13).

3. Medical conditions, such as respiratory or digestive problems, or medications that might contribute to depressive symptoms.

4. Social and environmental stressors that can make the disorder worse, such as job and housing troubles or having recently left a network of close friends.

5. A global assessment of the client's overall level of functioning in work, relationships, and leisure time, including whether the problem is of recent origin or of long duration and how incapacitating it is.

mental disorder Any behavior or emotional state that causes an individual great suffering or worry, is self-defeating or self-destructive, or is maladaptive and disrupts the person's relationships or the larger community.

Table 16.1	**Major Diagnostic Categories in the DSM-IV**

Disorders usually first diagnosed in infancy, childhood, or adolescence include mental retardation, attention deficit disorders (such as hyperactivity or an inability to concentrate), and developmental problems.

Delirium, dementia, amnesia, and other cognitive disorders are those resulting from brain damage, degenerative diseases such as syphilis or Alzheimer's, toxic substances, or drugs.

Substance-related disorders are problems associated with excessive use of or withdrawal from alcohol, amphetamines, caffeine, cocaine, hallucinogens, nicotine, opiates, or other drugs.

Schizophrenia and other psychotic disorders are disorders characterized by delusions, hallucinations, and severe disturbances in thinking and emotion.

Mood disorders include major depression, bipolar disorder (manic depression), and dysthymia (chronic depressed mood).

Anxiety disorders include generalized anxiety disorder, phobias, panic attacks with or without agoraphobia, posttraumatic stress disorder, and obsessive thoughts or compulsive rituals.

Eating disorders include anorexia nervosa (self-starvation because of an irrational fear of being or becoming fat) and bulimia nervosa (episodes of binge eating and vomiting).

Somatoform disorders involve physical symptoms (e.g., paralysis, heart palpitations, fatigue) for which no organic cause can be found. This category includes hypochondria (an extreme preoccupation with health and the unfounded conviction that one is ill) and conversion disorder (in which a physical symptom, such as a paralyzed arm or blindness, serves a psychological function).

Dissociative disorders include dissociative amnesia (in which important events cannot be remembered after a traumatic event) and dissociative identity disorder, characterized by the presence of two or more distinct identities or personalities.

Sexual and gender identity disorders include problems of sexual (gender) identity, such as transsexualism (wanting to be the other gender), problems of sexual performance (such as premature ejaculation or lack of orgasm), and paraphilias (needing unusual or bizarre imagery or acts for sexual arousal, as in sadomasochism or exhibitionism).

Impulse control disorders involve an inability to resist an impulse to perform some act that is harmful to the individual or to others, such as pathological gambling, stealing (kleptomania), setting fires (pyromania), or having violent rages.

Personality disorders are inflexible and maladaptive patterns that cause distress to the individual or impair the ability to function; they include paranoid, narcissistic, and antisocial personality disorders.

Additional conditions that may be a focus of clinical attention include "problems in living" such as bereavement, academic difficulties, spiritual problems, and acculturation problems.

Figure 16.1

THE RISING NUMBER OF DISORDERS IN THE DSM

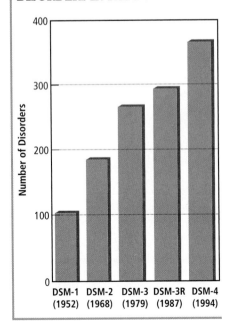

The DSM has had an extraordinary impact worldwide. Virtually all textbooks in psychiatry and psychology base their discussions of mental disorders on the DSM. Attorneys and judges often refer to the manual's list of mental disorders, even though the DSM warns that its categories "may not be wholly relevant to legal judgments." With each new edition of the manual, the number of mental disorders has grown (see Figure 16.1). The first edition, in 1952, was only 86 pages long and contained about 100 diagnoses. The DSM-IV, published in 1994 and as a slightly revised volume in 2000, is 900 pages long and contains nearly 400 diagnoses of mental disorder (Houts, 2002).

What is the reason for this explosion of "mental disorders"? Supporters of the new categories answer that it is important to distinguish disorders precisely in order to treat them properly. Critics point to an economic reason: Insurance companies require clinicians to assign their clients an appropriate DSM code number for the diagnosed disorder, which puts pressure on compilers of the manual to add more diagnoses so that physicians and psychologists will be compensated.

Problems with the DSM. Because of the DSM's powerful influence, critics maintain that it is important to be aware of its limitations and some inherent problems in the very effort to classify and label mental disorders:

1 *The danger of overdiagnosis.* "If you give a small boy a hammer," wrote Abraham Kaplan (1967), "it will turn out that everything he runs into needs pounding." Likewise, say critics, if you give mental health professionals a diagnostic label, it will turn out that everyone they run into has the symptoms of the new disorder.

Consider "attention deficit/hyperactivity disorder" (ADHD), a diagnostic label given to children (and adults) who are impulsive, messy, restless, and easily frustrated, and who have trouble concentrating. Since ADHD was added to the DSM, it has become the fastest-growing disorder in America, where it is diagnosed at least ten times as often as it is in Europe. It may reflect a true disorder in some cases, but critics fear that parents, teachers, and mental-health professionals are overusing this diagnosis, especially on boys, who make up 80 to 90 percent of all ADHD cases. The critics argue that normal boy behavior—being rambunctious, refusing to nap, being playful, not listening to teachers in school—is being pathologized (Panksepp, 1998).

2 *The power of diagnostic labels.* Being given a diagnosis reassures people who are seeking an explanation for their emotional symptoms or problems ("Whew! So *that's* what I've got!"). But it can also create a self-fulfilling prophecy: The client tries to conform to the assigned diagnosis, and the clinician interprets everything the client does as confirmation of the diagnosis (Maddux, 1996).

Moreover, once a person has been given a diagnosis, other people begin to see that person primarily in terms of the label; it sticks like lint. For example, when a rebellious, disobedient teenager is diagnosed as having "oppositional defiant disorder," people tend to see him as a person with a permanent, official disorder (something is wrong with his personality) and often fail to consider other explanations of his actions: Maybe he is defiant because he has been mistreated or his parents never listen to him. And once he is labeled, observers tend to ignore changes in his behavior and the times when he is not being defiant.

3 *The confusion of serious mental disorders with normal problems.* The DSM is not called "The Diagnostic and Statistical Manual of Mental Disorders and a Whole Bunch of Everyday Problems." Yet each edition of the DSM adds more everyday problems, including "disorder of written expression" (having trouble writing clearly), "mathematics disorder" (not doing well in math), "religious or spiritual problem," and "caffeine-induced sleep disorder" (which at least is easy to cure; just switch to decaf). Some critics fear that by lumping together such normal difficulties with true mental illnesses, such as schizophrenia, the DSM implies that everyday problems are comparable to disorders—and equally likely to require treatment (Houts, 2002; Kutchins & Kirk, 1997; Maddux, 1993).

4 *The illusion of objectivity and universality.* Finally, some psychologists argue that the whole enterprise of the DSM is a vain attempt to impose a veneer of science on an inherently subjective process

Critics say the **DSM** turns many normal behaviors into "disorders" or "disabilities."

NEWLY DISCOVERED LEARNING DISABILITIES

GO-CARTITIS
Instead of focussing on topic at hand, kid fantasizes about go-carts.

DOODLER'S SYNDROME
Child insists on drawing, thus completely shutting out teacher's voice.

What is a divisor? SALLY?

Harriet Tubman (on the left) poses with some of the people she helped to escape from slavery on her "underground railroad." Slaveholders welcomed the idea that Tubman and others who insisted on their freedom had a "mental disorder" called "drapetomania."

(Houts, 2002; Kutchins & Kirk, 1997; Maddux, 1993; Tiefer, 1995). Many decisions about what to include as a disorder, say these critics, are based not on empirical evidence but on group consensus. The problem is that group consensus often reflects prevailing attitudes and prejudices rather than objective evidence.

It is easy to identify these prejudices in past notions of "mental illness." For example, in the early years of the nineteenth century, a physician named Samuel Cartwright argued that many slaves were suffering from *drapetomania,* an urge to escape from slavery (Kutchins & Kirk, 1997; Landrine, 1988). Thus doctors could assure slave owners that a mental illness, not the intolerable condition of slavery, made slaves seek freedom. Today, of course, "drapetomania" seems foolish and cruel.

Over the years, psychiatrists have quite properly rejected many other "disorders" that reflected cultural prejudices and lacked empirical validation, such as lack of vaginal orgasm, childhood masturbation disorder, and homosexuality (Wakefield, 1992). But critics argue that many disorders in the DSM are just as affected by contemporary prejudices and values. Today you don't have a disorder if you want to have sex "too often" (once called, in women, "nymphomania"), but you do if you do not want to have sex often "enough" (hypoactive sexual desire disorder) (Groneman, 2000). Emotional problems allegedly associated with menstruation remain in the DSM, but behavioral problems associated with testosterone have never even been considered for inclusion. In short, critics maintain, many diagnoses still depend on a cultural consensus, not on empirical evidence, about what constitutes "normal behavior," as well as what constitutes a "mental disorder."

Advantages of the DSM. Defenders of the DSM point out that new studies are improving empirical support for many of the DSM's categories. They agree that the boundaries between "normality" and "mental disorder" are indeed fuzzy and often difficult to determine. They recognize that many psychological symptoms are not equally debilitating; difficulties fall along a continuum, ranging from mild to severe (Widiger & Clark, 2000). And they are developing other systems that have stronger empirical support for classifying mental disorders (Beutler & Malik, 2002).

Defenders argue, further, that when the manual is used correctly and diagnoses are made with valid objective tests, the DSM improves the reliability of diagnosis and increases agreement among clinicians (Wittchen et al., 1995). The DSM's categories help clinicians distinguish among disorders that might share certain symptoms (such as irritability or delusions) in order to select the most appropriate treatment (Kessler et al., 1994).

Moreover, the DSM-IV included, for the first time, a list of *culture-bound syndromes,* disorders that are specific to particular cultural contexts (see Table 16.2). The DSM acknowledges that these syndromes rarely overlap with DSM diagnostic categories, yet can cause great mental suffering in the cultures where they occur. At the same time, DSM defenders argue, some disorders are universal, although they might take different forms (take a look at the disorder of "brain fag" in Table 16.2!). All over the world, from the Inuit of Alaska to the Yorubas of Nigeria, some individuals have delusions, are severely depressed, suffer panic attacks, or cannot control their behavior. In every culture, such individuals are considered to have mental illnesses (Butcher, Lim, & Nezami, 1998; Kleinman, 1988).

Table 16.2	From Amok to Zar: Some Culture-Bound Syndromes	
Problem Name	**Where Recognized**	**Description**
Amok	Malaysia; similar patterns elsewhere	Brooding followed by a violent outburst; often precipitated by a slight or insult; seems to be prevalent only among men.
Ataque de nervios	Latin America and Mediterranean	An episode of uncontrollable shouting, crying, trembling, heat in chest rising to the head, verbal or physical aggression.
Boufée delirante	West Africa and Haiti	Sudden outburst of agitated and aggressive behavior, confusion, and mental and physical excitement.
Brain fag	West Africa	"Brain tiredness," a mental and physical reaction to the challenges of schooling.
Dhat	India; also in Sri Lanka and China	In males, severe anxiety and hypochondria associated with discharge of semen and feelings of exhaustion.
Falling-out or blacking out	Southern United States and Caribbean	Sudden collapse; eyes remain open but sightless; the victim hears but feels unable to move.
Ghost sickness	American Indian tribes	Preoccupation with death and the dead, with bad dreams, fainting, appetite loss, fear, hallucinations, etc.
Koro	Malaysia; related conditions in East Asia	Sudden intense anxiety that sexual organs will recede into body and possibly cause death.
Latah	Malaysia, Indonesia, Japan, Thailand	Hypersensitivity to sudden fright, often with mimicking of others, trancelike behavior.
Pibloktoq	Arctic and subarctic Eskimo communities	Episodes of extreme excitement of up to 30 minutes, during which the individual behaves irrationally or violently.
Qi-gong psychotic reaction	China	A short episode of mental symptoms after engaging in Chinese folk practice of qi-gong, or "exercise of vital energy."
Shin-byung	Korea	Syndrome of anxiety and bodily complaints followed by dissociation and possession by ancestral spirits.
Taijin kyofusho	Japan	An intense fear that the body, its parts, or its functions displease, embarrass or are offensive to others.
Zar	North Africa and Middle East	Belief in possession by a spirit, causing shouting, laughing, head banging, weeping, withdrawal, etc.

Source: DSM-IV

Dilemmas of Measurement

Clinical psychologists and psychiatrists usually arrive at a diagnosis by interviewing a patient and observing the person's behavior when he or she arrives at the office, hospital, or clinic (Luhrmann, 2000). But many also use psychological tests to help them decide on a diagnosis. Such tests are also commonly used in schools (e.g., to determine whether a child has a learning disorder or emotional problem) and in court settings (e.g., to try to determine which parent should have custody in a divorce case).

projective tests Psychological tests used to infer a person's motives, conflicts, and unconscious dynamics on the basis of the person's interpretations of ambiguous stimuli.

Rorschach Inkblot Test A projective personality test that requires respondents to interpret abstract, symmetrical inkblots.

A Rorschach inkblot. What do you see in it?

For years, many therapists used anatomically correct dolls as a projective test to determine whether a child had been sexually abused, but this practice has not been justified by empirical evidence.

Projective Tests. **Projective tests** are based on psychodynamic assumptions (see Chapter 13); they are designed to reveal unconscious motives, feelings, and conflicts. These tests consist of ambiguous pictures, sentences, or stories that the test taker interprets or completes. A child or adult may be asked to draw a person, a house, or some other object or to finish a sentence (such as "My father . . ." or "Women are . . ."). The assumption behind all projective tests is that the person's unconscious thoughts and feelings will be "projected" onto the test and revealed in the person's responses.

Projective tests can help clinicians establish rapport with their clients and encourage clients to open up about anxieties and conflicts they might be ashamed to discuss. But the evidence is overwhelming that they are too unreliable to be used, as they often currently are, for assessing personality traits or diagnosing mental disorders (Dawes, 1994; Lilienfeld, 1999). Different clinicians often interpret the same person's scores differently; they may be projecting their own beliefs and assumptions when they decide what a specific response means. The tests also have low validity, failing to measure what they claim to measure. One reason is that responses to a projective test are significantly affected by sleepiness, hunger, drugs, worry, verbal ability, the clinician's instructions, the clinician's own personality (friendly and warm, or cool and remote), and other events occurring that day (Anastasi, 1988; Lilienfeld, Wood, & Garb, 2000).

One of the most popular projectives is the **Rorschach Inkblot Test,** which was devised by Swiss psychiatrist Hermann Rorschach in 1921. It consists of ten cards with symmetrical abstract patterns, originally formed by spilling ink on paper and folding the paper in half. The test taker reports what he or she sees in the inkblots, and the clinician interprets the answers according to the symbolic meanings emphasized by psychodynamic theories. One kind of response, for example, might be interpreted as evidence of a person's dependency.

Although the Rorschach is widely used among clinicians, efforts to confirm its reliability and validity have repeatedly failed (Lilienfeld, Wood, & Garb, 2000). Clinicians often disagree with one another on what various answers mean, and test–retest reliability is also low. The Rorschach does not reliably diagnose depression, posttraumatic stress reactions, personality disorders, serious mental disorders, or evidence of sexual abuse (Garb, Wood, & Nezworski, 2000). In recent years, a scoring method called the Comprehensive System has become popular (Exner, 1993). But this method, too, has significant problems with reliability and validity. Claims of the system's success often come from Rorschach workshops where clinicians are taught how to use the test, which is hardly an impartial way of assessing it (Wood, Nezworski, & Stejskal, 1996).

Many psychotherapists use projective tests with children, to help those who have suffered traumatic experiences express feelings they cannot reveal verbally. But during the 1980s, some therapists began using projective methods for another purpose: to determine *whether* a child had been sexually abused. They claimed they could identify a child who had been abused by observing how the child played with "anatomically detailed" dolls (dolls with realistic genitals)—and that is how many of them testified in hundreds of court cases (Ceci & Bruck, 1995).

Unfortunately, these therapists did not test their beliefs by using a fundamental scientific procedure: comparison with a control group (see Chapter 2). They had not asked, "How do *nonabused* children play with these dolls?" When psychological scientists did ask this question and conducted controlled research to answer it, they found that large percentages of nonabused children are also fascinated with the doll's genitals. They will poke at them, grab them, pound sticks into a female doll's vagina, and do other things that alarm adults. The important conclusion was that you cannot reliably diagnose sexual abuse on the basis of children's doll play (Bruck et al., 1995; Koocher et al., 1995; Lilienfeld, Wood, & Garb, 2000; Poole & Lamb, 1998). You can see how a psychotherapist who had no understanding of the importance of empirically testing clinical observations and assumptions, and who did not understand the unreliability of projective tests, might end up making inferences about a child's behavior that were dangerously wrong.

Objective Tests. Many clinicians also use **objective tests (inventories)**. These are standardized questionnaires that ask about the test taker's behavior and feelings. Some inventories, such as the Beck Depression Inventory, the Spielberger State-Trait Anger Inventory, and the Taylor Manifest Anxiety Scale, reliably assess specific emotional problems. Inventories are generally more reliable and more valid than either projective methods or subjective clinical judgments based on observations and interviews (Anastasi & Urbina, 1997; Dawes, 1994).

"Rorschach! What's to become of you?"

Perhaps the most famous and widely used test for assessing personality disorders is the **Minnesota Multiphasic Personality Inventory (MMPI)**. The MMPI was developed in the 1930s by two psychiatrists who wanted a way to screen people with psychological disorders. The measure, developed by comparing the responses of people with various mental disorders to those of a control group who were not in treatment, consisted of ten categories, or *scales,* that identified such problems as depression, paranoia, schizophrenia, and introversion. Four additional *validity scales* indicated whether a test taker was likely to be lying, defensive, or evasive while answering the items. For example, if you tried to present a favorable but unrealistic image of yourself on nearly every item, your score on the lie scale would be high. Since the original MMPI was devised, additional scales have been added. In 1989, a major revision of the MMPI was released, the MMPI-2, with norms based on a sample that was more representative in terms of ethnicity, region, age, and gender (Butcher et al., 1989; Lucio et al., 1999).

Despite its popularity, the MMPI has some problems. Some critics have observed that the test's standards of "normalcy" still do not take into account some cultural differences. For example, Mexican, Puerto Rican, and Argentine respondents score differently from non-Hispanic Americans, on average, on the Masculinity–Femininity Scale (Cabiya et al., 2000). Latinos tend to be more traditional in their sex-role attitudes than Americans and Canadians, but this fact reflects cultural values, not emotional problems. In addition, norms for the MMPI-2 were based on samples in which minorities, the elderly, the poor, and the poorly educated were still underrepresented (Edwards & Edwards, 1991; Helmes & Reddon, 1993). Also, while the MMPI and other objective tests have good validity in diagnosing many mental disorders, they have a high rate of false positives—that is, they falsely label a person's responses as evidence of pathology (Guthrie & Mobley, 1994).

One review concluded that the MMPI is adequate if the test is used *only* to identify people with emotional problems (Parker, Hanson, & Hunsley, 1988). Yet the MMPI is often inappropriately used in business, industry, legal settings, and schools by persons who are not well trained in testing (or psychology). Overall, however, objective tests like the MMPI, particularly when used in combination, are far more reliable and valid than clinical interviews and projective tests (Meyer et al., 2001).

We turn now to a closer examination of some of the disorders described in the DSM. Of course we cannot cover all of them in one chapter, so we have singled out several that illustrate the range of psychological problems that afflict humanity. We begin with the most common and intensively studied: anxiety disorders, depression, antisocial personality disorder, and substance abuse. Then we will consider "multiple personality disorder," the fascinating story of how an extremely rare phenomenon became a large-scale epidemic. Finally, we turn to the mystery of schizophrenia, a debilitating mental illness that has severe consequences for those who suffer from it, for their families, and for society.

objective tests (inventories)
Standardized objective questionnaires requiring written responses; they typically include scales on which people are asked to rate themselves.

Minnesota Multiphasic Personality Inventory (MMPI) A widely used objective personality test.

WHAT'S AHEAD ▶

- **What is the difference between ordinary anxiety and an anxiety disorder?**
- **Why is the most disabling of all phobias known as the "fear of fear"?**
- **When is checking the stove before leaving home a sign of caution, and when does it signal a disorder?**

Anxiety Disorders

Anyone who is waiting for important news, or living in a situation that is unpredictable and uncontrollable, quite sensibly feels *anxiety*, a general state of apprehension or psychological tension. And anyone who is in a dangerous and unfamiliar situation, such as making a first parachute jump or being accosted by a hungry hippopotamus on the attack, quite sensibly feels flat-out fear. In the short run, these emotions are adaptive because they energize us to cope with danger. They ensure that we don't make that first jump without knowing how to operate the parachute, and that we get away from that hippo as fast as we can.

But in some individuals, fear and anxiety become detached from any actual danger, or these feelings continue even when danger and uncertainty are past. Such individuals may be suffering from *chronic anxiety,* marked by long-lasting feelings of apprehension and doom; *panic attacks,* short-lived but intense feelings of spontaneous anxiety; *phobias,* excessive fears of specific things or situations; or *obsessive–compulsive disorder,* in which repeated thoughts and rituals are used to ward off anxious feelings.

Anxiety and Panic

generalized anxiety disorder A continuous state of anxiety marked by feelings of worry and dread, apprehension, difficulties in concentration, and signs of motor tension.

The chief characteristic of **generalized anxiety disorder** is continuous, uncontrollable anxiety or worry—a feeling of foreboding and dread—that occurs on a majority of days during a six-month period and that is not brought on by physical causes such as disease, drugs, or drinking too much coffee. Symptoms include restlessness or feeling keyed up, difficulty concentrating, irritability, muscle tension and jitteriness, sleep disturbance, and unwanted, intrusive worries.

Some people suffer from generalized anxiety disorder without having lived through any specific anxiety-producing event. They may have a physiological tendency to experience anxiety symptoms—sweaty palms, a racing heart, shortness of breath—when they are in challenging or uncontrollable situations. As we saw in Chapter 13, temperamentally shy children and people with the personality trait of neuroticism (negative emotionality) are already predisposed to react with anxiety in novel situations. Other chronically anxious people may have a history, starting in childhood, of being unable to control or predict their environments (Barlow, 2000). Whatever the origins of their anxiety, people with generalized anxiety disorder have mental habits that foster their worries and keep their anxiety bubbling along; they perceive everything as an opportunity for disaster (McNally, 1996; Riskind et al., 2000).

Sometimes anxiety occurs in the aftermath of traumatic experiences: The September 11, 2001, attack on the World Trade Center and Pentagon left not only physical devastation but emotional devastation as well. People who survive sudden, unexpected bereavement (as did the families of the thousands of people who died that terrible day), or who live through uncontrollable and unpredictable dangers—such as war, rape, torture, or natural disasters—may suffer from **posttraumatic stress disorder (PTSD)**. Stress symptoms are entirely normal in the immediate aftermath of any crisis or trauma. PTSD is diagnosed only if the symptoms persist for 6 months or longer.

Typical symptoms of PTSD include reliving the trauma in recurrent, intrusive thoughts or dreams; "psychic numbing," a sense of detachment from others and an inability to feel happy or loving; and increased physiological arousal, reflected in insomnia, irritability, and impaired concentration. These symptoms can begin either immediately after a trauma or after a delay of many weeks or months; episodes may recur for months, years, or even decades (Breslau et al., 1998; Kessler et al., 1995). For example, after September 11, many people in Oklahoma City, where 168 people had died in a terrorist attack in 1995, found their anxieties and grief were rekindled. "Every time we see something devastating, it brings back the sleepless nights, the nightmares, the whole dang ball of wax," said one man whose daughter died in the bombing.

Most people who live through a traumatic experience, such as combat, rape, or a natural disaster, eventually recover. But why do some continue to have PTSD symptoms for many years? Animal research shows that exposure to severe and chronic stress can damage the hippocampus, producing death or atrophy of neurons. And, in fact, in many of the people who continue to suffer from PTSD, the hippocampus is significantly smaller than in those who recover (Sapolsky, 2001; Shin et al., 1997). So some researchers have concluded that severe trauma causes neuron damage or loss in the hippocampus, producing PTSD symptoms—impaired memory, recurrent fears, depression, and so forth.

But why wouldn't the trauma have the same effects on all victims? An intriguing possibility is that the lower hippocampal volume in PTSD sufferers is not a result of the disorder but a contributing cause—that it is a pre-existing condition that increases a person's vulnerability to PTSD. A team of researchers used MRIs to measure hippocampal volume in identical twins, only one of whom in each pair had been in combat in Vietnam. In one group of 17 twin pairs, the veterans had developed PTSD, and in another group of 23 twin pairs, the veterans had not. The severity of PTSD symptoms in the veterans was negatively correlated with their hippocampal volumes: The more symptoms, the smaller the hippocampus. Yet the identical twins *who had the same smaller hippocampi but who did not serve in combat* did not develop PTSD. This evidence suggests that people who suffer from a

posttraumatic stress disorder (PTSD) An anxiety disorder in which a person who has experienced a traumatic or life-threatening event has symptoms such as psychic numbing, reliving of the trauma, and increased physiological arousal.

This grief-stricken soldier has just learned that the body bag on the flight with him contains the remains of a close friend who was killed in action. Understandably, soldiers like him suffer posttraumatic stress symptoms. But why do most eventually recover, whereas others have PTSD for many years?

panic disorder An anxiety disorder in which a person experiences recurring panic attacks, periods of intense fear, and feelings of impending doom or death, accompanied by physiological symptoms such as rapid heart rate and dizziness.

trauma may have greater trouble recovering from it if they have smaller hippocampi to begin with (Gilbertson et al., in press).

Another kind of anxiety disorder is **panic disorder,** in which a person has recurring attacks of intense fear or panic, often with feelings of impending doom or death (McNally, 1998). These panic attacks may last from a few minutes to (more rarely) several hours. Symptoms include trembling and shaking, dizziness, chest pain or discomfort, heart palpitations, feelings of unreality, hot and cold flashes, sweating, and, as a result of all these physical reactions, a fear of dying, going crazy, or losing control. Many sufferers fear they are having a heart attack.

Although panic attacks seem to occur out of nowhere, they in fact usually occur in the aftermath of stress, prolonged emotion, specific worries, or frightening experiences (Beck, 1988; McNally, 1998). For example, a friend of ours was on a plane that was a target of a bomb threat while airborne at 33,000 feet. He coped beautifully at the time, but two weeks later, seemingly out of nowhere, he had a panic attack.

Such delayed attacks after life-threatening scares are common. The essential difference between people who develop panic disorder and those who do not lies in how they interpret their bodily reactions (Barlow, 2000; McNally, 1998). Healthy people who have occasional panic attacks see them correctly as a result of a passing crisis or period of stress, comparable to another person's migraines. But people who develop panic disorder regard the attack as a sign of illness or impending death, and they begin to live their lives in restrictive ways, trying to avoid future attacks. It is this self-imposed restriction that makes this disorder so difficult for its sufferers (and their families).

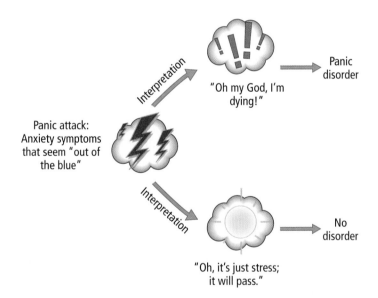

People who have panic disorder are found throughout the world, although culture influences the particular symptoms they experience (Barlow, Chorpita, & Turovsky, 1996). Feelings of choking or being smothered, numbness, and fear of dying are most common in Latin America and southern Europe; fear of public places is most common in northern Europe and America; and a fear of going crazy is more common in the Americas than in Europe. In Greenland, some fishermen suffer from "kayak-angst": a sudden attack of dizziness and fear that occurs while they are fishing in small, one-person kayaks (Amering & Katschnig, 1990).

Get Involved

What Scares You?

Everyone fears something. Stop for a moment to think about what you fear most. Is it heights? Snakes? Speaking in public? Ask yourself these questions: (1) How long have you feared this thing or situation? (2) How would you respond if you could not avoid this thing or situation? (3) How much would you be willing to rearrange your life to avoid this feared thing or situation? After considering these questions, would you regard your fear as a full-blown phobia or merely a normal source of apprehension?

Fears and Phobias

Are you afraid of bugs, snakes, or dogs? Are you vaguely uncomfortable with them or so afraid that you can't stand to be around one? A **phobia** is an exaggerated fear of a specific situation, activity, or thing. Some common phobias—such as fear of snakes, insects, heights (acrophobia), thunder (brontophobia), or enclosed spaces (claustrophobia)—may have evolved in human beings because these fears were adaptive for the species. Other, more idiosyncratic phobias, such as a fear of cats or the color purple (porphyrophobia), may be acquired through classical conditioning, as we saw in Chapter 7. Still other phobias, such as fear of dirt and germs (mysophobia) or of the number 13 (triskaidekaphobia), may reflect personality differences or cultural traditions. Whatever its source, a phobia is truly frightening and often incapacitating for its sufferer. It is not just a tendency to say "ugh" at tarantulas or skip the snake display at the zoo.

If you hate to get up in public to make a speech, you are not alone! Fear of public speaking is one of the most common social phobias, probably because so many people have the "speaker's nightmare" that the audience will be bored to death or go to sleep.

People who have a *social phobia* become extremely anxious in situations in which they will be observed by others—eating in a restaurant, speaking in front of a group or crowd, having to perform for others. They worry that they will do or say something that will be excruciatingly humiliating or embarrassing. Again, these phobias are more severe forms of the occasional shyness and social anxiety that everyone experiences. For people with a social phobia, the mere thought of going out on a date is scary enough to cause sweating, trembling, nausea, and an overwhelming feeling of inadequacy. So they don't go, increasing their fear and isolation.

By far the most disabling fear disorder is **agoraphobia.** In ancient Greece, the *agora* was the social, political, business, and religious center of town, the public meeting place away from home. The fundamental fear in agoraphobia is of being trapped in a crowded public place, where escape might be difficult or where help might be unavailable if the person has a panic attack. Individuals with agoraphobia report many specific fears—of being in a crowded movie theater, driving in traffic or tunnels, or going to parties—but the underlying fear is of being away from a safe place, usually home, or a familiar person.

Agoraphobia usually begins with a panic attack that seems to have no reason (McNally, 1998). The attack is so unexpected and scary that the agoraphobic-to-be begins to avoid situations that he or she thinks may provoke another one. For example, a woman we know had a panic attack while driving on a freeway. This was a perfectly normal posttraumatic response to the suicide of her husband a few weeks earlier. But thereafter she avoided freeways—as if the freeway, and not the suicide, had caused the attack. Because so many of the actions associated with agoraphobia arise as a mistaken effort to avoid a panic attack, psychologists regard agoraphobia as a "fear of fear" rather than a fear of places.

phobia An exaggerated, unrealistic fear of a specific situation, activity, or object.

agoraphobia A set of phobias, often set off by a panic attack, involving the basic fear of being away from a safe place or person.

Obsessions and Compulsions

Extreme hoarding is one form of obsessive–compulsive disorder. In this hoarder's apartment, nearly every inch of floor and furniture is covered with stuff—junk mail, wrapping paper, broken electric toothbrushes, old shopping lists, empty Kleenex boxes, and clothes—because the woman becomes extremely anxious at even the thought of throwing anything out. She herself is perfectly clean, and one place is uncluttered: the half of the bed she sleeps on.

obsessive–compulsive disorder (OCD) An anxiety disorder in which a person feels trapped in repetitive, persistent thoughts *(obsessions)* and repetitive, ritualized behaviors *(compulsions)* designed to reduce anxiety.

Obsessive–compulsive disorder (OCD) is characterized by recurrent, persistent, unwished-for thoughts or images (*obsessions*) or by repetitive, ritualized, stereotyped behaviors that the person feels must be carried out to avoid disaster (*compulsions*). Of course, many people have trivial compulsions and practice superstitious rituals; baseball players are famous for them. Obsessions and compulsions become a disorder when they become uncontrollable and interfere with a person's life.

Obsessive thoughts are often experienced as frightening or repugnant. For example, the person may have repetitive thoughts of killing a child, of becoming contaminated by a handshake, or of having unknowingly hurt someone in a traffic accident. Obsessive thoughts take many forms, but they are alike in reflecting maladaptive ways of reasoning and processing information.

People who suffer from compulsions likewise feel they have no control over them. The most common compulsions are hand washing, counting, touching, and checking. A woman *must* check the furnace, lights, locks, oven, and fireplace three times before she can sleep; or a man *must* wash his hands and face precisely eight times before he leaves the house. Most sufferers of OCD do not enjoy such rituals and realize that the behavior is senseless. But if they try to forgo the ritual, they feel mounting anxiety that is relieved only by giving in to it. For one young man with OCD, stairs became a treadmill he could not get off: "At first I'd walk up and down the stairs only three or four times," he recalled. "Later I had to run up and down 63 times in 45 minutes. If I failed, I had to start all over again from the beginning" (quoted in King, 1989).

Some cases of obsessive–compulsive disorder may involve a brain abnormality, because several parts of the brain are hyperactive in people with OCD (Schwartz et al., 1996). Normally, once danger is past or a person realizes that there is no cause for fear, the brain's alarm signal turns off. In people with OCD, however, false alarms keep clanging and the emotional networks keeping sending out mistaken "fear!" messages. The sufferer feels in a constant state of danger and tries repeatedly to reduce the resulting anxiety.

QUICK QUIZ

We hope you don't feel anxious about matching each term on the left with its description on the right.

1. social phobia — a. need to perform a ritual
2. generalized anxiety disorder — b. fear of fear; of being trapped with no way of escape
3. posttraumatic stress disorder — c. continuing sense of doom and worry
4. agoraphobia — d. repeated, unwanted thoughts
5. compulsion — e. fear of meeting new people
6. obsession — f. anxiety following a severe shock

Answers:

1.e 2.c 3.f 4.b 5.a 6.d

WHAT'S AHEAD▶

- How can you tell whether you have major depression or just the blues?
- What are the "poles" in bipolar disorder?
- How do some people think themselves into depression?

Mood Disorders

In the DSM, *mood disorders* include disturbances in mood ranging from extreme depression to extreme mania. Of course, most people feel sad from time to time, and also joyful. And most people, at some time in their lives, will know the wild grief that accompanies tragedy and bereavement. These feelings, however, are a far cry from the clinical disorders described by the DSM.

Depression

Anxiety, painful though it is, is at least a sign that a person is engaged in the future: It reflects the belief that *something bad will happen.* But depressed people feel burned out about the future: They are sure that *nothing good will ever happen.* Some people go through life with constant but low-grade unhappiness; they can do what they need to but nearly always report their mood as sad or "down in the dumps." Others, however, suffer from **major depression,** a serious mood disorder that involves emotional, behavioral, cognitive, and physical changes severe enough to disrupt a person's ordinary functioning. The writer William Styron, who fought and recovered from major depression, used the beginning of Dante's classic poem *The Divine Comedy* to convey his suffering:

> In the middle of the journey of our life
> I found myself in a dark wood.
> For I had lost the right path.

"For those who have dwelt in depression's dark wood," wrote Styron in *Darkness Visible,* "and known its inexplicable agony, the return from the abyss is not unlike the ascent of the poet, trudging upward and upward out of hell's black depths and at last emerging into what he saw as 'the shining world.'"

People with major depression feel despairing and hopeless. They may think often of death or suicide. They feel unable to get up and do things; it takes an enormous effort even to get dressed. Their thinking patterns feed their bleak moods. They exaggerate minor failings, ignore or discount positive events, and interpret any little thing that goes wrong as evidence that nothing will ever go right. Emotionally healthy people who are sad or grieving do not see themselves as completely worthless and unlovable.

Depression is accompanied by physical changes as well. The depressed person may overeat or stop eating, have difficulty falling asleep or sleeping through the night, have trouble concentrating, and feel tired all the time. Some sufferers have other physical reactions, such as inexplicable pain or headaches.

Major depression occurs two or three times as often among women as among men, all over the world (Culbertson, 1997). However, because women are more likely to talk about their feelings than men and more likely to seek help, depression in males may be underdiagnosed. Men who are depressed often try to mask the feeling by withdrawing, abusing drugs, or behaving violently (Canetto, 1992; Kessler et al., 1994). As one depression researcher put it, "Women think and men drink" (Nolen-Hoeksema, 1999).

major depression A mood disorder involving disturbances in emotion (excessive sadness), behavior (loss of interest in one's usual activities), cognition (thoughts of hopelessness), and body function (fatigue and loss of appetite).

Even people who are rich, successful, and adored by millions can suffer from major depression. The suicide of Nirvana's lead singer, Kurt Cobain, shocked and saddened his many fans.

Like many creative people, the great humorist Mark Twain suffered from bipolar disorder.

Bipolar Disorder

At the opposite pole from depression is *mania,* an abnormally high state of exhilaration. You might think it's impossible to feel too good, but mania is not the normal joy of being in love or winning the Pulitzer Prize. Instead of feeling fatigued and listless, the manic person is full of energy. Instead of feeling hopeless and powerless, the person feels full of ambitions, plans, and power. The depressed person speaks slowly and monotonously. The manic person speaks rapidly, dramatically, often with many jokes and puns. The depressed person has low self-esteem. The manic person has inflated self-esteem.

When people experience at least one episode of mania alternating with episodes of depression, they are said to have **bipolar disorder** (formerly called *manic-depressive disorder*). This is a much rarer problem than depression and distinctly different. Although more women than men suffer from depression, bipolar disorder occurs equally in both sexes. The great humorist Mark Twain had bipolar disorder, which he described as "periodical and sudden changes of mood . . . from deep melancholy to half-insane tempests and cyclones." Other writers, artists, musicians, and scientists have suffered from this disorder too (Jamison, 1992). During the "highs" many of these artists create their best work, but the price of the "lows" is disastrous relationships, bankruptcy, and sometimes suicide (Barondes, 1998).

Social and psychological explanations of bipolar disorder have not been supported. Therefore, most researchers believe that it results primarily from genetic or other biological abnormalities, although the precise genes and mechanisms are still unknown. In contrast, depression may have several different origins, as we are about to see.

Theories of Depression

The leading theories of depression emphasize four causes: biological factors, life experiences, problems with close attachments, and cognitive habits.

1 *Biological factors.* Studies of adopted children and twins support the notion that in many cases major depression is a moderately heritable disorder, particularly in women (Bierut et al., 1999; Kendler et al., 1993). However, the precise gene or genes involved have yet to be identified. One investigator compares his search to tracking down an enemy spy who is carrying a radio transmitter. Searchers know roughly where he is—the city and neighborhood—but not his street and number (Barondes, 1998).

How might genes exert their influence? For years, a leading hypothesis was that they create biochemical imbalances in neurotransmitters, specifically serotonin and norepinephrine. It was thought that depression is caused by a deficient production of one or both of these neurotransmitters. The main support for this idea was the fact that antidepressant drugs work by raising the levels of these neurotransmitters, but this explanation has proved to be too simple. Although antidepressants can be effective for many people (see Chapter 17), they take weeks to exert their effects, and by that time, surprisingly, the neurotransmitters have returned to their previous low levels (Davison & Neale, 2001). So when the drugs are effective, it must be because they are doing something else besides affecting neurotransmitter levels.

Brain scans suggest that many chronically depressed people have significant shrinkage of the hippocampus and amygdala, because of either cell loss or atrophy

bipolar disorder A mood disorder in which episodes of both depression and mania (excessive euphoria) occur.

of dendrites (Sapolsky, 2000; Sheline, 2000; Sheline et al., 1999). This damage may be due to excessive levels of the stress hormone cortisol. In depressed patients, the system that regulates reactions to stress is in overdrive; it doesn't shut down when it should, and it keeps overproducing cortisol (Plotsky, Owens, & Nemeroff, 1998).

2 *Life experiences.* Another line of investigation emphasizes the life experiences and social circumstances that might lead to stress and depression. For example, women may be more likely than men to suffer from depression in part because they have less satisfying work and family lives and lower status than men and face higher rates of discrimination, poverty, and sexual abuse (Klonoff, Landrine, & Campbell, 2000; Weiss, Longhurst, & Mazure, 1999). Mothers are especially vulnerable to depression: The more children a woman has, the more likely she is to become depressed, especially if she is unemployed (McGrath et al., 1990). Men are more likely than women to be both married and working full time, a combination of activities that is strongly associated with mental health and low rates of depression (Brown, 1993; Culbertson, 1997). Violence is also a risk factor for depression: Inner-city adolescents of both sexes who are exposed to high rates of violence report higher levels of depression and more attempts to commit suicide than those who are not subjected to constant violence in their lives or communities (Mazza & Reynolds, 1999).

Life experiences alone, however, fail to explain why *most* mothers, poor people, and even victims of violence do not become depressed. Nor do they explain why some people become depressed even though their lives are comfortable and secure.

3 *Problems with close attachments.* Depression can result from separations and losses, both past and present, and a history of insecure attachments (Weissman, Markowitz, & Klerman, 2000). Depressive episodes are frequently set off by disruption of a close relationship or the loss of friends and social networks. However, it also works the other way: Some relationships end *because* one partner is clinically depressed. Depressed people often seem demanding and "depressing" to family and friends, who in turn feel angry or sad when they cannot help the sufferer cheer up. Eventually, the depressed person's partner and friends may leave (Alloy et al., 1998; Coyne, 1990).

4 *Cognitive habits.* Depression involves specific, negative attributions, or ways of thinking about one's situation (Beck, 1991). Typically, depressed people believe that their situation is *permanent* ("Nothing good will ever happen to me") and *uncontrollable* ("I'm depressed because I'm ugly and horrible and I can't do anything about it"). Expecting nothing to get better, they do nothing to improve their lives and therefore remain unhappy.

Where do these beliefs come from? In the 1970s, the theory of *learned helplessness* held that people become depressed when their efforts to avoid pain or to control the environment consistently fail (Seligman, 1975). However, a fatal flaw with this theory was that not all depressed people have actually failed in their lives, and even living in painful or difficult situations does not make everyone depressed. The real problem for depressed people is not that they are *helpless* but

Source: Jacob Lawrence, Depression, 1950. Tempera on paper, 22 x 30⅝ in. (55.9 x 77.5 cm). Gift of David M. Solinger. Collection of Whitney Museum of American Art, New York. Photo by Geoffrey Clements.

Any doubt what emotion this painting conveys? The artist Jacob Lawrence has captured the body language of depression in the posture, downcast eyes, somber mood, and drooping heads and shoulders of his figures.

vulnerability–stress models Approaches that emphasize how individual vulnerabilities interact with external stresses or circumstances to produce mental disorders.

that they feel *hopeless* and pessimistic, believing that nothing good will ever happen to them and that they are powerless to change the future (Abramson, Metalsky, & Alloy, 1989; Seligman, 1991). For example, in a study of college students who were unhappy because they got worse grades than they expected, depression persisted only in those who had pessimistic attributions ("I'm stupid and always will be") *and* low self-esteem, resulting in hopelessness (Metalsky et al., 1993).

Another cognitive bad habit strongly associated with depression is *rumination*— brooding about everything that is wrong in your life, sitting alone thinking about how unmotivated you feel, and worrying that no one loves you. People who ruminate endlessly this way tend to have longer and more intense periods of depression than do those who are able to distract themselves, look outward, and seek solutions. Beginning in adolescence, women are more likely than men to develop a ruminating, introspective style, rehearsing the reasons for their unhappiness. This tendency contributes both to longer-lasting depressions in women and to the sex difference in reported rates (Nolen-Hoeksema, 2001; Nolen-Hoeksema & Girgus, 1994). People with ruminating cognitive styles that foster hopelessness are at greater risk of developing full-blown major depression than are people who think positively (Alloy et al., 1998; Chorpita & Barlow, 1998).

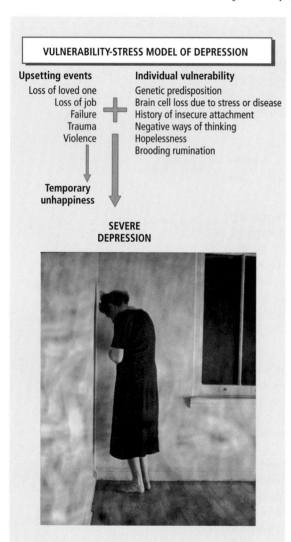

VULNERABILITY-STRESS MODEL OF DEPRESSION

Upsetting events	Individual vulnerability
Loss of loved one	Genetic predisposition
Loss of job	Brain cell loss due to stress or disease
Failure	History of insecure attachment
Trauma	Negative ways of thinking
Violence	Hopelessness
	Brooding rumination

Temporary unhappiness

SEVERE DEPRESSION

Today, most researchers realize that all of these potential causes of depression can also be effects. For example, high levels of cortisol may damage neurons and therefore lead to depression, but chronic episodes of depression are stressful and may boost levels of cortisol. Rumination may cause depression, but when you are depressed, gloomy thoughts come more easily. Having a rotten job may make you depressed, but when you're depressed, you may lack the energy to improve your working conditions.

Moreover, most researchers now emphasize the interactions among these factors. The **vulnerability–stress model** describes how individual vulnerabilities (in genetic predispositions or other biological factors, personality traits, or habits of thinking) combine with stressful events (such as sexual victimization, violence, or loss of a close relationship) to produce any given case of depression (Hankin & Abramson, 2001). Such an interactionist approach seems to best explain the sex difference in depression. In a longitudinal study of more than 1,000 adults, ages 25 to 75, women's greater likelihood of becoming depressed was due to a combination of ruminating and brooding about events; living under chronic work-and-family strain (such as having the burden of responsibility for housework and child care, along with their paid jobs); *and* having a low sense of mastery or control over their lives (Nolen-Hoeksema, Larson, & Grayson, 1999).

Interaction models are a big improvement over either–or theories of depression ("It's biological"; "It's psychological"). They explain why not everyone is equally vulnerable to depression, given a certain experience, gene, or biological disposition. By understanding the causes of depression as an interaction among an individual's biology, ways of thinking, and experiences, we can see why the same precipitating event, such as a minor setback or even the loss of a loved one, might produce normal sadness in one person and extreme depression in another.

QUICK QUIZ

Don't let another quiz make you vulnerable to depression!

1. Biological researchers find that depressed people have unusually high levels of the stress hormone _____ and cell damage in the _____.

2. Depressed people tend to believe that the reasons for their unhappiness are (a) controllable, (b) temporary, (c) internal, (d) caused by the situation.

3. Vulnerability–stress theories attribute depression to an interaction between _____ and _____.

 4. A news headline announces that a single gene has been identified as the cause of depression, but the article adds that other studies have failed to replicate this research. What might explain these contradictory findings?

Answers:

1. cortisol; hippocampus and amygdala 2. c 3. individual vulnerabilities; stressful events 4. The conflicting evidence may mean that if a genetic predisposition for depression exists, it is not due to a single gene but involves several genes working in the context of environmental events. It may mean that the right gene has not yet been identified. Or it may mean that genes are not a factor in any or all forms of depression.

WHAT'S AHEAD ▷

● **When does being self-centered become a disorder?**

● **What do a charming but heartless tycoon and a remorseless killer have in common?**

● **Why are some people seemingly incapable of feeling guilt and shame?**

Personality Disorders

Personality disorders involve unchanging, maladaptive traits that cause great distress or an inability to get along with others. The DSM-IV describes such a disorder as "an enduring pattern of inner experience and behavior that deviates markedly from the expectations of the individual's culture [and] is pervasive and inflexible." Personality disorders are unaffected by medical conditions, stress, or situations that temporarily induce a person to behave in ways that are out of character.

Problem Personalities

Personality disorders come in many varieties. For example, **narcissistic personality disorder** involves an exaggerated sense of self-importance and self-absorption. The word *narcissism* gets its name from the Greek myth of Narcissus, a beautiful young man who fell in love with his own image. Narcissistic individuals are preoccupied with fantasies of their own importance, power, and brilliance. They demand constant attention and admiration and feel entitled to special favors, without, however, being willing to reciprocate.

People with **borderline personality disorder** have a pervasive history of intense but unstable relationships in which they alternate between idealizing the partner and then devaluing the partner. They frantically try to avoid real or imagined abandonment by others, even if the "abandonment" is only a friend's brief vacation. They have profoundly unrealistic self-images. They are self-destructive and impulsive, often spending too much, abusing drugs, and threatening to commit suicide. And they are emotionally volatile, careening from anger to euphoria to anxiety.

Narcissus fell in love with his own image, and now he has a personality disorder named after him—just what a narcissist would expect!

personality disorders Rigid, maladaptive personality patterns that cause personal distress or an inability to get along with others.

narcissistic personality disorder A disorder characterized by an exaggerated sense of self-importance and self-absorption.

borderline personality disorder A disorder characterized by intense but unstable relationships, a fear of abandonment by others, an unrealistic self-image, and emotional volatility.

antisocial personality disorder (APD) A disorder characterized by antisocial behavior such as lying, stealing, manipulating others, and sometimes violence; and a lack of guilt, shame, and empathy. (Sometimes called *psychopathy* or *sociopathy*.)

Notice that although these descriptions evoke flashes of recognition ("I know that type!"), it is hard to know where value judgments end and a clear disorder begins (Maddux & Mundell, 1997). Cultures draw the line differently. For example, American society often encourages people to pursue dreams of unlimited success and ideal love, but such dreams might be considered signs of serious disturbance in a more group-oriented society. How would you distinguish between having a "narcissistic personality disorder" and being a normal member of a group or culture that encourages putting your own needs ahead of those of your family and friends and puts a premium on youth and beauty?

Antisocial Personality Disorder

Throughout history, societies have recognized and feared the few members in their midst who lack all human connection to anyone else—who can cheat, con, and kill without flinching. In the 1830s these individuals were said to be afflicted with "moral insanity," and in the twentieth century they came to be called "psychopaths" or "sociopaths." The DSM, in an effort to avoid such emotionally charged labels, now refers to **antisocial personality disorder (APD)**. APD occurs in only about 3 percent of all males and less than 1 percent of all females. Yet people with APD may account for more than half of all serious crimes committed in the United States (Hare, 1993).

Symptoms of APD. According to the DSM, people diagnosed with APD must meet at least three of seven criteria: (1) They repeatedly break the law; (2) they are deceitful, using aliases and lies to con others; (3) they are impulsive and unable to plan ahead; (4) they repeatedly get into physical fights or assaults; (5) they show reckless disregard for their own safety or that of others; (6) they are irresponsible, failing to meet obligations to others; and (7) they lack remorse for actions that harm others. They must also have had a *history* of these behavioral problems since childhood. As one researcher found, in people with APD, remorselessness and rule-breaking start early and take different forms at different ages: "biting and hitting at age 4, shoplifting and truancy at age 10, selling drugs and stealing cars at age 16, robbery and rape at age 22, and fraud and child abuse at age 30" (Moffitt, 1993).

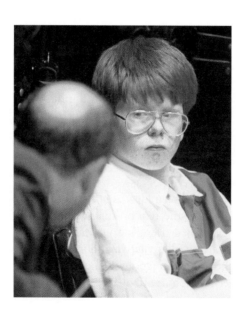 

Some people with APD are sadistic and violent from early in life. At age 13, Eric Smith (left) bludgeoned and strangled a 4-year-old boy to death. He was tried as an adult and sentenced to a prison term of nine years to life. But other people with APD use charm and elaborate scams to deceive and defraud. Babyfaced Christopher Rocancourt (right, wearing tie), shown with actor Mickey O'Rourke, conned celebrities and others into giving him money and doing him favors (some illegal) by adopting countless false identities, such as movie producer, cat burglar, diamond smuggler, or financier. After he was finally arrested on charges of passport counterfeiting, he persuaded authorities to free him on bond—and promptly jumped bail.

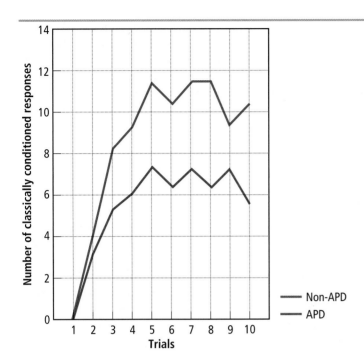

Figure 16.2
EMOTIONS AND ANTISOCIAL PERSONALITY DISORDER

In several experiments, people with antisocial personality disorder (APD) were slow to develop classically conditioned responses to anticipated danger, pain, or shock—responses that indicate normal anxiety (Hare, 1965). This deficit may be related to the ability of people with APD to behave in destructive ways without remorse or regard for the consequences (Hare, 1993).

However, not all violent people have APD; there are many motives that cause otherwise healthy people to commit crimes, even murder (see Chapter 8). Nor are all psychopaths violent. Some are sadistic, able to kill a pet, a child, or a random adult without a twinge of regret, but others direct their energies into con games or career advancement, abusing other people emotionally or economically rather than physically (Robins, Tipp, & Przybeck, 1991). The common quality of people with APD is that they completely lack conscience and empathy. If caught in a lie or a crime, they may seem sincerely sorry and promise to make amends, but it is all an act.

Causes of APD. Something certainly seems to be amiss in the normal emotional wiring of psychopaths—the wiring that allows all primates to feel connected to others of their kind. Researchers studying APD have proposed several possibilities for what might be awry.

1 *Abnormalities in the central nervous system.* Antisocial individuals do not respond physiologically to punishments the way other people do; this may be why they can behave fearlessly in situations that would scare others to death. Normally, when a person is anticipating danger, pain, or punishment, the electrical conductance of the skin changes, a classically conditioned response that indicates anxiety or fear. But people with APD are slow to develop such responses, which suggests that they are unable to feel the anxiety necessary for learning that their actions will have unpleasant consequences (see Figure 16.2). Their inability to feel emotional arousal—empathy, guilt, fear of punishment, and anxiety under stress—suggests some aberration in the central nervous system (Hare, 1965, 1996; Lykken, 1995; Raine et al., 2000). This abnormality distinguishes violent, antisocial teenagers who become career criminals from those who outgrow adolescent antisocial behavior. Boys who, at age 15, have low levels of physiological arousal are more likely to become criminal offenders by age 24. But antisocial adolescents who have normally high levels of arousal and whose responses can be classically conditioned do not usually get involved in a life of crime as adults (Raine & Liu, 1998).

2 *Genetically influenced problems with impulse control.* People who are antisocial, hyperactive, or impulsive may share a common inherited disorder involving an inability to control responses to frustration and provocation (Luengo et al., 1994; Raine, 1996). The biological children of parents with antisocial personality disorder, substance-abuse problems, or disorders involving an inability to control impulsive behavior are at greater than normal risk of developing these disorders themselves, even when these children are reared by others (Nigg & Goldsmith, 1994).

3 *Brain damage.* Another, more significant cause of antisocial personality disorder may be brain damage resulting from physical neglect, accidents, battering, or injury. Psychopaths arrested for vicious crimes are more likely than nonviolent criminals and noncriminals to have been severely battered as children (Lewis, 1992; Milner & McCanne, 1991; Raine et al., 2001).

One area of special interest to those studying APD is the prefrontal cortex, which, as we saw in Chapter 4, is responsible for planning and impulse control. One PET-scan study found that cold-blooded "predatory" murderers had less brain activity in this area than did men who murdered in the heat of passion or controls who had not murdered anybody (Raine et al., 1998). And in-depth analyses of two young adults whose prefrontal cortex was damaged in infancy—one was run over by a car when she was 15 months old, and the other had a brain tumor removed—showed that both grew up to be compulsive liars, thieves, and heartless rule-breakers. They could not hold jobs or plan for the future, could not distinguish right from wrong, and lacked empathy (Anderson et al., 1999).

Keep in mind, however, that not all psychopaths have injured brains, and that biological abnormalities alone are rarely enough to produce a psychopathic personality. As with depression and many other disorders, an individual's own vulnerability must be combined with outside experiences or stressors. For example, a study of more than 4,000 boys, followed from birth to age 18, found that many of those who became violent offenders had experienced two risk factors: (1) birth complications that caused damage to the prefrontal cortex, *and* (2) early maternal rejection. Their mothers had not wanted the pregnancy, and the babies were put in institutional care for at least four months during their first year. Although only 4.4 percent of the boys had both risk factors, these boys accounted for 18 percent of all violent crimes committed by the sample as a whole (Raine, Brennan, & Mednick, 1994).

Thus, according to the *vulnerability–stress model,* most individuals with APD develop the disorder when a biological vulnerability is combined with physical abuse, parental neglect, lack of love and contact comfort, environmental stresses, or living in a culture that rewards ruthlessness and hard-heartedness.

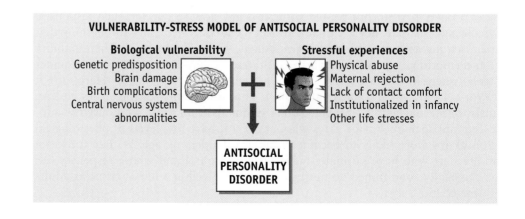

QUICK QUIZ

There is (as yet) no diagnosis of Test-Avoidance Personality Disorder, so take this quiz!

   A. Can you diagnose each of the following disorders?

   1. Ann can barely get out of bed in the morning. She feels that life is hopeless and despairs of ever feeling good about herself.

   2. Connie constantly feels a sense of impending doom; for days her heart has been beating rapidly, and she can't relax.

   3. Damon is totally absorbed in his own feelings and wishes.

   4. Edna has a long history of unstable relationships, emotional ups and downs, and an intense fear of being abandoned.

   B. What are three possible biological contributions to APD?

 C. Suppose you read about an unusually brutal assault committed by a gang member during a robbery. Should you assume that he has an antisocial personality disorder? Why or why not?

Answers:

A. 1. major depression 2. generalized anxiety disorder 3. narcissistic personality disorder 4. borderline personality disorder B. central nervous system abnormalities, genetically influenced problems with impulse control, and brain damage C. Behaving antisocially or even violently is not the same thing as having antisocial personality disorder. Many factors could have contributed to the gang member's violence, including conformity to norms of his fellow gang members, or his own fears or perceptions of danger during the robbery.

WHAT'S AHEAD

● **In what ways might genes contribute to alcoholism?**
● **Why is alcoholism more common in Ireland than in Italy?**
● **Why don't policies of abstinence from alcohol reduce problem drinking?**
● **If you take morphine to control chronic pain, does that mean you will become addicted to it?**

Drug Abuse and Addiction

Most people use drugs (legal, illegal, or prescription) in moderation and for short-lived effects, but some people depend too much on them and others abuse drugs even at the cost of their own health. The DSM-IV defines *substance abuse* as "a maladaptive pattern of substance use leading to clinically significant impairment or distress." Symptoms of such impairment include failure to hold a job, care for children, or complete schoolwork; use of the drug in hazardous situations (e.g., while driving a car or operating machinery); and frequent conflicts with others about use of the drug or as a result of using the drug.

In this section, focusing on the example of alcoholism, we will consider the two dominant approaches to understanding addiction and drug abuse—the biological model and the learning model—and then see how they might be reconciled.

Biology and Addiction

Are addicts people who just refuse to exert free will and moral responsibility, or are they suffering from a disease over which they have no control? Do they belong in prison or in treatment?

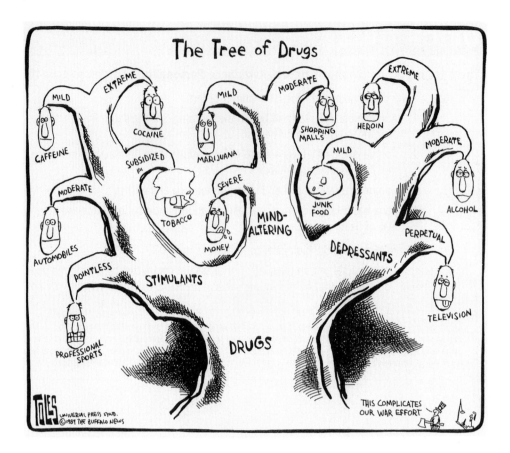

By poking fun at the things people do to make themselves feel better, this cartoon reminds us that many "addictions" are not biochemical.

The *biological model* holds that addiction, whether to alcohol or any other drug, is due primarily to a person's biochemistry, metabolism, and genetic predisposition. Most of the genetic evidence comes from twin and family studies of alcoholism. Evidence of an inherited vulnerability to alcohol is stronger for men than for women, but even this depends on the *kind* of alcoholism (Cloninger, 1990; Goodwin et al., 1994; McGue, 1999; Schuckit & Smith, 1996). For male alcoholics who begin drinking heavily in adulthood, genetic factors are only weakly involved, if at all. But there is a heritable component in the kind of alcoholism that begins in adolescence and is linked to impulsivity, antisocial behavior, and criminality (Bohman et al., 1987; McGue, 1999).

It is too simple to say that "genes cause alcoholism," but genes might contribute to traits or temperaments (such as impulsivity) that predispose a person to become alcoholic. Genes might also affect biochemical processes in the brain. For example, genetic factors may cause high levels of dopamine production in the limbic region, which is involved in pleasure, reward, and motivation, and these high dopamine levels may make some people more susceptible to alcohol or cause them to respond to it differently than others do (Reich et al., 1998; Schuckit & Smith, 1996). Genes may also affect how much a person needs to drink before feeling high. In an ongoing longitudinal study of 450 young men (half of whom had alcoholic fathers and half of whom did not), the men who at age 20 had to drink more than others to feel any reaction were at increased risk of becoming alcoholic within the decade. This was true regardless of their initial drinking habits or family history (Schuckit, 1998; Schuckit & Smith, 1996).

Virtually all geneticists agree that if heredity plays a role in alcoholism, more than one gene is involved and these genes interact in complex ways. Some people may inherit not only a general susceptibility to substance abuse but also a vulnerability to specific drugs—heroin, alcohol, cocaine, or nicotine (Tsuang et al., 2001). As with so many other disorders, however, tracking down such genes has been difficult. When one research team finds a likely candidate (e.g., Noble, 1998; Noble et al., 1991), that work is promptly contradicted by other teams (e.g., Baron, 1993; Edenberg et al., 1998).

The usual way of looking at the relationship between biological factors and addiction is to assume that the former somehow cause the latter. However, there is growing evidence that the relationship also works the other way: *Addictions can result from the abuse of drugs.* For example, heavy drinking alters brain function, reduces the level of painkilling endorphins, produces nerve damage, shrinks the cerebral cortex, and damages the liver. Heavy use of alcohol, cocaine, heroin, methamphetamine, or other drugs also reduces the number of receptors for dopamine, a neurotransmitter involved in the sensation of pleasure (Volkow et al., 2001). (See Figure 16.3.) These changes then create addiction: a craving for more of the drug. Thus drug abuse, which begins as a voluntary action, can turn into drug addiction, a compulsive behavior that the addict finds almost impossible to control.

Learning, Culture, and Addiction

The *learning model* examines the role of the person's environment, learning, and culture in encouraging or discouraging drug abuse and addiction. Four major findings underscore the importance of understanding social, psychological, and cultural factors:

1 *Addiction patterns vary according to cultural practices and the social environment.* Alcoholism is much more likely to occur in societies that forbid children to drink but condone drunkenness in adults (as in Ireland) than in societies that teach children how to drink responsibly and moderately but condemn adult drunkenness (as in Italy, Greece, and France). In cultures with low rates of alcoholism (except for those committed to a religious rule that forbids use of all psychoactive drugs), adults demonstrate correct drinking habits to their children, gradually introducing them to alcohol in safe family settings. Alcohol is not used as a rite of passage into adulthood, nor is it associated with masculinity and power (Peele & Brodsky, 1991; Vaillant, 1983). Abstainers are not sneered at, and

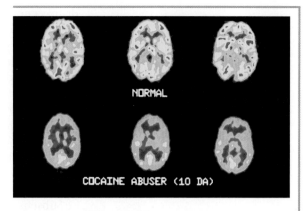

Figure 16.3

THE ADDICTED BRAIN

PET studies show that the brains of cocaine addicts have fewer receptors for dopamine, a neurotransmitter involved in pleasurable sensations. (The more yellow and red in the brain image, the more receptors.) The brains of people addicted to methamphetamine, alcohol, and even food show a similar dopamine deficiency (Volkow et al., 2001).

When children learn the rules of social drinking with their families, as at this Jewish family's seder, alcoholism rates are much lower than in cultures in which drinking occurs mainly in bars, or in privacy. Likewise, when marijuana is used as part of a religious tradition, as it is by members of the Rastafarian church in Jamaica, use of the "wisdom weed" does not lead to addiction or "harder" drugs.

drunkenness is not considered charming, comical, or manly; it is considered stupid or obnoxious.

Within a particular country, addiction rates can rise or fall rapidly in response to cultural changes. In colonial America, the average person actually drank two to three times the amount of liquor consumed today, yet alcoholism was not a serious problem. Drinking was a universally accepted social activity; families drank and ate together. Alcohol was believed to produce pleasant feelings and relaxation, and Puritan ministers endorsed its use (Critchlow, 1986). Then, between 1790 and 1830, when the American frontier was expanding, drinking came to symbolize masculine independence and toughness. The saloon became the place for drinking away from home. As people stopped drinking in moderation with their families, alcoholism rates shot up—as the learning model would predict.

Substance abuse and addiction problems also increase when people move from their own culture of origin into another that has different drinking rules (Westermeyer, 1995). For example, in most Latino cultures, such as those of Mexico and Puerto Rico, drinking and drunkenness are considered male activities. Thus Latina women tend to drink little, if at all, and they have few drinking problems—until they move into an Anglo environment, where their rates of alcoholism rise (Canino, 1994).

2 *Policies of total abstinence tend to increase rates of addiction rather than reduce them.* In the United States, the temperance movement of the early twentieth century held that drinking inevitably leads to drunkenness, and drunkenness to crime. The solution it won for the Prohibition years (1920 to 1933) was national abstinence. But this victory backfired: Again in accordance with the learning model, Prohibition reduced rates of per capita consumption, but it *increased* rates of alcoholism among those who did drink. Because people were denied the opportunity to learn to drink moderately, they drank excessively when given the chance (McCord, 1989).

3 *Not all addicts have withdrawal symptoms when they stop taking a drug.* When heavy users of a drug stop taking it, they often suffer such unpleasant symptoms as nausea, abdominal cramps, depression, and sleep problems, depending on the drug. But these symptoms are far from universal. During the Vietnam War, nearly 30 percent of American soldiers were taking heroin in doses far stronger than those available on the streets of U.S. cities. These men believed themselves to be addicted, and experts predicted a drug-withdrawal disaster among the returning veterans. It never materialized; over 90 percent of the men simply gave up the drug, without significant withdrawal pain, when they came home to new circumstances (Robins, Davis, & Goodwin, 1974; see Figure 16.4). Similarly, most people who are addicted to cigarettes, tranquilizers, or painkillers are able to stop taking these drugs, without outside help and without severe withdrawal symptoms (Prochaska, Norcross, & DiClemente, 1994).

4 *Addiction does not depend on properties of the drug alone but also on the reasons for taking it.* For example, addicts use drugs to escape from the real world, but people living with chronic pain use some of the same drugs, including morphine and other opiates, in order to function in the real world—and they do not become addicted (Portenoy, 1994). In a study of 100 hospital patients who had been given strong doses of narcotics for postoperative pain, 99 had no withdrawal symptoms upon leaving the hospital (Zinberg, 1974). And of 10,000 burn patients who received narcotics as part of their hospital care, not one became an addict (Perry & Heidrich, 1982).

In the case of alcohol, most people drink simply to be sociable, to conform to the group they are with, or to relax when they are stressed, and these people are unlikely to become addicted. The problem occurs when people drink in order to disguise or suppress their anxiety, depression, or fear, or when they drink alone in order to drown their sorrows and forget their worries (Cooper et al., 1995; Mohr et al.,

Figure 16.4
FAILURE OF THE ADDICTION PREDICTION

Three quarters of soldiers who had tested positive for drugs in Vietnam reported having been addicted during their term of duty (red bar). But far fewer reported post-Vietnam drug use (blue bar), and only a small number still showed narcotic dependency (green bar)—contrary to what the disease model would predict (Robins, Davis, & Goodwin, 1974).

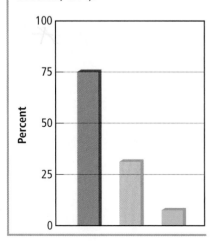

Get Involved ▣

Test Your Motives for Drinking

If you drink, why do you do so? Check all of the motives that apply to you:

____ to relax	____ to be sociable
____ to escape from worries	____ to cope with depression
____ to enhance a good meal	____ to get drunk and lose control
____ to conform to peers	____ to rebel against authority
____ to express anger or other uncomfortable feelings	____ to relieve boredom
	____ other (specify)

Do your reasons promote abuse or responsible use? How do you respond physically to alcohol? What have you learned about drinking from your family, your friends, and cultural messages? What do your answers tell you about your own vulnerability to addiction?

2001). College students who feel alienated and uninvolved with their studies are more likely than their happier peers to go binge drinking, with the conscious intention of getting drunk (Flacks & Thomas, 1998). In many cases, then, the decision to start abusing drugs depends more on the individual's motives than on the chemical properties of the drug itself.

Debating the Causes of Addiction

The biological and learning models both contribute to our understanding of drug use and addiction. Yet among many researchers and public-health professionals, these views are quite polarized (see Review 16.1). What we have here is a case of either–or thinking on a national scale, with passions running high because of the implications for the treatment of alcoholics and other addicts.

The argument is most heated in the debate over whether former alcoholics can learn to drink moderately without becoming intoxicated and dependent again on alcohol. Those who advocate the disease model say there is no such thing as a "former" alcoholic; once an addict has even a single drink, he or she will not be able to stop. In this view, problem drinkers who learn to cut back to social-drinking levels were never true alcoholics in the first place (Vaillant, 1995). Those who champion the learning model, on the other hand, argue that some problem drinkers can learn to drink moderately if they learn "safe drinking" skills, if they acquire other ways of coping with stress, and if they avoid friends and situations that pressure them to drink excessively (Marlatt, 1996; Marlatt et al., 1998; Vaillant, 1983).

How can we assess these two positions critically? Can we locate common ground between them? Because alcoholism and problem drinking occur for many reasons, neither model offers the only solution. Many alcoholics cannot learn to drink moderately, especially if they have been drinking heavily for many years—by which time, as we saw earlier, physiological changes in their brains and bodies may have turned them from drug abusers into drug addicts. On the other hand, for many people, total-abstinence groups like Alcoholics Anonymous do not work. According to its own surveys and those done independently, one-third to one-half of all people who join AA drop out. Many of these dropouts benefit from programs such as Rational Recovery, Moderation Management, and DrinkWise, which teach people how to drink moderately and keep their drinking under control (Marlatt, 1996; Peele & Brodsky, 1991; Rosenberg, 1993). (A few years ago a woman who founded

THINKING CRITICALLY

Avoid Emotional Reasoning

People disagree passionately about whether alcoholics can learn to drink moderately. How can we move beyond emotional reasoning on this contentious issue?

REVIEW 16.1	BIOLOGICAL AND LEARNING MODELS OF ADDICTION CONTRASTED

The biological and learning models of addiction differ in how they explain drug abuse and the solutions they propose:

The Biological Model	The Learning Model
Addiction is genetic, biological.	Addiction is a way of coping.
Once an addict, always an addict.	A person can grow beyond the need for alcohol or other drugs.
An addict must abstain from the drug forever.	Most problem drinkers can learn to drink in moderation.
A person is either addicted or not.	The degree of addiction will vary, depending on the situation.
The solution is medical treatment and membership in groups that reinforce one's permanent identity as a recovering addict.	The solution involves learning new coping skills and changing one's environment.
An addict needs the same treatment and group support forever.	Treatment lasts only until the person no longer abuses the drug.

Source: Adapted from Peele & Brodsky, 1991.

one of the moderation programs relapsed, became drunk, and got into a terrible car accident that made national news. Many people used this sad story to conclude that moderation programs "don't work," but of course one anecdote is not evidence of a program's failure—or of its success.)

So instead of asking, "Can addicts and problem drinkers learn to drink moderately?" we should ask, "What are the factors that make it more likely that someone can learn to control problem drinking?" Problem drinkers who are most likely to become moderate drinkers have a history of less severe dependence on the drug. They lead more stable lives, and have jobs and families. And they also believe that controlled drinking is possible, whereas alcoholics who believe that one drink will set them off—those who accept the alcoholics' creed, "first drink, then drunk"—are in fact more likely to behave that way (Rosenberg, 1993). Ironically, then, the course that alcoholism takes may reflect, in part, a person's belief in the disease model or the learning model.

As you can see, abuse and addiction reflect an interaction of physiology and psychology, person and culture. Problems with drugs are most likely to occur:

▶ When a person has a physiological vulnerability to a drug, or has been using a drug long enough to damage or cause changes in the brain;

▶ When a person believes that he or she has no control over the drug;

▶ When laws or customs encourage or teach people to take a drug in binges, and moderate use is neither encouraged nor taught;

▶ When a person comes to rely on a drug as a way of coping with problems, suppressing anger or fear, or relieving pain;

▶ When members of a person's peer group drink heavily or abuse other drugs.

QUICK QUIZ

If you are addicted to passing exams, answer these questions.

1. What is the most reasonable conclusion about the role of genes in alcoholism? (a) Without a key gene, a person cannot become alcoholic; (b) the presence of a key gene will almost always cause a person to become alcoholic; (c) genes may work in combination to increase a person's vulnerability to some kinds of alcoholism.

2. Which cultural practice is associated with *low* rates of alcoholism? (a) gradual introduction to drinking in family settings, (b) infrequent but binge drinking, (c) drinking as a rite of passage into adulthood, (d) policies of prohibition

3. In a national survey, 52 percent of American college students said they drink to get drunk and 42 percent said they usually binge when drinking. To reduce this problem, some schools and fraternities have instituted "zero tolerance" programs, permitting no alcohol at all. Others are trying "social norming," replacing norms that encourage binge drinking with norms that endorse moderate drinking. According to the research described in this section, which policies are more likely to work? Why or why not?

Answers:

1. c 2. a 3. Abstinence policies are likely to be much less effective than social-norming policies. Zero tolerance programs do not address the *reasons* that students binge, do not affect the student culture that fosters binge drinking, and do not teach students how to drink moderately.

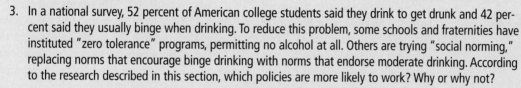

WHAT'S AHEAD

- Why are many clinicians and researchers skeptical about multiple personality disorder?
- Why did the number of "multiple personality" cases jump from a handful to many thousands in only a decade?

Dissociative Identity Disorder

Have you ever been out driving on a highway and suddenly realized you have lost all track of time and distance? This is a small but common everyday example of *dissociation,* a split in awareness: Part of you is driving the car and attending to other drivers, and part of you is daydreaming. Dissociation also occurs when we must deal with stress or shock and we feel temporarily cut off from ourselves—strange, dazed, or "unreal."

In dissociative disorders, however, consciousness, behavior, and identity are more severely split or altered, and the person cannot just "snap out of it." For example, one dissociative disorder is psychogenic amnesia, which we discussed in Chapter 10: In the aftermath of a shocking or harmful event, a person escapes the trauma by erasing it from memory (Cardeña et al., 1994). In this section we will examine one of the most controversial diagnoses ever to arise in psychiatry and psychology: **dissociative identity disorder,** popularly called *multiple personality disorder (MPD).* This disorder involves the apparent emergence, within one person, of two or more distinct identities, each with its own name, memories, preferences, and personality traits.

The MPD Controversy. Cases of multiple personality portrayed on TV, in popular books, and in films such as *The Three Faces of Eve* and *Sybil* have captivated

dissociative identity disorder A controversial disorder marked by the apparent appearance within one person of two or more distinct personalities, each with its own name and traits; commonly known as *multiple personality disorder (MPD).*

Popular books and films about multiple personality spawned countless imitators like *Lizzie*—and thousands of reported cases. According to critics, most of this increase was a result of unwitting therapist influence and sensational stories in the media (Acocella, 1999; Showalter, 1997).

the public for years. Among mental-health professionals, however, two competing views of MPD exist. On one side are those who think that MPD is common but often unrecognized or misdiagnosed. They believe the disorder originates in childhood as a means of coping with unspeakable, repeated traumas, such as torture (Gleaves, 1996; Kluft, 1993). In this view, the trauma produces a mental "splitting"; one personality emerges to handle everyday experiences, another to cope with the bad ones. MPD patients are frequently described as having lived for years with several personalities of which they were unaware, until hypnosis revealed them.

On the other side are those who believe that most cases of MPD are generated by clinicians themselves, knowingly or unknowingly, during their interactions with vulnerable clients who have other kinds of psychological problems (Ofshe & Watters, 1994). They point out that before 1980 only a handful of MPD cases had ever been diagnosed anywhere in the world; yet since 1980 *tens of thousands* of cases have been reported (see Table 16.3). Skeptics think such numbers are suspicious, a sign that the disorder is being wildly overdiagnosed by its proponents. How can this happen? Clinicians who deeply believe in the prevalence of MPD may actually be creating the disorder in their clients through suggestive (and unreliable) techniques like hypnosis, and also through the power of suggestion, sometimes bordering on coercion (Acocella 1999; McHugh, 1993; Merskey, 1992, 1995; Rieber, 1999; Spanos, 1996).

Table 16.3	**The Rise of Multiple Personality Disorder**
1789	An early case is reported of a young German woman with several "personalities" (including a French woman and a little boy).
1816	The first recorded case of "multiple personality" appears in the United States (Mary Reynolds).
1875	The condition is renamed "multiple personality" in France.
1886	Robert Louis Stevenson's *Dr. Jekyll and Mr. Hyde* popularizes the notion of two personalities in one body.
1800s–1960	**Cases begin to be reported worldwide.**
1957	*The Three Faces of Eve* is published and the film is released.
1960–1970	**8 cases are reported.**
1976	The movie *Sybil* is released.
1980	**The DSM includes the MPD diagnosis for the first time.**
1980	The book *Michelle Remembers* claims that "Satanic ritual abuse" is a leading cause of MPD.
1980–1991	Media coverage escalates in popular books and on talk shows that feature MPD "victims."
1985	Psychiatrist Richard Kluft claims to have treated 250 MPD patients.
By 1986	**6,000 cases are reported in North America.**
1987	The first MPD inpatient treatment unit is established at Rush Presbyterian Hospital in Chicago; others follow across the country.
By 1995	**More than 40,000 cases are reported in North America.**
1995	Diane Humenansky becomes the first psychiatrist found guilty of malpractice for inducing multiple personalities in a vulnerable patient.
1996–present	Other successful lawsuits are filed against major proponents of the MPD diagnosis and against treatment units in hospitals. Hospitals begin closing these units.

Sources: Acocella, 1999; Kenny, 1986; Loftus, 1996; Nathan, 1994; Pendergrast, 1995.

For example, psychiatrist Richard Kluft (1987) wrote that efforts to determine the presence of MPD—that is, to get the person to reveal a dissociated personality—may require "between 2 1/2 and 4 hours of continuous interviewing. Interviewees must be prevented from taking breaks to regain composure. . . . In one recent case of singular difficulty, the first sign of dissociation was noted in the 6th hour, and a definitive spontaneous switching of personalities occurred in the 8th hour." Mercy! After eight hours of "continuous interviewing" without a single break, how many of us wouldn't do what the interviewer wanted?

Clinicians who conduct such interrogations argue that they are merely *permitting* other personalities to reveal themselves. However, in numerous malpractice cases across the country, courts have ruled, on the basis of the testimony of scientific experts in psychiatry and psychology, that it is more likely that these clinicians were actively creating personalities through suggestion and sometimes outright intimidation (Loftus, 1996).

The Sociocognitive Explanation. No one disputes that some troubled, highly imaginative individuals can produce many different "personalities" when asked. The *sociocognitive explanation* of MPD holds that this phenomenon is simply an extreme form of the ability we all have to present different aspects of our personalities to others (Spanos, 1996). In this view, the diagnosis of MPD provides a culturally acceptable way for some troubled people to make sense of their problems (Kenny, 1986; Showalter, 1997). It allows them to account, for example, for sexual or criminal behavior that they now regret or find intolerably embarrassing; they can claim their "other personality did it." In turn, therapists who are looking for MPD reward such patients with attention and praise for revealing more and more personalities (Rieber, 1999).

> **THINKING CRITICALLY**
>
> **Consider Other Explanations**
>
> On the *Oprah* show, a man came on to talk about his new book, in which he described his 24 personalities, which emerged, he said, because he was sexually abused as a child. The book became a best-seller and was sold to the movies for more than $1 million. What else might explain how and why he developed "MPD"?

The story of the rise and fall of MPD offers an important lesson in critical thinking, because unskeptical media coverage of sensational MPD cases played a major role in fostering the rise of MPD diagnoses. When Canadian psychiatrist Harold Merskey (1992) reviewed the published cases of MPD, including Sybil's, he was unable to find a single one in which a patient developed MPD without being influenced by the therapist's suggestions or reports about the disorder in books and the media. MPD also became a lucrative business, benefitting hospitals that opened MPD clinics, therapists who had a new disorder to treat, and psychiatrists and patients who wrote best-selling books.

Of course, there have been legitimate examples of this rare disorder. But even the authors of *The Three Faces of Eve* became alarmed by the media hype and proliferation of questionable cases. Thirty years later, they reported that of the hundreds of possible MPD patients who had been referred to them in the intervening years, they thought only one was a genuine multiple personality (Thigpen & Cleckley, 1984). Each case, therefore, must be examined on its own merits. But the story of MPD teaches us to think critically about disorders that become trendy: to consider other explanations, to examine assumptions and biases, and to demand good evidence.

QUICK QUIZ

Any one of your personalities may answer this question.

Suppose you are on a jury in which the defendant, who killed six prostitutes, claims he suffers from multiple personality disorder. He has no memory of committing the murders, he says, and his psychiatrist testifies that the man has a true case of MPD. As a critical thinker, what questions would you want to ask about this defense? (By the way, this is a real case.)

Answer:

Some possible questions to ask: Was the diagnosis of MPD made *before* the man committed murder—that is, did he have a history of MPD or any other mental disorder—or did he conveniently "discover" his other personalities after being arrested? Is the psychiatrist a believer in MPD or a skeptic? Did any other psychiatrist or psychologist interview the defendant and agree on the diagnosis?

WHAT'S AHEAD

● **What's the difference between schizophrenia and a "split personality"?**
● **Is schizophrenia partly heritable?**
● **Could schizophrenia begin in the womb?**

Schizophrenia

schizophrenia A psychotic disorder or group of disorders marked by positive symptoms (e.g., delusions, hallucinations, disorganized and incoherent speech, and inappropriate behavior) and negative symptoms (e.g., emotional flatness and loss of motivation).

psychosis An extreme mental disturbance involving distorted perceptions and irrational behavior; it may have psychological or organic causes. (Plural: psychoses.)

To be schizophrenic is best summed up in a repeating dream that I have had since childhood. In this dream I am lying on a beautiful sunlit beach but my body is in pieces. . . . I realize that the tide is coming in and that I am unable to gather the parts of my dismembered body together to run away. . . . This to me is what schizophrenia feels like; being fragmented in one's personality and constantly afraid that the tide of illness will completely cover me. (Quoted in Rollin, 1980)

In 1911, Swiss psychiatrist Eugen Bleuler coined the term **schizophrenia** to describe cases in which the personality loses its unity. Contrary to popular belief, people with schizophrenia do *not* have a "split" or "multiple" personality. As this haunting quotation illustrates, schizophrenia is a fragmented condition in which words are split from meaning, actions from motives, perceptions from reality. It is an example of a **psychosis,** a mental condition that involves distorted perceptions of reality and an inability to function in most aspects of life.

Symptoms of Schizophrenia

Schizophrenia is the cancer of mental illness: elusive, complex, and varying in form. In general, schizophrenia produces two kinds of symptoms. *Active* or *positive* symptoms involve an exaggeration or distortion of normal thinking processes and behavior. These symptoms are called "positive" because they are *additions* to normal behavior; healthy people do not have delusions that their brains are receiving Martian signals. In contrast, *negative symptoms* involve the *loss* or absence of normal traits and abilities, such as the ability to speak fluently or take care of oneself.

The most common active symptoms include the following:

1 *Bizarre delusions,* such as the belief that dogs are extraterrestrials disguised as pets. Some people with schizophrenia have paranoid delusions, taking innocent events—a stranger's cough, a helicopter overhead—as evidence that the world is plotting against them. Some have delusions of identity, believing that they are Moses, Jesus, or another famous person. Some, like Margaret Mary Ray, whose story opened this chapter, have delusions that a celebrity loves them.

2 *Hallucinations and heightened sensory awareness.* Hallucinations are false sensory experiences that feel intensely real to the sufferer. They usually take the form of voices speaking odd, garbled words; a running conversation in the head; or two or more voices conversing with each other. Some are visual (e.g., seeing a celebrity in the mirror) or tactile (e.g., feeling insects crawling over the body). People with schizophrenia also have difficulty in filtering out sensory stimulation and distracting sounds, making it difficult for them to concentrate.

3 *Disorganized, incoherent speech,* consisting of an illogical jumble of ideas and symbols, linked by meaningless rhyming words or by remote associations called *word salads.* A patient of Bleuler's wrote, "Olive oil is an Arabian liquor-sauce which the Afghans, Moors and Moslems use in ostrich farming. The Indian plantain tree is the whiskey of the Parsees and Arabs. Barley, rice and sugar cane called

A common hallmark of schizophrenia is delusional thinking. Margaret Mary Ray suffered from the delusion that talk-show host David Letterman was in love with her.

artichoke, grow remarkably well in India. The Brahmins live as castes in Baluchistan. The Circassians occupy Manchuria and China. China is the Eldorado of the Pawnees" (Bleuler, 1911/1950).

4 *Grossly disorganized and inappropriate behavior,* which may range from child-like silliness to unpredictable and violent agitation. The person may wear three overcoats and gloves on a hot day, start collecting garbage, or hoard scraps of food.

In contrast to these positive symptoms, negative symptoms include loss of motivation; poverty of speech (making only brief, empty replies in conversation, because of diminished thought rather than an unwillingness to speak); and, most notably, emotional flatness—unresponsive facial expressions, poor eye contact, and diminished emotionality. Some people with schizophrenia completely withdraw into a private world, sitting for hours without moving, a condition called *catatonic stupor.* (Catatonic states may also produce frenzied, purposeless behavior that goes on for hours.) These negative symptoms may appear months before active ones do, and they often persist even when the active symptoms are in remission.

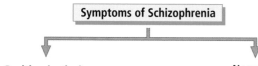

Symptoms of Schizophrenia

Positive (active):
Additions **to normal behavior**

Bizarre delusions
Hallucinations
Incoherent speech
(e.g., word salads)
Inappropriate/
disorganized behavior

Negative:
Losses **of normal abilities**

Loss of motivation
Emotional flatness
Impoverished speech
(e.g., brief, empty replies)
Social withdrawal

When people with schizophrenia are asked to draw pictures, their drawings are often distorted, lack color, include words, and reveal flat emotion. One patient was asked to copy a picture of flowers from a magazine (above). The initial result is shown below on the left. The drawing in the center shows improvement, and the drawing on the right shows how much the patient progressed after several months of treatment.

Schizophrenia typically emerges in late adolescence or early adulthood. In some individuals, schizophrenic symptoms appear suddenly. In others, the onset is more gradual; negative symptoms slowly emerge and friends and family report a slow change in personality. The person may stop working or bathing, become isolated and withdrawn, and start behaving in peculiar ways. The more breakdowns and relapses the individual has had, the poorer the chances for complete recovery. Yet many people suffering from this illness learn to control the symptoms, often with the help of antipsychotic medication (see Chapter 17), and are able to work and have good family relationships (Harding, Zubin, & Strauss, 1992).

The mystery of schizophrenia is that we could go on listing symptoms and variations all day and never finish. Some people with schizophrenia are almost completely impaired in all spheres; others do extremely well in certain areas. Still others have normal moments of lucidity in otherwise withdrawn lives. One adolescent crouched in a rigid catatonic posture in front of a television for the month of October; later, he was able to report on all the highlights of the World Series he had seen. A middle-aged man, hospitalized for 20 years, believing he was a prophet of God and that monsters were coming out of the walls, was able to interrupt his ranting to play a good game of chess (Wender & Klein, 1981).

Theories of Schizophrenia

Any disorder that has so many variations and symptoms will pose many problems for those trying to find its origins. Early psychodynamic and learning theories—that schizophrenia results from being raised by an erratic, cold, rejecting mother or from living in an unpredictable environment—have not been supported. Most researchers now believe that schizophrenia is caused by genetic predispositions that produce subtle abnormalities in the brain. These genetic predispositions, however, must interact with certain stressors in the environment during prenatal development, birth, and adolescence. Here is some evidence for this line of thinking.

1 *Genetic predispositions.* A person has a much greater risk of developing schizophrenia if an identical twin develops the disorder, even if the twins are reared apart (Gottesman, 1991, 1994). Children with one schizophrenic parent have a lifetime risk of 12 percent, and children with two schizophrenic parents have a lifetime risk of 35–46 percent, compared to a risk in the general population of only 1–2 percent (Goldstein, 1987). (See Figure 16.5.) In a Finnish study of identical twins, fully 83 percent of the variation in risk of becoming schizophrenic was due to combined genetic factors, and only 17 percent to unique environmental factors (Cannon et al., 1998).

Researchers all over the world are trying to track down the genes that might be involved in specific symptoms, such as hallucinations, sensitivity to sounds, and cognitive impairments (Blouin et al., 1998; Leonard et al., 1998; Tsuang, Stone, & Faraone, 2001). However, genes alone cannot predict who will develop the disorder; one identical twin may become schizophrenic and the other remain healthy.

2 *Structural brain abnormalities.* Some individuals with schizophrenia, especially those who have primarily negative symptoms, have decreased brain weight, a decrease in the volume of the temporal lobe or hippocampus, reduced numbers of

Figure 16.5

GENETIC VULNERABILITY TO SCHIZOPHRENIA

This graph, based on combined data from 40 European twin and adoption studies conducted over seven dacades, shows that the closer the genetic relationship to a person with schizophrenia, the higher the risk of developing the disorder. (Based on Gottesman, 1991.)

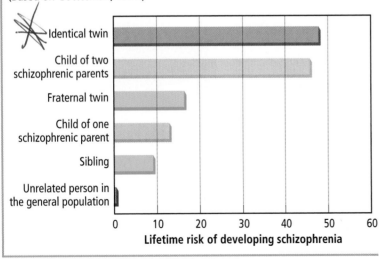

Lifetime risk of developing schizophrenia

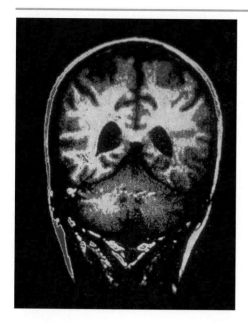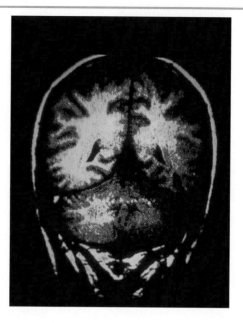

Figure 16.6
SCHIZOPHRENIA AND THE BRAIN

MRI scans show that a person with schizophrenia (left) is more likely than a healthy person (right) to have enlarged ventricles, or spaces, in the brain (see arrows) (Andreasen et al., 1994).

neurons in the prefrontal cortex, or enlargement of the *ventricles*, spaces in the brain that are filled with cerebrospinal fluid (see Figure 16.6) (Akbarian et al., 1996; Heinrichs, 1993; Zorrilla et al., 1997). Schizophrenics are also more likely than healthy individuals to have abnormalities in the thalamus, the traffic-control center that filters sensations and focuses attention (Andreasen et al., 1994; Gur et al., 1998). But, frustratingly, about one-fourth of all schizophrenics do not have these observable brain deficiencies.

3 *Neurotransmitter abnormalities.* Abnormalities in several neurotransmitters, including serotonin, glutamate, and dopamine, have been associated with schizophrenia. For example, many schizophrenics have high levels of activity in brain areas served by dopamine, and a particular kind of dopamine receptor is more common in their brains than in those of healthy people (Seeman, Guan, & Van Tol, 1993). And many schizophrenics also show disturbances in glutamate transmission between the thalamus and the cortex (Schwarcz et al., 2001). However, similar neurotransmitter abnormalities are also found in many other mental disorders, such as depression and alcoholism, making it difficult to know whether these abnormalities play a specific role in schizophrenia.

4 *Prenatal problems or birth complications.* Damage to the fetal brain significantly increases the likelihood of schizophrenia (and of other mental disorders). Such damage may occur if the mother suffers from malnutrition (Susser et al., 1996), if she gets an infectious virus during prenatal development (Mednick, Huttunen, & Machón, 1994), or if there are complications during birth that injure the baby's brain or deprive it of oxygen (Cannon et al., 2000; Rosso et al., 2000).

5 *Adolescent abnormalities in brain development.* The last factor contributing to schizophrenia occurs in adolescence, when the brain undergoes a natural pruning away of synapses in the brain. Normally, this pruning helps make the brain more efficient in handing the new challenges of adulthood. But it appears that schizophrenic brains aggressively prune away too many synapses, which may explain why the first full-blown schizophrenic episode typically occurs in adolescence or early adulthood. The reason is not yet known, but it may involve genetic dispositions, fetal brain damage, or stressful life experiences (McGlashan & Hoffman, 2000).

Thus the developmental pathway of schizophrenia looks like something of a relay. It starts with a genetic predisposition, which must combine with prenatal risk factors or birth complications, which then awaits events in adolescence—synaptic pruning within the brain or external stressors—as a trigger for the disease. This model explains why one identical twin may develop schizophrenia but not the other: Both may have the genetic susceptibility, but only one was exposed to flu or toxins in the womb or suffered from birth complications (Cannon et al., 2000). These factors may combine in different ways as well, explaining why some schizophrenics recover and others do not. The riddle of schizophrenia is likely to be several riddles, all waiting to be solved.

QUICK QUIZ

The following quiz is not a hallucination.

1. A patient with schizophrenia hears voices in her head when no one is around. Is this an example of a positive symptom or a negative one?
2. *True or false:* The vast majority of people with schizophrenia do not have a schizophrenic parent.

Answers:

1. positive 2. true

Mental Disorder and Personal Responsibility

We have come to the end of a long walk along the spectrum of psychological problems—from those that are normal conditions of life, such as occasional anxiety or "caffeine-induced sleep disorder," to mental disorders that can be severely disabling, such as schizophrenia.

One of the great debates generated by all diagnoses of mental disorder concerns the question of personal responsibility. In law and in everyday life, many people reach for a psychological reason to exonerate themselves of responsibility for their actions. Romance writer Janet Dailey who, when caught, admitted she had plagiarized whole passages from another writer's work, said she was suffering from "a psychological problem that I never even suspected I had." Before long, some students may claim that "Internet addiction disorder" was the reason they flunked out.

Such claims seem obvious excuses to avoid responsibility. On the other hand, consider the tragic story of Andrea Yates, a Texas woman who killed her five young children in a state of extreme despair. She had suffered from clinical depression and psychotic episodes for years and in her blackest depressions became mute and catatonic. She tried to kill herself twice. Her father, two brothers, and a sister had suffered different degrees of mental illness, including depression. Yates was overwhelmed by raising and home schooling all of her children by herself, with no help from her reportedly domineering husband, who permitted her two hours a week of personal time. Although she suffered a postpartum psychotic episode after the birth of their fourth child and a clinical psychologist warned against her having another, her husband refused to consider birth control, although not for religious reasons; "we want as many as nature will allow," he said (Yardley, 2001). Yates was eventually sentenced to life in prison.

Does Andrea Yates deserve our condemnation for her horrible acts of murder, or our pity? Was her punishment appropriate? Unquestionably, many people do suffer from mental disorders that make it difficult or even impossible for them to control their behavior. How can we distinguish impairments that legitimately reduce a per-

In March, 2002, Andrea Yates was convicted of the murder of her children and sentenced to life in prison. Do you agree that this was the appropriate punishment? Why or why not?

son's responsibility for his or her actions from unjustified excuses? This issue becomes especially urgent in civil and criminal cases when defendants use psychological diagnoses to try to exonerate themselves or excuse their behavior.

We noted at the beginning of this chapter that "insanity" refers only to the defendant's ability to know right from wrong at the time the crime was committed. It is used in only a tiny percentage of all criminal cases. But in some jurisdictions, a defendant may claim to have "diminished responsibility" for a crime. This claim does not *exonerate* the defendant, but it may result in reduced charges, for example from premeditated first-degree murder to manslaughter. A diminished-capacity defense holds that the defendant lacked the mental capacity to form a calculated and malicious plan but instead was impaired by mental illness or the great provocation of the situation. In some jurisdictions, diminished capacity and other mitigating factors are considered only at the sentencing phase, once the defendant has been found guilty.

When thinking about the relationship of mental disorder to personal responsibility, we face a dilemma. The law recognizes, rightly, that people who are mentally incompetent, delusional, or disturbed should not be judged by the same standards as mentally healthy individuals. At the same time, society has an obligation to protect its citizens from harm and to reject easy excuses for violations of the law. To balance these two positions, we need to find ways to ensure that people who commit crimes or behave reprehensibly face the consequences of their behavior. But we also must ensure that people who are suffering from psychological problems have the compassionate support of society in their search for help. After all, psychological problems of one kind or another are problems that all of us will have at some time in our lives.

THINKING CRITICALLY

Ask Questions

The legal system is based on the assumption of personal responsibility, but it also recognizes that some people cannot control their behavior. When does a mental disorder become an excuse to "get away with murder," and when does it truly diminish a person's responsibility?

Taking Psychology with You

WHEN A FRIEND IS SUICIDAL

Suicide can be frightening to those who find themselves fantasizing about it, and it is devastating to the family and friends of those who go through with it. In the United States, it is the ninth leading cause of death, far surpassing homicide. The suicide rate is highest among white men over the age of 65, but suicide rates have nearly tripled in the last 40 years among adolescents and young adults (Jamison, 1999).

Women are more likely than men to attempt suicide, primarily as a cry for help, whereas men are more likely to succeed, primarily as a result of hopelessness and despair. But this gender difference depends on culture and circumstances. In Finland, for example, more males than females attempt suicide; and in Canada and the United States, men in prison have high rates of attempted suicide (Canetto & Sakinofsky, 1998). Moreover, men's efforts to commit suicide are not always as obvious as those of women: Some men provoke confrontations with the police, hoping to be shot; some intentionally kill themselves in car accidents; and men are more likely than women to destroy themselves with drugs.

Because of the many widespread myths about suicide, it is important to become informed and know what to do in a crisis:

▶ *Take all suicide threats seriously.* Some people assume they can't do anything when a friend talks about committing suicide. "He'll just do it at another place, another time," they think. In fact, most suicides occur during an acute crisis. Once the person gets through the crisis, the desire to die fades. Most people who attempt to kill themselves once never do so again (Davison & Neale, 2001).

Others believe that if a friend is *talking* about committing suicide, he or she won't really *do* it. This belief also is false. More than 80 percent of young people who did commit suicide had communicated their intentions to someone else. Most people who are contemplating suicide are ambivalent: "I want to kill myself, but I don't want to be dead—at least not forever." Most suicidal people want relief from the terrible pain of feeling that nobody cares and that life is not worth living (Baumeister, 1990). Getting these thoughts and fears out in the open is an important first step.

▶ *Know the danger signs.* A person is at risk of trying to commit suicide if he or she has tried to do it before; has become withdrawn and listless; has a history of depression; reveals specific plans for carrying out the suicide or gives away cherished possessions; expresses no concern about religious prohibitions or the impact on family members; and has

access to a lethal method, such as a gun (Garland & Zigler, 1994).

▶ *Get involved: Ask questions, and help.* If you believe a friend is suicidal, do not be afraid to ask, "Are you thinking of suicide?" This question does not "put the idea" in anyone's mind. If your friend is contemplating the action, he or she will probably be relieved to talk about it, which in turn will reduce feelings of isolation and despair. Don't try to talk your friend out of it by debating whether suicide is right or wrong, and don't put on phony cheerfulness. If your friend's words scare you, say so. By allowing your friend to unburden his or her grief, you help the person get through the immediate crisis.

▶ *Do not leave your friend alone.* If necessary, get the person to a clinic

or a hospital emergency room, or call a local suicide hotline or the nationwide referral hotline, 1 (800) SUICIDE. Don't worry about doing the wrong thing. In an emergency, the worst thing you can do is nothing at all.

In her haunting book *Night Falls Fast: Understanding Suicide*, Kay Jamison (1999), a psychiatrist who suffers from bipolar disorder, explores this difficult subject from the standpoint both of a mental-health professional and a person who has "been there." In describing the aftermath of her own suicide attempt, she wrote: "I do know . . . that I should have been dead but was not—and that I was fortunate enough to be given another chance at life, which many others were not."

Summary

Defining and Diagnosing Disorder

▶ When defining *mental disorder,* mental health professionals emphasize the violation of cultural standards, whether the behavior is maladaptive for the individual or society, and the emotional suffering caused by the behavior.

▶ *The Diagnostic and Statistical Manual of Mental Disorders* (DSM), which is used throughout the world, is designed to provide objective criteria and categories for diagnosing mental disorder, using five *axes.* Critics argue that the diagnosis of mental disorders, unlike those of medical diseases, is inherently a subjective process that can never be entirely objective. They believe the DSM fosters overdiagnosis, overlooks the influence of diagnostic labels on clients and therapists, confuses serious mental illness with everyday problems in living, and creates an illusion of objectivity and universality.

▶ Supporters of the DSM believe that when the DSM criteria are used correctly and when empirically validated objective tests are used, reliability in diagnosis improves.

The DSM now lists many *culture-bound syndromes,* mental disorders that are specific to certain cultures. But many disorders, including depression and schizophrenia, are found all over the world.

▶ In diagnosing psychological disorders, clinicians often use *projective tests* such as the Rorschach Inkblot Test or, with children, the use of anatomically detailed dolls. These tests have low reliability and validity, creating problems when they are used in the legal arena or in diagnosing disorders. In general, *objective tests (inventories),* such as the *MMPI,* are more reliable and valid than projective ones.

Anxiety Disorders

▶ *Generalized anxiety disorder* involves continuous, chronic anxiety, with signs of nervousness, worry, and irritability. When anxiety results from exposure to uncontrollable or unpredictable danger, it can lead to *posttraumatic stress disorder,* which involves mentally reliving the trauma, "psychic numbing," and increased physiological arousal. *Panic disorder* involves sudden, intense attacks of profound fear, with feelings of impending doom. Panic attacks are common in the aftermath of stress or frightening experiences; those who go on to develop a disorder tend to interpret the attacks as a sign of impending disaster.

▶ *Phobias* are unrealistic fears of specific situations, activities, or things. Common *social phobias* include fears of speaking in public, using public restrooms, or being observed by others. *Agoraphobia,* the fear of being away from a safe place or person, is the most disabling phobia. It often begins with a panic attack, which the person tries to avoid in the future by staying close to "safe" places or people.

▶ *Obsessive–compulsive disorder (OCD)* involves recurrent, unwished-for thoughts or images (obsessions) and repetitive, ritualized behaviors (compulsions) that a person feels unable to control. Parts of the brain having to do with fear and response to threat are more active than normal in people with OCD.

Mood Disorders

▶ Symptoms of *major depression* include distorted thinking patterns, low self-esteem, physical ailments such as fatigue and loss of appetite, and prolonged grief and despair. Women are much more likely than men to suffer from major depression, but depression in men may be underdiagnosed. In *bipolar disorder,* a person experiences episodes of both depression and *mania* (excessive euphoria). It is equally common in both sexes.

▶ There are four leading contributions to depression. *Biological factors* include genetic predispositions and cell damage in the hippocampus and amygdala, possibly caused by elevated levels of the stress hormone cortisol. *Life experiences* related to depression include problems with work and family life, poverty, victimization, and experiences with violence. *Problems with close attachments*—such as breakups or a history of insecure attachment—can lead to depression. *Cognitive habits* also play an important role: believing that the origin of one's unhappiness is permanent and uncontrollable; feeling hopeless and pessimistic; and brooding or ruminating about one's problems. *Vulnerability–stress models* look at interactions between individual vulnerabilities (genetic dispositions, cognitive habits, and personality traits) and external stress and life experiences.

Personality Disorders

▶ *Personality disorders* are characterized by rigid, self-destructive traits that cause distress or an inability to get along with others. They include, among others, *narcissistic, borderline,* and *antisocial personality disorders.*

▶ A person with antisocial personality disorder lacks empathy and remorse, is unafraid of punishment, is impulsive and lacks self-control, and has a life history of behavioral problems. The disorder may stem from abnormalities in the central nervous system, genetically influenced problems with impulse control, or brain damage (for example, to the prefrontal cortex). These biological vulnerabilities often interact with stressful or violent environments to produce the disorder.

Drug Abuse and Addiction

▶ The effects of drugs depend on whether they are used moderately or are abused. Signs of *substance abuse* include impaired ability to work or get along with others, use of the drug in hazardous situations, recurrent arrests for drug use, and conflicts with others caused by drug use.

▶ According to the *biological model* of addiction, some people have a biological vulnerability to alcoholism and other addictions, due to a genetic factor that affects their metabolism, biochemistry, or personality traits. But heavy drug abuse also changes the brain in ways that make compulsive addiction more likely. For example, heavy use of alcohol, cocaine, and other drugs reduces the number of receptors for dopamine, making users crave more of the drug. Advocates of the *learning model* of addiction point out that addiction patterns vary according to culture, learning, and accepted practice; that many people can stop taking drugs without experiencing withdrawal symptoms; that drug abuse depends on the reasons for taking a drug; and that abuse increases when people are not taught moderate use.

▶ Although the biological and learning models are polarized on many issues, the evidence suggests that addiction and abuse result from an interaction between biological and psychological vulnerability and a person's culture, learning history, motives for taking a drug, and situation.

Dissociative Identity Disorder

▶ *Dissociation* is a split in consciousness and may temporarily occur under many normal conditions. In *dissociative identity disorder* (commonly called *multiple personality disorder,* or *MPD*), two or more distinct personalities and identities appear to exist within one person. Considerable controversy surrounds the validity and nature of MPD. Some clinicians think it is common, often goes undiagnosed, and originates in childhood trauma. Others have a *sociocognitive* explanation. They argue that most cases result from pressure and suggestion by clinicians who believe in the disorder, interacting with vulnerable patients who find MPD a plausible explanation for their problems. Media coverage of sensational alleged cases of MPD was a major contribution to the rise in the number of cases after 1980.

Schizophrenia

▶ *Schizophrenia* is a psychotic disorder involving *positive* or *active* symptoms (including delusions, hallucinations, disorganized speech called *word salads,* and inappropriate behavior) and *negative symptoms* (including loss of motivation, poverty of speech, emotional flatness, and *catatonic stupor*). Cases of schizophrenia vary in severity, duration, and prognosis.

▶ Schizophrenia appears to involve genetic predispositions that lead to structural brain abnormalities, such as enlarged ventricles and neurotransmitter abnormalities. However, genetic predispositions must interact with certain stressors in the environment during prenatal development (such as the mother's malnutrition or a prenatal viral infection), birth complications, and excessive pruning of synapses during adolescence.

Mental Disorder and Personal Responsibility

▶ The diagnosis of mental disorder raises important questions for issues of personal responsibility in the law and everyday life. When people claim to have a "mental disorder," psychologists and others struggle to decide whether the claim is an excuse for bad or destructive behavior, or whether these individuals truly have a disorder that reduces their ability to control their behavior.

Key Terms

insanity 580

mental disorder 581

Diagnostic and Statistical Manual of Mental Disorders (DSM) 581

culture-bound syndromes 584

projective tests 586

Rorschach Inkblot Test 586

objective tests (inventories) 587

Minnesota Multiphasic Personality Inventory (MMPI) 587

generalized anxiety disorder 588

posttraumatic stress disorder (PTSD) 589

panic disorder (panic attack) 590

phobia 591

social phobia 591

agoraphobia 591

obsessive–compulsive disorder (OCD) 592

mood disorder 593

major depression 593

mania 594

bipolar disorder 594

vulnerability–stress model of depression 596

personality disorders 597

narcissistic personality disorder 597

borderline personality disorder 597

antisocial personality disorder (APD) 598

vulnerability–stress model of APD 600

substance abuse 601

biological model of addiction 602

learning model of addiction 603

dissociation 607

dissociative identity disorder (multiple personality disorder, MPD) 607

sociocognitive explanation of MPD 609

schizophrenia 610

psychosis 610

positive and negative symptoms of schizophrenia 610

"word salad" 610

catatonic stupor 611

◄LOOKING BACK

- Is insanity the same thing as having a mental disorder? (p. 580)

- What are three approaches to defining "mental disorder"? (p. 580)

- Why is the standard guide to the diagnosis of mental disorders so controversial? (pp. 583–584)

- Why were slaves who dreamed of freedom once considered to be mentally ill? (p. 584)

- How reliable are "projective" tests like the famous and popular Rorschach Inkblot Test? (p. 586)

- What is the difference between ordinary anxiety and an anxiety disorder? (p. 588)

- Why is the most disabling of all phobias known as the "fear of fear"? (p. 591)

- When is checking the stove before leaving home a sign of caution, and when does it signal a disorder? (p. 592)

- How can you tell whether you have major depression or just the blues? (p. 593)

- What are the "poles" in bipolar disorder? (p. 594)

- How do some people think themselves into depression? (pp. 595–596)

- When does being self-centered become a disorder? (p. 597)

- What do a charming but heartless tycoon and a remorseless killer have in common? (p. 599)

- Why are some people seemingly incapable of feeling guilt and shame? (p. 599)

- In what ways might genes contribute to alcoholism? (p. 602)

- Why is alcoholism more common in Ireland than in Italy? (p. 603)

- Why don't policies of abstinence from alcohol reduce problem drinking? (p. 604)

- If you take morphine to control chronic pain, does that mean you will become addicted to it? (p. 604)

- Why are many clinicians and researchers skeptical about multiple personality disorder? (pp. 608–609)

- Why did the number of "multiple personality" cases jump from a handful to many thousands in only a decade? (p. 609)

- What's the difference between schizophrenia and a "split personality"? (p. 610)

- Is schizophrenia partly heritable? (p. 612)

- Could schizophrenia begin in the womb? (p. 613)

Go to **WWW.PRENHALL.COM/WADE for activities, practice tests, and review material.**

17

Approaches to Treatment and Therapy

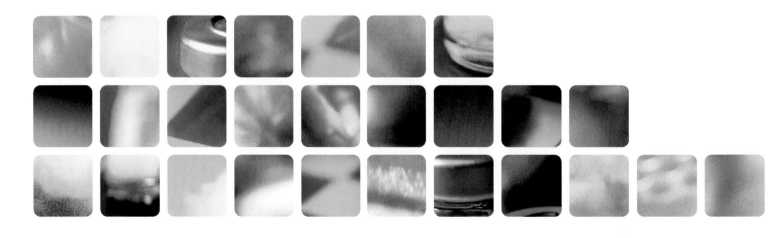

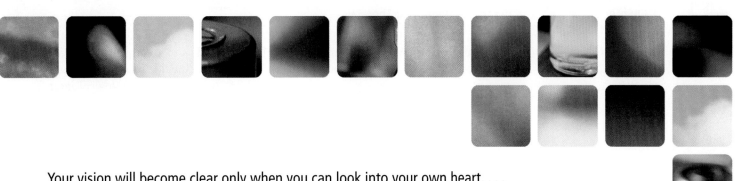

Your vision will become clear only when you can look into your own heart. . . .
Who looks outside, dreams; who looks inside, awakes.

CARL JUNG

In the aftermath of the attacks on the World Trade Center on September 11, 2001, many people across America developed emotional symptoms. Many were depressed and anxious. Some couldn't sleep. Many New Yorkers developed fears of leaving home, of riding in elevators, and of course of flying in planes. Firefighters, rescue workers, and families of the victims had recurring nightmares and flashbacks. The country had been through a shock, and if ever people understood what it meant to have "posttraumatic stress disorder," this was it.

And yet the miraculous thing is that the vast majority of people who experience a traumatic event—including combat during war, the sudden death of a loved one, or a natural disaster such as an earthquake or hurricane—recover from their immediate postshock symptoms and go on to lead normal lives. The two greatest allies in helping them do this are time, which does heal, and the support of friends.

For some people, however, time and friends are not enough, and they develop one or more of the disorders described in the previous chapter: depression, generalized anxiety disorder, specific phobias, or posttraumatic stress disorder. What kind of therapy might help them? People have many other problems too, ranging from normal life difficulties (such as marital conflict or fear of public speaking) to the delusions of schizophrenia. What kind of therapy might help them?

As we saw in Chapter 1, to become a licensed clinical psychologist, a person must have an advanced degree and a period of supervised training. However, the word *psychotherapist* is unregulated; anyone can set up any kind of program and call it "therapy"—and, by the thousands, they do! Increasingly in the United States and Canada, people can get credentialed as "experts" in various techniques and therapies—doing "hypnotherapy," diagnosing child sexual abuse, becoming a practitioner of some pop-psych method—simply by attending a weekend seminar or a training program lasting a week or two. To protect themselves as well as to get the best possible help when it is necessary, consumers need to be informed and know how to choose that help wisely.

In this chapter, we will evaluate two major approaches to treatment. *Biological treatments,* provided by psychiatrists or other physicians, include drugs or direct intervention in brain function. *Psychotherapy* covers an array of psychological interventions, including psychodynamic therapies, cognitive and behavior therapies, humanist therapies, and family or couples therapy. In addition to these major schools of psychotherapy, there are literally hundreds of offshoots and specialties. We will assess which kinds of therapy work best for which problems, which kinds of therapy are completely ineffective, and which ones carry a significant risk of harm to the client.

WHAT'S AHEAD

- **What kinds of drugs are used to treat psychological disorders?**
- **Are antidepressants always the best treatment for depression?**
- **Can mental disorders be cured by brain surgery?**
- **Why is "shock therapy" hailed by some clinicians but condemned by others?**

Biological Treatments for Mental Disorders

For hundreds of years, people have tried to find the origins of mental illness, attributing the causes at various times to evil spirits, pressure in the skull, disease, or bad environments. The contemporary mental-health world continues to alternate between viewing mental disorders as diseases that can be treated medically and as emotional problems that must be treated psychologically (Luhrmann, 2000). Today, biological explanations and treatments are in the ascendance. This is partly because of evidence that some disorders have a genetic component or involve a biochemical or neurological abnormality (see Chapter 16), and partly because economic and social forces are fostering biomedical solutions.

The Question of Drugs

The most commonly used biological treatment is medication. Because drugs are so widely prescribed these days, both for severe disorders such as schizophrenia and for more common problems such as anxiety and depression, consumers need to understand what these drugs are, how they can best be used, and their limitations.

Drugs Commonly Prescribed for Mental Disorders. The main classes of drugs used in the treatment of mental and emotional disorders are these:

1 **Antipsychotic drugs,** also called *neuroleptics*—older ones such as chlorpromazine (trade name Thorazine) and haloperidol (Haldol) and newer, "second-generation" ones such as clozapine (Clozaril)—are used in the treatment of schizophrenia and other psychoses. Many antipsychotic drugs block or reduce the sensitivity of brain receptors that respond to dopamine. Some also increase levels of serotonin, a neurotransmitter that inhibits dopamine activity.

Antipsychotic drugs can reduce the positive symptoms of schizophrenia, including agitation, delusions, and hallucinations, and they can shorten schizophrenic episodes. However, they offer little relief from (and may even worsen) negative symptoms, such as jumbled thoughts, difficulty concentrating, emotional flatness, or inability to interact with others (see Chapter 16). Although antipsychotic medica-

antipsychotic drugs Drugs used primarily in the treatment of schizophrenia and other psychotic disorders.

These photos show the effects of antipsychotic drugs on the symptoms of a young man with schizophrenia. In the photo on the left, he was unmedicated; in the photo on the right, he had taken medication. However, these drugs do not help all people with psychotic disorders.

tion allows many people to be released from hospitals, these individuals cannot always care for themselves, and they often fail to keep taking their medication because of its unpleasant side effects, including uncontrollable tremors (Luhrmann, 2000; Masand, 2000). And for many people with schizophrenia, even the newest drugs are still not effective (Valenstein, 1998).

2 Antidepressant drugs are used primarily in the treatment of depression, anxiety, phobias, and obsessive–compulsive disorder. *Monoamine oxidase inhibitors (MAOIs),* such as Nardil, elevate the level of norepinephrine and serotonin in the brain by blocking or inhibiting an enzyme that deactivates these neurotransmitters. *Tricyclic antidepressants,* such as Elavil, boost norepinephrine and serotonin levels by preventing the normal reabsorption, or "reuptake," of these substances by the cells that have released them. *Selective serotonin reuptake inhibitors (SSRIs),* such as Prozac, work on the same principle as the tricyclics but specifically target serotonin.

Antidepressants are nonaddictive, but they can produce some unpleasant physical reactions, including dry mouth, headaches, constipation, nausea, restlessness, gastrointestinal problems, weight gain, and, in as many as one-third of all patients, decreased sexual desire and blocked or delayed orgasm (Glenmullen, 2000). MAOIs interact with foods containing tyramine, a chemical found in cheese and beer, so dietary restrictions may be required.

Researchers hope to develop new antidepressants that will target other brain chemicals and produce fewer side effects. One drug in development, for example, targets receptors for a brain chemical called substance P, which helps transmit pain messages (Kramer et al., 1998). Others are studying herbs like St. John's wort, long used throughout Europe. A meta-analysis of clinical studies found that St. John's wort was more effective than placebo for milder forms of depression (Kim, Streltzer, & Goebert, 1999), but the efficacy of this herb remains in dispute.

3 Tranquilizers, such as Valium and Xanax, increase the activity of the neurotransmitter gamma-aminobutyric acid (GABA). Although they were developed to treat people with mild anxiety, they are often overprescribed by general physicians for patients who complain of any kind of mood disorder. Tranquilizers are not effective for depression. While they may help people with panic disorder and individuals who are having an acute anxiety attack (Ballenger et al., 1988), they are not considered the treatment of choice over a long period of time.

antidepressant drugs Drugs used primarily in the treatment of mood disorders, especially depression and anxiety.

tranquilizers Drugs commonly but often inappropriately prescribed for patients who complain of unhappiness, anxiety, or worry.

"Before Prozac, she loathed company."

lithium carbonate A drug frequently given to people suffering from bipolar disorder.

Symptoms almost always return if the medication is stopped, and a significant percentage of people who take tranquilizers overuse them and develop problems with withdrawal and tolerance (i.e., they need larger and larger doses).

4 A special category of drug, a salt called **lithium carbonate,** often helps people who suffer from bipolar disorder (depression alternating with euphoria) (Keck & McElroy, 1998). It may produce its effects by moderating levels of norepinephrine or by protecting brain cells from being overstimulated by another neurotransmitter, glutamate (Nonaka, Hough, & Chuang, 1998). Lithium must be given in exactly the right dose and bloodstream levels of the drug must be carefully monitored, because too little will not help and too much is toxic—even fatal. Once begun, lithium must be used continually, or discontinued very carefully, or the risk of recurrence rises (Suppes et al., 1991). Unfortunately, in some people, lithium produces short-term side effects (tremors) and long-term problems (kidney damage). Newer drugs for people with bipolar disorder include Tegretol, which is better tolerated by many people with bipolar disorder; another salt, Depakote (devalproex); and even some newer antipsychotics (Bowden et al., 2000; McElroy & Keck, 2000).

For a review of these drugs and their uses, see Review 17.1.

The increasing popularity of drugs as a method of treatment poses a problem for clinical psychologists, who, unlike psychiatrists, are not currently allowed to prescribe medication (except in New Mexico). Many psychologists are now lobbying for prescription rights, arguing that they should have access to the full range of treatment possibilities (DeLeon & Wiggins, 1996). But they have run into resistance from the medical profession, which argues that even if psychologists get more training, they will not be qualified to prescribe medication. Many psychologists, too, are concerned about the medicalizing of their field and want psychology to remain a distinct alternative to psychiatry (DeNelsky, 1996).

Some Cautions About Drug Treatments. Without question, drugs have rescued some people from emotional despair, suicide, obsessive-compulsive disorder, and panic attacks. They have enabled severely depressed or mentally disturbed people to function and respond to psychotherapy. Yet many psychiatrists and drug companies are trumpeting the benefits of medication without informing the public of its limitations, so a few words of caution are in order.

💡 **THINKING CRITICALLY**

Avoid Emotional Reasoning

A magazine announces that Prozac is "a breakthrough drug for depression." A headline announces that Clozaril is a "miracle cure" for people with schizophrenia. Such announcements always generate a lot of excitement. Why should people be cautious before concluding that a new drug is the miracle they are longing for it to be?

REVIEW 17.1	**DRUGS USED IN THE TREATMENT OF PSYCHOLOGICAL DISORDERS**			
Category	Antipsychotics (Neuroleptics)	Antidepressants	Tranquilizers	Lithium Carbonate
Examples	Thorazine Haldol Clozaril	Prozac (SSRI) Nardil (MAOI) Elavil (tricyclic)	Valium Xanax	
Used for	Schizophrenia Other psychoses	Depression Anxiety disorders Panic disorder Obsessive–compulsive disorder	Mood disorders Panic disorder	Bipolar disorder

1 *The placebo effect.* New drugs, like new psychotherapies, often promise quick and effective cures, as was the case with the arrival of Clozaril, Xanax, and Prozac. But the **placebo effect** (see Chapter 2) ensures that many people will respond positively to a new drug just because of the enthusiasm surrounding it and their own expectations that the drug will make them feel much better. After a while, when placebo effects decline, many drugs turn out to be neither as effective as promised nor as widely applicable. This has happened repeatedly with each new generation of tranquilizer and each new miracle antidepressant.

The belief that antidepressants are the treatment of choice for depression is widespread, so we were as surprised as anyone to discover the large amount of evidence questioning that belief (Antonuccio et al., 1999; Valenstein, 1998). In several large-scale meta-analyses, clinicians considered antidepressants helpful, yet the patients' ratings showed no advantage for the drugs beyond the placebo effect (Greenberg et al., 1992; Kirsch & Sapirstein, 1998; Moncrieff, 2001). Even Prozac, which arrived with much fanfare and enthusiasm, is not much more effective than the older generation of antidepressants (Greenberg et al., 1994).

2 *High relapse and dropout rates.* A person may have short-term success with antipsychotic or antidepressant drugs. However, in part because of their unpleasant side effects, half to two-thirds of people stop taking them (Glenmullen, 2000; Torrey, 1995). Individuals who take antidepressants without also learning how to cope with their problems are also more likely to relapse in the future (Antonuccio et al., 1999).

3 *Dosage problems.* The challenge with drugs is to find the *therapeutic window,* the amount that is enough but not too much. This problem is compounded by the fact that the same dose of a drug may be metabolized differently in men and women, old people and young people, and different ethnic groups (Willie et al., 1995). When psychiatrist Keh-Ming Lin moved from Taiwan to the United States, he was amazed to learn that the dosage of antipsychotic drugs given to American patients with schizophrenia was often 10 times higher than the dose for Chinese patients. In subsequent studies, Lin and his colleagues confirmed that Asian patients require significantly lower doses of the medication for optimal treatment (Lin, Poland, & Chien, 1990). Similarly, African-Americans suffering from depression or bipolar disorder seem to need lower dosages of tricyclic antidepressants and lithium than other ethnic groups do (Strickland et al., 1991, 1995). Groups may differ in the dosages they can tolerate because of variations in metabolic rates, amount of body fat, the number or type of drug receptors in the brain, or cultural practices such as smoking and eating habits.

4 *Long-term risks.* Antipsychotic drugs can have dangerous, even fatal consequences if taken for many years. About one-fourth of all adults who take these drugs, and fully one-third of elderly patients who do so, develop a neurological disorder called *tardive* (late-appearing) *dyskinesia,* which is characterized by hand tremors and other involuntary muscle movements (Saltz et al., 1991).

Antidepressants, in contrast, are assumed to be quite safe, but the effects of taking them for many years are still unknown (Glenmullen, 2000). The general public and even many physicians do not realize that new drugs are often tested on only a few hundred people for only a few weeks or months, even when the drug is one that patients might take for many years. For example, Clozapine was tested in controlled trials that lasted only six weeks (*FDA Drug Bulletin,* 1990), and none of the other second-generation antipsychotic drugs have been used long enough to determine their long-term risks (Gupta et al., 1999). Ritalin is given to many children diagnosed with attention deficit/hyperactivity disorder, but no studies have examined the drug's effect on children who take it for longer than 14 months (National Institutes of Health consensus report, November 19, 1998). Many physicians and the public, feeling reassured if a drug is effective in the short run, overlook the possibility of long-term dangers.

placebo effect The apparent success of a medication or treatment due to the patient's expectations or hopes rather than to the drug or treatment itself.

"I think the dosage needs adjusting. I'm not nearly as happy as the people in the ads."

These cautions are the reason that it is important to think critically about the popularity of an exclusively biological approach to mental disorders. Many American doctors prescribe drugs routinely, often without accompanying psychotherapy for the person's problems. The overprescription of drugs in the United States is partly a result of pressure from managed-care organizations, which prefer to pay for one patient visit for a prescription rather than ten visits for psychotherapy.

But it is also a result of advertising by drug companies, which are spending fortunes to study and market these highly profitable products. (In 1997 the U.S. Food and Drug Administration [FDA] permitted pharmaceutical companies to advertise directly to consumers, a practice still forbidden in Canada and Europe.) Most consumers do not realize that once a drug is approved by the FDA, doctors are then permitted to prescribe it for other conditions and to other populations than those on which it was originally tested. That is why antidepressants are now being marketed for social phobias; why Prozac, when its patent expired, was renamed Sarafem and marketed to women for "Premenstrual Dysphoric Disorder"; why Ritalin, widely used in the treatment of attention deficit disorder in school-aged children, is being prescribed for 2- and 3-year-olds; and why antipsychotics are being used for nonpsychotic disorders such as impulsive aggression.

Most worrisome for the future of impartial research, most of the researchers who are studying the effectiveness of medication have strong financial ties to the pharmaceutical industry, in the form of lucrative consulting fees, funding for studies, stock investments, and patents (Angell, 2000; Bodenheimer, 2000). Indeed, funding for some research is available only from pharmaceutical companies, which may require investigators to sign contracts allowing the company to determine whether, where, and when the research findings will be published. (Pfizer delayed publication of research it had sponsored showing that Viagra was ineffective for women; eventually, an independent Canadian study reported the same results [Tiefer, 2000].)

The overprescription of drugs for mood disorders in North America also occurs because of a common but mistaken assumption: that if a disorder appears to have biological origins or involve biochemical abnormalities, then biological treatments must be most appropriate. But in fact, changing your behavior and thoughts—through psychotherapy or other new experiences—can also change the way your brain functions. This point was dramatically illustrated in two PET-scan studies of people with obsessive–compulsive disorder. Among those who were taking Prozac, the metabolism of glucose in the brain improved, suggesting that the drug was having a beneficial effect. But exactly the *same* brain changes occurred in patients who were getting cognitive-behavior therapy and no medication (see Figure 17.1) (Baxter et al., 1992; Schwartz et al., 1996). And unlike antidepressants, cognitive-behavior therapy also restores depressed patients' brain-wave sleep patterns to normal (Thase et al., 1998).

In sum, consumers must think critically and carefully about the benefits and limitations of medication for psychological problems. Even when medication is clearly necessary, as it is for most cases of bipolar disorder, psychotherapy is almost always equally important. For example, a friend of a clinical psychologist we know said, "Lithium cuts out the highs as well as the lows. I don't miss the lows, but I gotta admit that there were some aspects of the highs that I do miss. It took me a while to accept that I had to give up those highs. Wanting to keep my job and my marriage helped!" (quoted in Davison & Neale, 2001). The drug alone could not have helped this man learn to live with his illness.

Figure 17.1

PSYCHOTHERAPY AND THE BRAIN

These PET scans show the brain of a person with obsessive-compulsive disorder before and after behavior therapy. Before therapy, the glucose metabolic rates in the right caudate nucleus (rCd) were elevated. After therapy, this area "calmed down," becoming less active, just as it did with medication (Schwartz et al., 1996).

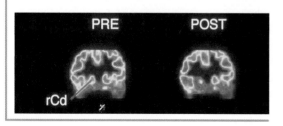

As you can see, drugs for mental disorders are neither totally miraculous nor totally worthless. Their effectiveness depends on the individual, the problem, and whether medication is combined with psychotherapy.

Surgery and Electroshock

For centuries, physicians treated mental illness by trying to change brain function directly. In the seventeenth century, for example, physicians tried to release the "psychic pressures" they believed were causing a person's symptoms by drilling holes in the person's skull. (It didn't work.) **Psychosurgery**—surgery designed to destroy selected areas of the brain thought to be responsible for emotional disorders or disturbed behavior—continued throughout most of the twentieth century.

The most famous form of modern psychosurgery was invented in 1935, when a Portuguese neurologist, Egas Moniz, drilled two holes into the skull of a mental patient and used a specially designed instrument to cut or crush nerve fibers running from the prefrontal lobes to other areas. This operation, called a *prefrontal lobotomy,* was supposed to reduce the patient's emotional symptoms without impairing intellectual ability. The procedure—which, incredibly, was never assessed or validated scientifically—was performed on tens of thousands of people. In America, the lobotomy was popularized by Walter Freeman, who personally performed more than 3,500 operations. Tragically, lobotomies left many patients apathetic, withdrawn, and unable to care for themselves (Valenstein, 1986). Yet Moniz won a Nobel Prize for his work.

Today, psychosurgery is rare, but some neurosurgeons have not given up on the effort to cure mental illness by operating on the brain. Some are performing cingulotomies (burning holes in the frontal lobes of the brain) on severely depressed or anxious patients whose symptoms have not responded to drugs or psychotherapy (Marino & Cosgrove, 1997). Cingulotomy is also being used as a method of last resort for intractable cases of obsessive–compulsive disorder; desperate, suicidal OCD patients sometimes plead to have the surgery. However, reports of success are anecdotal and no randomized controlled trials have been conducted on any of these forms of psychosurgery (Vertosick, 1997).

Another controversial procedure is **electroconvulsive therapy (ECT)**, or "shock therapy," which is used for the treatment of severe depression. An electrode is placed on one or both sides of the head, and a brief current is turned on. The current triggers a seizure that typically lasts one minute, causing the body to convulse. Today, unlike in the past, patients are given muscle relaxants and anesthesia, so they sleep through the procedure and their convulsions are minimized. ECT is sometimes used effectively on people who are suicidal, when there is a life-threatening risk of waiting for drugs or psychotherapy to help, although no one knows how or why it works (Davison & Neale, 2001). However, ECT is *ineffective* with other disorders, such as schizophrenia or alcoholism, though it is occasionally misused for these conditions.

ECT's supporters argue that it is foolish to deny suffering, depressed patients a way out of their misery, especially if their misery is making them suicidal. They cite research showing that when ECT is used properly, it is safe and effective and causes no long-term cognitive impairment, memory loss, or detectable brain damage (Devanand et al., 1994; Fink, 1999). Critics counter that ECT is often used improperly, and that it can in fact damage the brain (Breggin, 1991).

As the ECT controversy continues, researchers are looking for other, milder ways to electrically stimulate the brains of severely depressed individuals. One method described in Chapter 4, *transcranial magnetic stimulation (TMS),* involves the use of a pulsing magnetic coil held to a person's skull at the left prefrontal cortex. As we saw in Chapter 11, this area of the brain is less active in people with depression, and repeated TMS seems to give it a "boost." Researchers speculate that it also stimulates

psychosurgery Any surgical procedure that destroys selected areas of the brain believed to be involved in emotional disorders or disturbed behavior.

electroconvulsive therapy (ECT) A procedure used in cases of prolonged and severe major depression, in which a brief brain seizure is induced.

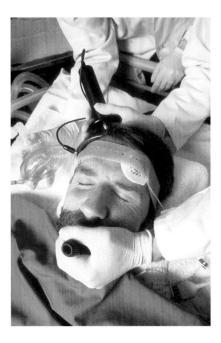

On the left, a man receives electroconvulsive therapy (ECT), which has been used successfully to treat suicidal depression. Supporters and critics continue to disagree about its potential for misuse or harm. On the right, Jordan Grafman, a cognitive neuroscientist, demonstrates the application of a newer and milder method, transcranial magnetic stimulation (TMS), on his colleague, neurologist Eric Wasserman.

the neural circuits of the limbic system. The patient is awake, and the procedure does not cause memory loss, seizures, or other side effects (Little et al., 2000; Wasserman & Lisanby, 2001). Compared to control patients who get a sham treatment without the stimulation, depressed patients given TMS treatments every day for two to four weeks are more likely to improve (George, 1998). This method is promising and safer than ECT, but no one yet really knows why it works or whether it will hold up in further research.

QUICK QUIZ

No amount of electric shock will stimulate test-taking ability.

A. Match these treatments with the problems for which they are typically used.

1. antipsychotic drugs
2. antidepressant drugs
3. lithium carbonate
4. electroconvulsive therapy

a. suicidal depression
b. bipolar disorder
c. schizophrenia
d. depression and anxiety
e. obsessive–compulsive disorder

B. Give four reasons that the public should be cautious about claims that drugs for psychological disorders are miracle cures.

 C. Jezebel has had occasional episodes of depression that seem to be getting worse. Her physician prescribes an antidepressant. Before taking it, what questions should Jezebel ask herself, and the doctor?

Answers:

A. 1. c 2. d, e 3. b 4. a B. Placebo effects are common; dropout and relapse rates are high; appropriate dosages can be difficult to determine and can vary by sex, age, and ethnicity; and some drugs have unknown or long-term risks. C. Has the physician prescribed the drug casually, without taking her full medical and psychological history? Has the physician considered other possible reasons for her depression? Would psychotherapy be appropriate, either with or without medication? Does the medication have any unpleasant side effects or long-term risks? Will the doctor continue to monitor her reactions to the drug on a regular basis?

WHAT'S AHEAD

- Why are psychodynamic therapies called "depth" therapies?
- How can therapies based on learning principles help you change your bad habits?
- How do cognitive therapists help people get rid of self-defeating thoughts?
- Why do humanist therapists focus on the "here and now" instead of the "why and how"?
- Why do family therapists prefer to treat families rather than individuals?

Kinds of Psychotherapy

All good psychotherapists want to help clients think about their lives in new ways and find solutions to the problems that plague them. In this section we will consider the major schools of psychotherapy, and to illustrate the philosophy and methods of each one, we will focus on a fictional fellow named Murray. Murray is a smart guy whose problem is all too familiar to many students: He procrastinates. He just can't seem to settle down and write his term papers. He keeps getting incompletes, and before long the incompletes turn to Fs. Why does Murray procrastinate, manufacturing his own misery? What kind of therapy might help him?

Psychodynamic Therapy

Sigmund Freud was the father of the "talking cure," as one of his patients called it. In his method of **psychoanalysis,** patients talk not about their immediate problems, but about their dreams, fantasies, and memories of childhood. Freud believed that intensive analysis of these dreams and memories would give patients insight into the unconscious reasons for their symptoms and unhappiness. With insight and emotional release, the person's symptoms would disappear.

In orthodox psychoanalysis, which is rarely practiced today, the client meets with the therapist as often as several times a week, for a period of years. The client lies on a sofa, with the analyst sitting out of view, and says whatever comes to mind without censoring, a technique called **free association.** (The popular image of therapy in cartoons and movies still often includes a person lying on a couch.) The analyst listens to the client's free associations and dreams, but rarely comments. There is no rush to solve the problem that brought the client into therapy. In fact, a person may come in complaining of a symptom such as anxiety or headaches, and the therapist may not get around to that symptom for months or even years. The analyst views the symptom as only the tip of the mental iceberg. Some traditional analysts do not attempt cures at all. The goal, they say, is understanding, not change.

Freud's psychoanalytic method has evolved into many different forms of **psychodynamic therapy,** which share the goal of exploring the unconscious dynamics of personality, such as defenses and conflicts (see Chapter 13). Proponents of these therapies often refer to them as "depth" therapies because the goal is to delve into the deep, unconscious processes believed to be the source of the patient's problems, rather than to concentrate on "superficial" symptoms and conscious beliefs.

A major element of all psychodynamic therapies, from Freudian to present forms, is **transference,** the client's transfer (displacement) of emotional elements of his or her inner life—usually feelings about the

psychoanalysis A method of "depth" psychotherapy emphasizing the exploration of unconscious motives and conflicts through free association to memories and dreams, in order to achieve insight.

free association In psychoanalysis, the process of saying freely whatever comes to mind in connection with dreams, memories, fantasies, or conflicts.

psychodynamic therapy Psychotherapies that explore the unconscious dynamics of personality, such as defenses and conflicts.

transference In psychodynamic therapies, a critical process in which the client transfers unconscious emotions or reactions onto the therapist.

"HAVE A COUPLE OF DREAMS, AND CALL ME IN THE MORNING."

Many popular TV shows and movies, such as *The Sopranos* and *Analyze This* (with Robert DeNiro as a mobster patient and Billy Crystal as his psychoanalyst), feature psychodynamic therapists. This is one reason that many people equate therapy with psychoanalysis.

parents—outward onto the analyst. Have you ever found yourself responding to a new acquaintance with unusually quick affection or dislike, and later realized it was because the person reminded you of a relative that you loved or loathed? That experience is similar to transference. In therapy, a woman who failed to resolve her Oedipal love for her father might believe she has fallen in love with the analyst. A man who is unconsciously angry at his mother for rejecting him might become furious with his analyst for going on vacation. Through analysis of transference in the therapy setting, psychodynamic therapists believe, clients can see their emotional conflicts in action, and thereby work through and resolve them.

As we saw in Chapter 13, a popular modern psychodynamic approach is based on *object-relations theory* (Greenberg & Mitchell, 1983). It holds that unconscious expectations and habits, established in early relations with important family members, reproduce themselves in adult relationships. As two object-relations analysts put it, "Experiences with our mother, father, siblings, and others form powerful impressions, like engravings on some inner wall of our psyche, which become the standards against which all other relationships are measured" (Dym & Glenn, 1993).

Today, most psychodynamic therapists reject the orthodox psychoanalytic approach, while retaining the key ideas of transference, probing for unconscious motives that stem from childhood experiences, and breaking through the client's unconscious defenses (Schafer, 1992; Westen, 1998). They sit facing the client, they participate more actively, and they are more goal-directed. Many practice time-limited therapy, consisting of 15, 20, or 25 sessions. Without delving into the client's entire history, the therapist listens to the client's problems and formulates the main issue (Groves, 1996). The rest of the therapy focuses on the person's self-defeating habits and recurring problems. For example, our friend Murray might gain the insight that he procrastinates as a way of expressing anger toward his parents. He might realize that he is angry because they insist that he study for a career he dislikes. Ideally, Murray will come to this insight by himself. If the analyst suggests it, Murray might feel too defensive to accept it.

Behavior and Cognitive Therapy

Unlike psychodynamic therapists, psychologists who practice behavior therapy or cognitive therapy would not worry much about Murray's past, his parents, or his unconscious anxieties. Psychologists who practice behavior therapy would get right to the problem: What are the reinforcers in Murray's environment that are maintaining his behavior? "Mur," they would say, "Forget about insight. You have lousy study habits." Psychologists who practice cognitive therapy would focus on helping Murray understand how his beliefs about studying, writing papers, and success are woefully unrealistic. Often, these two approaches are combined.

Behavioral Techniques. **Behavior therapy** is based on techniques derived from the behavioral principles of classical and operant conditioning that we discussed in Chapter 7. (You may want to review those principles before going on.) Here are some of these methods (Kazdin, 2001; Martin & Pear, 1999):

1 **Systematic desensitization.** Systematic desensitization is a step-by-step process of desensitizing a client to a feared object or experience. It is based on the classical-conditioning procedure of *counterconditioning*, in which a stimulus (such as a dog) for an unwanted response (such as fear) is paired with some other stimulus or situation that elicits a response incompatible with the undesirable one (see Chapter 7). In this case, the incompatible response is usually relaxation. The client learns to relax deeply while imagining or looking at a sequence of feared stimuli, arranged in a hierarchy ranging from

behavior therapy A form of therapy that applies principles and techniques of classical and operant conditioning to help people change self-defeating or problematic behaviors.

systematic desensitization In behavior therapy, a step-by-step process of desensitizing a client to a feared object or experience; it is based on the classical-conditioning procedure of counterconditioning.

the least frightening to the most frightening. The hierarchy itself is provided by the client. The sequence for a person who is terrified of spiders might be to read *Charlotte's Web,* then look at pictures of small, cute spiders, then pictures of tarantulas, then move on to observing a real spider, and so on. At each step the person must become relaxed and comfortable before going on. Eventually, the fear responses are extinguished.

2 **Exposure (flooding).** When people are afraid of some situation, object, or upsetting memory, they usually do everything they can to avoid confronting or thinking of it. Naturally, this only makes the fear worse. Exposure treatments are aimed at reversing this tendency. For example, a person who is trying to avoid thinking of a traumatic event might be asked to imagine the event over and over, until it no longer evokes the same degree of panic. Likewise, a person suffering from agoraphobia might be taken into the very situation that he or she fears most—a department store, say, or a subway—and would remain there, with the therapist, until the panic and anxiety declined. Notice how different this approach is from the psychodynamic one, in which the goal is to uncover the presumably unconscious reason that the agoraphobic feels afraid of going out.

In this "virtual reality" version of systematic desensitization, people with spider phobias are gradually exposed to computerized but extremely lifelike images of spiders in a realistic, three-dimensional environment.

Thanks to new computer technology, Virtual Reality (VR) devices permit behavior therapists to conduct exposure therapy and desensitization techniques in their offices. VR techniques have been used successfully in the treatment of several phobias, particularly of heights, flying, spiders, and driving (Wiederhold & Wiederhold, 2000).

3 **Behavioral records.** Before people can change their behavior, they have to identify the reinforcers (rewarding consequences) that are supporting their unwanted habits: attention from others, temporary relief from tension or unhappiness, or tangible rewards such as money or a good meal. One way to do this is for the client to keep a record of the behavior that he or she wishes to change. For example, a man who wants to curb his overeating may not be aware of how much he eats throughout the day to relieve tension; a behavioral record might show that he eats more junk food than he realized in the late afternoon. A mother might complain that her child "always" has temper tantrums; a behavioral record will show when, where, and with whom they occur. Once the unwanted behavior is identified, along with the reinforcers that have been maintaining it, a treatment program can be designed to change it. For instance, the man might find other ways to reduce stress and make sure that he is nowhere near junk food in the late afternoon. The mother can learn to respond to her child's tantrum not with her attention (or a cookie to buy silence), but with a time-out: Banishing the child to a corner where no positive reinforcers are available.

4 **Skills training.** It is not enough to tell someone "Don't be shy" if the person does not know how to make small talk with others, or "Don't yell" if the person does not know how to express feelings calmly. Therefore, some behavior therapists teach the skills a client might lack, by modeling these skills and also by asking the client to practice them in a role-playing situation. A shy person, for example, might learn how to converse in social settings by focusing on other people rather than on his or her own insecurity. Countless skills-training programs have been designed for parents who don't know how to discipline children, for people who don't know how to manage anger, for children and adults who don't know how to express their wishes

exposure (flooding) In behavior therapy, a method in which a person suffering from an anxiety disorder, such as a phobia or panic attacks, is taken directly into the feared situation until the anxiety subsides.

behavioral records In behavior therapy, a method of keeping careful data on the frequency and consequences of the behavior to be changed.

skills training In behavior therapy, an effort to teach the client skills that he or she may lack, as well as new, more constructive behaviors to replace self-defeating ones.

cognitive therapy A form of therapy designed to identify and change irrational, unproductive ways of thinking and hence to reduce negative emotions and their behavioral consequences; it is often combined with behavioral techniques.

Cognitive therapists encourage clients to emphasize the positive (the early sunny signs of spring) rather than always focusing on the negative (the lingering icy clutch of winter). Poet Michael Casey described the first daffodil that bravely rises through the snow as "a gleam of laughter in a sullen face."

clearly, and many other behavioral problems. Modeling and role-playing techniques have also been effective in teaching people with schizophrenia how to behave in social situations (Marder et al., 1996).

A behaviorist would treat Murray's procrastination in several ways. Murray might not know how he actually spends his time when he is avoiding his studies. Afraid that he hasn't time to do everything, he does nothing. Keeping a behavioral diary would let Murray know exactly how he spends his time, and how much time he should realistically allot to a project. Instead of having a vague, impossibly huge goal, such as "I'm going to reorganize my life," Murray would establish specific small goals, such as reading the two books necessary for an English paper and writing one page of an assignment. If Murray does not know how to write clearly, however, even writing one page might feel overwhelming; he might also need some skills training, such as a basic composition class. Most of all, the therapist would change the reinforcers that are maintaining Murray's "procrastination behavior"—perhaps the immediate gratification of partying with friends, or the temporary relief from a fear of failure—and replace them with reinforcers for getting the work done.

Cognitive Techniques. As we saw in Chapter 11, gloomy thoughts can generate an array of negative emotions and self-defeating behavior. The underlying premise of **cognitive therapy** is that constructive and rational thinking can do the opposite—get rid of anger, fear, and depression, and the downward spirals they can produce. This is not a new idea. It originated two thousand years ago, with the Stoic philosophers, and was popularized in the United States in the "mind cure" movement of the nineteenth century (Caplan, 1998).

Today, cognitive therapists help clients identify the beliefs and expectations that might be unnecessarily prolonging their unhappiness, conflicts, and other problems (Persons, Davidson, & Tompkins, 2001). Clients examine the evidence for their beliefs—say, that everyone is mean and selfish, that ambition is hopeless, or that love is doomed. They learn to consider other explanations for the behavior of people who annoy them: Perhaps their father's strict discipline was intended not to control but to protect them. By requiring people to identify their assumptions and biases, examine the evidence, and consider other interpretations, cognitive therapy, as you can see, teaches critical thinking!

One of the best-known contemporary schools of cognitive therapy is Albert Ellis's **rational emotive behavior therapy** (**REBT**) (Ellis, 1993; Ellis & Blau, 1998). In this approach, which reflects Ellis's own New York, no-nonsense, get-on-with-it attitude, the therapist uses rational arguments to directly challenge a client's unrealistic beliefs or expectations. Ellis has pointed out that people who are emotionally upset often *overgeneralize*: They decide that one annoying act by someone means that person is totally bad in every way, or that a normal mistake they made is evidence that they are rotten to the core. Many people also *catastrophize*, transforming a small problem into an international disaster: "I failed this test, and now I'll flunk out of school, and no one will ever like me, and even my cat will hate me, and I'll never get a job . . ." Ellis also observed that many people drive themselves crazy with unrealistic notions of what they "must" do. The therapist challenges these thoughts directly, showing the client why they are irrational and misguided.

Another leading form of cognitive therapy, devised by Aaron Beck (1976, 1991), avoids direct challenges to the client's beliefs. (His approach also reflects his personality; he is more easygoing and kindly in manner than Ellis.) Beck pioneered in the application of cognitive therapy for depression. As we saw in Chapter 16, depression often arises from specific, pessimistic ways of thinking—for example, that the sources of your misery are permanent and that nothing good will ever happen to you again. For Beck, these beliefs are not "irrational"; rather, they are unproductive or based on misinformation. A therapist using Beck's approach would encourage you to test your beliefs against the evidence. If you say, "But I *know* he's out to get me," the therapist might say, "Oh, yes? How do you know? Did he tell you, or are you reading his mind?"

A cognitive therapist might treat Murray's procrastination by having Murray write down his thoughts about work, read the thoughts as if someone else had said them, and then write a rational response to each one. This technique would encourage Murray to examine the validity of his assumptions and beliefs. Many procrastinators are perfectionists; if they cannot do something perfectly, they will not do it at all. Unable to accept their limitations, they set impossible standards and catastrophize:

rational emotive behavior therapy (REBT) A form of cognitive therapy devised by Albert Ellis, designed to challenge the client's unrealistic or irrational thoughts.

Negative thought	Rational response
If I don't get an A+ on this paper, my life will be ruined.	My life will be a lot worse if I keep getting incompletes. It's better to get a B or even a C than to do nothing at all.
My professor is going to think I'm an idiot when he reads this. I'll feel humiliated by his criticism.	He hasn't accused me of being an idiot yet. If he makes some criticisms, I can learn from them and do better next time.

Get Involved

Mind Over Mood

See whether cognitive-therapy techniques can help you control your moods. Think of a time recently when you felt a particularly strong emotion, such as depression, anger, or anxiety. On a piece of paper, record (1) the situation—who was there, what happened, and when; (2) the intensity of your feeling at the time, from weak to strong; and (3) the thoughts that were going through your mind (e.g., "She never cares about what I want to do"; "I hate being angry"; "He's going to leave me").

Now examine your thoughts. What is the worst thing that could happen if those thoughts are true? Are your thoughts accurate or are you "mind-reading" the other person's intentions and motives? Is there another way to think about this situation or the other person's behavior? If you practice this exercise repeatedly, you may learn how your thoughts affect your moods—and find out that you have more control over your feelings than you realized (Greenberger & Padesky, 1995).

humanist therapy A form of psychotherapy based on the philosophy of humanism, which starts from the assumption that people seek self-actualization and self-fulfillment; it emphasizes people's free will to change, not past conflicts.

client-centered (nondirective) therapy A humanist approach to therapy devised by Carl Rogers, which emphasizes the therapist's empathy with the client, the therapist's ability to see the world as the client does, and the use of unconditional positive regard.

existential therapy A form of therapy designed to help clients explore the meaning of existence and face the great questions of life, such as death, freedom, free will, alienation, and loneliness.

Strict behaviorists consider thoughts to be "behaviors" that are modifiable by learning principles; they do not regard thoughts as causes of behavior. But most psychologists believe that thoughts and behavior influence each other, which is why cognitive-behavior therapy is more common than either form alone.

Humanist and Existential Therapy

Humanist therapy, like its parent philosophy humanism, starts from the assumption that people seek self-actualization and self-fulfillment. The humanist therapist generally does not dig into past conflicts, but aims instead to help clients feel better about themselves and free themselves from self-imposed limits. (It was the humanists who changed the term for a person in therapy from "patient," which implies that the person is ill, to "client," which implies that the person simply has a problem.) Humanist therapists want to know how clients subjectively perceive their own situations, so they can help them develop the will and confidence to bring about change. That is why they explore what is going on "here and now," not the issues of "why and how."

In **client-centered (nondirective) therapy,** developed by Carl Rogers, the therapist's role is to listen to the client's needs in an accepting, nonjudgmental way and offer what Rogers called *unconditional positive regard* (see Chapter 13). Whatever the client's specific complaint is, the goal is to build the client's self-esteem and sense of acceptance, and help the client find a more productive way of seeing his or her problems. Thus a Rogerian might assume that Murray's procrastination masks his low self-regard, and that Murray is out of touch with his real feelings and wishes. Perhaps he is not passing his courses because he is trying to please his parents by majoring in prelaw, when he would secretly rather become an artist.

Rogers (1951, 1961) believed that effective therapists must be warm and genuine in expressing their feelings and respecting their clients. (He himself was.) For Rogers, *empathy,* the therapist's ability to understand and accept what the client says, is the crucial ingredient of successful therapy. The therapist shows a basic level of empathy by listening carefully and being able to restate accurately the client's remarks: "You tell me that you feel frustrated, Murray, because no matter how hard you try, you don't succeed." But the therapist shows advanced empathy by understanding the *meaning* of the client's remarks: "Working that hard without results must really make you unhappy and maybe make you feel a bit sorry for yourself." The therapist's support for the client, according to Rogers, will eventually be adopted by the client, who will become more self-accepting.

Existential therapy helps clients explore the meaning of existence and face with courage the great questions of life, such as death, freedom, free will, alienation from oneself and others, loneliness, and meaninglessness. Existential therapists, like humanist therapists, believe that our lives are not inevitably determined by our pasts or our circumstances—that we have the power to choose our own destinies. As Irvin Yalom (1989) explained, "The crucial first step in therapy is the patient's assumption of responsibility for his or her life predicament. As long as one believes that one's problems are caused by some force or agency outside oneself, there is no leverage in therapy."

Yalom argues that the goal of therapy is to help clients cope with the inescapable realities of life and death and the struggle for meaning. However grim our experiences may be, he believes, "they contain the seeds of wisdom and redemption." Perhaps the most remarkable example of a man able to find seeds of wisdom in a barren landscape was Victor Frankl (1905–1997), who developed a form of existential therapy after surviving a Nazi concentration camp. In that pit of horror, Frankl (1955) ob-

Humanist psychologist Carl Rogers emphasized the importance of the therapist's warmth and empathy, an idea that virtually all therapists now endorse.

Family therapist Alan Entin uses photographs to help people identify themes and problems in their family histories. When one woman was asked to talk about a photo of her parents (left), she began to cry; she felt that it revealed her father's alienation from her and the rest of his family. Does the picture on the right convey a happy cohesive family to you, or a divided one? Shortly after it was taken, the couple divorced; the father took custody of the children . . . and the mother kept the dog (Entin, 1992).

served, some people maintained their sanity because they were able to find meaning in the experience, shattering though it was.

Some observers believe that, ultimately, all therapies are existential. In different ways, therapy helps people determine what is important to them, what values guide them, and what changes they will have the courage to make. An existential therapist might help Murray think about the significance of his procrastination, what his ultimate goals in life are, and how he might find the strength to carry out his ambitions.

Family and Couples Therapy

Murray's situation is getting worse. His father has begun to call him Tomorrow Man, which upsets his mother, and his younger brother the math major has been calculating how much tuition money Murray's incompletes are costing. His older sister Isabel, the biochemist who never had an incomplete in her life, now proposes that all of them go to a family therapist. "Murray's not the only one in this family with complaints," she says.

Family therapists would maintain that Murray's problem developed in the context of his family, that it is sustained by the dynamics of his family, and that any change he makes will affect all members of his family (McDaniel, Lusterman, & Philpot, 2001). One leading family therapist, Salvador Minuchin (1984), compared the family to a kaleidoscope, a changing pattern of mosaics in which the pattern is larger than any one piece. In this view, efforts to isolate and treat one member of the family without the others are doomed. Only if all family members reveal their differing perceptions of each other can mistakes and misperceptions be identified. A teenager, for instance, may see his mother as crabby and nagging when actually she is tired and worried. A parent may see a child as rebellious when in fact the child is lonely and desperate for attention.

Family members are usually unaware of how they influence one another. By observing the entire family, the family therapist hopes to discover tensions and imbalances in power and communication. For example, in some families a child may have

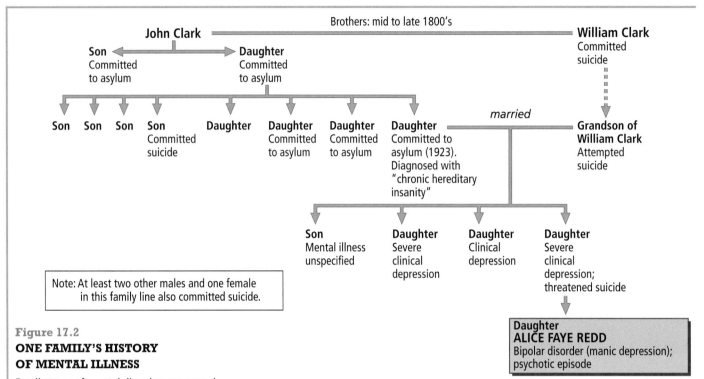

Brothers: mid to late 1800's

John Clark — William Clark
Committed suicide

Son
Committed to asylum ⟷ Daughter
Committed to asylum

Son | Son | Son | Son
Committed suicide | Daughter | Daughter
Committed to asylum | Daughter
Committed to asylum | Daughter
Committed to asylum (1923).
Diagnosed with "chronic hereditary insanity"

married

Grandson of William Clark
Attempted suicide

Son
Mental illness unspecified | Daughter
Severe clinical depression | Daughter
Clinical depression | Daughter
Severe clinical depression; threatened suicide

Note: At least two other males and one female in this family line also committed suicide.

Daughter
ALICE FAYE REDD
Bipolar disorder (manic depression); psychotic episode

Figure 17.2

ONE FAMILY'S HISTORY OF MENTAL ILLNESS

Family trees of mental disorders can reveal patterns across generations. (McGoldrick & Gerson, 1985). Alice Faye Redd was convicted of defrauding elderly investors of $10 million, money she then lost in lavish spending and extravagant investment schemes. Prosecution and defense psychiatrists agreed that she suffers from a form of manic depression (bipolar disorder). Alice Redd's daughter, Rebecca Hagelin, constructed this multi-generation family record of depression and suicide in an effort to have her mother committed for treatment, but the court sentenced Redd to 15 years in prison.

a chronic illness or a psychological problem, such as anorexia, that affects the workings of the whole family. One parent may become overinvolved with the sick child while the other parent retreats, and each may start blaming the other. The child, in turn, may cling to the illness as a way of expressing anger, keeping the parents together, getting the parents' attention, or asserting control (Luepnitz, 1988).

Some family therapists look for patterns of behavior across generations (Carter & McGoldrick, 1988; Kerr & Bowen, 1988). The therapist and client may create a family tree showing psychologically significant events across as many generations as possible (McGoldrick, Gerson, & Shellenberger, 1999). This method may reveal historical patterns, as you can see in Figure 17.2.

Even when it is not possible to treat the whole family, some therapists will treat individuals in a **family-systems perspective**, which recognizes that people's behavior in a family is as interconnected as that of two dancers (Bowen, 1978; Lerner, 1989). Clients learn that if they change in any way, even for the better, their families may protest noisily, or may send subtle messages that read, "Change back!" Why? Because when one family member changes, each of the others must change too. As the saying goes, it takes two to tango, and if one dancer stops, so must the other. But most people do not like change. They are comfortable with old patterns and habits, even those that cause them trouble. They want to keep dancing the same old dance, even if their feet hurt.

For example, one woman went to see family-systems therapist Harriet Lerner (1989) because she and her husband were arguing constantly. She wanted to go to graduate school and begin a career, and he kept insisting she had to stay home with their child. This was, Lerner showed the woman, not an argument about her career or their child, but about change in their family patterns: She wanted it, and he feared it. He was catastrophizing—if she goes to grad school, their child will suffer, she will find someone else, their marriage will end—but the real underlying fear, not misplaced, was that he would have to change his own behavior to accommodate the new arrangements. The child's expectations would have to change, too; mom wouldn't be there all the time. Lerner helped the woman formulate her own goals clearly, showed

family-systems perspective An approach to doing therapy with individuals or families by examining how each member forms part of a larger, interacting system.

her why any changes she made would evoke angry protest from the husband (protest designed to keep her from changing), and how she could make the changes that were so important for her in a way that might be more reassuring for him.

In this case, the husband was unwilling to go to therapy. Usually, when a couple is arguing frequently about issues that never seem to get resolved, they do best going together to *couples therapy*, which is designed to help couples understand and resolve the inevitable conflicts that occur in all relationships. Couples therapists generally insist on seeing both partners, so that they will hear both sides of the story. They cut through the blaming and attacking ("She never listens to me!" "He never does anything"!) and instead focus on helping the couple resolve, or learn to live with, their differences. As two psychologists specializing in couples therapy put it, "There are at least two sides to every conflict. No one partner is responsible for an interpersonal problem; both members contribute to it, usually unintentionally. . . . Crimes of the heart are usually misdemeanors, but our vulnerabilities make them feel like felonies" (Christensen & Jacobson, 2000).

Family and couples therapists may use psychodynamic, behavioral, cognitive, or humanist approaches in their work; they share only a focus on the family or the couple. In Murray's case, a family therapist would observe how Murray's procrastination fits his family dynamics. Perhaps it allows Murray to get his father's attention and his mother's sympathy. Perhaps it keeps Murray from facing his greatest fear: that if he does finish his work, it will not measure up to his father's high standards. The therapist will not only help Murray change his work habits, but will also help his family deal with a changed Murray.

Psychotherapy in Practice

The kinds of psychotherapy that we have discussed are all quite different in theory, and so are their techniques (see Review 17.2). Yet in practice, many psychotherapists take an *integrative approach*, drawing on methods and ideas from various schools and avoiding strong allegiances to any one theory. This flexibility enables them to treat clients with whatever methods are most appropriate and effective. For example, one approach to treating depression incorporates psychodynamic ideas about the role of unconscious forces in relationships, but the therapist plays an active role, does not dwell on a patient's dreams, and does not rely on free association. Instead, the therapist listens empathically, suggests behavioral changes, and focuses on solving problems in the individual's current, troubled relationships (Weissman, Markowitz, & Klerman, 2000).

All therapies, regardless of approach, share a key element: They replace a client's pessimistic or unrealistic story—the "story" each of us develops over time to explain our lives and problems—with one that is more hopeful or attainable (Freedman & Combs, 1996; Howard, 1991; Schafer, 1992). Some therapists explicitly focus on helping clients change their life stories and hence to change their own role in them. For example, therapist David Epston worked with an immigrant woman named Marisa, who had been abused and rejected all her life. "To tell a story about your life

REVIEW 17.2 THE MAJOR SCHOOLS OF THERAPY COMPARED

	Primary Goal	Methods
Psychodynamic		
Psychoanalytic	Insight into unconscious motives and feelings	Probing unconscious motives through dream analysis, free association, transference; several visits a week with little participation by analyst
Psychodynamic	Same, plus change in symptoms	Analyst more active and directive; therapy briefer
Cognitive-Behavioral		
Behavioral	Modification of self-defeating behaviors	Systematic desensitization, exposure (flooding), behavioral records, skills training
Cognitive	Modification of irrational or unvalidated beliefs	Direct challenge to unwarranted beliefs (catastrophizing, mind-reading) or appeals to see whether beliefs are supported by evidence
Humanist and Existential		
Humanist	Insight; self-acceptance and self-fulfillment; new, optimistic perceptions of self and world	Providing a safe, nonjudgmental setting in which to discuss life issues; use of empathy and unconditional positive regard by therapist
Existential	Acceptance of life's inevitable losses	Varies with therapist; philosophic discussions about meaning of life, client's goals, finding courage
Family and Couples		
Family	Modification of family patterns	May use any or all of the above methods to change family patterns that perpetuate problems
Couples	Resolution of conflicts, breaking out of destructive habits	May use any or all of the above methods to help the couple communicate better and resolve conflicts

turns it into a history," he told her, "one that can be left behind, and makes it easier for you to create a future of your own design" (quoted in O'Hanlon, 1994). Marisa came to see that she could tell a new story about her experiences. Instead of seeing the tragedies that had befallen her as evidence that she was a worthless victim, as she always had, she now saw the same events as evidence of her strength and endurance. "My life has a future now," she told him. "It will never be the same again."

QUICK QUIZ

Don't be a procrastinator like our friend Murray; take this quiz now.

Match each method or concept with the therapy associated with it.

1. transference
2. systematic desensitization
3. facing the fear of death
4. reappraisal of thoughts
5. unconditional positive regard
6. exposure to feared situation
7. avoidance of "catastrophizing"
8. analysis of generational patterns

a. cognitive therapy
b. psychodynamic therapy
c. humanist therapy
d. behavior therapy
e. family therapy
f. existential therapy

Answers:

1.b 2.d 3.f 4.a 5.c 6.d 7.a 8.e

WHAT'S AHEAD ▷

- **What is the "scientist–practitioner gap" and why has it been widening?**
- **What is the "therapeutic alliance," and why does it matter?**
- **What sorts of people make the best therapists and the best clients?**
- **Which form of psychotherapy is most likely to help if you are anxious or depressed?**
- **Under what conditions can psychotherapy be harmful?**

Evaluating Psychotherapy

Poor Murray! He is getting a little baffled by all these therapies. He wants to make a choice soon—no sense in procrastinating about that, too! Is there any scientific evidence, he wonders, that might help him decide which therapy will be best for him?

The Scientist–Practitioner Gap

Many psychotherapists believe that trying to evaluate psychotherapy using standard empirical methods is an exercise in futility: Numbers and graphs cannot possibly capture the complex exchange that takes place between a therapist and a client (Edelson, 1994; Elliott & Morrow-Bradley, 1994). Psychotherapy, they say, is an art that you acquire from clinical experience; it is not a science.

Scientific psychologists agree that research has little to say about the existential aims of therapy, such as helping people come to terms with illness and death or helping them choose which values to live by. But scientists are concerned that when therapists fail to keep up with empirical findings in the field—findings on the most beneficial methods for particular problems, on ineffective or potentially harmful tests and techniques, and on topics relevant to their practice, such as memory, hypnosis, and child development—their clients may suffer.

Over the years, the breach between scientists and therapists on this issue of the importance of research methods and findings has widened, creating what some psychologists call the *scientist–practitioner gap*. One reason for the growing split has been the rise of professional schools

> **THINKING CRITICALLY**
>
> **Don't Oversimplify**
>
> Many therapists believe that therapy is an art, not a science; many scientists believe that therapy must be evaluated scientifically or it can cause harm. Why is the "scientist–practitioner gap" widening, and how might it be bridged?

that are unconnected to academic psychology departments and that train students solely to do therapy (Dawes, 1994). Graduates of these schools sometimes know little about research methods or even about research assessing different therapy techniques.

The scientist–practitioner gap has also widened because of the proliferation of new therapies trying to get a foothold in a crowded market. New therapies are often started by a charismatic leader, who may or may not have professional training in psychology. They are then endorsed by enthusiastic practitioners who have been trained by the therapy's founder, usually in brief workshops that last a weekend or a week.

Some of these therapies are packaged and promoted without any scientific support at all (Beyerstein, 1999). For example, Thought Field Therapy (TFT), originated by Roger Callahan, assumes that emotional problems are caused by "perturbations" (disturbances) in "a subtle energy field" rather than by cognitions, environmental events, or chemical imbalances. Callahan claims he can successfully cure people on the phone, using his special patented Voice Technology™ method to assess their perturbations (Gallo, 1998). There is no solid empirical research to support these assumptions and claims, or to show that TFT offers anything other than a temporary placebo effect (Gaudiano & Herbert, 2000; McNally, 2001). Another popular therapy, Neurolinguistic Programming (NLP), claims to match people's learning styles with their "brain types" and thereby enhance their communication skills. The U.S. National Research Council concluded that there is no credible evidence for NLP's claims or methods (Druckman & Swets, 1988).

Other therapies repackage established techniques, using a new name and terminology. For example, Eye Movement Desensitization and Reprocessing (EMDR) is built on the tried-and-true desensitization and exposure techniques of behavior therapy for treating anxiety (Lohr, Tolin, & Lilienfeld, 1998). But EMDR's founder, Francine Shapiro (1995), added eye-movement exercises: Clients move their eyes from side to side, following the therapist's moving finger, while concentrating on the memory to be desensitized. Shapiro's (1994) explanation for why such eye movements work is that "The system may become unbalanced due to a trauma or through stress engendered during a developmental window, but once appropriately catalyzed and maintained in a dynamic state by EMDR, it transmutes information to a state of therapeutically appropriate resolution." (If you do not understand that, don't worry; we don't either.)

Thousands of therapists have been trained to do EMDR, and they have claimed success in treating everything from posttraumatic stress disorder and panic attacks to eating disorders and sexual dysfunction. Although EMDR has won endorsements from some prominent psychologists, there is no evidence from controlled studies that it is any better than standard exposure treatments (Goldstein et al., 2000; Lohr et al., 1999; Rosen, 1999). One clinical researcher who reviewed the evidence concluded that the eye movements that are supposedly essential to this technique do not constitute "anything more than pseudoscientific window dressing" (Lilienfeld, 1996).

Because of the proliferation of therapies, including many that are questionable at best, and because of economic pressures on insurers and rising health costs, psychotherapists are increasingly being called on to provide empirical assessments of therapy (Beutler, 2000). Which therapies are most effective, which therapies are best for which disorders, and which therapies are ineffective or potentially harmful? Hundreds of studies have been conducted to answer these questions.

The Therapeutic Alliance

Psychotherapy is, first and foremost, a relationship. Like all relationships, its success depends on the qualities that each person brings to the encounter. Successful therapy also depends on the bond the therapist and client establish between them, called the **therapeutic alliance.** When both parties respect and understand one another and agree on the goals of treatment, the client is more likely to improve.

Qualities of the Participants. Clients who are most likely to do well in therapy are, not surprisingly, motivated to improve and solve their problems (Orlinsky & Howard, 1994). They tend to have support from their families and a personal style of dealing actively with problems instead of avoiding them. Personality traits also influence whether a person will be able to change in therapy. As we saw in Chapter 13, some people are characteristically negative and bitter; others are more agreeable and positive, even in the midst of emotional crises. Hostile, negative individuals are more resistant to treatment and are less likely to benefit from it; so are people with long-standing personality problems or psychotic disorders (Kopta et al., 1994). The personality of the therapist affects the outcome of therapy, too, particularly the qualities that Carl Rogers praised: empathy, warmth, and genuineness. The most successful therapists make their clients feel respected, accepted, and understood (Orlinsky & Howard, 1994).

Culture and the Therapeutic Connection. Many therapists and clients establish successful therapeutic alliances in spite of coming from different backgrounds. But sometimes cultural differences cause misunderstandings that result from ignorance or prejudice (Comas-Díaz & Greene, 1994; Sue, 1998). For example, a lifetime of experience with racism may keep some African-Americans from revealing feelings that they believe a white therapist would not understand or accept. And black therapists frequently have to deal with clients who are bigoted or uncomfortable with them (Boyd-Franklin, 1989; Markowitz, 1993). Misunderstandings and prejudice may be a major reason that Asian-, Mexican-, and African-American clients are more likely to stay in therapy, and thus benefit from it, when their therapists' ethnicity matches their own (Sue, 1998). If such clients stay in therapy and do not drop out early, however, most are as likely to do as well with an "unmatched" therapist as with a matched one.

In establishing a bond with clients, therapists must distinguish normal cultural patterns from individual psychological problems (Pedersen et al., 1996). An Irish-American family therapist, Monica McGoldrick (1996), described some problems that are typical of Irish-American families. These problems arise from Irish history and religious beliefs, and they are deeply ingrained. "In general, the therapist cannot expect the family to turn

therapeutic alliance The bond of confidence and mutual understanding established between therapist and client, which allows them to work together to solve the client's problems.

Some psychotherapists fit their approach to the client's cultural background. For example, most Puerto Rican children know the tales of Juan Bobo (left), a foolish child ("bobo") who is always getting into trouble. The therapists on the right have adapted these stories for Puerto Rican children who are coping with new problems and temptations in America. The children and their mothers watch a videotape of the folktale, discuss it together, and role-play its major themes, such as controlling aggression and understanding right from wrong. This method has been more successful than traditional therapies in reducing the children's transitional anxieties and improving their attention spans and achievement motivation (Costantino & Malgady, 1996).

into a physically affectionate, emotionally intimate group, or to enjoy being in therapy very much," she observed. "The notion of Original Sin—that you are guilty before you are born—leaves them with a heavy sense of burden. Someone not sensitized to these issues may see this as pathological. It is not. But it is also not likely to change and the therapist should help the family tolerate this inner guilt rather than try to get rid of it."

More and more psychotherapists are becoming "sensitized to the issues" caused by cultural differences (Sue, 1998). For example, Latino and Asian clients are likely to react to a formal interview with a therapist with relative passivity and deference, leading some therapists to diagnose a shyness problem that is only a cultural norm. Latinos may respond to catastrophic stress with an *ataque de nervios,* a nervous attack of screaming, swooning, and agitation. Clinicians need to determine when this episode is a culturally influenced response and when it might be a sign of panic disorder (Costantino & Malgady, 1996). Similarly, *susto,* or "loss of the soul," is a common response in Latin American cultures to extreme grief or fright; the person believes that his or her soul has departed along with that of the deceased relative. A psychiatrist unfamiliar with this culturally determined response might conclude that the sufferer was delusional or psychotic (see Chapter 16).

Being aware of cultural differences, however, does not mean that the therapist should stereotype clients (Sue, 1998). Some Asians, after all, do have problems with excessive shyness, some Latinos do have emotional disorders, and some Irish do not carry burdens of guilt! It does mean that therapists must ensure that their clients find them to be trustworthy and effective; and it means that clients must be aware of their own prejudices, too.

When Therapy Helps

By now, Murray is really motivated to change. He just read a study showing that procrastinators not only get worse grades than other students, but also have more stress and illness during the semester (Tice & Baumeister, 1997). It is time to select a therapeutic approach. But how?

> **THINKING CRITICALLY**
>
> **Examine the Evidence**
>
> New therapies come along every week, it seems, often claiming remarkable, fast cures. Why should smart consumers examine the evidence for and against these therapies rather than be persuaded by enthusiastic testimonials?

Problems of Assessing Therapy. In studying the effectiveness of specific therapies, researchers must face a common problem: No matter what kind of therapy is involved, clients are motivated to tell you it worked. "Dr. Blitznik is a genius!" they will exclaim. "I would *never* have taken that job (or moved to Cincinnati, or found my true love) if it hadn't been for Dr. Blitznik! I was cured in a week!" Every kind of therapy ever devised, including TFT and EMDR, produces enthusiastic testimonials from people who feel it saved their lives.

The problem with testimonials is that none of us can be our own control group. How do people know they wouldn't have taken the job, moved to Cincinnati, or found true love anyway—maybe even sooner, if Dr. Blitznik had not kept them in treatment? Second, Dr. Blitznik's success could be due to the placebo effect (which we discussed earlier in this chapter in the context of new medications): The client's anticipation of success and the buzz about Dr. B.'s fabulous new method might be the active ingredients, rather than Dr. B.'s therapy itself. And third, notice that you never hear testimonials from the people who dropped out, who weren't helped, or who actually got worse.

So researchers cannot be satisfied with testimonials, no matter how glowing. They know that thanks to the *justification of effort* effect (see Chapter 9), people who have put time, money, and effort into something will tell you it was worth it. No one wants to say, "Yeah, I saw Dr. Blitznik for five years, and boy, was it ever a waste of time."

To guard against these problems, clinical researchers conduct **randomized controlled trials,** in which people with a given problem or disorder are randomly assigned to one or more treatment groups or to a control group. Sometimes the results have been surprising, even shocking. For example, in the aftermath of natural and human-made disasters, from earthquakes to terrorist attacks, disaster therapists often arrive on the scene to treat survivors for symptoms of trauma. Survivors are pressured or even required to attend one or more trauma-therapy sessions. The therapists' intentions are obviously well-meaning. But consider what the research shows about a popular intervention program called Critical Incident Stress Debriefing (CISD) (Gist & Lubin, 1999; Gist & Woodall, 1999). Its practitioners "debrief" people after a trauma, telling them what symptoms to expect and often encouraging them to vent their emotions. Yet independent assessments of CISD find that most people benefit just as much by simply talking with friends and other survivors. Sometimes the CISD intervention *slows* recovery, by preventing victims from drawing on their own wellsprings of resilience. And sometimes the intervention actually *harms* people because of the scientifically unsupported techniques the therapists use, such as having survivors keep ventilating their emotions without also learning good methods of coping.

Each school of therapy approaches problems differently. Empirical research helps determine which method is best suited for which problem.

You can see, then, why the careful assessment of psychotherapeutic claims and methods is so important. We turn now to the evidence showing the benefits of psychotherapy, and which therapies work best.

What Works? The APA's Division of Clinical Psychology convened a task force to assess the research evaluating specific methods for specific problems (Chambless et al., 1996, 1998). To qualify as an *empirically supported treatment*, a method had to have been tested repeatedly against a placebo or another treatment, and it had to have its efficacy demonstrated by at least two different investigators. Although the task force could not assess every therapy in existence, one key finding emerged clearly: For many problems and most emotional disorders, cognitive and behavior therapies are the method of choice. These therapies are particularly effective for the following problems:

▶ *Depression.* Cognitive therapy's greatest success has been in the treatment of mood disorders, especially depression. It is often more effective than antidepressant drugs alone, and people in cognitive therapy are also less likely than those on drugs to relapse when the treatment is over. The reason may be that the lessons learned in cognitive therapy last a long time, according to follow-ups done from 15 months to many years after treatment (Antonuccio et al., 1999; McNally, 1994; Seligman et al., 1999; Whisman, 1993).

   Cognitive therapy can even reduce the risk of developing depression. One intervention program targeted fifth- and sixth-grade children at risk of depression, teaching them to examine the evidence for and against their pessimistic beliefs and generate positive ways of coping. A control group of children did not get this training. As you can see in Figure 17.3, after the training, children in the intervention group had lower depression scores than did those in the control group at all four follow-up sessions, even two years later (Gillham et al., 1995).

▶ *Anxiety disorders.* Exposure techniques are more effective than any other treatment for posttraumatic stress disorder and agoraphobia. Systematic desensitization is usually all that is necessary in effectively treating specific phobias, such as fear of dogs or of public speaking. And cognitive-behavior therapy is often more effective than medication for panic disorder, generalized anxiety disorder, and obsessive–compulsive disorder (Kozak, Liebowitz, & Foa, 2000; Schwartz et al., 1996).

randomized controlled trials Research designed to determine the effectiveness of a new medication or form of therapy, in which people with a given problem or disorder are randomly assigned to one or more treatment groups or to a control group.

Figure 17.3

INOCULATING CHILDREN AGAINST DEPRESSION

This graph shows the percentage of children who were at moderate to high risk of depression (pretest), and their depression scores after a cognitive intervention (posttest) and during four follow-up assessments. Notice that the effects of the intervention were still strong two years later, as the children entered adolescence (Gillham et al., 1995).

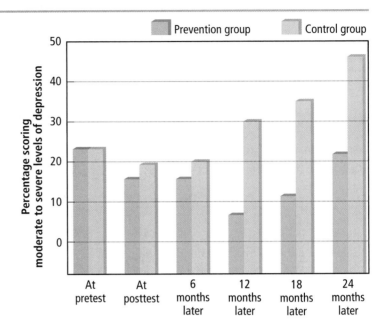

▶ *Anger and impulsive violence.* Cognitive therapy is often successful in reducing chronic anger, abusiveness, and hostility, and it also teaches people how to express anger more calmly and constructively (Deffenbacher et al., 1996, 1998; Kassinove, 1995). (However, many of the growing number of court-mandated "anger management programs" are run by people without specific training either in psychotherapy or cognitive-behavioral methods.)

▶ *Health problems.* Cognitive and behavior therapies are highly successful in helping people cope with pain, chronic fatigue syndrome, headaches, and irritable bowel syndrome; quit smoking or overcome other addictions; recover from eating disorders such as bulimia and binge eating; and manage other health problems (Butler et al., 1991; J. Skinner et al., 1990; Wilson & Fairburn, 1993).

▶ *Sleep disorders.* Cognitive-behavior therapy is as effective as medication in the short run for insomnia, circadian rhythm disorders, poor sleep habits, and other sleep problems; and it is more effective in the long run, because medications often make sleep disorders worse (Morin et al., 1999; Stepanski & Perlis, 2000).

▶ *Childhood and adolescent behavior problems.* Behavior therapy is the most effective treatment for behavior problems that range from bed-wetting to defiant rebelliousness, and even for problems that have biological origins, such as autism (Green, 1996). A meta-analysis of more than 100 studies of children and adolescents found that behavioral treatments worked better than others regardless of the child's age, the therapist's experience, or the specific problem (Weisz et al., 1995).

The APA task force also reported that young adults with schizophrenia are greatly helped by family intervention therapies that teach parents behavioral skills in dealing with their troubled children, and that educate the family in coping with the illness constructively (Chambless et al., 1998; Goldstein & Miklowitz, 1995). Nine studies found that in a two-year period, only 30 percent of the schizophrenic patients in such family intervention treatments relapsed, compared to 65 percent of those whose families were not involved. Family therapy, especially when designed to be culturally sensitive to the family's culture of origin, has also been shown to be effective for delinquent, aggressive adolescents (Dudley-Grant, 2001).

Of course, as the APA task force acknowledged, these important findings have limitations. Cognitive-behavior therapies are designed for specific, identifiable problems, but sometimes people seek therapy for less clearly defined reasons. They may wish to introspect about their feelings and lives, find solace and courage, or explore moral issues. Moreover, in spite of their many successes, behavior and cognitive therapies have had failures, especially with people unmotivated to carry out a behavioral or cognitive program or who have ingrained personality disorders and psychoses (Brody, 1990; Foa & Emmelkamp, 1983).

Special Problems and Populations. Some problems, and some clients, are immune to any single kind of therapy but may respond to *combined* methods. For example, people who have severe, recurrent depressions sometimes do better on a combination of antidepressants and psychotherapy than with either method alone (Keller et al., 2000; Thase et al., 1997). A promising treatment for sex offenders combines cognitive therapy, behavioral techniques, sex education, group therapy, and social-skills training (Abel et al., 1988; Kaplan, Morales, & Becker, 1993).

Some therapies are targeted for the problems of particular populations. For example, *rehabilitation psychologists* are concerned with the assessment and treatment of people who are physically disabled, temporarily or permanently, because of chronic pain, severe physical injuries, epilepsy, arthritis, cancer, addictions, or other conditions. They conduct research to find the best ways to teach disabled people to work and live independently, overcome motivational slumps, improve their sex lives, and follow healthy regimens. Their approach to treatment is flexible, often including behavior therapy, group counseling, job training, and community intervention. Because more people are surviving traumatic injuries and living long enough to develop chronic medical conditions, rehabilitation psychology is one of the fastest-growing areas of health care (Frank, Gluck, & Buckelew, 1990).

Some problems require more than one-on-one help from a psychotherapist. *Community psychologists* set up programs at a community level, often coordinating outpatient services at local clinics with support from family and friends. Some community interventions are designed to prevent psychological problems from developing in high-risk groups. Others are designed to help people in the aftermath of natural or human-made disasters (Gist & Lubin, 1999). Still other programs help people who have severe, chronic mental disorders, such as schizophrenia, and who need a comprehensive program to help them function. Although drugs are helpful, even essential, for such individuals, they are not sufficient; a drug can reduce symptoms but cannot teach the person how to get (or hold) a job. In some community interventions, mentally ill people live in a group home where they get counseling, job and skills training, and a support network. Other community approaches include family therapy, foster care and family home alternatives, and family support groups (Orford, 1992). Without these community approaches, many mentally ill people are treated at hospitals, released to the streets, and stop taking their medications. Their psychotic symptoms return, they are rehospitalized, and the revolving-door cycle continues (Luhrmann, 2000).

In sum, the factors contributing to successful therapy are qualities of the participants, the therapeutic alliance, and the specific methods of the therapy:

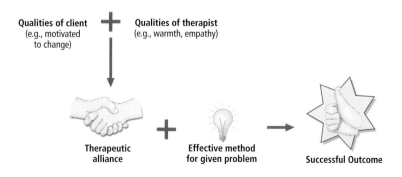

Qualities of client (e.g., motivated to change)   Qualities of therapist (e.g., warmth, empathy)

Therapeutic alliance   +   Effective method for given problem   →   Successful Outcome

When Therapy Harms

Candace Newmaker, age 10 (top), was smothered to death during a session of "rebirthing" therapy. The therapists, Julie Ponder and Connell Watkins (bottom), were convicted of reckless child abuse resulting in death, and were sentenced to 16 years in prison.

In May 2000, police arrested four people on charges of recklessly causing the death of 10-year-old Candace Newmaker during a session of "rebirthing" therapy. The procedure, which its proponents claim will help adopted children form attachments to their adoptive parents by "reliving" birth, was captured on closed circuit television as the girl's mother watched in a nearby room.

The child was completely wrapped in a blanket that supposedly simulated the womb, and was surrounded by large pillows. The therapists then pressed in on the pillows to simulate contractions and told the girl to push her way out of the blanket over her head. Candace repeatedly said that she could not breathe and felt she was going to die. But instead of unwrapping her, the therapists said, "You've got to push hard if you want to be born—or do you want to stay in there and die?"

Candace lost consciousness and was rushed to a local hospital, where she died the next day. Connell Watkins and Julie Ponder, unlicensed social workers who operated the counseling center, were sentenced to 16 years in prison for reckless child abuse resulting in death. Their two assistants, Brita St. Clair and Jack McDaniels, using the age-old "we were only following orders" excuse, were sentenced to 10 years' probation. "The defendants were neither trained or experienced," their attorney said. They "simply did what they were told to do"—which was to sit on the struggling child as she smothered to death.

Every treatment and intervention, including aspirin, carries risks, and so does psychotherapy. But the risks to clients increase when any of the following occurs:

1 *Sexual intimacies or other unethical behavior on the part of the therapist.* Movies often portray therapists who behave unethically, as if this were normal and acceptable practice. In *Prince of Tides,* for example, Barbra Streisand played a psychiatrist who becomes sexually involved with her client's brother, who then becomes her client too. In *Good Will Hunting,* Robin Williams played a therapist who reveals his own personal problems to his client and physically threatens him. Such films imply that the violation of therapist-client boundaries and even sexual relations are common, accepted, harmless practices. But they are prohibited by the APA's ethical guidelines.

Some therapists behave like cult leaders, persuading their clients that their mental health depends on staying in therapy and severing their connections to their "toxic" families (Mithers, 1994; Watters & Ofshe, 1999). Such "psychotherapy cults" are created by the therapist's use of techniques that foster the client's dependency and isolation, prevent the client from terminating therapy, and reduce the client's ability to think critically (see Chapter 8). In Pennsylvania in 1997, 13 former patients of a group practice called Genesis Associates filed lawsuits claiming that they had been victims of these techniques.

2 *Prejudice or cultural ignorance on the part of the therapist.* Some therapists may be prejudiced against their clients because of the client's gender, culture, religion, or sexual orientation. A therapist may try to induce the client to conform to the therapist's standards and values, even if they are not appropriate for the client or in the client's best interest (Brodsky, 1982; López, 1989). For example, for many years gay men and lesbians who entered therapy were told that homosexuality was a mental illness that could be cured. Some of the so-called treatments were harsh, such as shock applied to the genitals for "inappropriate" arousal. Other kinds of "reparative" therapies that supposedly turn gay men and lesbians into heterosexuals still surface from time to time. They are often promoted in campaigns by conservative Christians who believe that homosexuality is a sin, with testimonials from alleged converts. But there is no reliable empirical evidence from scientifically designed studies supporting these claims, and both the American Psychological Association and the American Psychiatric Association have gone on record opposing reparative therapies on ethical and scientific grounds.

3 *Inappropriate or coercive influence, which can create new problems for the client.* In a healthy therapeutic alliance, therapists and clients come to agree on an explanation for the client's problems. Of course, the therapist will influence this explanation, according to his or her training and philosophy. This is why Freudian patients have dreams of erotic symbols, patients in Jungian therapy have dreams of archetypes, and REBT clients, no doubt, dream of Albert Ellis telling them to quit being irrational! Some therapists, however, cross the line. They so zealously believe in the prevalence of certain problems or disorders that they actually induce the client to produce the symptoms they are looking for (McHugh, 1993; Merskey, 1995; Watters & Ofshe, 1999). Therapist influence, and sometimes downright coercion, is a likely reason for the huge numbers of people who were diagnosed with multiple personality disorder in the 1980s and 1990s (see Chapter 16) and for the epidemic of recovered memories of sexual abuse (see Chapter 10).

4 *The use of empirically unsupported, potentially dangerous techniques.* In Chapter 10 we saw that memory does not work like a videocamera or tape recorder; memories are not "buried" in the brain, awaiting magic methods to root them out. Yet many therapists claim that they can help clients accurately retrieve painful old memories. They use various unreliable methods to do so, including hypnosis, sodium amytal (a barbiturate misleadingly called "truth serum"), guided imagery, dream analysis, and other techniques that enhance the client's suggestibility (Mazzoni, Loftus, & Kirsch, 2001). For example, experimental research has found that when a therapist tells a client that his or her dreams are memories of something that really happened, suggestible clients begin to confuse their dreams with reality (Mazzoni et al., 1999). Many research psychologists are greatly concerned that a significant minority of registered, licensed psychotherapists—between one-fourth and one-third of them—have used one or more of these inappropriate techniques specifically to help clients "retrieve" memories of sexual abuse, as you can see in Figure 17.4 (Poole et al., 1995). Replications of this finding in the United States and Canada have shown that the percentages have not declined appreciably in recent years (Katz, 2001; Polusny & Follette, 1996; Nunez, Poole, & Memon, 2002).

The techniques used in "rebirthing" therapy are likewise unsupported by scientific research, even though many of rebirthing's practitioners have advanced degrees. This therapy was born in the 1970s, when its founder claimed he had reexperienced his own birth while taking a bath. (Many psychological problems, he somehow decided, can be

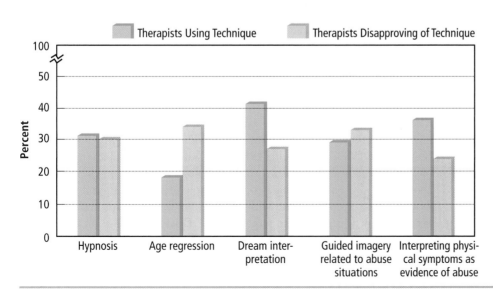

Figure 17.4

PSYCHOLOGISTS' ATTITUDES TOWARD THE USE OF SUGGESTIVE TECHNIQUES FOR RECOVERING MEMORIES OF SEXUAL ABUSE

Although suggestive techniques in psychotherapy can produce confabulation and false memories, between one-fourth and one-third of licensed clinical psychologists use these methods regularly "to help clients recall memories of sexual abuse." About the same percentages disapprove of using such techniques. (The rest neither use the methods nor disapprove of them.) The percentages are from two combined samples of American clinical psychologists with Ph.D.s, randomly drawn from names listed in the National Register of Health Service Providers in Psychology (Poole et al., 1995). The numbers have not changed appreciably in recent years (Katz, 2001; Nunez, Poole, & Memon, 2002).

traced to a traumatic experience in the womb or during birth.) But the basic assumptions of this method—that people can recover from trauma, insecure attachment, or other psychological problems by "reliving" their births—are completely contradicted by the vast research on infancy, attachment, memory, and posttraumatic stress disorder and its treatment. For that matter, why should anyone assume that the experience of being born is traumatic? Isn't it pretty nice to be let out of cramped quarters and see daylight and beaming parental faces?

To avoid these risks and benefit from what *good*, effective psychotherapy has to offer, people looking for the right therapy must become educated consumers.

QUICK QUIZ

Have you formed a therapeutic alliance with quizzes?

1. Which of the following is the most important predictor of successful therapy? (a) how long it lasts, (b) the insight it provides the client, (c) the bond between therapist and client, (d) whether the therapist and client are matched according to gender

2. In general, which type of psychotherapy is most effective for anxiety and depression?

3. What kind of psychologist is trained to help people cope with chronic illness or disability or recover from injury?

4. What are four possible sources of harm in psychotherapy?

5. Ferdie is spending too much time playing softball and not enough time studying, so he signs up for "sportaholic therapy (ST)." The therapist tells him the cure for his "addiction" is to quit softball cold turkey and tap his temples three times whenever he feels the urge to play. After a few months, Ferdie announces that ST isn't helping and he's going to stop coming. The therapist gives him testimonials of other clients who swear by ST, explaining that Ferdie's doubts are actually a sign that the therapy is working. What are some problems with this argument? (Bonus: What kind of therapy might help Ferdie manage his time better?)

Answers:

1. c 2. cognitive-behavior 3. rehabilitation psychologist 4. unethical behavior, prejudice or biased treatment, inappropriate or coercive influence, and the use of empirically unsupported techniques 5. The therapist has violated the principle of falsifiability (see Chapter 2). If Ferdie is helped by the treatment, that shows it works; if he is not helped, that still shows it works but Ferdie is "denying" its benefits. Also, Ferdie is not hearing testimonials from people who have dropped out of ST and were not helped by it. (Bonus: a good behavioral time-management program might help, so Ferdie can play softball *and* get other things done, too.)

The Value and Values of Psychotherapy

Modern psychotherapy has been of enormous value to many people. But in recent years, psychotherapists themselves have raised some important questions about the *values* inherent in what they do (Cushman, 1995; Hillman & Ventura, 1992; Wallach & Wallach, 1983; Zilbergeld, 1983). How much personal change is possible, and do some therapists promise their clients too much? Does psychotherapy, by encouraging people to look inward to their feelings and woes, foster a preoccupation with the self over relationships and the importance of contributing to the larger world? Does it promise unrealistic notions of endless happiness and complete self-fulfillment?

Many people in North America have an optimistic, can-do, let's-fix-this-fast attitude toward all problems, whether mental, physical, or social. In contrast, as discussed in Chapter 15, Eastern cultures have a less optimistic view

THINKING CRITICALLY

Ask Questions

The benefits of psychotherapy are well documented, but we can ask questions about its implicit messages. Does psychotherapy foster unrealistic expectations of personal change? Does it promote individualism at the expense of community and relationships?

of change and they tend to be more tolerant of events they regard as being outside of human control. In the Japanese practice of Morita therapy, therefore, clients are taught to accept
and live with their most troubling emotions, instead of trying
to eradicate these psychological weeds from the lawn of life
(Reynolds, 1987). Some Western psychotherapists now teach
techniques of mindful meditation and greater self-acceptance
instead of constant self-improvement (Kabat-Zinn, 1994).

Most people get all the help they need from talking things
over with good friends or with others who are in the same
situation they are. But if you have a persistent problem that
you do not know how to solve, one that causes you considerable unhappiness and that has lasted six months or more,
it may be time to look for help. As the research in this chapter suggests, consumers who are thinking about psychotherapy should consider these important matters:

THE SEVEN DWARFS AFTER THERAPY

▶ *Choosing a therapist.* Make sure you are dealing with a reputable individual with
appropriate credentials and training. (The therapists in Colorado had learned
"rebirthing" in a two-week training course. One of the members of the Colorado
Mental Health Grievance Board noted with dismay that her *hairdresser's* training
took 1,500 hours, whereas anyone could quickly become "certified" in a method
that could take a child's life.) Your school counseling center is a good place to
start. You might also seek out a university psychology clinic, where you can get
therapy with a graduate student in training; these students are closely supervised
and the fees will be lower. If you know the kind of therapy you want, check your
phone book; many therapists are listed according to the kind of therapy they do.

▶ *Choosing a therapy.* As we have seen, not all therapies are equally effective for
all problems. You should not spend four years in psychodynamic therapy for
panic attacks, which can generally be helped in a few sessions of cognitive-
behavior therapy. Likewise, as the APA task force recommends, if you have a
specific emotional problem, such as depression, anger, or anxiety, or if you are
coping with chronic health problems, look for a cognitive or behavior therapist.
However, if you just want to discuss your life with a wise and empathic person,
the kind of therapy may not matter so much.

▶ *Deciding when to leave.* For the common emotional problems of life, short-
term treatment is usually sufficient. About half of all people in therapy improve
within 8 to 11 sessions, and 76 percent improve within six months to a year;
after a year, further change is minimal (Howard et al., 1986; Kopta et al.,
1994). However, people with more severe mental disorders do often require
and benefit from continued therapeutic care (Shadish et al., 2000).

If you begin a time-limited treatment, such as 12 sessions of brief therapy or
a seven-session airplane-phobia program, you ought to stick with it to the end.
In unlimited therapy, however, you have the right to determine when enough is
enough, especially if the therapist has been unable to help you with your problem after a considerable length of time. If you have made a real effort to work
with a therapist and there has been no result after ample time and effort, the
reason could have as much to do with the treatment or therapist as with you.
But don't expect quick fixes. Successful therapy requires motivation, persistence,
a willingness to face possibly unwelcome truths, and the courage to change.

In the hands of an empathic and knowledgeable practitioner, psychotherapy can
help you make decisions and clarify your values and goals. It can teach you new skills
and new ways of thinking. It can help you get along better with your family and break

out of destructive family patterns. It can get you through bad times when no one seems to care or to understand what you are feeling. It can teach you how to manage depression, anxiety, and anger.

However, despite its many benefits, psychotherapy cannot transform you into someone you're not. It cannot turn an introvert into an extrovert. It cannot cure an emotional disorder overnight. It cannot provide a life without problems. And it is not intended to substitute for experience—for work that is satisfying, relationships that are sustaining, activities that are enjoyable. As Socrates knew, the unexamined life is not worth living. But as we would add, the unlived life is not worth examining.

Taking Psychology with You

HOW TO EVALUATE SELF-HELP GROUPS AND BOOKS

Not all psychological problems require the aid of a professional. Nowadays, thousands of programs and books are designed to help people help themselves. More than 2,000 self-help books are published every year, and an estimated 7 to 15 million adults belong to self-help groups. Do these books and groups help?

Self-help groups are available (on line and in person) for alcoholics, relatives of alcoholics, people suffering from depression, anorexia, or schizophrenia, women with breast cancer, parents of murdered children, diabetics, rape victims, stepparents, relatives of Alzheimer's patients, and people with just about any other concern you can think of (Davison, Pennebaker, & Dickerson, 2000). Members say that the primary benefits are the awareness that they are not alone, encouragement when they are feeling down, and help in feeling better about themselves.

Self-help groups offer understanding, empathy, and solutions to shared problems. Such groups can be reassuring and supportive in ways that family, friends, and psychotherapists sometimes may not be (Dunkel-Schetter, 1984). For example, people with disabilities face unique challenges that involve coping not only with physical problems but also with the condescen-

sion, hostility, and prejudice of many nondisabled people (Linton, 1998). Other disabled people, who share these challenges, can offer the right kind of empathy and useful advice.

Self-help groups do not provide psychotherapy and they are not designed to help people with serious psychological difficulties. They are not regulated by law or by professional standards, and they vary widely in their philosophies and methods. Some are accepting and tolerant, offering support and spiritual guidance. Others are confrontational and coercive, and members who disagree with the premises of the group may be made to feel deviant, crazy, or "in denial." If you choose to become part of a support group, be sure it falls in the first category.

As for self-help books, there is one for every problem, from how to toilet-train your children to how to find happiness in seven steps. When self-help books propose a specific, well-supported program for the reader to follow, they can actually be as effective as treatment administered by a therapist—*if* the reader follows through with the program (Christensen & Jacobson, 1994). Unfortunately, most books do not do

this. After serving as chair of the APA's Task Force on Self-Help Therapies, Gerald Rosen (1981) concluded, "Psychologists have published untested materials, advanced exaggerated claims, and accepted the use of misleading titles that encourage unrealistic expectations regarding outcome." (That was more than 20 years ago, and the situation is worse today.) The Task Force therefore offered consumers some guidelines for evaluating a self-help book:

▶ *The authors should be qualified,* which means that they have conducted good research or are thoroughly versed in the field. Personal accounts by people who have survived diffi-

Formal and informal support groups provide a setting for sharing concerns and exchanging constructive advice, as these men with AIDS are doing.

culties can be helpful and inspirational, of course, but an author's own experience is not grounds for generalizing to everyone.

▶ *The book's advice should be based on sound scientific theory,* not on the author's pseudoscientific theories, armchair observations, or political views. This criterion rules out, among other kinds of books, most of the love manuals in which the author's own lovelorn stories or tales of woe with the other sex become the basis of an entire philosophy of love, marriage, and happiness. *Men Are from Mars, Women Are from Venus,* by John Gray (whose "Ph.D." was from a mail-order, unaccredited college), is based on pure stereotyping; *Why Marriages Succeed or Fail,* by John Gottman (whose Ph.D. in psychology is from a prestigious university), is based on years of experimental research.

▶ *The book should not promise the impossible.* This lets out books that promise you perfect sex, total love, or high self-esteem in 30 days. It also lets out books or tapes that promote techniques whose effectiveness has been disconfirmed by research, such as dream analysis or "subliminal" tapes, discussed in Chapter 6.

▶ *The advice should be organized in a systematic program,* step by step, not as a vague pep talk to "take charge of your life" or "find love in your heart"; and the reader should be told how to evaluate his or her progress.

Some books do meet these criteria. One is *Changing for Good* (Prochaska, Norcross, & DiClemente, 1994), which describes the ingredients of effective change that apply to people in and out of therapy. But as long as people yearn for a magic bullet to cure their problems, quick-fix solutions will find a ready audience.

Summary

Biological Treatments for Mental Disorders

▶ Over the centuries, people trying to understand and treat psychological disorders have alternated between biological and psychological explanations. Today, biological treatments are in the ascendance because of research findings on the genetic and biological causes of some disorders, and because of economic and social factors.

▶ The medications most commonly prescribed for mental disorders include *antipsychotic drugs,* used in treating schizophrenia and other psychotic disorders; *antidepressants,* used in treating depression, anxiety disorders, and obsessive–compulsive disorder; *tranquilizers,* often prescribed for emotional problems; and *lithium carbonate,* a salt used to treat bipolar disorder. Antidepressants are generally more effective for mood disorders than are tranquilizers, which can become addictive.

▶ Drawbacks of drug treatment include the *placebo effect;* high dropout and relapse rates among people who take medications without also learning how to cope with their problems; the difficulty of finding the correct dose (the *therapeutic window*) for each individual, compounded by the fact that a person's ethnicity, sex, and age can influence a drug's effectiveness; and the long-term risks of medication, known and unknown. Medication can be helpful and can even save lives, but in an age where commercial interests are heavily invested in promoting drugs for psychological problems, the public is largely unaware of drugs' limitations. Medication should not be prescribed mindlessly and routinely, especially when non-drug therapies can work as well as drugs for many mood and behavioral problems. Also, the fact that a disorder appears to have biological origins or involve biochemical abnormalities does not mean that biological treatments are the only appropriate ones; psychotherapy can change brain patterns just as medication can.

▶ When drugs or psychotherapy have failed to help seriously disturbed people, some psychiatrists have intervened directly in the brain. *Psychosurgery,* which destroys selected areas of the brain thought to be responsible for a psychological problem, is rarely done today. *Electroconvulsive therapy* (ECT), in which a brief current is sent through the brain, has been used successfully to treat suicidal depression. However, controversy exists about its effects on the brain and the appropriateness of its use. A newer method, repeated *transcranial magnetic stimulation (TMS),* is showing promise in treating severe depression.

Kinds of Psychotherapy

▶ *Psychodynamic ("depth") therapies* include Freudian *psychoanalysis* and its modern variations, such as approaches based on *object-relations theory,* which explore unconscious dynamics. Freud used the technique of *free association* to try to uncover unconscious memories and help the patient achieve *insight*. Modern psychodynamic approaches share an emphasis on the importance of *transference* in therapy, the role of childhood experiences, and breaking through the patient's defenses.

▶ *Behavior and cognitive therapies* draw on principles of learning and cognition. They have different origins and use different techniques, but in practice are often combined. Behavior therapists use such methods as *systematic desensitization,* based on *counterconditioning; exposure (flooding); behavioral records;* and *skills training.* Cognitive therapists aim to change the irrational thoughts involved in negative emotions and self-defeating actions. Albert Ellis's *rational emotive behavior therapy (REBT)* and Aaron Beck's form of cognitive therapy are two leading approaches.

▶ *Humanist therapy* attempts to help people feel better about themselves by focusing on here-and-now issues and on the human capacity for self-fulfillment and self-actualization. Carl Rogers's *client-centered (nondirective) therapy* is the best-known of humanist approaches. Rogers emphasized the importance of the therapist's empathy and ability to provide *unconditional positive regard* to the client. *Existential therapy* helps people cope with philosophical dilemmas, such as the meaning of life and the fear of death. Both emphasize the human capacity for free will to overcome life's problems.

▶ *Family therapies* share the view that individual problems develop in the context of the whole family network. A family therapist may use psychodynamic, behavioral, cognitive, or humanist approaches, but they tend to share a *family-systems perspective,* understanding that any one person's behavior in the family affects everyone else. Some family therapists ask clients to identify patterns of behavior across generations. In *couples therapy,* the therapist sees both partners in a relationship to help them resolve ongoing quarrels and disputes.

▶ In practice, most therapists are *integrative,* drawing on many methods and ideas. Whatever their method, successful therapies share the goal of helping people form more adaptive "life stories."

Evaluating Psychotherapy

▶ A *scientist–practitioner gap* has developed because of the different assumptions held by researchers and many clinicians regarding the value of empirical research for doing psychotherapy and for assessing its effectiveness. The gap has led to a proliferation of scientifically unsupported psychotherapies. Because of this and because of economic pressures on insurers and rising

health costs, psychotherapists are increasingly being called on to provide empirical assessments of therapy.

▶ Successful therapy requires a *therapeutic alliance* between the therapist and the client, so that they understand each other and can work together. The clients who benefit most from psychotherapy are motivated to solve their problems; hostile, negative individuals are more resistant to treatment. For their part, good therapists are empathic, warm, and constructive. When therapist and client are of different ethnicities, both must try to avoid prejudice, misunderstanding, and stereotyping. The therapist must also be able to distinguish normal cultural patterns from signs of mental illness.

▶ In assessing the effectiveness of psychotherapy, researchers must control for the placebo effect (as with new medication) and the *justification of effort* effect. They rely on *randomized controlled trials* to determine which therapies are *empirically supported treatments.*

▶ Some therapies are demonstrably better than others for specific problems. Behavior therapy and cognitive-behavior therapy are the most effective for depression, anxiety disorders, anger problems, certain health problems and eating disorders, insomnia and other sleep disorders, and childhood and adolescent behavior problems. Family therapies are helpful for children and young adults with schizophrenia and for delinquent, aggressive adolescents.

▶ Some problems and target populations, such as people with severe depression or sex offenders, may respond best to combined therapeutic approaches. *Rehabilitation psychologists* are concerned with the assessment and treatment of people who are physically disabled. *Community psychologists* set up programs in the community to prevent and treat mental-health problems or help people cope in the aftermath of disaster.

▶ In some cases, therapy is harmful. The therapist may behave unethically, as by permitting a sexual relationship with the client. The therapist may be prejudiced against the client's gender, ethnicity, religion, or sexual orientation. The therapist may inadvertently create new disorders in the client through undue influence or suggestion. And the therapist may use empirically unsupported and potentially harmful techniques, such as unreliable methods of "retrieving" memories of abuse or of "rebirthing."

The Value and Values of Psychotherapy

▶ Therapists have pointed out that therapy often contains implicit cultural values, such as whether change is desirable and easy, or whether self-acceptance is a more realistic goal.

▶ Because of the growing number of unlicensed psychotherapists and the rise of new therapies whose methods and assumptions have little or no empirical validation, consumers need to choose a therapist carefully, select the kind of therapy best suited for their problems, and be realistic about what they expect of psychotherapy.

Key Terms

antipsychotic drugs (neuroleptics) 622

antidepressant drugs 623

   monoamine oxidase inhibitors (MAOIs) 623

   tricyclic antidepressants 623

   selective serotonin reuptake inhibitors (SSRIs) 623

tranquilizers 623

lithium carbonate 624

placebo effect 625

therapeutic window 625

tardive dyskinesia 625

psychosurgery 627

prefrontal lobotomy 627

electroconvulsive therapy (ECT) 627

transcranial magnetic stimulation (TMS) 627

psychoanalysis 629

free association 629

psychodynamic ("depth") therapies 629

transference 629

object-relations (psychodynamic) therapy 630

behavior therapy 630

systematic desensitization 630

counterconditioning 630

exposure (flooding) 631

behavioral records 631

skills training (modeling and role playing) 631

cognitive therapy 632

rational emotive behavior therapy (Ellis) 632

humanist therapy 634

client-centered (nondirective) therapy 634

unconditional positive regard 634

existential therapy 634

family therapy 635

family-systems perspective 636

couples therapy 637

integrative approach to psychotherapy 637

scientist–practitioner gap 639

therapeutic alliance 641

randomized controlled trials 642

empirically supported treatment 643

rehabilitation psychologists 645

community psychologists 645

◤OOKING BACK

- What kinds of drugs are used to treat psychological disorders? (pp. 622–624)

- Are antidepressants always the best treatment for depression? (p. 625)

- Can mental disorders be cured by brain surgery? (p. 627)

- Why is "shock therapy" hailed by some clinicians but condemned by others? (p. 627)

- Why are psychodynamic therapies called "depth" therapies? (p. 629)

- How can therapies based on learning principles help you change your bad habits? (pp. 630–632)

- How do cognitive therapists help people get rid of self-defeating thoughts? (pp. 632–633)

- Why do humanist therapists focus on the "here and now" instead of the "why and how"? (p. 634)

- Why do family therapists prefer to treat families rather than individuals? (p. 635)

- What is the "scientist-practitioner gap" and why has it been widening? (pp. 639–640)

- What is the "therapeutic alliance" and why does it matter? (p. 641)

- What sorts of people make the best therapists and the best clients? (p. 641)

- Which form of psychotherapy is most likely to help if you are anxious or depressed? (pp. 643–644)

- Under what conditions can psychotherapy be harmful? (pp. 646–648)

 **Go to** **WWW.PRENHALL.COM/WADE** **for activities, practice tests, and review material.**

Epilogue

TAKING PSYCHOLOGY WITH YOU

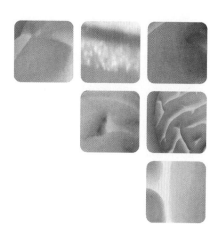

We [human beings] never stop investigating. We are never satisfied that we know enough to get by. Every question we answer leads on to another question. This has become the greatest survival trick of our species.

DESMOND MORRIS

You have come a long way since the beginning of this book. It is now time to stand back and ask yourself where you've been and what you've learned from the many studies, topics, and controversies that you have read about. What fundamental principles emerge, and how can you take them with you into your own life?

The Five Strands of Human Experience

In Chapter 1, we described five general perspectives on human behavior that guide the assumptions and methods of psychologists. Each of these perspectives on human experience offers questions to ask when trying to understand or change a particular aspect of your own life:

1 *Biological influences.* As physical creatures, we are influenced by our bodies and our brains. Physiology affects the rhythms of our lives, our perceptions of reality, our ability to learn, the intensity of our emotions, our temperaments, and in some cases our vulnerability to emotional disorder.

Thus, when you are distressed, you might want to start by asking yourself what might be going on in your body. Do you have a physical condition that might be affecting your behavior? Do you have a temperamental tendency to be easily aroused or to be calm? Are alcohol or other drugs altering your ability to make decisions or behave as you would like? Might an irregular schedule be disrupting your physical functions and impairing your efficiency? Are you under unusual pressures that increase your physical stress?

2 *Learning influences.* From the moment of birth, we begin learning and are exquisitely sensitive to our environments. What we do and how we do it are often a result of our learning histories and the specific situations we are in. We respond to the environment, and, in turn, our acts have consequences that influence future behavior. The right environment and rewards can help us cope better with disabilities, get along better with others, and even become more creative and happy. The wrong kind can foster boredom, hostility, and discontent.

So, as you analyze a situation, you will want to examine the contingencies and consequences governing your behavior and that of others. What rewards are maintaining your behavior? Of the many messages being aimed at you by television, books, parents, and teachers, which have the greatest influence? Who are your role models, the people you most admire and wish to emulate?

3 *Social and cultural influences.* Although most Westerners think of themselves as independent creatures, everyone conforms to some extent to the expectations and demands of others. Spouses, lovers, friends, bosses, parents, and perfect strangers "pull our strings" in ways we may not recognize. We conform to group pressures, obey authorities, and blossom or wilt in close relationships. Throughout life, we need "contact comfort"—sometimes in the literal touch or embrace of others and sometimes in shared experience or conversation. Further, we are all strongly influenced by our culture's norms and society's roles, which specify countless verbal and nonverbal rules governing the behavior of employers and employees, husbands and wives, parents and children, strangers and friends, and men and women. Whenever you find yourself wondering irritably why "*those* people are

behaving that way," chances are that a cultural difference or misunderstanding is at work.

So, in solving problems, you might think about the people in your life who are affecting you. Do your friends and relatives support you or hinder you in achieving your goals? How do your ethnicity and nationality affect you? What gender roles do they specify for you and your partners in close relationships, and what would happen if you ignored the norms of your role? Are your conflicts with others a result of cultural misunderstandings—due, for instance, to differing rules for expressing emotion?

4 *Cognitive influences.* Our species is, above all, the animal that explains things. These explanations may not always be realistic or sensible, but they continually influence our actions and choices. When you have a problem, ask yourself how you are framing the situation you are in. What biases might you bring to your assessment of the problem—e.g., the confirmation bias, the hindsight bias, the self-serving bias? Are your explanations of what is causing the problem reasonable? Have you checked them out to see if they are right or wrong? Are you wallowing in negative thoughts? Do you attribute your successes to luck but take all the blame for your failures—or do you take credit for your successes and blame everyone else for your failures? Are you responding to other people's expectations in a mindless way?

5 *Psychodynamic influences.* People are often unaware of the reasons they are getting themselves in trouble, just as they are unaware of the defense mechanisms they use to rationalize mistakes and protect self-esteem. If you find that you are repeating self-defeating patterns, expectations, and emotional reactions, you might want to consider why. Do other people "push your buttons" for reasons you cannot explain? Are you displacing feelings about your parents onto your friends or intimates? Are you carrying around "unfinished business" from childhood losses and hurts?

Keep in mind that no single one of these factors operates in isolation from the others. The forces that govern our behavior are as intertwined as strands of ivy on a wall, and it can be hard to see where one strand begins and another ends. This message, if enough people believed it, would probably put an end to the pop-psych industry, which promotes single, simple answers to real-life complexities. Some simplifiers of psychology try to reduce human problems to biochemical imbalances or genetic defects. Others argue that anyone can "fulfill any potential," regardless of biology or environment, and that solving problems is merely a matter of having enough determination.

In this book, we have tried to show that the concerns and dilemmas of life do not divide up neatly according to the chapters of an introductory psychology text (even ours). For example, to understand shyness or loneliness, you might consider whether you have a temperamental disposition toward introversion and shyness; your personal learning history; childhood experiences and what you observed from adult role models; how stress, diet, drugs, and sleep patterns might be affecting your mood; and whether you come from a culture that encourages or prohibits assertiveness. It may seem daunting to keep so many factors in mind. But once you get into the habit of seeing a situation from many points of view, relying on single-answer approaches will feel like wearing blinders. And it's a habit that will inoculate you against appealing pop-psych ideas that are unsupported by evidence.

Psychology in Your Life

If the theories and findings in this book are to be of long-lasting personal value to you, they must jump off the printed page and into your daily life. To give you some practice in applying them, let's consider an all-too-common problem—what to do when love is dwindling in a close relationship—and some ideas about where to look in this book for principles and findings that may shed light on it. Our list is far from exhaustive; feel free to come up with additional ideas.

Let's say you have been romantically involved with someone for a year. When the relationship began, you felt very much in love, and you thought your feelings were returned. But for a long time now, your partner's treatment of you has been anything but loving. In fact, your partner makes fun of your faults in front of others and yells at you about the slightest annoyance. Sometimes your partner ignores you for days on end, as if to punish you for some imagined wrong. Your friends advise you to leave the relationship, yet you can't shake the feeling that your partner really loves you. You still occasionally have a great time together, and your partner appears distressed whenever you threaten to leave. You wish you could either improve the relationship or get out, and your inability to act leaves you feeling angry and depressed.

Consider just a few of the topics covered in this book that contribute to understanding your problem and possibly resolving it:

▶ *Approach–avoidance conflicts* (Chapter 12) may help explain why you are both attracted to and repelled by this relationship, and why the closer you approach, the more you want to leave (and vice versa). When a goal is both attractive and painful, it is not unusual to feel uncertain and to vacillate about possible courses of action.

▶ *Intermittent reinforcement* (Chapter 7) may explain why you persist in apparently self-defeating behavior. If staying in the relationship brought *only* punishment or if your partner *always* ignored you, it would be easier to leave. But because your partner intermittently is kind and loving, your "staying around" behavior is rewarded, thereby becoming resistant to extinction.

▶ Past *observational learning* (Chapter 7) may help account for your present behavior. Perhaps your parents have a relationship like the one you are in, and their way of interacting is what you have learned to expect in your own relationships.

▶ If you have an *external locus of control* (Chapter 15), you feel that you cannot control what happens to you; you tend to feel that you are merely a victim of fate, chance, or the wishes of others. People with an internal locus of control feel more in charge of their lives and are less inclined to blame outside circumstances for their difficulties.

▶ *Cognitive-dissonance theory* (Chapter 9) suggests that you may be trying to keep your attitudes and behavior consistent. The cognition "I am in this relationship and choose to be with this person" is dissonant with "This person ignores and mistreats me." Because you are still unable to break up and alter the first cognition, you are working on the second cognition, hoping that your partner will change for the better.

▶ Research on *gender differences* finds that men and women often have different unstated rules about expressing emotion and different definitions of love (Chapters 11 and 12). Perhaps traditional gender roles are preventing you and your partner from communicating your true preferences and feelings.

▶ *Attribution theory* (Chapter 8) addresses the consequences of holding dispositional explanations of another person's behavior (it's due to something about the person) or situational explanations (it's due to something about the circumstances). Recall that unhappy couples tend to make dispositional attributions when the partner does something wrong or thoughtless ("My partner is mean"); happy couples look for situational attributions ("My partner is under a lot of pressure at work"). You might test possible reasons that your partner is treating you badly. Is the behavior characteristic of your partner in many situations—that is, it is typical of his or her personality—or might it be a temporary result of stress or something in the unique relationship with you?

Depending on the origins of your problem, you might choose to cope with the situation as it is; change your attributions about your partner; use learning principles to try to alter your own or your partner's behavior; consider how your perceptions and beliefs are affecting your emotions; seek psychotherapy, with or without your partner (Chapter 17); or leave the relationship.

Our example was an individual problem, but the applications of psychology extend beyond personal concerns to social ones, as we have seen throughout this book: disputes between neighbors and nations; prejudice and cross-cultural relations; the best ways to rear moral, considerate, and competent children; the formulation of social policies, such as ways of improving school performance or reducing drug abuse; and countless other issues.

Of course, research findings often change as new questions are asked, new methods become available, and new theories evolve. That is why the one chapter that may ultimately be most useful to you is the one you may have assumed to be least useful: Chapter 2, "How Psychologists Do Research." The best way to take psychology with you is to understand its basic ways of approaching problems and questions—that is, its principles of critical and scientific thinking. Old theories give way to new ones, dated results yield to contemporary ones, dead-end investigations halt and new directions are taken. But the methods of psychology continue, and critical thinking is their hallmark.

Appendix

STATISTICAL METHODS

Nineteenth-century English statesman Benjamin Disraeli reportedly once named three forms of dishonesty: "lies, damned lies, and statistics." It is certainly true that people can lie with the help of statistics. It happens all the time: Advertisers, politicians, and others with some claim to make either use numbers inappropriately or ignore certain critical ones. (When hearing that "four out of five doctors surveyed" recommended some product, have you ever wondered just how many doctors were surveyed and whether they were representative of all doctors?) People also use numbers to convey a false impression of certainty and objectivity when the true state of affairs is uncertainty or ignorance. But it is people, not statistics, that lie. When statistics are used correctly, they neither confuse nor mislead. On the contrary, they expose unwarranted conclusions, promote clarity and precision, and protect us from our own biases and blind spots.

If statistics are useful anywhere, it is in the study of human behavior. If human beings were all alike, and psychologists could specify all the influences on behavior, there would be no need for statistics. But any time we measure human behavior, we are going to wind up with different observations or scores for different individuals. Statistics can help us spot trends amid the diversity.

This appendix will introduce you to some basic statistical calculations used in psychology. Reading the appendix will not make you into a statistician, but it will acquaint you with some ways of organizing and assessing research data. If you suffer from a "number phobia," relax: You do not need to know much math to understand this material. However, you should have read Chapter 2, which discussed the rationale for using statistics and described various research methods. You may want to review the basic terms and concepts covered in that chapter. Be sure that you can define *hypothesis, sample, correlation, independent variable, dependent variable, random assignment, experimental group, control group, descriptive statistics, inferential statistics* and *test of statistical significance.* (Correlation coefficients, which are described in some detail in Chapter 2, will not be covered here.)

To read the tables in this appendix, you will also need to know the following symbols:

N = the total number of observations or scores in a set

X = an observation or score

Σ = the Greek capital letter sigma, read as "the sum of"

$\sqrt{}$ = the square root of

(*Note:* Boldfaced terms in this appendix are defined in the glossary at the end of the book.)

Organizing Data

Before we can discuss statistics, we need some numbers. Imagine that you are a psychologist and that you are interested in that most pleasing of human qualities, a sense of humor. You suspect that a well-developed funny bone can protect people from the negative emotional effects of stress. You already know that in the months following a stressful event, people who score high on sense-of-humor tests tend to feel less tense and moody than more sobersided individuals do. You realize, though, that this correlational evidence does not prove cause and effect. Perhaps people with a healthy sense of humor have other traits, such as flexibility or creativity, that act as the true stress buffers. To find out whether humor itself really softens the impact of stress, you do an experiment.

First, you randomly assign subjects to two groups, an experimental group and a control group. To keep our calculations simple, let's assume there are only 15 people per group. Each person individually views a silent film that most North Americans find fairly stressful, one showing Australian aboriginal boys undergoing a puberty rite involving genital mutilation. Subjects in the experimental group are instructed to make up a humorous monologue while watching the film. Those in the control group are told to make up a straightforward narrative. After the film, each person answers a mood questionnaire that measures current feelings of tension, depression, aggressiveness, and anxiety. A person's overall score on the questionnaire can range from 1 (no mood disturbance) to 7 (strong mood disturbance). This procedure provides you with 15 "mood disturbance" scores for each group. Have people who tried to be humorous reported less disturbance than those who did not?

Constructing a Frequency Distribution

Your first step might be to organize and condense the "raw data" (the obtained scores) by constructing a **frequency distribution** for each group. A frequency distribution shows how often each possible score actually occurred. To construct one, you first order all the possible scores from highest to lowest. (Our mood disturbance scores will be ordered from 7 to 1.) Then you tally how often each score was actually obtained. Table A.1 gives some hypothetical raw data for the

Table A.1 — Some Hypothetical Raw Data

These scores are for the hypothetical humor-and-stress study described in the text.

Experimental group	4,5,4,4,3,6,5,2,4,3,5,4,4,3,4
Control group	6,4,7,6,6,4,6,7,7,5,5,5,7,6,6

two groups, and Table A.2 shows the two frequency distributions based on these data. From these distributions you can see that the two groups differed. In the experimental group, the extreme scores of 7 and 1 did not occur at all, and the most common score was the middle one, 4. In the control group, a score of 7 occurred four times, the most common score was 6, and no one obtained a score lower than 4.

Because our mood scores have only seven possible values, our frequency distributions are quite manageable. Suppose, though, that your questionnaire had yielded scores that could range from 1 to 50. A frequency distribution with 50 entries would be cumbersome and might not reveal trends in the data clearly. A solution would be to construct a *grouped frequency distribution* by grouping adjacent scores into equal-sized *classes* or *intervals*. Each interval could cover, say, five scores (1–5, 6–10, 11–15, and so forth). Then you could tally the frequencies within each *interval*. This procedure would reduce the number of entries in each distribution from 50 to only 10, making the overall results much easier to grasp. However, information would be lost. For example, there would be no way of knowing how many people had a score of 43 versus 44.

Graphing the Data

As everyone knows, a picture is worth a thousand words. The most common statistical picture is a **graph**, a drawing that depicts numerical relationships. Graphs appear at several points in this book, and are routinely used by psychologists to convey their findings to others. From graphs, we can get a general impression of what the data are like, note the relative frequencies of different scores, and see which score was most frequent.

In a graph constructed from a frequency distribution, the possible score values are shown along a horizontal line (the *x-axis* of the graph) and frequencies along a vertical line (the *y-axis*), or vice versa. To construct a **histogram,** or **bar graph,** from our mood scores, we draw rectangles (bars) above each score, indicating the number of times it occurred by the rectangle's height (Figure A.1).

A slightly different kind of "picture" is provided by a **frequency polygon,** or **line graph.** In a frequency polygon, the frequency of each score is indicated by a dot placed directly over the score on the horizontal axis, at the appropriate height on the vertical axis. The dots for the various scores are then joined together by straight lines, as in Figure A.2. When necessary an "extra" score, with a frequency of zero, can be added at each end of the horizontal axis, so that the polygon will rest on this axis instead of floating above it.

Table A.2 — Two Frequency Distributions

The scores are from Table A.1.

Experimental Group			Control Group		
Mood Disturbance Score	Tally	Frequency	Mood Disturbance Score	Tally	Frequency
7		0	7	////	4
6	/	1	6	//// /	6
5	///	3	5	///	3
4	//// //	7	4	//	2
3	///	3	3		0
2	/	1	2		0
1		0	1		0
		$N = 15$			$N = 15$

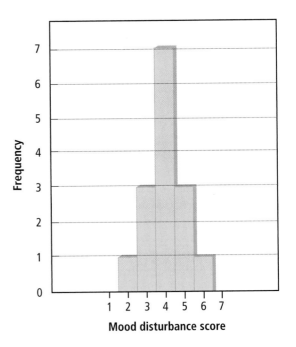

Figure A.1

A HISTOGRAM

This graph depicts the distribution of mood disturbance scores shown on the left side of Table A.2.

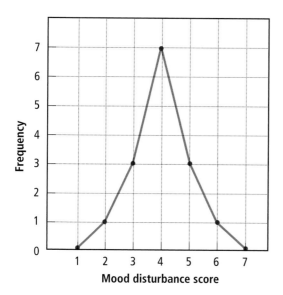

Figure A.2
A FREQUENCY POLYGON
This graph depicts the same data as Figure A.1.

A word of caution about graphs: They may either exaggerate or mask differences in the data, depending on which units are used on the vertical axis. The two graphs in Figure A.3, although they look quite different, actually depict the same data. Always read the units on the axes of a graph; otherwise, the shape of a histogram or frequency polygon may be misleading.

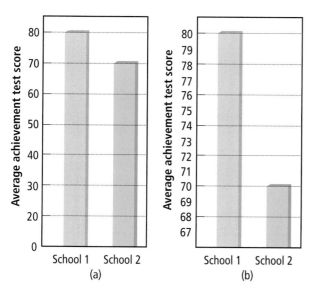

Figure A.3
SAME DATA, DIFFERENT IMPRESSIONS
These two graphs depict the same data, but have different units on the vertical axis.

Describing Data

Having organized your data, you are now ready to summarize and describe them. As you will recall from Chapter 2, procedures for doing so are known as **descriptive statistics**. In the following discussion, the word *score* will stand for any numerical observation.

Measuring Central Tendency

Your first step in describing your data might be to compute a **measure of central tendency** for each group. Measures of central tendency characterize an entire set of data in terms of a single representative number.

The Mean. The most popular measure of central tendency is the arithmetic mean, usually called simply the **mean**. It is often expressed by the symbol *M*. Most people are thinking of the mean when they say "average." We run across means all the time: in grade point averages, temperature averages, and batting averages. The mean is valuable to the psychologist because it takes all the data into account and it can be used in further statistical analyses. To compute the mean, you simply add up a set of scores and divide the total by the number of scores in the set. Recall that in mathematical notation, Σ means "the sum of," *X* stands for the individual scores, and *N* represents the total number of scores in a set. Thus the formula for calculating the mean is:

$$M = \frac{\Sigma X}{N}$$

Table A.3 shows how to compute the mean for our experimental group. Test your ability to perform this calculation by computing the mean for the control group yourself. (You can find the answer, along with other control group

Table A.3	**Calculating a Mean and a Median**

The scores are from the left side of Table A.1.

Mean (*M*)

$$M = \frac{4 + 5 + 4 + 4 + 3 + 6 + 5 + 2 + 4 + 3 + 5 + 4 + 4 + 3 + 4}{15}$$

$$= \frac{60}{15}$$

$$= 4$$

Median

Scores, in order: 2, 3, 3, 3, 4, 4, 4, [4,] 4, 4, 4, 5, 5, 5, 6

Median

statistics, on page A-7.) Later, we will describe how a psychologist would compare the two means statistically to see if there is a significant difference between them.

The Median. Despite its usefulness, sometimes the mean can be misleading, as we noted in Chapter 2. Suppose you piled some children on a seesaw in such a way that it was perfectly balanced, and then a 200-pound adult came and sat on one end. The center of gravity would quickly shift toward the adult. In the same way, one extremely high score can dramatically raise the mean (and one extremely low score can dramatically lower it). In real life, this can be a serious problem. For example, in the calculation of a town's mean income, one millionaire would offset hundreds of poor people. The mean income would be a misleading indication of the town's actual wealth.

When extreme scores occur, a more representative measure of central tendency is the **median**, or midpoint in a set of scores or observations ordered from highest to lowest. In any set of scores, the same *number* of scores falls above the median as below it. The median is not affected by extreme scores. If you were calculating the median income of that same town, the one millionaire would offset only one poor person.

When the number of scores in the set is odd, calculating the median is a simple matter of counting in from the ends to the middle. However, if the number of scores is even, there will be two middle scores. The simplest solution is to find the mean of those two scores and use that number as the median. (When the data are from a grouped frequency distribution, a more complicated procedure is required, one beyond the scope of this appendix.) In our experimental group, the median score is 4 (see Table A.3 again). What is it for the control group?

The Mode. A third measure of central tendency is the **mode**, the score that occurs most often. In our experimental group, the modal score is 4. In our control group, it is 6. In some distributions, all scores occur with equal frequency, and there is no mode. In others, two or more scores "tie" for the distinction of being most frequent. Modes are used less often than other measures of central tendency. They do not tell us anything about the other scores in the distribution; they often are not very "central"; and they tend to fluctuate from one random sample of a population to another more than either the median or the mean.

Measuring Variability

A measure of central tendency may or may not be highly representative of other scores in a distribution. To understand our results, we also need a **measure of variability** that will tell us whether our scores are clustered closely around the mean or widely scattered.

The Range. The simplest measure of variability is the **range**, which is found by subtracting the lowest score from the highest one. For our hypothetical set of mood disturbance scores, the range in the experimental group is 4 and in the control group it is 3. Unfortunately, though, simplicity is not always a virtue. The range gives us some information about variability but ignores all scores other than the highest and lowest ones.

The Standard Deviation. A more sophisticated measure of variability is the **standard deviation (SD)**. This statistic takes every score in the distribution into account. Loosely speaking, it gives us an idea of how much, on the average, scores in a distribution differ from the mean. If the scores were all the same, the standard deviation would be zero. The higher the standard deviation, the more variability there is among scores.

To compute the standard deviation, we must find out how much each individual score deviates from the mean. To do so we simply subtract the mean from each score. This gives us a set of *deviation scores*. Deviation scores for numbers above the mean will be positive, those for numbers below the mean will be negative, and the positive scores will exactly balance the negative ones. In other words, the sum of the deviation scores will be zero. That is a problem, since the next step in our calculation is to add. The solution is to *square* all the deviation scores (that is, to multiply each score by itself). This step gets rid of negative values. Then we can compute the average of the squared deviation scores by adding them up and dividing the sum by the number of scores (N). Finally, we take the square root of the result, which takes us from squared units of measurement back to the same units that were used originally (in this case, mood disturbance levels).

The calculations just described are expressed by the following formula:

$$SD = \sqrt{\frac{\Sigma(X - M)^2}{N}}$$

Table A.4 shows the calculations for computing the standard deviation for our experimental group. Try your hand at computing the standard deviation for the control group.

Remember, a large standard deviation signifies that scores are widely scattered, and that therefore the mean is not terribly typical of the entire population. A small standard deviation tells us that most scores are clustered near the mean, and that therefore the mean is representative. Suppose two classes took a psychology exam, and both classes had the same mean score, 75 out of a possible 100. From the means alone, you might conclude that the classes were similar in performance. But if Class A had a standard deviation of 3 and Class B had a standard deviation of 9, you would know that there was much more variability in performance in

Table A.4	**Calculating a Standard Deviation**	
Scores (X)	Deviation scores (X − M)	Squared deviation scores (X − M)²
6	2	4
5	1	1
5	1	1
5	1	1
4	0	0
4	0	0
4	0	0
4	0	0
4	0	0
4	0	0
3	−1	1
3	−1	1
3	−1	1
2	−2	4
	0	14

$$SD = \sqrt{\frac{\Sigma(X-M)^2}{N}} = \sqrt{\frac{14}{15}} = \sqrt{.93} = .97$$

Note: When data from a sample are used to estimate the standard deviation of the population from which the sample was drawn, division is by $N - 1$ instead of N, for reasons that will not concern us here.

Class B. This information could be useful to an instructor in planning lectures and making assignments.

Transforming Scores

Sometimes researchers do not wish to work directly with raw scores. They may prefer numbers that are more manageable, such as when the raw scores are tiny fractions. Or they may want to work with scores that reveal where a person stands relative to others. In such cases, raw scores can be transformed to other kinds of scores.

Percentile Scores. One common transformation converts each raw score to a **percentile score** (also called a *centile rank*). A percentile score gives the percentage of people who scored at or below a given raw score. Suppose you learn that you have scored 37 on a psychology exam. In the absence of any other information, you may not know whether to celebrate or cry. But if you are told that 37 is equivalent to a percentile score of 90, you know that you can be pretty proud of yourself; you have scored as well as, or higher than, 90 percent of those who have taken the test. On the other hand, if you are

told that 37 is equivalent to a percentile score of 50, you have scored only at the median—only as well as, or higher than, half of the other students. The highest possible percentile rank is 99, or more precisely, 99.99, because you can never do better than 100 percent of a group when you are a member of the group. (Can you say what the lowest possible percentile score is? The answer is on page A-7.) Standardized tests such as those described in previous chapters often come with tables that allow for the easy conversion of any raw score to the appropriate percentile score, based on data from a larger number of people who have already taken the test.

Percentile scores are easy to understand and easy to calculate. However, they also have a drawback: They merely rank people and do not tell us how far apart people are in terms of raw scores. Suppose you scored in the 50th percentile on an exam, June scored in the 45th, Tricia scored in the 20th, and Sean scored in the 15th. The difference between you and June may seem identical to that between Tricia and Sean (five percentiles). But in terms of raw scores you and June are probably more alike than Tricia and Sean, because exam scores usually cluster closely together around the midpoint of the distribution and are farther apart at the extremes. Because percentile scores do not preserve the spatial relationships in the original distribution of scores, they are inappropriate for computing many kinds of statistics. For example, they cannot be used to calculate means.

Z-scores. Another common transformation of raw scores is to **z-scores**, or **standard scores**. A z-score tells you how far a given raw score is above or below the mean, using the standard deviation as the unit of measurement. To compute a z-score, you subtract the mean of the distribution from the raw score and divide by the standard deviation:

$$z = \frac{X - M}{SD}$$

Unlike percentile scores, z-scores preserve the relative spacing of the original raw scores. The mean itself always corresponds to a z-score of zero, since it cannot deviate from itself. All scores above the mean have positive z-scores and all scores below the mean have negative ones. When the raw scores form a certain pattern called a *normal distribution* (to be described shortly), a z-score tells you how high or low the corresponding raw score was, relative to the other scores. If your exam score of 37 is equivalent to a z-score of +1.0, you have scored 1 standard deviation above the mean. Assuming a roughly normal distribution, that's pretty good, because in a normal distribution only about 16 percent of all scores fall at or above 1 standard deviation above the mean. But if your 37 is equivalent to a z-score of −1.0, you have scored 1 standard deviation below the mean—a poor score.

Z-scores are sometimes used to compare people's performance on different tests or measures. Say that Elsa earns a score of 64 on her first psychology test and Manuel, who is taking psychology from a different instructor, earns a 62 on his first test. In Elsa's class, the mean score is 50 and the standard deviation is 7, so Elsa's z-score is (64 − 50)/7 = 2.0. In Manuel's class, the mean is also 50, but the standard deviation is 6. Therefore, his z-score is also 2.0 [(62 − 50)/6]. Compared to their respective classmates, Elsa and Manuel did equally well. But be careful: This does not imply that they are equally able students. Perhaps Elsa's instructor has a reputation for giving easy tests and Manuel's for giving hard ones, so Manuel's instructor has attracted a more industrious group of students. In that case, Manuel faces stiffer competition than Elsa does, and even though he and Elsa have the same z-score, Manuel's performance may be more impressive.

You can see that comparing z-scores from different people or different tests must be done with caution. Standardized tests, such as IQ tests and various personality tests, use z-scores derived from a large sample of people assumed to be representative of the general population taking the tests. When two tests are standardized for similar populations, it is safe to compare z-scores on them. But z-scores derived from special samples, such as students in different psychology classes, may not be comparable.

Curves

In addition to knowing how spread out our scores are, we need to know the pattern of their distribution. At this point we come to a rather curious phenomenon. When researchers make a very large number of observations, many of the physical and psychological variables they study have a distribution that approximates a pattern called a **normal distribution.** (We say "approximates" because a perfect normal distribution is a theoretical construct and is not actually found in nature.) Plotted in a frequency polygon, a normal distribution has a symmetrical, bell-shaped form known as a **normal curve** (see Figure A.4).

A normal curve has several interesting and convenient properties. The right side is the exact mirror image of the left. The mean, median, and mode all have the same value and are at the exact center of the curve, at the top of the "bell." Most observations or scores cluster around the center of the curve, with far fewer out at the ends, or "tails" of the curve. Most important, as Figure A.4 shows, when standard deviations (or z-scores) are used on the horizontal axis of the curve, the percentage of scores falling between the mean and any given point on the horizontal axis is always the same. For example, 68.26 percent of the scores will fall between plus and minus 1 standard deviation from the mean; 95.44 percent of the scores will fall between plus and minus 2 standard deviations from the mean; and 99.74 percent of the scores will fall between plus and minus 3 stan-

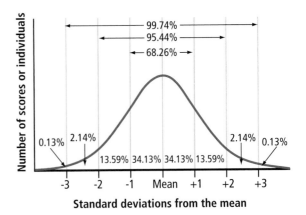

Figure A.4
A NORMAL CURVE

When standard deviations (or z-scores) are used along the horizontal axis of a normal curve, certain fixed percentages of scores fall between the mean and any given point. As you can see, most scores fall in the middle range (between +1 and −1 standard deviations from the mean).

dard deviations from the mean. These percentages hold for any normal curve, no matter what the size of the standard deviation. Tables are available showing the percentages of scores in a normal distribution that lie between the mean and various points (as expressed by z-scores).

The normal curve makes life easier for psychologists when they want to compare individuals on some trait or performance. For example, since IQ scores from a population form a roughly normal curve, the mean and standard deviation of a test are all the information you need in order to know how many people score above or below a particular score. On a test with a mean of 100 and a standard deviation of 15, about 68.26 percent of the population scores between 85 and 115—1 standard deviation below and 1 standard deviation above the mean (see Chapter 9).

Not all types of observations, however, are distributed normally. Some curves are lopsided, or *skewed*, with scores clustering at one end or the other of the horizontal axis (see Figure A.5). When the "tail" of the curve is longer on the right than on the left, the curve is said to be positively, or right, skewed. When the opposite is true, the curve is said to be negatively, or left, skewed. In experiments, reaction times typically form a right-skewed distribution. For example, if people must press a button whenever they hear some signal, most will react quite quickly; but a few will take an unusually long time, causing the right "tail" of the curve to be stretched out.

Knowing the shape of a distribution can be extremely valuable. Paleontologist Stephen Jay Gould (1985) has told how such information helped him cope with the news that he had a rare and serious form of cancer. Being a researcher, he immediately headed for the library to learn all he could about his disease. The first thing he found was that it was incurable, with a

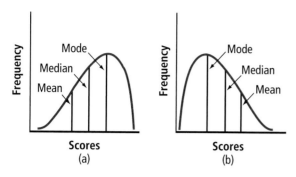

Figure A.5
SKEWED CURVES

Curve (a) is skewed negatively, to the left. Curve (b) is skewed positively, to the right. The direction of a curve's skewness is determined by the position of the long tail, not by the position of the bulge. In a skewed curve, the mean, median, and mode fall at different points.

median mortality of only eight months after discovery. Most people might have assumed that a "median mortality of eight months" means "I will probably be dead in eight months." But Gould realized that although half of all patients died within eight months, the other half survived longer than that. Since his disease had been diagnosed in its early stages, he was getting top-notch medical treatment, and he had a strong will to live, Gould figured he could reasonably expect to be in the half of the distribution that survived beyond eight months. Even more cheering, the distribution of deaths from the disease was right-skewed: The cases to the left of the median of eight months could only extend to zero months, but those to the right could stretch out for years. Gould saw no reason why he should not expect to be in the tip of that right-hand tail.

For Stephen Jay Gould, statistics, properly interpreted, were "profoundly nurturant and life-giving." They offered him hope and inspired him to fight his disease. The initial diagnosis was made in July of 1982. Gould remained professionally active for 20 more years. When he died in 2002, it was from an unrelated type of cancer.

ANSWERS TO QUESTIONS IN THIS CHAPTER:

Control group statistics:

$$\text{Mean} = \frac{\Sigma X}{N} = \frac{87}{15} = 5.8$$

$$\text{Median} = 6$$

$$\text{Standard Deviation} = \sqrt{\frac{\Sigma (X - M)^2}{N}} = \sqrt{\frac{14.4}{15}}$$

$$= \sqrt{.96} = .98$$

Lowest possible percentile score: 1 (or, more precisely, .01)

Drawing Inferences

Once data are organized and summarized, the next step is to ask whether they differ from what might have been expected purely by chance (see Chapter 2). A researcher needs to know whether it is safe to infer that the results from a particular sample of people are valid for the entire population from which the sample was drawn. **Inferential statistics** provide this information. They are used in both experimental and correlational studies.

The Null Versus the Alternative Hypothesis

In an experiment, the scientist must assess the possibility that his or her experimental manipulations will have no effect on the subjects' behavior. The statement expressing this possibility is called the **null hypothesis.** In our stress-and-humor study, the null hypothesis states that making up a funny commentary will not relieve stress any more than making up a straightforward narrative will. In other words, it predicts that the difference between the means of the two groups will not deviate significantly from zero. Any obtained difference will be due solely to chance fluctuations. In contrast, the **alternative hypothesis** (also called the *experimental* or *research hypothesis*) states that on the average the experimental group will have lower mood disturbance scores than the control group.

The null hypothesis and the alternative hypothesis cannot both be true. Our goal is to reject the null hypothesis. If our results turn out to be consistent with the null hypothesis, we will not be able to do so. If the data are inconsistent with the null hypothesis, we will be able to reject it with some degree of confidence. Unless we study the entire population, though, we will never be able to say that the alternative hypothesis has been proven. No matter how impressive our results are, there will always be some degree of uncertainty about the inferences we draw from them. Since we cannot prove the alternative hypothesis, we must be satisfied with showing that the null hypothesis is unreasonable.

Students are often surprised to learn that in traditional hypothesis testing it is the null hypothesis, not the alternative hypothesis, that is tested. After all, it is the alternative hypothesis that is actually of interest. But this procedure does make sense. The null hypothesis can be stated precisely and tested directly. In the case of our fictitious study, the null hypothesis predicts that the difference between the two means will be zero. The alternative hypothesis does not permit a precise prediction because we don't know how much the two means might differ (if, in fact, they do differ). Therefore, it cannot be tested directly.

Testing Hypotheses

Many computations are available for testing the null hypothesis. The choice depends on the design of the study, the size of the sample, and other factors. We will not cover any specific tests here. Our purpose is simply to introduce you to the kind of reasoning that underlies hypothesis testing. With that in mind, let us return once again to our data. For each of our two groups we have calculated a mean and a standard deviation. Now we want to compare the two sets of data to see if they differ enough for us to reject the null hypothesis. We wish to be reasonably certain that our observed differences did not occur entirely by chance.

What does it mean to be "reasonably certain"? How different from zero must our result be to be taken seriously? Imagine, for a moment, that we had infinite resources and could somehow repeat our experiment, each time using a new pair of groups, until we had "run" the entire population through the study. It can be shown mathematically that if only chance were operating, our various experimental results would form a normal distribution. This theoretical distribution is called "the sampling distribution of the difference between means," but since that is quite a mouthful, we will simply call it the *sampling distribution* for short. If the null hypothesis were true, the mean of the sampling distribution would be zero. That is, on the average, we would find no difference between the two groups. Often, though, because of chance influences or *random error,* we would get a result that deviated to one degree or another from zero. On rare occasions, the result would deviate a great deal from zero.

We cannot test the entire population, though. All we have are data from a single sample. We would like to know whether the difference between means that we actually obtained would be close to the mean of the theoretical sampling distribution (if we could test the entire population) or far away from it, out in one of the "tails" of the curve. Was our result highly likely to occur on the basis of chance alone or highly unlikely?

Before we can answer that question, we must have some precise way to measure distance from the mean of the sampling distribution. We must know exactly how far from the mean our obtained result must be to be considered "far away." If only we knew the standard deviation of the sampling distribution, we could use it as our unit of measurement. We don't know it, but fortunately, we can use the standard deviation of our *sample* to estimate it. (We will not go into the reasons that this is so.)

Now we are in business. We can look at the mean difference between our two groups and figure out how far it is (in terms of standard deviations) from the mean of the sampling distribution. As mentioned earlier, one of the convenient things about a normal distribution is that a certain fixed percentage of all observations falls between the mean of the distribution and any given point above or below the mean. These percentages are available from tables. Therefore, if we know the "distance" of our obtained result from the mean of the theoretical sampling distribution, we automatically know how likely our result is to have occurred strictly by chance.

To give a specific example, if it turns out that our obtained result is 2 standard deviations above the mean of the theoretical sampling distribution, we know that the probability of its having occurred by chance is less than 2.3 percent. If our result is 3 standard deviations above the mean of the sampling distribution, the probability of its having occurred by chance is less than .13 percent—less than 1 in 800. In either case, we might well suspect that our result did not occur entirely by chance after all. We would call the result **statistically significant.** (Psychologists usually consider any highly unlikely result to be of interest, no matter which direction it takes. In other words, the result may be in either "tail" of the sampling distribution.)

To summarize: Statistical significance means that if only chance were operating, our result would be highly improbable, so we are fairly safe in concluding that more than chance was operating—namely, the influence of our independent variable. We can reject the null hypothesis, and open the champagne. As we noted in Chapter 2, psychologists usually accept a finding as statistically significant if the likelihood of its occurring by chance is 5 percent or less (see Figure A.6). This cutoff point gives the researcher a reasonable chance of confirming reliable results as well as reasonable protection against accepting unreliable ones.

Some cautions are in order, though. As noted in Chapter 2, conventional tests of statistical significance have drawn serious criticisms in recent years. Statistically significant results are not always psychologically interesting or important. Further, statistical significance is related to the size of the sample. A large sample increases the likelihood of reliable results. But there is a trade-off: The larger the sample, the more probable it is that a small result having no practical importance will reach statistical significance. On the other hand, with the sample sizes typically used in psychological research, there is a good chance of falsely concluding that an experimental effect has not occurred when one actually has (Hunter, 1997). For these reasons, it is always useful to know how much of the total variability in scores was accounted for by the independent variable (the **effect size**). (The computations are not discussed here.) If only 3 percent of the variance was accounted for, then 97 percent was due either to chance factors or to systematic influences of which the researcher was unaware. Because human behavior is affected by so many factors, the amount of variability accounted for by a single psychological variable is often modest. But sometimes the effect size is considerable even when the results don't quite reach significance.

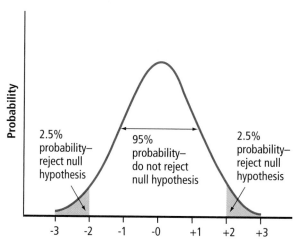

Figure A.6
STATISTICAL SIGNIFICANCE
This curve represents the theoretical sampling distribution discussed in the text. The curve is what we would expect by chance if we did our hypothetical stress-and-humor study many times, testing the entire population. If we used the conventional significance level of .05, we would regard our obtained result as significant only if the probability of getting a result that far from zero by chance (in either direction) totaled 5 percent or less. As shown, the result must fall far out in one of the tails of the sampling distribution. Otherwise, we cannot reject the null hypothesis.

Oh, by the way, to find out what experimental psychologists have learned about humor, stress, and health, see pp. 569–570 in Chapter 15. The study of humor turns out to be pretty complicated. The results depend on how you define "sense of humor," how you do the study, and what aspects of humor you are investigating. Researchers are learning that humor probably doesn't help people live longer, but it is more emotionally beneficial than moping around. So, when gravity gets you down, try a little levity.

Summary

1. When used correctly, statistics expose unwarranted conclusions, promote precision, and help researchers spot trends amid diversity.

2. Often, the first step in data analysis is to organize and condense data in a *frequency distribution*, a tally showing how often each possible score (or interval of scores) occurred. Such information can also be depicted in a *histogram* (bar graph) or a *frequency polygon* (line graph).

3. Descriptive statistics summarize and describe the data. *Central tendency* is measured by the *mean, median*, or, less frequently, the *mode*. Since a measure of central tendency

may or may not be highly representative of other scores in a distribution, it is also important to analyze variability. A large *standard deviation* means that scores are widely scattered about the mean; a small one means that most scores are clustered near the mean.

4. Raw scores can be transformed into other kinds of scores. *Percentile scores* indicate the percentage of people who scored at or below a given raw score. *Z-scores* (*standard scores*) indicate how far a given raw score is above or below the mean of the distribution.

5. Many variables have a distribution approximating a *normal distribution*, depicted as a *normal curve*. The normal curve has a convenient property: When standard deviations are used as the units on the horizontal axis, the percentage of scores falling between any two points on the horizontal axis is always the same. Not all types of observations are distributed normally, however. Some distributions are *skewed* to the left or right.

6. Inferential statistics can be used to test the *null hypothesis* and to tell a researcher whether a result differed significantly from what might have been expected purely by chance. Basically, hypothesis testing involves estimating where the obtained result would have fallen in a theoretical *sampling distribution* based on studies of the entire population in question. If the result would have been far out in one of the "tails" of the distribution, it is considered statistically significant. A statistically significant result may or may not be psychologically interesting or important, so many researchers also compute the *effect size*.

Key Terms

Glossary

absolute threshold   The smallest quantity of physical energy that can be reliably detected by an observer.

accommodation   In Piaget's theory, the process of modifying existing cognitive structures in response to experience and new information.

acculturation   The process by which members of minority groups come to identify with and feel part of the mainstream culture.

action potential   A brief change in electrical voltage that occurs between the inside and the outside of an axon when a neuron is stimulated; it serves to produce an electrical impulse.

activation–synthesis theory   The theory that dreaming results from the cortical synthesis and interpretation of neural signals triggered by activity in the lower part of the brain.

adrenal hormones   Hormones that are produced by the adrenal glands and that are involved in emotion and stress.

agoraphobia   A set of phobias, often set off by a panic attack, involving the basic fear of being away from a safe place or person.

algorithm   A problem-solving strategy guaranteed to produce a solution even if the user does not know how it works.

alternative hypothesis   An assertion that the independent variable in a study will have a certain predictable effect on the dependent variable; also called an *experimental* or *research hypothesis*.

amygdala [uh-MIG-dul-uh]   A brain structure involved in the arousal and regulation of emotion and the initial emotional response to sensory information.

anorexia nervosa   An eating disorder characterized by fear of being fat, a distorted body image, radically reduced consumption of food, and emaciation.

antidepressant drugs   Drugs used primarily in the treatment of mood disorders, especially depression and anxiety.

antipsychotic drugs   Drugs used primarily in the treatment of schizophrenia and other psychotic disorders.

antisocial personality disorder (APD)   A disorder characterized by antisocial behavior such as lying, stealing, manipulating others, and sometimes violence; and a lack of guilt, shame, and empathy. (Sometimes called *psychopathy* or *sociopathy*.)

applied psychology   The study of psychological issues that have direct practical significance; also, the application of psychological findings.

approach goals   Goals framed in terms of desired outcomes or experiences, such as learning to scuba dive.

archetypes [AR-ki-tipes]   Universal, symbolic images that appear in myths, art, stories, and dreams; to Jungians, they reflect the collective unconscious.

arithmetic mean   An average that is calculated by adding up a set of quantities and dividing the sum by the total number of quantities in the set.

assimilation   In Piaget's theory, the process of absorbing new information into existing cognitive structures.

attribution theory   The theory that people are motivated to explain their own and others' behavior by attributing causes of that behavior to a situation or disposition.

autonomic nervous system   The subdivision of the peripheral nervous system that regulates the internal organs and glands.

availability heuristic   The tendency to judge the probability of a type of event by how easy it is to think of examples or instances.

avoidance goals   Goals framed in terms of avoiding unpleasant experiences, such as trying not to look foolish in public.

axon   A neuron's extending fiber that conducts impulses away from the cell body and transmits them to other neurons.

bar graph   *See* histogram.

basic concepts   Concepts that have a moderate number of instances and that are easier to acquire than those having few or many instances.

basic psychology   The study of psychological issues in order to seek knowledge for its own sake rather than for its practical application.

behavior modification   The application of conditioning techniques to teach new responses or to reduce or eliminate maladaptive or problematic behavior.

behavior therapy   A form of therapy that applies principles and techniques of classical and operant conditioning to help people change self-defeating or problematic behaviors.

behavioral genetics   An interdisciplinary field of study concerned with the genetic bases of individual differences in behavior and personality.

behavioral records   In behavior therapy, a method of keeping careful data on the frequency and consequences of the behavior to be changed.

behaviorism   An approach to psychology that emphasizes the study of observable behavior and the role of the environment as a determinant of behavior.

binocular cues   Visual cues to depth or distance requiring two eyes.

biological perspective   A psychological approach that emphasizes bodily events and changes associated with actions, feelings, and thoughts.

biological rhythm   A periodic, more or less regular fluctuation in a biological system; may or may not have psychological implications.

bipolar disorder   A mood disorder in which episodes of both depression and mania (excessive euphoria) occur.

borderline personality disorder   A disorder characterized by intense but unstable relationships, a fear of abandonment by others, an unrealistic self-image, and emotional volatility.

brain stem   The part of the brain at the top of the spinal cord, consisting of the medulla and the pons.

brightness   Lightness or luminance; the dimension of visual experience related to the amount of light emitted from or reflected by an object.

bulimia   An eating disorder characterized by episodes of excessive eating (bingeing) followed by forced vomiting or use of laxatives (purging).

case study   A detailed description of a particular individual being studied or treated.

cell body   The part of the neuron that keeps it alive and determines whether it will fire.

central nervous system (CNS)   The portion of the nervous system consisting of the brain and spinal cord.

cerebellum   A brain structure that regulates movement and balance, and that is involved in the learning of certain kinds of simple responses.

cerebral cortex   A collection of several thin layers of cells covering the cerebrum; it is largely responsible for higher mental functions. *Cortex* is Latin for "bark" or "rind."

cerebral hemispheres   The two halves of the cerebrum.

cerebrum (suh-REE-brum)   The largest brain structure, consisting of the upper part of the brain; divided into two hemispheres, it is in charge of most sensory, motor, and cognitive processes. From the Latin for "brain."

childhood (infantile) amnesia   The inability to remember events and experiences that occurred during the first two or three years of life.

chromosomes   Within every cell, rod-shaped structures that carry the genes.

chunk   A meaningful unit of information; it may be composed of smaller units.

circadian [sur-CAY-dee-un] rhythm   A biological rhythm with a period (from peak to peak or trough to trough) of about 24 hours; from the Latin *circa*, "about," and *dies*, "a day."

classical conditioning   The process by which a previously neutral stimulus acquires the capacity to elicit a response through association with a stimulus that already elicits a similar or related response.

client-centered (nondirective) therapy   A humanist approach to therapy devised by Carl Rogers, which emphasizes the therapist's empathy with the client, the therapist's ability to see the world as the client does, and the use of unconditional positive regard.

cochlea [KOCK-lee-uh]   A snail-shaped, fluid-filled organ in the inner ear, containing the organ of Corti, where the receptors for hearing are located.

coefficient of correlation   A measure of correlation that ranges in value from −1.00 to +1.00.

cognitive dissonance   A state of tension that occurs when a person simultaneously holds two cognitions that are psychologically inconsistent, or when a person's belief is incongruent with his or her behavior.

cognitive ethology   The study of cognitive processes in nonhuman animals.

cognitive perspective   A psychological approach that emphasizes mental processes in perception, memory, language, problem solving, and other areas of behavior.

cognitive schema   An integrated mental network of knowledge, beliefs, and expectations concerning a particular topic or aspect of the world.

cognitive therapy   A form of therapy designed to identify and change irrational, unproductive ways of thinking and hence to reduce negative emotions and their behavioral consequences; it is often combined with behavioral techniques.

collective unconscious   In Jungian theory, the universal memories and experiences of humankind, represented in the symbols, stories, and images (archetypes) that occur across all cultures.

collectivist cultures   Cultures in which the self is regarded as embedded in relationships, and harmony with one's group is prized above individual goals and wishes.

concept   A mental category that groups objects, relations, activities, abstractions, or qualities having common properties.

conditioned response (CR)   The classical-conditioning term for a response that is elicited by a conditioned stimulus; it occurs after the conditioned stimulus is associated with an unconditioned stimulus.

conditioned stimulus (CS)   The classical-conditioning term for an initially neutral stimulus that comes to elicit a conditioned response after being associated with an unconditioned stimulus.

conditioning   A basic kind of learning that involves associations between environmental stimuli and the organism's responses.

cones   Visual receptors involved in color vision.

confabulation   Confusion of an event that happened to someone else with one that happened to you, or a belief that you remember something when it never actually happened.

confirmation bias   The tendency to look for or pay attention only to information that confirms one's own belief.

consciousness Awareness of oneself and the environment.

conservation The understanding that the physical properties of objects—such as the number of items in a cluster or the amount of liquid in a glass—can remain the same even when their form or appearance changes.

consolidation The process by which a long-term memory becomes durable and stable.

contact comfort In primates, the innate pleasure derived from close physical contact; it is the basis of the infant's first attachment.

continuous reinforcement A reinforcement schedule in which a particular response is always reinforced.

control condition In an experiment, a comparison condition in which subjects are not exposed to the same treatment as in the experimental condition.

convergence The turning inward of the eyes, which occurs when they focus on a nearby object.

corpus callosum [CORE-puhs cah-LOW-suhm] The bundle of nerve fibers connecting the two cerebral hemispheres.

correlation A measure of how strongly two variables are related to one another.

correlational study A descriptive study that looks for a consistent relationship between two phenomena.

counterconditioning In classical conditioning, the process of pairing a conditioned stimulus with a stimulus that elicits a response that is incompatible with an unwanted conditioned response.

critical thinking The ability and willingness to assess claims and make judgments on the basis of well-supported reasons and evidence, rather than emotion or anecdote.

cross-sectional study A study in which subjects of different ages are compared at a given time.

crystallized intelligence Cognitive skills and specific knowledge of information acquired over a lifetime; it is heavily dependent on education and tends to remain stable over the lifetime.

cue-dependent forgetting The inability to retrieve information stored in memory because of insufficient cues for recall.

culture A program of shared rules that govern the behavior of members of a community or society, and a set of values, beliefs, and attitudes shared by most members of that community.

dark adaptation A process by which visual receptors become maximally sensitive to dim light.

decay theory The theory that information in memory eventually disappears if it is not accessed; it applies better to short-term than to long-term memory.

declarative memories Memories of facts, rules, concepts, and events ("knowing that"); they include semantic and episodic memories.

deductive reasoning A form of reasoning in which a conclusion follows necessarily from certain premises; if the premises are true, the conclusion must be true.

deep processing In the encoding of information, the processing of meaning rather than simply the physical or sensory features of a stimulus.

defense mechanisms Methods used by the ego to prevent unconscious anxiety or threatening thoughts from entering consciousness.

deindividuation In groups or crowds, the loss of awareness of one's own individuality.

dendrites A neuron's branches that receive information from other neurons and transmit it toward the cell body.

dependent variable A variable that an experimenter predicts will be affected by manipulations of the independent variable.

depressants Drugs that slow down activity in the central nervous system.

descriptive methods Methods that yield descriptions of behavior but not necessarily causal explanations.

descriptive statistics Statistical procedures that organize and summarize research data.

dialectical reasoning A process in which opposing facts or ideas are weighed and compared, with a view to determining the best solution or resolving differences.

difference threshold The smallest difference in stimulation that can be reliably detected by an observer when two stimuli are compared; also called *just noticeable difference (jnd).*

diffusion of responsibility In organized or anonymous groups, the tendency of members to avoid taking responsibility for actions or decisions, assuming that others will do so.

discriminative stimulus A stimulus that signals when a particular response is likely to be followed by a certain type of consequence.

display rules Social and cultural rules that regulate when, how, and where a person may express (or must suppress) emotions.

dissociation A split in consciousness in which one part of the mind operates independently of others.

dissociative identity disorder A controversial disorder marked by the apparent appearance within one person of two or more distinct personalities, each with its own name and traits; commonly known as *multiple personality disorder (MPD).*

dizygotic twins *See* fraternal twins.

DNA (deoxyribonucleic acid) The chromosomal molecule that transfers genetic characteristics by way of coded instructions for the structure of proteins.

doctrine of specific nerve energies The principle that different sensory modalities exist because signals received by the sense organs stimulate different nerve pathways leading to different areas of the brain.

double-blind study An experiment in which neither the subjects nor the individuals running the study know which subjects are in the control group and which are in the experimental group until after the results are tallied.

effect size The amount of variance among scores in a study accounted for by the independent variable.

ego In psychoanalysis, the part of personality that represents reason, good sense, and rational self-control.

egocentric thinking Seeing the world from only your own point of view; the inability to take another person's perspective.

elaborative rehearsal Association of new information with already stored knowledge and analysis of the new information to make it memorable.

electroconvulsive therapy (ECT) A procedure used in cases of prolonged and severe major depression, in which a brief brain seizure is induced.

electroencephalogram (EEG) A recording of neural activity detected by electrodes.

emotion A state of arousal involving facial and bodily changes, brain activation, cognitive appraisals, subjective feelings, and tendencies toward action, all shaped by cultural rules.

emotion work Expression of an emotion that the person does not really feel, often because of a role requirement.

emotional intelligence The ability to identify your own and other people's emotions accurately, express your emotions clearly, and regulate emotions in yourself and others.

empirical Relying on or derived from observation, experimentation, or measurement.

endocrine glands Internal organs that produce hormones and release them into the bloodstream.

endogenous Generated from within rather than by external cues.

endorphins [en-DOR-fins] Chemical substances in the nervous system that are similar in structure and action to opiates; they are involved in pain reduction, pleasure, and memory, and are known technically as *endogenous opioid peptides*.

entrainment The synchronization of biological rhythms with external cues, such as fluctuations in daylight.

entrapment A gradual process in which individuals escalate their commitment to a course of action to justify their investment of time, money, or effort.

episodic memories Memories of personally experienced events and the contexts in which they occurred.

equilibrium The sense of balance.

ethnic identity A person's identification with a racial, religious, or ethnic group.

ethnocentrism The belief that one's own ethnic group, nation, or religion is superior to all others.

evolution A change in gene frequencies within a population over many generations; a mechanism by which genetically influenced characteristics of a population may change.

evolutionary psychology A field of psychology emphasizing evolutionary mechanisms that may help explain human commonalities in cognition, development, emotion, social practices, and other areas of behavior.

existential therapy A form of therapy designed to help clients explore the meaning of existence and face the great questions of life, such as death, freedom, free will, alienation, and loneliness.

experiment A controlled test of a hypothesis in which the researcher manipulates one variable to discover its effect on another.

experimenter effects Unintended changes in subjects' behavior due to cues inadvertently given by the experimenter.

explicit memory Conscious, intentional recollection of an event or of an item of information.

exposure (flooding) In behavior therapy, a method in which a person suffering from an anxiety disorder, such as a phobia or panic attacks, is taken directly into the feared situation until the anxiety subsides.

extinction The weakening and eventual disappearance of a learned response. In classical conditioning, it occurs when the conditioned stimulus is no longer paired with the unconditioned stimulus; in operant conditioning, it occurs when a response is no longer followed by a reinforcer.

extrinsic motivation The pursuit of an activity for external rewards, such as money or fame.

extrinsic reinforcers Reinforcers that are not inherently related to the activity being reinforced.

facial feedback The process by which the facial muscles send messages to the brain about the basic emotion being expressed.

factor analysis A statistical method for analyzing the intercorrelations among various measures or test scores; clusters of measures or scores that are highly correlated are assumed to measure the same underlying trait, ability, or aptitude (factor).

family-systems perspective An approach to doing therapy with individuals or families by examining how each member forms part of a larger, interacting system.

feature detectors Cells in the visual cortex that are sensitive to specific features of the environment.

feminist psychology A psychological approach that analyzes the influence of social inequities on gender relations and on the behavior of the two sexes.

field research Descriptive or experimental research conducted in a natural setting outside the laboratory.

fixed-interval schedule An intermittent schedule of reinforcement in which a reinforcer is delivered for the first response made after a fixed period of time has elapsed since the last reinforcer.

fixed-ratio schedule   An intermittent schedule of reinforcement in which reinforcement occurs only after a fixed number of responses.

fluid intelligence   The capacity for deductive reasoning and the ability to use new information to solve problems; it is relatively independent of education and tends to decline in old age.

fraternal (dizygotic) twins   Twins that develop from two separate eggs fertilized by different sperm; they are no more alike genetically than are any other pair of siblings.

free association   In psychoanalysis and other psychodynamic therapies, the process of saying freely whatever comes to mind in connection with dreams, memories, fantasies, or conflicts.

frequency distribution   A summary of how frequently each score in a set occurred.

frequency polygon (line graph)   A graph showing a set of points obtained by plotting score values against score frequencies; adjacent points are joined by straight lines.

frontal lobes   Lobes at the front of the brain's cerebral cortex; they contain areas involved in short-term memory, higher-order thinking, initiative, social judgment, and (in the left lobe, typically) speech production.

functionalism   An early psychological approach that emphasized the function or purpose of behavior and consciousness.

fundamental attribution error   The tendency, in explaining other people's behavior, to overestimate personality factors and underestimate the influence of the situation.

g factor   A general intellectual ability assumed by many theorists to underlie specific mental abilities and talents.

ganglion cells   Neurons in the retina of the eye, which gather information from receptor cells (by way of intermediate bipolar cells); their axons make up the optic nerve.

gate-control theory   The theory that the experience of pain depends in part on whether pain impulses get past a neurological "gate" in the spinal cord and thus reach the brain.

gender identity   The fundamental sense of being male or female; it is independent of whether the person conforms to the social and cultural rules of gender.

gender schema   A cognitive schema (mental network) of knowledge, beliefs, metaphors, and expectations about what it means to be male or female.

gender typing   The process by which children learn the abilities, interests, personality traits, and behaviors associated with being masculine or feminine in their culture.

general adaptation syndrome   According to Hans Selye, a series of physiological responses to stressors that occur in three phases: alarm, resistance, and exhaustion.

generalized anxiety disorder   A continuous state of anxiety marked by feelings of worry and dread, apprehension, difficulties in concentration, and signs of motor tension.

genes   The functional units of heredity; they are composed of DNA and specify the structure of proteins.

genetic marker   A segment of DNA that varies among individuals, has a known location on a chromosome, and can function as a genetic landmark for a gene involved in a physical or mental condition.

genome   The full set of genes in each cell of an organism (with the exception of sperm and egg cells).

Gestalt principles   Principles that describe the brain's organization of sensory information into meaningful units and patterns.

glia [GLY-uh or GLEE-uh]   Cells that support, nurture, and insulate neurons, remove debris when neurons die, enhance the formation and maintenance of synapses, and modify neuronal functioning.

graph   A drawing that depicts numerical relationships.

groupthink   In close-knit groups, the tendency for all members to think alike for the sake of harmony and to suppress disagreement.

heritability   A statistical estimate of the proportion of the total variance in some trait that is attributable to genetic differences among individuals within a group.

heuristic   A rule of thumb that suggests a course of action or guides problem solving but does not guarantee an optimal solution.

higher-order conditioning   In classical conditioning, a procedure in which a neutral stimulus becomes a conditioned stimulus through association with an already established conditioned stimulus.

hindsight bias   The tendency to overestimate one's ability to have predicted an event once the outcome is known; the "I knew it all along" phenomenon.

hippocampus   A brain structure involved in the storage of new information in memory.

histogram (bar graph)   A graph in which the heights (or lengths) of bars are proportional to the frequencies of individual scores or classes of scores in a distribution.

hormones   Chemical substances, secreted by organs called glands, that affect the functioning of other organs.

HPA (hypothalamus– pituitary–adrenal cortex) axis   A system activated to energize the body to respond to stressors. The hypothalamus sends chemical messengers to the pituitary, which in turn prompts the adrenal cortex to produce cortisol and other hormones.

hue   The dimension of visual experience specified by color names and related to the wavelength of light.

humanist psychology   A psychological approach that emphasizes personal growth, resilience, and the achievement of human potential, rather than the scientific understanding and assessment of behavior.

humanist therapy A form of psychotherapy based on the philosophy of humanism, which starts from the assumption that people seek self-actualization and self-fulfillment; it emphasizes people's free will to change, not past conflicts.

hypnosis A procedure in which the practitioner suggests changes in the sensations, perceptions, thoughts, feelings, or behavior of the subject.

hypothalamus A brain structure involved in emotions and drives vital to survival, such as fear, hunger, thirst, and reproduction; it regulates the autonomic nervous system.

hypothesis A statement that attempts to predict or to account for a set of phenomena; scientific hypotheses specify relationships among events or variables and are empirically tested.

id In psychoanalysis, the part of personality containing inherited psychic energy, particularly sexual and aggressive instincts.

identical (monozygotic) twins Twins that develop when a fertilized egg divides into two parts that develop into separate embryos.

implicit learning Learning that occurs when you acquire knowledge about something without being aware of how you did so and without being able to state exactly what it is you have learned.

implicit memory Unconscious retention in memory, as evidenced by the effect of a previous experience or previously encountered information on current thoughts or actions.

independent variable A variable that an experimenter manipulates.

individualist cultures Cultures in which the self is regarded as autonomous, and individual goals and wishes are prized above duty and relations with others.

induction A method of child rearing in which the parent appeals to the child's own resources, abilities, sense of responsibility, and feelings for others in correcting the child's misbehavior.

inductive reasoning A form of reasoning in which the premises provide support for a conclusion, but it is still possible for the conclusion to be false.

infantile amnesia *See* childhood amnesia.

inferential statistics Statistical procedures that allow researchers to draw inferences about how statistically meaningful a study's results are.

infradian [in-FRAY-dee-un] rhythm A biological rhythm that occurs less frequently than once a day; from the Latin for "below a day."

instinctive drift During operant learning, the tendency for an organism to revert to instinctive behavior.

intelligence An inferred characteristic of an individual, usually defined as the ability to profit from experience, acquire knowledge, think abstractly, act purposefully, or adapt to changes in the environment.

intelligence quotient (IQ) A measure of intelligence originally computed by dividing a person's mental age by his or her chronological age and multiplying the result by 100; it is now derived from norms provided for standardized intelligence tests.

intermittent (partial) schedule of reinforcement A reinforcement schedule in which a particular response is sometimes but not always reinforced.

internal desynchronization A state in which biological rhythms are not in phase (synchronized) with one another.

intrapsychic Within the mind (psyche) or self.

intrinsic motivation The pursuit of an activity for its own sake.

intrinsic reinforcers Reinforcers that are inherently related to the activity being reinforced.

just-world hypothesis The notion that many people need to believe that the world is fair and that justice is served; that bad people are punished and good people rewarded.

justification of effort The tendency of individuals to increase their liking for something that they have worked hard or suffered to attain; a common form of dissonance reduction.

kinesthesis [KIN-es-THEE-sís] The sense of body position and movement of body parts; also called kinesthesia.

language A system that combines meaningless elements such as sounds or gestures to form structured utterances that convey meaning.

language acquisition device According to many psycholinguists, an innate mental module that allows young children to develop language if they are exposed to an adequate sampling of conversation.

latent learning A form of learning that is not immediately expressed in an overt response; it occurs without obvious reinforcement.

lateralization Specialization of the two cerebral hemispheres for particular operations.

learning A relatively permanent change in behavior (or behavioral potential) due to experience.

learning perspective A psychological approach that emphasizes how the environment and experience affect a person's or animal's actions; it includes *behaviorism* and *social-cognitive learning theories*.

libido [li-BEE-do] In psychoanalysis, the psychic energy that fuels the life or sexual instincts of the id.

limbic system A group of brain areas involved in emotional reactions and motivated behavior.

line graph *See* frequency polygon.

linkage studies Studies that look for patterns of inheritance of genetic markers in large families in which a particular condition is common.

lithium carbonate A drug frequently given to people suffering from bipolar disorder.

localization of function Specialization of particular brain areas for particular functions.

locus of control A general expectation about whether the results of your actions are under your own control (internal locus) or beyond your control (external locus).

long-term memory (LTM) In the three-box model of memory, the memory system involved in the long-term storage of information.

long-term potentiation A long-lasting increase in the strength of synaptic responsiveness, thought to be a biological mechanism of long-term memory.

longitudinal study A study in which subjects are followed and periodically reassessed over a period of time.

loudness The dimension of auditory experience related to the intensity of a pressure wave.

lucid dream A dream in which the dreamer is aware of dreaming.

magnetic resonance imaging *See* MRI.

maintenance rehearsal Rote repetition of material in order to maintain its availability in memory.

major depression A mood disorder involving disturbances in emotion (excessive sadness), behavior (loss of interest in one's usual activities), cognition (thoughts of hopelessness), and body function (fatigue and loss of appetite).

mastery (learning) goals Goals framed in terms of increasing one's competence and skills.

mean *See* arithmetic mean.

measure of central tendency A number intended to characterize an entire set of data.

measure of variability A number that indicates how dispersed scores are around the mean of the distribution.

median A measure of central tendency; the value at the midpoint of a distribution of scores when the scores are ordered from highest to lowest.

medulla [muh-DUL-uh] A structure in the brain stem responsible for certain automatic functions, such as breathing and heart rate.

melatonin A hormone secreted by the pineal gland; it is involved in the regulation of circadian rhythms.

menarche [men-ARR-kee] The onset of menstruation.

menopause The cessation of menstruation and of the production of ova; it is usually a gradual process lasting up to several years.

mental age (MA) A measure of mental development expressed in terms of the average mental ability at a given age.

mental disorder Any behavior or emotional state that causes an individual great suffering or worry, is self-defeating or self-destructive, or is maladaptive and disrupts the person's relationships or the larger community.

mental image A mental representation that mirrors or resembles the thing it represents; mental images occur in many and perhaps all sensory modalities.

mental set A tendency to solve problems using procedures that worked before on similar problems.

meta-analysis A procedure for combining and analyzing data from many studies; it determines how much of the variance in scores across all studies can be explained by a particular variable.

metacognition The knowledge or awareness of one's own cognitive processes.

Minnesota Multiphasic Personality Inventory (MMPI) A widely used objective personality test.

mnemonics Strategies and tricks for improving memory, such as the use of a verse or a formula.

mode A measure of central tendency; the most frequently occurring score in a distribution.

monochronic cultures Cultures in which time is organized sequentially; schedules and deadlines are valued over people.

monocular cues Visual cues to depth or distance, which can be used by one eye alone.

monozygotic twins *See* identical twins.

motivation An inferred process within a person or animal that causes movement either toward a goal or away from an unpleasant situation.

MRI (magnetic resonance imaging) A method for studying body and brain tissue, using magnetic fields and special radio receivers.

multiple personality disorder (*See* dissociative identity disorder)

myelin sheath A fatty insulation that may surround the axon of a neuron.

narcissistic personality disorder A disorder characterized by an exaggerated sense of self-importance and self-absorption.

narcolepsy A sleep disorder involving sudden and unpredictable daytime attacks of sleepiness or lapses into REM sleep.

natural selection The evolutionary process in which individuals with genetically influenced traits that are adaptive in a particular environment tend to survive and to reproduce in greater numbers than do other individuals; as a result, their traits become more common in the population.

need for achievement A learned motive to meet personal standards of success and excellence in a chosen area.

need for affiliation The motive to associate with other people, as by seeking friends, companionship, or love.

negative correlation An association between increases in one variable and decreases in another.

negative reinforcement A reinforcement procedure in which a response is followed by the removal, delay, or decrease in intensity of an unpleasant stimulus; as a result, the response becomes stronger or more likely to occur.

nerve A bundle of nerve fibers (axons and sometimes dendrites) in the peripheral nervous system.

neurogenesis The production of new neurons from immature stem cells.

neuron A cell that conducts electrochemical signals; the basic unit of the nervous system; also called a nerve cell.

neurotransmitter A chemical substance that is released by a transmitting neuron at the synapse and that alters the activity of a receiving neuron.

nonconscious processes Mental processes occurring outside of and not available to conscious awareness.

nonshared environment Unique aspects of a person's environment and experience that are not shared with family members.

normal curve A symmetrical, bell-shaped frequency polygon representing a normal distribution.

normal distribution A theoretical frequency distribution having certain special characteristics. For example, the distribution is symmetrical; the mean, mode, and median all have the same value; and the farther a score is from the mean, the less the likelihood of obtaining it.

norms In test construction, established standards of performance.

norms (social) Rules that regulate human life, including social conventions, explicit laws, and implicit cultural standards.

null hypothesis An assertion that the independent variable in a study will have no effect on the dependent variable.

object permanence The understanding, which develops throughout the first year, that an object continues to exist even when you cannot see it or touch it.

object-relations school A psychodynamic approach that emphasizes the importance of the infant's first two years of life and the baby's formative relationships, especially with the mother.

objective tests (inventories) Standardized questionnaires requiring written responses; they typically include scales on which people are asked to rate themselves.

observational learning A process in which an individual learns new responses by observing the behavior of another (a model) rather than through direct experience; sometimes called vicarious conditioning.

observational study A study in which the researcher carefully and systematically observes and records behavior without interfering with the behavior; it may involve either naturalistic or laboratory observation.

obsessive–compulsive disorder (OCD) An anxiety disorder in which a person feels trapped in repetitive, persistent thoughts (*obsessions*) and repetitive, ritualized behaviors (*compulsions*) designed to reduce anxiety.

occipital [ahk-SIP-uh-tuhl] lobes Lobes at the lower back part of the brain's cerebral cortex; they contain areas that receive visual information.

Oedipus complex In psychoanalysis, a conflict occurring in the phallic (Oedipal) stage, in which a child desires the parent of the other sex and views the same-sex parent as a rival.

operant conditioning The process by which a response becomes more likely to occur or less so, depending on its consequences.

operational definition A precise definition of a term in a hypothesis, which specifies the operations for observing and measuring the process or phenomenon being defined.

operations In Piaget's theory, mental actions that are cognitively reversible.

opiates Drugs, derived from the opium poppy, that relieve pain and commonly produce euphoria.

opponent-process theory A theory of color perception that assumes that the visual system treats pairs of colors as opposing or antagonistic.

organ of Corti [core-tee] A structure in the cochlea containing hair cells that serve as the receptors for hearing.

panic disorder An anxiety disorder in which a person experiences recurring panic attacks, periods of intense fear, and feelings of impending doom or death, accompanied by physiological symptoms such as rapid heart rate and dizziness.

papillae [pa-PILL-ee] Knoblike elevations on the tongue, containing the taste buds. (Singular: papilla.)

parallel distributed processing (PDP) model A model of memory in which knowledge is represented as connections among thousands of interacting processing units, distributed in a vast network, and all operating in parallel.

parapsychology The study of purported psychic phenomena such as ESP and mental telepathy.

parasympathetic nervous system The subdivision of the autonomic nervous system that operates during relaxed states and that conserves energy.

parietal [puh-RYE-uh-tuhl] lobes Lobes at the top of the brain's cerebral cortex; they contain areas that receive information on pressure, pain, touch, and temperature.

pattern recognition The identification of a stimulus on the basis of information already contained in long-term memory.

percentile score A score that indicates the percentage of people who scored at or below a given raw score; also called *centile rank*.

perception The process by which the brain organizes and interprets sensory information.

perceptual constancy The accurate perception of objects as stable or unchanged despite changes in the sensory patterns they produce.

perceptual set A habitual way of perceiving, based on expectations.

performance goals Goals framed in terms of performing well in front of others, being judged favorably, and avoiding criticism.

peripheral nervous system (PNS) All portions of the nervous system outside the brain and spinal cord; it includes sensory and motor nerves.

personality A distinctive and relatively stable pattern of behavior, thoughts, motives, and emotions that characterizes an individual throughout life.

personality disorders Rigid, maladaptive personality patterns that cause personal distress or an inability to get along with others.

PET scan (positron-emission tomography) A method for analyzing biochemical activity in the brain, using injections of a glucoselike substance containing a radioactive element.

phobia An exaggerated, unrealistic fear of a specific situation, activity, or object.

phrenology The discredited theory that different brain areas account for character and personality traits, which can be "read" from bumps on the skull.

pitch The dimension of auditory experience related to the frequency of a pressure wave; the height or depth of a tone.

pituitary gland A small endocrine gland at the base of the brain, which releases many hormones and regulates other endocrine glands.

placebo An inactive substance or fake treatment used as a control in an experiment or given by a medical practitioner to a patient.

placebo effect The apparent success of a medication or treatment due to the patient's expectations or hopes rather than to the drug or treatment itself.

polychronic cultures Cultures in which time is organized horizontally; people tend to do several things at once and value relationships over schedules.

pons A structure in the brain stem involved in, among other things, sleeping, waking, and dreaming.

positive correlation An association between increases in one variable and increases in another—or between decreases in one and in another.

positive reinforcement A reinforcement procedure in which a response is followed by the presentation of, or increase in intensity of, a reinforcing stimulus; as a result, the response becomes stronger or more likely to occur.

positron-emission tomography *See* PET scan.

postdecision dissonance In the theory of cognitive dissonance, tension that occurs when you believe you may have made a bad decision.

posttraumatic stress disorder (PTSD) An anxiety disorder in which a person who has experienced a traumatic or life-threatening event has symptoms such as psychic numbing, reliving of the trauma, and increased physiological arousal.

power assertion A method of child rearing in which the parent uses punishment and authority to correct the child's misbehavior.

primary control An effort to modify reality by changing other people, the situation, or events; a "fighting back" philosophy.

primary emotions Emotions considered to be universal and biologically based; they generally include fear, anger, sadness, joy, surprise, disgust, and contempt.

primary punisher A stimulus that is inherently punishing; an example is electric shock.

primary reinforcer A stimulus that is inherently reinforcing, typically satisfying a physiological need; an example is food.

priming A method for measuring implicit memory in which a person reads or listens to information and is later tested to see whether the information affects performance on the same or another type of task.

principle of falsifiability The principle that a scientific theory must make predictions that are specific enough to expose the theory to the possibility of disconfirmation; that is, the theory must predict not only what will happen, but also what will not happen.

proactive interference Forgetting that occurs when previously stored material interferes with the ability to remember similar, more recently learned material.

procedural memories Memories for the performance of actions or skills ("knowing how").

projective tests Psychological tests used to infer a person's motives, conflicts, and unconscious dynamics on the basis of the person's interpretations of ambiguous stimuli.

proposition A unit of meaning that is made up of concepts and expresses a single idea.

prototype An especially representative example of a concept.

psychedelic drugs Consciousness-altering drugs that produce hallucinations, change thought processes, or disrupt the normal perception of time and space.

psychoactive drug A drug capable of influencing perception, mood, cognition, or behavior.

psychoanalysis A theory of personality and a method of psychotherapy, originally formulated by Sigmund Freud, which emphasizes unconscious motives and conflicts.

psychodynamic perspective A psychological approach that emphasizes unconscious dynamics within the individual, such as inner forces, conflicts, or the movement of instinctual energy.

psychodynamic theories Theories that explain behavior and personality in terms of unconscious energy dynamics within the individual.

psychodynamic therapy Psychotherapies that share the goal of exploring the unconscious dynamics of personality, such as defenses and conflicts.

psychogenic amnesia The partial or complete loss of memory (due to nonorganic causes) for threatening information or traumatic experiences.

psychological tests Procedures used to measure and evaluate personality traits, emotional states, aptitudes, interests, abilities, and values.

psychology The discipline concerned with behavior and mental processes and how they are affected by an organism's physical state, mental state, and external environment; the term is often represented by ψ, the Greek letter psi (usually pronounced "sy").

psychometrics The measurement of mental abilities, traits, and processes.

psychoneuroimmunology (PNI) The study of the relationships among psychology, the nervous and endocrine systems, and the immune system.

psychosis An extreme mental disturbance involving distorted perceptions and irrational behavior; it may have psychological or organic causes. (Plural: psychoses.)

psychosurgery Any surgical procedure that destroys selected areas of the brain believed to be involved in emotional disorders or disturbed behavior.

puberty The age at which a person becomes capable of sexual reproduction.

punishment The process by which a stimulus or event weakens or reduces the probability of the response that it follows.

random assignment A procedure for assigning people to experimental and control groups in which each individual has the same probability as any other of being assigned to a given group.

randomized controlled trials Research designed to determine the effectiveness of a new medication or form of therapy, in which people with a given problem or disorder are randomly assigned to one or more treatment groups or to a control group.

range A measure of the spread of scores, calculated by subtracting the lowest score from the highest score.

rapid eye movement (REM) sleep Sleep periods characterized by eye movement, loss of muscle tone, and dreaming.

rational emotive behavior therapy (REBT) A form of cognitive therapy devised by Albert Ellis, designed to challenge the client's unrealistic or irrational thoughts.

reasoning The drawing of conclusions or inferences from observations, facts, or assumptions.

recall The ability to retrieve and reproduce from memory previously encountered material.

reciprocal determinism In social-cognitive theories, the two-way interaction between aspects of the environment and aspects of the individual in the shaping of personality traits.

recognition The ability to identify previously encountered material.

reinforcement The process by which a stimulus or event strengthens or increases the probability of the response that it follows.

relearning method A method for measuring retention that compares the time required to relearn material with the time used in the initial learning of the material.

reliability In test construction, the consistency of scores derived from a test, from one time and place to another.

REM sleep *See* rapid eye movement sleep.

representative sample A group of subjects, selected from a population for study, which matches the population on important characteristics such as age and sex.

repression In psychoanalytic theory, the selective, involuntary pushing of threatening or upsetting information into the unconscious.

reticular activating system (RAS) A dense network of neurons found in the core of the brain stem; it arouses the cortex and screens incoming information.

retina Neural tissue lining the back of the eyeball's interior, which contains the receptors for vision.

retinal disparity The slight difference in lateral separation between two objects as seen by the left eye and the right eye.

retroactive interference Forgetting that occurs when recently learned material interferes with the ability to remember similar material stored previously.

rods Visual receptors that respond to dim light.

role A given social position that is governed by a set of norms for proper behavior.

Rorschach Inkblot Test A projective personality test that requires respondents to interpret abstract, symmetrical inkblots.

saturation Vividness or purity of color; the dimension of visual experience related to the complexity of light waves.

schizophrenia A psychotic disorder or group of disorders marked by positive symptoms (e.g., delusions, hallucinations, disorganized and incoherent speech, and inappropriate behavior) and negative symptoms (e.g., emotional flatness and loss of motivation).

seasonal affective disorder (SAD) A controversial disorder in which a person experiences depression during the winter and an improvement of mood in the spring.

secondary control   An effort to accept reality by changing your own attitudes, goals, or emotions; a "learn to live with it" philosophy.

secondary emotions   Emotions that develop with cognitive maturity and vary across individuals and cultures.

secondary punisher   A stimulus that has acquired punishing properties through association with other punishers.

secondary reinforcer   A stimulus that has acquired reinforcing properties through association with other reinforcers.

selective attention   The focusing of attention on selected aspects of the environment and the blocking out of others.

self-efficacy   A person's belief that he or she is capable of producing desired results, such as mastering new skills and reaching goals.

self-fulfilling prophecy   An expectation that comes true because of the tendency of the person holding it to act in ways that bring it about.

self-serving bias   The tendency, in explaining one's own behavior, to take credit for one's good actions and rationalize one's mistakes.

semantic memories   Memories of general knowledge, including facts, rules, concepts, and propositions.

semicircular canals   Sense organs in the inner ear that contribute to equilibrium by responding to rotation of the head.

sensation   The detection of physical energy emitted or reflected by physical objects; it occurs when energy in the external environment or the body stimulates receptors in the sense organs.

sense receptors   Specialized cells that convert physical energy in the environment or the body to electrical energy that can be transmitted as nerve impulses to the brain.

sensory adaptation   The reduction or disappearance of sensory responsiveness when stimulation is unchanging or repetitious.

sensory deprivation   The absence of normal levels of sensory stimulation.

sensory memory   A memory system that momentarily preserves extremely accurate images of sensory information.

separation anxiety   The distress that most children develop, at about 6 to 8 months of age, when their primary caregivers temporarily leave them with strangers.

serial-position effect   The tendency for recall of the first and last items on a list to surpass recall of items in the middle of the list.

set point   The genetically influenced weight range for an individual, maintained by biological mechanisms that regulate food intake, fat reserves, and metabolism.

sex hormones   Hormones that regulate the development and functioning of reproductive organs and that stimulate the development of male and female sexual characteristics; they include androgens, estrogens, and progesterone.

sex-typing   *See* gender typing.

sexual scripts   Sets of implicit rules that specify proper sexual behavior for a person in a given situation, varying with the person's age, culture, and gender.

shaping   An operant-conditioning procedure in which successive approximations of a desired response are reinforced.

short-term memory (STM)   In the three-box model of memory, a limited-capacity memory system involved in the retention of information for brief periods; it is also used to hold information retrieved from long-term memory for temporary use.

signal-detection theory   A psychophysical theory that divides the detection of a sensory signal into a sensory process and a decision process.

significance tests   Statistical tests that show how likely it is that a study's results occurred merely by chance.

single-blind study   An experiment in which subjects do not know whether they are in an experimental or a control group.

skills training   In behavior therapy, an effort to teach the client skills that he or she may lack, as well as new, more constructive behaviors to replace self-defeating ones.

sleep apnea   A disorder in which breathing briefly stops during sleep, causing the person to choke and gasp, and momentarily awaken.

social cognition   An area in social psychology concerned with social influences on thought, memory, perception, and other cognitive processes.

social identity   The part of a person's self-concept that is based on his or her identification with a nation, culture, or ethnic group or with gender or other roles in society.

social-cognitive theories   Theories that emphasize how behavior is learned and maintained through observation and imitation of others, positive consequences, and cognitive processes such as plans, expectations, and beliefs.

socialization   The processes by which children learn the behaviors, attitudes, and expectations required of them by their society or culture.

sociobiology   An interdisciplinary field that emphasizes evolutionary explanations of social behavior in animals, including human beings.

sociocultural perspective   A psychological approach that emphasizes social and cultural influences on behavior.

somatic nervous system   The subdivision of the peripheral nervous system that connects to sensory receptors and to skeletal muscles; sometimes called the *skeletal nervous system*.

source amnesia   The inability to distinguish what you originally experienced from what you heard or were told about an event later.

spinal cord   A collection of neurons and supportive tissue running from the base of the brain down the center of the back, protected by a column of bones (the spinal column).

spontaneous recovery   The reappearance of a learned response after its apparent extinction.

standard deviation (SD) A commonly used measure of variability that indicates the average difference between scores in a distribution and their mean; more precisely, the square root of the average squared deviation from the mean.

standardize In test construction, to develop uniform procedures for giving and scoring a test.

state-dependent memory The tendency to remember something when the rememberer is in the same physical or mental state as during the original learning or experience.

statistically significant A term used to refer to a result that is extremely unlikely to have occurred by chance.

stem cells Immature cells that renew themselves and have the potential to develop into mature cells; given encouraging environments, stem cells from early embryos can develop into any cell type.

stereotype A summary impression of a group, in which a person believes that all members of the group share a common trait or traits (positive, negative, or neutral).

stereotype threat A burden of doubt a person feels about his or her performance, due to negative stereotypes about his or her group's abilities.

stimulants Drugs that speed up activity in the central nervous system.

stimulus discrimination The tendency to respond differently to two or more similar stimuli. In classical conditioning, it occurs when a stimulus similar to the conditioned stimulus fails to evoke the conditioned response; in operant conditioning, it occurs when an organism learns to make a response in the presence of other, similar stimuli that differ from it on some dimension.

stimulus generalization After conditioning, the tendency to respond to a stimulus that resembles one involved in the original conditioning. In classical conditioning, it occurs when a stimulus that resembles the conditioned stimulus elicits the conditioned response; in operant conditioning, it occurs when a response that has been reinforced (or punished) in the presence of one stimulus occurs (or is suppressed) in the presence of other, similar stimuli.

structuralism An early psychological approach that emphasized the analysis of immediate experience into basic elements.

subconscious processes Mental processes occurring outside of conscious awareness but accessible to consciousness when necessary.

successive approximations In the operant-conditioning procedure of shaping, behaviors that are ordered in terms of increasing similarity or closeness to the desired response.

superego In psychoanalysis, the part of personality that represents conscience, morality, and social standards.

suprachiasmatic [soo-pruh-kye-az-MAT-ick] nucleus (SCN) An area of the brain containing a biological clock that governs circadian rhythms.

surveys Questionnaires and interviews that ask people directly about their experiences, attitudes, or opinions.

sympathetic nervous system The subdivision of the autonomic nervous system that mobilizes bodily resources and increases the output of energy during emotion and stress.

synapse The site where transmission of a nerve impulse from one nerve cell to another occurs; it includes the axon terminal, the synaptic cleft, and receptor sites in the membrane of the receiving cell.

synesthesia A condition in which stimulation of one sense also evokes another.

systematic desensitization In behavior therapy, a step-by-step process of desensitizing a client to a feared object or experience; it is based on the classical-conditioning procedure of counterconditioning.

tacit knowledge Strategies for success that are not explicitly taught but that instead must be inferred.

taste buds Nests of taste-receptor cells.

telegraphic speech A child's first word combinations, which omit (as a telegram did) unnecessary words.

temperaments Physiological dispositions to respond to the environment in certain ways; they are present in infancy and are assumed to be innate.

temporal lobes Lobes at the sides of the brain's cerebral cortex, just above the ears; they contain areas involved in hearing, memory, perception, emotion, and (in the left lobe, typically) language comprehension.

thalamus A brain structure that relays sensory messages to the cerebral cortex.

Thematic Apperception Test (TAT) A projective test that asks respondents to interpret a series of drawings showing scenes of people; usually scored for unconscious motives, such as the need for achievement, power, or affiliation.

theory An organized system of assumptions and principles that purports to explain a specified set of phenomena and their interrelationships.

theory of mind A system of beliefs about the way one's own mind and the minds of others work, and how cognitions and feelings affect behavior.

therapeutic alliance The bond of confidence and mutual understanding established between therapist and client, which allows them to work together to solve the client's problems.

timbre The distinguishing quality of a sound; the dimension of auditory experience related to the complexity of the pressure wave.

tolerance Increased resistance to a drug's effects accompanying continued use; as tolerance develops, larger doses are required to produce effects once brought about by smaller ones.

trait A characteristic of an individual, describing a habitual way of behaving, thinking, and feeling.

tranquilizers Drugs commonly but often inappropriately prescribed for patients who complain of unhappiness, anxiety, or worry.

transcranial magnetic stimulation (TMS) A method of stimulating brain cells, using a powerful magnetic field produced by a wire coil placed on a person's head; it can be used by researchers to temporarily inactivate neural circuits and is also being used therapeutically.

transference In psychodynamic therapies, a critical process in which the client transfers unconscious emotions or reactions, such as emotional feelings about his or her parents, onto the therapist.

triarchic theory of intelligence A theory of intelligence that emphasizes information-processing strategies, the ability to creatively transfer skills to new situations, and the practical application of intelligence.

trichromatic theory A theory of color perception that proposes three mechanisms in the visual system, each sensitive to a certain range of wavelengths; their interaction is assumed to produce all the different experiences of hue.

two-factor theory of emotion The theory that emotions depend on both physiological arousal and a cognitive interpretation of that arousal.

ultradian [ul-TRAY-dee-un] rhythm A biological rhythm that occurs more frequently than once a day; from the Latin for "beyond a day."

unconditional positive regard To Carl Rogers, love or support given to another person with no conditions attached.

unconditioned response (UR) The classical-conditioning term for a reflexive response elicited by a stimulus in the absence of learning.

unconditioned stimulus (US) The classical-conditioning term for a stimulus that elicits a reflexive response in the absence of learning.

validity The ability of a test to measure what it was designed to measure.

validity effect The tendency of people to believe that a statement is true or valid simply because it has been repeated many times.

variable-interval schedule An intermittent schedule of reinforcement in which a reinforcer is delivered for a response made after a variable period of time has elapsed since the last reinforcer.

variable-ratio schedule An intermittent schedule of reinforcement in which reinforcement occurs after a variable number of responses.

variables Characteristics of behavior or experience that can be measured or described by a numeric scale.

volunteer bias A shortcoming of findings derived from a sample of volunteers instead of a representative sample; the volunteers may differ from those who did not volunteer.

vulnerability–stress models Approaches that emphasize how individual vulnerabilities interact with external stresses or circumstances to produce mental disorders.

withdrawal symptoms Physical and psychological symptoms that occur when someone addicted to a drug stops taking it.

working memory In many models of memory, a memory system comprising short-term memory plus the mental processes that control retrieval of information from long-term memory and interpret that information appropriately for a given task.

z-score (standard score) A number that indicates how far a given raw score is above or below the mean, using the standard deviation of the distribution as the unit of measurement.

Bibliography

Abe, Jo Ann A., & Izard, Carroll E. (1999). A longitudinal study of emotion expression and personality relations in early development. *Journal of Personality and Social Psychology, 77,* 566–577.

Abel, Gene G.; Mittelman, Mary; Becker, Judith V.; et al. (1988). Predicting child molesters' response to treatment. *Annals of the New York Academy of Sciences, 528,* 223–234.

Abramovitch, Henry (1995). The nightmare of returning home: A case of acute onset nightmare disorder treated by lucid dreaming. *Israel Journal of Psychiatry and Related Sciences, 32,* 140–145.

Abrams, David B., & Wilson, G. Terence (1983). Alcohol, sexual arousal, and self-control. *Journal of Personality and Social Psychology, 45,* 188–198.

Abramson, Lyn Y.; Metalsky, Gerald I.; & Alloy, Lauren B. (1989). Hopelessness depression: A theory-based subtype of depression. *Psychological Review, 96,* 358–372.

Acocella, Joan (1999). *Creating hysteria: Women and multiple personality disorder.* San Francisco: Jossey-Bass.

Adams, James L. (1986). *Conceptual blockbusting: A guide to better ideas* (3rd ed.). Boston: Addison-Wesley.

Ader, Robert (1997). The role of conditioning. In A. Harrington (ed.), *The placebo effect: An interdisciplinary exploration.* Cambridge, MA: Harvard University Press.

Ader, Robert (2000). True or false: The placebo effect as seen in drug studies is definitive proof that the mind can bring about clinically relevant changes in the body: The placebo effect: If it's all in your head, does that mean you only think you feel better? *Advances in Mind-Body Medicine, 16,* 7–11.

Ader, Robert (2001). Psychoneuroimmunology. *Current Directions in Psychological Science, 10,* 94–98.

Adler, Nancy E.; Boyce, Thomas; Chesney, Margaret A.; et al. (1994). Socioeconomic status and health: The challenge of the gradient. *American Psychologist, 49,* 15–24.

Adolphs, Ralph (2001). Emotion, social cognition, and the human brain. Invited address presented at the annual meeting of the American Psychological Society, Toronto.

Affleck, Glenn; Tennen, Howard; Croog, Sydney; & Levine, Sol (1987). Causal attribution, perceived control, and recovery from a heart attack. *Journal of Social and Clinical Psychology, 5,* 339–355.

Ainsworth, Mary D. S. (1973). The development of infant–mother attachment. In B. M. Caldwell & H. N. Ricciuti (eds.), *Review of child development research* (Vol. 3). Chicago: University of Chicago Press.

Ainsworth, Mary D. S. (1979). Infant–mother attachment. *American Psychologist, 34,* 932–937.

Akbarian, Schahram; Kim, J. J.; Potkin, Steven G.; et al. (1996). Maldistribution of interstitial neurons in prefrontal white matter of the brains of schizophrenic patients. *Archives of General Psychiatry, 53,* 425–436.

Albee, George W. (1985, February). The answer is prevention. *Psychology Today,* 60–64.

Alkon, Daniel L. (1989). Memory storage and neural systems. *Scientific American, 261,* 42–50.

Allen, Laura S., & Gorski, Robert A. (1992). Sexual orientation and the size of the anterior commissure in the human brain. *Proceedings of the National Academy of Sciences, 89,* 7199–7202.

Allison, David B.; & Faith, Myles S. (1997). Issues in mapping genes for eating disorders. *Psychopharmacology Bulletin, 33,* 359–368.

Allison, David B., & Heshka, Stanley (1993). Emotion and eating in obesity? A critical analysis. *International Journal of Eating Disorders, 13,* 289–295.

Alloy, Lauren B.; Fedderly, Sharon S.; Kennedy-Moore, Eileen; & Cohan, Catherine L. (1998). Dysphoria and social interaction: An integration of behavioral confirmation and interpersonal perspectives. *Journal of Personality and Social Psychology, 74,* 1566–1579.

Allport, Gordon W. (1937). *Personality: A psychological interpretation.* New York: Holt, Rinehart and Winston.

Allport, Gordon W. (1954/1979). *The nature of prejudice.* Reading, MA: Addison-Wesley.

Allport, Gordon W. (1961). *Pattern and growth in personality.* New York: Holt, Rinehart and Winston.

Amabile, Teresa M. (1983). *The social psychology of creativity.* New York: Springer-Verlag.

Amabile, Teresa M.; Phillips, Elise D.; & Collins, Mary Ann (1993). Creativity by contract: Social influences on the creativity of professional artists. Paper presented at the annual meeting of the American Psychological Association, Toronto, Canada.

Amato, Paul R. (1994). Life-span adjustment of children to their parents' divorce. *Social Forces, 73,* 895–915.

Amato, Paul R.; & Keith, Bruce (1991). Parental divorce and the well-being of children: A meta-analysis. *Psychological Bulletin, 110,* 26–46.

Ambert, Anne-Marie (1997). *Parents, children, and adolescents: Interactive relationships and development in context.* New York: Haworth Press.

American Psychiatric Association (1994). *The diagnostic and statistical manual of mental disorders* (4th ed.). Washington, DC: American Psychiatric Association.

American Psychiatric Association (2000). *The diagnostic and statistical manual of mental disorders, IV-TR.* Washington, DC: American Psychiatric Association.

Amering, Michaela, & Katschnig, Heinz (1990). Panic attacks and panic disorder in cross-cultural perspective. *Psychiatric Annals, 20,* 511–516.

Anastasi, Anne (1988). *Psychological testing* (6th ed.). New York: Macmillan.

Anastasi, Anne, & Urbina, Susan (1997). *Psychological testing* (7th ed.). Upper Saddle River, NJ: Prentice Hall.

Anderson, Adam K., & Phelps, Elizabeth A. (2000). Expression without recognition: Contributions of the human amygdala to emotional communication. *Psychological Science, 11,* 106–111.

Anderson, Craig A., & Bushman, Brad J. (2001). Effects of violent video games on aggressive behavior, aggressive cognition, aggressive affect, physiological arousal, and prosocial behavior: A meta-analytic review of the scientific literature. *Psychological Science, 12:* 353–359.

Anderson, John R. (1990). *The adaptive nature of thought.* Hillsdale, NJ: Erlbaum.

Anderson, S. W.; Bechara, A.; Damasio, H.; Tranel, D.; & Damasio, A. R. (1999). Impairment of social and moral behavior related to early damage in human prefrontal cortex. *Nature Neuroscience, 2,* 1032–1037.

Andreasen, Nancy C.; Arndt, Stephan; Swayze, Victor, II; et al. (1994). Thalamic abnormalities in schizophrenia visualized through magnetic resonance image averaging. *Science, 266,* 294–298.

Angell, Marcia (2000, May 18). Is academic medicine for sale? [Editorial] *New England Journal of Medicine, 342,* 1516–1518.

Angell, Marcia, & Kassirer, Jerome P. (1998, September 17). Alternative medicine: The risks of untested and unregulated remedies [editorial]. *The New England Journal of Medicine, 339,* 839–841.

Angier, Natalie (2000, November 7). Who is fat? It depends on culture. *The New York Times,* Science Times, D1–2.

Antonova, Irina; Arancio, Ottavio; Trillat, Anne-Cecile; et al. (2001). Rapid increase in clusters of presynaptic proteins at onset of long-lasting potentiation. *Science, 294,* 1547–1550.

Antonuccio, David O.; Danton, William G.; & DeNelsky, Garland Y.; et al. (1999). Raising questions about antidepressants. *Psychotherapy and Psychosomatics, 68,* 3–14.

APA Commission on Violence and Youth (1993). *Violence and youth: Psychology's response.* Washington, DC: American Psychological Association.

APA Research Office (1998). *APA doctorate employment survey, 1996.* Washington, DC: American Psychological Association.

Arendt, Hannah (1963). *Eichmann in Jerusalem: A report on the banality of evil.* New York: Viking.

Arendt, Josephine; Skene, Debra J.; Middleton, B.; et al. (1997). Efficacy of melatonin treatment in jet lag, shift work, and blindness. *Journal of Biological Rhythms, 12,* 604–617.

Arkes, Hal R. (1993). Some practical judgment and decision-making research. In N. J. Castellan, Jr., et al. (eds.), *Individual and group decision making: Current issues.* Hillsdale, NJ: Erlbaum.

Arkes, Hal R.; Boehm, Lawrence E.; & Xu, Gang (1991). The determinants of judged validity. *Journal of Experimental Social Psychology, 27,* 576–605.

Arkes, Hal R.; Faust, David; Guilmette, Thomas J.; & Hart, Kathleen (1988). Eliminating the hindsight bias. *Journal of Applied Psychology, 73,* 305–307.

Arnett, Jeffrey J. (1999). Adolescent storm and stress, reconsidered. *American Psychologist, 54,* 317–326.

Arnett, Jeffrey J. (2000). Emerging adulthood: A theory of development from the late teens through the twenties. *American Psychologist, 55,* 469–480.

Aron, Arthur, & Westbay, Lori (1996). Dimensions of the prototype of love. *Journal of Personality and Social Psychology, 70,* 535–551.

Aron, Arthur; Aron, Elaine N.; & Allen, Joselyn (1998). Motivations for unreciprocated love. *Personality and Social Psychology Bulletin, 24,* 787–796.

Aronson, Elliot (1998). Dissonance, hypocrisy, and the self concept. In J. E. Harmon-Jones and J. Mills (eds.), *Cognitive dissonance: Progress on a pivotal theory in social psychology.* Washington: American Psychological Association.

Aronson, Elliot (1999a). Dissonance, hypocrisy, and the self concept. In J. E. Harmon-Jones and J. Mills (eds.), *Cognitive dissonance: Progress on a pivotal theory in social psychology.* Washington: American Psychological Association.

Aronson, Elliot (1999b). *The social animal* (8th ed.). New York: Freeman.

Aronson, Elliot, & Mills, Judson (1959). The effect of severity of initiation on liking for a group. *Journal of Abnormal and Social Psychology, 59,* 177–181.

Aronson, Elliot, & Patnoe, Shelley (1997). *Cooperation in the classroom: The jigsaw method.* New York: Longman.

Aronson, Elliot; Wilson, Timothy D.; & Akert, Robin A. (2002). *Social psychology* (4th ed.). Upper Saddle River, NJ: Prentice Hall.

Aronson, Joshua, & Salinas, Moises F. (1997). Stereotype threat, attribution ambiguity, and Latino underperformance. Unpublished manuscript, University of Texas, Austin.

Arroyo, Carmen G., & Zigler, Edward (1995). Racial identity, academic achievement, and the psychological well-being of economically disadvantaged adolescents. *Journal of Personality and Social Psychology, 69,* 903–914.

Arsenijevic, D.; Onuma, H.; Pecqueur, C.; et al. (2000, December 26). Disruption of the uncoupling protein-2 gene in mice reveals a role in immunity and reactive oxygen species production. *Nature Genetics, 4,* 387–388.

Asch, Solomon E. (1952). *Social psychology.* Englewood Cliffs, NJ: Prentice-Hall.

Asch, Solomon E. (1965). Effects of group pressure upon the modification and distortion of judgments. In H. Proshansky & B. Seidenberg (eds.), *Basic studies in social psychology.* New York: Holt, Rinehart and Winston.

Aserinsky, Eugene, & Kleitman, Nathaniel (1955). Two types of ocular motility occurring in sleep. *Journal of Applied Physiology, 8,* 1–10.

Ashrof, H. (2001). U.S. expert group rejects link between MMR and autism. *Lancet, 359:* 1341.

Aspinwall, Lisa G., & Brunhart, Susanne M. (1996). Distinguishing optimism from denial: Optimistic beliefs predict attention to health threats. *Personality and Social Psychology Bulletin, 22,* 993–1003.

Aspinwall, Lisa G., & Taylor, Shelley E. (1997). A stitch in time: Self-regulation and proactive coping. *Psychological Bulletin, 121,* 417–436.

Atkinson, John W. (ed.) (1958). *Motives in fantasy, action, and society.* Princeton, NJ: Van Nostrand.

Atkinson, Richard C., & Shiffrin, Richard M. (1968). Human memory: A proposed system and its control processes. In K. W. Spence & J. T. Spence (eds.), *The psychology of learning and motivation: Vol. 2. Advances in research and theory.* New York: Academic Press.

Atkinson, Richard C., & Shiffrin, Richard M. (1971, August). The control of short-term memory. *Scientific American, 225*(2), 82–90.

AuBuchon, Peter G., & Calhoun, Karen S. (1985). Menstrual cycle symptomatology: The role of social expectancy and experimental demand characteristics. *Psychosomatic Medicine, 47,* 35–45.

Axel, Richard (1995, October). The molecular logic of smell. *Scientific American,* 154–159.

Azrin, Nathan H., & Foxx, Richard M. (1974). *Toilet training in less than a day.* New York: Simon & Schuster.

Azuma, Hiroshi (1984). Secondary control as a heterogeneous category. *American Psychologist, 39,* 970–971.

Baddeley, Alan D. (1992). Working memory. *Science, 255,* 556–559.

Bahill, A. Terry, & Karnavas, William J. (1993). The perceptual illusion of baseball's rising fastball and breaking curveball. *Journal of Experimental Psychology: Human Perception & Performance, 19,* 3–14.

Bahrick, Harry P. (1984). Semantic memory content in permastore: Fifty years of memory for Spanish learned in school. *Journal of Experimental Psychology: General, 113,* 1–29.

Bahrick, Harry P.; Bahrick, Phyllis O.; & Wittlinger, Roy P. (1975). Fifty years of memory for names and faces: A cross-sectional approach. *Journal of Experimental Psychology: General, 104,* 54–75.

Bailey, J. Michael, & Pillard, Richard C. (1995). Genetics of human sexual orientation. *Annual Review of Sex Research, 6,* 126–150.

Bailey, J. Michael, & Zucker, Kenneth J. (1995). Childhood sex-typed behavior and sexual orientation: A conceptual analysis and quantitative review. *Developmental Psychology, 31,* 43–55.

Bailey, J. Michael; Bobrow, David; Wolfe, Marilyn; & Mikach, Sarah (1995). Sexual orientation of adult sons of gay fathers. *Developmental Psychology, 31,* 124–129.

Bailey, J. Michael; Dunne, Michael P.; & Martin, Nicholas G. (2000). Genetic and environmental influences on sexual orientation and its correlates in an Australian twin sample. *Journal of Personality and Social Psychology, 78,* 524–536.

Bailey, J. Michael; Gaulin, Steven; Agyei, Yvonne; & Gladue, Brian A. (1994). Effects of gender and sexual orientation on evolutionarily relevant aspects of human mating psychology. *Journal of Personality and Social Psychology, 66,* 1081–1093.

Baillargeon, Renée (1994). How do infants learn about the physical world? *Current Directions in Psychological Science, 5,* 133–140.

Baillargeon, Renée (1999). Young infants' expectations about hidden objects: A reply to three challenges. *Developmental Science, 2,* 115–163.

Baker, Mark C. (2001). *The atoms of language: The mind's hidden rules of grammar.* New York: Basic Books.

Baker, Robert A. (1992). *Hidden memories: Voices and visions from within.* Buffalo, NY: Prometheus.

Ballenger, James C.; Burrows, Graham D.; DuPont, Robert L.; et al. (1988). Alprazolam in panic disorder and agoraphobia: Results from a multicenter trial. *Archives of General Psychiatry, 45,* 413–421.

Baltes, Paul B., & Graf, Peter (1996). Psychological aspects of aging: Facts and frontiers. In D. Magnusson (ed.), *The lifespan development of individuals.* Cambridge, England: Cambridge University Press.

Baltes, Paul B.; Sowarka, Doris; & Kliegl, Reinhold (1989). Cognitive training research on fluid intelligence in old age: What can older adults achieve by themselves? *Psychology and Aging, 4,* 217–221.

Bancroft, John; Sherwin, Barbara B.; Alexander, G. M.; et al. (1991). Oral contraceptives, androgens, and the sexuality of young women: II. The role of androgens. *Archives of Sexual Behavior, 20,* 121–135.

Bandura, Albert (1977). *Social learning theory.* Englewood Cliffs, NJ: Prentice-Hall.

Bandura, Albert (1986). *Social foundations of thought and action: A social cognitive theory.* Englewood Cliffs, NJ: Prentice-Hall.

Bandura, Albert (1997). *Self-efficacy: The exercise of control.* New York: Freeman.

Bandura, Albert (1999). Moral disengagement in the perpetration of inhumanities. *Personality and Social Psychology Review, 3,* 193–209.

Bandura, Albert (2001). Social cognitive theory: An agentic perspective. *Annual Review of Psychology, 52,* 1–26. Palo Alto, CA: Annual Reviews.

Bandura, Albert; Caprara, Gian Vittorio; Barbaranelli, Claudio; Pastorelli, Concetta; & Regalia, Camillo (2001). Sociocognitive self-regulatory mechanisms governing transgressive behavior. *Journal of Personality and Social Psychology, 80,* 125–135.

Bandura, Albert; Ross, Dorothea; & Ross, Sheila A. (1963). Vicarious reinforcement and imitative learning. *Journal of Abnormal and Social Psychology, 67,* 601–607.

Banks, Martin S. (with Philip Salapatek) (1984). Infant visual perception. In P. Mussen (series ed.), M. M. Haith & J. J. Campos (vol. eds.), *Handbook of child psychology: Vol. II. Infancy and developmental psychobiology* (4th ed.). New York: Wiley.

Barash, David P. (2001, April 20). Deflating the myth of monogamy. *The Chronicle of Higher Education,* B16–B17.

Barash, David P., & Lipton, Judith Eve (2001). *The myth of monogamy: Fidelity and infidelity in animals and people.* New York: W. H. Freeman.

Barber, Theodore X. (1979). Suggested ("hypnotic") behavior: The trance paradigm versus an alternative paradigm. In E. Fromm & R. E. Shor (eds.), *Hypnosis: Developments in research and new perspectives* (2nd ed.). New York: Aldine.

Barbuto, J. E. (1997). A critique of the Myers-Briggs Type Indicator and its operationalization of Carl Jung's psychological types. *Psychological Reports, 80,* 611–625.

Bargh, John A. (1999, January 29). The most powerful manipulative messages are hiding in plain sight. *The Chronicle of Higher Education,* B6.

Barinaga, Marcia (1992). Challenging the "no new neurons" dogma. *Science, 255,* 1646.

Barlow, David H. (2000). Unraveling the mysteries of anxiety and its disorders from the perspective of emotion theory. *American Psychologist, 55,* 1247–1263.

Barlow, David H.; Chorpita, Bruce F.; & Turovsky, Julia (1996). Fear, panic, anxiety, and disorders of emotion. In D. A. Hope et al. (eds.), *Nebraska Symposium on Motivation, 1995: Perspectives on anxiety, panic, and fear.* Lincoln, NE: University of Nebraska Press.

Baron, Miron (1993). The D2 dopamine receptor gene and alcoholism: A tempest in a wine cup? *Biological Psychiatry, 34,* 821–823.

Baron-Cohen, S., & Harrison, J. E. (eds.) (1997). *Synaesthesia: Classic and contemporary readings.* Cambridge, MA: Blackwell.

Barondes, Samuel H. (1998). *Mood genes: Hunting for origins of mania and depression.* New York: Freeman.

Barone, David F.; Maddux, James E.; & Snyder, C. R. (1997). *Social cognitive psychology: History and current domains.* New York: Plenum Press.

Barrish, Barbara M. (1996). The relationship of remembered parental physical punishment to adolescent self-concept. *Dissertation Abstracts International, Section B, 57,* 2171.

Barron, Kenneth S., & Harackiewicz, Judith M. (2001). Achievement goals and optimal motivation: Testing multiple goal models. *Journal of Personality and Social Psychology, 80,* 706–722.

Barsky, S. H.; Roth, M. D.; Kleerup, E. C.; Simmons, M.; & Tashkin, D. P. (1998). Histopathologic and molecular alterations in bronchial epithelium in habitual smokers of marijuana, cocaine, and/or tobacco. *Journal of the National Cancer Institute, 90,* 1198–1205.

Bartlett, Frederic C. (1932). *Remembering.* Cambridge, England: Cambridge University Press.

Bartoshuk, Linda M. (1993). Genetic and pathological taste variation: What can we learn from animal models and human disease? In D. J. Chadwick, J. Marsh, & J. Goode (eds.), *The molecular basis of smell and taste transduction.* CIBA Foundation Symposia Series, No. 179. New York: Wiley.

Bartoshuk, Linda M. (1998). Born to burn: Genetic variation in taste. Paper presented at the annual meeting of the American Psychological Association, San Francisco.

Bartoshuk, Linda M.; Duffy, V. B.; Lucchina, L. A.; et al. (1998). PROP (6-n-propylthiouracil) supertasters and the saltiness of NaCl. *Annals of the New York Academy of Sciences, 855,* 793–796.

Bashore, Theodore R.; Ridderinkhof, K. Richard; & van der Molen, Maurits W. (1997). The decline of cognitive processing speed in old age. *Current Directions in Psychological Science, 6,* 163–169.

Basic Behavioral Science Task Force of the National Advisory Mental Health Council (1996). Basic behavioral science research for mental health: Vulnerability and resilience. *American Psychologist, 51,* 22–28.

Bassetti, C.; Vella, S.; Donati, F.; et al. (2000). SPECT during sleepwalking. *Lancet, 356,* 484–485.

Basson, R.; McInnis, R.; Smith, M.; Hodgson, G.; & Koppiker, N. (2002). Efficacy and safety of sildenafil citrate in women with sexual dysfunction associated with female sexual arousal disorder. *Journal of Women's Health and Gender Based Medicine, 11,* 339–349.

Bauer, Patricia J., & Dow, Gina Annunziato (1994). Episodic memory in 16- and 20-month-old children: Specifics are generalized but not forgotten. *Developmental Psychology, 30,* 403–417.

Baumeister, Roy F. (1990). Suicide as escape from self. *Psychological Review, 97,* 90–113.

Baumeister, Roy F. (2000). Gender differences in erotic plasticity: The female sex drive as socially flexible and responsive. *Psychological Bulletin, 126,* 347–374.

Baumeister, Roy F., & Bratslavsky, Ellen (1999). Passion, intimacy, and time: Passionate love as a function of change in intimacy. *Personality and Social Psychology Review, 3,* 49–67.

Baumeister, Roy F.; Catanese, Kathleen R.; & Vohs, Kathleen D. (2001). Is there a gender difference in strength of sex drive? Theoretical views, conceptual distinctions, and a review of relevant evidence. *Personality and Social Psychology Review, 5,* 242–273.

Baumeister, Roy F.; Dale, Karen; & Sommer, Kristin L. (1998). Freudian defense mechanisms and empirical findings in modern social psychology: Reaction formation, projection, displacement, undoing, isolation, sublimation, and denial. *Journal of Personality, 66,* 1081–1124.

Baumeister, Roy F.; Stillwell, Arlene M.; & Heatherton, Todd F. (1994). Guilt: An interpersonal approach. *Psychological Bulletin, 115,* 243–267.

Baumeister, Roy F.; Stillwell, Arlene M.; & Wotman, Sara R. (1990). Victim and perpetrator accounts of interpersonal conflict: Autobiographical narratives about anger. *Journal of Personality and Social Psychology, 59,* 994–1005.

Baumrind, Diana (1989). Rearing competent children. In W. Damon (ed.), *Child development today and tomorrow.* San Francisco: Jossey-Bass.

Baumrind, Diana (1991). Parenting styles and adolescent development. In R. Lerner, A. C. Petersen, & J. Brooks-Gunn (eds.), *The encyclopedia of adolescence.* New York: Garland.

Baumrind, Diana (1995). Commentary on sexual orientation: Research and social policy implications. *Developmental Psychology, 31,* 130–136.

Baumrind, Diana; Larzelere, Robert E.; & Cowan, Philip (2002). Ordinary physical punishment—Is it harmful? Commentary on Gershoff's Review. *Psychological Bulletin, 128,* in press.

Baxter, Lewis R.; Schwartz, Jeffrey M.; Bergman, Kenneth S.; et al. (2002). Caudate glucose metabolic rate changes with both drug and behavior therapy for obsessive–compulsive disorder. *Archives of General Psychiatry, 49,* 681–689.

Baynes, Kathleen; Eliassen, James C.; Lutsep, Helmi L; & Gazzaniga, Michael S. (1998). Modular organization of cognitive systems masked by interhemispheric integration. *Science, 280,* 902–905.

Bechara, Antoine; Dermas, Hanna; Tranel, Daniel; & Damasio, Antonio R. (1997). Deciding advantageously before knowing the advantageous strategy. *Science, 275,* 1293–1294.

Beck, Aaron T. (1976). *Cognitive therapy and the emotional disorders.* New York: International Universities Press.

Beck, Aaron T. (1988). Cognitive approaches to panic disorder: Theory and therapy. In S. Rachman & J. D. Maser (eds.), *Panic: Psychological perspectives.* Hillsdale, NJ: Erlbaum.

Beck, Aaron T. (1991). Cognitive therapy: A 30-year retrospective. *American Psychologist, 46,* 368–375.

Becker, Anne E. (1999). Paper presented at the annual meeting of the American Psychiatric Association, Washington, DC.

Beckerman, Stephen; Lizarralde, Roberto; Ballew, Carol; et al. (1998). The Barí partible paternity project: Preliminary results. *Current Anthropology, 39,* 164–167.

Beer, Jeremy M.; Arnold, Richard D.; & Loehlin, John C. (1998). Genetic and environmental influences on MMPI factor scales: Joint model fitting to twin and adoption data. *Journal of Personality and Social Psychology, 74,* 818–827.

Bekenstein, Jonathan W., & Lothman, Eric W. (1993). Dormancy of inhibitory interneurons in a model of temporal lobe epilepsy. *Science, 259,* 97–100.

Bell, Derrick (1992). *Faces at the bottom of the well: The permanence of racism.* New York: Basic Books.

Belsky, Jay; Campbell, Susan B.; Cohn, Jeffrey F.; & Moore, Ginger (1996). Instability of infant parent attachment security. *Developmental Psychology, 32,* 921–924.

Belsky, Jay; Hsieh, Kuang-Hua; & Crnic, Keith (1996). Infant positive and negative emotionality: One dimension or two? *Developmental Psychology, 32,* 289–298.

Bem, Daryl J., & Honorton, Charles (1994). Does psi exist? Replicable evidence for an anomalous process of information transfer. *Psychological Bulletin, 115,* 4–18.

Bem, Sandra L. (1993). *The lenses of gender.* New Haven, CT: Yale University Press.

Benedetti, Fabrizio, & Levi-Montalcini, Rita (2001). Opioid and non-opioid mechanisms of placebo analgesia. Paper presented at the annual meeting of the American Psychological Society, Toronto.

Benet-Martínez, Verónica, & Waller, Niels G. (1997). Further evidence for the cross-cultural generality of the Big Seven factor model: Indigenous and imported Spanish personality constructs. *Journal of Personality, 65,* 567–598.

Benjamin, Ludy T., Jr. (1998). Why Gorgeous George, and not Wilhelm Wundt, was the founder of psychology: A history of popular psychology in America. Invited address presented at the National Institute on the Teaching of Psychology, St. Petersburg Beach.

Benjamin, Ludy T., Jr. (2003). Why can't psychology get a stamp? *Journal of Applied Psychoanalytic Studies,* in press.

Bereiter, Carl, & Bird, Marlene (1985). Use of thinking aloud in identification and teaching of reading comprehension strategies. *Cognition and Instruction, 2,* 131–156.

Berenbaum, Sheri A., & Snyder, Elizabeth (1995). Early hormonal influences on childhood sex-typed activity and playmate preferences: Implications for the development of sexual orientation. *Developmental Psychology, 31,* 31–42.

Berger, F.; Gage, F. H.; & Vijayaraghavan, S. (1998). Nicotinic receptor-induced apoptotic cell death of hippocampal progenitor cells. *Journal of Neuroscience, 18,* 6871–6881.

Berkman, Lisa F.; Leo-Summers, L.; & Horwitz, R. I. (1992). Emotional support and survival after myocardial infarction: A prospective, population-based study of the elderly. *Annals of Internal Medicine, 117,* 1003–1009.

Berkman, Lisa F., & Syme, S. Leonard (1979). Social networks, host resistance, and mortality: A nine-year follow-up study of Alameda County residents. *American Journal of Epidemiology, 109,* 186–204.

Berko, Jean (1958). The child's learning of English morphology. *Word, 14,* 150–177.

Berkowitz, Leonard (1999). Evil is more than banal: Situationism and the concept of evil. *Personality and Social Psychology Review, 3,* 246–253.

Berkowitz, Marvin W., & Grych, John H. (2000). Early character development and education. *Early Education & Development, 11,* 55–72.

Bernhardt, Paul C; Dabbs, James M., Jr.; Fielden, Julie A.; & Lutter, Candice D. (1998). Testosterone changes during vicarious experiences of winning and losing among fans at sporting events. *Physiology & Behavior, 65,* 59–62.

Bernieri, Frank J.; Davis, Janet M.; Rosenthal, Robert; & Knee, C. Raymond (1991). *Interactional synchrony and the social affordance of rapport: A validation study.* Unpublished manuscript, Oregon State University, Corvallis.

Bernieri, Frank J.; Davis, Janet M.; Rosenthal, Robert; & Knee, C. Raymond (1994). Interactional synchrony and rapport: Measuring synchrony in displays devoid of sound and facial affect. *Personality and Social Psychology Bulletin, 20,* 303–311.

Bernieri, Frank J.; Gillis, John S.; Davis, Janet M.; & Grahe, Jon E. (1996). Dyad rapport and the accuracy of its judgment across situations: A lens model analysis. *Journal of Personality and Social Psychology, 71,* 110–129.

Berry, John W. (1994). Acculturative stress. In W. J. Lonner & R. S. Malpass (eds.), *Psychology and culture.* Needham Heights, MA: Allyn & Bacon.

Berscheid, Ellen, & Reis, Harry T. (1998). Attraction and close relationships. In D. T. Gilbert, S. T. Fiske, & G. Lindzey (eds.), *The handbook of social psychology, Vol. 2* (4th ed.). New York: McGraw-Hill.

Best, Joel (2001). *Damned lies and statistics*. Berkeley: University of California Press.

Bettelheim, Bruno (1967). *The empty fortress*. New York: Free Press.

Beutler, Larry E. (2000). David and Goliath: When empirical and clinical standards of practice meet. *American Psychologist, 55*, 997–1007.

Beutler, Larry E., & Malik, Mary L. (eds.) (2002). *Rethinking the DSM: A psychological perspective*. Washington, DC: American Psychological Association.

Beyerstein, Barry L. (1996). Graphology. In G. Stein (ed.), *The encyclopedia of the paranormal*. Amherst, NY: Prometheus Books.

Beyerstein, Barry L. (1999). Fringe psychotherapies: The public at risk. In W. Sampson (ed.), *A Guide to Alternative Medicine*. London: Gordon and Breech.

Bierut, Laura Jean; Heath, Andrew C.; Bucholz, Kathleen K.; et al. (1999). Major depressive disorder in a community-based twin sample: Are there different genetic contributions for men and women? *Archives of General Psychiatry, 56*, 557–563.

Birdwhistell, Ray L. (1970). *Kinesics and context: Essays on body motion communication*. Philadelphia: University of Pennsylvania Press.

Birkhead, Tim (2001). *Promiscuity: An evolutionary history of sperm competition*. Cambridge, MA: Harvard University Press.

Bishop, Katherine M., & Wahlsten, Douglas (1997). Sex differences in the human corpus callosum: Myth or reality? *Neuroscience and Biobehavioral Reviews, 21*, 581–601.

Bjork, Daniel W. (1993). *B. F. Skinner: A life*. New York: Basic Books.

Bjork, Elizabeth L.; Bjork, Robert A.; & Anderson, M. C. (1998). Varieties of goal-directed forgetting. In J. M. Golding & C. M. MacLoed (eds.), *Intentional forgetting*. Mahway, NJ: Erlbaum.

Bjork, Robert A. (October, 2000). Human factors 101: How about just trying things out? *APS Observer, 13,* 3, 30.

Blackmore, Susan (2001, March/April). Giving up the ghosts: End of a personal quest. *Skeptical Inquirer*, p. 25.

Blagrove, Mark (1996). Problems with the cognitive psychological modeling of dreaming. *Journal of Mind and Behavior, 17,* 99–134.

Blakemore, Colin, & Cooper, Grahame F. (1970). Development of the brain depends on the visual environment. *Nature, 228,* 477–478.

Blanton, Hart; Buunk, Bram P.; Gibbons, Frederick X.; & Kuyper, Hans (1999). When better-than-others compare upward. *Journal of Personality and Social Psychology, 76*, 420–430.

Blass, Thomas (1993). What we know about obedience: Distillations from 30 years of research on the Milgram paradigm. Paper presented at the annual meeting of the American Psychological Association, Toronto.

Blass, Thomas (ed.) (2000). *Obedience to authority: Current perspectives on the Milgram paradigm*. Mahwah, NJ: Erlbaum.

Blatt, Sidney J.; Auerbach, John S.; & Levy, Kenneth N. (1997). Mental representations in personality development, psychopathology, and the therapeutic process. *Review of General Psychology, 1,* 351–374.

Blazer, Dan G.; Kessler, Ronald C.; & Swartz, Marvin S. (1998). Epidemiology of recurrent major and minor depression with a seasonal pattern: The National Comorbidity Survey. *British Journal of Psychiatry, 172,* 164–167.

Bleuler, Eugen (1911/1950). *Dementia praecox or the group of schizophrenias*. New York: International Universities Press.

Bliss, T. V., & Collingridge, G. L. (1993). A synaptic model of memory: Long-term potentiation in the hippocampus. *Nature, 361*(6407), 31–39.

Blouin, J. L; Dombroski, B. A.; Nath, S. K.; et al. (1998). Schizophrenia susceptibility loci on chromosomes 13q32 and 8p21. *Nature Genetics, 20,* 70–73.

Blum, Deborah (1997). *Sex on the brain: The biological differences between men and women*. New York: Viking.

Bodenheimer, Thomas (2000, May 18). Uneasy alliance—clinical investigators and the pharmaceutical industry [Health policy report]. *New England Journal of Medicine, 342,* 1539–1544.

Boesch, Cristophe (1991). Teaching among wild chimpanzees. *Animal Behavior, 41,* 530–532.

Bohannon, John N., & Stanowicz, Laura (1988). The issue of negative evidence: Adult responses to children's language errors. *Developmental Psychology, 24,* 684–689.

Bohannon, John N., & Symons, Victoria (1988). *Conversational conditions of children's imitation*. Paper presented at the biennial Conference on Human Development, Charleston, South Carolina.

Bohman, Michael; Cloninger, R.; Sigvardsson, S.; & von Knorring, Anne-Liis (1987). The genetics of alcoholisms and related disorders. *Journal of Psychiatric Research, 21,* 447–452.

Bolger, Niall; Foster, Mark; Vinokur, Amiram D.; & Ng, Rosanna (1996). Close relationships and adjustment to a life crisis: The case of breast cancer. *Journal of Personality and Social Psychology, 70,* 283–294.

Bolshakov, Vadim Y., & Siegelbaum, Steven A. (1994). Postsynaptic induction and presynaptic expression of hippocampal long-term depression. *Science, 264,* 1148–1152.

Bond, Rod, & Smith, Peter B. (1996). Culture and conformity: A meta-analysis of studies using Asch's (1952b, 1956) line judgment task. *Psychological Bulletin, 119,* 111–137.

Bonnet, Michael H. (1990). The perception of sleep onset in insomniacs and normal sleepers. In R. R. Bootzin, J. F. Kihlstrom, & D. L. Schacter (eds.), *Sleep and cognition*. Washington, DC: American Psychological Association.

Bordo, Susan (2000). *The male body*. New York: Farrar, Straus and Giroux.

Boring, Edward G. (1923, June 6). Tests test it. *New Republic*, p. 35.

Boring, Edwin G. (1953). A history of introspection. *Psychological Bulletin, 50,* 169–187.

Borkenau, Peter; Riemann, Rainer; Angleitner, Alois; & Spinath, Frank M. (2001). Genetic and environmental influences on observed personality: Evidence from the German observational study of adult twins. *Journal of Personality and Social Psychology, 80,* 655–668.

Bornstein, Robert F.; Leone, Dean R.; & Galley, Donna J. (1987). The generalizability of subliminal mere exposure effects: Influence of stimuli perceived without awareness on social behavior. *Journal of Personality and Social Psychology, 53,* 1070–1079.

Bosworth, Hayden B., & Schaie, K. Warner (1999). Survival effects in cognitive function, cognitive style, and sociodemographic variables in the Seattle Longitudinal Study. *Experimental Aging Research, 25,* 121–139.

Bothwell, R. K., Deffenbacher, K. A., & Brigham, J. C. (1987). Correlation of eyewitness accuracy and confidence: Optimality hypothesis revised. *Journal of Applied Psychology, 72,* 691–698.

Bouchard, Claude; Tremblay, A.; Despres, J. P.; et al. (1990, May 24). The response to long-term overfeeding in identical twins. *New England Journal of Medicine, 322,* 1477–1482.

Bouchard, Thomas J., Jr. (1995). Nature's twice-told tale: Identical twins reared apart—what they tell us about human individuality. Paper presented at the annual meeting of the Western Psychological Association, Los Angeles.

Bouchard, Thomas J., Jr. (1997a). The genetics of personality. In K. Blum & E. P. Noble (eds.), *Handbook of psychiatric genetics*. Boca Raton, FL: CRC Press.

Bouchard, Thomas J., Jr. (1997b). IQ similarity in twins reared apart: Findings and responses to critics. In R. J. Sternberg & E. Grigorenko (eds.),

Intelligence: Heredity and environment. New York: Cambridge University Press.

Bouchard, Thomas J., Jr., & McGue, Matthew (1981). Familial studies of intelligence: A review. *Science, 212,* 1055–1058.

Bousfield, W. A. (1953). The occurrence of clustering in the recall of randomly arranged associates. *Journal of General Psychology, 49,* 229–240.

Bowden, Charles L.; Calabrese, Joseph R.; McElroy, Susan L.; et al. (2000). A randomized, placebo-controlled 12-month trial or divalproex and lithium in treatment of outpatients with bipolar I disorder. *Archives of General Psychiatry, 57,* 481–489.

Bowen, Murray (1978). *Family therapy in clinical practice.* New York: Jason Aronson.

Bower, Bruce (1998, February 21). All fired up: Perception may dance to the beat of collective neuronal rhythms. *Science news, 153,* 120–121.

Bower, Gordon H., & Clark, M. C. (1969). Narrative stories as mediators of serial learning. *Psychonomic Science, 14,* 181–182.

Bowers, Kenneth S.; Regehr, Glenn; Balthazard, Claude; & Parker, Kevin (1990). Intuition in the context of discovery. *Cognitive Psychology, 22,* 72–110.

Bowlby, John (1969). *Attachment and loss. Vol. 1. Attachment.* New York: Basic Books.

Bowlby, John (1973). *Attachment and loss: Vol. 2. Separation.* New York: Basic Books.

Boyd-Franklin, Nancy (1989). *Black families in therapy: A multisystems approach.* New York: Guilford.

Boysen, Sarah T., & Berntson, Gary G. (1989). Numerical competence in a chimpanzee *(Pan troglodytes). Journal of Comparative Psychology, 103,* 23–31.

Bradford, John M., & Pawlak, Anne (1993). Effects of cyproterone acetate on sexual arousal patterns of pedophiles. *Archives of Sexual Behavior, 22,* 629–641.

Brainerd, C. J.; Reyna, V. F.; & Brandse, E. (1995). Are children's false memories more persistent than their true memories? *Psychological Science, 6,* 359–364.

Brannon, Elizabeth M., & Terrace, Herbert S. (1998). Ordering of the numerosities 1 to 9 by monkeys. *Science, 282,* 746–749.

Brauer, Markus; Wasel, Wolfgang; & Niedenthal, Paula (2000). Implicit and explicit components of prejudice. *Review of General Psychology, 4,* 79–101.

Braun, Kathryn A.; Ellis, Rhiannon; & Loftus, Elizabeth F. (2002). Make my memory: How advertising can change our memories of the past. *Psychology & Marketing, 19,* 1–23.

Braungert, J. M.; Plomin, Robert; DeFries, J. C.; & Fulker, D. W. (1992). Genetic influence on tester-rated infant temperament as assessed by Bayley's Infant Behavior Record: Nonadoptive and adoptive siblings and twins. *Developmental Psychology, 28,* 40–47.

Brazelton, Timony R.; Rossi, Fabio M.; Keshet, Gilmor I.; & Blau, Helen M. (2000). From marrow to brain: expression of neuronal phenotypes in adult mice. *Science, 290,* 1775–1779.

Breggin, Peter R. (1991). *Toxic psychiatry.* New York: St. Martin's Press.

Brehm, Jack W. (1999). The intensity of emotion. *Personality and Social Psychology Review, 3,* 2–22.

Breland, Keller, & Breland, Marian (1961). The misbehavior of organisms. *American Psychologist, 16,* 681–684.

Brennan, Patricia A., & Mednick, Sarnoff A. (1994). Learning theory approach to the deterrence of criminal recidivism. *Journal of Abnormal Psychology, 103,* 430–440.

Breslau, Naomi; Kessler, Ronald C.; Chilcoat, Howard D.; et al. (1998). Trauma and posttraumatic stress disorder in the community: The 1996 Detroit area survey of trauma. *Archives of General Psychiatry, 55,* 626–632.

Brewer, James; Zhao, Zuo; Desmond, John E.; et al. (1998). Making memories: Brain activity that predicts how well visual experience will be remembered. *Science, 281,* 1185–1187.

Brewer, Marilynn B., & Gardner, Wendi (1996). Who is this "we"? Levels of collective identity and self representations. *Journal of Personality and Social Psychology, 71,* 83–93.

Briggs, John (1984, December). The genius mind. *Science Digest, 92(12),* 74–77, 102–103.

Brissette, Ian; Scheier, Michael F.; & Carver, Charles S. (2002). The role of optimism in social network development, coping, and psychological adjustment during a life transition. *Journal of Personality and Social Psychology, 82,* 102–111.

Brockner, Joel, & Rubin, Jeffrey Z. (1985). *Entrapment in escalating conflicts: A social psychological analysis.* New York: Springer-Verlag.

Brodsky, Annette M. (1982). Sex, race, and class issues in psychotherapy research. In J. H. Harvey & M. M. Parks (eds.), *Psychotherapy research and behavior change: Vol. 1. The APA Master Lecture Series.* Washington, DC: American Psychological Association.

Brody, Leslie (1999). *Gender, emotion and the family.* Cambridge, MA: Harvard University Press.

Brody, Nathan (1990). Behavior therapy versus placebo: Comment on Bowers and Clum's meta-analysis. *Psychological Bulletin, 107,* 106–109.

Bronfenbrenner, Urie (1995). Developmental ecology through space and time: A future perspective. In P. Moen, G. H. Elder, Jr., et al. (eds.), *Examining lives in context: Perspectives on the ecology of human development.* Washington, DC: American Psychological Association.

Brooks-Gunn, J. (1986). Differentiating premenstrual symptoms and syndromes. *Psychosomatic Medicine, 48,* 385–387.

Brown, George W. (1993). Life events and affective disorder: Replications and limitations. *Psychosomatic Medicine, 55,* 248–259.

Brown, Robert, & Middlefell, Robert (1989). Fifty-five years of cocaine dependence [letter]. *British Journal of Addiction, 84,* 946.

Brown, Roger (1986). *Social psychology* (2nd ed.). New York: Free Press.

Brown, Roger, & Kulik, James (1977). Flashbulb memories. *Cognition, 5,* 73–99.

Brown, Roger, & McNeill, David (1966). The "tip of the tongue" phenomenon. *Journal of Verbal Learning and Verbal Behavior, 5,* 325–337.

Brown, Roger; Cazden, Courtney; & Bellugi, Ursula (1969). The child's grammar from I to III. In J. P. Hill (ed.), *Minnesota Symposium on Child Psychology* (Vol. 2). Minneapolis: University of Minnesota Press.

Brown, Ryan P., & Josephs, Robert A. (1999). A burden of proof: Stereotype relevance and gender differences in math performance. *Journal of Personality and Social Psychology, 76,* 246–257.

Brown, Steven P. (1996). A meta-analysis and review of organizational research on job involvement. *Psychological Bulletin, 120,* 235–255.

Brownell, Kelly D., & Rodin, Judith (1994). The dieting maelstrom: Is it possible and advisable to lose weight? *American Psychologist, 49,* 781–791.

Browning, James R.; Hatfield, Elaine; Kessler, Debra; & Levine, Tim (2000). Sexual motives, gender, and sexual behavior. *Archives of Sexual Behavior, 29,* 135–153.

Bruck, Maggie; Ceci, Stephen J.; Francoeur, E.; & Renick, A. (1995). Anatomically detailed dolls do not facilitate preschoolers' reports of a pediatric examination involving genital touching. *Journal of Experimental Psychology: Applied, 1,* 95–109.

Bruer, John T. (1999). *The myth of the first three years.* New York: Free Press.

Brumberg, Joan J. (2000). *Fasting girls: The history of anorexia nervosa.* New York: Vintage.

Buck, Linda, & Axel, Richard (1991). A novel multigene family may encode odorant receptors: A molecular basis for odor recognition. *Cell, 65,* 175–187.

Buck, Ross (1984). *The communication of emotion.* New York: Guilford Press.

Budiansky, Stephen (1998). *If a lion could talk: Animal intelligence and the evolution of consciousness.* New York: Free Press.

Bukowski, William M. (2001). Friendship and the worlds of childhood. In D. W. Nangle & C. A. Erdley (eds.), *The role of friendship in psychological adjustment.* New directions for child and adolescent development, No. 91. San Francisco, CA: Jossey-Bass.

Burgess, Cheryl A.; Kirsch, Irving; Shane, Howard; et al. (1998). Facilitated communication as an ideomotor response. *Psychological Science, 9,* 71–74.

Burke, Deborah M.; MacKay, Donald G.; Worthley, Joanna S.; & Wade, Elizabeth (1991). On the tip of the tongue: What causes word finding failures in young and older adults? *Journal of Memory and Language, 30,* 237–246.

Burke, Phyllis (1996). *Gender shock.* New York: Basic Books.

Bursik, Krisanne (1998). Moving beyond gender differences: Gender role comparisons of manifest dream content. *Sex Roles, 38,* 203–214.

Bushman, Brad J. (1995). Moderating role of trait aggressiveness in the effects of violent media on aggression. *Journal of Personality and Social Psychology, 69,* 950–960.

Bushman, Brad J., & Anderson, Craig A. (2001). Media violence and the American public: Scientific facts versus media misinformation. *American Psychologist, 56,* 477–489.

Bushman, Brad J.; Baumeister, Roy; & Stack, Angela D. (1999). Catharsis, aggression, and persuasive influence: Self-fulfilling or self-defeating prophecies? *Journal of Personality and Social Psychology, 76,* 367–376.

Buss, David M. (1994). *The evolution of desire: Strategies of human mating.* New York: Basic Books.

Buss, David M. (1995). Evolutionary psychology: A new paradigm for psychological science. *Psychological Inquiry, 6,* 1–30.

Buss, David M. (1996). Sexual conflict: Can evolutionary and feminist perspectives converge? In D. M. Buss & N. Malamuth (eds.), *Sex, power, conflict: Evolutionary and feminist perspectives.* New York: Oxford University Press.

Buss, David M. (1999). *Evolutionary psychology: The new science of the mind.* Boston: Allyn and Bacon.

Bussey, Kay, & Bandura, Albert (1992). Self-regulatory mechanisms governing gender development. *Child Development, 63,* 1236–1250.

Butcher, James N.; Dahlstrom, W. Grant; Graham, John R.; Tellegen, Auke; & Kaemmer, Beverly (1989). *Minnesota Multiphasic Personality Inventory-II: Manual for administration and scoring.* Minneapolis: University of Minnesota Press.

Butcher, James N.; Lim, Jeeyoung; & Nezami, Elahe (1998). Objective study of abnormal personality in cross-cultural settings: The MMPI-2. *Journal of Cross-Cultural Psychology, 29,* 189–211.

Butler, S.; Chalder, T.; Ron, M.; et al. (1991). Cognitive behaviour therapy in chronic fatigue syndrome. *Journal of Neurology, Neurosurgery & Psychiatry, 54,* 153–158.

Buunk, Bram; Angleitner, Alois; Oubaid, Viktor; & Buss, David M. (1996). Sex differences in jealousy in evolutionary and cultural perspective: Tests from the Netherlands, Germany, and the United States. *Psychological Science, 7,* 359–363.

Byne, William (1993). Sexual orientation and brain structure: Adding up the evidence. Paper presented at the annual meeting of the International Academy of Sex Research, Pacific Grove, CA.

Byne, William (1995). Science and belief: Psychobiological research on sexual orientation. *Journal of Homosexuality, 28,* 303–344.

Cabiya, Jose J.; Lucio, Emilia; Chavira, Denise A.; et al. (2000). MMPI-2 scores of Puerto Rican, Mexican, and U.S. Latino college students: A research note. *Psychological Reports, 87,* 266–268.

Cachelin, Fary M.; Veisel, Catherine; Barzegarnazari, Emilia; & Striegel-Moore, Ruth H. (2000). Disordered eating, acculturation, and treatment-seeking in a community sample of Hispanic, Asian, Black, and White women. *Psychology of Women Quarterly, 24,* 244–253.

Cahill, Larry; Haier, Richard J.; White, N. S.; et al. (2001). Sex-related differences in amygdala activity during emotionally influenced memory storage. *Neurbiology of Learning and Memory, 75,* 1–9.

Cahill, Larry; Prins, Bruce; Weber, Michael; & McGaugh, James L. (1994). ß-adrenergic activation and memory for emotional events. *Nature, 371,* 702–704.

Calder, A. J.; Keane, J.; Manes, F.; Antoun, N.; & Young, A. W. (2000). Impaired recognition and experience of disgust following brain injury. *Nature Neuroscience, 3,* 1077–1078.

Campbell, Frances A., & Ramey, Craig T. (1995). Cognitive and school outcomes for high risk students at middle adolescence: Positive effects of early intervention. *American Educational Research Journal, 32,* 743–772.

Campbell, Jennifer; Trapnell, Paul D.; Heine, Steven J.; et al. (1996). Self-concept clarity: Measurement, personality correlates, and cultural boundaries. *Journal of Personality and Social Psychology, 70,* 141–156.

Campbell, Joseph (1949/1968). *The hero with 1,000 faces* (2nd ed.). Princeton, NJ: Princeton University Press.

Campbell, W. Keith, & Sedikides, Constantine (1999). Self-threat magnifies the self-serving bias: A meta-analytic integration. *Review of General Psychology, 3,* 23–43.

Cancian, Francesca M. (1987). *Love in America: Gender and self-development.* Cambridge, England: Cambridge University Press.

Canetto, Silvia S. (1992). Suicide attempts and substance abuse: Similarities and differences. *Journal of Psychology, 125,* 605–620.

Canetto, Silvia S., & Sakinofsky, Isaac (1998). The gender paradox in suicide. *Suicide and Life-Threatening Behavior, 28,* 1–23.

Canino, Glorisa (1994). Alcohol use and misuse among Hispanic women: Selected factors, processes, and studies. *International Journal of the Addictions, 29,* 1083–1100.

Cannon, Tyrone D.; Huttunen, Matti O.; Loennqvist, Jouko; et al. (2000). The inheritance of neuropsychological dysfunction in twins discordant for schizophrenia. *American Journal of Human Genetics, 67,* 369–382.

Cannon, Tyrone D.; Kaprio, Jaakko; Loennqvist, Jouko; Huttunen, Matti O.; & Koskenvuo, Markku (1998). The genetic epidemiology of schizophrenia in a Finnish twin cohort: A population-based modeling study. *Archives of General Psychiatry, 55,* 67–74.

Chance, Paul (1989, November). The other 90%. *Psychology Today,* 20–21.

Caplan, Eric (1998). *Mind games: American culture and the birth of psychotherapy.* (See Chapter 4: Inventing psychotherapy: The American Mind Cure movement, 1830–1900.) Berkeley: University of California Press.

Carani, C.; Bancroft, J.; Granata, A.; et al. (1992). Testosterone and erectile function, nocturnal penile tumescence and rigidity, and erectile response to visual erotic stimuli in hypogonadal and eugonadal men. *Psychoneuroendocrinology, 17,* 647–654.

Cardeña, Etzel; Lewis-Fernández, Roberto; Bear, David; et al. (1994). Dissociative disorders. In *DSM-IV Sourcebook.* Washington, DC: American Psychiatric Press.

Carroll, James M., & Russell, James A. (1996). Do facial expressions signal specific emotions? Judging emotion from the face in context. *Journal of Personality and Social Psychology, 70,* 203–218.

Carskadon, Mary A.; Mitler, Merrill M.; & Dement, William C. (1974). A comparison of insomniacs and normals: Total sleep time and sleep latency. *Sleep Research, 3,* 130 [Abstract].

Carstensen, Laura L.; Pasupathi, Monisha; Mayr, Ulrich; & Nesselroade, John R. (2000). Emotional experience in everyday life across the adult life span. *Journal of Personality and Social Psychology, 79,* 644–655.

Carter, Betty, & McGoldrick, Monica (eds.) (1988). *The changing family life cycle: A framework for family therapy* (2nd ed.). New York: Gardner Press.

Cartwright, Rosalind D. (1990). A network model of dreams. In R. R. Bootzin, J. F. Kihlstrom, & D. L. Schacter (eds.), *Sleep and cognition.* Washington, DC: American Psychological Association.

Cartwright, Rosalind D. (1996). Dreams and adaptations to divorce. In D. Barrett (ed.), Trauma and dreams. Cambridge: Harvard University Press.

Cartwright, Rosalind D.; Young, Michael A.; Mercer, Patricia; & Bears, Michael (1998). Role of REM sleep and dream variables in the prediction of remission from depression. *Psychiatry Research, 80,* 249–255.

Carver, Charles S. (1998). Resilience and thriving: Issues, models, and linkages. *Journal of Social Issues, 54,* 245–266.

Carver, Charles S., & Baird, Eryn (1998). The American dream revisited: Is it *what* you want or *why* you want it that matters? *Psychological Science, 9,* 289–292.

Carver, Charles S., & Scheier, Michael F. (1999). Optimism. In C. R. Snyder (ed.), *Coping: The psychology of what works.* New York: Oxford University Press.

Carver, Charles S.; Pozo, Christina; Harris, Suzanne D.; et al. (1993). How coping mediates the effect of optimism on distress: A study of women with early stage breast cancer. *Journal of Personality and Social Psychology, 65,* 375–390.

Caspi, Avshalom (2000). The child is father of the man: Personality continuities from childhood to adulthood. *Journal of Personality and Social Psychology, 78,* 158–172.

Caspi, Avshalom, & Moffitt, Terrie E. (1991). Individual differences are accentuated during periods of social change: The sample case of girls at puberty. *Journal of Personality and Social Psychology, 61,* 157–168.

Cattell, Raymond B. (1965). *The scientific analysis of personality.* Baltimore, MD: Penguin.

Cattell, Raymond B. (1973). *Personality and mood by questionnaire.* San Francisco: Jossey-Bass.

Ceci, Stephen J. (1996). *On intelligence: A bioecological treatise on intellectual development.* Cambridge, MA: Harvard University Press.

Ceci, Stephen J., & Bruck, Maggie (1995). *Jeopardy in the courtroom: A scientific analysis of children's testimony.* Washington, DC: American Psychological Association.

Cejka, Mary Ann, & Eagly, Alice H. (1999). Gender-stereotypic images of occupations correspond to the sex segregation of employment. *Personality and Social Psychology Bulletin, 25,* 413–423.

Cermak, Laird S., & Craik, Fergus I. M. (eds.) (1979). *Levels of processing in human memory.* Hillsdale, NJ: Erlbaum.

Cervone, Daniel (1997). Social-cognitive mechanisms and personality coherence. *Psychological Science, 8,* 43–50.

Cervone, Daniel, & Shoda, Yuichi (1999). Beyond traits in the study of personality coherence. *Current Directions in Psychological Science, 8,* 27–32.

Chabris, Christopher F.; Steele, Kenneth M.; Bella, Simone Dalla; et al. (1999). Prelude or requiem for the "Mozart effect"? *Nature, 400,* 826–828.

Chambless, Dianne L., & members of the Division 12 Task Force (1996). An update on empirically validated therapies. *The Clinical Psychologist, 49,* 5–18.

Chambless, Dianne L.; and the Task Force on Psychological Interventions (1998). Update on empirically validated therapies II. *The Clinical Psychologist, 51,* 3–16.

Chance, June E., & Goldstein, Alvin G. (1995). The other-race effect in eyewitness identification. In S. L. Sporer, G. Koehnken, & R. S. Malpass (eds.), *Psychological issues in eyewitness identification.* Hillsdale, NJ: Erlbaum.

Chance, Paul (1999). *Learning and behavior* (4th ed.). Pacific Grove: Brooks/Cole.

Chandra, R. K. (2001). Effect of vitamin and trace-element supplementation on cognitive function in elderly subjects. *Nutrition, 17,* 709–712.

Chang, Edward C. (1998). Dispositional optimism and primary and secondary appraisal of a stressor. *Journal of Personality and Social Psychology, 74,* 1109–1120.

Charles, Susan T.; Reynolds, Chandra A.; & Gatz, Margaret (2001). Age-related differences and change in positive and negative affect over 23 years. *Journal of Personality and Social Psychology, 80,* 136–151.

Chaudhari, Nirupa ; Landin, A. M.; & Roper, S. D. (2000). A metabotropic glutamate receptor variant functions as a taste receptor. *Nature Neuroscience, 3,* 113–119

Chaves, J. F. (1989). Hypnotic control of clinical pain. In N. P. Spanos & J. F. Chaves (eds.), *Hypnosis: The cognitive-behavioral perspective.* Buffalo, NY: Prometheus Books.

Chehab, Farid F.; Mounzih, K.; Lu, R.; & Lim, M. E. (1997, January 3). Early onset of reproductive function in normal female mice treated with leptin. *Science, 275,* 88–90.

Cheney, Dorothy L., & Seyfarth, Robert M. (1985). Vervet monkey alarm calls: Manipulation through shared information? *Behavior, 94,* 150–166.

Cheng, Cecilia (2001). Assessing coping flexibility in real-life and laboratory settings: A multimethod approach. *Journal of Personality and Social Psychology, 80,* 814–833.

Chipuer, Heather M.; Rovine, Michael J.; & Plomin, Robert (1990). LISREL modeling: Genetic and environmental influences on IQ revisited. *Intelligence, 14,* 11–29.

Cho, Kwangwook (2001). Chronic "jet lag" produces temporal lobe atrophy and spatial cognitive deficits. *Nature Neuroscience, 4,* 567–568.

Chodorow, Nancy (1978). *The reproduction of mothering.* Berkeley: University of California Press.

Chodorow, Nancy (1992). *Feminism and psychoanalytic theory.* New Haven, CT: Yale University Press.

Choi, Incheol, & Nisbett, Richard (2000). Cultural psychology of surprise: Holistic theories and recognition of contradiction. *Journal of Personality and Social Psychology, 79,* 890–905.

Choi, Incheol; Nisbett, Richard E.; & Norenzayan, Ara (1999). Causal attribution across cultures: Variation and universality. *Psychological Bulletin, 125,* 47–63.

Chomsky, Noam (1957). *Syntactic structures.* The Hague, Netherlands: Mouton.

Chomsky, Noam (1980). Initial states and steady states. In M. Piatelli-Palmerini (ed.), *Language and learning: The debate between Jean Piaget and Noam Chomsky.* Cambridge, MA: Harvard University Press.

Chorney, M. J.; Chorney, K.; Seese, N.; et al. (1998). A quantitative trait locus associated with cognitive ability in children. *Psychological Science, 9,* 159–166.

Chorpita, Bruce F., & Barlow, David H. (1998). The development of anxiety: The role of control in the early environment. *Psychological Bulletin, 124,* 3–21.

Chrisler, Joan C. (2000). PMS as a culture-bound syndrome. In J. C. Chrisler, C. Golden, & P. D. Rozee (eds.), *Lectures on the psychology of women* (2nd ed.). New York: McGraw-Hill.

Christensen, Andrew, & Jacobson, Neil S. (1994). Who (or what) can do psychotherapy: The status and challenge of nonprofessional therapies. *Psychological Science, 5,* 8–14.

Christensen, Andrew, & Jacobson, Neil S. (2000) *Reconcilable differences.* New York: Guilford.

Christensen, Larry, & Burrows, Ross (1990). Dietary treatment of depression. *Behavior Therapy, 21,* 183–194.

Church, A. Timothy, & Lonner, Walter J. (1998). The cross-cultural perspective in the study of personality: Rationale and current research. *Journal of Cross-Cultural Psychology, 29,* 32–62.

Cialdini, Robert B. (1993). *Influence: The psychology of persuasion.* New York: Quill/Morrow.

Cialdini, Robert B.; Trost, Melanie R.; & Newsom, Jason T. (1995). Preference for consistency: The development of a valid measure and the discovery of surprising behavioral implications. *Journal of Personality and Social Psychology, 69,* 318–328.

Cinque, Guglielmo (1999). *Adverbs and functional heads: A cross-linguistic approach.* New York: Oxford University Press.

Cioffi, Delia, & Holloway, James (1993). Delayed costs of suppressed pain. *Journal of Personality and Social Psychology, 64,* 274–282.

Cioffi, Frank (1998). *Freud and the question of pseudoscience.* Chicago, IL: Open Court.

Clark, Margaret S.; Milberg, Sandra; & Erber, Ralph (1987). Arousal state dependent memory: Evidence and some implications for understanding social judgments and social behavior. In K. Fiedler & J. P. Forgas (eds.), *Affect, cognition and social behavior.* Toronto, Canada: Hogrefe.

Clark, Rodney; Anderson, Norman B.; Clark, Vernessa R.; & Williams, David R. (1999). Racism as a stressor for African Americans: A biopsychosocial model. *American Psychologist, 54,* 805–816.

Clarke, Peter, & Evans, Susan H. (1998). *Surviving modern medicine.* Rutgers, NJ: Rutgers University Press.

Cloninger, C. Robert (1990). *The genetics and biology of alcoholism.* Cold Springs Harbor, ME: Cold Springs Harbor Press.

Clopton, Nancy A., & Sorell, Gwendolyn T. (1993). Gender differences in moral reasoning: Stable or situational? *Psychology of Women Quarterly, 17,* 85–101.

Coats, Erik J.; Janoff-Bulman, Ronnie; & Alpert, Nancy (1996). Approach versus avoidance goals: Differences in self-evaluation and well-being. *Personality and Social Psychology Bulletin, 22,* 1057–1067.

Cohen, David B. (1999). *Stranger in the nest: Do parents really shape their child's personality, intelligence, or character?* New York: Wiley.

Cohen, Dov (1998). Culture, social organization, and patterns of violence. *Journal of Personality and Social Psychology, 75,* 408–419.

Cohen, Dov (2001). Cultural variation: Considerations and implications. *Psychological Bulletin, 127,* 451–471.

Cohen, Dov; Nisbett, Richard E.; Bowdle, Brian F.; & Schwarz, Norbert (1996). Insult, aggression, and the Southern culture of honor: An "experimental ethnography." *Journal of Personality and Social Psychology, 70,* 945–960.

Cohen, Jonathan D., & Tong, Frank (2001). The face of controversy. *Science, 293,* 2405–2407.

Cohen, Sheldon, & Herbert, Tracy B. (1996). Health psychology: psychological factors and physical disease from the perspective of human psychoneuroimmunology. *Annual Review of Psychology, 47,* 113–142.

Cohen, Sheldon; Doyle, W. J.; Skoner, D. P.; et al. (1997). Social ties and susceptibility to the common cold. *Journal of the American Medical Association, 277,* 1940–1944.

Cohen, Sheldon; Evans, Gary W.; Krantz, David S.; & Stokols, Daniel (1980). Physiological, motivational, and cognitive effects of aircraft noise on children. *American Psychologist, 35,* 231–243.

Cohen, Sheldon; Frank, Ellen; Doyle, William J.; et al. (1998). Types of stressors that increase susceptibility to the common cold in healthy adults. *Health Psychology, 17,* 214–223.

Cohen, Sheldon; Tyrrell, David A.; & Smith, Andrew P. (1993). Negative life events, perceived stress, negative affect, and susceptibility to the common cold. *Journal of Personality and Social Psychology, 64,* 131–140.

Cohn, Lawrence D. (1991). Sex differences in the course of personality development: A meta-analysis. *Psychological Bulletin, 109,* 252–266.

Cole, Michael, & Cole, Sheila R. (1993). *The development of children* (2nd ed.). New York: Freeman.

Collaer, Marcia L., & Hines, Melissa (1995). Human behavioral sex differences: A role for gonadal hormones during early development? *Psychological Bulletin, 118,* 55–107.

Collins, Allan M., & Loftus, Elizabeth F. (1975). A spreading-activation theory of semantic processing. *Psychological Review, 82,* 407–428.

Collins, Barry E., & Brief, Diana E. (1995). Using person-perception vignette methodologies to uncover the symbolic meanings of teacher behaviors in the Milgram paradigm. *Journal of Social Issues, 51,* 89–106.

Collins, Rebecca L. (1996). For better or worse: The impact of upward social comparison on self-evaluations. *Psychological Bulletin, 119,* 51–69.

Collins, W. Andrew; Maccoby, Eleanor E.; Steinberg, Laurence; Hetherington, E. Mavis; & Bornstein, Marc H. (2000). Contemporary research on parenting: The case of nature *and* nurture. *American Psychologist, 55,* 218–232.

Colman, Andrew (1991). Crowd psychology in South African murder trials. *American Psychologist, 46,* 1071–1079.

Comas-Díaz, Lillian, & Greene, Beverly (1994). *Women of color: Integrating ethnic and gender identities in psychotherapy.* New York: Guilford.

Comuzzie, Anthony G., & Allison, David B. (1998). The search for human obesity genes. *Science, 280,* 1374–1377.

Conroy, John (2000). *Unspeakable acts, ordinary people: The dynamics of torture.* New York: Knopf.

Conway, Martin A., & Pleydell-Pearce, Christopher W. (2000). The construction of autobiographical memories in the self-memory system. *Psychological Review, 107,* 261–288.

Cooper, M. Lynne; Frone, Michael R.; Russell, Marcia; & Mudar, Pamela (1995). Drinking to regulate positive and negative emotions: A motivational model of alcohol use. *Journal of Personality and Social Psychology, 69,* 990–1005.

Cooper, M. Lynne; Shapiro, Cheryl M.; & Powers, Anne M. (1998). Motivations for sex and risky sexual behavior among adolescents and young adults: A functional perspective. *Journal of Personality and Social Psychology, 75,* 1528–1558.

Copi, Irving M., & Burgess-Jackson, Keith (1992). *Informal logic* (2nd ed.). New York: Macmillan.

Coren, Stanley (1996). Daylight saving time and traffic accidents. *New England Journal of Medicine, 334,* 924.

Corkin, Suzanne (1984). Lasting consequences of bilateral medial temporal lobectomy: Clinical course and experimental findings in H. M. *Seminars in Neurology, 4,* 249–259.

Corkin, Suzanne; Amaral, David G.; Gonzalez, R. Gilberto; et al. (1997). H. M.'s medial temporal lobe lesion: Findings from magnetic resonance imaging. Journal of *Neuroscience, 17,* 3964–3979.

Cornelius, Randolph R. (1991). Gregorio Marañon's two-factor theory of emotion. *Personality and Social Psychology Bulletin, 17,* 65–69.

Cose, Ellis (1994). *The rage of a privileged class.* New York: HarperCollins.

Cosmides, Leda; Tooby, John; & Barkow, Jerome H. (1992) Introduction: Evolutionary psychology and conceptual integration. In J. H. Barkow, L. Cosmides, & J. Tooby (eds.), *The adapted mind: Evolutionary psychology and the generation of culture.* New York: Oxford University Press.

Costa, Paul T., Jr., & McCrae, Robert R. (1994). "Set like plaster"? Evidence for the stability of adult personality. In R. Heatherton & J. Weinberger (eds.), *Can personality change?* Washington, DC: American Psychological Association.

Costa, Paul T., Jr.; McCrae, Robert R.; Martin, Thomas A.; et al. (1999). Personality development from adolescence through adulthood: Further cross-cultural comparisons of age differences. In V. J. Molfese & D. Molfese (eds.), *Temperament and personality development across the life span.* Hillsdale, NJ: Erlbaum.

Costantino, Giuseppe, & Malgady, Robert G. (1996). Culturally sensitive treatment: Cuento and hero/heroine modeling therapies for Hispanic children and adolescents. In E. D. Hibbs & P. S. Jensen (eds.), *Psychosocial treatments for child and adolescent disorders: Empirically based strategies for clinical practice.* Washington, DC: American Psychological Association.

Council, J. R.; Kirsch, Irving; & Grant, D. L. (1996). Imagination, expectancy and hypnotic responding. In R. G. Kunzendorf, N. K. Spanos, & B. J. Wallace (eds.), *Hypnosis and imagination.* Amityville, NY: Baywood.

Courtney, J. G.; Longnecker, M. P.; Theorell, T.; & Gerhardsson de Verdier, M. (1993). Stressful life events and the risk of colorectal cancer. *Epidemiology, 4,* 407–414.

Cowan, Nelson (2001). The magical number 4 in short-term memory: A reconsideration of mental storage capacity. *Behavioral and Brain Sciences, 24,* 87–185.

Cowen, Emory L.; Wyman, Peter A.; Work, William C.; & Parker, Gayle R. (1990). The Rochester Child Resilience Project (RCRP): Overview and summary of first year findings. *Development and Psychopathology, 2,* 193–212.

Coyne, J. C. (1990). Interpersonal processes in depression. In G. I. Keitner (ed.), *Depression and families: Impact and treatment.* Washington, DC: American Psychiatric Press.

Craik, Fergus I. M. & Lockhart, Robert (1972). Levels of processing: A framework for memory research. *Journal of Verbal Learning and Verbal Behavior, 11,* 671–684.

Craik, Fergus I. M., & Tulving, Endel (1975). Depth of processing and the retention of words in episodic memory. *Journal of Experimental Psychology: General, 104,* 268–294.

Crair, Michael C.; Gillespie, Deda C.; & Stryker, Michael P. (1998). The role of visual experience in the development of columns in cat visual cortex. *Science, 279,* 566–570.

Cramer, Phebe (2000). Defense mechanisms in psychology today: Further processes for adaptation. *American Psychologist, 55,* 637–646.

Crandall, Christian S., & Martinez, Rebecca (1996). Culture, ideology, and antifat attitudes. *Personality and Social Psychology Bulletin, 22,* 1165–1176.

Crawford, Mary, & Marecek, Jeanne (1989). Psychology constructs the female: 1968–1988. *Psychology of Women Quarterly, 13,* 147–165.

Crews, Frederick (ed.) (1998). *Unauthorized Freud: Doubters confront a legend.* New York: Viking.

Crick, Francis, & Mitchison, Graeme (1995). REM sleep and neural nets. *Behavioural Brain Research, 69,* 147–155.

Critchlow, Barbara (1986). The powers of John Barleycorn: Beliefs about the effects of alcohol on social behavior. *American Psychologist, 41,* 751–764.

Critser, Greg (2002). *Supersize.* New York: Houghton-Mifflin.

Croizen, Jean-Claude, & Claire, Theresa (1998). Extending the concept of stereotype threat to social class: The intellectual underperformance of students from low socioeconomic backgrounds. *Personality and Social Psychology Bulletin, 24,* 588–594.

Cronbach, Lee (1990). *Essentials of psychological testing* (5th ed.). New York: Harper & Row.

Cross, William E. (1991). *Shades of Black: Diversity in African-American identity.* Philadelphia, PA: Temple University Press.

Crowley, Thomas J.; MacDonald, Marilyn J.; Whitmore, Elizabeth A.; & Mikulich, Susan K. (1998). Cannabis dependence, withdrawal and reinforcing effects among adolescents with conduct symptoms and substance use disorders. *Drug and Alcohol Dependence, 50,* 27–37.

Csikszentmihalyi, Mihaly, & Larson, Reed (1984). *Being adolescent: Conflict and growth in the teenage years.* New York: Basic Books.

Culbertson, Frances M. (1997). Depression and gender: An international review. *American Psychologist, 52,* 25–31.

Cunningham, Michael R.; Roberts, A. R.; Barbee, A. P.; Druen, P. B.; & Wu, C. (1995). "Their ideas of beauty are, on the whole, the same as ours": Consistency and variability in the cross-cultural perception of female physical attractiveness. *Journal of Personality and Social Psychology, 68,* 261–279.

Cunningham, William A.; Preacher, Kristopher J.; & Banaji, Mahzarin R. (2001). Implicit attitude measures: Consistency, stability, and convergent validity. *Psychological Science, 12,* 163–170.

Currie, Elliot (1998). Crime and punishment in America. New York: Henry Holt.

Curtiss, Susan (1977). *Genie: A psycholinguistic study of a modern-day "wild child."* New York: Academic Press.

Curtiss, Susan (1982). Developmental dissociations of language and cognition. In L. Obler & D. Fein (eds.), *Exceptional language and linguistics.* New York: Academic Press.

Cushman, Philip (1995). *Constructing the self, constructing America: A cultural history of psychotherapy.* New York: Addison-Wesley.

Cvetkovich, George T., & Earle, Timothy C. (1994). Risk and culture. In W. J. Lonner & R. Malpass (eds.), *Psychology and culture.* Boston: Allyn & Bacon.

Czeisler, Charles A.; Duffy, Jeanne F.; Shanahan, Theresa L.; et al. (1999). Stability, precision, and near-24-hour period of the human circadian pacemaker. *Science, 284,* 2177–2181.

Dabbs, James M., Jr. (2000). *Heroes, rogues, and lovers: Testosterone and behavior.* New York: McGraw-Hill.

Dabbs, James M., Jr.; Alford, Elizabeth Carriere; & Fielden, Julie A. (1998). Trial lawyers and testosterone: Blue-collar talent in a white-collar world. *Journal of Applied Social Psychology, 28,* 84–94.

Dabbs, James M., Jr.; Carr, Timothy S.; Frady, Robert L.; & Riad, Jasmin K. (1995). Testosterone, crime, and misbehavior among 692 male prison inmates. *Personality and Individual Differences, 18,* 627–633.

Dabbs, James M., Jr.; Hargrove, Marian F.; & Heusel, Colleen (1996). Testosterone differences among college fraternities: Well-behaved vs. rambunctious. *Personality and Individual Differences, 20,* 157–161.

Dabbs, James M., Jr.; Strong, Rebecca; & Milun, Rhonda (1997). Exploring the mind of testosterone: A beeper study. *Journal of Research in Personality, 31,* 577–587.

Dadds, Mark R.; Bovbjerg, Dana H.; Redd, William H.; & Cutmore, Tim R. H. (1997). Imagery in human classical conditioning. *Psychological Bulletin, 122,* 89–103.

Dalton, K. S.; Morris, D. L.; Delanoy, D. I.; et al. (1996). Security measures in an automated ganzfeld system. *Journal of Parapsychology, 60,* 129–147.

Daly, Martin, & Wilson, Margo (1983). *Sex, evolution, and behavior* (2nd ed.). Belmont, CA: Wadsworth.

Damasio, Antonio R. (1994). *Descartes' error: Emotion, reason, and the human brain*. New York: Grosset/Putnam.

Damasio, Antonio R.; (1996). A neural basis for lexical retrieval. *Nature, 380*, 499–505.

Damasio, A. R.; Grabowski, T. J.; Bechara, A.; et al. (2000). Subcortical and cortical brain activity during the feeling of self-generated emotions. *Nature Neuroscience, 3*, 1049–1056.

Damasio, Hanna; Grabowski, Thomas J.; Frank, Randall; et al. (1994). The return of Phineas Gage: Clues about the brain from the skull of a famous patient. *Science, 264*, 1102–1105.

Damasio, Hanna; Grabowski, Thomas J.; Tranel, Daniel; et al. (1996). A neural basis for lexical retrieval. *Nature, 380*, 499–505.

Damon, William (1995). *Greater expectations*. New York: Free Press.

Danner, Deborah D.; Snowdon, David A.; & Friesen, Wallace V. (2001). Positive emotions in early life and longevity: Findings from the nun study. *Journal of Personality and Social Psychology, 80*, 804–813.

Darley, John M. (1995). Constructive and destructive obedience: A taxonomy of principal agent relationships. In A. G. Miller, B. E. Collins, & D. E. Brief (eds.), Perspectives on obedience to authority: The legacy of the Milgram experiments. *Journal of Social Issues, 51*(3), 125–154.

Darwin, Charles (1859). *On the origin of species*. [A facsimile of the first edition, edited by Ernst Mayer, 1964.] Cambridge, MA: Harvard University Press.

Darwin, Charles (1872/1965). *The expression of the emotions in man and animals*. Chicago: The University of Chicago Press.

Darwin, Charles (1874). *The descent of man and selection in relation to sex* (2nd ed.). New York: Hurst.

Dasen, Pierre R. (1994). Culture and cognitive development from a Piagetian perspective. In W. J. Lonner & R. S. Malpass (eds.), *Psychology and culture*. Needham Heights, MA: Allyn & Bacon.

Daum, Irene, & Schugens, Markus M. (1996). On the cerebellum and classical conditioning. *Psychological Science, 5*, 58–61.

Davey, Graham C. (1992). Classical conditioning and the acquisition of human fears and phobias: A review and synthesis of the literature. *Advances in Behaviour Research and Therapy, 14*, 29–66.

Davidson, Richard J.; Abercrombie, H.; Nitschke, J. B.; & Putnam, K. (1999). Regional brain function, emotion, and disorders of emotion. *Current Opinion in Neurobiology, 9*, 228–234.

Davidson, Richard J., & Henriques, Jeffrey B. (2000). Regional brain function in sadness and depression. In J. Borod (ed.), *The neuropsychology of emotion*. New York: Oxford University Press.

Davidson, Richard J.; Jackson, Daren C.; & Kalin, Ned H. (2000). Emotion, plasticity, context, and regulation: Perspectives from affective neuroscience. *Psychological Bulletin, 126*, 890–909.

Davies, Michaela; Stankov, Lazar; & Roberts, Richard D. (1998). Emotional intelligence: In search of an elusive construct. *Journal of Personality and Social Psychology, 75*, 989–1015.

Davis, B. E.; Moon, R. Y.; Sachs, H. C.; & Ottolini, M. C. (1998). Effects of sleep position on infant motor development. *Pediatrics, 102*, 1135–1140.

Davis, Christopher G.; Nolen-Hoeksema, Susan; & Larson, Judith (1998). Making sense of loss and benefiting from the experience: Two construals of meaning. *Journal of Personality and Social Psychology, 75*, 561–574.

Davis, Karen D.; Kiss, Z. H.; Luo, L.; et al. (1998). Phantom sensations generated by thalamic microstimulation. *Nature, 391*, 385–387.

Davis, Penelope J. (1999). Gender differences in autobiographical memory for childhood emotional experiences. *Journal of Personality and Social Psychology, 76*, 498–510.

Davis, T. L. (1995). Gender differences in masking negative emotions: Ability or motivation? *Developmental Psychology, 31*, 660–667.

Davison, Gerald C., & Neale, John M. (2001). Abnormal psychology (8th ed.). New York: Wiley.

Davison, Kathryn P.; Pennebaker, James W.; & Dickerson, Sally S. (2000). Who talks? The social psychology of illness support groups. *American Psychologist, 55*, 205–217.

Dawes, Robyn M. (1994). *House of cards: Psychology and psychotherapy built on myth*. New York: Free Press.

Dawson, Drew; Lack, Leon; & Morris, Mary (1993). Phase resetting of the human circadian pacemaker with use of a single pulse of bright light. *Chronobiology International, 10*, 94–102.

Dawson, Neal V.; Arkes, Hal R.; Siciliano, C.; et al. (1988). Hindsight bias: An impediment to accurate probability estimation in clinicopathologic conferences. *Medical Decision Making, 8*(4), 259–264.

de Bono, Edward (1985). *de Bono's thinking course*. New York: Facts on File.

de Lacoste-Utamsing, Christine, & Holloway, Ralph L. (1982). Sexual dimorphism in the human corpus callosum. *Science, 216*, 1431–1432.

de Rivera, Joseph (1989). Comparing experiences across cultures: Shame and guilt in America and Japan. *Hiroshima Forum for Psychology, 14*, 13–20.

De Robertis, Michael M., & Delaney, Paul A. (2000). A second survey of the attitudes of university students to astrology and astronomy. *Journal of the Royal Astronomical Society of Canada, 94*, 112–122.

de Waal, Frans (1997, July). Are we in anthropodenial? *Discover*, 50–53.

de Waal, Frans (2001a). *The ape and the sushi master: Cultural reflections by a primatologist*. New York: Basic Books.

de Waal, Frans (2001b). Inevitability of evolutionary psychology and the limitations of adaptationism: Lessons from the other primates. Invited address at the annual meeting of the American Psychological Association, San Francisco.

De Wolff, Marianne, & van IJzendoorn, Marinus H. (1997). Sensitivity and attachment: A meta-analysis on parental antecedents of infant attachment. *Child Development, 68*, 571–591.

Dean, Geoffrey (1992). The bottom line: Effect size. In B. Beyerstein & D. Beyerstein (eds.), *The write stuff: Evaluations of graphology-The study of handwriting analysis*. Buffalo, NY: Prometheus Books.

Deaux, Kay (1985). Sex and gender. *Annual Review of Psychology, 36*, 49–81.

Deci, Edward L.; Koestner, Richard; & Ryan, Richard M. (1999). A meta-analytic review of experiments examining the effects of extrinsic rewards on intrinsic motivation. *Psychological Bulletin, 125*, 627–668.

Deci, Edward L., & Ryan, Richard M. (1985). *Intrinsic motivation and self-determination of human behavior*. New York: Plenum.

Deci, Edward L., & Ryan, Richard M. (1987). The support of autonomy and the control of behavior. *Journal of Personality and Social Psychology, 53*, 1024–1037.

Deffenbacher, Jerry L.; Dahlen, Eric R.; Lynch, Rebekah S.; et al. (1998). Application of Beck's cognitive therapy to general anger reduction. Paper presented at the annual meeting of the American Psychological Association, San Francisco.

Deffenbacher, Jerry L.; Oetting, Eugene R.; Lynch, Rebekah S.; & Morris, Chad D. (1996). The expression of anger and its consequences. *Behaviour Research and Therapy, 34*, 575–590.

Dehaene, S.; Spelke, E.; Pinel, P; et al. (1999). Sources of mathematical thinking: Behavioral and brain-imaging evidence. *Science, 284*, 970–974.

DeLeon, Patrick H., & Wiggins, Jack G., Jr. (1996). Prescription privileges for psychologists. *American Psychologist, 51*, 225–229.

Dement, William (1978). *Some must watch while some must sleep.* New York: Norton.

Dement, William (1992). *The sleepwatchers.* Stanford, CA: Stanford Alumni Association.

DeNelsky, Garland Y. (1996). The case against prescription privileges for psychologists. *American Psychologist, 51*, 207–212.

Dennett, Daniel C. (1991). *Consciousness explained.* Boston: Little, Brown.

DePaulo, Bella M. (1992). Nonverbal behavior and self-presentation. *Psychological Bulletin, 111*, 203–243.

DeValois, Russell L., & DeValois, Karen K. (1975). Neural coding of color. In E. C. Carterette & M. P. Friedman (eds.), *Handbook of perception* (Vol. 5). New York: Academic Press.

Devanand, Devangere P.; Dwork, Andrew J.; Hutchinson, Edward R.; et al. (1994). Does ECT alter brain structure? *American Journal of Psychiatry, 151*, 957–970.

Devlin, B.; Daniels, Michael; & Roeder, Kathryn (1997). The heritability of IQ. *Nature, 388*, 468–471.

Dewsbury, Donald A. (1996). Animal research: Getting in and getting out. *The General Psychologist, 32*, 19–25.

Di Blas, Lisa, & Forzi, Mario (1999). Refining a descriptive structure of personality attributes in the Italian language: The abridged Big Three circumplex structure. *Journal of Personality and Social Psychology, 76*, 451–481.

di Leonardo, Micaela (1987). The female world of cards and holidays: Women, families, and the work of kinship. *Signs, 12*, 1–20.

Diamond, Marian C. (1993, Winter–Spring). An optimistic view of the aging brain. *Generations, 17*, 31–33.

Dickinson, Alyce M. (1989). The detrimental effects of extrinsic reinforcement on "intrinsic motivation." *The Behavior Analyst, 12*, 1–15.

Dien, Dora S. (1982). A Chinese perspective on Kohlberg's theory of moral development. *Developmental Review, 2*, 331–341.

Dien, Dora S. (1999). Chinese authority-directed orientation and Japanese peer-group orientation: Questioning the notion of collectivism. *Review of General Psychology, 3*, 372–385.

Digman, John M. (1996). The curious history of the five-factor model. In J. S. Wiggins (ed.), *The five-factor model of personality: Theoretical perspectives.* New York: Guilford Press.

Digman, John M., & Shmelyov, Alexander G. (1996). The structure of temperament and personality in Russian children. *Journal of Personality and Social Psychology, 71*, 341–351.

Dimberg, Ulf; Thunberg, Monika; & Elmehed, Kurt (2000). Unconscious facial reactions to emotional facial expressions. *Psychological Science, 11*, 86–89.

Dinges, David F.; Whitehouse, Wayne G.; Orne, Emily C.; Powell, John W.; Orne, Martin T.; & Erdelyi, Matthew H. (1992). Evaluating hypnotic memory enhancement (hypermnesia and reminiscence) using multitrial forced recall. *Journal of Experimental Psychology: Learning, Memory, and Cognition, 18*, 1139–1147.

Dion, Kenneth L., & Dion, Karen K. (1993). Gender and ethnocultural comparisons in styles of love. *Psychology of Women Quarterly, 17*, 463–474.

Dixon, L. B.; Sundquist, J.; Winkleby, M. (2000, September 15). Differences in energy, nutrient, and food intakes in a US sample of Mexican-American women and men: Findings from the Third National Health and Nutrition Examination Survey, 1988–1994. *American Journal of Epidemiology, 152*, 548–557.

Doering, Charles H.; Brodie, H. K. H.; Kraemer, H. C.; Becker, H. B.; & Hamburg, D. A. (1974). Plasma testosterone levels and psychologic measures in men over a 2-month period. In R. C. Friedman, R. M. Richard, & R. L. Vande Wiele (eds.), *Sex differences in behavior.* New York: Wiley.

Doering, Stephan; Katzlberger, Florian; Rumpold, Gerhard; et al. (2000). Videotape preparation of patients before hip replacement surgery reduces stress. *Psychosomatic Medicine, 62*, 365–373.

Dollard, John, & Miller, Neal E. (1950). *Personality and psychotherapy: An analysis in terms of learning, thinking, and culture.* New York: McGraw-Hill.

Dolnick, Edward (1990, July). What dreams are (really) made of. *The Atlantic Monthly, 226*, 41–45, 48–53, 56–58, 60–61.

Domhoff, G. William (1996). *Finding meaning in dreams: A quantitative approach.* New York: Plenum.

Doty, Richard M.; Peterson, Bill E.; & Winter, David G. (1991). Threat and authoritarianism in the United States, 1978–1987. *Journal of Personality and Social Psychology, 61*, 629–640.

Dovidio, John F. (2001). On the nature of contemporary prejudice: The third wave. *Journal of Social Issues*, in press.

Dovidio, John F., & Gaertner, Samuel L. (2000). Aversive racism and selection decisions: 1989 and 1999. *Psychological Science, 11*, 315–319.

Dovidio, John F.; Gaertner, Samuel L.; & Validzic, Ana (1998). Intergroup bias: Status, differentiation, and a common in-group identity. *Journal of Personality and Social Psychology, 75*, 109–120.

Drayna, Dennis; Manichaikul, Ani; de Lange, Marlies; et al. (2001). Genetic correlates of musical pitch recognition in humans. *Science, 291*, 1969–1972.

Drevets, W. C. (2000). Neuroimaging studies of mood disorders. *Biological Psychiatry, 48*, 813–829.

Drieschner, K., & Lange, A. (1999). A review of cognitive factors in the etiology of rape: Theories, empirical studies, and implications. *Clinical Psychology Review, 19*, 57–77.

Druckman, Daniel, & Swets, John A. (eds.) (1988). *Enhancing human performance: Issues, theories, and techniques.* Washington, DC: National Academy Press.

Dudley-Grant, G. Rita (2001). Eastern Caribbean family psychology with conduct-disordered adolescents from the Virgin Islands. *American Psychologist, 56*, 47–57.

Duncan, Paula D.; Ritter, Philip L.; Dornbusch, Sanford M.; et al. (1985). The effects of pubertal timing on body image, school behavior, and deviance. *Journal of Youth and Adolescence, 14*, 227–235.

Dunkel-Schetter, Christine (1984). Social support and cancer: Findings based on patient interviews and their implications. *Journal of Social Issues, 40*(4), 77–98.

Dweck, Carol S. (1992). The study of goals in psychology. *Psychological Science, 3*, 165–167.

Dweck, Carol S., & Sorich, Lisa A. (1999). Mastery-oriented thinking. In C. R. Snyder (ed.), *Coping: The psychology of what works.* New York: Oxford University Press.

Dym, Barry, & Glenn, Michael L. (1993). *Couples: Exploring and understanding the cycles of intimate relationships.* New York: HarperCollins.

Eagly, Alice H., & Wood, Wendy (1999). The origins of sex differences in human behavior: Evolved dispositions versus social roles. *American Psychologist, 54*, 408–423.

Eastman, Charmane I.; Young, Michael A.; Fogg, Louis F.; et al. (1998). Bright light treatment of winter depression: A placebo-controlled trial. *Achives of General Psychiatry, 55*, 883–889.

Ebbinghaus, Hermann M. (1885/1913). *Memory: A contribution to experimental psychology* (H. A. Ruger & C. E. Bussenius, trans.). New York: Teachers College Press, Columbia University.

Eberlin, Michael; McConnachie, Gene; Ibel, Stuart; & Volpe, Lisa (1993). Facilitated communication: A failure to replicate the phenomenon. *Journal of Autism and Developmental Disorders, 23,* 507–530.

Eccles, Jacquelynne S.; Midgley, Carol; Wigfield, Allan; et al. (1993). Development during adolescence: The impact of stage- environment fit on young adolescents' experiences in schools and in families. *American Psychologist, 48,* 90–101.

Eckensberger, Lutz H. (1994). Moral development and its measurement across cultures. In W. J. Lonner & R. Malpass (eds.), *Psychology and culture.* Needham Heights, MA: Allyn & Bacon.

Edelson, Marshall (1994). Can psychotherapy research answer this psychotherapist's questions? In P. F. Talley, H. H. Strupp, & S. F. Butler (eds.), *Psychotherapy research and practice: Bridging the gap.* New York: Basic Books.

Edenberg, Howard J.; Foroud, Tatiana; Koller, D. L.; et al. (1998). A family-based analysis of the association of the dopamine D2 receptor (DRD2) with alcoholism. *Alcohol Clinical and Experimental Research, 22,* 505–512.

Edwards, Kari, & Smith, Edward E. (1996). A disconfirmation bias in the evaluation of arguments. *Journal of Personality and Social Psychology, 71,* 5–24.

Edwards, Lynne K., & Edwards, Allen L. (1991). A principal-components analysis of the Minnesota Multiphasic Personality Inventory Factor Scales. *Journal of Personality and Social Psychology, 60,* 766–772.

Efran, Jay S.; Greene, Mitchell A.; & Gordon, Don E. (1998, March/April). Lessons of the new genetics: Finding the right fit for our clients. *Family Therapy Networker, 22,* 26–41.

Ehrenreich, Barbara (1978). *For her own good: 150 years of the experts' advice to women.* New York: Doubleday.

Ehrenreich, Barbara (2001, June 4). What are they probing for? [Essay.] *Time,* p. 86.

Eich, E., & Hyman, R. (1992). Subliminal self-help. In D. Druckman & R. A. Bjork (eds.), *In the mind's eye: Enhancing human performance.* Washington, DC: National Academy Press.

Eisenberg, Nancy (1995). Prosocial development: A multifaceted model. In W. M. Kurtines & J. L. Gewirtz (eds.), *Moral development: An introduction.* Boston: Allyn & Bacon.

Eisenberg, Nancy; Fabes, Richard A.; Murphy, Bridget; et al. (1996). The relations of children's dispositional empathy-related responding to their emotionality, regulation, and social functioning. *Developmental Pschology, 32,* 195–209.

Eisenberger, Robert, & Cameron, Judy (1996). Detrimental effects of reward: Reality or myth? *American Psychologist, 51,* 1153–1166.

Eisenberger, Robert, & Cameron, Judy (1998). Reward, intrinsic interest, and creativity: New findings. [Comment.] *American Psychologist, 53,* 676–679.

Eisenberger, Robert; Armeli, Stephen; & Pretz, Jean (1998). Can the promise of reward increase creativity? *Journal of Personality and Social Psychology, 74,* 704–714.

Ekman, Paul (1994). Strong evidence for universals in facial expressions: A reply to Russell's mistaken critique. *Psychological Bulletin, 115,* 268–287.

Ekman, Paul (1997). What we have learned by measuring facial behavior. In P. Ekman & E. L. Rosenberg (eds.), *What the face reveals.* Oxford, England: Oxford University Press.

Ekman, Paul, & Heider, Karl G. (1988). The universality of a contempt expression: A replication. *Motivation and Emotion, 12,* 303–308.

Ekman, Paul; Friesen, Wallace V.; & O'Sullivan, Maureen (1988). Smiles when lying. *Journal of Personality and Social Psychology, 54,* 414–420.

Ekman, Paul; Friesen, Wallace V.; O'Sullivan, Maureen; et al. (1987). Universals and cultural differences in the judgments of facial expression of emotion. *Journal of Personality and Social Psychology, 53,* 712–717.

Elliot, Andrew J., & McGregor, Holly A. (2001). A 2 X 2 achievement goal framework. *Journal of Personality and Social Psychology, 80,* 501–519.

Elliot, Andrew J., & Sheldon, Kennon M. (1998). Avoidance personal goals and the personality-illness relationship. *Journal of Personality and Social Psychology, 75,* 1282–1299.

Elliott, Robert, & Morrow-Bradley, Cheryl (1994). Developing a working marriage between psychotherapists and psychotherapy researchers: Identifying shared purposes. In P. F. Talley, H. H. Strupp, & S. F. Butler (eds.), *Psychotherapy research and practice: Bridging the gap.* New York: Basic Books.

Ellis, Albert (1993). Changing rational-emotive therapy (RET) to rational emotive behavior therapy (REBT). *Behavior Therapist, 16,* 257–258.

Ellis, Albert, & Blau, S. (1998). Rational emotive behavior therapy. *Directions in Clinical and Counseling Psychology, 8,* 41–56.

Ellison, Carol R. (2000). *Women's sexualities.* Oakland, CA: New Harbinger.

Emery, C. Eugene, Jr. (2001, January/February). Cracked crystal balls? Psychic's predictions for past year a litany of prognostive failures. *Skeptical Inquirer,* 7–8.

Emery, Robert E., & Laumann-Billings, Lisa (1998). An overview of the nature, causes, and consequences of abusive family relationships. *American Psychologist, 53,* 121–135.

Emmons, Robert A., & King, Laura A. (1988). Conflict among personal strivings: Immediate and long-term implications for psychological and physical well-being. *Journal of Personality and Social Psychology, 54,* 1040–1048.

Englander-Golden, Paula; Whitmore, Mary R.; & Dienstbier, Richard A. (1978). Menstrual cycle as focus of study and self-reports of moods and behavior. *Motivation and Emotion, 2,* 75–86.

Entin, Alan D. (1992). Family photographs: Visual icons and emotional history. Paper presented at the annual meeting of the American Psychological Association, Washington, DC.

Epstein, Seymour (1994). Integration of the cognitive and the psychodynamic unconscious. *American Psychologist, 49,* 709–724.

Ericksen, Julia A., & Steffen, Sally A. (1999). *Kiss and tell: Surveying sex in the twentieth century.* Cambridge, MA: Harvard University Press.

Erikson, Erik H. (1950/1963). *Childhood and society* (2nd ed.). New York: Norton.

Erikson, Erik H. (1982). *The life cycle completed.* New York: Norton.

Eriksson, P. S.; Perfilieva, E; Bjork-Eriksson, T.; et al. (1998). Neurogenesis in the adult human hippocampus. *Nature Medicine, 4,* 1313–1317.

Eron, Leonard D. (1995). *Media violence: How it affects kids and what can be done about it.* Invited address presented at the annual meeting of the American Psychological Association, New York.

Ervin-Tripp, Susan (1964). Imitation and structural change in children's language. In E. H. Lenneberg (ed.), *New directions in the study of language.* Cambridge, MA: MIT Press.

Escera, Carles; Cilveti, Robert; & Grau, Carles (1992). Ultradian rhythms in cognitive operations: Evidence from the P300 component of the event-related potentials. *Medical Science Research, 20,* 137–138.

Esparza, J.; Fox, C.; Harper, I. T.; et al. (2000, January 24). Daily energy expenditure in Mexican and USA Pima Indians: Low physical activity as a possible cause of obesity. *International Journal of Obesity and Related Metabolic Disorders, 1,* 55–59.

Evans, Christopher (1984). *Landscapes of the night* (edited and completed by Peter Evans). New York: Viking.

Evans, Gary W.; Bullinger, Monika; & Hygge, Staffan (1998). Chronic noise exposure and physiological response: A prospective study of children living under environmental stress. *Psychological Science, 9,* 75–77.

Evans, Gary W.; Lepore, Stephen J.; & Allen, Karen Mata (2000). Cross-cultural differences in tolerance for crowding: Fact or fiction? *Journal of Personality and Social Psychology, 79,* 204–210.

Evans, Gary W.; Lepore, Stephen J.; & Schroeder, Alex (1996). The role of interior design elements in human responses to crowding. *Journal of Personality and Social Psychology, 70,* 41–46.

Ewart, Craig K. (1995). Self-efficacy and recovery from heart attack. In J. E. Maddux (ed.), *Self-efficacy, adaptation, and adjustment: Theory, research, and application.* New York: Plenum.

Ewart, Craig K., & Kolodner, Kenneth B. (1994). Negative affect, gender, and expressive style predict elevated ambulatory blood pressure in adolescents. *Journal of Personality and Social Psychology, 66,* 596–605.

Exner, John E. (1993). *The Rorschach: A comprehensive system: Vol. 1. Basic foundations* (3rd ed.). New York: Wiley.

Eyer, Diane E. (1992). *Mother-infant bonding: A scientific fiction.* New Haven, CT: Yale University Press.

Eyferth, Klaus (1961). [The performance of different groups of the children of occupation forces on the Hamburg-Wechsler Intelligence Test for Children.] *Archiv für die Gesamte Psychologie, 113,* 222–241.

Eysenck, Hans J. (1993). Prediction of cancer and coronary heart disease mortality by means of a personality inventory: Results of a 15-year follow-up study. *Psychological Reports, 72,* 499–516.

Fagan, Joseph F., III (1992). Intelligence: A theoretical viewpoint. *Current Directions in Psychological Science, 1,* 82–86.

Fagot, Beverly I. (1985). Beyond the reinforcement principle: Another step toward understanding sex role development. *Developmental Psychology, 2,* 1097–1104.

Fagot, Beverly I. (1993, June). Gender role development in early childhood: Environmental input, internal construction. Invited address presented at the annual meeting of the International Academy of Sex Research, Monterey, CA.

Fagot, Beverly I.; Hagan, R.; Leinbach, Mary D.; & Kronsberg, S. (1985). Differential reactions to assertive and communicative acts of toddler boys and girls. *Child Development, 56,* 1499–1505.

Fagot, Beverly I., & Leinbach, Mary D. (1993). Gender-role development in young children: From discrimination to labeling. *Developmental Review, 13,* 205–224.

Falk, Ruma, & Greenbaum, Charles W. (1995). Significance tests die hard: The amazing persistence of a probabilistic misconception. *Theory & Psychology, 5*(1), 75–98.

Fancher, Robert T. (1995). *Cultures of healing.* New York: W. H. Freeman.

Fausto-Sterling, Anne (1997). Beyond difference: A biologist's perspective. *Journal of Social Issues, 53,* 233–258.

Fazio, Russell H.; Jackson, Joni R.; Dunton, Bridget C.; & Williams, Carol J. (1995). Variability in automatic activation as an unobtrusive measure of racial attitudes: A bona fide pipeline? *Journal of Personality and Social Psychology, 69,* 1013–1027.

FDA Drug Bulletin (1990, April). Two new psychiatric drugs. 20(1), 9.

Feather, N. T. (1966). Effects of prior success and failure on expectations of success and subsequent performance. *Journal of Personality and Social Psychology, 3,* 287–298.

Feeney, Judith A., & Noller, Patricia (1990). Attachment style as a predictor of adult romantic relationships. *Journal of Personality and Social Psychology, 58,* 281–291.

Fehr, Beverley (1993). How do I love thee . . . Let me consult my prototype. In S. Duck (ed.), *Individuals in relationships* (Vol. 1). Newbury Park, CA: Sage.

Fehr, Beverley; Baldwin, Mark; Collins, Lois; et al. (1999). Anger in close relationships: An interpersonal script analysis. *Personality and Social Psychology Bulletin, 25,* 299–312.

Fein, Steven, & Spencer, Steven J. (1997). Prejudice as self-image maintenance: Affirming the self through derogating others. *Journal of Personality and Social Psychology, 73,* 31–44.

Feingold, Alan (1988). Cognitive gender differences are disappearing. *American Psychologist, 43,* 95–103.

Fernald, Anne, & Mazzie, Claudia (1991). Prosody and focus in speech to infants and adults. *Developmental Psychology, 27,* 209–221.

Fernandez, Ephrem, & Turk, Dennis C. (1992). Sensory and affective components of pain: Separation and synthesis. *Psychological Bulletin, 112,* 205–217.

Fernández-Dols, José-Miguel, & Ruiz-Belda, María-Angeles (1995). Are smiles a sign of happiness? Gold medal winners at the Olympic games. *Journal of Personality and Social Psychology, 69,* 1113–1119.

Fernea, Elizabeth, & Fernea, Robert (1994). Cleanliness and culture. In W. J. Lonner & Malpass (eds.), *Psychology and culture.* Boston: Allyn & Bacon.

Festinger, Leon (1957). *A theory of cognitive dissonance.* Evanston, IL: Row, Peterson.

Festinger, Leon (1980). Looking backward. In L. Festinger (ed.), *Retrospections on social psychology.* New York: Oxford University Press.

Festinger, Leon, & Carlsmith, J. Merrill (1959). Cognitive consequences of forced compliance. *Journal of Abnormal and Social Psychology, 58,* 203–210.

Festinger, Leon; Pepitone, Albert; & Newcomb, Theodore (1952). Some consequences of deindividuation in a group. *Journal of Abnormal and Social Psychology, 47,* 382–389.

Festinger, Leon; Riecken, Henry W.; & Schachter, Stanley (1956). *When prophecy fails.* Minneapolis: University of Minnesota Press.

Field, Tiffany M. (1998). Massage therapy effects. *American Psychologist, 53,* 1270–1281.

Field, Tiffany M. (2001). Massage therapy facilitates weight gain in preterm infants. *Current Directions in Psychological Science, 10,* 51–54.

Fields, Howard (1991). Depression and pain: A neurobiological model. *Neuropsychiatry, Neuropsychology, and Behavioral Neurology, 4,* 83–92.

Fiez, J. A. (1996). Cerebellar contributions to cognition. *Neuron, 16,* 13–15.

Fink, Max (1999). *Electroshock: Restoring the mind.* New York: Oxford University Press.

Fischer, Agneta H. (1993). Sex differences in emotionality: Fact or stereotype? *Feminism & Psychology, 3,* 303–318.

Fischer, Ann R.; Tokar, David M.; Good, Glenn E.; & Snell, Andrea F. (1998). More on the structure of male role norms. *Psychology of Women Quarterly, 22,* 135–155.

Fischer, Pamela C.; Smith, Randy J.; Leonard, Elizabeth; et al. (1993). Sex differences on affective dimensions: Continuing examination. *Journal of Counseling and Development, 71,* 440–443.

Fischhoff, Baruch (1975). Hindsight is not equal to foresight: The effect of outcome knowledge on judgment under uncertainty. *Journal of Experimental Psychology: Human Perception and Performance, 1,* 288–299.

Fishbein, Harold D. (1996). *Peer prejudice and discrimination.* Boulder, CO: Westview Press.

Fisher, P. J.; Turic, D.; McGuffin, P.; et al. (1999). DNA pooling identifies QTLs for general cognitive ability in children on chromosome 4. *Human Molecular Genetics, 8,* 915–922.

Fisher, Ronald J. (1994). Generic principles for resolving intergroup conflict. *Journal of Social Issues, 50,* 47–66.

Fisher, S., & Greenberg, R. (1996). Freud scientifically appraised. New York: John Wiley.

Fiske, Susan T. (1993). Controlling other people: The impact of power on stereotyping. *American Psychologist, 48,* 621–628.

Fivush, Robyn, & Hamond, Nina R. (1991). Autobiographical memory across the school years: Toward reconceptualizing childhood amnesia. In

R. Fivush & J. A. Hudson (eds.), *Knowing and remembering in young children*. New York: Cambridge University Press.

Flacks, Richard, & Thomas, Scott L. (1998, November 27). Among affluent students, a culture of disengagement. *Chronicle of Higher Education*, A48.

Flavell, John H. (1996). Piaget's legacy. *Psychological Science, 7*, 200–203.

Flavell, John H. (1999). Cognitive development: Children's knowledge about the mind. *Annual Review of Psychology, 50*, 21–45.

Fleeson, William (2001). Toward a structure- and process-integrated view of personality: Traits as density distributions of states. *Journal of Personality and Social Psychology, 80*, 1011–1027.

Flett, Gordon L.; Hewitt, Paul L.; Blankstein, Kirk R.; & Gray, Lisa (1998). Psychological distress and the frequency of perfectionistic thinking. *Journal of Personality and Social Psychology, 75*, 1363–1381.

Flor, Herta; Kerns, Robert D.; & Turk, Dennis C. (1987). The role of spouse reinforcement, perceived pain, and activity levels of chronic pain patients. *Journal of Psychosomatic Research, 31*, 251–259.

Flynn, James R. (1987). Massive IQ gains in 14 nations: What IQ tests really measure. *Psychological Bulletin, 95*, 29–51.

Flynn, James R. (1999). Searching for justice: the discovery of IQ gains over time. *American Psychologist, 54*, 5–20.

Foa, Edna, & Emmelkamp, Paul (eds.) (1983). *Failures in behavior therapy*. New York: Wiley.

Fogelman, Eva (1994). *Conscience and courage: Rescuers of Jews during the Holocaust*. New York: Anchor Books.

Folkman, Susan, & Moskowitz, Judith T. (2000). Positive affect and the other side of coping. *American Psychologist, 55*, 647–654.

Ford, D. E.; Mead, L. A.; Chang, P. P.; et al. (1998). Depression is a risk factor for coronary artery disease in men: the precursors study. *Archives of Internal Medicine, 158*, 1422–1426.

Fordham, Signithia (1991, Spring). Racelessness in private schools: Should we deconstruct the racial and cultural identity of African-American adolescents? *Teachers College Record, 92*, 470–484.

Forgas, Joseph P. (1998). On being happy and mistaken: Mood effects on the fundamental attribution error. *Journal of Personality and Social Psychology, 75*, 318–331.

Forgas, Joseph P., & Bond, Michael H. (1985). Cultural influences on the perception of interaction episodes. *Personality and Social Psychology Bulletin, 11*, 75–88.

Foulkes, D. (1962). Dream reports from different states of sleep. *Journal of Abnormal and Social Psychology, 65*, 14–25.

Fouts, Roger S. (with Stephen T. Mills) (1997). *Next of kin: What chimpanzees have taught me about who we are*. New York: Morrow.

Fouts, Roger S., & Rigby, Randall L. (1977). Man-chimpanzee communication. In T. A. Seboek (ed.), *How animals communicate*. Bloomington: University of Indiana Press.

Fox, Nathan A., & Davidson, Richard J. (1988). Patterns of brain electrical activity during facial signs of emotion in 10-month-old infants. *Developmental Psychology, 24*, 230–236.

Frank, Mark G., & Stennett, Janine (2001). The forced-choice paradigm and the perception of facial expressions of emotion. *Journal of Personality and Social Psychology, 80*, 75–85.

Frank, Robert G.; Gluck, John P.; & Buckelew, Susan P. (1990). Rehabilitation: Psychology's greatest opportunity? *American Psychologist, 45*, 757–761.

Frankl, Victor E. (1955). *The doctor and the soul: An introduction to logotherapy*. New York: Knopf.

Franz, Carol E. (1997). Stability and change in the transition to midlife: A longitudinal study of midlife adults. In M. E. Lachman & J. B. James (eds.), *Multiple paths of midlife development*. Chicago: University of Chicago Press.

Frasure-Smith, Nancy; Lesperance, F.; Juneau, M.; Talajic, M.; & Bourassa, M. G. (1999). Gender, depression, and one-year prognosis after myocardial infarction. *Psychosomatic Medicine, 61*, 26–37.

Fredrickson, Barbara L. (2001). The role of positive emotions in positive psychology. *American Psychologist, 56*, 218–226.

Freedman, Hill, & Combs, Gene (1996). *Narrative therapy*. New York: Norton.

Freedman, Jonathan L. (1988). Television violence and aggression: What the evidence shows. In S. Oskamp (ed.), *Television as a social issue (Applied Social Psychology Annual*, Vol. 8). Newbury Park, CA: Sage.

Freud, Anna (1967). *Ego and the mechanisms of defense (The writings of Anna Freud, Vol. 2)* (rev. ed.). New York: International Universities Press.

Freud, Sigmund (1900/1953). The interpretation of dreams. In J. Strachey (ed.), *The standard edition of the complete psychological works of Sigmund Freud* (Vols. 4 and 5). London: Hogarth Press.

Freud, Sigmund (1905). Three essays on the theory of sexuality. In J. Strachey (ed.), *Standard edition* (Vol. 7).

Freud, Sigmund (1905a). Fragment of an analysis of a case of hysteria. In J. Strachey (ed. and trans.), *Standard edition of the complete psychological works of Sigmund Freud* (Vol. 7).

Freud, Sigmund (1920/1960). *A general introduction to psychoanalysis* (Joan Riviere, trans.). New York: Washington Square Press.

Freud, Sigmund (1923/1962). *The ego and the id* (Joan Riviere, trans.). New York: Norton.

Freud, Sigmund (1924a). The dissolution of the Oedipus complex. In J. Strachey (ed.), *Standard edition* (Vol. 19).

Freud, Sigmund (1924b). Some psychical consequences of the anatomical distinction between the sexes. In J. Strachey (ed.), *Standard edition* (Vol. 19).

Freud, Sigmund (1961). *Letters of Sigmund Freud, 1873–1939*. Edited by Ernst L. Freud. London: Hogarth Press.

Fridlund, Alan J. (1994). *Human facial expression: An evolutionary view*. San Diego: Academic Press.

Friedman, Meyer, & Rosenman, Ray (1974). *Type A behavior and your heart*. New York: Knopf.

Friedrich, William; Fisher, Jennifer; Broughton, Daniel; et al. (1998). Normative sexual behavior in children: A contemporary sample. *Pediatrics, 101*, 1–8. See also http://www.pediatrics.org/cgi/content/full/101/4/e9.

Frijda, Nico H. (1988). The laws of emotion. *American Psychologist, 43*, 349–358.

Frome, Pamela M., & Eccles, Jacquelynne S. (1998). Parents' influence on children's achievement-related perceptions. *Journal of Personality and Social Psychology, 74*, 435–452.

Frye, Richard E.; Schwartz, B. S.; & Doty, Richard L. (1990). Dose-related effects of cigarette smoking on olfactory function. *Journal of the American Medical Association, 263*, 1233–1236.

Fuchs, C. S.; Stampfer, M. J.; Colditz, G. A.; et al. (1995, May 11). Alcohol consumption and mortality among women. *New England Journal of Medicine, 332*, 1245–1250.

Furedy, John J. (1996). The North American polygraph and psychophysiology: Disinterested, uninterested, and interested perspectives. *International Journal of Psychophysiology, 21*, 97–105.

Gaertner, Samuel L.; Mann, Jeffrey A.; Dovidio, John F.; et al. (1990). How does cooperation reduce intergroup bias? *Journal of Personality and Social Psychology, 59*, 692–704.

Gage, Fred H.; Kempermann, G.; Palmer, T. D.; et al. (1998). Multipotent progenitor cells in the adult dentate gyrus. *Journal of Neurobiology, 36*, 249–266.

Gagnon, John, & Simon, William (1973). *Sexual conduct: The social sources of human sexuality*. Chicago: Aldine.

Galanter, Eugene (1962). Contemporary psychophysics. In R. Brown, E. Galanter, H. Hess, & G. Mandler (eds.), *New directions in psychology*. New York: Holt, Rinehart and Winston.

Galanter, Marc (1989). *Cults: Faith, healing, and coercion*. New York: Oxford University Press.

Gallant, Jack L.; Braun, Jochen; & Van Essen, David C. (1993). Selectivity for polar, hyperbolic, and Cartesian gratings in macaque visual cortex. *Science, 259*, 100–103.

Gallant, Sheryle J.; Hamilton, Jean A.; Popiel, Debra A.; et al. (1991). Daily moods and symptoms: Effects of awareness of study focus, gender, menstrual-cycle phase, and day of the week. *Health Psychology, 10*, 180–189.

Gallo, Fred (1998). *Energy therapies*. Washington, DC: American Psychological Association.

Gallo, Linda C., & Eastman, Charmane I. (1993). Circadian rhythms during gradually delaying and advancing sleep and light schedules. *Physiology and Behavior, 53*, 119–126.

Gallo, Vittorio, & Chittajallu, Ramesh (2001). Unwrapping glial cells from the synapse: What lies inside? *Science, 292*, 872–873.

Galotti, Kathleen (1989). Approaches to studying formal and everyday reasoning. *Psychological Bulletin, 105*, 331–351.

Gangestad, Steven W., & Simpson, Jeffry A. (2000). The evolution of human mating: Trade-offs and strategic pluralism. *Behavioral and Brain Sciences, 23*, 1–72.

Gao, Jia-Hong; Parsons, Lawrence M.; Bower, James M.; et al. (1996). Cerebellum implicated in sensory acquisition and discrimination rather than motor control. *Science, 272*, 545–547.

Garb, Howard N.; Wood, James M.; & Nezworski, M. Teresa (2000). Projective techniques and the detection of child sexual abuse. *Child Maltreatment, 5*, 161–168.

Garbarino, James, & Bedard, Claire (2001). *Parents under siege*. New York: The Free Press.

Garcia, John, & Gustavson, Carl R. (1997, January). Carl R. Gustavson (1946–1996): Pioneering wildlife psychologist. *APS Observer*, pp. 34–35.

Garcia, John, & Koelling, Robert A. (1966). Relation of cue to consequence in avoidance learning. *Psychonomic Science, 4*, 23–124.

Garcia-Marques, Leonel, & Mackie, Diane M. (1999). The impact of stereotype-incongruent information on perceptive group variability and stereotype change. *Journal of Personality and Social Psychology, 77*, 979–990.

Gardner, Howard (1983). *Frames of mind: The theory of multiple intelligences*. New York: Basic Books.

Gardner, Howard (1993). Creating minds. New York: Basic Books.

Gardner, Howard (1995). Perennial antinomies and perpetual redrawings: Is there progress in the study of mind? In R. L. Solso & D. W. Massar (eds.), *The science of the mind: 2001 and beyond*. New York: Oxford University Press.

Gardner, R. Allen, & Gardner, Beatrice T. (1969). Teaching sign language to a chimpanzee. *Science, 165*, 664–672.

Garland, Ann F., & Zigler, Edward (1994). Adolescent suicide prevention: Current research and social policy implications. *American Psychologist, 48*, 169–182.

Garmezy, Norman (1991). Resilience and vulnerability to adverse developmental outcomes associated with poverty. *American Behavioral Scientist, 34*, 416–430.

Garry, Maryanne, & Loftus, Elizabeth F. (2000). Imagination inflation is not a statistical artifact. Paper presented at the annual meeting of the American Psychological & Law Society, New Orleans.

Garry, Maryanne; Manning, Charles G.; & Loftus, Elizabeth F. (1996). Imagination inflation: Imagining a childhood event inflates confidence that it occurred. *Psychonomic Bulletin & Review, 3*, 208–214.

Garven, Sena; Wood, James M.; Malpass, Roy S.; & Shaw, John S., III (1998). More than suggestion: The effect of interviewing techniques from the McMartin Preschool case. *Journal of Applied Psychology, 83*, 347–359.

Gaudiano, Brandon A., & Herbert, James D. (2000, July/August). Can we really tap our problems away? A critical analysis of Thought Field Therapy. *Skeptical Inquirer*, 29–33, 36.

Gauthier, Irene; Skudlarksi, P.; Gore, J. C.; & Anderson, A. W. (2000). Expertise for cars and birds recruits brain areas involved in face recognition. *Nature Neuroscience, 3*, 191–197.

Gauthier, Irene; Tarr, M. J.; Anderson A. W.; et al. (1999). Activation of the middle fusiform "face area" increases with expertise in recognizing novel objects. *Nature Neuroscience, 2*, 568–573.

Gawande, Atul (1998, September 21). The pain perplex. *The New Yorker*, 86, 88, 90, 92–94.

Gawande, Atul (2001, July 9). The man who couldn't stop eating. *The New Yorker*, 66–75.

Gay, Peter (1988). *Freud: A life for our time*. New York: Norton.

Gaziano, J. Michael, & Hennekens, Charles (1995, July 1). Royal colleges' advice on alcohol consumption [editorial]. *British Medical Journal, 311*, 3–4.

Gazzaniga, Michael S. (1967). The split brain in man. *Scientific American, 217*(2), 24–29.

Gazzaniga, Michael S. (1983). Right hemisphere language following brain bisection: A 20-year perspective. *American Psychologist, 38*, 525–537.

Gazzaniga, Michael S. (1985). *The social brain: Discovering the networks of the mind*. New York: Basic Books.

Gazzaniga, Michael S. (1988). *Mind matters*. Boston: Houghton Mifflin.

Gazzaniga, Michael S. (1998). *The mind's past*. Berkeley, CA: University of California Press.

Geary, David C. (1995). Reflections of evolution and culture in children's cognition: Implications for mathematical development and instruction. *American Psychologist, 50*, 24–37.

George, Mark S. (1998). Why would you ever want to?: Toward understanding the antidepressant effect of prefrontal rTMS. *Human Psychopharmacology Clinical & Experimental, 13*, 307–313.

Gershoff, Elizabeth T. (2002). Parental corporal punishment and associated child behaviors and experiences: A meta-analytic and theoretical review. *Psychological Bulletin, 128*, in press.

Gibson, Eleanor, & Walk, Richard (1960). The "visual cliff." *Scientific American, 202*, 80–92.

Gilbertson, Mark W.; Shenton, Martha E.; Ciszewski, Aleksandra; et al. (in press). Hippocampal volume as a vulnerability factor for chronic posttraumatic stress disorder: MRI evidence from monozygotic twins discordant for combat exposure.

Gillham, Jane E.; Reivich, Karen J.; Jaycox, Lisa H.; & Seligman, Martin E. P. (1995). Prevention of depressive symptoms in schoolchildren: A two-year follow-up. *Psychological Science, 6*, 343–351.

Gilligan, Carol (1982). *In a different voice*. Cambridge, MA: Harvard University Press.

Gilmore, David D. (1990). *Manhood in the making: Cultural concepts of masculinity*. New Haven, CT: Yale University Press.

Gist, Richard, & Lubin, Bernard (eds.) (1999). *Response to disaster: Psychosocial, community, and ecological approaches*. Philadelphia, PA: Brunner/Mazel (Taylor & Francis).

Gist, Richard, & Woodall, S. Joseph (1999). There are no simple solutions to complex problems: The rise and fall of Critical Incident Stress Debriefing as a response to occupational stress in the fire service. In R. Gist & B. Lubin (eds.), *Response to disaster: Psychosocial, community, and ecological approaches*. Philadelphia, PA: Brunner/Mazel (Taylor & Francis).

Gladue, Brian A. (1994). The biopsychology of sexual orientation. *Current Directions in Psychological Science, 3,* 150–154.

Glanzer, Murray, & Cunitz, Anita R. (1966). Two storage mechanisms in free recall. *Journal of Verbal Learning and Verbal Behavior, 5,* 351–360.

Glassner, Barry (2001, October 26). The fate of false fears. *Chronicle of Higher Education,* B16–18.

Gleaves, David H. (1996). The sociocognitive model of dissociative identity disorder: A reexamination of the evidence. *Psychological Bulletin, 120,* 42–59.

Glenmullen, Joseph (2000). *Prozac backlash: Overcoming the dangers of Prozac, Zoloft, Paxil, and other antidepressants with safe, effective alternatives.* New York: Simon & Schuster.

Glick, Peter, & Fiske, Susan T. (2001). An ambivalent alliance: Hostile and benevolent sexism as complementary justifications for gender inequality. *American Psychologist, 56,* 109–118.

Glick, Peter; Fiske, Susan T.; Mladinic, Antonio; et al. (2000). Beyond prejudice as simple antipathy: Hostile and benevolent sexism across cultures. *Journal of Personality and Social Psychology, 79,* 763–775.

Gobodo-Madikizela, Pumla (1994). The notion of the "collective" in South African "political" murder cases: The "deindividuation" argument revisited. Paper presented to the biennial conference of the American Psychology and Law Society, Santa Fe, NM.

Gold, Paul E. (1987). Sweet memories. *American Scientist, 75,* 151–155.

Goldin-Meadow, S., & Mylander, C. (1998). Spontaneous sign systems created by deaf children in two cultures. *Nature, 391,* 279–281.

Goldman-Rakic, Patricia S. (1996). Opening the mind through neurobiology. Invited address at the annual meeting of the American Psychological Association, Toronto, Canada.

Goldstein, Alan J.; de Beurs, Edwin; Chambless, Dianne L.; & Wilson, Kimberly A. (2000). EMDR for panic disorder with agoraphobia: Comparison with waiting list and credible attention-placebo control conditions. *Journal of Consulting and Clinical Psychology, 68,* 947–956.

Goldstein, Michael J. (1987). Psychosocial issues. *Schizophrenia Bulletin, 13*(1), 157–171.

Goldstein, Michael, & Miklowitz, David (1995). The effectiveness of psychoeducational family therapy in the treatment of schizophrenic disorders. *Journal of Marital and Family Therapy, 21,* 361–376.

Goleman, Daniel (1995). *Emotional intelligence.* New York: Bantam.

Golub, Sharon (1992). *Periods: From menarche to menopause.* Newbury Park, CA: Sage.

Goodman, Gail S.; Qin, Jianjian; Bottoms, Bette L.; & Shaver, Phillip R. (1995). *Characteristics and sources of allegations of ritualistic child abuse.* Final report to the National Center on Child Abuse and Neglect, Washington, DC. [Executive summary and complete report available from NCCAN, 1-800-394-3366.]

Goodwin, Donald W.; Knop, Joachim; Jensen, Per; et al. (1994). Thirty-year follow-up of men at high risk for alcoholism. In T. F. Babor & V. M. Hesselbrock (eds.), *Types of alcoholics: Evidence from clinical, experimental, and genetic research.* New York: New York Academy of Sciences.

Goodwin, P. J.; Leszcz, M.; Ennis, M.; et al. (2001, December 13). The effect of group psychosocial support on survival in metastatic breast cancer. *New England Journal of Medicine, 345,* 1719–1726.

Goodwyn, Susan, & Acredolo, Linda (1998). Encouraging symbolic gestures: A new perspective on the relationship between gesture and speech. In J. Iverson & S. Goldin-Meadow (eds.), *The nature and functions of gesture in children's communication.* San Francisco: Jossey-Bass.

Gopnik, Alison; Meltzoff, Andrew N.; & Kuhl, Patricia K. (1999). *The scientist in the crib.* New York: Morrow.

Gopnik, Myrna; Choi, Sooja; & Baumberger, Therese (1996). Cross-linguistic differences in early semantic and cognitive development. *Cognitive Development, 11,* 197–227.

Gopnik, Myrna, & Goad, Heather (1997). What underlies inflectional error patterns in genetic dysphasia? *Journal of Neurolinguistics, 10,* 109–137.

Gore, P. M., & Rotter, Julian B. (1963). A personality correlate of social action. *Journal of Personality, 31,* 58–64.

Goren, C. C.; Sarty, J.; & Wu, P. Y. (1975). Visual following and pattern discrimination of face-like stimuli by newborn infants. *Pediatrics, 56,* 544–549.

Gorn, Gerald J. (1982). The effects of music in advertising on choice behavior: A classical conditioning approach. *Journal of Marketing, 46,* 94–101.

Gosling, Samuel D. (2001). From mice to men: What can we learn about personality from animal research? *Psychological Bulletin, 127,* 45–86.

Gosling, Samuel D., & John, Oliver P. (1999). Personality dimensions in nonhuman animals: A cross-species review. *Current Directions in Psychological Science, 8,* 69–75.

Gottesman, Irving I. (1991). *Schizophrenia genesis: The origins of madness.* New York: Freeman.

Gottesman, Irving I. (1994). Perils and pleasures of genetic psychopathology. Distinguished Scientist Award address presented at the annual meeting of the American Psychological Association, Los Angeles.

Gottman, John (1994, May/June). Why marriages fail. *The Family Therapy Networker,* 40–48.

Gould, Elizabeth; Beylin, A; Tanapat, Patima; et al. (1999). Learning enhances adult neurogenesis in the hippocampal formation. *Nature Neuroscience, 2,* 260–265.

Gould, Elizabeth; Reeves, Alison J.; Graziano, Michael S. A.; & Gross, Charles G. (1999). Neurogenesis in the neocortex of adult primates. *Science, 286,* 548–552.

Gould, Elizabeth; Tanapat, Patima; McEwen, Bruce S.; et al. (1998). Proliferation of granule cell precursors in the dentate gyrus of adult monkeys is diminished by stress. *Proceedings of the National Academy of Science, 95,* 3168–3171.

Gould, Stephen Jay (1985). The median isn't the message. *Discover, 6,* 40–42.

Gould, Stephen Jay (1987). *An urchin in the storm.* New York: W. W. Norton.

Gould, Stephen Jay (1994, November 28). Curveball. [Review of *The Bell Curve,* by Richard J. Herrnstein and Charles Murray.] *New Yorker,* 139–149.

Gould, Stephen Jay (1996). *The mismeasure of man* (rev. ed.). New York: Norton.

Gourevich, Philip (1998). *We wish to inform you that tomorrow we will be killed with our families: Stories from Rwanda.* New York: Farrar, Straus & Giroux.

Graf, Peter, & Schacter, Daniel A. (1985). Implicit and explicit memory for new associations in normal and amnesic subjects. *Journal of Experimental Psychology: Learning, Memory, and Cognition, 11,* 501–518.

Graham, Jill W. (1986). Principled organizational dissent: A theoretical essay. *Research in Organizational Behavior, 8,* 1–52.

Graham, Sandra (1994). Motivation in African Americans. *Review of Educational Research, 64,* 55–117.

Grandin, Temple (1996). *Thinking in pictures and other reports from my life with autism.* New York: Doubleday.

Green, Gina (1996a). Behavioral treatment of autistic persons: A review of research from 1980 to the present. *Research in Developmental Disabilities, 17,* 433–465.

Green, Gina (1996b). Early behavioral intervention for autism: What does research tell us? In C. Maurice, G. Green, & S. C. Luce (Eds.), *Behavioral Intervention for Young Children with Autism*. Austin, TX: PRO-ED.

Greenberg, Jay, & Mitchell, Stephen A. (1983). *Object relations in psychoanalytic theory*. Cambridge, MA: Harvard University Press.

Greenberg, Roger P.; Bornstein, Robert F.; Greenberg, Michael D.; & Fisher, Seymour (1992). A meta-analysis of antidepressant outcome under "blinder" conditions. *Journal of Consulting and Clinical Psychology, 60*, 664–669.

Greenberg, Roger P.; Bornstein, Robert F.; Zborowski, Michael J.; et al. (1994). A meta-analysis of fluoxetine outcome in the treatment of depression. *Journal of Nervous and Mental Disease, 182*, 547–551.

Greenberger, Dennis, & Padesky, Christine A. (1995). *Mind over mood: A cognitive therapy treatment manual for clients*. New York: Guilford.

Greene, Robert L. (1986). Sources of recency effects in free recall. *Psychological Bulletin, 99*, 221–228.

Greenfield, Patricia (1976). Cross-cultural research and Piagetian theory: Paradox and progress. In K. F. Riegel & J. A. Meacham (eds.), *The developing individual in a changing world: Vol. 1. Historical and cultural issues*. The Hague, Netherlands: Mouton.

Greenough, William T. (1984). Structural correlates of information storage in the mammalian brain: A review and hypothesis. *Trends in Neurosciences, 7*, 229–233.

Greenough, William T., & Anderson, Brenda J. (1991). Cerebellar synaptic plasticity: Relation to learning vs. neural activity. *Annals of the New York Academy of Sciences, 627*, 231–247.

Greenough, William T., & Black, James E. (1992). Induction of brain structure by experience: Substrates for cognitive development. In M. Gunnar & C. A. Nelson (eds.), *Behavioral developmental neuroscience: Vol. 24. Minnesota Symposia on Child Psychology*. Hillsdale, NJ: Erlbaum.

Greenough, William T.; Cohen, N. J.; & Juraska, J. M. (1999). New neurons in old brains: Learning to survive? *Nature Neuroscience, 2*, 203–205.

Greenwald, Anthony G.; Draine, Sean C.; & Abrams, Richard L. (1996). Three cognitive markers of unconscious semantic activation. *Science, 273*, 1699–1702.

Greenwald, Anthony G.; McGhee, Debbie E.; & Schwartz, Jordan L. K. (1998). Measuring individual differences in implicit cognition: The Implicit Association Test. *Journal of Personality and Social Psychology, 74*, 1464–1480.

Greenwald, Anthony G.; Spangenberg, Eric R.; Pratkanis, Anthony R.; & Eskenazi, Jay (1991). Double-blind tests of subliminal self-help audiotapes. *Psychological Science, 2*, 119–122.

Gregory, Richard L. (1963). Distortion of visual space as inappropriate constancy scaling. *Nature, 199*, 678–679.

Griffin, Donald R. (1992). *Animal minds*. Chicago: University of Chicago Press.

Grigorenko, Elena L., & Sternberg, Robert J. (1998). Dynamic testing. *Psychological Bulletin, 124*, 75–111.

Grinspoon, Lester, & Bakalar, James B. (1993). *Marihuana, the forbidden medicine*. New Haven, CT: Yale University Press.

Gronbaek, M.; Deis, A.; Sorensen, T. I.; Becker, U.; Schnohr, P.; & Jensen, G. (1995, May 6). Mortality associated with moderate intakes of wine, beer, or spirits. *British Medical Journal, 310*, 1165–1169.

Groneman, Carol (2000). *Nymphomania: A history*. New York: Norton.

Gross, C. G. (2000). Neurogenesis in the adult brain: death of a dogma. *Nature Review of Neuroscience, 1*, 67–73.

Gross, James J. (1998). The emerging field of emotion regulation: An integrative review. *Review of General Psychology, 2*, 271–299.

Grossman, Michele, & Wood, Wendy (1993). Sex differences in intensity of emotional experience: A social role interpretation. *Journal of Personality and Social Psychology, 65*, 1010–1022.

Groves, James E. (ed.) (1996). *Essential papers on short-term dynamic therapy*. New York: New York University Press.

Gruber, Barry L.; Hersh, Stephen P.; Hall, Nicholas R.; et al. (1993). Immunological responses of breast cancer patients to behavioral interventions. *Biofeedback and Self-Regulation, 18*, 1–22.

Guglielmi, R. Sergio (1999). Psychophysiological assessment of prejudice: Past research, current status, and future directions. *Personality and Social Psychology Review, 3*, 123–157.

Guilford, J. P. (1988). Some changes in the structure-of-intellect model. *Educational and Psychological Measurement, 48*, 1–4.

Gupta, S.; Mosnik, D.; Black, D. W.; et al. (1999). Tardive dyskinesia: Review of treatments past, present, and future. *Annals of Clinical Psychiatry, 11*, 257–266.

Gur, R. C.; Turetsky, B. I.; Matsui, M.; et al. (1999). Sex differences in brain gray and white matter in healthy young adults: correlations with cognitive performance. *Journal of Neuroscience, 19*, 4065–4072.

Gur, R. E.; Maany, V.; Mozley, P. D.; et al. (1998). Subcortical MRI volumes in neuroleptic-naive and treated patients with schizophrenia. *American Journal of Psychiatry, 155*, 1711–1717.

Guralnick, M. J. (ed.) (1997). *The effectiveness of early intervention*. Baltimore: Brookes.

Gustavson, Carl R.; Garcia, John; Hankins, Walter G.; & Rusiniak, Kenneth W. (1974). Coyote predation control by aversive conditioning. *Science, 184*, 581–583.

Gustavson, Carl R.; Kelly, Daniel J.; Sweeney, Michael; & Garcia, John (1976). Pre-lithium aversions I: Coyotes and wolves. *Behavioral Biology, 17*, 61–72.

Guthrie, Paul C., & Mobley, Brenda D. (1994). A comparison of the differential diagnostic efficiency of three personality disorder inventories. *Journal of Clinical Psychology, 50*, 656–665.

Guthrie, Robert (1976). *Even the rat was white: A historical view of psychology*. New York: Harper & Row.

Gwiazda, Jane; Thorn, Frank; Bauer, Joseph; & Held, Richard (1993). Emmetropization and the progression of manifest refraction in children followed from infancy to puberty. *Clinical Vision Sciences, 8*, 337–344.

Haber, Ralph N. (1970, May). How we remember what we see. *Scientific American, 222*, 104–112.

Haimov, I., & Lavie, P. (1996). Melatonin—A soporific hormone. *Current Directions in Psychological Science, 5*, 106–111.

Halaas, Jeffrey L.; Gajiwala, Ketan S.; Maffei, Margherita; et al. (1995). Weight-reducing effects of the plasma protein encoded by the *obese* gene. *Science, 269*, 543–546.

Hall, C. S.; Domhoff, G. W.; Thick, K. A.; & Weesner, K. E. (1982). The dreams of college men and women in 1950 and 1980: A comparison of dream content and sex differences. *Sleep, 5*, 188–194.

Hall, Edward T. (1959). *The silent language*. Garden City, NY: Doubleday.

Hall, Edward T. (1976). *Beyond culture*. New York: Anchor.

Hall, Edward T. (1983). *The dance of life: The other dimension of time*. Garden City, NY: Anchor Press/Doubleday.

Hall, Edward T., & Hall, Mildred R. (1987). *Hidden differences: Doing business with the Japanese*. Garden City, NY: Anchor Press/Doubleday.

Hall, Edward T., & Hall, Mildred R. (1990). *Understanding cultural differences*. Yarmouth, ME: Intercultural Press.

Hall, G. Stanley (1899). A study of anger. *American Journal of Psychology, 10*, 516–591.

Hall, Judith A. (1987). On explaining gender differences: The case of non-verbal communication. In P. Shaver & C. Hendrick (eds.), *Sex and gender: Review of Personality and Social Psychology* (Vol. 7). Beverly Hills, CA: Sage.

Halliday, G. (1993). Examination dreams. *Perceptual and Motor Skills, 77,* 489–490.

Halpern, Diane (1995). *Thought and knowledge: An introduction to critical thinking* (3rd ed.). Hillsdale, NJ: Erlbaum.

Halpern, Diane (1998). Teaching critical thinking for transfer across domains. *American Psychologist, 53,* 449–455.

Hamer, Dean H.; Hu, Stella; Magnuson, Victoria L.; et al. (1993). A linkage between DNA markers on the X chromosome and male sexual orientation. *Science, 261,* 321–327.

Haney, Craig, & Zimbardo, Philip (1998). The past and future of U.S. prison policy: Twenty-five years after the Stanford Prison Experiment. *American Psychologist, 53,* 709–727.

Haney, Craig; Banks, Curtis; & Zimbardo, Philip (1973). Interpersonal dynamics in a simulated prison. *International Journal of Criminology and Penology, 1,* 69–97.

Hankin, Benjamin L., & Abramson, Lyn Y. (2001). Development of gender differences in depression: An elaborated cognitive vulnerability-transactional stress theory. *Psychological Bulletin, 127,* 773–796.

Hardie, Elizabeth A. (1997). PMS in the workplace: Dispelling the myth of cyclic function. Journal of *Occupational and Organizational Psychology, 70,* 97–102.

Harding, Courtenay M.; Zubin, Joseph; & Strauss, John S. (1992). Chronicity in schizophrenia: Revisited. *British Journal of Psychiatry, 161*(Suppl. 18), 27–37.

Hare, Robert D. (1965). Temporal gradient of fear arousal in psychopaths. *Journal of Abnormal Psychology, 70,* 442–445.

Hare, Robert D. (1993). *Without conscience: The disturbing world of the psychopaths among us.* New York: Pocket Books.

Hare, Robert D. (1996). *Psychopathy: A clinical construct whose time has come.* Criminal Justice and Behavior, 23, *24–54.*

Hare Mustin, Rachel T. (1991). Sex, lies, and headaches: The problem is power. In T. J. Goodrich (ed.), *Women and power: Perspectives for therapy.* New York: Norton.

Hare-Mustin, Rachel T., & Marecek, Jeanne (1990). Gender and the meaning of difference: Postmodernism and psychology. In R. Hare-Mustin & J. Maracek (eds.), *Psychology and the construction of gender.* New Haven, CT: Yale University Press.

Haritos-Fatouros, Mika (1988). The official torturer: A learning model for obedience to the authority of violence. *Journal of Applied Social Psychology, 18,* 1107–1120.

Harkins, Stephen G., & Szymanski, Kate (1989). Social loafing and group evaluation. *Journal of Personality and Social Psychology, 56,* 934–941.

Harlow, Harry F. (1958). The nature of love. *American Psychologist, 13,* 673–685.

Harlow, Harry F., & Harlow, Margaret K. (1966). Learning to love. *American Scientist, 54,* 244–272.

Harlow, Harry F.; Harlow, Margaret K.; & Meyer, D. R. (1950). Learning motivated by a manipulation drive. *Journal of Experimental Psychology, 40,* 228–234.

Harmon-Jones, Eddie, & Allen, John J. B. (1998). Anger and frontal brain activity: EEG asymmetry consistent with approach motivation despite negative affective valence. *Journal of Personality and Social Psychology, 74,* 1310–1316.

Harmon-Jones, Eddie, & Sigelman, Jonathan (2001). State anger and prefrontal brain activity: Evidence that insult-related relative left-prefrontal activation is associated with experienced anger and aggression. *Journal of Personality and Social Psychology, 80,* 797–803.

Harris, Judith R. (1998). *The nurture assumption.* New York: The Free Press.

Harris, Judith R. (2000). Context-specific learning, personality, and birth order. *Current Directions in Psychological Science, 9,* 174–177.

Hart, John, Jr.; Berndt, Rita S.; & Caramazza, Alfonso (1985, August 1). Category-specific naming deficit following cerebral infarction. *Nature, 316,* 339–340.

Hartup, William (1999). Peer experience and its developmental significance. In M. Bennett (ed.), *Developmental Psychology: Achievements and prospects.* Philadelphia, PA: Psychology Press.

Hatfield, Elaine, & Rapson, Richard L. (1996). *Love and sex: Cross-cultural perspectives.* Boston: Allyn & Bacon.

Hatfield, Elaine; Cacioppo, John T.; & Rapson, Richard L. (1994). *Emotional contagion.* New York: Cambridge University Press.

Hauser, Marc (2000). *Wild minds: What animals really think.* New York: Holt.

Haut, Jennifer S.; Beckwith, Bill E.; Petros, Thomas V.; & Russell, Sue (1989). Gender differences in retrieval from long-term memory following acute intoxication with ethanol. *Physiology and Behavior, 45,* 1161–1165.

Hawkins, Scott A., & Hastie, Reid (1990). Hindsight: Biased judgments of past events after the outcomes are known. *Psychological Bulletin, 107,* 311–327.

Haxby, James V.; Gobbini, M. Ida; Furey, Maura L.; et al. (2001). Distributed and overlapping representations of faces and objects in ventral temporal cortex. *Science, 293,* 2425–2430.

Hayman, Ronald (2001). *A life of Jung.* New York: W. W. Norton.

Hazan, Cindy, & Diamond, Lisa M. (2000). The place of attachment in human mating. *Review of General Psychology, 4,* 186–204.

Hazan, Cindy, & Shaver, Phillip R. (1987). Romantic love conceptualized as an attachment process. *Journal of Personality and Social Psychology, 52,* 511–524.

Hazan, Cindy, & Shaver, Phillip R. (1994). Attachment as an organizational framework for research on close relationships. *Psychological Inquiry, 5,* 1–22.

Hébert, Richard (September, 2001). Code overload: Doing a number on memory. *APS Observer, 14,* 1, 7–11.

Hebl, Michelle R., & Heatherton, Todd F. (1998). The stigma of obesity in women: The difference in black and white. *Personality and Social Psychology Bulletin, 24,* 417–426.

Hecht, Marvin A., & LaFrance, Marianne (1998). License or obligation to smile: The effect of power and sex on amount and type of smiling. *Personality and Social Psychology Bulletin, 24,* 1332–1342.

Heinrichs, R. Walter (1993). Schizophrenia and the brain: Conditions for a neuropsychology of madness. *American Psychologist, 48,* 221–233.

Heller, Wendy, & Nitschke, Jack B. (1997). Regional brain activity in emotion: A framework for understanding cognition in depression. *Cognition & Emotion, 11,* 637–661.

Heller, Wendy; Nitschke, Jack B.; Miller, Gregory A. (1998). Lateralization in emotion and emotional disorders. *Current Directions in Psychological Science, 7,* 26–32.

Helmes, Edward, & Reddon, John R. (1993). A perspective on developments in assessing psychopathology: A critical review of the MMPI and MMPI-2. *Psychological Bulletin, 113,* 453–471.

Helson, Ravenna, & McCabe, Laurel (1993). The social clock project in middle age. In B. F. Turner & L. E. Troll (eds.), *Women growing older.* Newbury Park, CA: Sage.

Helson, Ravenna, & Srivastava, Sanjay (2001). Three paths of adult development: Conservers, seekers, and achievers. *Journal of Personality and Social Psychology, 80,* 995–1010.

Helson, Ravenna; Roberts, Brent; & Agronick, Gail (1995). Enduringness and change in creative personality and the prediction of occupational creativity. *Journal of Personality and Social Psychology, 6,* 1173–1183.

Hendrix, William H.; Steel, Robert P.; Leap, Terry L.; & Summers, Timothy P. (1991). Development of a stress-related health promotion model: Antecedents and organizational effectiveness outcomes. *Journal of Social Behavior and Personality, 6,* 141–162.

Henley, Nancy (1995). Body politics revisited: What do we know today? In P. J. Kalbfleisch & M. J. Cody (eds.), *Gender, power, and communication in human relationships.* Hillsdale, NJ: Erlbaum.

Herdt, Gilbert (1984). *Ritualized homosexuality in Melanesia.* Berkeley: University of California Press.

Herek, Gregory M. (1999). Interpersonal contact and sexual prejudice. Paper presented at the annual meeting of the American Psychological Society, Denver.

Herek, Gregory M., & Capitanio, J. P. (1996). "Some of my best friends": Intergroup contact, concealable stigma, and heterosexuals' attitudes toward gay men and lesbians. *Personality and Social Psychology Bulletin, 22,* 412–424.

Herman, John H. (1992). Transmutative and reproductive properties of dreams: Evidence for cortical modulation of brainstem generators. In J. Antrobus & M. Bertini (eds.), *The neuropsychology of dreaming.* Hillsdale, NJ: Erlbaum.

Herman, Judith (1992). *Trauma and recovery.* New York: Basic Books.

Hilts, Philip J. (1995). *Memory's ghost: The strange tale of Mr. M. and the nature of memory.* New York: Simon & Schuster.

Herman, Louis M. (1987). Receptive competencies of language-trained animals. In J. S. Rosenblatt, C. Beer, M. C. Busnel, & P. J. B. Slater (eds.), *Advances in the study of behavior* (Vol. 17). Petaluma, CA: Academic Press.

Herman, Louis M., & Morrel-Samuels, Palmer (1996). Knowledge acquisition and asymmetry between language comprehension and production: Dolphins and apes as general models for animals. In M. Bekoff & D. Jamieson et al. (eds.), *Readings in animal cognition.* Cambridge, MA: MIT Press.

Herman, Louis M.; Kuczaj, Stan A.; & Holder, Mark D. (1993). Responses to anomalous gestural sequences by a language-trained dolphin: Evidence for processing of semantic relations and syntactic information. *Journal of Experimental Psychology: General, 122,* 184–194.

Heron, Woodburn (1957). The pathology of boredom. *Scientific American, 196*(1), 52–56.

Herrnstein, Richard J., & Murray, Charles (1994). *The bell curve: Intelligence and class structure in American life.* New York: Free Press.

Herz, Rachel S., & Cupchik, Gerald C. (1995). The emotional distinctiveness of odor-evoked memories. *Chemical Senses, 20,* 517–528.

Hicks, Robert D. (1991). The police model of satanism crime. In J. T. Richardson, J. Best, & D. G. Bromley (eds.), *The satanism scare.* New York: Aldine de Gruyter.

Higgins, E. Tory (1998). Promotion and prevention: Regulatory focus as a motivational principle. *Advances in Experimental Social Psychology, 30,* 1–46.

Hilgard, Ernest R. (1977). *Divided consciousness: Multiple controls in human thought and action.* New York: Wiley-Interscience.

Hilgard, Ernest R. (1986). *Divided consciousness: Multiple controls in human thought and action* (2nd ed.). New York: Wiley.

Hill, Harlan F.; Chapman, C. Richard; Kornell, Judy A.; et al. (1990). Self-administration of morphine in bone marrow transplant patients reduces drug requirement. *Pain, 40,* 121–129.

Hill, James O., & Peters, John C. (1998). Environmental contributions to the obesity epidemic. *Science, 280,* 1371–1374.

Hill, L.; Craig, I. W.; Ball, D. M.; et al. (1999). DNA pooling and dense marker maps: A systematic search for genes for cognitive ability. *NeuroReport, 10,* 843–848.

Hillman, James, & Ventura, Michael (1992). *We've had a hundred years of psychotherapy—and the world's getting worse.* San Francisco: HarperCollins.

Hines, Terence M. (1998). Comprehensive review of biorhythm theory. *Psychological Reports, 83,* 19–64.

Hirsch, Helmut V. B., & Spinelli, D. N. (1970). Visual experience modifies distribution of horizontally and vertically oriented receptive fields in cats. *Science, 168,* 869–871.

Hirst, William; Neisser, Ulric; & Spelke, Elizabeth (1978, January). Divided attention. *Human Nature, 1,* 54–61.

Hobson, J. Allan (1988). *The dreaming brain.* New York: Basic Books.

Hobson, J. Allan (1990). Activation, input source, and modulation: A neurocognitive model of the state of the brain mind. In R. R. Bootzin, J. F. Kihlstrom, & D. L. Schacter (eds.), *Sleep and cognition.* Washington, DC: American Psychological Association.

Hobson, J. Allan; Pace-Schott, Edward F.; & Stickgold, Robert (2000). Dreaming and the brain: Toward a cognitive neuroscience of consicous states. *Behavioral and Brain Sciences, 23,* 793–842, 904–1018, 1083–1121.

Hochschild, Arlie (1983). *The managed heart.* Berkeley: University of California Press.

Hockett, Charles F. (1960). The origins of speech. *Scientific American, 203,* 89–96.

Hodges, Ernest V. E., & Perry, David G. (1999). Personal and interpersonal antecedents and consequences of victimization by peers. *Journal of Personality and Social Psychology, 76,* 677–685.

Hoffman, Martin L. (1990). Empathy and justice motivation. *Motivation and Emotion, 14,* 151–172.

Hoffman, Martin L. (1994). Discipline and internalization. *Developmental Psychology, 30,* 26–28.

Hoffrage, Ulrich; Hertwig, Ralph; & Gigerenzer, Gerd (2000). Hindsight bias: A by-product of knowledge updating? *Journal of Experimental Psychology: Learning, Memory, & Cognition, 26,* 566–581.

Hofstede, Geert, & Bond, Michael H. (1988). The Confucius connection: From cultural roots to economic growth. *Organizational Dynamics,* 5–21.

Holden, Constance (1997). Thumbs up for acupuncture. [News report.] *Science, 278,* 1231.

Holden, George W., & Miller, Pamela C. (1999). Enduring and different: A meta-analysis of the similarity in parents' child rearing. *Psychological Bulletin, 125,* 223–254.

Holmes, David S. (1990). The evidence for repression: An examination of sixty years of research. In J. L. singer (ed.), *Repression and dissociation.* Chicago: University of Chicago Press.

Honts, Charles R. (1994). Psychophysiological detection of deception. *Current Directions in Psychological Science, 3,* 77–82.

Hooker, Evelyn (1957). The adjustment of the male overt homosexual. *Journal of Projective Techniques, 21,* 18–31.

Hoon, M. A.; Adler, E.; Lindemeier, J.; et al. (1999). Putative mammalian taste receptors: a class of taste-specific GPCRs with distinct topographic selectivity. *Cell, 96,* 541–551.

Horgan, John (1995, November). Get smart, take a test: A long-term rise in IQ scores baffles intelligence experts. *Scientific American, 273,* 12,14.

Horney, Karen (1926/1973). The flight from womanhood. *The International Journal of Psycho-Analysis, 7,* 324–339. Reprinted in J. B. Miller (ed.), *Psychoanalysis and women.* New York: Brunner/Mazel, 1973.

Hornstein, Gail (1992). The return of the repressed: Psychology's problematic relations with psychoanalysis, 1909–1960. *American Psychologist, 47,* 254–263.

Hotz, Robert Lee (2000, November 29). Women use more of brain when listening, study says. *Los Angeles Times,* A1, A18–19.

House, James S.; Landis, Karl R.; & Umberson, Debra (1988, July 19). Social relationships and health. *Science, 241,* 540–545.

Houts, Arthur C. (2002). Discovery, invention, and the expansion of the modern *Diagnostic and Statistical Manuals of Mental Disorders.* In L. E. Beutler & M. L. Malik (eds.), *Rethinking the DSM: A psychological perspective.* Washington, DC: American Psychological Association.

Howard, George S. (1991). Culture tales: A narrative approach to thinking, cross-cultural psychology, and psychotherapy. *American Psychologist, 46,* 187–197.

Howard, Kenneth; Kopta, S. Mark; Krause, Merton S.; & Orlinsky, David (1986). The dose–effect relationship in psychotherapy. *American Psychologist, 41,* 159–164.

Howe, Mark L., & Courage, Mary L. (1993). On resolving the enigma of infantile amnesia. *Psychological Bulletin, 113,* 305–326.

Howe, Mark L.; Courage, Mary L.; & Peterson, Carole (1994). How can I remember when "I" wasn't there? Long-term retention of traumatic experiences and emergence of the cognitive self. *Consciousness and Cognition, 3,* 327–355.

Hrdy, Sarah B. (1988). Empathy, polyandry, and the myth of the coy female. In R. Bleier (ed.), *Feminist approaches to science.* New York: Pergamon.

Hrdy, Sarah B. (1994). What do women want? In T. A. Bass (ed.), *Reinventing the future: Conversations with the world's leading scientists.* Reading, MA: Addison-Wesley.

Hrdy, Sarah B. (1999). *Mother nature.* New York: Pantheon.

Hu, S.; Pattatucci, A. M.; Patterson C.; et al. (1995). Linkage between sexual orientation and chromosome Xq28 in males but not in females. *Nature Genetics, 11,* 248–256.

Huang, L.; Shanker, Y. G.; Dubauskaite, J.; et al. (1999). Ggamma13 colocalizes with gustducin in taste receptor cells and mediates IP3 responses to bitter denatonium. *Nature Neuroscience, 2,* 1055–1062.

Hubel, David H., & Wiesel, Torsten N. (1962). Receptive fields, binocular interaction and functional architecture in the cat's visual cortex. *Journal of Physiology* (London), *160,* 106–154.

Hubel, David H., & Wiesel, Torsten N. (1968). Receptive fields and functional architecture of monkey striate cortex. *Journal of Physiology* (London), *195,* 215–243.

Hultsch, David F.; Hertzog, Christopher; Small, Brent J.; & Dixon, Roger A. (1999). Use it or lose it: Engaged lifestyle as a buffer of cognitive decline in aging? *Psychology and Aging, 14,* 245–263.

Hunt, Morton M. (1959/1967). *The natural history of love.* New York: Minerva Press.

Hunter, John E. (1997). Needed: A ban on the significance test. *Psychological Science, 8,* 3–7.

Huntington's Disease Collaborative Research Group (1993). A novel gene containing a trinucleotide repeat that is expanded and unstable on Huntington's disease chromosomes. *Cell, 72,* 971–983.

Hupka, Ralph B. (1981). Cultural determinants of jealousy. *Alternative Lifestyles, 4,* 310–356.

Hupka, Ralph B. (1991). The motive for the arousal of romantic jealousy. In P. Salovey (ed.), *The psychology of jealousy and envy.* New York: Guilford Press.

Hupka, Ralph B.; Lenton, Alison P.; & Hutchison, Keith A. (1999). Universal development of emotion categories in natural language. *Journal of Personality and Social Psychology, 77,* 247–278.

Hur, Yoon-Mi; Bouchard, Thomas J., Jr.; & Lykken, David T. (1998). Genetic and environmental influence on morningness-eveningness. *Personality and Individual Differences, 25,* 917–925.

Hur, Yoon-Mi; McGue, Matt; & Iacono, William G. (1998). The structure of self-concept in female preadolescent twins: A behavioral genetic approach. *Journal of Personality and Social Psychology, 74,* 1069–1077.

Hyde, Janet S. (2000). A gendered brain? [Review of *Sex and cognition,* by Doreen Kimura.] *Journal of Sex Research, 37,* 191.

Hyde, Janet S.; Fennema, Elizabeth; & Lamon, Susan J. (1990). Gender differences in mathematics performance: A meta-analysis. *Psychological Bulletin, 107,* 139–155.

Hyde, Janet S., & Linn, Marcia C. (1988). Gender differences in verbal ability: A meta-analysis. *Psychological Bulletin, 104,* 53–69.

Hyman, Ira E., Jr., & Pentland, Joel (1996). The role of mental imagery in the creation of false childhood memories. *Journal of Memory and Language, 35,* 101–117.

Hyman, Ray (1994). Anomaly or artifact? Comments on Bem and Honorton. *Psychological Bulletin, 115,* 25–27.

Iacono, William G., & Lykken, David T. (1997). The scientific status of research on polygraph techniques: The case against polygraph tests. In D. L. Faigman, D. Kaye, M. J. Saks, & J. Sanders (eds.), *Modern scientific evidence: The law and science of expert testimony.* St. Paul, MN: West.

Ikonomidou, Chrysanthy; Bittigau, Petra; Ishimaru, Masahiko J.; et al. (2000, February 11). Ethanol-induced apoptotic neurodegeneration and fetal alcohol syndrome. *Science, 287,* 1056–1060.

Inglehart, Ronald (1990). *Culture shift in advanced industrial society.* Princeton, NJ: Princeton University Press.

Inglis, James, & Lawson, J. S. (1981). Sex differences in the effects of unilateral brain damage on intelligence. *Science, 212,* 693–695.

Ingram, J. L.; Stodgell, C. J.; Hyman, S. L.; et al. (2000). Discovery of allelic variants of HOXA1 and HOXB1: genetic susceptibility to autism spectrum disorders. *Teratology, 62,* 393–405.

Inzlicht, Michael, & Ben-Zeev, Talia (2000). A threatening intellectual environment: Why females are susceptible to experiencing problem-solving deficits in the presence of males. *Psychological Science, 11,* 365–371.

Irvine, Janice M. (1990). *Disorders of desire: Sex and gender in modern American sexology.* Philadelphia: Temple University Press.

Islam, Mir Rabiul, & Hewstone, Miles (1993). Intergroup attributions and affective consequences in majority and minority groups. *Journal of Personality and Social Psychology, 64,* 936–950.

Izard, Carroll E. (1990). Facial expressions and the regulation of emotions. *Journal of Personality and Social Psychology, 58,* 487–498.

Izard, Carroll E. (1994a). Four systems for emotion activation: Cognitive and noncognitive processes. *Psychological Review, 100,* 68–90.

Izard, Carroll E. (1994b). Innate and universal facial expressions: Evidence from developmental and cross-cultural research. *Psychological Bulletin, 115,* 288–299.

Jacobsen, Paul B; Bovbjerg, Dana H.; Schwartz, Marc D.; et al. (1995). Conditioned emotional distress in women receiving chemotherapy for breast cancer. *Journal of Consulting & Clinical Psychology, 63,* 108–114.

Jacobson, John W., Mulick, James A.; & Schwartz, Allan A. (1995). The history of facilitated communication: Science, pseudoscience, and anti-science. *American Psychologist, 50,* 750–765.

Jaffe, Joseph; Beebe, Beatrice; Feldstein, Stanley; Crown, Cynthia L.; & Jasnow, Michael D. (2001). Rhythms of dialogue in infancy: Coordinated timing in development. *Monographs of the Society for Research in Child Development, 66*(2), Serial No. 265.

Jaffee, Sara, & Hyde, Janet S. (2000). Gender differences in moral orientation: A meta-analysis. *Psychological Bulletin, 126,* 703–726.

James, Jacquelyn B., & Lewkowicz, Corinne J. (1997). Themes of power and affiliation across time. In M. E. Lachman & J. B. James (eds.), *Multiple paths of midlife development*. Chicago: University of Chicago Press.

James, William (1890/1950). *Principles of psychology* (Vol. 1). New York: Dover.

James, William (1902/1936). *The varieties of religious experience*. New York: Modern Library.

Jamison, Kay (1992). *Touched with fire: Manic depressive illness and the artistic temperament*. New York: Free Press.

Jamison, Kay (1999). *Night falls fast: Understanding suicide*. New York: Knopf.

Jancke, Lutz; Schlaug, Gottfried; & Steinmetz, Helmuth (1997). Hand skill asymmetry in professional musicians. *Brain and Cognition, 34*, 424–432.

Jang, Kerry L.; Hu, Stella; Livesley, W. John; et al. (2001). Covariance structure of neuroticism and agreeableness: A twin and molecular genetic analysis of the role of the serotonin transporter gene. *Journal of Personality and Social Psychology, 81*, 295–304.

Jang, Kerry L.; McCrae, Robert R.; Angleitner, Alois; et al. (1998). Heritability of facet-level traits in a cross-cultural twin sample: Support for a hierarchical model of personality. *Journal of Personality and Social Psychology, 74*, 1556–1565.

Janis, Irving L. (1982). *Groupthink: Psychological studies of policy decisions and fiascoes* (2nd ed.). Boston: Houghton Mifflin.

Janis, Irving L. (1989). *Crucial decisions: Leadership in policymaking and crisis management*. New York: Free Press.

Janis, Irving L.; Kaye, Donald; & Kirschner, Paul (1965). Facilitating effects of "eating-while-reading" on responsiveness to persuasive communications. *Journal of Personality and Social Psychology, 1*, 181–186.

Jenkins, John G., & Dallenbach, Karl M. (1924). Obliviscence during sleep and waking. *American Journal of Psychology, 35*, 605–612.

Jenkins, Sharon Rae (1994). Need for power and women's careers over 14 years: Structural power, job satisfaction, and motive change. *Journal of Personality and Social Psychology, 66*, 155–165.

Jensen, Arthur R. (1969). How much can we boost IQ and scholastic achievement? *Harvard Educational Review, 39*, 1–123.

Jensen, Arthur R. (1981). *Straight talk about mental tests*. New York: Free Press.

Jensen, Arthur R. (1998). *The g factor: The science of mental ability*. Westport, CT: Praeger/Greenwood.

Johnson, Marcia K. (1995). The relation between memory and reality. Paper presented at the annual meeting of the American Psychological Association, New York.

Johnson, Mark H.; Dziurawiec, Suzanne; Ellis, Hadyn; & Morton, John (1991). Newborns' preferential tracking of face-like stimuli and its subsequent decline. *Cognition, 40*, 1–19.

Johnson, Robert, & Downing, Leslie (1979). Deindividuation and valence of cues: Effects of prosocial and antisocial behavior. *Journal of Personality and Social Psychology, 37*, 1532–1538.

Joiner, Thomas E. (1994). Contagious depression: Existence, specificity to depressed symptoms, and the role of reassurance seeking. *Journal of Personality and Social Psychology, 67*, 287–296.

Jones, Edward E. (1990). *Interpersonal perception*. New York: Macmillan.

Jones, James M. (1991). Psychological models of race: What have they been and what should they be? In J. D. Goodchilds (ed.), *Psychological perspectives on human diversity in America*. Washington, DC: American Psychological Association.

Jones, James M. (1997). *Prejudice and racism* (2nd ed.). New York: McGraw-Hill.

Jones, Mary Cover (1924). A laboratory study of fear: The case of Peter. *Pedagogical Seminary, 31*, 308–315.

Jones, Steve (1994). *The language of genes*. New York: Anchor/Doubleday.

Jones, Steve (2000). *Darwin's ghost: "The Origin of Species" updated*. New York: Random House.

Jordan, B. D.; Relkin, N. R.; Ravdin, L. D.; et al. (1997). Apolipoprotein E epsilon 4 associated with chronic traumatic brain injury in boxing. *Journal of the American Medical Association, 278*, 136–140.

Jorgensen, Randall S.; Johnson, Blair T.; Kolodziej, Monika E.; & Schreer, George E. (1996). Elevated blood pressure and personality: A meta-analytic review. *Psychological Bulletin, 120*, 293–320.

Judd, Charles M.; Park, Bernadette; Ryan, Carey S.; et al. (1995). Stereotypes and ethnocentrism: Diverging interethnic perceptions of African American and white American youth. *Journal of Personality and Social Psychology, 69*, 460–481.

Judge, Timothy A.; Thoresen, Carl J.; Bono, Joyce E.; & Patton, Gregory K. (2001). The job satisfaction-job performance relationship: A qualitative and quantitative review. *Psychological Bulletin, 127*, 376–407.

Jung, Carl (1967). *Collected works*. Princeton, NJ: Princeton University Press.

Jusczyk, Peter W. (1997). Finding and remembering words: Some beginnings by English-learning infants. *Current Directions in Psychological Science, 6*, 170–174.

Just, Marcel A.; Carpenter, Patricia A.; Keller, T. A.; et al. (2001). Interdependence of nonoverlapping cortical systems in dual cognitive tasks. *NeuroImage, 14*, 417–426.

Kabat-Zinn, Jon (1994). *Wherever you go, there you are: Mindfulness meditation in everyday life*. New York: Hyperion.

Kagan, Jerome (1984). *The nature of the child*. New York: Basic Books.

Kagan, Jerome (1989). *Unstable ideas: Temperament, cognition, and self*. Cambridge, MA: Harvard University Press.

Kagan, Jerome (1993). The meanings of morality. *Psychological Science, 4*, 353, 357–360.

Kagan, Jerome (1994). *Galen's prophecy: Temperament in human nature*. New York: Basic Books.

Kagan, Jerome (1997). Temperament and the reactions to unfamiliarity. *Child Development, 68*, 139–143.

Kagan, Jerome (1998a). How we become what we are. Paper presented at the annual meeting of the Family Therapy Network Symposium, Washington, DC.

Kagan, Jerome (1998b). *Three seductive ideas*. Cambridge, MA: Harvard University Press.

Kagan, Jerome; Kearsley, Richard B.; & Zelazo, Philip R. (1978). *Infancy: Its place in human development*. Cambridge, MA: Harvard University Press.

Kahneman, Daniel, & Treisman, Anne (1984). Changing views of attention and automaticity. In R. Parasuraman, D. R. Davies, & J. Beatty (eds.), *Varieties of attention*. New York: Academic Press.

Kameda, Tatsuya, & Sugimori, Shinkichi (1993). Psychological entrapment in group decision making: An assigned decision rule and a groupthink phenomenon. *Journal of Personality and Social Psychology, 65*, 282–292.

Kandel, Eric R., & Schwartz, James H. (1982). Molecular biology of learning: Modulation of transmitter release. *Science, 218*, 433–443.

Kanin, Eugene J. (1985). Date rapists: Differential sexual socialization and relative deprivation. *Archives of Sexual Behavior, 14*, 219–231.

Kanter, Rosabeth M. (1977/1993). *Men and women of the corporation*. New York: Basic Books.

Kanwisher, Nancy (2000). Domain specificity in face perception. *Nature Neuroscience, 3*, 759.

Kaplan, Abraham (1967). A philosophical discussion of normality. *Archives of General Psychiatry, 17,* 325–330.

Kaplan, Meg S.; Morales, Miguel; & Becker, Judith V. (1993). The impact of verbal satiation of adolescent sex offenders: A preliminary report. *Journal of Child Sexual Abuse, 2,* 81–88.

Karasek, Robert, & Theorell, Tores (1990). *Healthy work: Stress, productivity, and the reconstruction of working life.* New York: Basic Books.

Karau, Steven J., & Williams, Kipling D. (1993). Social loafing: A meta-analytic review and theoretical integration. *Journal of Personality and Social Psychology, 65,* 681–706.

Karney, Benjamin, & Bradbury, Thomas N. (2000). Attributions in marriage: State or trait? A growth curve analysis. *Journal of Personality and Social Psychology, 78,* 295–309.

Karni, Avi; Tanne, David; Rubenstein, Barton S.; Askenasy, Jean J. M.; & Sagi, Dov (1994). Dependence on REM sleep of overnight improvement of a perceptual skill. *Science, 265,* 679–682.

Karraker, Katherine H.; Vogel, Dena A.; & Lake, Margaret A. (1995). Parents' gender-stereotyped perceptions of newborns: The eye of the beholder revisited. *Sex Roles, 33,* 687–701.

Kashima, Yoshihisa; Yamaguchi, Susumu; Kim, Uichol; et al. (1995). Culture, gender, and self: A perspective from individualism–collectivism research. *Journal of Personality and Social Psychology, 69,* 925–937.

Kasser, Tim, & Ryan, Richard M. (1996). Further examining the American dream: Correlates of financial success as a central life aspiration. *Personality and Social Psychology Bulletin, 22,* 280–287.

Kasser, Tim, & Ryan, Richard M. (2001). Be careful what you wish for: Optimal functioning and the relative attainment of intrinsic and extrinsic goals. In P. Schmuck & K. M. Sheldon (eds.), *Life goals and well-being.* Lengerich, Germany: Pabst Science Publishers.

Kassinove, Howard (ed.) (1995). *Anger disorders: Definition, diagnosis, treatment.* Washington, DC: Taylor & Francis.

Katigbak, Marcia S.; Church, A. Timothy; & Akamine, Toshio X. (1996). Cross-cultural generalizability of personality dimensions: Relating indigenous and imported dimensions in two cultures. *Journal of Personality and Social Psychology, 70,* 99–114.

Katigbak, Marcia S.; Church, A. Timothy; Guanzon-Lapeña, Ma. Angeles; et al. (2002). Are indigenous personality dimensions culture specific? Philippine inventories and the Five-Factor model. *Journal of Personality and Social Psychology, 82,* 89–101.

Katz, Phyllis A., & Ksansnak, Keith R. (1994). Developmental aspects of gender role flexibility and traditionality in middle childhood and adolescence. *Developmental Psychology, 30,* 272–282.

Katz, Stuart, & Lautenschlager, Gary J. (1994). Answering reading comprehension items without passages on the SAT-I, the ACT, and the GRE. *Educational Assessment, 2,* 295–308.

Katz, Zender (2001). Canadian psychologists' education, trauma history, and the recovery of memories of childhood sexual abuse. (Doctoral Dissertation, Simon Fraser University, 2001.) *Dissertations Abstracts International, 61,* 3848.

Kaufman, Joan, & Zigler, Edward (1987). Do abused children become abusive parents? *American Journal of Orthopsychiatry, 57,* 186–192.

Kazdin, Alan E. (2001). *Behavior modification in applied settings* (6th ed.). Belmont, CA: Wadsworth.

Keane, M. M.; Gabrieli, J. D. E.; & Corkin, S. (1987). Multiple relations between fact-learning and priming in global amnesia. *Society for Neuroscience Abstracts, 13,* 1454.

Keating, Caroline F. (1994). World without words: Messages from face and body. In W. J. Lonner & R. Malpass (eds.), *Psychology and culture.* Needham Heights, MA: Allyn & Bacon.

Keck, Paul E., Jr., & McElroy, Susan L. (1998). Pharmacological treatment of bipolar disorders. In P. E. Nathan & J. M. Gorman (eds.), *A guide to treatments that work.* New York: Oxford University Press.

Keen, Sam (1986). *Faces of the enemy: Reflections of the hostile imagination.* San Francisco: Harper & Row.

Keller, Martin B.; McCullough, James P.; Klein, Daniel N.; et al. (2000, May 18). A comparison of nefazodone, the cognitive behavioral-analysis system of psychotherapy, and their combination for the treatment of chronic depression. *New England Journal of Medicine, 342,* 1462–1470.

Kelly, Anita E. (1999). Revealing personal secrets. *Current Directions in Psychological Science, 8,* 105–109.

Kelly, Dennis (1981). Disorders of sleep and consciousness. In E. Kandel & J. Schwartz (eds.), *Principles of neural science.* New York: Elsevier-North Holland.

Kelman, Herbert C., & Hamilton, V. Lee (1989). *Crimes of obedience: Toward a social psychology of authority and responsibility.* New Haven, CT: Yale University Press.

Keltner, Dacher, & Anderson, Cameron (2000). Saving face for Darwin: The functions and uses of embarrassment. *Current Directions in Psychological Science, 9,* 187–192.

Kempermann, G.; Brandon, E. P.; & Gage, F. H. (1998). Environmental stimulation of 120/SvJ mice causes increased cell proliferation and neurogenesis in the adult dentate gyrus. *Current Biology, 8,* 939–942.

Kendall [no first name] (1999). Women in Lesotho and the (Western) construction of homophobia. In E. Blackwood & S. E. Wieringa (eds.), *Female desires: Same-sex relations and transgender practices across cultures.* New York: Columbia University Press.

Kendler, Kenneth S.; Pedersen, Nancy; Johnson, Lars; Neale, Michael C.; & Mathie, A. (1993). A Swedish pilot twin study of affective illness, including hospital and population-ascertained subsamples. *Archives of General Psychiatry, 50,* 699–706.

Kennedy-Moore, Eileen, & Watson, Jeanne C. (2001). How and when does emotional expression help? *Review of General Psychology, 5,* 187–212.

Kenny, Michael G. (1986). *The passion of Ansel Bourne: Multiple personality in American culture.* Washington, DC: Smithsonian Press.

Kenrick, Douglas T.; Sundie, Jill M.; Nicastle, Lionel D.; & Stone, Gregory O. (2001). Can one ever be too wealthy or too chaste? Searching for nonlinearities in mate judgment. *Journal of Personality and Social Psychology, 80,* 462–471.

Kenrick, Douglas T., & Trost, Melanie R. (1993). The evolutionary perspective. In A. E. Beall & R. J. Sternberg (eds.), *The psychology of gender.* New York: Guilford Press.

Kephart, William M. (1967). Some correlates of romantic love. *Journal of Marriage and the Family, 29,* 470–474.

Kerr, Michael E., & Bowen, Murray (1988). *Family evaluation: An approach based on Bowen theory.* New York: Norton.

Kessler, Ronald C.; McGonagle, Katherine A.; Zhao, Shanyang; et al. (1994). Lifetime and 12-month prevalence of DSM-III-R psychiatric disorders in the United States: Results from the National Comorbidity Survey. *Archives of General Psychiatry, 51,* 8–19.

Kessler, Ronald C.; Sonnega, A.; Bromet, E.; et al. (1995). Posttraumatic stress disorder in the National Comorbidity Survey. *Archives of General Psychiatry, 52,* 1048–1060.

Kiecolt-Glaser, Janice K.; Garner, Warren; Speicher, Carl; et al. (1985a). Psychosocial modifiers of immunocompetence in medical students. *Psychosomatic Medicine, 46,* 7–14.

Kiecolt-Glaser, Janice K.; Glaser, Ronald; Williger, D.; et al. (1985b). Psychosocial enhancement of immunocompetence in a geriatric population. *Health Psychology, 4,* 25–41.

Kiecolt-Glaser, Janice K.; Malarkey, William B.; Chee, MaryAnn; et al. (1993). Negative behavior during marital conflict is associated with immunological down-regulation. *Psychosomatic Medicine, 55,* 395–409.

Kiecolt-Glaser, Janice K., & Newton, Tamara L. (2001). Marriage and health: His and hers. *Psychological Bulletin, 127,* 472–503.

Kiecolt-Glaser, Janice K.; Page, Gayle G.; Marucha, Phillip T.; et al. (1998). Psychological influences on surgical recovery: Perspectives from psychoneuroimmunology. *American Psychologist, 53,* 1209–1218.

Kihlstrom, John F. (1994). Hypnosis, delayed recall, and the principles of memory. *International Journal of Clinical and Experimental Hypnosis, 40,* 337–345.

Kihlstrom, John F. (1995). *From a subject's point of view: The experiment as conversation and collaboration between investigator and subject.* Invited address presented at the annual meeting of the American Psychological Society, New York.

Kihlstrom, John F. (1998). Dissociations and dissociation theory in hypnosis: Comment on Kirsch and Lynn (1998). *Psychological Bulletin, 123,* 186–191.

Kihlstrom, John F.; Barnhardt, Terrence M.; & Tataryn, Douglas J. (1992). The psychological unconscious: Found, lost, and regained. *American Psychologist, 47,* 788–791.

Kihlstrom, John F., & Harackiewicz, Judith M. (1982). The earliest recollection: A new survey. *Journal of Personality, 50,* 134–148.

Kim, Hannah L.; Streltzer, Jon; & Goebert, Deborah (1999). St. John's wort for depression: A meta-analysis of well-defined clinical trials. *Journal of Nervous and Mental Diseases, 187,* 532–538.

Kim, Heejung, & Markus, Hazel Rose (1999). Deviance or uniqueness, harmony or conformity? A cultural analysis. *Journal of Personality and Social Psychology, 77,* 785–800.

Kim, Karl H. S.; Relkin, Norman R.; Lee, Kyoung-Min; & Hirsch, Joy (1997). Distinct cortical areas associated with native and second languages. *Nature, 388,* 171–174.

Kimmel, Michael (1995). *Manhood in America: A cultural history.* New York: Free Press.

King, M., & Woollett, E. (1997). Sexually assaulted males: 115 men consulting a counseling service. *Archives of Sexual Behavior, 26,* 579–588.

King, Pamela (1989, October). The chemistry of doubt. *Psychology Today,* 58, 60.

King, Patricia M., & Kitchener, Karen S. (1994). *Developing reflective judgment: Understanding and promoting intellectual growth and critical thinking in adolescents and adults.* San Francisco: Jossey Bass.

Kinsey, Alfred C.; Pomeroy, Wardell B.; & Martin, Clyde E. (1948). *Sexual behavior in the human male.* Philadelphia: Saunders.

Kinsey, Alfred C.; Pomeroy, Wardell B.; & Martin, Clyde E. (1948). *Sexual behavior in the human male.* Philadelphia: Saunders.

Kinsey, Alfred C.; Pomeroy, Wardell B.; Martin, Clyde E.; & Gebhard, Paul H. (1953). *Sexual behavior in the human female.* Philadelphia: Saunders.

Kirkpatrick, Lee A., & Davis, Keith A. (1994). Attachment style, gender, and relationship stability: A longitudinal analysis. *Journal of Personality and Social Psychology, 66,* 502–512.

Kirsch, Irving (1997). Response expectancy theory and application: A decennial review. *Applied and Preventive Psychology, 6,* 69–70.

Kirsch, Irving, & Lynn, Steven J. (1995). The altered state of hypnosis: Changes in the theoretical landscape. *American Psychologist, 50,* 846–858.

Kirsch, Irving, & Lynn, Steven J. (1998). Dissociation theories of hypnosis. *Psychological Bulletin, 123,* 100–113.

Kirsch, Irving; Montgomery, G.; & Sapirstein, G. (1995). Hypnosis as an adjunct to cognitive behavioral psychotherapy: A meta-analysis. *Journal of Consulting and Clinical Psychology, 63,* 214–220.

Kirsch, Irving, & Sapirstein, Guy (1998). Listening to Prozac but hearing placebo: A meta-analysis of antidepressant medication. *Prevention & Treatment, 1, Article 0002a,* posted electronically June 26, 1998 on the website of the American Psychological Association.

Kirsch, Irving; Silva, Christopher E.; Carone, James E.; Johnston, J. Dennis; & Simon, B. (1989). The surreptitious observation design: An experimental paradigm for distinguishing artifact from essence in hypnosis. *Journal of Abnormal Psychology, 98,* 132–136.

Kirschbaum, C.; Prussner, J. C.; & Stone, A. A. (1995). Persistent high cortisol responses to repeated psychological stress in a subpopulation of healthy men. *Psychosomatic Medicine, 57,* 468–474.

Kitayama, Shinobu, & Markus, Hazel R. (1994). Introduction to cultural psychology and emotion research. In S. Kitayama & H. R. Markus (eds.), *Emotion and culture: Empirical studies of mutual influence.* Washington, DC: American Psychological Association.

Kitchener, Karen S., & King, Patricia M. (1990). The Reflective Judgment Model: Ten years of research. In M. L. Commons (ed.), *Models and methods in the study of adolescent and adult thought: Vol. 2. Adult development.* Westport, CT: Greenwood Press.

Kitchener, Karen S.; Lynch, Cindy L.; Fischer, Kurt W.; & Wood, Phillip K. (1993). Developmental range of reflective judgment: The effect of contextual support and practice on developmental stage. *Developmental Psychology, 29,* 893–906.

Kitzinger, Celia, & Wilkinson, Sue (1995). Transitions from heterosexuality to lesbianism: The discursive production of lesbian identities. *Developmental Psychology, 31,* 95–104.

Kleim, J. A.; Swain, R. A.; Armstrong, K. A.; et al. (1998). Selective synaptic plasticity within the cerebellar cortex following complex motor skill learning. *Neurobiology of Learning and Memory, 69,* 274–289.

Klein, Raymond, & Armitage, Roseanne (1979). Rhythms in human performance: 1 1/2-hour oscillations in cognitive style. *Science, 204,* 1326–1328.

Klein, Stanley B., & Kihlstrom, John F. (1998). On bridging the gap between social-personality psychology and neuropsychology. *Personality and Social Psychology Review, 2,* 228–242.

Kleinke, Chris L.; Peterson, Thomas R.; & Rutledge, Thomas R. (1998). Effects of self-generated facial expressions on mood. *Journal of Personality and Social Psychology, 74,* 272–279.

Kleinman, Arthur (1988). *Rethinking psychiatry: From cultural category to personal experience.* New York: Free Press.

Kleinmuntz, Benjamin, & Szucko, Julian J. (1984, March 29). A field study of the fallibility of polygraph lie detection. *Nature, 308,* 449–450.

Klima, Edward S., & Bellugi, Ursula (1966). Syntactic regularities in the speech of children. In J. Lyons & R. J. Wales (eds.), *Psycholinguistics papers.* Edinburgh, Scotland: Edinburgh University Press.

Klimoski, R. (1992). Graphology and personnel selection. In B. Beyerstein & D. Beyerstein (eds.), *The write stuff: Evaluations of graphology-The Study of handwriting analysis.* Buffalo, NY: Prometheus Books.

Klohnen, Eva C., & Bera, Stephan (1998). Behavioral and experiential patterns of avoidantly and securely attached women across adulthood: A 31-year longitudinal perspective. *Journal of Personality and Social Psychology, 74,* 211–223.

Klonoff, Elizabeth A.; Landrine, Hope; & Campbell, Robin (2000). Sexist discrimination may account for well-known gender differences in psychiatric symptoms. *Psychology of Women Quarterly, 24,* 93–99.

Kluft, Richard P. (1987). The simulation and dissimulation of multiple personality disorder. *American Journal of Clinical Hypnosis, 30,* 104–118.

Kluft, Richard P. (1993). Multiple personality disorders. In D. Spiegel (ed.), *Dissociative disorders: A clinical review.* Lutherville, MD: Sidran.

Knight, Raymond A.; Prentky, Robert A.; & Cerce, David D. (1994). The development, reliability, and validity of an inventory for the multidimensional assessment of sex and aggression. *Criminal Justice and Behavior, 21*, 72–94.

Kohlberg, Lawrence (1964). Development of moral character and moral ideology. In M. Hoffman & L. W. Hoffman (eds.), *Review of child development research*. New York: Russell Sage Foundation.

Kohlberg, Lawrence (1984). *Essays on moral development: Vol. 2. The psychology of moral development: The nature and validity of moral stages.* San Francisco: Harper & Row.

Köhler, Wolfgang (1925). *The mentality of apes.* New York: Harcourt, Brace.

Köhler, Wolfgang (1959). *Gestalt psychology today.* Presidential address to the American Psychological Association, Cincinnati. [Reprinted in E. R. Hilgard (ed.), *American psychology in historical perspective: Addresses of the presidents of the American Psychological Association, 1892–1977.* Washington, DC: American Psychological Association, 1978.]

Kohn, Melvin, & Schooler, Carmi (1983). *Work and personality: An inquiry into the impact of social stratification.* Norwood, NJ: Ablex.

Kolb, Bryan, & Whishaw, Ian Q. (1998). Brain plasticity and behavior. *Annual Review of Psychology, 49*, 43–64.

Koocher, Gerald P.; Goodman, Gail S.; White, C. Sue; et al. (1995). Psychological science and the use of anatomically detailed dolls in child sexual-abuse assessments. *Psychological Bulletin, 118*, 199–222.

Kopta, Stephen M.; Howard, Kenneth I.; Lowry, Jenny L.; & Beutler, Larry E. (1994). Patterns of symptomatic recovery in psychotherapy. *Journal of Consulting and Clinical Psychology, 62*, 1009–1016.

Korn, James H. (1998). *Illusions of reality: A history of deception in social psychology.* New York: State University of New York Press.

Koski, Lilah R., & Shaver, Phillip R. (1997). Attachment and relationship satisfaction across the lifespan. In R. J. Sternberg & M. Hojjat (eds.), *Satisfaction in close relationships.* New York: Guilford.

Koss, Mary P. (1993). Rape: Scope, impact, interventions, and public policy responses. *American Psychologist, 48*, 1062–1069.

Kosslyn, Stephen M. (1980). *Image and mind.* Cambridge, MA: Harvard University Press.

Kosslyn, Stephen M.; Pascual-Leone, A.; Felician, O.; et al. (1999). The role of area 17 in visual imagery: convergent evidence from PET and rTMS. *Science, 284*, 167–170.

Kozak, Michael J.; Liebowitz, Michael R.; & Foa, Edna B. (2000). Cognitive-behavior therapy and pharmacotherapy for OCD: The NIMH-sponsored collaborative study. In W.K. Goodman, M. Rudorfer, & J. Maser (eds.), *Treatment challenges in obsessive compulsive disorder.* Mahwah, NJ: Erlbaum.

Kramer, M. S.; Cutler, N.; Feighner, J.; et al. (1998). Distinct mechanism for antidepressant activity by blockade of central substance P receptors. *Science, 281*, 1640–1645.

Krantz, David S., & Manuck, Stephen B. (1984). Acute psychophysiologic reactivity and risk of cardiovascular disease: A review and methodological critique. *Psychological Bulletin, 96*, 435–464.

Kreps, Bonnie (1990). *Subversive thoughts, authentic passions.* San Francisco: Harper & Row.

Krieger, Nancy, & Sidney, S. (1996). Racial discrimination and blood pressure: The CARDIA study of young black and white adults. *American Journal of Public Health, 86*, 1370–1378.

Kring, Ann M., & Gordon, Albert H. (1998). Sex differences in emotion: Expression, experience, and physiology. *Journal of Personality and Social Psychology, 74*, 686–703.

Kripke, Daniel F. (1974). Ultradian rhythms in sleep and wakefulness. In E. D. Weitzman (ed.), *Advances in sleep research* (Vol. 1). Flushing, NY: Spectrum.

Kroll, Barry M. (1992). *Teaching hearts and minds: College students reflect on the Vietnam War in literature.* Carbondale: Southern Illinois University Press.

Krueger, Robert F. (2000). Phenotypic, genetic, and nonshared environmental parallels in the structure of personality: A view from the Multidimensional Personality Questionnaire. *Journal of Personality and Social Psychology, 79*, 1057–1067.

Krueger, Robert F.; Hicks, Brian M.; & McGue, Matt (2001). Altruism and antisocial behavior: Independent tendencies, unique personality correlates, distinct etiologies. *Psychological Science, 12*, 397–402.

Kruger, Justin, & Dunning, David (1999). Unskilled and unaware of it: How difficulties in recognizing one's own incompetence lead to inflated self-assessments. *Journal of Personality and Social Psychology, 77*, 1121–1134.

Krupa, David J.; Thompson, Judith K.; & Thompson, Richard F. (1993). Localization of a memory trace in the mammalian brain. *Science, 260*, 989–991.

Kuhl, Patricia K.; Andruski, Jean E.; Chistovich, Inna A.; et al. (1997, August 1). Cross-language analysis of phonetic units in language addressed to infants. *Science, 277*, 684–686.

Kuhl, Patricia K.; Williams, Karen A.; Lacerda, Francisco; et al. (1992, January 31). Linguistic experience alters phonetic perception in infants by 6 months of age. *Science, 255*, 606–608.

Kuhn, Deanna (2000). Metacognitive development. *Current Directions in Psychological Science, 9*, 178–182.

Kuhn, Deanna; Weinstock, Michael; & Flaton, Robin (1994). How well do jurors reason? Competence dimensions of individual variation in a juror reasoning task. *Psychological Science, 5*, 289–296.

Kunda, Ziva (1990). The case for motivated reasoning. *Psychological Bulletin, 108*, 480–498.

Kutchins, Herb, & Kirk, Stuart A. (1997). *Making us crazy: DSM. The psychiatric bible and the creation of mental disorders.* New York: Free Press.

LaBerge, Stephen (1986). *Lucid dreaming.* New York: Ballantine Books.

LaBerge, Stephen, & Levitan, Lynne (1995). Validity established of Dream-Light cues for eliciting lucid dreaming. *Dreaming: Journal of the Association for the Study of Dreams, 5*, 159–168.

Lachman, Margie E., & Weaver, Suzanne L. (1998). The sense of control as a moderator of social class differences in health and well-being. *Journal of Personality and Social Psychology, 74*, 763–773.

Lachman, Sheldon J. (1996). Processes in perception: Psychological transformations of highly structured stimulus material. *Perceptual and Motor Skills, 83*, 411–418.

Lai, Cecilia S. L.; Fisher, Simon E.; Hurst, Jane A.; et al. (2001). A forkhead-domain gene is mutated in a severe speech and language disorder. *Nature, 413*, 519–523.

Laird, James D. (1974). Self-attribution of emotion: The effects of expressive behavior on the quality of emotional experience. *Journal of Personality and Social Psychology, 29*, 475–486.

Lakoff, Robin T. (1990). *Talking power.* New York: Basic Books.

Lakoff, Robin T., & Coyne, James C. (1993). *Father knows best: The use and abuse of power in Freud's case of "Dora."* New York: Teachers College Press.

Lamb, Sharon (2002). *The secret lives of girls.* New York: The Free Press.

Landrine, Hope (1988). Revising the framework of abnormal psychology. In P. Bronstein & K. Quina (eds.), *Teaching a psychology of people.* Washington, DC: American Psychological Association.

Lang, Frieder R., & Heckhausen, Jutta (2001). Perceived control over development and subjective well-being: Differential benefits across adulthood. *Journal of Personality and Social Psychology, 81*, 509–523.

Lang, Peter (1995). The emotion probe: Studies of motivation and attention. *American Psychologist, 50*, 372–385.

Langer, Ellen J. (1983). *The psychology of control.* Beverly Hills, CA: Sage.

Langer, Ellen J. (1989). *Mindfulness.* Reading, MA: Addison-Wesley.

Langer, Ellen J. (1997). *The power of mindful learning.* Reading, MA: Addison-Wesley.

Langer, Ellen J.; Blank, Arthur; & Chanowitz, Benzion (1978). The mindlessness of ostensibly thoughtful action: The role of placebic information in interpersonal interaction. *Journal of Personality and Social Psychology, 36,* 635–642.

Lanphear, B. P.; Hornung, R.; Ho, M.; et al. (2002). Environmental lead exposure during early childhood. *Journal of Pediatrics, 140,* 49–47.

Latané, Bibb; Williams, Kipling; & Harkins, Stephen (1979). Many hands make light the work: The causes and consequences of social loafing. *Journal of Personality and Social Psychology, 37,* 822–832.

Laudenslager, Mark L. (1988). The psychology of loss: Lessons from humans and nonhuman primates. *Journal of Social Issues, 44,* 19–36.

Laumann, Edward O., & Gagnon John H. (1995). A sociological perspective on sexual action. In R. G. Parker & J. H. Gagnon (eds.), *Conceiving sexuality: Approaches to sex research in a postmodern world.* New York: Routledge.

Laumann, Edward O.; Gagnon, John H.; Michael, Robert T.; & Michaels, Stuart (1994). *The social organization of sexuality.* Chicago: University of Chicago Press.

Laurence, J. R., & Perry, C. (1988). *Hypnosis, will, and memory: A psycholegal history.* New York: Guilford Press.

Laursen, Brett, & Collins, W. Andrew (1994). Interpersonal conflict during adolescence. *Psychological Bulletin, 115,* 197–209.

Lavie, Peretz (1976). Ultradian rhythms in the perception of two apparent motions. *Chronobiologia, 3,* 21–218.

Lazarus, Richard S. (2000a, Spring). Reason and our emotions: A hard sell. *The General Psychologist, 35,* 16–20.

Lazarus, Richard S. (2000b). Toward better research on stress and coping. *American Psychologist, 55,* 665–673.

Lazarus, Richard S., & Folkman, Susan (1984). *Stress, appraisal, and coping.* New York: Springer.

LeDoux, Joseph E. (1996). *The emotional brain.* New York: Simon & Schuster.

Lee, Tatia M. C.; Blashko, Carl A.; Janzen, Henry L.; et al. (1997). Pathophysiological mechanism of seasonal affective disorder. *Journal of Affective Disorders, 46,* 25–38.

Lehman, Adam K., & Rodin, Judith (1989). Styles of self-nurturance and disordered eating. *Journal of Consulting and Clinical Psychology, 57,* 117–122.

Leibel, Rudolph L.; Rosenbaum, Michael; & Hirsch, Jules (1995). Changes in energy expenditure resulting from altered body weight. *New England Journal of Medicine, 332,* 621–628.

Lemieux, Robert, & Hale, Jerold L. (2000). Intimacy, passion, and commitment among married individuals: Further testing of the Triangular Theory of Love. *Psychological Reports, 87,* 941–948.

Lenneberg, Eric H. (1967). *Biological foundations of language.* New York: Wiley.

Lent, James R. (1968, June). Mimosa cottage: Experiment in hope. *Psychology Today,* 51–58.

Leonard, S.; Gault, J.; Moore, T.; et al. (1998, July 10). Further investigation of a chromosome 15 locus in schizophrenia: Analysis of affected sibpairs from the NIMH Genetics Initiative. *American Journal of Medical Genetics, 81,* 308–312.

Lepore, Stephen J.; Ragan, Jennifer D.; & Jones, Scott (2000). Talking facilitates cognitive-emotional processes of adaptation to an acute stressor. *Journal of Personality and Social Psychology, 78,* 499–508.

Lepore, Stephen J.; Silver, Roxanne C.; Wortman, Camille B.; & Wayment, Heidi A. (1996). Social constraints, intrusive thoughts, and depressive symptoms among bereaved mothers. *Journal of Personality and Social Psychology, 70,* 271–282.

Lepowsky, Maria (1994). *Fruit of the motherland: Gender in an egalitarian society.* New York: Columbia University Press.

Lepper, Mark R.; Greene, David; & Nisbett, Richard E. (1973). Undermining children's intrinsic interest with extrinsic rewards. *Journal of Personality and Social Psychology, 28,* 129–137.

Leproult, Rachel; Copinschi, Georges; Buxton, Orfeu; & Van Cauter, Eve (1997). Sleep loss results in an elevation of cortisol levels the next evening. *Sleep, 20,* 865–870.

Leproult, Rachel; Van Reeth, Olivier; Byrne, Maria M.; et al. (1997). Sleepiness, performance, and neuroendocrine function during sleep deprivation: Effects of exposure to bright light or exercise. *Journal of Biological Rhythms, 12,* 245–258.

Lerner, Harriet G. (1989). *The dance of intimacy.* New York: Harper & Row.

Lerner, Jennifer S.; Goldberg, Julie H.; & Tetlock, Philip E. (1998). Sober second thought: The effects of accountability, anger, and authoritarianism on attributions of responsibility. *Personality and Social Psychology Bulletin, 24,* 563–574.

Lerner, Melvin J. (1980). *The belief in a just world: A fundamental delusion.* New York: Plenum.

Lesch, Klaus-Peter; Bengel, Dietmar; Heils, Armin; et al. (1996). Association of anxiety-related traits with a polymorphism in the serotonin transporter gene regulatory region. *Science, 274,* 1527–1531.

Lester, Barry M.; LaGasse, Linda L.; & Seifer, Ronald (1998, October 23). Cocaine exposure and children: The meaning of subtle effects. *Science, 282,* 633–634.

LeVay, Simon (1991). A difference in hypothalamic structure between heterosexual and homosexual men. *Science, 253,* 1034–1037.

Levenson, Robert W. (1992). Autonomic nervous system differences among emotions. *Psychological Science, 3,* 23–27.

Levenson, Robert W.; Carstensen, Laura L.; & Gottman, John M. (1994). Influence of age and gender on affect, physiology, and their interrelations: A study of long-term marriages. *Journal of Personality & Social Psychology, 67,* 56–68.

Levenson, Robert W.; Ekman, Paul; & Friesen, Wallace V. (1990). Voluntary facial action generates emotion-specific autonomic nervous system activity. *Psychophysiology, 27,* 363–384.

Levenstein, Susan; Ackerman, S.; Kiecolt-Glaser, Janice K.; & Dubois, A. (1999, January 6). Stress and peptic ulcer disease. *Journal of the American Medical Association, 281,* 10–11.

Levin, Daniel T. (2000). Race as a visual feature: Using visual search and perceptual discrimination tasks to understand face categories and the cross-race recognition deficit. *Journal of Experimental Psychology: General, 129,* 559–574.

Levine, James A.; Eberhardt, Norman L.; & Jensen, Michael D. (1999, January 8). Role of nonexercise activity thermogenesis in resistance to fat gain in humans. *Science, 283,* 212–214.

Levine, Joseph, & Suzuki, David (1993). *The secret of life: Redesigning the living world.* Boston: WGBH Educational Foundation.

Levine, Judith (2002). *Harmful to minors.* Minneapolis: University of Minnesota Press.

Levine, Robert V.; Martinez, Todd S.; Brase, Gary; & Sorenson, Kerry (1994). Helping in 36 U.S. cities. *Journal of Personality and Social Psychology, 67,* 69–82.

Levy, Becca. (1996). Improving memory in old age through implicit self-stereotyping. *Journal of Personality and Social Psychology, 71,* 1092–1107.

Levy, David A. (1997). *Tools of critical thinking: Metathoughts for psychology*. Boston: Allyn & Bacon.

Levy, Jerre; Trevarthen, Colwyn; & Sperry, Roger W. (1972). Perception of bilateral chimeric figures following hemispheric deconnection. *Brain, 95*, 61–78.

Levy, Kenneth N.; Blatt, Sidney J.; & Shaver, Phillip R. (1998). Attachment styles are parental representations. *Journal of Personality and Social Psychology, 74*, 407–419.

Levy, Robert I. (1984). The emotions in comparative perspective. In K. R. Scherer & P. Ekman (eds.), *Approaches to emotion*. Hillsdale, NJ: Erlbaum.

Lewin, Kurt (1948). *Resolving social conflicts*. New York: Harper.

Lewis, Dorothy O. (1992). From abuse to violence: Psychophysiological consequences of maltreatment. *Journal of the American Academy of Child and Adolescent Psychiatry, 31*, 383–391.

Lewis, Michael (1997). *Altering fate: Why the past does not predict the future*. New York: Guilford Press.

Lewontin, Richard C. (1970). Race and intelligence. *Bulletin of the Atomic Scientists, 26*(3), 2–8.

Lewontin, Richard C. (2001, March 5). Genomania: A disorder of modern biology and medicine. Invited address at the University of California, Los Angeles.

Lewontin, Richard C.; Rose, Steven; & Kamin, Leon J. (1984). *Not in our genes: Biology, ideology, and human nature*. New York: Pantheon.

Lewy, Alfred J.; Ahmed, Saeeduddin; Jackson, Jeanne L.; & Sack, Robert L. (1992). Melatonin shifts human circadian rhythms according to a phase response curve. *Chronobiology International, 9*, 380–392.

Lewy, Alfred J.; Ahmed, Saeeduddin; & Sack, Robert L. (1995). Phase shifting the human circadian clock using melatonin. *Behavior and Brain Research, 73*, 131–134.

Lewy, Alfred J.; Bauer, Vance K.; Cutler, Neil L.; et al. (1998). Morning vs. evening light treatment of patients with winter depression. *Archives of General Psychiatry, 55*, 890–896.

Lichtenstein, Sarah; Slovic, Paul; Fischhoff, Baruch; et al. (1978). Judged frequency of lethal events. *Journal of Experimental Psychology: Human Learning and Memory, 4*, 551–578.

Lickona, Thomas (1983). *Raising good children*. New York: Bantam.

Lieberman, Matthew (2000). Intuition: A social cognitive neuroscience approach. *Psychological Bulletin, 126*, 109–137.

Liepert, J.; Bauder, H.; Miltner, W. H.; et al. (2000). Treatment-induced cortical reorganization after stroke in humans. *Stroke, 31*, 1210–1216.

Lightdale, Jenifer R., & Prentice, Deborah A. (1994). Rethinking sex differences in aggression: Aggressive behavior in the absence of social roles. *Personality and Social Psychology Bulletin, 20*, 34–44.

Lilienfeld, Scott O. (1993, Fall). Do "honesty" tests really measure honesty? *Skeptical Inquirer, 18*, 32–41.

Lilienfeld, Scott O. (1996, January/February). EMDR treatment: Less than meets the eye? *Skeptical Inquirer*, 25–31.

Lilienfeld, Scott O. (1999, September/October). Projective measures of personality and psychopathology: How well do they work? *Skeptical Inquirer*, 32–39.

Lilienfeld, Scott O.; Wood, James M.; & Garb, Howard N. (2000). The scientific status of projective techniques. *Psychological Science in the Public Interest, 1*, 27–66.

Lillard, Angeline S. (1998). Ethnopsychologies: Cultural variations in theories of mind. *Psychological Bulletin, 123*, 3–32.

Lin, Keh-Ming; Poland, Russell E.; & Chien, C. P. (1990). Ethnicity and psychopharmacology: Recent findings and future research directions. In E. Sorel (ed.), *Family, culture, and psychobiology*. New York: Legas.

Lin, L.; Hungs, M.; & Mignot, E. (2001). Narcolepsy and the HLA region. *Journal of Neuroimmunology, 117*, 9–20.

Linday, Linda A. (1994). Maternal reports of pregnancy, genital, and related fantasies in preschool and kindergarten children. *Journal of the American Academy of Child and Adolescent Psychiatry, 33*, 416–423.

Lindsay, D. Stephen, & Read, J. D. (1994). Psychotherapy and memories of childhood sexual abuse: A cognitive perspective. *Applied Cognitive Psychology, 8*, 281–338.

Linton, Marigold (1978). Real-world memory after six years: An in vivo study of very long-term memory. In M. M. Gruneberg, P. E. Morris, & R. N. Sykes (eds.), *Practical aspects of memory*. London: Academic Press.

Linton, Simi (1998). *Claiming disability: Knowledge and identity*. New York: New York University Press.

Linville, P. W.; Fischer, G. W.; & Fischhoff, B. (1992). AIDS risk perceptions and decision biases. In J. B. Pryor & G. D. Reeder (eds.), *The social psychology of HIV infection*. Hillsdale, NJ: Erlbaum.

Lissner, L.; Odell, P. M.; D'Agostino, R. B.; et al. (1991, June 27). Variability of body weight and health outcomes in the Framingham population. *New England Journal of Medicine, 324*, 1839–1844.

Little, John T.; Kimbrell, Tim A.; Wassermann, Eric M.; et al. (2000). Cognitive effects of 1- and 20-hertz repetitive transcranial magnetic stimulation in depression: Preliminary report. *Neuropsychiatry, Neuropsychology, & Behavioral Neurology, 13*, 119–124.

Locher, R.; Suter, P. M.; & Vetter, W. (1998). Ethanol suppresses smooth muscle cell proliferation in the postprandial state: a new antiatherosclerotic mechanism of ethanol? *American Journal of Clinical Nutrition, 67*, 338–341.

Locke, Edwin A., & Latham, Gary P. (1990). Work motivation and satisfaction: Light at the end of the tunnel. *Psychological Science, 1*, 240–246.

Locke, Edwin A.; Shaw, Karyll; Saari, Lise; & Latham, Gary (1981). Goal-setting and task performance: 1969–1980. *Psychological Bulletin, 90*, 125–152.

Loehlin, John C. (1992). *Genes and environment in personality development*. Newbury Park CA: Sage.

Loehlin, John C.; Horn, J. M.; & Willerman, L. (1996). Heredity, environment, and IQ in the Texas adoption study. In R. J. Sternberg & E. Grigorenko (eds.), *Intelligence: Heredity and environment*. New York: Cambridge University Press.

Loewen, E. Ruth; Shaw, Raymond J.; & Craik, Fergus I. (1990). Age differences in components of metamemory. *Experimental Aging Research, 16*(1–2), 43–48.

Loftus, Elizabeth F. (1980). *Memory*. Reading, MA: Addison-Wesley.

Loftus, Elizabeth F. (1996). Memory distortion and false memory creation. *Bulletin of the American Academy of Psychiatry and the Law, 24*, 281–295.

Loftus, Elizabeth F., & Greene, Edith (1980). Warning: Even memory for faces may be contagious. *Law and Human Behavior, 4*, 323–334.

Loftus, Elizabeth F., & Ketcham, Katherine (1994). *The myth of repressed memory*. New York: St. Martin's Press.

Loftus, Elizabeth F., & Palmer, John C. (1974). Reconstruction of automobile destruction: An example of the interaction between language and memory. *Journal of Verbal Learning and Verbal Behavior, 13*, 585–589.

Loftus, Elizabeth F., & Pickrell, Jacqueline E. (1995). The formation of false memories. *Psychiatric Annals, 25*, 720–725.

Loftus, Elizabeth F., & Zanni, Guido (1975). Eyewitness testimony: The influence of the wording of a question. *Bulletin of the Psychonomic Society, 5*, 86–88.

Loftus, Elizabeth F.; Miller, David G.; & Burns, Helen J. (1978). Semantic integration of verbal information into a visual memory. *Journal of Experimental Psychology: Human Learning and Memory, 4*, 19–31.

Lohr, Jeffrey M.; Montgomery, Robert W.; Lilienfeld, Scott O.; & Tolin, David F. (1999). Pseudoscience and the commercial promotion of trauma treatments. In R. Gist & B. Lubin (eds.), *Response to disaster: Psychosocial, community, and ecological approaches.* Philadelphia, PA: Brunner/Mazel (Taylor & Francis).

Lohr, Jeffrey M.; Tolin, D. F.; & Lilienfeld, Scott O. (1998). Efficacy of Eye Movement Desensitization and Reprocessing: Implications for behavior therapy. *Behavior Therapy, 29,* 123–156.

Lonner, Walter J. (1995). Culture and human diversity. In E. Trickett, R. Watts, & D. Birman (eds.), *Human diversity: Perspectives on people in context.* San Francisco: Jossey-Bass.

Lopez, N. L; Bonenberger, J. L; & Schneider, H. G. (2001). Parental disciplinary history, current levels of empathy, and moral reasoning in young adults. *North American Journal of Psychology, 3,* 193–204.

López, Steven R. (1989). Patient variable biases in clinical judgment: Conceptual overview and methodological considerations. *Psychological Bulletin, 106,* 184–203.

López, Steven R. (1995). Testing ethnic minority children. In B. B. Wolman (ed.), *The encyclopedia of psychology, psychiatry, and psychoanalysis.* New York: Holt.

Lott, Bernice, & Maluso, Diane (1993). The social learning of gender. In A. E. Beall & R. J. Sternberg (eds.), *The psychology of gender.* New York: Guilford Press.

Louie, Therese A. (1999). Decision makers' hindsight bias after making favorable and unfavorable feedback. *Journal of Applied Psychology, 84,* 29–41.

Lovaas, O. Ivar (1977). *The autistic child: Language development through behavior modification.* New York: Halsted Press.

Lovaas, O. Ivar; Schreibman, Laura; & Koegel, Robert L. (1974). A behavior modification approach to the treatment of autistic children. *Journal of Autism and Childhood Schizophrenia, 4,* 111–129.

Lucchina, L. A.; Curtis, O. F.; Putnam, P.; et al. (1998). Psychophysical measurement of 6-n-propylthiouracil (PROP) taste perception. *Annals of the New York Academy of Sciences, 855,* 816–819.

Lucio-G.M., Emilia; Palacios, Hugo; Duran, Consuelo; Butcher, James N. (1999). MMPI-2 with Mexican psychiatric inpatients: Basic and content scales. *Journal of Clinical Psychology, 1999,* 1541–1552.

Luengo, M. A.; Carrillo-de-la-Peña, M. T.; Otero, J. M.; & Romero, E. (1994). A short-term longitudinal study of impulsivity and antisocial behavior. *Journal of Personality and Social Psychology, 66,* 542–548.

Luepnitz, Deborah A. (1988). *The family interpreted: Feminist theory in clinical practice.* New York: Basic Books.

Lugaresi, Elio; Medori, R.; Montagna, P.; et al. (1986, October 16). Fatal familial insomnia and dysautonomia with selective degeneration of thalamic nuclei. *New England Journal of Medicine, 315,* 997–1003.

Luhrmann, T. M. (2000). *Of two minds: the growing disorder in American psychiatry.* New York: Knopf.

Luria, Alexander R. (1968). *The mind of a mnemonist* (L. Soltaroff, trans.). New York: Basic Books.

Luria, Alexander R. (1980). *Higher cortical functions in man* (2nd rev. ed.). New York: Basic Books.

Lutz, Catherine (1988). *Unnatural emotions.* Chicago: University of Chicago Press.

Lyketsos, C. G.; Hoover, D. R.; Guccione, M.; et al. (1993). Depressive symptoms as predictors of medical outcomes in HIV infection: Multicenter AIDS Cohort Study. *Journal of the American Medical Association, 270,* 2563–2567.

Lykken, David T. (1981). *A tremor in the blood: Uses and abuses of the lie detector.* New York: McGraw-Hill.

Lykken, David T. (1995). *The antisocial personalities.* Hillsdale, NJ: Erlbaum.

Lykken, David T., & Tellegen, Auke (1996). Happiness is a stochastic phenomenon. *Psychological Science, 7,* 186–189.

Lynn, Steven Jay; Rhue, Judith W.; & Weekes, John R. (1990). Hypnotic involuntariness: A social cognitive analysis. *Psychological Review, 97,* 69–184.

Lytton, Hugh, & Romney, David M. (1991). Parents' differential socialization of boys and girls: A meta-analysis. *Psychological Bulletin, 109,* 267–296.

Lyubomirsky, Sonja; Caldwell, Nicole D.; & Nolen-Hoeksema, Susan (1998). Effects of ruminative and distracting responses to depressed mood on retrieval of autobiographical memories. *Journal of Personality and Social Psychology, 75,* 166–177.

Maas, James B. (1998). *Power sleep.* New York: Villard.

MacArthur Foundation Research Network on Successful Midlife Development (1999). Report of latest findings (Orville G. Brim, director; 2145 14th Avenue, Vero Beach, FL 32960).

Maccoby, Eleanor E. (1998). *The two sexes: Growing up apart, coming together.* Cambridge, MA: Belknap Press/Harvard University Press.

MacKavey, William R.; Malley, Janet E.; & Stewart, Abigail, J. (1991). Remembering autobiographically consequential experiences: Content analysis of psychologists' accounts of their lives. *Psychology and Aging, 6,* 50–59.

MacKinnon, Donald W. (1968). Selecting students with creative potential. In P. Heist (ed.), *The creative college student: An unmet challenge.* San Francisco: Jossey-Bass.

MacLean, Paul (1993). Cerebral evolution of emotion. In M. Lewis & J. M. Haviland (eds.), *Handbook of emotions.* New York: Guilford Press.

Macmillan, Malcolm (2000). *An odd kind of fame: Stories of Phineas Gage.* Cambridge: MIT Press, 2000.

Macrae, C. Neil; Milne, Alan B.; & Bodenhausen, Galen V. (1994). Stereotypes as energy-saving devices: A peek inside the cognitive toolbox. *Journal of Personality and Social Psychology, 66,* 37–47.

Maddux, James E. (1993, Summer). The mythology of psychopathology: A social cognitive view of deviance, difference, and disorder. *General Psychologist, 29,* 34–45.

Maddux, James E. (ed.) (1995). *Self-efficacy, adaptation, and adjustment: Theory, research, and application.* New York: Plenum.

Maddux, James E. (1996). The social-cognitive construction of difference and disorder. In D. F. Barone, J. E. Maddux, & C. R. Snyder (eds.), *Social cognitive psychology: History and current domains.* New York: Plenum.

Maddux, James E., & Mundell, Clare E. (1997). Disorders of personality. In V. Derlega, B. Winstead, & W. Jones (eds.), *Personality: Contemporary theory and research* (2nd ed.). Chicago: Nelson-Hall.

Maguire, Eleanor A.; Gadian, David G.; Johnsrude, Ingrid S.; et al. (2000). Navigation-related structural change in the hippocampi of taxi drivers. *Proceedings of the National Academy of Sciences, 97,* 4398–4403.

Major, Brenda; Spencer, Steven; Schmader, Toni; et al. (1998). Coping with negative stereotypes about intellectual performance: The role of psychological disengagement. *Personality and Social Psychology Bulletin, 24,* 34–50.

Maki, Pauline M.; & Resnick, Susan M. (2000). Longitudinal effects of estrogen replacement therapy on PET cerebral blood flow and cognition. *Neurobiology of Aging, 21,* 373–383.

Malamuth, Neil M.; Linz, Daniel; Heavey, Christopher L.; et al. (1995). Using the confluence model of sexual aggression to predict men's conflict with women: A 10-year follow-up study. *Journal of Personality and Social Psychology, 69,* 353–369.

Malamuth, Neil, & Dean, Karol (1990). Attraction to sexual aggression. In A. Parrot & L. Bechhofer (eds.), *Acquaintance rape: The hidden crime.* Newark, NJ: Wiley.

Malaspina, Dolores (2001). Paternal factors and schizophrenia risk: De novo mutations and imprinting. *Schizophrenia Bulletin, 27,* 379–393.

Malenka, Robert C., & Nicoll, Roger A. (1999). Long-term potentiation—a decade of progress? *Science, 285,* 1870–1874.

Malinosky-Rummell, Robin, & Hansen, David J. (1993). Long-term consequences of childhood physical abuse. *Psychological Bulletin, 114,* 68–79.

Malnic, B.; Hirono, J.; Sato, T.; & Buck, L. B. (1999). Combinatorial receptor codes for odors. *Cell, 96,* 713–723.

Manning, Carol A.; Hall, J. L.; & Gold, Paul E. (1990). Glucose effects on memory and other neuropsychological tests in elderly humans. *Psychological Science, 1,* 307–311.

Manning, Carol A.; Ragozzino, Michael E.; & Gold, Paul E. (1993). Glucose enhancement of memory in patients with probable senile dementia of the Alzheimer's type. *Neurobiology of Aging, 14,* 523–528.

Mansfield, Elizabeth D., & McAdams, Dan P. (1996). Generativity and themes of agency and community in adult autobiography. *Personality and Social Psychology Bulletin, 22,* 721–731.

Maquet, Pierre (2001). The role of sleep in learning and memory. *Science, 294,* 1048–1052.

Maquet, Pierre; Laereys, S.; Peigneux, P.; et al. (2000). Experience-dependent changes in cerebral activation during human REM sleep. *Nature Neuroscience, 8,* 831–836.

Marcus, G. F.; Vijayan, S.; Rao, S. Bandi; & Vishton, P. M. (1999, January 1). Rule learning by seven-month-old infants. *Science, 283,* 77–79.

Marcus, Gary F. (1999). *The algebraic mind.* Cambridge, MA: MIT Press.

Marcus, Gary F.; Pinker, Steven; Ullman, Michael; et al. (1992). Overregularization in language acquisition. *Monographs of the Society for Research in Child Development, 57* (Serial No. 228), 1–182.

Marcus, Gary F.; Vijayan, S.; Rao, S. Bandi; & Vishton, P. M. (1999). Rule learning by seven-month-old infants. *Science, 283,* 77–80.

Marcus-Newhall, Amy; Pedersen, William C.; Carlson, Mike; & Miller, Norman (2000). Displaced aggression is alive and well: A meta-analytic review. *Journal of Personality and Social Psychology, 78,* 670–689.

Marder, Stephen R.; Wirshing, William C.; Mintz, Jim; et al. (1996). Two-year outcome of social-skills training and group psychotherapy for outpatients with schizophrenia. *American Journal of Psychiatry, 153,* 1585–1592.

Marino, Raul, Jr., & Cosgrove, G. Rees (1997). Neurosurgical treatment of neuropsychiatric illness. *Psychiatric Clinics of North America, 20,* 933–943.

Markowitz, Laura M. (1993, July/August). Walking the walk. *Family Therapy Networker,* 19–31.

Markus, Hazel R., & Kitayama, Shinobu (1991). Culture and the self: Implications for cognition, emotion, and motivation. *Psychological Review, 98,* 224–253.

Markus, Rob; Panhuysen, Geert; Tuiten, Adriaan; & Koppeschaar, Hans (2000). Effects of food on cortisol and mood in vulnerable subjects under controllable and uncontrollable stress. *Physiology and Behavior, 70,* 333–342.

Marlatt, G. Alan (1996). Models of relapse and relapse prevention: A commentary. *Experimental and Clinical Psychopharmacology, 4,* 55–60.

Marlatt, G. Alan; Baer, John S.; Kivlahan, Daniel R.; et al. (1998). Screening and brief intervention for high-risk college student drinkers. *Journal of Consulting and Clinical Psychology, 66,* 604–615.

Marlatt, G. Alan, & Rohsenow, Damaris J. (1980). Cognitive processes in alcohol use: Expectancy and the balanced placebo design. In N. K. Mello (ed.), *Advances in substance abuse* (Vol. 1). Greenwich, CT: JAI Press.

Marriott, Bernadette M. (ed.) (1994). *Food components to enhance performance.* Washington, DC: National Academy Press.

Marshall, Grant N.; Wortman, Camille B.; Vickers, Ross R., Jr.; et al. (1994). The five-factor model of personality as a framework for personality health research. *Journal of Personality and Social Psychology, 67,* 278–286.

Martin, Garry, & Pear, Joseph (1999). *Behavior modification: What it is and how to do it* (6th ed.). Upper Saddle River, NJ: Prentice Hall.

Martin, Rod A. (2001). Humor, laughter, and physical health: Methodological issues and research findings. *Psychological Bulletin, 127,* 504–519.

Martin, Rod A., & Dobbin, James P. (1988). Sense of humor, hassles, and immunoglobulin A: Evidence for a stress-moderating effect of humor. *International Journal of Psychiatry in Medicine, 18,* 93–105.

Martin, Stacia K., & Eastman, Charmane I. (1998). Medium-intensity light produces circadian rhythm adaption to simulated night-shift work. *Sleep, 21,* 154–165.

Martino, Gail, & Marks, Lawrence E. (2001). Synesthesia: Strong and weak. *Current Directions in Psychological Science, 10,* 61–69.

Maruta, T.; Colligan R. C.; Malinchoc, M.; & Offord, K. P. (2000). Optimists vs. pessimists: Survival rate among medical patients over a 30-year period. *Mayo Clinic Proceedings, 75,* 140–143.

Masand, P. S. (2000). Side effects of antipsychotics in the elderly. *Journal of Clinical Psychiatry, 61*(suppl. 8), 43–49.

Maslow, Abraham H. (1970). *Motivation and personality* (2nd ed.). New York: Harper & Row.

Maslow, Abraham H. (1971). *The farther reaches of human nature.* New York: Viking.

Masten, Ann S. (2001). Ordinary magic: Resilience processes in development. *American Psychologist, 56,* 227–238.

Masten, Ann S., & Coatsworth, J. Douglas (1998). The development of competence in favorable and unfavorable environments. *American Psychologist, 53,* 205–220.

Masters, William H., & Johnson, Virginia E. (1966). *Human sexual response.* Boston: Little, Brown.

Masuda, Takahiko, & Nisbett, Richard E. (2001). Attending holistically versus analytically: Comparing the context sensitivity of Japanese and Americans. *Journal of Personality and Social Psychology, 81,* 922–934.

Matarazzo, Joseph (1984). Behavioral immunogens and pathogens in health and illness. In B. L. Hammonds & C. J. Scheirer (eds.), *Psychology and health: The master lecture series* (Vol. 3). Washington, DC: American Psychological Association.

Mather, Mara; Shafir, Eldar; & Johnson, Marcia K. (2000). Misremembrance of options past: Source monitoring and choice. *Psychological Science, 11,* 132–138.

Matsumoto, David (1996). *Culture and psychology.* Pacific Grove, CA: Brooks-Cole.

Matthews, John (ed.) (1994). *McGill working papers in linguistics* (Vol. 10 [1 & 2]). [Special Issue: Linguistic aspects of familial language impairment.] Montreal, Quebec: McGill University.

Matthews, Karen A.; Wing, Rena R.; Kuller, Lewis H.; et al. (1990). Influences of natural menopause on psychological characteristics and symptoms of middle-aged healthy women. *Journal of Consulting and Clinical Psychology, 58,* 345–351.

Maurer, Daphne; Lewis, Terri L.; Brent, Henry P.; & Levin, Alex V. (1999). Rapid improvement in the acuity of infants after visual input. *Science, 286,* 108–110.

Mawhinney, T. C. (1990). Decreasing intrinsic "motivation" with extrinsic rewards: Easier said than done. *Journal of Organizational Behavior Management, 11,* 175–191.

Max, M.; Shanker, Y. G.; Huang, L.; et al. (2001). Tas1r3, encoding a new candidate taste receptor, is allelic to the sweet responsiveness locus Sac. *Nature Genetics, 28,* 58–63.

Maxfield, Michael, & Widom, Cathy S. (1996). The cycle of violence. Revisited 6 years later. *Archives of Pediatric and Adolescent Medicine, 150,* 390–395.

Mayberry, Rachel I., & Nicoladis, Elena (2000). Gesture reflects language development: Evidence from bilingual children. *Current Directions in Psychological Science, 9,* 192–196.

Mayer, John D.; McCormick, Laura J.; & Strong, Sara E. (1995). Mood-congruent memory and natural mood: New evidence. *Personality and Social Psychology Bulletin, 21,* 736–746.

Mayer, John D., & Salovey, Peter (1997). What is emotional intelligence? In P. Salovey & D. Sluyter (eds.), *Emotional development and emotional intelligence: Implications for educators.* New York: Basic Books.

Mayeux, R.; Ottman, R.; Maestre, G.; et al. (1998). Synergistic effects of traumatic head injury and apolipoprotein-epsilon in patients with Alzheimer's disease. *Neurology, 45,* 555–557.

Mazur, Allen, & Lamb, Theodore A. (1980). Testosterone, status, and mood in human males. *Hormones and Behavior, 14,* 236–246.

Mazza, James J., & Reynolds, William M. (1999). Exposure to violence in young inner-city adolescents: Relationships with suicidal ideation, depression, and PTSD symptomatology. *Journal of Abnormal Child Psychology, 27,* 203–213.

Mazzoni, Giuliana A.; Loftus, Elizabeth F.; & Kirsch, Irving (2001). Changing beliefs about implausible autobiographical events: A little plausibility goes a long way. *Journal of Experimental Psychology: Applied, 7,* 51–59.

Mazzoni, Giuliana A.; Loftus, Elizabeth F.; Seitz, Aaron; & Lynn, Steven J. (1999). Changing beliefs and memories through dream interpretation. *Applied Cognitive Psychology, 13,* 125–144.

McClearn, Gerald E.; Johanson, Boo; Berg, Stig; et al. (1997). Substantial genetic influence on cognitive abilities in twins 80 or more years old. *Science, 176,* 1560–1563.

McClelland, David C. (1961). *The achieving society.* New York: Free Press.

McClelland, David C. (1987). Characteristics of successful entrepreneurs. *Journal of Creative Behavior, 3,* 219–233.

McClelland, David C.; Atkinson, John W.; Clark, Russell A.; & Lowell, Edgar L. (1953). *The achievement motive.* New York: Appleton-Century-Crofts.

McClelland, James L. (1994). The organization of memory: A parallel distributed processing perspective. *Revue Neurologique, 150,* 570–579.

McClintock, Martha K., & Herdt, Gilbert (1996). Rethinking puberty: The development of sexual attraction. *Current Directions in Psychological Science, 6,* 178–183.

McConnell, James V. (1962). Memory transfer through cannibalism in planarians. *Journal of Neuropsychiatry, 3* (Monograph Supplement 1).

McCord, Joan (1989). Another time, another drug. Paper presented at conference on Vulnerability to the Transition from Drug Use to Abuse and Dependence, Rockville, MD.

McCord, Joan (1992). The Cambridge-Somerville study: A pioneering longitudinal-experimental study of delinquency prevention. In J. McCord & R. E. Tremblay (eds.), *Preventing antisocial behavior: Interventions from birth through adolescence.* New York: Guilford Press.

McCrae, Robert R. (1987). Creativity, divergent thinking, and openness to experience. *Journal of Personality and Social Psychology, 52,* 1258–1265.

McCrae, Robert R., & Costa, Paul T., Jr. (1988). Do parental influences matter? A reply to Halverson. *Journal of Personality, 56,* 445–449.

McCrae, Robert R.; Costa, Paul T., Jr.; Ostendorf, Fritz; et al. (2000). Nature over nurture: Temperament, personality, and life span development. *Journal of Personality and Social Psychology, 78,* 173–186.

McDaniel, Susan H.; Lusterman, Don-David; & Philpot, Carol L. (eds.) (2001). *Casebook for integrating family therapy: An ecosystemic approach.* Washington, DC: American Psychological Association.

McDonough, Laraine, & Mandler, Jean M. (1994). Very long-term recall in infancy. *Memory, 2,* 339–352.

McElroy, Susan L., & Keck, Paul E., Jr. (2000). Pharmacologic agents for the treatment of acute bipolar mania. *Biological Psychiatry, 48,* 539–557.

McEwen, Bruce S. (1998). Protective and damaging effects of stress mediators. *New England Journal of Medicine, 338,* 171–179.

McEwen, Bruce S. (2000). Allostasis and allostatic load: Implications for neuropsychopharmacology. *Neuropsychopharmacology 22,* 108–124.

McFarland, Cathy, & Alvaro, Celeste (2000). The impact of motivation on temporal comparisons: Coping with traumatic events by perceiving personal growth. *Journal of Personality and Social Psychology, 79,* 327–343.

McFarlane, Jessica; Martin, Carol L.; & Williams, Tannis M. (1988). Mood fluctuations: Women versus men and menstrual versus other cycles. *Psychology of Women Quarterly, 12,* 201–223.

McFarlane, Jessica M., & Williams, Tannis M. (1994). Placing premenstrual syndrome in perspective. *Psychology of Women Quarterly, 18,* 339–373.

McGaugh, James L. (1990). Significance and remembrance: The role of neuromodulatory systems. *Psychological Science, 1,* 15–25.

McGinnis, Michael, & Foege, William (1993, November 10). Actual causes of death in the United States. *Journal of the American Medical Association, 270,* 2207–2212.

McGlashan, Thomas H., & Hoffman, Ralph E. (2000). Schizophrenia as a disorder of developmentally reduced synaptic connectivity. *Archives of General Psychiatry, 57,* 637–648.

McGlone, Jeannette (1978). Sex differences in functional brain asymmetry. *Cortex, 14,* 122–128.

McGlynn, Susan M. (1990). Behavioral approaches to neuropsychological rehabilitation. *Psychological Bulletin, 108,* 420–441.

McGoldrick, Monica (1996). Irish families. In M. McGoldrick, J. Giordano, & J. K. Pearce (eds.), *Ethnicity and family therapy* (2nd ed.). New York: Guilford.

McGoldrick, Monica; Gerson, Randy; & Shellenberger, Sylvia (1999). *Genograms: Assessment and intervention* (2nd ed.). New York: W. W. Norton.

McGrath, Ellen; Keita, Gwendolyn P.; Strickland, Bonnie; & Russo, Nancy F. (eds.) (1990). *Women and depression: Risk factors and treatment issues.* Washington, DC: American Psychological Association.

McGregor, Ian, & Holmes, John G. (1999). How storytelling shapes memory and impressions of relationship events over time. *Journal of Personality and Social Psychology, 76,* 403–419.

McGregor, Ian, & Little, Brian R. (1998). Personal projects, happiness, and meaning: On doing well and being yourself. *Journal of Personality and Social Psychology, 74,* 494–512.

McGregor, Jock (1997). The icon of postmodernity. Retrieved 9/3/01 from http://www.studyofmadonna.com/articles.htm.

McGue, Matt (1999). The behavioral genetics of alcoholism. *Current Directions in Psychological Science, 8,* 109–115.

McGue, Matt, & Lykken, David T. (1992). Genetic influence on risk of divorce. *Psychological Science, 3,* 368–373.

McGue, Matt; Bouchard, Thomas J., Jr.; Iacono, William G.; & Lykken, David T. (1993). Behavioral genetics of cognitive ability: A life-span perspective. In R. Plomin & G. E. McClearn (eds.), *Nature, nurture, and psychology.* Washington, DC: American Psychological Association.

McHugh, Paul R. (1993, December). Psychotherapy awry. *American Scholar,* 17–30.

McKee, Richard D., & Squire, Larry R. (1992). Equivalent forgetting rates in long-term memory for diencephalic and medial temporal lobe amnesia. *Journal of Neuroscience, 12,* 3765–3772.

McKee, Richard D., & Squire, Larry R. (1993). On the development of declarative memory. *Journal of Experimental Psychology: Learning, Memory, and Cognition, 19,* 397–404.

McKim, Margaret K.; Cramer, Kenneth M.; Stuart, Barbara; & O'Connor, Deborah L. (1999). Infant care decisions and attachment security: The Canadian Transition to Child Care Study. *Canadian Journal of Behavioural Science, 31,* 92–106.

McKinlay, John B.; McKinlay, Sonja M.; & Brambilla, Donald (1987). The relative contributions of endocrine changes and social circumstances to depression in mid-aged women. *Journal of Health and Social Behavior, 28,* 345–363.

McLeod, Beverly (1985, March). Real work for real pay. *Psychology Today,* 42–44, 46, 48–50.

McNally, Richard J. (1994). *Panic disorder: A critical analysis.* New York: Guilford.

McNally, Richard J. (1996). Cognitive bias in the anxiety disorders. In D. A. Hope et al. (eds.), *Nebraska Symposium on Motivation, 1995: Perspectives on anxiety, panic, and fear.* Lincoln, NE: University of Nebraska Press.

McNally, Richard J. (1998). Panic attacks. In *Encyclopedia of mental health* (Vol. 3). New York: Academic Press.

McNally, Richard J. (2001). Tertullian's motto and Callahan's method [Invited commentary]. *Journal of Clinical Psychology, 57,* 1171–1174.

McNally, Richard J. (2003). *Remembering trauma.* Cambridge, MA: Harvard University Press.

McNaughton, B. L., & Morris, R. G. M. (1987). Hippocampal synaptic enhancement and information storage within a distributed memory system. *Trends in Neuroscience, 10,* 408–415.

McNeill, David (1966). Developmental psycholinguistics. In F. L. Smith & G. A. Miller (eds.), *The genesis of language: A psycholinguistic approach.* Cambridge, MA: MIT Press.

McSweeney, Frances K., & Swindell, Samantha (1999). General-process theories of motivation revisited: The role of habituation. *Psychological Bulletin, 125,* 437–457.

Mealey, Linda (1996). Evolutionary psychology: The search for evolved mental mechanisms underlying complex human behavior. In J. P. Hurd (ed.), *Investigating the biological foundations of human morality* (Vol. 37). Lewiston, NY: Edwin Mellen Press.

Mealey, Linda (2000). *Sex differences: Developmental and evolutionary strategies.* San Diego: Academic Press.

Medawar, Peter B. (1979). *Advice to a young scientist.* New York: Harper & Row.

Medawar, Peter B. (1982). *Pluto's republic.* Oxford, England: Oxford University Press.

Mednick, Martha T. (1989). On the politics of psychological constructs: Stop the bandwagon, I want to get off. *American Psychologist, 44,* 1118–1123.

Mednick, Sarnoff A. (1962). The associative basis of the creative process. *Psychological Review, 69,* 220–232.

Mednick, Sarnoff A.; Huttunen, Matti O.; & Machón, Ricardo (1994). Prenatal influenza infections and adult schizophrenia. *Schizophrenia Bulletin, 20,* 263–267.

Medvec, Victoria H.; Madey, Scott F.; & Gilovich, Thomas (1995). When less is more: Counterfactual thinking and satisfaction among Olympic medalists. *Journal of Personality and Social Psychology, 69,* 603–610.

Meeus, Wim H. J., & Raaijmakers, Quinten A. W. (1995). Obedience in modern society: The Utrecht studies. In A. G. Miller, B. E. Collins, & D. E. Brief (eds.), *Perspectives on obedience to authority: The legacy of the Milgram experiments. Journal of Social Issues, 51*(3), 155–175.

Meindl, James R., & Lerner, Melvin J. (1985). Exacerbation of extreme responses to an out-group. *Journal of Personality and Social Psychology, 47,* 71–84.

Meltzoff, Andrew N., & Gopnik, Alison (1993). The role of imitation in understanding persons and developing a theory of mind. In S. Baron-Cohen, H. Tager-Flusberg, & D. Cohen (eds.), *Understanding other minds.* New York: Oxford University Press.

Melzack, Ronald (1992, April). Phantom limbs. *Scientific American, 266,* 120–126. [Reprinted in the special issue *Mysteries of the Mind,* 1997.]

Melzack, Ronald (1993). Pain: Past, present and future. *Canadian Journal of Experimental Psychology, 47,* 615–629.

Melzack, Ronald, & Wall, Patrick D. (1965). Pain mechanisms: A new theory. *Science, 13,* 971–979.

Mennella, Julie A.; Jagnow, C. P.; & Beauchamp, Gary K. (2001). Prenatal and postnatal flavor learning by human infants. *Pediatrics, 107,* E88.

Menon, Tanya; Morris, Michael W.; Chiu, Chi-yue; & Hone, Ying-yi (1999). Culture and the construal of agency: Attribution to individual versus group dispositions. *Journal of Personality and Social Psychology, 76,* 701–717.

Merikle, Philip M., & Skanes, Heather E. (1992). Subliminal self-help audiotapes: A search for placebo effects. *Journal of Applied Psychology, 77,* 772–776.

Merrill, L. L.; Newell, C. E.; Milner, J. S.; et al. (1998). Prevalence of premilitary adult sexual victimization and aggression in a Navy recruit sample. *Military Medicine, 163,* 209–212.

Merskey, Harold (1992). The manufacture of personalities: The production of MPD. *British Journal of Psychiatry, 160,* 327–340.

Merskey, Harold (1995). The manufacture of personalities: The production of multiple personality disorder. In L. M. Cohen, J. N. Berzoff, & M. R. Elin (eds.), *Dissociative identity disorder: Theoretical and treatment controversies.* Northvale, NJ: Aronson.

Merton, Robert K. (1948). The self-fulfilling prophecy. *Antioch Review, 8,* 193–210.

Mesquita, Batja (2001). Emotions in collectivist and individualist contexts. *Journal of Personality and Social Psychology, 80,* 68–74.

Mesquita, Batja, & Frijda, Nico H. (1992). Cultural variations in emotions: A review. *Psychological Bulletin, 112,* 179–204.

Metalsky, Gerald I.; Joiner, Thomas E., Jr.; Hardin, Tammy S.; & Abramson, Lyn Y. (1993). Depressive reactions to failure in a naturalistic setting: A test of the hopelessness and self-esteem theories of depression. *Journal of Abnormal Psychology, 102,* 101–109.

Meyer, Gregory J.; Finn, Stephen E.; Eyde, Lorraine D.; et al. (2001). Psychological testing and psychological assessment. *American Psychologist, 56,* 128–165.

Meyer-Bahlburg, Heino F. L.; Ehrhardt, Anke A.; Rosen, Laura R.; et al. (1995). Prenatal estrogens and the development of homosexual orientation. *Developmental Psychology, 31,* 12–21.

Mickelson, Kristin D.; Kessler, Ronald C.; & Shaver, Phillip R. (1997). Adult attachment in a nationally representative sample. *Journal of Personality and Social Psychology, 73,* 1092–1106.

Milgram, Stanley (1963). Behavioral study of obedience. *Journal of Abnormal and Social Psychology, 67,* 371–378.

Milgram, Stanley (1974). *Obedience to authority: An experimental view.* New York: Harper & Row.

Miller, George A. (1956). The magical number seven, plus or minus two: Some limits on our capacity for processing information. *Psychological Review, 63,* 81–97.

Miller, George A. (1969, December). On turning psychology over to the unwashed. *Psychology Today,* 53–55, 66–68, 70, 72, 74.

Miller, Gregory E., & Cohen, Sheldon (2001). Psychological interventions and the immune system: A meta-analytic review and critique. *Health Psychology, 20,* 47–63.

Miller, Inglis J., & Reedy, Frank E. (1990). Variations in human taste bud density and taste intensity perception. *Physiology and Behavior, 47,* 1213–1219.

Miller, Joan G.; Bersoff, David M.; & Harwood, Robin L. (1990). Perceptions of social responsibilities in India and in the United States: Moral imperatives or personal decisions? *Journal of Personality and Social Psychology, 58,* 33–47.

Miller, Neal E. (1978). Biofeedback and visceral learning. *Annual Review of Psychology, 29,* 421–452.

Miller, Todd Q.; Smith, Timothy W.; Turner, Charles W.; et al. (1996). A meta-analytic review of research on hostility and physical health. *Psychological Bulletin, 119,* 322–348.

Miller-Jones, Dalton (1989). Culture and testing. *American Psychologist, 44,* 360–366.

Milner, Brenda (1970). Memory and the temporal regions of the brain. In K. H. Pribram & D. E. Broadbent (eds.), *Biology of memory.* New York: Academic Press.

Milner, J. S., & McCanne, T. R. (1991). Neuropsychological correlates of physical child abuse. In J. S. Milner (ed.), *Neuropsychology of aggression.* Norwell, MA: Kluwer Academic.

Milton, Julie, & Wiseman, Richard (1999). Does Psi exist? Lack of replication of an anomalous process of information transfer. *Psychological Bulletin, 125,* 387–391.

Milton, Julie, & Wiseman, Richard (2001). Does psi exist? Reply to Storm and Ertel (2001). *Psychological Bulletin, 127,* 434–438.

Minuchin, Salvador (1984). *Family kaleidoscope.* Cambridge, MA: Harvard University Press.

Mischel, Walter (1973). Toward a cognitive social learning reconceptualization of personality. *Psychological Review, 80,* 252–253.

Mischel, Walter, & Shoda, Yuichi (1995). A cognitive affective system theory of personality: Reconceptualizing situations, dispositions, dynamics, and invariance in personality structures. *Psychological Review, 102,* 246–268.

Mischel, Walter, & Shoda, Yuichi (1995). A cognitive affective system theory of personality: Reconceptualizing situations, dispositions, dynamics, and invariance in personality structures. *Psychological Review, 102,* 246–268.

Mishkin, M.; Suzuki, W. A.; Gadian, D. G.; & Vargha-Khadem, F. (1997). Hierarchical organization of cognitive memory. *Philosophical Transactions of the Royal Society of London, B: Biological Science, 352,* 1461–1467.

Mishkin, Mortimer, & Appenzeller, Tim (1987). The anatomy of memory. *Scientific American, 256,* 80–89.

Mistry, Jayanthi, & Rogoff, Barbara (1994). Remembering in cultural context. In W. J. Lonner & R. Malpass (eds.), *Psychology and culture.* Needham Heights, MA: Allyn & Bacon.

Mitchell, D.;, & Gingras, G. (1998). Visual recovery after monocular deprivation is driven by absolute, rather than relative, visually evoked activity levels. *Current Biology, 8,* 1179, R897.

Mithers, Carol L. (1994). *Reasonable insanity: A true story of the seventies.* Reading, MA: Addison-Wesley.

Modigliani, Andre, & Rochat, François (1995). The role of interaction sequences and the timing of resistance in shaping obedience and defiance to authority. In A. G. Miller, B. E. Collins, & D. E. Brief (eds.), *Perspectives on obedience to authority: The legacy of the Milgram experiments. Journal of Social Issues, 51*(3), 107–125.

Moen, Phyllis (2001). Gender, age and the life course. In R. H. Binstock & L. K. George (eds.), *Handbook of aging and the social sciences* (5ᵗʰ ed.). San Diego, CA: Academic Press.

Moen, Phyllis, & Wethington, Elaine (1999). Midlife development in a life course context. In S. L. Willis & J. E. Reid (eds.), *Life in the middle: Psychological and social development in middle age.* San Diego, CA: Academic Press.

Moffitt, Terrie E. (1993). Adolescence-limited and life-course-persistent antisocial behavior: A developmental taxonomy. *Psychological Review, 100,* 674–701.

Mohr, Cynthia; Armeli, Stephen; Tennen, Howard; et al. (2001). Daily interpersonal experiences, context, and alcohol consumption: Crying in your beer and toasting good times. *Journal of Personality and Social Psychology, 80,* 489–500.

Monahan, Jennifer L.; Murphy, Sheila T.; & Zajonc, R. B. (2000). Subliminal mere exposure: Specific, general, and diffuse effects. *Psychological Science, 11,* 462–466.

Moncrieff, Joanna (2001). Are antidepressants overrated? A review of methodological problems in antidepressant trials. *Journal of Nervous and Mental Disease, 189,* 288–295.

Montagner, Hubert (1985). Approache ethologique des systems à interaction du nouveau né et du jeune enfant. [An ethological approach of the interaction systems of the infant and the young child.] *Neuropsychiatrie de l'Enfance et de l'Adolescence, 33,* 59–71.

Montmayeur, J. P.; Liberies, S. D.; Matsunami, H.; & Buck, L. B. (2001). A candidate taste receptor gene near a sweet taste locus. *Nature Neuroscience, 4,* 492–498.

Moore, Robert Y. (1997). Circadian rhythms: Basic neurobiology and clinical applications. *Annual Review of Medicine, 48,* 253–266.

Moore, Timothy E. (1992, Spring). Subliminal perception: Facts and fallacies. *Skeptical Inquirer, 16,* 273–281.

Moore, Timothy E. (1995). Subliminal self-help auditory tapes: An empirical test of perceptual consequences. *Canadian Journal of Behavioural Science, 27,* 9–20.

Moore, Timothy E., & Pepler, Debra J. (1998). Correlates of adjustment in children at risk. In G. W. Holden, R. Geffner, et al. (eds.), *Children exposed to marital violence: Theory, research, and applied issues.* Washington, DC: American Psychological Association.

Moorhead, Gregory; Ference, Richard; & Neck, Chris P. (1991). Group decision fiascoes continue: Space shuttle Challenger and a revised groupthink framework. *Human Relations, 44,* 539–550.

Morelli, Gilda A.; Rogoff, Barbara; Oppenheim, David; & Goldsmith, Denise (1992). Cultural variation in infants' sleeping arrangements: Questions of independence. *Developmental Psychology, 28,* 604–613.

Morin, Charles M.; Colecchi, C.; Stone, J.; Sood, R.; & Brink, D. (1999). Behavioral and pharmacological therapies for late-life insomnia: A randomized controlled trial. *Journal of the American Medical Association, 281,* 991–999.

Morley, S.; Eccleston, C.; & Williams, A. C. deC. (1999). Systematic review and meta-analysis of randomized controlled trials of cognitive behavioural therapy for chronic pain in adults, excluding headache. *Pain, 80,* 1–13.

Morris, Michael W., & Peng, Kaiping (1994). Culture and cause: American and Chinese attributions for social and physical events. *Journal of Personality and Social Psychology, 67,* 949–971.

Morrison, Ann M., & Von Glinow, Mary Ann (1990). Women and minorities in management. *American Psychologist, 45,* 200–208.

Moscovici, Serge (1985). Social influence and conformity. In G. Lindzey & E. Aronson (eds.), *Handbook of social psychology* (Vol. 2, 3rd ed.). New York: Random House.

Moscovitch, Morris; Winocur, Gordon; & Behrmann, Marlene (1997). What is special about face recognition? Nineteen experiments on a person with visual object agnosia and dyslexia but normal face recognition. *Journal of Cognitive Neuroscience, 9,* 555–604.

Moskowitz, Eva (2001). *In therapy we trust.* Baltimore, MD: Johns Hopkins University Press.

Mozell, Maxwell M.; Smith, Bruce P., Smith, Paul E.; Sullivan, Richard L.; & Swender, Philip (1969). Nasal chemoreception in flavor identification. *Archives of Otolaryngology, 90,* 367–373.

Mroczek, Daniel K., & Kolarz, Christian M. (1998). The effect of age on positive and negative affect: A developmental perspective on happiness. *Journal of Personality and Social Psychology, 75,* 1333–1349.

Muehlenhard, Charlene L., & Cook, Stephen (1988). Men's self-reports of unwanted sexual activity. *Journal of Sex Research, 24,* 58–72.

Mueller, Claudia M., & Dweck, Carol S. (1998). Praise for intelligence can undermine children's motivation and performance. *Journal of Personality and Social Psychology, 75,* 33–52.

Mulick, James (1994, November/December). The non-science of facilitated communication. *Science Agenda* (APA newsletter), 8–9.

Müller, Ralph-Axel; Courchesne, Eric; & Allen, Greg (1998). The cerebellum: So much more. [Letter.] *Science, 282,* 879–880.

Murphy, Sheila T.; Monahan, Jennifer L.; & Zajonc, R. B. (1995). Additivity of nonconscious affect: Combined effects of priming and exposure. *Journal of Personality and Social Psychology, 69,* 589–602.

Myers, Ronald E., & Sperry, R. W. (1953). Interocular transfer of a visual form discrimination habit in cats after section of the optic chiasm and corpus callosum. *Anatomical Record, 115,* 351–352.

Nash, Michael R. (1987). What, if anything, is regressed about hypnotic age regression? A review of the empirical literature. *Psychological Bulletin, 102,* 42–52.

Nash, Michael R. (1994). Memory distortion and sexual trauma: The problem of false negatives and false positives. International *Journal of Clinical and Experimental Hypnosis, 42,* 346–362.

Nash, Michael R. (2001, July). The truth and the hype of hypnosis. *Scientific American, 285,* 46–49, 52–55.

Nash, Michael R., & Nadon, Robert (1997). Hypnosis. In D. L. Faigman, D. Kaye, M. J. Saks, & J. Sanders (eds.), *Modern scientific evidence: The law and science of expert testimony.* St. Paul, MN: West.

Nathan, Debbie (1994, Fall). Dividing to conquer? Women, men, and the making of multiple personality disorder. *Social Text, 40,* 77–114.

National Science Board (2000). *Science & engineering indicators 2000.* Chapter 8: Science and technology: Attitudes and public understanding. Arlington, VA: National Science Foundation. [A reprint of the relevant section of this chapter can be found in the January/February 2001 issue of *Skeptical Inquirer,* pp. 12–15.]

National Victim Center & Crime Victims Research and Treatment Center (1992). *Rape in America: A report to the nation.* Fort Worth, TX: National Victim Center.

Needleman, Herbert L.; Riess, Julie A.; Tobin, Michael J.; et al. (1996). Bone lead levels and delinquent behavior. *Journal of the American Medical Association, 275,* 363–369.

Neher, Andrew (1996). Jung's theory of archetypes: A critique. *Journal of Humanistic Psychology, 36,* 61–91.

Neisser, Ulric, & Harsch, Nicole (1992). Phantom flashbulbs: False recollections of hearing the news about *Challenger.* In E. Winograd & U. Neisser (eds.), *Affect and accuracy in recall: Studies of "flashbulb memories."* New York: Cambridge University Press.

Neisser, Ulric (ed.) (1998). *The rising curve: Long-term gains in IQ and related measures.* Washington, DC: American Psychological Association.

Neitz, Maureen, & Neitz, Jay (1995). Numbers and ratios of visual pigment genes for normal red-green color vision. *Science, 267,* 1013–1016.

Nelson, Thomas O., & Dunlosky, John (1991). When people's judgments of learning (JOLs) are extremely accurate at predicting subsequent recall: The "delayed JOL effect." *Psychological Science, 2,* 267–270.

Nelson, Thomas O., & Leonesio, R. Jacob (1988). Allocation of self-paced study time and the "labor in vain effect." *Journal of Experimental Psychology: Learning, Memory, and Cognition, 14,* 676–686.

Netting, Jessa (2001, April 7). Gray matters: Neurons get top billing, but lesser-known brain cells also star. *Science News, 159,* 222–223.

Neugarten, Bernice (1979). Time, age, and the life cycle. *American Journal of Psychiatry, 136,* 887–894.

Neumann, Roland, & Strack, Fritz (2000). "Mood contagion": The automatic transfer of mood between persons. *Journal of Personality and Social Psychology, 79,* 211–223.

Newcombe, Nora S.; Drummey, Anna B.; Fox, Nathan A.; et al. (2000). Remembering early childhood: How much, how, and why (or why not). *Current Directions in Psychological Science, 9,* 55–58.

Newman, Leonard S., & Baumeister, Roy F. (1996). Toward an explanation of the UFO abduction phenomenon: Hypnotic elaboration, extraterrestrial sadomasochism, and spurious memories. *Psychological Inquiry, 7,* 99–126.

Newman, Lucille F., & Buka, Stephen (1991, Spring). Clipped wings. *American Educator,* 27–33, 42.

Nezu, Arthur M.; Nezu, Christine M.; & Blissett, Sonia E. (1988). Sense of humor as a moderator of the relation between stressful events and psychological distress: A prospective analysis. *Journal of Personality and Social Psychology, 54,* 520–525.

NICHD Early Child Care Research Network (1997). The effects of infant-child care on infant-mother attachment security (Results of the NICHD study of early child care). *Child Development, 68,* 860–879.

NICHD Early Child Care Research Network (2001). Further explorations of the detected effects of quantity of early child care on socio-emotional adjustment. Paper presented at the biennial meetings of the Society for Research on Child Development, Minneapolis.

Nickerson, Raymond A., & Adams, Marilyn Jager (1979). Long-term memory for a common object. *Cognitive Psychology, 11,* 287–307.

Nickerson, Raymond S. (1998). Confirmation bias: A ubiquitous phenomenon in many guises. *Review of General Psychology, 2,* 175–220.

Nigg, Joel T., & Goldsmith, H. Hill (1994). Genetics of personality disorders: Perspectives from personality and psychopathology research. *Psychological Bulletin, 115,* 346–380.

NIH Technology Assessment Panel on Integration of Behavioral and Relaxation Approaches into the Treatment of Chronic Pain and Insomnia (1996). *Journal of the American Medical Association, 276,* 313–318.

Nisbett, Richard E. (1993). Violence and U.S. regional culture. *American Psychologist, 48,* 441–449.

Nisbett, Richard E., & Ross, Lee (1980). *Human inference: Strategies and shortcomings of social judgment.* Englewood Cliffs, NJ: Prentice-Hall.

Noble, Ernest P. (1998, August 28). DRD2 gene and alcoholism. *Science, 281,* 1287–1288.

Noble, Ernest P.; Blum, Kenneth; Ritchie, T.; Montgomery, A.; & Sheridan, P. J. (1991). Allelic association of the D2 dopamine receptor gene with receptor-binding characteristics in alcoholism. *Archives of General Psychiatry, 48,* 648–654.

Nolen-Hoeksema, Susan (1999). Women think and men drink. Paper presented at the annual meeting of the American Psychological Association, Boston.

Nolen-Hoeksema, Susan (2001). Gender differences in depression. *Current Directions in Psychological Science, 10,* 173–176.

Nolen-Hoeksema, Susan, & Girgus, Joan S. (1994). The emergence of gender differences in depression during adolescence. *Psychological Bulletin, 115,* 424–443.

Nolen-Hoeksema, Susan; Larson, Judith; & Grayson, Carla (1999). Explaining the gender difference in depressive symptoms. *Journal of Personality and Social Psychology, 77,* 1061–1072.

Nonaka, S.; Hough, C. J.; & Chuang, De-Maw (1998, March 3). Chronic lithium treatment robustly protects neurons in the central nervous system against excitotoxicity by inhibiting N-methyl-D-aspartate receptor-mediated calcium influx. *Proceedings of the National Academy of Sciences, 95,* 2642–2647.

Norem, Julie K. (2001). *The positive power of negative thinking.* New York: Basic Books.

Norman, Donald A. (1988). *The psychology of everyday things.* New York: Basic Books.

Nowicki, Stephen, & Strickland, Bonnie R. (1973). A locus of control scale for children. *Journal of Consulting Psychology, 40,* 148–154.

Nunez, Narina; Poole, Debra A.; & Memon, Amina (2002). Psychology's two cultures revisited: Implications for the integration of science with practice. *Scientific Review of Mental Health Practice, 1.*

Nyberg, Lars; Habib, Reza; McIntosh, Anthony R.; & Tulving, Endel. (2000). Reactivation of encoding-related brain activity during memory retrieval. *Proceedings of the National Academy of Sciences, 97,* 11120–11124.

Ó Scalaidhe, Séamas P.; Wilson, Fraser A. W.; & Goldman-Rakic, Patricia S. (1997). A real segregation of face-processing neurons in prefrontal cortex. *Science, 278,* 1135–1138.

O'Hanlon, Bill (1994, November/December). The third wave. *Family Therapy Networker,* 18–29.

O'Leary, Virginia E.; Alday, C. Sloan; & Ickovics, Jeannette R. (1998). Models of life change and posttraumatic growth. In R. G. Tedeschi & C. L. Park (eds.), *Posttraumatic growth: Positive changes in the aftermath of crisis.* Mahwah, NJ: Erlbaum.

O'Rahilly, Ronan, & Müller, Fabiola (2001). *Human embryology and teratology.* New York: Wiley.

Oatley, Keith (1990). Do emotional states produce irrational thinking? In K. J. Gilhooly, M. T. G. Keane, R. H. Logie, & G. Erdos (eds.), *Lines of thinking* (Vol. 2). New York: Wiley.

Oatley, Keith, & Duncan, Elaine (1994). The experience of emotions in everyday life. *Cognition and Emotion, 8,* 369–381.

Oatley, Keith, & Jenkins, Jennifer M. (1996). *Understanding emotions.* Cambridge, MA: Blackwell.

Ofshe, Richard J., & Watters, Ethan (1994). *Making monsters: False memory, psychotherapy, and sexual hysteria.* New York: Scribners.

Ogden, Jenni A., & Corkin, Suzanne (1991). Memories of H. M. In W. C. Abraham, M. C. Corballis, & K. G. White (eds.), *Memory mechanisms: A tribute to G. V. Goddard.* Hillsdale, NJ: Erlbaum.

Öhman, Arne, & Mineka, Susan (2001). Fears, phobias, and preparedness: Toward an evolved module of fear and fear learning. *Psychological Review, 108,* 483–522.

Okonkwo, Rachel U. N. (1997). Moral development and culture in Kohlberg's theory: A Nigerian (Igbo) evidence. *IFE Psychologia: An International Journal, 5,* 117–128.

Olds, James (1975). Mapping the mind onto the brain. In F. G. Worden, J. P. Swazy, & G. Adelman (eds.), *The neurosciences: Paths of discovery.* Cambridge, MA: Colonial Press.

Olds, James, & Milner, Peter (1954). Positive reinforcement produced by electrical stimulation of septal area and other regions of the rat brain. *Journal of Comparative and Physiological Psychology, 47,* 419–429.

Oliver, Mary Beth, & Hyde, Janet S. (1993). Gender differences in sexuality: A meta-analysis. *Psychological Bulletin, 114,* 29–51.

Olson, James M.; Vernon, Philip A.; Harris, Julie Aitken; & Jang, Kerry L. (2001). The heritability of attitudes: A study of twins. *Journal of Personality and Social Psychology, 80,* 845–850.

Olujic, M. B. (1998). Embodiment of terror: Gendered violence in peacetime and wartime in Croatia and Bosnia-Herzegovina. *Medical Anthropology Quarterly, 12,* 31–50.

Orford, Jim (1992). *Community psychology: Theory and practice.* New York: Wiley.

Orlinsky, David E., & Howard, Kenneth I. (1994). Unity and diversity among psychotherapies: A comparative perspective. In B. Bongar & L. E. Beutler (eds.), *Foundations of psychotherapy: Theory, research, and practice.* New York: Oxford University Press.

O'Sullivan, Lucia F.; Byers, E. Sandra; & Finkelman, Larry (1998). A comparison of male and female college students' experiences of sexual coercion. *Psychology of Women Quarterly, 22,* 177–195.

Overeem, S.; Mignot, E.; Gert van Dijk, J.; & Lammers, G. J. (2001). Narcolepsy: clinical features, new pathophysiologic insights, and future perspectives. *Journal of Clinical Neurophysiology, 18,* 78–105.

Page, Gayle G.; Ben-Eliyahu, Shamgar; Yirmiya, Raz; & Liebeskind, John C. (1993). Morphine attenuates surgery-induced enhancement of metastatic colonization in rats. *Pain, 54,* 21–28.

Paik, Haejung, & Comstock, George (1994). The effects of television violence on antisocial behavior: A meta-analysis. *Communicataion Research, 21,* 516–546.

Palmer, T. D.; Schartz, P. H.; Taupin, P.; et al. (2001). Cell culture. Progenitor cells from human brain after death. *Nature, 411,* 42–43.

Panksepp, Jaak (1998). Attention deficit hyperactivity disorders, psychostimulants, and intolerance of childhood playfulness: A tragedy in the making? *Current Directions in Psychological Science, 7,* 91–98.

Panksepp, Jaak; Herman, B. H.; Vilberg, T.; et al. (1980). Endogenous opioids and social behavior. *Neuroscience and Biobehavioral Reviews, 4,* 473–487.

Park, Robert L. (1999, July 12). Liars never break a sweat. *The New York Times,* op-ed page.

Park, Robert L. (2000). *Voodoo science: The road from foolishness to fraud.* New York: Oxford University Press.

Parker, A. (2000). A review of the Ganzfeld work at Gotheburg University. *Journal of the Society for Psychical Research, 62,* 114–137.

Parker, Elizabeth S.; Birnbaum, Isabel M.; & Noble, Ernest P. (1976). Alcohol and memory: Storage and state dependency. *Journal of Verbal Learning and Verbal Behavior, 15,* 691–702.

Parker, Gwendolyn M. (1997). *Trespassing: My sojourn in the halls of privilege.* Boston: Houghton Mifflin.

Parker, Kevin C. H.; Hanson, R. Karl; & Hunsley, John (1988). MMPI, Rorschach, and WAIS: A meta-analytic comparison of reliability, stability, and validity. *Psychological Bulletin, 103,* 367–373.

Parlee, Mary B. (1994). The social construction of premenstrual syndrome: A case study of scientific discourse as cultural contestation. In M. G. Winkler & L. B. Cole (eds.), *The good body: Asceticism in contemporary culture.* New Haven, CT: Yale University Press.

Parlee, Mary B. (1982). Changes in moods and activation levels during the menstrual cycle in experimentally naive subjects. *Psychology of Women Quarterly, 7,* 119–131.

Parsons, Michael W., & Gold, Paul E. (1992). Glucose enhancement of memory in elderly humans: An inverted-U dose response curve. *Neurobiology of Aging, 13,* 401–404.

Pasupath, Monisha (2001). The social construction of the personal past and its implications for adult development. *Psychological Bulletin, 127,* 651–672.

Patterson, Charlotte J. (1992). Children of lesbian and gay parents. *Child Development, 63,* 1025–1042.

Patterson, Charlotte J. (1995). Sexual orientation and human development: An overview. *Developmental Psychology, 31,* 3–11.

Patterson, Francine, & Linden, Eugene (1981). *The education of Koko.* New York: Holt, Rinehart and Winston.

Patterson, Gerald R.; Forgatch, Marion S.; Yoerger, Karen L.; & Stoolmiller, Mike (1998). Variables that initiate and maintain an early-onset trajectory for juvenile offending. *Development and Psychopathology, 10,* 531–547.

Patterson, Gerald R.; Reid, John; & Dishion, Thomas (1992). *Antisocial boys.* Eugene, OR: Castalia.

Paul, Richard W. (1984, September). Critical thinking: Fundamental to education for a free society. *Educational Leadership,* 4–14.

Paunonen, Sampo V. (1998). Hierarchical organization of personality and prediction of behavior. *Journal of Personality and Social Psychology, 74,* 538–556.

Paunonen, Sampo V., & Ashton, Michael C. (2001). Big Five factors and facets and the prediction of behavior. *Journal of Personality and Social Psychology, 81,* 524–539.

Pavlov, Ivan P. (1927). *Conditioned reflexes* (G. V. Anrep, Trans.). London: Oxford University Press.

Pearlin, Leonard (1982). Discontinuities in the study of aging. In T. K. Hareven & K. J. Adams (eds.), *Aging and life course transitions: An interdisciplinary perspective.* New York: Guilford.

Pedersen, Paul B.; Draguns, Juris G.; Lonner, Walter J.; & Trimble, Joseph E. (eds.) (1996). *Counseling across cultures* (4th ed.). Thousand Oaks, CA: Sage.

Peele, Stanton, & Brodsky, Archie, with Mary Arnold (1991). *The truth about addiction and recovery.* New York: Simon & Schuster.

Pellegrini, Anthony D., & Galda, Lee (1993). Ten years after: A reexamination of symbolic play and literacy research. *Reading Research Quarterly, 28,* 163–175.

Pendergrast, Mark (1995). *Victims of memory* (2nd ed.). Hinesburg, VT: Upper Access Press.

Peng, Kaiping, & Nisbett, Richard E. (1999). Culture, dialectics, and reasoning about contradiction. *American Psychologist, 54,* 741–754.

Pennebaker, James W. (1997). Writing about emotional experiences as a therapeutic process. *Psychological Science, 8,* 162–166.

Pennebaker, James W.; Colder, Michelle; & Sharp, Lisa K. (1990). Accelerating the coping process. *Journal of Personality and Social Psychology, 58,* 528–527.

Pennebaker, James W.; Kiecolt-Glaser, Janice; & Glaser, Ronald (1988). Disclosure of traumas and immune function: Health implications for psychotherapy. *Journal of Consulting and Clinical Psychology, 56,* 239–245.

Penninx, B. W.; Guralnik, J. M.; Pahor, M.; et al. (1998). Chronically depressed mood and cancer risk in older persons. *Journal of the National Cancer Institute, 90,* 1888–1893.

Peplau, Letitia A., & Conrad, Eva (1989). Beyond nonsexist research: The perils of feminist methods in psychology. *Psychology of Women Quarterly, 13,* 379–400.

Peplau, Letitia A., & Spalding, Leah R. (2000). The close relationships of lesbians, gay men and bisexuals. In C. Hendrick & S. Hendrick (eds.), *Close relationships: A sourcebook.* Thousand Oaks, CA: Sage.

Peplau, Letitia A.; Spalding, Leah R.; Conley, Terri D.; & Veniegas, Rosemary C. (2000). The development of sexual orientation in women. *Annual Review of Sex Research, 10,* 70–99.

Pepperberg, Irene (2000). *The Alex studies: Cognitive and communicative abilities of grey parrots.* Cambridge, MA: Harvard University Press.

Perloff, Robert (1992, Summer). "Where ignorance is bliss, 'tis folly to be wise." *The General Psychologist Newsletter, 28,* 34.

Perry, Samuel W., & Heidrich, George (1982). Management of pain during debridement: A survey of U.S. burn units. *Pain, 13,* 267–280.

Persons, Jacqueline; Davidson, Joan; & Tompkins, Michael A. (2001). *Essential components of cognitive-behavior therapy for depression.* Washington, DC: American Psychological Association.

Pert, Candace B., & Snyder, Solomon H. (1973). Opiate receptor: Demonstration in nervous tissue. *Science, 179,* 1011–1014.

Pesetsky, David (1999). Introduction to symposium: "Grammar: What's innate?" Paper presented at the annual meeting of the American Association for the Advancement of Science, Anaheim.

Peterson, Christopher (2000). The future of optimism. *American Psychologist, 55,* 44–55.

Peterson, Christopher; Seligman, Martin E. P.; Yurko, Karen H.; et al. (1998). Catastrophizing and untimely death. *Psychological Science, 9,* 127–130.

Peterson, Lloyd R., & Peterson, Margaret J. (1959). Short-term retention of individual verbal items. *Journal of Experimental Psychology, 58,* 193–198.

Petrie, Keith J.; Booth, Roger J.; & Pennebaker, James W. (1998). The immunological effects of thought suppression. *Journal of Personality and Social Psychology, 75,* 1264–1272.

Pettigrew, Thomas F. (1997). Generalized intergroup contact effects on prejudice. *Personality and Social Psychology Bulletin, 23,* 173–185.

Pettigrew, Thomas F. (1998). Intergroup contact theory. *Annual Review of Psychology, 49,* 65–85. Palo Alto, CA: Annual Reviews.

Pfungst, Oskar (1911/1965). *Clever Hans (The horse of Mr. von Osten): A contribution to experimental animal and human psychology.* New York: Holt, Rinehart and Winston.

Phillips, D. P.; Ruth, T. E.; & Wagner, L. M. (1993, November 6). Psychology and survival. *Lancet, 342*(8880), 1142–1145.

Phillips, Michael (1999, October 15). Problems with the polygraph [Letter]. *Science, 286,* 413.

Phillips, Micheal D.; Lowe, M. J.; Lurito, J. T.; et al. (2001). Temporal lobe activation demonstrates sex-based differences during passive listening. *Radiology, 220,* 202–207.

Phinney, Jean S. (1990). Ethnic identity in adolescents and adults: Review of research. *Psychological Bulletin, 108,* 499–514.

Phinney, Jean S. (1996). When we talk about American ethnic groups, what do we mean? *American Psychologist, 51,* 918–927.

Piaget, Jean (1929/1960). *The child's conception of the world.* Paterson, NJ: Littlefield, Adams.

Piaget, Jean (1932). *The moral judgment of the child.* New York: Macmillan.

Piaget, Jean (1952a). *The origins of intelligence in children.* New York: International Universities Press.

Piaget, Jean (1952b). Play, dreams, and imitation in childhood. New York: W. W. Norton.

Piaget, Jean (1984). Piaget's theory. In P. Mussen (series ed.) & W. Kessen (vol. ed.), *Handbook of child psychology: Vol. 1. History, theory, and methods* (4th ed.). New York: Wiley.

Pincus, Tamar, & Morley, Stephen (2001). Cognitive-processing bias in chronic pain: A review and integration. *Psychological Bulletin, 127,* 599–617.

Pinel, John P. J.; Assanand, Sunaina; & Lehman, Darrin R. (2000). Hunger, eating, and ill health. *American Psychologist, 55,* 1105–1116.

Pinker, Steven (1994). *The language instinct: How the mind creates language.* New York: Morrow.

Pinker, Steven (1997). *How the mind works.* New York: Norton.

Pinker, Steven (1999). *Words and rules: The ingredients of language.* New York: Basic Books.

Pittenger, David J. (1993). The utility of the Myers-Briggs Type Indicator. *Review of Educational Research, 63,* 467–488.

Plant, E. Ashby, & Devine, Patricia G. (1998). Internal and external motivation to respond without prejudice. *Journal of Personality and Social Psychology, 75,* 811–832.

Plant, E. Ashby; Hyde, Janet S.; Keltner, Dacher; & Devine, Patricia G. (2000). The gender stereotyping of emotions. *Psychology of Women Quarterly, 24,* 81–92.

Plomin, Robert (1989). Environment and genes: Determinants of behavior. *American Psychologist, 44,* 105–111.

Plomin, Robert, & Crabbe, John (2000). DNA. *Psychological Bulletin, 126*, 806–828.

Plomin, Robert, & DeFries, John C. (1985). *Origins of individual differences in infancy: The Colorado Adoption Project.* New York: Academic Press.

Plomin, Robert; Corley, Robin; DeFries, J. C.; & Fulker, D. W. (1990). Individual differences in television viewing in early childhood: Nature as well as nurture. *Psychological Science, 1*, 371–377.

Plomin, Robert; DeFries, John C.; McClearn, Gerald E.; & McGuffin, Peter (2001). *Behavioral genetics* (4th ed.). New York: Worth.

Plotsky, Paul M.; Owens, Michael J.; & Nemeroff, Charles B. (1998). Psychoneuroendocrinology of depression: Hypothalamic-pituitary-adrenal axis. *Psychoneuroendocrinology, 21*, 293–307.

Plous, Scott L. (1996). Attitudes toward the use of animals in psychological research and education: Results from a national survey of psychologists. *American Psychologist, 51*, 1167–1180.

Plous, Scott, & Herzog, Harold A. (1999). Should the AWA cover rats, mice, and birds? The results of an IACUC survey. *Lab Animal, 28*, 38–40.

Polefrone, Joanna M., & Manuck, Stephen B. (1987). Gender differences in cardiovascular and neuroendocrine response to stressors. In R. C. Barnett, L. Biener, & G. K. Baruch (eds.), *Gender and stress.* New York: Free Press.

Pollak, Richard (1997). *The creation of Dr. B: A biography of Bruno Bettelheim.* New York: Simon & Schuster.

Polusny, Melissa A., & Follette, Victoria M. (1996). Remembering childhood sexual abuse: A national survey of psychologists' clinical practices, beliefs, and personal experiences. *Professional Psychology: Research and Practice, 27*, 41–52.

Poole, Debra A. (1995). Strolling fuzzy-trace theory through eyewitness testimony (or vice versa). *Learning and Individual Differences, 7*, 87–93.

Poole, Debra A., & Lamb, Michael E. (1998). *Investigative interviews of children.* Washington, DC: American Psychological Association.

Poole, Debra A.; Lindsay, D. Stephen; Memon, Amina; & Bull, Ray (1995). Psychotherapy and the recovery of memories of childhood sexual abuse: U.S. and British practitioners' opinions, practices, and experiences. *Journal of Consulting and Clinical Psychology, 63*, 426–437.

Pope, Harrison G., & Katz, David L. (1992). Psychiatric effects of anabolic steroids. *Psychiatric Annals, 22*, 24–29.

Pope, Harrison G., Jr.,; Phillips, Katharine A.; & Olivardia, Roberto (2000). *The Adonis complex: The secret crisis of male body obsession.* New York: Free Press.

Pope, Kenneth S. (1996). Memory, abuse, and science: Questioning claims about the false memory syndrome epidemic. *American Psychologist, 51*, 957–974.

Portenoy, Russell K. (1994). Opioid therapy for chronic nonmalignant pain: Current status. In H. L. Fields & J. C. Liebeskind (eds.), *Progress in pain research and management. Pharmacological approaches to the treatment of chronic pain: Vol. 1.* Seattle: International Association for the Study of Pain.

Postmes, Tom, & Spears, Russell (1998). Deindividuation and antinormative behavior: A meta-analysis. *Psychological Bulletin, 123*, 238–259.

Postmes, Tom; Spears, Russell; & Cihangir, Sezgin (2001). Quality of decision making and group norms. *Journal of Personality and Social Psychology, 80*, 918–930.

Potter, W. James (1987). Does television viewing hinder academic achievement among adolescents? *Human Communication Research, 14*, 27–46.

Poulin-Dubois, Diane; Serbin, Lisa A.; Kenyon, Brenda; & Derbyshire, Alison (1994). Infants' intermodal knowledge about gender. *Developmental Psychology, 30*, 436–442.

Povinelli, Daniel J. (2000). *Folk physics for apes: The chimpanzee's theory of how the world works.* Oxford: Oxford University Press.

Powell, Russell A., & Boer, Douglas P. (1995). Did Freud misinterpret reported memories of sexual abuse as fantasies? *Psychological Reports, 77*, 563–570.

Pratkanis, Anthony, & Aronson, Elliot (1992). *Age of propaganda: The everyday use and abuse of persuasion.* New York: Freeman.

Pratt, L. A.; Ford, D. E.; Crum, R. M.; et al. (1996, December 15). Depression, psychotropic medication, and risk of myocardial infarction: Prospective data from the Baltimore ECA follow-up. *Circulation, 94*, 3123–3129.

Premack, David, & Premack, Ann James (1983). *The mind of an ape.* New York: Norton.

Press, Gary A.; Amaral, David G.; & Squire, Larry R. (1989, September 7). Hippocampal abnormalities in amnesic patients revealed by high-resolution magnetic resonance imaging. *Nature, 341*, 54–57.

Prochaska, James O.; Norcross, John C.; & DiClemente, Carlo C. (1994). *Changing for good.* New York: Morrow.

Pryor, Karen (1999). *Don't shoot the dog: The new art of teaching and training* (rev. ed). New York: Bantam.

Punamaeki, Raija-Leena, & Joustie, Marja (1998). The role of culture, violence, and personal factors affecting dream content. *Journal of Cross-Cultural Psychology, 29*, 320–342.

Pynoos, R. S., & Nader, K. (1989). Children's memory and proximity to violence. *Journal of the American Academy of Child and Adolescent Psychiatry, 28*, 236–241.

Pyszczynski, Tom; Greenberg, Jeff; & Solomon, Sheldon (2000). Proximal and distal defense: A new perspective on unconscious motivation. *Current Directions in Psychological Science, 9*, 156–160.

Quinn, Diane M., & Spencer, Steven J. (2001). The interference of stereotype threat with women's generation of mathematical problem-solving strategies. *Journal of Social Issues, 57*, 55–71.

Radetsky, Peter (1991, April). The brainiest cells alive. *Discover, 12*, 82–85, 88, 90.

Räikkönen, Katri; Matthews, Karen A.; Flory, Janine D.; et al. (1999). Effects of optimism, pessimism, and trait anxiety on ambulatory blood pressure and mood during everyday life. *Journal of Personality and Social Psychology, 76*, 104–113.

Raine, Adrian (1996). Autonomic nervous system factors underlying disinhibited, antisocial, and violent behavior. Biosocial perspectives and treatment implications. *Annals of the New York Academy of Sciences, 794*, 46–59.

Raine, Adrian; Brennan, Patricia; & Mednick, Sarnoff A. (1994). Birth complications combined with early maternal rejection at age one year predispose to violent crime at age 18 years. *Archives of General Psychiatry, 51*, 984–988.

Raine, Adrian; Lencz, Todd; Bihrle, Susan; LaCasse, Lori; & Colletti, Patrick (2000). Reduced prefrontal gray matter volume and reduced autonomic activity in antisocial personality disorder. *Archives of General Psychiatry, 57*, 119–127.

Raine, Adrian, & Liu, Jiang-Hong (1998). Biological predispositions to violence and their implications for biosocial treatment and prevention. *Psychology, Crime & Law, 4*, 107–125.

Raine, Adrian; Meloy, J. R.; Bihrle, S.; et al. (1998). Reduced prefrontal and increased subcortical brain functioning assessed using positron emission tomography in predatory and affective murderers. *Behavioral Science and Law, 16*, 319–332.

Raine, Adrian; Park, Sohee; Lencz, Todd; et al. (2001). Reduced right hemisphere activation in severely abused violent offenders during a working memory task: An fMRI study. *Aggressive Behavior, 27*, 111–129.

Ramey, Craig T., & Ramey, Sharon Landesman (1998). Early intervention and early experience. *American Psychologist, 53*, 109–120.

Rapkin, Andrea J.; Chang, Li C.; & Reading, Anthony E. (1988). Comparison of retrospective and prospective assessment of premenstrual symptoms. *Psychological Reports, 62,* 55–60.

Raskin, David C.; Honts, Charles R.; & Kircher, John C. (1997). The scientific status of research on polygraph techniques: The case for polygraph tests. In D. L. Faigman, D. Kaye, M. J. Saks, & J. Sanders (eds.), *Modern scientific evidence: The law and science of expert testimony.* St. Paul, MN: West.

Raso, Jack (1996, July/August). Alternative health education and pseudo-credentialing. *Skeptical Inquirer,* 39–45.

Rathbun, Constance; DiVirgilio, Letitia; & Waldfogel, Samuel (1958). A restitutive process in children following radical separation from family and culture. *American Journal of Orthopsychiatry, 28,* 408–415.

Rauschecker, Josef P. (1999). Making brain circuits listen. *Science, 285,* 1686–1687.

Ravussin, Eric; Lillioja, Stephen; Knowler, William; et al. (1988). Reduced rate of energy expenditure as a risk factor for body-weight gain. *New England Journal of Medicine, 318,* 467–472.

Rawsthorne, Laird J., & Elliot, Andrew J. (1999). Achievement goals and intrinsic motivation: A meta-analytic review. *Personality and Social Psychology Review, 3,* 326–344.

Raynor, Hollie A., & Epstein, Leonard H. (2001). Dietary variety, energy regulation, and obesity. *Psychological Bulletin, 127,* 325–341.

Reber, Paul J.; Stark, Craig E. L.; & Squire, Larry R. (1998). Contrasting cortical activity associated with category memory and recognition memory. *Learning & Memory, 5,* 420–428.

Redd, W.H.; Dadds, M.R.; Futterman, A.D.; Taylor, K.; & Bovbjerg, D. (1993). Nausea induced by mental images of chemotherapy. *Cancer, 72,* 629–636.

Redelmeier, Donald A., & Tversky, Amos (1996). On the belief that arthritis pain is related to the weather. *Proceedings of the National Academy of Sciences, 93,* 2895–2896.

Reed, Geoffrey M. (1990). Stress, coping, and psychological adaptation in a sample of gay and bisexual men with AIDS. Unpublished doctoral dissertation, University of California, Los Angeles.

Reed, Geoffrey M.; Kemeny, Margaret E.; Taylor, Shelley E.; et al. (1994). Realistic acceptance as a predictor of decreased survival time in gay men with AIDS. *Health Psychology, 13,* 299–307.

Reedy, F. E.; Bartoshuk, L. M.; Miller, I. J.; Duffy, V. B.; Lucchina, L.; & Yanagisawa, K. (1993). Relationships among papillae, taste pores, and 6-n-propylthiouracil (PROP) suprathreshold taste sensitivity. *Chemical Senses, 18,* 618–619.

Regard, Marianne, & Landis, Theodor (1997). "Gourmand syndrome": Eating passion associated with right anterior lesions. *Neurology, 48,* 1185–1190.

Reich, Theodore; Edenberg, Howard J.; Goate, Alison; et al. (1998, May 8). Genome-wide search for genes affecting the risk for alcohol dependence. *American Journal of Medical Genetics, 81,* 207–215.

Reid, R. L. (1991). Premenstrual syndrome. *New England Journal of Medicine, 324,* 1208–1210.

Reiss, Diana, & Marino, Lori (2001). Mirror self-recognition in the bottlenose dolphin: A case of cognitive convergence. *Proceedings of the National Academy of Science, 98,* 5937–5942.

Reneman, Liesbeth; Lavalaye, Jules; Schmand, Ben; et al. (2001). Cortical serotonin transporter density and verbal memory in individuals who stopped using 3,4-methylenedioxymethamphetamine (MDMA or "ecstasy"). *Archives of General Psychology, 58,* 901–906.

Rescorla, Robert A. (1988). Pavlovian conditioning: It's not what you think it is. *American Psychologist, 43,* 151–160.

Rest, James; Narváez, Darcia; Bebeau, Muriel J.; & Thoma, Stephen J. (1999). Postconventional moral thinking: A neo-Kohlbergian approach. Hillsdale, NJ: Erlbaum.

Restak, Richard (1983, October). Is free will a fraud? *Science Digest, 91*(10), 52–55.

Restak, Richard M. (1994). *The modular brain.* New York: Macmillan.

Reuter-Lorenz, Patricia A.; Jonides, John; Smith, Edward E.; et al. (2000). Age differences in the frontal lateralization of verbal and spatial working memory revealed by PET. *Journal of Cognitive Neuroscience, 12,* 174–187.

Reuter-Lorenz, Patricia A.; Stanczak, Louise; & Miller, Andrea C. (1999). Neural recruitment and cognitive aging: Two hemispheres are better than one, especially as you age. *Psychological Science, 10,* 494–500.

Reynolds, Brent A., & Weiss, Samuel (1992). Generation of neurons and astrocytes from isolated cells of the adult mammalian central nervous system. *Science, 255,* 1707–1710.

Reynolds, David K. (1987). *Water bears no scars: Japanese lifeways for personal growth.* New York: Morrow.

Rice, George; Anderson, Carol; Risch, Neil; & Ebers, George (1999, April 23). Male homosexuality: Absence of linkage to microsatellite markers at Xq28. *Science, 284,* 665–667.

Rice, Mabel L. (1990). Preschoolers' QUIL: Quick incidental learning of words. In G. Conti-Ramsden & C. E. Snow (eds.), *Children's language* (Vol. 7). Hillsdale, NJ: Erlbaum.

Richards, Jane M., & Gross, James J. (2000). Emotion regulation and memory: The cognitive costs of keeping one's cool. *Journal of Personality and Social Psychology, 79,* 410–424.

Richards, Ruth L. (1991). Everyday creativity and the arts. Paper presented at the annual meeting of the American Psychological Association, San Francisco.

Richardson, John T. E. (ed.) (1992). *Cognition and the menstrual cycle.* New York: Springer-Verlag.

Richardson-Klavehn, Alan, & Bjork, Robert A. (1988). Measures of memory. *Annual Review of Psychology, 39,* 475–543.

Ridley-Johnson, Robyn; Cooper, Harris; & Chance, June (1983). The relation of children's television viewing to school achievement and I.Q. *Journal of Educational Research, 76,* 294–297.

Rieber, Robert W. (1999). Hypnosis, false memory and multiple personality: A trinity of affinity. *History of Psychiatry, 10*(37, Pt. 1), 3–11.

Riessman, Catherine K. (1990). *Divorce talk.* New Brunswick, NJ: Rutgers University Press.

Riley, Vernon; Spackman, Darrel; & Santisteban, George (1975). The role of physiological stress on breast tumor incidence in mice. *Proceedings of the American Association of Cancer Research, 16,* 152.

Rind, Bruce, & Tromovitch, Philip (1997). A meta-analytic review of findings from national samples on psychological correlates of child sexual abuse. *Journal of Sex Research, 34,* 237–255.

Rind, Bruce; Tromovitch, Philip; & Bauserman, Robert (1998). A meta-analytic examination of assumed properties of child sexual abuse using college samples. *Psychological Bulletin, 124,* 22–53.

Riskind, John H.; Williams, Nathan L.; Gessner, Theodore L.; et al. (2000). The looming maladaptive style: Anxiety, danger, and schematic processing. *Journal of Personality and Social Psychology, 79,* 837–852.

Roberts, Brent W.; Caspi, Avshalom; & Moffitt, Terrie E. (2001). The kids are alright: Growth and stability in personality development from adolescence to adulthood. *Journal of Personality and Social Psychology, 81,* 670–683.

Roberts, Brent W., & DelVecchio, Wendy F. (2000). The rank-order consistency of personality traits from childhood to old age: A quantitative review of longitudinal studies. *Psychological Bulletin, 126,* 3–25.

Robins, Lee N.; Davis, Darlene H.; & Goodwin, Donald W. (1974). Drug use by U.S. Army enlisted men in Vietnam: A follow-up on their return home. *American Journal of Epidemiology, 99,* 235–249.

Robins, Lee N.; Tipp, Jayson; & Przybeck, Thomas R. (1991). Antisocial personality. In L. N. Robins & D. A. Regier (eds.), *Psychiatric disorders in America.* New York: Free Press.

Robins, Richard W., & Beer, Jennifer S. (2001). Positive illusions about the self: Short-term benefits and long-term costs. *Journal of Personality and Social Psychology, 80,* 340–352.

Robins, Richard W.; Gosling, Samuel D.; & Craik, Kenneth H. (1999). An empirical analysis of trends in psychology. *American Psychologist, 54,* 117–128.

Robinson, Thomas N. (1999, October 27). Reducing children's television viewing to prevent obesity: A randomized controlled trial. *Journal of the American Medical Association, 282,* 1561–1567.

Robinson, Thomas; Wilde, M. L.; Navracruz, L. C.; et al (2001). Effects of reducing children's television and video game use on aggressive behavior: a randomized controlled trial. *Archives of Pediatric and Adolescent Medicine, 155,* 13–14.

Rocha, Beatriz A.; Scearce-Levie, Kimberly; Lucas, Jose J.; et al. (1998). Increased vulnerability to cocaine in mice lacking the serotonin-1B receptor. *Nature, 393,* 175–178.

Rodriguez, Paul; Wiles, Janet; & Elman, Jeffrey L. (1999). A recurrent neural network that learns to count. *Connection Science, 11,* 5–40.

Roediger, Henry L., & McDermott, Kathleen B. (1995). Creating false memories: Remembering words not presented in lists. *Journal of Experimental Psychology; Learning, Memory, & Cognition, 21,* 803–814.

Roediger, Henry L. (1990). Implicit memory: Retention without remembering. *American Psychologist, 45,* 1043–1056.

Rogers, Carl (1951). *Client-centered therapy: Its current practice, implications, and theory.* Boston: Houghton Mifflin.

Rogers, Carl (1961). *On becoming a person.* Boston: Houghton Mifflin.

Rogers, Ronald W., & Prentice-Dunn, Steven (1981). Deindividuation and anger-mediated interracial aggression: Unmasking regressive racism. *Journal of Personality and Social Psychology, 41,* 63–73.

Rollin, Henry (ed.) (1980). *Coping with schizophrenia.* London: Burnett.

Rosch, Eleanor H. (1973). Natural categories. *Cognitive Psychology, 4,* 328–350.

Rose, Suzanna; Zand, Debra; & Cini, Marie A. (1993). Lesbian courtship scripts. In E. D. Rothblum & K. A. Brehony (eds.), *Boston marriages.* Amherst: University of Massachusetts Press.

Roseman, Ira J.; Wiest, Cynthia; & Swartz, Tamara S. (1994). Phenomenology, behaviors, and goals differentiate discrete emotions. *Journal of Personality and Social Psychology, 67,* 206–221.

Rosen, Gerald M. (1981). Guidelines for the review of do-it-yourself treatment books. *Contemporary Psychology, 26,* 189–191.

Rosen, Gerald M. (1999). Treatment fidelity and research on Eye Movement Desensitization and Reprocessing (EMDR). *Journal of Anxiety Disorders, 13,* 173–184.

Rosen, R. D. (1977). *Psychobabble.* New York: Atheneum.

Rosenberg, Harold (1993). Prediction of controlled drinking by alcoholics and problem drinkers. *Psychological Bulletin, 113,* 129–139.

Rosenthal, Norman E. (1998). *Winter blues: Seasonal affective disorder: What it is and how to overcome it.* New York: Guilford Press.

Rosenthal, Robert (1966). *Experimenter effects in behavioral research.* New York: Appleton-Century-Crofts.

Rosenthal, Robert (1994). Interpersonal expectancy effects: A 30-year perspective. *Current Directions in Psychological Science, 3,* 176–179.

Rosenzweig, Mark R. (1984). Experience, memory, and the brain. *American Psychologist, 39,* 365–376.

Rosso, Isabelle M.; Cannon, Tyrone D.; Huttunen, Tiia; et al. (2000). Obstetric risk factors for early-onset schizophrenia in a Finnish birth cohort. *American Journal of Psychiatry, 157,* 801–807.

Roth, David L.; & Holmes, David S. (1985). Influence of physical fitness in determining the impact of stressful life events on physical and psychologic health. *Psychosomatic Medicine, 47,* 164–173.

Rothbart, Mary K.; Ahadi, Stephan A.; & Evans, David E. (2000). Temperament and personality: Origins and outcomes. *Journal of Personality and Social Psychology, 78,* 122–135.

Rothbaum, Fred M.; Weisz, John R.; & Snyder, Samuel S. (1982). Changing the world and changing the self: A two-process model of perceived control. *Journal of Personality and Social Psychology, 42,* 5–37.

Rothbaum, Fred; Weisz, John; Pott, Martha; et al. (2000). Attachment and culture: Security in the United States and Japan. *American Psychologist, 55,* 1093–1104.

Rothman, Barbara K. (1989). *Recreating motherhood: Ideology and technology in a patriarchal society.* New York: W. W. Norton.

Rotter, Julian B. (1990). Internal versus external control of reinforcement: A case history of a variable. *American Psychologist, 45,* 489–493.

Rovee-Collier, Carolyn (1993). The capacity for long-term memory in infancy. *Current Directions in Psychological Science, 2,* 130–135.

Rowe, John W., & Kahn, Robert L. (1998). *Successful aging.* New York: Pantheon.

Rowe, Walter F. (1993, Winter). Psychic detectives: A critical examination. *Skeptical Inquirer, 17,* 159–165.

Roy, Mark P.; Steptoe, Andrew; & Kirschbaum, Clemens (1998). Life events and social support as moderators of individual differences in cardiovascular and cortisol reactivity. *Journal of Personality and Social Psychology, 75,* 1273–1281.

Rozin, Paul; Lowery, Laura; & Ebert, Rhonda (1994). Varieties of disgust faces and the structure of disgust. *Journal of Personality and Social Psychology, 66,* 870–881.

Rubin, Jeffrey Z. (1994). Models of conflict management. *Journal of Social Issues, 50,* 33–45.

Ruggiero, Vincent R. (1988). *Teaching thinking across the curriculum.* New York: Harper & Row.

Ruggiero, Vincent R. (1997). *The art of thinking: A guide to critical and creative thought* (5th ed.). New York: HarperCollins.

Ruitenberg, A.; van Swieten, J. C.; Witteman, J. C.; et al. (2002). Alcohol consumption and risk of dementia: the Rotterdam Study. *Lancet, 359,* 281–286.

Rumbaugh, Duane M. (1977). *Language learning by a chimpanzee: The Lana project.* New York: Academic Press.

Rumbaugh, Duane M.; Savage-Rumbaugh, E. Sue; & Pate, James L. (1988). Addendum to "Summation in the chimpanzee (*Pan troglodytes*)." *Journal of Experimental Psychology: Animal Behavior Processes, 14,* 118–120.

Rumelhart, David E., & McClelland, James L. (1987). Learning the past tenses of English verbs: Implicit rules or parallel distributed processing. In B. MacWhinney (ed.), *Mechanisms of language acquisition.* Hillsdale, NJ: Erlbaum.

Rumelhart, David E.; McClelland, James L.; & the PDP Research Group (1986). *Parallel distributed processing: Explorations in the microstructure of cognition* (Vols. 1 and 2). Cambridge, MA: MIT Press.

Rushton, J. Philippe (1988). Race differences in behavior: A review and evolutionary analysis. *Personality and Individual Differences, 9,* 1009–1024.

Russell, Diana E. H. (1990). *Rape in marriage* (rev. ed.). Bloomington: Indiana University Press.

Russell, James A., & Fehr, Beverley (1994). Fuzzy concepts in a fuzzy hierarchy: Varieties of anger. *Journal of Personality and Social Psychology, 67,* 186–205.

Rusting, Cheryl L., & Nolen-Hoeksema, Susan (1998). Regulating responses of anger: Effects of rumination and distraction on angry mood. *Journal of Personality and Social Psychology, 74,* 790–803.

Rutter, Michael; Pickles, Andrew; Murray, Robin; & Eaves, Lindon (2001). Testing hypotheses on specific environmental causal effects on behavior. *Psychological Bulletin, 127,* 291–324.

Ryan, Richard M.; Chirkov, Valery I.; Little, Todd D.; et al. (1999). The American dream in Russia: Extrinsic aspirations and well-being in two cultures. *Personality and Social Psychology Bulletin, 25,* 1509–1524.

Ryder, Andrew G.; Alden, Lynn E.; & Paulhus, Delroy L. (2000). Is acculturation unidimensional or bidimensional? A head-to-head comparison in the prediction of personality, self-identity, and adjustment. *Journal of Personality and Social Psychology, 79,* 49–65.

Rymer, Russ (1993). *Genie: An abused child's flight from silence.* New York: HarperCollins.

Saarni, Carolyn (1989). Children's understanding of strategic control of emotional expression in social transactions. In C. Saarni & P. L. Harris (eds.), *Children's understanding of emotion.* Cambridge, England: Cambridge University Press.

Sack, Robert L., & Lewy, Alfred J. (1997). Melatonin as a chronobiotic: Treatment of circadian desynchrony in night workers and the blind. *Journal of Biological Rhythms, 12,* 595–603.

Sacks, Oliver (1985). *The man who mistook his wife for a hat and other clinical tales.* New York: Simon & Schuster.

Saffran, J. R.; Aslin, R. N.; & Newport, E. L. (1996). Statistical learning by 8-month-old infants. *Science, 274,* 1926–1928.

Sagan, Eli (1988). *Freud, women, and morality: The psychology of good and evil.* New York: Basic Books.

Sahley, Christie L.; Rudy, Jerry W.; & Gelperin, Alan (1981). An analysis of associative learning in a terrestrial mollusk: 1. Higher-order conditioning, blocking, and a transient US preexposure effect. *Journal of Comparative Physiology, 144,* 1–8.

Salovey, Peter; Rothman, Alexander J.; Detweiler, Jerusha B.; & Steward, Wayne T. (2000). Emotional states and physical health. *American Psychologist, 55,* 110–121.

Salthouse, Timothy A. (1998). The what and where of cognitive aging. Address presented at the annual meeting of the American Psychological Association, San Francisco.

Saltz, Bruce L.; Woerner, M. G.; Kane, J. M.; et al. (1991, November 6). Prospective study of tardive dyskinesia incidence in the elderly. *Journal of the American Medical Association, 266*(17), 2402–2406.

Samelson, Franz (1979). Putting psychology on the map: Ideology and intelligence testing. In A. R. Buss (ed.), *Psychology in social context.* New York: Irvington.

Sameroff, Arnold J.; Seifer, Ronald; Barocas, Ralph; et al. (1987). Intelligence quotient scores of 4-year-old children: Social-environmental risk factors. *Pediatrics, 79,* 343–350.

Sanchez-Ramos, J. R.; Song, S.; Kamath, S. G.; et al. (2001). Expression of neural markers in human umbilical cord blood. *Experimental Neurology, 171,* 109–115.

Sapolsky, Robert M. (1997). *The trouble with testosterone.* New York: Touchstone.

Sapolsky, Robert M. (2000). The possibility of neurotoxicity in the hippocampus in major depression: A primer on neuron death. *Biological Psychiatry, 48,* 755–765.

Sapolsky, Robert M. (2001). Atrophy of the hippocampus in posttraumatic stress disorder: How and when? *Hippocampus, 11,* 90–91.

Sarbin, Theodore R. (1991). Hypnosis: A fifty year perspective. *Contemporary Hypnosis, 8,* 1–15.

Saucier, Gerard (2000). Isms and the structure of social attitudes. *Journal of Personality and Social Psychology, 78,* 366–385.

Savage-Rumbaugh, Sue, & Lewin, Roger (1994). *Kanzi: The ape at the brink of the human mind.* New York: Wiley.

Savage-Rumbaugh, Sue; Shanker, Stuart; & Taylor, Talbot (1998). *Apes, language and the human mind.* New York: Oxford University Press.

Saxe, Leonard (1994). Detection of deception: Polygraph and integrity tests. *Current Directions in Psychological Science, 3,* 69–73.

Scarr, Sandra (1993). Biological and cultural diversity: The legacy of Darwin for development. *Child Development, 64,* 1333–1353.

Scarr, Sandra, & Weinberg, Robert A. (1994). Educational and occupational achievement of brothers and sisters in adoptive and biologically related families. *Behavioral Genetics, 24,* 301–325.

Scarr, Sandra; Pakstis, Andrew J.; Katz, Soloman H.; & Barker, William B. (1977). Absence of a relationship between degree of white ancestry and intellectual skill in a black population. *Human Genetics, 39,* 69–86.

Schachter, Stanley, & Singer, Jerome E. (1962). Cognitive, social, and physiological determinants of emotional state. *Psychological Review, 69,* 379–399.

Schacter, Daniel L. (1996). *Searching for memory: The brain, the mind, and the past.* New York: Basic Books.

Schacter, Daniel L. (1999). The seven sins of memory: Insights from psychology and cognitive neuroscience. *American Psychologist, 54,* 182–203.

Schacter, Daniel L. (2001). *The seven sins of memory: How the mind forgets and remembers.* Boston: Houghton Mifflin.

Schacter, Daniel L.; Chiu, C.-Y. Peter; & Ochsner, Kevin N. (1993). Implicit memory: A selective review. *Annual Review of Neuroscience, 16,* 159–182.

Schafer, Roy (1992). *Retelling a life: Narration and dialogue in psychoanalysis.* New York: Basic Books.

Schaie, K. Warner (1993). The Seattle longitudinal studies of adult intelligence. *Current Directions in Psychological Science, 2,* 171–175.

Schaie, K. Warner, & Willis, Sherry L. (2002). *Adult development and aging* (5th ed.). Upper Saddle River, NJ: Prentice Hall.

Schaie, K. Warner, & Zuo, Yan-Ling (2001). Family environments and cognitive functioning. In R. J. Sternberg & E. Grigorenko (eds.), *Cognitive development in context.* Hillsdale, NJ: Erlbaum.

Schank, Roger, with Peter Childers (1988). *The creative attitude.* New York: Macmillan.

Scherer, Klaus R. (1997). The role of culture in emotion-antecedent appraisal. *Journal of Personality and Social Psychology, 73,* 902–922.

Scheufele, Peter M. (2000). Effects of progressive relaxation and classical music on measurements of attention, relaxation, and stress responses. *Journal of Behavioral Medicine, 23,* 207–228.

Schlossberg, Nancy K., & Robinson, Susan P. (1996). *Going to plan B.* New York: Simon & Schuster/Fireside.

Schmelz, M.; Schmidt, R.; Bickel, A.; et al. (1997). Specific C-receptors for itch in human skin. *Journal of Neuroscience, 17,* 8003–8008.

Schmolck, H.; Buffalo, E. A.; & Squire, L. R. (2000). Memory distortions develop over time: Recollections of the O. J. Simpson trial verdict after 15 and 32 months. *Psychological Science, 11,* 39–45.

Schneider, Edward L. (1999, February 5). Aging in the third millennium. *Science, 283,* 796–797.

Schneider, Sandra L. (2001). In search of realistic optimism: Meaning, knowledge, and warm fuzziness. *American Psychologist, 56,* 250–263.

Schnell, Lisa, & Schwab, Martin E. (1990, January 18). Axonal regeneration in the rat spinal cord produced by an antibody against myelin-associated neurite growth inhibitors. *Nature, 343,* 269–272.

Schuckit, Marc A. (1998). Relationship among genetic, environmental, and psychological variables in predicting alcoholism. Invited address presented at the annual meeting of the American Psychological Association, San Francisco.

Schuckit, Marc A., & Smith, T. L. (1996). An 8-year follow-up of 450 sons of alcoholic and control subjects. *Archives of General Psychiatry, 53,* 202–210.

Schulz, Richard, & Decker, Susan (1985). Long-term adjustment to physical disability: The role of social support, perceived control, and self-blame. *Journal of Personality and Social Psychology, 48,* 1162–1172.

Schulz, Richard; Beach, S. R.; Ives, D. G.; et al. (2000). Association between depression and mortality in older adults: The Cardiovascular Health Study. *Archives of Internal Medicine, 160,* 1761–1768.

Schuman, Howard, & Scott, Jacqueline (1989). Generations and collective memories. *American Journal of Sociology, 54,* 359–381.

Schwarcz, Robert; Rassaoulpour, Arash; Wu, Hui-Qiu; et al. (2001). Increased cortical kynurenate content in schizophrenia. *Biological Psychiatry, 50,* 521–530.

Schwartz, Jeffrey; Stoessel, Paula W.; Baxter, Lewis R.; et al. (1996). Systematic changes in cerebral glucose metabolic rate after successful behavior modification treatment of obsessive–compulsive disorder. *Archives of General Psychiatry, 53,* 109–113.

Sears, Pauline, & Barbee, Ann H. (1977). Career and life satisfactions among Terman's gifted women. In J. C. Stanley, W. C. George, & C. H. Solano (eds.), *The gifted and the creative: A fifty-year perspective.* Baltimore, MD: Johns Hopkins University Press.

Seeman, Philip; Guan, Hong-chang; & Van Tol, Hubert H. (1993). Dopamine D4 receptors elevated in schizophrenia. *Nature, 365,* 441–445.

Segal, Julius (1986). *Winning life's toughest battles.* New York: McGraw-Hill.

Segall, Marshall H. (1994). A cross-cultural research contribution to unraveling the nativist/empiricist controversy. In W. J. Lonner & R. Malpass (eds.), *Psychology and culture.* Needham Heights, MA: Allyn & Bacon.

Segall, Marshall H.; Campbell, Donald T.; & Herskovits, Melville J. (1966). *The influence of culture on visual perception.* Indianapolis: Bobbs-Merrill.

Segall, Marshall H.; Dasan, Pierre R.; Berry, John W.; & Poortinga, Ype H. (1999). *Human behavior in global perspective: An introduction to cross-cultural psychology* (2nd ed.). Boston, MA: Allyn & Bacon.

Segall, Marshall H.; Lonner, Walter J.; & Berry, John W. (1998). Cross-cultural psychology as a scholarly discipline: On the flowering of culture in behavioral research. *American Psychologist, 53,* 1101–1110.

Segerstrom, Suzanne C.; Taylor, Shelley E.; Kemeny, Margaret E.; & Fahey, John L. (1998). Optimism is associated with mood, coping, and immune change in response to stress. *Journal of Personality and Social Psychology, 74,* 1646–1655.

Seidenberg, Mark S. (1997). Language acquisition and use: Learning and applying probabilistic constraints. *Science, 275,* 1599–1603.

Seidenberg, Mark S., & Petitto, Laura A. (1979). Signing behavior in apes: A critical review. *Cognition, 7,* 177–215.

Seidlitz, Larry, & Diener, Edward (1998). Sex differences in the recall of affective experiences. *Journal of Personality and Social Psychology, 74,* 262–271.

Seifer, Ronald; Schiller, Masha; Sameroff, Arnold; et al. (1996). Attachment, maternal sensitivity, and infant temperament during the first year of life. *Developmental Psychology, 32,* 12–25.

Sekuler, Robert, & Blake, Randolph (1994). *Perception* (3rd ed.). New York: Knopf.

Seligman, Martin E. P. (1975). *Helplessness: On depression, development, and death.* San Francisco: Freeman.

Seligman, Martin E. P. (1991). *Learned optimism.* New York: Knopf.

Seligman, Martin E. P., & Csikszentmihaly, Mihaly (2000). Positive psychology: An introduction. *American Psychologist, 55,* 5–14.

Seligman, Martin E. P., & Hager, Joanne L. (1972, August). Biological boundaries of learning: The sauce-béarnaise syndrome. *Psychology Today,* 59–61, 84–87.

Seligman, Martin E. P.; Schulman, Peter; DeRubeis, Robert J.; & Hollon, Steven D. (1999). The prevention of depression and anxiety. *Prevention & Treatment, 2,* electronic posting December 21, 1999 on the website of the American Psychological Association.

Selye, Hans (1956). *The stress of life.* New York: McGraw-Hill.

Senghas, Ann, & Coppola, Marie (2001). Children creating language: How Nicaraguan Sign Language acquired a spatial grammar. *Psychological Science, 12,* 323–328.

Serbin, Lisa A.; Powlishta, Kimberly K.; & Gulko, Judith (1993). The development of sex typing in middle childhood. *Monographs of the Society for Research in Child Development, 58*(2), Serial No. 232, v-74.

Serpell, Robert (1994). The cultural construction of intelligence. In W. J. Lonner & R. S. Malpass (eds.), *Psychology and culture.* Needham Heights, MA: Allyn & Bacon.

Seydel, Caroline (2002). How neurons know that it's c-c-c-c-cold outside. *Science, 295,* 1451–1452.

Shadish, William R.; Matt, Georg E.; Navarro, Ana M.; & Phillips, Glenn (2000). The effects of psychological therapies under clinically representative conditions: A meta-analysis. *Psychological Bulletin, 126,* 512–529.

Shapiro, Deane H.; Schwartz, Carolyn E.; & Astin, John A. (1996). Controlling ourselves, controlling our world. *American Psychologist, 51,* 1213–1230.

Shapiro, Francine (1994). EMDR: In the eye of a paradigm shift. *Behavior Therapist, 17,* 153–156.

Shapiro, Francine (1995). *Eye movement desensitization and reprocessing: Basic principles, protocols, and procedures.* New York: Guilford.

Shatz, Marilyn, & Gelman, Rochel (1973). The development of communication skills: Modifications in the speech of young children as a function of the listener. *Monographs of the Society for Research in Child Development, 38.*

Shaver, Phillip R., & Hazan, Cindy (1993). Adult romantic attachment: Theory and evidence. In D. Perlman & W. H. Jones (eds.), *Advances in personal relationships* (Vol. 4). London: Kingsley.

Shaver, Phillip R.; Wu, Shelley; & Schwartz, Judith C. (1992). Cross-cultural similarities and differences in emotion and its representation: A prototype approach. In M. S. Clark (ed.), *Review of Personality and Social Psychology* (Vol. 13). Newbury Park, CA: Sage.

Shaw, Daniel S.; Keenan, Kate; & Vondra, Joan I. (1994). Developmental precursors of externalizing behavior: Ages 1 to 3. *Developmental Psychology, 30,* 355–364.

Shaywitz, Bennett A.; Shaywitz, Sally E.; Pugh, Kenneth R.; et al. (1995). Sex differences in the functional organization of the brain for language. *Nature, 373,* 607–609.

Shea, Chrisopher (2001, September). White man can't contextualize. *Lingua Franca,* 44–47, 49–51.

Sheldon, Kennon M., & Elliot, Andrew J. (1999). Goal striving, need satisfaction, and longitudinal well-being: The self-concordance model. *Journal of Personality and Social Psychology, 76,* 482–497.

Sheldon, Kennon M., & Houser-Marko, Linda (2001). Self-concordance, goal attainment, and the pursuit of happiness: Can there be an upward spiral? *Journal of Personality and Social Psychology, 80,* 152–165.

Sheldon, Kennon M.; Elliot, Andrew J.; Kim, Youngmee; & Kasser, Tim (2001). What is satisfying about satisfying events? Testing 10 candidate psychological needs. *Journal of Personality and Social Psychology, 80,* 325–339.

Sheline, Yvette I. (2000). 3D MRI studies of neuroanatomic changes in unipolar major depression: The role of stress and medical comorbidity. *Biological Psychiatry, 48,* 791–800.

Sheline, Yvette I.; Sanghavi, Milan; Mintun, Mark A.; & Gado, Mokhtar H. (1999). Depression duration but not age predicts hippocampal volume loss in medically healthy women with recurrent major depression. *Journal of Neuroscience, 19,* 5034–5043.

Shepard, Roger N., & Metzler, Jacqueline (1971). Mental rotation of three-dimensional objects. *Science, 171,* 701–703.

Shepperd, James A. (1995). Remedying motivation and productivity loss in collective settings. *Current Directions in Psychological Science, 4,* 131–140.

Sherif, Muzafer (1958). Superordinate goals in the reduction of intergroup conflicts. *American Journal of Sociology, 63,* 349–356.

Sherif, Muzafer; Harvey, O. J.; White, B. J.; Hood, William; & Sherif, Carolyn (1961). *Intergroup conflict and cooperation: The Robbers Cave experiment.* Norman: University of Oklahoma Institute of Intergroup Relations.

Sherman, Bonnie R., & Kunda, Ziva (1989). Motivated evaluation of scientific evidence. Paper presented at the annual meeting of the American Psychological Society, Arlington, VA.

Sherman, Jeffrey W., & Bessenoff, Gayle R. (1999). Stereotypes as source-monitoring cues: On the interaction between episodic and semantic memory. *Psychological Science, 10,* 106–110.

Shermer, Michael (1997). *Why people believe weird things: Pseudoscience, superstition, and other confusions of our time.* New York: Freeman.

Sherwin, Barbara B. (1998a). Estrogen and cognitive functioning in women. *Proceedings of the Society for Experimental Biological Medicine, 217,* 17–22.

Sherwin, Barbara B. (1998b). Use of combined estrogen-androgen preparations in the postmenopause: Evidence from clinical studies. *International Journal of Fertility & Women's Medicine, 43,* 98–103.

Shields, Stephanie (2002). *Gender and the social meaning of emotion.* Cambridge, MA: Cambridge University Press.

Shields, Stephanie A. (1975). Functionalism, Darwinism, and the psychology of women: A study in social myth. *American Psychologist, 30,* 739–754.

Shih, Margaret; Pittinsky, Todd L.; & Ambady, Nalini (1999). Stereotype susceptibility: Identity salience and shifts in quantitative performance. *Psychological Science, 10,* 80–83.

Shin, Lisa M.; Kosslyn, Stephen M.; McNally, Richard J.; et al. (1997). Visual imagery and perception in posttraumatic stress disorder. *Archives of General Psychiatry, 54,* 233–241.

Showalter, Elaine (1997). *Hystories: Hysterical epidemics and modern culture.* New York: Columbia University Press.

Shweder, Richard A.; Mahapatra, Manamohan; & Miller, Joan G. (1990). Culture and moral development. In J. W. Stigler, R. A. Shweder, & G. Herdt (eds.), *Cultural psychology: Essays on comparative human development.* Cambridge, England: Cambridge University Press.

Sidanius, Jim; Pratto, Felicia; & Bobo, Lawrence (1996). Racism, conservatism, affirmative action, and intellectual sophistication: A matter of principled conservatism or group dominance? *Journal of Personality and Social Psychology, 70,* 476–490.

Siegel, Alan B. (1991). *Dreams that can change your life.* Los Angeles: Tarcher.

Siegel, Judith M. (1990). Stressful life events and use of physician services among the elderly: The moderating role of pet ownership. *Journal of Personality and Social Psychology, 58,* 1081–1086.

Siegel, Ronald K. (1989). *Intoxication: Life in pursuit of artificial paradise.* New York: Dutton.

Siegler, Robert S. (1996). *Emerging minds: The process of change in children's thinking.* New York: Oxford University Press.

Siegler, Robert S. (2001). Cognition, instruction, and the quest for meaning. In S. M. Carver & D. Klahr (eds.), *Cognition and instruction: Twenty-five years of progress.* Mahwah, NJ: Erlbaum.

Silverman, J. G.; Raj, A.; Mucci, L. A.; & Hathaway, J. E. (2001, August 1). Dating violence against adolescent girls and associated substance use, unhealthy weight control, sexual risk behavior, pregnancy, and suicidality. *Journal of the American Medical Association, 286,* 572–579.

Silverstein, Brett, & Perlick, Deborah (1995). *The cost of competence: Why inequality causes depression, eating disorders, and illness in women.* New York: Oxford University Press.

Silverstein, Brett; Peterson, Barbara; & Perdue, Lauren (1986). Some correlates of the thin standard of bodily attractiveness in women. *International Journal of Eating Disorders, 5,* 145–155.

Sims, Ethan A. (1974). Studies in human hyperphagia. In G. Bray & J. Bethune (eds.), *Treatment and management of obesity.* New York: Harper & Row.

Sinclair, Lisa, & Kunda, Ziva (1999). Reactions to a Black professional: Motivated inhibition and activation of conflicting stereotypes. *Journal of Personality and Social Psychology, 77,* 885–904.

Singer, Margaret T.; Temerlin, Maurice K.; & Langone, Michael D. (1990). Psychotherapy cults. *Cultic Studies Journal, 7,* 101–125.

Singh, Devendra; Vidaurri, Melody; Zambarano, Robert J.; & Dabbs, James M., Jr. (1999). Lesbian erotic role identification: Behavioral, morphological, and hormonal correlates. *Journal of Personality and Social Psychology, 76,* 1035–1049.

Skinner, B. F. (1938). *The behavior of organisms: An experimental analysis.* New York: Appleton-Century-Crofts.

Skinner, B. F. (1948). Superstition in the pigeon. *Journal of Experimental Psychology, 38,* 168–172.

Skinner, B. F. (1948/1976). *Walden Two.* New York: Macmillan.

Skinner, B. F. (1956). A case history in the scientific method. *American Psychologist, 11,* 221–233.

Skinner, B. F. (1961, November). Teaching machines. *Scientific American,* 91–102.

Skinner, B. F. (1972). The operational analysis of psychological terms. In B. F. Skinner, *Cumulative record* (3rd ed.). New York: Appleton-Century-Crofts.

Skinner, B. F. (1990). Can psychology be a science of mind? *American Psychologist, 45,* 1206–1210.

Skinner, B. F., & Vaughan, Margaret (1984). *Enjoy old age.* New York: W. W. Norton.

Skinner, Ellen A. (1996). A guide to constructs of control. *Journal of Personality and Social Psychology, 71,* 549–570.

Skinner, J. B.; Erskine, A.; Pearce, S. A.; et al. (1990). The evaluation of a cognitive behavioural treatment programme in outpatients with chronic pain. *Journal of Psychosomatic Research, 34,* 13–19.

Skreslet, Paula (1987, November 30). The prizes of first grade. *Newsweek,* 8.

Slade, Pauline (1984). Premenstrual emotional changes in normal women: Fact or fiction? *Journal of Psychosomatic Research, 28,* 1–7.

Slavin, Robert E., & Cooper, Robert (1999). Improving intergroup relations: Lessons learned from cooperative learning programs. *Journal of Social Issues, 55,* 647–663.

Slobin, Daniel I. (ed.) (1985). *The cross-linguistic study of language acquisition* (Vols. 1 and 2). Hillsdale, NJ: Erlbaum.

Slobin, Daniel I. (ed.) (1991). *The cross-linguistic study of language acquisition* (Vol. 3). Hillsdale, NJ: Erlbaum.

Slotkin, Theodore A. (1998). Fetal nicotine or cocaine exposure: Which one is worse? *Journal of Pharmacology and Experimental Therapeutics, 285,* 931–945.

Smith, Carlyle (1995). Sleep states and memory processes. *Behavioural Brain Research, 69,* 137–145.

Smith, Carolyn A.; Lizotte, Alan J.; Thornberry, Terence P.; et al. (1997). Resilient youth: Identifying factors that prevent high-risk youth from engaging in delinquency and drug use. In J. Hagan (ed.), *Delinquency and disrepute in the life course.* Greenwich, CT: JAI Press.

Smith, David N. (1998). The psychocultural roots of genocide: Legitimacy and crisis in Rwanda. *American Psychologist, 53,* 743–753.

Smith, Larissa L., & Reise, Steven P. (1998). Gender differences on negative affectivity: An IRT study of differential item functioning on the Multidimensional Personality Questionnaire Stress Reaction Scale. *Journal of Personality and Social Psychology, 75,* 1350–1362.

Smith, Michael D.; Keltner, Dacher; & Gonzaga, Gian C. (1998). Love and desire: New evidence for distinct displays of emotion. Paper presented at the annual meeting of the American Psychological Association, San Francisco.

Smith, Peter B., & Bond, Michael H. (1994). *Social psychology across cultures: Analysis and perspectives.* Boston: Allyn & Bacon.

Smith, Timothy W.; Limon, Jeffery P.; Gallo, Linda C.; & Ngu, Le Q. (1996). Interpersonal control and cardiovascular reactivity: Goals, behavioral expression, and the moderating effects of sex. *Journal of Personality and Social Psychology, 70,* 1012–1024.

Smither, Robert D. (1998). *The psychology of work and human performance* (3ʳᵈ ed.). New York: Longman.

Smyth, Joshua M., & Pennebaker, James W. (1999). Sharing one's story: Translating emotional experiences into words as a coping tool. In C. R. Snyder (ed.), *Coping: The psychology of what works.* New York: Oxford University Press.

Snidman, Nancy; Kagan, Jerome; Riordan, Linda; et al. (1995). Cardiac function and behavioral reactivity during infancy. *Psychophysiology, 32,* 199–207.

Snodgrass, Sara E. (1985). Women's intuition: The effect of subordinate role on interpersonal sensitivity. *Journal of Personality and Social Psychology, 49,* 146–155.

Snodgrass, Sara E. (1992). Further effects of role versus gender on interpersonal sensitivity. *Journal of Personality and Social Psychology, 62,* 154–158.

Snodgrass, Sara E.; Hecht, Marvin A.; & Ploutz-Snyder, Robert (1998). Interpersonal sensitivity: Expressivity or perceptivity? *Journal of Personality and Social Psychology, 74,* 238–249.

Snow, Barry R; Pinter, Isaac; Gusmorino, Paul; et al. (1986). Sex differences in chronic pain: Incidence and causal mechanisms. Paper presented at the annual meeting of the American Psychological Association, Washington, DC.

Snowdon, Charles T. (1997). The "nature" of sex differences: Myths of male and female. In P.A. Gowaty (ed.), *Feminism and evolutionary biology.* New York: Chapman and Hall.

Snyder, C. R., & Shenkel, Randee J. (1975, March). The P. T. Barnum effect. *Psychology Today,* 52–54.

Snyder, James J., & Patterson, Gerald R. (1995). Individual differences in social aggression: A test of a reinforcer model of socialization in the natural environment. *Behavior Therapy, 26,* 371–391.

Solms, Mark (2000). "The new neuropsychology of sleep: Implications for psychoanalysis": Comment on J. Allan Hobson and Edward Pace-Schott's response. *Neuro-psychoanalysis, 2,* 193–201.

Solomon, Jennifer C. (1996). Humor and aging well: A laughing matter or a matter of laughing? *American Behavioral Scientist, 39,* 249–271.

Solomon, Paul R. (1979). Science and television commercials: Adding relevance to the research methodology course. *Teaching of Psychology, 6,* 26–30.

Solomon, Robert C. (1994). *About love.* Lanham, MD: Littlefield Adams.

Somer, Oya, & Goldberg, Lewis R. (1999). The structure of Turkish trait-descriptive adjectives. *Journal of Personality and Social Psychology, 76,* 431–450.

Sommer, Robert (1969). *Personal space: The behavioral basis of design.* Englewood Cliffs, NJ: Prentice-Hall.

Sommer, Robert (1977, January). Toward a psychology of natural behavior. *APA Monitor.* (Reprinted in *Readings in psychology 78/79.* Guilford, CT: Dushkin, 1978.)

Sorce, James F.; Emde, Robert N.; Campos, Joseph; & Klinnert, Mary D. (1985). Maternal emotional signaling: Its effect on the visual cliff behavior of 1-year-olds. *Developmental Psychology, 21,* 195–200.

Spanos, Nicholas P. (1991). A sociocognitive approach to hypnosis. In S. J. Lynn & J. W. Rhue (eds.), *Theories of hypnosis: Current models and perspectives.* New York: Guilford Press.

Spanos, Nicholas P. (1996). *Multiple identities and false memories: A sociocognitive perspective.* Washington, DC: American Psychological Association.

Spanos, Nicholas P.; Burgess, Cheryl A.; Roncon, Vera; et al. (1993). Surreptitiously observed hypnotic responding in simulators and in skill-trained and untrained high hypnotizables. *Journal of Personality and Social Psychology, 65,* 391–398.

Spanos, Nicholas P.; Menary, Evelyn; Gabora, Natalie J.; et al. (1991). Secondary identity enactments during hypnotic past-life regression: A sociocognitive perspective. *Journal of Personality and Social Psychology, 61,* 308–320.

Spanos, Nicholas P.; Stenstrom, Robert J.; & Johnson, Joseph C. (1988). Hypnosis, placebo, and suggestion in the treatment of warts. *Psychosomatic Medicine, 50,* 245–260.

Spear, Linda P. (2000). Neurobiological changes in adolescence. *Current Directions in Psychological Science, 9,* 111–114.

Spearman, Charles (1927). *The abilities of man.* London: Macmillan.

Spelke, Elizabeth S. (2000). Core knowledge. *American Psychologist, 55,* 1233–1243.

Spence, Janet T. (1985). Gender identity and its implications for concepts of masculinity and femininity. In T. Sonderegger (ed.), *Nebraska Symposium on Motivation, 1984.* Lincoln, NE: University of Nebraska Press.

Spencer, M. B., & Dornbusch, Sanford M. (1990). Ethnicity. In S. S. Feldman & G. R. Elliott (eds.), *At the threshold: The developing adolescent.* Cambridge, MA: Harvard University Press.

Sperling, George (1960). The information available in brief visual presentations. *Psychological Monographs, 74*(498).

Sperry, Roger W. (1964). The great cerebral commissure. *Scientific American, 210*(1), 42–52.

Sperry, Roger W. (1982). Some effects of disconnecting the cerebral hemispheres. *Science, 217,* 1223–1226.

Spiegel, D.; Bloom, J. R.; Kraemer, H. C.; Gottheil, E. (1989, October 14). Effect of psychosocial treatment on survival of patients with metastatic breast cancer. *Lancet, 2,* 888–891.

Spilich, George J.; June, Lorraine; & Renner, Judith (1992). Cigarette smoking and cognitive performance. *British Journal of Addiction, 87,* 113–126.

Spitz, Herman H. (1997). *Nonconscious movements: From mystical messages to facilitated communication.* Mahwah, NJ: Erlbaum.

Sporer, Siegfried L.; Penrod, Steven; Read, Don; & Cutler, Brian (1995). Choosing, confidence, and accuracy: A meta-analysis of the confidence-accuracy relation in eyewitness identification studies. *Psychological Bulletin, 118,* 315–327.

Sprecher, Susan; Sullivan, Quintin; & Hatfield, Elaine (1994). Mate selection preferences: Gender differences examined in a national sample. *Journal of Personality and Social Psychology, 66,* 1074–1080.

Spring, Bonnie; Chiodo, June; & Bowen, Deborah J. (1987). Carbohydrates, tryptophan, and behavior: A methodological review. *Psychological Bulletin, 102,* 234–256.

Springer, Sally P., & Deutsch, Georg (1998). Left brain, right brain: *Perspectives from cognitive neuroscience.* New York: Freeman.

Squier, Leslie H., & Domhoff, G. William (1998). The presentation of dreaming and dreams in introductory psychology textbooks: A critical examination with suggestions for textbook authors and course instructors. *Dreaming, 8,* 149–168.

Squire, Larry R. (1987). *Memory and the brain.* New York: Oxford University Press.

Squire, Larry R., & Zola-Morgan, Stuart (1991). The medial temporal lobe memory system. *Science, 253,* 1380–1386.

Squire, Larry R.; Ojemann, Jeffrey G.; Miezin, Francis M.; et al. (1992). Activation of the hippocampus in normal humans: A functional anatomical study of memory. *Proceedings of the National Academy of Science, 89,* 1837–1841.

Srivastava, Abhishek; Locke, Edwin A.; & Bartol, Kathryn M. (2001). Money and subjective well-being: It's not the money, it's the motives. *Journal of Personality and Social Psychology, 80,* 959–971.

Staats, Carolyn K., & Staats, Arthur W. (1957). Meaning established by classical conditioning. *Journal of Experimental Psychology, 54,* 74–80.

Stadler, Michael A., & Frensch, Peter A. (1998). *Handbook of implicit learning.* Thousand Oaks, CA: Sage.

Stajkovic, Alexander D., & Luthans, Fred (1998). Self-efficacy and work-related performance: A meta-analysis. *Psychological Bulletin, 124,* 240–261.

Stam, Henderikus J. (1989). From symptom relief to cure: Hypnotic interventions in cancer. In N. P. Spanos & J. F. Chaves (eds.), *Hypnosis: The cognitive-behavioral perspective.* Buffalo, NY: Prometheus Books.

Stanovich, Keith (1996). *How to think straight about psychology* (4th ed.). New York: HarperCollins.

Staples, Brent (1994). *Parallel time.* New York: Pantheon.

Staples, Susan L. (1996). Human response to environmental noise: Psychological research and public policy. *American Psychologist, 51,* 143–150.

Stapley, Janice C., & Haviland, Jeannette M. (1989). Beyond depression: Gender differences in normal adolescents' emotional experiences. *Sex Roles, 20,* 295–308.

Stattin, Haken, & Magnusson, David (1990). *Pubertal maturation in female development.* Hillsdale, NJ: Erlbaum.

Staub, Ervin (1996). Cultural–social roots of violence. *American Psychologist, 51,* 117–132.

Staub, Ervin (1999). The roots of evil: Social conditions, culture, personality, and basic human needs. *Personality and Social Psychology Review, 3,* 179–192.

Staudinger, Ursula M.; Fleeson, William; & Baltes, Paul B. (1999). Predictors of subjective physical health and global well-being: Similarities and differences between the United States and Germany. *Journal of Personality and Social Psychology, 76,* 305–319.

Stearns, Peter N. (1997). *Fat history: Bodies and beauty in the modern West.* New York: New York University Press.

Steele, Claude M. (1992, April). Race and the schooling of Black Americans. *Atlantic Monthly,* 68–78.

Steele, Claude M. (1997). A threat in the air: How stereotypes shape intellectual identity and performance. *American Psychologist, 52,* 613–629.

Steele, Claude M., & Aronson, Joshua (1995). Stereotype threat and the intellectual test performance of African-Americans. *Journal of Personality and Social Psychology, 69,* 797–811.

Steinberg, Laurence D. (1990). Interdependence in the family: Autonomy, conflict and harmony in the parent-adolescent relationship. In S. S. Feldman & G. R. Elliott (eds.), *At the threshold: The developing adolescent.* Cambridge, MA: Harvard University Press.

Steinberg, Laurence D.; Dornbusch, Sanford M.; & Brown, B. Bradford (1992). Ethnic differences in adolescent achievement: An ecological Stern, Daniel (1985). *The interpersonal world of the infant.* New York: Basic Books.

Steiner, Robert A. (1989). *Don't get taken!* El Cerrito, CA: Wide-Awake Books.

Stenberg, Craig R., & Campos, Joseph (1990). The development of anger expressions in infancy. In N. Stein, B. Leventhal, & T. Trabasso (eds.), *Psychological and biological approaches to emotion.* Hillsdale, NJ: Erlbaum.

Stepanski, Edward, & Perlis, Michael (2000). Behavioral sleep medicine: An emerging subspecialty in health psychology. *Journal of Psychosomatic Research, 49,* 343–347.

Stephan, K. M.; Fink, G. R.; Passingham, R. E.; et al. (1995). Functional anatomy of the mental representation of upper movements in healthy subjects. *Journal of Neurophysiology, 73,* 373–386.

Stephan, Walter G. (1999). *Reducing prejudice and stereotyping in schools.* New York: Teachers College Press.

Stephan, Walter G.; Ageyev, Vladimir; Coates-Shrider, Lisa; et al. (1994). On the relationship between stereotypes and prejudice: An international study. *Personality and Social Psychology Bulletin, 20,* 277–284.

Stern, Marilyn, & Karraker, Katherine H. (1989). Sex stereotyping of infants: A review of gender labeling studies. *Sex Roles, 20,* 501–522.

Sternberg, Robert J. (1988). *The triarchic mind: A new theory of human intelligence.* New York: Viking.

Sternberg, Robert J. (1997). Construct validation of a triangular love scale. *European Journal of Social Psychology, 27,* 313–335.

Sternberg, Robert J., & Wagner, Richard K. (1989). Individual differences in practical knowledge and its acquisition. In P. Ackerman, R. J. Sternberg, & R. Glaser (eds.), *Individual differences.* New York: Freeman.

Sternberg, Robert J.; Forsythe, George B.; Hedlund, Jennifer; et al. (2000). *Practical intelligence in everyday life.* New York: Cambridge University Press.

Sternberg, Robert J.; Wagner, Richard K.; Williams, Wendy M.; & Horvath, Joseph A. (1995). Testing common sense. *American Psychologist, 50,* 912–927.

Stevenson, Harold W.; Chen, Chuansheng; & Lee, Shin-ying (1993, January 1). Mathematics achievement of Chinese, Japanese, and American children: Ten years later. *Science, 259,* 53–58.

Stevenson, Harold W., & Stigler, James W. (1992). *The learning gap.* New York: Summit.

Stewart, Abigail J., & Ostrove, Joan M. (1998). Women's personality in middle age: Gender, history, and midcourse corrections. *American Psychologist, 53,* 1185–1194.

Stewart, Abigail J., & Vandewater, Elizabeth A. (1999). "If I had it to do over again . . .": Midlife review, midcourse corrections, and women's well-being in midlife. *Journal of Personality and Social Psychology, 76,* 270–283.

Stimpson, Catherine (1996, Winter). Women's studies and its discontents. *Dissent, 43,* 67–75.

Stoch, M. B., & Smythe, P. M. (1963). Does undernutrition during infancy inhibit brain growth and subsequent intellectual development? *Archives of Diseases in Childhood, 38,* 546–552.

Strack, Fritz; Martin, Leonard L.; & Stepper, Sabine (1988). Inhibiting and facilitating conditions of the human smile: A nonobtrusive test of the facial-feedback hypothesis. *Journal of Social and Personality Psychology, 54,* 768–777.

Strahan, Erin J.; Spencer, Steven J.; & Zanna, Mark P. (in press). Subliminal priming and persuasion: Striking while the iron is hot. *Journal of Experimental Social Psychology.*

Straus, Murray A., & Kantor, Glenda Kaufman (1994). Corporal punishment of adolescents by parents: A risk factor in the epidemiology of depression, suicide, alcohol abuse, child abuse, and wife beating. *Adolescence, 29,* 543–561.

Strayer, David L., & Johnston, William A. (2001). Driven to distraction: Dual-task studies of simulated driving and conversing on a cellular telephone. *Psychological Science, 12,* 462–466.

Streissguth, Ann P.; Barr, Helen M.; Bookstein, Fred L.; et al. (1999). The long-term neurocognitive consequences of prenatal alcohol exposure: A 14-year study. *Psychological Science, 10,* 186–190.

Strickland, Bonnie R. (1989). Internal–external control expectancies: From contingency to creativity. *American Psychologist, 44,* 1–12.

Strickland, Tony L.; Lin, Keh-Ming; Fu, Paul; et al. (1995). Comparison of lithium ratio between African-American and Caucasian bipolar patients. *Biological Psychiatry, 37,* 325–330.

Strickland, Tony L.; Ranganath, Vijay; Lin, Keh-Ming; et al. (1991). Psychopharmacological considerations in the treatment of black American populations. *Psychopharmacology Bulletin, 27,* 441–448.

Stroebe, Margaret; Strobe, Wolfgang; & Schut, Henk (2001). Gender differences in adjustment to bereavement: An empirical and theoretical review. *Review of General Psychology, 5,* 62–83.

Strupp, Hans H., & Binder, Jeffrey (1984). *Psychotherapy in a new key.* New York: Basic Books.

Stunkard, Albert J. (ed.) (1980). *Obesity.* Philadelphia: Saunders.

Stunkard, Albert J.; Harris, J. R.; Pedersen, N. L.; & McClearn, G. E. (1990, May 24). The body-mass index of twins who have been reared apart. *New England Journal of Medicine, 322,* 1483–1487.

Suddendorf, Thomas, & Whiten, Andrew (2001). Mental evolution and development: Evidence for secondary representation in children, great apes, and other animals. *Psychological Bulletin, 127,* 629–650.

Sue, Stanley (1998). In search of cultural competence in psychotherapy and counseling. *American Psychologist, 53,* 440–448.

Suedfeld, Peter (1975). The benefits of boredom: Sensory deprivation reconsidered. *American Scientist, 63*(1), 60–69.

Suinn, Richard M. (2001). The terrible twos—Anger and anxiety. *American Psychologist, 56,* 27–36.

Sullivan, M. J.; Stanish, W.; Waite, H.; et al. (1998). Catastrophizing, pain, and disability in patients with soft-tissue injuries. *Pain, 77,* 253–260.

Sulloway, Frank J. (1992). *Freud, biologist of the mind: Beyond the psychoanalytic legend* (rev. ed.). Cambridge, MA: Harvard University Press.

Sundquist, J., & Winkleby, M. (2000, June). Country of birth, acculturation status and abdominal obesity in a national sample of Mexican-American women and men. *International Journal of Epidemiology, 29,* 470–477.

Suomi, Stephen J. (1991). Uptight and laid-back monkeys: Individual differences in the response to social challenges. In S. Branch, W. Hall, & J. E. Dooling (eds.), *Plasticity of development.* Cambridge, MA: MIT Press.

Super, Charles A., & Harkness, Sara (1994). The developmental niche. In W. J. Lonner & R. Malpass (eds.), *Psychology and culture.* Needham Heights, MA: Allyn & Bacon.

Suppes, Trisha; Baldessarini, Ross J.; Faedda, Gianni L.; & Tohen, Mauricio (1991). Risk of recurrence following discontinuation of lithium treatment in bipolar disorder. *Archives of General Psychiatry, 48,* 1082–1087.

Susman, Elizabeth J.; Inoff-Germain, Gale; Nottelmann, Editha D.; et al. (1987). Hormones, emotional dispositions, and aggressive attributes in young adolescents. *Child Development, 58,* 1114–1134.

Susser, Ezra; Neugebauer, Richard; Hoek, Hans W.; et al. (1996). Schizophrenia after prenatal famine: Further evidence. *Archives of General Psychiatry, 53,* 25–31.

Swain, Scott (1989). Covert intimacy: Closeness in men's friendships. In B. J. Risman & P. Schwartz (eds.), *Gender in intimate relationships.* Belmont, CA: Wadsworth.

Symons, Donald (1979). *The evolution of human sexuality.* New York: Oxford University Press.

Tajfel, Henri; Billig, M. G.; Bundy, R. P.; & Flament, C. (1971). Social categorization and intergroup behavior. *European Journal of Social Psychology, 1,* 149–178.

Tajfel, Henri, & Turner, John C. (1986). The social identity theory of intergroup behavior. In S. Worchel & W. G. Austin (eds.), *Psychology of intergroup relations.* Chicago: Nelson-Hall.

Tangney, June P.; Wagner, Patricia E.; Hill-Barlow, Deborah; et al. (1996). Relation of shame and guilt to constructive versus destructive responses to anger across the lifespan. *Journal of Personality and Social Psychology, 70,* 797–809.

Tartter, Vivien C. (1986). *Language processes.* New York: Holt, Rinehart and Winston.

Taubes, Gary (1998). As obesity rates rise, experts struggle to explain why. *Science, 280,* 1367–1368.

Tavris, Carol (1989). *Anger: The misunderstood emotion* (rev. ed.). New York: Simon & Schuster/Touchstone.

Taylor, Donald M., & Porter, Lana E. (1994). A multicultural view of stereotyping. In W. J. Lonner & R. Malpass (eds.), *Psychology and culture.* Needham Heights, MA: Allyn & Bacon.

Taylor, Eugene (2001). Positive psychology and humanistic psychology: A reply to Seligman. *Journal of Humanistic Psychology, 41,* 13–29.

Taylor, Shelley E., & Brown, Jonathon D. (1994). Positive illusions and well-being revisited: Separating fact from fiction. *Psychological Bulletin, 116,* 21–27.

Taylor, Shelley E., & Lobel, Marci (1989). Social comparison activity under threat: Downward evaluation and upward contacts. *Psychological Review, 96,* 569–575.

Taylor, Shelley E.; Kemeny, Margaret E.; Reed, Geoffrey M.; Bower, Julienne E.; & Gruenewald, Tara L. (2000a). Psychological resources, positive illusions, and health. *American Psychologist, 55,* 99–109.

Taylor, Shelley E.; Klein, Laura C.; Lewis, Brian P.; et al. (2000b). Biobehavioral responses to stress in females: Tend-and-befriend, not fight-or-flight. *Psychological Review, 107,* 411–429.

Taylor, Shelley E.; Lichtman, Rosemary R.; & Wood, Joanne V. (1984). Attributions, beliefs about control, and adjustment to breast cancer. *Journal of Personality and Social Psychology, 46,* 489–502.

Taylor, Shelley E.; Repetti, Rena; & Seeman, Teresa (1997). Health psychology: What is an unhealthy environment and how does it get under the skin? *Annual Review of Psychology* (Vol. 48). Palo Alto, CA: Annual Reviews.

Tellegen, Auke, & Waller, Niels G. (in press). Exploring personality through test construction: Development of the Multidimensional Personality Questionnaire. In S. R. Briggs & J. M. Cheek (eds.), *Personality measures: Development and evaluation* (Vol. 1). Greenwich, CT: JAI Press.

Terman, Lewis M., & Oden, Melita H. (1959). *Genetic studies of genius: Vol. 5. The gifted group at mid-life.* Stanford, CA: Stanford University Press.

Terman, Michael; Terman, Jiuan Su; & Ross, Donald C. (1998). A controlled trial of timed bright light and negative air ionization for treatment of winter depression. *Archives of General Psychiatry, 55,* 875–882.

Terrace, H. S. (1985). In the beginning was the "name." *American Psychologist, 40,* 1011–1028.

Thannickal, T. C.; Moore, R. Y.; Nienhuis, R.; et al. (2000). Reduced number of hypocretin neurons in human narcolepsy. *Neuron, 27,* 469–474.

Thase, Michael E.; Fasiczka, Amy L.; Berman, Susan R.; et al. (1998). Electroencephalographic sleep profiles before and after cognitive behavior therapy of depression. *Archives of General Psychiatry, 55*, 138–144.

Thase, Michael E.; Greenhouse, Joel B.; Frank, Ellen; et al. (1997). Treatment of major depression with psychotherapy or psychotherapy-pharmacotherapy combinations. *Archives of General Psychiatry, 54*, 1009–1015.

Thigpen, Corbett H., & Cleckley, Hervey M. (1984). On the incidence of multiple personality disorder: A brief communication. *International Journal of Clinical and Experimental Hypnosis, 32*, 63–66.

Thomassen, R.; van Schaick, H. W.; & Blansjaar, B. A. (1998). Prevalence of dementia over age 100. *Neurology, 50*, 283–286

Thompson, Clara (1943/1973). Penis envy in women. *Psychiatry, 6*, 123–125. Reprinted in J. B. Miller (ed.), *Psychoanalysis and women.* New York: Brunner/Mazel, 1973.

Thompson, Richard F. (1983). Neuronal substrates of simple associative learning: Classical conditioning. *Trends in Neurosciences, 6*, 270–275.

Thompson, Richard F. (1986). The neurobiology of learning and memory. *Science, 233*, 941–947.

Thompson, Richard F., & Kosslyn, Stephen M. (2000). Neural systems activated during visual mental imagery: A review and meta-analyses. In A. W. Toga & J. C. Mazziotta (eds.), *Brain mapping: The systems.* San Diego, CA: Academic Press.

Thompson, Ross A., & Nelson, Charles A. (2001). Developmental science and the media: Early brain development. *American Psychologist, 56*, 5–15.

Thompson, Suzanne C.; Nanni, Christopher; & Levine, Alexandra (1994). Primary versus secondary and central versus consequence-related control in HIV-positive men. *Journal of Personality and Social Psychology, 67*, 540–547.

Thorndike, Edward L. (1898). Animal intelligence: An experimental study of the associative processes in animals. *Psychological Review Monograph Supplement, 2* (Whole No. 8).

Thorndike, Edward L. (1903). *Educational psychology.* New York: Columbia University Teachers College.

Thorne, Avril (2000). Personal memory telling and personality development. *Personality and Social Psychology Review, 4*, 45–56.

Thornhill, Randy, & Palmer, Craig T. (2000). *A natural history of rape: Biological bases of sexual coercion.* Cambridge, MA: MIT Press.

Thorsteinsson, Einar B.; James, Jack E.; & Gregg, M. Elizabeth (1998). Effects of video-relayed social support on hemodynamic reactivity and salivary cortisol during laboratory-based behavioral challenge. *Health Psychology, 17*, 436–444.

Thun, M. J.; Peto, R.; Lopez, A. D.; et al. (1997). Alcohol consumption and mortality among middle-aged and elderly U.S. adults. *New England Journal of Medicine, 337*, 1705–1714.

Tice, Dianne M., & Baumeister, Roy F. (1997). Longitudinal study of procrastination, performance, stress, and health: The costs and benefits of dawdling. *Pscyhological Science, 8*, 454–458.

Tiedens, Larissa Z. (2001). Anger and advancement versus sadness and subjugation: The effect of negative emotion expressions on social status conferral. *Journal of Personality and Social Psychology, 80*, 86–94.

Tiefer, Leonore (1995). *Sex is not a natural act and other essays.* Boulder, CO: Westview Press.

Tiefer, Leonore (2000). Sexology and the pharmaceutical industry: The threat of co-optation. *Journal of Sex Research, 37*, 273–283.

Timmers, Monique; Fischer, Agneta H.; & Manstead, Antony S. R. (1998). Gender differences in motives for regulating emotions. *Personality and Social Psychology Bulletin, 24*, 974–985.

Todes, Daniel P. (1997). From the machine to the ghost within: Pavlov's transition from digestive physiology to conditioned reflexes. *American Psychologist, 52*, 947–955.

Tolman, Edward C. (1938). The determiners of behavior at a choice point. *Psychological Review, 45*, 1–35.

Tolman, Edward C., & Honzik, Chase H. (1930). Introduction and removal of reward and maze performance in rats. *University of California Publications in Psychology, 4*, 257–275.

Toma, J. G.; Akhavan, M.; Frenandes, K. J.; et al. (2001). Isolation of multipotent adult stem cells from the dermis of mammalian skin. *Nature Cell Biology, 3*, 778–784.

Tomasello, Michael (2000). Culture and cognitive development. *Current Directions in Psychological Science, 9*, 37–40.

Torrey, E. Fuller (1995). *Surviving schizophrenia* (3rd ed.). New York: Harper Perennial.

Totterdell, Peter; Kellett, Steve; Teuchmann, Katja; & Briner, Rob B. (1998). Evidence of mood linkage in work groups. *Journal of Personality and Social Psychology, 74*, 1504–1515.

Travis, John (2000). Snap, crackle, and feel good? Magnetic fields that map the brain may also treat its disorders. *Science News.*

Triandis, Harry C. (1994). *Culture and social behavior.* New York: McGraw-Hill.

Triandis, Harry C. (1995). *Individualism and collectivism.* Boulder, CO: Westview Press.

Triandis, Harry C. (1996). The psychological measurement of cultural syndromes. *American Psychologist, 51*, 407–415.

Trivers, Robert (1972). Parental investment and sexual selection. In B. Campbell (ed.), *Sexual selection and the descent of man.* New York: Aldine de Gruyter.

Tronick, Edward Z.; Morelli, Gilda A.; & Ivey, Paula K. (1992). The Efe forager infant and toddler's pattern of social relationships: Multiple and simultaneous. *Developmental Psychology, 28*, 568–577.

Tsuang, Ming T.; Bar, Jessica L.; Harley, Rebecca M.; Lyons, Michael J. (2001). The Harvard Twin Study of Substance Abuse: What we have learned. *Harvard Review of Psychiatry, 9*, 267–279.

Tsuang, Ming T.; Stone, William S.; & Faraone, Stephen V. (2001). Genes, environment and schizophrenia. *British Journal of Psychiatry, 178*(Suppl. 40), s18–s24.

Tulving, Endel (1985). How many memory systems are there? *American Psychologist, 40*, 385–398.

Turkheimer, Eric (2000). Three laws of behavior genetics and what they mean. *Current Directions in Psychological Science, 9*, 160–164.

Turner, C. F.; Ku, L.; Rogers, S. M.; et al. (1998). Adolescent sexual behavior, drug use, and violence: Increased reporting with computer survey technology. *Science, 280*, 867–873.

Tversky, Amos, & Kahneman, Daniel (1973). Availability: A heuristic for judging frequency and probability. *Cognitive Psychology, 5*, 207–232.

Tversky, Amos, & Kahneman, Daniel (1981). The framing of decisions and the psychology of choice. *Science, 211*, 453–458.

Twenge, Jean (2000). The age of anxiety? Birth cohort change in anxiety and neuroticism, 1952–1993. *Journal of Personality and Social Psychology, 79*, 1007–1021.

Tyler, Tom R. (1997). The psychology of legitimacy: A relational perspective on voluntary deference to authorities. *Personality and Social Psychology Review, 1*, 323–345.

Uchino, Bert N.; Cacioppo, John T.; & Kiecolt-Glaser, Janice K. (1996). The relationship between social support and physiological processes: A review with emphasis on underlying mechanisms and implications for health. *Psychological Bulletin, 119*, 488–531.

Uchino, Bert N.; Cacioppo, John T.; Malarkey, William; & Glaser, Ronald (1995). Individual differences in cardiac sympathetic control predict endocrine and immune responses to acute psychological stress. *Journal of Personality and Social Psychology, 69,* 736–743.

Ullian, Erik M.; Sapperstein, Stephanie K.; Christopherson, Karen S.; & Barres, Ben A. (2001). Control of synapse number by glia. *Science, 291,* 657–661.

Usher, JoNell A., & Neisser, Ulric (1993). Childhood amnesia and the beginnings of memory for four early life events. *Journal of Experimental Psychology: General, 122,* 155–165.

Vaillant, George E. (1983). *The natural history of alcoholism: Causes, patterns, and paths to recovery.* Cambridge, MA: Harvard University Press.

Vaillant, George E. (1995). *The natural history of alcoholism revisited.* Cambridge, MA: Harvard University Press.

Vaillant, George E. (ed.) (1992). *Ego mechanisms of defense.* Washington, DC: American Psychiatric Press.

Valenstein, Elliot (1986). *Great and desperate cures: The rise and decline of psychosurgery and other radical treatments for mental illness.* New York: Basic Books.

Valenstein, Elliot (1998). *Blaming the brain: The truth about drugs and mental health.* New York: The Free Press.

Valian, Virginia (1998). *Why so slow? The advancement of women.* Cambridge, MA: MIT Press.

Van Boven, Leaf; Kamada, Akiko; & Gilovich, Thomas (1999). The perceiver as perceived: Everyday intuitions about the correspondence bias. *Journal of Personality and Social Psychology, 77,* 1188–1199.

Van Cantfort, Thomas E., & Rimpau, James B. (1982). Sign language studies with children and chimpanzees. *Sign Language Studies, 34,* 15–72.

Van de Castle, R. (1994). *Our dreaming mind.* New York: Ballantine Books.

van Praag, H.; Kempermann, G.; & Gage, F. H. (1999). Running increases cell proliferation and neurogenesis in the adult mouse dentate gyrus. *Nature Neuroscience, 2,* 266–270.

Vandello, Joseph A., & Cohen, Dov (1999). Patterns of individualism and collectivism across the United States. *Journal of Personality and Social Psychology, 77,* 279–292.

Vandenberg, Brian (1985). Beyond the ethology of play. In A. Gottfried & C. C. Brown (eds.), *Play interactions.* Lexington, MA: Lexington Books.

Vastag, B. (2001). Congressional autism hearings continue: No evidence MMR vaccine causes disorder. *Journal of the American Medical Association, 285:* 2567–2569.

Verhaeghen, Paul, & Salthouse, Timothy A. (1997). Meta-analyses of age-cognition relations in adulthood: Estimates of linear and nonlinear age effects and structural models. *Psychological Bulletin, 122,* 231–249.

Vertosick, Frank T. (1997, October). Lobotomy's back. *Discover,* 66–72.

Vila, J., & Beech, H. R. (1980). Premenstrual symptomatology: An interaction hypothesis. *British Journal of Social and Clinical Psychology, 19,* 73–80.

Vita, A. J.; Terry, R. B.; Hubert, H. B.; & Fries, J. F. (1998). Aging, health risks, and cumulative disability. *New England Journal of Medicine, 338,* 1035–1041.

Volkow, Nora D.; Chang, Linda; Wang, Gene-Jack; et al. (2001). Association of dopamine transporter reduction with psychomotor impairment in methamphetamine abusers. *American Journal of Psychiatry, 158,* 377–382.

Von Lang, Jochen, & Sibyll, Claus (eds.) (1984). *Eichmann interrogated: Transcripts from the archives of the Israeli police.* New York: Random House.

Voyer, Daniel; Voyer, Susan; & Bryden, M. P. (1995). Magnitude of sex differences in spatial abilities: A meta-analysis and consideration of critical variables. *Psychological Bulletin, 117,* 250–270.

Vroon, Piet (1997). *Smell: The secret seducer.* [Trans. by Paul Vincent.] New York: Farrar, Straus & Giroux.

Vygotsky, Lev (1962). *Thought and language.* Cambridge, MA: MIT Press.

Vygotsky, Lev (1978). *Mind in society: The development of higher psychological processes.* Cambridge, MA: Harvard University Press. (Originals published in 1930, 1933, and 1935.)

Wadden, Thomas A.; Foster, G. D.; Letizia, K. A.; & Mullen, J. L. (1990, August 8). Long-term effects of dieting on resting metabolic rate in obese outpatients. *Journal of the American Medical Association, 264,* 707–711.

Wagenaar, Willem A. (1986). My memory: A study of autobiographical memory over six years. *Cognitive Psychology, 18,* 225–252.

Wagner, Anthony D.; Schacter, Daniel L.; Rotte, Michael; et al. (1998). Building memories: Remembrance and forgetting of verbal experiences as predicted by brain activity. *Science, 281,* 1188–1191.

Wakefield, Jerome C. (1992). Disorder as harmful dysfunction: A conceptual critique of DSM-III-R's definition of mental disorder. *Psychological Review, 99,* 232–247.

Walker, Anne (1994). Mood and well-being in consecutive menstrual cycles: Methodological and theoretical implications. *Psychology of Women Quarterly, 18,* 271–290.

Walker, Lawrence J.; de Vries, Brian; & Trevethan, Shelley D. (1987). Moral stages and moral orientations in real-life and hypothetical dilemmas. *Child Development, 58,* 842–858.

Walker-Andrews, Arlene S. (1997). Infants' perception of expressive behaviors: Differentiation of multimodal information. *Psychological Bulletin, 121,* 437–456.

Wallach, Michael A., & Wallach, Lise (1983). *Psychology's sanction for selfishness: The error of egoism in theory and therapy.* New York: Freeman.

Wallbott, Harald G.; Ricci-Bitti, Pio; & Bänninger-Huber, Eva (1986). Non-verbal reactions to emotional experiences. In K. R. Scherer, H. G. Wallbott, & A. B. Summerfield (eds.), *Experiencing emotion: A cross-cultural study.* Cambridge, England: Cambridge University Press.

Waller, Niels G.; Kojetin, Brian A.; Bouchard, Thomas J., Jr.; et al. (1990). Genetic and environmental influences on religious interests, attitudes, and values: A study of twins reared apart and together. *Psychological Science, 1,* 138–142.

Wallerstein, Judith; Lewis, Julia; and Blakeslee, Sandra (2000). *The unexpected legacy of divorce: A 25-year landmark study.* New York: Hyperion.

Walsh, B. Timothy, & Devlin, Michael J. (1998). Eating disorders: Progress and problems. *Science, 280,* 1387–1390.

Wandersman, Abraham, & Nation, Maury (1998). Urban neighborhoods and mental health: Psychological contributions to understanding toxicity, resilience, and interventions. *American Psychologist, 53,* 647–656.

Wang, Alvin Y.; Thomas, Margaret H.; & Ouellette, Judith A. (1992). The keyword mnemonic and retention of second-language vocabulary words. *Journal of Educational Psychology, 84,* 520–528.

Wang, Qi (2001). Culture effects on adults' earliest childhood recollection and self-description: Implications for the relation between memory and the self. *Journal of Personality and Social Psychology, 81,* 220–233.

Wark, Gillian R., & Krebs, Dennis (1996). Gender and dilemma differences in real-life moral judgment. *Developmental Psychology, 32,* 220–230.

Warren, Gayle H., & Raynes, Anthony E. (1972). Mood changes during three conditions of alcohol intake. *Quarterly Journal of Studies on Alcohol, 33,* 979–989.

Washburn, David A., & Rumbaugh, Duane M. (1991). Ordinal judgments of numerical symbols by macaques (*Macaca mulatta*). *Psychological Science, 2,* 190–193.

Wasserman, Eric W., & Lisanby, Sarah H. (2001). Therapeutic application of repetitive transcranial magnetic stimulation: A review. *Clinical Neurophysiology, 112,* 1367–1377.

Watson, David; Hubbard, Brock; & Wiese, David (2000). Self-other agreement in personality and affectivity: The role of acquaintanceship, trait visibility, and assumed similarity. *Journal of Personality and Social Psychology, 78,* 546–558.

Watson, John B. (1925). *Behaviorism.* New York: Norton.

Watson, John B., & Rayner, Rosalie (1920). Conditioned emotional reactions. *Journal of Experimental Psychology, 3,* 1–14.

Watters, Ethan, & Ofshe, Richard (1999). *Therapy's delusions.* New York: Scribner.

Webb, Wilse B., & Cartwright, Rosalind D. (1978). Sleep and dreams. In M. Rosenzweig & L. Porter (eds.), *Annual Review of Psychology, 29,* 223–252.

Webster, Richard (1995). *Why Freud was wrong.* New York: Basic Books.

Wechsler, David (1955). *Manual for the Wechsler Adult Intelligence Scale.* New York: Psychological Corporation.

Wegner, Daniel M., & Gold, Daniel B. (1995). Fanning old flames: Emotional and cognitive effects of suppressing thoughts of a past relationship. *Journal of Personality and Social Psychology, 68,* 782–792.

Weil, Andrew T. (1972/1986). *The natural mind: A new way of looking at drugs and the higher consciousness.* Boston: Houghton Mifflin.

Weil, Andrew T. (1974a, June). Parapsychology: Andrew Weil's search for the true Geller. *Psychology Today,* 45–50.

Weil, Andrew T. (1974b, July). Parapsychology: Andrew Weil's search for the true Geller: Part II. The letdown. *Psychology Today,* 74–78, 82.

Weiner, Bernard (1986). *An attributional theory of motivation and emotion.* New York: Springer-Verlag.

Weiss, Erica; Longhurst, James G.; & Mazure, Carolyn M. (1999). Childhood sexual abuse as a risk factor for depression in women: Psychological and neurological correlates. *American Journal of Psychiatry, 156,* 816–828.

Weissman, Myrna M.; Markowitz, John C.; & Klerman, Gerald L. (2000). *Comprehensive guide to interpersonal psychotherapy.* New York: Basic Books.

Weisz, John R.; Weiss, Bahr; Han, Susan S.; et al. (1995). Effects of psychotherapy with children and adolescents revisited: A meta-analysis of treatment outcome studies. *Psychological Bulletin, 117,* 450–468.

Weitzenhoffer, André M. (1996). Catalepsy tests: What do they tell us? *International Journal of Clinical and Experimental Hypnosis, 44,* 307–323.

Wellenkamp, Jane (1995). Cultural similarities and differences regarding emotional disclosure: Some examples from Indonesia and the Pacific. In J. W. Pennebaker (ed.), *Emotion, disclosure, and health.* Washington, DC: American Psychological Association.

Wells, Gary L.; Small, Mark; Penrod, Steven; et al. (1998). Eyewitness identification procedures: Recommendations for lineups and photospreads. *Law and Human Behavior, 22,* 602–647.

Wender, Paul H., & Klein, Donald F. (1981). *Mind, mood, and medicine: A guide to the new biopsychiatry.* New York: Farrar, Straus and Giroux.

Werner, Emmy E. (1989). High-risk children in young adulthood: A longitudinal study from birth to 32 years. *American Journal of Orthopsychiatry, 59,* 72–81.

Werner, Peter; Pitt, D.; & Raine, C. S. (2001). Multiple sclerosis: altered glutamate homeostasis in lesions correlates with aligodendrocyte and axonal damage. Annals of Neurology, 50, 169–180.

West, Melissa O., & Prinz, Ronald J. (1987). Parental alcoholism and childhood psychopathology. *Psychological Bulletin, 102,* 204–218.

Westen, Drew (1998). The scientific legacy of Sigmund Freud: Toward a psychodynamically informed psychological science. *Psychological Bulletin, 124,* 333–371.

Westen, Drew, & Shedler, Jonathan (1999). Revising and assessing axis II, Part II: Toward an empirically based and clinically useful classification of personality disorders. *American Journal of Psychiatry, 156,* 273–285.

Westermeyer, Joseph (1995). Cultural aspects of substance abuse and alcoholism: Assessment and management. *Psychiatric Clinics of North America, 18,* 589–605.

Wethington, Elaine (2000). Expecting stress: Americans and the "midlife crisis." *Motivation & Emotion, 24,* 85–103.

Wheeler, David L. (1998, September 11). Neuroscientists take stock of brain-imaging studies. *Chronicle of Higher Education,* A20–A21.

Wheeler, Mark E.; Petersen, Steven E.; & Buckner, Randy L. (2000). Memory's echo: Vivid remembering reactivates sensory-specific cortex. *Proceedings of the National Academy of Sciences, 97*(20), 11125–11129.

Whisman, Mark A. (1993). Mediators and moderators of change in cognitive therapy of depression. *Psychological Bulletin, 114,* 248–265.

Whitam, Frederick L.; Diamond, Milton; & Martin, James (1993). Homosexual orientation in twins: A report on 61 pairs and 3 triplet sets. *Archives of Sexual Behavior, 22,* 187–206.

Whitehouse, W. G.; Dinges, D. F.; Orne, E. C.; & Orne, M. T. (1988). Hypnotic hypermnesia: Enhanced memory accessibility or report bias? *Journal of Abnormal Psychology, 97,* 289–295.

Whiting, Beatrice B., & Edwards, Carolyn P. (1988). *Children of different worlds: The formation of social behavior.* Cambridge, MA: Harvard University Press.

Whiting, Beatrice, & Whiting, John (1975). *Children of six cultures.* Cambridge, MA: Harvard University Press.

Wickelgren, Ingrid (1997). Estrogen stakes claim to cognition. *Science, 276,* 675–678.

Widiger, Thomas, & Clark, Lee Anna (2000). Toward DSM-V and the classification of psychopathology. *Psychological Bulletin, 126,* 946–963.

Wiederhold, Brenda K., & Wiederhold, Mark D. (2000). Lessons learned from 600 virtual reality sessions. *CyberPsychology & Behavior, 3,* 393–400.

Wiggins, Jerry S. (ed.) (1996). *The five-factor model of personality: Theoretical perspectives.* New York: Guilford Press.

Williams, Janice E.; Paton, Catherine C.; Siegler, Ilene C.; et al. (2000). Anger proneness predicts coronary heart disease risk. *Circulation, 101,* 2034–2039.

Williams, Kipling D., & Karau, Steven J. (1991). Social loafing and social compensation: The effects of expectations of co-worker performance. *Journal of Personality and Social Psychology, 61,* 570–581.

Williams, Redford B., Jr.; Barefoot, John C.; & Shekelle, Richard B. (1985). The health consequences of hostility. In M. A. Chesney & R. H. Rosenman (eds.), *Anger and hostility in cardiovascular and behavioral disorders.* New York: Hemisphere.

Willie, Charles V.; Rieker, Patricia P.; Kramer, Bernard M.; & Brown, Bertram S. (eds.) (1995). *Mental health, racism, and sexism* (rev. ed.). Pittsburgh: University of Pittsburgh Press.

Willis, Sherry L. (1987). Cognitive training and everyday competence. In K. W. Schaie (ed.), *Annual review of gerontology and geriatrics* (Vol. 7). New York: Springer.

Wilner, Daniel; Walkley, Rosabelle; & Cook, Stuart (1955). *Human relations in interracial housing.* Minneapolis: University of Minnesota Press.

Wilson, Edward O. (1975). *Sociobiology: The new synthesis.* Cambridge, MA: Belknap/Harvard University Press.

Wilson, Edward O. (1978). *On human nature.* Cambridge, MA: Harvard University Press.

Wilson, G. Terence, & Fairburn, Christopher G. (1993). Cognitive treatments for eating disorders. *Journal of Consulting and Clinical Psychology, 61,* 261–269.

Wilson, Matthew A., & Louie, Kenway (2001). Temporally structured replay of awake hippocampal ensemble activity during rapid eye movement sleep. *Neuron, 29,* 145–156.

Wilson, Timothy D.; Lindsey, S.; & Schooler, T. Y. (2000). A model of dual attitudes. *Psychological Review, 107,* 101–126.

Winick, Myron; Meyer, Knarig Katchadurian; & Harris, Ruth C. (1975). Malnutrition and environmental enrichment by early adoption. *Science, 190,* 1173–1175.

Winnicott, D. W. (1957/1990). *Home is where we start from.* New York: Norton.

Winslade, William J. (1998). *Confronting traumatic brain injury: Devastation, hope, and healing.* New Haven: Yale University Press.

Wispé, Lauren G., & Drambarean, Nicholas C. (1953). Physiological need, word frequency, and visual duration thresholds. *Journal of Experimental Psychology, 46,* 25–31.

Witelson, Sandra F.; Glazer, I. I.; & Kigar, D. L. (1994). Sex differences in numerical density of neurons in human auditory association cortex. *Society for Neuroscience Abstracts, 30* (Abstr. No. 582.12).

Witelson, Sandra; Kigar, D. L.; & Harvey, T. (1999). The exceptional brian of Albert Einstein. *Lancet, 353,* 2149–2153.

Wittchen, Hans-Ulrich; Kessler, Ronald C.; Zhao, Shanyang; & Abelson, Jamie (1995). Reliability and clinical validity of UM-CIDI DSM-III-R generalized anxiety disorder. *Journal of Psychiatric Research, 29,* 95–110.

Wittig, Michele A., & Grant-Thompson, Sheila (1998). The utility of Allport's conditions of intergroup contact for predicting perceptios of improved racial attitudes and beliefs. *Journal of Social Issues, 54,* 795–812.

Witvliet, Charlotte vanOyen; Ludwig, Thomas E.; & Vander Laan, Kelly L. (2001). Granting forgiveness or harboring grudges: Implications for emotion, physiology, and health. *Psychological Science, 12,* 117–123.

Wolfson, Amy R., and Carskadon, Mary A. (1998). Sleep schedules and daytime functioning in adolescents. *Child Development, 69,* 875–887.

Wood, James M.; Nezworski, Teresa; & Stejskal, William J. (1996). The comprehensive system for the Rorschach: A critical examination. *Psychological Science, 7,* 3–10.

Wood, Joanne V.; Michela, John L.; & Giordano, Caterina (2000). Downward comparison in everyday life: Reconciling self-enhancement models with the mood-cognition priming model. *Journal of Personality and Social Psychology, 79,* 563–579.

Wood, Wendy; Lundgren, Sharon; Ouellette, Judith A.; et al. (1994). Minority influence: A meta-analytic review of social influence processes. *Psychological Bulletin, 115,* 323–345.

Woodbury, D.; Schwarz, E. J; Prockop, D. J.; & Black, I. B. (2000). Adult rat and human bone marrow stromal cells differentiate into neurons. *Journal of Neuroscience Research, 61,* 364–370.

Woody, Erik Z., & Bowers, Kenneth S. (1994). A frontal assault on dissociated control. In S. J. Lynn & J. W. Rhue (eds.), *Dissociation: Clinical, theoretical and research perspectives.* New York: Guilford.

Woody, Erik Z., & Sadler, Pamela (1998). On reintegrating dissociated theories: Comment on Kirsch and Lynn (1998). *Psychological Bulletin, 123,* 192–197.

Wooley, Susan; Wooley, O. Wayne; & Dyrenforth, Susan (1979). Theoretical, practical, and social issues in behavioral treatments of obesity. *Journal of Applied Behavior Analysis, 12,* 3–25.

Wulsin, L. R.; Vaillant, G. E.; & Wells, V. E. (1999). A systematic review of the mortality of depression. *Psychosomatic Medicine, 61,* 6–17.

Wurtman, Richard J. (1982). Nutrients that modify brain function. *Scientific American, 264*(4), 50–59.

Wurtman, Richard J., & Lieberman, Harris R. (eds.) (1982–1983). Research strategies for assessing the behavioral effects of foods and nutrients. *Journal of Psychiatric Research, 17*(2) [whole issue].

Wygant, Steven A. (1997). Moral reasoning about real-life dilemmas: Paradox in research using the Defining Issues Test. *Personality and Social Psychology Bulletin, 23,* 1022–1033.

Yalom, Irvin D. (1989). *Love's executioner and other tales of psychotherapy.* New York: Basic Books.

Yang, Kuo-shu, & Bond, Michael H. (1990). Exploring implicit personality theories with indigenous or imported constructs: The Chinese case. *Journal of Personality and Social Psychology, 58,* 1087–1095.

Yapko, Michael (1994). *Suggestions of abuse: True and false memories of childhood sexual trauma.* New York: Simon & Schuster.

Yardley, Jim (2001, September 8). Despair plagued mother held in children's deaths. *The New York Times,* A16.

Yazigi, R. A.; Odem, R. R.; & Polakoski, K. L. (1991, October 9). Demonstration of specific binding of cocaine to human spermatozoa. *Journal of the American Medical Association, 266*(14), 1956–1959.

Yoder, Janice D., & Kahn, Arnold S. (1993). Working toward an inclusive psychology of women. *American Psychologist, 48,* 846–850.

Young, Malcolm P., & Yamane, Shigeru (1992). Sparse population coding of faces in the inferotemporal cortex. *Science, 256,* 1327–1331.

Young-Eisendrath, Polly (1993). *You're not what I expected: Learning to love the opposite sex.* New York: Morrow.

Yzerbyt, Vincent Y.; Corneille, Olivier; Dumont, Muriel; & Hahn, Kirstin (2001). The dispositional inference strikes back: Situational focus and dispositional suppression in causal attribution. *Journal of Personality and Social Psychology, 81,* 365–376.

Zahn-Waxler, Carolyn (1996). Environment, biology, and culture: Implications for adolescent development. *Developmental Psychology, 32,* 571–573.

Zajonc, Robert B. (1968). Attitudinal effects of mere exposure. *Journal of Personality and Social Psychology, 9,* Monograph Supplement 2, 1–27.

Zelicoff, Alan P. (2001, July/August). Polygraphs and the national labs: Dangerous ruse undermines national security. *Skeptical Inquirer,* 21–23.

Zhang, Yiying; Proenca, Ricardo; Maffei, Margherita; et al. (1994). Positional cloning of the mouse obese gene and its human homologue. *Nature, 372*(6505), 425–432.

Zhu, L. X.; Sharma, S.; Stolina, M.; et al. (2000). Delta-9-tetrahydrocannabinol inhibits antitumor immunity by a CB2 receptor-mediated, cytokine-dependent pathway. *Journal of Immunology, 165,* 373–380.

Zilbergeld, Bernie (1983). *The shrinking of America: Myths of psychological change.* Boston: Little, Brown.

Zilbergeld, Bernie (1992). *The new male sexuality.* New York: Bantam.

Zimbardo, Philip G. (1970). The human choice: Individuation, reason, and order versus deindividuation, impulse, and chaos. In W. J. Arnold & D. Levine (eds.), *Nebraska Symposium on Motivation, 1969.* Lincoln, NE: University of Nebraska Press.

Zimbardo, Philip G., & Leippe, Michael R. (1991). *The psychology of attitude change and social influence.* New York: McGraw-Hill.

Zimmer, Lynn, & Morgan, John P. (1997). *Marijuana myths, marijuana fact: A review of the scientific evidence.* New York: Lindesmith Center.

Zinberg, Norman (1974). The search for rational approaches to heroin use. In P. G. Bourne (ed.), *Addiction.* New York: Academic Press.

Zorrilla, L. T.; Cannon, T. D.; Kronenberg, S.; et al. (1997, December 15). Structural brain abnormalities in schizophrenia: A family study. *Biological Psychiatry, 42,* 1080–1086.

Zurbriggen, Eileen L. (2000). Social motives and cognitive power-sex associations: Predictors of aggressive sexual behavior. *Journal of Personality and Social Psychology, 78,* 559–581.

Credits

Text, Table, and Figure Credits

CHAPTER 2 *Page 38:* Figure 2.1, (a) Jose L. Pelaez, Inc./Corbis/Stock Market, (b) Unicorn Stock Photos; *p. 48:* Figure 2.2, (a & b) From *Understanding Statistics*, 1ˢᵗ edition, by R.L.D. Wright Copyright © 1976. Reprinted with permission of Brooks/Cole, an imprint of the Wadsworth Group, a division of Thomson Learning. Fax 800 730–2215, (c) *Introduction To The Practice of Statistics* by David S. Moore & George P. McCabe 1989, 1993, 1999 by W.H. Freeman and Company. Used with permission.

CHAPTER 3 *Page 71:* Figure 3.1, (L) Photo Researchers, Inc., (R) Macmillan Publishers; *p. 84:* Figure 3.2, (R) Reuters/Fred Prouser/Getty Images, Inc.

CHAPTER 4 *Page 117:* Figure 4.8, (a) Hank Morgan/Science Source/Photo Researchers, Inc., (b) Michael E. Phelps/Mazziotta UCLA School of Medicine, (c) Howard Sochurek, Inc.; *p. 123:* Figure 4.12, from Kim, Relkin, Lee, & Hirsch, "Nature" 388, 171–174 (1997). Courtesy of Dr. Joy Hirsch, Head, fMRI Laboratory Memorial Sloan-Kettering Cancer Center; *p. 124:* (a) The Warren Anatomical Museum, Francis A. Countway Library of Medicine, Harvard Medical School, (b) from: Damasio H, Grabowski T, Frank R, Galaburda AM, Damasio AR: "The Return of Phineas Gage: Clues about the brain from a famous patient." *Science*, 264: 1102–1105, 1994. Department of Neurology and Image Analysis Facility, University of Iowa; *p. 133:* Figure 4.16, Michael D. Phillips/Radiology Society of North America.

CHAPTER 5 *Page 155:* Figure 5.3, Figure from "Physiology of sleep and dreaming" by Dennis Kelly from *Principles Of Neural Science*, Copyright © 1981, reproduced with permission of The McGraw-Hill Companies; *p. 174:* Excerpt from *Encounters: A Psychologist Reveals Case Studies Of Abduction By Extraterrestrials* by Edith Fiore. Copyright © 1989 by Doubleday. Reprinted with permission.

CHAPTER 6 *Page 195:* Figure 6.5, Greebles created by Isabel Gauthier (Vanderbilt University), Scott Yu and Michael J. Tarr; *p. 197:* Figure 6.6, M.C. Escher's "Circle Limit IV" Copyright © 2001 Cordon Art B.V.–Baarn-Holland. All rights reserved; *p. 202:* Figure 6.8, Josef Albers, "Plate VI-3 from 'Interaction of Color'". Copyright © Josef Albers Foundation/Yale University Press. Copyright © 2000 The Josef and Anni Albers Foundation/Artists Rights Society (ARS), New York; *p. 205:* Table 6.1, Table from "Sound intensity levels in the environment." Reprinted by permission of the Academy of Otolaryngology-Head and Neck Surgery, Washington, D.C.; *p. 211:* Figure 6.13, From "Taste Test" from *Archives of Otolaryngology*, 90, pp. 367–73, 1969. Copyright © 1969 American Medical Association. Reprinted by permission; *p. 215:* Figure 6.14, (L) Joseph Campos.

CHAPTER 7 *Page 230:* Figure 7.1, (L) The Granger Collection; *p. 232:* Figure 7.2, Figure from "Acquisition and extinction of a salivary response" by Ivan P. Pavlov from *Conditioned Reflexes*, trans. G.V. Anrep. Copyright © 1927. Reprinted by permission of Oxford University Press, Oxford, England; *p. 244:* Figure 7.4, (R) Joe McNally Photography; *p. 247:* Figure 7.5, Adapted from "Teaching Machines" by B.F. Skinner in *Scientific American*, November 1961, p. 96. Reprinted with permission; *p. 255:* Figure 7.6, Reprinted with permission from *Psychology Today Magazine*, Copyright © 1974 Sussex Publishers, Inc.; *p. 257:* Figure 7.7, From *Introduction and removal of reward and maze performance in rats* by E.C. Tolman and C.H. Honzik from PSYCHOLOGY, 4, 1930.

CHAPTER 8 *Page 115:* Figure 8.1, Copyright © 1965 by Stanley Milgram. From the film OBEDIENCE, distributed by Penn State Media Sales; *p. 145:* Figure 8.4, Cunningham, William A.; Preacher, Kristopher J.; and Banaji, Mahzarin R. "Implicit Attitude Measures: Consistency, Stability, and Convergent Validity," *Psychological Science*, 12, p. 165. Copyright © 2001 Blackwell Publishers Ltd. Reprinted with permission.

CHAPTER 9 *Page 318:* Table 9.1, Copyright © 1989 by the American Psychological Association. Adapted with permission; *p. 319:* Excerpt from King, Patricia M. and Kitchener, Karen Strohm, *Developing Reflective Judgment: Understanding and Promoting Intellectual Growth and Critical Thinking In Adolescents and Adults.* Copyright © 1994 Jossey-Bass Inc., Publishers. This material is used by permission of John Wiley & Sons, Inc.; *p. 328:* Figure 9.2, (R) Copyright © Corbis; *p. 332:* Table 9.2, Table from *Sample Items from the Stanford-Binet Intelligence Scale* by Lewis M. Terman and Maud A. Merrill. Copyright © 1973 by Houghton Mifflin Company. Reprinted by permission of Riverside Publishing Co.; *p. 333:* Figure 9.4, Figure from "Performance tasks on the Weschler tests" by Lee J. Cronbach from *Essentials of Psychological Testing*, 4ᵗʰ edition, p. 208. Copyright © 1984 by HarperCollins Publishers. Reprinted by permission; *p. 343:* Figure 9.6, From "Knowledge of Number: Its Evolution and Ontogeny" by Susan Carey in *Science*, 282, 23 October 1998, p. 641. Reprinted by permission of Elizabeth Brannon.

CHAPTER 10 *Page 359:* Figure 10.1, Dr. Elizabeth Loftus; *p. 361:* Figure 10.2, Figure from "Serial Position Effect" in *Memory* by Elizabeth Loftus, 1980, p. 25. Copyright © 1980 by Addison Wesley Publishing Company. Reprinted by permission; *p. 374:* Figure 10.7, Fig. 3, from Reber, PJ, Stark, CEL & Squire, LR (1998). Contrasting cortical activity associated with category memory and recognition memory. Learning & Memory, 5, p. 420–428; *p. 380:* Figure 10.9, (b) Reprinted by permission from *Psychology Today Magazine*. Copyright © 1970 (Sussex Publishers, Inc.); *p. 381:* Figure 10.10, Loftus EF, Miller DG, Burns HJ, (1978). Semantic integration of verbal information into a visual memory. *Journal of Experimental Psychology; Human Learning and Memory*, 4, 19–31.

Photographs and Cartoons

Phototake NYC; *p. 112:* AP/Wide World Photos; *p. 113:* Sidney Harris; *p. 115:* Keith Brofsky/Getty Images, Inc./PhotoDisc, Inc.; *p. 116:* Photo Lennart Nilsson/Albert Bonniers Forlag AB; *p. 131:* Rainbow; *p. 132:* Sidney Harris; *p. 134:* Jennifer Berman/Jennifer K. Berman.

CHAPTER 5 *Page 140:* Bill Frymire/Masterfile Corporation; *p. 143:* (L) Tom Ives/Corbis/Sygma, (R) Tom Ives/Corbis/Sygma; *p. 144:* Magnum Photos, Inc.; *p. 145:* Sidney Harris; *p. 146:* Bryan and Cherry Alexander; *p. 147:* PhotoEdit; *p. 149:* Copyright © The New Yorker Collection 1999 William Haefeli from cartoonbank.com. All rights reserved; *p. 151:* (L) Photo Researchers, Inc., (TR) Jessica Offir/Jessica T. Offir, (BR) R. Hutchings/PhotoEdit; *p. 154:* (T) Chandoha Photography, (B) Chandoha Photography; *p. 156:* Copyright © The New Yorker Collection 1973 Dana Fradon from cartoonbank.com. All rights reserved; *p. 158:* (L) Photo Researchers, Inc., (R) Photo Researchers, Inc., (B) Photo Researchers, Inc.; *p. 163:* (L) Woodfin Camp & Associates, (C) Photo Researchers, Inc., (R) Kal Muller/Woodfin Camp & Associates; *p. 166:* Science Source/Photo Researchers; *p. 168:* (L) Index Stock Imagery, Inc., (R) The Image Works; *p. 169:* (L) The Granger Collection, (R) The Granger Collection; *p. 171:* Bookstaver/AP/Wide World Photos; *p. 172:* Sidney Harris; *p. 173:* Ernest R. Hilgard.

CHAPTER 6 *Page 180:* Bill Brooks/Masterfile Corporation; *p. 185:* (L) Gary Retherford, (R) Gary Retherford; *p. 188:* (L) National Library of Medicine, (R) National Library of Medicine; *p. 189:* Corbis/Sygma; *p. 194:* Giuseppe Arcimboldo (1527–93), "Vertumnus (Emperor Rudolf II)," 1590. Oil on wood, 70,5 x 57,5 cm. Stocklosters Slott, Sweden; *p. 200:* (L) Roy Schneider/Corbis/Stock Market, (T) Erik Svesson/Corbis/Stock Market, (B) Photo Researchers, Inc.; *p. 201:* (TL) Nicholas Desciose/Photo Researchers, Inc., (BL) Cameramann International, (TR) Topham/The Image Works, (BR) Copyright Barrie Rokeach 2002. All rights reserved; *p. 207:* Molly Webster/Copyright © 1982. Reprinted with permission of Discover Magazine, 11/82p92; *p. 211:* Chris Lisle/Corbis; *p. 213:* Steve Simoneau/AP/Wide World Photos; *p. 214:* M. Grecco/Stock Boston; *p. 217:* (L) Bill Steber/Nashville Tennessean, (R) Bill Steber/Nashville Tennessean; *p. 222:* Culver Pictures.

CHAPTER 7 *Page 228:* Allan Davey/Masterfile Corporation; *p. 235:* Getty Images Inc.; *p. 238:* The Image Works; *p. 240:* Reprinted with special permission of King Features Syndicate; *p. 248:* (L) Stephen Ferry/Getty Images, Inc., (R) Guide Horse Foundation; *p. 249:* Courtesy of The Dominion Post; *p. 251:* Jim Gensheimer/San Jose Mercury News; *p. 252:* D. Young-Wolff/PhotoEdit; *p. 253:* Peter Glass/Peter Glass Photography; *p. 256:* Copyright © The New Yorker Collection 1986 Lee Lorenz from cartoonbank.com. All rights reserved; *p. 259:* Albert Bandura, D. Ross & S.A. Ross, Imitation of film-mediated aggressive models. *Journal of Abnormal and Social Psychology, 1963, 66.* P.8; *p. 260:* Andrew Lichtenstein/Corbis/Sygma.

CHAPTER 8 *Page 110:* Pierre Tremblay; *p. 112:* (L) AP/Wide World Photos, (C) Getty Images, Inc., (R) Corbis/Sygma; *p. 113:* Giuliano Colliva/Getty Images, Inc.; *p. 114:* Robert Azzi/Woodfin Camp & Associates; *p. 116:* Stanley Milgram/Alexandra Milgram; *p. 117:* Copyright © Bettman/Corbis; *p. 118:* David Harvey/ National Geo-

graphic Society; *p. 119:* AP/Wide World Photos; *p. 123:* Getty Images, Inc.; *p. 124:* Copyright © The New Yorker Collection 2001 Lee Lorenz from cartoonbank.com. All rights reserved; *p. 125:* (T) PhotoEdit, (B) A. Ramey/PhotoEdit; *p. 127:* The Sankei Shimbun; *p. 129:* (L) Alex Webb/Magnum Photos, Inc., (R) AP/Wide World Photos; *p. 130:* Sidney Harris; *p. 132:* The Image Works; *p. 133:* Philip G. Zimbardo, Inc.; *p. 134:* AP/Wide World Photos; *p. 135:* (L) Dawson-Coy/SIPA Press, (R) Shelly Katz Photographer; *p. 137:* (T) Tony Freeman/PhotoEdit, (C) Tony Freeman/PhotoEdit, (B) Tony Freeman/PhotoEdit; *p. 140:* (L) United States Holocaust Memorial Museum; (C) AP/Wide World Photos, (R) Copley News Service; *p. 142:* (L) National Archives and Records Information, (C) Getty Images, Inc., (R) Stock Boston; *p. 143:* (TL) Steve Kagan/Photo Researchers, Inc., (BL) Courtesy of the Library of Congress; (TR) Corbis, (BR) Dana Stone, Richmond, VA; *p. 146:* A. Ramey/PhotoEdit.

CHAPTER 9 *Page 310:* Bill Frymire/Masterfile Corporation; *p. 312:* Stock Boston; *p. 313:* (L) Carlos Alvarez/Getty Images Inc., (C) Corbis/Sygma, (R) Copyright © Corbis; *p. 314:* Spencer Grant/PhotoEdit; *p. 315:* Copyright © 1996 by Jennifer Berman; *p. 316:* "Copyright © 201-785-Zits Partnership. Reprinted with special permission of King Features"; *p. 318:* AP/Wide World Photos; *p. 321* Copyright © 1999 by Jennifer Berman; *p. 322:* (T) Malcolm Hancock, (B)James Watt/Animals/Earth Scenes; *p. 330:* Laura Dwight/PhotoEdit; *p. 334:* Gary Conner/PhotoEdit; *p. 337:* (L) Photo Researchers, Inc., (C) Peter Vadnai/Corbis/Stock Market, (R) Michael Okoniewski/Getty Images Inc.; *p. 338:* Eric R. Berndt/Unicorn Stock Photos; *p. 341:* Jeff Foott Productions; *p. 342:* (L) SuperStock, Inc., (C) SuperStock, Inc., (R) SuperStock Inc.; *p. 345:* (T) Georgia State University/LRC, (BR) Michael Goldman Photography; *p. 346:* The Granger Collection, New York.

CHAPTER 10 *Page 352:* Bill Frymire/Masterfile Corporation; *p. 354:* HO/Burlington Police Department; *p. 355:* Frank Siteman/Stock Boston; *p. 356:* (T) AP/Wide World Photos; (B) Sidney Harris; *p. 358:* James Shaffer/PhotoEdit; *p. 362:* From "Rudolph the Red-Nosed Reindeer" by Robert L. May. Copyright © 1967, 1939 by Robert L. May, published Modern Curriculum Press. Used by permission of Pearson Education, Inc. All rights reserved. For online information for other Pearson Education, Inc. publications go to Internet website http://www.pearsoned.com; *p. 363:* Susan Mansfield; *p. 366:* Travis Gering; *p. 367:* Photo Researchers, Inc.; *p. 368:* Hank deLespinasse/Hank deLespinasse Studios, Inc.; *p. 370:* Jerry Jacka Photography; *p. 373:* Copyright © 1995 by Jennifer Berman; *p. 376:* Wasyl Szrodzinski/Photo Researchers, Inc.; *p. 378:* Sidney Harris; *p. 381:* (TR) The Image Works; *p. 383:* Picture Desk, Inc./Kobal Collection; *p. 384:* Photofest; *p. 386:* Courtesy of Carolyn Rovee-Collier; *p. 388:* Chuck Burton/AP/Wide World Photos.

CHAPTER 11 *Page 394:* Masterfile Corporation; *p. 397:* OSF/Clive Bromhall/Animals Animals/Earth Scenes; *p. 399:* Heidi S. Mario; *p. 400:* (L) Corbis/Sygma, (R) Wally McNamee; *p. 401:* David Matsumoto and Paul Ekman, Human Interaction Laboratory, University of California, San Francisco; *p. 404:* Tony Freeman/PhotoEdit; *p. 406:* Sidney Harris; *p. 409:* Duomo Photography Incorporated; *p. 410:* Laura Dwight Photography; *p. 413:* Peter

Beck/Corbis/Stock Market; *p. 412:* (L) Stock Boston, (R) Photo Researchers, Inc.; *p. 414:* (TL) Universitatsbiblio thek Heidelberg, (BR) Magnum Photos, Inc.; *p. 415:* Paul Brown/Rex Features USA Ltd.; *p. 416:* Index Stock Imagery, Inc.; *p. 418:* Copyright © Charles Barsotti from cartoonbank.com. All rights reserved; *p. 419:* (TR) W. Hill, Jr./The Image Works, (BL) Janice Rubin, (BR) Joel Gordon Photography; *p. 420:* (L) William Karel/Corbis/Sygma, (R) Tannenbaum/Corbis/Sygma; *p. 423:* BIZARRO Copyright © 1999 by Dan Piraro. Reprinted with permission of UNIVERSAL PRESS SYNDICATE. All rights reserved.

CHAPTER 12 *Page 426:* Daryl Benson/Masterfile Corporation; *p. 430:* (TL) Photo Researchers, Inc., (TR) Dennis Stock/Magnum Photos, Inc., (BL) Remi Banali/Gamma Press USA, Inc.; *p. 431:* Index Stock Imagery, Inc.; *p. 433:* (TL) Getty Images, Inc., (C) Michael Caulfield/AP/Wide World Photos, (TR) Frank Siteman/ Stock Boston, (BR) Phil McCarten/PhotoEdit; *p. 434:* William Thompson/Index Stock Imagery, Inc.; *p. 436:* Getty Images, Inc.; *p. 439:* Magnum Photos, Inc.; *p. 440:* Getty Images, Inc.; *p. 442:* Kinsey Inst. For Research–Sex, Gender and Reproduction; *p. 443:* (L) Getty Images, Inc., (C) Chris Harvey/Getty Images Inc., (R) Carol Ford/Getty Images, Inc.; *p. 444:* Rachel Epstein/PhotoEdit; *p. 445:* Unicorn Stock Photos; *p. 446:* (L) John Eastcott/Yva Momatiuk/ Woodfin Camp & Associates, (R) Cassy Cohen/PhotoEdit; *p. 447:* Corbis; *p. 450:* (L) Courtesy of the Library of Congress, (LC) Corbis, (RC) Flip Schulke/Black Star, (R) Corbis; *p. 451:* (L) Corbis/Sygma, (LC) Marvin Koner/Black Star, (RC) Corbis/Sygma, (R) Carol Halebian/Getty Images, Inc.; *p. 454:* Index Stock Imagery, Inc.

CHAPTER 13 *Page 464:* Mark Tomalty/Masterfile Corporation; *p. 468:* Catherine Karnow/Woodfin Camp & Associates; *p. 471:* Sidney Harris; *p. 472:* (L) The Image Works, (R) Dr. Stephen J. Suomi; *p. 473:* Peter Byron, Photographer; *p. 477:* Richard Hutchings/PhotoEdit; *p. 479:* (L) Marcel Thomas/Cashew1digitalfotos.com, (R) AP/Wide World Photos; *p. 481:* (L) Woodfin Camp & Associates, (R) Timothy Eagan/Woodfin Camp & Associates; *p. 485:* (L) Alison Wright/Stock Boston, (R) Betsy Lee; *p. 486:* Courtesy of A.W. Freud et al./Collection of the Library of Congress; *p. 487:* Sidney Harris; *p. 489:* Innervisions; *p. 491:* Photofest; *p. 492:* Donna Day/Getty Images, Inc.; *p. 493:* Getty Images, Inc.; *p. 494:* AP/Wide World Photos; *p. 495:* Dennis Budd Gray/Stock Boston.

CHAPTER 14 *Page 502:* Bill Frymire/Masterfile Corporation; *p. 504:* (L) UPI/Corbis, (C) Popperfoto/Getty Images, Inc., (R) Corbis; *p. 505:* Copyright © Baby Blues Partnership. Reprinted with special permission of King Features Syndicate; *p. 507:* Picture Press Bild-und Textagentur GmbH, Munich, Germany; *p. 508:* Doris Pinney Brenner; *p. 509:* Folio, Inc., *p. 510:* Lawrence Migdale/Pix; *p. 511:* Mark H. Johnson/Department of Psychology, Birkbeck College, London; *p. 513:* (T) Laura Dwight Photography, (B) Erika Stone; *p. 518* Jackie Curtis; *p. 519:* Photo Researchers, Inc.; *p. 521:* AP/World Wide Photos; *p. 523:* (L) PhotEdit, (R) PhotoEdit; *p. 525:* (L) The Granger Collection, New York, (R) National Anthropological Archives/Smithsonian Institution; *p. 526:* Laura Dwight Photography; *p. 527:* (L) Getty Images, Inc., (R) Index Stock Imagery, Inc.; *p. 529:* Richard Hutchings/Photo Researchers, Inc.; *p. 530:* (T) Copyright © 201-785-Zits Partnership. Reprinted with special permission of King Features; (B) TimePix; *p. 531:* COMMITTED reprinted by permission of United Features Syndicate, Inc.; *p. 532:* (L) Robert Frerck/Odyssey Productions, Inc., (R) Joel Gordon/Joel Gordon Photography; *p. 534:* Index Stock Imagery, Inc.; *p. 535:* (L) AP/Wide World Photos, (C) AP/Wide World Photos, (R) Albert Einstein™ licensed by the Hebrew University of Jerusalem, represented by the Roger Richman Agency, Inc., Beverly Hills, California; *p. 536:* (L) National Enquirer, (R) PhotoEdit; *p. 538:* Theo Westenberger Photography; *p. 540:* (L) Charles Gupton/Corbis/Stock Market, (R) Abigail Heyman; *p. 542:* Barritt/Getty Images, Inc.

CHAPTER 15 *Page 548:* Paul Terpanjian/Masterfile Corporation; *p. 554:* R. Wahlstrom/Getty Images, Inc.; *p. 555:* Juergen Berger, Max-Planck Institute/Science Photo Library/Photo Researchers, Inc.; *p. 558:* Amana America, Inc.; *p. 561:* National Baseball Hall of Fame Library, Cooperstown, N.Y.; *p. 563:* Angel Franco/New York Times Pictures; *p. 564:* (L) The Image Bank, (R) the mage Bank; *p. 568:* Malcolm Hancock; *p. 569:* MGM (Courtesy Kobal); *p. 570:* Arnold Gold/The Image Works; *p. 571:* (TR) Getty Images, Inc., (BL) Getty Images, Inc.

CHAPTER 16 *Page 578:* Nora Good/Masterfile Corporation; *p. 581:* (L) The Image Works, (C) Art Wolfe/Getty Images, Inc., (R) Les Stone/Corbis/Sygma; *p. 583:* Detail from original reprinted by permission. Copyright © The New Yorker Collection 2001 Roz Chast from cartoonbank.com. All rights reserved; *p. 584:* Sophia Smith Collection, Smith College; *p. 586:* (T) Yoav Levy/Phototake NYC, (B) Corbis; *p. 587:* Sidney Harris; *p. 589:* David Turnley/ Corbis; *p. 591:* SuperStock, Inc.; *p. 592:* Michael Lutsky/Washington Post; *p. 593:* Mick Hutson/Retna Ltd. USA; *p. 594:* AP/Wide World Photos; *p. 596:* Alfred Gescheidt/Getty Images, Inc.; *p. 597:* Corbis; *p. 598:* (L) Karen Garber-Corning Leader/SIPA Press, (R) Don Camp/ Getty Images, Inc.; *p. 603:* (BL) Leland Bobbe/Getty Images, Inc., (BR) Matrix International, Inc.; *p. 608:* Photofest/Jagarts; *p. 610:* Bob Child/AP/Wide World Photos; *p. 611:* Al Vercoutere; *p. 614:* AP/Wide World Photos.

CHAPTER 17 *Page 620:* Chris McElcheran/Masterfile Corporation; *p. 623:* (T) Alvin H. Perlmutter Inc., (B) Copyright © The New Yorker Collection 1993 Lee Lorenz from cartoonbank.com. All rights reserved; *p. 626:* Copyright © The New Yorker Collection 2001 Barbara Smaller from cartoonbank.com. All rights reserved; *p. 628:* (L) Photo Researchers, Inc., (R) Dr. Jordan Grafman, Eric M. Wassermann/"Brain Stimulation Unit, National Institute of Neurological Disorders and Stroke, National Institutes of Health"; *p. 629:* Sidney Harris; *p. 630:* Photofest; *p. 631:* University of Washington HIT Lab/Mary Levin; *p. 632:* H. Armstrong Roberts; *p. 634:* Michael Newman/PhotoEdit; *p. 635:* Courtesy of Alan Entin, Ph.D., family psychologist; *p. 640:* Sidney Harris; *p. 641:* (L) Courtesy of Dr. Guiseppe Constantino, (R) Xan Lopez; *p. 643:* Sidney Harris; *p. 646:* (T) AP/Wide World Photos, (B) AP/Wide World Photos; *p. 649:* Copyright © The New Yorker Collection 1993 Mike Twohy from cartoonbank.com. All rights reserved; *p. 650:* Michael Schumann/Corbis/SABA Press Photos, Inc.

Name Index

Subject Index